MW00509576

Aeronautics and Space Title 14 Volume 1

United States National Archives and Records Administration Federal Register Office

This work has been selected by scholars as being culturally important, and is part of the knowledge base of civilization as we know it. This work was reproduced from the original artifact, and remains as true to the original work as possible. Therefore, you will see the original copyright references, library stamps (as most of these works have been housed in our most important libraries around the world), and other notations in the work.

This work is in the public domain in the United States of America, and possibly other nations. Within the United States, you may freely copy and distribute this work, as no entity (individual or corporate) has a copyright on the body of the work.

As a reproduction of a historical artifact, this work may contain missing or blurred pages, poor pictures, errant marks, etc. Scholars believe, and we concur, that this work is important enough to be preserved, reproduced, and made generally available to the public. We appreciate your support of the preservation process, and thank you for being an important part of keeping this knowledge alive and relevant.

14

Parts 1 to 59
Revised as of January 1, 2003

Aeronautics and Space

Containing a codification of documents
of general applicability and future effect

As of January 1, 2003

With Ancillaries

Published by:
Office of the Federal Register
National Archives and Records
Administration

A Special Edition of the Federal Register

Code of Federal Regulations

U.S. GOVERNMENT PRINTING OFFICE
WASHINGTON : 2003

For sale by the Superintendent of Documents, U.S. Government Printing Office
Internet: bookstore.gpo.gov Phone: toll free (866) 512-1800; DC area (202) 512-1800
Fax: (202) 512-2250 Mail: Stop SSOP, Washington, DC 20402–0001

Table of Contents

Cite this Code: CFR

To cite the regulations in this volume use title, part and section number. Thus, 14 CFR 1.1 refers to title 14, part 1, section 1.

Explanation

The Code of Federal Regulations is a codification of the general and permanent rules published in the Federal Register by the Executive departments and agencies of the Federal Government. The Code is divided into 50 titles which represent broad areas subject to Federal regulation. Each title is divided into chapters which usually bear the name of the issuing agency. Each chapter is further subdivided into parts covering specific regulatory areas.

Each volume of the Code is revised at least once each calendar year and issued on a quarterly basis approximately as follows:

Title 1 through Title 16...as of January 1
Title 17 through Title 27 ....as of April 1
Title 28 through Title 41 ....as of July 1
Title 42 through Title 50 ....as of October 1

The appropriate revision date is printed on the cover of each volume.

LEGAL STATUS

The contents of the Federal Register are required to be judicially noticed (44 U.S.C. 1507). The Code of Federal Regulations is prima facie evidence of the text of the original documents (44 U.S.C. 1510).

HOW TO USE THE CODE OF FEDERAL REGULATIONS

The Code of Federal Regulations is kept up to date by the individual issues of the Federal Register. These two publications must be used together to determine the latest version of any given rule.

To determine whether a Code volume has been amended since its revision date (in this case, January 1, 2003), consult the "List of CFR Sections Affected (LSA)," which is issued monthly, and the "Cumulative List of Parts Affected," which appears in the Reader Aids section of the daily Federal Register. These two lists will identify the Federal Register page number of the latest amendment of any given rule.

EFFECTIVE AND EXPIRATION DATES

Each volume of the Code contains amendments published in the Federal Register since the last revision of that volume of the Code. Source citations for the regulations are referred to by volume number and page number of the Federal Register and date of publication. Publication dates and effective dates are usually not the same and care must be exercised by the user in determining the actual effective date. In instances where the effective date is beyond the cut-off date for the Code a note has been inserted to reflect the future effective date. In those instances where a regulation published in the Federal Register states a date certain for expiration, an appropriate note will be inserted following the text.

OMB CONTROL NUMBERS

The Paperwork Reduction Act of 1980 (Pub. L. 96–511) requires Federal agencies to display an OMB control number with their information collection request.

Many agencies have begun publishing numerous OMB control numbers as amendments to existing regulations in the CFR. These OMB numbers are placed as close as possible to the applicable recordkeeping or reporting requirements.

OBSOLETE PROVISIONS

Provisions that become obsolete before the revision date stated on the cover of each volume are not carried. Code users may find the text of provisions in effect on a given date in the past by using the appropriate numerical list of sections affected. For the period before January 1, 2001, consult either the List of CFR Sections Affected, 1949–1963, 1964–1972, 1973–1985, or 1986–2000, published in 11 separate volumes. For the period beginning January 1, 2001, a "List of CFR Sections Affected" is published at the end of each CFR volume.

INCORPORATION BY REFERENCE

What is incorporation by reference? Incorporation by reference was established by statute and allows Federal agencies to meet the requirement to publish regulations in the Federal Register by referring to materials already published elsewhere. For an incorporation to be valid, the Director of the Federal Register must approve it. The legal effect of incorporation by reference is that the material is treated as if it were published in full in the Federal Register (5 U.S.C. 552(a)). This material, like any other properly issued regulation, has the force of law.

What is a proper incorporation by reference? The Director of the Federal Register will approve an incorporation by reference only when the requirements of 1 CFR part 51 are met. Some of the elements on which approval is based are:

(a) The incorporation will substantially reduce the volume of material published in the Federal Register.

(b) The matter incorporated is in fact available to the extent necessary to afford fairness and uniformity in the administrative process.

(c) The incorporating document is drafted and submitted for publication in accordance with 1 CFR part 51.

Properly approved incorporations by reference in this volume are listed in the Finding Aids at the end of this volume.

What if the material incorporated by reference cannot be found? If you have any problem locating or obtaining a copy of material listed in the Finding Aids of this volume as an approved incorporation by reference, please contact the agency that issued the regulation containing that incorporation. If, after contacting the agency, you find the material is not available, please notify the Director of the Federal Register, National Archives and Records Administration, Washington DC 20408, or call (202) 741–6010.

CFR INDEXES AND TABULAR GUIDES

A subject index to the Code of Federal Regulations is contained in a separate volume, revised annually as of January 1, entitled CFR INDEX AND FINDING AIDS. This volume contains the Parallel Table of Statutory Authorities and Agency Rules (Table I). A list of CFR titles, chapters, and parts and an alphabetical list of agencies publishing in the CFR are also included in this volume.

An index to the text of "Title 3—The President" is carried within that volume.

The Federal Register Index is issued monthly in cumulative form. This index is based on a consolidation of the "Contents" entries in the daily Federal Register.

A List of CFR Sections Affected (LSA) is published monthly, keyed to the revision dates of the 50 CFR titles.

REPUBLICATION OF MATERIAL

There are no restrictions on the republication of material appearing in the Code of Federal Regulations.

INQUIRIES

For a legal interpretation or explanation of any regulation in this volume, contact the issuing agency. The issuing agency's name appears at the top of odd-numbered pages.

For inquiries concerning CFR reference assistance, call 202–741–6000 or write to the Director, Office of the Federal Register, National Archives and Records Administration, Washington, DC 20408 or e-mail info@fedreg.nara.gov.

SALES

The Government Printing Office (GPO) processes all sales and distribution of the CFR. For payment by credit card, call toll free, 866–512–1800 or DC area, 202–512–1800, M–F, 8 a.m. to 4 p.m. e.s.t. or fax your order to 202–512–2250, 24 hours a day. For payment by check, write to the Superintendent of Documents, Attn: New Orders, P.O. Box 371954, Pittsburgh, PA 15250–7954. For GPO Customer Service call 202–512–1803.

ELECTRONIC SERVICES

The full text of the Code of Federal Regulations, The United States Government Manual, the Federal Register, Public Laws, Public Papers, Weekly Compilation of Presidential Documents and the Privacy Act Compilation are available in electronic format at www.access.gpo.gov/nara ("GPO Access"). For more information, contact Electronic Information Dissemination Services, U.S. Government Printing Office. Phone 202–512–1530, or 888–293–6498 (toll-free). E-mail, gpoaccess@gpo.gov.

The Office of the Federal Register also offers a free service on the National Archives and Records Administration's (NARA) World Wide Web site for public law numbers, Federal Register finding aids, and related information. Connect to NARA's web site at www.nara.gov/fedreg. The NARA site also contains links to GPO Access.

RAYMOND A. MOSLEY,
Director,
Office of the Federal Register.

January 1, 2003.

THIS TITLE

Title 14—AERONAUTICS AND SPACE is composed of five volumes. The parts in these volumes are arranged in the following order: parts 1–59, 60–139, 140–199, 200–1199, and part 1200–End. The first three volumes containing parts 1–199 are comprised of chapter I—Federal Aviation Administration, Department of Transportation (DOT). The fourth volume containing parts 200–1199 is comprised of chapter II—Office of the Secretary, DOT (Aviation Proceedings) and chapter III—Commercial Space Transportation, Federal Aviation Administration, DOT. The fifth volume containing part 1200–End is comprised of chapter V—National Aeronautics and Space Administration and chapter VI—Air Transportation System Stabilization. The contents of these volumes represent all current regulations codified under this title of the CFR as of January 1, 2003.

Would you like to know. . .

if any changes have been made to the *Code of Federal Regulations* or what documents have been published in the *Federal Register* without reading the *Federal Register* every day? If so, you may wish to subscribe to the *LSA* (List of CFR Sections Affected), the *Federal Register Index,* or both.

LSA
The *LSA* (List of CFR Sections Affected) is designed to lead users of the *Code of Federal Regulations* to amendatory actions published in the *Federal Register.* The *LSA* is issued monthly in cumulative form. Entries indicate the nature of the changes—such as revised, removed, or corrected. $31 per year.

Federal Register Index
The index, covering the contents of the daily *Federal Register,* is issued monthly in cumulative form. Entries are carried primarily under the names of the issuing agencies. Significant subjects are carried as cross-references. $28 per year.

A finding aid is included in each publication which lists *Federal Register* page numbers with the date of publication in the *Federal Register.*

- -

Superintendent of Documents Subscription Order Form

Order Processing Code:
*5421

❑ **YES,** send me the following indicated subscriptions for one year:

____ **LSA (List of CFR Sections Affected),** (LCS) for $31 per year.

____ **Federal Register Index** (FRSU) $28 per year.

The total cost of my order is $ _____.
Price is subject to change. International customers please add 25%.

_____
Company or personal name

_____
Street address

_____
City, State, ZIP code

_____
Daytime phone with area code

_____
Purchase order No.   (optional)

(Includes regular shipping and handling.)

For privacy check box below:
❑ Do not make my name available to other mailers

Check method of payment:
❑ Check payable to Superintendent of Documents
❑ GPO Deposit Account ⬚⬚⬚⬚⬚⬚⬚–⬚
❑ VISA ❑ MasterCard ⬚⬚⬚⬚ (expiration date)

_____
Credit card No.   (must be 20 digits)

Thank you for your order!

_____
Authorizing signature   7/00

Mail To: Superintendent of Documents
P.O. Box 371954
Pittsburgh, PA 15250-7954

Fax your orders (202) 512-2250
Phone your orders (202) 512-1800

Title 14—Aeronautics and Space

(This book contains parts 1 to 59)

CROSS REFERENCES: Department of the Air Force; Use of Air Force installations by other than U.S. Department of Defense aircraft: See National Defense, 32 CFR Part 855.
Federal Communications Commission, aviation services: See Telecommunication, 47 CFR Part 87.

CHAPTER I—FEDERAL AVIATION ADMINISTRATION, DEPARTMENT OF TRANSPORTATION

3

SUBCHAPTER A—DEFINITIONS

PART 1—DEFINITIONS AND ABBREVIATIONS

AUTHORITY: 49 U.S.C. 106(g), 40113, 44701.

§ 1.1 General definitions.

As used in Subchapters A through K of this chapter, unless the context requires otherwise:

Administrator means the Federal Aviation Administrator or any person to whom he has delegated his authority in the matter concerned.

Aerodynamic coefficients means non-dimensional coefficients for aerodynamic forces and moments.

Air carrier means a person who undertakes directly by lease, or other arrangement, to engage in air transportation.

Air commerce means interstate, overseas, or foreign air commerce or the transportation of mail by aircraft or any operation or navigation of aircraft within the limits of any Federal airway or any operation or navigation of aircraft which directly affects, or which may endanger safety in, interstate, overseas, or foreign air commerce.

Aircraft means a device that is used or intended to be used for flight in the air.

Aircraft engine means an engine that is used or intended to be used for propelling aircraft. It includes turbosuperchargers, appurtenances, and accessories necessary for its functioning, but does not include propellers.

Airframe means the fuselage, booms, nacelles, cowlings, fairings, airfoil surfaces (including rotors but excluding propellers and rotating airfoils of engines), and landing gear of an aircraft and their accessories and controls.

Airplane means an engine-driven fixed-wing aircraft heavier than air, that is supported in flight by the dynamic reaction of the air against its wings.

Airport means an area of land or water that is used or intended to be used for the landing and takeoff of aircraft, and includes its buildings and facilities, if any.

Airship means an engine-driven lighter-than-air aircraft that can be steered.

Air traffic means aircraft operating in the air or on an airport surface, exclusive of loading ramps and parking areas.

Air traffic clearance means an authorization by air traffic control, for the purpose of preventing collision between known aircraft, for an aircraft to proceed under specified traffic conditions within controlled airspace.

Air traffic control means a service operated by appropriate authority to promote the safe, orderly, and expeditious flow of air traffic.

Air transportation means interstate, overseas, or foreign air transportation or the transportation of mail by aircraft.

Alert Area. An alert area is established to inform pilots of a specific area wherein a high volume of pilot training or an unusual type of aeronautical activity is conducted.

Alternate airport means an airport at which an aircraft may land if a landing at the intended airport becomes inadvisable.

Altitude engine means a reciprocating aircraft engine having a rated takeoff power that is producible from sea level to an established higher altitude.

Appliance means any instrument, mechanism, equipment, part, apparatus, appurtenance, or accessory, including communications equipment, that is used or intended to be used in operating or controlling an aircraft in flight, is installed in or attached to the aircraft, and is not part of an airframe, engine, or propeller.

Approved, unless used with reference to another person, means approved by the Administrator.

Area navigation (RNAV) means a method of navigation that permits aircraft operations on any desired course within the coverage of station-referenced navigation signals or within the limits of self-contained system capability.

Area navigation low route means an area navigation route within the airspace extending upward from 1,200 feet above the surface of the earth to, but not including, 18,000 feet MSL.

Area navigation high route means an area navigation route within the airspace extending upward from, and including, 18,000 feet MSL to flight level 450.

Armed Forces means the Army, Navy, Air Force, Marine Corps, and Coast Guard, including their regular and reserve components and members serving without component status.

Autorotation means a rotorcraft flight condition in which the lifting rotor is driven entirely by action of the air when the rotorcraft is in motion.

Auxiliary rotor means a rotor that serves either to counteract the effect of the main rotor torque on a rotorcraft or to maneuver the rotorcraft about one or more of its three principal axes.

Balloon means a lighter-than-air aircraft that is not engine driven, and that sustains flight through the use of either gas buoyancy or an airborne heater.

Brake horsepower means the power delivered at the propeller shaft (main drive or main output) of an aircraft engine.

Calibrated airspeed means the indicated airspeed of an aircraft, corrected for position and instrument error. Calibrated airspeed is equal to true airspeed in standard atmosphere at sea level.

Canard means the forward wing of a canard configuration and may be a fixed, movable, or variable geometry surface, with or without control surfaces.

Canard configuration means a configuration in which the span of the forward wing is substantially less than that of the main wing.

Category:

(1) As used with respect to the certification, ratings, privileges, and limitations of airmen, means a broad classification of aircraft. Examples include: airplane; rotorcraft; glider; and lighter-than-air; and

(2) As used with respect to the certification of aircraft, means a grouping of aircraft based upon intended use or operating limitations. Examples in-

clude: transport, normal, utility, acrobatic, limited, restricted, and provisional.

Category A, with respect to transport category rotorcraft, means multiengine rotorcraft designed with engine and system isolation features specified in Part 29 and utilizing scheduled takeoff and landing operations under a critical engine failure concept which assures adequate designated surface area and adequate performance capability for continued safe flight in the event of engine failure.

Category B, with respect to transport category rotorcraft, means single-engine or multiengine rotorcraft which do not fully meet all Category A standards. Category B rotorcraft have no guaranteed stay-up ability in the event of engine failure and unscheduled landing is assumed.

Category II operations, with respect to the operation of aircraft, means a straight-in ILS approach to the runway of an airport under a Category II ILS instrument approach procedure issued by the Administrator or other appropriate authority.

Category III operations, with respect to the operation of aircraft, means an ILS approach to, and landing on, the runway of an airport using a Category III ILS instrument approach procedure issued by the Administrator or other appropriate authority.

Category IIIa operations, an ILS approach and landing with no decision height (DH), or a DH below 100 feet (30 meters), and controlling runway visual range not less than 700 feet (200 meters).

Category IIIb operations, an ILS approach and landing with no DH, or with a DH below 50 feet (15 meters), and controlling runway visual range less than 700 feet (200 meters), but not less than 150 feet (50 meters).

Category IIIc operations, an ILS approach and landing with no DH and no runway visual range limitation.

Ceiling means the height above the earth's surface of the lowest layer of clouds or obscuring phenomena that is reported as "broken", "overcast", or "obscuration", and not classified as "thin" or "partial".

Civil aircraft means aircraft other than public aircraft.

Class:

(1) As used with respect to the certification, ratings, privileges, and limitations of airmen, means a classification of aircraft within a category having similar operating characteristics. Examples include: single engine; multiengine; land; water; gyroplane; helicopter; airship; and free balloon; and

(2) As used with respect to the certification of aircraft, means a broad grouping of aircraft having similar characteristics of propulsion, flight, or landing. Examples include: airplane; rotorcraft; glider; balloon; landplane; and seaplane.

Clearway means:

(1) For turbine engine powered airplanes certificated after August 29, 1959, an area beyond the runway, not less than 500 feet wide, centrally located about the extended centerline of the runway, and under the control of the airport authorities. The clearway is expressed in terms of a clearway plane, extending from the end of the runway with an upward slope not exceeding 1.25 percent, above which no object nor any terrain protrudes. However, threshold lights may protrude above the plane if their height above the end of the runway is 26 inches or less and if they are located to each side of the runway.

(2) For turbine engine powered airplanes certificated after September 30, 1958, but before August 30, 1959, an area beyond the takeoff runway extending no less than 300 feet on either side of the extended centerline of the runway, at an elevation no higher than the elevation of the end of the runway, clear of all fixed obstacles, and under the control of the airport authorities.

Climbout speed, with respect to rotorcraft, means a referenced airspeed which results in a flight path clear of the height-velocity envelope during initial climbout.

Commercial operator means a person who, for compensation or hire, engages in the carriage by aircraft in air commerce of persons or property, other than as an air carrier or foreign air carrier or under the authority of Part 375 of this title. Where it is doubtful that an operation is for "compensation or hire", the test applied is whether the carriage by air is merely incidental to the person's other business or is, in itself, a major enterprise for profit.

Controlled airspace means an airspace of defined dimensions within which air traffic control service is provided to IFR flights and to VFR flights in accordance with the airspace classification.

NOTE: Controlled airspace is a generic term that covers Class A, Class B, Class C, Class D, and Class E airspace.

Controlled Firing Area. A controlled firing area is established to contain activities, which if not conducted in a controlled environment, would be hazardous to nonparticipating aircraft.

Crewmember means a person assigned to perform duty in an aircraft during flight time.

Critical altitude means the maximum altitude at which, in standard atmosphere, it is possible to maintain, at a specified rotational speed, a specified power or a specified manifold pressure. Unless otherwise stated, the critical altitude is the maximum altitude at which it is possible to maintain, at the maximum continuous rotational speed, one of the following:

(1) The maximum continuous power, in the case of engines for which this power rating is the same at sea level and at the rated altitude.

(2) The maximum continuous rated manifold pressure, in the case of engines, the maximum continuous power of which is governed by a constant manifold pressure.

Critical engine means the engine whose failure would most adversely affect the performance or handling qualities of an aircraft.

Decision height, with respect to the operation of aircraft, means the height at which a decision must be made, during an ILS or PAR instrument approach, to either continue the approach or to execute a missed approach.

Equivalent airspeed means the calibrated airspeed of an aircraft corrected for adiabatic compressible flow for the particular altitude. Equivalent airspeed is equal to calibrated airspeed in standard atmosphere at sea level.

Extended over-water operation means—

(1) With respect to aircraft other than helicopters, an operation over water at a horizontal distance of more

7

than 50 nautical miles from the nearest shoreline; and

(2) With respect to helicopters, an operation over water at a horizontal distance of more than 50 nautical miles from the nearest shoreline and more than 50 nautical miles from an offshore heliport structure.

External load means a load that is carried, or extends, outside of the aircraft fuselage.

External-load attaching means means the structural components used to attach an external load to an aircraft, including external-load containers, the backup structure at the attachment points, and any quick-release device used to jettison the external load.

Final takeoff speed means the speed of the airplane that exists at the end of the takeoff path in the en route configuration with one engine inoperative.

Fireproof—

(1) With respect to materials and parts used to confine fire in a designated fire zone, means the capacity to withstand at least as well as steel in dimensions appropriate for the purpose for which they are used, the heat produced when there is a severe fire of extended duration in that zone; and

(2) With respect to other materials and parts, means the capacity to withstand the heat associated with fire at least as well as steel in dimensions appropriate for the purpose for which they are used.

Fire resistant—

(1) With respect to sheet or structural members means the capacity to withstand the heat associated with fire at least as well as aluminum alloy in dimensions appropriate for the purpose for which they are used; and

(2) With respect to fluid-carrying lines, fluid system parts, wiring, air ducts, fittings, and powerplant controls, means the capacity to perform the intended functions under the heat and other conditions likely to occur when there is a fire at the place concerned.

Flame resistant means not susceptible to combustion to the point of propagating a flame, beyond safe limits, after the ignition source is removed.

Flammable, with respect to a fluid or gas, means susceptible to igniting readily or to exploding.

Flap extended speed means the highest speed permissible with wing flaps in a prescribed extended position.

Flash resistant means not susceptible to burning violently when ignited.

Flightcrew member means a pilot, flight engineer, or flight navigator assigned to duty in an aircraft during flight time.

Flight level means a level of constant atmospheric pressure related to a reference datum of 29.92 inches of mercury. Each is stated in three digits that represent hundreds of feet. For example, flight level 250 represents a barometric altimeter indication of 25,000 feet; flight level 255, an indication of 25,500 feet.

Flight plan means specified information, relating to the intended flight of an aircraft, that is filed orally or in writing with air traffic control.

Flight time means:

(1) Pilot time that commences when an aircraft moves under its own power for the purpose of flight and ends when the aircraft comes to rest after landing; or

(2) For a glider without self-launch capability, pilot time that commences when the glider is towed for the purpose of flight and ends when the glider comes to rest after landing.

Flight visibility means the average forward horizontal distance, from the cockpit of an aircraft in flight, at which prominent unlighted objects may be seen and identified by day and prominent lighted objects may be seen and identified by night.

Foreign air carrier means any person other than a citizen of the United States, who undertakes directly, by lease or other arrangement, to engage in air transportation.

Foreign air commerce means the carriage by aircraft of persons or property for compensation or hire, or the carriage of mail by aircraft, or the operation or navigation of aircraft in the conduct or furtherance of a business or vocation, in commerce between a place in the United States and any place outside thereof; whether such commerce moves wholly by aircraft or partly by aircraft and partly by other forms of transportation.

Foreign air transportation means the carriage by aircraft of persons or property as a common carrier for compensation or hire, or the carriage of mail by aircraft, in commerce between a place in the United States and any place outside of the United States, whether that commerce moves wholly by aircraft or partly by aircraft and partly by other forms of transportation.

Forward wing means a forward lifting surface of a canard configuration or tandem-wing configuration airplane. The surface may be a fixed, movable, or variable geometry surface, with or without control surfaces.

Glider means a heavier-than-air aircraft, that is supported in flight by the dynamic reaction of the air against its lifting surfaces and whose free flight does not depend principally on an engine.

Ground visibility means prevailing horizontal visibility near the earth's surface as reported by the United States National Weather Service or an accredited observer.

Go-around power or thrust setting means the maximum allowable inflight power or thrust setting identified in the performance data.

Gyrodyne means a rotorcraft whose rotors are normally engine-driven for takeoff, hovering, and landing, and for forward flight through part of its speed range, and whose means of propulsion, consisting usually of conventional propellers, is independent of the rotor system.

Gyroplane means a rotorcraft whose rotors are not engine-driven, except for initial starting, but are made to rotate by action of the air when the rotorcraft is moving; and whose means of propulsion, consisting usually of conventional propellers, is independent of the rotor system.

Helicopter means a rotorcraft that, for its horizontal motion, depends principally on its engine-driven rotors.

Heliport means an area of land, water, or structure used or intended to be used for the landing and takeoff of helicopters.

Idle thrust means the jet thrust obtained with the engine power control level set at the stop for the least thrust position at which it can be placed.

IFR conditions means weather conditions below the minimum for flight under visual flight rules.

IFR over-the-top, with respect to the operation of aircraft, means the operation of an aircraft over-the-top on an IFR flight plan when cleared by air traffic control to maintain "VFR conditions" or "VFR conditions on top".

Indicated airspeed means the speed of an aircraft as shown on its pitot static airspeed indicator calibrated to reflect standard atmosphere adiabatic compressible flow at sea level uncorrected for airspeed system errors.

Instrument means a device using an internal mechanism to show visually or aurally the attitude, altitude, or operation of an aircraft or aircraft part. It includes electronic devices for automatically controlling an aircraft in flight.

Interstate air commerce means the carriage by aircraft of persons or property for compensation or hire, or the carriage of mail by aircraft, or the operation or navigation of aircraft in the conduct or furtherance of a business or vocation, in commerce between a place in any State of the United States, or the District of Columbia, and a place in any other State of the United States, or the District of Columbia; or between places in the same State of the United States through the airspace over any place outside thereof; or between places in the same territory or possession of the United States, or the District of Columbia.

Interstate air transportation means the carriage by aircraft of persons or property as a common carrier for compensation or hire, or the carriage of mail by aircraft in commerce:

(1) Between a place in a State or the District of Columbia and another place in another State or the District of Columbia;

(2) Between places in the same State through the airspace over any place outside that State; or

(3) Between places in the same possession of the United States;

Whether that commerce moves wholly by aircraft of partly by aircraft and partly by other forms of transportation.

Intrastate air transportation means the carriage of persons or property as a

9

common carrier for compensation or hire, by turbojet-powered aircraft capable of carrying thirty or more persons, wholly within the same State of the United States.

Kite means a framework, covered with paper, cloth, metal, or other material, intended to be flown at the end of a rope or cable, and having as its only support the force of the wind moving past its surfaces.

Landing gear extended speed means the maximum speed at which an aircraft can be safely flown with the landing gear extended.

Landing gear operating speed means the maximum speed at which the landing gear can be safely extended or retracted.

Large aircraft means aircraft of more than 12,500 pounds, maximum certificated takeoff weight.

Lighter-than-air aircraft means aircraft that can rise and remain suspended by using contained gas weighing less than the air that is displaced by the gas.

Load factor means the ratio of a specified load to the total weight of the aircraft. The specified load is expressed in terms of any of the following: aerodynamic forces, inertia forces, or ground or water reactions.

Long-range communication system (LRCS). A system that uses satellite relay, data link, high frequency, or another approved communication system which extends beyond line of sight.

Long-range navigation system (LRNS). An electronic navigation unit that is approved for use under instrument flight rules as a primary means of navigation, and has at least one source of navigational input, such as inertial navigation system, global positioning system, Omega/very low frequency, or Loran C.

Mach number means the ratio of true airspeed to the speed of sound.

Main rotor means the rotor that supplies the principal lift to a rotorcraft.

Maintenance means inspection, overhaul, repair, preservation, and the replacement of parts, but excludes preventive maintenance.

Major alteration means an alteration not listed in the aircraft, aircraft engine, or propeller specifications—

(1) That might appreciably affect weight, balance, structural strength, performance, powerplant operation, flight characteristics, or other qualities affecting airworthiness; or

(2) That is not done according to accepted practices or cannot be done by elementary operations.

Major repair means a repair:

(1) That, if improperly done, might appreciably affect weight, balance, structural strength, performance, powerplant operation, flight characteristics, or other qualities affecting airworthiness; or

(2) That is not done according to accepted practices or cannot be done by elementary operations.

Manifold pressure means absolute pressure as measured at the appropriate point in the induction system and usually expressed in inches of mercury.

Maximum speed for stability characteristics, V_{FC}/M_{FC} means a speed that may not be less than a speed midway between maximum operating limit speed (V_{MO}/M_{MO}) and demonstrated flight diving speed (V_{DF}/M_{DF}), except that, for altitudes where the Mach number is the limiting factor, M_{FC} need not exceed the Mach number at which effective speed warning occurs.

Medical certificate means acceptable evidence of physical fitness on a form prescribed by the Administrator.

Military operations area. A military operations area (MOA) is airspace established outside Class A airspace to separate or segregate certain nonhazardous military activities from IFR Traffic and to identify for VFR traffic where theses activities are conducted.

V_A means design maneuvering speed.

V_B means design speed for maximum gust intensity.

V_C means design cruising speed.

V_D means design diving speed.

V_{DF}/M_{DF} means demonstrated flight diving speed.

V_{EF} means the speed at which the critical engine is assumed to fail during takeoff.

V_F means design flap speed.

V_{FC}/M_{FC} means maximum speed for stability characteristics.

V_{FE} means maximum flap extended speed.

V_H means maximum speed in level flight with maximum continuous power.

V_{LE} means maximum landing gear extended speed.

V_{LO} means maximum landing gear operating speed.

V_{LOF} means lift-off speed.

V_{MC} means minimum control speed with the critical engine inoperative.

V_{MO}/M_{MO} means maximum operating limit speed.

V_{MU} means minimum unstick speed.

V_{NE} means never-exceed speed.

V_{NO} means maximum structural cruising speed.

V_R means rotation speed.

V_S means the stalling speed or the minimum steady flight speed at which the airplane is controllable.

Minimum descent altitude means the lowest altitude, expressed in feet above mean sea level, to which descent is authorized on final approach or during circle-to-land maneuvering in execution of a standard instrument approach procedure, where no electronic glide slope is provided.

Minor alteration means an alteration other than a major alteration.

Minor repair means a repair other than a major repair.

Navigable airspace means airspace at and above the minimum flight altitudes prescribed by or under this chapter, including airspace needed for safe takeoff and landing.

Night means the time between the end of evening civil twilight and the beginning of morning civil twilight, as published in the American Air Almanac, converted to local time.

Nonprecision approach procedure means a standard instrument approach procedure in which no electronic glide slope is provided.

Operate, with respect to aircraft, means use, cause to use or authorize to use aircraft, for the purpose (except as provided in §91.13 of this chapter) of air navigation including the piloting of aircraft, with or without the right of legal control (as owner, lessee, or otherwise).

Operational control, with respect to a flight, means the exercise of authority over initiating, conducting or terminating a flight.

Overseas air commerce means the carriage by aircraft of persons or property for compensation or hire, or the carriage of mail by aircraft, or the operation or navigation of aircraft in the conduct or furtherance of a business or vocation, in commerce between a place in any State of the United States, or the District of Columbia, and any place in a territory or possession of the United States; or between a place in a territory or possession of the United States, and a place in any other territory or possession of the United States.

Overseas air transportation means the carriage by aircraft of persons or property as a common carrier for compensation or hire, or the carriage of mail by aircraft, in commerce:

(1) Between a place in a State or the District of Columbia and a place in a possession of the United States; or

(2) Between a place in a possession of the United States and a place in another possession of the United States; whether that commerce moves wholly by aircraft or partly by aircraft and partly by other forms of transportation.

Over-the-top means above the layer of clouds or other obscuring phenomena forming the ceiling.

Parachute means a device used or intended to be used to retard the fall of a body or object through the air.

Person means an individual, firm, partnership, corporation, company, association, joint-stock association, or governmental entity. It includes a trustee, receiver, assignee, or similar representative of any of them.

Pilotage means navigation by visual reference to landmarks.

Pilot in command means the person who:

(1) Has final authority and responsibility for the operation and safety of the flight;

(2) Has been designated as pilot in command before or during the flight; and

(3) Holds the appropriate category, class, and type rating, if appropriate, for the conduct of the flight.

Pitch setting means the propeller blade setting as determined by the blade angle measured in a manner, and at a radius, specified by the instruction manual for the propeller.

Positive control means control of all air traffic, within designated airspace, by air traffic control.

Powered-lift means a heavier-than-air aircraft capable of vertical takeoff, vertical landing, and low speed flight that depends principally on engine-driven lift devices or engine thrust for lift during these flight regimes and on nonrotating airfoil(s) for lift during horizontal flight.

Precision approach procedure means a standard instrument approach procedure in which an electronic glide slope is provided, such as ILS and PAR.

Preventive maintenance means simple or minor preservation operations and the replacement of small standard parts not involving complex assembly operations.

Prohibited area. A prohibited area is airspace designated under part 73 within which no person may operate an aircraft without the permission of the using agency.

Propeller means a device for propelling an aircraft that has blades on an engine-driven shaft and that, when rotated, produces by its action on the air, a thrust approximately perpendicular to its plane of rotation. It includes control components normally supplied by its manufacturer, but does not include main and auxiliary rotors or rotating airfoils of engines.

Public aircraft means an aircraft used only for the United States Government, or owned and operated (except for commercial purposes), or exclusively leased for at least 90 continuous days, by a government (except the United States Government), including a State, the District of Columbia, or a territory or possession of the United States, or political subdivision of that government; but does not include a government-owned aircraft transporting property for commercial purposes, or transporting passengers other than transporting (for other than commercial purposes) crewmembers or other persons aboard the aircraft whose presence is required to perform, or is associated with the performance of, a governmental function such as firefighting, search and rescue, law enforcement, aeronautical research, or biological or geological resource management; or transporting (for other than commercial purposes) persons aboard the aircraft if the aircraft is operated by the Armed Forces or an intelligence agency of the United States. An aircraft described in the preceding sentence shall, notwithstanding any limitation relating to use of the aircraft for commercial purposes, be considered to be a public aircraft for the purposes of this Chapter without regard to whether the aircraft is operated by a unit of government on behalf of another unit of government, pursuant to a cost reimbursement agreement between such units of government, if the unit of government on whose behalf the operation is conducted certifies to the Administrator of the Federal Aviation Administration that the operation was necessary to respond to a significant and imminent threat to life or property (including natural resources) and that no service by a private operator was reasonably available to meet the threat.

Rated 30-second OEI power, with respect to rotorcraft turbine engines, means the approved brake horsepower developed under static conditions at specified altitudes and temperatures within the operating limitations established for the engine under part 33 of this chapter, for continued one-flight operation after the failure of one engine in multiengine rotorcraft, limited to three periods of use no longer than 30 seconds each in any one flight, and followed by mandatory inspection and prescribed maintenance action.

Rated 2-minute OEI power, with respect to rotorcraft turbine engines, means the approved brake horsepower developed under static conditions at specified altitudes and temperatures within the operating limitations established for the engine under part 33 of this chapter, for continued one-flight operation after the failure of one engine in multiengine rotorcraft, limited to three periods of use no longer than 2 minutes each in any one flight, and followed by mandatory inspection and prescribed maintenance action.

Rated continuous OEI power, with respect to rotorcraft turbine engines, means the approved brake horsepower developed under static conditions at specified altitudes and temperatures within the operating limitations established for the engine under Part 33 of this chapter, and limited in use to the time required to complete the flight after the failure of one engine of a multiengine rotorcraft.

Rated maximum continuous augmented thrust, with respect to turbojet engine type certification, means the approved jet thrust that is developed statically or in flight, in standard atmosphere at a specified altitude, with fluid injection or with the burning of fuel in a separate combustion chamber, within the engine operating limitations established under Part 33 of this chapter, and approved for unrestricted periods of use.

Rated maximum continuous power, with respect to reciprocating, turbopropeller, and turboshaft engines, means the approved brake horsepower that is developed statically or in flight, in standard atmosphere at a specified altitude, within the engine operating limitations established under Part 33, and approved for unrestricted periods of use.

Rated maximum continuous thrust, with respect to turbojet engine type certification, means the approved jet thrust that is developed statically or in flight, in standard atmosphere at a specified altitude, without fluid injection and without the burning of fuel in a separate combustion chamber, within the engine operating limitations established under Part 33 of this chapter, and approved for unrestricted periods of use.

Rated takeoff augmented thrust, with respect to turbojet engine type certification, means the approved jet thrust that is developed statically under standard sea level conditions, with fluid injection or with the burning of fuel in a separate combustion chamber, within the engine operating limitations established under Part 33 of this chapter, and limited in use to periods of not over 5 minutes for takeoff operation.

Rated takeoff power, with respect to reciprocating, turbopropeller, and turboshaft engine type certification, means the approved brake horsepower that is developed statically under standard sea level conditions, within the engine operating limitations estab-

lished under Part 33, and limited in use to periods of not over 5 minutes for takeoff operation.

Rated takeoff thrust, with respect to turbojet engine type certification, means the approved jet thrust that is developed statically under standard sea level conditions, without fluid injection and without the burning of fuel in a separate combustion chamber, within the engine operating limitations established under Part 33 of this chapter, and limited in use to periods of not over 5 minutes for takeoff operation.

Rated 30-minute OEI power, with respect to rotorcraft turbine engines, means the approved brake horsepower developed under static conditions at specified altitudes and temperatures within the operating limitations established for the engine under Part 33 of this chapter, and limited in use to a period of not more than 30 minutes after the failure of one engine of a multiengine rotorcraft.

Rated 2½-minute OEI power, with respect to rotorcraft turbine engines, means the approved brake horsepower developed under static conditions at specified altitudes and temperatures within the operating limitations established for the engine under Part 33 of this chapter, and limited in use to a period of not more than 2½ minutes after the failure of one engine of a multiengine rotorcraft.

Rating means a statement that, as a part of a certificate, sets forth special conditions, privileges, or limitations.

Reference landing speed means the speed of the airplane, in a specified landing configuration, at the point where it descends through the 50 foot height in the determination of the landing distance.

Reporting point means a geographical location in relation to which the position of an aircraft is reported.

Restricted area. A restricted area is airspace designated under Part 73 within which the flight of aircraft, while not wholly prohibited, is subject to restriction.

RNAV way point (W/P) means a predetermined geographical position used for route or instrument approach definition or progress reporting purposes that is defined relative to a VORTAC station position.

Rocket means an aircraft propelled by ejected expanding gases generated in the engine from self-contained propellants and not dependent on the intake of outside substances. It includes any part which becomes separated during the operation.

Rotorcraft means a heavier-than-air aircraft that depends principally for its support in flight on the lift generated by one or more rotors.

Rotorcraft-load combination means the combination of a rotorcraft and an external-load, including the external-load attaching means. Rotorcraft-load combinations are designated as Class A, Class B, Class C, and Class D, as follows:

(1) *Class A rotorcraft-load combination* means one in which the external load cannot move freely, cannot be jettisoned, and does not extend below the landing gear.

(2) *Class B rotorcraft-load combination* means one in which the external load is jettisonable and is lifted free of land or water during the rotorcraft operation.

(3) *Class C rotorcraft-load combination* means one in which the external load is jettisonable and remains in contact with land or water during the rotorcraft operation.

(4) *Class D rotorcraft-load combination* means one in which the external-load is other than a Class A, B, or C and has been specifically approved by the Administrator for that operation.

Route segment means a part of a route. Each end of that part is identified by:

(1) A continental or insular geographical location; or

(2) A point at which a definite radio fix can be established.

Sea level engine means a reciprocating aircraft engine having a rated takeoff power that is producible only at sea level.

Second in command means a pilot who is designated to be second in command of an aircraft during flight time.

Show, unless the context otherwise requires, means to show to the satisfaction of the Administrator.

Small aircraft means aircraft of 12,500 pounds or less, maximum certificated takeoff weight.

Special VFR conditions mean meteorological conditions that are less than those required for basic VFR flight in controlled airspace and in which some aircraft are permitted flight under visual flight rules.

Special VFR operations means aircraft operating in accordance with clearances within controlled airspace in meteorological conditions less than the basic VFR weather minima. Such operations must be requested by the pilot and approved by ATC.

Standard atmosphere means the atmosphere defined in U.S. Standard Atmosphere, 1962 (Geopotential altitude tables).

Stopway means an area beyond the takeoff runway, no less wide than the runway and centered upon the extended centerline of the runway, able to support the airplane during an aborted takeoff, without causing structural damage to the airplane, and designated by the airport authorities for use in decelerating the airplane during an aborted takeoff.

Takeoff power:

(1) With respect to reciprocating engines, means the brake horsepower that is developed under standard sea level conditions, and under the maximum conditions of crankshaft rotational speed and engine manifold pressure approved for the normal takeoff, and limited in continuous use to the period of time shown in the approved engine specification; and

(2) With respect to turbine engines, means the brake horsepower that is developed under static conditions at a specified altitude and atmospheric temperature, and under the maximum conditions of rotor shaft rotational speed and gas temperature approved for the normal takeoff, and limited in continuous use to the period of time shown in the approved engine specification.

Takeoff safety speed means a referenced airspeed obtained after lift-off at which the required one-engine-inoperative climb performance can be achieved.

Takeoff thrust, with respect to turbine engines, means the jet thrust that is developed under static conditions at a specific altitude and atmospheric temperature under the maximum conditions of rotorshaft rotational speed and gas temperature approved for the normal takeoff, and limited in continuous use to the period of time shown in the approved engine specification.

Tandem wing configuration means a configuration having two wings of similar span, mounted in tandem.

TCAS I means a TCAS that utilizes interrogations of, and replies from, airborne radar beacon transponders and provides traffic advisories to the pilot.

TCAS II means a TCAS that utilizes interrogations of, and replies from airborne radar beacon transponders and provides traffic advisories and resolution advisories in the vertical plane.

TCAS III means a TCAS that utilizes interrogation of, and replies from, airborne radar beacon transponders and provides traffic advisories and resolution advisories in the vertical and horizontal planes to the pilot.

Time in service, with respect to maintenance time records, means the time from the moment an aircraft leaves the surface of the earth until it touches it at the next point of landing.

True airspeed means the airspeed of an aircraft relative to undisturbed air. True airspeed is equal to equivalent airspeed multiplied by $(\rho 0/\rho)^{1/2}$.

Traffic pattern means the traffic flow that is prescribed for aircraft landing at, taxiing on, or taking off from, an airport.

Type:

(1) As used with respect to the certification, ratings, privileges, and limitations of airmen, means a specific make and basic model of aircraft, including modifications thereto that do not change its handling or flight characteristics. Examples include: DC–7, 1049, and F–27; and

(2) As used with respect to the certification of aircraft, means those aircraft which are similar in design. Examples include: DC–7 and DC–7C; 1049G and 1049H; and F–27 and F–27F.

(3) As used with respect to the certification of aircraft engines means those engines which are similar in design. For example, JT8D and JT8D–7 are engines of the same type, and JT9D–3A and JT9D–7 are engines of the same type.

United States, in a geographical sense, means (1) the States, the District of Columbia, Puerto Rico, and the posses-sions, including the territorial waters, and (2) the airspace of those areas.

United States air carrier means a citizen of the United States who undertakes directly by lease, or other arrangement, to engage in air transportation.

VFR over-the-top, with respect to the operation of aircraft, means the operation of an aircraft over-the-top under VFR when it is not being operated on an IFR flight plan.

Warning area. A warning area is airspace of defined dimensions, extending from 3 nautical miles outward from the coast of the United States, that contains activity that may be hazardous to nonparticipating aircraft. The purpose of such warning areas is to warn nonparticipating pilots of the potential danger. A warning area may be located over domestic or international waters or both.

Winglet or tip fin means an out-of-plane surface extending from a lifting surface. The surface may or may not have control surfaces.

[Doc. No. 1150, 27 FR 4588, May 15, 1962]

EDITORIAL NOTE: For FEDERAL REGISTER citations affecting §1.1, see the List of CFR Sections Affected, which appears in the Finding Aids section of the printed volume and on GPO Access.

§1.2 Abbreviations and symbols.

In Subchapters A through K of this chapter:

AGL means above ground level.

ALS means approach light system.

ASR means airport surveillance radar.

ATC means air traffic control.

CAS means calibrated airspeed.

CAT II means Category II.

CONSOL or *CONSOLAN* means a kind of low or medium frequency long range navigational aid.

DH means decision height.

DME means distance measuring equipment compatible with TACAN.

EAS means equivalent airspeed.

FAA means Federal Aviation Administration.

FM means fan marker.

GS means glide slope.

HIRL means high-intensity runway light system.

IAS means indicated airspeed.

ICAO means International Civil Aviation Organization.

IFR means instrument flight rules.

ILS means instrument landing system.

IM means ILS inner marker.

INT means intersection.

LDA means localizer-type directional aid.

LFR means low-frequency radio range.

LMM means compass locator at middle marker.

LOC means ILS localizer.

LOM means compass locator at outer marker.

M means mach number.

MAA means maximum authorized IFR altitude.

MALS means medium intensity approach light system.

MALSR means medium intensity approach light system with runway alignment indicator lights.

MCA means minimum crossing altitude.

MDA means minimum descent altitude.

MEA means minimum en route IFR altitude.

MM means ILS middle marker.

MOCA means minimum obstruction clearance altitude.

MRA means minimum reception altitude.

MSL means mean sea level.

NDB(ADF) means nondirectional beacon (automatic direction finder).

NOPT means no procedure turn required.

OEI means one engine inoperative.

OM means ILS outer marker.

PAR means precision approach radar.

RAIL means runway alignment indicator light system.

RBN means radio beacon.

RCLM means runway centerline marking.

RCLS means runway centerline light system.

REIL means runway end identification lights.

'RR'' means low or medium frequency radio range station.

RVR means runway visual range as measured in the touchdown zone area.

SALS means short approach light system.

SSALS means simplified short approach light system.

SSALSR means simplified short approach light system with runway alignment indicator lights.

TACAN means ultra-high frequency tactical air navigational aid.

TAS means true airspeed.

TCAS means a traffic alert and collision avoidance system.

TDZL means touchdown zone lights.

TVOR means very high frequency terminal omnirange station.

V_A means design maneuvering speed.

V_B means design speed for maximum gust intensity.

V_C means design cruising speed.

V_D means design diving speed.

V_{DF}/M_{DF} means demonstrated flight diving speed.

V_{EF} means the speed at which the critical engine is assumed to fail during takeoff.

V_F means design flap speed.

V_{FC}/M_{FC} means maximum speed for stability characteristics.

V_{FE} means maximum flap extended speed.

V_{FTO} means final takeoff speed.

V_H means maximum speed in level flight with maximum continuous power.

V_{LE} means maximum landing gear extended speed.

V_{LO} means maximum landing gear operating speed.

V_{LOF} means lift-off speed.

V_{MC} means minimum control speed with the critical engine inoperative.

V_{MO}/M_{MO} means maximum operating limit speed.

V_{MU} means minimum unstick speed.

V_{NE} means never-exceed speed.

V_{NO} means maximum structural cruising speed.

V_R means rotation speed.

V_{REF} means reference landing speed.

V_S means the stalling speed or the minimum steady flight speed at which the airplane is controllable.

V_{S0} means the stalling speed or the minimum steady flight speed in the landing configuration.

V_{S1} means the stalling speed or the minimum steady flight speed obtained in a specific configuration.

V_{SR} means reference stall speed.

V_{SR0} means reference stall speed in the landing configuration.

V_{SR1} means reference stall speed in a specific configuration.

V_{SW} means speed at which onset of natural or artificial stall warning occurs.

V_{TOSS} means takeoff safety speed for Category A rotorcraft.

V_X means speed for best angle of climb.

V_Y means speed for best rate of climb.

V_1 means the maximum speed in the takeoff at which the pilot must take the first action (e.g., apply brakes, reduce thrust, deploy speed brakes) to stop the airplane within the accelerate-stop distance. V_1 also means the minimum speed in the takeoff, following a failure of the critical engine at V_{EF}, at which the pilot can continue the takeoff and achieve the required height above the takeoff surface within the takeoff distance.

V_2 means takeoff safety speed.

V_{2min} means minimum takeoff safety speed.

VFR means visual flight rules.

VHF means very high frequency.

VOR means very high frequency omnirange station.

VORTAC means collocated VOR and TACAN.

[Doc. No. 1150, 27 FR 4590, May 15, 1962]

EDITORIAL NOTE: For FEDERAL REGISTER citations affecting §1.2, see the List of CFR Sections Affected, which appears in the Finding Aids section of the printed volume and on GPO Access.

§1.3 Rules of construction.

(a) In Subchapters A through K of this chapter, unless the context requires otherwise:

(1) Words importing the singular include the plural;

(2) Words importing the plural include the singular; and

(3) Words importing the masculine gender include the feminine.

(b) In Subchapters A through K of this chapter, the word:

(1) *Shall* is used in an imperative sense;

(2) *May* is used in a permissive sense to state authority or permission to do the act prescribed, and the words "no person may * * *" or "a person may not * * *" mean that no person is required, authorized, or permitted to do the act prescribed; and

(3) *Includes* means "includes but is not limited to".

[Doc. No. 1150, 27 FR 4590, May 15, 1962, as amended by Amdt. 1–10, 31 FR 5055, Mar. 29, 1966]

SUBCHAPTER B—PROCEDURAL RULES

PART 11—GENERAL RULEMAKING PROCEDURES

Subpart A—Rulemaking Procedures

AUTHORITY: 49 U.S.C. 106(g), 40101, 40103, 40105, 40109, 40113, 44110, 44502, 44701–44702, 44711, and 46102.

SOURCE: Docket No. 1999–6622, 65 FR 50863, Aug. 21, 2000, unless otherwise noted.

EDITORIAL NOTE: Nomenclature changes to part 11 appear at 61 FR 18052, April 24, 1996.

Subpart A—Rulemaking Procedures

§ 11.1 To what does this part apply?

This part applies to the issuance, amendment, and repeal of any regulation for which FAA ("we") follows public rulemaking procedures under the Administrative Procedure Act ("APA") (5 U.S.C. 553).

DEFINITION OF TERMS

§ 11.3 What is an advance notice of proposed rulemaking?

An advance notice of proposed rulemaking (ANPRM) tells the public that FAA is considering an area for rulemaking and requests written comments on the appropriate scope of the rulemaking or on specific topics. An advance notice of proposed rulemaking may or may not include the text of potential changes to a regulation.

§ 11.5 What is a notice of proposed rulemaking?

A notice of proposed rulemaking (NPRM) proposes FAA's specific regulatory changes for public comment and contains supporting information. It includes proposed regulatory text.

§ 11.7 What is a supplemental notice of proposed rulemaking?

On occasion, FAA may decide that it needs more information on an issue, or that we should take a different approach than we proposed. Also, we may want to follow a commenter's suggestion that goes beyond the scope of the original proposed rule. In these cases, FAA may issue a supplemental notice of proposed rulemaking (SNPRM) to give the public an opportunity to comment further or to give us more information.

§ 11.9 What is a final rule?

A final rule sets out new or revised requirements and their effective date. It also may remove requirements. When preceded by an NPRM, a final rule will also identify significant substantive issues raised by commenters in response to the NPRM and will give the agency's response.

§ 11.11 What is a final rule with request for comments?

A final rule with request for comment is a rule that the FAA issues in final (with an effective date) that invites public comment on the rule. We usually do this when we have not first issued an ANPRM or NPRM, because we have found that doing so would be impracticable, unnecessary, or contrary to the public interest. We give our reasons for our determination in the preamble. The comment period often ends after the effective date of the rule. A final rule not preceded by an ANPRM or NPRM is commonly called an "immediately adopted final rule." We invite comments on these rules only if we think that we will receive useful information. For example, we would not invite comments when we are just making an editorial clarification or correction.

§ 11.13 What is a direct final rule?

A direct final rule is a type of final rule with request for comments. Our reason for issuing a direct final rule without an NPRM is that we would not expect to receive any adverse comments, and so an NPRM is unnecessary. However, to be certain that we are correct, we set the comment period to end before the effective date. If we receive an adverse comment or notice of intent to file an adverse comment, we then withdraw the final rule before it becomes effective and may issue an NPRM.

§ 11.15 What is a petition for exemption?

A petition for exemption is a request to FAA by an individual or entity asking for relief from the requirements of a current regulation.

§ 11.17 What is a petition for rulemaking?

A petition for rulemaking is a request to FAA by an individual or entity asking the FAA to adopt, amend, or repeal a regulation.

§ 11.19 What is a special condition?

A special condition is a regulation that applies to a particular aircraft design. The FAA issues special conditions when we find that the airworthiness regulations for an aircraft, aircraft engine, or propeller design do not contain adequate or appropriate safety standards, because of a novel or unusual design feature.

GENERAL

§ 11.21 What are the most common kinds of rulemaking actions for which FAA follows the Administrative Procedure Act?

FAA follows the Administrative Procedure Act (APA) procedures for these common types of rules:

(a) Rules found in the Code of Federal Regulations;

(b) Airworthiness directives issued under part 39 of this chapter; and

(c) Airspace Designations issued under various parts of this chapter.

§ 11.23 Does FAA follow the same procedures in issuing all types of rules?

Yes, in general, FAA follows the same procedures for all rule types. There are some differences as to which FAA official has authority to issue each type, and where you send petitions for FAA to adopt, amend, or repeal each type. Assume that the procedures in this subpart apply to all rules, except where we specify otherwise.

§ 11.25 How does FAA issue rules?

(a) The FAA uses APA rulemaking procedures to adopt, amend, or repeal regulations. To propose or adopt a new regulation, or to change a current regulation, FAA will issue one or more of the following documents. We publish these rulemaking documents in the FEDERAL REGISTER unless we name and personally serve a copy of a rule on every person subject to it. We also make all documents available to the public by posting them in the Department of Transportation's electronic docket at http://dms.dot.gov.

(1) An advance notice of proposed rulemaking (ANPRM).

(2) A notice of proposed rulemaking (NPRM).

(3) A supplemental notice of proposed rulemaking (SNPRM).

(4) A final rule.

(5) A final rule with request for comments.

(6) A direct final rule.

(b) Each of the rulemaking documents in paragraph (a) of this section generally contains the following information:

(1) The topic involved in the rulemaking document.

(2) FAA's legal authority for issuing the rulemaking document.

(3) How interested persons may participate in the rulemaking proceeding (for example, by filing written comments or making oral presentations at a public meeting).

(4) Whom to call if you have questions about the rulemaking document.

(5) The date, time, and place of any public meetings FAA will hold to discuss the rulemaking document.

(6) The docket number and regulation identifier number (RIN) for the rulemaking proceeding.

§ 11.27 Are there other ways FAA collects specific rulemaking recommendations before we issue an NPRM?

Yes, the FAA obtains advice and recommendations from rulemaking advisory committees. One of these committees is the Aviation Rulemaking Advisory Committee (ARAC), which is a formal standing committee comprised of representatives of aviation associations and industry, consumer groups, and interested individuals. In conducting its activities, ARAC complies with the Federal Advisory Committee Act and the direction of FAA. We task ARAC with providing us with recommended rulemaking actions dealing with specific areas and problems. If we accept an ARAC recommendation to change an FAA rule, we ordinarily publish an NPRM using the procedures in this part. The FAA may establish other rulemaking advisory committees as needed to focus on specific issues for a limited period of time.

§ 11.29 May FAA change its regulations without first issuing an ANPRM or NPRM?

The FAA normally adds or changes a regulation by issuing a final rule after an NPRM. However, FAA may adopt, amend, or repeal regulations without first issuing an ANPRM or NPRM in the following situations:

(a) We may issue a final rule without first requesting public comment if, for good cause, we find that an NPRM is impracticable, unnecessary, or contrary to the public interest. We place that finding and a brief statement of the reasons for it in the final rule. For example, we may issue a final rule in response to a safety emergency.

(b) If an NPRM would be unnecessary because we do not expect to receive adverse comment, we may issue a direct final rule.

§ 11.31 How does FAA process direct final rules?

(a) A direct final rule will take effect on a specified date unless FAA receives an adverse comment or notice of intent to file an adverse comment within the comment period—generally 60 days after the direct final rule is published in the FEDERAL REGISTER. An adverse comment explains why a rule would be inappropriate, or would be ineffective or unacceptable without a change. It may challenge the rule's underlying premise or approach. Under the direct final rule process, we do not consider the following types of comments to be adverse:

(1) A comment recommending another rule change, in addition to the change in the direct final rule at issue. We consider the comment adverse, however, if the commenter states why the direct final rule would be ineffective without the change.

(2) A frivolous or insubstantial comment.

(b) If FAA has not received an adverse comment or notice of intent to file an adverse comment, we will publish a confirmation document in the FEDERAL REGISTER, generally within 15 days after the comment period closes. The confirmation document tells the public the effective date of the rule.

(c) If we receive an adverse comment or notice of intent to file an adverse comment, we will advise the public by publishing a document in the FEDERAL REGISTER before the effective date of the direct final rule. This document may withdraw the direct final rule in whole or in part. If we withdraw a direct final rule because of an adverse comment, we may incorporate the commenter's recommendation into another direct final rule or may publish a notice of proposed rulemaking.

§ 11.33 How can I track FAA's rulemaking activities?

The best ways to track FAA's rulemaking activities are with the docket number or the regulation identifier number.

(a) *Docket number.* We assign a docket number to each rulemaking proceeding. Each rulemaking document FAA issues in a particular rulemaking proceeding, as well as public comments on the proceeding, will display the same docket number. This number allows you to search DOT's Docket Management System (DMS) for information on most rulemaking proceedings. You can view and copy docket materials during regular business hours at the U.S. Department of Transportation, Plaza Level 401, 400 7th Street, SW., Washington, DC 20590–0001. Or you can view and download docketed materials through the Internet at http://dms.dot.gov. If you can't find the material in the electronic docket, contact the person listed under **FOR FURTHER INFORMATION CONTACT** in the document you are interested in.

(b) *Regulation identifier number.* DOT publishes a semiannual agenda of all current and projected DOT rulemakings, reviews of existing regulations, and completed actions. This semiannual agenda appears in the Unified Agenda of Federal Regulations, published in the FEDERAL REGISTER in April and October of each year. The semiannual agenda tells the public about DOT's—including FAA's—regulatory activities. DOT assigns a regulation identifier number (RIN) to each individual rulemaking proceeding in the semiannual agenda. This number appears on all rulemaking documents published in the FEDERAL REGISTER and makes it easy for you to track those rulemaking proceedings in both the FEDERAL REGISTER and the semiannual regulatory agenda.

§ 11.35 Does FAA include sensitive security information and proprietary information in the Docket Management System (DMS)?

(a) *Sensitive security information.* You should not submit sensitive security information to the rulemaking docket, unless you are invited to do so in our request for comments. If we ask for this information, we will tell you in the specific document how to submit this information, and we will provide a separate non-public docket for it. For all proposed rule changes involving civil aviation security, we review comments as we receive them, before they are placed in the docket. If we find that a comment contains sensitive security information, we remove that information before placing the comment in the general docket.

(b) *Proprietary information.* When we are aware of proprietary information filed with a comment, we do not place it in the docket. We hold it in a separate file to which the public does not have access, and place a note in the docket that we have received it. If we receive a request to examine or copy this information, we treat it as any other request under the Freedom of Information Act (5 U.S.C. 552). We process such a request under the DOT procedures found in 49 CFR part 7.

§ 11.37 Where can I find information about an Airworthiness Directive, an airspace designation, or a petition handled in a region?

The FAA includes most documents concerning Airworthiness Directives, airspace designations, or petitions handled in a region in the electronic docket. If the information isn't in the docket, contact the person listed under **FOR FURTHER INFORMATION CONTACT** in the FEDERAL REGISTER document about the action.

§ 11.38 What public comment procedures does the FAA follow for Special Conditions?

Even though the Administrative Procedure Act does not require notice and comment for rules of particular applicability, FAA does publish proposed special conditions for comment. In the following circumstances we may not invite comment before we issue a special condition. If we don't, we will invite comment when we publish the final special condition.

(a) The FAA considers prior notice to be impracticable if issuing a design approval would significantly delay delivery of the affected aircraft. We consider such a delay to be contrary to the public interest.

(b) The FAA considers prior notice to be unnecessary if we have provided previous opportunities to comment on substantially identical proposed special conditions, and we are satisfied that new comments are unlikely.

§ 11.39 How may I participate in FAA's rulemaking process?

You may participate in FAA's rulemaking process by doing any of the following:

(a) File written comments on any rulemaking document that asks for comments, including an ANPRM, NPRM, SNPRM, a final rule with request for comments, or a direct final rule. Follow the directions for commenting found in each rulemaking document.

(b) Ask that we hold a public meeting on any rulemaking, and participate in any public meeting that we hold.

(c) File a petition for rulemaking that asks us to adopt, amend, or repeal a regulation.

§ 11.40 Can I get more information about a rulemaking?

You can contact the person listed under **FOR FURTHER INFORMATION CONTACT** in the preamble of a rule. That person can explain the meaning and intent of a proposed rule, the technical aspects of a document, the terminology in a document, and can tell you our published schedule for the rulemaking process. We cannot give you information that is not already available to other members of the public. Department of Transportation policy on oral communications with the public during rulemaking appears in appendix 1 of this part.

WRITTEN COMMENTS

§ 11.41 Who may file comments?

Anyone may file written comments about proposals and final rules that request public comments.

§ 11.43 What information must I put in my written comments?

(a) Your written comments must be in English and must contain the following:

(1) The docket number of the rulemaking document you are commenting

on, clearly set out at the beginning of your comments.

(2) Your name and mailing address, and, if you wish, other contact information, such as a fax number, telephone number, or e-mail address.

(3) Your information, views, or arguments, following the instructions for participation in the rulemaking document on which you are commenting.

(b) You should also include all material relevant to any statement of fact or argument in your comments, to the extent that the material is available to you and reasonable for you to submit. Include a copy of the title page of the document. Whether or not you submit a copy of the material to which you refer, you should indicate specific places in the material that support your position.

§ 11.45 Where and when do I file my comments?

(a) Send your comments to the location specified in the rulemaking document on which you are commenting. If you are asked to send your comments to the Docket Management System, you may send them in either of the following ways:

(1) By mail to: U.S. Department of Transportation, Docket Management System, 400 7th Street, SW., Plaza Level 401, Washington, DC 20591.

(2) Through the Internet to http://dms.dot.gov/.

(3) In any other manner designated by FAA.

(b) Make sure that your comments reach us by the deadline set out in the rulemaking document on which you are commenting. We will consider late-filed comments to the extent possible only if they do not significantly delay the rulemaking process.

(c) We may reject your paper or electronic comments if they are frivolous, abusive, or repetitious. We may reject comments you file electronically if you do not follow the electronic filing instructions at the Docket Management System web site.

§ 11.47 May I ask for more time to file my comments?

Yes, if FAA grants your request for more time to file comments, we grant all persons the same amount of time.

We will notify the public of the extension by a document in the FEDERAL REGISTER. If FAA denies your request, we will notify you of the denial. To ask for more time, you must file a written or electronic request for extension at least 10 days before the end of the comment period. Your letter or message must—

(a) Show the docket number of the rule at the top of the first page;

(b) State, at the beginning, that you are requesting an extension of the comment period;

(c) Show that you have good cause for the extension and that an extension is in the public interest;

(d) Be sent to the address specified for comments in the rulemaking document on which you are commenting.

PUBLIC MEETINGS AND OTHER
PROCEEDINGS

§ 11.51 May I request that FAA hold a public meeting on a rulemaking action?

Yes, you may request that we hold a public meeting. FAA holds a public meeting when we need more than written comments to make a fully informed decision. Submit your written request to the address specified in the rulemaking document on which you are commenting. Specify at the top of your letter or message that you are requesting that the agency hold a public meeting. Submit your request no later than 30 days after our rulemaking notice. If we find good cause for a meeting, we will notify you and publish a notice of the meeting in the FEDERAL REGISTER.

§ 11.53 What takes place at a public meeting?

A public meeting is a non-adversarial, fact-finding proceeding conducted by an FAA representative. Public meetings are announced in the FEDERAL REGISTER. We invite interested persons to attend and to present their views to the agency on specific issues. There are no formal pleadings and no adverse parties, and any regulation issued afterward is not necessarily based exclusively on the record of the meeting.

PETITIONS FOR RULEMAKING AND FOR EXEMPTION

§ 11.61 May I ask FAA to adopt, amend, or repeal a regulation, or grant relief from the requirements of a current regulation?

(a) Using a petition for rulemaking, you may ask FAA to add a new regulation to title 14 of the Code of Federal Regulations (14 CFR) or ask FAA to amend or repeal a current regulation in 14 CFR.

(b) Using a petition for exemption, you may ask FAA to grant you relief from current regulations in 14 CFR.

§ 11.63 How and to whom do I submit my petition for rulemaking or petition for exemption?

(a) For paper submissions, send the original signed copy of your petition for rulemaking or exemption to this address: U.S. Department of Transportation, Docket Management System, 400 7th Street, SW., Room PL 401, Washington, DC 20591-0001.

(b) For electronic submissions, submit your petition to FAA through the Internet using the Docket Management System web site at this Internet address: http://dms.dot.gov/.

(c) In the future, FAA may designate other means by which you can submit petitions.

(d) Submit your petition for exemption 120 days before you need the exemption to take effect.

§ 11.71 What information must I include in my petition for rulemaking?

(a) You must include the following information in your petition for rulemaking:

(1) Your name and mailing address and, if you wish, other contact information such as a fax number, telephone number, or e-mail address.

(2) An explanation of your proposed action and its purpose.

(3) The language you propose for a new or amended rule, or the language you would remove from a current rule.

(4) An explanation of why your proposed action would be in the public interest.

(5) Information and arguments that support your proposed action, including relevant technical and scientific data available to you.

(6) Any specific facts or circumstances that support or demonstrate the need for the action you propose.

(b) In the process of considering your petition, we may ask that you provide information or data available to you about the following:

(1) The costs and benefits of your proposed action to society in general, and identifiable groups within society in particular.

(2) The regulatory burden of your proposed action on small businesses, small organizations, small governmental jurisdictions, and Indian tribes.

(3) The recordkeeping and reporting burdens of your proposed action and whom the burdens would affect.

(4) The effect of your proposed action on the quality of the natural and social environments.

§ 11.73 How does FAA process petitions for rulemaking?

After we have determined the disposition of your petition, we will contact you in writing about our decision. The FAA may respond to your petition for rulemaking in one of the following ways:

(a) If we determine that your petition justifies our taking the action you suggest, we may issue an NPRM or ANPRM. We will do so no later than 6 months after the date we receive your petition. In making our decision, we consider:

(1) The immediacy of the safety or security concerns you raise;

(2) The priority of other issues the FAA must deal with; and

(3) The resources we have available to address these issues.

(b) If we have issued an ANPRM or NPRM on the subject matter of your petition, we will consider your arguments for a rule change as a comment in connection with the rulemaking proceeding. We will not treat your petition as a separate action.

(c) If we have begun a rulemaking project in the subject area of your petition, we will consider your comments and arguments for a rule change as part of that project. We will not treat your petition as a separate action.

(d) If we have tasked ARAC to study the general subject area of your petition, we will ask ARAC to review and evaluate your proposed action. We will not treat your petition as a separate action.

(e) If we determine that the issues you identify in your petition may have merit, but do not address an immediate safety concern or cannot be addressed because of other priorities and resource constraints, we may dismiss your petition. Your comments and arguments for a rule change will be placed in a database, which we will examine when we consider future rulemaking.

§ 11.75 Does FAA invite public comment on petitions for rulemaking?

Generally, FAA does not invite public comment on petitions for rulemaking.

§ 11.77 Is there any additional information I must include in my petition for designating airspace?

In petitions asking FAA to establish, amend, or repeal a designation of airspace, including special use airspace, you must include all the information specified by § 11.71 and also:

(a) The location and a description of the airspace you want assigned or designated;

(b) A complete description of the activity or use to be made of that airspace, including a detailed description of the type, volume, duration, time, and place of the operations to be conducted in the area;

(c) A description of the air navigation, air traffic control, surveillance, and communication facilities available and to be provided if we grant the designation; and

(d) The name and location of the agency, office, facility, or person who would have authority to permit the use of the airspace when it was not in use for the purpose to which you want it assigned.

§ 11.81 What information must I include in my petition for an exemption?

You must include the following information in your petition for an exemption and submit it to FAA as soon as you know you need an exemption.

(a) Your name and mailing address and, if you wish, other contact information such as a fax number, telephone number, or e-mail address;

(b) The specific section or sections of 14 CFR from which you seek an exemption;

(c) The extent of relief you seek, and the reason you seek the relief;

(d) The reasons why granting your request would be in the public interest; that is, how it would benefit the public as a whole;

(e) The reasons why granting the exemption would not adversely affect safety, or how the exemption would provide a level of safety at least equal to that provided by the rule from which you seek the exemption;

(f) A summary we can publish in the FEDERAL REGISTER, stating:

(1) The rule from which you seek the exemption; and

(2) A brief description of the nature of the exemption you seek;

(g) Any additional information, views or arguments available to support your request; and

(h) If you want to exercise the privileges of your exemption outside the United States, the reason why you need to do so.

§ 11.83 How can I operate under an exemption outside the United States?

If you want to be able to operate under your exemption outside the United States, you must request this when you petition for relief and give us the reason for this use. If you do not provide your reason or we determine that it does not justify this relief, we will limit your exemption to use within the United States. Before we extend your exemption for use outside the United States, we will verify that the exemption would be in compliance with the Standards of the International Civil Aviation Organization (ICAO). If it would not, but we still believe it would be in the public interest to allow you to do so, we will file a difference with ICAO. However, a foreign country still may not allow you to operate in that country without meeting the ICAO standard.

§ 11.85 Does FAA invite public comment on petitions for exemption?

Yes, FAA publishes information about petitions for exemption in the FEDERAL REGISTER. The information includes—

(a) The docket number of the petition;

(b) The citation to the rule or rules from which the petitioner requested relief;

(c) The name of the petitioner;

(d) The petitioner's summary of the action requested and the reasons for requesting it; and

(e) A request for comments to assist FAA in evaluating the petition.

§ 11.87 Are there circumstances in which FAA may decide not to publish a summary of my petition for exemption?

The FAA may not publish a summary of your petition for exemption and request comments if you present or we find good cause why we should not delay action on your petition. The factors we consider in deciding not to request comment include:

(a) Whether granting your petition would set a precedent.

(b) Whether the relief requested is identical to exemptions granted previously.

(c) Whether our delaying action on your petition would affect you adversely.

(d) Whether you filed your petition in a timely manner.

§ 11.89 How much time do I have to submit comments to FAA on a petition for exemption?

The FAA states the specific time allowed for comments in the FEDERAL REGISTER notice about the petition. We usually allow 20 days to comment on a petition for exemption.

§ 11.91 How does FAA inform me of its decision on my petition for exemption?

(a) The FAA will notify you in writing about its decision on your petition.

(b) The FAA publishes a summary in the FEDERAL REGISTER that includes—

(1) The docket number of your petition;

(2) Your name;

(3) The citation to the rules from which you requested relief;

(4) A brief description of the general nature of the relief requested;

(5) Whether FAA granted or denied the request;

(6) The date of FAA's decision; and

(7) An exemption number.

§ 11.101 May I ask FAA to reconsider my petition for rulemaking or petition for exemption if it is denied?

Yes, you may petition FAA to reconsider your petition denial. You must submit your request to the address to which you sent your original petition, and FAA must receive it within 60 days after we issued the denial. For us to accept your petition, show the following:

(a) That you have a significant additional fact and why you did not present it in your original petition;

(b) That we made an important factual error in our denial of your original petition; or

(c) That we did not correctly interpret a law, regulation, or precedent.

Subpart B—Paperwork Reduction Act Control Numbers

§ 11.201 Office of Management and Budget (OMB) control numbers assigned under the Paperwork Reduction Act.

(a) The Paperwork Reduction Act of 1995 (44 U.S.C. 3501–3520) requires FAA to get approval from OMB for our information collection activities, and to list a record of those approvals in the FEDERAL REGISTER. This subpart lists the control numbers OMB assigned to FAA's information collection activities.

(b) The table listing OMB control numbers assigned to FAA's information collection activities follows:

14 CFR part or section identified and described	Current OMB control number
Part 14	2120–0539
Part 17	2120–0632
Part 21	2120–0018, 2120–0552
Part 34	2120–0508
Part 39	2120–0056
Part 43	2120–0020
Part 45	2120–0508
Part 47	2120–0024, 2120–0042
Part 49	2120–0043
Part 61	2120–0021, 2120–0034, 2120–0543, 2120–0571

14 CFR part or section identified and described	Current OMB control number
Part 63	2120–0007
Part 65	2120–0022, 2120–0535, 2120–0571, 2120–0648
Part 67	2120–0034, 2120–0543
Part 77	2120–0001
Part 91	2120–0005, 2120–0026, 2120–0027, 2120–0573, 2120–0606, 2120–0620, 2120–0631, 2120–0651
Part 93	2120–0524, 2120–0606, 2120–0639
Part 101	2120–0027
Part 105	2120–0027, 2120–0641
Part 107	2120–0075, 2120–0554, 2120–0628
Part 108	2120–0098, 2120–0554, 2120–0577, 2120–0628, 2120–0642
Part 109	2120–0505
Part 119	2120–0593
Part 121	2120–0008, 2120–0028, 2120–0535, 2120–0571, 2120–0600, 2120–0606, 2120–0614, 2120–0616, 2120–0631, 2120–0651, 2120–0653
Part 125	2120–0028, 2120–0085, 2120–0616, 2120–0651
Part 129	2120–0028, 2120–0536, 2120–0616, 2120–0638
Part 133	2120–0044
Part 135	2120–0003, 2120–0028, 2120–0039, 2120–0535, 2120–0571, 2120–0600, 2120–0606, 2120–0614, 2120–0616, 2120–0620, 2120–0631, 2120–0653
Part 137	2120–0049
Part 139	2120–0045, 2120–0063
Part 141	2120–0009
Part 142	2120–0570
Part 145	2120–0003, 2120–0010, 2120–0571
Part 147	2120–0040
Part 150	2120–0517
Part 157	2120–0036
Part 158	2120–0557
Part 161	2120–0563
Part 171	2120–0014
Part 183	2120–0033, 2120–0604
Part 193	2120–0646
Part 198	2120–0514
Part 400	2120–0643, 2120–0644, 0649
Part 401	2120–0608
Part 440	2120–0601
SFAR 36	2120–0507
SFAR 71	2120–0620

[Doc. No. 1999–6622, 65 FR 50863, Aug. 21, 2000, as amended by Amdt. 11–47, 67 FR 9553, Mar. 1, 2002]

APPENDIX 1 TO PART 11—ORAL COMMUNICATIONS WITH THE PUBLIC DURING RULEMAKING

1. What is an ex parte contact?

"Ex parte" is a Latin term that means "one sided," and indicates that not all par-

ties to an issue were present when it was discussed. An ex parte contact involving rulemaking is any communication between FAA and someone outside the government regarding a specific rulemaking proceeding, before that proceeding closes. A rulemaking proceeding does not close until we publish the final rule or withdraw the NPRM. Because an ex parte contact excludes other interested persons, including the rest of the public, from the communication, it may give an unfair advantage to one party, or appear to do so.

2. Are written comments to the docket ex parte contacts?

Written comments submitted to the docket are not ex parte contacts because they are available for inspection by all members of the public.

3. What is DOT policy on ex parte contacts?

It is DOT policy to provide for open development of rules and to encourage full public participation in rulemaking actions. In addition to providing opportunity to respond in writing to an NPRM and to appear and be heard at a hearing, DOT policy encourages agencies to contact the public directly when we need factual information to resolve questions of substance. It also encourages DOT agencies to be receptive to appropriate contacts from persons affected by or interested in a proposed action. But under some circumstances an ex parte contact could affect the basic openness and fairness of the rulemaking process. Even the appearance of impropriety can affect public confidence in the process. For this reason, DOT policy sets careful guidelines for these contacts. The kind of ex parte contacts permitted and the procedures we follow depend on when the contact occurs in the rulemaking process.

4. What kinds of ex parte contacts does DOT policy permit before we issue an ANPRM, NPRM, Supplemental NPRM, or immediately adopted final rule?

The DOT policy authorizes ex parte contacts that we need to obtain technical and economic information. We need this information to decide whether to issue a regulation and what it should say. Each contact that influences our development of the regulation is noted in the preamble. For multiple contacts that are similar, we may provide only a general discussion. For contacts not discussed in the preamble, we place a report discussing each contact or group of related contacts in the rulemaking docket when it is opened.

5. Does DOT policy permit ex parte contacts during the comment period?

No, during the comment period, the public docket is available for written comments

27

from any member of the public. These comments can be examined and responded to by any interested person. Because this public forum is available, DOT policy discourages ex parte contacts during the comment period. They are not necessary to collect the information the agency needs to make its decision.

6. What if the FAA believes it needs to meet with members of the public to discuss the proposal?

If the FAA determines that it would be helpful to invite members of the public to make oral presentations to it regarding the proposal, we will announce a public meeting in the FEDERAL REGISTER.

7. Are any oral contacts concerning the proposal permitted during the comment period?

If you contact the agency with questions regarding the proposal during the comment period, we can only provide you with information that has already been made available to the general public. If you contact the agency to discuss the proposal, you will be told that the proper avenue of communication during the comment period is a written communication to the docket.

8. If a substantive ex parte contact does occur during the comment period, what does FAA do?

While FAA tries to ensure that FAA personnel and the public are aware of DOT policy, substantive ex parte contacts do occasionally occur, for example, at meetings not intended for that purpose. In such a case, we place a summary of the contact and a copy of any materials provided at the meeting in the rulemaking docket. We encourage participants in such a meeting to file written comments in the docket.

9. Does DOT policy permit ex parte contacts the comment period has closed?

DOT policy strongly discourages ex parte contacts initiated by commenters to discuss their position on the proposal once the comment period has closed. Such a contact at this time would be improper, since other interested persons would not have an opportunity to respond. If we need further information regarding a comment in the docket, we may request this from a commenter. A record of this contact and the information provided is placed in the docket. If we need to make other contacts to update factual information, such as economic data, we will disclose this information in the final rule docket or in the economic studies accompanying it, which are available in the docket.

10. What if FAA needs to meet with interested persons to discuss the proposal after the comment period has closed?

If FAA determines that it would be helpful to meet with a person or group after the close of the comment period to discuss a course of action to be taken, we will announce the meeting in the FEDERAL REGISTER. We will also consider reopening the comment period. If an inappropriate ex parte contact does occur after the comment period closes, a summary of the contact and a copy of any material distributed during meeting will be placed in the docket if it could be seen as influencing the rulemaking process.

11. Under what circumstances will FAA reopen the comment period?

If we receive an ex parte communication after the comment period has closed that could substantially influence the rulemaking, we may reopen the comment period. DOT policy requires the agency to carefully consider whether the substance of the contact will give the commenter an unfair advantage, since the rest of the public may not see the record of the contact in the docket. When the substance of a proposed rule is significantly changed as a result of such an oral communication, DOT policy and practice requires that the comment period be reopened by issuing a supplemental NPRM in which the reasons for the change are discussed.

12. What if I have important information for FAA and the comment period is closed?

You may always provide FAA with written information after the close of the comment period and it will be considered if time permits. Because contacts after the close of the comment may not be seen by other interested persons, if they substantially and specifically influence the FAA's decision, we may need to reopen the comment period.

PART 13—INVESTIGATIVE AND ENFORCEMENT PROCEDURES

Subpart A—Investigative Procedures

Subpart I—Flight Operational Quality Assurance Programs

AUTHORITY: 18 U.S.C. 6002; 28 U.S.C. 2461 (note); 49 U.S.C. 106(g), 5121–5124, 40113–40114, 44103–44106, 44702–44703, 44709–44710, 44713, 46101–46110, 46301–46316, 46501–46502, 46504–46507, 47106, 47111, 47122, 47306, 47531–47532.

SOURCE: Docket No. 18884, 44 FR 63723, Nov. 5, 1979, unless otherwise noted.

Subpart A—Investigative Procedures

§ 13.1 Reports of violations.

(a) Any person who knows of a violation of the Federal Aviation Act of 1958, as amended, the Hazardous Materials Transportation Act relating to the transportation or shipment by air of hazardous materials, the Airport and Airway Development Act of 1970, the Airport and Airway Improvement Act of 1982, the Airport and Airway Improvement Act of 1982 as amended by the Airport and Airway Safety and Capacity Expansion Act of 1987, or any rule, regulation, or order issued thereunder, should report it to appropriate personnel of any FAA regional or district office.

(b) Each report made under this section, together with any other information the FAA may have that is relevant to the matter reported, will be reviewed by FAA personnel to determine the nature and type of any additional investigation or enforcement action the FAA will take.

[Doc. No. 18884, 44 FR 63723, Nov. 5, 1979, as amended by Amdt. 13–17, 53 FR 33783, Aug. 31, 1988]

§ 13.3 Investigations (general).

(a) Under the Federal Aviation Act of 1958, as amended, (49 U.S.C. 1301 *et seq.*), the Hazardous Materials Transportation Act (49 U.S.C. 1801 *et seq.*), the Airport and Airway Development Act of 1970 (49 U.S.C. 1701 *et seq.*), the Airport and Airway Improvement Act of 1982 (49 U.S.C. 2201 *et seq.*), the Airport and Airway Improvement Act of 1982 (as amended, 49 U.S.C. App. 2201 *et seq.*, Airport and Airway Safety and Capacity Expansion Act of 1987), and the Regulations of the Office of the Secretary of Transportation (49 CFR 1 *et seq.*), the Administrator may conduct investigations, hold hearings, issue subpoenas, require the production of relevant documents, records, and property, and take evidence and depositions.

(b) For the purpose of investigating alleged violations of the Federal Aviation Act of 1958, as amended the Hazardous Materials Transportation Act, the Airport and Airway Development Act of 1970, the Airport and Airway Improvement Act of 1982, the Airport and Airway Improvement Act of 1982 as amended by the Airport and Airway Safety and Capacity Expansion Act of 1987, or any rule, regulation, or order issued thereunder, the Administrator's authority has been delegated to the various services and or offices for matters within their respective areas for all routine investigations. When the compulsory processes of sections 313 and 1004 (49 U.S.C. 1354 and 1484) of the Federal Aviation Act, or section 109 of the Hazardous Materials Transportation Act (49 U.S.C. 1808) are invoked, the Administrator's authority has been delegated to the Chief Counsel, the Deputy Chief Counsel, each Assistant Chief Counsel, each Regional Counsel, the Aeronautical Center Counsel, and the Technical Center Counsel.

(c) In conducting formal investigations, the Chief Counsel, the Deputy Chief Counsel, each Assistant Chief Counsel, each Regional Counsel, the Aeronautical Center Counsel, and the Technical Center Counsel may issue an order of investigation in accordance with Subpart F of this part.

(d) A complaint against the sponsor, proprietor, or operator of a Federally-assisted airport involving violations of the legal authorities listed in § 16.1 of this chapter shall be filed in accordance with the provisions of part 16 of this chapter, except in the case of complaints, investigations, and proceedings initiated before December 16, 1996, the effective date of part 16 of this chapter.

[Doc. No. 18884, 44 FR 63723, Nov. 5, 1979, as amended by Amdt. 13–17, 53 FR 33783, Aug. 31, 1988; 53 FR 35255, Sept. 12, 1988; Amdt. 13–19, 54 FR 39290, Sept. 25, 1989; Amdt. 13–27, 61 FR 54004, Oct. 16, 1996; Amdt. 13–29, 62 FR 46865, Sept. 4, 1997]

§13.5 Formal complaints.

(a) Any person may file a complaint with the Administrator with respect to anything done or omitted to be done by any person in contravention of any provision of any Act or of any regulation or order issued under it, as to matters within the jurisdiction of the Administrator. This section does not apply to complaints against the Administrator or employees of the FAA acting within the scope of their employment.

(b) Complaints filed under this section must—

(1) Be submitted in writing and identified as a complaint filed for the purpose of seeking an appropriate order or other enforcement action;

(2) Be submitted to the Federal Aviation Administration, Office of the Chief Counsel, Attention: Enforcement Docket (AGC–10), 800 Independence Avenue, S.W., Washington, DC 20591;

(3) Set forth the name and address, if known, of each person who is the subject of the complaint and, with respect to each person, the specific provisions of the Act or regulation or order that the complainant believes were violated;

(4) Contain a concise but complete statement of the facts relied upon to substantiate each allegation;

(5) State the name, address and telephone number of the person filing the complaint; and

(6) Be signed by the person filing the complaint or a duly authorized representative.

(c) Complaints which do not meet the requirements of paragraph (b) of this section will be considered reports under §13.1.

(d) Complaints which meet the requirements of paragraph (b) of this section will be docketed and a copy mailed to each person named in the complaint.

(e) Any complaint filed against a member of the Armed Forces of the United States acting in the performance of official duties shall be referred to the Secretary of the Department concerned for action in accordance with the procedures set forth in §13.21 of this part.

(f) The person named in the complaint shall file an answer within 20 days after service of a copy of the complaint.

(g) After the complaint has been answered or after the allotted time in which to file an answer has expired, the Administrator shall determine if there are reasonable grounds for investigating the complaint.

(h) If the Administrator determines that a complaint does not state facts which warrant an investigation or action, the complaint may be dismissed without a hearing and the reason for the dismissal shall be given, in writing, to the person who filed the complaint and the person named in the complaint.

(i) If the Administrator determines that reasonable grounds exist, an informal investigation may be initiated or an order of investigation may be issued in accordance with Subpart F of this part, or both. Each person named in the complaint shall be advised which official has been delegated the responsibility under §13.3(b) or (c) for conducting the investigation.

(j) If the investigation substantiates the allegations set forth in the complaint, a notice of proposed order may be issued or other enforcement action taken in accordance with this part.

(k) The complaint and other pleadings and official FAA records relating to the disposition of the complaint are maintained in current docket form in the Enforcement Docket (AGC–10), Office of the Chief Counsel, Federal Aviation Administration, 800 Independence Avenue, S.W., Washington, D. C. 20591. Any interested person may examine any docketed material at that office, at any time after the docket is established, except material that is ordered withheld from the public under applicable law or regulations, and may obtain a photostatic or duplicate copy upon paying the cost of the copy.

(Secs. 313(a), 314(a), 601 through 610, and 1102 of the Federal Aviation Act of 1958 (49 U.S.C. 1354(a), 1421 through 1430, 1502); sec. 6(c), Dept. of Transportation Act (49 U.S.C. 1655(c)))

[Doc. No 13–14, 44 FR 63723, Nov. 5, 1979; as amended by Amdt. 13–16, 45 FR 35307, May 27, 1980; Amdt. 13–19, 54 FR 39290, Sept. 25, 1989]

§ 13.7 Records, documents and reports.

Each record, document and report that the Federal Aviation Regulations require to be maintained, exhibited or submitted to the Administrator may be used in any investigation conducted by the Administrator; and, except to the extent the use may be specifically limited or prohibited by the section which imposes the requirement, the records, documents and reports may be used in any civil penalty action, certificate action, or other legal proceeding.

Subpart B—Administrative Actions

§ 13.11 Administrative disposition of certain violations.

(a) If it is determined that a violation or an alleged violation of the Federal Aviation Act of 1958, or an order or regulation issued under it, or of the Hazardous Materials Transportation Act, or an order or regulation issued under it, does not require legal enforcement action, an appropriate official of the FAA field office responsible for processing the enforcement case or other appropriate FAA official may take administrative action in disposition of the case.

(b) An administrative action under this section does not constitute a formal adjudication of the matter, and may be taken by issuing the alleged violator—

(1) A "Warning Notice" which recites available facts and information about the incident or condition and indicates that it may have been a violation; or

(2) A "Letter of Correction" which confirms the FAA decision in the matter and states the necessary corrective action the alleged violator has taken or agrees to take. If the agreed corrective action is not fully completed, legal enforcement action may be taken.

Subpart C—Legal Enforcement Actions

§ 13.13 Consent orders.

(a) At any time before the issuance of an order under this subpart, the official who issued the notice and the person subject to the notice may agree to dispose of the case by the issuance of a consent order by the official.

(b) A proposal for a consent order, submitted to the official who issued the notice, under this section must include—

(1) A proposed order;

(2) An admission of all jurisdictional facts;

(3) An express waiver of the right to further procedural steps and of all rights to judicial review; and

(4) An incorporation by reference of the notice and an acknowledgment that the notice may be used to construe the terms of the order.

(c) If the issuance of a consent order has been agreed upon after the filing of a request for hearing in accordance with Subpart D of this part, the proposal for a consent order shall include a request to be filed with the Hearing Officer withdrawing the request for a hearing and requesting that the case be dismissed.

§ 13.15 Civil penalties: Federal Aviation Act of 1958, as amended, involving an amount in controversy in excess of $50,000; an in rem action; seizure of aircraft; or injunctive relief.

(a) The following penalties apply to persons who violate the Federal Aviation Act of 1958, as amended:

(1) Any person who violates any provision of Title III, V, VI, or XII of the Federal Aviation Act of 1958, as amended, or any rule, regulation, or order issued thereunder, is subject to a civil penalty of not more than the amount specified in the Act for each violation in accordance with section 901 of the Federal Aviation Act of 1958, as amended (49 U.S.C. 1471, *et seq.*).

(2) Any person who violates section 404(d) of the Federal Aviation Act of

1958, as amended, or any rule, regulation, or order issued thereunder, is subject to a civil penalty of not more than the amount specified in the Act for each violation in accordance with section 404(d) or section 901 of the Federal Aviation Act of 1958, as amended (49 U.S.C. 1374, 1471, *et seq.*).

(3) Any person who operates aircraft for the carriage of persons or property for compensation or hire (other than an airman serving in the capacity of an airman) is subject to a civil penalty of not more than $10,000 for each violation of Title III, VI, or XII of the Federal Aviation Act of 1958, as amended, or any rule, regulation, or order issued thereunder, occurring after December 30, 1987, in accordance with section 901 of the Federal Aviation Act of 1958, as amended (49 U.S.C. 1471 *et seq.*).

(b) The authority of the Administrator, under section 901 of the Federal Aviation Act of 1958, as amended, to propose a civil penalty for a violation of that Act, or a rule, regulation, or order issued thereunder, and the ability to refer cases to the United States Attorney General, or the delegate of the Attorney General, for prosecution of civil penalty actions proposed by the Administrator, involving an amount in controversy in excess of $50,000, an *in rem* action, seizure of aircraft subject to lien, or suit for injunctive relief, or for collection of an assessed civil penalty, is delegated to the Chief Counsel, the Assistant Chief Counsel, Enforcement, the Assistant Chief Counsel, Regulations, the Assistant Chief Counsel, Europe, Africa, and Middle East Area Office, the Regional Counsel, the Aeronautical Center Counsel, and the Technical Center Counsel.

(c) The Administrator may compromise any civil penalty, proposed in accordance with section 901 of the Federal Aviation Act of 1958, as amended, involving an amount in controversy in excess of $50,000, an *in rem* action, seizure of aircraft subject to lien, or suit for injunctive relief, prior to referral of the civil penalty action to the United States Attorney General, or the delegate of the Attorney General, for prosecution.

(1) The Administrator, through the Chief Counsel, the Assistant Chief Counsel, Enforcement, the Assistant Chief Counsel, Regulations, the Assistant Chief Counsel, Europe, Africa, and Middle East Area Office, the Regional Counsel, the Aeronautical Center Counsel, and the Technical Center Counsel sends a civil penalty letter to the person charged with a violation of the Federal Aviation Act of 1958, as amended, or a rule, regulation, or order issued thereunder. The civil penalty letter contains a statement of the charges, the applicable law, rule, regulation, or order, the amount of civil penalty that the Administrator will accept in full settlement of the action or an offer to compromise the civil penalty.

(2) Not later than 30 days after receipt of the civil penalty letter, the person charged with a violation may present any material or information in answer to the charges to the agency attorney, either orally or in writing, that may explain, mitigate, or deny the violation or that may show extenuating circumstances. The Administrator will consider any material or information submitted in accordance with this paragraph to determine whether the person is subject to a civil penalty or to determine the amount for which the Administrator will compromise the action.

(3) If the person charged with the violation offers to compromise for a specific amount, that person shall send a certified check or money order for that amount, payable to the Federal Aviation Administration, to the agency attorney. The Chief Counsel, the Assistant Chief Counsel, Enforcement, the Assistant Chief Counsel, Regulations, the Assistant Chief Counsel, Europe, Africa, and Middle East Area Office, the Regional Counsel, the Aeronautical Center Counsel, or the Technical Center Counsel may accept the certified check or money order or may refuse and return the certified check or money order.

(4) If the offer to compromise is accepted by the Administrator, the agency attorney will send a letter to the person charged with the violation stating that the certified check or money order is accepted in full settlement of the civil penalty action.

(5) If the parties cannot agree to compromise the civil penalty action or

the offer to compromise is rejected and the certified check or money order submitted in compromise is returned, the Administrator may refer the civil penalty action to the United States Attorney General, or the delegate of the Attorney General, to begin proceedings in a United States District Court, pursuant to the authority in section 903 of the Federal Aviation Act, as amended (49 U.S.C. 1473), to prosecute and collect the civil penalty.

[Amdt. 13–18, 53 FR 34653, Sept. 7, 1988, as amended by Amdt. 13–20, 55 FR 15128, Apr. 20, 1990; Amdt. 13–29, 62 FR 46865, Sept. 4, 1997]

§ 13.16 Civil penalties: Federal Aviation Act of 1958, involving an amount in controversy not exceeding $50,000; Hazardous Materials Transportation Act.

(a) *General.* The following penalties apply to persons who violate the Federal Aviation Act of 1958, as amended, and the Hazardous Materials Transportation Act:

(1) Any person who violates any provision of title III, V, VI, or XII of the Federal Aviation Act of 1958, as amended, or any rule, regulation, or order issued thereunder, is subject to a civil penalty of not more than the amount specified in the Act for each violation in accordance with section 901 of the Federal Aviation Act, of 1958, as amended (49 U.S.C. 1471, *et seq.*).

(2) Any person who violates section 404(d) of the Federal Aviation Act of 1958, as amended, or any rule, regulation, or order issued thereunder, is subject to a civil penalty of not more than the amount specified in the Act for each violation in accordance with section 404(d) or section 901 of the Federal Aviation Act of 1958, as amended (49 U.S.C. 1374, 1471, *et seq.*).

(3) Any person who operates aircraft for the carriage of persons or property for compensation or hire (other than an airman serving in the capacity of an airman) is subject to a civil penalty of not more than $10,000 for each violation of title III, VI, or XII of the Federal Aviation Act of 1958, as amended, or any rule, regulation, or order issued thereunder, occurring after December 30, 1987, in accordance with section 901 of the Federal Aviation Act of 1958, as amended (49 U.S.C. 1471, *et seq.*).

(4) Any person who knowingly commits an act in violation of the Hazardous Materials Transportation Act, or any rule, regulation, or order issued thereunder, is subject to a civil penalty of not more than $10,000 for each violation in accordance with section 901 of the Federal Aviation Act of 1958, as amended, and section 110 of the Hazardous Materials Transportation Act (49 U.S.C. 1471 and 1809, *et seq.*). An order assessing civil penalty for a violation under the Hazardous Materials Transportation Act, or a rule, regulation, or order issued thereunder, will be issued only after consideration of—

(i) The nature and circumstances of the violation;

(ii) The extent and gravity of the violation;

(iii) The person's degree of culpability;

(iv) The person's history of prior violations;

(v) The person's ability to pay the civil penalty;

(vi) The effect on the person's ability to continue in business; and

(vii) Such other matters as justice may require.

(b) *Order assessing civil penalty.* An order assessing civil penalty may be issued for a violation described in paragraph (a) of this section, or as otherwise provided by statute, after notice and opportunity for a hearing. A person charged with a violation may be subject to an order assessing civil penalty in the following circumstances:

(1) An order assessing civil penalty may be issued if a person charged with a violation submits or agrees to submit a civil penalty for a violation.

(2) An order assessing civil penalty may be issued if a person charged with a violation does not request a hearing under paragraph (e)(2)(ii) of this section within 15 days after receipt of a final notice of proposed civil penalty.

(3) Unless an appeal is filed with the FAA decisionmaker in a timely manner, an initial decision or order of an administrative law judge shall be considered an order assessing civil penalty if an administrative law judge finds that an alleged violation occurred and determines that a civil penalty, in an amount found appropriate by the administrative law judge, is warranted.

34

(4) Unless a petition for review is filed with a U.S. Court of Appeals in a timely manner, a final decision and order of the Administrator shall be considered an order assessing civil penalty if the FAA decisionmaker finds that an alleged violation occurred and a civil penalty is warranted.

(c) *Delegation of authority.* The authority of the Administrator, under section 901 and section 905 of the Federal Aviation Act of 1958, as amended, and section 110 of the Hazardous Materials Transportation Act, to initiate and assess civil penalties for a violation of those Acts, or a rule, regulation, or order issued thereunder, is delegated to the Deputy Chief Counsel, the Assistant Chief Counsel, Enforcement, the Assistant Chief Counsel, Regulations, the Assistant Chief Counsel, Europe, Africa, and Middle East Area Office, each Regional Counsel, the Aeronautical Center Counsel, and the Technical Center Counsel. The authority of the Administrator to refer cases to the Attorney General of the United States, or the delegate of the Attorney General, for the collection of civil penalties, is delegated to the Chief Counsel, the Deputy Chief Counsel, the Assistant Chief Counsel, Enforcement, the Assistant Chief Counsel, Regulations, the Assistant Chief Counsel, Europe, Africa, and Middle East Area Office, each Regional Counsel, the Aeronautical Center Counsel, and the Technical Center Counsel.

(d) *Notice of proposed civil penalty.* A civil penalty action is initiated by sending a notice of proposed civil penalty to the person charged with a violation of the Federal Aviation Act of 1958, as amended, the Hazardous Materials Transportation Act, or a rule, regulation, or order issued thereunder. A notice of proposed civil penalty will be sent to the individual charged with a violation or to the president of the corporation or company charged with a violation. In response to a notice of proposed civil penalty, a corporation or company may designate in writing another person to receive documents in that civil penalty action. The notice of proposed civil penalty contains a statement of the charges and the amount of the proposed civil penalty. Not later than 30 days after receipt of the notice of proposed civil penalty, the person charged with a violation shall—

(1) Submit the amount of the proposed civil penalty or an agreed-upon amount, in which case either an order assessing civil penalty or compromise order shall be issued in that amount;

(2) Submit to the agency attorney one of the following:

(i) Written information, including documents and witness statements, demonstrating that a violation of the regulations did not occur or that a penalty or the amount of the penalty is not warranted by the circumstances.

(ii) A written request to reduce the proposed civil penalty, the amount of reduction, and the reasons and any documents supporting a reduction of the proposed civil penalty, including records indicating a financial inability to pay or records showing that payment of the proposed civil penalty would prevent the person from continuing in business.

(iii) A written request for an informal conference to discuss the matter with the agency attorney and to submit relevant information or documents; or

(3) Request a hearing in which case a complaint shall be filed with the hearing docket clerk.

(e) *Final notice of proposed civil penalty.* A final notice of proposed civil penalty may be issued after participation in informal procedures provided in paragraph (d)(2) of this section or failure to respond in a timely manner to a notice of proposed civil penalty. A final notice of proposed civil penalty will be sent to the individual charged with a violation, to the president of the corporation or company charged with a violation, or a person previously designated in writing by the individual, corporation, or company to receive documents in that civil penalty action. If not previously done in response to a notice of proposed civil penalty, a corporation or company may designate in writing another person to receive documents in that civil penalty action. The final notice of proposed civil penalty contains a statement of the charges and the amount of the proposed civil penalty and, as a result of information submitted to the agency attorney during informal procedures, may modify an allegation or a proposed civil penalty contained in a notice of proposed civil penalty.

(1) A final notice of proposed civil penalty may be issued—

(i) If the person charged with a violation fails to respond to the notice of proposed civil penalty within 30 days after receipt of that notice; or

(ii) If the parties participated in any informal procedures under paragraph (d)(2) of this section and the parties have not agreed to compromise the action or the agency attorney has not agreed to withdraw the notice of proposed civil penalty.

(2) Not later than 15 days after receipt of the final notice of proposed civil penalty, the person charged with a violation shall do one of the following—

(i) Submit the amount of the proposed civil penalty or an agreed-upon amount, in which case either an order assessing civil penalty or a compromise order shall be issued in that amount; or

(ii) Request a hearing in which case a complaint shall be filed with the hearing docket clerk.

(f) *Request for a hearing.* Any person charged with a violation may request a hearing, pursuant to paragraph (d)(3) or paragraph (e)(2)(ii) of this section, to be conducted in accordance with the procedures in subpart G of this part. A person requesting a hearing shall file a written request for a hearing with the hearing docket clerk (Hearing Docket, Federal Aviation Administration, 800 Independence Avenue, SW., Room 924A, Washington, DC 20591, Attention: Hearing Docket Clerk) and shall mail a copy of the request to the agency attorney. The request for a hearing may be in the form of a letter but must be dated and signed by the person requesting a hearing. The request for a hearing may be typewritten or may be legibly handwritten.

(g) *Hearing.* If the person charged with a violation requests a hearing pursuant to paragraph (d)(3) or paragraph (e)(2)(ii) of this section, the original complaint shall be filed with the hearing docket clerk and a copy shall be sent to the person requesting the hearing. The procedural rules in subpart G of this part apply to the

hearing and any appeal. At the close of the hearing, the administrative law judge shall issue, either orally on the record or in writing, an initial decision, including the reasons for the decision, that contains findings or conclusions on the allegations contained, and the civil penalty sought, in the complaint.

(h) *Appeal.* Either party may appeal the administrative law judge's initial decision to the FAA decisionmaker pursuant to the procedures in subpart G of this part. If a party files a notice of appeal pursuant to § 13.233 of subpart G, the effectiveness of the initial decision is stayed until a final decision and order of the Administrator have been entered on the record. The FAA decisionmaker shall review the record and issue a final decision and order of the Administrator that affirm, modify, or reverse the initial decision. The FAA decisionmaker may assess a civil penalty but shall not assess a civil penalty in an amount greater than that sought in the complaint.

(i) *Payment.* A person shall pay a civil penalty by sending a certified check or money order, payable to the Federal Aviation Administration, to the agency attorney.

(j) *Collection of civil penalties.* If a person does not pay a civil penalty imposed by an order assessing civil penalty or a compromise order within 60 days after service of the order, the Administrator may refer the order to the United States Attorney General, or the delegate of the Attorney General, to begin proceedings to collect the civil penalty. The action shall be brought in a United States District Court, pursuant to the authority in section 903 of the Federal Aviation Act of 1958, as amended (49 U.S.C. 1473), or section 110 of the Hazardous Materials Transportation Act (49 U.S.C. 1809).

(k) *Exhaustion of administrative remedies.* A party may only petition for review of a final decision and order of the Administrator to the courts of appeals of the United States or the United States Court of Appeals for the District of Columbia pursuant to section 1006 of the Federal Aviation Act of 1958, as amended. Neither an initial decision or order issued by an administrative law judge, that has not been appealed to the FAA decisionmaker, nor an order compromising a civil penalty action constitutes a final order of the Administrator for the purposes of judicial appellate review under section 1006 of the Federal Aviation Act of 1958, as amended.

(1) *Compromise.* The FAA may compromise any civil penalty action initiated in accordance with section 901 and section 905 of the Federal Aviation Act of 1958, as amended, involving an amount in controversy not exceeding $50,000, or any civil penalty action initiated in accordance with section 901 of the Federal Aviation Act of 1958, as amended, and section 110 of the Hazardous Materials Transportation Act, at any time before referring the action to the United States Attorney for collection.

(1) An agency attorney may compromise any civil penalty action where a person charged with a violation agrees to pay a civil penalty and the FAA agrees to make no finding of violation. Pursuant to such agreement, a compromise order shall be issued, stating:

(i) The person agrees to pay a civil penalty.

(ii) The FAA makes no finding of a violation.

(iii) The compromise order shall not be used as evidence of a prior violation in any subsequent civil penalty proceeding or certificate action proceeding.

(2) An agency attorney may compromise the amount of any civil penalty proposed in a notice, assessed in an order, or imposed in a compromise order.

[Amdt. 13–21, 55 FR 27574, July 3, 1990; 55 FR 29293, July 18, 1990; 55 FR 31027, July 30, 1990; Amdt. 13–29, 62 FR 46865, Sept. 4, 1997]

§ 13.17 Seizure of aircraft.

(a) Under section 903 of the Federal Aviation Act of 1958 (49 U.S.C. 1473), a State or Federal law enforcement officer, or a Federal Aviation Administration safety inspector, authorized in an order of seizure issued by the Regional Administrator of the region, or by the Chief Counsel, may summarily seize an aircraft that is involved in a violation for which a civil penalty may be imposed on its owner or operator.

(b) Each person seizing an aircraft under this section shall place it in the nearest available and adequate public storage facility in the judicial district in which it was seized.

(c) The Regional Administrator or Chief Counsel, without delay, sends a written notice and a copy of this section, to the registered owner of the seized aircraft, and to each other persons shown by FAA records to have an interest in it, stating the—

(1) Time, date, and place of seizure;

(2) Name and address of the custodian of the aircraft;

(3) Reasons for the seizure, including the violations believed, or judicially determined, to have been committed; and

(4) Amount that may be tendered as—

(i) A compromise of a civil penalty for the alleged violation; or

(ii) Payment for a civil penalty imposed by a Federal court for a proven violation.

(d) The Chief Counsel, or the Regional Counsel or Assistant Chief Counsel for the region or area in which an aircraft is seized under this section, immediately sends a report to the United States District Attorney for the judicial district in which it was seized, requesting the District Attorney to institute proceedings to enforce a lien against the aircraft.

(e) The Regional Administrator or Chief Counsel directs the release of a seized aircraft whenever—

(1) The alleged violator pays a civil penalty or an amount agreed upon in compromise, and the costs of seizing, storing, and maintaining the aircraft;

(2) The aircraft is seized under an order of a Federal Court in proceedings in rem to enforce a lien against the aircraft, or the United States District Attorney for the judicial district concerned notifies the FAA that the District Attorney refuses to institute those proceedings; or

(3) A bond in the amount and with the sureties prescribed by the Chief Counsel, the Regional Counsel, or the Assistant Chief Counsel is deposited, conditioned on payment of the penalty, or the compromise amount, and the

costs of seizing, storing, and maintaining the aircraft.

[Doc. No. 18884, 44 FR 63723, Nov. 5, 1979, as amended by Amdt. 13-19, 54 FR 39290, Sept. 25, 1989; Amdt. 13-29, 62 FR 46865, Sept. 4, 1997]

§ 13.19 Certificate action.

(a) Under section 609 of the Federal Aviation Act of 1958 (49 U.S.C. 1429), the Administrator may reinspect any civil aircraft, aircraft engine, propeller, appliance, air navigation facility, or air agency, and may re-examine any civil airman. Under section 501(e) of the FA Act, any Certificate of Aircraft Registration may be suspended or revoked by the Administrator for any cause that renders the aircraft ineligible for registration.

(b) If, as a result of such a reinspection re-examination, or other investigation made by the Administrator under section 609 of the FA Act, the Administrator determines that the public interest and safety in air commerce requires it, the Administrator may issue an order amending, suspending, or revoking, all or part of any type certificate, production certificate, airworthiness certificate, airman certificate, air carrier operating certificate, air navigation facility certificate, or air agency certificate. This authority may be exercised for remedial purposes in cases involving the Hazardous Materials Transportation Act (49 U.S.C. 1801 et seq.) or regulations issued under that Act. This authority is also exercised by the Chief Counsel, the Assistant Chief Counsel, Enforcement, the Assistant Chief Counsel, Regulations, the Assistant Chief Counsel, Europe, Africa, and Middle East Area Office, each Regional Counsel, and the Aeronautical Center Counsel. If the Administrator finds that any aircraft registered under Part 47 of this chapter is ineligible for registration or if the holder of a Certificate of Aircraft Registration has refused or failed to submit AC Form 8050-73, as required by § 47.51 of this chapter, the Administrator issues an order suspending or revoking that certificate. This authority as to aircraft found ineligible for registration is also exercised by each Regional Counsel, the Aeronautical Center Counsel, and the Assistant Chief Counsel, Europe, Africa, and Middle East Area Office.

(c) Before issuing an order under paragraph (b) of this section, the Chief Counsel, the Assistant Chief Counsel, Enforcement, the Assistant Chief Counsel, Regulations, the Assistant Chief Counsel, Europe, Africa, and Middle East Area Office, each Regional Counsel, or the Aeronautical Center Counsel advises the certificate holder of the charges or other reasons upon which the Administrator bases the proposed action and, except in an emergency, allows the holder to answer any charges and to be heard as to why the certificate should not be amended, suspended, or revoked. The holder may, by checking the appropriate box on the form that is sent to the holder with the notice of proposed certificate action, elect to—

(1) Admit the charges and surrender his or her certificate;

(2) Answer the charges in writing;

(3) Request that an order be issued in accordance with the notice of proposed certificate action so that the certificate holder may appeal to the National Transportation Safety Board, if the charges concerning a matter under Title VI of the FA Act;

(4) Request an opportunity to be heard in an informal conference with the FAA counsel; or

(5) Request a hearing in accordance with Subpart D of this part if the charges concern a matter under Title V of the FA Act.

Except as provided in § 13.35(b), unless the certificate holder returns the form and, where required, an answer or motion, with a postmark of not later than 15 days after the date of receipt of the notice, the order of the Administrator is issued as proposed. If the certificate holder has requested an informal conference with the FAA counsel and the charges concern a matter under Title V of the FA Act, the holder may after that conference also request a formal hearing in writing with a postmark of not later than 10 days after the close of the conference. After considering any information submitted by the certificate holder, the Chief Counsel, the Assistant Chief Counsel for Regulations and Enforcement, the Regional Counsel concerned, or the Aeronautical Center

Counsel (as to matters under Title V of the FA Act) issues the order of the Administrator, except that if the holder has made a valid request for a formal hearing on a matter under Title V of the FA Act initially or after an informal conference, Subpart D of this part governs further proceedings.

(d) Any person whose certificate is affected by an order issued under this section may appeal to the National Transportation Safety Board. If the certificate holder files an appeal with the Board, the Administrator's order is stayed unless the Administrator advises the Board that an emergency exists and safety in air commerce requires that the order become effective immediately. If the Board is so advised, the order remains effective and the Board shall finally dispose of the appeal within 60 days after the date of the advice. This paragraph does not apply to any person whose Certificate of Aircraft Registration is affected by an order issued under this section.

[Doc. No. 13–14, 44 FR 63723, Nov. 5, 1979, as amended by Amdt. 13–15, 45 FR 20773, Mar. 31, 1980; Amdt. 13–19, 54 FR 39290, Sept. 25, 1989; Amdt. 13–29, 62 FR 46865, Sept. 4, 1997]

§ 13.20 Orders of compliance, cease and desist orders, orders of denial, and other orders.

(a) This section applies to orders of compliance, cease and desist orders, orders of denial, and other orders issued by the Administrator to carry out the provisions of the Federal Aviation Act of 1958, as amended, the Hazardous Materials Transportation Act, the Airport and Airway Development Act of 1970, and the Airport and Airway Improvement Act of 1982, or the Airport and Airway Improvement Act of 1982 as amended by the Airport and Airway Safety and Capacity Expansion Act of 1987. This section does not apply to orders issued pursuant to section 602 or section 609 of the Federal Aviation Act of 1958, as amended.

(b) Unless the Administrator determines that an emergency exists and safety in air commerce requires the immediate issuance of an order under this section, the person subject to the order shall be provided with notice prior to issuance.

(c) Within 30 days after service of the notice, the person subject to the order may reply in writing or request a hearing in accordance with Subpart D of this part.

(d) If a reply is filed, as to any charges not dismissed or not subject to a consent order, the person subject to the order may, within 10 days after receipt of notice that the remaining charges are not dismissed, request a hearing in accordance with Subpart D of this part.

(e) Failure to request a hearing within the period provided in paragraphs (c) or (d) of this section—

(1) Constitutes a waiver of the right to appeal and the right to a hearing, and

(2) Authorizes the official who issued the notice to find the facts to be as alleged in the notice, or as modified as the official may determine necessary based on any written response, and to issue an appropriate order, without further notice or proceedings.

(f) If a hearing is requested in accordance with paragraph (c) or (d) of this section, the procedure of Subpart D of this part applies. At the close of the hearing, the Hearing Officer, on the record or subsequently in writing, shall set forth findings and conclusions and the reasons therefor, and either—

(1) Dismiss the notice; or

(2) Issue an order.

(g) Any party to the hearing may appeal from the order of the Hearing Officer by filing a notice of appeal with the Administrator within 20 days after the date of issuance of the order.

(h) If a notice of appeal is not filed from the order issued by a Hearing Officer, such order is the final agency order.

(i) Any person filing an appeal authorized by paragraph (g) of this section shall file an appeal brief with the Administrator within 40 days after the date of issuance of the order, and serve a copy on the other party. A reply brief must be filed within 20 days after service of the appeal brief and a copy served on the appellant.

(j) On appeal the Administrator reviews the available record of the proceeding, and issues an order dismissing, reversing, modifying or affirming the order. The Administrator's order includes the reasons for the Administrator's action.

(k) For good cause shown, requests for extensions of time to file any document under this section may be granted by—

(1) The official who issued the order, if the request is filed prior to the designation of a Hearing Officer; or

(2) The Hearing Officer, if the request is filed prior to the filing of a notice of appeal; or

(3) The Administrator, if the request is filed after the filing of a notice of appeal.

(l) Except in the case of an appeal from the decision of a Hearing Officer, the authority of the Administrator under this section is also exercised by the Chief Counsel, Deputy Chief Counsel, each Assistant Chief Counsel, each Regional Counsel, and the Aeronautical Center Counsel (as to matters under Title V of the Federal Aviation Act of 1958).

(m) Filing and service of documents under this section shall be accomplished in accordance with § 13.43; and the periods of time specified in this section shall be computed in accordance with § 13.44.

[Doc. No. 18884, 44 FR 63723, Nov. 5, 1979, as amended by Amdt. 13–17, 53 FR 33783, Aug. 31, 1988; Amdt. 13–19, 54 FR 39290, Sept. 25, 1989; Amdt. 13–29, 62 FR 46865, Sept. 4, 1997]

§ 13.21 Military personnel.

If a report made under this part indicates that, while performing official duties, a member of the Armed Forces, or a civilian employee of the Department of Defense who is subject to the Uniform Code of Military Justice (10 U.S.C. Ch. 47), has violated the Federal Aviation Act of 1958, or a regulation or order issued under it, the Chief Counsel, the Assistant Chief Counsel, Enforcement, the Assistant Chief Counsel, Regulations, the Assistant Chief Counsel, Europe, Africa, and Middle East Area Office, each Regional Counsel, and the Aeronautical Center Counsel send a copy of the report to the appropriate military authority for such disciplinary action as that authority considers appropriate and a report to the Administrator thereon.

[Doc. No. 18884, 44 FR 63723, Nov. 5, 1979, as amended by Amdt. 13–19, 54 FR 39290, Sept. 25, 1989; Amdt. 13–29, 62 FR 46866, Sept. 4, 1997]

§ 13.23 Criminal penalties.

(a) Sections 902 and 1203 of the Federal Aviation Act of 1958 (49 U.S.C. 1472 and 1523), provide criminal penalties for any person who knowingly and willfully violates specified provisions of that Act, or any regulation or order issued under those provisions. Section 110(b) of the Hazardous Materials Transportation Act (49 U.S.C. 1809(b)) provides for a criminal penalty of a fine of not more than $25,000, imprisonment for not more than five years, or both, for any person who willfully violates a provision of that Act or a regulation or order issued under it.

(b) If an inspector or other employee of the FAA becomes aware of a possible violation of any criminal provision of the Federal Aviation Act of 1958 (except a violation of section 902 (i) through (m) which is reported directly to the Federal Bureau of Investigation), or of the Hazardous Materials Transportation Act, relating to the transportation or shipment by air of hazardous materials, he or she shall report it to the Office of the Chief Counsel or the Regional Counsel or Assistant Chief Counsel for the region or area concerned. If appropriate, that office refers the report to the Department of Justice for criminal prosecution of the offender. If such an inspector or other employee becomes aware of a possible violation of a Federal statute that is within the investigatory jurisdiction of another Federal agency, he or she shall immediately report it to that agency according to standard FAA practices.

[Doc. No. 18884, 44 FR 63723, Nov. 5, 1979, as amended by Amdt. 13–19, 54 FR 39290, Sept. 25, 1989; Amdt. 13–29, 62 FR 46866, Sept. 4, 1997]

§ 13.25 Injunctions.

(a) Whenever it is determined that a person has engaged, or is about to engage, in any act or practice constituting a violation of the Federal Aviation Act of 1958, or any regulation or order issued under it for which the

FAA exercises enforcement responsibility, or, with respect to the transportation or shipment by air of any hazardous materials, in any act or practice constituting a violation of the Hazardous Materials Transportation Act, or any regulation or order issued under it for which the FAA exercises enforcement responsibility, the Chief Counsel, the Assistant Chief Counsel, Enforcement, the Assistant Chief Counsel, Regulations, the Assistant Chief Counsel, Europe, Africa, and Middle East Area Office, each Regional Counsel, and the Aeronautical Center Counsel may request the United States Attorney General, or the delegate of the Attorney General, to bring an action in the appropriate United States District Court for such relief as is necessary or appropriate, including mandatory or prohibitive injunctive relief, interim equitable relief, and punitive damages, as provided by section 1007 of the Federal Aviation Act of 1958 (49 U.S.C. 1487) and section 111(a) of the Hazardous Materials Transportation Act (49 U.S.C. 1810).

(b) Whenever it is determined that there is substantial likelihood that death, serious illness, or severe personal injury, will result from the transportation by air of a particular hazardous material before an order of compliance proceeding, or other administrative hearing or formal proceeding to abate the risk of the harm can be completed, the Chief Counsel, the Assistant Chief Counsel, Enforcement, the Assistant Chief Counsel, Regulations, the Assistant Chief Counsel, Europe, Africa, and Middle East Area Office, each Regional Counsel, and the Aeronautical Center Counsel may bring, or request the United States Attorney General to bring, an action in the appropriate United States District Court for an order suspending or restricting the transportation by air of the hazardous material or for such other order as is necessary to eliminate or ameliorate the imminent hazard, as provided by section 111(b) of the Hazardous Materials Transportation Act (49 U.S.C. 1810).

[Doc. No. 18884, 44 FR 63723, Nov. 5, 1979, as amended by Amdt. 13–19, 54 FR 39290, Sept. 25, 1989; Amdt. 13–29, 62 FR 46866, Sept. 4, 1997]

§ 13.27 Final order of Hearing Officer in certificate of aircraft registration proceedings.

(a) If, in proceedings under section 501(b) of the Federal Aviation Act of 1958 (49 USC 1401), the Hearing Officer determines that the holder of the Certificate of Aircraft Registration has refused or failed to submit AC Form 8050–73, as required by § 47.51 of this chapter, or that the aircraft is ineligible for a Certificate of Aircraft Registration, the Hearing Officer shall suspend or revoke the respondent's certificate, as proposed in the notice of proposed certificate action.

(b) If the final order of the Hearing Officer makes a decision on the merits, it shall contain a statement of the findings and conclusions of law on all material issues of fact and law. If the Hearing Officer finds that the allegations of the notice have been proven, but that no sanction is required, the Hearing Officer shall make appropriate findings and issue an order terminating the notice. If the Hearing Officer finds that the allegations of the notice have not been proven, the Hearing Officer shall issue an order dismissing the notice. If the Hearing Officer finds it to be equitable and in the public interest, the Hearing Officer shall issue an order terminating the proceeding upon payment by the respondent of a civil penalty in an amount agreed upon by the parties.

(c) If the order is issued in writing, it shall be served upon the parties.

[Doc. No. 13–14, 44 FR 63723, Nov. 5, 1979; as amended by Amdt. 13–15, 45 FR 20773, Mar. 31, 1980]

§ 13.29 Civil penalties: Streamlined enforcement procedures for certain security violations.

This section may be used, at the agency's discretion, in enforcement actions involving individuals presenting dangerous or deadly weapons for screening at airports or in checked baggage where the amount of the proposed civil penalty is less than $5,000. In these cases, sections 13.16(a), 13.16(c), and 13.16 (f) through (l) of this chapter are used, as well as paragraphs (a) through (d) of this section:

(a) *Delegation of authority.* The authority of the Administrator, under 49

U.S.C. 46301, to initiate the assessment of civil penalties for a violation of 49 U.S.C. Subtitle VII, or a rule, regulation, or order issued thereunder, is delegated to the regional Civil Aviation Security Division Manager and the regional Civil Aviation Security Deputy Division Manager for the purpose of issuing notices of violation in cases involving violations of 49 U.S.C. Subtitle VII and the FAA's regulations by individuals presenting dangerous or deadly weapons for screening at airport checkpoints or in checked baggage. This authority may not be delegated below the level of the regional Civil Aviation Security Deputy Division Manager.

(b) *Notice of violation.* A civil penalty action is initiated by sending a notice of violation to the person charged with the violation. The notice of violation contains a statement of the charges and the amount of the proposed civil penalty. Not later than 30 days after receipt of the notice of violation, the person charged with a violation shall:

(1) Submit the amount of the proposed civil penalty or an agreed-upon amount, in which case either an order assessing a civil penalty or a compromise order shall be issued in that amount; or

(2) Submit to the agency attorney identified in the material accompanying the notice any of the following:

(i) Written information, including documents and witness statements, demonstrating that a violation of the regulations did not occur or that a penalty or the penalty amount is not warranted by the circumstances; or

(ii) A written request to reduce the proposed civil penalty, the amount of reduction, and the reasons and any documents supporting a reduction of the proposed civil penalty, including records indicating a financial inability to pay or records showing that payment of the proposed civil penalty would prevent the person from continuing in business; or

(iii) A written request for an informal conference to discuss the matter with an agency attorney and submit relevant information or documents; or

(3) Request a hearing in which case a complaint shall be filed with the hearing docket clerk.

(c) *Final notice of violation and civil penalty assessment order.* A final notice of violation and civil penalty assessment order ("final notice and order") may be issued after participation in any informal proceedings as provided in paragraph (b)(2) of this section, or after failure of the respondent to respond in a timely manner to a notice of violation. A final notice and order will be sent to the individual charged with a violation. The final notice and order will contain a statement of the charges and the amount of the proposed civil penalty and, as a result of information submitted to the agency attorney during any informal procedures, may reflect a modified allegation or proposed civil penalty.

A final notice and order may be issued—

(1) If the person charged with a violation fails to respond to the notice of violation within 30 days after receipt of that notice; or

(2) If the parties participated in any informal procedures under paragraph (b)(2) of this section and the parties have not agreed to compromise the action or the agency attorney has not agreed to withdraw the notice of violation.

(d) *Order assessing civil penalty.* An order assessing civil penalty may be issued after notice and opportunity for a hearing. A person charged with a violation may be subject to an order assessing civil penalty in the following circumstances:

(1) An order assessing civil penalty may be issued if a person charged with a violation submits, or agrees to submit, the amount of civil penalty proposed in the notice of violation.

(2) An order assessing civil penalty may be issued if a person charged with a violation submits, or agrees to submit, an agreed-upon amount of civil penalty that is not reflected in either the notice of violation or the final notice and order.

(3) The final notice and order becomes (and contains a statement so indicating) an order assessing a civil penalty when the person charged with a violation submits the amount of the proposed civil penalty that is reflected in the final notice and order.

(4) The final notice and order becomes (and contains a statement so indicating) an order assessing a civil penalty 16 days after receipt of the final notice and order, *unless* not later than 15 days after receipt of the final notice and order, the person charged with a violation does one of the following—

(i) Submits an agreed-upon amount of civil penalty that is not reflected in the final notice and order, in which case an order assessing civil penalty or a compromise order shall be issued in that amount; or

(ii) Requests a hearing in which case a complaint shall be filed with the hearing docket clerk.

(5) Unless an appeal is filed with the FAA decisionmaker in a timely manner, an initial decision or order of an administrative law judge shall be considered an order assessing civil penalty if an administrative law judge finds that an alleged violation occurred and determines that a civil penalty, in an amount found to be appropriate by the administrative law judge, is warranted.

(6) Unless a petition for review is filed with a U.S. Court of Appeals in a timely manner, a final decision and order of the Administrator shall be considered an order assessing civil penalty if the FAA decisionmaker finds that an alleged violation occurred and a civil penalty is warranted.

[Doc. No. 27873, 61 FR 44155, Aug. 28, 1996]

Subpart D—Rules of Practice for FAA Hearings

§ 13.31   Applicability.

This subpart applies to proceedings in which a hearing has been requested in accordance with §§ 13.19(c)(5), 13.20(c), 13.20(d), 13.75(a)(2), 13.75(b), or 13.81(e).

[Amdt. 13–18, 53 FR 34655, Sept. 7, 1988]

§ 13.33   Appearances.

Any party to a proceeding under this subpart may appear and be heard in person or by attorney.

§ 13.35   Request for hearing.

(a) A request for hearing must be made in writing to the Hearing Docket, Room 924A, Federal Aviation Administration, 800 Independence Avenue, S.W., Washington, D.C. 20591. It must describe briefly the action proposed by the FAA, and must contain a statement that a hearing is requested. A copy of the request for hearing and a copy of the answer required by paragraph (b) of this section must be served on the official who issued the notice of proposed action.

(b) An answer to the notice of proposed action must be filed with the request for hearing. All allegations in the notice not specifically denied in the answer are deemed admitted.

(c) Within 15 days after service of the copy of the request for hearing, the official who issued the notice of proposed action forwards a copy of that notice, which serves as the complaint, to the Hearing Docket.

[Doc. No. 18884, 44 FR 63723, Nov. 5, 1979, as amended by Amdt. 13–19, 54 FR 39290, Sept. 25, 1989]

§ 13.37   Hearing Officer's powers.

Any Hearing Officer may—

(a) Give notice concerning, and hold, prehearing conferences and hearings;

(b) Administrator oaths and affirmations;

(c) Examine witnesses;

(d) Adopt procedures for the submission of evidence in written form;

(e) Issue subpoenas and take depositions or cause them to be taken;

(f) Rule on offers of proof;

(g) Receive evidence;

(h) Regulate the course of the hearing;

(i) Hold conferences, before and during the hearing, to settle and simplify issues by consent of the parties;

(j) Dispose of procedural requests and similar matters; and

(k) Issue decisions, make findings of fact, make assessments, and issue orders, as appropriate.

§ 13.39   Disqualification of Hearing Officer.

If disqualified for any reason, the Hearing Officer shall withdraw from the case.

§ 13.41 [Reserved]

§ 13.43 Service and filing of pleadings, motions, and documents.

(a) Copies of all pleadings, motions, and documents filed with the Hearing Docket must be served upon all parties to the proceedings by the person filing them.

(b) Service may be made by personal delivery or by mail.

(c) A certificate of service shall accompany all documents when they are tendered for filing and shall consist of a certificate of personal delivery or a certificate of mailing, executed by the person making the personal delivery or mailing the document.

(d) Whenever proof of service by mail is made, the date of mailing or the date as shown on the postmark shall be the date of service, and where personal service is made, the date of personal delivery shall be the date of service.

(e) The date of filing is the date the document is actually received.

§ 13.44 Computation of time and extension of time.

(a) In computing any period of time prescribed or allowed by this subpart, the date of the act, event, default, notice or order after which the designated period of time begins to run is not to be included in the computation. The last day of the period so computed is to be included unless it is a Saturday, Sunday, or legal holiday for the FAA, in which event the period runs until the end of the next day which is neither a Saturday, Sunday nor a legal holiday.

(b) Upon written request filed with the Hearing Docket and served upon all parties, and for good cause shown, a Hearing Officer may grant an extension of time to file any documents specified in this subpart.

§ 13.45 Amendment of notice and answer.

At any time more than 10 days before the date of hearing, any party may amend his or her notice, answer, or other pleading, by filing the amendment with the Hearing Officer and serving a copy of it on each other party. After that time, amendments may be allowed only in the discretion of the Hearing Officer. If an amendment to an initial pleading has been allowed, the Hearing Officer shall allow the other parties a reasonable opportunity to answer.

§ 13.47 Withdrawal of notice or request for hearing.

At any time before the hearing, the FAA counsel may withdraw the notice of proposed action, and the party requesting the hearing may withdraw the request for hearing.

§ 13.49 Motions.

(a) *Motion to dismiss for insufficiency.* A respondent who requests a formal hearing may, in place of an answer, file a motion to dismiss for failure of the allegations in the notice of proposed action to state a violation of the FA Act or of this chapter or to show lack of qualification of the respondent. If the Hearing Officer denies the motion, the respondent shall file an answer within 10 days.

(b) [Reserved]

(c) *Motion for more definite statement.* The certificate holder may, in place of an answer, file a motion that the allegations in the notice be made more definite and certain. If the Hearing Officer grants the motion, the FAA counsel shall comply within 10 days after the date it is granted. If the Hearing Officer denies the motion the certificate holder shall file an answer within 10 days after the date it is denied.

(d) *Motion for judgment on the pleadings.* After the pleadings are closed, either party may move for a judgment on the pleadings.

(e) *Motion to strike.* Upon motion of either party, the Hearing Officer may order stricken, from any pleadings, any insufficient allegation or defense, or any immaterial, impertinent, or scandalous matter.

(f) *Motion for production of documents.* Upon motion of any party showing good cause, the Hearing Officer may, in the manner provided by Rule 34, Federal Rules of Civil Procedure, order any party to produce any designated document, paper, book, account, letter, photograph, object, or other tangible thing, that is not privileged, that constitutes or contains evidence relevant to the subject matter of the hearings, and that is in the party's possession, custody, or control.

(g) *Consolidation of motions.* A party who makes a motion under this section shall join with it all other motions that are then available to the party. Any objection that is not so raised is considered to be waived.

(h) *Answers to motions.* Any party may file an answer to any motion under this section within 5 days after service of the motion.

§ 13.51 Intervention.

Any person may move for leave to intervene in a proceeding and may become a party thereto, if the Hearing Officer, after the case is sent to the Hearing Officer for hearing, finds that the person may be bound by the order to be issued in the proceedings or has a property or financial interest that may not be adequately represented by existing parties, and that the intervention will not unduly broaden the issues or delay the proceedings. Except for good cause shown, a motion for leave to intervene may not be considered if it is filed less than 10 days before the hearing.

§ 13.53 Depositions.

After the respondent has filed a request for hearing and an answer, either party may take testimony by deposition in accordance with section 1004 of the Federal Aviation Act of 1958 (49 U.S.C. 1484) or Rule 26, Federal Rules of Civil Procedure.

§ 13.55 Notice of hearing.

The Hearing Officer shall set a reasonable date, time, and place for the hearing, and shall give the parties adequate notice thereof and of the nature of the hearing. Due regard shall be given to the convenience of the parties with respect to the place of the hearing.

§ 13.57 Subpoenas and witness fees.

(a) The Hearing Officer to whom a case is assigned may, upon application by any party to the proceeding, issue subpoenas requiring the attendance of witnesses or the production of documentary or tangible evidence at a hearing or for the purpose of taking depositions. However, the application for producing evidence must show its general relevance and reasonable scope. This paragraph does not apply to the attendance of FAA employees or to the production of documentary evidence in the custody of such an employee at a hearing.

(b) A person who applies for the production of a document in the custody of an FAA employee must follow the procedure in § 13.49(f). A person who applies for the attendance of an FAA employee must send the application, in writing, to the Hearing Officer setting forth the need for that employee's attendance.

(c) A witness in a proceeding under this subpart is entitled to the same fees and mileage as is paid to a witness in a court of the United States under comparable circumstances. The party at whose instance the witness is subpoenaed or appears shall pay the witness fees.

(d) Notwithstanding the provisions of paragraph (c) of this section, the FAA pays the witness fees and mileage if the Hearing Officer who issued the subpoena determines, on the basis of a written request and good cause shown, that—

(1) The presence of the witness will materially advance the proceeding; and

(2) The party at whose instance the witness is subpoenaed would suffer a serious hardship if required to pay the witness fees and mileage.

§ 13.59 Evidence.

(a) Each party to a hearing may present the party's case or defense by oral or documentary evidence, submit evidence in rebuttal, and conduct such cross-examination as may be needed for a full disclosure of the facts.

(b) Except with respect to affirmative defenses and orders of denial, the burden of proof is upon the FAA counsel.

(c) The Hearing Officer may order information contained in any report or document filed or in any testimony given pursuant to this subpart withheld from public disclosure when, in the judgment of the Hearing Officer, disclosure would adversely affect the interests of any person and is not required in the public interest or is not otherwise required by statute to be made available to the public. Any person may make written objection to the public disclosure of such information, stating the ground for such objection.

§ 13.61 Argument and submittals.

The Hearing Officer shall give the parties adequate opportunity to present arguments in support of motions, objections, and the final order. The Hearing Officer may determine whether arguments are to be oral or written. At the end of the hearing the Hearing Officer may, in the discretion of the Hearing Officer, allow each party to submit written proposed findings and conclusions and supporting reasons for them.

§ 13.63 Record.

The testimony and exhibits presented at a hearing, together with all papers, requests, and rulings filed in the proceedings are the exclusive basis for the issuance of an order. Either party may obtain a transcript from the official reporter upon payment of the fees fixed therefor.

Subpart E—Orders of Compliance Under the Hazardous Materials Transportation Act

§ 13.71 Applicability.

Whenever the Chief Counsel, the Assistant Chief Counsel, Enforcement, the Assistant Chief Counsel, Europe, Africa, and Middle East Area Office, or a Regional Counsel has reason to believe that a person is engaging in the transportation or shipment by air of hazardous materials in violation of the Hazardous Materials Transportation Act, or any regulation or order issued under it for which the FAA exercises enforcement responsibility, and the circumstances do not require the issuance of an order of immediate compliance, he may conduct proceedings pursuant to section 109 of that Act (49 U.S.C. 1808) to determine the nature and extent of the violation, and may thereafter issue an order directing compliance.

[Doc. No. 18884, 44 FR 63723, Nov. 5, 1979, as amended by Amdt. 13-19, 54 FR 39290, Sept. 25, 1989; Amdt. 13-29, 62 FR 46866, Sept. 4, 1997]

§ 13.73 Notice of proposed order of compliance.

A compliance order proceeding commences when the Chief Counsel, the Assistant Chief Counsel, Enforcement, the Assistant Chief Counsel, Europe, Africa, and Middle East Area Office, or a Regional Counsel sends the alleged violator a notice of proposed order of compliance advising the alleged violator of the charges and setting forth the remedial action sought in the form of a proposed order of compliance.

[Doc. No. 18884, 44 FR 63723, Nov. 5, 1979, as amended by Amdt. 13-19, 54 FR 39290, Sept. 25, 1989; Amdt. 13-29, 62 FR 46866, Sept. 4, 1997]

§ 13.75 Reply or request for hearing.

(a) Within 30 days after service upon the alleged violator of a notice of proposed order of compliance, the alleged violator may—

(1) File a reply in writing with the official who issued the notice; or

(2) Request a hearing in accordance with Subpart D of this part.

(b) If a reply is filed, as to any charges not dismissed or not subject to a consent order of compliance, the alleged violator may, within 10 days after receipt of notice that the remaining charges are not dismissed, request a hearing in accordance with Subpart D of this part.

(c) Failure of the alleged violator to file a reply or request a hearing within the period provided in paragraph (a) or (b) of this section—

(1) Constitutes a waiver of the right to a hearing and the right to an appeal, and

(2) Authorizes the official who issued the notice to find the facts to be as alleged in the notice and to issue an appropriate order directing compliance, without further notice or proceedings.

§ 13.77 Consent order of compliance.

(a) At any time before the issuance of an order of compliance, the official who issued the notice and the alleged violator may agree to dispose of the case by the issuance of a consent order of compliance by the official.

(b) A proposal for a consent order submitted to the official who issued the notice under this section must include—

(1) A proposed order of compliance;

(2) An admission of all jurisdictional facts;

(3) An express waiver of right to further procedural steps and of all rights to judicial review;

(4) An incorporation by reference of the notice and an acknowledgement that the notice may be used to construe the terms of the order of compliance; and

(5) If the issuance of a consent order has been agreed upon after the filing of a request for hearing in accordance with Subpart D of this part, the proposal for a consent order shall include a request to be filed with the Hearing Officer withdrawing the request for a hearing and requesting that the case be dismissed.

§13.79 Hearing.

If an alleged violator requests a hearing in accordance with §13.75, the procedure of Subpart D of this part applies. At the close of the hearing, the Hearing Officer, on the record or subsequently in writing, sets forth the Hearing Officer's findings and conclusion and the reasons therefor, and either—

(a) Dismisses the notice of proposed order of compliance; or

(b) Issues an order of compliance.

§13.81 Order of immediate compliance.

(a) Notwithstanding §§13.73 through 13.79, the Chief Counsel, the Assistant Chief Counsel, Enforcement, the Assistant Chief Counsel, Europe, Africa, and Middle East Area Office, or a Regional Counsel may issue an order of immediate compliance, which is effective upon issuance, if the person who issues the order finds that—

(1) There is strong probability that a violation is occurring or is about to occur;

(2) The violation poses a substantial risk to health or to safety of life or property; and

(3) The public interest requires the avoidance or amelioration of that risk through immediate compliance and waiver of the procedures afforded under §§13.73 through 13.79.

(b) An order of immediate compliance is served promptly upon the person against whom the order is issued by telephone or telegram, and a written statement of the relevant facts and the legal basis for the order, including the findings required by paragraph (a) of this section, is served promptly by personal service or by mail.

(c) The official who issued the order of immediate compliance may rescind or suspend the order if it appears that the criteria set forth in paragraph (a) of this section are no longer satisfied, and, when appropriate, may issue a notice of proposed order of compliance under §13.73 in lieu thereof.

(d) If at any time in the course of a proceeding commenced in accordance with §13.73 the criteria set forth in paragraph (a) of this section are satisfied, the official who issued the notice may issue an order of immediate compliance, even if the period for filing a reply or requesting a hearing specified in §13.75 has not expired.

(e) Within three days after receipt of service of an order of immediate compliance, the alleged violator may request a hearing in accordance with Subpart D of this part and the procedure in that subpart will apply except that—

(1) The case will be heard within fifteen days after the date of the order of immediate compliance unless the alleged violator requests a later date;

(2) The order will serve as the complaint; and

(3) The Hearing Officer shall issue his decision and order dismissing, reversing, modifying, or affirming the order of immediate compliance on the record at the close of the hearing.

(f) The filing of a request for hearing in accordance with paragraph (e) of this section does not stay the effectiveness of an order of immediate compliance.

(g) At any time after an order of immediate compliance has become effective, the official who issued the order may request the United States Attorney General, or the delegate of the Attorney General, to bring an action for appropriate relief in accordance with §13.25.

[Doc. No. 18884, 44 FR 63723, Nov. 5, 1979, as amended by Amdt. 13–19, 54 FR 39290, Sept. 25, 1989; Amdt. 13–29, 62 FR 46866, Sept. 4, 1997]

§ 13.83 Appeal.

(a) Any party to the hearing may appeal from the order of the Hearing Officer by filing a notice of appeal with the Administrator within 20 days after the date of issuance of the order.

(b) Any person against whom an order of immediate compliance has been issued in accordance with § 13.81 or the official who issued the order of immediate compliance may appeal from the order of the Hearing Officer by filing a notice of appeal with the Administrator within three days after the date of issuance of the order by the Hearing Officer.

(c) Unless the Administrator expressly so provides, the filing of a notice of appeal does not stay the effectiveness of an order of immediate compliance.

(d) If a notice of appeal is not filed from the order of compliance issued by a Hearing Officer, such order is the final agency order of compliance.

(e) Any person filing an appeal authorized by paragraph (a) of this section shall file an appeal brief with the Administrator within 40 days after the date of the issuance of the order, and serve a copy on the other party. Any reply brief must be filed within 20 days after service of the appeal brief. A copy of the reply brief must be served on the appellant.

(f) Any person filing an appeal authorized by paragraph (b) of this section shall file an appeal brief with the Administrator with the notice of appeal and serve a copy on the other party. Any reply brief must be filed within 3 days after receipt of the appeal brief. A copy of the reply brief must be served on the appellant.

(g) On appeal the Administrator reviews the available record of the proceeding, and issues an order dismissing, reversing, modifying or affirming the order of compliance or the order of immediate compliance. The Administrator's order includes the reasons for the action.

(h) In cases involving an order of immediate compliance, the Administrator's order on appeal is issued within ten days after the filing of the notice of appeal.

§ 13.85 Filing, service and computation of time.

Filing and service of documents under this subpart shall be accomplished in accordance with § 13.43 except service of orders of immediate compliance under § 13.81(b); and the periods of time specified in this subpart shall be computed in accordance with § 13.44.

§ 13.87 Extension of time.

(a) The official who issued the notice of proposed order of compliance, for good cause shown, may grant an extension of time to file any document specified in this subpart, except documents to be filed with the Administrator.

(b) Extensions of time to file documents with the Administrator may be granted by the Administrator upon written request, served upon all parties, and for good cause shown.

Subpart F—Formal Fact-Finding Investigation Under an Order of Investigation

§ 13.101 Applicability.

(a) This subpart applies to fact-finding investigations in which an order of investigation has been issued under § 13.3(c) or § 13.5(i) of this part.

(b) This subpart does not limit the authority of duly designated persons to issue subpoenas, administer oaths, examine witnesses and receive evidence in any informal investigation as provided for in sections 313 and 1004(a) of the Federal Aviation Act (49 U.S.C. 1354 and 1484(a)) and section 109(a) of the Hazardous Materials Transportation Act (49 U.S.C. 1808(a)).

§ 13.103 Order of investigation.

The order of investigation—

(a) Defines the scope of the investigation by describing the information sought in terms of its subject matter or its relevancy to specified FAA functions;

(b) Sets forth the form of the investigation which may be either by individual deposition or investigative proceeding or both; and

(c) Names the official who is authorized to conduct the investigation and serve as the Presiding Officer.

§13.105 Notification.

Any person under investigation and any person required to testify and produce documentary or physical evidence during the investigation will be advised of the purpose of the investigation, and of the place where the investigative proceeding or deposition will be convened. This may be accomplished by a notice of investigation or by a subpoena. A copy of the order of investigation may be sent to such persons, when appropriate.

§13.107 Designation of additional parties.

(a) The Presiding Officer may designate additional persons as parties to the investigation, if in the discretion of the Presiding Officer, it will aid in the conduct of the investigation.

(b) The Presiding Officer may designate any person as a party to the investigation if that person—

(1) Petitions the Presiding Officer to participate as a party; and

(2) Is so situated that the disposition of the investigation may as a practical matter impair the ability to protect that person's interest unless allowed to participate as a party, and

(3) Is not adequately represented by existing parties.

§13.109 Convening the investigation.

The investigation shall be conducted at such place or places designated by the Presiding Officer, and as convenient to the parties involved as expeditious and efficient handling of the investigation permits.

§13.111 Subpoenas.

(a) Upon motion of the Presiding Officer, or upon the request of a party to the investigation, the Presiding Officer may issue a subpoena directing any person to appear at a designated time and place to testify or to produce documentary or physical evidence relating to any matter under investigation.

(b) Subpoenas shall be served by personal service, or upon an agent designated in writing for the purpose, or by registered or certified mail addressed to such person or agent. Whenever service is made by registered or certified mail, the date of mailing shall be considered as the time when service is made.

(c) Subpoenas shall extend in jurisdiction throughout the United States or any territory or possession thereof.

§13.113 Noncompliance with the investigative process.

If any person fails to comply with the provisions of this subpart or with any subpoena or order issued by the Presiding Officer or the designee of the Presiding Officer, judicial enforcement may be initiated against that person under applicable statutes.

§13.115 Public proceedings.

(a) All investigative proceedings and depositions shall be public unless the Presiding Officer determines that the public interest requires otherwise.

(b) The Presiding Officer may order information contained in any report or document filed or in any testimony given pursuant to this subpart withheld from public disclosure when, in the judgment of the Presiding Officer, disclosure would adversely affect the interests of any person and is not required in the public interest or is not otherwise required by statute to be made available to the public. Any person may make written objection to the public disclosure of such information, stating the grounds for such objection.

§13.117 Conduct of investigative proceeding or deposition.

(a) The Presiding Officer or the designee of the Presiding Officer may question witnesses.

(b) Any witness may be accompanied by counsel.

(c) Any party may be accompanied by counsel and either the party or counsel may—

(1) Question witnesses, provided the questions are relevant and material to the matters under investigation and would not unduly impede the progress of the investigation; and

(2) Make objections on the record and argue the basis for such objections.

(d) Copies of all notices or written communications sent to a party or witness shall upon request be sent to that person's attorney of record.

§ 13.119 Rights of persons against self-incrimination.

(a) Whenever a person refuses, on the basis of a privilege against self-incrimination, to testify or provide other information during the course of any investigation conducted under this subpart, the Presiding Officer may, with the approval of the Attorney General of the United States, issue an order requiring the person to give testimony or provide other information. However, no testimony or other information so compelled (or any information directly or indirectly derived from such testimony or other information) may be used against the person in any criminal case, except in a prosecution for perjury, giving a false statement, or otherwise failing to comply with the order.

(b) The Presiding Officer may issue an order under this section if—

(1) The testimony or other information from the witness may be necessary to the public interest; and

(2) The witness has refused or is likely to refuse to testify or provide other information on the basis of a privilege against self-incrimination.

(c) Immunity provided by this section will not become effective until the person has refused to testify or provide other information on the basis of a privilege against self-incrimination, and an order under this section has been issued. An order, however, may be issued prospectively to become effective in the event of a claim of the privilege.

§ 13.121 Witness fees.

All witnesses appearing shall be compensated at the same rate as a witness appearing before a United States District Court.

§ 13.123 Submission by party to the investigation.

(a) During an investigation conducted under this subpart, a party may submit to the Presiding Officer—

(1) A list of witnesses to be called, specifying the subject matter of the expected testimony of each witness, and

(2) A list of exhibits to be considered for inclusion in the record.

(b) If the Presiding Officer determines that the testimony of a witness or the receipt of an exhibit in accordance with paragraph (a) of this section will be relevant, competent and material to the investigation, the Presiding Officer may subpoena the witness or use the exhibit during the investigation.

§ 13.125 Depositions.

Depositions for investigative purposes may be taken at the discretion of the Presiding Officer with reasonable notice to the party under investigation. Such depositions shall be taken before the Presiding Officer or other person authorized to administer oaths and designated by the Presiding Officer. The testimony shall be reduced to writing by the person taking the deposition, or under the direction of that person, and where possible shall then be subscribed by the deponent. Any person may be compelled to appear and testify and to produce physical and documentary evidence.

§ 13.127 Reports, decisions and orders.

The Presiding Officer shall issue a written report based on the record developed during the formal investigation, including a summary of principal conclusions. A summary of principal conclusions shall be prepared by the official who issued the order of investigation in every case which results in no action, or no action as to a particular party to the investigation. All such reports shall be furnished to the parties to the investigation and filed in the public docket. Insertion of the report in the Public Docket shall constitute "entering of record" and publication as prescribed by section 313(b) of the Federal Aviation Act.

§ 13.129 Post-investigation action.

A decision on whether to initiate subsequent action shall be made on the basis of the record developed during the formal investigation and any other information in the possession of the Administrator.

§ 13.131 Other procedures.

Any question concerning the scope or conduct of a formal investigation not covered in this subpart may be ruled on by the Presiding Officer on motion of the Presiding Officer, or on the motion of a party or a person testifying or producing evidence.

Subpart G—Rules of Practice in FAA Civil Penalty Actions

Source: Amdt. 13–21, 55 FR 27575, July 3, 1990, unless otherwise noted.

§ 13.201 Applicability.

(a) This subpart applies to the following actions:

(1) A civil penalty action in which a complaint has been issued for an amount not exceeding $50,000 for a violation arising under the Federal Aviation Act of 1958, as amended (49 U.S.C. 1301, *et seq.*), or a rule, regulation, or order issued thereunder.

(2) A civil penalty action in which a complaint has been issued for a violation arising under the Federal Aviation Act of 1958, as amended (49 U.S.C. 1471, *et seq.*) and the Hazardous Materials Transportation Act (49 U.S.C. 1801 *et seq.*), or a rule, regulation, or order issued thereunder.

(b) This subpart applies only to proceedings initiated after September 7, 1988. All other cases, hearings, or other proceedings pending or in progress before September 7, 1988, are not affected by the rules in this subpart.

(c) Notwithstanding the provisions of paragraph (a) of this section, the United States district courts shall have exclusive jurisdiction of any civil penalty action initiated by the Administrator:

(1) Which involves an amount in controversy in excess of $50,000;

(2) Which is an *in rem* action or in which an *in rem* action based on the same violation has been brought;

(3) Regarding which an aircraft subject to lien has been seized by the United States; and

(4) In which a suit for injunctive relief based on the violation giving rise to the civil penalty has also been brought.

§ 13.202 Definitions.

Administrative law judge means an administrative law judge appointed pursuant to the provisions of 5 U.S.C. 3105.

Agency attorney means the Deputy Chief Counsel, the Assistant Chief Counsel, Enforcement, the Assistant Chief Counsel, Regulations, the Assistant Chief Counsel, Europe, Africa, and Middle East Area Office, each Regional Counsel, the Aeronautical Center Counsel, or the Technical Center Counsel, or an attorney on the staff of the Assistant Chief Counsel, Enforcement, the Assistant Chief Counsel, Regulations, the Assistant Chief Counsel, Europe, Africa, and Middle East Area Office, each Regional Counsel, the Aeronautical Center Counsel, or the Technical Center Counsel who prosecutes a civil penalty action. An agency attorney shall not include:

(1) The Chief Counsel, the Assistant Chief Counsel for Litigation, or the Special Counsel and Director of Civil Penalty Adjudications; or

(2) Any attorney on the staff of either the Assistant Chief Counsel for Litigation or the Special Counsel and Director of Civil Penalty Adjudications who advises the FAA decisionmaker regarding an initial decision or any appeal to the FAA decisionmaker; or

(3) Any attorney who is supervised in a civil penalty action by a person who provides such advice to the FAA decisionmaker in that action or a factually-related action.

Attorney means a person licensed by a state, the District of Columbia, or a territory of the United States to practice law or appear before the courts of that state or territory.

Complaint means a document issued by an agency attorney alleging a violation of the Federal Aviation Act of 1958, as amended, or a rule, regulation, or order issued thereunder, or the Hazardous Materials Transportation Act, or a rule, regulation, or order issued thereunder that has been filed with the hearing docket after a hearing has been requested pursuant to § 13.16(d)(3) or § 13.16(e)(2)(ii) of this part.

FAA decisionmaker means the Administrator of the Federal Aviation Administration, acting in the capacity of the decisionmaker on appeal, or any person to whom the Administrator has delegated the Administrator's decision-making authority in a civil penalty action. As used in this subpart, the FAA decisionmaker is the official authorized to issue a final decision and order of the Administrator in a civil penalty action.

Mail includes U.S. certified mail, U.S. registered mail, or use of an overnight express courier service.

Order assessing civil penalty means a document that contains a finding of violation of the Federal Aviation Act of 1958, as amended, or a rule, regulation, or order issued thereunder, or the Hazardous Materials Transportation Act, or a rule, regulation, or order issued thereunder and may direct payment of a civil penalty. Unless an appeal is filed with the FAA decisionmaker in a timely manner, an initial decision or order of an administrative law judge shall be considered an order assessing civil penalty if an administrative law judge finds that an alleged violation occurred and determines that a civil penalty, in an amount found appropriate by the administrative law judge, is warranted. Unless a petition for review is filed with a U.S. Court of Appeals in a timely manner, a final decision and order of the Administrator shall be considered an order assessing civil penalty if the FAA decisionmaker finds that an alleged violation occurred and a civil penalty is warranted.

Party means the respondent or the Federal Aviation Administration (FAA).

Personal delivery includes hand-delivery or use of a contract or express messenger service. "Personal delivery" does not include the use of Government interoffice mail service.

Pleading means a complaint, an answer, and any amendment of these documents permitted under this subpart.

Properly addressed means a document that shows an address contained in agency records, a residential, business, or other address submitted by a person on any document provided under this subpart, or any other address shown by other reasonable and available means.

Respondent means a person, corporation, or company named in a complaint.

[Amdt. 13–21, 55 FR 27575, July 3, 1990, as amended by Amdt. 13–24, 58 FR 50241, Sept. 24, 1993; Amdt. 13–29, 62 FR 46866, Sept. 4, 1997]

§ 13.203 Separation of functions.

(a) Civil penalty proceedings, including hearings, shall be prosecuted by an agency attorney.

(b) An agency employee engaged in the performance of investigative or prosecutorial functions in a civil penalty action shall not, in that case or a factually-related case, participate or give advice in a decision by the administrative law judge or by the FAA decisionmaker on appeal, except as counsel or a witness in the public proceedings.

(c) The Chief Counsel, the Assistant Chief Counsel for Litigation, the Special Counsel and Director of Civil Penalty Adjudications, or an attorney on the staff of either the Assistant Chief Counsel for Litigation or the Special Counsel and Director of Civil Penalty Adjudications, will advise the FAA decisionmaker regarding an initial decision or any appeal of a civil penalty action to the FAA decisionmaker.

[Amdt. 13–21, 55 FR 27575, July 3, 1990, as amended by Amdt. 13–24, 58 FR 50241, Sept. 24, 1993]

§ 13.204 Appearances and rights of parties.

(a) Any party may appear and be heard in person.

(b) Any party may be accompanied, represented, or advised by an attorney or representative designated by the party and may be examined by that attorney or representative in any proceeding governed by this subpart. An attorney or representative who represents a party may file a notice of appearance in the action, in the manner provided in § 13.210 of this subpart, and shall serve a copy of the notice of appearance on each party, in the manner provided in § 13.211 of this subpart, before participating in any proceeding governed by this subpart. The attorney or representative shall include the name, address, and telephone number of the attorney or representative in the notice of appearance.

(c) Any person may request a copy of a document upon payment of reasonable costs. A person may keep an original document, data, or evidence, with the consent of the administrative law judge, by substituting a legible copy of the document for the record.

§ 13.205 Administrative law judges.

(a) *Powers of an administrative law judge.* In accordance with the rules of this subpart, an administrative law judge may:

(1) Give notice of, and hold, pre-hearing conferences and hearings;

(2) Administer oaths and affirmations;

(3) Issue subpoenas authorized by law and issue notices of deposition requested by the parties;

(4) Rule on offers of proof;

(5) Receive relevant and material evidence;

(6) Regulate the course of the hearing in accordance with the rules of this subpart;

(7) Hold conferences to settle or to simplify the issues by consent of the parties;

(8) Dispose of procedural motions and requests; and

(9) Make findings of fact and conclusions of law, and issue an initial decision.

(b) *Limitations on the power of the administrative law judge.* The administrative law judge shall not issue an order of contempt, award costs to any party, or impose any sanction not specified in this subpart. If the administrative law judge imposes any sanction not specified in this subpart, a party may file an interlocutory appeal of right with the FAA decisionmaker pursuant to §13.219(c)(4) of this subpart. This section does not preclude an administrative law judge from issuing an order that bars a person from a specific proceeding based on a finding of obstreperous or disruptive behavior in that specific proceeding.

(c) *Disqualification.* The administrative law judge may disqualify himself or herself at any time. A party may file a motion, pursuant to §13.218(f)(6), requesting that an administrative law judge be disqualified from the proceedings.

[Amdt. 13–21, 55 FR 27575, July 3, 1990; 55 FR 29293, July 18, 1990]

§13.206 Intervention.

(a) A person may submit a motion for leave to intervene as a party in a civil penalty action. Except for good cause shown, a motion for leave to intervene shall be submitted not later than 10 days before the hearing.

(b) If the administrative law judge finds that intervention will not unduly broaden the issues or delay the proceedings, the administrative law judge may grant a motion for leave to intervene if the person will be bound by any order or decision entered in the action or the person has a property, financial, or other legitimate interest that may not be addressed adequately by the parties. The administrative law judge may determine the extent to which an intervenor may participate in the proceedings.

§13.207 Certification of documents.

(a) *Signature required.* The attorney of record, the party, or the party's representative shall sign each document tendered for filing with the hearing docket clerk, the administrative law judge, the FAA decisionmaker on appeal, or served on each party.

(b) *Effect of signing a document.* By signing a document, the attorney of record, the party, or the party's representative certifies that the attorney, the party, or the party's representative has read the document and, based on reasonable inquiry and to the best of that person's knowledge, information, and belief, the document is—

(1) Consistent with these rules;

(2) Warranted by existing law or that a good faith argument exists for extension, modification, or reversal of existing law; and

(3) Not unreasonable or unduly burdensome or expensive, not made to harass any person, not made to cause unnecessary delay, not made to cause needless increase in the cost of the proceedings, or for any other improper purpose.

(c) *Sanctions.* If the attorney of record, the party, or the party's representative signs a document in violation of this section, the administrative law judge or the FAA decisionmaker shall:

(1) Strike the pleading signed in violation of this section;

(2) Strike the request for discovery or the discovery response signed in violation of this section and preclude further discovery by the party;

(3) Deny the motion or request signed in violation of this section;

(4) Exclude the document signed in violation of this section from the record;

(5) Dismiss the interlocutory appeal and preclude further appeal on that issue by the party who filed the appeal until an initial decision has been entered on the record; or

(6) Dismiss the appeal of the administrative law judge's initial decision to the FAA decisionmaker.

§ 13.208 Complaint.

(a) *Filing.* The agency attorney shall file the original and one copy of the complaint with the hearing docket clerk, or may file a written motion pursuant to § 13.218(f)(2)(i) of this subpart instead of filing a complaint, not later than 20 days after receipt by the agency attorney of a request for hearing.

The agency attorney should suggest a location for the hearing when filing the complaint.

(b) *Service.* An agency attorney shall personally deliver or mail a copy of the complaint on the respondent, the president of the corporation or company named as a respondent, or a person designated by the respondent to accept service of documents in the civil penalty action.

(c) *Contents.* A complaint shall set forth the facts alleged, any regulation allegedly violated by the respondent, and the proposed civil penalty in sufficient detail to provide notice of any factual or legal allegation and proposed civil penalty.

(d) *Motion to dismiss allegations or complaint.* Instead of filing an answer to the complaint, a respondent may move to dismiss the complaint, or that part of the complaint, alleging a violation that occurred on or after August 2, 1990, and more than 2 years before an agency attorney issued a notice of proposed civil penalty to the respondent.

(1) An administrative law judge may not grant the motion and dismiss the complaint or part of the complaint if the administrative law judge finds that the agency has shown good cause for any delay in issuing the notice of proposed civil penalty.

(2) If the agency fails to show good cause for any delay, an administrative law judge may dismiss the complaint, or that part of the complaint, alleging a violation that occurred more than 2 years before an agency attorney issued

the notice of proposed civil penalty to the respondent.

(3) A party may appeal the administrative law judge's ruling on the motion to dismiss the complaint or any part of the complaint in accordance with § 13.219(b) of this subpart.

[Admt. 13–21, 55 FR 27575, July 3, 1990, as amended by Admt. 13–22, 55 FR 31176, Aug. 1, 1990]

§ 13.209 Answer.

(a) *Writing required.* A respondent shall file a written answer to the complaint, or may file a written motion pursuant to § 13.208(d) or § 13.218(f)(1–4) of this subpart instead of filing an answer, not later than 30 days after service of the complaint. The answer may be in the form of a letter but must be dated and signed by the person responding to the complaint. An answer may be typewritten or may be legibly handwritten.

(b) *Filing and address.* A person filing an answer shall personally deliver or mail the original and one copy of the answer for filing with the hearing docket clerk, not later than 30 days after service of the complaint, to the Hearing Docket, Federal Aviation Administration, 800 Independence Avenue, SW., Room 924A, Washington, DC 20591, Attention: Hearing Docket Clerk. The person filing an answer should suggest a location for the hearing when filing the answer.

(c) *Service.* A person filing an answer shall serve a copy of the answer on the agency attorney who filed the complaint.

(d) *Contents.* An answer shall specifically state any affirmative defense that the respondent intends to assert at the hearing. A person filing an answer may include a brief statement of any relief requested in the answer.

(e) *Specific denial of allegations required.* A person filing an answer shall admit, deny, or state that the person is without sufficient knowledge or information to admit or deny, each numbered paragraph of the complaint. Any statement or allegation contained in the complaint that is not specifically denied in the answer may be deemed an admission of the truth of that allegation. A general denial of the complaint is deemed a failure to file an answer.

(f) *Failure to file answer.* A person's failure to file an answer without good cause shall be deemed an admission of the truth of each allegation contained in the complaint.

§ 13.210 Filing of documents.

(a) *Address and method of filing.* A person tendering a document for filing shall personally deliver or mail the signed original and one copy of each document to the Hearing Docket, Federal Aviation Administration, 800 Independence Avenue, SW., Room 924A, Washington, DC 20591, Attention: Hearing Docket Clerk. A person shall serve a copy of each document on each party in accordance with § 13.211 of this subpart.

(b) *Date of filing.* A document shall be considered to be filed on the date of personal delivery; or if mailed, the mailing date shown on the certificate of service, the date shown on the postmark if there is no certificate of service, or other mailing date shown by other evidence if there is no certificate of service or postmark.

(c) *Form.* Each document shall be typewritten or legibly handwritten.

(d) *Contents.* Unless otherwise specified in this subpart, each document must contain a short, plain statement of the facts on which the person's case rests and a brief statement of the action requested in the document.

[Amdt. 13–21, 55 FR 27575, July 3, 1990; 55 FR 29293, July 18, 1990]

§ 13.211 Service of documents.

(a) *General.* A person shall serve a copy of any document filed with the Hearing Docket on each party at the time of filing. Service on a party's attorney of record or a party's designated representative may be considered adequate service on the party.

(b) *Type of service.* A person may serve documents by personal delivery or by mail.

(c) *Certificate of service.* A person may attach a certificate of service to a document tendered for filing with the hearing docket clerk. A certificate of service shall consist of a statement, dated and signed by the person filing the document, that the document was personally delivered or mailed to each party on a specific date.

(d) *Date of service.* The date of service shall be the date of personal delivery; or if mailed, the mailing date shown on the certificate of service, the date shown on the postmark if there is no certificate of service, or other mailing date shown by other evidence if there is no certificate of service or postmark.

(e) *Additional time after service by mail.* Whenever a party has a right or a duty to act or to make any response within a prescribed period after service by mail, or on a date certain after service by mail, 5 days shall be added to the prescribed period.

(f) *Service by the administrative law judge.* The administrative law judge shall serve a copy of each document including, but not limited to, notices of prehearing conferences and hearings, rulings on motions, decisions, and orders, upon each party to the proceedings by personal delivery or by mail.

(g) *Valid service.* A document that was properly addressed, was sent in accordance with this subpart, and that was returned, that was not claimed, or that was refused, is deemed to have been served in accordance with this subpart. The service shall be considered valid as of the date and the time that the document was deposited with a contract or express messenger, the document was mailed, or personal delivery of the document was refused.

(h) *Presumption of service.* There shall be a presumption of service where a party or a person, who customarily receives mail, or receives it in the ordinary course of business, at either the person's residence or the person's principal place of business, acknowledges receipt of the document.

§ 13.212 Computation of time.

(a) This section applies to any period of time prescribed or allowed by this subpart, by notice or order of the administrative law judge, or by any applicable statute.

(b) The date of an act, event, or default, after which a designated time period begins to run, is not included in a computation of time under this subpart.

(c) The last day of a time period is included in a computation of time unless it is a Saturday, Sunday, or a legal holiday. If the last day of the time period is a Saturday, Sunday, or legal holiday, the time period runs until the end of the next day that is not a Saturday, Sunday, or legal holiday.

§ 13.213 Extension of time.

(a) *Oral requests.* The parties may agree to extend for a reasonable period the time for filing a document under this subpart. If the parties agree, the administrative law judge shall grant one extension of time to each party. The party seeking the extension of time shall submit a draft order to the administrative law judge to be signed by the administrative law judge and filed with the hearing docket clerk. The administrative law judge may grant additional oral requests for an extension of time where the parties agree to the extension.

(b) *Written motion.* A party shall file a written motion for an extension of time with the administrative law judge not later than 7 days before the document is due unless good cause for the late filing is shown. A party filing a written motion for an extension of time shall serve a copy of the motion on each party. The administrative law judge may grant the extension of time if good cause for the extension is shown.

(c) *Failure to rule.* If the administrative law judge fails to rule on a written motion for an extension of time by the date the document was due, the motion for an extension of time is deemed granted for no more than 20 days after the original date the document was to be filed.

§ 13.214 Amendment of pleadings.

(a) *Filing and service.* A party shall file the amendment with the administrative law judge and shall serve a copy of the amendment on all parties to the proceeding.

(b) *Time.* A party shall file an amendment to a complaint or an answer within the following:

(1) Not later than 15 days before the scheduled date of a hearing, a party may amend a complaint or an answer without the consent of the administrative law judge.

(2) Less than 15 days before the scheduled date of a hearing, the administrative law judge may allow amendment of a complaint or an answer only for good cause shown in a motion to amend.

(c) *Responses.* The administrative law judge shall allow a reasonable time, but not more than 20 days from the date of filing, for other parties to respond if an amendment to a complaint, answer, or other pleading has been filed with the administrative law judge.

§ 13.215 Withdrawal of complaint or request for hearing.

At any time before or during a hearing, an agency attorney may withdraw a complaint or a party may withdraw a request for a hearing without the consent of the administrative law judge. If an agency attorney withdraws the complaint or a party withdraws the request for a hearing and the answer, the administrative law judge shall dismiss the proceedings under this subpart with prejudice.

§ 13.216 Waivers.

Waivers of any rights provided by statute or regulation shall be in writing or by stipulation made at a hearing and entered into the record. The parties shall set forth the precise terms of the waiver and any conditions.

§ 13.217 Joint procedural or discovery schedule.

(a) *General.* The parties may agree to submit a schedule for filing all prehearing motions, a schedule for conducting discovery in the proceedings, or a schedule that will govern all prehearing motions and discovery in the proceedings.

(b) *Form and content of schedule.* If the parties agree to a joint procedural or discovery schedule, one of the parties shall file the joint schedule with the administrative law judge, setting forth the dates to which the parties have agreed, and shall serve a copy of the joint schedule on each party.

(1) The joint schedule may include, but need not be limited to, requests for discovery, any objections to discovery

requests, responses to discovery requests to which there are no objections, submission of prehearing motions, responses to prehearing motions, exchange of exhibits to be introduced at the hearing, and a list of witnesses that may be called at the hearing.

(2) Each party shall sign the original joint schedule to be filed with the administrative law judge.

(c) *Time.* The parties may agree to submit all prehearing motions and responses and may agree to close discovery in the proceedings under the joint schedule within a reasonable time before the date of the hearing, but not later than 15 days before the hearing.

(d) *Order establishing joint schedule.* The administrative law judge shall approve the joint schedule filed by the parties. One party shall submit a draft order establishing a joint schedule to the administrative law judge to be signed by the administrative law judge and filed with the hearing docket clerk.

(e) *Disputes.* The administrative law judge shall resolve disputes regarding discovery or disputes regarding compliance with the joint schedule as soon as possible so that the parties may continue to comply with the joint schedule.

(f) *Sanctions for failure to comply with joint schedule.* If a party fails to comply with the administrative law judge's order establishing a joint schedule, the administrative law judge may direct that party to comply with a motion to discovery request or, limited to the extent of the party's failure to comply with a motion or discovery request, the administrative law judge may:

(1) Strike that portion of a party's pleadings;

(2) Preclude prehearing or discovery motions by that party;

(3) Preclude admission of that portion of a party's evidence at the hearing, or

(4) Preclude that portion of the testimony of that party's witnesses at the hearing.

§ 13.218   Motions.

(a) *General.* A party applying for an order or ruling not specifically provided in this subpart shall do so by motion. A party shall comply with the requirements of this section when filing a motion with the administrative law judge. A party shall serve a copy of each motion on each party.

(b) *Form and contents.* A party shall state the relief sought by the motion and the particular grounds supporting that relief. If a party has evidence in support of a motion, the party shall attach any supporting evidence, including affidavits, to the motion.

(c) *Filing of motions.* A motion made prior to the hearing must be in writing. Unless otherwise agreed by the parties or for good cause shown, a party shall file any prehearing motion, and shall serve a copy on each party, not later than 30 days before the hearing. Motions introduced during a hearing may be made orally on the record unless the administrative law judge directs otherwise.

(d) *Answers to motions.* Any party may file an answer, with affidavits or other evidence in support of the answer, not later than 10 days after service of a written motion on that party. When a motion is made during a hearing, the answer may be made at the hearing on the record, orally or in writing, within a reasonable time determined by the administrative law judge.

(e) *Rulings on motions.* The administrative law judge shall rule on all motions as follows:

(1) *Discovery motions.* The administrative law judge shall resolve all pending discovery motions not later than 10 days before the hearing.

(2) *Prehearing motions.* The administrative law judge shall resolve all pending prehearing motions not later than 7 days before the hearing. If the administrative law judge issues a ruling or order orally, the administrative law judge shall serve a written copy of the ruling or order, within 3 days, on each party. In all other cases, the administrative law judge shall issue rulings and orders in writing and shall serve a copy of the ruling or order on each party.

(3) *Motions made during the hearing.* The administrative law judge may issue rulings and orders on motions made during the hearing orally. Oral rulings or orders on motions must be made on the record.

(f) *Specific motions.* A party may file the following motions with the administrative law judge:

(1) *Motion to dismiss for insufficiency.* A respondent may file a motion to dismiss the complaint for insufficiency instead of filing an answer. If the administrative law judge denies the motion to dismiss the complaint for insufficiency, the respondent shall file an answer not later than 10 days after service of the administrative law judge's denial of the motion. A motion to dismiss the complaint for insufficiency must show that the complaint fails to state a violation of the Federal Aviation Act of 1958, as amended, or a rule, regulation, or order issued thereunder, or a violation of the Hazardous Materials Transportation Act, or a rule, regulation, or order issued thereunder.

(2) *Motion to dismiss.* A party may file a motion to dismiss, specifying the grounds for dismissal. If an administrative law judge grants a motion to dismiss in part, a party may appeal the administrative law judge's ruling on the motion to dismiss under §13.219(b) of this subpart.

(i) *Motion to dismiss a request for a hearing.* An agency attorney may file a motion to dismiss a request for a hearing instead of filing a complaint. If the motion to dismiss is not granted, the agency attorney shall file the complaint and shall serve a copy of the complaint on each party not later than 10 days after service of the administrative law judge's ruling or order on the motion to dismiss. If the motion to dismiss is granted and the proceedings are terminated without a hearing, the respondent may file an appeal pursuant to §13.233 of this subpart. If required by the decision on appeal, the agency attorney shall file a complaint and shall serve a copy of the complaint on each party not later than 10 days after service of the decision on appeal.

(ii) *Motion to dismiss a complaint.* A respondent may file a motion to dismiss a complaint instead of filing an answer. If the motion to dismiss is not granted, the respondent shall file an answer and shall serve a copy of the answer on each party not later than 10 days after service of the administrative law judge's ruling or order on the motion to dismiss. If the motion to dismiss is

granted and the proceedings are terminated without a hearing, the agency attorney may file an appeal pursuant to §13.233 of this subpart. If required by the decision on appeal, the respondent shall file an answer and shall serve a copy of the answer on each party not later than 10 days after service of the decision on appeal.

(3) *Motion for more definite statement.* A party may file a motion for more definite statement of any pleading which requires a response under this subpart. A party shall set forth, in detail, the indefinite or uncertain allegations contained in a complaint or response to any pleading and shall submit the details that the party believes would make the allegation or response definite and certain.

(i) *Complaint.* A respondent may file a motion requesting a more definite statement of the allegations contained in the complaint instead of filing an answer. If the administrative law judge grants the motion, the agency attorney shall supply a more definite statement not later than 15 days after service of the ruling granting the motion. If the agency attorney fails to supply a more definite statement, the administrative law judge shall strike the allegations in the complaint to which the motion is directed. If the administrative law judge denies the motion, the respondent shall file an answer and shall serve a copy of the answer on each party not later than 10 days after service of the order of denial.

(ii) *Answer.* An agency attorney may file a motion requesting a more definite statement if an answer fails to respond clearly to the allegations in the complaint. If the administrative law judge grants the motion, the respondent shall supply a more definite statement not later than 15 days after service of the ruling on the motion. If the respondent fails to supply a more definite statement, the administrative law judge shall strike those statements in the answer to which the motion is directed. The respondent's failure to supply a more definite statement may be deemed an admission of unanswered allegations in the complaint.

(4) *Motion to strike.* Any party may make a motion to strike any insufficient allegation or defense, or any redundant, immaterial, or irrelevant matter in a pleading. A party shall file a motion to strike with the administrative law judge and shall serve a copy on each party before a response is required under this subpart or, if a response is not required, not later than 10 days after service of the pleading.

(5) *Motion for decision.* A party may make a motion for decision, regarding all or any part of the proceedings, at any time before the administrative law judge has issued an initial decision in the proceedings. The administrative law judge shall grant a party's motion for decision if the pleadings, depositions, answers to interrogatories, admissions, matters that the administrative law judge has officially noticed, or evidence introduced during the hearing show that there is no genuine issue of material fact and that the party making the motion is entitled to a decision as a matter of law. The party making the motion for decision has the burden of showing that there is no genuine issue of material fact disputed by the parties.

(6) *Motion for disqualification.* A party may file a motion for disqualification with the administrative law judge and shall serve a copy on each party. A party may file the motion at any time after the administrative law judge has been assigned to the proceedings but shall make the motion before the administrative law judge files an initial decision in the proceedings.

(i) *Motion and supporting affidavit.* A party shall state the grounds for disqualification, including, but not limited to, personal bias, pecuniary interest, or other factors showing disqualification, in the motion for disqualification. A party shall submit an affidavit with the motion for disqualification that sets forth, in detail, the matters alleged to constitute grounds for disqualification.

(ii) *Answer.* A party shall respond to the motion for disqualification not later than 5 days after service of the motion for disqualification.

(iii) *Decision on motion for disqualification.* The administrative law judge shall render a decision on the motion for disqualification not later than 15 days after the motion has been filed. If the administrative law judge finds that the motion for disqualification and supporting affidavit show a basis for disqualification, the administrative law judge shall withdraw from the proceedings immediately. If the administrative law judge finds that disqualification is not warranted, the administrative law judge shall deny the motion and state the grounds for the denial on the record. If the administrative law judge fails to rule on a party's motion for disqualification within 15 days after the motion has been filed, the motion is deemed granted.

(iv) *Appeal.* A party may appeal the administrative law judge's denial of the motion for disqualification in accordance with § 13.219(b) of this subpart.

§ 13.219 Interlocutory appeals.

(a) *General.* Unless otherwise provided in this subpart, a party may not appeal a ruling or decision of the administrative law judge to the FAA decisionmaker until the initial decision has been entered on the record. A decision or order of the FAA decisionmaker on the interlocutory appeal does not constitute a final order of the Administrator for the purposes of judicial appellate review under section 1006 of the Federal Aviation Act of 1958, as amended.

(b) *Interlocutory appeal for cause.* If a party files a written request for an interlocutory appeal for cause with the administrative law judge, or orally requests an interlocutory appeal for cause, the proceedings are stayed until the administrative law judge issues a decision on the request. If the administrative law judge grants the request, the proceedings are stayed until the FAA decisionmaker issues a decision on the interlocutory appeal. The administrative law judge shall grant an interlocutory appeal for cause if a party shows that delay of the appeal would be detrimental to the public interest or would result in undue prejudice to any party.

(c) *Interlocutory appeals of right.* If a party notifies the administrative law judge of an interlocutory appeal of right, the proceedings are stayed until the FAA decisionmaker issues a decision on the interlocutory appeal. A party may file an interlocutory appeal with the FAA decisionmaker, without the consent of the administrative law judge, before an initial decision has been entered in the case of:

(1) A ruling or order by the administrative law judge barring a person from the proceedings.

(2) Failure of the administrative law judge to dismiss the proceedings in accordance with § 13.215 of this subpart.

(3) A ruling or order by the administrative law judge in violation of § 13.205(b) of this subpart.

(d) *Procedure.* A party shall file a notice of interlocutory appeal, with supporting documents, with the FAA decisionmaker and the hearing docket clerk, and shall serve a copy of the notice and supporting documents on each party and the administrative law judge, not later than 10 days after the administrative law judge's decision forming the basis of an interlocutory appeal of right or not later than 10 days after the administrative law judge's decision granting an interlocutory appeal for cause, whichever is appropriate. A party shall file a reply brief, if any, with the FAA decisionmaker and serve a copy of the reply brief on each party, not later than 10 days after service of the appeal brief. The FAA decisionmaker shall render a decision on the interlocutory appeal, on the record and as a part of the decision in the proceedings, within a reasonable time after receipt of the interlocutory appeal.

(e) The FAA decisionmaker may reject frivolous, repetitive, or dilatory appeals, and may issue an order precluding one or more parties from making further interlocutory appeals in a proceeding in which there have been frivolous, repetitive, or dilatory interlocutory appeals.

[Amdt. 13–21, 55 FR 27575, July 3, 1990, as amended by Amdt. 13–23, 55 FR 45983, Oct. 31, 1990]

§ 13.220 Discovery.

(a) *Initiation of discovery.* Any party may initiate discovery described in this section, without the consent or approval of the administrative law judge, at any time after a complaint has been filed in the proceedings.

(b) *Methods of discovery.* The following methods of discovery are permitted under this section: depositions on oral examination or written questions of any person; written interrogatories directed to a party; requests for production of documents or tangible items to any person; and requests for admission by a party. A party is not required to file written interrogatories and responses, requests for production of documents or tangible items and responses, and requests for admission and response with the administrative law judge or the hearing docket clerk. In the event of a discovery dispute, a party shall attach a copy of these documents in support of a motion made under this section.

(c) *Service on the agency.* A party shall serve each discovery request directed to the agency or any agency employee on the agency attorney of record.

(d) *Time for response to discovery requests.* Unless otherwise directed by this subpart or agreed by the parties, a party shall respond to a request for discovery, including filing objections to a request for discovery, not later than 30 days of service of the request.

(e) *Scope of discovery.* Subject to the limits on discovery set forth in paragraph (f) of this section, a party may discover any matter that is not privileged and that is relevant to the subject matter of the proceeding. A party may discover information that relates to the claim or defense of any party including the existence, description, nature, custody, condition, and location of any document or other tangible item and the identity and location of any person having knowledge of discoverable matter. A party may discover facts known, or opinions held, by an expert who any other party expects to call to testify at the hearing. A party has no ground to object to a discovery request on the basis that the information sought would not be admissible at the hearing if the information sought during discovery is reasonably calculated to lead to the discovery of admissible evidence.

(f) *Limiting discovery.* The administrative law judge shall limit the frequency and extent of discovery permitted by this section if a party shows that—

(1) The information requested is cumulative or repetitious;

(2) The information requested can be obtained from another less burdensome and more convenient source;

(3) The party requesting the information has had ample opportunity to obtain the information through other discovery methods permitted under this section; or

(4) The method or scope of discovery requested by the party is unduly burdensome or expensive.

(g) *Confidential orders.* A party or person who has received a discovery request for information that is related to a trade secret, confidential or sensitive material, competitive or commercial information, proprietary data, or information on research and development, may file a motion for a confidential order with the administrative law judge and shall serve a copy of the motion for a confidential order on each party.

(1) The party or person making the motion must show that the confidential order is necessary to protect the information from disclosure to the public.

(2) If the administrative law judge determines that the requested material is not necessary to decide the case, the administrative law judge shall preclude any inquiry into the matter by any party.

(3) If the administrative law judge determines that the requested material may be disclosed during discovery, the administrative law judge may order that the material may be discovered and disclosed under limited conditions or may be used only under certain terms and conditions.

(4) If the administrative law judge determines that the requested material is necessary to decide the case and that a confidential order is warranted, the administrative law judge shall provide:

(i) An opportunity for review of the document by the parties off the record;

(ii) Procedures for excluding the information from the record; and

(iii) Order that the parties shall not disclose the information in any manner and the parties shall not use the information in any other proceeding.

(h) *Protective orders.* A party or a person who has received a request for discovery may file a motion for protective order with the administrative law judge and shall serve a copy of the motion for protective order on each party. The party or person making the motion must show that the protective order is necessary to protect the party or the person from annoyance, embarrassment, oppression, or undue burden or expense. As part of the protective order, the administrative law judge may:

(1) Deny the discovery request;

(2) Order that discovery be conducted only on specified terms and conditions, including a designation of the time or place for discovery or a determination of the method of discovery; or

(3) Limit the scope of discovery or preclude any inquiry into certain matters during discovery.

(i) *Duty to supplement or amend responses.* A party who has responded to a discovery request has a duty to supplement or amend the response, as soon as the information is known, as follows:

(1) A party shall supplement or amend any response to a question requesting the identity and location of any person having knowledge of discoverable matters.

(2) A party shall supplement or amend any response to a question requesting the identity of each person who will be called to testify at the hearing as an expert witness and the subject matter and substance of that witness' testimony.

(3) A party shall supplement or amend any response that was incorrect when made or any response that was correct when made but is no longer correct, accurate, or complete.

(j) *Depositions.* The following rules apply to depositions taken pursuant to this section:

(1) *Form.* A deposition shall be taken on the record and reduced to writing. The person being deposed shall sign the deposition unless the parties agree to waive the requirement of a signature.

(2) *Administration of oaths.* Within the United States, or a territory or possession subject to the jurisdiction of the United States, a party shall take a deposition before a person authorized to administer oaths by the laws of the

United States or authorized by the law of the place where the examination is held. In foreign countries, a party shall take a deposition in any manner allowed by the Federal Rules of Civil Procedure.

(3) *Notice of deposition.* A party shall serve a notice of deposition, stating the time and place of the deposition and the name and address of each person to be examined, on the person to be deposed, on the administrative law judge, on the hearing docket clerk, and on each party not later than 7 days before the deposition. A party may serve a notice of deposition less than 7 days before the deposition only with consent of the administrative law judge. If a subpoena *duces tecum* is to be served on the person to be examined, the party shall attach a copy of the subpoena *duces tecum* that describes the materials to be produced at the deposition to the notice of deposition.

(4) *Use of depositions.* A party may use any part or all of a deposition at a hearing authorized under this subpart only upon a showing of good cause. The deposition may be used against any party who was present or represented at the deposition or who had reasonable notice of the deposition.

(k) *Interrogatories.* A party, the party's attorney, or the party's representative may sign the party's responses to interrogatories. A party shall answer each interrogatory separately and completely in writing.If a party objects to an interrogatory, the party shall state the objection and the reasons for the objection. An opposing party may use any part or all of a party's responses to interrogatories at a hearing authorized under this subpart to the extent that the response is relevant, material, and not repetitious.

(1) A party shall not serve more than 30 interrogatories to each other party. Each subpart of an interrogatory shall be counted as a separate interrogatory.

(2) A party shall file a motion for leave to serve additional interrogatories on a party with the administrative law judge before serving additional interrogatories on a party. The administrative law judge shall grant the motion only if the party shows good cause for the party's failure to inquire about the information previously and that

the information cannot reasonably be obtained using less burdensome discovery methods or be obtained from other sources.

(1) *Requests for admission.* A party may serve a written request for admission of the truth of any matter within the scope of discovery under this section or the authenticity of any document described in the request. A party shall set forth each request for admission separately. A party shall serve copies of documents referenced in the request for admission unless the documents have been provided or are reasonably available for inspection and copying.

(1) *Time.* A party's failure to respond to a request for admission, in writing and signed by the attorney or the party, not later than 30 days after service of the request, is deemed an admission of the truth of the statement or statements contained in the request for admission. The administrative law judge may determine that a failure to respond to a request for admission is not deemed an admission of the truth if a party shows that the failure was due to circumstances beyond the control of the party or the party's attorney.

(2) *Response.* A party may object to a request for admission and shall state the reasons for objection. A party may specifically deny the truth of the matter or describe the reasons why the party is unable to truthfully deny or admit the matter. If a party is unable to deny or admit the truth of the matter, the party shall show that the party has made reasonable inquiry into the matter or that the information known to, or readily obtainable by, the party is insufficient to enable the party to admit or deny the matter. A party may admit or deny any part of the request for admission. If the administrative law judge determines that a response does not comply with the requirements of this rule or that the response is insufficient, the matter is deemed admitted.

(3) *Effect of admission.* Any matter admitted or deemed admitted under this section is conclusively established for the purpose of the hearing and appeal.

(m) *Motion to compel discovery.* A party may make a motion to compel discovery if a person refuses to answer a question during a deposition, a party fails or refuses to answer an interrogatory, if a person gives an evasive or incomplete answer during a deposition or when responding to an interrogatory, or a party fails or refuses to produce documents or tangible items. During a deposition, the proponent of a question may complete the deposition or may adjourn the examination before making a motion to compel if a person refuses to answer.

(n) *Failure to comply with a discovery order or order to compel.* If a party fails to comply with a discovery order or an order to compel, the administrative law judge, limited to the extent of the party's failure to comply with the discovery order or motion to compel, may:

(1) Strike that portion of a party's pleadings;

(2) Preclude prehearing or discovery motions by that party;

(3) Preclude admission of that portion of a party's evidence at the hearing; or

(4) Preclude that portion of the testimony of that party's witnesses at the hearing.

[Amdt. 13–21, 55 FR 27575, July 3, 1990, as amended by Amdt. 13–23, 55 FR 45983, Oct. 31, 1990]

§ 13.221 Notice of hearing.

(a) *Notice.* The administrative law judge shall give each party at least 60 days notice of the date, time, and location of the hearing.

(b) *Date, time, and location of the hearing.* The administrative law judge to whom the proceedings have been assigned shall set a reasonable date, time, and location for the hearing. The administrative law judge shall consider the need for discovery and any joint procedural or discovery schedule submitted by the parties when determining the hearing date. The administrative law judge shall give due regard to the convenience of the parties, the location where the majority of the witnesses reside or work, and whether the location is served by a scheduled air carrier.

(c) *Earlier hearing.* With the consent of the administrative law judge, the parties may agree to hold the hearing on an earlier date than the date specified in the notice of hearing.

§ 13.222 Evidence.

(a) *General.* A party is entitled to present the party's case or defense by oral, documentary, or demonstrative evidence, to submit rebuttal evidence, and to conduct any cross-examination that may be required for a full and true disclosure of the facts.

(b) *Admissibility.* A party may introduce any oral, documentary, or demonstrative evidence in support of the party's case or defense. The administrative law judge shall admit any oral, documentary, or demonstrative evidence introduced by a party but shall exclude irrelevant, immaterial, or unduly repetitious evidence.

(c) *Hearsay evidence.* Hearsay evidence is admissible in proceedings governed by this subpart. The fact that evidence submitted by a party is hearsay goes only to the weight of the evidence and does not affect its admissibility.

§ 13.223 Standard of proof.

The administrative law judge shall issue an initial decision or shall rule in a party's favor only if the decision or ruling is supported by, and in accordance with, the reliable, probative, and substantial evidence contained in the record. In order to prevail, the party with the burden of proof shall prove the party's case or defense by a preponderance of reliable, probative, and substantial evidence.

§ 13.224 Burden of proof.

(a) Except in the case of an affirmative defense, the burden of proof is on the agency.

(b) Except as otherwise provided by statute or rule, the proponent of a motion, request, or order has the burden of proof.

(c) A party who has asserted an affirmative defense has the burden of proving the affirmative defense.

§ 13.225 Offer of proof.

A party whose evidence has been excluded by a ruling of the administrative law judge may offer the evidence for the record on appeal.

§ 13.226 Public disclosure of evidence.

(a) The administrative law judge may order that any information contained in the record be withheld from public disclosure. Any person may object to disclosure of information in the record by filing a written motion to withhold specific information with the administrative law judge and serving a copy of the motion on each party. The party shall state the specific grounds for nondisclosure in the motion.

(b) The administrative law judge shall grant the motion to withhold information in the record if, based on the motion and any response to the motion, the administrative law judge determines that disclosure would be detrimental to aviation safety, disclosure would not be in the public interest, or that the information is not otherwise required to be made available to the public.

§ 13.227 Expert or opinion witnesses.

An employee of the agency may not be called as an expert or opinion witness, for any party other than the FAA, in any proceeding governed by this subpart. An employee of a respondent may not be called by an agency attorney as an expert or opinion witness for the FAA in any proceeding governed by this subpart to which the respondent is a party.

§ 13.228 Subpoenas.

(a) *Request for subpoena.* A party may obtain a subpoena to compel the attendance of a witness at a deposition or hearing or to require the production of documents or tangible items from the hearing docket clerk. The hearing docket clerk shall deliver the subpoena, signed by the hearing docket clerk or an administrative law judge but otherwise in blank, to the party. The party shall complete the subpoena, stating the title of the action and the date and time for the witness' attendance or production of documents or items. The party who obtained the subpoena shall serve the subpoena on the witness.

(b) *Motion to quash or modify the subpoena.* A party, or any person upon whom a subpoena has been served, may file a motion to quash or modify the subpoena with the administrative law judge at or before the time specified in the subpoena for compliance. The applicant shall describe, in detail, the basis for the application to quash or modify the supoena including, but not limited to, a statement that the testimony, document, or tangible evidence is not relevant to the proceeding, that the subpoena is not reasonably tailored to the scope of the proceeding, or that the subpoena is unreasonable and oppressive. A motion to quash or modify the subpoena will stay the effect of the subpoena pending a decision by the administrative law judge on the motion.

(c) *Enforcement of subpoena.* Upon a showing that a person has failed or refused to comply with a subpoena, a party may apply to the local Federal district court to seek judicial enforcement of the subpoena in accordance with section 1004 of the Federal Aviation Act of 1958, as amended.

§ 13.229 Witness fees.

(a) *General.* Unless otherwise authorized by the administrative law judge, the party who applies for a subpoena to compel the attendance of a witness at a deposition or hearing, or the party at whose request a witness appears at a deposition or hearing, shall pay the witness fees described in this section.

(b) *Amount.* Except for an employee of the agency who appears at the direction of the agency, a witness who appears at a deposition or hearing is entitled to the same fees and mileage expenses as are paid to a witness in a court of the United States in comparable circumstances.

§ 13.230 Record.

(a) *Exclusive record.* The transcript of all testimony in the hearing, all exhibits received into evidence, and all motions, applications, requests, and rulings shall constitute the exclusive record for decision of the proceedings and the basis for the issuance of any orders in the proceeding. Any proceedings regarding the disqualification of an administrative law judge shall be included in the record.

(b) *Examination and copying of record.* Any person may examine the record at the Hearing Docket, Federal Aviation Administration, 800 Independence Avenue, SW., Room 924A, Washington, DC

20591. Any person may have a copy of the record after payment of reasonable costs to copy the record.

§ 13.231 Argument before the administrative law judge.

(a) *Arguments during the hearing.* During the hearing, the administrative law judge shall give the parties a reasonable opportunity to present arguments on the record supporting or opposing motions, objections, and rulings if the parties request an opportunity for argument. The administrative law judge may request written arguments during the hearing if the administrative law judge finds that submission of written arguments would be reasonable.

(b) *Final oral argument.* At the conclusion of the hearing and before the administrative law judge issues an initial decision in the proceedings, the parties are entitled to submit oral proposed findings of fact and conclusions of law, exceptions to rulings of the administrative law judge, and supporting arguments for the findings, conclusions, or exceptions. At the conclusion of the hearing, a party may waive final oral argument.

(c) *Posthearing briefs.* The administrative law judge may request written posthearing briefs before the administrative law judge issues an initial decision in the proceedings if the administrative law judge finds that submission of written arguments would be reasonable. If a party files a written posthearing brief, the party shall include proposed findings of fact and conclusions of law, exceptions to rulings of the administrative law judge, and supporting arguments for the findings, conclusions, or exceptions. The administrative law judge shall give the parties a reasonable opportunity, not more than 30 days after receipt of the transcript, to prepare and submit the briefs.

§ 13.232 Initial decision.

(a) *Contents.* The administrative law judge shall issue an initial decision at the conclusion of the hearing. In each oral or written decision, the administrative law judge shall include findings of fact and conclusions of law, and the grounds supporting those findings and conclusions, upon all material issues of fact, the credibility of witnesses, the applicable law, any exercise of the administrative law judge's discretion, the amount of any civil penalty found appropriate by the administrative law judge, and a discussion of the basis for any order issued in the proceedings. The administrative law judge is not required to provide a written explanation for rulings on objections, procedural motions, and other matters not directly relevant to the substance of the initial decision. If the administrative law judge refers to any previous unreported or unpublished initial decision, the administrative law judge shall make copies of that initial decision available to all parties and the FAA decisionmaker.

(b) *Oral decision.* Except as provided in paragraph (c) of this section, at the conclusion of the hearing, the administrative law judge shall issue the initial decision and order orally on the record.

(c) *Written decision.* The administrative law judge may issue a written initial decision not later than 30 days after the conclusion of the hearing or submission of the last posthearing brief if the administrative law judge finds that issuing a written initial decision is reasonable. The administrative law judge shall serve a copy of any written initial decision on each party.

(d) *Order assessing civil penalty.* Unless appealed pursuant to § 13.233 of this subpart, the initial decision issued by the administrative law judge shall be considered an order assessing civil penalty if the administrative law judge finds that an alleged violation occurred and determines that a civil penalty, in an amount found appropriate by the administrative law judge, is warranted.

§ 13.233 Appeal from initial decision.

(a) *Notice of appeal.* A party may appeal the initial decision, and any decision not previously appealed pursuant to § 13.219, by filing a notice of appeal with the FAA decisionmaker. A party shall file the notice of appeal with the Federal Aviation Administration, 800 Independence Avenue, SW., Room 924A, Washington, DC 20591, Attention: Appellate Docket Clerk. A party shall file the notice of appeal not later than 10 days after entry of the oral initial decision on the record or service of the written initial decision on the parties and shall serve a copy of the notice of appeal on each party.

(b) *Issues on appeal.* A party may appeal only the following issues:

(1) Whether each filing of fact is supported by a preponderance of reliable, probative, and substantial evidence;

(2) Whether each conclusion of law is made in accordance with applicable law, precedent, and public policy; and

(3) Whether the administrative law judge committed any prejudicial errors during the hearing that support the appeal.

(c) *Perfecting an appeal.* Unless otherwise agreed by the parties, a party shall perfect an appeal, not later than 50 days after entry of the oral initial decision on the record or service of the written initial decision on the party, by filing an appeal brief with the FAA decisionmaker.

(1) *Extension of time by agreement of the parties.* The parties may agree to extend the time for perfecting the appeal with the consent of the FAA decisionmaker. If the FAA decisionmaker grants an extension of time to perfect the appeal, the appellate docket clerk shall serve a letter confirming the extension of time on each party.

(2) *Written motion for extension.* If the parties do not agree to an extension of time for perfecting an appeal, a party desiring an extension of time may file a written motion for an extension with the FAA decisionmaker and shall serve a copy of the motion on each party. The FAA decisionmaker may grant an extension if good cause for the extension is shown in the motion.

(d) *Appeal briefs.* A party shall file the appeal brief with the FAA decisionmaker and shall serve a copy of the appeal brief on each party.

(1) A party shall set forth, in detail, the party's specific objections to the initial decision or rulings in the appeal brief. A party also shall set forth, in detail, the basis for the appeal, the reasons supporting the appeal, and the relief requested in the appeal. If the party relies on evidence contained in the record for the appeal, the party shall specifically refer to the pertinent evidence contained in the transcript in the appeal brief.

(2) The FAA decisionmaker may dismiss an appeal, on the FAA decisionmaker's own initiative or upon motion of any other party, where a party has filed a notice of appeal but fails to perfect the appeal by timely filing an appeal brief with the FAA decisionmaker.

(e) *Reply brief.* Unless otherwise agreed by the parties, any party may file a reply brief with the FAA decisionmaker not later than 35 days after the appeal brief has been served on that party. The party filing the reply brief shall serve a copy of the reply brief on each party. If the party relies on evidence contained in the record for the reply, the party shall specifically refer to the pertinent evidence contained in the transcript in the reply brief.

(1) *Extension of time by agreement of the parties.* The parties may agree to extend the time for filing a reply brief with the consent of the FAA decisionmaker. If the FAA decisionmaker grants an extension of time to file the reply brief, the appellate docket clerk shall serve a letter confirming the extension of time on each party.

(2) *Written motion for extension.* If the parties do not agree to an extension of time for filing a reply brief, a party desiring an extension of time may file a written motion for an extension with the FAA decisionmaker and shall serve a copy of the motion on each party. The FAA decisionmaker may grant an extension if good cause for the extension is shown in the motion.

(f) *Other briefs.* The FAA decisionmaker may allow any person to submit an *amicus curiae* brief in an appeal of an initial decision. A party may not file more than one appeal brief or reply brief. A party may petition the FAA decisionmaker, in writing, for leave to file an additional brief and shall serve a copy of the petition on each party. The party may not file the additional brief with the petition. The FAA decisionmaker may grant leave to file an additional brief if the party demonstrates good cause for allowing additional argument on the appeal. The FAA decisionmaker will allow a reasonable time for the party to file the additional brief.

(g) *Number of copies.* A party shall file the original appeal brief or the original reply brief, and two copies of the brief, with the FAA decisionmaker.

(h) *Oral argument.* The FAA decisionmaker has sole discretion to permit oral argument on the appeal. On the FAA decisionmaker's own initiative or upon written motion by any party, the FAA decisionmaker may find that oral argument will contribute substantially to the development of the issues on appeal and may grant the parties an opportunity for oral argument.

(i) *Waiver of objections on appeal.* If a party fails to object to any alleged error regarding the proceedings in an appeal or a reply brief, the party waives any objection to the alleged error. The FAA decisionmaker is not required to consider any objection in an appeal brief or any argument in the reply brief if a party's objection is based on evidence contained on the record and the party does not specifically refer to the pertinent evidence from the record in the brief.

(j) *FAA decisionmaker's decision on appeal.* The FAA decisionmaker will review the briefs on appeal and the oral argument, if any, to determine if the administrative law judge committed prejudicial error in the proceedings or that the initial decision should be affirmed, modified, or reversed. The FAA decisionmaker may affirm, modify, or reverse the initial decision, make any necessary findings, or may remand the case for any proceedings that the FAA decisionmaker determines may be necessary.

(1) The FAA decisionmaker may raise any issue, on the FAA decisionmaker's own initiative, that is required for proper disposition of the proceedings. The FAA decisionmaker will give the parties a reasonable opportunity to submit arguments on the new issues before making a decision on appeal. If an issue raised by the FAA decisionmaker requires the consideration of additional testimony or evidence, the FAA decisionmaker will remand the case to the administrative law judge for further proceedings and an initial decision related to that issue. If an issue raised by the FAA decisionmaker is solely an issue of law or the issue was addressed at the hearing but was not raised by a party in the briefs on appeal, a remand of the case to the ad-

ministrative law judge for further proceedings is not required but may be provided in the discretion of the FAA decisionmaker.

(2) The FAA decisionmaker will issue the final decision and order of the Administrator on appeal in writing and will serve a copy of the decision and order on each party. Unless a petition for review is filed pursuant to §13.235, a final decision and order of the Administrator shall be considered an order assessing civil penalty if the FAA decisionmaker finds that an alleged violation occurred and a civil penalty is warranted.

(3) A final decision and order of the Administrator after appeal is precedent in any other civil penalty action. Any issue, finding or conclusion, order, ruling, or initial decision of an administrative law judge that has not been appealed to the FAA decisionmaker is not precedent in any other civil penalty action.

§ 13.234 Petition to reconsider or modify a final decision and order of the FAA decisionmaker on appeal.

(a) *General.* Any party may petition the FAA decisionmaker to reconsider or modify a final decision and order issued by the FAA decisionmaker on appeal from an initial decision. A party shall file a petition to reconsider or modify with the FAA decisionmaker not later than 30 days after service of the FAA decisionmaker's final decision and order on appeal and shall serve a copy of the petition on each party. The FAA decisionmaker will not reconsider or modify an initial decision and order issued by an administrative law judge that has not been appealed by any party to the FAA decisionmaker.

(b) *Form and number of copies.* A party shall file a petition to reconsider or modify, in writing, with the FAA decisionmaker. The party shall file the original petition with the FAA decisionmaker and shall serve a copy of the petition on each party.

(c) *Contents.* A party shall state briefly and specifically the alleged errors in the final decision and order on appeal, the relief sought by the party, and the grounds that support, the petition to reconsider or modify.

(1) If the petition is based, in whole or in part, on allegations regarding the consequences of the FAA decisionmaker's decision, the party shall describe these allegations and shall describe, and support, the basis for the allegations.

(2) If the petition is based, in whole or in part, on new material not previously raised in the proceedings, the party shall set forth the new material and include affidavits of prospective witnesses and authenticated documents that would be introduced in support of the new material. The party shall explain, in detail, why the new material was not discovered through due diligence prior to the hearing.

(d) *Repetitious and frivolous petitions.* The FAA decisionmaker will not consider repetitious or frivolous petitions. The FAA decisionmaker may summarily dismiss repetitious or frivolous petitions to reconsider or modify.

(e) *Reply petitions.* Any other party may reply to a petition to reconsider or modify, not later than 10 days after service of the petition on that party, by filing a reply with the FAA decisionmaker. A party shall serve a copy of the reply on each party.

(f) *Effect of filing petition.* Unless otherwise ordered by the FAA decisionmaker, filing of a petition pursuant to this section will not stay or delay the effective date of the FAA decisionmaker's final decision and order on appeal and shall not toll the time allowed for judicial review.

(g) *FAA decisionmaker's decision on petition.* The FAA decisionmaker has sole discretion to grant or deny a petition to reconsider or modify. The FAA decisionmaker will grant or deny a petition to reconsider or modify within a reasonable time after receipt of the petition or receipt of the reply petition, if any. The FAA decisionmaker may affirm, modify, or reverse the final decision and order on appeal, or may remand the case for any proceedings that the FAA decisionmaker determines may be necessary.

[Amdt. 13–21, 55 FR 27575, July 3, 1990; 55 FR 29293, July 18, 1990; Amdt. 13–23, 55 FR 45983, Oct. 31, 1990]

§ 13.235 Judicial review of a final decision and order.

A person may seek judicial review of a final decision and order of the Administrator as provided in section 1006 of the Federal Aviation Act of 1958, as amended. A party seeking judicial review of a final decision and order shall file a petition for review not later than 60 days after the final decision and order has been served on the party.

Subpart H—Civil Monetary Penalty Inflation Adjustment

SOURCE: Docket No. 28762, 61 FR 67445, Dec. 20, 1996, unless otherwise noted.

§ 13.301 Scope and purpose.

(a) This subpart provides a mechanism for the regular adjustment for inflation of civil monetary penalties in conformity with the Federal Civil Penalties Inflation Adjustment Act of 1990, 28 U.S.C. 2461 (note), as amended by the Debt Collection Improvement Act of 1996, Public Law 104–134, April 26, 1996, in order to maintain the deterrent effect of civil monetary penalties and to promote compliance with the law. This subpart also sets out the current adjusted maximum civil monetary penalties or range of minimum and maximum civil monetary penalties for each statutory civil penalty subject to the FAA's jurisdiction.

(b) Each adjustment to the maximum civil monetary penalty or the range of minimum and maximum civil monetary penalties, as applicable, made in accordance with this subpart applies prospectively from the date it becomes effective to actions initiated under this part, notwithstanding references to a specific maximum civil monetary penalty or range of minimum and maximum civil monetary penalties contained elsewhere in this part.

§ 13.303 Definitions.

(a) *Civil Monetary Penalty* means any penalty, fine, or other sanction that:

(1) Is for a specific monetary amount as provided by Federal law or has a maximum amount provided by Federal law;

(2) Is assessed or enforced by the FAA pursuant to Federal law; and

(3) Is assessed or enforced pursuant to an administrative proceeding or a civil action in the Federal courts.

(b) *Consumer Price Index* means the Consumer Price Index for all urban consumers published by the Department of Labor.

§ 13.305 Cost of living adjustments of civil monetary penalties.

(a) Except for the limitation to the initial adjustment to statutory maximum civil monetary penalties or range of minimum and maximum civil monetary penalties set forth in paragraph (c) of this section, the inflation adjustment under this subpart is determined by increasing the maximum civil monetary penalty or range of minimum and maximum civil monetary penalty for each civil monetary penalty by the cost-of-living adjustment. Any increase determined under paragraph (a) of this section is rounded to the nearest:

(1) Multiple of $10 in the case of penalties less than or equal to $100;

(2) Multiple of $100 in the case of penalties greater than $100 but less than or equal to $1,000;

(3) Multiple of $1,000 in the case of penalties greater than $1,000 but less than or equal to $10,000;

(4) Multiple of $5,000 in the case of penalties greater than $10,000 but less than or equal to $100,000;

(5) Multiple of $10,000 in the case of penalties greater than $100,000 but less than or equal to $200,000; and

(6) Multiple of $25,000 in the case of penalties greater than $200,000.

(b) For purposes of paragraph (a) of this section, the term "cost-of-living adjustment" means the percentage (if any) for each civil monetary penalty by which the Consumer Price Index for the month of June of the calendar year preceding the adjustment exceeds the Consumer Price Index for the month of June of the calendar year in which the amount of such civil monetary penalty was last set or adjusted pursuant to law.

(c) *Limitation on initial adjustment.* The initial adjustment of maximum civil penalty or range of minimum and maximum civil monetary penalties made pursuant to this subpart does not exceed 10 percent of the statutory maximum civil penalty before an adjustment under this subpart is made. This limitation applies only to the initial adjustment, effective on January 21, 1997.

(d) *Inflation adjustment.* Minimum and maximum civil monetary penalties within the jurisdiction of the FAA are adjusted for inflation as follows: Minimum and Maximum Civil Penalties— Adjusted for Inflation, Effective March 13, 2002.

United States Code citation	Civil monetary penalty description	Minimum penalty amount	New adjusted minimum penalty amount	Maximum penalty amount when last set or adjusted pursuant to law	New or Adjusted Maximum penalty amount
49 U.S.C. 5123(a)	Violations of hazardous materials transportation law, regulations, or orders..	$250 per violation adjusted 1/27/1997.	$250 per violation.	$27,500 per violation adjusted 1/21/1997.	$30,000 per violation, adjusted effective 3/30/02.
49 U.S.C. 46301(a)(1)	Violations of statutory provisions listed in 49 U.S.C. 46301(a)(1), regulations prescribed, or orders issued under those provisions..	N/A	N/A	$1,100 per violation, adjusted 1/21/1997.	$1,100 per violation, adjusted 1/21/1997.
49 U.S.C. 46301(a)(2)	Violations of statutory provisions listed in 49 USC 46301(a)(2), regulations prescribed, or orders issued under those provisions by a person operating an aircraft for the transportation of passengers or property for compensation.	N/A	N/A	$11,000 per violation, adjusted 1/21/1997.	$11,000 per violation, adjusted 1/21/1997.
49 U.S.C. 46301(a)(3)(A)	Violations of statutory provisions listed in 49 U.S.C. 46301(a)(1), regulations prescribed, or orders issued under those provisions relating to the transportation of hazardous materials by air..	N/A	N/A	$11,000 per violation, adjusted 1/21/1997.	$11,000 per violation, adjusted 1/21/1997.

United States Code citation	Civil monetary penalty description	Minimum penalty amount	New adjusted minimum penalty amount	Maximum penalty amount when last set or adjusted pursuant to law	New or Adjusted Maximum penalty amount
49 U.S.C. 46301(a)(3)(B)	Violations of statutory provisions listed in 49 U.S.C. 46301(a)(1), regulations prescribed, or orders issued under those provisions relating to the registration or recordation under chapter 441 of Title 49, United States Code, or an aircraft not used to provide air transportation..	N/A	N/A	$11,000 per violation, adjusted 1/21/1997.	$11,000 per violation, adjusted 1/21/1997.
49 U.S.C. 46301(a)(3)(C)	Violations of 49 U.S.C. 44718(d), or regulations prescribed or orders issued under it, relating to limiting construction or establishment of landfills.	N/A	N/A	$10,000, set 10/9/1996.	$10,000, set 10/9/1996.
49 U.S.C. 46301(a)(3)(D)	Violations of 49 U.S.C. 44725, or regulations prescribed or orders issued under it, relating to the safe disposal of life-limited aircraft parts.	N/A	N/A	$10,000, adopted 4/5/2000.	$10,000, adopted 4/5/2000.
49 U.S.C. 46301(b)	Tampering with a smoke alarm device..	N/A	N/A	$2,200 per violation, adjusted 1/21/1997.	$2,200 per violation, adjusted 1/21/1997.
49 U.S.C. 46302	Knowingly providing false information about alleged violations involving the special aircraft jurisdiction of the United States..	N/A	N/A	$11,000 per violation, adjusted 1/21/1997.	$11,000 per violation adjusted 1/21/1997.
49 U.S.C. 46303	Carrying a concealed dangerous weapon.	N/A	N/A	$11,000 per violation, adjusted 1/21/1997.	$11,000 per violation, adjusted 1/21/1997.
49 U.S.C. 46318	Interference with cabin or flight crew ..	N/A	N/A	$25,000 per violation, adopted 4/5/2000.	$25,000 per violation, adopted 4/5/2000.

[61 FR 67445, Dec. 20, 1996, as amended by Amdt. 13–28, 62 FR 4134, Jan. 29, 1997; 67 FR 6366, Feb. 11, 2002]

Subpart I—Flight Operational Quality Assurance Programs

§ 13.401 Flight Operational Quality Assurance Program: Prohibition against use of data for enforcement purposes.

(a) *Applicability*. This section applies to any operator of an aircraft who operates such aircraft under an approved Flight Operational Quality Assurance (FOQA) program.

(b) *Definitions*. For the purpose of this section, the terms—

(1) *Flight Operational Quality Assurance (FOQA) program* means an FAA-approved program for the routine collection and analysis of digital flight data gathered during aircraft operations, including data currently collected pursuant to existing regulatory provisions, when such data is included in an approved FOQA program.

(2) *FOQA data* means any digital flight data that has been collected from an individual aircraft pursuant to an FAA-approved FOQA program, regardless of the electronic format of that data.

(3) *Aggregate FOQA data* means the summary statistical indices that are associated with FOQA event categories, based on an analysis of FOQA data from multiple aircraft operations.

(c) *Requirements*. In order for paragraph (e) of this section to apply, the operator must submit, maintain, and adhere to a FOQA Implementation and Operation Plan that is approved by the Administrator and which contains the following elements:

(1) A description of the operator's plan for collecting and analyzing flight

recorded data from line operations on a routine basis, including identification of the data to be collected;

(2) Procedures for taking corrective action that analysis of the data indicates is necessary in the interest of safety;

(3) Procedures for providing the FAA with aggregate FOQA data;

(4) Procedures for informing the FAA as to any corrective action being undertaken pursuant to paragraph (c)(2) of this section.

(d) *Submission of aggregate data.* The operator will provide the FAA with aggregate FOQA data in a form and manner acceptable to the Administrator.

(e) *Enforcement.* Except for criminal or deliberate acts, the Administrator will not use an operator's FOQA data or aggregate FOQA data in an enforcement action against that operator or its employees when such FOQA data or aggregate FOQA data is obtained from a FOQA program that is approved by the Administrator.

(f) *Disclosure.* FOQA data and aggregate FOQA data, if submitted in accordance with an order designating the information as protected under part 193 of this chapter, will be afforded the nondisclosure protections of part 193 of this chapter.

(g) *Withdrawal of program approval.* The Administrator may withdraw approval of a previously approved FOQA program for failure to comply with the requirements of this chapter. Grounds for withdrawal of approval may include, but are not limited to—

(1) Failure to implement corrective action that analysis of available FOQA data indicates is necessary in the interest of safety; or

(2) Failure to correct a continuing pattern of violations following notice by the agency; or also

(3) Willful misconduct or willful violation of the FAA regulations in this chapter.

[Doc. No. FAA–2000–7554, 66 FR 55048, Oct. 31, 2001; Amdt. 13–30, 67 FR 31401, May 9, 2002]

PART 14—RULES IMPLEMENTING THE EQUAL ACCESS TO JUSTICE ACT OF 1980

Subpart A—General Provisions

AUTHORITY: 5 U.S.C. 504; 49 U.S.C. 106(f), 40113, 46104 and 47122.

SOURCE: 54 FR 46199, Nov. 1, 1989, unless otherwise noted.

Subpart A—General Provisions

§ 14.01 Purpose of these rules.

The Equal Access to Justice Act, 5 U.S.C. 504 (the Act), provides for the award of attorney fees and other expenses to eligible individuals and entities who are parties to certain administrative proceedings (adversary adjudications) before the Federal Aviation Administration (FAA). An eligible party may receive an award when it prevails over the FAA, unless the agency's position in the proceeding was substantially justified or special circumstances make an award unjust. The rules in this part describe the parties eligible for awards and the proceedings that are covered. They also explain how to apply for awards, and the procedures and standards that the FAA Decisionmaker will use to make them. As used hereinafter, the term "agency" applies to the FAA.

§ 14.02 Proceedings covered.

(a) The Act applies to certain adversary adjudications conducted by the FAA under 49 CFR part 17 and the Acquisition Management System (AMS). These are adjudications under 5 U.S.C. 554, in which the position of the FAA is represented by an attorney or other representative who enters an appearance and participates in the proceeding. This subpart applies to proceedings under 49 U.S.C. 46301, 46302, and 46303 and to the Default Adjudicative Process under part 17 of this chapter and the AMS.

(b) If a proceeding includes both matters covered by the Act and matters specifically excluded from coverage, any award made will include only fees and expenses related to covered issues.

(c) Fees and other expenses may not be awarded to a party for any portion of the adversary adjudication in which such party has unreasonably protracted the proceedings.

[54 FR 46199, Nov. 1, 1989, as amended by Amdt. 14–03, 64 FR 32935, June 18, 1999]

§ 14.03 Eligibility of applicants.

(a) To be eligible for an award of attorney fees and other expenses under the Act, the applicant must be a party to the adversary adjudication for which it seeks an award. The term "party" is defined in 5 U.S.C. 504(b)(1)(B) and 5 U.S.C. 551(3). The applicant must show that it meets all conditions or eligibility set out in this subpart.

(b) The types of eligible applicants are as follows:

(1) An individual with a net worth of not more than $2 million at the time the adversary adjudication was initiated;

(2) The sole owner of an unincorporated business who has a net worth of not more than $7 million, including both personal and business interests, and not more than 500 employees at the time the adversary adjudication was initiated;

(3) A charitable or other tax-exempt organization described in section 501(c)(3) of the Internal Revenue Code (26 U.S.C. 501(c)(3)) with not more than 500 employees at the time the adversary adjudication was initiated; and

(4) A cooperative association as defined in section 15(a) of the Agricultural Marketing Act (12 U.S.C. 1141j(a)) with not more than 500 employees at the time the adversary adjudication was initiated; and

(5) Any other partnership, corporation, association, or public or private organization with a net worth of not more than $7 million and not more than 500 employees at the time the adversary adjudication was initiated.

(c) For the purpose of eligibility, the net worth and number of employees of an applicant shall be determined as of the date the proceeding was initiated.

(d) An applicant who owns an unincorporated business will be considered an "individual" rather than a "sole owner of an unincorporated business" if the issues on which the applicant prevails are related primarily to personal interests rather than to business interest.

(e) The employees of an applicant include all persons who regularly perform services for remuneration for the applicant, under the applicant's direction and control. Part-time employees shall be included on a proportional basis.

(f) The net worth and number of employees of the applicant and all of its affiliates shall be aggregated to determine eligibility. Any individual, corporation, or other entity that directly or indirectly controls or owns a majority of the voting shares or other interest of the applicant, or any corporation or other entity of which the applicant directly or indirectly owns or controls a majority of the voting shares or other interest, will be considered an affiliate for purposes of this part, unless the ALJ or adjudicative officer determines that such treatment would be unjust and contrary to the purposes of the Act in light of the actual relationship between the affiliated entities. In addition, the ALJ or adjudicative officer may determine that financial relationships of the applicant, other than those described in this paragraph, constitute special circumstances that would make an award unjust.

(g) An applicant that participates in a proceeding primarily on behalf of one or more other persons or entities that would be ineligible if not itself eligible for an award.

[54 FR 46199, Nov. 1, 1989, as amended by Amdt. 14–03, 64 FR 32935, June 18, 1999]

§14.04 Standards for awards.

(a) A prevailing applicant may receive an award for attorney fees and other expenses incurred in connection with a proceeding, or in a significant and discrete substantive portion of the proceeding, unless the position of the agency over which the applicant has prevailed was substantially justified. Whether or not the position of the FAA was substantially justified shall be determined on the basis of the record (including the record with respect to the action or failure to act by the agency upon which the civil action is based) which was made in the civil action for which fees and other expenses are sought. The burden of proof that an award should not be made to an eligible prevailing applicant is on the agency counsel, who may avoid an award by showing that the agency's position was reasonable in law and fact.

(b) An award will be reduced or denied if the applicant has unduly or unreasonably protracted the proceeding or if special circumstances make the award sought unjust.

§14.05 Allowance fees and expenses.

(a) Awards will be based on rates customarily charged by persons engaged in the business of acting as attorneys, agents, and expert witnesses, even if the services were made available without charge or at a reduced rate to the applicant.

(b) No award for the fee of an attorney or agent under this part may exceed $125 per hour, or such rate as prescribed by 5 U.S.C. 504. No award to compensate an expert witness may exceed the highest rate at which the agency pays expert witnesses. However, an award may also include the reasonable expenses of the attorney, agent, or witness as a separate item, if the attorney, agent, or witness ordinarily charges clients separately for such expenses.

(c) In determining the reasonableness of the fee sought for an attorney, agent, or expert witness, the ALJ or adjudicative officer shall consider the following:

(1) If the attorney, agent, or witness is in private practice, his or her customary fee for similar services, or if an employee of the applicant, the fully allocated cost of the services;

(2) The prevailing rate for similar services in the community in which the attorney, agent, or witness ordinarily performs services;

(3) The time actually spent in the representation of the applicant;

(4) The time reasonably spent in light of the difficulty or complexity of the issues in the proceeding; and

(5) Such other factors as may bear on the value of the services provided.

(d) The reasonable cost of any study, analysis, engineering report, test, project, or similar matter prepared on behalf of a party may be awarded, to the extent that the charge for the service does not exceed the prevailing rate for similar services, and the study or other matter was necessary for preparation of the applicant's case.

(e) Fees may be awarded only for work performed after the issuance of a complaint, or in the Default Adjudicative Process for a protest or contract dispute under part 17 of this chapter and the AMS.

[Amdt. 13–18, 53 FR 34655, Sept. 7, 1988, as amended by Amdt. 14–1, 55 FR 15131, Apr. 20, 1990; Amdt. 14–03, 64 FR 32935, June 18, 1999]

Subpart B—Information Required From Applicants

§14.10 Contents of application.

(a) An application for an award of fees and expenses under the Act shall identify the applicant and the proceeding for which an award is sought. The application shall show that the applicant has prevailed and identify the position of the agency in the proceeding that the applicant alleges was not substantially justified. Unless the applicant is an individual, the application shall also state the number of employees of the applicant and describe briefly the type and purpose of its organization or business.

(b) The application shall also include a statement that the applicant's net worth does not exceed $2 million (if an individual) or $7 million (for all other applicants, including their affiliates) at the time the adversary adjudication was initiated. However, an applicant may omit this statement if:

(1) It attaches a copy of a ruling by the Internal Revenue Service that it qualifies as an organization described in section 501(c)(3) of the Internal Revenue Code (26 U.S.C. 501(c)(3)), or in the case of a tax-exempt organization not required to obtain a ruling from the Internal Revenue Service on its exempt status, a statement that describes the basis for the applicant's belief that it qualifies under such section; or

(2) It states that it is a cooperative association as defined in section 15(a) of the Agricultural Marketing Act (12 U.S.C. 1141j(a)).

(c) The application shall state the amount of fees and expenses for which an award is sought.

(d) The application may also include any other matters that the applicant wishes this agency to consider in determining whether and in what amount an award should be made.

(e) The application shall be signed by the applicant or an authorized officer or attorney for the applicant. It shall also contain or be accompanied by a written verification under oath or under penalty of perjury that the information provided in the application is true and correct.

(f) If the applicant is a partnership, corporation, association, organization, or sole owner of an unincorporated business, the application shall state that the applicant did not have more than 500 employees at the time the adversary adjudication was initiated, giving the number of its employees and describing briefly the type and purpose of its organization or business.

§ 14.11 Net worth exhibit.

(a) Each applicant except a qualified tax-exempt organization or cooperative association must provide with its application a detailed exhibit showing the net worth of the applicant and any affiliates when the proceeding was initiated. If any individual, corporation, or other entity directly or indirectly

controls or owns a majority of the voting shares or other interest of the applicant, or if the applicant directly or indirectly owns or controls a majority of the voting shares or other interest of any corporation or other entity, the exhibit must include a showing of the net worth of all such affiliates or of the applicant including the affiliates. The exhibit may be in any form convenient to the applicant that provides full disclosure of the applicant's and its affiliates' assets and liabilities and is sufficient to determine whether the applicant qualifies under the standards in this part. The administrative law judge may require an applicant to file additional information to determine the eligibility for an award.

(b) The net worth exhibit shall describe any transfers of assets from, or obligations incurred by, the applicant or any affiliate, occurring in the one-year period prior to the date on which the proceeding was initiated, that reduced the net worth of the applicant and its affiliates below the applicable net worth ceiling. If there were no such transactions, the applicant shall so state.

(c) Ordinarily, the net worth exhibit will be included in the public record of the proceeding. However, an applicant that objects to public disclosure of the net worth exhibit, or any part of it, may submit that portion of the exhibit directly to the ALJ or adjudicative officer in a sealed envelope labeled "Confidential Financial Information," accompanied by a motion to withhold the information.

(1) The motion shall describe the information sought to be withheld and explain, in detail, why it should be exempt under applicable law or regulation, why public disclosure would adversely affect the applicant, and why disclosure is not required in the public interest.

(2) The net worth exhibit shall be served on the FAA counsel, but need not be served on any other party to the proceeding.

(3) If the ALJ or adjudicative officer finds that the net worth exhibit, or any part of it, should not be withheld from disclosure, it shall be placed in the public record of the proceeding. Otherwise, any request to inspect or copy

the exhibit shall be disposed of in accordance with the FAA's established procedures.

[54 FR 46199, Nov. 1, 1989, as amended by Amdt. 14–03, 64 FR 32935, June 18, 1999]

§ 14.12 Documentation of fees and expenses.

The application shall be accompanied by full documentation of the fees and expenses, including the cost of any study, analysis, engineering report, test, project or similar matter, for which an award is sought. A separate itemized statement shall be submitted for each professional firm or individual whose services are covered by the application, showing the hours spent in connection with the proceedings by each individual, a description of the specific services performed, the rate at which each fee has been computed, any expenses for which reimbursement is sought, the total amount claimed, and the total amount paid or payable by the applicant or by any other person or entity for the services provided. The administrative law judge may require the applicant to provide vouchers, receipts, or other substantiation for any expenses claimed.

Subpart C—Procedures for Considering Applications

§ 14.20 When an application may be filed.

(a) An application may be filed whenever the applicant has prevailed in the proceeding, but in no case later than 30 days after the FAA Decisionmaker's final disposition of the proceeding, or service of the order of the Administrator in a proceeding under the AMS.

(b) If review or reconsideration is sought or taken of a decision to which an applicant believes it has prevailed, proceedings for the award of fees shall be stayed pending final disposition of the underlying controversy.

(c) For purposes of this part, final disposition means the later of:

(1) Under part 17 of this chapter and the AMS, the date on which the order of the Administrator is served;

(2) The date on which an unappealed initial decision becomes administratively final;

(3) Issuance of an order disposing of any petitions for reconsideration of the FAA Decisionmaker's final order in the proceeding;

(4) If no petition for reconsideration is filed, the last date on which such a petition could have been filed; or

(5) Issuance of a final order or any other final resolution of a proceeding, such as a settlement or voluntary dismissal, which is not subject to a petition for reconsideration.

[54 FR 46199, Nov. 1, 1989, as amended by Amdt. 14–03, 64 FR 32936, June 18, 1999]

§ 14.21 Filing and service of documents.

Any application for an award or other pleading or document related to an application shall be filed and served on all parties to the proceeding in the same manner as other pleadings in the proceeding, except as provided in § 14.11(b) for confidential financial information. Where the proceeding was held under part 17 of this chapter and the AMS, the application shall be filed with the FAA's attorney and with the Office of Dispute Resolution for Acquisition.

[Doc. No. FAA–1998–4379, 64 FR 32936, June 18, 1999]

§ 14.22 Answer to application.

(a) Within 30 days after service of an application, counsel representing the agency against which an award is sought may file an answer to the application. Unless agency counsel requests an extension of time for filing or files a statement of intent to negotiate under paragraph (b) of the section, failure to file an answer within the 30-day period may be treated as a consent to the award requested.

(b) If the FAA's counsel and the applicant believe that the issues in the fee application can be settled, they may jointly file a statement of their intent to negotiate a settlement. The filing of this statement shall extend the time for filing an answer for an additional 30 days, and further extensions may be granted by the ALJ or adjudicative officer upon request by the FAA's counsel and the applicant.

(c) The answer shall explain in detail any objections to the award requested and identify the facts relied on in support of agency counsel's position. If the answer is based on any alleged facts not already in the record of the proceeding, agency counsel shall include with the answer either supporting affidavits or a request for further proceedings under § 14.26.

[54 FR 46199, Nov. 1, 1989, as amended by Amdt. 14–03, 64 FR 32936, June 18, 1999]

§ 14.23 Reply.

Within 15 days after service of an answer, the applicant may file a reply. If the reply is based on any alleged facts not already in the record of the proceeding, the applicant shall include with the reply either supporting affidavits or a request for further proceedings under § 14.26.

§ 14.24 Comments by other parties.

Any party to a proceeding other than the applicant and the FAA's counsel may file comments on an application within 30 days after it is served, or on an answer within 15 days after it is served. A commenting party may not participate further in proceedings on the application unless the ALJ or adjudicative officer determines that the public interest requires such participation in order to permit full exploration of matters raised in the comments.

[Doc. No. FAA–1998–4379, 64 FR 32936, June 18, 1999]

§ 14.25 Settlement.

The applicant and agency counsel may agree on a proposed settlement of the award before final action on the application, either in connection with a settlement of the underlying proceeding, or after the underlying proceeding has been concluded. If a prevailing party and agency counsel agree on a proposed settlement of an award before an application has been filed, the application shall be filed with the proposed settlement.

§ 14.26 Further proceedings.

(a) Ordinarily the determination of an award will be made on the basis of the written record; however, on request of either the applicant or agency counsel, or on his or her own initiative, the ALJ or adjudicative officer assigned to the matter may order further proceedings, such as an informal conference, oral argument, additional written submissions, or an evidentiary hearing. Such further proceedings shall be held only when necessary for full and fair resolution of the issues arising from the application and shall be conducted as promptly as possible.

(b) A request that the administrative law judge order further proceedings under this section shall specifically identify the information sought or the disputed issues and shall explain why the additional proceedings are necessary to resolve the issues.

[54 FR 46199, Nov. 1, 1989, as amended by Amdt. 14–03, 64 FR 32936, June 18, 1999]

§ 14.27 Decision.

(a) The ALJ shall issue an initial decision on the application within 60 days after completion of proceedings on the application.

(b) An adjudicative officer in a proceeding under part 17 of this chapter and the AMS shall prepare a findings and recommendations for the Office of Dispute Resolution for Acquisition.

(c) A decision under paragraph (a) or (b) of this section shall include written findings and conclusions on the applicant's eligibility and status as prevailing party and an explanation of the reasons for any difference between the amount requested and the amount awarded. The decision shall also include, if at issue, findings on whether the FAA's position was substantially justified, or whether special circumstances make an award unjust.

[Doc. No. FAA–1998–4379, 64 FR 32936, June 18, 1999]

§ 14.28 Review by FAA decisionmaker.

(a) In proceedings other than those under part 17 of this chapter and the AMS, either the applicant or the FAA counsel may seek review of the initial decision on the fee application. Additionally, the FAA Decisionmaker may decide to review the decision on his/her own initiative. If neither the applicant nor the FAA's counsel seeks review within 30 days after the decision is issued, it shall become final. Whether to review a decision is a matter within the discretion of the FAA Decision-maker. If review is taken, the FAA Decisionmaker will issue a final decision on the application or remand the application to the ALJ who issue the initial fee award determination for further proceedings.

(b) In proceedings under part 17 of this chapter and the AMS, the adjudicative officer shall prepare findings and recommendations for the Office of Dispute Resolution for Acquisition with recommendations as to whether or not an award should be made, the amount of the award, and the reasons therefor. The Office of Dispute Resolution for Acquisition shall submit a recommended order to the Administrator after the completion of all submissions related to the EAJA application. Upon the Administrator's action, the order shall become final, and may be reviewed under 49 U.S.C. 46110.

[Doc. No. FAA–1998–4379, 64 FR 32936, June 18, 1999]

§ 14.29 Judicial review.

If an applicant is dissatisfied with the determination of fees and other expenses made under this subsection, pursuant 5 U.S.C. 504(c)(2), that applicant may, within thirty (30) days after the determination is made, appeal the determination to the court of the United States having jurisdiction to review the merits of the underlying decision of the FAA adversary adjudication. The court's determination on any appeal heard under this paragraph shall be based solely on the factual record made before the FAA. The court may modify the determination of fees and other expenses only if the court finds that the failure to make an award of fees and other expenses, or the calculation of the amount of the award, was unsupported by substantial evidence.

§ 14.30 Payment of award.

An applicant seeking payment of an award shall submit to the disbursing official of the FAA a copy of the FAA Decisionmaker's final decision granting the award, accompanied by a statement that the applicant will not seek review of the decision in the United States courts. Applications for award grants in cases involving the FAA shall

be sent to: The Office of Accounting and Audit, AAA–1, Federal Aviation Administration, 800 Independence Avenue, SW., Washington, DC 20591. The agency will pay the amount awarded to the applicant within 60 days, unless judicial review of the award or of the underlying decision of the adversary adjudication has been sought by the applicant or any other party to the proceeding.

PART 15—ADMINISTRATIVE CLAIMS UNDER FEDERAL TORT CLAIMS ACT

Subpart A—General Procedures

Sec.
15.1   Scope of regulations.
15.3   Administrative claim, when presented; appropriate office.
15.5   Administrative claim, who may file.
15.7   Administrative claims; evidence and information to be submitted.
15.9   Investigation and examination.

Subpart B—Indemnification Under Section 1118 of the Federal Aviation Act of 1958

15.101   Applicability.
15.103   Exclusions.
15.105   Filing of requests for indemnification.
15.107   Notification requirements.
15.109   Settlements.
15.111   Conduct of litigation.
15.113   Indemnification agreements.
15.115   Payment.

AUTHORITY: 5 U.S.C. 301; 28 U.S.C. 2672, 2675; 49 U.S.C. 106(g), 40113, 44721.

Subpart A—General Procedures

SOURCE: Docket No. 25264, 52 FR 18171, May 13, 1987, unless otherwise noted.

§ 15.1 Scope of regulations.

(a) These regulations apply to claims asserted under the Federal Tort Claims Act, as amended, for money damages against the United States for injury to, or loss of property, or for personal injury or death, caused by the negligent or wrongful act or omission of an employee of the FAA acting within the scope of office or employment. The regulations in this part supplement the Attorney General's regulations in 28 CFR Part 14, as amended. The regulations in 28 CFR Part 14, as amended, and the regulations in this part apply to consideration by the FAA of administrative claims under the Federal Tort Claims Act.

§ 15.3 Administrative claim, when presented; appropriate office.

(a) A claim is deemed to have been presented when the FAA receives, at a place designated in paragraph (b) of this section, an executed Standard Form 95 or other written notification of an incident, accompanied by a claim for money damages in a sum certain for injury to, or loss of, property or for personal injury or death, alleged to have occurred by reason of the incident. A claim which should have been presented to the FAA but which was mistakenly filed with another Federal agency, is deemed presented to the FAA on the date the claim is received by the FAA at a place designated in paragraph (b) of this section. A claim addressed to, or filed with, the FAA by mistake will be transferred to the appropriate Federal agency, if that agency can be determined, or returned to the claimant.

(b) Claims shall be delivered or mailed to the Assistant Chief Counsel, Litigation Division, AGC–400, Federal Aviation Administration, 800 Independence Avenue, SW., Washington, DC 20591, or alternatively, may be mailed or delivered to the Regional Counsel in any of the FAA Regional Offices or the Assistant Chief Counsel, Europe, Africa, and Middle East Area Office.

(d) A claim presented in accordance with this section may be amended by the claimant at any time prior to final FAA action or prior to the exercise of the claimant's option, under 28 U.S.C. 2675(a), to deem the agency's failure to make a final disposition of his or her claim within 6 months after it was filed as a final denial. Each amendment to a claim shall be submitted in writing and signed by the claimant or the claimant's duly authorized agent or legal representative. Upon the timely filing of an amendment to a pending claim, the FAA has 6 months thereafter in which to make a final disposition of the claim as amended, and the claimant's option under 28 U.S.C. 2675(a) does

not accrue until 6 months after the filing of the amendment.

[Doc. No. 18884, 44 FR 63723, Nov. 5, 1979, as amended by Amdt. 15–1, 54 FR 39290, Sept. 25, 1989; Amdt. 15–4, 62 FR 46866, Sept. 4, 1997]

§ 15.5 Administrative claim, who may file.

(a) A claim for injury to, or loss of, property may be presented by the owner of the property interest which is the subject of the claim or by the owner's duly authorized agent or legal representative.

(b) A claim for personal injury may be presented by the injured person or that person's duly authorized agent or legal representative.

(c) A claim based on death may be presented by the executor or administrator of the decedent's estate or by any other person legally entitled to assert such a claim under applicable State law.

(d) A claim for loss wholly compensated by an insurer with the rights of a subrogee may be presented by the insurer. A claim for loss partially compensated by an insurer with the rights of a subrogee may be presented by the insurer or the insured individually, as their respective interest appear, or jointly. Whenever an insurer presents a claim asserting the rights of a subrogee, it shall present with its claim appropriate evidence that it has the rights of a subrogee.

(e) A claim presented by an agent or legal representative shall be presented in the name of the claimant, be signed by the agent or legal representative, show the title or legal capacity of the person signing, and be accompanied by evidence of authority to present a claim on behalf of the claimant as agent, executor, administrator, parent, guardian, or other representative.

§ 15.7 Administrative claims; evidence and information to be submitted.

(a) *Death.* In support of a claim based on death, the claimant may be required to submit the following evidence or information:

(1) An authenticated death certificate or other competent evidence showing cause of death, date of death, and age of the decedent.

(2) The decedent's employment or occupation at time of death, including monthly or yearly salary or earnings (if any), and the duration of last employment or occupation.

(3) Full names, addresses, birth dates, kinship, and marital status of the decedent's survivors, including identification of those survivors who were dependent for support upon the decedent at the time of death.

(4) Degree of support afforded by the decedent to each survivor dependent upon decedent for support at the time of death.

(5) Decedent's general, physical, and mental conditions before death.

(6) Itemized bills for medical and burial expenses incurred by reason of the incident causing death or itemized receipts of payment for such expenses.

(7) If damages for pain and suffering prior to death are claimed, a physician's detailed statement specifying the injuries suffered, duration of pain and suffering, any drugs administered for pain, and the decedent's physical condition in the interval between injury and death.

(8) Any other evidence or information which may have a bearing on either the responsibility of the United States for the death or the amount of damages claimed.

(b) *Personal injury.* In support of a claim for personal injury, including pain and suffering, the claimant may be required to submit the following evidence or information:

(1) A written report by the attending physician or dentist setting forth the nature and extent of the injuries, nature and extent of treatment, any degree of temporary or permanent disability, the prognosis, period of hospitalization, and any diminished earning capacity.

(2) In addition to the report required by paragraph (b)(1) of this section, the claimant may be required to submit to a physical or mental examination by a physician employed by the FAA or another Federal agency. A copy of the report of the examining physician is made available to the claimant upon the claimant's written request if the claimant has, upon request, furnished the report required by paragraph (b)(1), and has made or agrees to make available to the FAA any other physician's reports previously or thereafter made on the physical or mental condition which is the subject matter of the claim.

(3) Itemized bills for medical, dental, and hospital expenses incurred or itemized receipts of payment for such expenses.

(4) If the prognosis reveals the necessity for future treatment, a statement of expected expenses for such treatment.

(5) If a claim is made for loss of time from employment, a written statement from the claimant's employer showing actual time lost from employment, whether the claimant is a full or part-time employee, and wages or salary actually lost.

(6) If a claim is made for loss of income and the claimant is self-employed, documentary evidence showing the amount of earnings actually lost.

(7) Any other evidence or information which may have a bearing on the responsibility of the United States for the personal injury or the damages claimed.

(c) *Property damage.* In support of a claim for injury to or loss of property, real or personal, the claimant may be required to submit the following evidence or information:

(1) Proof of ownership of the property interest which is the subject of the claim.

(2) A detailed statement of the amount claimed with respect to each item of property.

(3) An itemized receipt of payment for necessary repairs or itemized written estimates of the cost of such repairs.

(4) A statement listing date of purchase, purchase price, and salvage value, where repair is not economical.

(5) Any other evidence or information which may have a bearing on either the responsibility of the United States for the injury to or loss of property or the damages claimed.

§15.9 Investigation and examination.

The FAA may investigate a claim or conduct a physical examination of a claimant. The FAA may request any other Federal agency to investigate a claim or conduct a physical examination of a claimant and provide a report of the investigation or examination to the FAA.

Subpart B—Indemnification Under Section 1118 of the Federal Aviation Act of 1958

Source: Amdt. 15-2, 55 FR 18710, May 3, 1990, unless otherwise noted.

§ 15.101 Applicability.

This subpart prescribes procedural requirements for the indemnification of a publisher of aeronautical charts or maps under section 1118 of the Federal Aviation Act of 1958, as amended, when the publisher incurs liability as a result of publishing—

(a) A chart or map accurately depicting a defective or deficient flight procedure or airway that was promulgated by the FAA; or

(b) Aeronautical data that—

(1) Is visually displayed in the cockpit of an aircraft; and

(2) When visually displayed, accurately depicts a defective or deficient flight procedure or airway promulgated by the FAA.

§ 15.103 Exclusions.

A publisher that requests indemnification under this part will not be indemnified if—

(a) The complaint filed against the publisher, or demand for payment against the publisher, first occurred before December 19, 1985;

(b) The publisher does not negotiate a good faith settlement;

(c) The publisher does not conduct a good faith defense;

(d) The defective or deficient flight procedure or airway—

(1) Was not promulgated by the FAA;

(2) Was not accurately depicted on the publisher's chart or map;

(3) Was not accurately displayed on a visual display in the cockpit, or

(4) Was obviously defective or deficient;

(e) The publisher does not give notice as required by § 15.107 of this part and that failure is prejudicial to the Government; or

(f) The publisher does not appeal a lower court's decision pursuant to a request by the Administrator under § 15.111(d)(2) of this part.

§ 15.105 Filing of requests for indemnification.

A request for indemnification under this part—

(a) May be filed by—

(1) A publisher described in § 15.101 of this part; or

(2) The publisher's duly authorized agent or legal representative;

(b) Shall be filed with the Chief Counsel, Federal Aviation Administration, 800 Independence Avenue SW., Washington, DC 20591; and

(c) Shall state the basis for the publisher's assertion that indemnification under this part is required.

§ 15.107 Notification requirements.

A request for indemnification will not be considered by the FAA unless the following conditions are met:

(a) The publisher must notify the Chief Counsel of the FAA, within the time limits prescribed in paragraph (b) or (c) of this section, of the publisher's first receipt of a demand for payment, or service of a complaint in any proceeding, federal or state, in which it appears that indemnification under this part may be required.

(b) For each complaint filed, or demand for payment made, on or after December 19, 1985, and before June 4, 1990, the notice required by paragraph (a) of this section must be received by the FAA on or before July 2, 1990.

(c) For each complaint filed, or demand for payment made, on or after June 4, 1990, the notice required by paragraph (a) of this section must be received by the FAA within 60 days after the day the publisher first receives the demand for payment or service of the complaint.

(d) Within 5 days after the day a judgment is rendered against the publisher in any proceeding, or within 30 days of the denial of an appeal, whichever is later, the publisher must notify the FAA Chief Counsel that—

(1) There is an adverse judgment against the publisher; and

(2) The publisher has a claim for indemnification against the FAA arising out of that judgment.

§ 15.109　Settlements.

(a) A publisher may not settle a claim with another party, for which the publisher has sought, or intends to seek, indemnification under this part, unless—

(1) The publisher submits a copy of the proposed settlement, and a statement justifying the settlement, to the Chief Counsel of the FAA; and

(2) The Administrator and where necessary, the appropriate official of the Department of Justice, approves the proposed settlement.

(3) The publisher submits a signed release that clearly releases the United States from any further liability to the publisher and the claimant.

(b) If the Administrator does not approve the proposed settlement, the Administrator will—

(1) So notify the publisher by registered mail within 60 days of receipt of the proposed settlement; and

(2) Explain why the request for indemnification was not approved.

(c) If the Administrator approves the proposed settlement, the Administrator will so notify the publisher by registered mail within 60 days after the FAA's receipt of the proposed settlement.

(d) If the Administrator does not have sufficient information to approve or disapprove the proposed settlement, the Administrator will request, within 60 days after receipt of the proposed settlement, the additional information needed to make a determination.

§ 15.111　Conduct of litigation.

(a) If a lawsuit is filed against the publisher and the publisher has sought, or intends to seek, indemnification under this part, the publisher shall—

(1) Give notice as required by § 15.107 of this part;

(2) If requested by the United States—

(i) Implead the United States as a third-party defendant in the action; and

(ii) Arrange for the removal of the action to Federal Court;

(3) Promptly provide any additional information requested by the United States; and

(4) Cooperate with the United States in the defense of the lawsuit.

(b) If the lawsuit filed against the publisher results in a proposed settlement, the publisher shall submit that proposed settlement to the FAA for approval in accordance with § 15.109 of this part.

(c) If the lawsuit filed against the publisher results in a judgment against the publisher and the publisher has sought, or intends to seek, indemnification under this part as a result of the adverse judgment, the publisher shall—

(1) Give notice to the FAA as required by § 15.107(d) of this part;

(2) Submit a copy of the trial court's decision to the FAA Chief Counsel not more than 5 business days after the adverse judgment is rendered; and

(3) If an appeal is taken from the adverse judgment, submit a copy of the appellate decision to the FAA Chief Counsel not more than 30 days after that decision is rendered.

(d) Within 60 days after receipt of the trial court's decision, the Administrator by registered mail will—

(1) Notify the publisher that indemnification is required under this part;

(2) Request that the publisher appeal the trial court's adverse decision; or

(3) Notify the publisher that it is not entitled to indemnification under this part and briefly state the basis for the denial.

§ 15.113　Indemnification agreements.

(a) Upon a finding of the Administrator that indemnification is required under this part, and after obtaining the concurrence of the United States Department of Justice, the FAA will promptly enter into an indemnification agreement providing for the payment of the costs specified in paragraph (c) of this section.

(b) The indemnification agreement will be signed by the Chief Counsel and the publisher.

(c) The FAA will indemnify the publisher for—

(1) Compensatory damages awarded by the court against the publisher;

(2) Reasonable costs and fees, including reasonable attorney fees at a rate not to exceed that permitted under the Equal Access to Justice Act (5 U.S.C. 504), and any postjudgment interest, if

the publisher conducts a good faith defense, or pursues a good faith appeal, at the request, or with the concurrence, of the FAA.

(d) Except as otherwise provided in this section, the FAA will not indemnify the publisher for—

(1) Punitive or exemplary damages;

(2) Civil or criminal fines or any other litigation sanctions;

(3) Postjudgment interest;

(4) Costs;

(5) Attorney fees; or

(6) Other incidental expenses.

(e) The indemnification agreement must provide that the Government will be subrogated to all claims or rights of the publisher, including third-party claims, cross-claims, and counterclaims.

§ 15.115 Payment.

After execution of the indemnification agreement, the FAA will submit the agreement to the United States Department of Justice and request payment, in accordance with the agreement, from the Judgment Fund.

PART 16—RULES OF PRACTICE FOR FEDERALLY-ASSISTED AIRPORT ENFORCEMENT PROCEEDINGS

Subpart A—General Provisions

Subpart B—General Rules Applicable to Complaints, Proceedings Initiated by the FAA, and Appeals

Subpart C—Special Rules Applicable to Complaints

Subpart D—Special Rules Applicable to Proceedings Initiated by the FAA

Subpart E—Proposed Orders of Compliance

Subpart F—Hearings

Subpart G—Initial Decisions, Orders and Appeals

Subpart H—Judicial Review

Subpart I—Ex Parte Communications

AUTHORITY: 49 U.S.C. 106(g), 322, 1110, 1111, 1115, 1116, 1718 (a) and (b), 1719, 1723, 1726, 1727, 40103(e), 40113, 40116, 44502(b), 46101, 46104, 46110, 47104, 47106(e), 47107, 47108, 47111(d), 47122, 47123–47125, 47151–47153, 48103.

SOURCE: Docket No. 27783, 61 FR 54004, October 16, 1996, unless otherwise noted.

Subpart A—General Provisions

§16.1 Applicability and description of part.

(a) *General.* The provisions of this part govern all proceedings involving Federally-assisted airports, except for disputes between U.S. and foreign air carriers and airport proprietors concerning the reasonableness of airport fees covered by 14 CFR part 302, whether the proceedings are instituted by order of the FAA or by filing with the FAA a complaint, under the following authorities:

(1) 49 U.S.C. 40103(e), prohibiting the grant of exclusive rights for the use of any landing area or air navigation facility on which Federal funds have been expended (formerly section 308 of the Federal Aviation Act of 1958, as amended).

(2) Requirements of the Anti-Head Tax Act, 49 U.S.C. 40116.

(3) The assurances contained in grant-in-aid agreements issued under the Federal Airport Act of 1946, 49 U.S.C. 1101 *et seq* (repealed 1970).

(4) The assurances contained in grant-in-aid agreements issued under the Airport and Airway Development Act of 1970, as amended, 49 U.S.C. 1701 *et seq.*

(5) The assurances contained in grant-in-aid agreements issued under the Airport and Airway Improvement Act of 1982 (AAIA), as amended, 49 U.S.C. 47101 *et seq.*, specifically section 511(a), 49 U.S.C. 47107(a) and (b).

(6) Section 505(d) of the Airport and Airway Improvement Act of 1982, as amended, 49 U.S.C. 47113.

(7) Obligations contained in property deeds for property transferred pursuant to section 16 of the Federal Airport Act (49 U.S.C. 1115), section 23 of the Airport and Airway Development Act (49 U.S.C. 1723), or section 516 of the Airport and Airway Improvement Act (49 U.S.C. 47125).

(8) Obligations contained in property deeds for property transferred under the Surplus Property Act (49 U.S.C. 47151–47153).

(b) *Other agencies.* Where a grant assurance concerns a statute, executive order, regulation, or other authority that provides an administrative process for the investigation or adjudication of complaints by a Federal agency other than the FAA, persons shall use the administrative process established by those authorities. Where a grant assurance concerns a statute, executive order, regulation, or other authority that enables a Federal agency other than the FAA to investigate, adjudicate, and enforce compliance under those authorities on its own initiative, the FAA may defer to that Federal agency.

(c) *Other enforcement.* If a complaint or action initiated by the FAA involves a violation of the 49 U.S.C. subtitle VII or FAA regulations, except as specified in paragraphs (a)(1) and (a)(2) of this section, the FAA may take investigative and enforcement action under 14 CFR part 13, "Investigative and Enforcement Procedures."

(d) *Effective date.* This part applies to a complaint filed with the FAA and to an investigation initiated by the FAA on or after December 16, 1996.

§16.3 Definitions.

Terms defined in the Acts are used as so defined. As used in this part:

Act means a statute listed in §16.1 and any regulation, agreement, or document of conveyance issued or made under that statute.

Agency attorney means the Deputy Chief Counsel; the Assistant Chief Counsel and attorneys in the Airports/Environmental Law Division of the Office of the Chief Counsel; the Assistant Chief Counsel and attorneys in an FAA region or center who represent the FAA during the investigation of a complaint or at a hearing on a complaint, and who prosecute on behalf of the FAA, as appropriate. An agency attorney shall not include the Chief Counsel; the Assistant Chief Counsel for Litigation, or any attorney on the staff of the Assistant Chief Counsel for Litigation, who advises the Associate Administrator regarding an initial decision of the hearing officer or any appeal to the Associate Administrator or who is supervised in that action by a person who provides such advice in an action covered by this part.

Agency employee means any employee of the U.S. Department of Transportation.

Associate Administrator means the Associate Administrator for Airports or a designee.

Complainant means the person submitting a complaint.

Complaint means a written document meeting the requirements of this part filed with the FAA by a person directly and substantially affected by anything allegedly done or omitted to be done by any person in contravention of any provision of any Act, as defined in this section, as to matters within the jurisdiction of the Administrator.

Director means the Director of the Office of Airport Safety and Standards.

Director's determination means the initial determination made by the Director following an investigation, which is a non-final agency decision.

File means to submit written documents to the FAA for inclusion in the Part 16 Airport Proceedings Docket or to a hearing officer.

Final decision and order means a final agency decision that disposes of a complaint or determines a respondent's compliance with any Act, as defined in this section, and directs appropriate action.

Hearing officer means an attorney designated by the FAA in a hearing order to serve as a hearing officer in a hearing under this part. The following are not designated as hearing officers: the Chief Counsel and Deputy Chief Counsel; the Assistant Chief Counsel and attorneys in the FAA region or center in which the noncompliance has allegedly occurred or is occurring; the Assistant Chief Counsel and attorneys in the Airports and Environmental Law Division of the FAA Office of the Chief Counsel; and the Assistant Chief Counsel and attorneys in the Litigation Division of the FAA Office of Chief Counsel.

Initial decision means a decision made by the hearing officer in a hearing under subpart F of this part.

Mail means U.S. first class mail; U.S. certified mail; and U.S. express mail.

Noncompliance means anything done or omitted to be done by any person in contravention of any provision of any Act, as defined in this section, as to

matters within the jurisdiction of the Administrator.

Party means the complainant(s) and the respondent(s) named in the complaint and, after an initial determination providing an opportunity for hearing is issued under § 16.31 and subpart E of this part, the agency.

Person in addition to its meaning under 49 U.S.C. 40102(a)(33), includes a public agency as defined in 49 U.S.C. 47102(a)(15).

Personal delivery means hand delivery or overnight express delivery service.

Respondent means any person named in a complaint as a person responsible for noncompliance.

Sponsor means:

(1) Any public agency which, either individually or jointly with one or more other public agencies, has received Federal financial assistance for airport development or planning under the Federal Airport Act, Airport and Airway Development Act or Airport and Airway Improvement Act;

(2) Any private owner of a public-use airport that has received financial assistance from the FAA for such airport; and

(3) Any person to whom the Federal Government has conveyed property for airport purposes under section 13(g) of the Surplus Property Act of 1944, as amended.

§ 16.5 Separation of functions.

(a) Proceedings under this part, including hearings under subpart F of this part, will be prosecuted by an agency attorney.

(b) After issuance of an initial determination in which the FAA provides the opportunity for a hearing, an agency employee engaged in the performance of investigative or prosecutorial functions in a proceeding under this part will not, in that case or a factually related case, participate or give advice in an initial decision by the hearing officer, or a final decision by the Associate Administrator or designee on written appeal, and will not, except as counsel or as witness in the public proceedings, engage in any substantive communication regarding that case or a related case with the hearing officer, the Associate Administrator on written appeal, or agency employees advising those officials in that capacity.

(c) The Chief Counsel, the Assistant Chief Counsel for Litigation, or an attorney on the staff of the Assistant Chief Counsel for Litigation advises the Associate Administrator regarding an initial decision, an appeal, or a final decision regarding any case brought under this part.

Subpart B—General Rules Applicable to Complaints, Proceedings Initiated by the FAA, and Appeals

§ 16.11 Expedition and other modification of process.

(a) Under the authority of 49 U.S.C. 40113 and 47121, the Director may conduct investigations, issue orders, and take such other actions as are necessary to fulfill the purposes of this part, including the extension of any time period prescribed where necessary or appropriate for a fair and complete hearing of matters before the agency.

(b) Notwithstanding any other provision of this part, upon finding that circumstances require expedited handling of a particular case or controversy, the Director may issue an order directing any of the following prior to the issuance of the Director's determination:

(1) Shortening the time period for any action under this part consistent with due process;

(2) If other adequate opportunity to respond to pleadings is available, eliminating the reply, rebuttal, or other actions prescribed by this part;

(3) Designating alternative methods of service; or

(4) Directing such other measures as may be required.

§ 16.13 Filing of documents.

Except as otherwise provided in this part, documents shall be filed with the FAA during a proceeding under this part as follows:

(a) *Filing address.* Documents to be filed with the FAA shall be filed with the Office of the Chief Counsel, Attention: FAA Part 16 Airport Proceedings Docket, AGC–610, Federal Aviation Administration, 800 Independence Ave., SW., Washington, DC, 20591. Documents to be filed with a hearing officer shall be filed at the address stated in the hearing order.

(b) *Date and method of filing.* Filing of any document shall be by personal delivery or mail as defined in this part, or by facsimile (when confirmed by filing on the same date by one of the foregoing methods). Unless the date is shown to be inaccurate, documents to be filed with the FAA shall be deemed to be filed on the date of personal delivery, on the mailing date shown on the certificate of service, on the date shown on the postmark if there is no certificate of service, on the send date shown on the facsimile (provided filing has been confirmed through one of the foregoing methods), or on the mailing date shown by other evidence if there is no certificate of service and no postmark.

(c) *Number of copies.* Unless otherwise specified, an executed original and three copies of each document shall be filed with the FAA Part 16 Airport Proceedings Docket. Copies need not be signed, but the name of the person signing the original shall be shown. If a hearing order has been issued in the case, one of the three copies shall be filed with the hearing officer. If filing by facsimile, the facsimile copy does not constitute one of the copies required under this section.

(d) *Form.* Documents filed with the FAA shall be typewritten or legibly printed. In the case of docketed proceedings, the document shall include the docket number of the proceeding on the front page.

(e) *Signing of documents and other papers.* The original of every document filed shall be signed by the person filing it or the person's duly authorized representative. The signature shall serve as a certification that the signer has read the document and, based on reasonable inquiry and to the best of the signer's knowledge, information, and belief, the document is—

(1) Consistent with this part;

(2) Warranted by existing law or that a good faith argument exists for extension, modification, or reversal of existing law; and

(3) Not interposed for any improper purpose, such as to harass or to cause unnecessary delay or needless increase

in the cost of the administrative process.

(f) *Designation of person to receive service.* The initial document filed by any person shall state on the first page the name, post office address, telephone number, and facsimile number, if any, of the person(s) to be served with documents in the proceeding. If any of these items change during the proceeding, the person shall promptly file notice of the change with the FAA Part 16 Airport Proceedings Docket and the hearing officer and shall serve the notice on all parties.

(g) *Docket numbers.* Each submission identified as a complaint under this part by the submitting person will be assigned a docket number.

§ 16.15 Service of documents on the parties and the agency.

Except as otherwise provided in this part, documents shall be served as follows:

(a) *Who must be served.* Copies of all documents filed with the FAA Part 16 Airport Proceedings Docket shall be served by the persons filing them on all parties to the proceeding. A certificate of service shall accompany all documents when they are tendered for filing and shall certify concurrent service on the FAA and all parties. Certificates of service shall be in substantially the following form:

I hereby certify that I have this day served the foregoing [name of document] on the following persons at the following addresses and facsimile numbers (if also served by facsimile) by [specify method of service]:

[list persons, addresses, facsimile numbers]

Dated this ____ day of ____, 19___.
[signature], for [party]

(b) *Method of service.* Except as otherwise agreed by the parties and the hearing officer, the method of service is the same as set forth in § 16.13(b) for filing documents.

(c) *Where service shall be made.* Service shall be made to the persons identified in accordance with § 16.13(f). If no such person has been designated, service shall be made on the party.

(d) *Presumption of service.* There shall be a presumption of lawful service—

(1) When acknowledgment of receipt is by a person who customarily or in the ordinary course of business re-

ceives mail at the address of the party or of the person designated under § 16.13(f); or

(2) When a properly addressed envelope, sent to the most current address submitted under § 16.13(f), has been returned as undeliverable, unclaimed, or refused.

(e) *Date of service.* The date of service shall be determined in the same manner as the filing date under § 16.13(b).

§ 16.17 Computation of time.

This section applies to any period of time prescribed or allowed by this part, by notice or order of the hearing officer, or by an applicable statute.

(a) The date of an act, event, or default, after which a designated time period begins to run, is not included in a computation of time under this part.

(b) The last day of a time period is included in a computation of time unless it is a Saturday, Sunday, or legal holiday for the FAA, in which case, the time period runs until the end of the next day that is not a Saturday, Sunday, or legal holiday.

(c) Whenever a party has the right or is required to do some act within a prescribed period after service of a document upon the party, and the document is served on the party by mail, 3 days shall be added to the prescribed period.

§ 16.19 Motions.

(a) *General.* An application for an order or ruling not otherwise specifically provided for in this part shall be by motion. Unless otherwise ordered by the agency, the filing of a motion will not stay the date that any action is permitted or required by this part.

(b) *Form and contents.* Unless made during a hearing, motions shall be made in writing, shall state with particularity the relief sought and the grounds for the relief sought, and shall be accompanied by affidavits or other evidence relied upon. Motions introduced during hearings may be made orally on the record, unless the hearing officer directs otherwise.

(c) *Answers to motions.* Except as otherwise provided in this part, or except when a motion is made during a hearing, any party may file an answer in support of or in opposition to a motion, accompanied by affidavits or other evidence relied upon, provided that the answer to the motion is filed within 10 days after the motion has been served upon the person answering, or any other period set by the hearing officer. Where a motion is made during a hearing, the answer and the ruling thereon may be made at the hearing, or orally or in writing within the time set by the hearing officer.

Subpart C—Special Rules Applicable to Complaints

§16.21 Pre-complaint resolution.

(a) Prior to filing a complaint under this part, a person directly and substantially affected by the alleged noncompliance shall initiate and engage in good faith efforts to resolve the disputed matter informally with those individuals or entities believed responsible for the noncompliance. These efforts at informal resolution may include, without limitation, at the parties' expense, mediation, arbitration, or the use of a dispute resolution board, or other form of third party assistance. The FAA Airports District Office, FAA Airports Field Office, or FAA Regional Airports Division responsible for administering financial assistance to the respondent airport proprietor, will be available upon request to assist the parties with informal resolution.

(b) A complaint under this part will not be considered unless the person or authorized representative filing the complaint certifies that substantial and reasonable good faith efforts to resolve the disputed matter informally prior to filing the complaint have been made and that there appears no reasonable prospect for timely resolution of the dispute. This certification shall include a brief description of the party's efforts to obtain informal resolution but shall not include information on monetary or other settlement offers made but not agreed upon in writing by all parties.

§16.23 Complaints, answers, replies, rebuttals, and other documents.

(a) A person directly and substantially affected by any alleged noncompliance may file a complaint with the Administrator. A person doing business with an airport and paying fees or rentals to the airport shall be considered directly and substantially affected by alleged revenue diversion as defined in 49 U.S.C. 47107(b).

(b) Complaints filed under this part shall—

(1) State the name and address of each person who is the subject of the complaint and, with respect to each person, the specific provisions of each Act that the complainant believes were violated;

(2) Be served, in accordance with §16.15, along with all documents then available in the exercise of reasonable diligence, offered in support of the complaint, upon all persons named in the complaint as persons responsible for the alleged action(s) or omission(s) upon which the complaint is based;

(3) Provide a concise but complete statement of the facts relied upon to substantiate each allegation; and

(4) Describe how the complainant was directly and substantially affected by the things done or omitted to be done by the respondents.

(c) Unless the complaint is dismissed pursuant to §16.25 or §16.27, the FAA notifies the complainant and respondents in writing within 20 days after the date the FAA receives the complaint that the complaint has been docketed and that respondents are required to file an answer within 20 days of the date of service of the notification.

(d) The respondent shall file an answer within 20 days of the date of service of the FAA notification.

(e) The complainant may file a reply within 10 days of the date of service of the answer.

(f) The respondent may file a rebuttal within 10 days of the date of service of the complainant's reply.

(g) The answer, reply, and rebuttal shall, like the complaint, be accompanied by supporting documentation upon which the parties rely.

(h) The answer shall deny or admit the allegations made in the complaint or state that the person filing the document is without sufficient knowledge or information to admit or deny an allegation, and shall assert any affirmative defense.

(i) The answer, reply, and rebuttal shall each contain a concise but complete statement of the facts relied upon to substantiate the answers, admissions, denials, or averments made.

(j) The respondent's answer may include a motion to dismiss the complaint, or any portion thereof, with a supporting memorandum of points and authorities. If a motion to dismiss is filed, the complainant may respond as part of its reply notwithstanding the 10-day time limit for answers to motions in § 16.19(c).

§ 16.25 Dismissals.

Within 20 days after the receipt of the complaint, the Director will dismiss a complaint, or any claim made in a complaint, with prejudice if:

(a) It appears on its face to be outside the jurisdiction of the Administrator under the Acts listed in § 16.1;

(b) On its face it does not state a claim that warrants an investigation or further action by the FAA; or

(c) The complainant lacks standing to file a complaint under §§ 16.3 and 16.23. The Director's dismissal will include the reasons for the dismissal.

§ 16.27 Incomplete complaints.

If a complaint is not dismissed pursuant to § 16.25 of this part, but is deficient as to one or more of the requirements set forth in § 16.21 or § 16.23(b), the Director will dismiss the complaint within 20 days after receiving it. Dismissal will be without prejudice to the refiling of the complaint after amendment to correct the deficiency. The Director's dismissal will include the reasons for the dismissal.

§ 16.29 Investigations.

(a) If, based on the pleadings, there appears to be a reasonable basis for further investigation, the FAA investigates the subject matter of the complaint.

(b) The investigation may include one or more of the following, at the sole discretion of the FAA:

(1) A review of the written submissions or pleadings of the parties, as supplemented by any informal investigation the FAA considers necessary and by additional information furnished by the parties at FAA request.

In rendering its initial determination, the FAA may rely entirely on the complaint and the responsive pleadings provided under this subpart. Each party shall file documents that it considers sufficient to present all relevant facts and argument necessary for the FAA to determine whether the sponsor is in compliance.

(2) Obtaining additional oral and documentary evidence by use of the agency's authority to compel production of such evidence under section 313 Aviation Act, 49 U.S.C. 40113 and 46104, and section 519 of the Airport and Airway Improvement Act, 49 U.S.C. 47122. The Administrator's statutory authority to issue compulsory process has been delegated to the Chief Counsel, the Deputy Chief Counsel, the Assistant Chief Counsel for Airports and Environmental Law, and each Assistant Chief Counsel for a region or center.

(3) Conducting or requiring that a sponsor conduct an audit of airport financial records and transactions as provided in 49 U.S.C. 47107 and 47121.

§ 16.31 Director's determinations after investigations.

(a) After consideration of the pleadings and other information obtained by the FAA after investigation, the Director will render an initial determination and provide it to each party by certified mail within 120 days of the date the last pleading specified in § 16.23 was due.

(b) The Director's determination will set forth a concise explanation of the factual and legal basis for the Director's determination on each claim made by the complainant.

(c) A party adversely affected by the Director's determination may appeal the initial determination to the Associate Administrator as provided in § 16.33.

(d) If the Director's determination finds the respondent in noncompliance and proposes the issuance of a compliance order, the initial determination will include notice of opportunity for a hearing under subpart F of this part, if such an opportunity is provided by the FAA. The respondent may elect or waive a hearing as provided in subpart E of this part.

§ 16.33 Final decisions without hearing.

(a) The Associate Administrator will issue a final decision on appeal from the Director's determination, without a hearing, where—

(1) The complaint is dismissed after investigation;

(2) A hearing is not required by statute and is not otherwise made available by the FAA; or

(3) The FAA provides opportunity for a hearing to the respondent and the respondent waives the opportunity for a hearing as provided in subpart E of this part.

(b) In the cases described in paragraph (a) of this section, a party adversely affected by the Director's determination may file an appeal with the Associate Administrator within 30 days after the date of service of the initial determination.

(c) A reply to an appeal may be filed with the Associate Administrator within 20 days after the date of service of the appeal.

(d) The Associate Administrator will issue a final decision and order within 60 days after the due date of the reply.

(e) If no appeal is filed within the time period specified in paragraph (b) of this section, the Director's determination becomes the final decision and order of the FAA without further action. A Director's determination that becomes final because there is no administrative appeal is not judicially reviewable.

Subpart D—Special Rules Applicable to Proceedings Initiated by the FAA

§ 16.101 Basis for the initiation of agency action.

The FAA may initiate its own investigation of any matter within the applicability of this part without having received a complaint. The investigation may include, without limitation, any of the actions described in § 16.29(b).

§ 16.103 Notice of investigation.

Following the initiation of an investigation under § 16.101, the FAA sends a notice to the person(s) subject to investigation. The notice will set forth the areas of the agency's concern and the reasons therefor; request a response to the notice within 30 days of the date of service; and inform the respondent that the FAA will, in its discretion, invite good faith efforts to resolve the matter.

§ 16.105 Failure to resolve informally.

If the matters addressed in the FAA notices are not resolved informally, the FAA may issue a Director's determination under § 16.31.

Subpart E—Proposed Orders of Compliance

§ 16.109 Orders terminating eligibility for grants, cease and desist orders, and other compliance orders.

This section applies to initial determinations issued under § 16.31 that provide the opportunity for a hearing.

(a) The agency will provide the opportunity for a hearing if, in the Director's determination, the agency proposes to issue an order terminating eligibility for grants pursuant to 49 U.S.C. 47106(e) and 47111(d), an order suspending the payment of grant funds, an order withholding approval of any new application to impose a passenger facility charge pursuant to section 112 of the Federal Aviation Administration Act of 1994, 49 U.S.C. 47111(e), a cease and desist order, an order directing the refund of fees unlawfully collected, or any other compliance order issued by the Administrator to carry out the provisions of the Acts, and required to be issued after notice and opportunity for a hearing. In cases in which a hearing is not required by statute, the FAA may provide opportunity for a hearing at its discretion.

(b) In a case in which the agency provides the opportunity for a hearing, the Director's determination issued under § 16.31 will include a statement of the availability of a hearing under subpart F of this part.

(c) Within 20 days after service of a Director's determination under § 16.31 and paragraph (b) of this section, a person subject to the proposed compliance order may—

(1) Request a hearing under subpart F of this part;

(2) Waive hearing and appeal the Director's determination in writing to the Associate Administrator, as provided in § 16.33;

(3) File, jointly with a complainant, a motion to withdraw the complaint and to dismiss the proposed compliance action; or

(4) Submit, jointly with the agency attorney, a proposed consent order under § 16.243(e).

(d) If the respondent fails to request a hearing or to file an appeal in writing within the time periods provided in paragraph (c) of this section, the Director's determination becomes final.

Subpart F—Hearings

§ 16.201 Notice and order of hearing.

(a) If a respondent is provided the opportunity for hearing in an initial determination and does not waive hearing, the Deputy Chief Counsel within 10 days after the respondent elects a hearing will issue and serve on the respondent and complainant a hearing order. The hearing order will set forth:

(1) The allegations in the complaint, or notice of investigation, and the chronology and results of the investigation preliminary to the hearing;

(2) The relevant statutory, judicial, regulatory, and other authorities;

(3) The issues to be decided;

(4) Such rules of procedure as may be necessary to supplement the provisions of this part;

(5) The name and address of the person designated as hearing officer, and the assignment of authority to the hearing officer to conduct the hearing in accordance with the procedures set forth in this part; and

(6) The date by which the hearing officer is directed to issue an initial decision.

(b) Where there are no genuine issues of material fact requiring oral examination of witnesses, the hearing order may contain a direction to the hearing officer to conduct a hearing by submission of briefs and oral argument without the presentation of testimony or other evidence.

§ 16.202 Powers of a hearing officer.

In accordance with the rules of this subpart, a hearing officer may:

(a) Give notice of, and hold, prehearing conferences and hearings;

(b) Administer oaths and affirmations;

(c) Issue subpoenas authorized by law and issue notices of deposition requested by the parties;

(d) Limit the frequency and extent of discovery;

(e) Rule on offers of proof;

(f) Receive relevant and material evidence;

(g) Regulate the course of the hearing in accordance with the rules of this part to avoid unnecessary and duplicative proceedings in the interest of prompt and fair resolution of the matters at issue;

(h) Hold conferences to settle or to simplify the issues by consent of the parties;

(i) Dispose of procedural motions and requests;

(j) Examine witnesses; and

(k) Make findings of fact and conclusions of law, and issue an initial decision.

§ 16.203 Appearances, parties, and rights of parties.

(a) *Appearances.* Any party may appear and be heard in person.

(1) Any party may be accompanied, represented, or advised by an attorney licensed by a State, the District of Columbia, or a territory of the United States to practice law or appear before the courts of that State or territory, or by another duly authorized representative.

(2) An attorney, or other duly authorized representative, who represents a party shall file a notice of appearance in accordance with § 16.13.

(b) *Parties and agency participation.*

(1) The parties to the hearing are the respondent (s) named in the hearing order, the complainant(s), and the agency.

(2) Unless otherwise specified in the hearing order, the agency attorney will serve as prosecutor for the agency from the date of issuance of the Director's determination providing an opportunity for hearing.

§ 16.207 Intervention and other participation.

(a) A person may submit a motion for leave to intervene as a party. Except for good cause shown, a motion for leave to intervene shall be submitted not later than 10 days after the notice of hearing and hearing order.

(b) If the hearing officer finds that intervention will not unduly broaden the issues or delay the proceedings and, if the person has a property or financial interest that may not be addressed adequately by the parties, the hearing officer may grant a motion for leave to intervene. The hearing officer may determine the extent to which an intervenor may participate in the proceedings.

(c) Other persons may petition the hearing officer for leave to participate in the hearing. Participation is limited to the filing of post-hearing briefs and reply to the hearing officer and the Associate Administrator. Such briefs shall be filed and served on all parties in the same manner as the parties' post hearing briefs are filed.

(d) Participation under this section is at the discretion of the FAA, and no decision permitting participation shall be deemed to constitute an expression by the FAA that the participant has such a substantial interest in the proceeding as would entitle it to judicial review of such decision.

§ 16.209 Extension of time.

(a) *Extension by oral agreement.* The parties may agree to extend for a reasonable period of time for filing a document under this part. If the parties agree, the hearing officer shall grant one extension of time to each party. The party seeking the extension of time shall submit a draft order to the hearing officer to be signed by the hearing officer and filed with the hearing docket. The hearing officer may grant additional oral requests for an extension of time where the parties agree to the extension.

(b) *Extension by motion.* A party shall file a written motion for an extension of time with the hearing officer not later than 7 days before the document is due unless good cause for the late filing is shown. A party filing a written motion for an extension of time shall serve a copy of the motion on each party.

(c) *Failure to rule.* If the hearing officer fails to rule on a written motion for an extension of time by the date the document was due, the motion for an extension of time is deemed denied.

(d) *Effect on time limits.* In a hearing required by section 519(b) of the Airport and Airways Improvement Act, as amended in 1987, 49 U.S.C. 47106(e) and 47111(d), the due date for the hearing officer's initial decision and for the final agency decision are extended by the length of the extension granted by the hearing officer only if the hearing officer grants an extension of time as a result of an agreement by the parties as specified in paragraph (a) of this section or, if the hearing officer grants an extension of time as a result of the sponsor's failure to adhere to the hearing schedule. In any other hearing, an extension of time granted by the hearing officer for any reason extends the due date for the hearing officer's initial decision and for the final agency decision by the length of time of the hearing officer's decision.

§ 16.211 Prehearing conference.

(a) *Prehearing conference notice.* The hearing officer schedules a prehearing conference and serves a prehearing conference notice on the parties promptly after being designated as a hearing officer.

(1) The prehearing conference notice specifies the date, time, place, and manner (in person or by telephone) of the prehearing conference.

(2) The prehearing conference notice may direct the parties to exchange proposed witness lists, requests for evidence and the production of documents in the possession of another party, responses to interrogatories, admissions, proposed procedural schedules, and proposed stipulations before the date of the prehearing conference.

(b) *The prehearing conference.* The prehearing conference is conducted by telephone or in person, at the hearing officer's discretion. The prehearing conference addresses matters raised in the prehearing conference notice and such other matters as the hearing officer determines will assist in a prompt, full and fair hearing of the issues.

(c) *Prehearing conference report.* At the close of the prehearing conference, the hearing officer rules on any requests for evidence and the production of documents in the possession of other parties, responses to interrogatories, and admissions; on any requests for depositions; on any proposed stipulations; and on any pending applications for subpoenas as permitted by § 16.219. In addition, the hearing officer establishes the schedule, which shall provide for the issuance of an initial decision not later than 110 days after issuance of the Director's determination order unless otherwise provided in the hearing order.

§ 16.213 Discovery.

(a) Discovery is limited to requests for admissions, requests for production of documents, interrogatories, and depositions as authorized by § 16.215.

(b) The hearing officer shall limit the frequency and extent of discovery permitted by this section if a party shows that—

(1) The information requested is cumulative or repetitious;

(2) The information requested may be obtained from another less burdensome and more convenient source;

(3) The party requesting the information has had ample opportunity to obtain the information through other discovery methods permitted under this section; or

(4) The method or scope of discovery requested by the party is unduly burdensome or expensive.

§ 16.215 Depositions.

(a) *General.* For good cause shown, the hearing officer may order that the testimony of a witness may be taken by deposition and that the witness produce documentary evidence in connection with such testimony. Generally, an order to take the deposition of a witness is entered only if:

(1) The person whose deposition is to be taken would be unavailable at the hearing;

(2) The deposition is deemed necessary to perpetuate the testimony of the witness; or

(3) The taking of the deposition is necessary to prevent undue and excessive expense to a party and will not result in undue burden to other parties or in undue delay.

(b) *Application for deposition.* Any party desiring to take the deposition of a witness shall make application therefor to the hearing officer in writing, with a copy of the application served on each party. The application shall include:

(1) The name and residence of the witness;

(2) The time and place for the taking of the proposed deposition;

(3) The reasons why such deposition should be taken; and

(4) A general description of the matters concerning which the witness will be asked to testify.

(c) *Order authorizing deposition.* If good cause is shown, the hearing officer, in his or her discretion, issues an order authorizing the deposition and specifying the name of the witness to be deposed, the location and time of the deposition and the general scope and subject matter of the testimony to be taken.

(d) *Procedures for deposition.*

(1) Witnesses whose testimony is taken by deposition shall be sworn or shall affirm before any questions are put to them. Each question propounded shall be recorded and the answers of the witness transcribed verbatim.

(2) Objections to questions or evidence shall be recorded in the transcript of the deposition. The interposing of an objection shall not relieve the witness of the obligation to answer questions, except where the answer would violate a privilege.

(3) The written transcript shall be subscribed by the witness, unless the parties by stipulation waive the signing, or the witness is ill, cannot be found, or refuses to sign. The reporter shall note the reason for failure to sign.

§ 16.217 Witnesses.

(a) Each party may designate as a witness any person who is able and willing to give testimony that is relevant and material to the issues in the hearing case, subject to the limitation set forth in paragraph (b) of this section.

(b) The hearing officer may exclude testimony of witnesses that would be irrelevant, immaterial, or unduly repetitious.

(c) Any witness may be accompanied by counsel. Counsel representing a nonparty witness has no right to examine the witness or otherwise participate in the development of testimony.

§ 16.219   Subpoenas.

(a) *Request for subpoena.* A party may apply to the hearing officer, within the time specified for such applications in the prehearing conference report, for a subpoena to compel testimony at a hearing or to require the production of documents only from the following persons:

(1) Another party;

(2) An officer, employee, or agent of another party;

(3) Any other person named in the complaint as participating in or benefiting from the actions of the respondent alleged to have violated any Act;

(4) An officer, employee, or agent of any other person named in the complaint as participating in or benefiting from the actions of the respondent alleged to have violated any Act.

(b) *Issuance and service of subpoena.*

(1) The hearing officer issues the subpoena if the hearing officer determines that the evidence to be obtained by the subpoena is relevant and material to the resolution of the issues in the case.

(2) Subpoenas shall be served by personal service, or upon an agent designated in writing for the purpose, or by certified mail, return receipt addressed to such person or agent. Whenever service is made by registered or certified mail, the date of mailing shall be considered as the time when service is made.

(3) A subpoena issued under this part is effective throughout the United States or any territory or possession thereof.

(c) *Motions to quash or modify subpoena.*

(1) A party or any person upon whom a subpoena has been served may file a motion to quash or modify the subpoena with the hearing officer at or before the time specified in the subpoena for the filing of such motions. The applicant shall describe in detail the basis for the application to quash or modify the subpoena including, but not

limited to, a statement that the testimony, document, or tangible evidence is not relevant to the proceeding, that the subpoena is not reasonably tailored to the scope of the proceeding, or that the subpoena is unreasonable and oppressive.

(2) A motion to quash or modify the subpoena stays the effect of the subpoena pending a decision by the hearing officer on the motion.

§ 16.221   Witness fees.

(a) The party on whose behalf a witness appears is responsible for paying any witness fees and mileage expenses.

(b) Except for employees of the United States summoned to testify as to matters related to their public employment, witnesses summoned by subpoena shall be paid the same fees and mileage expenses as are paid to a witness in a court of the United States in comparable circumstances.

§ 16.223   Evidence.

(a) *General.* A party may submit direct and rebuttal evidence in accordance with this section.

(b) *Requirement for written testimony and evidence.* Except in the case of evidence obtained by subpoena, or in the case of a special ruling by the hearing officer to admit oral testimony, a party's direct and rebuttal evidence shall be submitted in written form in advance of the oral hearing pursuant to the schedule established in the hearing officer's prehearing conference report. Written direct and rebuttal fact testimony shall be certified by the witness as true and correct. Subject to the same exception (for evidence obtained by subpoena or subject to a special ruling by the hearing officer), oral examination of a party's own witness is limited to certification of the accuracy of written evidence, including correction and updating, if necessary, and reexamination following cross-examination by other parties.

(c) *Subpoenaed testimony.* Testimony of witnesses appearing under subpoena may be obtained orally.

(d) *Cross-examination.* A party may conduct cross-examination that may be required for disclosure of the facts, subject to control by the hearing officer for fairness, expedition and exclusion of extraneous matters.

(e) *Hearsay evidence.* Hearsay evidence is admissible in proceedings governed by this part. The fact that evidence is hearsay goes to the weight of evidence and does not affect its admissibility.

(f) *Admission of evidence.* The hearing officer admits evidence introduced by a party in support of its case in accordance with this section, but may exclude irrelevant, immaterial, or unduly repetitious evidence.

(g) *Expert or opinion witnesses.* An employee of the FAA or DOT may not be called as an expert or opinion witness for any party other than the agency except as provided in Department of Transportation regulations at 49 CFR part 9.

§ 16.225 Public disclosure of evidence.

(a) Except as provided in this section, the hearing shall be open to the public.

(b) The hearing officer may order that any information contained in the record be withheld from public disclosure. Any person may object to disclosure of information in the record by filing a written motion to withhold specific information with the hearing officer. The person shall state specific grounds for nondisclosure in the motion.

(c) The hearing officer shall grant the motion to withhold information from public disclosure if the hearing officer determines that disclosure would be in violation of the Privacy Act, would reveal trade secrets or privileged or confidential commercial or financial information, or is otherwise prohibited by law.

§ 16.227 Standard of proof.

The hearing officer shall issue an initial decision or shall rule in a party's favor only if the decision or ruling is supported by, and in accordance with, reliable, probative, and substantial evidence contained in the record and is in accordance with law.

§ 16.229 Burden of proof.

(a) The burden of proof of noncompliance with an Act or any regulation, order, agreement or document of conveyance issued under the authority of an Act is on the agency.

(b) Except as otherwise provided by statute or rule, the proponent of a motion, request, or order has the burden of proof.

(c) A party who has asserted an affirmative defense has the burden of proving the affirmative defense.

§ 16.231 Offer of proof.

A party whose evidence has been excluded by a ruling of the hearing officer may offer the evidence on the record when filing an appeal.

§ 16.233 Record.

(a) *Exclusive record.* The transcript of all testimony in the hearing, all exhibits received into evidence, all motions, applications requests and rulings, and all documents included in the hearing record shall constitute the exclusive record for decision in the proceedings and the basis for the issuance of any orders.

(b) *Examination and copy of record.* Any interested person may examine the record at the Part 16 Airport Proceedings Docket, AGC-600, Federal Aviation Administration, 800 Independence Avenue, SW., Washington, DC 20591. Any person may have a copy of the record after payment of reasonable costs for search and reproduction of the record.

§ 16.235 Argument before the hearing officer.

(a) *Argument during the hearing.* During the hearing, the hearing officer shall give the parties reasonable opportunity to present oral argument on the record supporting or opposing motions, objections, and rulings if the parties request an opportunity for argument. The hearing officer may direct written argument during the hearing if the hearing officer finds that submission of written arguments would not delay the hearing.

(b) *Posthearing briefs.* The hearing officer may request or permit the parties to submit posthearing briefs. The hearing officer may provide for the filing of simultaneous reply briefs as well, if such filing will not unduly delay the issuance of the hearing officer's initial decision. Posthearing briefs shall include proposed findings of fact and conclusions of law; exceptions to rulings of the hearing officer; references to the record in support of the findings of fact; and supporting arguments for the proposed findings, proposed conclusions, and exceptions.

§16.237 Waiver of procedures.

(a) The hearing officer shall waive such procedural steps as all parties to the hearing agree to waive before issuance of an initial decision.

(b) Consent to a waiver of any procedural step bars the raising of this issue on appeal.

(c) The parties may not by consent waive the obligation of the hearing officer to enter an initial decision on the record.

Subpart G—Initial Decisions, Orders and Appeals

§16.241 Initial decisions, order, and appeals.

(a) The hearing officer shall issue an initial decision based on the record developed during the proceeding and shall send the initial decision to the parties not later than 110 days after the Director's determination unless otherwise provided in the hearing order.

(b) Each party adversely affected by the hearing officer's initial decision may file an appeal with the Associate Administrator within 15 days of the date the initial decision is issued. Each party may file a reply to an appeal within 10 days after it is served on the party. Filing and service of appeals and replies shall be by personal delivery.

(c) If an appeal is filed, the Associate Administrator reviews the entire record and issues a final agency decision and order within 30 days of the due date of the reply. If no appeal is filed, the Associate Administrator may take review of the case on his or her own motion. If the Associate Administrator finds that the respondent is not in compliance with any Act or any regulation, agreement, or document of conveyance issued or made under such Act, the final agency order includes a statement of corrective action, if appropriate, and identifies sanctions for continued noncompliance.

(d) If no appeal is filed, and the Associate Administrator does not take review of the initial decision on the Associate Administrator's own motion, the initial decision shall take effect as the final agency decision and order on the sixteenth day after the actual date the initial decision is issued.

(e) The failure to file an appeal is deemed a waiver of any rights to seek judicial review of an initial decision that becomes a final agency decision by operation of paragraph (d) of this section.

(f) If the Associate Administrator takes review on the Associate Administrator's own motion, the Associate Administrator issues a notice of review by the sixteenth day after the actual date the initial decision is issued.

(1) The notice sets forth the specific findings of fact and conclusions of law in the initial decision that are subject to review by the Associate Administrator.

(2) Parties may file one brief on review to the Associate Administrator or rely on their posthearing briefs to the hearing officer. Briefs on review shall be filed not later than 10 days after service of the notice of review. Filing and service of briefs on review shall be by personal delivery.

(3) The Associate Administrator issues a final agency decision and order within 30 days of the due date of the briefs on review. If the Associate Administrator finds that the respondent is not in compliance with any Act or any regulation, agreement or document of conveyance issued under such Act, the final agency order includes a statement of corrective action, if appropriate, and identifies sanctions for continued noncompliance.

§16.243 Consent orders.

(a) The agency attorney and the respondents may agree at any time before the issuance of a final decision and order to dispose of the case by issuance of a consent order. Good faith efforts to resolve a complaint through issuance of a consent order may continue throughout the administrative process. Except as provided in §16.209, such efforts may not serve as the basis for extensions of the times set forth in this part.

(b) A proposal for a consent order, specified in paragraph (a) of this section, shall include:

(1) A proposed consent order;

(2) An admission of all jurisdictional facts;

(3) An express waiver of the right to further procedural steps and of all rights of judicial review; and

(4) The hearing order, if issued, and an acknowledgment that the hearing order may be used to construe the terms of the consent order.

(c) If the issuance of a consent order has been agreed upon by all parties to the hearing, the proposed consent order shall be filed with the hearing officer, along with a draft order adopting the consent decree and dismissing the case, for the hearing officer's adoption.

(d) The deadline for the hearing officer's initial decision and the final agency decision is extended by the amount of days elapsed between the filing of the proposed consent order with the hearing officer and the issuance of the hearing officer's order continuing the hearing.

(e) If the agency attorney and sponsor agree to dispose of a case by issuance of a consent order before the FAA issues a hearing order, the proposal for a consent order is submitted jointly to the official authorized to issue a hearing order, together with a request to adopt the consent order and dismiss the case. The official authorized to issue the hearing order issues the consent order as an order of the FAA and terminates the proceeding.

Subpart H—Judicial Review

§ 16.247 Judicial review of a final decision and order.

(a) A person may seek judicial review, in a United States Court of Appeals, of a final decision and order of the Associate Administrator as provided in 49 U.S.C. 46110 or section 519(b)(4) of the Airport and Airway Improvement Act of 1982, as amended, (AAIA), 49 U.S.C. 47106(d) and 47111(d). A party seeking judicial review of a final decision and order shall file a petition for review with the Court not later than 60 days after a final decision and order under the AAIA has been served on the party or within 60 days

after the entry of an order under 49 U.S.C. 40101 et seq.

(b) The following do not constitute final decisions and orders subject to judicial review:

(1) An FAA decision to dismiss a complaint without prejudice, as set forth in § 16.27;

(2) A Director's determination;

(3) An initial decision issued by a hearing officer at the conclusion of a hearing;

(4) A Director's determination or an initial decision of a hearing officer that becomes the final decision of the Associate Administrator because it was not appealed within the applicable time periods provided under §§ 16.33(b) and 16.241(b).

Subpart I—Ex Parte Communications

§ 16.301 Definitions.

As used in this subpart:

Decisional employee means the Administrator, Deputy Administrator, Associate Administrator, Director, hearing officer, or other FAA employee who is or who may reasonably be expected to be involved in the decisional process of the proceeding.

Ex parte communication means an oral or written communication not on the public record with respect to which reasonable prior notice to all parties is not given, but it shall not include requests for status reports on any matter or proceeding covered by this part, or communications between FAA employees who participate as parties to a hearing pursuant to 16.203(b) of this part and other parties to a hearing.

§ 16.303 Prohibited ex parte communications.

(a) The prohibitions of this section shall apply from the time a proceeding is noticed for hearing unless the person responsible for the communication has knowledge that it will be noticed, in which case the prohibitions shall apply at the time of the acquisition of such knowledge.

(b) Except to the extent required for the disposition of ex parte matters as authorized by law:

(1) No interested person outside the FAA and no FAA employee participating as a party shall make or knowingly cause to be made to any decisional employee an ex parte communication relevant to the merits of the proceeding;

(2) No FAA employee shall make or knowingly cause to be made to any interested person outside the FAA an ex parte communication relevant to the merits of the proceeding; or

(3) Ex parte communications regarding solely matters of agency procedure or practice are not prohibited by this section.

§ 16.305 Procedures for handling ex parte communications.

A decisional employee who receives or who makes or knowingly causes to be made a communication prohibited by § 16.303 shall place in the public record of the proceeding:

(a) All such written communications;

(b) Memoranda stating the substance of all such oral communications; and

(c) All written responses, and memoranda stating the substance of all oral responses, to the materials described in paragraphs (a) and (b) of this section.

§ 16.307 Requirement to show cause and imposition of sanction.

(a) Upon receipt of a communication knowingly made or knowingly caused to be made by a party in violation of § 16.303, the Associate Administrator or his designee or the hearing officer may, to the extent consistent with the interests of justice and the policy of the underlying statutes, require the party to show cause why his or her claim or interest in the proceeding should not be dismissed, denied, disregarded, or otherwise adversely affected on account of such violation.

(b) The Associate Administrator may, to the extent consistent with the interests of justice and the policy of the underlying statutes administered by the FAA, consider a violation of this subpart sufficient grounds for a decision adverse to a party who has knowingly committed such violation or knowingly caused such violation to occur.

PART 17—PROCEDURES FOR PROTESTS AND CONTRACTS DISPUTES

Subpart A—General

Subpart B—Protests

Subpart C—Contract Disputes

Subpart D—Alternative Dispute Resolution

Subpart E—Default Adjudicative Process

Subpart F—Finality and Review

AUTHORITY: 5 U.S.C. 570–581, 49 U.S.C. 106(f)(2), 40110, 40111, 40112, 46102, 46014, 46105, 46109, and 46110.

SOURCE: Docket No. FAA–1998–4379, 64 FR 32936, June 18, 1999, unless otherwise noted.]

Subpart A—General

§ 17.1 Applicability.

This part applies to all protests or contract disputes against the FAA that are brought on or after June 28, 1999, with the exception of those contract disputes arising under or related to FAA contracts entered into prior to April 1, 1996.

§ 17.3 Definitions.

(a) *Accrual* mean to come into existence as a legally enforceable claim.

(b) *Accrual of a contract claim* means that all events relating to a claim have occurred which fix liability of either the government or the contractor and permit assertion of the claim, regardless of when the claimant actually discovered those events. For liability to be fixed, some injury must have occurred. Monetary damages need not have been incurred, but if the claim is for money, such damages must be capable of reasonable estimation. The accrual of a claim or the running of the limitations period may be tolled on such equitable grounds as where the office of Dispute Resolution for Acquisition determines that there has been active concealment or fraud or where it finds that the facts were inherently unknowable.

(c) *Acquisition Management System* (AMS) establishes the policies, guiding principles, and internal procedures for the FAA's acquisition system.

(d) *Administrator* means the Administrator of the Federal Aviation Administration.

(e) *Alternative Dispute Resolution* (ADR) is the primary means of dispute resolution that would be employed by the FAA's Office of Dispute Resolution for Acquisition. See Appendix A of this part.

(f) *Compensated Neutral* refers to an impartial third party chosen by the parties to act as a facilitator, mediator, or arbitrator functioning to resolve the protest or contract dispute under the auspices of the Office of Dispute Resolution for Acquisition. The parties pay equally for the services of a Compensated Neutral, unless otherwise agreed to by the parties. A Dispute Resolution Officer (DRO) or Neutral cannot be a Compensated Neutral.

(g) *Contract dispute*, as used in this part, means a written request to the Office of Dispute Resolution for Acquisition seeking resolution, under an existing FAA contract subject to the AMS, of a claim for the payment of money in a sum certain, the adjustment or interpretation of contract terms, or for other relief arising under, relating to or involving an alleged breach of that contract. A contract dispute does not require, as a prerequisite, the issuance of a Contracting Officer final decision. Contract disputes for purposes of ADR only may also involve contracts not subject to the AMS.

(h) *Default Adjudicative Process* is an adjudicative process used to resolve protests or contract disputes where the parties cannot achieve resolution through informal communication or the use of ADR. The Default Adjudicative Process is conducted by a DRO or Special Master selected by the Office of Dispute Resolution for Acquisition to serve as "adjudicative officers," as that term is used in part 14 of this chapter.

(i) *Discovery* is the procedure where opposing parties in a protest or contract dispute may, either voluntarily or to the extent directed by the Office of Dispute Resolution for Acquisition, obtain testimony from, or documents and information held by, other parties or non-parties.

(j) *Dispute Resolution Officer* (DRO) is a licensed attorney reporting to the Office of Dispute Resolution for Acquisition. The term DRO can include the Director of the Office of Dispute Resolution for Acquisition, Office of Dispute Resolution for Acquisition staff attorneys or other FAA attorneys assigned to the Office of Dispute Resolution for Acquisition.

(k) *An interested party*, in the context of a bid protest, is one whose direct economic interest has been or would be affected by the award or failure to award an FAA contract. Proposed subcontractors are not "interested parties" within this definition and are not eligible to submit protests to the Office of Dispute Resolution for Acquisition.

(l) An *intervenor* is an interested party other than the protester whose participation in a protest is allowed by the Office of Dispute Resolution for Acquisition. For a post-award protest, the awardee of the contract that is the subject of the protest shall be allowed, upon request, to participate as an intervenor in the protest. In such a protest, no other interested parties shall be allowed to participate as intervenors.

(m) *Neutral* refers to an impartial third party in the ADR process chosen by the Office of Dispute Resolution for Acquisition to act as a facilitator, mediator, arbitrator, or otherwise to resolve a protest or contract dispute. A Neutral can be a DRO or a person not an employee of the FAA who serves on behalf of the Office of Dispute Resolution for Acquisition.

(n) The *Office of Dispute Resolution for Acquisition* (ODRA), under the direction of the Director, acts on behalf of the Administrator to manage the FAA Dispute Resolution Process, and to recommend action to be the Administrator on matters concerning protests or contract disputes.

(o) *Parties* include the protester(s) or (in the case of a contract dispute) the contractor, the FAA, and any intervenor(s).

(p) *Product Team*, as used in these rules, refers to the FAA organization(s) responsible for the procurement activity, without regard to funding source, and includes the Contracting Officer (CO) and assigned FAA legal counsel, when the FAA organization(s) represent(s) the FAA as a party to a protest or contract dispute before the Office of Dispute Resolution for Acquisition. The CO is responsible for all Product Team communications with and submissions to the Office of Dispute Resolution for Acquisition through assigned FAA counsel.

(q) *Screening Information Request* (SIR) means a request by the FAA for documentation, information, presentations, proposals, or binding offers concerning an approach to meeting potential acquisition requirements established by the FAA. The purpose of a SIR is for the FAA to obtain information needed for it to proceed with a source selection decision and contract award.

(r) A *Special Master* is an attorney, usually with extensive adjudicative experience, who has been assigned by the Office of Dispute Resolution for Acquisition to act as its finder of fact, and to make findings and recommendations based upon AMS policy and applicable law and authorities in the Default Adjudicative Process.

§17.5 Delegation of authority.

(a) The authority of the Administrator to conduct dispute resolution proceedings concerning acquisition matters, is delegated to the Director of the Office of Dispute Resolution for Acquisition.

(b) The Director of the Office of Dispute Resolution for Acquisition may redelegate to Special Masters and DROs such delegated authority in paragraph (a) of this section as is deemed necessary by the Director for efficient resolution of an assigned protest or contract dispute, including the imposition of sanctions or other disciplinary actions.

§17.7 Filing and computation of time.

(a) Filing of a protest or contract dispute may be accomplished by mail, overnight delivery, hand delivery, or by facsimile. A protest or contract dispute is considered to be filed on the date it is received by the Office of Dispute Resolution for Acquisition during normal business hours. The Office of Dispute Resolution for Acquisition's normal business hours are from 8:30 a.m. to 5 p.m. est or edt, whichever is in use. A protest or contract dispute received via mail, after the time period prescribed for filing, shall not be considered timely filed even though it may be postmarked within the time period prescribed for filing.

(b) Submissions to the Office of Dispute Resolution for Acquisition after the initial filing of a contract dispute may be accomplished by any means available in paragraph (a) of this section. Submissions to the Office of Dispute Resolution for Acquisition after the initial filing of a protest may only be accomplished by overnight delivery, hand delivery or facsimile.

(c) The time limits stated in this part are calculated in business days, which exclude weekends and Federal holidays. In computing time, the day of the event beginning a period of time shall not be included. If the last day of a period falls on a weekend or a Federal holiday, the first business day following the weekend or holiday shall be considered the last day of the period.

§ 17.9 Protective orders.

(a) The Office of Dispute Resolution for Acquisition may issue protective orders addressing the treatment of protected information, either at the request of a party or upon its own initiative. Such information may include proprietary, confidential, or source-selection-sensitive material, or other information the release of which could result in a competitive advantage to one or more firms.

(b) The terms of the Office of Dispute Resolution for Acquisition's standard protective order may be altered to suit particular circumstances, by negotiation of the parties, subject to the approval of the Office of Dispute Resolution for Acquisition. The protective order establishes procedures for application for access to protected information, identification and safeguarding of that information, and submission of redacted copies of documents omitting protected information.

(c) After a protective order has been issued, counsel or consultants retained by counsel appearing on behalf of a party may apply for access to the material under the order by submitting an application to the Office of Dispute Resolution for Acquisition, with copies furnished simultaneously to all parties. The application shall establish that the applicant is not involved in competitive decisionmaking for any firm that could gain a competitive advantage from access to the protected information and that the applicant will diligently protect any protected information received from inadvertent disclosure. Objections to an applicant's admission shall be raised within two (2) days of the application, although the Office of Dispute Resolution for Acquisition may consider objections raised after that time for good cause.

(d) Any violation of the terms of a protective order may result in the imposition of sanctions or the taking of the actions as the Office of Dispute Resolution for Acquisition deems appropriate.

(e) The parties are permitted to agree upon what material is to be covered by a protective order, subject to approval by the Office of Dispute Resolution for Acquisition.

Subpart B—Protests

§ 17.11 Matters not subject to protest.

The following matters may not be protested before the Office of Dispute Resolution for Acquisition:

(a) FAA purchases from or through, state, local, and tribal governments and public authorities;

(b) FAA purchases from or through other federal agencies;

(c) Grants;

(d) Cooperative agreements;

(e) Other transactions which do not fall into the category of procurement contracts subject to the AMS.

§ 17.13 Dispute resolution process for protests.

(a) Protests concerning FAA SIRs or contract awards shall be resolved pursuant to this part.

(b) The offeror initially should attempt to resolve any issues concerning potential protests with the CO. The CO, in coordination with FAA legal counsel, will make reasonable efforts to answer questions promptly and completely, and, where possible, to resolve concerns or controversies.

(c) Offerors or prospective offerors shall file a protest with the Office of Dispute Resolution for Acquisition in accordance with § 17.15. The protest time limitations set forth in § 17.15 will not be extended by attempts to resolve a potential protest with the CO. Other than the time limitations specified in § 17.15 for the filing of protests, the Office of Dispute Resolution for Acquisition retains the discretion to modify any time constraints imposed in connection with protests.

(d) In accordance with § 17.17, the Office of Dispute Resolution for Acquisition shall convene a status conference for the protest. Under the procedures set forth in that section, the parties generally will either decide to utilize Alternative Dispute Resolution (ADR) techniques to resolve the protest, pursuant to subpart D of this part, or they will proceed under the Default Adjudicative Process set forth in subpart E of this part. However, as provided in §17.31(c), informal ADR techniques may be utilized simultaneously with ongoing adjudication.

(e) The Office of Dispute Resolution for Acquisition Director shall designate Dispute Resolution Officers (DROs) or Special Masters for protests.

(f) Multiple protests concerning the same SIR, solicitation, or contract award may be consolidated at the discretion of the Office of Dispute Resolution for Acquisition, and assigned to a single DRO or Special Master for adjudication.

(g) Procurement activities, and, where applicable, contractor performance pending resolution of a protest shall continue during the pendency of a protest, unless there is a compelling reason to suspend or delay all or part of the procurement activities. Pursuant to §§17.15(d) and 17.17(b), the Office of Dispute Resolution for Acquisition may recommend suspension of award or delay of contract performance, in whole or in part, for a compelling reason. A decision to suspend or delay procurement activities or contractor performance would be made in writing by the FAA Administrator or the Administrator's delegee.

§17.15 Filing a protest.

(a) Only an interested party may file a protest, and shall initiate a protest by filing a written protest with the Office of Dispute Resolution for Acquisition within the times set forth below, or the protest shall be dismissed as untimely:

(1) Protests based upon alleged improprieties in a solicitation or a SIR that are apparent prior to bid opening or the time set for receipt of initial proposals shall be filed prior to bid opening or the time set for the receipt of initial proposals.

(2) In procurements where proposals are requested, alleged improprieties that do not exist in the initial solicitation, but which are subsequently incorporated into the solicitation, must be protested not later than the next closing time for receipt of proposals following the incorporation;

(3) For protests other than those related to alleged solicitation improprieties, the protest must be filed on the later of the following two dates:

(i) Not later than seven (7) business days after the date the protester knew or should have known of the grounds for the protest; or

(ii) If the protester has requested a post-award debriefing from the FAA Product Team, not later than five (5) business days after the date on which the Product Team holds that debriefing.

(b) Protest shall be filed at:

(1) Office of Dispute Resolution for Acquisition, AGC–70, Federal Aviation Administration, 400 7th Street, SW., Room 8332, Washington, DC 20590, Telephone: (202) 366–6400, Facsimile: (202) 366–7400; or

(2) Other address as shall be published from time to time in the FEDERAL REGISTER.

(c) A Protest shall be in writing, and set forth:

(1) The protester's name, address, telephone number, and facsimile (FAX) number;

(2) The name, address, telephone number, and FAX number of a person designated by the protester (Protester Designee), and who shall be duly authorized to represent the protester, to be the point of contact;

(3) The SIR number or, if available, the contract number and the name of the CO;

(4) The basis for the protester's status as an interested party;

(5) The facts supporting the timeliness of the protest;

(6) Whether the protester requests a protective order, the material to be protected, and attach a redacted copy of that material;

(7) A detailed statement of both the legal and factual grounds of the protest, and attach one (1) copy of each relevant document;

(8) The remedy or remedies sought by the protester, as set forth in §17.21;

(9) The signature of the Protester Designee, or another person duly authorized to represent the protester.

(d) If the protester wishes to request a suspension or delay of the procurement, in whole or in part, and believes there are compelling reasons that, if known to the FAA, would cause the FAA to suspend or delay the procurement because of the protested action, the protester shall:

(1) Set forth each such compelling reason, supply all facts supporting the protester's position, identify each person with knowledge of the facts supporting each compelling reason, and identify all documents that support each compelling reason.

(2) Clearly identify any adverse consequences to the protester, the FAA, or any interested party, should the FAA not suspend or delay the procurement.

(e) At the same time as filing the protest with the Office of Dispute Resolution for Acquisition, the protester shall serve a copy of the protest on the CO and any other official designated in the SIR for receipt of protests by means reasonably calculated to be received by the CO on the same day as it is to be received by the Office of Dispute Resolution for Acquisition. The protest shall include a signed statement from the protester, certifying to the Office of Dispute Resolution for Acquisition the manner of service, date, and time when a copy of the protest was served on the CO and other designated official(s).

(f) Upon receipt of the protest, the CO shall inform the Office of Dispute Resolution for Acquisition of the names, addresses, and telephone and facsimile numbers of the awardee and/or other interested parties, if known, and shall, in such notice, designate a person as the point of contact for the Office of Dispute Resolution for Acquisition by facsimile. The CO shall also notify the awardee and/or interested parties in writing of the existence of the protest the same day as the CO provides the foregoing information to the Office of Dispute Resolution for Acquisition. The awardee and/or interested parties shall notify the ODRA in writing, of their interest in participating in the protest as intervenors within two (2) business days of receipt of the CO's notification, and shall, in such notice, designate a person as the point of contact for the ODRA. Such notice may be submitted to the ODRA by facsimile.

(g) The Office of Dispute Resolution for Acquisition has discretion to designate the parties who shall participate

in the protest as intervenors. For awarded contracts, only the awardee may participate as an intervenor.

[Doc. No. FAA–1998–4379, 64 FR 32936, June 18, 1999; 64 FR 47362, Aug. 31, 1999]

§ 17.17 Initial protest procedures.

(a) If, as part of a protest, the protester requests a suspension or delay of procurement, in whole or in part, pursuant to § 17.15(d), the Product Team shall submit a response to the request to the Office of Dispute Resolution for Acquisition within two (2) business days of receipt of the protest. Copies of the response shall be furnished to the protester and any intervenor(s) so as to be received within the same two (2) business days. The protester and any intervenor(s) shall have the opportunity of providing additional comments on the response within an additional period of two (2) business days. Based on its review of such submissions, the Office of Dispute Resolution for Acquisition, in its discretion, may recommend such suspension or delay to the Administrator or the Administrator's designee.

(b) Within five (5) business days of the filing of a protest, or as soon thereafter as practicable, the Office of Dispute Resolution for Acquisition shall convene a status conference to—

(1) Review procedures;

(2) Identify and develop issues related to summary dismissal and suspension recommendations;

(3) Handle issues related to protected information and the issuance of any needed protective order;

(4) Encourage the parties to use ADR;

(5) Conduct or arrange for early neutral evaluation of the protest by a DRO or Neutral or Compensated Neutral, at the discretion of the Office of Dispute Resolution for Acquisition and/or based upon the agreement or request of any party(ies) seeking such evaluation; and

(6) For any other reason deemed appropriate by the DRO or by the Office of Dispute Resolution for Acquisition.

(c) On the fifth business day following the status conference, the Product Team and protester will file with the Office of Dispute Resolution for Acquisition—

(1) A joint statement that they have decided to pursue ADR proceedings in

lieu of adjudication in order to resolve the protest; or

(2) Joint or separate written explanations as to why ADR proceedings will not be used and why the Default Adjudicative Process will be needed..

(d) Should the Product Team and protester elect to utilize ADR proceedings to resolve the protest, they will agree upon the neutral to conduct the ADR proceedings (either an Office of Dispute Resolution for Acquisition-designated Neutral or a Compensated Neutral of their own choosing) pursuant to §17.33(c), and shall execute and file with the Office of Dispute Resolution for Acquisition a written ADR agreement within five (5) business days after the status conference. Agreement of any intervenor(s) to the use of ADR or the resolution of a dispute through ADR shall not be required.

(e) Should the Product Team or protester indicate at the status conference that ADR proceedings will not be used, then within ten (10) business days following the status conference, the Product Team will file with the Office of Dispute Resolution for Acquisition a Product Team Response to the protest. The Office of Dispute Resolution for Acquisition may alter the schedule for filing of the Product Team Response to accommodate the requirements of a particular protest.

(f) The Product Team Response shall consist of a written chronological statement of pertinent facts, and a written presentation of applicable legal or other defenses. The Product Team Response shall cite to and be accompanied by all relevant documents, which shall be chronologically indexed and tabbed. A copy of the response shall be furnished so as to be received by the protester and any intervenor(s) on the same date it is filed with the Office of Dispute Resolution for Acquisition, if practicable, but in any event no later than one (1) business day after the date if it is filed with the Office of Dispute Resolution for Acquisition. In all cases, the Product Team shall indicate the method of service used.

(g) Should the parties pursue ADR proceedings under subpart D of this part and fail to achieve a complete resolution of the protest via ADR, the Office of Dispute Resolution for Acquisi-

tion, upon notification of that fact by any of the parties, shall designate a DRO or Special Master for purposes of adjudication under subpart E of this part, and the DRO or Special Master shall convene a status conference, wherein he/she shall establish a schedule for the filing of the Product Team Response and further submissions.

(h) Upon submission of the Product Team Response, the protest will proceed under the Default Adjudicative Process pursuant to §17.37.

(i) The time limitations of this section maybe be extended by the Office of Dispute Resolution for Acquisition for good cause.

§ 17.19 **Dismissal or summary decision of protests.**

(a) At any time during the protest, any party may request, by motion to the Office of Dispute Resolution for Acquisition, that—

(1) The protest, or any count or portion of a protest, be dismissed for lack of jurisdiction, if the protester fails to establish that the protest is timely, or that the protester has no standing to pursue the protest;

(2) The protest, or any count or portion of a protest, be dismissed, if frivolous or without basis in fact or law, or for failure to state a claim upon which relief may be had;

(3) A summary decision be issued with respect to the protest, or any count or portion of a protest, if:

(i) The undisputed material facts demonstrate a rational basis for the Product Team action or inaction in question, and there are no other material facts in dispute that would overcome a finding of such a rational basis; or

(ii) The undisputed material facts demonstrate, that no rational basis exists for the Product Team action or inaction in question, and there are no material facts in dispute that would overcome a finding of the lack of such a rational basis.

(b) In connection with any request for dismissal or summary decision, the Office of Dispute Resolution for Acquisition shall consider any material facts in dispute, in a light most favorable to the party against whom the request is made.

(c) Either upon motion by a party or on its own initiative, the Office of Dispute Resolution for Acquisition may, at any time, exercise its discretion to:

(1) Recommend to the Administrator dismissal or the issuance of a summary decision with respect to the entire protest;

(2) Dismiss the entire protest or issue a summary decision with respect to the entire protest, if delegated that authority by the Administrator; or

(3) Dismiss or issue a summary decision with respect to any count or portion of a protest.

(d) A dismissal or summary decision regarding the entire protest by either the Administrator, or the Office of Dispute Resolution for Acquisition by delegation, shall be construed as a final agency order. A dismissal or summary decision that does not resolve all counts or portions of a protest shall not constitute a final agency order, unless and until such dismissal or decision is incorporated or otherwise adopted in a decision by the Administrator (or the Office of Dispute Resolution for Acquisition, by delegation) regarding the entire protest.

(e) Prior to recommending or entering either a dismissal or a summary decision, either in whole or in part, the Office of Dispute Resolution for Acquisition shall afford all parties against whom the dismissal or summary decision is to be entered the opportunity to respond to the proposed dismissal or summary decision.

§ 17.21 Protest remedies.

(a) The Office of Dispute Resolution for Acquisition has broad discretion to recommend remedies for a successful protest that are consistent with the AMS and applicable statutes. Such remedies may include, but are not limited to one or more, or a combination of, the following—

(1) Amend the SIR;

(2) Refrain from exercising options under the contract;

(3) Issue a new SIR;

(4) Require recompetition;

(5) Terminate an existing contract for the FAA's convenience;

(6) Direct an award to the protester;

(7) Award bid and proposal costs; or

(8) Any combination of the above remedies, or any other action consistent with the AMS that is appropriate under the circumstances.

(b) In determining the appropriate recommendation, the Office of Dispute Resolution for Acquisition should consider the circumstances surrounding the procurement or proposed procurement including, but not limited to: the nature of the procurement deficiency; the degree of prejudice to other parties or to the integrity of the acquisition system; the good faith of the parties; the extent of performance completed; the cost of any proposed remedy to the FAA; the urgency of the procurement; and the impact of the recommendation on the FAA.

(c) Attorney's fees of a prevailing protester are allowable to the extent permitted by the Equal Access to Justice Act, 5 U.S.C. 504(a)(1)(EAJA).

Subpart C—Contract Disputes

§ 17.23 Dispute resolution process for contract disputes.

(a) All contract disputes arising under contracts subject to the AMS shall be resolved under this subpart.

(b) Contractors shall file contract disputes with the Office of Dispute Resolution for Acquisition and the CO pursuant to § 17.25.

(c) After filing the contract dispute, the contractor should seek informal resolution with the CO:

(1) The CO, with the advice of FAA legal counsel, has full discretion to settle contract disputes, except where the matter involves fraud;

(2) The parties shall have up to twenty (20) business days within which to resolve the dispute informally, and may contact the Office of Dispute Resolution for Acquisition for assistance in facilitating such a resolution; and

(3) If no informal resolution is achieved during the twenty (20) business day period, the parties shall file joint or separate statements with the Office of Dispute Resolution for Acquisition pursuant to § 17.27.

(d) If informal resolution of the contract dispute appears probable, the Office of Dispute Resolution for Acquisition shall extend the time for the filing of the joint statement under § 17.27 for up to an additional twenty (20) business days, upon joint request of the CO and contractor.

(e) The Office of Dispute Resolution for Acquisition shall hold a status conference with the parties within ten (10) business days after receipt of the joint statement required by §17.27, or as soon thereafter as is practicable, in order to establish the procedures to be utilized to resolve the contract dispute.

(f) The Office of Dispute Resolution for Acquisition has broad discretion to recommend remedies for a successful contract dispute, that are consistent with the AMS and applicable law.

§17.25 Filing a contract dispute.

(a) Contract disputes are to be in writing and shall contain:

(1) The contractor's name, address, telephone and fax numbers and the name, address, telephone and fax numbers of the contractor's legal representative(s) (if any) for the contract dispute;

(2) The contract number and the name of the Contracting Officer;

(3) A detailed chronological statement of the facts and of the legal grounds for the contractor's positions regarding each element or count of the contract dispute (i.e., broken down by individual claim item), citing to relevant contract provisions and documents and attaching copies of those provisions and documents;

(4) All information establishing that the contract dispute was timely filed;

(5) A request for a specific remedy, and if a monetary remedy is requested, a sum certain must be specified and pertinent cost information and documentation (e.g., invoices and cancelled checks) attached, broken down by individual claim item and summarized; and

(6) The signature of a duly authorized representative of the initiating party.

(b) Contract disputes shall be filed by mail, in person, by overnight delivery or by facsimile at the following address:

(1) Office of Dispute Resolution for Acquisition, AGC–70, Federal Aviation Administration, 400 7th Street, SW., Room 8332, Washington, DC 20590, Telephone: (202) 366–6400, Facsimile: (202) 366–7400; or

(2) Other address as shall be published from time to time in the FEDERAL REGISTER.

(c) A contract dispute against the FAA shall be filed with the Office of Dispute Resolution for Acquisition within two (2) years of the accrual of the contract claim involved. A contract dispute by the FAA against a contractor (excluding contract disputes alleging warranty issues, fraud or latent defects) likewise shall be filed within two (2) years after the accrual of the contract claim. If an underlying contract entered into prior to the effective date of this part provides for time limitations for filing of contract disputes with The Office of Dispute Resolution for Acquisition which differ from the aforesaid two (2) year period, the limitation periods in the contract shall control over the limitation period of this section. In no event will either party be permitted to file with the Office of Dispute Resolution for Acquisition a contract dispute seeking an equitable adjustment or other damages after the contractor has accepted final contract payment, with the exception of FAA claims related to warranty issues, gross mistakes amounting to fraud or latent defects. FAA claims against the contractor based on warranty issues must be filed within the time specified under applicable contract warranty provisions. Any FAA claims against the contractor based on gross mistakes amounting to fraud or latent defects shall be filed with the Office of Dispute Resolution for Acquisition within two (2) years of the date on which the FAA knew or should have known of the presence of the fraud or latent defect.

(d) A party shall serve a copy of the contract dispute upon the other party, by means reasonably calculated to be received on the same day as the filing is to be received by the Office of Dispute Resolution for Acquisition.

§17.27 Submission of joint or separate statements.

(a) If the matter has not been resolved informally, the parties shall file joint or separate statements with the

Office of Dispute Resolution for Acquisition no later than twenty (20) business days after the filing of the contract dispute. The Office of Dispute Resolution for Acquisition may extend this time, pursuant to § 17.23(d).

(b) The statement(s) shall include either—

(1) A joint request for ADR, and an executed ADR agreement, pursuant to § 17.33(d), specifying which ADR techniques will be employed; or

(2) Written explanation(s) as to why ADR proceedings will not be used and why the Default Adjudicative Process will be needed.

(c) Such statements shall be directed to the following address:

(1) Office of Dispute Resolution for Acquisition, AGC–70, Federal Aviation Administration, 400 7th Street, SW., Room 8332, Washington, DC 20590, Telephone: (202) 366–6400, Facsimile: (202) 366–7400; or

(2) Other address as shall be published from time to time in the FEDERAL REGISTER.

(d) The submission of a statement which indicates that ADR will not be utilized will not in any way preclude the parties from engaging in informal ADR techniques with the Office of Dispute Resolution for Acquisition (neutral evaluation and/or informal mediation) concurrently with ongoing adjudication under the Default Adjudicative Process, pursuant to § 17.31(c).

§ 17.29 Dismissal or summary decision of contract disputes.

(a) Any party may request, by motion to the Office of Dispute Resolution for Acquisition, that a contract dispute be dismissed, or that a count or portion of a contract dispute be stricken, if:

(1) It was not timely filed with the Office of Dispute Resolution for Acquisition;

(2) It was filed by a subcontractor;

(3) It fails to state a matter upon which relief may be had; or

(4) It involves a matter not subject to the jurisdiction of the Office of Dispute Resolution for Acquisition.

(b) In connection with any request for dismissal of a contract dispute, or to strike a count or portion thereof, the Office of Dispute Resolution for Acquisition should consider any material facts in dispute in a light most favorable to the party against whom the request for dismissal is made.

(c) At any time, whether pursuant to a motion or request or on its own initiative and at its discretion, the Office of Dispute Resolution for Acquisition may—

(1) Dismiss or strike a count or portion of a contract dispute;

(2) Recommend to the Administrator that the entire contract dispute be dismissed; or

(3) With delegation from the Administrator, dismiss the entire contract dispute.

(d) An order of dismissal of the entire contract dispute, issued either by the Administrator or by the Office of Dispute Resolution for Acquisition where delegation exists, on the grounds set forth in this section, shall constitute a final agency order. An Office of Dispute Resolution for Acquisition order dismissing or striking a count or portion of a contract dispute shall not constitute a final agency order, unless and until such Office of Dispute Resolution for Acquisition order is incorporated or otherwise adopted in a decision of the Administrator or the Administrator's delegee.

(e) Prior to recommending or entering either a dismissal or a summary decision, either in whole or in part, the Office of Dispute Resolution for Acquisition shall afford all parties against whom the dismissal or summary decision is to be entered the opportunity to respond to a proposed dismissal or summary decision.

Subpart D—Alternative Dispute Resolution

§ 17.31 Use of alternative dispute resolution.

(a) The Office of Dispute Resolution for Acquisition shall encourage the parties to utilize ADR as their primary means to resolve protests and contract disputes.

(b) The parties shall make a good faith effort to explore ADR possibilities in all cases and to employ ADR in every appropriate case. The Office of Dispute Resolution for Acquisition will encourage use of ADR techniques such as mediation, neutral evaluation, or minitrials, or variations of these techniques as agreed by the parties and approved by the Office of Dispute Resolution for Acquisition. The Office of Dispute Resolution for Acquisition shall assign a DRO to explore ADR options with the parties and to arrange for an early neutral evaluation of the merits of a case, if requested by any party.

(c) The Default Adjudicative Process will be used where the parties cannot achieve agreement on the use of ADR; or where ADR has been employed but has not resolved all pending issues in dispute; or where the Office of Dispute Resolution for Acquisition concludes that ADR will not provide an expeditious means of resolving a particular dispute. Even where the Default Adjudicative Process is to be used, the Office of Dispute Resolution for Acquisition, with the parties consent, may employ informal ADR techniques concurrently with and in parallel to adjudication.

§17.33 Election of alternative dispute resolution process.

(a) The Office of Dispute Resolution for Acquisition will make its personnel available to serve as Neutrals in ADR proceedings and, upon request by the parties, will attempt to make qualified non-FAA personnel available to serve as Neutrals through neutral-sharing programs and other similar arrangements. The parties may elect to employ a mutually Compensated Neutral, if the parties agree as to how the costs of any such Compensated Neutral are to be shared.

(b) The parties using an ADR process to resolve a protest shall submit an executed ADR agreement containing the information outlined in paragraph (d) of this section to the Office of Dispute Resolution for Acquisition within five (5) business days after the Office of Dispute Resolution for Acquisition conducts a status conference pursuant to §17.17(c). The Office of Dispute Resolution for Acquisition may extend this time for good cause.

(c) The parties using an ADR process to resolve a contract dispute shall submit an executed ADR agreement containing the information outlined in paragraph (d) of this section to the Office of Dispute Resolution for Acquisi-

tion as part of the joint statement specified under §17.27.

(d) The parties to a protest or contract dispute who elect to use ADR must submit to the Office of Dispute Resolution for Acquisition an ADR agreement setting forth:

(1) The type of ADR technique(s) to be used;

(2) The agreed-upon manner of using the ADR process; and

(3) Whether the parties agree to use a Neutral through The Office of Dispute Resolution for Acquisition or to use a Compensated Neutral of their choosing, and, if a Compensated Neutral is to be used, how the cost of the Compensated Neutral's services will be shared.

(e) Non-binding ADR techniques are not mutually exclusive, and may be used in combination if the parties agree that a combination is most appropriate to the dispute. The techniques to be employed must be determined in advance by the parties and shall be expressly described in their ADR agreement. The agreement may provide for the use of any fair and reasonable ADR technique that is designed to achieve a prompt resolution of the matter. An ADR agreement for non-binding ADR shall provide for a termination of ADR proceedings and the commencement of adjudication under the Default Adjudicative Process, upon the election of any party. Notwithstanding such termination, the parties may still engage with the Office of Dispute Resolution for Acquisition in ADR techniques (neutral evaluation and/or informal mediation) concurrently with adjudication, pursuant to §17.31(c).

(f) Binding arbitration may be permitted by the Office of Dispute Resolution for Acquisition on a case-by-case basis; and shall be subject to the provisions of 5 U.S.C. 575(a), (b), and (c), and any other applicable law. Arbitration that is binding on the parties, subject to the Administrator's right to approve or disapprove the arbitrator's decision, may also be permitted.

(g) For protests, the ADR process shall be completed within twenty (20) business days from the filing of an executed ADR agreement with the Office of Dispute Resolution for Acquisition unless the parties request, and are granted an extension of time from the Office of Dispute Resolution for Acquisition.

(h) For contract disputes, the ADR process shall be completed within forty (40) business days from the filing of an executed ADR agreement with the Office of Dispute Resolution for Acquisition, unless the parties request, and are granted an extension of time from the Office of Dispute Resolution for Acquisition.

(i) The parties shall submit to the Office of Dispute Resolution for Acquisition an agreed-upon protective order, if necessary, in accordance with the requirements of § 17.9.

§ 17.35 Selection of neutrals for the alternative dispute resolution process.

(a) In connection with the ADR process, the parties may select a Compensated Neutral acceptable to both, or may request the Office of Dispute Resolution for Acquisition to provide the services of a DRO or other Neutral.

(b) In cases where the parties select a Compensated Neutral who is not familiar with Office of Dispute Resolution for Acquisition procedural matters, the parties or Compensated Neutral may request the Office of Dispute Resolution for Acquisition for the services of a DRO to advise on such matters.

Subpart E—Default Adjudicative Process

§ 17.37 Default adjudicative process for protests.

(a) Other than for the resolution of preliminary or dispositive matters, the Default Adjudicative Process for protests will commence upon the submission of the Product Team Response to the Office of Dispute Resolution for Acquisition, pursuant to § 17.17.

(b) The Director of the Office of Dispute Resolution for Acquisition shall select a DRO or a Special Master to conduct fact-finding proceedings and to provide findings and recommendations concerning some or all of the matters in controversy.

(c) The DRO or Special Master may prepare procedural orders for the proceedings as deemed appropriate; and may require additional submissions from the parties. As a minimum, the protester and any intervenor(s) must submit to the Office of Dispute Resolution for Acquisition written comments with respect to the Product Team Response within five (5) business days of the Response having been filed with the Office of Dispute Resolution for Acquisition or within five (5) business days of their receipt of the Response, whichever is later. Copies of such comments shall be provided to the other participating parties by the same means and on the same date as they are furnished to the Office of Dispute Resolution for Acquisition.

(d) The DRO or Special Master may convene the parties and/or their representatives, as needed, to pursue the Default Adjudicative Process.

(e) If, in the sole judgment of the DRO or Special Master, the parties have presented written material sufficient to allow the protest to be decided on the record presented, the DRO or Special Master shall have the discretion to decide the protest on that basis.

(f) The parties may engage in voluntary discovery with one another and, if justified, with non-parties, so as to obtain information relevant to the allegations of the protest. The DRO or Special Master may also direct the parties to exchange, in an expedited manner, relevant, non-privileged documents. Where justified, the DRO or Special Master may direct the taking of deposition testimony, however, the FAA dispute resolution process does not contemplate extensive discovery. The DRO or Special Master shall manage the discovery process, including limiting its length and availability, and shall establish schedules and deadlines for discovery, which are consistent with time frames established in this part and with the FAA policy of providing fair and expeditious dispute resolution.

(g) The DRO or Special Master may conduct hearings, and may limit the hearings to the testimony of specific witnesses and/or presentations regarding specific issues. The DRO or Special Master shall control the nature and conduct of all hearings, including the sequence and extent of any testimony. Hearings will be conducted:

(1) Where the DRO or Special Master determines that there are complex factual issues in dispute that cannot adequately or efficiently be developed solely by means of written presentations and/or that resolution of the controversy will be dependent on his/her assessment of the credibility of statements provided by individuals with first-hand knowledge of the facts; or

(2) Upon request of any party to the protest, unless the DRO or Special Master finds specifically that a hearing is unnecessary and that no party will be prejudiced by limiting the record in the adjudication to the parties' written submissions. All witnesses at any such hearing shall be subject to cross-examination by the opposing party and to questioning by the DRO or Special Master.

(h) The Director of the Office of Dispute Resolution for Acquisition may review the status of any protest in the Default Adjudicative Process with the DRO or Special Master during the pendency of the process.

(i) Within thirty (30) business days of the commencement of the Default Adjudicative Process, or at the discretion of the Office of Dispute Resolution for Acquisition, the DRO or Special Master will submit findings and recommendations to the Office of Dispute Resolution for Acquisition that shall contain the following:

(1) Findings of fact;

(2) Application of the principles of the AMS, and any applicable law or authority to the findings of fact;

(3) A recommendation for a final FAA order; and

(4) If appropriate, suggestions for future FAA action.

(j) In arriving at findings and recommendations relating to protests, the DRO or Special Master shall consider whether or not the Product Team actions in question had a rational basis, and whether or not the Product Team decision under question was arbitrary, capricious or an abuse of discretion. Findings of fact underlying the recommendations must be supported by substantial evidence.

(k) The DRO or Special Master has broad discretion to recommend a remedy that is consistent with §17.21.

(l) A DRO or Special Master shall submit findings and recommendations only to the Director of the Office of Dispute Resolution for Acquisition. The findings and recommendations will be released to the parties and to the public, only upon issuance of the final FAA order in the case. Should an Office of Dispute Resolution for Acquisition protective order be issued in connection with the protest, a redacted version of the findings and recommendations, omitting any protected information, shall be prepared wherever possible and released to the public along with a copy of the final FAA order. Only persons admitted by the Office of Dispute Resolution for Acquisition under the protective order and Government personnel shall be provided copies of the unredacted findings and recommendations.

(m) The time limitations set forth in this section may be extended by the Office of Dispute Resolution for Acquisition for good cause.

§17.39 Default adjudicative process for contract disputes.

(a) The Default Adjudicative Process for contract disputes will commence on the latter of:

(1) The parties' submission to the Office of Dispute Resolution for Acquisition of a joint statement pursuant to §17.27 which indicates that ADR will not be utilized; or

(2) The parties' submission to the Office of Dispute Resolution for Acquisition of notification by any party that the parties have not settled some or all of the dispute issues via ADR, and it is unlikely that they can do so within the time period allotted and/or any reasonable extension.

(b) Within twenty (2) business days of the commencement of the Default Adjudicative Process, the Product Team shall prepare and submit to the Office of Dispute Resolution for Acquisition, with a copy to the contractor, a chronologically arranged and indexed Dispute File, containing all documents which are relevant to the facts and issues in dispute. The contractor will be entitled to supplement such a Dispute File with additional documents.

(c) The Director of the Office of Dispute Resolution for Acquisition shall assign a DRO or a Special Master to conduct fact-finding proceedings and provide findings and recommendations concerning the issues in dispute.

(d) The Director of the Office of Dispute Resolution for Acquisition may delegate authority to the DRO or Special Master to conduct a Status Conference within ten (10) business days of the commencement of the Default Adjudicative Process, and, may further delegate to the DRO or Special Master the authority to issue such orders or decisions to promote the efficient resolution of the contract dispute.

(e) At any such Status Conference, or as necessary during the Default Adjudicative Process, the DRO or Special Master will:

(1) Determine the appropriate amount of discovery required to resolve the dispute;

(2) Review the need for a protective order, and if one is needed, prepare a protective order pursuant to § 17.9;

(3) Determine whether any issue can be stricken; and

(4) Prepare necessary procedural orders for the proceedings.

(f) At a time or at times determined by the DRO or Special Master, and in advance of the decision of the case, the parties shall make final submissions to the Office of Dispute Resolution for Acquisition and to the DRO or Special Master, which submissions shall include the following:

(1) A joint statement of the issues;

(2) A joint statement of undisputed facts related to each issue;

(3) Separate statements of disputed facts related to each issue, with appropriate citations to documents in the Dispute File, to pages of transcripts of any hearing or deposition, or to any affidavit or exhibit which a party may wish to submit with its statement;

(4) Separate legal analyses in support of the parties' respective positions on disputed issues.

(g) Each party shall serve a copy of its final submission on the other party by means reasonable calculated so that the other party receives such submissions on the same day it is received by the Office of Dispute Resolution for Acquisition.

(h) The DRO or Special Master may decide the contract dispute on the basis of the record and the submissions referenced in this section, or may, in the DRO or Special Master's discretion, allow the parties to make additional presentations in writing. The DRO or Special Master may conduct hearings, and may limit the hearings to the testimony of specific witnesses and/or presentations regarding specific issues. The DRO or Special Master shall control the nature and conduct of all hearings, including the sequence and extent of any testimony. Hearings on the record shall be conducted by the ODRA:

(1) Where the DRO or Special Master determines that there are complex factual issues in dispute that cannot adequately or efficiently be developed solely by means of written presentations and/or that resolution of the controversy will be dependent on his/her assessment of the credibility of statements provided by individuals with first-hand knowledge of the facts; or

(2) Upon request of any party to the contract dispute, unless the DRO or Special Master finds specifically that a hearing is unnecessary and that no party will be prejudiced by limiting the record in the adjudication to the parties written submissions. All witnesses at any such hearing shall be subject to cross-examination by the opposing party and to questioning by the DRO or Special Master.

(i) The DRO or Special Master shall prepare findings and recommendations within thirty (30) business days from receipt of the final submissions of the parties, unless that time is extended by the Officer of Dispute Resolution for Acquisition for good cause. The findings and recommendations shall contain findings of fact, application of the principles of the AMS and other law or authority applicable to the findings of fact, a recommendation for a final FAA order, and, if appropriate, suggestions for future FAA action.

(j) As a party of the findings and recommendations, the DRO or Special Master shall review the disputed issue or issues in the context of the contract, any applicable law and the AMS. Any finding of fact set forth in the fundings and recommendation must be supported by substantial evidence.

(k) The Director of the Office of Dispute Resolution for Acquisition may review the status of any contract dispute in the Default Adjudicative Process with the DRO or Special Master during the pendency of the process.

(l) A DRO or Special Master shall submit findings and recommendations only to the Director of the Office of Dispute Resolution for Acquisition. The findings and recommendations will be released to the parties and to the public, upon issuance of the final FAA order in the case. Should an Office of Dispute Resolution for Acquisition protective order be issued in connection with the contract dispute, a redacted version of the findings and recommendations omitting any protected information, shall be prepared wherever possible and released to the public along with a copy of the final FAA order. Only persons admitted by the Office of Dispute Resolution for Acquisition under the protective order and Government personal shall be provided copies of the unredacted findings and recommendation.

(m) The time limitations set forth in this section may be extended by the Office of Dispute Resolution for Acquisition for good cause.

(n) Attorneys fees of a qualified prevailing contractor are allowable to the extent permitted by the EAJA, 5 U.S.C. 504 (a)(1).

[Doc. No. FAA–1998–4379, 64 FR 32936, June 18, 1999; 64 FR 47362, Aug. 31, 1999]

Subpart F—Finality and Review

§ 17.41 Final orders.

All final FAA orders regarding protests or connect disputes under this part are to be issued by the FAA Administrator or by a delegee of the Administrator.

§ 17.43 Judicial review.

(a) A protestor or contractor may seek of a final FAA order, pursuant to 49 U.S.C. 46110, only after the administrative remedies of this part have been exhausted.

(b) A copy of the petition for review shall be filed with the Office of Dispute Resolution for Acquisition and the FAA Chief Counsel on the date that the petition for review is filed with the appropriate circuit court of appeals.

§ 17.45 Conforming amendments.

The FAA shall amend pertinent provisions of the AMS, standard contract forms and clauses, and any guidance to contracting officials, so as to conform to the provisions of this part.

APPENDIX A TO PART 17—ALTERNATIVE DISPUTE RESOLUTION (ADR)

A. The FAA dispute resolution procedures encourage the parties to protests and contract disputes to use ADR as the primary means to resolve protests and contract disputes, pursuant to the Administrative Dispute Resolution Act of 1996, Pub. L. 104–320, 5 U.S.C. 570–579, and Department of Transportation and FAA policies to utilize ADR to the maximum extent practicable. Under the procedures presented in this part, the Office of Dispute Resolution for Acquisition would encourage parties to consider ADR techniques such as case evaluation, mediation, or arbitration.

B. ADR encompasses a number of processes and techniques for resolving protests or contract disputes. The most commonly used types include:

(1) *Mediation.* The Neutral or Compensated Neutral ascertains the needs and interests of both parties and facilitates discussions between or among the parties and an amicable resolution of their differences, seeking approaches to bridge the gaps between the parties' respective positions. The Neutral or Compensated Neutral can meet with the parties separately, conduct joint meetings with the parties' representatives, or employ both methods in appropriate cases.

(2) *Neutral Evaluation.* At any stage during the ADR process, as the parties may agree, the Neutral or Compensated Neutral will provide a candid assessment and opinion of the strengths and weaknesses of the parties' positions as to the facts and law, so as to facilitate further discussion and resolution.

(3) *Minitrial.* The minitrial resembles adjudication, but is less formal. It is used to provide an efficient process for airing and resolving more complex, fact-intensive disputes. The parties select principal representatives who should be senior officials of their respective organizations, having authority to negotiate a complete settlement. It is preferable that the principals be individuals who were not directly involved in the events leading to the dispute and who, thus, may be able to maintain a degree of impartiality during the proceeding. In order to maintain such impartiality, the principals typically serve as "judges" over the mini-trial proceeding together with the Neutral or Compensated Neutral. The proceeding is aimed at

informing the principal representatives and the Neutral or Compensated Neutral of the underlying bases of the parties' positions. Each party is given the opportunity and responsibility to present its position. The presentations may be made through the parties' counsel and/or through some limited testimony of fact witnesses or experts, which may be subject to cross-examination or rebuttal. Normally, witnesses are not sworn in and transcripts are not made of the proceedings. Similarly, rules of evidence are not directly applicable, though it is recommended that the Neutral or Compensated Neutral be provided authority by the parties' ADR agreement to exclude evidence which is not relevant to the issues in dispute, for the sake of an efficient proceeding. Frequently, minitrials are followed either by direct one-on-one negotiations by the parties' principals or by meetings between the Neutral/Compensated Neutral and the parties' principals, at which the Neutral/Compensated Neutral may offer his or her views on the parties' positions (*i.e.*, Neutral Evaluation) and/or facilitate negotiations and ultimate resolution via Mediation.

SUBCHAPTER C—AIRCRAFT

PART 21—CERTIFICATION PROCE-DURES FOR PRODUCTS AND PARTS

AUTHORITY: 42 U.S.C. 7572; 49 U.S.C. 106(g), 40105, 40113, 44701–44702, 44707, 44709, 44711, 44713, 44715, 45303.

EDITORIAL NOTE: For miscellaneous amendments to cross references in this Part 21 see Amdt. 21–10, 31 FR 9211, July 6, 1966.

SPECIAL FEDERAL AVIATION REGULATION No. 88—FUEL TANK SYSTEM FAULT TOLERANCE EVALUATION REQUIREMENTS

1. *Applicability.* This SFAR applies to the holders of type certificates, and supplemental type certificates that may affect the airplane fuel tank system, for turbine-powered transport category airplanes, provided the type certificate was issued after January 1, 1958, and the airplane has either a maximum type certificated passenger capacity of 30 or more, or a maximum type certificated payload capacity of 7,500 pounds or more. This SFAR also applies to applicants for type certificates, amendments to a type certificate, and supplemental type certificates affecting the fuel tank systems for those airplanes identified above, if the application was filed before June 6, 2001, the effective date of this SFAR, and the certificate was not issued before June 6, 2001.

2. *Compliance:* Each type certificate holder, and each supplemental type certificate holder of a modification affecting the airplane fuel tank system, must accomplish the following within the compliance times specified in paragraph (e) of this section:

(a) Conduct a safety review of the airplane fuel tank system to determine that the design meets the requirements of §§ 25.901 and 25.981(a) and (b) of this chapter. If the current design does not meet these requirements, develop all design changes to the fuel tank system that are necessary to meet these requirements. The FAA (Aircraft Certification Office (ACO), or office of the Transport Airplane Directorate, having cognizance over the type certificate for the affected airplane) may grant an extension of the 18-month compliance time for development of design changes if:

(1) The safety review is completed within the compliance time;

(2) Necessary design changes are identified within the compliance time; and

(3) Additional time can be justified, based on the holder's demonstrated aggressiveness in performing the safety review, the complexity of the necessary design changes, the availability of interim actions to provide an acceptable level of safety, and the resulting level of safety.

(b) Develop all maintenance and inspection instructions necessary to maintain the design features required to preclude the existence or development of an ignition source within the fuel tank system of the airplane.

(c) Submit a report for approval to the FAA Aircraft Certification Office (ACO), or office of the Transport Airplane Directorate, having cognizance over the type certificate for the affected airplane, that:

(1) Provides substantiation that the airplane fuel tank system design, including all necessary design changes, meets the requirements of §§ 25.901 and 25.981(a) and (b) of this chapter; and

(2) Contains all maintenance and inspection instructions necessary to maintain the design features required to preclude the existence or development of an ignition source within the fuel tank system throughout the operational life of the airplane.

(d) The Aircraft Certification Office (ACO), or office of the Transport Airplane Directorate, having cognizance over the type certificate for the affected airplane, may approve a report submitted in accordance with paragraph 2(c) if it determines that any provisions of this SFAR not complied with are compensated for by factors that provide an equivalent level of safety.

(e) Each type certificate holder must comply no later than December 6, 2002, or within 18 months after the issuance of a type certificate for which application was filed before June 6, 2001, whichever is later; and each supplemental type certificate holder of a modification affecting the airplane fuel tank system must comply no later than June 6, 2003, or within 18 months after the issuance of a supplemental type certificate for which application was filed before June 6, 2001, whichever is later.

[Doc. No. 1999–6411, 66 FR 23129, May 7, 2001, as amended by Amdt. 21–82, 67 FR 57493, Sept. 10, 2002; 67 FR 70809, Nov. 26, 2002; Amdt. 21–82, 67 FR 72833, Dec. 9, 2002]

Subpart A—General

§21.1 Applicability.

(a) This part prescribes—

(1) Procedural requirements for the issue of type certificates and changes to those certificates; the issue of production certificates; the issue of airworthiness certificates; and the issue of export airworthiness approvals.

(2) Rules governing the holders of any certificate specified in paragraph (a)(1) of this section; and

(3) Procedural requirements for the approval of certain materials, parts, processes, and appliances.

(b) For the purposes of this part, the word "product" means an aircraft, aircraft engine, or propeller. In addition, for the purposes of Subpart L only, it includes components and parts of aircraft, of aircraft engines, and of propellers; also parts, materials, and appliances, approved under the Technical Standard Order system.

[Doc. No. 5085, 29 FR 14563, Oct. 24, 1964, as amended by Amdt. 21–2, 30 FR 8465, July 2, 1965; Amdt. 21–6, 30 FR 11379, Sept. 8, 1965]

§ 21.2 Falsification of applications, reports, or records.

(a) No person shall make or cause to be made—

(1) Any fraudulent or intentionally false statement on any application for a certificate or approval under this part;

(2) Any fraudulent or intentionally false entry in any record or report that is required to be kept, made, or used to show compliance with any requirement for the issuance or the exercise of the privileges of any certificate or approval issued under this part;

(3) Any reproduction for a fraudulent purpose of any certificate or approval issued under this part.

(4) Any alteration of any certificate or approval issued under this part.

(b) The commission by any person of an act prohibited under paragraph (a) of this section is a basis for suspending or revoking any certificate or approval issued under this part and held by that person.

[Doc. No. 23345, 57 FR 41367, Sept. 9, 1992]

§ 21.3 Reporting of failures, malfunctions, and defects.

(a) Except as provided in paragraph (d) of this section, the holder of a Type Certificate (including a Supplemental Type Certificate), a Parts Manufacturer Approval (PMA), or a TSO authorization, or the licensee of a Type Certificate shall report any failure, malfunction, or defect in any product, part, process, or article manufactured by it that it determines has resulted in

any of the occurrences listed in paragraph (c) of this section.

(b) The holder of a Type Certificate (including a Supplemental Type Certificate), a Parts Manufacturer Approval (PMA), or a TSO authorization, or the licensee of a Type of Certificate shall report any defect in any product, part, or article manufactured by it that has left its quality control system and that it determines could result in any of the occurrences listed in paragraph (c) of this section.

(c) The following occurrences must be reported as provided in paragraphs (a) and (b) of this section:

(1) Fires caused by a system or equipment failure, malfunction, or defect.

(2) An engine exhaust system failure, malfunction, or defect which causes damage to the engine, adjacent aircraft structure, equipment, or components.

(3) The accumulation or circulation of toxic or noxious gases in the crew compartment or passenger cabin.

(4) A malfunction, failure, or defect of a propeller control system.

(5) A propeller or rotorcraft hub or blade structural failure.

(6) Flammable fluid leakage in areas where an ignition source normally exists.

(7) A brake system failure caused by structural or material failure during operation.

(8) A significant aircraft primary structural defect or failure caused by any autogenous condition (fatigue, understrength, corrosion, etc.).

(9) Any abnormal vibration or buffeting caused by a structural or system malfunction, defect, or failure.

(10) An engine failure.

(11) Any structural or flight control system malfunction, defect, or failure which causes an interference with normal control of the aircraft for which derogates the flying qualities.

(12) A complete loss of more than one electrical power generating system or hydraulic power system during a given operation of the aircraft.

(13) A failure or malfunction of more than one attitude, airspeed, or altitude instrument during a given operation of the aircraft.

(d) The requirements of paragraph (a) of this section do not apply to—

(1) Failures, malfunctions, or defects that the holder of a Type Certificate (including a Supplemental Type Certificate), Parts Manufacturer Approval (PMA), or TSO authorization, or the licensee of a Type Certificate—

(i) Determines were caused by improper maintenance, or improper usage;

(ii) Knows were reported to the FAA by another person under the Federal Aviation Regulations; or

(iii) Has already reported under the accident reporting provisions of Part 430 of the regulations of the National Transportation Safety Board.

(2) Failures, malfunctions, or defects in products, parts, or articles manufactured by a foreign manufacturer under a U.S. Type Certificate issued under §21.29 or §21.617, or exported to the United States under §21.502.

(e) Each report required by this section—

(1) Shall be made to the Aircraft Certification Office in the region in which the person required to make the report is located within 24 hours after it has determined that the failure, malfunction, or defect required to be reported has occurred. However, a report that is due on a Saturday or a Sunday may be delivered on the following Monday and one that is due on a holiday may be delivered on the next workday;

(2) Shall be transmitted in a manner and form acceptable to the Administrator and by the most expeditious method available; and

(3) Shall include as much of the following information as is available and applicable:

(i) Aircraft serial number.

(ii) When the failure, malfunction, or defect is associated with an article approved under a TSO authorization, the article serial number and model designation, as appropriate.

(iii) When the failure, malfunction, or defect is associated with an engine or propeller, the engine or propeller serial number, as appropriate.

(iv) Product model.

(v) Identification of the part, component, or system involved. The identification must include the part number.

(vi) Nature of the failure, malfunction, or defect.

(f) Whenever the investigation of an accident or service difficulty report shows that an article manufactured under a TSO authorization is unsafe because of a manufacturing or design defect, the manufacturer shall, upon request of the Administrator, report to the Administrator the results of its investigation and any action taken or proposed by the manufacturer to correct that defect. If action is required to correct the defect in existing articles, the manufacturer shall submit the data necessary for the issuance of an appropriate airworthiness directive to the Manager of the Aircraft Certification Office for the geographic area of the FAA regional office in the region in which it is located.

[Amdt. 21–36, 35 FR 18187, Nov. 28, 1970, as amended by Amdt. 21–37, 35 FR 18450, Dec. 4, 1970; Amdt. 21–50, 45 FR 38346, June 9, 1980; Amdt. 21–67, 54 FR 39291, Sept. 25, 1989]

§ 21.5 Airplane or Rotorcraft Flight Manual.

(a) With each airplane or rotorcraft that was not type certificated with an Airplane or Rotorcraft Flight Manual and that has had no flight time prior to March 1, 1979, the holder of a Type Certificate (including a Supplemental Type Certificate) or the licensee of a Type Certificate shall make available to the owner at the time of delivery of the aircraft a current approved Airplane or Rotorcraft Flight Manual.

(b) The Airplane or Rotorcraft Flight Manual required by paragraph (a) of this section must contain the following information:

(1) The operating limitations and information required to be furnished in an Airplane or Rotorcraft Flight Manual or in manual material, markings, and placards, by the applicable regulations under which the airplane or rotorcraft was type certificated.

(2) The maximum ambient atmospheric temperature for which engine cooling was demonstrated must be stated in the performance information section of the Flight Manual, if the applicable regulations under which the aircraft was type certificated do not require ambient temperature on engine cooling operating limitations in the Flight Manual.

[Amdt. 21–46, 43 FR 2316, Jan. 16, 1978]

Subpart B—Type Certificates

SOURCE: Docket No. 5085, 29 FR 14564, Oct. 24, 1964, unless otherwise noted.

§ 21.11 Applicability.

This subpart prescribes—

(a) Procedural requirements for the issue of type certificates for aircraft, aircraft engines, and propellers; and

(b) Rules governing the holders of those certificates.

§ 21.13 Eligibility.

Any interested person may apply for a type certificate.

[Amdt. 21-25, 34 FR 14068, Sept. 5, 1969]

§ 21.15 Application for type certificate.

(a) An application for a type certificate is made on a form and in a manner prescribed by the Administrator and is submitted to the appropriate Aircraft Certification Office.

(b) An application for an aircraft type certificate must be accompanied by a three-view drawing of that aircraft and available preliminary basic data.

(c) An application for an aircraft engine type certificate must be accompanied by a description of the engine design features, the engine operating characteristics, and the proposed engine operating limitations.

[Doc. No. 5085, 29 FR 14564, Oct. 24, 1964, as amended by Amdt. 21-40, 39 FR 35459, Oct. 1, 1974; Amdt. 21-67, 54 FR 39291, Sept. 25, 1989]

§ 21.16 Special conditions.

If the Administrator finds that the airworthiness regulations of this subchapter do not contain adequate or appropriate safety standards for an aircraft, aircraft engine, or propeller because of a novel or unusual design feature of the aircraft, aircraft engine or propeller, he prescribes special conditions and amendments thereto for the product. The special conditions are issued in accordance with Part 11 of this chapter and contain such safety standards for the aircraft, aircraft engine or propeller as the Administrator finds necessary to establish a level of safety equivalent to that established in the regulations.

[Amdt. 21-19, 32 FR 17851, Dec. 13, 1967; as amended by Amdt. 21-51, 45 FR 60170, Sept. 11, 1980]

§ 21.17 Designation of applicable regulations.

(a) Except as provided in § 23.2, § 25.2, § 27.2, § 29.2 and in parts 34 and 36 of this chapter, an applicant for a type certificate must show that the aircraft, aircraft engine, or propeller concerned meets—

(1) The applicable requirements of this subchapter that are effective on the date of application for that certificate unless—

(i) Otherwise specified by the Administrator; or

(ii) Compliance with later effective amendments is elected or required under this section; and

(2) Any special conditions prescribed by the Administrator.

(b) For special classes of aircraft, including the engines and propellers installed thereon (e.g., gliders, airships, and other nonconventional aircraft), for which airworthiness standards have not been issued under this subchapter, the applicable requirements will be the portions of those other airworthiness requirements contained in Parts 23, 25, 27, 29, 31, 33, and 35 found by the Administrator to be appropriate for the aircraft and applicable to a specific type design, or such airworthiness criteria as the Administrator may find provide an equivalent level of safety to those parts.

(c) An application for type certification of a transport category aircraft is effective for 5 years and an application for any other type certificate is effective for 3 years, unless an applicant shows at the time of application that his product requires a longer period of time for design, development, and testing, and the Administrator approves a longer period.

(d) In a case where a type certificate has not been issued, or it is clear that a type certificate will not be issued, within the time limit established under paragraph (c) of this section, the applicant may—

(1) File a new application for a type certificate and comply with all the provisions of paragraph (a) of this section applicable to an original application; or

(2) File for an extension of the original application and comply with the applicable airworthiness requirements of this subchapter that were effective on a date, to be selected by the applicant, not earlier than the date which precedes the date of issue of the type certificate by the time limit established under paragraph (c) of this section for the original application.

(e) If an applicant elects to comply with an amendment to this subchapter that is effective after the filing of the application for a type certificate, he must also comply with any other amendment that the Administrator finds is directly related.

(f) For primary category aircraft, the requirements are:

(1) The applicable airworthiness requirements contained in parts 23, 27, 31, 33, and 35 of this subchapter, or such other airworthiness criteria as the Administrator may find appropriate and applicable to the specific design and intended use and provide a level of safety acceptable to the Administrator.

(2) The noise standards of part 36 applicable to primary category aircraft.

[Doc. No. 5085, 29 FR 14564, Oct. 24, 1964, as amended by Amdt. 21–19, 32 FR 17851, Dec. 13, 1967; Amdt. 21–24, 34 FR 364, Jan. 10, 1969; Amdt. 21–42, 40 FR 1033, Jan. 6, 1975; Amdt. 21–58, 50 FR 46877, Nov. 13, 1985; Amdt. 21–60, 52 FR 8042, Mar. 13, 1987; Amdt. 21–68, 55 FR 32860, Aug. 10, 1990; Amdt. 21–69, 56 FR 41051, Aug. 16, 1991; Amdt. 21–70, 57 FR 41367, Sept. 9, 1992]

§21.19 Changes requiring a new type certificate.

Each person who proposes to change a product must apply for a new type certificate if the Administrator finds that the proposed change in design, power, thrust, or weight is so extensive that a substantially complete investigation of compliance with the applicable regulations is required.

[Doc. No. 28903, 65 FR 36265, June 7, 2000]

§21.21 Issue of type certificate: normal, utility, acrobatic, commuter, and transport category aircraft; manned free balloons; special classes of aircraft; aircraft engines; propellers.

An applicant is entitled to a type certificate for an aircraft in the normal, utility, acrobatic, commuter, or transport category, or for a manned free balloon, special class of aircraft, or an aircraft engine or propeller, if—

(a) The product qualifies under §21.27; or

(b) The applicant submits the type design, test reports, and computations necessary to show that the product to be certificated meets the applicable airworthiness, aircraft noise, fuel venting, and exhaust emission requirements of the Federal Aviation Regulations and any special conditions prescribed by the Administrator, and the Administrator finds—

(1) Upon examination of the type design, and after completing all tests and inspections, that the type design and the product meet the applicable noise, fuel venting, and emissions requirements of the Federal Aviation Regulations, and further finds that they meet the applicable airworthiness requirements of the Federal Aviation Regulations or that any airworthiness provisions not complied with are compensated for by factors that provide an equivalent level of safety; and

(2) For an aircraft, that no feature or characteristic makes it unsafe for the category in which certification is requested.

[Doc. No. 5085, 29 FR 14564, Oct. 24, 1964, as amended by Amdt. 21–15, 32 FR 3735, Mar. 4, 1967; Amdt. 21–27, 34 FR 18368, Nov. 18, 1969; Amdt. 21–60, 52 FR 8042, Mar. 13, 1987; Amdt. 21–68, 55 FR 32860, Aug. 10, 1990]

§21.23 [Reserved]

§21.24 Issuance of type certificate: primary category aircraft.

(a) The applicant is entitled to a type certificate for an aircraft in the primary category if—

(1) The aircraft—

(i) Is unpowered; is an airplane powered by a single, naturally aspirated engine with a 61-knot or less V$_{so}$ stall speed as defined in § 23.49; or is a rotor-craft with a 6-pound per square foot main rotor disc loading limitation, under sea level standard day conditions;

(ii) Weighs not more than 2,700 pounds; or, for seaplanes, not more than 3,375 pounds;

(iii) Has a maximum seating capacity of not more than four persons, including the pilot; and

(iv) Has an unpressurized cabin.

(2) The applicant has submitted—

(i) Except as provided by paragraph (c) of this section, a statement, in a form and manner acceptable to the Administrator, certifying that: the applicant has completed the engineering analysis necessary to demonstrate compliance with the applicable airworthiness requirements; the applicant has conducted appropriate flight, structural, propulsion, and systems tests necessary to show that the aircraft, its components, and its equipment are reliable and function properly; the type design complies with the airworthiness standards and noise requirements established for the aircraft under § 21.17(f); and no feature or characteristic makes it unsafe for its intended use;

(ii) The flight manual required by § 21.5(b), including any information required to be furnished by the applicable airworthiness standards;

(iii) Instructions for continued airworthiness in accordance with § 21.50(b); and

(iv) A report that: summarizes how compliance with each provision of the type certification basis was determined; lists the specific documents in which the type certification data information is provided; lists all necessary drawings and documents used to define the type design; and lists all the engineering reports on tests and computations that the applicant must retain and make available under § 21.49 to substantiate compliance with the applicable airworthiness standards.

(3) The Administrator finds that—

(i) The aircraft complies with those applicable airworthiness requirements approved under § 21.17(f) of this part; and

(ii) The aircraft has no feature or characteristic that makes it unsafe for its intended use.

(b) An applicant may include a special inspection and preventive maintenance program as part of the aircraft's type design or supplemental type design.

(c) For aircraft manufactured outside of the United States in a country with which the United States has a bilateral airworthiness agreement for the acceptance of these aircraft, and from which the aircraft is to be imported into the United States—

(1) The statement required by paragraph (a)(2)(i) of this section must be made by the civil airworthiness authority of the exporting country; and

(2) The required manuals, placards, listings, instrument markings, and documents required by paragraphs (a) and (b) of this section must be submitted in English.

[Doc. No. 23345, 57 FR 41367, Sept. 9, 1992; as amended by Amdt. 21–75, 62 FR 62808, Nov. 25, 1997]

§ 21.25 Issue of type certificate: Restricted category aircraft.

(a) An applicant is entitled to a type certificate for an aircraft in the restricted category for special purpose operations if he shows compliance with the applicable noise requirements of Part 36 of this chapter, and if he shows that no feature or characteristic of the aircraft makes it unsafe when it is operated under the limitations prescribed for its intended use, and that the aircraft—

(1) Meets the airworthiness requirements of an aircraft category except those requirements that the Administrator finds inappropriate for the special purpose for which the aircraft is to be used; or

(2) Is of a type that has been manufactured in accordance with the requirements of and accepted for use by, an Armed Force of the United States and has been later modified for a special purpose.

(b) For the purposes of this section, "special purpose operations" includes—

(1) Agricultural (spraying, dusting, and seeding, and livestock and predatory animal control);

(2) Forest and wildlife conservation;

(3) Aerial surveying (photography, mapping, and oil and mineral exploration);

(4) Patrolling (pipelines, power lines, and canals);

(5) Weather control (cloud seeding);

(6) Aerial advertising (skywriting, banner towing, airborne signs and public address systems); and

(7) Any other operation specified by the Administrator.

[Doc. No. 5085, 29 FR 14564, Oct. 24, 1964, as amended by Amdt. 21–42, 40 FR 1033, Jan. 6, 1975]

§21.27 Issue of type certificate: surplus aircraft of the Armed Forces.

(a) Except as provided in paragraph (b) of this section an applicant is entitled to a type certificate for an aircraft in the normal, utility, acrobatic, commuter, or transport category that was designed and constructed in the United States, accepted for operational use, and declared surplus by, an Armed Force of the United States, and that is shown to comply with the applicable certification requirements in paragraph (f) of this section.

(b) An applicant is entitled to a type certificate for a surplus aircraft of the Armed Forces of the United States that is a counterpart of a previously type certificated civil aircraft, if he shows compliance with the regulations governing the original civil aircraft type certificate.

(c) Aircraft engines, propellers, and their related accessories installed in surplus Armed Forces aircraft, for which a type certificate is sought under this section, will be approved for use on those aircraft if the applicant shows that on the basis of the previous military qualifications, acceptance, and service record, the product provides substantially the same level of airworthiness as would be provided if the engines or propellers were type certificated under Part 33 or 35 of the Federal Aviation Regulations.

(d) The Administrator may relieve an applicant from strict compliance with a specific provision of the applicable requirements in paragraph (f) of this section, if the Administrator finds that the method of compliance proposed by the applicant provides substantially the same level of airworthiness and that strict compliance with those regulations would impose a severe burden on the applicant. The Administrator may use experience that was satisfactory to an Armed Force of the United States in making such a determination.

(e) The Administrator may require an applicant to comply with special conditions and later requirements than those in paragraphs (c) and (f) of this section, if the Administrator finds that compliance with the listed regulations would not ensure an adequate level of airworthiness for the aircraft.

(f) Except as provided in paragraphs (b) through (e) of this section, an applicant for a type certificate under this section must comply with the appropriate regulations listed in the following table:

Type of aircraft	Date accepted for operational use by the Armed Forces of the United States	Regulations that apply [1]
Small reciprocating-engine powered airplanes	Before May 16, 1956	CAR Part 3, as effective May 15, 1956.
	After May 15, 1956	CAR Part 3, or FAR Part 23.
Small turbine engine-powered airplanes	Before Oct. 2, 1959	CAR Part 3, as effective Oct. 1, 1959.
	After Oct. 1, 1959	CAR Part 3 or FAR Part 23.
Commuter category airplanes	After (Feb. 17, 1987) FAR Part 23 as of (Feb. 17, 1987)..	
Large reciprocating-engine powered airplanes	Before Aug. 26, 1955	CAR Part 4b, as effective Aug. 25, 1955.
	After Aug. 25, 1959	CAR Part 4b or FAR Part 25.
Large turbine engine-powered airplanes	Before Oct. 2, 1959	CAR Part 4b, as effective Oct. 1, 1959.
	After Oct. 1, 1959	CAR Part 4b or FAR Part 25.
Rotorcraft with maximum certificated takeoff weight of:		
6,000 pounds or less	Before Oct. 2, 1959	CAR Part 6, as effective Oct. 1, 1959.
	After Oct. 1, 1959	CAR Part 6, or FAR Part 27.
Over 6,000 pounds	Before Oct. 2, 1959	CAR Part 7, as effective Oct. 1, 1959.
	After Oct. 1, 1959	CAR Part 7, or FAR Part 29.

[1] Where no specific date is listed, the applicable regulations are those in effect on the date that the first aircraft of the particular model was accepted for operational use by the Armed Forces.

[Doc. No. 5085, 29 FR 14564, Oct. 24, 1964, as amended by Amdt. 21–59, 52 FR 1835, Jan. 15, 1987; 52 FR 7262, Mar. 9, 1987]

§ 21.29 Issue of type certificate: import products.

(a) A type certificate may be issued for a product that is manufactured in a foreign country with which the United States has an agreement for the acceptance of these products for export and import and that is to be imported into the United States if—

(1) The country in which the product was manufactured certifies that the product has been examined, tested, and found to meet—

(i) The applicable aircraft noise, fuel venting and exhaust emissions requirements of this subchapter as designated in § 21.17, or the applicable aircraft noise, fuel venting and exhaust emissions requirements of the country in which the product was manufactured, and any other requirements the Administrator may prescribe to provide noise, fuel venting and exhaust emission levels no greater than those provided by the applicable aircraft noise, fuel venting, and exhaust emission requirements of this subchapter as designated in § 21.17; and

(ii) The applicable airworthiness requirements of this subchapter as designated in § 21.17, or the applicable airworthiness requirements of the country in which the product was manufactured and any other requirements the Administrator may prescribe to provide a level of safety equivalent to that provided by the applicable airworthiness requirements of this subchapter as designated in § 21.17;

(2) The applicant has submitted the technical data, concerning aircraft noise and airworthiness, respecting the product required by the Administrator; and

(3) The manuals, placards, listings, and instrument markings required by the applicable airworthiness (and noise, where applicable) requirements are presented in the English language.

(b) A product type certificated under this section is considered to be type certificated under the noise standards of part 36, and the fuel venting and exhaust emission standards of part 34, of the Federal Aviation Regulations where compliance therewith is certified under paragraph (a)(1)(i) of this section, and under the airworthiness standards of that part of the Federal Aviation Regulations with which compliance is certified under paragraph (a)(1)(ii) of this section or to which an equivalent level of safety is certified under paragraph (a)(1)(ii) of this section.

[Amdt. 21–27, 34 FR 18363, Nov. 18, 1969, as amended by Amdt. 21–68, 55 FR 32860, Aug. 10, 1990; 55 FR 37287, Sept. 10, 1990]

§ 21.31 Type design.

The type design consists of—

(a) The drawings and specifications, and a listing of those drawings and specifications, necessary to define the configuration and the design features of the product shown to comply with the requirements of that part of this subchapter applicable to the product;

(b) Information on dimensions, materials, and processes necessary to define the structural strength of the product;

(c) The Airworthiness Limitations section of the Instructions for Continued Airworthiness as required by Parts 23, 25, 27, 29, 31, 33, and 35 of this chapter or as otherwise required by the Administrator; and as specified in the applicable airworthiness criteria for special classes of aircraft defined in § 21.17(b); and

(d) For primary category aircraft, if desired, a special inspection and preventive maintenance program designed to be accomplished by an appropriately rated and trained pilot-owner.

(e) Any other data necessary to allow, by comparison, the determination of the airworthiness, noise characteristics, fuel venting, and exhaust emissions (where applicable) of later products of the same type.

[Doc. No. 5085, 29 FR 14564, Oct. 24, 1964, as amended by Amdt. 21–27, 34 FR 18363, Nov. 18, 1969; Amdt. 21–51, 45 FR 60170, Sept. 11, 1980; Amdt. 21–60, 52 FR 8042, Mar. 13, 1987; Amdt. 21–68, 55 FR 32860, Aug. 10, 1990; Amdt. 21–70, 57 FR 41368, Sept. 9, 1992]

§21.33 Inspection and tests.

(a) Each applicant must allow the Administrator to make any inspection and any flight and ground test necessary to determine compliance with the applicable requirements of the Federal Aviation Regulations. However, unless otherwise authorized by the Administrator—

(1) No aircraft, aircraft engine, propeller, or part thereof may be presented to the Administrator for test unless compliance with paragraphs (b)(2) through (b)(4) of this section has been shown for that aircraft, aircraft engine, propeller, or part thereof; and

(2) No change may be made to an aircraft, aircraft engine, propeller, or part thereof between the time that compliance with paragraphs (b)(2) through (b)(4) of this section is shown for that aircraft, aircraft engine, propeller, or part thereof and the time that it is presented to the Administrator for test.

(b) Each applicant must make all inspections and tests necessary to determine—

(1) Compliance with the applicable airworthiness, aircraft noise, fuel venting, and exhaust emission requirements;

(2) That materials and products conform to the specifications in the type design;

(3) That parts of the products conform to the drawings in the type design; and

(4) That the manufacturing processes, construction and assembly conform to those specified in the type design.

[Doc. No. 5085, 29 FR 14564, Oct. 24, 1964, as amended by Amdt. 21–17, 32 FR 14926, Oct. 28, 1967; Amdt. 21–27, 34 FR 18363, Nov. 18, 1969; Amdt. 21–44, 41 FR 55463, Dec. 20, 1976; Amdt. 21–68, 55 FR 32860, Aug. 10, 1990; Amdt. 21–68, 55 FR 32860, Aug. 10, 1990]

§21.35 Flight tests.

(a) Each applicant for an aircraft type certificate (other than under §§21.24 through 21.29) must make the tests listed in paragraph (b) of this section. Before making the tests the applicant must show—

(1) Compliance with the applicable structural requirements of this subchapter;

(2) Completion of necessary ground inspections and tests;

(3) That the aircraft conforms with the type design; and

(4) That the Administrator received a flight test report from the applicant (signed, in the case of aircraft to be certificated under Part 25 [New] of this chapter, by the applicant's test pilot) containing the results of his tests.

(b) Upon showing compliance with paragraph (a) of this section, the applicant must make all flight tests that the Administrator finds necessary—

(1) To determine compliance with the applicable requirements of this subchapter; and

(2) For aircraft to be certificated under this subchapter, except gliders and except airplanes of 6,000 lbs. or less maximum certificated weight that are to be certificated under Part 23 of this chapter, to determine whether there is reasonable assurance that the aircraft, its components, and its equipment are reliable and function properly.

(c) Each applicant must, if practicable, make the tests prescribed in paragraph (b)(2) of this section upon the aircraft that was used to show compliance with—

(1) Paragraph (b)(1) of this section; and

(2) For rotorcraft, the rotor drive endurance tests prescribed in §27.923 or §29.923 of this chapter, as applicable.

(d) Each applicant must show for each flight test (except in a glider or a manned free balloon) that adequate provision is made for the flight test crew for emergency egress and the use of parachutes.

(e) Except in gliders and manned free balloons, an applicant must discontinue flight tests under this section until he shows that corrective action has been taken, whenever—

(1) The applicant's test pilot is unable or unwilling to make any of the required flight tests; or

(2) Items of noncompliance with requirements are found that may make additional test data meaningless or that would make further testing unduly hazardous.

(f) The flight tests prescribed in paragraph (b)(2) of this section must include—

(1) For aircraft incorporating turbine engines of a type not previously used in a type certificated aircraft, at least 300 hours of operation with a full complement of engines that conform to a type certificate; and

(2) For all other aircraft, at least 150 hours of operation.

[Doc. No. 5085, 29 FR 14564, Oct. 24, 1964, as amended by Amdt. 21–40, 39 FR 35459, Oct. 1, 1974; Amdt. 21–51, 45 FR 60170, Sept. 11, 1980; Amdt. 21–70, 57 FR 41368, Sept. 9, 1992]

§ 21.37 Flight test pilot.

Each applicant for a normal, utility, acrobatic, commuter, or transport category aircraft type certificate must provide a person holding an appropriate pilot certificate to make the flight tests required by this part.

[Doc. No. 5085, 29 FR 14564, Oct. 24, 1964, as amended by Amdt. 21–59, 52 FR 1835, Jan. 15, 1987]

§ 21.39 Flight test instrument calibration and correction report.

(a) Each applicant for a normal, utility, acrobatic, commuter, or transport category aircraft type certificate must submit a report to the Administrator showing the computations and tests required in connection with the calibration of instruments used for test purposes and in the correction of test results to standard atmospheric conditions.

(b) Each applicant must allow the Administrator to conduct any flight tests that he finds necessary to check the accuracy of the report submitted under paragraph (a) of this section.

[Doc. No. 5085, 29 FR 14564, Oct. 24, 1964, as amended by Amdt. 21–59, 52 FR 1835, Jan. 15, 1987]

§ 21.41 Type certificate.

Each type certificate is considered to include the type design, the operating limitations, the certificate data sheet, the applicable regulations of this subchapter with which the Administrator records compliance, and any other conditions or limitations prescribed for the product in this subchapter.

§ 21.43 Location of manufacturing facilities.

Except as provided in § 21.29, the Administrator does not issue a type certificate if the manufacturing facilities for the product are located outside of the United States, unless the Administrator finds that the location of the manufacturer's facilities places no undue burden on the FAA in administering applicable airworthiness requirements.

§ 21.45 Privileges.

The holder or licensee of a type certificate for a product may—

(a) In the case of aircraft, upon compliance with §§ 21.173 through 21.189, obtain airworthiness certificates;

(b) In the case of aircraft engines or propellers, obtain approval for installation or certified aircraft;

(c) In the case of any product, upon compliance with §§ 21.133 through 21.163, obtain a production certificate for the type certificated product;

(d) Obtain approval of replacement parts for that product.

§ 21.47 Transferability.

A type certificate may be transferred to or made available to third persons by licensing agreements. Each grantor shall, within 30 days after the transfer of a certificate or execution or termination of a licensing agreement, notify in writing the appropriate Aircraft Certification Office. The notification must state the name and address of the transferee or licensee, date of the transaction, and in the case of a licensing agreement, the extent of authority granted the licensee.

[Doc. No. 5085, 29 FR 14564, Oct. 24, 1964, as amended by Amdt. 21–67, 54 FR 39291, Sept. 25, 1989]

§ 21.49 Availability.

The holder of a type certificate shall make the certificate available for examination upon the request of the Administrator or the National Transportation Safety Board.

[Doc. No. 5085, 29 FR 14564, Oct. 24, 1964, as amended by Doc. No. 8084, 32 FR 5769, Apr. 11, 1967]

§21.50 Instructions for continued airworthiness and manufacturer's maintenance manuals having airworthiness limitations sections.

(a) The holder of a type certificate for a rotorcraft for which a Rotorcraft Maintenance Manual containing an "Airworthiness Limitations" section has been issued under §27.1529 (a)(2) or §29.1529 (a)(2) of this chapter, and who obtains approval of changes to any replacement time, inspection interval, or related procedure in that section of the manual, shall make those changes available upon request to any operator of the same type of rotorcraft.

(b) The holder of a design approval, including either the type certificate or supplemental type certificate for an aircraft, aircraft engine, or propeller for which application was made after January 28, 1981, shall furnish at least one set of complete Instructions for Continued Airworthiness, prepared in accordance with §§23.1529, 25.1529, 27.1529, 29.1529, 31.82, 33.4, or 35.4 of this chapter, or as specified in the applicable airworthiness criteria for special classes of aircraft defined in §21.17(b), as applicable, to the owner of each type of aircraft, aircraft engine, or propeller upon its delivery, or upon issuance of the first standard airworthiness certificate for the affected aircraft, whichever occurs later, and thereafter make those instructions available to any other person required by this chapter to comply with any of the terms of these instructions. In addition, changes to the Instructions for Continued Airworthiness shall be made available to any person required by this chapter to comply with any of those instructions.

[Amdt. No. 21–23, 33 FR 14105, Sept. 18, 1968, as amended by Amdt. No 21–51, 45 FR 60170, Sept. 11, 1980; Amdt. 21–60, 52 FR 8042, Mar. 13, 1987]

§21.51 Duration.

A type certificate is effective until surrendered, suspended, revoked, or a termination date is otherwise established by the Administrator.

§21.53 Statement of conformity.

(a) Each applicant must submit a statement of conformity (FAA Form 317) to the Administrator for each aircraft engine and propeller presented to the Administrator for type certification. This statement of conformity must include a statement that the aircraft engine or propeller conforms to the type design therefor.

(b) Each applicant must submit a statement of conformity to the Administrator for each aircraft or part thereof presented to the Administrator for tests. This statement of conformity must include a statement that the applicant has complied with §21.33(a) (unless otherwise authorized under that paragraph).

[Amdt. 21–17, 32 FR 14926, Oct. 28, 1967]

Subpart C—Provisional Type Certificates

Source: Docket No. 5085, 29 FR 14566, Oct. 24, 1964, unless otherwise noted.

§21.71 Applicability.

This subpart prescribes—

(a) Procedural requirements for the issue of provisional type certificates, amendments to provisional type certificates, and provisional amendments to type certificates; and

(b) Rules governing the holders of those certificates.

§21.73 Eligibility.

(a) Any manufacturer of aircraft manufactured within the United States who is a United States citizen may apply for Class I or Class II provisional type certificates, for amendments to provisional type certificates held by him, and for provisional amendments to type certificates held by him.

(b) Any manufacturer of aircraft manufactured in a foreign country with which the United States has an agreement for the acceptance of those aircraft for export and import may apply for a Class II provisional type certificate, for amendments to provisional type certificates held by him, and for provisional amendments to type certificates held by him.

(c) An aircraft engine manufacturer who is a United States citizen and who has altered a type certificated aircraft by installing different type certificated aircraft engines manufactured by him within the United States may apply for a Class I provisional type certificate for the aircraft, and for amendments to Class I provisional type certificates held by him, if the basic aircraft, before alteration, was type certificated in the normal, utility, acrobatic, commuter, or transport category.

[Doc. No. 5085, 29 FR 14566, Oct. 24, 1964, as amended by Amdt. 21–12, 31 FR 13380, Oct. 15, 1966; Amdt. 21–59, 52 FR 1836, Jan. 15, 1987]

§ 21.75 Application.

Applications for provisional type certificates, for amendments thereto, and for provisional amendments to type certificates must be submitted to the Manager of the Aircraft Certification Office for the geographic area in which the applicant is located (or in the case of European, African, Middle East Region, the Manager, Aircraft Engineering Division), and must be accompanied by the pertinent information specified in this subpart.

[Amdt. 21–67, 54 FR 39291, Sept. 25, 1989]

§ 21.77 Duration.

(a) Unless sooner surrendered, superseded, revoked, or otherwise terminated, provisional type certificates and amendments thereto are effective for the periods specified in this section.

(b) A Class I provisional type certificate is effective for 24 months after the date of issue.

(c) A Class II provisional type certificate is effective for twelve months after the date of issue.

(d) An amendment to a Class I or Class II provisional type certificate is effective for the duration of the amended certificate.

(e) A provisional amendment to a type certificate is effective for six months after its approval or until the amendment of the type certificate is approved, whichever is first.

[Doc. No. 5085, 29 FR 14566, Oct. 24, 1964 as amended by Amdt. 21–7, 30 FR 14311, Nov. 16, 1965]

§ 21.79 Transferability.

Provisional type certificates are not transferable.

§ 21.81 Requirements for issue and amendment of Class I provisional type certificates.

(a) An applicant is entitled to the issue or amendment of a Class I provisional type certificate if he shows compliance with this section and the Administrator finds that there is no feature, characteristic, or condition that would make the aircraft unsafe when operated in accordance with the limitations established in paragraph (e) of this section and in § 91.317 of this chapter.

(b) The applicant must apply for the issue of a type or supplemental type certificate for the aircraft.

(c) The applicant must certify that—

(1) The aircraft has been designed and constructed in accordance with the airworthiness requirements applicable to the issue of the type or supplemental type certificate applied for;

(2) The aircraft substantially meets the applicable flight characteristic requirements for the type or supplemental type certificate applied for; and

(3) The aircraft can be operated safely under the appropriate operating limitations specified in paragraph (a) of this section.

(d) The applicant must submit a report showing that the aircraft had been flown in all maneuvers necessary to show compliance with the flight requirements for the issue of the type or supplemental type certificate applied for, and to establish that the aircraft can be operated safely in accordance with the limitations contained in this subchapter.

(e) The applicant must establish all limitations required for the issue of the type or supplemental type certificate applied for, including limitations on weights, speeds, flight maneuvers, loading, and operation of controls and equipment unless, for each limitation not so established, appropriate operating restrictions are established for the aircraft.

(f) The applicant must establish an inspection and maintenance program for the continued airworthiness of the aircraft.

(g) The applicant must show that a prototype aircraft has been flown for at least 50 hours under an experimental certificate issued under §§ 21.191 through 21.195, or under the auspices of an Armed Force of the United States. However, in the case of an amendment to a provisional type certificate, the Administrator may reduce the number of required flight hours.

[Doc. No. 5085, 29 FR 14566, Oct. 24, 1964, as amended by Amdt. 21–66, 54 FR 34329, Aug. 18, 1989]

§ 21.83 Requirements for issue and amendment of Class II provisional type certificates.

(a) An applicant who manufactures aircraft within the United States is entitled to the issue or amendment of a Class II provisional type certificate if he shows compliance with this section and the Administrator finds that there is no feature, characteristic, or condition that would make the aircraft unsafe when operated in accordance with the limitations in paragraph (h) of this section, and §§ 91.317 and 121.207 of this chapter.

(b) An applicant who manufactures aircraft in a country with which the United States has an agreement for the acceptance of those aircraft for export and import is entitled to the issue or amendment of a Class II provisional type certificate if the country in which the aircraft was manufactured certifies that the applicant has shown compliance with this section, that the aircraft meets the requirements of paragraph (f) of this section and that there is no feature, characteristic, or condition that would make the aircraft unsafe when operated in accordance with the limitations in paragraph (h) of this section and §§ 91.317 and 121.207 of this chapter.

(c) The applicant must apply for a type certificate, in the transport category, for the aircraft.

(d) The applicant must hold a U.S. type certificate for at least one other aircraft in the same transport category as the subject aircraft.

(e) The FAA's official flight test program or the flight test program conducted by the authorities of the country in which the aircraft was manufactured, with respect to the issue of a type certificate for that aircraft, must be in progress.

(f) The applicant or, in the case of a foreign manufactured aircraft, the country in which the aircraft was manufactured, must certify that—

(1) The aircraft has been designed and constructed in accordance with the airworthiness requirements applicable to the issue of the type certificate applied for;

(2) The aircraft substantially complies with the applicable flight characteristic requirements for the type certificate applied for; and

(3) The aircraft can be operated safely under the appropriate operating limitations in this subchapter.

(g) The applicant must submit a report showing that the aircraft has been flown in all maneuvers necessary to show compliance with the flight requirements for the issue of the type certificate and to establish that the aircraft can be operated safely in accordance with the limitations in this subchapter.

(h) The applicant must prepare a provisional aircraft flight manual containing all limitations required for the issue of the type certificate applied for, including limitations on weights, speeds, flight maneuvers, loading, and operation of controls and equipment unless, for each limitation not so established, appropriate operating restrictions are established for the aircraft.

(i) The applicant must establish an inspection and maintenance program for the continued airworthiness of the aircraft.

(j) The applicant must show that a prototype aircraft has been flown for at least 100 hours. In the case of an amendment to a provisional type certificate, the Administrator may reduce the number of required flight hours.

[Amdt. 21–12, 31 FR 13386, Oct. 15, 1966, as amended by Amdt. 21–66, 54 FR 34329, Aug. 18, 1989]

§ 21.85 Provisional amendments to type certificates.

(a) An applicant who manufactures aircraft within the United States is entitled to a provisional amendment to a type certificate if he shows compliance with this section and the Administrator finds that there is no feature, characteristic, or condition that would make the aircraft unsafe when operated under the appropriate limitations contained in this subchapter.

(b) An applicant who manufactures aircraft in a foreign country with which the United States has an agreement for the acceptance of those aircraft for export and import is entitled to a provisional amendment to a type certificate if the country in which the aircraft was manufactured certifies that the applicant has shown compliance with this section, that the aircraft meets the requirements of paragraph (e) of this section and that there is no feature, characteristic, or condition that would make the aircraft unsafe when operated under the appropriate limitations contained in this subchapter.

(c) The applicant must apply for an amendment to the type certificate.

(d) The FAA's official flight test program or the flight test program conducted by the authorities of the country in which the aircraft was manufactured, with respect to the amendment of the type certificate, must be in progress.

(e) The applicant or, in the case of foreign manufactured aircraft, the country in which the aircraft was manufactured, must certify that—

(1) The modification involved in the amendment to the type certificate has been designed and constructed in accordance with the airworthiness requirements applicable to the issue of the type certificate for the aircraft;

(2) The aircraft substantially complies with the applicable flight characteristic requirements for the type certificate; and

(3) The aircraft can be operated safely under the appropriate operating limitations in this subchapter.

(f) The applicant must submit a report showing that the aircraft incorporating the modifications involved has been flown in all maneuvers necessary to show compliance with the flight requirements applicable to those modifications and to establish that the aircraft can be operated safely in accordance with the limitations specified in §§ 91.317 and 121.207 of this chapter.

(g) The applicant must establish and publish, in a provisional aircraft flight manual or other document and on appropriate placards, all limitations required for the issue of the type certificate applied for, including weight, speed, flight maneuvers, loading, and operation of controls and equipment, unless, for each limitation not so established, appropriate operating restrictions are established for the aircraft.

(h) The applicant must establish an inspection and maintenance program for the continued airworthiness of the aircraft.

(i) The applicant must operate a prototype aircraft modified in accordance with the corresponding amendment to the type certificate for the number of hours found necessary by the Administrator.

[Amdt. 21–12, 31 FR 13388, Oct. 15, 1966, as amended by Amdt. 21–66, 54 FR 34329, Aug. 18, 1989]

Subpart D—Changes to Type Certificates

SOURCE: Docket No. 5085, 29 FR 14567, Oct. 24, 1964, unless otherwise noted.

§ 21.91 Applicability.

This subpart prescribes procedural requirements for the approval of changes to type certificates.

§ 21.93 Classification of changes in type design.

(a) In addition to changes in type design specified in paragraph (b) of this section, changes in type design are classified as minor and major. A "minor change" is one that has no appreciable effect on the weight, balance, structural strength, reliability, operational characteristics, or other characteristics affecting the airworthiness of the product. All other changes are "major changes" (except as provided in paragraph (b) of this section).

(b) For the purpose of complying with Part 36 of this chapter, and except as provided in paragraphs (b)(2), (b)(3), and (b)(4) of this section, any voluntary change in the type design of an aircraft that may increase the noise levels of that aircraft is an "acoustical change" (in addition to being a minor or major change as classified in paragraph (a) of this section) for the following aircraft:

(1) Transport category large airplanes.

(2) Jet (Turbojet powered) airplanes (regardless of category). For airplanes to which this paragraph applies, "acoustical changes" do not include changes in type design that are limited to one of the following—

(i) Gear down flight with one or more retractable landing gear down during the entire flight, or

(ii) Spare engine and nacelle carriage external to the skin of the airplane (and return of the pylon or other external mount), or

(iii) Time-limited engine and/or nacelle changes, where the change in type design specifies that the airplane may not be operated for a period of more than 90 days unless compliance with the applicable acoustical change provisions of Part 36 of this chapter is shown for that change in type design.

(3) Propeller driven commuter category and small airplanes in the primary, normal, utility, acrobatic, transport, and restricted categories, except for airplanes that are:

(i) Designated for "agricultural aircraft operations" (as defined in §137.3 of this chapter, effective January 1, 1966) to which §36.1583 of this chapter does not apply, or

(ii) Designated for dispensing fire fighting materials to which §36.1583 of this chapter does not apply, or

(iii) U.S. registered, and that had flight time prior to January 1, 1955 or

(iv) Land configured aircraft reconfigured with floats or skis. This reconfiguration does not permit further exception from the requirements of this section upon any acoustical change not enumerated in §21.93(b).

(4) Helicopters except:

(i) Those helicopters that are designated exclusively:

(A) For "agricultural aircraft operations", as defined in §137.3 of this chapter, as effective on January 1, 1966;

(B) For dispensing fire fighting materials; or

(C) For carrying external loads, as defined in §133.1(b) of this chapter, as effective on December 20, 1976.

(ii) Those helicopters modified by installation or removal of external equipment. For purposes of this paragraph, "external equipment" means any in-

strument, mechanism, part, apparatus, appurtenance, or accessory that is attached to, or extends from, the helicopter exterior but is not used nor is intended to be used in operating or controlling a helicopter in flight and is not part of an airframe or engine. An "acoustical change" does not include:

(A) Addition or removal of external equipment;

(B) Changes in the airframe made to accommodate the addition or removal of external equipment, to provide for an external load attaching means, to facilitate the use of external equipment or external loads, or to facilitate the safe operation of the helicopter with external equipment mounted to, or external loads carried by, the helicopter;

(C) Reconfiguration of the helicopter by the addition or removal of floats and skis;

(D) Flight with one or more doors and/or windows removed or in an open position; or

(E) Any changes in the operational limitations placed on the helicopter as a consequence of the addition or removal of external equipment, floats, and skis, or flight operations with doors and/or windows removed or in an open position.

(c) For purposes of complying with part 34 of this chapter, any voluntary change in the type design of the airplane or engine which may increase fuel venting or exhaust emissions is an "emissions change."

[Amdt. 21–27, 34 FR 18363, Nov. 18, 1969, as amended by Amdt. 21–42, 40 FR 1033, Jan. 6, 1975; Amdt. 21–47, 43 FR 28419, June 29, 1978; Amdt. 21–56, 47 FR 758, Jan. 7, 1982; Amdt. 21–61, 53 FR 3539, Feb. 5, 1988; Amdt. 21–62, 53 FR 16365, May 6, 1988; Amdt. 21–63, 53 FR 47399, Nov. 22, 1988; Amdt. 21–68, 55 FR 32860, Aug. 10, 1990; Amdt. 21–70, 57 FR 41368, Sept. 9, 1992; Amdt. 21–73, 61 FR 20699, May 7, 1996; 61 FR 57002, Nov. 5, 1996; Amdt. 21–81, 67 FR 45211, July 8, 2002]

§21.95 Approval of minor changes in type design.

Minor changes in a type design may be approved under a method acceptable to the Administrator before submitting to the Administrator any substantiating or descriptive data.

§ 21.97 Approval of major changes in type design.

(a) In the case of a major change in type design, the applicant must submit substantiating data and necessary descriptive data for inclusion in the type design.

(b) Approval of a major change in the type design of an aircraft engine is limited to the specific engine configuration upon which the change is made unless the applicant identifies in the necessary descriptive data for inclusion in the type design the other configurations of the same engine type for which approval is requested and shows that the change is compatible with the other configurations.

[Amdt. 21–40, 39 FR 35459, Oct. 1, 1974]

§ 21.99 Required design changes.

(a) When an Airworthiness Directive is issued under Part 39 the holder of the type certificate for the product concerned must—

(1) If the Administrator finds that design changes are necessary to correct the unsafe condition of the product, and upon his request, submit appropriate design changes for approval; and

(2) Upon approval of the design changes, make available the descriptive data covering the changes to all operators of products previously certificated under the type certificate.

(b) In a case where there are no current unsafe conditions, but the Administrator or the holder of the type certificate finds through service experience that changes in type design will contribute to the safety of the product, the holder of the type certificate may submit appropriate design changes for approval. Upon approval of the changes, the manufacturer shall make information on the design changes available to all operators of the same type of product.

[Doc. No. 5085, 29 FR 14567, Oct. 24, 1964, as amended by Amdt. 21–3, 30 FR 8826, July 24, 1965]

§ 21.101 Designation of applicable regulations.

(a) An applicant for a change to a type certificate must show that the changed product complies with the airworthiness requirements applicable to the category of the product in effect on the date of the application for the change and with parts 34 and 36 of this chapter. Exceptions are detailed in paragraphs (b) and (c) of this section.

(b) If paragraphs (b)(1), (2), or (3) of this section apply, an applicant may show that the changed product complies with an earlier amendment of a regulation required by paragraph (a) of this section, and of any other regulation the Administrator finds is directly related. However, the earlier amended regulation may not precede either the corresponding regulation incorporated by reference in the type certificate, or any regulation in §§ 23.2, 25.2, 27.2, or 29.2 of this chapter that is related to the change. The applicant may show compliance with an earlier amendment of a regulation for any of the following:

(1) A change that the Administrator finds not to be significant. In determining whether a specific change is significant, the Administrator considers the change in context with all previous relevant design changes and all related revisions to the applicable regulations incorporated in the type certificate for the product. Changes that meet one of the following criteria are automatically considered significant:

(i) The general configuration or the principles of construction are not retained.

(ii) The assumptions used for certification of the product to be changed do not remain valid.

(2) Each area, system, component, equipment, or appliance that the Administrator finds is not affected by the change.

(3) Each area, system, component, equipment, or appliance that is affected by the change, for which the Administrator finds that compliance with a regulation described in paragraph (a) of this section would not contribute materially to the level of safety of the changed product or would be impractical.

(c) An applicant for a change to an aircraft (other than a rotorcraft) of 6,000 pounds or less maximum weight, or to a non-turbine rotorcraft of 3,000 pounds or less maximum weight may show that the changed product complies with the regulations incorporated by reference in the type certificate. However, if the Administrator finds that the change is significant in an area, the Administrator may designate compliance with an amendment to the regulation incorporated by reference in the type certificate that applies to the change and any regulation that the Administrator finds is directly related, unless the Administrator also finds that compliance with that amendment or regulation would not contribute materially to the level of safety of the changed product or would be impractical.

(d) If the Administrator finds that the regulations in effect on the date of the application for the change do not provide adequate standards with respect to the proposed change because of a novel or unusual design feature, the applicant must also comply with special conditions, and amendments to those special conditions, prescribed under the provisions of §21.16, to provide a level of safety equal to that established by the regulations in effect on the date of the application for the change.

(e) An application for a change to a type certificate for a transport category aircraft is effective for 5 years, and an application for a change to any other type certificate is effective for 3 years. If the change has not been approved, or if it is clear that it will not be approved under the time limit established under this paragraph, the applicant may do either of the following:

(1) File a new application for a change to the type certificate and comply with all the provisions of paragraph (a) of this section applicable to an original application for a change.

(2) File for an extension of the original application and comply with the provisions of paragraph (a) of this section. The applicant must then select a new application date. The new application date may not precede the date the change is approved by more than the time period established under this paragraph (e).

(f) For aircraft certificated under §§21.17(b), 21.24, 21.25, and 21.27 the airworthiness requirements applicable to the category of the product in effect on the date of the application for the change include each airworthiness re-

quirement that the Administrator finds to be appropriate for the type certification of the aircraft in accordance with those sections.

[Doc. No. 28903, 65 FR 36266, June 7, 2000]

Subpart E—Supplemental Type Certificates

SOURCE: Docket No. 5085, 29 FR 14568, Oct. 24, 1964, unless otherwise noted.

§21.111 Applicability.

This subpart prescribes procedural requirements for the issue of supplemental type certificates.

§21.113 Requirement of supplemental type certificate.

Any person who alters a product by introducing a major change in type design, not great enough to require a new application for a type certificate under §21.19, shall apply to the Administrator for a supplemental type certificate, except that the holder of a type certificate for the product may apply for amendment of the original type certificate. The application must be made in a form and manner prescribed by the Administrator.

§21.115 Applicable requirements.

(a) Each applicant for a supplemental type certificate must show that the altered product meets applicable requirements specified in §21.101 and, in the case of an acoustical change described in §21.93(b), show compliance with the applicable noise requirements of part 36 of this chapter and, in the case of an emissions change described in §21.93(c), show compliance with the applicable fuel venting and exhaust emissions requirements of part 34 of this chapter.

(b) Each applicant for a supplemental type certificate must meet §§21.33 and 21.53 with respect to each change in the type design.

[Amdt. 21–17, 32 FR 14927, Oct. 28, 1967, as amended by Amdt. 21–42, 40 FR 1033, Jan. 6, 1975; Amdt. 21–52A, 45 FR 79009, Nov. 28, 1980; Amdt. 21–61, 53 FR 3540, Feb. 5, 1988; Amdt. 21–68, 55 FR 32860, Aug. 10, 1990; Amdt. 21–71, 57 FR 42854, Sept. 16, 1992; Amdt. 21–77, 65 FR 36266, June 7, 2000]

§ 21.117 Issue of supplemental type certificates.

(a) An applicant is entitled to a supplemental type certificate if he meets the requirements of §§ 21.113 and 21.115.

(b) A supplemental type certificate consists of—

(1) The approval by the Administrator of a change in the type design of the product; and

(2) The type certificate previously issued for the product.

§ 21.119 Privileges.

The holder of a supplemental type certificate may—

(a) In the case of aircraft, obtain airworthiness certificates;

(b) In the case of other products, obtain approval for installation on certificated aircraft; and

(c) Obtain a production certificate for the change in the type design that was approved by that supplemental type certificate.

Subpart F—Production Under Type Certificate Only

SOURCE: Docket No. 5085, 29 FR 14568, Oct. 24, 1964, unless otherwise noted.

§ 21.121 Applicability.

This subpart prescribes rules for production under a type certificate only.

§ 21.123 Production under type certificate.

Each manufacturer of a product being manufactured under a type certificate only shall—

(a) Make each product available for inspection by the Administrator;

(b) Maintain at the place of manufacture the technical data and drawings necessary for the Administrator to determine whether the product and its parts conform to the type design;

(c) Except as otherwise authorized by the Aircraft Certification Directorate Manager for the geographic area which the manufacturer is located, for products manufactured more than 6 months after the date of issue of the type certificate, establish and maintain an approved production inspection system that insures that each product con-

forms to the type design and is in condition for safe operation; and

(d) Upon the establishment of the approved production inspection system (as required by paragraph (c) of this section) submit to the Administrator a manual that describes that system and the means for making the determinations required by § 21.125(b).

[Doc. No. 5085, 29 FR 14568, Oct. 24, 1964, as amended by Amdt. 21–34, 35 FR 13008, Aug. 15, 1970; Amdt. 21–51, 45 FR 60170, Sept. 11, 1980; Amdt. 21–67, 54 FR 39291, Sept. 25, 1989]

§ 21.125 Production inspection system: Materials Review Board.

(a) Each manufacturer required to establish a production inspection system by § 21.123(c) shall—

(1) Establish a Materials Review Board (to include representatives from the inspection and engineering departments) and materials review procedures; and

(2) Maintain complete records of Materials Review Board action for at least two years.

(b) The production inspection system required in § 21.123(c) must provide a means for determining at least the following:

(1) Incoming materials, and bought or subcontracted parts, used in the finished product must be as specified in the type design data, or must be suitable equivalents.

(2) Incoming materials, and bought or subcontracted parts, must be properly identified if their physical or chemical properties cannot be readily and accurately determined.

(3) Materials subject to damage and deterioration must be suitably stored and adequately protected.

(4) Processes affecting the quality and safety of the finished product must be accomplished in accordance with acceptable industry or United States specifications.

(5) Parts and components in process must be inspected for conformity with the type design data at points in production where accurate determinations can be made.

(6) Current design drawings must be readily available to manufacturing and inspection personnel, and used when necessary.

(7) Design changes, including material substitutions, must be controlled and approved before being incorporated in the finished product.

(8) Rejected materials and parts must be segregated and identified in a manner that precludes installation in the finished product.

(9) Materials and parts that are withheld because of departures from design data or specifications, and that are to be considered for installation in the finished product, must be processed through the Materials Review Board. Those materials and parts determined by the Board to be serviceable must be properly identified and reinspected if rework or repair is necessary. Materials and parts rejected by the Board must be marked and disposed of to ensure that they are not incorporated in the final product.

(10) Inspection records must be maintained, identified with the completed product where practicable, and retained by the manufacturer for at least two years.

§21.127 Tests: aircraft.

(a) Each person manufacturing aircraft under a type certificate only shall establish an approved production flight test procedure and flight check-off form, and in accordance with that form, flight test each aircraft produced.

(b) Each production flight test procedure must include the following:

(1) An operational check of the trim, controllability, or other flight characteristics to establish that the production aircraft has the same range and degree of control as the prototype aircraft.

(2) An operational check of each part or system operated by the crew while in flight to establish that, during flight, instrument readings are within normal range.

(3) A determination that all instruments are properly marked, and that all placards and required flight manuals are installed after flight test.

(4) A check of the operational characteristics of the aircraft on the ground.

(5) A check on any other items peculiar to the aircraft being tested that can best be done during the ground or flight operation of the aircraft.

§21.128 Tests: aircraft engines.

(a) Each person manufacturing aircraft engines under a type certificate only shall subject each engine (except rocket engines for which the manufacturer must establish a sampling technique) to an acceptable test run that includes the following:

(1) Break-in runs that include a determination of fuel and oil consumption and a determination of power characteristics at rated maximum continuous power or thrust and, if applicable, at rated takeoff power or thrust.

(2) At least five hours of operation at rated maximum continuous power or thrust. For engines having a rated takeoff power or thrust higher than rated maximum continuous power or thrust, the five-hour run must include 30 minutes at rated takeoff power or thrust.

(b) The test runs required by paragraph (a) of this section may be made with the engine appropriately mounted and using current types of power and thrust measuring equipment.

[Doc. No. 5085, 29 FR 14568, Oct. 24, 1964, as amended by Amdt. 21–5, 32 FR 3735, Mar. 4, 1967]

§21.129 Tests: propellers.

Each person manufacturing propellers under a type certificate only shall give each variable pitch propeller an acceptable functional test to determine if it operates properly throughout the normal range of operation.

§21.130 Statement of conformity.

Each holder or licensee of a type certificate only, for a product manufactured in the United States, shall, upon the initial transfer by him of the ownership of such product manufactured under that type certificate, or upon application for the original issue of an aircraft airworthiness certificate or an aircraft engine or propeller airworthiness approval tag (FAA Form 8130–3), give the Administrator a statement of conformity (FAA Form 317). This statement must be signed by an authorized person who holds a responsible position in the manufacturing organization, and must include—

(a) For each product, a statement that the product conforms to its type certificate and is in condition for safe operation;

(b) For each aircraft, a statement that the aircraft has been flight checked; and

(c) For each aircraft engine or variable pitch propeller, a statement that the engine or propeller has been subjected by the manufacturer to a final operational check.

However, in the case of a product manufactured for an Armed Force of the United States, a statement of conformity is not required if the product has been accepted by that Armed Force.

[Amdt. 21–25, 34 FR 14068, Sept. 5, 1969]

Subpart G—Production Certificates

SOURCE: Docket No. 5085, 29 FR 14569, Oct. 24, 1964, unless otherwise noted.

§ 21.131 Applicability.

This subpart prescribes procedural requirements for the issue of production certificates and rules governing the holders of those certificates.

§ 21.133 Eligibility.

(a) Any person may apply for a production certificate if he holds, for the product concerned, a—

(1) Current type certificate;

(2) Right to the benefits of that type certificate under a licensing agreement; or

(3) Supplemental type certificate.

(b) Each application for a production certificate must be made in a form and manner prescribed by the Administrator.

§ 21.135 Requirements for issuance.

An applicant is entitled to a production certificate if the Administrator finds, after examination of the supporting data and after inspection of the organization and production facilities, that the applicant has complied with §§ 21.139 and 21.143.

§ 21.137 Location of manufacturing facilities.

The Administrator does not issue a production certificate if the manufacturing facilities concerned are located outside the United States, unless the Administrator finds no undue burden on the United States in administering the applicable requirements of the Federal Aviation Act of 1958 or of the Federal Aviation Regulations.

§ 21.139 Quality control.

The applicant must show that he has established and can maintain a quality control system for any product, for which he requests a production certificate, so that each article will meet the design provisions of the pertinent type certificate.

§ 21.143 Quality control data requirements; prime manufacturer.

(a) Each applicant must submit, for approval, data describing the inspection and test procedures necessary to ensure that each article produced conforms to the type design and is in a condition for safe operation, including as applicable—

(1) A statement describing assigned responsibilities and delegated authority of the quality control organization, together with a chart indicating the functional relationship of the quality control organization to management and to other organizational components, and indicating the chain of authority and responsibility within the quality control organization;

(2) A description of inspection procedures for raw materials, purchased items, and parts and assemblies produced by manufacturers' suppliers including methods used to ensure acceptable quality of parts and assemblies that cannot be completely inspected for conformity and quality when delivered to the prime manufacturer's plant;

(3) A description of the methods used for production inspection of individual parts and complete assemblies, including the identification of any special manufacturing processes involved, the means used to control the processes, the final test procedure for the complete product, and, in the case of aircraft, a copy of the manufacturer's production flight test procedures and checkoff list;

(4) An outline of the materials review system, including the procedure for recording review board decisions and disposing of rejected parts;

(5) An outline of a system for informing company inspectors of current changes in engineering drawings, specifications, and quality control procedures; and

(6) A list or chart showing the location and type of inspection stations.

(b) Each prime manufacturer shall make available to the Administrator information regarding all delegation of authority to suppliers to make major inspections of parts or assemblies for which the prime manufacturer is responsible.

[Doc. No. 5085, 29 FR 14569, Oct. 24, 1964, as amended by Amdt. 21–51, 45 FR 60170, Sept. 11, 1980]

§21.147 Changes in quality control system.

After the issue of a production certificate, each change to the quality control system is subject to review by the Administrator. The holder of a production certificate shall immediately notify the Administrator, in writing of any change that may affect the inspection, conformity, or airworthiness of the product.

§21.149 Multiple products.

The Administrator may authorize more than one type certificated product to be manufactured under the terms of one production certificate, if the products have similar production characteristics.

§21.151 Production limitation record.

A production limitation record is issued as part of a production certificate. The record lists the type certificate of every product that the applicant is authorized to manufacture under the terms of the production certificate.

§21.153 Amendment of the production certificates.

The holder of a production certificate desiring to amend it to add a type certificate or model, or both, must apply therefor in a form and manner prescribed by the Administrator. The applicant must comply with the applicable requirements of §§21.139, 21.143, and 21.147.

§21.155 Transferability.

A production certificate is not transferable.

§21.157 Inspections and tests.

Each holder of a production certificate shall allow the Administrator to make any inspections and tests necessary to determine compliance with the applicable regulations in this subchapter.

§21.159 Duration.

A production certificate is effective until surrendered, suspended, revoked, or a termination date is otherwise established by the Administrator, or the location of the manufacturing facility is changed.

§21.161 Display.

The holder of a production certificate shall display it prominently in the main office of the factory in which the product concerned is manufactured.

§21.163 Privileges.

(a) The holder of a production certificate may—

(1) Obtain an aircraft airworthiness certificate without further showing, except that the Administrator may inspect the aircraft for conformity with the type design; or

(2) In the case of other products, obtain approval for installation on type certificated aircraft.

(b) Notwithstanding the provisions of §147.3 of this chapter, the holder of a production certificate for a primary category aircraft, or for a normal, utility, or acrobatic category aircraft of a type design that is eligible for a special airworthiness certificate in the primary category under §21.184(c), may—

(1) Conduct training for persons in the performance of a special inspection and preventive maintenance program approved as a part of the aircraft's type design under §21.24(b), provided the training is given by a person holding a mechanic certificate with appropriate airframe and powerplant ratings issued under part 65 of this chapter; and

(2) Issue a certificate of competency to persons successfully completing the approved training program, provided the certificate specifies the aircraft make and model to which the certificate applies.

[Doc. No. 23345, 57 FR 41368, Sept. 9, 1992]

§ 21.165 Responsibility of holder.

The holder of a production certificate shall—

(a) Maintain the quality control system in conformity with the data and procedures approved for the production certificate; and

(b) Determine that each part and each completed product, including primary category aircraft assembled under a production certificate by another person from a kit provided by the holder of the production certificate, submitted for airworthiness certification or approval conforms to the approved design and is in a condition for safe operation.

[Doc. No. 5085, 29 FR 14569, Oct. 24, 1964, as amended by Amdt. 21–64, 53 FR 48521, Dec. 1, 1988; Amdt. 21–70, 57 FR 41368, Sept. 9, 1992]

Subpart H—Airworthiness Certificates

SOURCE: Docket No. 5085, 29 FR 14569, Oct. 24, 1964, unless otherwise noted.

§ 21.171 Applicability.

This subpart prescribes procedural requirements for the issue of airworthiness certificates.

§ 21.173 Eligibility.

Any registered owner of a U.S.-registered aircraft (or the agent of the owner) may apply for an airworthiness certificate for that aircraft. An application for an airworthiness certificate must be made in a form and manner acceptable to the Administrator, and may be submitted to any FAA office.

[Amdt. 21–26, 34 FR 15244, Sept. 30, 1969]

§ 21.175 Airworthiness certificates: classification.

(a) Standard airworthiness certificates are airworthiness certificates issued for aircraft type certificated in the normal, utility, acrobatic, com-muter, or transport category, and for manned free balloons, and for aircraft designated by the Administrator as special classes of aircraft.

(b) Special airworthiness certificates are primary, restricted, limited, and provisional airworthiness certificates, special flight permits, and experimental certificates.

[Amdt. 21–21, 33 FR 6858, May 7, 1968, as amended by Amdt. 21–60, 52 FR 8043, Mar. 13, 1987; Amdt. 21–70, 57 FR 41368, Sept. 9, 1992]

§ 21.177 Amendment or modification.

An airworthiness certificate may be amended or modified only upon application to the Administrator.

§ 21.179 Transferability.

An airworthiness certificate is transferred with the aircraft.

§ 21.181 Duration.

(a) Unless sooner surrendered, suspended, revoked, or a termination date is otherwise established by the Administrator, airworthiness certificates are effective as follows:

(1) Standard airworthiness certificates, special airworthiness certificates—primary category, and airworthiness certificates issued for restricted or limited category aircraft are effective as long as the maintenance, preventive maintenance, and alterations are performed in accordance with Parts 43 and 91 of this chapter and the aircraft are registered in the United States.

(2) A special flight permit is effective for the period of time specified in the permit.

(3) An experimental certificate for research and development, showing compliance with regulations, crew training, or market surveys is effective for one year after the date of issue or renewal unless a shorter period is prescribed by the Administrator. The duration of amateur-built, exhibition, and air-racing experimental certificates will be unlimited unless the Administrator finds for good cause that a specific period should be established.

(b) The owner, operator, or bailee of the aircraft shall, upon request, make it available for inspection by the Administrator.

(c) Upon suspension, revocation, or termination by order of the Administrator of an airworthiness certificate, the owner, operator, or bailee of an aircraft shall, upon request, surrender the certificate to the Administrator.

[Amdt. 21–21, 33 FR 6858, May 7, 1968, as amended by Amdt. 21–49, 44 FR 46781, Aug. 9, 1979; Amdt. 21–70, 57 FR 41368, Sept. 9, 1992]

§21.182 Aircraft identification.

(a) Except as provided in paragraph (b) of this section, each applicant for an airworthiness certificate under this subpart must show that his aircraft is identified as prescribed in §45.11.

(b) Paragraph (a) of this section does not apply to applicants for the following:

(1) A special flight permit.

(2) An experimental certificate for an aircraft that is not amateur-built or kit-built.

(3) A change from one airworthiness classification to another, for an aircraft already identified as prescribed in §45.11.

[Amdt. 21–13, 32 FR 188, Jan. 10, 1967, as amended by Amdt. 21–51, 45 FR 60170, Sept. 11, 1980; Amdt. 21–70, 57 FR 41368, Sept. 9, 1992]

§21.183 Issue of standard airworthiness certificates for normal, utility, acrobatic, commuter, and transport category aircraft; manned free balloons; and special classes of aircraft.

(a) *New aircraft manufactured under a production certificate.* An applicant for a standard airworthiness certificate for a new aircraft manufactured under a production certificate is entitled to a standard airworthiness certificate without further showing, except that the Administrator may inspect the aircraft to determine conformity to the type design and condition for safe operation.

(b) *New aircraft manufactured under type certificate only.* An applicant for a standard airworthiness certificate for a new aircraft manufactured under a type certificate only is entitled to a standard airworthiness certificate upon presentation, by the holder or licensee of the type certificate, of the statement of conformity prescribed in §21.130 if the Administrator finds after inspection that the aircraft conforms to the type design and is in condition for safe operation.

(c) *Import aircraft.* An applicant for a standard airworthiness certificate for an import aircraft type certificated in accordance with §21.29 is entitled to an airworthiness certificate if the country in which the aircraft was manufactured certifies, and the Administrator finds, that the aircraft conforms to the type design and is in condition for safe operation.

(d) *Other aircraft.* An applicant for a standard airworthiness certificate for aircraft not covered by paragraphs (a) through (c) of this section is entitled to a standard airworthiness certificate if—

(1) He presents evidence to the Administrator that the aircraft conforms to a type design approved under a type certificate or a supplemental type certificate and to applicable Airworthiness Directives;

(2) The aircraft (except an experimentally certificated aircraft that previously had been issued a different airworthiness certificate under this section) has been inspected in accordance with the performance rules for 100-hour inspections set forth in §43.15 of this chapter and found airworthy by—

(i) The manufacturer;

(ii) The holder of a repair station certificate as provided in Part 145 of this chapter;

(iii) The holder of a mechanic certificate as authorized in Part 65 of this chapter; or

(iv) The holder of a certificate issued under Part 121 of this chapter, and having a maintenance and inspection organization appropriate to the aircraft type; and

(3) The Administrator finds after inspection, that the aircraft conforms to the type design, and is in condition for safe operation.

(e) *Noise requirements.* Notwithstanding all other provisions of this section, the following must be complied with for the original issuance of a standard airworthiness certificate:

(1) For transport category large airplanes and jet (turbojet powered) airplanes that have not had any flight time before the dates specified in

§ 36.1(d), no standard airworthiness certificate is originally issued under this section unless the Administrator finds that the type design complies with the noise requirements in § 36.1(d) in addition to the applicable airworthiness requirements in this section. For import airplanes, compliance with this paragraph is shown if the country in which the airplane was manufactured certifies, and the Administrator finds, that § 36.1(d) (or the applicable airplane noise requirements of the country in which the airplane was manufactured and any other requirements the Administrator may prescribe to provide noise levels no greater than those provided by compliance with § 36.1(d)) and paragraph (c) of this section are complied with.

(2) For normal, utility, acrobatic, commuter, or transport category propeller driven small airplanes (except for those airplanes that are designed for "agricultural aircraft operations" (as defined in § 137.3 of this chapter, as effective on January 1, 1966) or for dispensing fire fighting materials to which § 36.1583 of this chapter does not apply) that have not had any flight time before the applicable date specified in Part 36 of this chapter, no standard airworthiness certificate is originally issued under this section unless the applicant shows that the type design complies with the applicable noise requirements of Part 36 of this chapter in addition to the applicable airworthiness requirements in this section. For import airplanes, compliance with this paragraph is shown if the country in which the airplane was manufactured certifies, and the Administrator finds, that the applicable requirements of Part 36 of this chapter (or the applicable airplane noise requirements of the country in which the airplane was manufactured and any other requirements the Administrator may prescribe to provide noise levels no greater than those provided by compliance with the applicable requirements of Part 36 of this chapter) and paragraph (c) of this section are complied with.

(f) *Passenger emergency exit requirements.* Notwithstanding all other provisions of this section, each applicant for issuance of a standard airworthiness certificate for a transport category airplane manufactured after October 16, 1987, must show that the airplane meets the requirements of § 25.807(c)(7) in effect on July 24, 1989. For the purposes of this paragraph, the date of manufacture of an airplane is the date the inspection acceptance records reflect that the airplane is complete and meets the FAA-approved type design data.

(g) *Fuel venting and exhaust emission requirements.* Notwithstanding all other provisions of this section, and irrespective of the date of application, no airworthiness certificate is issued, on and after the dates specified in part 34 for the airplanes specified therein, unless the airplane complies with the applicable requirements of that part.

[Amdt. 21–17, 32 FR 14927, Oct. 28, 1967, as amended by Amdt. 21–20, 33 FR 3055, Feb. 16, 1968; Amdt. 21–25, 34 FR 14068, Sept. 5, 1969; Amdt. 21–42, 40 FR 1033, Jan. 6, 1975; Amdt. 21–47, 43 FR 28419, June 29, 1978; Amdt. 21–52, 45 FR 67066, Oct. 9, 1980; Amdt. 21–59, 52 FR 1836, Jan. 15, 1987; Amdt. 21–60, 52 FR 8043, Mar. 13, 1987; Amdt. 21–65, 54 FR 26695, June 23, 1989; Amdt. 21–68, 55 FR 32860, Aug. 10, 1990; Amdt. 21–79, 66 FR 21065, Apr. 27, 2001; Amdt. 21–81, 67 FR 45211, July 8, 2002]

§ 21.184 **Issue of special airworthiness certificates for primary category aircraft.**

(a) *New primary category aircraft manufactured under a production certificate.* An applicant for an original, special airworthiness certificate-primary category for a new aircraft that meets the criteria of § 21.24(a)(1), manufactured under a production certificate, including aircraft assembled by another person from a kit provided by the holder of the production certificate and under the supervision and quality control of that holder, is entitled to a special airworthiness certificate without further showing, except that the Administrator may inspect the aircraft to determine conformity to the type design and condition for safe operation.

(b) *Imported aircraft.* An applicant for a special airworthiness certificate-primary category for an imported aircraft type certificated under § 21.29 is entitled to a special airworthiness certificate if the civil airworthiness authority of the country in which the aircraft was manufactured certifies, and the

Administrator finds after inspection, that the aircraft conforms to an approved type design that meets the criteria of §21.24(a)(1) and is in a condition for safe operation.

(c) *Aircraft having a current standard airworthiness certificate.* An applicant for a special airworthiness certificate-primary category, for an aircraft having a current standard airworthiness certificate that meets the criteria of §21.24(a)(1), may obtain the primary category certificate in exchange for its standard airworthiness certificate through the supplemental type certification process. For the purposes of this paragraph, a current standard airworthiness certificate means that the aircraft conforms to its approved normal, utility, or acrobatic type design, complies with all applicable airworthiness directives, has been inspected and found airworthy within the last 12 calendar months in accordance with §91.409(a)(1) of this chapter, and is found to be in a condition for safe operation by the Administrator.

(d) *Other aircraft.* An applicant for a special airworthiness certificate-primary category for an aircraft that meets the criteria of §21.24(a)(1), and is not covered by paragraph (a), (b), or (c) of this section, is entitled to a special airworthiness certificate if—

(1) The applicant presents evidence to the Administrator that the aircraft conforms to an approved primary, normal, utility, or acrobatic type design, including compliance with all applicable airworthiness directives;

(2) The aircraft has been inspected and found airworthy within the past 12 calendar months in accordance with §91.409(a)(1) of this chapter and;

(3) The aircraft is found by the Administrator to conform to an approved type design and to be in a condition for safe operation.

(e) *Multiple-category airworthiness certificates* in the primary category and any other category will not be issued; a primary category aircraft may hold only one airworthiness certificate.

[Doc. No. 23345, 57 FR 41368, Sept. 9, 1992, as amended by Amdt. 21–70, 57 FR 43776, Sept. 22, 1992]

§21.185 Issue of airworthiness certificates for restricted category aircraft.

(a) *Aircraft manufactured under a production certificate or type certificate only.* An applicant for the original issue of a restricted category airworthiness certificate for an aircraft type certificated in the restricted category, that was not previously type certificated in any other category, must comply with the appropriate provisions of §21.183.

(b) *Other aircraft.* An applicant for a restricted category airworthiness certificate for an aircraft type certificated in the restricted category, that was either a surplus aircraft of the Armed Forces or previously type certificated in another category, is entitled to an airworthiness certificate if the aircraft has been inspected by the Administrator and found by him to be in a good state of preservation and repair and in a condition for safe operation.

(c) *Import aircraft.* An applicant for the original issue of a restricted category airworthiness certificate for an import aircraft type certificated in the restricted category only in accordance with §21.29 is entitled to an airworthiness certificate if the country in which the aircraft was manufactured certifies, and the Administrator finds, that the aircraft conforms to the type design and is in a condition for safe operation.

(d) *Noise requirements.* For propeller-driven small airplanes (except airplanes designed for "agricultural aircraft operations," as defined in §137.3 of this chapter, as effective on January 1, 1966, or for dispensing fire fighting materials) that have not had any flight time before the applicable date specified in Part 36 of this chapter, and notwithstanding the other provisions of this section, no original restricted category airworthiness certificate is issued under this section unless the Administrator finds that the type design complies with the applicable noise requirements of Part 36 of this chapter in addition to the applicable airworthiness requirements of this section. For import airplanes, compliance with this paragraph is shown if the country in which the airplane was manufactured certifies, and the Administrator finds, that the applicable requirements of

Part 36 of this chapter (or the applicable airplane noise requirements of the country in which the airplane was manufactured and any other requirements the Administrator may prescribe to provide noise levels no greater than those provided by compliance with the applicable requirements of Part 36 of this chapter) and paragraph (c) of this section are complied with.

[Amdt. 21–10, 31 FR 9211, July 6, 1966; as amended by Amdt. 21–32, 35 FR 10202, June 23, 1970; Amdt. 21–42, 40 FR 1034, Jan. 6, 1975]

§ 21.187 Issue of multiple airworthiness certification.

(a) An applicant for an airworthiness certificate in the restricted category, and in one or more other categories except primary category, is entitled to the certificate, if—

(1) He shows compliance with the requirements for each category, when the aircraft is in the configuration for that category; and

(2) He shows that the aircraft can be converted from one category to another by removing or adding equipment by simple mechanical means.

(b) The operator of an aircraft certificated under this section shall have the aircraft inspected by the Administrator, or by a certificated mechanic with an appropriate airframe rating, to determine airworthiness each time the aircraft is converted from the restricted category to another category for the carriage of passengers for compensation or hire, unless the Administrator finds this unnecessary for safety in a particular case.

(c) The aircraft complies with the applicable requirements of part 34.

[Doc. No. 5085, 29 FR 14569, Oct. 24, 1964, as amended by Amdt. 21–68, 55 FR 32860, Aug. 10, 1990; Amdt. 21–70, 57 FR 41369, Sept. 9, 1992]

§ 21.189 Issue of airworthiness certificate for limited category aircraft.

(a) An applicant for an airworthiness certificate for an aircraft in the limited category is entitled to the certificate when—

(1) He shows that the aircraft has been previously issued a limited category type certificate and that the aircraft conforms to that type certificate; and

(2) The Administrator finds, after inspection (including a flight check by the applicant), that the aircraft is in a good state of preservation and repair and is in a condition for safe operation.

(b) The Administrator prescribes limitations and conditions necessary for safe operation.

[Doc. No. 5085, 29 FR 14570, Oct. 24, 1964, as amended by Amdt. 21–4, 30 FR 9437, July 29, 1965]

§ 21.191 Experimental certificates.

Experimental certificates are issued for the following purposes:

(a) *Research and development.* Testing new aircraft design concepts, new aircraft equipment, new aircraft installations, new aircraft operating techniques, or new uses for aircraft.

(b) *Showing compliance with regulations.* Conducting flight tests and other operations to show compliance with the airworthiness regulations including flights to show compliance for issuance of type and supplemental type certificates, flights to substantiate major design changes, and flights to show compliance with the function and reliability requirements of the regulations.

(c) *Crew training.* Training of the applicant's flight crews.

(d) *Exhibition.* Exhibiting the aircraft's flight capabilities, performance, or unusual characteristics at air shows, motion picture, television, and similar productions, and the maintenance of exhibition flight proficiency, including (for persons exhibiting aircraft) flying to and from such air shows and productions.

(e) *Air racing.* Participating in air races, including (for such participants) practicing for such air races and flying to and from racing events.

(f) *Market surveys.* Use of aircraft for purposes of conducting market surveys, sales demonstrations, and customer crew training only as provided in § 21.195.

(g) *Operating amateur-built aircraft.* Operating an aircraft the major portion of which has been fabricated and assembled by persons who undertook the construction project solely for their own education or recreation.

(h) *Operating kit-built aircraft.* Operating a primary category aircraft that meets the criteria of §21.24(a)(1) that was assembled by a person from a kit manufactured by the holder of a production certificate for that kit, without the supervision and quality control of the production certificate holder under §21.184(a).

[Amdt. 21–21, 38 FR 6858, May 7, 1968, as amended by Amdt. 21–57, 49 FR 39651, Oct. 9, 1984; Amdt. 21–70, 57 FR 41369, Sept. 9, 1992]

§21.193 Experimental certificates: general.

An applicant for an experimental certificate must submit the following information:

(a) A statement, in a form and manner prescribed by the Administrator setting forth the purpose for which the aircraft is to be used.

(b) Enough data (such as photographs) to identify the aircraft.

(c) Upon inspection of the aircraft, any pertinent information found necessary by the Administrator to safeguard the general public.

(d) In the case of an aircraft to be used for experimental purposes—

(1) The purpose of the experiment;

(2) The estimated time or number of flights required for the experiment;

(3) The areas over which the experiment will be conducted; and

(4) Except for aircraft converted from a previously certificated type without appreciable change in the external configuration, three-view drawings or three-view dimensioned photographs of the aircraft.

§21.195 Experimental certificates: Aircraft to be used for market surveys, sales demonstrations, and customer crew training.

(a) A manufacturer of aircraft manufactured within the United States may apply for an experimental certificate for an aircraft that is to be used for market surveys, sales demonstrations, or customer crew training.

(b) A manufacturer of aircraft engines who has altered a type certificated aircraft by installing different engines, manufactured by him within the United States, may apply for an experimental certificate for that aircraft to be used for market surveys, sales demonstrations, or customer crew training, if the basic aircraft, before alteration, was type certificated in the normal, acrobatic, commuter, or transport category.

(c) A person who has altered the design of a type certificated aircraft may apply for an experimental certificate for the altered aircraft to be used for market surveys, sales demonstrations, or customer crew training if the basic aircraft, before alteration, was type certificated in the normal, utility, acrobatic, or transport category.

(d) An applicant for an experimental certificate under this section is entitled to that certificate if, in addition to meeting the requirements of §21.193—

(1) He has established an inspection and maintenance program for the continued airworthiness of the aircraft; and

(2) He shows that the aircraft has been flown for at least 50 hours, or for at least 5 hours if it is a type certificated aircraft which has been modified.

[Amdt. 21–21, 33 FR 6858, May 7, 1968, as amended by Amdt. 21–28, 35 FR 2818, Feb. 11, 1970; Amdt. 21–57, 49 FR 39651, Oct. 9, 1984; Amdt. 21–59, 52 FR 1836, Jan. 15, 1987]

§21.197 Special flight permits.

(a) A special flight permit may be issued for an aircraft that may not currently meet applicable airworthiness requirements but is capable of safe flight, for the following purposes:

(1) Flying the aircraft to a base where repairs, alterations, or maintenance are to be performed, or to a point of storage.

(2) Delivering or exporting the aircraft.

(3) Production flight testing new production aircraft.

(4) Evacuating aircraft from areas of impending danger.

(5) Conducting customer demonstration flights in new production aircraft that have satisfactorily completed production flight tests.

(b) A special flight permit may also be issued to authorize the operation of an aircraft at a weight in excess of its maximum certificated takeoff weight for flight beyond the normal range over water, or over land areas where adequate landing facilities or appropriate fuel is not available. The excess weight that may be authorized under this paragraph is limited to the additional fuel, fuel-carrying facilities, and navigation equipment necessary for the flight.

(c) Upon application, as prescribed in §§ 121.79 and 135.17 of this chapter, a special flight permit with a continuing authorization may be issued for aircraft that may not meet applicable airworthiness requirements but are capable of safe flight for the purpose of flying aircraft to a base where maintenance or alterations are to be performed. The permit issued under this paragraph is an authorization, including conditions and limitations for flight, which is set forth in the certificate holder's operations specifications. The permit issued under this paragraph may be issued to—

(1) Certificate holders authorized to conduct operations under Part 121 of this chapter; or

(2) Certificate holders authorized to conduct operations under Part 135 for those aircraft they operate and maintain under a continuous airworthiness maintenance program prescribed by § 135.411 (a)(2) or (b) of that part.

The permit issued under this paragraph is an authorization, including any conditions and limitations for flight, which is set forth in the certificate holder's operations specifications.

[Doc. No. 5085, 29 FR 14570, Oct. 24, 1964, as amended by Amdt. 21–21, 33 FR 6859, May 7, 1968; Amdt. 21—51, 45 FR 60170, Sept. 11, 1980; Amdt. 21–54, 46 FR 37878, July 23, 1981; Amdt. 21–79, 66 FR 21066, Apr. 27, 2001]

§ 21.199 Issue of special flight permits.

(a) Except as provided in § 21.197(c), an applicant for a special flight permit must submit a statement in a form and manner prescribed by the Administrator, indicating—

(1) The purpose of the flight.

(2) The proposed itinerary.

(3) The crew required to operate the aircraft and its equipment, e.g., pilot, co-pilot, navigator, etc.

(4) The ways, if any, in which the aircraft does not comply with the applicable airworthiness requirements.

(5) Any restriction the applicant considers necessary for safe operation of the aircraft.

(6) Any other information considered necessary by the Administrator for the purpose of prescribing operating limitations.

(b) The Administrator may make, or require the applicant to make appropriate inspections or tests necessary for safety.

[Doc. No. 5085, 29 FR 14570, Oct. 24, 1964, as amended by Amdt. 21–21, 33 FR 6859, May 7, 1968; Amdt. 21–22, 33 FR 11901, Aug. 22, 1968]

Subpart I—Provisional Airworthiness Certificates

Source: Docket No. 5085, 29 FR 14571, Oct. 24, 1964, unless otherwise noted.

§ 21.211 Applicability.

This subpart prescribes procedural requirements for the issue of provisional airworthiness certificates.

§ 21.213 Eligibility.

(a) A manufacturer who is a United States citizen may apply for a Class I or Class II provisional airworthiness certificate for aircraft manufactured by him within the U.S.

(b) Any holder of an air carrier operating certificate under Part 121 of this chapter who is a United States citizen may apply for a Class II provisional airworthiness certificate for transport category aircraft that meet either of the following:

(1) The aircraft has a current Class II provisional type certificate or an amendment thereto.

(2) The aircraft has a current provisional amendment to a type certificate that was preceded by a corresponding Class II provisional type certificate.

(c) An aircraft engine manufacturer who is a United States citizen and who has altered a type certificated aircraft by installing different type certificated engines, manufactured by him within the United States, may apply for a Class I provisional airworthiness certificate for that aircraft, if the basic aircraft, before alteration, was type certificated in the normal, utility, acrobatic, commuter, or transport category.

[Doc. No. 5085, 29 FR 14571, Oct. 24, 1964, as amended by Amdt. 21–59, 52 FR 1836, Jan. 15, 1987; Amdt. 21–79, 66 FR 21066, Apr. 27, 2001]

§21.215 Application.

Applications for provisional airworthiness certificates must be submitted to the Manufacturing Inspection District Office in the geographic area in which the manufacturer or air carrier is located. The application must be accompanied by the pertinent information specified in this subpart.

[Amdt. 21–67, 54 FR 39291, Sept. 25, 1989; 54 FR 52872, Dec. 22, 1989]

§21.217 Duration.

Unless sooner surrendered, superseded, revoked, or otherwise terminated, provisional airworthiness certificates are effective for the duration of the corresponding provisional type certificate, amendment to a provisional type certificate, or provisional amendment to the type certificate.

§21.219 Transferability.

Class I provisional airworthiness certificates are not transferable. Class II provisional airworthiness certificates may be transferred to an air carrier eligible to apply for a certificate under §21.213(b).

§21.221 Class I provisional airworthiness certificates.

(a) Except as provided in §21.225, an applicant is entitled to a Class I provisional airworthiness certificate for an aircraft for which a Class I provisional type certificate has been issued if—

(1) He meets the eligibility requirements of §21.213 and he complies with this section; and

(2) The Administrator finds that there is no feature, characteristic or condition of the aircraft that would make the aircraft unsafe when operated in accordance with the limitations established in §§21.81(e) and 91.317 of this subchapter.

(b) The manufacturer must hold a provisional type certificate for the aircraft.

(c) The manufacturer must submit a statement that the aircraft conforms to the type design corresponding to the provisional type certificate and has been found by him to be in safe operating condition under all applicable limitations.

(d) The aircraft must be flown at least five hours by the manufacturer.

(e) The aircraft must be supplied with a provisional aircraft flight manual or other document and appropriate placards containing the limitations established by §§21.81(e) and 91.317.

[Doc. No. 5085, 29 FR 14571, Oct. 24, 1964, as amended by Amdt. 21–66, 54 FR 34329, Aug. 18, 1989]s

§21.223 Class II provisional airworthiness certificates.

(a) Except as provided in §21.225, an applicant is entitled to a Class II provisional airworthiness certificate for an aircraft for which a Class II provisional type certificate has been issued if—

(1) He meets the eligibility requirements of §21.213 and he complies with this section; and

(2) The Administrator finds that there is no feature, characteristic, or condition of the aircraft that would make the aircraft unsafe when operated in accordance with the limitations established in §§21.83(h), 91.317, and 121.207 of this chapter.

(b) The applicant must show that a Class II provisional type certificate for the aircraft has been issued to the manufacturer.

(c) The applicant must submit a statement by the manufacturer that the aircraft has been manufactured under a quality control system adequate to ensure that the aircraft conforms to the type design corresponding with the provisional type certificate.

(d) The applicant must submit a statement that the aircraft has been found by him to be in a safe operating condition under the applicable limitations.

(e) The aircraft must be flown at least five hours by the manufacturer.

(f) The aircraft must be supplied with a provisional aircraft flight manual containing the limitations established by §§21.83(h), 91.317, and 121.207 of this chapter.

[Doc. No. 5085, 29 FR 14571, Oct. 24, 1964, as amended by Amdt. 21–12, 31 FR 13389, Oct. 15, 1966; Amdt. 21–66, 54 FR 34329, Aug. 18, 1989]

§ 21.225 Provisional airworthiness certificates corresponding with provisional amendments to type certificates.

(a) An applicant is entitled to a Class I or a Class II provisional airworthiness certificate, for an aircraft, for which a provisional amendment to the type certificate has been issued, if—

(1) He meets the eligibility requirements of § 21.213 and he complies with this section; and

(2) The Administrator finds that there is no feature, characteristic, or condition of the aircraft, as modified in accordance with the provisionally amended type certificate, that would make the aircraft unsafe when operated in accordance with the applicable limitations established in §§ 21.85(g), 91.317, and 121.207 of this chapter.

(b) The applicant must show that the modification was made under a quality control system adequate to ensure that the modification conforms to the provisionally amended type certificate.

(c) The applicant must submit a statement that the aircraft has been found by him to be in a safe operating condition under the applicable limitations.

(d) The aircraft must be flown at least five hours by the manufacturer.

(e) The aircraft must be supplied with a provisional aircraft flight manual or other document and appropriate placards containing the limitations required by §§ 21.85(g), 91.317, and 121.207 of this chapter.

[Doc. No. 5085, 29 FR 14571, Oct. 24, 1964, as amended by Amdt. 21–12, 31 FR 13389, Oct. 15, 1966; Amdt. 21–66, 54 FR 34329, Aug. 18, 1989]

Subpart J—Delegation Option Authorization Procedures

SOURCE: Amdt. 21–5, 30 FR 11375, Sept. 8, 1965, unless otherwise noted.

§ 21.231 Applicability.

This subpart prescribes procedures for—

(a) Obtaining and using a delegation option authorization for type, production, and airworthiness certification (as applicable) of—

(1) Small airplanes and small gliders;

(2) Commuter category airplanes;

(3) Normal category rotorcraft;

(4) Turbojet engines of not more than 1,000 pounds thrust;

(5) Turbopropeller and reciprocating engines of not more than 500 brake horsepower; and

(6) Propellers manufactured for use on engines covered by paragraph (a)(4) of this section; and

(b) Issuing airworthiness approval tags for engines, propellers, and parts of products covered by paragraph (a) of this section.

[Amdt. 21–5, 30 FR 11375, Sept. 8, 1965, as amended by Amdt. 21–59, 52 FR 1836, Jan. 15, 1987]

§ 21.235 Application.

(a) An application for a delegation option authorization must be submitted, in a form and manner prescribed by the Administrator, to the Aircraft Certification Office for the area in which the manufacturer is located.

(b) The application must include the names, signatures, and titles of the persons for whom authorization to sign airworthiness certificates, repair and alteration forms, and inspection forms is requested.

[Doc. No. 5085, 29 FR 14574, Oct. 24, 1964, as amended by Amdt. 21–67, 54 FR 39291, Sept. 25, 1989]

§ 21.239 Eligibility.

To be eligible for a delegation option authorization, the applicant must—

(a) Hold a current type certificate, issued to him under the standard procedures, for a product type certificated under the same part as the products for which the delegation option authorization is sought;

(b) Hold a current production certificate issued under the standard procedures;

(c) Employ a staff of engineering, flight test, production and inspection personnel who can determine compliance with the applicable airworthiness requirements of this chapter; and

(d) Meet the requirements of this subpart.

§ 21.243 Duration.

A delegation option authorization is effective until it is surrendered or the

144

Administrator suspends, revokes, or otherwise terminates it.

§21.245 Maintenance of eligibility.

The holder of a delegation option authorization shall continue to meet the requirements for issue of the authorization or shall notify the Administrator within 48 hours of any change (including a change of personnel) that could affect the ability of the holder to meet those requirements.

§21.247 Transferability.

A delegation option authorization is not transferable.

§21.249 Inspections.

Upon request, each holder of a delegation option authorization and each applicant shall let the Administrator inspect his organization, facilities, product, and records.

§21.251 Limits of applicability.

(a) Delegation option authorizations apply only to products that are manufactured by the holder of the authorization.

(b) Delegation option authorizations may be used for—

(1) Type certification;

(2) Changes in the type design of products for which the manufacturer holds, or obtains, a type certificate;

(3) The amendment of a production certificate held by the manufacturer to include additional models or additional types for which he holds or obtains a type certificate; and

(4) The issue of—

(i) Experimental certificates for aircraft for which the manufacturer has applied for a type certificate or amended type certificate under §21.253, to permit the operation of those aircraft for the purpose of research and development, crew training, market surveys, or the showing of compliance with the applicable airworthiness requirements;

(ii) Airworthiness certificates (other than experimental certificates) for aircraft for which the manufacturer holds a type certificate and holds or is in the process of obtaining a production certificate;

(iii) Airworthiness approval tags (FAA Form 8130–3) for engines and pro-

pellers for which the manufacturer holds a type certificate and holds or is in the process of obtaining a production certificate; and

(iv) Airworthiness approval tags (FAA Form 8130–3) for parts of products covered by this section.

(c) Delegation option procedures may be applied to one or more types selected by the manufacturer, who must notify the FAA of each model, and of the first serial number of each model manufactured by him under the delegation option procedures. Other types or models may remain under the standard procedures.

(d) Delegation option authorizations are subject to any additional limitations prescribed by the Administrator after inspection of the applicant's facilities or review of the staff qualifications.

[Amdt. 21–5, 30 FR 11375, Sept. 8, 1965, as amended by Amdt. 21–31, 35 FR 7292, May 9, 1970; Amdt. 21–43, 40 FR 2576, Jan. 14, 1975]

§21.253 Type certificates: application.

(a) To obtain, under the delegation option authorization, a type certificate for a new product or an amended type certificate, the manufacturer must submit to the Administrator—

(1) An application for a type certificate (FAA Form 312);

(2) A statement listing the airworthiness requirements of this chapter (by part number and effective date) that the manufacturer considers applicable;

(3) After determining that the type design meets the applicable requirements, a statement certifying that this determination has been made;

(4) After placing the required technical data and type inspection report in the technical data file required by §21.293(a)(1)(i), a statement certifying that this has been done;

(5) A proposed type certificate data sheet; and

(6) An Aircraft Flight Manual (if required) or a summary of required operating limitations and other information necessary for safe operation of the product.

§21.257 Type certificates: issue.

An applicant is entitled to a type certificate for a product manufactured under a delegation option authorization if the Administrator finds that the product meets the applicable airworthiness, noise, fuel venting, and exhaust emission requirements (including applicable acoustical change or emissions change requirements in the case of changes in type design).

[Amdt. 21-68, 55 FR 32860, Aug. 10, 1990]

§ 21.261 Equivalent safety provisions.

The manufacturer shall obtain the Administrator's concurrence on the application of all equivalent safety provisions applied under § 21.21.

§ 21.267 Production certificates.

To have a new model or new type certificate listed on his production certificate (issued under Subpart G of this part), the manufacturer must submit to the Administrator—

(a) An application for an amendment to the production certificate;

(b) After determining that the production certification requirements of Subpart G, with respect to the new model or type, are met, a statement certifying that this determination has been made;

(c) A statement identifying the type certificate number under which the product is being manufactured; and

(d) After placing the manufacturing and quality control data required by § 21.143 with the data required by § 21.293(a)(1)(ii), a statement certifying that this has been done.

§ 21.269 Export airworthiness approvals.

The manufacturer may issue export airworthiness approvals.

§ 21.271 Airworthiness approval tags.

(a) A manufacturer may issue an airworthiness approval tag (FAA Form 8130-3) for each engine and propeller covered by § 21.251(b)(4), and may issue an airworthiness approval tag for parts of each product covered by that section, if he finds, on the basis of inspection and operation tests, that those products conform to a type design for which he holds a type certificate and are in condition for safe operation.

(b) When a new model has been included on the Production Limitation Record, the production certification number shall be stamped on the engine or propeller identification data place instead of issuing an airworthiness approval tag.

[Amdt. 21-5, 30 FR 11375, Sept. 8, 1965, as amended by Amdt. 21-43, 40 FR 2577, Jan. 14, 1975]

§ 21.273 Airworthiness certificates other than experimental.

(a) The manufacturer may issue an airworthiness certificate for aircraft manufactured under a delegation option authorization if he finds, on the basis of the inspection and production flight check, that each aircraft conforms to a type design for which he holds a type certificate and is in a condition for safe operation.

(b) The manufacturer may authorize any employee to sign airworthiness certificates if that employee is in direct—

(1) Performs, or is in direct charge of, the inspection specified in paragraph (a) of this section; and

(2) Is listed on the manufacturer's application for the delegation option authorization, or on amendments thereof.

[Amdt. 21-5, 30 FR 11375, Sept. 8, 1965, as amended by Amdt. 21-18, 32 FR 15472, Nov. 7, 1967]

§ 21.275 Experimental certificates.

(a) The manufacturer shall, before issuing an experimental certificate, obtain from the Administration any limitations and conditions that the Administrator considers necessary for safety.

(b) For experimental certificates issued by the manufacturer, under this subpart, for aircraft for which the manufacturer holds the type certificate and which have undergone changes to the type design requiring flight test, the manufacturer may prescribe any operating limitations that he considers necessary.

§ 21.277 Data review and service experience.

(a) If the Administrator finds that a product for which a type certificate was issued under this subpart does not meet the applicable airworthiness requirements, or that an unsafe feature or characteristic caused by a defect in design or manufacture exists, the manufacturer, upon notification by the Administrator, shall investigate the matter and report to the Administrator the results of the investigation and the action, if any, taken or proposed.

(b) If corrective action by the user of the product is necessary for safety because of any noncompliance or defect specified in paragraph (a) of this section, the manufacturer shall submit the information necessary for the issue of an Airworthiness Directive under Part 39.

§ 21.289 Major repairs, rebuilding and alteration.

For types covered by a delegation option authorization, a manufacturer may—

(a) After finding that a major repair or major alteration meets the applicable airworthiness requirements of this chapter, approve that repair or alteration; and

(b) Authorize any employee to execute and sign FAA Form 337 and make required log book entries if that employee—

(1) Inspects, or is in direct charge of inspecting, the repair, rebuilding, or alteration; and

(2) Is listed on the application for the delegation option authorization, or on amendments thereof.

§ 21.293 Current records.

(a) The manufacturer shall maintain at his factory, for each product type certificated under a delegation option authorization, current records containing the following:

(1) For the duration of the manufacturing operating under the delegation option authorization—

(i) A technical data file that includes the type design drawings, specifications, reports on tests prescribed by this part, and the original type inspection report and amendments to that report;

(ii) The data (including amendments) required to be submitted with the original application for each production certificate; and

(iii) A record of any rebuilding and alteration performed by the manufacturer on products manufactured under the delegation option authorization.

(2) For 2 years—

(i) A complete inspection record for each product manufactured, by serial number, and data covering the processes and tests to which materials and parts are subjected; and

(ii) A record of reported service difficulties.

(b) The records and data specified in paragraph (a) of this section shall be—

(1) Made available, upon the Administrator's request, for examination by the Administrator at any time; and

(2) Identified and sent to the Administrator as soon as the manufacturer no longer operates under the delegation option procedures.

Subpart K—Approval of Materials, Parts, Processes, and Appliances

SOURCE: Docket No. 5085, 29 FR 14574, Oct. 24, 1964, unless otherwise noted.

§ 21.301 Applicability.

This subpart prescribes procedural requirements for the approval of certain materials, parts, processes, and appliances.

§ 21.303 Replacement and modification parts.

(a) Except as provided in paragraph (b) of this section, no person may produce a modification or replacement part for sale for installation on a type certificated product unless it is produced pursuant to a Parts Manufacturer Approval issued under this subpart.

(b) This section does not apply to the following:

(1) Parts produced under a type or production certificate.

(2) Parts produced by an owner or operator for maintaining or altering his own product.

(3) Parts produced under an FAA Technical Standard Order.

(4) Standard parts (such as bolts and nuts) conforming to established industry or U.S. specifications.

(c) An application for a Parts Manufacturer Approval is made to the Manager of the Aircraft Certification Office for the geographic area in which the manufacturing facility is located and must include the following:

(1) The identity of the product on which the part is to be installed.

(2) The name and address of the manufacturing facilities at which these parts are to be manufactured.

(3) The design of the part, which consists of—

(i) Drawings and specifications necessary to show the configuration of the part; and

(ii) Information on dimensions, materials, and processes necessary to define the structural strength of the part.

(4) Test reports and computations necessary to show that the design of the part meets the airworthiness requirements of the Federal Aviation Regulations applicable to the product on which the part is to be installed, unless the applicant shows that the design of the part is identical to the design of a part that is covered under a type certificate. If the design of the part was obtained by a licensing agreement, evidence of that agreement must be furnished.

(d) An applicant is entitled to a Parts Manufacturer Approval for a replacement or modification part if—

(1) The Administrator finds, upon examination of the design and after completing all tests and inspections, that the design meets the airworthiness requirements of the Federal Aviation Regulations applicable to the product on which the part is to be installed; and

(2) He submits a statement certifying that he has established the fabrication inspection system required by paragraph (h) of this section.

(e) Each applicant for a Parts Manufacturer Approval must allow the Administrator to make any inspection or test necessary to determine compliance with the applicable Federal Aviation Regulations. However, unless otherwise authorized by the Administrator—

(1) No part may be presented to the Administrator for an inspection or test unless compliance with paragraphs (f)(2) through (4) of this section has been shown for that part; and

(2) No change may be made to a part between the time that compliance with paragraphs (f)(2) through (4) of this section is shown for that part and the time that the part is presented to the Administrator for the inspection or test.

(f) Each applicant for a Parts Manufacturer Approval must make all inspections and tests necessary to determine—

(1) Compliance with the applicable airworthiness requirements;

(2) That materials conform to the specifications in the design;

(3) That the part conforms to the drawings in the design; and

(4) That the fabrication processes, construction, and assembly conform to those specified in the design.

(g) The Administrator does not issue a Parts Manufacturer Approval if the manufacturing facilities for the part are located outside of the United States, unless the Administrator finds that the location of the manufacturing facilities places no burden on the FAA in administering applicable airworthiness requirements.

(h) Each holder of a Parts Manufacturer Approval shall establish and maintain a fabrication inspection system that ensures that each completed part conforms to its design data and is safe for installation on applicable type certificated products. The system shall include the following:

(1) Incoming materials used in the finished part must be as specified in the design data.

(2) Incoming materials must be properly identified if their physical and chemical properties cannot otherwise be readily and accurately determined.

(3) Materials subject to damage and deterioration must be suitably stored and adequately protected.

(4) Processes affecting the quality and safety of the finished product must be accomplished in accordance with acceptable specifications.

(5) Parts in process must be inspected for conformity with the design data at points in production where accurate determination can be made. Statistical quality control procedures may be employed where it is shown that a satisfactory level of quality will be maintained for the particular part involved.

(6) Current design drawings must be readily available to manufacturing and inspection personnel, and used when necessary.

(7) Major changes to the basic design must be adequately controlled and approved before being incorporated in the finished part.

(8) Rejected materials and components must be segregated and identified in such a manner as to preclude their use in the finished part.

(9) Inspection records must be maintained, identified with the completed part, where practicable, and retained in the manufacturer's file for a period of at least 2 years after the part has been completed.

(i) A Parts Manufacturer Approval issued under this section is not transferable and is effective until surrendered or withdrawn or otherwise terminated by the Administrator.

(j) The holder of a Parts Manufacturer Approval shall notify the FAA in writing within 10 days from the date the manufacturing facility at which the parts are manufactured is relocated or expanded to include additional facilities at other locations.

(k) Each holder of a Parts Manufacturer Approval shall determine that each completed part conforms to the design data and is safe for installation on type certificated products.

[Amdt. 21–38, 37 FR 10659, May 26, 1972, as amended by Amdt. 21–41, 39 FR 41965, Dec. 4, 1974; Amdt. 21–67, 54 FR 39291, Sept. 25, 1989]

§ 21.305 Approval of materials, parts, processes, and appliances.

Whenever a material, part, process, or appliance is required to be approved under this chapter, it may be approved—

(a) Under a Parts Manufacturer Approval issued under § 21.303;

(b) Under a Technical Standard Order issued by the Administrator. Advisory Circular 20–110 contains a list of Technical Standard Orders that may be used to obtain approval. Copies of the Advisory Circular may be obtained from the U.S. Department of Transportation, Publication Section (M–443.1), Washington, D.C. 20590;

(c) In conjunction with type certification procedures for a product; or

(d) In any other manner approved by the Administrator.

[Amdt. 21–38, 37 FR 10659, May 26, 1972, as amended by Amdt. 21–50, 45 FR 38346, June 9, 1980]

Subpart L—Export Airworthiness Approvals

SOURCE: Amdt. 21–2, 30 FR 8465, July 2, 1965, unless otherwise noted.

§ 21.321 Applicability.

(a) This subpart prescribes—

(1) Procedural requirements for the issue of export airworthiness approvals; and

(2) Rules governing the holders of those approvals.

(b) For the purposes of this subpart—

(1) A Class I product is a complete aircraft, aircraft engine, or propeller, which—

(i) Has been type certificated in accordance with the applicable Federal Aviation Regulations and for which Federal Aviation Specifications or type certificate data sheets have been issued; or

(ii) Is identical to a type certificated product specified in paragraph (b)(1)(i) of this section in all respects except as is otherwise acceptable to the civil aviation authority of the importing state.

(2) A Class II product is a major component of a Class I product (e.g., wings, fuselages, empennage assemblies, landing gears, power transmissions, control surfaces, etc), the failure of which would jeopardize the safety of a Class I product; or any part, material, or appliance, approved and manufactured under the Technical Standard Order (TSO) system in the "C" series.

(3) A Class III product is any part or component which is not a Class I or Class II product and includes standard parts, i.e., those designated as AN, NAS, SAE, etc.

(4) The words "newly overhauled" when used to describe a product means that the product has not been operated or placed in service, except for functional testing, since having been overhauled, inspected and approved for return to service in accordance with the applicable Federal Aviation Regulations.

[Amdt. 21–2, 30 FR 11375, July 2, 1965, as amended by Amdt. 21–48, 44 FR 15649, Mar. 15, 1979]

§ 21.323 Eligibility.

(a) Any exporter or his authorized representative may obtain an export airworthiness approval for a Class I or Class II product.

(b) Any manufacturer may obtain an export airworthiness approval for a Class III product if the manufacturer—

(1) Has in his employ a designated representative of the Administrator who has been authorized to issue that approval; and

(2) Holds for that product—

(i) A production certificate;

(ii) An approved production inspection system;

(iii) An FAA Parts Manufacturer Approval (PMA); or

(iv) A Technical Standard Order authorization.

§ 21.325 Export airworthiness approvals.

(a) *Kinds of approvals.* (1) Export airworthiness approval of Class I products is issued in the form of Export Certificates of Airworthiness, FAA Form 8130–4. Such a certificate does not authorize the operation of aircraft.

(2) Export airworthiness approval of Class II and III products is issued in the form of Airworthiness Approval Tags, FAA Form 8130–3.

(b) *Products which may be approved.* Export airworthiness approvals are issued for—

(1) New aircraft that are assembled and that have been flight-tested, and other Class I products located in the United States, except that export airworthiness approval may be issued for any of the following without assembly or flight-test:

(i) A small airplane type certificated under Part 3 or 4a of the Civil Air Regulations, or Part 23 of the Federal Aviation Regulations, and manufactured under a production certificate;

(ii) A glider type certificated under § 21.23 of this part and manufactured under a production certificate; or

(iii) A normal category rotorcraft type certificated under Part 6 of the Civil Air Regulations or Part 27 of the Federal Aviation Regulations and manufactured under a production certificate.

(2) Used aircraft possessing a valid U.S. airworthiness certificate, or other used Class I products that have been maintained in accordance with the applicable CAR's or FAR's and are located in a foreign country, if the Administrator finds that the location places no undue burden upon the FAA in administering the provisions of this regulation.

(3) Class II and III products that are manufactured and located in the United States.

(c) *Export airworthiness approval exceptions.* If the export airworthiness approval is issued on the basis of a written statement by the importing state as provided for in § 21.327(e)(4), the requirements that are not met and the differences in configuration, if any, between the product to be exported and the related type certificated product, are listed on the export airworthiness approval as exceptions.

[Amdt. 21–2, 30 FR 8465, July 2, 1965, as amended by Amdt. 21–14, 32 FR 2999, Feb. 17, 1967; Amdt. 21–43, 40 FR 2577, Jan. 14, 1975; Amdt. 21–48, 44 FR 15649, Mar. 15, 1979]

§ 21.327 Application.

(a) Except as provided in paragraph (b) of this section, an application for export airworthiness approval for a Class I or Class II product is made on a form and in a manner prescribed by the Administrator and is submitted to the appropriate Flight Standards District Office or to the nearest international field office.

(b) A manufacturer holding a production certificate may apply orally to the appropriate Flight Standards District Office or the nearest international field office for export airworthiness approval of a Class II product approved under his production certificate.

(c) Application for export airworthiness approval of Class III products is made to the designated representative of the Administrator authorized to issue those approvals.

(d) A separate application must be made for—

(1) Each aircraft;

(2) Each engine and propeller, except that one application may be made for more than one engine or propeller, if all are of the same type and model and are exported to the same purchaser and country; and

(3) Each type of Class II product, except that one application may be used for more than one type of Class II product when—

(i) They are separated and identified in the application as to the type and model of the related Class I product; and

(ii) They are to be exported to the same purchaser and country.

(e) Each application must be accompanied by a written statement from the importing country that will validate the export airworthiness approval if the product being exported is—

(1) An aircraft manufactured outside the United States and being exported to a country with which the United States has a reciprocal agreement concerning the validation of export certificates;

(2) An unassembled aircraft which has not been flight-tested;

(3) A product that does not meet the special requirement of the importing country; or

(4) A product that does not meet a requirement specified in §§ 21.329, 21.331, or 21.333, as applicable, for the issuance of an export airworthiness approval. The written statement must list the requirements not met.

(f) Each application for export airworthiness approval of a Class I product must include, as applicable:

(1) A Statement of Conformity, FAA Form 8130-9, for each new product that has not been manufactured under a production certificate.

(2) A weight and balance report, with a loading schedule when applicable, for each aircraft in accordance with Part 43 of this chapter. For transport aircraft and commuter category airplanes this report must be based on an actual weighing of the aircraft within the preceding twelve months, but after any major repairs or alterations to the aircraft. Changes in equipment not classed as major changes that are made after the actual weighing may be accounted for on a "computed" basis and the report revised accordingly. Manufacturers of new nontransport category airplanes, normal category rotorcraft, and gliders may submit reports having computed weight and balance data, in place of an actual weighing of the aircraft, if fleet weight control procedures approved by the FAA have been established for such aircraft. In such a case, the following statement must be entered in each report: "The weight and balance data shown in this report are computed on the basis of Federal Aviation Administration approved procedures for establishing fleet weight averages." The weight and balance report must include an equipment list showing weights and moment arms of all required and optional items of equipment that are included in the certificated empty weight.

(3) A maintenance manual for each new product when such a manual is required by the applicable airworthiness rules.

(4) Evidence of compliance with the applicable airworthiness directives. A suitable notation must be made when such directives are not complied with.

(5) When temporary installations are incorporated in an aircraft for the purpose of export delivery, the application form must include a general description of the installations together with a statement that the installation will be removed and the aircraft restored to the approved configuration upon completion of the delivery flight.

(6) Historical records such as aircraft and engine log books, repair and alteration forms, etc., for used aircraft and newly overhauled products.

(7) For products intended for overseas shipment, the application form must describe the methods used, if any, for the preservation and packaging of such products to protect them against corrosion and damage while in transit or storage. The description must also indicate the duration of the effectiveness of such methods.

(8) The Airplane or Rotorcraft Flight Manual when such material is required by the applicable airworthiness regulations for the particular aircraft.

(9) A statement as to the date when title passed or is expected to pass to a foreign purchaser.

(10) The data required by the special requirements of the importing country.

[Amdt. 21-2, 30 FR 8465, July 2, 1965, as amended by Doc. No. 8084, 32 FR 5769, Apr. 11, 1967; Amdt. 21-48, 44 FR 15650, Mar. 15, 1979; Amdt. 21-59, 52 FR 1836, Jan. 15, 1987]

§ 21.329 Issue of export certificates of airworthiness for Class I products.

An applicant is entitled to an export certificate of airworthiness for a Class I product if that applicant shows at the time the product is submitted to the Administrator for export airworthiness approval that it meets the requirements of paragraphs (a) through (f) of this section, as applicable, except as provided in paragraph (g) of this section:

(a) New or used aircraft manufactured in the United States must meet the airworthiness requirement for a standard U.S. airworthiness certificate under § 21.183, or meet the airworthiness certification requirements for a "restricted" airworthiness certificate under § 21.185.

(b) New or used aircraft manufactured outside the United States must have a valid U.S. standard airworthiness certificate.

(c) Used aircraft must have undergone an annual type inspection and be approved for return to service in accordance with Part 43 of this chapter. The inspection must have been performed and properly documented within 30 days before the date the application is made for an export certificate of airworthiness. In complying with this paragraph, consideration may be given to the inspections performed on an aircraft maintained in accordance with a continuous airworthiness maintenance program under Part 121 of this chapter or a progressive inspection program under Part 91 of this chapter, within the 30 days prior to the date the application is made for an export certificate of airworthiness.

(d) New engines and propellers must conform to the type design and must be in a condition for safe operation.

(e) Used engines and propellers which are not being exported as part of a certificated aircraft must have been newly overhauled.

(f) The special requirements of the importing country must have been met.

(g) A product need not meet a requirement specified in paragraphs (a) through (f) of this section, as applicable, if acceptable to the importing country and the importing country in-

dicates that acceptability in accordance with § 21.327(e)(4) of this part.

[Amdt. 21–2, 30 FR 8465, July 2, 1965, as amended by Amdt. 21–8, 31 FR 2421, Feb. 5, 1966; Amdt. 21–9, 31 FR 3336, Mar. 3, 1966; Amdt. 21–48, 44 FR 15650, Mar. 15, 1979; Amdt. 21–79, 66 FR 21066, Apr. 27, 2001]

§ 21.331 Issue of airworthiness approval tags for Class II products.

(a) An applicant is entitled to an export airworthiness approval tag for Class II products if that applicant shows, except as provided in paragraph (b) of this section, that—

(1) The products are new or have been newly overhauled and conform to the approved design data;

(2) The products are in a condition for safe operation;

(3) The products are identified with at least the manufacturer's name, part number, model designation (when applicable), and serial number or equivalent; and

(4) The products meet the special requirements of the importing country.

(b) A product need not meet a requirement specified in paragraph (a) of this section if acceptable to the importing country and the importing country indicates that acceptability in accordance with § 21.327(e)(4) of this part.

[Amdt. 21–2, 30 FR 8465, July 2, 1965, as amended by Amdt. 21–48, 44 FR 15650, Mar. 15, 1979]

§ 21.333 Issue of export airworthiness approval tags for Class III products.

(a) An applicant is entitled to an export airworthiness approval tag for Class III products if that applicant shows, except as provided in paragraph (b) of this section, that—

(1) The products conform to the approved design data applicable to the Class I or Class II product of which they are a part;

(2) The products are in a condition for safe operation; and

(3) The products comply with the special requirements of the importing country.

(b) A product need not meet a requirement specified in paragraph (a) of this section if acceptable to the importing country and the importing country indicates that acceptability in accordance with §21.327(e)(4) of this part.

[Amdt. 21–2, 30 FR 8465, July 2, 1965, as amended by Amdt. 21–48, 44 FR 15650, Mar. 15, 1979]

§21.335 Responsibilities of exporters.

Each exporter receiving an export airworthiness approval for a product shall—

(a) Forward to the air authority of the importing country all documents and information necessary for the proper operation of the products being exported, e.g., Flight Manuals, Maintenance Manuals, Service Bulletins, and assembly instructions, and such other material as is stipulated in the special requirements of the importing country. The documents, information, and material may be forwarded by any means consistent with the special requirements of the importing country;

(b) Forward the manufacturer's assembly instructions and an FAA-approved flight test checkoff form to the air authority of the importing country when unassembled aircraft are being exported. These instructions must be in sufficient detail to permit whatever rigging, alignment, and ground testing is necessary to ensure that the aircraft will conform to the approved configuration when assembled;

(c) Remove or cause to be removed any temporary installation incorporated on an aircraft for the purpose of export delivery and restore the aircraft to the approved configuration upon completion of the delivery flight;

(d) Secure all proper foreign entry clearances from all the countries involved when conducting sales demonstrations or delivery flights; and

(e) When title to an aircraft passes or has passed to a foreign purchaser—

(1) Request cancellation of the U.S. registration and airworthiness certificates, giving the date of transfer of title, and the name and address of the foreign owner;

(2) Return the Registration and Airworthiness Certificates, AC Form 8050.3 and FAA Form 8100–2, to the FAA; and

(3) Submit a statement certifying that the United States' identification and registration numbers have been removed from the aircraft in compliance with §45.33.

[Amdt. 21–2, 30 FR 8465, July 2, 1965, as amended by Amdt. 21–48, 44 FR 15650, Mar. 15, 1979]

§21.337 Performance of inspections and overhauls.

Unless otherwise provided for in this subpart, each inspection and overhaul required for export airworthiness approval of Class I and Class II products must be performed and approved by one of the following:

(a) The manufacturer of the product.

(b) An appropriately certificated domestic repair station.

(c) An appropriately certificated foreign repair station having adequate overhaul facilities, and maintenance organization appropriate to the product involved, when the product is a Class I product located in a foreign country and an international office of Flight Standards Service has approved the use of such foreign repair station.

(d) The holder of an inspection authorization as provided in Part 65 of this chapter.

(e) An air carrier, when the product is one that the carrier has maintained under its own or another air carrier's continuous airworthiness maintenance program and maintenance manuals as provided in Part 121 of this chapter.

(f) A commercial operator, when the product is one that the operator has maintained under its continuous airworthiness maintenance program and maintenance manual as provided in Part 121 of this chapter.

[Amdt. 21–2, 30 FR 8465, July 2, 1965, as amended by Amdt. 21–8, 31 FR 2421, Feb. 5, 1966; Amdt. 21–79, 66 FR 21066, Apr. 27, 2001]

§21.339 Special export airworthiness approval for aircraft.

A special export certificate of airworthiness may be issued for an aircraft located in the United States that is to be flown to several foreign countries for the purpose of sale, without returning the aircraft to the United States for the certificate if—

(a) The aircraft possesses either—

(1) A standard U.S. certificate of airworthiness; or

(2) A special U.S. certificate of airworthiness in the restricted category issued under § 21.185;

(b) The owner files an application as required by § 21.327 except that items 3 and 4 of the application (FAA Form 8130-1) need not be completed;

(c) The aircraft is inspected by the Administrator before leaving the United States and is found to comply with all the applicable requirements;

(d) A list of foreign countries in which it is intended to conduct sales demonstrations, together with the expected dates and duration of such demonstration, is included in the application;

(e) For each prospective importing country, the applicant shows that—

(1) He has met that country's special requirements, other than those requiring that documents, information, and materials be furnished; and

(2) He has the documents, information, and materials necessary to meet the special requirements of that country; and

(f) All other requirements for the issuance of a Class I export certificate of airworthiness are met.

[Amdt. 21-12, 31 FR 12565, Sept. 23, 1966, as amended by Amdt. 21-43, 40 FR 2577, Jan. 14, 1975; Amdt. 21-55, 46 FR 44737, Sept. 8, 1981]

Subpart M—Designated Alteration Station Authorization Procedures

SOURCE: Amdt. 21-6, 30 FR 11379, Sept. 8, 1965; 30 FR 11849, Sept. 16, 1965, unless otherwise noted.

§ 21.431 Applicability.

(a) This subpart prescribes Designated Alteration Station (DAS) authorization procedures for—

(1) Issuing supplemental type certificates;

(2) Issuing experimental certificates; and

(3) Amending standard airworthiness certificates.

(b) This subpart applies to domestic repair stations, air carriers, commercial operators of large aircraft, and manufacturers of products.

[Amdt. 21-6, 30 FR 11379, Sept. 8, 1965; 30 FR 11849, Sept. 16, 1965, as amended by Amdt. 21-74, 62 FR 13253, Mar. 19, 1997]

§ 21.435 Application.

The applicant for a DAS authorization must submit an application, in writing and signed by an official of the applicant, to the Aircraft Certification Office responsible for the geographic area in which the applicant is located. The application must contain—

(a) The repair station certificate number held by the repair station applicant, and the current ratings covered by the certificate;

(b) The air carrier or commercial operator operating certificate number held by the air carrier or commercial operator applicant, and the products that it may operate and maintain under the certificate;

(c) A statement by the manufacturer applicant of the products for which he holds the type certificate;

(d) The names, signatures, and titles of the persons for whom authorization to issue supplemental type certificates or experimental certificates, or amend airworthiness certificates, is requested; and

(e) A description of the applicant's facilities, and of the staff with which compliance with § 21.439(a)(4) is to be shown.

[Amdt. 21-6, 30 FR 11379, Sept. 8, 1965; 30 FR 11849, Sept. 16, 1965, as amended by Amdt. 21-67, 54 FR 39291, Sept. 25, 1989]

§ 21.439 Eligibility.

(a) To be eligible for a DAS authorization, the applicant must—

(1) Hold a current domestic repair station certificate under Part 145, or air carrier or commercial operator operating certificate under Part 121;

(2) Be a manufacturer of a product for which it has alteration authority under § 43.3(i) of this subchapter;

(3) Have adequate maintenance facilities and personnel, in the United States, appropriate to the products that it may operate and maintain under its certificate; and

(4) Employ, or have available, a staff of engineering, flight test, and inspection personnel who can determine compliance with the applicable airworthiness requirements of this chapter.

(b) At least one member of the staff required by paragraph (a)(4) of this section must have all of the following qualifications:

(1) A thorough working knowledge of the applicable requirements of this chapter.

(2) A position, on the applicant's staff, with authority to establish alteration programs that ensure that altered products meet the applicable requirements of this chapter.

(3) At least one year of satisfactory experience in direct contact with the FAA (or its predecessor agency (CAA)) while processing engineering work for type certification or alteration projects.

(4) At least eight years of aeronautical engineering experience (which may include the one year required by paragraph (b)(3) of this section).

(5) The general technical knowledge and experience necessary to determine that altered products, of the types for which a DAS authorization is requested, are in condition for safe operation.

§ 21.441 Procedure manual.

(a) No DAS may exercise any authority under this subpart unless it submits, and obtains approval of, a procedure manual containing—

(1) The procedures for issuing STCs; and

(2) The names, signatures, and responsibilities of officials and of each staff member required by §21.439(a)(4), identifying those persons who—

(i) Have authority to make changes in procedures that require a revision to the procedure manual; and

(ii) Are to conduct inspections (including conformity and compliance inspections) or approve inspection reports, prepare or approve data, plan or conduct tests, approve the results of tests, amend airworthiness certificates, issue experimental certificates, approve changes to operating limitations or Aircraft Flight Manuals, and sign supplemental type certificates.

(b) No DAS may continue to perform any DAS function affected by any change in facilities or staff necessary to continue to meet the requirements of §21.439, or affected by any change in procedures from those approved under paragraph (a) of this section, unless that change is approved and entered in the manual. For this purpose, the manual shall contain a log-of-revisions page with space for the identification of each revised item, page, or date, and the signature of the person approving the change for the Administrator.

§ 21.443 Duration.

(a) A DAS authorization is effective until it is surrendered or the Administrator suspends, revokes, or otherwise terminates it.

(b) The DAS shall return the authorization certificate to the Administrator when it is no longer effective.

§ 21.445 Maintenance of eligibility.

The DAS shall continue to meet the requirements for issue of the authorization or shall notify the Administrator within 48 hours of any change (including a change of personnel) that could affect the ability of the DAS to meet those requirements.

§ 21.447 Transferability.

A DAS authorization is not transferable.

§ 21.449 Inspections.

Upon request, each DAS and each applicant shall let the Administrator inspect his facilities, products, and records.

§ 21.451 Limits of applicability.

(a) DAS authorizations apply only to products—

(1) Covered by the ratings of the repair station applicant;

(2) Covered by the operating certificate and maintenance manual of the air carrier or commercial operator applicant; and

(3) For which the manufacturer applicant has alteration authority under §43.3(i) of this subchapter.

(b) DAS authorizations may be used for—

(1) The issue of supplemental type certificates;

(2) The issue of experimental certificates for aircraft that—

(i) Are altered by the DAS under a supplemental type certificate issued by the DAS; and

(ii) Require flight tests in order to show compliance with the applicable airworthiness requirements of this chapter; and

(3) The amendment of standard airworthiness certificates for aircraft altered under this subpart.

(c) DAS authorizations are subject to any additional limitations prescribed by the Administrator after inspection of the applicant's facilities or review of the staff qualifications.

(d) Notwithstanding any other provision of this subpart, a DAS may not issue a supplemental type certificate involving the exhaust emissions change requirements of part 34 or the acoustical change requirements of part 36 of this chapter until the Administrator finds that those requirements are met.

[Amdt. 21-6, 30 FR 11379, Sept. 8, 1965; 30 FR 11849, Sept. 16, 1965, as amended by Amdt. 21-42, 40 FR 1034, Jan. 6, 1975; Amdt. 21-68, 55 FR 32860, Aug. 10, 1990]

§ 21.461 Equivalent safety provisions.

The DAS shall obtain the Administrator's concurrence on the application of all equivalent safety provisions applied under § 21.21.

§ 21.463 Supplemental type certificates.

(a) For each supplemental type certificate issued under this subpart, the DAS shall follow the procedure manual prescribed in § 21.441 and shall, before issuing the certificate—

(1) Submit to the Administrator a statement describing—

(i) The type design change;

(ii) The airworthiness requirements of this chapter (by part and effective date) that the DAS considers applicable; and

(iii) The proposed program for meeting the applicable airworthiness requirements;

(2) Find that each applicable airworthiness requirement is met; and

(3) Find that the type of product for which the STC is to be issued, as modified by the supplemental type design data upon which the STC is based, is of proper design for safe operation.

(b) Within 30 days after the date of issue of the STC, the DAS shall submit to the Administrator—

(1) Two copies of the STC;

(2) One copy of the design data approved by the DAS and referred to in the STC;

(3) One copy of each inspection and test report; and

(4) Two copies of each revision to the Aircraft Flight Manual or to the operating limitations, and any other information necessary for safe operation of the product.

§ 21.473 Airworthiness certificates other than experimental.

For each amendment made to a standard airworthiness certificate under this subpart, the DAS shall follow the procedure manual prescribed in § 21.441 and shall, before making that amendment—

(a) Complete each flight test necessary to meet the applicable airworthiness requirements of this chapter;

(b) Find that each applicable airworthiness requirement of this chapter is met; and

(c) Find that the aircraft is in condition for safe operation.

§ 21.475 Experimental certificates.

The DAS shall, before issuing an experimental certificate, obtain from the Administrator any limitations and conditions that the Administrator considers necessary for safety.

§ 21.477 Data review and service experience.

(a) If the Administrator finds that a product for which an STC was issued under this subpart does not meet the applicable airworthiness requirements, or that an unsafe feature or characteristic caused by a defect in design or manufacture exists, the DAS, upon notification by the Administrator, shall investigate the matter and report to the Administrator the results of the investigation and the action, if any, taken or proposed.

(b) If corrective action by the user of the product is necessary for safety because of any noncompliance or defect specified in paragraph (a) of this section, the DAS shall submit the information necessary for the issue of an Airworthiness Directive under Part 39.

§ 21.493 Current records.

(a) The DAS shall maintain, at its facility, current records containing—

(1) For each product for which it has issued an STC under this subpart, a technical data file that includes any data and amendments thereto (including drawings, photographs, specifications, instructions, and reports) necessary for the STC;

(2) A list of products by make, model, manufacturer's serial number and, if applicable, any FAA identification, that have been altered under the DAS authorization; and

(3) A file of information from all available sources on alteration difficulties of products altered under the DAS authorization.

(b) The records prescribed in paragraph (a) of this section shall be—

(1) Made available by the DAS, upon the Administrator's request, for examination by the Administrator at any time; and

(2) In the case of the data file prescribed in paragraph (a)(1) of this section, identified by the DAS and sent to the Administrator as soon as the DAS no longer operates under this subpart.

Subpart N—Approval of Engines, Propellers, Materials, Parts, and Appliances: Import

§21.500 Approval of engines and propellers.

Each holder or licensee of a U.S. type certificate for an aircraft engine or propeller manufactured in a foreign country with which the United States has an agreement for the acceptance of those products for export and import, shall furnish with each such aircraft engine or propeller imported into this country, a certificate of airworthiness for export issued by the country of manufacture certifying that the individual aircraft engine or propeller—

(a) Conforms to its U.S. type certificate and is in condition for safe operation; and

(b) Has been subjected by the manufacturer to a final operational check.

[Amdt. 21–25, 34 FR 14068, Sept. 5, 1969]

§21.502 Approval of materials, parts, and appliances.

(a) A material, part, or appliance, manufactured in a foreign country with which the United States has an agreement for the acceptance of those materials, parts, or appliances for export and import, is considered to meet the requirements for approval in the Federal Aviation Regulations when the country of manufacture issues a certificate of airworthiness for export certifying that the individual material, part, or appliance meets those requirements, unless the Administrator finds, based on the technical data submitted under paragraph (b) of this section, that the material, part, or appliance is otherwise not consistent with the intent of the Federal Aviation Regulations.

(b) An applicant for approval of a material, part, or appliance must, upon request, submit to the Administrator any technical data respecting that material, part, or appliance.

[Amdt. 21–25, 34 FR 14068, Sept. 5, 1969]

Subpart O—Technical Standard Order Authorizations

SOURCE: Docket No. 19589, 45 FR 38346, June 9, 1980, unless otherwise noted.

§21.601 Applicability.

(a) This subpart prescribes—

(1) Procedural requirements for the issue of Technical Standard Order authorizations;

(2) Rules governing the holders of Technical Standard Order authorizations; and

(3) Procedural requirements for the issuance of a letter of Technical Standard Order design approval.

(b) For the purpose of this subpart—

(1) A Technical Standard Order (referred to in this subpart as "TSO") is issued by the Administrator and is a minimum performance standard for specified articles (for the purpose of this subpart, articles means materials, parts, processes, or appliances) used on civil aircraft.

(2) A TSO authorization is an FAA design and production approval issued to the manufacturer of an article which has been found to meet a specific TSO.

(3) A letter of TSO design approval is an FAA design approval for a foreign-manufactured article which has been

found to meet a specific TSO in accordance with the procedures of § 21.617.

(4) An article manufactured under a TSO authorization, an FAA letter of acceptance as described in § 21.603(b), or an appliance manufactured under a letter of TSO design approval described in § 21.617 is an approved article or appliance for the purpose of meeting the regulations of this chapter that require the article to be approved.

(5) An article manufacturer is the person who controls the design and quality of the article produced (or to be produced, in the case of an application), including the parts of them and any processes or services related to them that are procured from an outside source.

(c) The Administrator does not issue a TSO authorization if the manufacturing facilities for the product are located outside of the United States, unless the Administrator finds that the location of the manufacturer's facilities places no undue burden on the FAA in administering applicable airworthiness requirements.

§ 21.603 TSO marking and privileges.

(a) Except as provided in paragraph (b) of this section and § 21.617(c), no person may identify an article with a TSO marking unless that person holds a TSO authorization and the article meets applicable TSO performance standards.

(b) The holder of an FAA letter of acceptance of a statement of conformance issued for an article before July 1, 1962, or any TSO authorization issued after July 1, 1962, may continue to manufacture that article without obtaining a new TSO authorization but shall comply with the requirements of §§ 21.3, 21.607 through 21.615, 21.619, and 21.621.

(c) Notwithstanding paragraphs (a) and (b) of this section, after August 6, 1976, no person may identify or mark an article with any of the following TSO numbers:

(1) TSO-C18, -C18a, -C18b, -C18c.

(2) TSO-C24.

(3) TSO-C33.

(4) TSO-C61 or C61a.

§ 21.605 Application and issue.

(a) The manufacturer (or an authorized agent) shall submit an application for a TSO authorization, together with the following documents, to the Manager of the Aircraft Certification Office for the geographic area in which the applicant is located:

(1) A statement of conformance certifying that the applicant has met the requirements of this subpart and that the article concerned meets the applicable TSO that is effective on the date of application for that article.

(2) One copy of the technical data required in the applicable TSO.

(3) A description of its quality control system in the detail specified in § 21.143. In complying with this section, the applicant may refer to current quality control data filed with the FAA as part of a previous TSO authorization application.

(b) When a series of minor changes in accordance with § 21.611 is anticipated, the applicant may set forth in its application the basic model number of the article and the part number of the components with open brackets after it to denote that suffix change letters or numbers (or combinations of them) will be added from time to time.

(c) After receiving the application and other documents required by paragraph (a) of this section to substantiate compliance with this part, and after a determination has been made of its ability to produce duplicate articles under this part, the Administrator issues a TSO authorization (including all TSO deviations granted to the applicant) to the applicant to identify the article with the applicable TSO marking.

(d) If the application is deficient, the applicant must, when requested by the Administrator, submit any additional information necessary to show compliance with this part. If the applicant fails to submit the additional information within 30 days after the Administrator's request, the application is denied and the applicant is so notified.

(e) The Administrator issues or denies the application within 30 days after its receipt or, if additional information has been requested, within 30 days after receiving that information.

[Doc. No. 19589, 45 FR 38346, June 9, 1980, as amended by Amdt. 21–67, 54 FR 39291, Sept. 25, 1989]

§21.607 General rules governing holders of TSO authorizations.

Each manufacturer of an article for which a TSO authorization has been issued under this part shall—

(a) Manufacture the article in accordance with this part and the applicable TSO;

(b) Conduct all required tests and inspections and establish and maintain a quality control system adequate to ensure that the article meets the requirements of paragraph (a) of this section and is in condition for safe operation;

(c) Prepare and maintain, for each model of each article for which a TSO authorization has been issued, a current file of complete technical data and records in accordance with §21.613; and

(d) Permanently and legibly mark each article to which this section applies with the following information:

(1) The name and address of the manufacturer.

(2) The name, type, part number, or model designation of the article.

(3) The serial number or the date of manufacture of the article or both.

(4) The applicable TSO number.

§21.609 Approval for deviation.

(a) Each manufacturer who requests approval to deviate from any performance standard of a TSO shall show that the standards from which a deviation is requested are compensated for by factors or design features providing an equivalent level of safety.

(b) The request for approval to deviate, together with all pertinent data, must be submitted to the Manager of the Aircraft Certification Office for the geographic area in which the manufacturer is located. If the article is manufactured in another country, the request for approval to deviate, together with all pertinent data, must be submitted through the civil aviation authority in that country to the FAA.

[Doc. No. 19589, 45 FR 38346, June 9, 1980, as amended by Amdt. 21–67, 54 FR 39291, Sept. 25, 1989]

§21.611 Design changes.

(a) *Minor changes by the manufacturer holding a TSO authorization.* The manufacturer of an article under an authorization issued under this part may make minor design changes (any change other than a major change) without further approval by the Administrator. In this case, the changed article keeps the original model number (part numbers may be used to identify minor changes) and the manufacturer shall forward to the appropriate Aircraft Certification Office for the geographic area, any revised data that are necessary for compliance with §21.605(b).

(b) *Major changes by manufacturer holding a TSO authorization.* Any design change by the manufacturer that is extensive enough to require a substantially complete investigation to determine compliance with a TSO is a major change. Before making such a change, the manufacturer shall assign a new type or model designation to the article and apply for an authorization under §21.605.

(c) *Changes by person other than manufacturer.* No design change by any person (other than the manufacturer who submitted the statement of conformance for the article) is eligible for approval under this part unless the person seeking the approval is a manufacturer and applies under §21.605(a) for a separate TSO authorization. Persons other than a manufacturer may obtain approval for design changes under Part 43 or under the applicable airworthiness regulations.

[Doc. No. 19589, 45 FR 38346, June 9, 1980, as amended by Amdt. 21–67, 54 FR 39291, Sept. 25, 1989]

§21.613 Recordkeeping requirements.

(a) *Keeping the records.* Each manufacturer holding a TSO authorization under this part shall, for each article manufactured under that authorization, keep the following records at its factory:

(1) A complete and current technical data file for each type or model article, including design drawings and specifications.

(2) Complete and current inspection records showing that all inspections

and tests required to ensure compliance with this part have been properly completed and documented.

(b) *Retention of records.* The manufacturer shall retain the records described in paragraph (a)(1) of this section until it no longer manufactures the article. At that time, copies of these records shall be sent to the Administrator. The manufacturer shall retain the records described in paragraph (a)(2) of this section for a period of at least 2 years.

§ 21.615 FAA inspection.

Upon the request of the Administrator, each manufacturer of an article under a TSO authorization shall allow the Administrator to—

(a) Inspect any article manufactured under that authorization;

(b) Inspect the manufacturer's quality control system;

(c) Witness any tests;

(d) Inspect the manufacturing facilities; and

(e) Inspect the technical data files on that article.

§ 21.617 Issue of letters of TSO design approval: import appliances.

(a) A letter of TSO design approval may be issued for an appliance that is manufactured in a foreign country with which the United States has an agreement for the acceptance of these appliances for export and import and that is to be imported into the United States if—

(1) The country in which the appliance was manufactured certifies that the appliance has been examined, tested, and found to meet the applicable TSO designated in § 21.305(b) or the applicable performance standards of the country in which the appliance was manufactured and any other performance standards the Administrator may prescribe to provide a level of safety equivalent to that provided by the TSO designated in § 21.305(b); and

(2) The manufacturer has submitted one copy of the technical data required in the applicable performance standard through its civil aviation authority.

(b) The letter of TSO design approval will be issued by the Administrator and must list any deviation granted to the manufacturer under § 21.609.

(c) After the Administrator has issued a letter of TSO design approval and the country of manufacture issues a Certificate of Airworthiness for Export as specified in § 21.502(a), the manufacturer shall be authorized to identify the appliance with the TSO marking requirements described in § 21.607(d) and in the applicable TSO. Each appliance must be accompanied by a Certificate of Airworthiness for Export as specified in § 21.502(a) issued by the country of manufacture.

§ 21.619 Noncompliance.

The Administrator may, upon notice, withdraw the TSO authorization or letter of TSO design approval of any manufacturer who identifies with a TSO marking an article not meeting the performance standards of the applicable TSO.

§ 21.621 Transferability and duration.

A TSO authorization or letter of TSO design approval issued under this part is not transferable and is effective until surrendered, withdrawn, or otherwise terminated by the Administrator.

PART 23—AIRWORTHINESS STANDARDS: NORMAL, UTILITY, ACROBATIC, AND COMMUTER CATEGORY AIRPLANES

SPECIAL FEDERAL AVIATION REGULATION NO. 23

Subpart A—General

Sec.
23.1 Applicability.
23.2 Special retroactive requirements.
23.3 Airplane categories.

Subpart B—Flight

GENERAL

23.21 Proof of compliance.
23.23 Load distribution limits.
23.25 Weight limits.
23.29 Empty weight and corresponding center of gravity.
23.31 Removable ballast.
23.33 Propeller speed and pitch limits.

PERFORMANCE

23.45 General.
23.49 Stalling period.
23.51 Takeoff speeds.
23.53 Takeoff performance.

AIRPLANE FLIGHT MANUAL AND APPROVED
MANUAL MATERIAL

AUTHORITY: 49 U.S.C. 106(g), 40113, 44701–
44702, 44704.

SOURCE: Docket No. 4080, 29 FR 17955, Dec.
18. 1964; 30 FR 258, Jan. 9, 1965, unless otherwise noted.

SPECIAL FEDERAL AVIATION REGULATION
No. 23

1. *Applicability.* An applicant is entitled to
a type certificate in the normal category for
a reciprocating or turbopropeller multiengine powered small airplane that is to be certificated to carry more than 10 occupants
and that is intended for use in operations
under Part 135 of the Federal Aviation Regulations if he shows compliance with the applicable requirements of Part 23 of the Federal Aviation Regulations, as supplemented
or modified by the additional airworthiness
requirements of this regulation.

2. *References.* Unless otherwise provided, all
references in this regulation to specific sections of Part 23 of the Federal Aviation Regulations are those sections of Part 23 in effect on March 30, 1967.

FLIGHT REQUIREMENTS

3. *General.* Compliance must be shown with
the applicable requirements of Subpart B of
Part 23 of the Federal Aviation Regulations
in effect on March 30, 1967, as supplemented
or modified in sections 4 through 10 of this
regulation.

PERFORMANCE

4. *General.* (a) Unless otherwise prescribed
in this regulation, compliance with each applicable performance requirement in sections
4 through 7 of this regulation must be shown
for ambient atmospheric conditions and still
air.

(b) The performance must correspond to
the propulsive thrust available under the
particular ambient atmospheric conditions
and the particular flight condition. The
available propulsive thrust must correspond
to engine power or thrust, not exceeding the
approved power or thrust less—
(1) Installation losses; and
(2) The power or equivalent thrust absorbed by the accessories and services appropriate to the particular ambient atmospheric
conditions and the particular flight condition.
(c) Unless otherwise prescribed in this regulation, the applicant must select the takeoff, en route, and landing configurations for
the airplane.
(d) The airplane configuration may vary
with weight, altitude, and temperature, to
the extent they are compatible with the operating procedures required by paragraph (e)
of this section.
(e) Unless otherwise prescribed in this regulation, in determining the critical engine
inoperative takeoff performance, the accelerate-stop distance, takeoff distance,
changes in the airplane's configuration,
speed, power, and thrust, must be made in
accordance with procedures established by
the applicant for operation in service.
(f) Procedures for the execution of balked
landings must be established by the applicant and included in the Airplane Flight
Manual.
(g) The procedures established under paragraphs (e) and (f) of this section must—
(1) Be able to be consistently executed in
service by a crew of average skill;
(2) Use methods or devices that are safe
and reliable; and
(3) Include allowance for any time delays,
in the execution of the procedures, that may
reasonably be expected in service.
5. *Takeoff*—(a) *General.* The takeoff speeds
described in paragraph (b), the accelerate-
stop distance described in paragraph (c), and
the takeoff distance described in paragraph
(d), must be determined for—
(1) Each weight, altitude, and ambient
temperature within the operational limits
selected by the applicant;
(2) The selected configuration for takeoff;
(3) The center of gravity in the most unfavorable position;
(4) The operating engine within approved
operating limitation; and
(5) Takeoff data based on smooth, dry,
hard-surface runway.
(b) *Takeoff speeds.* (1) The decision speed V_1
is the calibrated airspeed on the ground at
which, as a result of engine failure or other
reasons, the pilot is assumed to have made a
decision to continue or discontinue the takeoff. The speed V_1 must be selected by the applicant but may not be less than—
(i) 1.10 V_{s1};
(ii) 1.10 V_{MC};

(iii) A speed that permits acceleration to V_1 and stop in accordance with paragraph (c) allowing credit for an overrun distance equal to that required to stop the airplane from a ground speed of 35 knots utilizing maximum braking; or

(iv) A speed at which the airplane can be rotated for takeoff and shown to be adequate to safely continue the takeoff, using normal piloting skill, when the critical engine is suddenly made inoperative.

(2) Other essential takeoff speeds necessary for safe operation of the airplane must be determined and shown in the Airplane Flight Manual.

(c) *Accelerate-stop distance.* (1) The accelerate-stop distance is the sum of the distances necessary to—

(i) Accelerate the airplane from a standing start to V_1; and

(ii) Decelerate the airplane from V_1 to a speed not greater than 35 knots, assuming that in the case of engine failure, failure of the critical engine is recognized by the pilot at the speed V_1. The landing gear must remain in the extended position and maximum braking may be utilized during deceleration.

(2) Means other than wheel brakes may be used to determine the accelerate-stop distance if that means is available with the critical engine inoperative and—

(i) Is safe and reliable;

(ii) Is used so that consistent results can be expected under normal operating conditions; and

(iii) Is such that exceptional skill is not required to control the airplane.

(d) *All engines operating takeoff distance.* The all engine operating takeoff distance is the horizontal distance required to takeoff and climb to a height of 50 feet above the takeoff surface according to procedures in FAR 23.51(a).

(e) *One-engine-inoperative takeoff.* The maximum weight must be determined for each altitude and temperature within the operational limits established for the airplane, at which the airplane has takeoff capability after failure of the critical engine at or above V_1 determined in accordance with paragraph (b) of this section. This capability may be established—

(1) By demonstrating a measurably positive rate of climb with the airplane in the takeoff configuration, landing gear extended; or

(2) By demonstrating the capability of maintaining flight after engine failure utilizing procedures prescribed by the applicant.

6. *Climb*—(a) *Landing climb: All-engines-operating.* The maximum weight must be determined with the airplane in the landing configuration, for each altitude, and ambient temperature within the operational limits established for the airplane and with the most unfavorable center of gravity and out-

of-ground effect in free air, at which the steady gradient of climb will not be less than 3.3 percent, with:

(1) The engines at the power that is available 8 seconds after initiation of movement of the power or thrust controls from the mimimum flight idle to the takeoff position.

(2) A climb speed not greater than the approach speed established under section 7 of this regulation and not less than the greater of 1.05_{MC} or $1.10V_{S1}$.

(b) *En route climb, one-engine-inoperative.* (1) the maximum weight must be determined with the airplane in the en route configuration, the critical engine inoperative, the remaining engine at not more than maximum continuous power or thrust, and the most unfavorable center of gravity, at which the gradient at climb will be not less than—

(i) 1.2 percent (or a gradient equivalent to $0.20 V_{so}2$, if greater) at 5,000 feet and an ambient temperature of 41 °F. or

(ii) 0.6 percent (or a gradient equivalent to $0.01 V_{so}2$, if greater) at 5,000 feet and ambient temperature of 81 °F.

(2) The minimum climb gradient specified in subdivisions (i) and (ii) of subparagraph (1) of this paragraph must vary linearly between 41 °F. and 81 °F. and must change at the same rate up to the maximum operational temperature approved for the airplane.

7. *Landing.* The landing distance must be determined for standard atmosphere at each weight and altitude in accordance with FAR 23.75(a), except that instead of the gliding approach specified in FAR 23.75(a)(1), the landing may be preceded by a steady approach down to the 50-foot height at a gradient of descent not greater than 5.2 percent (3°) at a calibrated airspeed not less than 1.3_{s1}.

TRIM

8. *Trim*—(a) *Lateral and directional trim.* The airplane must maintain lateral and directional trim in level flight at a speed of V_h or V_{MO}/M_{MO}, whichever is lower, with landing gear and wing flaps retracted.

(b) *Longitudinal trim.* The airplane must maintain longitudinal trim during the following conditions, except that it need not maintain trim at a speed greater than V_{MO}/M_{MO}:

(1) In the approach conditions specified in FAR 23.161(c)(3) through (5), except that instead of the speeds specified therein, trim must be maintained with a stick force of not more than 10 pounds down to a speed used in showing compliance with section 7 of this regulation or $1.4 V_{s1}$ whichever is lower.

(2) In level flight at any speed from V_H or V_{MO}/M_{MO}, whichever is lower, to either V_z or $1.4 V_{s1}$, with the landing gear and wing flaps retracted.

9. *Static longitudinal stability.* (a) In showing compliance with the provisions of FAR 23.175(b) and with paragraph (b) of this section, the airspeed must return to within ±7½ percent of the trim speed.

(b) *Cruise stability.* The stick force curve must have a stable slope for a speed range of ±50 knots from the trim speed except that the speeds need not exceed V_{FC}/M_{FC} or be less than 1.4 V_{s1}. This speed range will be considered to begin at the outer extremes of the friction band and the stick force may not exceed 50 pounds with—

(i) Landing gear retracted;

(ii) Wing flaps retracted;

(iii) The maximum cruising power as selected by the applicant as an operating limitation for turbine engines or 75 percent of maximum continuous power for reciprocating engines except that the power need not exceed that required at V_{MO}/M_{MO}:

(iv) Maximum takeoff weight; and

(v) The airplane trimmed for level flight with the power specified in subparagraph (iii) of this paragraph.

V_{FC}/M_{FC} may not be less than a speed midway between V_{MO}/M_{MO} and V_{DF}/M_{DF}, except that, for altitudes where Mach number is the limiting factor, M_{FC} need not exceed the Mach number at which effective speed warning occurs.

(c) *Climb stability. For turbopropeller powered airplanes only.* In showing compliance with FAR 23.175(a), an applicant must in lieu of the power specified in FAR 23.175(a)(4), use the maximum power or thrust selected by the applicant as an operating limitation for use during climb at the best rate of climb speed except that the speed need not be less than 1.4 V_{s1}.

STALLS

10. *Stall warning.* If artificial stall warning is required to comply with the requirements of FAR 23.207, the warning device must give clearly distinguishable indications under expected conditions of flight. The use of a visual warning device that requires the attention of the crew within the cockpit is not acceptable by itself.

CONTROL SYSTEMS

11. *Electric trim tabs.* The airplane must meet the requirements of FAR 23.677 and in addition it must be shown that the airplane is safely controllable and that a pilot can perform all the maneuvers and operations necessary to effect a safe landing following any probable electric trim tab runaway which might be reasonably expected in service allowing for appropriate time delay after pilot recognition of the runaway. This demonstration must be conducted at the critical airplane weights and center of gravity positions.

INSTRUMENTS: INSTALLATION

12. *Arrangement and visibility.* Each instrument must meet the requirements of FAR 23.1321 and in addition—

(a) Each flight, navigation, and powerplant instrument for use by any pilot must be plainly visible to him from his station with the minimum practicable deviation from his normal position and line of vision when he is looking forward along the flight path.

(b) The flight instruments required by FAR 23.1303 and by the applicable operating rules must be grouped on the instrument panel and centered as nearly as practicable about the vertical plane of each pilot's forward vision. In addition—

(1) The instrument that most effectively indicates the attitude must be on the panel in the top center position;

(2) The instrument that most effectively indicates airspeed must be adjacent to and directly to the left of the instrument in the top center position;

(3) The instrument that most effectively indicates altitude must be adjacent to and directly to the right of the instrument in the top center position; and

(4) The instrument that most effectively indicates direction of flight must be adjacent to and directly below the instrument in the top center position.

13. *Airspeed indicating system.* Each airspeed indicating system must meet the requirements of FAR 23.1323 and in addition—

(a) Airspeed indicating instruments must be of an approved type and must be calibrated to indicate true airspeed at sea level in the standard atmosphere with a mimimum practicable instrument calibration error when the corresponding pilot and static pressures are supplied to the instruments.

(b) The airspeed indicating system must be calibrated to determine the system error, i.e., the relation between IAS and CAS, in flight and during the accelerate takeoff ground run. The ground run calibration must be obtained between 0.8 of the mimimum value of V_1 and 1.2 times the maximum value of V_1, considering the approved ranges of altitude and weight. The ground run calibration will be determined assuming an engine failure at the mimimum value of V_1.

(c) The airspeed error of the installation excluding the instrument calibration error, must not exceed 3 percent or 5 knots whichever is greater, throughout the speed range from V_{MO} to 1.3S_1 with flaps retracted and from 1.3 VS_O to V_{FE} with flaps in the landing position.

(d) Information showing the relationship between IAS and CAS must be shown in the Airplane Flight Manual.

14. *Static air vent system.* The static air vent system must meet the requirements of FAR 23.1325. The altimeter system calibration

must be determined and shown in the Airplane Flight Manual.

OPERATING LIMITATIONS AND INFORMATION

15. *Maximum operating limit speed V_{MO}/M_{MO}.* Instead of establishing operating limitations based on V_{ME} and V_{NO}, the applicant must establish a maximum operating limit speed V_{MO}/M_{MO} in accordance with the following:

(a) The maximum operating limit speed must not exceed the design cruising speed Vc and must be sufficiently below V_D/M_D or V_{DF}/M_{DF} to make it highly improbable that the latter speeds will be inadvertently exceeded in flight.

(b) The speed Vmo must not exceed 0.8 V_D/M_D or 0.8 V_{DF}/M_{DF} unless flight demonstrations involving upsets as specified by the Administrator indicates a lower speed margin will not result in speeds exceeding V_D/M_D or V_{DF}. Atmospheric variations, horizontal gusts, and equipment errors, and airframe production variations will be taken into account.

16. *Minimum flight crew.* In addition to meeting the requirements of FAR 23.1523, the applicant must establish the minimum number and type of qualified flight crew personnel sufficient for safe operation of the airplane considering—

(a) Each kind of operation for which the applicant desires approval;

(b) The workload on each crewmember considering the following:

(1) Flight path control.

(2) Collision avoidance.

(3) Navigation.

(4) Communications.

(5) Operation and monitoring of all essential aircraft systems.

(6) Command decisions; and

(c) The accessibility and ease of operation of necessary controls by the appropriate crewmember during all normal and emergency operations when at his flight station.

17. *Airspeed indicator.* The airspeed indicator must meet the requirements of FAR 23.1545 except that, the airspeed notations and markings in terms of V_{NO} and V_{NE} must be replaced by the V_{MO}/M_{MO} notations. The airspeed indicator markings must be easily read and understood by the pilot. A placard adjacent to the airspeed indicator is an acceptable means of showing compliance with the requirements of FAR 23.1545(c).

AIRPLANE FLIGHT MANUAL

18. *General.* The Airplane Flight Manual must be prepared in accordance with the requirements of FARs 23.1583 and 23.1587, and in addition the operating limitations and performance information set forth in sections 19 and 20 must be included.

19. *Operating limitations.* The Airplane Flight Manual must include the following limitations—

(a) *Airspeed limitations.* (1) The maximum operating limit speed V_{MO}/M_{MO} and a statement that this speed limit may not be deliberately exceeded in any regime of flight (climb, cruise, or descent) unless a higher speed is authorized for flight test or pilot training;

(2) If an airspeed limitation is based upon compressibility effects, a statement to this effect and information as to any symptoms, the probable behavior of the airplane, and the recommended recovery procedures; and

(3) The airspeed limits, shown in terms of V_{MO}/M_{MO} instead of V_{NO} and V_{NE}.

(b) *Takeoff weight limitations.* The maximum takeoff weight for each airport elevation, ambient temperature, and available takeoff runway length within the range selected by the applicant. This weight may not exceed the weight at which:

(1) The all-engine operating takeoff distance determined in accordance with section 5(d) or the accelerate-stop distance determined in accordance with section 5(c), whichever is greater, is equal to the available runway length;

(2) The airplane complies with the one-engine-inoperative takeoff requirements specified in section 5(e); and

(3) The airplane complies with the one-engine-inoperative en route climb requirements specified in section 6(b), assuming that a standard temperature lapse rate exists from the airport elevation to the altitude of 5,000 feet, except that the weight may not exceed that corresponding to a temperature of 41 °F at 5,000 feet.

20. *Performance information.* The Airplane Flight Manual must contain the performance information determined in accordance with the provisions of the performance requirements of this regulation. The information must include the following:

(a) Sufficient information so that the takeoff weight limits specified in section 19(b) can be determined for all temperatures and altitudes within the operation limitations selected by the applicant.

(b) The conditions under which the performance information was obtained, including the airspeed at the 50-foot height used to determine landing distances.

(c) The performance information (determined by extrapolation and computed for the range of weights between the maximum landing and takeoff weights) for—

(1) Climb in the landing configuration; and

(2) Landing distance.

(d) Procedure established under section 4 of this regulation related to the limitations and information required by this section in the form of guidance material including any relevant limitations or information.

(e) An explanation of significant or unusual flight or ground handling characteristics of the airplane.

(f) Airspeeds, as indicated airspeeds, corresponding to those determined for takeoff in accordance with section 5(b).

21. *Maximum operating altitudes.* The maximum operating altitude to which operation is permitted, as limited by flight, structural, powerplant, functional, or equipment characteristics, must be specified in the Airplane Flight Manual.

22. *Stowage provision for Airplane Flight Manual.* Provision must be made for stowing the Airplane Flight Manual in a suitable fixed container which is readily accessible to the pilot.

23. *Operating procedures.* Procedures for restarting turbine engines in flight (including the effects of altitude) must be set forth in the Airplane Flight Manual.

AIRFRAME REQUIREMENTS

FLIGHT LOADS

24. *Engine torque.* (a) Each turbopropeller engine mount and its supporting structure must be designed for the torque effects of—

(1) The conditions set forth in FAR 23.361(a).

(2) The limit engine torque corresponding to takeoff power and propeller speed, multiplied by a factor accounting for propeller control system malfunction, including quick feathering action, simultaneously with 1 *g* level flight loads. In the absence of a rational analysis, a factor of 1.6 must be used.

(b) The limit torque is obtained by multiplying the mean torque by a factor of 1.25.

25. *Turbine engine gyroscopic loads.* Each turbopropeller engine mount and its supporting structure must be designed for the gyroscopic loads that result, with the engines at maximum continuous r.p.m., under either—

(a) The conditions prescribed in FARs 23.351 and 23.423; or

(b) All possible combinations of the following:

(1) A yaw velocity of 2.5 radius per second.

(2) A pitch velocity of 1.0 radians per second.

(3) A normal load factor of 2.5.

(4) Maximum continuous thrust.

26. *Unsymmetrical loads due to engine failure.* (a) Turbopropeller powered airplanes must be designed for the unsymmetrical loads resulting from the failure of the critical engine including the following conditions in combination with a single malfunction of the propeller drag limiting system, considering the probable pilot corrective action on the flight controls.

(1) At speeds between V_{MC} and V_D, the loads resulting from power failure because of fuel flow interruption are considered to be limit loads.

(2) At speeds between V_{MC} and V_C, the loads resulting from the disconnection of the engine compressor from the turbine or from loss of the turbine blades are considered to be ultimate loads.

(3) The time history of the thrust decay and drag buildup occurring as a result of the prescribed engine failures must be substantiated by test or other data applicable to the particular engine-propeller combination.

(4) The timing and magnitude of the probable pilot corrective action must be conservatively estimated, considering the characteristics of the particular engine-propeller-airplane combination.

(b) Pilot corrective action may be assumed to be initiated at the time maximum yawing velocity is reached, but not earlier than two seconds after the engine failure. The magnitude of the corrective action may be based on the control forces specified in FAR 23.397 except that lower forces may be assumed where it is shown by analysis or test that these forces can control the yaw and roll resulting from the prescribed engine failure conditions.

GROUND LOADS

27. *Dual wheel landing gear units.* Each dual wheel landing gear unit and its supporting structure must be shown to comply with the following:

(a) *Pivoting.* The airplane must be assumed to pivot about one side of the main gear with the brakes on that side locked. The limit vertical load factor must be 1.0 and the coefficient of friction 0.8. This condition need apply only to the main gear and its supporting structure.

(b) *Unequal tire inflation.* A 60–40 percent distribution of the loads established in accordance with FAR 23.471 through FAR 23.483 must be applied to the dual wheels.

(c) *Flat tire.* (1) Sixty percent of the loads specified in FAR 23.471 through FAR 23.483 must be applied to either wheel in a unit.

(2) Sixty percent of the limit drag and side loads and 100 percent of the limit vertical load established in accordance with FARs 23.493 and 23.485 must be applied to either wheel in a unit except that the vertical load need not exceed the maximum vertical load in paragraph (c)(1) of this section.

FATIGUE EVALUATION

28. *Fatigue evaluation of wing and associated structure.* Unless it is shown that the structure, operating stress levels, materials, and expected use are comparable from a fatigue standpoint to a similar design which has had substantial satisfactory service experience, the strength, detail design, and the fabrication of those parts of the wing, wing carry-through, and attaching structure whose failure would be catastrophic must be evaluated under either—

(a) A fatigue strength investigation in which the structure is shown by analysis, tests, or both to be able to withstand the repeated loads of variable magnitude expected in service; or

(b) A fail-safe strength investigation in which it is shown by analysis, tests, or both that catastrophic failure of the structure is not probable after fatigue, or obvious partial failure, of a principal structural element, and that the remaining structure is able to withstand a static ultimate load factor of 75 percent of the critical limit load factor at V_c. These loads must be multiplied by a factor of 1.15 unless the dynamic effects of failure under static load are otherwise considered.

DESIGN AND CONSTRUCTION

29. *Flutter.* For Multiengine turbopropeller powered airplanes, a dynamic evaluation must be made and must include—

(a) The significant elastic, inertia, and aerodynamic forces associated with the rotations and displacements of the plane of the propeller; and

(b) Engine-propeller-nacelle stiffness and damping variations appropriate to the particular configuration.

LANDING GEAR

30. *Flap operated landing gear warning device.* Airplanes having retractable landing gear and wing flaps must be equipped with a warning device that functions continuously when the wing flaps are extended to a flap position that activates the warning device to give adequate warning before landing, using normal landing procedures, if the landing gear is not fully extended and locked. There may not be a manual shut off for this warning device. The flap position sensing unit may be installed at any suitable location. The system for this device may use any part of the system (including the aural warning device) provided for other landing gear warning devices.

PERSONNEL AND CARGO ACCOMMODATIONS

31. *Cargo and baggage compartments.* Cargo and baggage compartments must be designed to meet the requirements of FAR 23.787 (a) and (b), and in addition means must be provided to protect passengers from injury by the contents of any cargo or baggage compartment when the ultimate forward inertia force is 9g.

32. *Doors and exits.* The airplane must meet the requirements of FAR 23.783 and FAR 23.807 (a)(3), (b), and (c), and in addition:

(a) There must be a means to lock and safeguard each external door and exit against opening in flight either inadvertently by persons, or as a result of mechanical failure. Each external door must be operable from both the inside and the outside.

(b) There must be means for direct visual inspection of the locking mechanism by

crewmembers to determine whether external doors and exits, for which the initial opening movement is outward, are fully locked. In addition, there must be a visual means to signal to crewmembers when normally used external doors are closed and fully locked.

(c) The passenger entrance door must qualify as a floor level emergency exit. Each additional required emergency exit except floor level exits must be located over the wing or must be provided with acceptable means to assist the occupants in descending to the ground. In addition to the passenger entrance door:

(1) For a total seating capacity of 15 or less, an emergency exit as defined in FAR 23.807(b) is required on each side of the cabin.

(2) For a total seating capacity of 16 through 23, three emergency exits as defined in 23.807(b) are required with one on the same side as the door and two on the side opposite the door.

(d) An evacuation demonstration must be conducted utilizing the maximum number of occupants for which certification is desired. It must be conducted under simulated night conditions utilizing only the emergency exits on the most critical side of the aircraft. The participants must be representative of average airline passengers with no prior practice or rehearsal for the demonstration. Evacuation must be completed within 90 seconds.

(e) Each emergency exit must be marked with the word "Exit" by a sign which has white letters 1 inch high on a red background 2 inches high, be self-illuminated or independently internally electrically illuminated, and have a minimum luminescence (brightness) of at least 160 microlamberts. The colors may be reversed if the passenger compartment illumination is essentially the same.

(f) Access to window type emergency exits must not be obstructed by seats or seat backs.

(g) The width of the main passenger aisle at any point between seats must equal or exceed the values in the following table.

Total seating capacity	Minimum main passenger aisle width	
	Less than 25 inches from floor	25 inches and more from floor
10 through 23	9 inches	15 inches.

MISCELLANEOUS

33. *Lightning strike protection.* Parts that are electrically insulated from the basic airframe must be connected to it through lightning arrestors unless a lightning strike on the insulated part—

(a) Is improbable because of shielding by other parts; or

(b) Is not hazardous.

34. *Ice protection.* If certification with ice protection provisions is desired, compliance with the following requirements must be shown:

(a) The recommended procedures for the use of the ice protection equipment must be set forth in the Airplane Flight Manual.

(b) An analysis must be performed to establish, on the basis of the airplane's operational needs, the adequacy of the ice protection system for the various components of the airplane. In addition, tests of the ice protection system must be conducted to demonstrate that the airplane is capable of operating safely in continuous maximum and intermittent maximum icing conditions as described in FAR 25, appendix C.

(c) Compliance with all or portions of this section may be accomplished by reference, where applicable because of similarity of the designs, to analysis and tests performed by the applicant for a type certificated model.

35. *Maintenance information.* The applicant must make available to the owner at the time of delivery of the airplane the information he considers essential for the proper maintenance of the airplane. That information must include the following:

(a) Description of systems, including electrical, hydraulic, and fuel controls.

(b) Lubrication instructions setting forth the frequency and the lubricants and fluids which are to be used in the various systems.

(c) Pressures and electrical loads applicable to the various systems.

(d) Tolerances and adjustments necessary for proper functioning.

(e) Methods of leveling, raising, and towing.

(f) Methods of balancing control surfaces.

(g) Identification of primary and secondary structures.

(h) Frequency and extent of inspections necessary to the proper operation of the airplane.

(i) Special repair methods applicable to the airplane.

(j) Special inspection techniques, including those that require X-ray, ultrasonic, and magnetic particle inspection.

(k) List of special tools.

PROPULSION

GENERAL

36. *Vibration characteristics.* For turbopropeller powered airplanes, the engine installation must not result in vibration characteristics of the engine exceeding those established during the type certification of the engine.

37. *In-flight restarting of engine.* If the engine on turbopropeller powered airplanes cannot be restarted at the maximum cruise altitude, a determination must be made of the altitude below which restarts can be consistently accomplished. Restart information must be provided in the Airplane Flight Manual.

38. *Engines*—(a) *For turbopropeller powered airplanes.* The engine installation must comply with the following requirements:

(1) *Engine isolation.* The powerplants must be arranged and isolated from each other to allow operation, in at least one configuration, so that the failure or malfunction of any engine, or of any system that can affect the engine, will not—

(i) Prevent the continued safe operation of the remaining engines; or

(ii) Require immediate action by any crewmember for continued safe operation.

(2) *Control of engine rotation.* There must be a means to individually stop and restart the rotation of any engine in flight except that engine rotation need not be stopped if continued rotation could not jeopardize the safety of the airplane. Each component of the stopping and restarting system on the engine side of the firewall, and that might be exposed to fire, must be at least fire resistant. If hydraulic propeller feathering systems are used for this purpose, the feathering lines must be at least fire resistant under the operating conditions that may be expected to exist during feathering.

(3) *Engine speed and gas temperature control devices.* The powerplant systems associated with engine control devices, systems, and instrumentation must provide reasonable assurance that those engine operating limitations that adversely affect turbine rotor structural integrity will not be exceeded in service.

(b) *For reciprocating-engine powered airplanes.* To provide engine isolation, the powerplants must be arranged and isolated from each other to allow operation, in at least one configuration, so that the failure or malfunction of any engine, or of any system that can affect that engine, will not—

(1) Prevent the continued safe operation of the remaining engines; or

(2) Require immediate action by any crewmember for continued safe operation.

39. *Turbopropeller reversing systems.* (a) Turbopropeller reversing systems intended for ground operation must be designed so that no single failure or malfunction of the system will result in unwanted reverse thrust under any expected operating condition. Failure of structural elements need not be considered if the probability of this kind of failure is extremely remote.

(b) Turbopropeller reversing systems intended for in-flight use must be designed so that no unsafe condition will result during normal operation of the system, or from any failure (or reasonably likely combination of failures) of the reversing system, under any anticipated condition of operation of the airplane. Failure of structural elements need not be considered if the probability of this kind of failure is extremely remote.

171

(c) Compliance with this section may be shown by failure analysis, testing, or both for propeller systems that allow propeller blades to move from the flight low-pitch position to a position that is substantially less than that at the normal flight low-pitch stop position. The analysis may include or be supported by the analysis made to show compliance with the type certification of the propeller and associated installation components. Credit will be given for pertinent analysis and testing completed by the engine and propeller manufacturers.

40. *Turbopropeller drag-limiting systems.* Turbopropeller drag-limiting systems must be designed so that no single failure or malfunction of any of the systems during normal or emergency operation results in propeller drag in excess of that for which the airplane was designed. Failure of structural elements of the drag-limiting systems need not be considered if the probability of this kind of failure is extremely remote.

41. *Turbine engine powerplant operating characteristics.* For turbopropeller powered airplanes, the turbine engine powerplant operating characteristics must be investigated in flight to determine that no adverse characteristics (such as stall, surge, or flameout) are present to a hazardous degree, during normal and emergency operation within the range of operating limitations of the airplane and of the engine.

42. *Fuel flow.* (a) For turbopropeller powered airplanes—

(1) The fuel system must provide for continuous supply of fuel to the engines for normal operation without interruption due to depletion of fuel in any tank other than the main tank; and

(2) The fuel flow rate for turbopropeller engine fuel pump systems must not be less than 125 percent of the fuel flow required to develop the standard sea level atmospheric conditions takeoff power selected and included as an operating limitation in the Airplane Flight Manual.

(b) For reciprocating engine powered airplanes, it is acceptable for the fuel flow rate for each pump system (main and reserve supply) to be 125 percent of the takeoff fuel consumption of the engine.

FUEL SYSTEM COMPONENTS

43. *Fuel pumps.* For turbopropeller powered airplanes, a reliable and independent power source must be provided for each pump used with turbine engines which do not have provisions for mechanically driving the main pumps. It must be demonstrated that the pump installations provide a reliability and durability equivalent to that provided by FAR 23.991(a).

44. *Fuel strainer or filter.* For turbopropeller powered airplanes, the following apply:

(a) There must be a fuel strainer or filter between the tank outlet and the fuel metering device of the engine. In addition, the fuel strainer or filter must be—

(1) Between the tank outlet and the engine-driven positive displacement pump inlet, if there is an engine-driven positive displacement pump;

(2) Accessible for drainage and cleaning and, for the strainer screen, easily removable; and

(3) Mounted so that its weight is not supported by the connecting lines or by the inlet or outlet connections of the strainer or filter itself.

(b) Unless there are means in the fuel system to prevent the accumulation of ice on the filter, there must be means to automatically maintain the fuel flow if ice-clogging of the filter occurs; and

(c) The fuel strainer or filter must be of adequate capacity (with respect to operating limitations established to insure proper service) and of appropriate mesh to insure proper engine operation, with the fuel contaminated to a degree (with respect to particle size and density) that can be reasonably expected in service. The degree of fuel filtering may not be less than that established for the engine type certification.

45. *Lightning strike protection.* Protection must be provided against the ignition of flammable vapors in the fuel vent system due to lightning strikes.

COOLING

46. *Cooling test procedures for turbopropeller powered airplanes.* (a) Turbopropeller powered airplanes must be shown to comply with the requirements of FAR 23.1041 during takeoff, climb en route, and landing stages of flight that correspond to the applicable performance requirements. The cooling test must be conducted with the airplane in the configuration and operating under the conditions that are critical relative to cooling during each stage of flight. For the cooling tests a temperature is "stabilized" when its rate of change is less than 2 °F. per minute.

(b) Temperatures must be stabilized under the conditions from which entry is made into each stage of flight being investigated unless the entry condition is not one during which component and engine fluid temperatures would stabilize, in which case, operation through the full entry condition must be conducted before entry into the stage of flight being investigated in order to allow temperatures to reach their natural levels at the time of entry. The takeoff cooling test must be preceded by a period during which the powerplant component and engine fluid temperatures are stabilized with the engines at ground idle.

(c) Cooling tests for each stage of flight must be continued until—

(1) The component and engine fluid temperatures stabilize;

(2) The stage of flight is completed; or

(3) An operating limitation is reached.

INDUCTION SYSTEM

47. *Air induction.* For turbopropeller powered airplanes—

(a) There must be means to prevent hazardous quantities of fuel leakage or overflow from drains, vents, or other components of flammable fluid systems from entering the engine intake system; and

(b) The air inlet ducts must be located or protected so as to minimize the ingestion of foreign matter during takeoff, landing, and taxiing.

48. *Induction system icing protection.* For turbopropeller powered airplanes, each turbine engine must be able to operate throughout its flight power range without adverse effect on engine operation or serious loss of power or thrust, under the icing conditions specified in appendix C of FAR 25. In addition, there must be means to indicate to appropriate flight crewmembers the functioning of the powerplant ice protection system.

49. *Turbine engine bleed air systems.* Turbine engine bleed air systems of turbopropeller powered airplanes must be investigated to determine—

(a) That no hazard to the airplane will result if a duct rupture occurs. This condition must consider that a failure of the duct can occur anywhere between the engine port and the airplane bleed service; and

(b) That if the bleed air system is used for direct cabin pressurization, it is not possible for hazardous contamination of the cabin air system to occur in event of lubrication system failure.

EXHAUST SYSTEM

50. *Exhaust system drains.* Turbopropeller engine exhaust systems having low spots or pockets must incorporate drains at such locations. These drains must discharge clear of the airplane in normal and ground attitudes to prevent the accumulation of fuel after the failure of an attempted engine start.

POWERPLANT CONTROLS AND ACCESSORIES

51. *Engine controls.* If throttles or power levers for turbopropeller powered airplanes are such that any position of these controls will reduce the fuel flow to the engine(s) below that necessary for satisfactory and safe idle operation of the engine while the airplane is in flight, a means must be provided to prevent inadvertent movement of the control into this position. The means provided must incorporate a positive lock or stop at this idle position and must require a separate and distinct operation by the crew to displace the control from the normal engine operating range.

52. *Reverse thrust controls.* For turbopropeller powered airplanes, the propeller reverse thrust controls must have a means to prevent their inadvertent operation. The means must have a positive lock or stop at the idle position and must require a separate and distinct operation by the crew to displace the control from the flight regime.

53. *Engine ignition systems.* Each turbopropeller airplane ignition system must be considered an essential electrical load.

54. *Powerplant accessories.* The powerplant accessories must meet the requirements of FAR 23.1163, and if the continued rotation of any accessory remotely driven by the engine is hazardous when malfunctioning occurs, there must be means to prevent rotation without interfering with the continued operation of the engine.

POWERPLANT FIRE PROTECTION

55. *Fire detector system.* For turbopropeller powered airplanes, the following apply:

(a) There must be a means that ensures prompt detection of fire in the engine compartment. An overtemperature switch in each engine cooling air exit is an acceptable method of meeting this requirement.

(b) Each fire detector must be constructed and installed to withstand the vibration, inertia, and other loads to which it may be subjected in operation.

(c) No fire detector may be affected by any oil, water, other fluids, or fumes that might be present.

(d) There must be means to allow the flight crew to check, in flight, the functioning of each fire detector electric circuit.

(e) Wiring and other components of each fire detector system in a fire zone must be at least fire resistant.

56. *Fire protection, cowling and nacelle skin.* For reciprocating engine powered airplanes, the engine cowling must be designed and constructed so that no fire originating in the engine compartment can enter, either through openings or by burn through, any other region where it would create additional hazards.

57. *Flammable fluid fire protection.* If flammable fluids or vapors might be liberated by the leakage of fluid systems in areas other than engine compartments, there must be means to—

(a) Prevent the ignition of those fluids or vapors by any other equipment; or

(b) Control any fire resulting from that ignition.

EQUIPMENT

58. *Powerplant instruments.* (a) The following are required for turbopropeller airplanes:

(1) The instruments required by FAR 23.1305 (a)(1) through (4), (b)(2) and (4).

(2) A gas temperature indicator for each engine.

(3) Free air temperature indicator.

173

(4) A fuel flowmeter indicator for each engine.

(5) Oil pressure warning means for each engine.

(6) A torque indicator or adequate means for indicating power output for each engine.

(7) Fire warning indicator for each engine.

(8) A means to indicate when the propeller blade angle is below the low-pitch position corresponding to idle operation in flight.

(9) A means to indicate the functioning of the ice protection system for each engine.

(b) For turbopropeller powered airplanes, the turbopropeller blade position indicator must begin indicating when the blade has moved below the flight low-pitch position.

(c) The following instruments are required for reciprocating-engine powered airplanes:

(1) The instruments required by FAR 23.1305.

(2) A cylinder head temperature indicator for each engine.

(3) A manifold pressure indicator for each engine.

Systems and Equipments

GENERAL

59. Function and installation. The systems and equipment of the airplane must meet the requirements of FAR 23.1301, and the following:

(a) Each item of additional installed equipment must—

(1) Be of a kind and design appropriate to its intended function;

(2) Be labeled as to its identification, function, or operating limitations, or any applicable combination of these factors, unless misuse or inadvertent actuation cannot create a hazard;

(3) Be installed according to limitations specified for that equipment; and

(4) Function properly when installed.

(b) Systems and installations must be designed to safeguard against hazards to the aircraft in the event of their malfunction or failure.

(c) Where an installation, the functioning of which is necessary in showing compliance with the applicable requirements, requires a power supply, such installation must be considered an essential load on the power supply, and the power sources and the distribution system must be capable of supplying the following power loads in probable operation combinations and for probable durations:

(1) All essential loads after failure of any prime mover, power converter, or energy storage device.

(2) All essential loads after failure of any one engine on two-engine airplanes.

(3) In determining the probable operating combinations and durations of essential loads for the power failure conditions described in subparagraphs (1) and (2) of this paragraph, it is permissible to assume that the power loads are reduced in accordance with a monitoring procedure which is consistent with safety in the types of operations authorized.

60. Ventilation. The ventilation system of the airplane must meet the requirements of FAR 23.831, and in addition, for pressurized aircraft the ventilating air in flight crew and passenger compartments must be free of harmful or hazardous concentrations of gases and vapors in normal operation and in the event of reasonably probable failures or malfunctioning of the ventilating, heating, pressurization, or other systems, and equipment. If accumulation of hazardous quantities of smoke in the cockpit area is reasonably probable, smoke evacuation must be readily accomplished.

Electrical Systems and Equipment

61. General. The electrical systems and equipment of the airplane must meet the requirements of FAR 23.1351, and the following:

(a) *Electrical system capacity.* The required generating capacity, and number and kinds of power sources must—

(1) Be determined by an electrical load analysis, and

(2) Meet the requirements of FAR 23.1301.

(b) *Generating system.* The generating system includes electrical power sources, main power busses, transmission cables, and associated control, regulation, and protective devices. It must be designed so that—

(1) The system voltage and frequency (as applicable) at the terminals of all essential load equipment can be maintained within the limits for which the equipment is designed, during any probable operating conditions;

(2) System transients due to switching, fault clearing, or other causes do not make essential loads inoperative, and do not cause a smoke or fire hazard;

(3) There are means, accessible in flight to appropriate crewmembers, for the individual and collective disconnection of the electrical power sources from the system; and

(4) There are means to indicate to appropriate crewmembers the generating system quantities essential for the safe operation of the system, including the voltage and current supplied by each generator.

62. Electrical equipment and installation. Electrical equipment controls, and wiring must be installed so that operation of any one unit or system of units will not adversely affect the simultaneous operation of to the safe operation.

63. Distribution system. (a) For the purpose of complying with this section, the distribution system includes the distribution busses, their associated feeders and each control and protective device.

(b) Each system must be designed so that essential load circuits can be supplied in the event of reasonably probable faults or open circuits, including faults in heavy current carrying cables.

(c) If two independent sources of electrical power for particular equipment or systems are required by this regulation, their electrical energy supply must be insured by means such as duplicate electrical equipment, throwover switching, or multichannel or loop circuits separately routed.

64. *Circuit protective devices.* The circuit protective devices for the electrical circuits of the airplane must meet the requirements of FAR 23.1357, and in addition circuits for loads which are essential to safe operation must have individual and exclusive circuit protection.

[Doc. No. 8070, 34 FR 189, Jan. 7, 1969, as amended by SFAR 23–1, 34 FR 20176, Dec. 24, 1969; 35 FR 1102, Jan. 28, 1970]

Subpart A—General

§23.1 Applicability.

(a) This part prescribes airworthiness standards for the issue of type certificates, and changes to those certificates, for airplanes in the normal, utility, acrobatic, and commuter categories.

(b) Each person who applies under Part 21 for such a certificate or change must show compliance with the applicable requirements of this part.

[Doc. No. 4080, 29 FR 17955, Dec. 18, 1964, as amended by Amdt. 23–34, 52 FR 1825, Jan. 15, 1987]

§23.2 Special retroactive requirements.

(a) Notwithstanding §§21.17 and 21.101 of this chapter and irrespective of the type certification basis, each normal, utility, and acrobatic category airplane having a passenger seating configuration, excluding pilot seats, of nine or less, manufactured after December 12, 1986, or any such foreign airplane for entry into the United States must provide a safety belt and shoulder harness for each forward- or aft-facing seat which will protect the occupant from serious head injury when subjected to the inertia loads resulting from the ultimate static load factors prescribed in §23.561(b)(2) of this part, or which will provide the occupant protection specified in §23.562 of this part when that section is applicable to the airplane. For other seat orientations, the seat/restraint system must be de-signed to provide a level of occupant protection equivalent to that provided for forward- or aft-facing seats with a safety belt and shoulder harness installed.

(b) Each shoulder harness installed at a flight crewmember station, as required by this section, must allow the crewmember, when seated with the safety belt and shoulder harness fastened, to perform all functions necessary for flight operations.

(c) For the purpose of this section, the date of manufacture is:

(1) The date the inspection acceptance records, or equivalent, reflect that the airplane is complete and meets the FAA approved type design data; or

(2) In the case of a foreign manufactured airplane, the date the foreign civil airworthiness authority certifies the airplane is complete and issues an original standard airworthiness certificate, or the equivalent in that country.

[Amdt. 23–36, 53 FR 30812, Aug. 15, 1988]

§23.3 Airplane categories.

(a) The normal category is limited to airplanes that have a seating configuration, excluding pilot seats, of nine or less, a maximum certificated takeoff weight of 12,500 pounds or less, and intended for nonacrobatic operation. Nonacrobatic operation includes:

(1) Any maneuver incident to normal flying;

(2) Stalls (except whip stalls); and

(3) Lazy eights, chandelles, and steep turns, in which the angle of bank is not more than 60 degrees.

(b) The utility category is limited to airplanes that have a seating configuration, excluding pilot seats, of nine or less, a maximum certificated takeoff weight of 12,500 pounds or less, and intended for limited acrobatic operation. Airplanes certificated in the utility category may be used in any of the operations covered under paragraph (a) of this section and in limited acrobatic operations. Limited acrobatic operation includes:

(1) Spins (if approved for the particular type of airplane); and

(2) Lazy eights, chandelles, and steep turns, or similar maneuvers, in which the angle of bank is more than 60 degrees but not more than 90 degrees.

(c) The acrobatic category is limited to airplanes that have a seating configuration, excluding pilot seats, of nine or less, a maximum certificated takeoff weight of 12,500 pounds or less, and intended for use without restrictions, other than those shown to be necessary as a result of required flight tests.

(d) The commuter category is limited to propeller-driven, multiengine airplanes that have a seating configuration, excluding pilot seats, of 19 or less, and a maximum certificated takeoff weight of 19,000 pounds or less. The commuter category operation is limited to any maneuver incident to normal flying, stalls (except whip stalls), and steep turns, in which the angle of bank is not more than 60 degrees.

(e) Except for commuter category, airplanes may be type certificated in more than one category if the requirements of each requested category are met.

[Doc. No. 4080, 29 FR 17955, Dec. 18, 1964, as amended by Amdt. 23–4, 32 FR 5934, Apr. 14, 1967; Amdt. 23–34, 52 FR 1825, Jan. 15, 1987; 52 FR 34745, Sept. 14, 1987; Amdt. 23–50, 61 FR 5183, Feb. 9, 1996]

Subpart B—Flight

General

§ 23.21 Proof of compliance.

(a) Each requirement of this subpart must be met at each appropriate combination of weight and center of gravity within the range of loading conditions for which certification is requested. This must be shown—

(1) By tests upon an airplane of the type for which certification is requested, or by calculations based on, and equal in accuracy to, the results of testing; and

(2) By systematic investigation of each probable combination of weight and center of gravity, if compliance cannot be reasonably inferred from combinations investigated.

(b) The following general tolerances are allowed during flight testing. However, greater tolerances may be allowed in particular tests:

Item	Tolerance
Weight	+5%, −10%.

Item	Tolerance
Critical items affected by weight	+5%, −1%.
C.G	±7% total travel.

§ 23.23 Load distribution limits.

(a) Ranges of weights and centers of gravity within which the airplane may be safely operated must be established. If a weight and center of gravity combination is allowable only within certain lateral load distribution limits that could be inadvertently exceeded, these limits must be established for the corresponding weight and center of gravity combinations.

(b) The load distribution limits may not exceed any of the following:

(1) The selected limits;

(2) The limits at which the structure is proven; or

(3) The limits at which compliance with each applicable flight requirement of this subpart is shown.

[Doc. No. 26269, 58 FR 42156, Aug. 6, 1993]

§ 23.25 Weight limits.

(a) *Maximum weight.* The maximum weight is the highest weight at which compliance with each applicable requirement of this part (other than those complied with at the design landing weight) is shown. The maximum weight must be established so that it is—

(1) Not more than the least of—

(i) The highest weight selected by the applicant; or

(ii) The design maximum weight, which is the highest weight at which compliance with each applicable structural loading condition of this part (other than those complied with at the design landing weight) is shown; or

(iii) The highest weight at which compliance with each applicable flight requirement is shown, and

(2) Not less than the weight with—

(i) Each seat occupied, assuming a weight of 170 pounds for each occupant for normal and commuter category airplanes, and 190 pounds for utility and acrobatic category airplanes, except that seats other than pilot seats may be placarded for a lesser weight; and

(A) Oil at full capacity, and

(B) At least enough fuel for maximum continuous power operation of at least 30 minutes for day-VFR approved airplanes and at least 45 minutes for night-VFR and IFR approved airplanes; or

(ii) The required minimum crew, and fuel and oil to full tank capacity.

(b) *Minimum weight.* The minimum weight (the lowest weight at which compliance with each applicable requirement of this part is shown) must be established so that it is not more than the sum of—

(1) The empty weight determined under §23.29;

(2) The weight of the required minimum crew (assuming a weight of 170 pounds for each crewmember); and

(3) The weight of—

(i) For turbojet powered airplanes, 5 percent of the total fuel capacity of that particular fuel tank arrangement under investigation, and

(ii) For other airplanes, the fuel necessary for one-half hour of operation at maximum continuous power.

[Doc. No. 4080, 29 FR 17955, Dec. 18, 1964, as amended by Amdt. 23–7, 34 FR 13086, Aug. 13, 1969; Amdt. 23–21, 43 FR 2317, Jan. 16, 1978; Amdt. 23–34, 52 FR 1825, Jan. 15, 1987; Amdt. 23–45, 58 FR 42156, Aug. 6, 1993; Amdt. 23–50, 61 FR 5183, Feb. 9, 1996]

§23.29 Empty weight and corresponding center of gravity.

(a) The empty weight and corresponding center of gravity must be determined by weighing the airplane with—

(1) Fixed ballast;

(2) Unusable fuel determined under §23.959; and

(3) Full operating fluids, including—

(i) Oil;

(ii) Hydraulic fluid; and

(iii) Other fluids required for normal operation of airplane systems, except potable water, lavatory precharge water, and water intended for injection in the engines.

(b) The condition of the airplane at the time of determining empty weight must be one that is well defined and can be easily repeated.

[Doc. No. 4080, 29 FR 17955, Dec. 18, 1964; 30 FR 258, Jan. 9, 1965, as amended by Amdt. 23–21, 43 FR 2317, Jan. 16, 1978]

§23.31 Removable ballast.

Removable ballast may be used in showing compliance with the flight requirements of this subpart, if—

(a) The place for carrying ballast is properly designed and installed, and is marked under §23.1557; and

(b) Instructions are included in the airplane flight manual, approved manual material, or markings and placards, for the proper placement of the removable ballast under each loading condition for which removable ballast is necessary.

[Doc. No. 4080, 29 FR 17955, Dec. 18, 1964; 30 FR 258, Jan. 9, 1965, as amended by Amdt. 23–13, 37 FR 20023, Sept. 23, 1972]

§23.33 Propeller speed and pitch limits.

(a) *General.* The propeller speed and pitch must be limited to values that will assure safe operation under normal operating conditions.

(b) *Propellers not controllable in flight.* For each propeller whose pitch cannot be controlled in flight—

(1) During takeoff and initial climb at the all engine(s) operating climb speed specified in §23.65, the propeller must limit the engine r.p.m., at full throttle or at maximum allowable takeoff manifold pressure, to a speed not greater than the maximum allowable takeoff r.p.m.; and

(2) During a closed throttle glide, at V_{NE}, the propeller may not cause an engine speed above 110 percent of maximum continuous speed.

(c) *Controllable pitch propellers without constant speed controls.* Each propeller that can be controlled in flight, but that does not have constant speed controls, must have a means to limit the pitch range so that—

(1) The lowest possible pitch allows compliance with paragraph (b)(1) of this section; and

(2) The highest possible pitch allows compliance with paragraph (b)(2) of this section.

(d) *Controllable pitch propellers with constant speed controls.* Each controllable pitch propeller with constant speed controls must have—

(1) With the governor in operation, a means at the governor to limit the maximum engine speed to the maximum allowable takeoff r.p.m.; and

(2) With the governor inoperative, the propeller blades at the lowest possible pitch, with takeoff power, the airplane stationary, and no wind, either—

(i) A means to limit the maximum engine speed to 103 percent of the maximum allowable takeoff r.p.m., or

(ii) For an engine with an approved overspeed, a means to limit the maximum engine and propeller speed to not more than the maximum approved overspeed.

[Doc. No. 4080, 29 FR 17955, Dec. 18, 1964, as amended by Amdt. 23–45, 58 FR 42156, Aug. 6, 1993; Amdt. 23–50, 61 FR 5183, Feb. 9, 1996]

PERFORMANCE

§ 23.45 General.

(a) Unless otherwise prescribed, the performance requirements of this part must be met for—

(1) Still air and standard atmosphere; and

(2) Ambient atmospheric conditions, for commuter category airplanes, for reciprocating engine-powered airplanes of more than 6,000 pounds maximum weight, and for turbine engine-powered airplanes.

(b) Performance data must be determined over not less than the following ranges of conditions—

(1) Airport altitudes from sea level to 10,000 feet; and

(2) For reciprocating engine-powered airplanes of 6,000 pounds, or less, maximum weight, temperature from standard to 30 °C above standard; or

(3) For reciprocating engine-powered airplanes of more than 6,000 pounds maximum weight and turbine engine-powered airplanes, temperature from standard to 30 °C above standard, or the maximum ambient atmospheric temperature at which compliance with the cooling provisions of § 23.1041 to § 23.1047 is shown, if lower.

(c) Performance data must be determined with the cowl flaps or other means for controlling the engine cooling air supply in the position used in the cooling tests required by § 23.1041 to § 23.1047.

(d) The available propulsive thrust must correspond to engine power, not exceeding the approved power, less—

(1) Installation losses; and

(2) The power absorbed by the accessories and services appropriate to the particular ambient atmospheric conditions and the particular flight condition.

(e) The performance, as affected by engine power or thrust, must be based on a relative humidity:

(1) Of 80 percent at and below standard temperature; and

(2) From 80 percent, at the standard temperature, varying linearly down to 34 percent at the standard temperature plus 50 °F.

(f) Unless otherwise prescribed, in determining the takeoff and landing distances, changes in the airplane's configuration, speed, and power must be made in accordance with procedures established by the applicant for operation in service. These procedures must be able to be executed consistently by pilots of average skill in atmospheric conditions reasonably expected to be encountered in service.

(g) The following, as applicable, must be determined on a smooth, dry, hard-surfaced runway—

(1) Takeoff distance of § 23.53(b);

(2) Accelerate-stop distance of § 23.55;

(3) Takeoff distance and takeoff run of § 23.59; and

(4) Landing distance of § 23.75.

NOTE: The effect on these distances of operation on other types of surfaces (for example, grass, gravel) when dry, may be determined or derived and these surfaces listed in the Airplane Flight Manual in accordance with § 23.1583(p).

(h) For commuter category airplanes, the following also apply:

(1) Unless otherwise prescribed, the applicant must select the takeoff, enroute, approach, and landing configurations for the airplane.

(2) The airplane configuration may vary with weight, altitude, and temperature, to the extent that they are compatible with the operating procedures required by paragraph (h)(3) of this section.

(3) Unless otherwise prescribed, in determining the critical-engine-inoperative takeoff performance, takeoff flight path, and accelerate-stop distance, changes in the airplane's configuration, speed, and power must be made in accordance with procedures established by the applicant for operation in service.

(4) Procedures for the execution of discontinued approaches and balked landings associated with the conditions prescribed in §23.67(c)(4) and §23.77(c) must be established.

(5) The procedures established under paragraphs (h)(3) and (h)(4) of this section must—

(i) Be able to be consistently executed by a crew of average skill in atmospheric conditions reasonably expected to be encountered in service;

(ii) Use methods or devices that are safe and reliable; and

(iii) Include allowance for any reasonably expected time delays in the execution of the procedures.

[Doc. No. 27807, 61 FR 5184, Feb. 9, 1996]

§23.49 Stalling period.

(a) V_{SO} and V_{S1} are the stalling speeds or the minimum steady flight speeds, in knots (CAS), at which the airplane is controllable with—

(1) For reciprocating engine-powered airplanes, the engine(s) idling, the throttle(s) closed or at not more than the power necessary for zero thrust at a speed not more than 110 percent of the stalling speed;

(2) For turbine engine-powered airplanes, the propulsive thrust not greater than zero at the stalling speed, or, if the resultant thrust has no appreciable effect on the stalling speed, with engine(s) idling and throttle(s) closed;

(3) The propeller(s) in the takeoff position;

(4) The airplane in the condition existing in the test, in which V_{SO} and V_{S1} are being used;

(5) The center of gravity in the position that results in the highest value of V_{SO} and V_{S1}; and

(6) The weight used when V_{SO} and V_{S1} are being used as a factor to determine compliance with a required performance standard.

(b) V_{SO} and V_{S1} must be determined by flight tests, using the procedure and meeting the flight characteristics specified in §23.201.

(c) Except as provided in paragraph (d) of this section, V_{SO} and V_{S1} at maximum weight must not exceed 61 knots for—

(1) Single-engine airplanes; and

(2) Multiengine airplanes of 6,000 pounds or less maximum weight that cannot meet the minimum rate of climb specified in §23.67(a)(1) with the critical engine inoperative.

(d) All single-engine airplanes, and those multiengine airplanes of 6,000 pounds or less maximum weight with a V_{SO} of more than 61 knots that do not meet the requirements of §23.67(a)(1), must comply with §23.562(d).

[Doc. No. 27807, 61 FR 5184, Feb. 9, 1996]

§23.51 Takeoff speeds.

(a) For normal, utility, and acrobatic category airplanes, rotation speed, V_R, is the speed at which the pilot makes a control input, with the intention of lifting the airplane out of contact with the runway or water surface.

(1) For multiengine landplanes, V_R, must not be less than the greater of 1.05 V_{MC}; or 1.10 V_{S1};

(2) For single-engine landplanes, V_R, must not be less than V_{S1}; and

(3) For seaplanes and amphibians taking off from water, V_R, may be any speed that is shown to be safe under all reasonably expected conditions, including turbulence and complete failure of the critical engine.

(b) For normal, utility, and acrobatic category airplanes, the speed at 50 feet above the takeoff surface level must not be less than:

(1) or multiengine airplanes, the highest of—

(i) A speed that is shown to be safe for continued flight (or emergency landing, if applicable) under all reasonably expected conditions, including turbulence and complete failure of the critical engine;

(ii) 1.10 V_{MC}; or

(iii) 1.20 V_{S1}.

(2) For single-engine airplanes, the higher of—

(i) A speed that is shown to be safe under all reasonably expected conditions, including turbulence and complete engine failure; or

(ii) 1.20 V_{S1}.

(c) For commuter category airplanes, the following apply:

(1) V_1 must be established in relation to V_{EF} as follows:

(i) V_{EF} is the calibrated airspeed at which the critical engine is assumed to fail. V_{EF} must be selected by the applicant but must not be less than 1.05 V_{MC} determined under §23.149(b) or, at the

179

option of the applicant, not less than V_{MCG} determined under § 23.149(f).

(ii) The takeoff decision speed, V_1, is the calibrated airspeed on the ground at which, as a result of engine failure or other reasons, the pilot is assumed to have made a decision to continue or discontinue the takeoff. The takeoff decision speed, V_1, must be selected by the applicant but must not be less than V_{EF} plus the speed gained with the critical engine inoperative during the time interval between the instant at which the critical engine is failed and the instant at which the pilot recognizes and reacts to the engine failure, as indicated by the pilot's application of the first retarding means during the accelerate-stop determination of § 23.55.

(2) The rotation speed, V_R, in terms of calibrated airspeed, must be selected by the applicant and must not be less than the greatest of the following:

(i) V_1;

(ii) 1.05 V_{MC} determined under § 23.149(b);

(iii) 1.10 V_{S1}; or

(iv) The speed that allows attaining the initial climb-out speed, V_2, before reaching a height of 35 feet above the takeoff surface in accordance with § 23.57(c)(2).

(3) For any given set of conditions, such as weight, altitude, temperature, and configuration, a single value of V_R must be used to show compliance with both the one-engine-inoperative takeoff and all-engines-operating takeoff requirements.

(4) The takeoff safety speed, V_2, in terms of calibrated airspeed, must be selected by the applicant so as to allow the gradient of climb required in § 23.67 (c)(1) and (c)(2) but mut not be less than 1.10 V_{MC} or less than 1.20 V_{S1}.

(5) The one-engine-inoperative takeoff distance, using a normal rotation rate at a speed 5 knots less than V_R, established in accordance with paragraph (c)(2) of this section, must be shown not to exceed the corresponding one-engine-inoperative takeoff distance, determined in accordance with § 23.57 and § 23.59(a)(1), using the established V_R. The takeoff, otherwise performed in accordance with § 23.57, must be continued safely from the point at which the airplane is 35 feet above the takeoff

surface and at a speed not less than the established V_2 minus 5 knots.

(6) The applicant must show, with all engines operating, that marked increases in the scheduled takeoff distances, determined in accordance with § 23.59(a)(2), do not result from over-rotation of the airplane or out-of-trim conditions.

[Doc. No. 27807, 61 FR 5184, Feb. 9, 1996]

§ 23.53 Takeoff performance.

(a) For normal, utility, and acrobatic category airplanes, the takeoff distance must be determined in accordance with paragraph (b) of this section, using speeds determined in accordance with § 23.51 (a) and (b).

(b) For normal, utility, and acrobatic category airplanes, the distance required to takeoff and climb to a height of 50 feet above the takeoff surface must be determined for each weight, altitude, and temperature within the operational limits established for takeoff with—

(1) Takeoff power on each engine;

(2) Wing flaps in the takeoff position(s); and

(3) Landing gear extended.

(c) For commuter category airplanes, takeoff performance, as required by §§ 23.55 through 23.59, must be determined with the operating engine(s) within approved operating limitations.

[Doc. No. 27807, 61 FR 5185, Feb. 9, 1996]

§ 23.55 Accelerate-stop distance.

For each commuter category airplane, the accelerate-stop distance must be determined as follows:

(a) The accelerate-stop distance is the sum of the distances necessary to—

(1) Accelerate the airplane from a standing start to V_{EF} with all engines operating;

(2) Accelerate the airplane from V_{EF} to V_1, assuming the critical engine fails at V_{EF}; and

(3) Come to a full stop from the point at which V_1 is reached.

(b) Means other than wheel brakes may be used to determine the accelerate-stop distances if that means—

(1) Is safe and reliable;

(2) Is used so that consistent results can be expected under normal operating conditions; and

(3) Is such that exceptional skill is not required to control the airplane.

[Amdt. 23–34, 52 FR 1826, Jan. 15, 1987, as amended by Amdt. 23–50, 61 FR 5185, Feb. 9, 1996]

§23.57 Takeoff path.

For each commuter category airplane, the takeoff path is as follows:

(a) The takeoff path extends from a standing start to a point in the takeoff at which the airplane is 1500 feet above the takeoff surface at or below which height the transition from the takeoff to the enroute configuration must be completed; and

(1) The takeoff path must be based on the procedures prescribed in §23.45;

(2) The airplane must be accelerated on the ground to V_{EF} at which point the critical engine must be made inoperative and remain inoperative for the rest of the takeoff; and

(3) After reaching V_{EF}, the airplane must be accelerated to V_2.

(b) During the acceleration to speed V_2, the nose gear may be raised off the ground at a speed not less than V_R. However, landing gear retraction must not be initiated until the airplane is airborne.

(c) During the takeoff path determination, in accordance with paragraphs (a) and (b) of this section—

(1) The slope of the airborne part of the takeoff path must not be negative at any point;

(2) The airplane must reach V_2 before it is 35 feet above the takeoff surface, and must continue at a speed as close as practical to, but not less than V_2, until it is 400 feet above the takeoff surface;

(3) At each point along the takeoff path, starting at the point at which the airplane reaches 400 feet above the takeoff surface, the available gradient of climb must not be less than—

(i) 1.2 percent for two-engine airplanes;

(ii) 1.5 percent for three-engine airplanes;

(iii) 1.7 percent for four-engine airplanes; and

(4) Except for gear retraction and automatic propeller feathering, the airplane configuration must not be changed, and no change in power that requires action by the pilot may be made, until the airplane is 400 feet above the takeoff surface.

(d) The takeoff path to 35 feet above the takeoff surface must be determined by a continuous demonstrated takeoff.

(e) The takeoff path to 35 feet above the takeoff surface must be determined by synthesis from segments; and

(1) The segments must be clearly defined and must be related to distinct changes in configuration, power, and speed;

(2) The weight of the airplane, the configuration, and the power must be assumed constant throughout each segment and must correspond to the most critical condition prevailing in the segment; and

(3) The takeoff flight path must be based on the airplane's performance without utilizing ground effect.

[Amdt. 23–34, 52 FR 1827, Jan. 15, 1987, as amended by Amdt. 23–50, 61 FR 5185, Feb. 9, 1996]

§23.59 Takeoff distance and takeoff run.

For each commuter category airplane, the takeoff distance and, at the option of the applicant, the takeoff run, must be determined.

(a) Takeoff distance is the greater of—

(1) The horizontal distance along the takeoff path from the start of the takeoff to the point at which the airplane is 35 feet above the takeoff surface as determined under §23.57; or

(2) With all engines operating, 115 percent of the horizontal distance from the start of the takeoff to the point at which the airplane is 35 feet above the takeoff surface, determined by a procedure consistent with §23.57.

(b) If the takeoff distance includes a clearway, the takeoff run is the greater of—

(1) The horizontal distance along the takeoff path from the start of the takeoff to a point equidistant between the liftoff point and the point at which the airplane is 35 feet above the takeoff surface as determined under §23.57; or

(2) With all engines operating, 115 percent of the horizontal distance from the start of the takeoff to a point equidistant between the liftoff point and the point at which the airplane is 35

feet above the takeoff surface, determined by a procedure consistent with § 23.57.

[Amdt. 23–34, 52 FR 1827, Jan. 15, 1987, as amended by Amdt. 23–50, 61 FR 5185, Feb. 9, 1996]

§ 23.61 Takeoff flight path.

For each commuter category airplane, the takeoff flight path must be determined as follows:

(a) The takeoff flight path begins 35 feet above the takeoff surface at the end of the takeoff distance determined in accordance with § 23.59.

(b) The net takeoff flight path data must be determined so that they represent the actual takeoff flight paths, as determined in accordance with § 23.57 and with paragraph (a) of this section, reduced at each point by a gradient of climb equal to—

(1) 0.8 percent for two-engine airplanes;

(2) 0.9 percent for three-engine airplanes; and

(3) 1.0 percent for four-engine airplanes.

(c) The prescribed reduction in climb gradient may be applied as an equivalent reduction in acceleration along that part of the takeoff flight path at which the airplane is accelerated in level flight.

[Amdt. 23–34, 52 FR 1827, Jan. 15, 1987]

§ 23.63 Climb: General.

(a) Compliance with the requirements of §§ 23.65, 23.66, 23.67, 23.69, and 23.77 must be shown—

(1) Out of ground effect; and

(2) At speeds that are not less than those at which compliance with the powerplant cooling requirements of §§ 23.1041 to 23.1047 has been demonstrated; and

(3) Unless otherwise specified, with one engine inoperative, at a bank angle not exceeding 5 degrees.

(b) For normal, utility, and acrobatic category reciprocating engine-powered airplanes of 6,000 pounds or less maximum weight, compliance must be shown with § 23.65(a), § 23.67(a), where appropriate, and § 23.77(a) at maximum takeoff or landing weight, as appropriate, in a standard atmosphere.

(c) For normal, utility, and acrobatic category reciprocating engine-powered airplanes of more than 6,000 pounds maximum weight, and turbine engine-powered airplanes in the normal, utility, and acrobatic category, compliance must be shown at weights as a function of airport altitude and ambient temperature, within the operational limits established for takeoff and landing, respectively, with—

(1) Sections 23.65(b) and 23.67(b) (1) and (2), where appropriate, for takeoff, and

(2) Section 23.67(b)(2), where appropriate, and § 23.77(b), for landing.

(d) For commuter category airplanes, compliance must be shown at weights as a function of airport altitude and ambient temperature within the operational limits established for takeoff and landing, respectively, with—

(1) Sections 23.67(c)(1), 23.67(c)(2), and 23.67(c)(3) for takeoff; and

(2) Sections 23.67(c)(3), 23.67(c)(4), and 23.77(c) for landing.

[Doc. No. 27807, 61 FR 5186, Feb. 9, 1996]

§ 23.65 Climb: All engines operating.

(a) Each normal, utility, and acrobatic category reciprocating engine-powered airplane of 6,000 pounds or less maximum weight must have a steady climb gradient at sea level of at least 8.3 percent for landplanes or 6.7 percet for seaplanes and amphibians with—

(1) Not more than maximum continuous power on each engine;

(2) The landing gear retracted;

(3) The wing flaps in the takeoff position(s); and

(4) A climb speed not less than the greater of 1.1 V_{MC} and 1.2 V_{S1} for multi-engine airplanes and not less than 1.2 V_{S1} for single—engine airplanes.

(b) Each normal, utility, and acrobatic category reciprocating engine-powered airplane of more than 6,000 pounds maximum weight and turbine engine-powered airplanes in the normal, utility, and acrobatic category must have a steady gradient of climb after takeoff of at least 4 percent with

(1) Take off power on each engine;

(2) The landing gear extended, except that if the landing gear can be retracted in not more than sven seconds, the test may be conducted with the gear retracted;

(3) The wing flaps in the takeoff position(s); and

(4) A climb speed as specified in §23.65(a)(4).

[Doc. No. 27807, 61 FR 5186, Feb. 9, 1996]

§23.66 Takeoff climb: One-engine inoperative.

For normal, utility, and acrobatic category reciprocating engine-powered airplanes of more than 6,000 pounds maximum weight, and turbine engine-powered airplanes in the normal, utility, and acrobatic category, the steady gradient of climb or descent must be determined at each weight, altitude, and ambient temperature within the operational limits established by the applicant with—

(a) The critical engine inoperative and its propeller in the position it rapidly and automatically assumes;

(b) The remaining engine(s) at takeoff power;

(c) The landing gear extended, except that if the landing gear can be retracted in not more than seven seconds, the test may be conducted with the gear retracted;

(d) The wing flaps in the takeoff position(s):

(e) The wings level; and

(f) A climb speed equal to that achieved at 50 feet in the demonstration of §23.53.

[Doc. No. 27807, 61 FR 5186, Feb. 9, 1996]

§23.67 Climb: One engine inoperative.

(a) For normal, utility, and acrobatic category reciprocating engine-powered airplanes of 6,000 pounds or less maximum weight, the following apply:

(1) Except for those airplanes that meet the requirements prescribed in §23.562(d), each airplane with a V_{SO} of more than 61 knots must be able to maintain a steady climb gradient of at least 1.5 percent at a pressure altitude of 5,000 feet with the—

(i) Critical engine inoperative and its propeller in the minimum drag position;

(ii) Remaining engine(s) at not more than maximum continuous power;

(iii) Landing gear retracted;

(iv) Wing flaps retracted; and

(v) Climb speed not less than $1.2 V_{S1}$.

(2) For each airplane that meets the requirements prescribed in §23.562(d), or that has a V_{SO} of 61 knots or less, the steady gradient of climb or descent at a pressure altitude of 5,000 feet must be determined with the—

(i) Critical engine inoperative and its propeller in the minimum drag position;

(ii) Remaining engine(s) at not more than maximum continuous power;

(iii) Landing gear retracted;

(iv) Wing flaps retracted; and

(v) Climb speed not less than $1.2V_{S1}$.

(b) For normal, utility, and acrobatic category reciprocating engine-powered airplanes of more than 6,000 pounds maximum weight, and turbine engine-powered airplanes in the normal, utility, and acrobatic category—

(1) The steady gradient of climb at an altitude of 400 feet above the takeoff must be measurably positive with the—

(i) Critical engine inoperative and its propeller in the minimum drag position;

(ii) Remaining engine(s) at takeoff power;

(iii) Landing gear retracted;

(iv) Wing flaps in the takeoff position(s); and

(v) Climb speed equal to that achieved at 50 feet in the demonstration of §23.53.

(2) The steady gradient of climb must not be less than 0.75 percent at an altitude of 1,500 feet above the takeoff surface, or landing surface, as appropriate, with the—

(i) Critical engine inoperative and its propeller in the minimum drag position;

(ii) Remaining engine(s) at not more than maximum continuous power;

(iii) Landing gear retracted;

(iv) Wing flaps retracted; and

(v) Climb speed not less than $1.2 V_{S1}$.

(c) For commuter category airplanes, the following apply:

(1) *Takeoff; landing gear extended.* The steady gradient of climb at the altitude of the takeoff surface must be measurably positive for two-engine airplanes, not less than 0.3 percent for three-engine airplanes, or 0.5 percent for four-engine airplanes with—

(i) The critical engine inoperative and its propeller in the position it rapidly and automatically assumes;

(ii) The remaining engine(s) at take-off power;

(iii) The landing gear extended, and all landing gear doors open;

(iv) The wing flaps in the takeoff position(s);

(v) The wings level; and

(vi) A climb speed equal to V_2.

(2) *Takeoff; landing gear retracted.* The steady gradient of climb at an altitude of 400 feet above the takeoff surface must be not less than 2.0 percent of two-engine airplanes, 2.3 percent for three-engine airplanes, and 2.6 percent for four-engine airplanes with—

(i) The critical engine inoperative and its propeller in the position it rapidly and automatically assumes;

(ii) The remaining engine(s) at take-off power;

(iii) The landing gear retracted;

(iv) The wing flaps in the takeoff position(s);

(v) A climb speed equal to V_2.

(3) *Enroute.* The steady gradient of climb at an altitude of 1,500 feet above the takeoff or landing surface, as appropriate, must be not less than 1.2 percent for two-engine airplanes, 1.5 percent for three-engine airplanes, and 1.7 percent for four-engine airplanes with—

(i) The critical engine inoperative and its propeller in the minimum drag position;

(ii) The remaining engine(s) at not more than maximum continuous power;

(iii) The landing gear retracted;

(iv) The wing flaps retracted; and

(v) A climb speed not less than 1.2 V_{S1}.

(4) *Discontinued approach.* The steady gradient of climb at an altitude of 400 feet above the landing surface must be not less than 2.1 percent for two-engine airplanes, 2.4 percent for three-engine airplanes, and 2.7 percent for four-engine airplanes, with—

(i) The critical engine inoperative and its propeller in the minimum drag position;

(ii) The remaining engine(s) at take-off power;

(iii) Landing gear retracted;

(iv) Wing flaps in the approach position(s) in which V_{S1} for these position(s) does not exceed 110 percent of the V_{S1} for the related all-engines-operated landing position(s); and

(v) A climb speed established in connection with normal landing procedures but not exceeding 1.5 V_{S1}.

[Doc. No. 27807, 61 FR 5186, Feb. 9, 1996]

§ 23.69 Enroute climb/descent.

(a) *All engines operating.* The steady gradient and rate of climb must be determined at each weight, altitude, and ambient temperature within the operational limits established by the applicant with—

(1) Not more than maximum continuous power on each engine;

(2) The landing gear retracted;

(3) The wing flaps retracted; and

(4) A climb speed not less than 1.3 V_{S1}.

(b) *One engine inoperative.* The steady gradient and rate of climb/descent must be determined at each weight, altitude, and ambient temperature within the operational limits established by the applicant with—

(1) The critical engine inoperative and its propeller in the minimum drag position;

(2) The remaining engine(s) at not more than maximum continuous power;

(3) The landing gear retracted;

(4) The wing flaps retracted; and

(5) A climb speed not less than 1.2 V_{S1}.

[Doc. No. 27807, 61 FR 5187, Feb. 9, 1996]

§ 23.71 Glide: Single-engine airplanes.

The maximum horizontal distance traveled in still air, in nautical miles, per 1,000 feet of altitude lost in a glide, and the speed necessary to achieve this must be determined with the engine inoperative, its propeller in the minimum drag position, and landing gear and wing flaps in the most favorable available position.

[Doc. No. 27807, 61 FR 5187, Feb. 9, 1996]

§ 23.73 Reference landing approach speed.

(a) For normal, utility, and acrobatic category reciprocating engine-powered airplanes of 6,000 pounds or less maximum weight, the reference landing approach speed, V_{REF}, must not be less than the greater of V_{MC}, determined in

§23.149(b) with the wing flaps in the most extended takeoff position, and 1.3 V_{SO}.

(b) For normal, utility, and acrobatic category reciprocating engine-powered airplanes of more than 6,000 pounds maximum weight, and turbine engine-powered airplanes in the normal, utility, and acrobatic category, the reference landing approach speed, V_{REF}, must not be less than the greater of V_{MC}, determined in §23.149(c), and 1.3 V_{SO}.

(c) For commuter category airplanes, the reference landing approach speed, V_{REF}, must not be less than the greater of 1.05 V_{MC}, determined in §23.149(c), and 1.3 V_{SO}.

[Doc. No. 27807, 61 FR 5187, Feb. 9, 1996]

§23.75 Landing distance.

The horizontal distance necessary to land and come to a complete stop from a point 50 feet above the landing surface must be determined, for standard temperatures at each weight and altitude within the operational limits established for landing, as follows:

(a) A steady approach at not less than V_{REF}, determined in accordance with §23.73 (a), (b), or (c), as appropriate, must be maintained down to the 50 foot height and—

(1) The steady approach must be at a gradient of descent not greater than 5.2 percent (3 degrees) down to the 50-foot height.

(2) In addition, an applicant may demonstrate by tests that a maximum steady approach gradient steeper than 5.2 percent, down to the 50-foot height, is safe. The gradient must be established as an operating limitation and the information necessary to display the gradient must be available to the pilot by an appropriate instrument.

(b) A constant configuration must be maintained throughout the maneuver.

(c) The landing must be made without excessive vertical acceleration or tendency to bounce, nose over, ground loop, porpoise, or water loop.

(d) It must be shown that a safe transition to the balked landing conditions of §23.77 can be made from the conditions that exist at the 50 foot height, at maximum landing weight, or at the maximum landing weight for altitude

and temperature of §23.63 (c)(2) or (d)(2), as appropriate.

(e) The brakes must be used so as to not cause excessive wear of brakes or tires.

(f) Retardation means other than wheel brakes may be used if that means—

(1) Is safe and reliable; and

(2) Is used so that consistent results can be expected in service.

(g) If any device is used that depends on the operation of any engine, and the landing distance would be increased when a landing is made with that engine inoperative, the landing distance must be determined with that engine inoperative unless the use of other compensating means will result in a landing distance not more than that with each engine operating.

[Amdt. 23–21, 43 FR 2318, Jan. 16, 1978, as amended by Amdt. 23–34, 52 FR 1828, Jan. 15, 1987; Amdt. 23–42, 56 FR 351, Jan. 3, 1991; Amdt. 23–50, 61 FR 5187, Feb. 9, 1996]

§23.77 Balked landing.

(a) Each normal, utility, and acrobatic category reciprocating engine-powered airplane at 6,000 pounds or less maximum weight must be able to maintain a steady gradient of climb at sea level of at least 3.3 percent with—

(1) Takeoff power on each engine;

(2) The landing gear extended;

(3) The wing flaps in the landing position, except that if the flaps may safely be retracted in two seconds or less without loss of altitude and without sudden changes of angle of attack, they may be retracted; and

(4) A climb speed equal to V_{REF}, as defined in §23.73(a).

(b) Each normal, utility, and acrobatic category reciprocating engine-powered airplane of more than 6,000 pounds maximum weight and each normal, utility, and acrobatic category turbine engine-powered airplane must be able to maintain a steady gradient of climb of at least 2.5 percent with—

(1) Not more than the power that is available on each engine eight seconds after initiation of movement of the power controls from minimum flight-idle position;

(2) The landing gear extended;

(3) The wing flaps in the landing position; and

(4) A climb speed equal to V_{REF}, as defined in §23.73(b).

(c) Each commuter category airplane must be able to maintain a steady gradient of climb of at least 3.2 percent with—

(1) Not more than the power that is available on each engine eight seconds after initiation of movement of the power controls from the minimum flight idle position;

(2) Landing gear extended;

(3) Wing flaps in the landing position; and

(4) A climb speed equal to V_{REF}, as defined in §23.73(c).

[Doc. No. 27807, 61 FR 5187, Feb. 9, 1996]

FLIGHT CHARACTERISTICS

§ 23.141 General.

The airplane must meet the requirements of §§23.143 through 23.253 at all practical loading conditions and operating altitudes for which certification has been requested, not exceeding the maximum operating altitude established under §23.1527, and without requiring exceptional piloting skill, alertness, or strength.

[Doc. No. 26269, 58 FR 42156, Aug. 6, 1993]

CONTROLLABILITY AND
MANEUVERABILITY

§ 23.143 General.

(a) The airplane must be safely controllable and maneuverable during all flight phases including—

(1) Takeoff;

(2) Climb;

(3) Level flight;

(4) Descent;

(5) Go-around; and

(6) Landing (power on and power off) with the wing flaps extended and retracted.

(b) It must be possible to make a smooth transition from one flight condition to another (including turns and slips) without danger of exceeding the limit load factor, under any probable operating condition (including, for multiengine airplanes, those conditions normally encountered in the sudden failure of any engine).

(c) If marginal conditions exist with regard to required pilot strength, the control forces necessary must be deter-

mined by quantitative tests. In no case may the control forces under the conditions specified in paragraphs (a) and (b) of this section exceed those prescribed in the following table:

Values in pounds force applied to the relevant control	Pitch	Roll	Yaw
(a) For temporary application:			
Stick	60	30	....
Wheel (Two hands on rim)	75	50	....
Wheel (One hand on rim)	50	25	....
Rudder Pedal	....	....	150
(b) For prolonged application	10	5	20

[Doc. No, 4080, 29 FR 17955, Dec. 18, 1964, as amended by Amdt. 23–14, 38 FR 31819, Nov. 19, 1973; Amdt. 23–17, 41 FR 55464, Dec. 20, 1976; Amdt. 23–45, 58 FR 42156, Aug. 6, 1993; Amdt. 23–50, 61 FR 5188, Feb. 9, 1996]

§ 23.145 Longitudinal control.

(a) With the airplane as nearly as possible in trim at 1.3 V_{S1}, it must be possible, at speeds below the trim speed, to pitch the nose downward so that the rate of increase in airspeed allows prompt acceleration to the trim speed with—

(1) Maximum continuous power on each engine;

(2) Power off; and

(3) Wing flap and landing gear—

(i) retracted, and

(ii) extended.

(b) Unless otherwise required, it must be possible to carry out the following maneuvers without requiring the application of single-handed control forces exceeding those specified in §23.143(c). The trimming controls must not be adjusted during the maneuvers:

(1) With the landing gear extended, the flaps retracted, and the airplanes as nearly as possible in trim at 1.4 V_{S1}, extend the flaps as rapidly as possible and allow the airspeed to transition from 1.4V_{S1} to 1.4 $V_{SO\leq}$

(i) With power off; and

(ii) With the power necessary to maintain level flight in the initial condition.

(2) With landing gear and flaps extended, power off, and the airplane as nearly as possible in trim at 1.3 V_{SO}, quickly apply takeoff power and retract the flaps as rapidly as possible to the recommended go around setting and allow the airspeed to transition from 1.3 V_{SO} to 1.3 V_{S1}. Retract the gear

when a positive rate of climb is established.

(3) With landing gear and flaps extended, in level flight, power necessary to attain level flight at 1.1 V_{SO}, and the airplane as nearly as possible in trim, it must be possible to maintain approximately level flight while retracting the flaps as rapidly as possible with simultaneous application of not more than maximum continuous power. If gated flat positions are provided, the flap retraction may be demonstrated in stages with power and trim reset for level flight at 1.1 V_{S1}, in the initial configuration for each stage—

(i) From the fully extended position to the most extended gated position;

(ii) Between intermediate gated positions, if applicable; and

(iii) From the least extended gated position to the fully retracted position.

(4) With power off, flaps and landing gear retracted and the airplane as nearly as possible in trim at 1.4 V_{S1}, apply takeoff power rapidly while maintaining the same airspeed.

(5) With power off, landing gear and flaps extended, and the airplane as nearly as possible in trim at V_{REF}, obtain and maintain airspeeds between 1.1 V_{SO}, and either 1.7 V_{SO} or V_{FE}, whichever is lower without requiring the application of two-handed control forces exceeding those specified in § 23.143(c).

(6) With maximum takeoff power, landing gear retracted, flaps in the takeoff position, and the airplane as nearly as possible in trim at V_{FE} appropriate to the takeoff flap position, retract the flaps as rapidly as possible while maintaining constant speed. At speeds above V_{MO}/M_{MO}, and up to the maximum speed shown under § 23.251, a maneuvering capability of 1.5 g must be demonstrated to provide a margin to recover from upset or inadvertent speed increase.

(d) It must be possible, with a pilot control force of not more than 10 pounds, to maintain a speed of not more than V_{REF} during a power-off glide with landing gear and wing flaps extended, for any weight of the airplane, up to and including the maximum weight.

(e) By using normal flight and power controls, except as otherwise noted in paragraphs (e)(1) and (e)(2) of this section, it must be possible to establish a zero rate of descent at an attitude suitable for a controlled landing without exceeding the operational and structural limitations of the airplane, as follows:

(1) For single-engine and multiengine airplanes, without the use of the primary longitudinal control system.

(2) For multiengine airplanes—

(i) Without the use of the primary directional control; and

(ii) If a single failure of any one connecting or transmitting link would affect both the longitudinal and directional primary control system, without the primary longitudinal and directional control system.

[Doc. No. 26269, 58 FR 42157, Aug. 6, 1993; Amdt. 23-45, 58 FR 51970, Oct. 5, 1993, as amended by Amdt. 23-50, 61 FR 5188, Feb. 9, 1996]

§ 23.147 Directional and lateral control.

(a) For each multiengine airplane, it must be possible, while holding the wings level within five degrees, to make sudden changes in heading safely in both directions. This ability must be shown at 1.4 V_{S1} with heading changes up to 15 degrees, except that the heading change at which the rudder force corresponds to the limits specified in § 23.143 need not be exceeded, with the—

(1) Critical engine inoperative and its propeller in the minimum drag position;

(2) Remaining engines at maximum continuous power;

(3) Landing gear—

(i) Retracted; and

(ii) Extended; and

(4) Flaps retracted.

(b) For each multiengine airplane, it must be possible to regain full control of the airplane without exceeding a bank angle of 45 degrees, reaching a dangerous attitude or encountering dangerous characteristics, in the event of a sudden and complete failure of the critical engine, making allowance for a delay of two seconds in the initiation of recovery action appropriate to the situation, with the airplane initially in trim, in the following condition:

(1) Maximum continuous power on each engine;

(2) The wing flaps retracted;

(3) The landing gear retracted;

(4) A speed equal to that at which compliance with § 23.69(a) has been shown; and

(5) All propeller controls in the position at which compliance with § 23.69(a) has been shown.

(c) For all airplanes, it must be shown that the airplane is safely controllable without the use of the primary lateral control system in any all-engine configuration(s) and at any speed or altitude within the approved operating envelope. It must also be shown that the airplane's flight characteristics are not impaired below a level needed to permit continued safe flight and the ability to maintain attitudes suitable for a controlled landing without exceeding the operational and structural limitations of the airplane. If a single failure of any one connecting or transmitting link in the lateral control system would also cause the loss of additional control system(s), compliance with the above requirement must be shown with those additional systems also assumed to be inoperative.

[Doc. No. 27807, 61 FR 5188, Feb. 9, 1996]

§ 23.149 Minimum control speed.

(a) V_{MC} is the calibrated airspeed at which, when the critical engine is suddenly made inoperative, it is possible to maintain control of the airplane with that engine still inoperative, and thereafter maintain straight flight at the same speed with an angle of bank of not more than 5 degrees. The method used to simulate critical engine failure must represent the most critical mode of powerplant failure expected in service with respect to controllability.

(b) V_{MC} for takeoff must not exceed 1.2 V_{S1}, where V_{S1} is determined at the maximum takeoff weight. V_{MC} must be determined with the most unfavorable weight and center of gravity position and with the airplane airborne and the ground effect negligible, for the takeoff configuration(s) with—

(1) Maximum available takeoff power initially on each engine;

(2) The airplane trimmed for takeoff;

(3) Flaps in the takeoff position(s);

(4) Landing gear retracted; and

(5) All propeller controls in the recommended takeoff position throughout.

(c) For all airplanes except reciprocating engine-powered airplanes of 6,000 pounds or less maximum weight, the conditions of paragraph (a) of this section must also be met for the landing configuration with—

(1) Maximum available takeoff power initially on each engine;

(2) The airplane trimmed for an approach, with all engines operating, at V_{REF}, at an approach gradient equal to the steepest used in the landing distance demonstration of § 23.75;

(3) Flaps in the landing position;

(4) Landing gear extended; and

(5) All propeller controls in the position recommended for approach with all engines operating.

(d) A minimum speed to intentionally render the critical engine inoperative must be established and designated as the safe, intentional, one-engine-inoperative speed, V_{SSE}.

(e) At V_{MC}, the rudder pedal force required to maintain control must not exceed 150 pounds and it must not be necessary to reduce power of the operative engine(s). During the maneuver, the airplane must not assume any dangerous attitude and it must be possible to prevent a heading change of more than 20 degrees.

(f) At the option of the applicant, to comply with the requirements of § 23.51(c)(1), V_{MCG} may be determined. V_{MCG} is the minimum control speed on the ground, and is the calibrated airspeed during the takeoff run at which, when the critical engine is suddenly made inoperative, it is possible to maintain control of the airplane using the rudder control alone (without the use of nosewheel steering), as limited by 150 pounds of force, and using the lateral control to the extent of keeping the wings level to enable the takeoff to be safely continued. In the determination of V_{MCG}, assuming that the path of the airplane accelerating with all engines operating is along the centerline of the runway, its path from the point at which the critical engine is made inoperative to the point at which recovery to a direction parallel to the centerline is completed may not deviate more than 30 feet laterally from the centerline at any point. V_{MCG} must be established with—

(1) The airplane in each takeoff configuration or, at the option of the applicant, in the most critical takeoff configuration;

(2) Maximum available takeoff power on the operating engines;

(3) The most unfavorable center of gravity;

(4) The airplane trimmed for takeoff; and

(5) The most unfavorable weight in the range of takeoff weights.

[Doc. No. 27807, 61 FR 5189, Feb. 9, 1996]

§ 23.151 Acrobatic maneuvers.

Each acrobatic and utility category airplane must be able to perform safely the acrobatic maneuvers for which certification is requested. Safe entry speeds for these maneuvers must be determined.

§ 23.153 Control during landings.

It must be possible, while in the landing configuration, to safely complete a landing without exceeding the one-hand control force limits specified in § 23.143(c) following an approach to land—

(a) At a speed of V_{REF} minus 5 knots;

(b) With the airplane in trim, or as nearly as possible in trim and without the trimming control being moved throughout the maneuver;

(c) At an approach gradient equal to the steepest used in the landing distance demonstration of § 23.75; and

(d) With only those power changes, if any, that would be made when landing normally from an approach at V_{REF}.

[Doc. No. 27807, 61 FR 5189, Feb. 9, 1996]

§ 23.155 Elevator control force in maneuvers.

(a) The elevator control force needed to achieve the positive limit maneuvering load factor may not be less than:

(1) For wheel controls, W/100 (where W is the maximum weight) or 20 pounds, whichever is greater, except that it need not be greater than 50 pounds; or

(2) For stick controls, W/140 (where W is the maximum weight) or 15 pounds,

whichever is greater, except that it need not be greater than 35 pounds.

(b) The requirement of paragraph (a) of this section must be met at 75 percent of maximum continuous power for reciprocating engines, or the maximum continuous power for turbine engines, and with the wing flaps and landing gear retracted—

(1) In a turn, with the trim setting used for wings level flight at V_O; and

(2) In a turn with the trim setting used for the maximum wings level flight speed, except that the speed may not exceed V_{NE} or V_{MO}/M_{MO}, whichever is appropriate.

(c) There must be no excessive decrease in the gradient of the curve of stick force versus maneuvering load factor with increasing load factor.

[Amdt. 23–14, 38 FR 31819, Nov. 19, 1973; 38 FR 32784, Nov. 28, 1973, as amended by Amdt. 23–45, 58 FR 42158, Aug. 6, 1993; Amdt. 23–50, 61 FR 5189 Feb. 9, 1996]

§ 23.157 Rate of roll.

(a) *Takeoff*. It must be possible, using a favorable combination of controls, to roll the airplane from a steady 30-degree banked turn through an angle of 60 degrees, so as to reverse the direction of the turn within:

(1) For an airplane of 6,000 pounds or less maximum weight, 5 seconds from initiation of roll; and

(2) For an airplane of over 6,000 pounds maximum weight,

$$(W+500)/1,300$$

seconds, but not more than 10 seconds, where W is the weight in pounds.

(b) The requirement of paragraph (a) of this section must be met when rolling the airplane in each direction with—

(1) Flaps in the takeoff position;

(2) Landing gear retracted;

(3) For a single-engine airplane, at maximum takeoff power; and for a multiengine airplane with the critical engine inoperative and the propeller in the minimum drag position, and the other engines at maximum takeoff power; and

(4) The airplane trimmed at a speed equal to the greater of 1.2 V_{S1} or 1.1 V_{MC}, or as nearly as possible in trim for straight flight.

(c) *Approach.* It must be possible, using a favorable combination of controls, to roll the airplane from a steady 30-degree banked turn through an angle of 60 degrees, so as to reverse the direction of the turn within:

(1) For an airplane of 6,000 pounds or less maximum weight, 4 seconds from initiation of roll; and

(2) For an airplane of over 6,000 pounds maximum weight,

(W+2,800)/2,200

seconds, but not more than 7 seconds, where W is the weight in pounds.

(d) The requirement of paragraph (c) of this section must be met when rolling the airplane in each direction in the following conditions—

(1) Flaps in the landing position(s);

(2) Landing gear extended;

(3) All engines operating at the power for a 3 degree approach; and

(4) The airplane trimmed at V_{REF}.

[Amdt. 23–14, 38 FR 31819, Nov. 19, 1973, as amended by Amdt. 23–45, 58 FR 42158, Aug. 6, 1993; Amdt. 23–50, 61 FR 5189, Feb. 9, 1996]

TRIM

§ 23.161 Trim.

(a) *General.* Each airplane must meet the trim requirements of this section after being trimmed and without further pressure upon, or movement of, the primary controls or their corresponding trim controls by the pilot or the automatic pilot. In addition, it must be possible, in other conditions of loading, configuration, speed and power to ensure that the pilot will not be unduly fatigued or distracted by the need to apply residual control forces exceeding those for prolonged application of § 23.143(c). This applies in normal operation of the airplane and, if applicable, to those conditions associated with the failure of one engine for which performance characteristics are established.

(b) *Lateral and directional trim.* The airplane must maintain lateral and directional trim in level flight with the landing gear and wing flaps retracted as follows:

(1) For normal, utility, and acrobatic category airplanes, at a speed of 0.9 V_H, V_C, or V_{MO}/M_O, whichever is lowest; and

(2) For commuter category airplanes, at all speeds from 1.4 V_{S1} to the lesser of V_H or V_{MO}/M_{MO}.

(c) *Longitudinal trim.* The airplane must maintain longitudinal trim under each of the following conditions:

(1) A climb with—

(i) Takeoff power, landing gear retracted, wing flaps in the takeoff position(s), at the speeds used in determining the climb performance required by § 23.65; and

(ii) Maximum continuous power at the speeds and in the configuration used in determining the climb performance required by § 23.69(a).

(2) Level flight at all speeds from the lesser of V_H and either V_{NO} or V_{MO}/M_{MO} (as appropriate), to 1.4 V_{S1}, with the landing gear and flaps retracted.

(3) A descent at V_{NO} or V_{MO}/M_{MO}, whichever is applicable, with power off and with the landing gear and flaps retracted.

(4) Approach with landing gear extended and with—

(i) A 3 degree angle of descent, with flaps retracted and at a speed of 1.4 V_{S1};

(ii) A 3 degree angle of descent, flaps in the landing position(s) at V_{REF}; and

(iii) An approach gradient equal to the steepest used in the landing distance demonstrations of § 23.75, flaps in the landing position(s) at V_{REF}.

(d) In addition, each multiple airplane must maintain longitudinal and directional trim, and the lateral control force must not exceed 5 pounds at the speed used in complying with § 23.67(a), (b)(2), or (c)(3), as appropriate, with—

(1) The critical engine inoperative, and if applicable, its propeller in the minimum drag position;

(2) The remaining engines at maximum continuous power;

(3) The landing gear retracted;

(4) Wing flaps retracted; and

(5) An angle of bank of not more than five degrees.

(e) In addition, each commuter category airplane for which, in the determination of the takeoff path in accordance with § 23.57, the climb in the takeoff configuration at V_2 extends beyond 400 feet above the takeoff surface, it must be possible to reduce the longitudinal and lateral control forces to 10 pounds and 5 pounds, respectively, and the directional control force must not exceed 50 pounds at V_2 with—

(1) The critical engine inoperative and its propeller in the minimum drag position;

(2) The remaining engine(s) at take-off power;

(3) Landing gear retracted;

(4) Wing flaps in the takeoff position(s); and

(5) An angle of bank not exceeding 5 degrees.

[Doc. No. 4080, 29 FR 17955, Dec. 18, 1964, as amended by Amdt. 23–21, 43 FR 2318, Jan. 16, 1978; Amdt. 23–34, 52 FR 1828, Jan. 15, 1987; Amdt. 23–42, 56 FR 351, Jan. 3, 1991; 56 FR 5455, Feb. 11, 1991; Amdt. 23–50, 61 FR 5189, Feb. 9, 1996]

STABILITY

§23.171 General.

The airplane must be longitudinally, directionally, and laterally stable under §§23.173 through 23.181. In addition, the airplane must show suitable stability and control "feel" (static stability) in any condition normally encountered in service, if flight tests show it is necessary for safe operation.

§23.173 Static longitudinal stability.

Under the conditions specified in §23.175 and with the airplane trimmed as indicated, the characteristics of the elevator control forces and the friction within the control system must be as follows:

(a) A pull must be required to obtain and maintain speeds below the specified trim speed and a push required to obtain and maintain speeds above the specified trim speed. This must be shown at any speed that can be obtained, except that speeds requiring a control force in excess of 40 pounds or speeds above the maximum allowable speed or below the minimum speed for steady unstalled flight, need not be considered.

(b) The airspeed must return to within the tolerances specified for applicable categories of airplanes when the control force is slowly released at any speed within the speed range specified in paragraph (a) of this section. The applicable tolerances are—

(1) The airspeed must return to within plus or minus 10 percent of the original trim airspeed; and

(2) For commuter category airplanes, the airspeed must return to within plus or minus 7.5 percent of the original trim airspeed for the cruising condition specified in §23.175(b).

(c) The stick force must vary with speed so that any substantial speed change results in a stick force clearly perceptible to the pilot.

[Doc. No. 4080, 29 FR 17955, Dec. 18, 1964, as amended by Amdt. 23–14, 38 FR 31820 Nov. 19, 1973; Amdt. 23–34, 52 FR 1828, Jan. 15, 1987]

§23.175 Demonstration of static longitudinal stability.

Static longitudinal stability must be shown as follows:

(a) *Climb.* The stick force curve must have a stable slope at speeds between 85 and 115 percent of the trim speed, with—

(1) Flaps retracted;

(2) Landing gear retracted;

(3) Maximum continuous power; and

(4) The airplane trimmed at the speed used in determining the climb performance required by §23.69(a).

(b) *Cruise.* With flaps and landing gear retracted and the airplane in trim with power for level flight at representative cruising speeds at high and low altitudes, including speeds up to V_{NO} or V_{MO}/M_{MO}, as appropriate, except that the speed need not exceed V_H—

(1) For normal, utility, and acrobatic category airplanes, the stick force curve must have a stable slope at all speeds within a range that is the greater of 15 percent of the trim speed plus the resulting free return speed range, or 40 knots plus the resulting free return speed range, above and below the trim speed, except that the slope need not be stable—

(i) At speeds less than 1.3 V_{S1}; or

(ii) For airplanes with V_{NE} established under §23.1505(a), at speeds greater than V_{NE}; or

(iii) For airplanes with V_{MO}/M_{MO} established under §23.1505(c), at speeds greater than V_{FC}/M_{FC}.

(2) For commuter category airplanes, the stick force curve must have a stable slope at all speeds within a range of 50 knots plus the resulting free return speed range, above and below the trim

speed, except that the slope need not be stable—

(i) At speeds less than 1.4 V_{S1}; or

(ii) At speeds greater than V_{FC}/M_{FC}; or

(iii) At speeds that require a stick force greater than 50 pounds.

(c) *Landing.* The stick force curve must have a stable slope at speeds between 1.1 V_{S1} and 1.8 V_{S1} with—

(1) Flaps in the landing position;

(2) Landing gear extended; and

(3) The airplane trimmed at—

(i) V_{REF}, or the minimum trim speed if higher, with power off; and

(ii) V_{REF} with enough power to maintain a 3 degree angle of descent.

[Doc. No. 27807, 61 FR 5190, Feb. 9, 1996]

§ 23.177 Static directional and lateral stability.

(a) The static directional stability, as shown by the tendency to recover from a wings level sideslip with the rudder free, must be positive for any landing gear and flap position appropriate to the takeoff, climb, cruise, approach, and landing configurations. This must be shown with symmetrical power up to maximum continuous power, and at speeds from 1.2 V_{S1} up to the maximum allowable speed for the condition being investigated. The angel of sideslip for these tests must be appropriate to the type of airplane. At larger angles of sideslip, up to that at which full rudder is used or a control force limit in § 23.143 is reached, whichever occurs first, and at speeds from 1.2 V_{S1} to V_O, the rudder pedal force must not reverse.

(b) The static lateral stability, as shown by the tendency to raise the low wing in a sideslip, must be positive for all landing gear and flap positions. This must be shown with symmetrical power up to 75 percent of maximum continuous power at speeds above 1.2 V_{S1} in the take off configuration(s) and at speeds above 1.3 V_{S1} in other configurations, up to the maximum allowable speed for the configuration being investigated, in the takeoff, climb, cruise, and approach configurations. For the landing configuration, the power must be that necessary to maintain a 3 degree angle of descent in coordinated flight. The static lateral stability must not be negative at 1.2 V_{S1} in

the takeoff configuration, or at 1.3 V_{S1} in other configurations. The angle of sideslip for these tests must be appropriate to the type of airplane, but in no case may the constant heading sideslip angle be less than that obtainable with a 10 degree bank, or if less, the maximum bank angle obtainable with full rudder deflection or 150 pound rudder force.

(c) Paragraph (b) of this section does not apply to acrobatic category airplanes certificated for inverted flight.

(d) In straight, steady slips at 1.2 V_{S1} for any landing gear and flap positions, and for any symmetrical power conditions up to 50 percent of maximum continuous power, the aileron and rudder control movements and forces must increase steadily, but not necessarily in constant proportion, as the angle of sideslip is increased up to the maximum appropriate to the type of airplane. At larger slip angles, up to the angle at which full rudder or aileron control is used or a control force limit contained in § 23.143 is reached, the aileron and rudder control movements and forces must not reverse as the angle of sideslip is increased. Rapid entry into, and recovery from, a maximum sideslip considered appropriate for the airplane must not result in uncontrollable flight characteristics.

[Doc. No. 27807, 61 FR 5190, Feb. 9, 1996]

§ 23.181 Dynamic stability.

(a) Any short period oscillation not including combined lateral-directional oscillations occurring between the stalling speed and the maximum allowable speed appropriate to the configuration of the airplane must be heavily damped with the primary controls—

(1) Free; and

(2) In a fixed position.

(b) Any combined lateral-directional oscillations ("Dutch roll") occurring between the stalling speed and the maximum allowable speed appropriate to the configuration of the airplane must be damped to 1/10 amplitude in 7 cycles with the primary controls—

(1) Free; and

(2) In a fixed position.

(c) If it is determined that the function of a stability augmentation system, reference § 23.672, is needed to meet the flight characteristic requirements of this part, the primary control requirements of paragraphs (a)(2) and (b)(2) of this section are not applicable to the tests needed to verify the acceptability of that system.

(d) During the conditions as specified in §23.175, when the longitudinal control force required to maintain speeds differing from the trim speed by at least plus and minus 15 percent is suddenly released, the response of the airplane must not exhibit any dangerous characteristics nor be excessive in relation to the magnitude of the control force released. Any long-period oscillation of flight path, phugoid oscillation, that results must not be so unstable as to increase the pilot's workload or otherwise endanger the airplane.

[Amdt. 23–21, 43 FR 2318, Jan. 16, 1978, as amended by Amdt. 23–45, 58 FR 42158, Aug. 6, 1993]

STALLS

§23.201 Wings level stall.

(a) It must be possible to produce and to correct roll by unreversed use of the rolling control and to produce and to correct yaw by unreversed use of the directional control, up to the time the airplane stalls.

(b) The wings level stall characteristics must be demonstrated in flight as follows: Starting from a speed at least 10 knots above the stall speed, the elevator control must be pulled back so that the rate of speed reduction will not exceed one knot per second until a stall is produced, as shown by either:

(1) An uncontrollable downward pitching motion of the airplane;

(2) A downward pitching motion of the airplane that results from the activation of a stall avoidance device (for example, stick pusher); or

(3) The control reaching the stop.

(c) Normal use of elevator control for recovery is allowed after the downward pitching motion of paragraphs (b)(1) or (b)(2) of this section has unmistakably been produced, or after the control has been held against the stop for not less than the longer of two seconds or the time employed in the minimum steady slight speed determination of §23.49.

(d) During the entry into and the recovery from the maneuver, it must be possible to prevent more than 15 degrees of roll or yaw by the normal use of controls.

(e) Compliance with the requirements of this section must be shown under the following conditions:

(1) *Wing flaps.* Retracted, fully extended, and each intermediate normal operating position.

(2) *Landing gear.* Retracted and extended.

(3) *Cowl flaps.* Appropriate to configuration.

(4) *Power:*

(i) Power off; and

(ii) 75 percent of maximum continuous power. However, if the power-to-weight ratio at 75 percent of maximum continuous power result in extreme nose-up attitudes, the test may be carried out with the power required for level flight in the landing configuration at maximum landing weight and a speed of 1.4 V_{SO}, except that the power may not be less than 50 percent of maximum continuous power.

(5) *Trim.* The airplane trimmed at a speed as near 1.5 V_{S1} as practicable.

(6) *Propeller.* Full increase r.p.m. position for the power off condition.

[Doc. No. 27807, 61 FR 5191, Feb. 9, 1996]

§23.203 Turning flight and accelerated turning stalls.

Turning flight and accelerated turning stalls must be demonstrated in tests as follows:

(a) Establish and maintain a coordinated turn in a 30 degree bank. Reduce speed by steadily and progressively tightening the turn with the elevator until the airplane is stalled, as defined in §23.201(b). The rate of speed reduction must be constant, and—

(1) For a turning flight stall, may not exceed one knot per second; and

(2) For an accelerated turning stall, be 3 to 5 knots per second with steadily increasing normal acceleration.

(b) After the airplane has stalled, as defined in §23.201(b), it must be possible to regain wings level flight by normal use of the flight controls, but without increasing power and without—

(1) Excessive loss of altitude;

(2) Undue pitchup;

(3) Uncontrollable tendency to spin;

(4) Exceeding a bank angle of 60 degrees in the original direction of the

turn or 30 degrees in the opposite direction in the case of turning flight stalls;

(5) Exceeding a bank angle of 90 degrees in the original direction of the turn or 60 degrees in the opposite direction in the case of accelerated turning stalls; and

(6) Exceeding the maximum permissible speed or allowable limit load factor.

(c) Compliance with the requirements of this section must be shown under the following conditions:

(1) *Wing flaps:* Retracted, fully extended, and each intermediate normal operating position;

(2) *Landing gear:* Retracted and extended;

(3) *Cowl flaps:* Appropriate to configuration;

(4) *Power:*

(i) Power off; and

(ii) 75 percent of maximum continuous power. However, if the power-to-weight ratio at 75 percent of maximum continuous power results in extreme nose-up attitudes, the test may be carried out with the power required for level flight in the landing configuration at maximum landing weight and a speed of 1.4 V_{SO}, except that the power may not be less than 50 percent of maximum continuous power.

(5) *Trim:* The airplane trimmed at a speed as near 1.5 V_{S1} as practicable.

(6) *Propeller.* Full increase rpm position for the power off condition.

[Amdt. 23–14, 38 FR 31820, Nov. 19, 1973, as amended by Amdt. 23–45, 58 FR 42159, Aug. 6, 1993; Amdt. 23–50, 61 FR 5191, Feb. 9, 1996]

§ 23.207 Stall warning.

(a) There must be a clear and distinctive stall warning, with the flaps and landing gear in any normal position, in straight and turning flight.

(b) The stall warning may be furnished either through the inherent aerodynamic qualities of the airplane or by a device that will give clearly distinguishable indications under expected conditions of flight. However, a visual stall warning device that requires the attention of the crew within the cockpit is not acceptable by itself.

(c) During the stall tests required by § 23.201(b) and § 23.203(a)(1), the stall warning must begin at a speed exceeding the stalling speed by a margin of not less than 5 knots and must continue until the stall occurs.

(d) When following procedures furnished in accordance with § 23.1585, the stall warning must not occur during a takeoff with all engines operating, a takeoff continued with one engine inoperative, or during an approach to landing.

(e) During the stall tests required by § 23.203(a)(2), the stall warning must begin sufficiently in advance of the stall for the stall to be averted by pilot action taken after the stall warning first occurs.

(f) For acrobatic category airplanes, an artificial stall warning may be mutable, provided that it is armed automatically during takeoff and rearmed automatically in the approach configuration.

[Amdt. 23–7, 34 FR 13087, Aug. 13, 1969, as amended by Amdt. 23–45, 58 FR 42159, Aug. 6, 1993; Amdt. 23–50, 61 FR 5191, Feb. 9, 1996]

SPINNING

§ 23.221 Spinning.

(a) *Normal category airplanes.* A single-engine, normal category airplane must be able to recover from a one-turn spin or a three-second spin, whichever takes longer, in not more than one additional turn after initiation of the first control action for recovery, or demonstrate compliance with the optional spin resistant requirements of this section.

(1) The following apply to one turn or three second spins:

(i) For both the flaps-retracted and flaps-extended conditions, the applicable airspeed limit and positive limit maneuvering load factor must not be exceeded;

(ii) No control forces or characteristic encountered during the spin or recovery may adversely affect prompt recovery;

(iii) It must be impossible to obtain unrecoverable spins with any use of the flight or engine power controls either at the entry into or during the spin; and

(iv) For the flaps-extended condition, the flaps may be retracted during the recovery but not before rotation has ceased.

(2) At the applicant's option, the airplane may be demonstrated to be spin resistant by the following:

(i) During the stall maneuver contained in §23.201, the pitch control must be pulled back and held against the stop. Then, using ailerons and rudders in the proper direction, it must be possible to maintain wings-level flight within 15 degrees of bank and to roll the airplane from a 30 degree bank in one direction to a 30 degree bank in the other direction;

(ii) Reduce the airplane speed using pitch control at a rate of approximately one knot per second until the pitch control reaches the stop; then, with the pitch control pulled back and held against the stop, apply full rudder control in a manner to promote spin entry for a period of seven seconds or through a 360 degree heading change, whichever occurs first. If the 360 degree heading change is reached first, it must have taken no fewer than four seconds. This maneuver must be performed first with the ailerons in the neutral position, and then with the ailerons deflected opposite the direction of turn in the most adverse manner. Power and airplane configuration must be set in accordance with §23.201(e) without change during the maneuver. At the end of seven seconds or a 360 degree heading change, the airplane must respond immediately and normally to primary flight controls applied to regain coordinated, unstalled flight without reversal of control effect and without exceeding the temporary control forces specified by §23.143(c); and

(iii) Compliance with §§23.201 and 23.203 must be demonstrated with the airplane in uncoordinated flight, corresponding to one ball width displacement on a slip-skid indicator, unless one ball width displacement cannot be obtained with full rudder, in which case the demonstration must be with full rudder applied.

(b) *Utility category airplanes.* A utility category airplane must meet the requirements of paragraph (a) of this section. In addition, the requirements of paragraph (c) of this section and §23.807(b)(7) must be met if approval for spinning is requested.

(c) *Acrobatic category airplanes.* An acrobatic category airplane must meet the spin requirements of paragraph (a) of this section and §23.807(b)(6). In addition, the following requirements must be met in each configuration for which approval for spinning is requested:

(1) The airplane must recover from any point in a spin up to and including six turns, or any greater number of turns for which certification is requested, in not more than one and one-half additional turns after initiation of the first control action for recovery. However, beyond three turns, the spin may be discontinued if spiral characteristics appear.

(2) The applicable airspeed limits and limit maneuvering load factors must not be exceeded. For flaps-extended configurations for which approval is requested, the flaps must not be retracted during the recovery.

(3) It must be impossible to obtain unrecoverable spins with any use of the flight or engine power controls either at the entry into or during the spin.

(4) There must be no characteristics during the spin (such as excessive rates of rotation or extreme oscillatory motion) that might prevent a successful recovery due to disorientation or incapacitation of the pilot.

[Doc. No. 27807, 61 FR 5191, Feb. 9, 1996]

GROUND AND WATER HANDLING CHARACTERISTICS

§23.231 Longitudinal stability and control.

(a) A landplane may have no uncontrollable tendency to nose over in any reasonably expected operating condition, including rebound during landing or takeoff. Wheel brakes must operate smoothly and may not induce any undue tendency to nose over.

(b) A seaplane or amphibian may not have dangerous or uncontrollable porpoising characteristics at any normal operating speed on the water.

§23.233 Directional stability and control.

(a) A 90 degree cross-component of wind velocity, demonstrated to be safe for taxiing, takeoff, and landing must be established and must be not less than $0.2 V_{SO}$.

(b) The airplane must be satisfactorily controllable in power-off landings at normal landing speed, without using brakes or engine power to maintain a straight path until the speed has decreased to at least 50 percent of the speed at touchdown.

(c) The airplane must have adequate directional control during taxiing.

(d) Seaplanes must demonstrate satisfactory directional stability and control for water operations up to the maximum wind velocity specified in paragraph (a) of this section.

[Doc. No. 4080, 29 FR 17955, Dec. 18, 1964, as amended by Amdt. 23–45, 58 FR 42159, Aug. 6, 1993; Amdt. 23–50, 61 FR 5192, Feb. 9, 1996]

§ 23.235 Operation on unpaved surfaces.

The airplane must be demonstrated to have satisfactory characteristics and the shock-absorbing mechanism must not damage the structure of the airplane when the airplane is taxied on the roughest ground that may reasonably be expected in normal operation and when takeoffs and landings are performed on unpaved runways having the roughest surface that may reasonably be expected in normal operation.

[Doc. No. 27807, 61 FR 5192, Feb. 9, 1996]

§ 23.237 Operation on water.

A wave height, demonstrated to be safe for operation, and any necessary water handling procedures for seaplanes and amphibians must be established.

[Doc. No. 27807, 61 FR 5192, Feb. 9, 1996]

§ 23.239 Spray characteristics.

Spray may not dangerously obscure the vision of the pilots or damage the propellers or other parts of a seaplane or amphibian at any time during taxiing, takeoff, and landing.

MISCELLANEOUS FLIGHT REQUIREMENTS

§ 23.251 Vibration and buffeting.

There must be no vibration or buffeting severe enough to result in structural damage, and each part of the airplane must be free from excessive vibration, under any appropriate speed and power conditions up to V_D/M_D. In addition, there must be no buffeting in any normal flight condition severe enough to interfere with the satisfactory control of the airplane or cause excessive fatigue to the flight crew. Stall warning buffeting within these limits is allowable.

[Doc. No. 26269, 58 FR 42159, Aug. 6, 1993]

§ 23.253 High speed characteristics.

If a maximum operating speed V_{MO}/M_{MO} is established under § 23.1505(c), the following speed increase and recovery characteristics must be met:

(a) Operating conditions and characteristics likely to cause inadvertent speed increases (including upsets in pitch and roll) must be simulated with the airplane trimmed at any likely speed up to V_{MO}/M_{MO}. These conditions and characteristics include gust upsets, inadvertent control movements, low stick force gradients in relation to control friction, passenger movement, leveling off from climb, and descent from Mach to airspeed limit altitude.

(b) Allowing for pilot reaction time after occurrence of the effective inherent or artificial speed warning specified in § 23.1303, it must be shown that the airplane can be recovered to a normal attitude and its speed reduced to V_{MO}/M_{MO}, without—

(1) Exceeding V_D/M_D, the maximum speed shown under § 23.251, or the structural limitations; or

(2) Buffeting that would impair the pilot's ability to read the instruments or to control the airplane for recovery.

(c) There may be no control reversal about any axis at any speed up to the maximum speed shown under § 23.251. Any reversal of elevator control force or tendency of the airplane to pitch, roll, or yaw must be mild and readily controllable, using normal piloting techniques.

[Amdt. 23–7, 34 FR 13087, Aug. 13, 1969; as amended by Amdt. 23–26, 45 FR 60170, Sept. 11, 1980; Amdt. 23–45, 58 FR 42160, Aug. 6, 1993; Amdt. 23–50, 61 FR 5192, Feb. 9, 1996]

Subpart C—Structure

GENERAL

§ 23.301 Loads.

(a) Strength requirements are specified in terms of limit loads (the maximum loads to be expected in service) and ultimate loads (limit loads multiplied by prescribed factors of safety). Unless otherwise provided, prescribed loads are limit loads.

(b) Unless otherwise provided, the air, ground, and water loads must be placed in equilibrium with inertia forces, considering each item of mass in the airplane. These loads must be distributed to conservatively approximate or closely represent actual conditions. Methods used to determine load intensities and distribution on canard and tandem wing configurations must be validated by flight test measurement unless the methods used for determining those loading conditions are shown to be reliable or conservative on the configuration under consideration.

(c) If deflections under load would significantly change the distribution of external or internal loads, this redistribution must be taken into account.

(d) Simplified structural design criteria may be used if they result in design loads not less than those prescribed in §§ 23.331 through 23.521. For airplane configurations described in appendix A, § 23.1, the design criteria of appendix A of this part are an approved equivalent of §§ 23.321 through 23.459. If appendix A of this part is used, the entire appendix must be substituted for the corresponding sections of this part.

[Doc. No. 4080, 29 FR 17955, Dec. 18, 1964; 30 FR 258, Jan. 9, 1965, as amended by Amdt. 23-28, 47 FR 13315, Mar. 29, 1982; Amdt. 23-42, 56 FR 352, Jan. 3, 1991; Amdt. 23-48, 61 FR 5143, Feb. 9, 1996]

§ 23.302 Canard or tandem wing configurations.

The forward structure of a canard or tandem wing configuration must:

(a) Meet all requirements of subpart C and subpart D of this part applicable to a wing; and

(b) Meet all requirements applicable to the function performed by these surfaces.

[Amdt. 23-42, 56 FR 352, Jan. 3, 1991]

§ 23.303 Factor of safety.

Unless otherwise provided, a factor of safety of 1.5 must be used.

§ 23.305 Strength and deformation.

(a) The structure must be able to support limit loads without detrimental, permanent deformation. At any load up to limit loads, the deformation may not interfere with safe operation.

(b) The structure must be able to support ultimate loads without failure for at least three seconds, except local failures or structural instabilities between limit and ultimate load are acceptable only if the structure can sustain the required ultimate load for at least three seconds. However when proof of strength is shown by dynamic tests simulating actual load conditions, the three second limit does not apply.

[Doc. No. 4080, 29 FR 17955, Dec. 18, 1964, as amended by Amdt. 23-45, 58 FR 42160, Aug. 6, 1993]

§ 23.307 Proof of structure.

(a) Compliance with the strength and deformation requirements of § 23.305 must be shown for each critical load condition. Structural analysis may be used only if the structure conforms to those for which experience has shown this method to be reliable. In other cases, substantiating load tests must be made. Dynamic tests, including structural flight tests, are acceptable if the design load conditions have been simulated.

(b) Certain parts of the structure must be tested as specified in Subpart D of this part.

FLIGHT LOADS

§ 23.321 General.

(a) Flight load factors represent the ratio of the aerodynamic force component (acting normal to the assumed longitudinal axis of the airplane) to the weight of the airplane. A positive flight load factor is one in which the aerodynamic force acts upward, with respect to the airplane.

(b) Compliance with the flight load requirements of this subpart must be shown—

(1) At each critical altitude within the range in which the airplane may be expected to operate;

(2) At each weight from the design minimum weight to the design maximum weight; and

(3) For each required altitude and weight, for any practicable distribution of disposable load within the operating limitations specified in §§ 23.1583 through 23.1589.

(c) When significant, the effects of compressibility must be taken into account.

[Doc. No. 4080, 29 FR 17955, Dec. 18, 1964, as amended by Amdt. 23–45, 58 FR 42160, Aug. 6, 1993]

§ 23.331 Symmetrical flight conditions.

(a) The appropriate balancing horizontal tail load must be accounted for in a rational or conservative manner when determining the wing loads and linear inertia loads corresponding to any of the symmetrical flight conditions specified in §§ 23.333 through 23.341.

(b) The incremental horizontal tail loads due to maneuvering and gusts must be reacted by the angular inertia of the airplane in a rational or conservative manner.

(c) Mutual influence of the aerodynamic surfaces must be taken into account when determining flight loads.

[Doc. No. 4080, 29 FR 17955, Dec. 18, 1964; 30 FR 258, Jan. 9, 1965, as amended by Amdt. 23–42, 56 FR 352, Jan. 3, 1991]

§ 23.333 Flight envelope.

(a) *General.* Compliance with the strength requirements of this subpart must be shown at any combination of airspeed and load factor on and within the boundaries of a flight envelope (similar to the one in paragraph (d) of this section) that represents the envelope of the flight loading conditions specified by the maneuvering and gust criteria of paragraphs (b) and (c) of this section respectively.

(b) *Maneuvering envelope.* Except where limited by maximum (static) lift coefficients, the airplane is assumed to

be subjected to symmetrical maneuvers resulting in the following limit load factors:

(1) The positive maneuvering load factor specified in § 23.337 at speeds up to V_D;

(2) The negative maneuvering load factor specified in § 23.337 at V_C; and

(3) Factors varying linearly with speed from the specified value at V_C to 0.0 at V_D for the normal and commuter category, and −1.0 at V_D for the acrobatic and utility categories.

(c) *Gust envelope.* (1) The airplane is assumed to be subjected to symmetrical vertical gusts in level flight. The resulting limit load factors must correspond to the conditions determined as follows:

(i) Positive (up) and negative (down) gusts of 50 f.p.s. at V_C must be considered at altitudes between sea level and 20,000 feet. The gust velocity may be reduced linearly from 50 f.p.s. at 20,000 feet to 25 f.p.s. at 50,000 feet.

(ii) Positive and negative gusts of 25 f.p.s. at V_D must be considered at altitudes between sea level and 20,000 feet. The gust velocity may be reduced linearly from 25 f.p.s. at 20,000 feet to 12.5 f.p.s. at 50,000 feet.

(iii) In addition, for commuter category airplanes, positive (up) and negative (down) rough air gusts of 66 f.p.s. at VB must be considered at altitudes between sea level and 20,000 feet. The gust velocity may be reduced linearly from 66 f.p.s. at 20,000 feet to 38 f.p.s. at 50,000 feet.

(2) The following assumptions must be made:

(i) The shape of the gust is—

$$U = \frac{U_{de}}{2}\left(1 - \text{COS}\,\frac{2\pi s}{25C}\right)$$

Where—

s=Distance penetrated into gust (ft.);
C=Mean geometric chord of wing (ft.); and
Ude=Derived gust velocity referred to in subparagraph (1) of this section.

(ii) Gust load factors vary linearly with speed between V_C and V_D.

(d) *Flight envelope.*

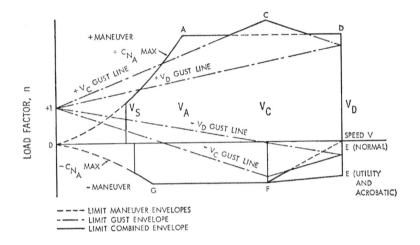

LIMIT MANEUVER ENVELOPES
LIMIT GUST ENVELOPE
LIMIT COMBINED ENVELOPE

[Doc. No. 4080, 29 FR 17955, Dec. 18, 1964, as amended by Amdt. 23–7, 34 FR 13087, Aug. 13, 1969; Amdt. 23–34, 52 FR 1829, Jan. 15, 1987]

§23.335 Design airspeeds.

Except as provided in paragraph (a)(4) of this section, the selected design airspeeds are equivalent airspeeds (EAS).

(a) *Design cruising speed, V_C.* For V_C the following apply:

(1) Where W/S'=wing loading at the design maximum takeoff weight, V_c (in knots) may not be less than—

(i) $33 \sqrt{(W/S)}$ (for normal, utility, and commuter category airplanes);

(ii) $36 \sqrt{(W/S)}$ (for acrobatic category airplanes).

(2) For values of *W/S* more than 20, the multiplying factors may be decreased linearly with *W/S* to a value of 28.6 where *W/S*=100.

(3) V_C need not be more than $0.9 \, V_H$ at sea level.

(4) At altitudes where an M_D is established, a cruising speed M_C limited by compressibility may be selected.

(b) *Design dive speed V_D.* For V_D, the following apply:

(1) V_D/M_D may not be less than 1.25 V_C/M_C; and

(2) With $V_{C \ min}$, the required minimum design cruising speed, V_D (in knots) may not be less than—

(i) 1.40 $V_{c \ min}$ (for normal and commuter category airplanes);

(ii) 1.50 $V_{C \ min}$ (for utility category airplanes); and

(iii) 1.55 $V_{C \ min}$ (for acrobatic category airplanes).

(3) For values of *W/S* more than 20, the multiplying factors in paragraph (b)(2) of this section may be decreased linearly with *W/S* to a value of 1.35 where *W/S*=100.

(4) Compliance with paragraphs (b)(1) and (2) of this section need not be shown if V_D/M_D is selected so that the minimum speed margin between V_C/M_C and V_D/M_D is the greater of the following:

(i) The speed increase resulting when, from the initial condition of stabilized flight at V_C/M_C, the airplane is assumed to be upset, flown for 20 seconds along a flight path 7.5° below the initial path, and then pulled up with a load factor of 1.5 (0.5 g. acceleration increment). At least 75 percent maximum continuous power for reciprocating engines, and maximum cruising power for turbines, or, if less, the power required for V_C/M_C for both kinds of engines, must be assumed until the pullup is initiated, at which point power reduction and pilot-controlled drag devices may be used; and either—

199

(ii) Mach 0.05 for normal, utility, and acrobatic category airplanes (at altitudes where M_D is established); or

(iii) Mach 0.07 for commuter category airplanes (at altitudes where M_D is established) unless a rational analysis, including the effects of automatic systems, is used to determine a lower margin. If a rational analysis is used, the minimum speed margin must be enough to provide for atmospheric variations (such as horizontal gusts), and the penetration of jet streams or cold fronts), instrument errors, airframe production variations, and must not be less than Mach 0.05.

(c) *Design maneuvering speed V_A.* For V_A, the following applies:

(1) V_A may not be less than $V_S\sqrt{n}$ where—

(i) V_S is a computed stalling speed with flaps retracted at the design weight, normally based on the maximum airplane normal force coefficients, C_{NA}; and

(ii) n is the limit maneuvering load factor used in design

(2) The value of V_A need not exceed the value of V_C used in design.

(d) *Design speed for maximum gust intensity, V_B.* For V_B, the following apply:

(1) V_B may not be less than the speed determined by the intersection of the line representing the maximum positive lift, C_{NMAX}, and the line representing the rough air gust velocity on the gust V-n diagram, or $V_{S1}\sqrt{n_g}$, whichever is less, where:

(i) n_g the positive airplane gust load factor due to gust, at speed V_C (in accordance with § 23.341), and at the particular weight under consideration; and

(ii) V_{S1} is the stalling speed with the flaps retracted at the particular weight under consideration.

(2) V_B need not be greater than V_C.

[Doc. No. 4080, 29 FR 17955, Dec. 18, 1964, as amended by Amdt. 23–7, 34 FR 13088, Aug. 13, 1969; Amdt. 23–16, 40 FR 2577, Jan. 14, 1975; Amdt. 23–34, 52 FR 1829, Jan. 15, 1987; Amdt. 23–24, 52 FR 34745, Sept. 14, 1987; Amdt. 23–48, 61 FR 5143, Feb. 9, 1996]

§ 23.337 Limit maneuvering load factors.

(a) The positive limit maneuvering load factor n may not be less than—

(1) $2.1 + (24,000 \div (W+10,000))$ for normal and commuter category airplanes,

where W=design maximum takeoff weight, except that n need not be more than 3.8;

(2) 4.4 for utility category airplanes; or

(3) 6.0 for acrobatic category airplanes.

(b) The negative limit maneuvering load factor may not be less than—

(1) 0.4 times the positive load factor for the normal utility and commuter categories; or

(2) 0.5 times the positive load factor for the acrobatic category.

(c) Maneuvering load factors lower than those specified in this section may be used if the airplane has design features that make it impossible to exceed these values in flight.

[Doc. No. 4080, 29 FR 17955, Dec. 18, 1964, as amended by Amdt. 23–7, 34 FR 13088, Aug. 13, 1969; Amdt. 23–34, 52 FR 1829, Jan. 15, 1987; Amdt. 23–48, 61 FR 5144, Feb. 9, 1996]

§ 23.341 Gust loads factors.

(a) Each airplane must be designed to withstand loads on each lifting surface resulting from gusts specified in § 23.333(c).

(b) The gust load for a canard or tandem wing configuration must be computed using a rational analysis, or may be computed in accordance with paragraph (c) of this section, provided that the resulting net loads are shown to be conservative with respect to the gust criteria of § 23.333(c).

(c) In the absence of a more rational analysis, the gust load factors must be computed as follows—

$$n = 1 + \frac{K_g\, U_{de}\, V\, a}{498\,(W/S)}$$

Where—

$K_g = 0.88\mu_g/5.3 + \mu_g$ = gust alleviation factor;

$\mu_g = 2(W/S)/\rho\, Ca g$ = airplane mass ratio;

U_{de} = Derived gust velocities referred to in § 23.333(c) (f.p.s.);

ρ = Density of air (slugs/cu.ft.);

W/S = Wing loading (p.s.f.) due to the applicable weight of the airplane in the particular load case.

W/S = Wing loading (p.s.f.);

C = Mean geometric chord (ft.);

g = Acceleration due to gravity (ft./sec.²)

V = Airplane equivalent speed (knots); and

a = Slope of the airplane normal force coefficient curve C_{NA} per radian if the gust loads are applied to the wings and horizontal tail surfaces simultaneously by a rational method. The wing lift curve slope C_L per radian may be used when the gust load is applied to the wings only and the horizontal tail gust loads are treated as a separate condition.

[Amdt. 23–7, 34 FR 13088, Aug. 13, 1969, as amended by Amdt. 23–42, 56 FR 352, Jan. 3, 1991; Amdt. 23–48, 61 FR 5144, Feb. 9, 1996]

§23.343 Design fuel loads.

(a) The disposable load combinations must include each fuel load in the range from zero fuel to the selected maximum fuel load.

(b) If fuel is carried in the wings, the maximum allowable weight of the airplane without any fuel in the wing tank(s) must be established as "maximum zero wing fuel weight," if it is less than the maximum weight.

(c) For commuter category airplanes, a structural reserve fuel condition, not exceeding fuel necessary for 45 minutes of operation at maximum continuous power, may be selected. If a structural reserve fuel condition is selected, it must be used as the minimum fuel weight condition for showing compliance with the flight load requirements prescribed in this part and—

(1) The structure must be designed to withstand a condition of zero fuel in the wing at limit loads corresponding to:

(i) Ninety percent of the maneuvering load factors defined in §23.337, and

(ii) Gust velocities equal to 85 percent of the values prescribed in §23.333(c).

(2) The fatigue evaluation of the structure must account for any increase in operating stresses resulting from the design condition of paragraph (c)(1) of this section.

(3) The flutter, deformation, and vibration requirements must also be met with zero fuel in the wings.

[Doc. No. 27805, 61 FR 5144, Feb. 9, 1996]

§23.345 High lift devices.

(a) If flaps or similar high lift devices are to be used for takeoff, approach or landing, the airplane, with the flaps fully extended at V_F, is assumed to be subjected to symmetrical maneuvers and gusts within the range determined by—

(1) Maneuvering, to a positive limit load factor of 2.0; and

(2) Positive and negative gust of 25 feet per second acting normal to the flight path in level flight.

(b) V_F must be assumed to be not less than 1.4 V_S or 1.8 V_{SF}, whichever is greater, where—

(1) V_S is the computed stalling speed with flaps retracted at the design weight; and

(2) V_{SF} is the computed stalling speed with flaps fully extended at the design weight.

(3) If an automatic flap load limiting device is used, the airplane may be designed for the critical combinations of airspeed and flap position allowed by that device.

(c) In determining external loads on the airplane as a whole, thrust, slipstream, and pitching acceleration may be assumed to be zero.

(d) The flaps, their operating mechanism, and their supporting structures, must be designed to withstand the conditions prescribed in paragraph (a) of this section. In addition, with the flaps fully extended at V_F, the following conditions, taken separately, must be accounted for:

(1) A head-on gust having a velocity of 25 feet per second (EAS), combined with propeller slipstream corresponding to 75 percent of maximum continuous power; and

(2) The effects of propeller slipstream corresponding to maximum takeoff power.

[Doc. No. 27805, 61 FR 5144, Feb. 9, 1996]

§23.347 Unsymmetrical flight conditions.

(a) The airplane is assumed to be subjected to the unsymmetrical flight conditions of §§23.349 and 23.351. Unbalanced aerodynamic moments about the center of gravity must be reacted in a rational or conservative manner, considering the principal masses furnishing the reacting inertia forces.

(b) Acrobatic category airplanes certified for flick maneuvers (snap roll) must be designed for additional asymmetric loads acting on the wing and the horizontal tail.

[Doc. No. 4080, 29 FR 17955, Dec. 18, 1964, as amended by Amdt. 23–48, 61 FR 5144, Feb. 9, 1996]

§ 23.349 Rolling conditions.

The wing and wing bracing must be designed for the following loading conditions:

(a) Unsymmetrical wing loads appropriate to the category. Unless the following values result in unrealistic loads, the rolling accelerations may be obtained by modifying the symmetrical flight conditions in § 23.333(d) as follows:

(1) For the acrobatic category, in conditions A and F, assume that 100 percent of the semispan wing airload acts on one side of the plane of symmetry and 60 percent of this load acts on the other side.

(2) For normal, utility, and commuter categories, in Condition A, assume that 100 percent of the semispan wing airload acts on one side of the airplane and 75 percent of this load acts on the other side.

(b) The loads resulting from the aileron deflections and speeds specified in § 23.455, in combination with an airplane load factor of at least two thirds of the positive maneuvering load factor used for design. Unless the following values result in unrealistic loads, the effect of aileron displacement on wing torsion may be accounted for by adding the following increment to the basic airfoil moment coefficient over the aileron portion of the span in the critical condition determined in § 23.333(d):

$$\Delta c_m = -0.01\delta$$

where—

Δc_m is the moment coefficient increment; and
δ is the down aileron deflection in degrees in the critical condition.

[Doc. No. 4080, 29 FR 17955, Dec. 18, 1964, as amended by Amdt. 23–7, 34 FR 13088, Aug. 13, 1969; Amdt. 23–34, 52 FR 1829, Jan. 15, 1987; Amdt. 23–48, 61 FR 5144, Feb. 9, 1996]

§ 23.351 Yawing conditions.

The airplane must be designed for yawing loads on the vertical surfaces resulting from the loads specified in §§ 23.441 through 23.445.

[Doc. No. 4080, 29 FR 17955, Dec. 18, 1964; 30 FR 258, Jan. 9, 1965, as amended by Amdt. 23–42, 56 FR 352, Jan. 3, 1991]

§ 23.361 Engine torque.

(a) Each engine mount and its supporting structure must be designed for the effects of—

(1) A limit engine torque corresponding to takeoff power and propeller speed acting simultaneously with 75 percent of the limit loads from flight condition A of § 23.333(d);

(2) A limit engine torque corresponding to maximum continuous power and propeller speed acting simultaneously with the limit loads from flight condition A of § 23.333(d); and

(3) For turbopropeller installations, in addition to the conditions specified in paragraphs (a)(1) and (a)(2) of this section, a limit engine torque corresponding to takeoff power and propeller speed, multiplied by a factor accounting for propeller control system malfunction, including quick feathering, acting simultaneously with 1g level flight loads. In the absence of a rational analysis, a factor of 1.6 must be used.

(b) For turbine engine installations, the engine mounts and supporting structure must be designed to withstand each of the following:

(1) A limit engine torque load imposed by sudden engine stoppage due to malfunction or structural failure (such as compressor jamming).

(2) A limit engine torque load imposed by the maximum acceleration of the engine.

(c) The limit engine torque to be considered under paragraph (a) of this section must be obtained by multiplying the mean torque by a factor of—

(1) 1.25 for turbopropeller installations;

(2) 1.33 for engines with five or more cylinders; and

(3) Two, three, or four, for engines with four, three, or two cylinders, respectively.

[Amdt. 23–26, 45 FR 60171, Sept. 11, 1980, as amended by Amdt. 23–45, 58 FR 42160, Aug. 6, 1993]

§ 23.363 Side load on engine mount.

(a) Each engine mount and its supporting structure must be designed for a limit load factor in a lateral direction, for the side load on the engine mount, of not less than—

(1) 1.33, or

(2) One-third of the limit load factor for flight condition A.

(b) The side load prescribed in paragraph (a) of this section may be assumed to be independent of other flight conditions.

§23.365 Pressurized cabin loads.

For each pressurized compartment, the following apply:

(a) The airplane structure must be strong enough to withstand the flight loads combined with pressure differential loads from zero up to the maximum relief valve setting.

(b) The external pressure distribution in flight, and any stress concentrations, must be accounted for.

(c) If landings may be made with the cabin pressurized, landing loads must be combined with pressure differential loads from zero up to the maximum allowed during landing.

(d) The airplane structure must be strong enough to withstand the pressure differential loads corresponding to the maximum relief valve setting multiplied by a factor of 1.33, omitting other loads.

(e) If a pressurized cabin has two or more compartments separated by bulkheads or a floor, the primary structure must be designed for the effects of sudden release of pressure in any compartment with external doors or windows. This condition must be investigated for the effects of failure of the largest opening in the compartment. The effects of intercompartmental venting may be considered.

§23.367 Unsymmetrical loads due to engine failure.

(a) Turbopropeller airplanes must be designed for the unsymmetrical loads resulting from the failure of the critical engine including the following conditions in combination with a single malfunction of the propeller drag limiting system, considering the probable pilot corrective action on the flight controls:

(1) At speeds between V_{MC} and V_D, the loads resulting from power failure because of fuel flow interruption are considered to be limit loads.

(2) At speeds between V_{MC} and V_C, the loads resulting from the disconnection of the engine compressor from the turbine or from loss of the turbine blades are considered to be ultimate loads.

(3) The time history of the thrust decay and drag buildup occurring as a result of the prescribed engine failures must be substantiated by test or other data applicable to the particular engine-propeller combination.

(4) The timing and magnitude of the probable pilot corrective action must be conservatively estimated, considering the characteristics of the particular engine-propeller-airplane combination.

(b) Pilot corrective action may be assumed to be initiated at the time maximum yawing velocity is reached, but not earlier than 2 seconds after the engine failure. The magnitude of the corrective action may be based on the limit pilot forces specified in §23.397 except that lower forces may be assumed where it is shown by analysis or test that these forces can control the yaw and roll resulting from the prescribed engine failure conditions.

[Amdt. 23–7, 34 FR 13089, Aug. 13, 1969]

§23.369 Rear lift truss.

(a) If a rear lift truss is used, it must be designed to withstand conditions of reversed airflow at a design speed of—

V=8.7 $\sqrt{(W/S)}$ + 8.7 (knots), where W/S=wing loading at design maximum takeoff weight.

(b) Either aerodynamic data for the particular wing section used, or a value of C_L equalling -0.8 with a chordwise distribution that is triangular between a peak at the trailing edge and zero at the leading edge, must be used.

[Doc. No. 4080, 29 FR 17955, Dec. 18, 1964, as amended by Amdt. 23–7, 34 FR 13089, Aug. 13, 1969; 34 FR 17509, Oct. 30, 1969; Amdt. 23–45, 58 FR 42160, Aug. 6, 1993; Amdt. 23–48, 61 FR 5145, Feb. 9, 1996]

§23.371 Gyroscopic and aerodynamic loads.

(a) Each engine mount and its supporting structure must be designed for the gyroscopic, inertial, and aerodynamic loads that result, with the engine(s) and propeller(s), if applicable, at maximum continuous r.p.m., under either:

(1) The conditions prescribed in §23.351 and §23.423; or

(2) All possible combinations of the following—

(i) A yaw velocity of 2.5 radians per second;

(ii) A pitch velocity of 1.0 radian per second;

(iii) A normal load factor of 2.5; and

(iv) Maximum continuous thrust.

(b) For airplanes approved for aerobatic maneuvers, each engine mount and its supporting structure must meet the requirements of paragraph (a) of this section and be designed to withstand the load factors expected during combined maximum yaw and pitch velocities.

(c) For airplanes certificated in the commuter category, each engine mount and its supporting structure must meet the requirements of paragraph (a) of this section and the gust conditions specified in § 23.341 of this part.

[Doc. No. 27805, 61 FR 5145, Feb. 9, 1996]

§ 23.373 Speed control devices.

If speed control devices (such as spoilers and drag flaps) are incorporated for use in enroute conditions—

(a) The airplane must be designed for the symmetrical maneuvers and gusts prescribed in §§ 23.333, 23.337, and 23.341, and the yawing maneuvers and lateral gusts in §§ 23.441 and 23.443, with the device extended at speeds up to the placard device extended speed; and

(b) If the device has automatic operating or load limiting features, the airplane must be designed for the maneuver and gust conditions prescribed in paragraph (a) of this section at the speeds and corresponding device positions that the mechanism allows.

[Amdt. 23-7, 34 FR 13089, Aug. 13, 1969]

CONTROL SURFACE AND SYSTEM LOADS

§ 23.391 Control surface loads.

The control surface loads specified in §§ 23.397 through 23.459 are assumed to occur in the conditions described in §§ 23.331 through 23.351.

[Doc. No. 4080, 29 FR 17955, Dec. 18, 1964, as amended by Amdt. 23-48, 61 FR 5145, Feb. 9, 1996]

§ 23.393 Loads parallel to hinge line.

(a) Control surfaces and supporting hinge brackets must be designed to withstand inertial loads acting parallel to the hinge line.

(b) In the absence of more rational data, the inertial loads may be assumed to be equal to KW, where—

(1) K=24 for vertical surfaces;

(2) K=12 for horizontal surfaces; and

(3) W=weight of the movable surfaces.

[Doc. No. 27805, 61 FR 5145, Feb. 9, 1996]

§ 23.395 Control system loads.

(a) Each flight control system and its supporting structure must be designed for loads corresponding to at least 125 percent of the computed hinge moments of the movable control surface in the conditions prescribed in §§ 23.391 through 23.459. In addition, the following apply:

(1) The system limit loads need not exceed the higher of the loads that can be produced by the pilot and automatic devices operating the controls. However, autopilot forces need not be added to pilot forces. The system must be designed for the maximum effort of the pilot or autopilot, whichever is higher. In addition, if the pilot and the autopilot act in opposition, the part of the system between them may be designed for the maximum effort of the one that imposes the lesser load. Pilot forces used for design need not exceed the maximum forces prescribed in § 23.397(b).

(2) The design must, in any case, provide a rugged system for service use, considering jamming, ground gusts, taxiing downwind, control inertia, and friction. Compliance with this subparagraph may be shown by designing for loads resulting from application of the minimum forces prescribed in § 23.397(b).

(b) A 125 percent factor on computed hinge moments must be used to design elevator, aileron, and rudder systems. However, a factor as low as 1.0 may be used if hinge moments are based on accurate flight test data, the exact reduction depending upon the accuracy and reliability of the data.

(c) Pilot forces used for design are assumed to act at the appropriate control grips or pads as they would in flight, and to react at the attachments of the control system to the control surface horns.

[Doc. No. 4080, 29 FR 17955, Dec. 18, 1964, as amended by Amdt. 23–7, 34 FR 13089, Aug. 13, 1969]

§23.397 Limit control forces and torques.

(a) In the control surface flight loading condition, the airloads on movable surfaces and the corresponding deflections need not exceed those that would result in flight from the application of any pilot force within the ranges specified in paragraph (b) of this section. In applying this criterion, the effects of control system boost and servo-mechanisms, and the effects of tabs must be considered. The automatic pilot effort must be used for design if it alone can produce higher control surface loads than the human pilot.

(b) The limit pilot forces and torques are as follows:

Control	Maximum forces or torques for design weight, weight equal to or less than 5,000 pounds [1]	Minimum forces or torques [2]
Aileron:		
Stick	67 lbs	40 lbs.
Wheel [3]	50 D in.-lbs [4]	40 D in.-lbs.[4]
Elevator:		
Stick	167 lbs	100 lbs.
Wheel (symmetrical)	200 lbs	100 lbs.
Wheel (unsymmetrical) [5]	....	100 lbs.
Rudder	200 lbs	150 lbs.

[1] For design weight (W) more than 5,000 pounds, the specified maximum values must be increased linearly with weight to 1.18 times the specified values at a design weight of 12,500 pounds and for commuter category airplanes, the specified values must be increased linearly with weight to 1.35 times the specified values at a design weight of 19,000 pounds.

[2] If the design of any individual set of control systems or surfaces makes these specified minimum forces or torques inapplicable, values corresponding to the present hinge moments obtained under §23.415, but not less than 0.6 of the specified minimum forces or torques, may be used.

[3] The critical parts of the aileron control system must also be designed for a single tangential force with a limit value of 1.25 times the couple force determined from the above criteria.

[4] D=wheel diameter (inches).

[5] The unsymmetrical force must be applied at one of the normal handgrip points on the control wheel.

[Doc. No. 4080, 29 FR 17955, Dec. 18, 1964, as amended by Amdt. 23–7, 34 FR 13089, Aug. 13, 1969; Amdt. 23–17, 41 FR 55464, Dec. 20, 1976; Amdt. 23–34, 52 FR 1829, Jan. 15, 1987; Amdt. 23–45, 58 FR 42160, Aug. 6, 1993]

§23.399 Dual control system.

(a) Each dual control system must be designed to withstand the force of the pilots operating in opposition, using individual pilot forces not less than the greater of—

(1) 0.75 times those obtained under §23.395; or

(2) The minimum forces specified in §23.397(b).

(b) Each dual control system must be designed to withstand the force of the pilots applied together, in the same direction, using individual pilot forces not less than 0.75 times those obtained under §23.395.

[Doc. No. 27805, 61 FR 5145, Feb. 9, 1996]

§23.405 Secondary control system.

Secondary controls, such as wheel brakes, spoilers, and tab controls, must be designed for the maximum forces that a pilot is likely to apply to those controls.

§23.407 Trim tab effects.

The effects of trim tabs on the control surface design conditions must be accounted for only where the surface loads are limited by maximum pilot effort. In these cases, the tabs are considered to be deflected in the direction that would assist the pilot. These deflections must correspond to the maximum degree of "out of trim" expected at the speed for the condition under consideration.

§23.409 Tabs.

Control surface tabs must be designed for the most severe combination of airspeed and tab deflection likely to be obtained within the flight envelope for any usable loading condition.

§23.415 Ground gust conditions.

(a) The control system must be investigated as follows for control surface loads due to ground gusts and taxiing downwind:

(1) If an investigation of the control system for ground gust loads is not required by paragraph (a)(2) of this section, but the applicant elects to design a part of the control system of these loads, these loads need only be carried from control surface horns through the

nearest stops or gust locks and their supporting structures.

(2) If pilot forces less than the minimums specified in § 23.397(b) are used for design, the effects of surface loads due to ground gusts and taxiing downwind must be investigated for the entire control system according to the formula:

H=K c S q

where—

H=limit hinge moment (ft.-lbs.);

c=mean chord of the control surface aft of the hinge line (ft.);

S=area of control surface aft of the hinge line (sq. ft.);

q=dynamic pressure (p.s.f.) based on a design speed not less than $14.6 \sqrt{(W/S)} + 14.6$ (f.p.s.) where W/S=wing loading at design maximum weight, except that the design speed need not exceed 88 (f.p.s.);

K=limit hinge moment factor for ground gusts derived in paragraph (b) of this section. (For ailerons and elevators, a positive value of K indicates a moment tending to depress the surface and a negative value of K indicates a moment tending to raise the surface).

(b) The limit hinge moment factor K for ground gusts must be derived as follows:

Surface	K	Position of controls
(a) Aileron	0.75	Control column locked lashed in mid-position.
(b) Aileron	±0.50	Ailerons at full throw; + moment on one aileron, − moment on the other.
(c) Elevator	±0.75	(c) Elevator full up (−).
(d) Elevator	....	(d) Elevator full down (+).
(e) Rudder	±0.75	(e) Rudder in neutral.
(f) Rudder	....	(f) Rudder at full throw.

(c) At all weights between the empty weight and the maximum weight declared for tie-down stated in the appropriate manual, any declared tie-down points and surrounding structure, control system, surfaces and associated gust locks, must be designed to withstand the limit load conditions that exist when the airplane is tied down and that result from wind speeds of up to 65 knots horizontally from any direction.

[Doc. No. 4080, 29 FR 17955, Dec. 18, 1964, as amended by Amdt. 23-7, 34 FR 13089, Aug. 13, 1969; Amdt. 23-45, 58 FR 42160, Aug. 6, 1993; Amdt. 23-48, 61 FR 5145, Feb. 9, 1996]

HORIZONTAL STABILIZING AND BALANCING SURFACES

§ 23.421 Balancing loads.

(a) A horizontal surface balancing load is a load necessary to maintain equilibrium in any specified flight condition with no pitching acceleration.

(b) Horizontal balancing surfaces must be designed for the balancing loads occurring at any point on the limit maneuvering envelope and in the flap conditions specified in § 23.345.

[Doc. No. 4080, 29 FR 17955, Dec. 18, 1964, as amended by Amdt. 23-7, 34 FR 13089, Aug. 13, 1969; Amdt. 23-42, 56 FR 352, Jan. 3, 1991]

§ 23.423 Maneuvering loads.

Each horizontal surface and its supporting structure, and the main wing of a canard or tandem wing configuration, if that surface has pitch control, must be designed for the maneuvering loads imposed by the following conditions:

(a) A sudden movement of the pitching control, at the speed V_A, to the maximum aft movement, and the maximum forward movement, as limited by the control stops, or pilot effort, whichever is critical.

(b) A sudden aft movement of the pitching control at speeds above V_A, followed by a forward movement of the pitching control resulting in the following combinations of normal and angular acceleration:

Condition	Normal acceleration (n)	Angular acceleration (radian/sec₂)
Nose-up pitching	1.0	$+39n_m \div V \times (n_m - 1.5)$
Nose-down pitching	n_m	$-39n_m \div V \times (n_m - 1.5)$

where—

(1) n_m=positive limit maneuvering load factor used in the design of the airplane; and

(2) V=initial speed in knots.

The conditions in this paragraph involve loads corresponding to the loads that may occur in a "checked maneuver" (a maneuver in which the pitching control is suddenly displaced in one direction and then suddenly moved in the opposite direction). The deflections and timing of the "checked maneuver" must avoid exceeding the limit maneuvering load factor. The total horizontal surface load for both nose-up and nose-down pitching conditions is the sum of the balancing loads at V and the specified value of the normal load factor n, plus the maneuvering load increment due to the specified value of the angular acceleration.

[Amdt. 23–42, 56 FR 353, Jan. 3, 1991; 56 FR 5455, Feb. 11, 1991]

§23.425 Gust loads.

(a) Each horizontal surface, other than a main wing, must be designed for loads resulting from—

(1) Gust velocities specified in §23.333(c) with flaps retracted; and

(2) Positive and negative gusts of 25 f.p.s. nominal intensity at V_F corresponding to the flight conditions specified in §23.345(a)(2).

(b) [Reserved]

(c) When determining the total load on the horizontal surfaces for the conditions specified in paragraph (a) of this section, the initial balancing loads for steady unaccelerated flight at the pertinent design speeds V_F, V_C, and V_D must first be determined. The incremental load resulting from the gusts must be added to the initial balancing load to obtain the total load.

(d) In the absence of a more rational analysis, the incremental load due to the gust must be computed as follows only on airplane configurations with aft-mounted, horizontal surfaces, unless its use elsewhere is shown to be conservative:

$$\Delta L_{ht} = \frac{K_g U_{de} V a_{ht} S_{ht}}{498}\left(1 - \frac{d\varepsilon}{d\alpha}\right)$$

where—

ΔL_{ht}=Incremental horizontal tailload (lbs.);
K_g=Gust alleviation factor defined in §23.341;
U_{de}=Derived gust velocity (f.p.s.);
V=Airplane equivalent speed (knots);
a_{ht}=Slope of aft horizontal lift curve (per radian)
S_{ht}=Area of aft horizontal lift surface (ft²); and

$$\left(1 - \frac{d\varepsilon}{d\alpha}\right) = \text{Downwash factor}$$

[Doc. No. 4080, 29 FR 17955, Dec. 18, 1964, as amended by Amdt. 23–7, 34 FR 13089 Aug. 13, 1969; Amdt. 23–42, 56 FR 353, Jan. 3, 1991]

§23.427 Unsymmetrical loads.

(a) Horizontal surfaces other than main wing and their supporting structure must be designed for unsymmetrical loads arising from yawing and slipstream effects, in combination with the loads prescribed for the flight conditions set forth in §§23.421 through 23.425.

(b) In the absence of more rational data for airplanes that are conventional in regard to location of engines, wings, horizontal surfaces other than main wing, and fuselage shape:

(1) 100 percent of the maximum loading from the symmetrical flight conditions may be assumed on the surface on one side of the plane of symmetry; and

(2) The following percentage of that loading must be applied to the opposite side:

Percent=100−10 (n−1), where n is the specified positive maneuvering load factor, but this value may not be more than 80 percent.

(c) For airplanes that are not conventional (such as airplanes with horizontal surfaces other than main wing having appreciable dihedral or supported by the vertical tail surfaces) the surfaces and supporting structures must be designed for combined vertical and horizontal surface loads resulting from each prescribed flight condition taken separately.

[Amdt. 23–14, 38 FR 31820, Nov. 19, 1973, as amended by Amdt. 23–42, 56 FR 353, Jan. 3, 1991]

VERTICAL SURFACES

§23.441 Maneuvering loads.

(a) At speeds up to V_A, the vertical surfaces must be designed to withstand the following conditions. In computing the loads, the yawing velocity may be assumed to be zero:

(1) With the airplane in unaccelerated flight at zero yaw, it is assumed that the rudder control is suddenly displaced to the maximum deflection, as limited by the control stops or by limit pilot forces.

(2) With the rudder deflected as specified in paragraph (a)(1) of this section, it is assumed that the airplane yaws to the overswing sideslip angle. In lieu of a rational analysis, an overswing angle

equal to 1.5 times the static sideslip angle of paragraph (a)(3) of this section may be assumed.

(3) A yaw angle of 15 degrees with the rudder control maintained in the neutral position (except as limited by pilot strength).

(b) For commuter category airplanes, the loads imposed by the following additional maneuver must be substantiated at speeds from V_A to V_D/M_D. When computing the tail loads—

(1) The airplane must be yawed to the largest attainable steady state sideslip angle, with the rudder at maximum deflection caused by any one of the following:

(i) Control surface stops;

(ii) Maximum available booster effort;

(iii) Maximum pilot rudder force as shown below:

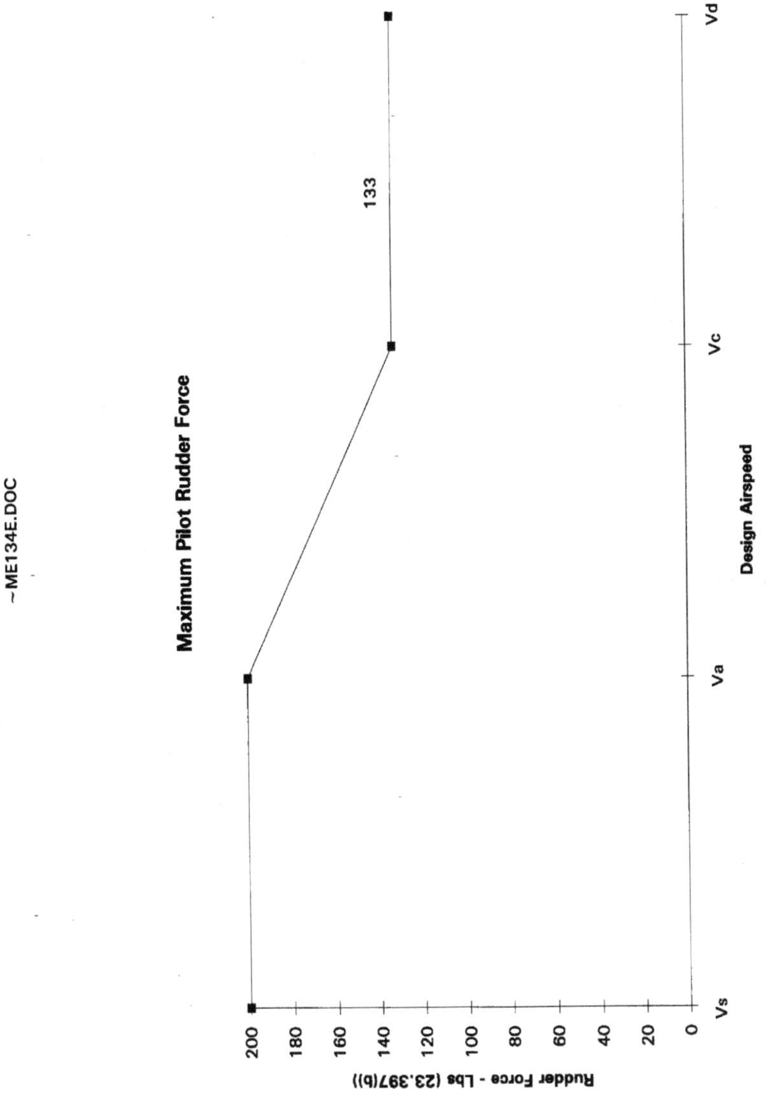

~ME134E.DOC

Maximum Pilot Rudder Force

133

200
180
160
140
120
100
80
60
40
20
0

Rudder Force - Lbs (23.397(b))

Vs　　Va　　　　　　Vc　　　　Vd

Design Airspeed

(2) The rudder must be suddenly displaced from the maximum deflection to the neutral position.

(c) The yaw angles specified in paragraph (a)(3) of this section may be reduced if the yaw angle chosen for a particular speed cannot be exceeded in—

(1) Steady slip conditions;

(2) Uncoordinated rolls from steep banks; or

(3) Sudden failure of the critical engine with delayed corrective action.

[Doc. No. 4080, 29 FR 17955, Dec. 18, 1964, as amended by Amdt. 23-7, 34 FR 13090, Aug. 13, 1969; Amdt. 23-14, 38 FR 31821, Nov. 19, 1973; Amdt. 23-28, 47 FR 13315, Mar. 29, 1982; Amdt. 23-42, 56 FR 353, Jan. 3, 1991; Amdt. 23-48, 61 FR 5145, Feb. 9, 1996]

§ 23.443 Gust loads.

(a) Vertical surfaces must be designed to withstand, in unaccelerated flight at speed V_C, lateral gusts of the values prescribed for V_C in § 23.333(c).

(b) In addition, for commuter category airplanes, the airplane is assumed to encounter derived gusts normal to the plane of symmetry while in unaccelerated flight at V_B, V_C, V_D, and V_F. The derived gusts and airplane speeds corresponding to these conditions, as determined by §§ 23.341 and 23.345, must be investigated. The shape of the gust must be as specified in § 23.333(c)(2)(i).

(c) In the absence of a more rational analysis, the gust load must be computed as follows:

$$L_{vt} = \frac{K_{gt} \, U_{de} \, V \, a_{vt} \, S_{vt}}{498}$$

Where—

L_{vt}=Vertical surface loads (lbs.);

$$k_{gt} = \frac{0.88 \, \mu_{gt}}{5.3 + \mu_{gt}} = \text{gust alleviation factor;}$$

$$\mu_{gt} = \frac{2W}{\rho \, c_t \, g \, a_{vt} \, S_{vt}} \frac{K^2}{l_{vt}} = \text{lateral mass ratio;}$$

U_{de}=Derived gust velocity (f.p.s.);
ρ=Air density (slugs/cu.ft.);
W=the applicable weight of the airplane in the particular load case (lbs.);
S_{vt}=Area of vertical surface (ft.²);
$\check{c}_{\leq t}$=Mean geometric chord of vertical surface (ft.);
a_{vt}=Lift curve slope of vertical surface (per radian);
K=Radius of gyration in yaw (ft.);
l_{vt}=Distance from airplane c.g. to lift center of vertical surface (ft.);
g=Acceleration due to gravity (ft./sec.²); and

V=Equivalent airspeed (knots).

[Amdt. 23-7, 34 FR 13090, Aug. 13, 1969, as amended by Amdt. 23-34, 52 FR 1830, Jan. 15, 1987; 52 FR 7262, Mar. 9, 1987; Amdt. 23-24, 52 FR 34745, Sept. 14, 1987; Amdt. 23-42, 56 FR 353, Jan. 3, 1991; Amdt. 23-48, 61 FR 5147, Feb. 9, 1996]

§ 23.445 Outboard fins or winglets.

(a) If outboard fins or winglets are included on the horizontal surfaces or wings, the horizontal surfaces or wings must be designed for their maximum load in combination with loads induced by the fins or winglets and moments or forces exerted on the horizontal surfaces or wings by the fins or winglets.

(b) If outboard fins or winglets extend above and below the horizontal surface, the critical vertical surface loading (the load per unit area as determined under §§ 23.441 and 23.443) must be applied to—

(1) The part of the vertical surfaces above the horizontal surface with 80 percent of that loading applied to the part below the horizontal surface; and

(2) The part of the vertical surfaces below the horizontal surface with 80 percent of that loading applied to the part above the horizontal surface.

(c) The end plate effects of outboard fins or winglets must be taken into account in applying the yawing conditions of §§ 23.441 and 23.443 to the vertical surfaces in paragraph (b) of this section.

(d) When rational methods are used for computing loads, the maneuvering loads of § 23.441 on the vertical surfaces and the one-g horizontal surface load, including induced loads on the horizontal surface and moments or forces exerted on the horizontal surfaces by the vertical surfaces, must be applied simultaneously for the structural loading condition.

[Doc. No. 4080, 29 FR 17955, Dec. 18, 1964, as amended by Amdt. 23-14, 38 FR 31821, Nov. 19, 1973; Amdt. 23-42, 56 FR 353, Jan. 3, 1991]

AILERONS AND SPECIAL DEVICES

§ 23.455 Ailerons.

(a) The ailerons must be designed for the loads to which they are subjected—

(1) In the neutral position during symmetrical flight conditions; and

(2) By the following deflections (except as limited by pilot effort), during unsymmetrical flight conditions:

(i) Sudden maximum displacement of the aileron control at V_A. Suitable allowance may be made for control system deflections.

(ii) Sufficient deflection at V_C, where V_C is more than V_A, to produce a rate of roll not less than obtained in paragraph (a)(2)(i) of this section.

(iii) Sufficient deflection at V_D to produce a rate of roll not less than one-third of that obtained in paragraph (a)(2)(i) of this section.

(b) [Reserved]

[Doc. No. 4080, 29 FR 17955, Dec. 18, 1964, as amended by Amdt. 23–7, 34 FR 13090, Aug. 13, 1969; Amdt. 23–42, 56 FR 353, Jan. 3, 1991]

§23.459 Special devices.

The loading for special devices using aerodynamic surfaces (such as slots and spoilers) must be determined from test data.

GROUND LOADS

§23.471 General.

The limit ground loads specified in this subpart are considered to be external loads and inertia forces that act upon an airplane structure. In each specified ground load condition, the external reactions must be placed in equilibrium with the linear and angular inertia forces in a rational or conservative manner.

§23.473 Ground load conditions and assumptions.

(a) The ground load requirements of this subpart must be complied with at the design maximum weight except that §§23.479, 23.481, and 23.483 may be complied with at a design landing weight (the highest weight for landing conditions at the maximum descent velocity) allowed under paragraphs (b) and (c) of this section.

(b) The design landing weight may be as low as—

(1) 95 percent of the maximum weight if the minimum fuel capacity is enough for at least one-half hour of operation at maximum continuous power plus a capacity equal to a fuel weight which is the difference between the design maximum weight and the design landing weight; or

(2) The design maximum weight less the weight of 25 percent of the total fuel capacity.

(c) The design landing weight of a multiengine airplane may be less than that allowed under paragraph (b) of this section if—

(1) The airplane meets the one-engine-inoperative climb requirements of §23.67(b)(1) or (c); and

(2) Compliance is shown with the fuel jettisoning system requirements of §23.1001.

(d) The selected limit vertical inertia load factor at the center of gravity of the airplane for the ground load conditions prescribed in this subpart may not be less than that which would be obtained when landing with a descent velocity (V), in feet per second, equal to $4.4 (W/S)^{1/4}$, except that this velocity need not be more than 10 feet per second and may not be less than seven feet per second.

(e) Wing lift not exceeding two-thirds of the weight of the airplane may be assumed to exist throughout the landing impact and to act through the center of gravity. The ground reaction load factor may be equal to the inertia load factor minus the ratio of the above assumed wing lift to the airplane weight.

(f) If energy absorption tests are made to determine the limit load factor corresponding to the required limit descent velocities, these tests must be made under §23.723(a).

(g) No inertia load factor used for design purposes may be less than 2.67, nor may the limit ground reaction load factor be less than 2.0 at design maximum weight, unless these lower values will not be exceeded in taxiing at speeds up to takeoff speed over terrain as rough as that expected in service.

[Doc. No. 4080, 29 FR 17955, Dec. 18, 1964, as amended by Amdt. 23–7, 34 FR 13090, Aug. 13, 1969; Amdt. 23–28, 47 FR 13315, Mar. 29, 1982; Amdt. 23–45, 58 FR 42160, Aug. 6, 1993; Amdt. 23–48, 61 FR 5147, Feb. 9, 1996]

§23.477 Landing gear arrangement.

Sections 23.479 through 23.483, or the conditions in appendix C, apply to airplanes with conventional arrangements of main and nose gear, or main and tail gear.

§ 23.479 Level landing conditions.

(a) For a level landing, the airplane is assumed to be in the following attitudes:

(1) For airplanes with tail wheels, a normal level flight attitude.

(2) For airplanes with nose wheels, attitudes in which—

(i) The nose and main wheels contact the ground simultaneously; and

(ii) The main wheels contact the ground and the nose wheel is just clear of the ground.

The attitude used in paragraph (a)(2)(i) of this section may be used in the analysis required under paragraph (a)(2)(ii) of this section.

(b) When investigating landing conditions, the drag components simulating the forces required to accelerate the tires and wheels up to the landing speed (spin-up) must be properly combined with the corresponding instantaneous vertical ground reactions, and the forward-acting horizontal loads resulting from rapid reduction of the spin-up drag loads (spring-back) must be combined with vertical ground reactions at the instant of the peak forward load, assuming wing lift and a tire-sliding coefficient of friction of 0.8. However, the drag loads may not be less than 25 percent of the maximum vertical ground reactions (neglecting wing lift).

(c) In the absence of specific tests or a more rational analysis for determining the wheel spin-up and spring-back loads for landing conditions, the method set forth in appendix D of this part must be used. If appendix D of this part is used, the drag components used for design must not be less than those given by appendix C of this part.

(d) For airplanes with tip tanks or large overhung masses (such as turbo-propeller or jet engines) supported by the wing, the tip tanks and the structure supporting the tanks or overhung masses must be designed for the effects of dynamic responses under the level landing conditions of either paragraph (a)(1) or (a)(2)(ii) of this section. In evaluating the effects of dynamic re-

sponse, an airplane lift equal to the weight of the airplane may be assumed.

[Doc. No. 4080, 29 FR 17955, Dec. 18, 1964, as amended by Amdt. 23–17, 41 FR 55464, Dec. 20, 1976; Amdt. 23–45, 58 FR 42160, Aug. 6, 1993]

§ 23.481 Tail down landing conditions.

(a) For a tail down landing, the airplane is assumed to be in the following attitudes:

(1) For airplanes with tail wheels, an attitude in which the main and tail wheels contact the ground simultaneously.

(2) For airplanes with nose wheels, a stalling attitude, or the maximum angle allowing ground clearance by each part of the airplane, whichever is less.

(b) For airplanes with either tail or nose wheels, ground reactions are assumed to be vertical, with the wheels up to speed before the maximum vertical load is attained.

§ 23.483 One-wheel landing conditions.

For the one-wheel landing condition, the airplane is assumed to be in the level attitude and to contact the ground on one side of the main landing gear. In this attitude, the ground reactions must be the same as those obtained on that side under § 23.479.

§ 23.485 Side load conditions.

(a) For the side load condition, the airplane is assumed to be in a level attitude with only the main wheels contacting the ground and with the shock absorbers and tires in their static positions.

(b) The limit vertical load factor must be 1.33, with the vertical ground reaction divided equally between the main wheels.

(c) The limit side inertia factor must be 0.83, with the side ground reaction divided between the main wheels so that—

(1) 0.5 (W) is acting inboard on one side; and

(2) 0.33 (W) is acting outboard on the other side.

(d) The side loads prescribed in paragraph (c) of this section are assumed to be applied at the ground contact point and the drag loads may be assumed to be zero.

[Doc. No. 4080, 29 FR 17955, Dec. 18, 1964, as amended by Amdt. 23–45, 58 FR 42160, Aug. 6, 1993]

§23.493 Braked roll conditions.

Under braked roll conditions, with the shock absorbers and tires in their static positions, the following apply:

(a) The limit vertical load factor must be 1.33.

(b) The attitudes and ground contacts must be those described in §23.479 for level landings.

(c) A drag reaction equal to the vertical reaction at the wheel multiplied by a coefficient of friction of 0.8 must be applied at the ground contact point of each wheel with brakes, except that the drag reaction need not exceed the maximum value based on limiting brake torque.

§23.497 Supplementary conditions for tail wheels.

In determining the ground loads on the tail wheel and affected supporting structures, the following apply:

(a) For the obstruction load, the limit ground reaction obtained in the tail down landing condition is assumed to act up and aft through the axle at 45 degrees. The shock absorber and tire may be assumed to be in their static positions.

(b) For the side load, a limit vertical ground reaction equal to the static load on the tail wheel, in combination with a side component of equal magnitude, is assumed. In addition—

(1) If a swivel is used, the tail wheel is assumed to be swiveled 90 degrees to the airplane longitudinal axis with the resultant ground load passing through the axle;

(2) If a lock, steering device, or shimmy damper is used, the tail wheel is also assumed to be in the trailing position with the side load acting at the ground contact point; and

(3) The shock absorber and tire are assumed to be in their static positions.

(c) If a tail wheel, bumper, or an energy absorption device is provided to show compliance with §23.925(b), the following apply:

(1) Suitable design loads must be established for the tail wheel, bumper, or energy absorption device; and

(2) The supporting structure of the tail wheel, bumper, or energy absorption device must be designed to withstand the loads established in paragraph (c)(1) of this section.

[Doc. No. 4080, 29 FR 17955, Dec. 18, 1964, as amended by Amdt. 23–48, 61 FR 5147, Feb. 9, 1996]

§23.499 Supplementary conditions for nose wheels.

In determining the ground loads on nose wheels and affected supporting structures, and assuming that the shock absorbers and tires are in their static positions, the following conditions must be met:

(a) For aft loads, the limit force components at the axle must be—

(1) A vertical component of 2.25 times the static load on the wheel; and

(2) A drag component of 0.8 times the vertical load.

(b) For forward loads, the limit force components at the axle must be—

(1) A vertical component of 2.25 times the static load on the wheel; and

(2) A forward component of 0.4 times the vertical load.

(c) For side loads, the limit force components at ground contact must be—

(1) A vertical component of 2.25 times the static load on the wheel; and

(2) A side component of 0.7 times the vertical load.

(d) For airplanes with a steerable nose wheel that is controlled by hydraulic or other power, at design takeoff weight with the nose wheel in any steerable position, the application of 1.33 times the full steering torque combined with a vertical reaction equal to 1.33 times the maximum static reaction on the nose gear must be assumed. However, if a torque limiting device is installed, the steering torque can be reduced to the maximum value allowed by that device.

(e) For airplanes with a steerable nose wheel that has a direct mechanical connection to the rudder pedals, the mechanism must be designed to withstand the steering torque for the maximum pilot forces specified in § 23.397(b).

[Doc. No. 4080, 29 FR 17955, Dec. 18, 1964, as amended by Amdt. 23–48, 61 FR 5147, Feb. 9, 1996]

§ 23.505 Supplementary conditions for skiplanes.

In determining ground loads for skiplanes, and assuming that the airplane is resting on the ground with one main ski frozen at rest and the other skis free to slide, a limit side force equal to 0.036 times the design maximum weight must be applied near the tail assembly, with a factor of safety of 1.

[Amdt. 23–7, 34 FR 13090, Aug. 13, 1969]

§ 23.507 Jacking loads.

(a) The airplane must be designed for the loads developed when the aircraft is supported on jacks at the design maximum weight assuming the following load factors for landing gear jacking points at a three-point attitude and for primary flight structure jacking points in the level attitude:

(1) Vertical-load factor of 1.35 times the static reactions.

(2) Fore, aft, and lateral load factors of 0.4 times the vertical static reactions.

(b) The horizontal loads at the jack points must be reacted by inertia forces so as to result in no change in the direction of the resultant loads at the jack points.

(c) The horizontal loads must be considered in all combinations with the vertical load.

[Amdt. 23–14, 38 FR 31821, Nov. 19, 1973]

§ 23.509 Towing loads.

The towing loads of this section must be applied to the design of tow fittings and their immediate attaching structure.

(a) The towing loads specified in paragraph (d) of this section must be considered separately. These loads must be applied at the towing fittings and must act parallel to the ground. In addition:

(1) A vertical load factor equal to 1.0 must be considered acting at the center of gravity; and

(2) The shock struts and tires must be in there static positions.

(b) For towing points not on the landing gear but near the plane of symmetry of the airplane, the drag and side tow load components specified for the auxiliary gear apply. For towing points located outboard of the main gear, the drag and side tow load components specified for the main gear apply. Where the specified angle of swivel cannot be reached, the maximum obtainable angle must be used.

(c) The towing loads specified in paragraph (d) of this section must be reacted as follows:

(1) The side component of the towing load at the main gear must be reacted by a side force at the static ground line of the wheel to which the load is applied.

(2) The towing loads at the auxiliary gear and the drag components of the towing loads at the main gear must be reacted as follows:

(i) A reaction with a maximum value equal to the vertical reaction must be applied at the axle of the wheel to which the load is applied. Enough airplane inertia to achieve equilibrium must be applied.

(ii) The loads must be reacted by airplane inertia.

(d) The prescribed towing loads are as follows, where W is the design maximum weight:

Tow point	Position	Load		
		Magnitude	No.	Direction
Main gear	....	0.225W	1	Forward, parallel to drag axis.
			2	Forward, at 30° to drag axis.
			3	Aft, parallel to drag axis.
			4	Aft, at 30° to drag axis.
Auxiliary gear	Swiveled forward	0.3W	5	Forward.
			6	Aft.
	Swiveled aft	0.3W	7	Forward.
			8	Aft.

Tow point	Position	Load		
		Magnitude	No.	Direction
	Swiveled 45° from forward	0.15W	9	Forward, in plane of wheel.
			10	Aft, in plane of wheel.
	Swiveled 45° from aft	0.15W	11	Forward, in plane of wheel.
			12	Aft, in plane of wheel.

[Amdt. 23–14, 38 FR 31821, Nov. 19, 1973]

§23.511 Ground load; unsymmetrical loads on multiple-wheel units.

(a) *Pivoting loads.* The airplane is assumed to pivot about on side of the main gear with—

(1) The brakes on the pivoting unit locked; and

(2) Loads corresponding to a limit vertical load factor of 1, and coefficient of friction of 0.8 applied to the main gear and its supporting structure.

(b) *Unequal tire loads.* The loads established under §§23.471 through 23.483 must be applied in turn, in a 60/40 percent distribution, to the dual wheels and tires in each dual wheel landing gear unit.

(c) *Deflated tire loads.* For the deflated tire condition—

(1) 60 percent of the loads established under §§23.471 through 23.483 must be applied in turn to each wheel in a landing gear unit; and

(2) 60 percent of the limit drag and side loads, and 100 percent of the limit vertical load established under §§23.485 and 23.493 or lesser vertical load obtained under paragraph (c)(1) of this section, must be applied in turn to each wheel in the dual wheel landing gear unit.

[Amdt. 23–7, 34 FR 13090, Aug. 13, 1969]

WATER LOADS

§23.521 Water load conditions.

(a) The structure of seaplanes and amphibians must be designed for water loads developed during takeoff and landing with the seaplane in any attitude likely to occur in normal operation at appropriate forward and sinking velocities under the most severe sea conditions likely to be encountered.

(b) Unless the applicant makes a rational analysis of the water loads, §§23.523 through 23.537 apply.

[Doc. No. 4080, 29 FR 17955, Dec. 18, 1964, as amended by Amdt. 23–45, 58 FR 42160, Aug. 6, 1993; Amdt. 23–48, 61 FR 5147, Feb. 9, 1996]

§23.523 Design weights and center of gravity positions.

(a) *Design weights.* The water load requirements must be met at each operating weight up to the design landing weight except that, for the takeoff condition prescribed in §23.531, the design water takeoff weight (the maximum weight for water taxi and takeoff run) must be used.

(b) *Center of gravity positions.* The critical centers of gravity within the limits for which certification is requested must be considered to reach maximum design loads for each part of the seaplane structure.

[Doc. No. 26269, 58 FR 42160, Aug. 6, 1993]

§23.525 Application of loads.

(a) Unless otherwise prescribed, the seaplane as a whole is assumed to be subjected to the loads corresponding to the load factors specified in §23.527.

(b) In applying the loads resulting from the load factors prescribed in §23.527, the loads may be distributed over the hull or main float bottom (in order to avoid excessive local shear loads and bending moments at the location of water load application) using pressures not less than those prescribed in §23.533(c).

(c) For twin float seaplanes, each float must be treated as an equivalent hull on a fictitious seaplane with a weight equal to one-half the weight of the twin float seaplane.

(d) Except in the takeoff condition of §23.531, the aerodynamic lift on the

215

seaplane during the impact is assumed to be ⅔ of the weight of the seaplane.

[Doc. No. 26269, 58 FR 42161, Aug. 6, 1993; 58 FR 51970, Oct. 5, 1993]

§ 23.527 Hull and main float load factors.

(a) Water reaction load factors n_w must be computed in the following manner:

(1) For the step landing case

$$n_w = \frac{C_1 V_{SO}^2}{\left(Tan^{\frac{2}{3}}\beta\right)W^{\frac{1}{3}}}$$

(2) For the bow and stern landing cases

$$n_w = \frac{C_1 V_{SO}^2}{\left(Tan^{\frac{2}{3}}\beta\right)W^{\frac{1}{3}}} \times \frac{K_1}{\left(1+r_x^2\right)^{\frac{2}{3}}}$$

(b) The following values are used:

(1) n_w=water reaction load factor (that is, the water reaction divided by seaplane weight).

(2) C_1=empirical seaplane operations factor equal to 0.012 (except that this factor may not be less than that necessary to obtain the minimum value of step load factor of 2.33).

(3) V_{SO}=seaplane stalling speed in knots with flaps extended in the appropriate landing position and with no slipstream effect.

(4) β=Angle of dead rise at the longitudinal station at which the load factor is being determined in accordance with figure 1 of appendix I of this part.

(5) W=seaplane landing weight in pounds.

(6) K_1=empirical hull station weighing factor, in accordance with figure 2 of appendix I of this part.

(7) r_x=ratio of distance, measured parallel to hull reference axis, from the center of gravity of the seaplane to the hull longitudinal station at which the load factor is being computed to the radius of gyration in pitch of the seaplane, the hull reference axis being a straight line, in the plane of symmetry, tangential to the keel at the main step.

(c) For a twin float seaplane, because of the effect of flexibility of the attachment of the floats to the seaplane, the factor K_1 may be reduced at the bow and stern to 0.8 of the value shown in figure 2 of appendix I of this part. This reduction applies only to the design of the carrythrough and seaplane structure.

[Doc. No. 26269, 58 FR 42161, Aug. 6, 1993; 58 FR 51970, Oct. 5, 1993]

§ 23.529 Hull and main float landing conditions.

(a) *Symmetrical step, bow, and stern landing.* For symmetrical step, bow, and stern landings, the limit water reaction load factors are those computed under § 23.527. In addition—

(1) For symmetrical step landings, the resultant water load must be applied at the keel, through the center of gravity, and must be directed perpendicularly to the keel line;

(2) For symmetrical bow landings, the resultant water load must be applied at the keel, one-fifth of the longitudinal distance from the bow to the step, and must be directed perpendicularly to the keel line; and

(3) For symmetrical stern landings, the resultant water load must be applied at the keel, at a point 85 percent of the longitudinal distance from the step to the stern post, and must be directed perpendicularly to the keel line.

(b) *Unsymmetrical landing for hull and single float seaplanes.* Unsymmetrical step, bow, and stern landing conditions must be investigated. In addition—

(1) The loading for each condition consists of an upward component and a side component equal, respectively, to 0.75 and 0.25 tan β times the resultant load in the corresponding symmetrical landing condition; and

(2) The point of application and direction of the upward component of the load is the same as that in the symmetrical condition, and the point of application of the side component is at the same longitudinal station as the upward component but is directed inward perpendicularly to the plane of symmetry at a point midway between the keel and chine lines.

(c) *Unsymmetrical landing; twin float seaplanes.* The unsymmetrical loading consists of an upward load at the step of each float of 0.75 and a side load of 0.25 tan β at one float times the step landing load reached under § 23.527. The side load is directed inboard, perpendicularly to the plane of symmetry midway between the keel and chine lines of the float, at the same longitudinal station as the upward load.

[Doc. No. 26269, 58 FR 42161, Aug. 6, 1993]

§ 23.531 Hull and main float takeoff condition.

For the wing and its attachment to the hull or main float—

(a) The aerodynamic wing lift is assumed to be zero; and

(b) A downward inertia load, corresponding to a load factor computed from the following formula, must be applied:

$$n = \frac{C_{TO} V_{S1}{}^2}{\left(\mathrm{Tan}^{\frac{2}{3}} \beta \right) W^{\frac{1}{3}}}$$

Where—

n=inertia load factor;
C_{TO}=empirical seaplane operations factor equal to 0.004;
V_{S1}=seaplane stalling speed (knots) at the design takeoff weight with the flaps extended in the appropriate takeoff position;
β=angle of dead rise at the main step (degrees); and
W=design water takeoff weight in pounds.

[Doc. No. 26269, 58 FR 42161, Aug. 6, 1993]

§ 23.533 Hull and main float bottom pressures.

(a) *General.* The hull and main float structure, including frames and bulkheads, stringers, and bottom plating, must be designed under this section.

(b) *Local pressures.* For the design of the bottom plating and stringers and their attachments to the supporting structure, the following pressure distributions must be applied:

(1) For an unflared bottom, the pressure at the chine is 0.75 times the pressure at the keel, and the pressures between the keel and chine vary linearly, in accordance with figure 3 of appendix I of this part. The pressure at the keel (p.s.i.) is computed as follows:

$$P_K = \frac{C_2 K_2 V_{S1}{}^2}{\mathrm{Tan}\, \beta_k}$$

where—

P_k=pressure (p.s.i.) at the keel;
C_2=0.00213;
K_2=hull station weighing factor, in accordance with figure 2 of appendix I of this part;
V_{S1}=seaplane stalling speed (knots) at the design water takeoff weight with flaps extended in the appropriate takeoff position; and
β_K=angle of dead rise at keel, in accordance with figure 1 of appendix I of this part.

(2) For a flared bottom, the pressure at the beginning of the flare is the same as that for an unflared bottom, and the pressure between the chine and the beginning of the flare varies linearly, in accordance with figure 3 of appendix I of this part. The pressure distribution is the same as that prescribed in paragraph (b)(1) of this section for an unflared bottom except that the pressure at the chine is computed as follows:

$$P_{ch} = \frac{C_3 K_2 V_{S1}{}^2}{\mathrm{Tan}\, \beta}$$

where—

P_{ch}=pressure (p.s.i.) at the chine;
C_3=0.0016;
K_2=hull station weighing factor, in accordance with figure 2 of appendix I of this part;
V_{S1}=seaplane stalling speed (knots) at the design water takeoff weight with flaps extended in the appropriate takeoff position; and
β=angle of dead rise at appropriate station.

The area over which these pressures are applied must simulate pressures occurring during high localized impacts on the hull or float, but need not extend over an area that would induce critical stresses in the frames or in the overall structure.

(c) *Distributed pressures.* For the design of the frames, keel, and chine structure, the following pressure distributions apply:

(1) Symmetrical pressures are computed as follows:

$$P = \frac{C_4 K_2 V_{SO}{}^2}{\mathrm{Tan}\, \beta}$$

where—

P=pressure (p.s.i.);
C_4=0.078 C_1 (with C_1 computed under § 23.527);
K_2=hull station weighing factor, determined in accordance with figure 2 of appendix I of this part;

V_{so}=seaplane stalling speed (knots) with landing flaps extended in the appropriate position and with no slipstream effect; and
β=angle of dead rise at appropriate station.

(2) The unsymmetrical pressure distribution consists of the pressures prescribed in paragraph (c)(1) of this section on one side of the hull or main float centerline and one-half of that pressure on the other side of the hull or main float centerline, in accordance with figure 3 of appendix I of this part.

(3) These pressures are uniform and must be applied simultaneously over the entire hull or main float bottom. The loads obtained must be carried into the sidewall structure of the hull proper, but need not be transmitted in a fore and aft direction as shear and bending loads.

[Doc. No. 26269, 58 FR 42161, Aug. 6, 1993; 58 FR 51970, Oct. 5, 1993]

§ 23.535 Auxiliary float loads.

(a) *General.* Auxiliary floats and their attachments and supporting structures must be designed for the conditions prescribed in this section. In the cases specified in paragraphs (b) through (e) of this section, the prescribed water loads may be distributed over the float bottom to avoid excessive local loads, using bottom pressures not less than those prescribed in paragraph (g) of this section.

(b) *Step loading.* The resultant water load must be applied in the plane of symmetry of the float at a point three-fourths of the distance from the bow to the step and must be perpendicular to the keel. The resultant limit load is computed as follows, except that the value of L need not exceed three times the weight of the displaced water when the float is completely submerged:

$$L = \frac{C_5 V_{SO}^2 W^{\frac{2}{3}}}{\mathrm{Tan}^{\frac{2}{3}} \beta_S \left(1 + r_y^2\right)^{\frac{2}{3}}}$$

where—

L=limit load (lbs.);
C_5=0.0053;
V_{so}=seaplane stalling speed (knots) with landing flaps extended in the appropriate position and with no slipstream effect;
W=seaplane design landing weight in pounds;

βs=angle of dead rise at a station ¾ of the distance from the bow to the step, but need not be less than 15 degrees; and
r_y=ratio of the lateral distance between the center of gravity and the plane of symmetry of the float to the radius of gyration in roll.

(c) *Bow loading.* The resultant limit load must be applied in the plane of symmetry of the float at a point one-fourth of the distance from the bow to the step and must be perpendicular to the tangent to the keel line at that point. The magnitude of the resultant load is that specified in paragraph (b) of this section.

(d) *Unsymmetrical step loading.* The resultant water load consists of a component equal to 0.75 times the load specified in paragraph (a) of this section and a side component equal to 0.025 tan β times the load specified in paragraph (b) of this section. The side load must be applied perpendicularly to the plane of symmetry of the float at a point midway between the keel and the chine.

(e) *Unsymmetrical bow loading.* The resultant water load consists of a component equal to 0.75 times the load specified in paragraph (b) of this section and a side component equal to 0.25 tan β times the load specified in paragraph (c) of this section. The side load must be applied perpendicularly to the plane of symmetry at a point midway between the keel and the chine.

(f) *Immersed float condition.* The resultant load must be applied at the centroid of the cross section of the float at a point one-third of the distance from the bow to the step. The limit load components are as follows:

$$\text{vertical} = PgV$$

$$\text{aft} = \frac{C_X PV^{\frac{2}{3}} (KV_{SO})^2}{2}$$

$$\text{side} = \frac{C_Y PV^{\frac{2}{3}} (KV_{SO})^2}{2}$$

where—

P=mass density of water (slugs/ft.³)
V=volume of float (ft.³);
C_x=coefficient of drag force, equal to 0.133;
C_y=coefficient of side force, equal to 0.106;

K=0.8, except that lower values may be used if it is shown that the floats are incapable of submerging at a speed of 0.8 V_{so} in normal operations;

V_{so}=seaplane stalling speed (knots) with landing flaps extended in the appropriate position and with no slipstream effect; and

g=acceleration due to gravity (ft/sec²).

(g) *Float bottom pressures.* The float bottom pressures must be established under §23.533, except that the value of K_2 in the formulae may be taken as 1.0. The angle of dead rise to be used in determining the float bottom pressures is set forth in paragraph (b) of this section.

[Doc. No. 26269, 58 FR 42162, Aug. 6, 1993; 58 FR 51970, Oct. 5, 1993]

§23.537 Seawing loads.

Seawing design loads must be based on applicable test data.

[Doc. No. 26269, 58 FR 42163, Aug. 6, 1993]

EMERGENCY LANDING CONDITIONS

§23.561 General.

(a) The airplane, although it may be damaged in emergency landing conditions, must be designed as prescribed in this section to protect each occupant under those conditions.

(b) The structure must be designed to give each occupant every reasonable chance of escaping serious injury when—

(1) Proper use is made of the seats, safety belts, and shoulder harnesses provided for in the design;

(2) The occupant experiences the static inertia loads corresponding to the following ultimate load factors—

(i) Upward, 3.0g for normal, utility, and commuter category airplanes, or 4.5g for acrobatic category airplanes;

(ii) Forward, 9.0g;

(iii) Sideward, 1.5g; and

(iv) Downward, 6.0g when certification to the emergency exit provisions of §23.807(d)(4) is requested; and

(3) The items of mass within the cabin, that could injure an occupant, experience the static inertia loads corresponding to the following ultimate load factors—

(i) Upward, 3.0g;

(ii) Forward, 18.0g; and

(iii) Sideward, 4.5g.

(c) Each airplane with retractable landing gear must be designed to protect each occupant in a landing—

(1) With the wheels retracted;

(2) With moderate descent velocity; and

(3) Assuming, in the absence of a more rational analysis—

(i) A downward ultimate inertia force of 3 *g;* and

(ii) A coefficient of friction of 0.5 at the ground.

(d) If it is not established that a turnover is unlikely during an emergency landing, the structure must be designed to protect the occupants in a complete turnover as follows:

(1) The likelihood of a turnover may be shown by an analysis assuming the following conditions—

(i) The most adverse combination of weight and center of gravity position;

(ii) Longitudinal load factor of 9.0g;

(iii) Vertical load factor of 1.0g; and

(iv) For airplanes with tricycle landing gear, the nose wheel strut failed with the nose contacting the ground.

(i) Maximum weight;

(ii) Most forward center of gravity position;

(iii) Longitudinal load factor of 9.0g;

(iv) Vertical load factor of 1.0g; and

(v) For airplanes with tricycle landing gear, the nose wheel strut failed with the nose contacting the ground.

(2) For determining the loads to be applied to the inverted airplane after a turnover, an upward ultimate inertia load factor of 3.0g and a coefficient of friction with the ground of 0.5 must be used.

(e) Except as provided in §23.787(c), the supporting structure must be designed to restrain, under loads up to those specified in paragraph (b)(3) of this section, each item of mass that could injure an occupant if it came loose in a minor crash landing.

[Doc. No. 4080, 29 FR 17955, Dec. 18, 1964, as amended by Amdt. 23–7, 34 FR 13090, Aug. 13, 1969; Amdt. 23–24, 52 FR 34745, Sept. 14, 1987; Amdt. 23–36, 53 FR 30812, Aug. 15, 1988; Amdt. 23–46, 59 FR 25772, May 17, 1994; Amdt. 23–48, 61 FR 5147, Feb. 9, 1996]

§ 23.562 Emergency landing dynamic conditions.

(a) Each seat/restraint system for use in a normal, utility, or acrobatic category airplane must be designed to protect each occupant during an emergency landing when—

(1) Proper use is made of seats, safety belts, and shoulder harnesses provided for in the design; and

(2) The occupant is exposed to the loads resulting from the conditions prescribed in this section.

(b) Except for those seat/restraint systems that are required to meet paragraph (d) of this section, each seat/restraint system for crew or passenger occupancy in a normal, utility, or acrobatic category airplane, must successfully complete dynamic tests or be demonstrated by rational analysis supported by dynamic tests, in accordance with each of the following conditions. These tests must be conducted with an occupant simulated by an anthropomorphic test dummy (ATD) defined by 49 CFR Part 572, Subpart B, or an FAA-approved equivalent, with a nominal weight of 170 pounds and seated in the normal upright position.

(1) For the first test, the change in velocity may not be less than 31 feet per second. The seat/restraint system must be oriented in its nominal position with respect to the airplane and with the horizontal plane of the airplane pitched up 60 degrees, with no yaw, relative to the impact vector. For seat/restraint systems to be installed in the first row of the airplane, peak deceleration must occur in not more than 0.05 seconds after impact and must reach a minimum of 19g. For all other seat/restraint systems, peak deceleration must occur in not more than 0.06 seconds after impact and must reach a minimum of 15g.

(2) For the second test, the change in velocity may not be less than 42 feet per second. The seat/restraint system must be oriented in its nominal position with respect to the airplane and with the vertical plane of the airplane yawed 10 degrees, with no pitch, relative to the impact vector in a direction that results in the greatest load on the shoulder harness. For seat/restraint systems to be installed in the first row of the airplane, peak decelera-

tion must occur in not more than 0.05 seconds after impact and must reach a minimum of 26g. For all other seat/restraint systems, peak deceleration must occur in not more than 0.06 seconds after impact and must reach a minimum of 21g.

(3) To account for floor warpage, the floor rails or attachment devices used to attach the seat/restraint system to the airframe structure must be preloaded to misalign with respect to each other by at least 10 degrees vertically (i.e., pitch out of parallel) and one of the rails or attachment devices must be preloaded to misalign by 10 degrees in roll prior to conducting the test defined by paragraph (b)(2) of this section.

(c) Compliance with the following requirements must be shown during the dynamic tests conducted in accordance with paragraph (b) of this section:

(1) The seat/restraint system must restrain the ATD although seat/restraint system components may experience deformation, elongation, displacement, or crushing intended as part of the design.

(2) The attachment between the seat/restraint system and the test fixture must remain intact, although the seat structure may have deformed.

(3) Each shoulder harness strap must remain on the ATD's shoulder during the impact.

(4) The safety belt must remain on the ATD's pelvis during the impact.

(5) The results of the dynamic tests must show that the occupant is protected from serious head injury.

(i) When contact with adjacent seats, structure, or other items in the cabin can occur, protection must be provided so that the head impact does not exceed a head injury criteria (HIC) of 1,000.

(ii) The value of HIC is defined as—

$$HIC = \left\{ (t_2 - t_1) \left[\frac{1}{(t_2 - t_1)} \int_{t_1}^{t_2} a(t)dt \right]^{2.5} \right\}_{Max}$$

Where:

t_1 is the initial integration time, expressed in seconds, t_2 is the final integration time, expressed in seconds, $(t_2 - t_1)$ is the time duration of the major head impact, expressed in seconds, and $a(t)$ is the resultant deceleration at the center of gravity of the head form expressed as a multiple of g (units of gravity).

(iii) Compliance with the HIC limit must be demonstrated by measuring the head impact during dynamic testing as prescribed in paragraphs (b)(1) and (b)(2) of this section or by a separate showing of compliance with the head injury criteria using test or analysis procedures.

(6) Loads in individual shoulder harness straps may not exceed 1,750 pounds. If dual straps are used for retaining the upper torso, the total strap loads may not exceed 2,000 pounds.

(7) The compression load measured between the pelvis and the lumbar spine of the ATD may not exceed 1,500 pounds.

(d) For all single-engine airplanes with a V_{SO} of more than 61 knots at maximum weight, and those multiengine airplanes of 6,000 pounds or less maximum weight with a V_{SO} of more than 61 knots at maximum weight that do not comply with §23.67(a)(1);

(1) The ultimate load factors of §23.561(b) must be increased by multiplying the load factors by the square of the ratio of the increased stall speed to 61 knots. The increased ultimate load factors need not exceed the values reached at a V_{SO} of 79 knots. The upward ultimate load factor for acrobatic category airplanes need not exceed 5.0g.

(2) The seat/restraint system test required by paragraph (b)(1) of this section must be conducted in accordance with the following criteria:

(i) The change in velocity may not be less than 31 feet per second.

(ii)(A) The peak deceleration (g_p) of 19g and 15g must be increased and multiplied by the square of the ratio of the increased stall speed to 61 knots:

$$g_p = 19.0 \ (V_{SO}/61)^2 \ \text{or} \ g_p = 15.0 \ (V_{SO}/61)^2$$

(B) The peak deceleration need not exceed the value reached at a V_{SO} of 79 knots.

(iii) The peak deceleration must occur in not more than time (t_r), which must be computed as follows:

$$t_r = \frac{31}{32.2 \left(g_p\right)} = \frac{.96}{g_p}$$

where—

g_p=The peak deceleration calculated in accordance with paragraph (d)(2)(ii) of this section

t_r=The rise time (in seconds) to the peak deceleration.

(e) An alternate approach that achieves an equivalent, or greater, level of occupant protection to that required by this section may be used if substantiated on a rational basis.

[Amdt. 23–36, 53 FR 30812, Aug. 15, 1988, as amended by Amdt. 23–44, 58 FR 38639, July 19, 1993; Amdt. 23–50, 61 FR 5192, Feb. 9, 1996]

FATIGUE EVALUATION

§23.571 Metallic pressurized cabin structures.

For normal, utility, and acrobatic category airplanes, the strength, detail design, and fabrication of the metallic structure of the pressure cabin must be evaluated under one of the following:

(a) A fatigue strength investigation in which the structure is shown by tests, or by analysis supported by test evidence, to be able to withstand the repeated loads of variable magnitude expected in service; or

(b) A fail safe strength investigation, in which it is shown by analysis, tests, or both that catastrophic failure of the structure is not probable after fatigue failure, or obvious partial failure, of a principal structural element, and that the remaining structures are able to withstand a static ultimate load factor of 75 percent of the limit load factor at V_C, considering the combined effects of normal operating pressures, expected external aerodynamic pressures, and flight loads. These loads must be multiplied by a factor of 1.15 unless the dynamic effects of failure under static load are otherwise considered.

(c) The damage tolerance evaluation of §23.573(b).

[Doc. No. 4080, 29 FR 17955, Dec. 18, 1964, as amended by Amdt. 23–14, 38 FR 31821, Nov. 19, 1973; Amdt. 23–45, 58 FR 42163, Aug. 6, 1993; Amdt. 23–48, 61 FR 5147, Feb. 9, 1996]

§23.572 Metallic wing, empennage, and associated structures.

(a) For normal, utility, and acrobatic category airplanes, the strength, detail design, and fabrication of those parts of the airframe structure whose failure would be catastrophic must be evaluated under one of the following unless it is shown that the structure, operating stress level, materials and expected uses are comparable, from a fatigue standpoint, to a similar design that has had extensive satisfactory service experience:

(1) A fatigue strength investigation in which the structure is shown by tests, or by analysis supported by test evidence, to be able to withstand the repeated loads of variable magnitude expected in service; or

(2) A fail-safe strength investigation in which it is shown by analysis, tests, or both, that catastrophic failure of the structure is not probable after fatigue failure, or obvious partial failure, of a principal structural element, and that the remaining structure is able to withstand a static ultimate load factor of 75 percent of the critical limit load factor at V_c. These loads must be multiplied by a factor of 1.15 unless the dynamic effects of failure under static load are otherwise considered.

(3) The damage tolerance evaluation of § 23.573(b).

(b) Each evaluation required by this section must—

(1) Include typical loading spectra (e.g. taxi, ground-air-ground cycles, maneuver, gust);

(2) Account for any significant effects due to the mutual influence of aerodynamic surfaces; and

(3) Consider any significant effects from propeller slipstream loading, and buffet from vortex impingements.

[Amdt. 23–7, 34 FR 13090, Aug. 13, 1969, as amended by Amdt. 23–14, 38 FR 31821, Nov. 19, 1973; Amdt. 23–34, 52 FR 1830, Jan. 15, 1987; Amdt. 23–38, 54 FR 39511, Sept. 26, 1989; Amdt. 23–45, 58 FR 42163, Aug. 6, 1993; Amdt. 23–48, 61 FR 5147, Feb. 9, 1996]

§ 23.573 Damage tolerance and fatigue evaluation of structure.

(a) *Composite airframe structure.* Composite airframe structure must be evaluated under this paragraph instead of §§ 23.571 and 23.572. The applicant must evaluate the composite airframe structure, the failure of which would result in catastrophic loss of the airplane, in each wing (including canards, tandem wings, and winglets), empennage, their carrythrough and attaching structure,

moveable control surfaces and their attaching structure fuselage, and pressure cabin using the damage-tolerance criteria prescribed in paragraphs (a)(1) through (a)(4) of this section unless shown to be impractical. If the applicant establishes that damage-tolerance criteria is impractical for a particular structure, the structure must be evaluated in accordance with paragraphs (a)(1) and (a)(6) of this section. Where bonded joints are used, the structure must also be evaluated in accordance with paragraph (a)(5) of this section. The effects of material variability and environmental conditions on the strength and durability properties of the composite materials must be accounted for in the evaluations required by this section.

(1) It must be demonstrated by tests, or by analysis supported by tests, that the structure is capable of carrying ultimate load with damage up to the threshold of detectability considering the inspection procedures employed.

(2) The growth rate or no-growth of damage that may occur from fatigue, corrosion, manufacturing flaws or impact damage, under repeated loads expected in service, must be established by tests or analysis supported by tests.

(3) The structure must be shown by residual strength tests, or analysis supported by residual strength tests, to be able to withstand critical limit flight loads, considered as ultimate loads, with the extent of detectable damage consistent with the results of the damage tolerance evaluations. For pressurized cabins, the following loads must be withstood:

(i) Critical limit flight loads with the combined effects of normal operating pressure and expected external aerodynamic pressures.

(ii) The expected external aerodynamic pressures in 1g flight combined with a cabin differential pressure equal to 1.1 times the normal operating differential pressure without any other load.

(4) The damage growth, between initial detectability and the value selected for residual strength demonstrations, factored to obtain inspection intervals, must allow development of an

inspection program suitable for application by operation and maintenance personnel.

(5) For any bonded joint, the failure of which would result in catastrophic loss of the airplane, the limit load capacity must be substantiated by one of the following methods—

(i) The maximum disbonds of each bonded joint consistent with the capability to withstand the loads in paragraph (a)(3) of this section must be determined by analysis, tests, or both. Disbonds of each bonded joint greater than this must be prevented by design features; or

(ii) Proof testing must be conducted on each production article that will apply the critical limit design load to each critical bonded joint; or

(iii) Repeatable and reliable non-destructive inspection techniques must be established that ensure the strength of each joint.

(6) Structural components for which the damage tolerance method is shown to be impractical must be shown by component fatigue tests, or analysis supported by tests, to be able to withstand the repeated loads of variable magnitude expected in service. Sufficient component, subcomponent, element, or coupon tests must be done to establish the fatigue scatter factor and the environmental effects. Damage up to the threshold of detectability and ultimate load residual strength capability must be considered in the demonstration.

(b) *Metallic airframe structure.* If the applicant elects to use §23.571(a)(3) or §23.572(a)(3), then the damage tolerance evaluation must include a determination of the probable locations and modes of damage due to fatigue, corrosion, or accidental damage. The determination must be by analysis supported by test evidence and, if available, service experience. Damage at multiple sites due to fatigue must be included where the design is such that this type of damage can be expected to occur. The evaluation must incorporate repeated load and static analyses supported by test evidence. The extent of damage for residual strength evaluation at any time within the operational life of the airplane must be consistent with the initial detectability and subsequent growth under repeated loads. The residual strength evaluation must show that the remaining structure is able to withstand critical limit flight loads, considered as ultimate, with the extent of detectable damage consistent with the results of the damage tolerance evaluations. For pressurized cabins, the following load must be withstood:

(1) The normal operating differential pressure combined with the expected external aerodynamic pressures applied simultaneously with the flight loading conditions specified in this part, and

(2) The expected external aerodynamic pressures in 1g flight combined with a cabin differential pressure equal to 1.1 times the normal operating differential pressure without any other load.

[Doc. No. 26269, 58 FR 42163, Aug. 6, 1993; 58 FR 51970, Oct. 5, 1993, as amended by Amdt. 23–48, 61 FR 5147, Feb. 9, 1996]

§23.574 Metallic damage tolerance and fatigue evaluation of commuter category airplanes.

For commuter category airplanes—

(a) *Metallic damage tolerance.* An evaluation of the strength, detail design, and fabrication must show that catastrophic failure due to fatigue, corrosion, defects, or damage will be avoided throughout the operational life of the airplane. This evaluation must be conducted in accordance with the provisions of §23.573, except as specified in paragraph (b) of this section, for each part of the structure that could contribute to a catastrophic failure.

(b) *Fatigue (safe-life) evaluation.* Compliance with the damage tolerance requirements of paragraph (a) of this section is not required if the applicant establishes that the application of those requirements is impractical for a particular structure. This structure must be shown, by analysis supported by test evidence, to be able to withstand the repeated loads of variable magnitude expected during its service life without detectable cracks. Appropriate safe-life scatter factors must be applied.

[Doc. No. 27805, 61 FR 5148, Feb. 9, 1996]

§ 23.575 Inspections and other procedures.

Each inspection or other procedure, based on an evaluation required by §§ 23.571, 23.572, 23.573 or 23.574, must be established to prevent catastrophic failure and must be included in the Limitations Section of the Instructions for Continued Airworthiness required by § 23.1529.

[Doc. No. 27805, 61 FR 5148, Feb. 9, 1996]

Subpart D—Design and Construction

§ 23.601 General.

The suitability of each questionable design detail and part having an important bearing on safety in operations, must be established by tests.

§ 23.603 Materials and workmanship.

(a) The suitability and durability of materials used for parts, the failure of which could adversely affect safety, must—

(1) Be established by experience or tests;

(2) Meet approved specifications that ensure their having the strength and other properties assumed in the design data; and

(3) Take into account the effects of environmental conditions, such as temperature and humidity, expected in service.

(b) Workmanship must be of a high standard.

[Doc. No. 4080, 29 FR 17955, Dec. 18, 1964, as amended by Amdt. 23-17, 41 FR 55464, Dec. 20, 1976; Amdt. 23-23, 43 FR 50592, Oct. 10, 1978]

§ 23.605 Fabrication methods.

(a) The methods of fabrication used must produce consistently sound structures. If a fabrication process (such as gluing, spot welding, or heat-treating) requires close control to reach this objective, the process must be performed under an approved process specification.

(b) Each new aircraft fabrication method must be substantiated by a test program.

[Doc. No. 4080, 29 FR 17955, Dec. 18, 1964; 30 FR 258, Jan. 9, 1965, as amended by Amdt. 23-23, 43 FR 50592, Oct. 10, 1978]

§ 23.607 Fasteners.

(a) Each removable fastener must incorporate two retaining devices if the loss of such fastener would preclude continued safe flight and landing.

(b) Fasteners and their locking devices must not be adversely affected by the environmental conditions associated with the particular installation.

(c) No self-locking nut may be used on any bolt subject to rotation in operation unless a non-friction locking device is used in addition to the self-locking device.

[Doc. No. 27805, 61 FR 5148, Feb. 9, 1996]

§ 23.609 Protection of structure.

Each part of the structure must—

(a) Be suitably protected against deterioration or loss of strength in service due to any cause, including—

(1) Weathering;

(2) Corrosion; and

(3) Abrasion; and

(b) Have adequate provisions for ventilation and drainage.

§ 23.611 Accessibility provisions.

For each part that requires maintenance, inspection, or other servicing, appropriate means must be incorporated into the aircraft design to allow such servicing to be accomplished.

[Doc. No. 27805, 61 FR 5148, Feb. 9, 1996]

§ 23.613 Material strength properties and design values.

(a) Material strength properties must be based on enough tests of material meeting specifications to establish design values on a statistical basis.

(b) Design values must be chosen to minimize the probability of structural failure due to material variability. Except as provided in paragraph (e) of this section, compliance with this paragraph must be shown by selecting design values that ensure material strength with the following probability:

(1) Where applied loads are eventually distributed through a single member within an assembly, the failure of which would result in loss of structural integrity of the component; 99 percent probability with 95 percent confidence.

(2) For redundant structure, in which the failure of individual elements would result in applied loads being safely distributed to other load carrying members; 90 percent probability with 95 percent confidence.

(c) The effects of temperature on allowable stresses used for design in an essential component or structure must be considered where thermal effects are significant under normal operating conditions.

(d) The design of the structure must minimize the probability of catastrophic fatigue failure, particularly at points of stress concentration.

(e) Design values greater than the guaranteed minimums required by this section may be used where only guaranteed minimum values are normally allowed if a "premium selection" of the material is made in which a specimen of each individual item is tested before use to determine that the actual strength properties of that particular item will equal or exceed those used in design.

[Doc. No. 4080, 29 FR 17955, Dec. 18, 1964; 30 FR 258, Jan. 9, 1965, as amended by Amdt. 23–23, 43 FR 50592, Oct. 30, 1978; Amdt. 23–45, 58 FR 42163, Aug. 6, 1993]

§ 23.619 Special factors.

The factor of safety prescribed in § 23.303 must be multiplied by the highest pertinent special factors of safety prescribed in §§ 23.621 through 23.625 for each part of the structure whose strength is—

(a) Uncertain;

(b) Likely to deteriorate in service before normal replacement; or

(c) Subject to appreciable variability because of uncertainties in manufacturing processes or inspection methods.

[Amdt. 23–7, 34 FR 13091, Aug. 13, 1969]

§ 23.621 Casting factors.

(a) *General.* The factors, tests, and inspections specified in paragraphs (b) through (d) of this section must be applied in addition to those necessary to establish foundry quality control. The inspections must meet approved specifications. Paragraphs (c) and (d) of this section apply to any structural castings except castings that are pressure tested as parts of hydraulic or other fluid systems and do not support structural loads.

(b) *Bearing stresses and surfaces.* The casting factors specified in paragraphs (c) and (d) of this section—

(1) Need not exceed 1.25 with respect to bearing stresses regardless of the method of inspection used; and

(2) Need not be used with respect to the bearing surfaces of a part whose bearing factor is larger than the applicable casting factor.

(c) *Critical castings.* For each casting whose failure would preclude continued safe flight and landing of the airplane or result in serious injury to occupants, the following apply:

(1) Each critical casting must either—

(i) Have a casting factor of not less than 1.25 and receive 100 percent inspection by visual, radiographic, and either magnetic particle, penetrant or other approved equivalent non-destructive inspection method; or

(ii) Have a casting factor of not less than 2.0 and receive 100 percent visual inspection and 100 percent approved non-destructive inspection. When an approved quality control procedure is established and an acceptable statistical analysis supports reduction, non-destructive inspection may be reduced from 100 percent, and applied on a sampling basis.

(2) For each critical casting with a casting factor less than 1.50, three sample castings must be static tested and shown to meet—

(i) The strength requirements of § 23.305 at an ultimate load corresponding to a casting factor of 1.25; and

(ii) The deformation requirements of § 23.305 at a load of 1.15 times the limit load.

(3) Examples of these castings are structural attachment fittings, parts of flight control systems, control surface hinges and balance weight attachments, seat, berth, safety belt, and fuel and oil tank supports and attachments, and cabin pressure valves.

(d) *Non-critical castings.* For each casting other than those specified in paragraph (c) or (e) of this section, the following apply:

(1) Except as provided in paragraphs (d)(2) and (3) of this section, the casting

factors and corresponding inspections must meet the following table:

Casting factor	Inspection
2.0 or more	100 percent visual.
Less than 2.0 but more than 1.5.	100 percent visual, and magnetic particle or penetrant or equivalent nondestructive inspection methods.
1.25 through 1.50	100 percent visual, magnetic particle or penetrant, and radiographic, or approved equivalent nondestructive inspection methods.

(2) The percentage of castings inspected by nonvisual methods may be reduced below that specified in subparagraph (d)(1) of this section when an approved quality control procedure is established.

(3) For castings procured to a specification that guarantees the mechanical properties of the material in the casting and provides for demonstration of these properties by test of coupons cut from the castings on a sampling basis—

(i) A casting factor of 1.0 may be used; and

(ii) The castings must be inspected as provided in paragraph (d)(1) of this section for casting factors of "1.25 through 1.50" and tested under paragraph (c)(2) of this section.

(e) *Non-structural castings.* Castings used for non-structural purposes do not require evaluation, testing or close inspection.

[Doc. No. 4080, 29 FR 17955, Dec. 18, 1964, as amended by Amdt. 23–45, 58 FR 42164, Aug. 6, 1993]

§ 23.623 Bearing factors.

(a) Each part that has clearance (free fit), and that is subject to pounding or vibration, must have a bearing factor large enough to provide for the effects of normal relative motion.

(b) For control surface hinges and control system joints, compliance with the factors prescribed in §§ 23.657 and 23.693, respectively, meets paragraph (a) of this section.

[Amdt. 23–7, 34 FR 13091, Aug. 13, 1969]

§ 23.625 Fitting factors.

For each fitting (a part or terminal used to join one structural member to another), the following apply:

(a) For each fitting whose strength is not proven by limit and ultimate load tests in which actual stress conditions are simulated in the fitting and surrounding structures, a fitting factor of at least 1.15 must be applied to each part of—

(1) The fitting;

(2) The means of attachment; and

(3) The bearing on the joined members.

(b) No fitting factor need be used for joint designs based on comprehensive test data (such as continuous joints in metal plating, welded joints, and scarf joints in wood).

(c) For each integral fitting, the part must be treated as a fitting up to the point at which the section properties become typical of the member.

(d) For each seat, berth, safety belt, and harness, its attachment to the structure must be shown, by analysis, tests, or both, to be able to withstand the inertia forces prescribed in § 23.561 multiplied by a fitting factor of 1.33.

[Doc. No. 4080, 29 FR 17955, Dec. 18, 1964, as amended by Amdt. 23–7, 34 FR 13091, Aug. 13, 1969]

§ 23.627 Fatigue strength.

The structure must be designed, as far as practicable, to avoid points of stress concentration where variable stresses above the fatigue limit are likely to occur in normal service.

§ 23.629 Flutter.

(a) It must be shown by the methods of paragraph (b) and either paragraph (c) or (d) of this section, that the airplane is free from flutter, control reversal, and divergence for any condition of operation within the limit V-n envelope and at all speeds up to the speed specified for the selected method. In addition—

(1) Adequate tolerances must be established for quantities which affect flutter, including speed, damping, mass balance, and control system stiffness; and

(2) The natural frequencies of main structural components must be determined by vibration tests or other approved methods.

(b) Flight flutter tests must be made to show that the airplane is free from flutter, control reversal and divergence and to show that—

(1) Proper and adequate attempts to induce flutter have been made within the speed range up to V_D;

(2) The vibratory response of the structure during the test indicates freedom from flutter;

(3) A proper margin of damping exists at V_D; and

(4) There is no large and rapid reduction in damping as V_D is approached.

(c) Any rational analysis used to predict freedom from flutter, control reversal and divergence must cover all speeds up to 1.2 V_D.

(d) Compliance with the rigidity and mass balance criteria (pages 4–12), in Airframe and Equipment Engineering Report No. 45 (as corrected) "Simplified Flutter Prevention Criteria" (published by the Federal Aviation Administration) may be accomplished to show that the airplane is free from flutter, control reversal, or divergence if—

(1) V_D/M_D for the airplane is less than 260 knots (EAS) and less than Mach 0.5,

(2) The wing and aileron flutter prevention criteria, as represented by the wing torsional stiffness and aileron balance criteria, are limited in use to airplanes without large mass concentrations (such as engines, floats, or fuel tanks in outer wing panels) along the wing span, and

(3) The airplane—

(i) Does not have a T-tail or other unconventional tail configurations;

(ii) Does not have unusual mass distributions or other unconventional design features that affect the applicability of the criteria, and

(iii) Has fixed-fin and fixed-stabilizer surfaces.

(e) For turbopropeller-powered airplanes, the dynamic evaluation must include—

(1) Whirl mode degree of freedom which takes into account the stability of the plane of rotation of the propeller and significant elastic, inertial, and aerodynamic forces, and

(2) Propeller, engine, engine mount, and airplane structure stiffness and damping variations appropriate to the particular configuration.

(f) Freedom from flutter, control reversal, and divergence up to V_D/M_D must be shown as follows:

(1) For airplanes that meet the criteria of paragraphs (d)(1) through (d)(3) of this section, after the failure, malfunction, or disconnection of any single element in any tab control system.

(2) For airplanes other than those described in paragraph (f)(1) of this section, after the failure, malfunction, or disconnection of any single element in the primary flight control system, any tab control system, or any flutter damper.

(g) For airplanes showing compliance with the fail-safe criteria of §§23.571 and 23.572, the airplane must be shown by analysis to be free from flutter up to V_D/M_D after fatigue failure, or obvious partial failure, of a principal structural element.

(h) For airplanes showing compliance with the damage tolerance criteria of §23.573, the airplane must be shown by analysis to be free from flutter up to V_D/M_D with the extent of damage for which residual strength is demonstrated.

(i) For modifications to the type design that could affect the flutter characteristics, compliance with paragraph (a) of this section must be shown, except that analysis based on previously approved data may be used alone to show freedom from flutter, control reversal and divergence, for all speeds up to the speed specified for the selected method.

[Amdt. 23–23, 43 FR 50592, Oct. 30, 1978, as amended by Amdt. 23–31, 49 FR 46867, Nov. 28, 1984; Amdt. 23–45, 58 FR 42164, Aug. 6, 1993; 58 FR 51970, Oct. 5, 1993; Amdt. 23–48, 61 FR 5148, Feb. 9, 1996]

WINGS

§23.641 Proof of strength.

The strength of stressed-skin wings must be proven by load tests or by combined structural analysis and load tests.

CONTROL SURFACES

§ 23.651 Proof of strength.

(a) Limit load tests of control surfaces are required. These tests must include the horn or fitting to which the control system is attached.

(b) In structural analyses, rigging loads due to wire bracing must be accounted for in a rational or conservative manner.

§ 23.655 Installation.

(a) Movable surfaces must be installed so that there is no interference between any surfaces, their bracing, or adjacent fixed structure, when one surface is held in its most critical clearance positions and the others are operated through their full movement.

(b) If an adjustable stabilizer is used, it must have stops that will limit its range of travel to that allowing safe flight and landing.

[Doc. No. 4080, 29 FR 17955, Dec. 18, 1964, as amended by Amdt. 23–45, 58 FR 42164, Aug. 6, 1993]

§ 23.657 Hinges.

(a) Control surface hinges, except ball and roller bearing hinges, must have a factor of safety of not less than 6.67 with respect to the ultimate bearing strength of the softest material used as a bearing.

(b) For ball or roller bearing hinges, the approved rating of the bearing may not be exceeded.

[Doc. No. 4080, 29 FR 17955, Dec. 18, 1964, as amended by Amdt. 23–48, 61 FR 5148, Feb. 9, 1996]

§ 23.659 Mass balance.

The supporting structure and the attachment of concentrated mass balance weights used on control surfaces must be designed for—

(a) 24 g normal to the plane of the control surface;

(b) 12 g fore and aft; and

(c) 12 g parallel to the hinge line.

CONTROL SYSTEMS

§ 23.671 General.

(a) Each control must operate easily, smoothly, and positively enough to allow proper performance of its functions.

(b) Controls must be arranged and identified to provide for convenience in operation and to prevent the possibility of confusion and subsequent inadvertent operation.

§ 23.672 Stability augmentation and automatic and power-operated systems.

If the functioning of stability augmentation or other automatic or power-operated systems is necessary to show compliance with the flight characteristics requirements of this part, such systems must comply with § 23.671 and the following:

(a) A warning, which is clearly distinguishable to the pilot under expected flight conditions without requiring the pilot's attention, must be provided for any failure in the stability augmentation system or in any other automatic or power-operated system that could result in an unsafe condition if the pilot was not aware of the failure. Warning systems must not activate the control system.

(b) The design of the stability augmentation system or of any other automatic or power-operated system must permit initial counteraction of failures without requiring exceptional pilot skill or strength, by either the deactivation of the system or a failed portion thereof, or by overriding the failure by movement of the flight controls in the normal sense.

(c) It must be shown that, after any single failure of the stability augmentation system or any other automatic or power-operated system—

(1) The airplane is safely controllable when the failure or malfunction occurs at any speed or altitude within the approved operating limitations that is critical for the type of failure being considered;

(2) The controllability and maneuverability requirements of this part are met within a practical operational flight envelope (for example, speed, altitude, normal acceleration, and airplane configuration) that is described in the Airplane Flight Manual (AFM); and

(3) The trim, stability, and stall characteristics are not impaired below a

level needed to permit continued safe flight and landing.

[Doc. No. 26269, 58 FR 42164, Aug. 6, 1993]

§ 23.673 Primary flight controls.

Primary flight controls are those used by the pilot for the immediate control of pitch, roll, and yaw.

[Doc. No. 4080, 29 FR 17955, Dec. 18, 1964, as amended by Amdt. 23–48, 61 FR 5148, Feb. 9, 1996]

§ 23.675 Stops.

(a) Each control system must have stops that positively limit the range of motion of each movable aerodynamic surface controlled by the system.

(b) Each stop must be located so that wear, slackness, or takeup adjustments will not adversely affect the control characteristics of the airplane because of a change in the range of surface travel.

(c) Each stop must be able to withstand any loads corresponding to the design conditions for the control system.

[Amdt. 23–17, 41 FR 55464, Dec. 20, 1976]

§ 23.677 Trim systems.

(a) Proper precautions must be taken to prevent inadvertent, improper, or abrupt trim tab operation. There must be means near the trim control to indicate to the pilot the direction of trim control movement relative to airplane motion. In addition, there must be means to indicate to the pilot the position of the trim device with respect to both the range of adjustment and, in the case of lateral and directional trim, the neutral position. This means must be visible to the pilot and must be located and designed to prevent confusion. The pitch trim indicator must be clearly marked with a position or range within which it has been demonstrated that take-off is safe for all center of gravity positions and each flap position approved for takeoff.

(b) Trimming devices must be designed so that, when any one connecting or transmitting element in the primary flight control system fails, adequate control for safe flight and landing is available with—

(1) For single-engine airplanes, the longitudinal trimming devices; or

(2) For multiengine airplanes, the longitudinal and directional trimming devices.

(c) Tab controls must be irreversible unless the tab is properly balanced and has no unsafe flutter characteristics. Irreversible tab systems must have adequate rigidity and reliability in the portion of the system from the tab to the attachment of the irreversible unit to the airplane structure.

(d) It must be demonstrated that the airplane is safely controllable and that the pilot can perform all maneuvers and operations necessary to effect a safe landing following any probable powered trim system runaway that reasonably might be expected in service, allowing for appropriate time delay after pilot recognition of the trim system runaway. The demonstration must be conducted at critical airplane weights and center of gravity positions.

[Doc. No. 4080, 29 FR 17955, Dec. 18, 1964, as amended by Amdt. 23–7, 34 FR 13091, Aug. 13, 1969; Amdt. 23–34, 52 FR 1830, Jan. 15, 1987; Amdt. 23–42, 56 FR 353, Jan. 3, 1991; Amdt. 23–49, 61 FR 5165, Feb. 9, 1996]

§ 23.679 Control system locks.

If there is a device to lock the control system on the ground or water:

(a) There must be a means to—

(1) Give unmistakable warning to the pilot when lock is engaged; or

(2) Automatically disengage the device when the pilot operates the primary flight controls in a normal manner.

(b) The device must be installed to limit the operation of the airplane so that, when the device is engaged, the pilot receives unmistakable warning at the start of the takeoff.

(c) The device must have a means to preclude the possibility of it becoming inadvertently engaged in flight.

[Doc. No. 26269, 58 FR 42164, Aug. 6, 1993]

§ 23.681 Limit load static tests.

(a) Compliance with the limit load requirements of this part must be shown by tests in which—

(1) The direction of the test loads produces the most severe loading in the control system; and

(2) Each fitting, pulley, and bracket used in attaching the system to the main structure is included.

(b) Compliance must be shown (by analyses or individual load tests) with the special factor requirements for control system joints subject to angular motion.

§ 23.683 Operation tests.

(a) It must be shown by operation tests that, when the controls are operated from the pilot compartment with the system loaded as prescribed in paragraph (b) of this section, the system is free from—

(1) Jamming;

(2) Excessive friction; and

(3) Excessive deflection.

(b) The prescribed test loads are—

(1) For the entire system, loads corresponding to the limit airloads on the appropriate surface, or the limit pilot forces in § 23.397(b), whichever are less; and

(2) For secondary controls, loads not less than those corresponding to the maximum pilot effort established under § 23.405.

[Doc. No. 4080, 29 FR 17955, Dec. 18, 1964, as amended by Amdt. 23–7, 34 FR 13091, Aug. 13, 1969]

§ 23.685 Control system details.

(a) Each detail of each control system must be designed and installed to prevent jamming, chafing, and interference from cargo, passengers, loose objects, or the freezing of moisture.

(b) There must be means in the cockpit to prevent the entry of foreign objects into places where they would jam the system.

(c) There must be means to prevent the slapping of cables or tubes against other parts.

(d) Each element of the flight control system must have design features, or must be distinctively and permanently marked, to minimize the possibility of incorrect assembly that could result in malfunctioning of the control system.

[Doc. No. 4080, 29 FR 17955, Dec. 18, 1964, as amended by Amdt. 23–17, 41 FR 55464, Dec. 20, 1976]

§ 23.687 Spring devices.

The reliability of any spring device used in the control system must be es-

tablished by tests simulating service conditions unless failure of the spring will not cause flutter or unsafe flight characteristics.

§ 23.689 Cable systems.

(a) Each cable, cable fitting, turnbuckle, splice, and pulley used must meet approved specifications. In addition—

(1) No cable smaller than ⅛ inch diameter may be used in primary control systems;

(2) Each cable system must be designed so that there will be no hazardous change in cable tension throughout the range of travel under operating conditions and temperature variations; and

(3) There must be means for visual inspection at each fairlead, pulley, terminal, and turnbuckle.

(b) Each kind and size of pulley must correspond to the cable with which it is used. Each pulley must have closely fitted guards to prevent the cables from being misplaced or fouled, even when slack. Each pulley must lie in the plane passing through the cable so that the cable does not rub against the pulley flange.

(c) Fairleads must be installed so that they do not cause a change in cable direction of more than three degrees.

(d) Clevis pins subject to load or motion and retained only by cotter pins may not be used in the control system.

(e) Turnbuckles must be attached to parts having angular motion in a manner that will positively prevent binding throughout the range of travel.

(f) Tab control cables are not part of the primary control system and may be less than ⅛ inch diameter in airplanes that are safely controllable with the tabs in the most adverse positions.

[Doc. No. 4080, 29 FR 17955, Dec. 18, 1964, as amended by Amdt. 23–7, 34 FR 13091, Aug. 13, 1969]

§ 23.691 Artificial stall barrier system.

If the function of an artificial stall barrier, for example, stick pusher, is used to show compliance with § 23.201(c), the system must comply with the following:

(a) With the system adjusted for operation, the plus and minus airspeeds at which downward pitching control will be provided must be established.

(b) Considering the plus and minus airspeed tolerances established by paragraph (a) of this section, an airspeed must be selected for the activation of the downward pitching control that provides a safe margin above any airspeed at which any unsatisfactory stall characteristics occur.

(c) In addition to the stall warning required §23.07, a warning that is clearly distinguishable to the pilot under all expected flight conditions without requiring the pilot's attention, must be provided for faults that would prevent the system from providing the required pitching motion.

(d) Each system must be designed so that the artificial stall barrier can be quickly and positively disengaged by the pilots to prevent unwanted downward pitching of the airplane by a quick release (emergency) control that meets the requirements of §23.1329(b).

(e) A preflight check of the complete system must be established and the procedure for this check made available in the Airplane Flight Manual (AFM). Preflight checks that are critical to the safety of the airplane must be included in the limitations section of the AFM.

(f) For those airplanes whose design includes an autopilot system:

(1) A quick release (emergency) control installed in accordance with §23.1329(b) may be used to meet the requirements of paragraph (d), of this section, and

(2) The pitch servo for that system may be used to provide the stall downward pitching motion.

(g) In showing compliance with §23.1309, the system must be evaluated to determine the effect that any announced or unannounced failure may have on the continued safe flight and landing of the airplane or the ability of the crew to cope with any adverse conditions that may result from such failures. This evaluation must consider the hazards that would result from the airplane's flight characteristics if the system was not provided, and the hazard that may result from unwanted downward pitching motion, which

could result from a failure at airspeeds above the selected stall speed.

[Doc. No. 27806, 61 FR 5165, Feb. 9, 1996]

§23.693 Joints.

Control system joints (in push-pull systems) that are subject to angular motion, except those in ball and roller bearing systems, must have a special factor of safety of not less than 3.33 with respect to the ultimate bearing strength of the softest material used as a bearing. This factor may be reduced to 2.0 for joints in cable control systems. For ball or roller bearings, the approved ratings may not be exceeded.

§23.697 Wing flap controls.

(a) Each wing flap control must be designed so that, when the flap has been placed in any position upon which compliance with the performance requirements of this part is based, the flap will not move from that position unless the control is adjusted or is moved by the automatic operation of a flap load limiting device.

(b) The rate of movement of the flaps in response to the operation of the pilot's control or automatic device must give satisfactory flight and performance characteristics under steady or changing conditions of airspeed, engine power, and attitude.

(c) If compliance with §23.145(b)(3) necessitates wing flap retraction to positions that are not fully retracted, the wing flap control lever settings corresponding to those positions must be positively located such that a definite change of direction of movement of the lever is necessary to select settings beyond those settings.

[Doc. No. 4080, 29 FR 17955, Dec. 18, 1964, as amended by Amdt. 23–49, 61 FR 5165, Feb. 9, 1996]

§23.699 Wing flap position indicator.

There must be a wing flap position indicator for—

(a) Flap installations with only the retracted and fully extended position, unless—

(1) A direct operating mechanism provides a sense of "feel" and position (such as when a mechanical linkage is employed); or

(2) The flap position is readily determined without seriously detracting from other piloting duties under any flight condition, day or night; and

(b) Flap installation with intermediate flap positions if—

(1) Any flap position other than retracted or fully extended is used to show compliance with the performance requirements of this part; and

(2) The flap installation does not meet the requirements of paragraph (a)(1) of this section.

§ 23.701 Flap interconnection.

(a) The main wing flaps and related movable surfaces as a system must—

(1) Be synchronized by a mechanical interconnection between the movable flap surfaces that is independent of the flap drive system; or by an approved equivalent means; or

(2) Be designed so that the occurrence of any failure of the flap system that would result in an unsafe flight characteristic of the airplane is extremely improbable; or

(b) The airplane must be shown to have safe flight characteristics with any combination of extreme positions of individual movable surfaces (mechanically interconnected surfaces are to be considered as a single surface).

(c) If an interconnection is used in multiengine airplanes, it must be designed to account for the unsummetrical loads resulting from flight with the engines on one side of the plane of symmetry inoperative and the remaining engines at takeoff power. For single-engine airplanes, and multiengine airplanes with no slipstream effects on the flaps, it may be assumed that 100 percent of the critical air load acts on one side and 70 percent on the other.

[Doc. No. 4080, 29 FR 17955, Dec. 18, 1964, as amended by Amdt. 23–14, 38 FR 31821, Nov. 19, 1973; Amdt. 23–42, 56 FR 353, Jan. 3, 1991; 56 FR 5455, Feb. 11, 1991; Amdt. 23–49, 61 FR 5165, Feb. 9, 1996]

§ 23.703 Takeoff warning system.

For commuter category airplanes, unless it can be shown that a lift or longitudinal trim device that affects the takeoff performance of the aircraft would not give an unsafe takeoff configuration when selection out of an approved takeoff position, a takeoff warning system must be installed and meet the following requirements:

(a) The system must provide to the pilots an aural warning that is automatically activated during the initial portion of the takeoff role if the airplane is in a configuration that would not allow a safe takeoff. The warning must continue until—

(1) The configuration is changed to allow safe takeoff, or

(2) Action is taken by the pilot to abandon the takeoff roll.

(b) The means used to activate the system must function properly for all authorized takeoff power settings and procedures and throughout the ranges of takeoff weights, altitudes, and temperatures for which certification is requested.

[Doc. No. 27806, 61 FR 5166, Feb. 9, 1996]

LANDING GEAR

§ 23.721 General.

For commuter category airplanes that have a passenger seating configuration, excluding pilot seats, of 10 or more, the following general requirements for the landing gear apply:

(a) The main landing-gear system must be designed so that if it fails due to overloads during takeoff and landing (assuming the overloads to act in the upward and aft directions), the failure mode is not likely to cause the spillage of enough fuel from any part of the fuel system to consitute a fire hazard.

(b) Each airplane must be designed so that, with the airplane under control, it can be landed on a paved runway with any one or more landing-gear legs not extended without sustaining a structural component failure that is likely to cause the spillage of enough fuel to consitute a fire hazard.

(c) Compliance with the provisions of this section may be shown by analysis or tests, or both.

[Amdt. 23–34, 52 FR 1830, Jan. 15, 1987]

§ 23.723 Shock absorption tests.

(a) It must be shown that the limit load factors selected for design in accordance with § 23.473 for takeoff and landing weights, respectively, will not be exceeded. This must be shown by energy absorption tests except that analysis based on tests conducted on a landing gear system with identical energy absorption characteristics may be used for increases in previously approved takeoff and landing weights.

(b) The landing gear may not fail, but may yield, in a test showing its reserve energy absorption capacity, simulating a descent velocity of 1.2 times the limit descent velocity, assuming wing lift equal to the weight of the airplane.

[Doc. No. 4080, 29 FR 17955, Dec. 18, 1964; 30 FR 258, Jan. 9, 1965, as amended by Amdt. 23–23, 43 FR 50593, Oct. 30, 1978; Amdt. 23–49, 61 FR 5166, Feb. 9, 1996]

§ 23.725 Limit drop tests.

(a) If compliance with § 23.723(a) is shown by free drop tests, these tests must be made on the complete airplane, or on units consisting of wheel, tire, and shock absorber, in their proper relation, from free drop heights not less than those determined by the following formula:

h (inches)=3.6 (W/S) ½

However, the free drop height may not be less than 9.2 inches and need not be more than 18.7 inches.

(b) If the effect of wing lift is provided for in free drop tests, the landing gear must be dropped with an effective weight equal to

$$W_e = W \frac{\left[h + (1-L)d \right]}{(h+d)}$$

where—

W_e=the effective weight to be used in the drop test (lbs.);

h=specified free drop height (inches);

d=deflection under impact of the tire (at the approved inflation pressure) plus the vertical component of the axle travel relative to the drop mass (inches);

$W=W_M$ for main gear units (lbs), equal to the static weight on that unit with the airplane in the level attitude (with the nose wheel clear in the case of nose wheel type airplanes);

$W=W_T$ for tail gear units (lbs.), equal to the static weight on the tail unit with the airplane in the tail-down attitude;

$W=W_N$ for nose wheel units lbs.), equal to the vertical component of the static reaction that would exist at the nose wheel, assuming that the mass of the airplane acts at the center of gravity and exerts a force of 1.0 g downward and 0.33 g forward; and

L= the ratio of the assumed wing lift to the airplane weight, but not more than 0.667.

(c) The limit inertia load factor must be determined in a rational or conservative manner, during the drop test, using a landing gear unit attitude, and applied drag loads, that represent the landing conditions.

(d) The value of d used in the computation of W_e in paragraph (b) of this section may not exceed the value actually obtained in the drop test.

(e) The limit inertia load factor must be determined from the drop test in paragraph (b) of this section according to the following formula:

$$n = n_j \frac{W_e}{W} + L$$

where—

n_j=the load factor developed in the drop test (that is, the acceleration (dv/dt) in gs recorded in the drop test) plus 1.0; and

W_e, W, and L are the same as in the drop test computation.

(f) The value of n determined in accordance with paragraph (e) may not be more than the limit inertia load factor used in the landing conditions in § 23.473.

[Doc. No. 4080, 29 FR 17955, Dec. 18, 1964, as amended by Amdt. 23–7, 34 FR 13091, Aug. 13, 1969; Amdt. 23–48, 61 FR 5148, Feb. 9, 1996]

§ 23.726 Ground load dynamic tests.

(a) If compliance with the ground load requirements of §§ 23.479 through 23.483 is shown dynamically by drop test, one drop test must be conducted that meets § 23.725 except that the drop height must be—

(1) 2.25 times the drop height prescribed in § 23.725(a); or

(2) Sufficient to develop 1.5 times the limit load factor.

(b) The critical landing condition for each of the design conditions specified in §§ 23.479 through 23.483 must be used for proof of strength.

[Amdt. 23–7, 34 FR 13091, Aug. 13, 1969]

§ 23.727 Reserve energy absorption drop test.

(a) If compliance with the reserve energy absorption requirement in § 23.723(b) is shown by free drop tests, the drop height may not be less than 1.44 times that specified in § 23.725.

(b) If the effect of wing lift is provided for, the units must be dropped with an effective mass equal to $W_e=Wh/(h+d)$, when the symbols and other details are the same as in § 23.725.

[Doc. No. 4080, 29 FR 17955, Dec. 18, 1964, as amended by Amdt. 23–7, 34 FR 13091, Aug. 13, 1969]

§ 23.729 Landing gear extension and retraction system.

(a) *General.* For airplanes with retractable landing gear, the following apply:

(1) Each landing gear retracting mechanism and its supporting structure must be designed for maximum flight load factors with the gear retracted and must be designed for the combination of friction, inertia, brake torque, and air loads, occurring during retraction at any airspeed up to 1.6 V_{S1} with flaps retracted, and for any load factor up to those specified in § 23.345 for the flaps-extended condition.

(2) The landing gear and retracting mechanism, including the wheel well doors, must withstand flight loads, including loads resulting from all yawing conditions specified in § 23.351, with the landing gear extended at any speed up to at least 1.6 V_{S1} with the flaps retracted.

(b) *Landing gear lock.* There must be positive means (other than the use of hydraulic pressure) to keep the landing gear extended.

(c) *Emergency operation.* For a landplane having retractable landing gear that cannot be extended manually, there must be means to extend the landing gear in the event of either—

(1) Any reasonably probable failure in the normal landing gear operation system; or

(2) Any reasonably probable failure in a power source that would prevent the operation of the normal landing gear operation system.

(d) *Operation test.* The proper functioning of the retracting mechanism must be shown by operation tests.

(e) *Position indicator.* If a retractable landing gear is used, there must be a landing gear position indicator (as well as necessary switches to actuate the indicator) or other means to inform the pilot that each gear is secured in the extended (or retracted) position. If switches are used, they must be located and coupled to the landing gear mechanical system in a manner that prevents an erroneous indication of either "down and locked" if each gear is not in the fully extended position, or "up and locked" if each landing gear is not in the fully retracted position.

(f) *Landing gear warning.* For landplanes, the following aural or equally effective landing gear warning devices must be provided:

(1) A device that functions continuously when one or more throttles are closed beyond the power settings normally used for landing approach if the landing gear is not fully extended and locked. A throttle stop may not be used in place of an aural device. If there is a manual shutoff for the warning device prescribed in this paragraph, the warning system must be designed so that when the warning has been suspended after one or more throttles are closed, subsequent retardation of any throttle to, or beyond, the position for normal landing approach will activate the warning device.

(2) A device that functions continuously when the wing flaps are extended beyond the maximum approach flap position, using a normal landing procedure, if the landing gear is not fully extended and locked. There may not be a manual shutoff for this warning device. The flap position sensing unit may be installed at any suitable location. The system for this device may use any part of the system (including the aural warning device) for the device required in paragraph (f)(1) of this section.

(g) *Equipment located in the landing gear bay.* If the landing gear bay is used as the location for equipment other than the landing gear, that equipment must be designed and installed to minimize damage from items such as a tire burst, or rocks, water, and slush that may enter the landing gear bay.

[Doc. No. 4080, 29 FR 17955, Dec. 18, 1964, as amended by Amdt. 23–7, 34 FR 13091, Aug. 13, 1969; Amdt. 23–21, 43 FR 2318, Jan. 1978; Amdt. 23–26, 45 FR 60171, Sept. 11, 1980; Amdt. 23–45, 58 FR 42164, Aug. 6, 1993; Amdt. 23–49, 61 FR 5166, Feb. 9, 1996]

§ 23.731   Wheels.

(a) The maximum static load rating of each wheel may not be less than the corresponding static ground reaction with—

(1) Design maximum weight; and

(2) Critical center of gravity.

(b) The maximum limit load rating of each wheel must equal or exceed the maximum radial limit load determined under the applicable ground load requirements of this part.

[Doc. No. 4080, 29 FR 17955, Dec. 18, 1964, as amended by Amdt. 23–45, 58 FR 42165, Aug. 6, 1993]

§ 23.733   Tires.

(a) Each landing gear wheel must have a tire whose approved tire ratings (static and dynamic) are not exceeded—

(1) By a load on each main wheel tire) to be compared to the static rating approved for such tires) equal to the corresponding static ground reaction under the design maximum weight and critical center of gravity; and

(2) By a load on nose wheel tires (to be compared with the dynamic rating approved for such tires) equal to the reaction obtained at the nose wheel, assuming the mass of the airplane to be concentrated at the most critical center of gravity and exerting a force of 1.0 W downward and 0.31 W forward (where W is the design maximum weight), with the reactions distributed to the nose and main wheels by the principles of statics and with the drag reaction at the ground applied only at wheels with brakes.

(b) If specially constructed tires are used, the wheels must be plainly and conspicuously marked to that effect. The markings must include the make, size, number of plies, and identification marking of the proper tire.

(c) Each tire installed on a retractable landing gear system must, at the maximum size of the tire type expected in service, have a clearance to surrounding structure and systems that is adequate to prevent contact between the tire and any part of the structure of systems.

[Doc. No. 4080, 29 FR 17955, Dec. 18, 1964, as amended by Amdt. 23–7, 34 FR 13092, Aug. 13, 1969; Amdt. 23–17, 41 FR 55464, Dec. 20, 1976; Amdt. 23–45, 58 FR 42165, Aug. 6, 1993]

§ 23.735   Brakes.

(a) Brakes must be provided. The landing brake kinetic energy capacity rating of each main wheel brake assembly must not be less than the kinetic energy absorption requirements determined under either of the following methods:

(1) The brake kinetic energy absorption requirements must be based on a conservative rational analysis of the sequence of events expected during landing at the design landing weight.

(2) Instead of a rational analysis, the kinetic energy absorption requirements for each main wheel brake assembly may be derived from the following formula:

$$KE = 0.0443 \, WV^2/N$$

where—

KE=Kinetic energy per wheel (ft.-lb.);
W=Design landing weight (lb.);
V=Airplane speed in knots. V must be not less than $V_S\sqrt{}$, the poweroff stalling speed of the airplane at sea level, at the design landing weight, and in the landing configuration; and
N=Number of main wheels with brakes.

(b) Brakes must be able to prevent the wheels from rolling on a paved runway with takeoff power on the critical engine, but need not prevent movement of the airplane with wheels locked.

(c) During the landing distance determination required by § 23.75, the pressure on the wheel braking system must not exceed the pressure specified by the brake manufacturer.

(d) If antiskid devices are installed, the devices and associated systems must be designed so that no single probable malfunction or failure will result in a hazardous loss of braking ability or directional control of the airplane.

(e) In addition, for commuter category airplanes, the rejected takeoff brake kinetic energy capacity rating of each main wheel brake assembly must not be less than the kinetic energy absorption requirements determined under either of the following methods—

(1) The brake kinetic energy absorption requirements must be based on a conservative rational analysis of the sequence of events expected during a rejected takeoff at the design takeoff weight.

(2) Instead of a rational analysis, the kinetic energy absorption requirements for each main wheel brake assembly may be derived from the following formula—

$$KE = 0.0443\ WV^2N$$

where,

KE=Kinetic energy per wheel (ft.-lbs.);
W=Design takeoff weight (lbs.);
V=Ground speed, in knots, associated with the maximum value of V_1 selected in accordance with § 23.51(c)(1);
N=Number of main wheels with brakes.

[Amdt. 23–7, 34 FR 13092, Aug. 13, 1969, as amended by Amdt. 23–24, 44 FR 68742, Nov. 29, 1979; Amdt. 23–42, 56 FR 354, Jan. 3, 1991; Amdt. 23–49, 61 FR 5166, Feb. 9, 1996]

§ 23.737 Skis.

The maximum limit load rating for each ski must equal or exceed the maximum limit load determined under the applicable ground load requirements of this part.

[Doc. No. 26269, 58 FR 42165, Aug. 6, 1993]

§ 23.745 Nose/tail wheel steering.

(a) If nose/tail wheel steering is installed, it must be demonstrated that its use does not require exceptional pilot skill during takeoff and landing, in crosswinds, or in the event of an engine failure; or its use must be limited to low speed maneuvering.

(b) Movement of the pilot's steering control must not interfere with the retraction or extension of the landing gear.

[Doc. No. 27806, 61 FR 5166, Feb. 9, 1996]

FLOATS AND HULLS

§ 23.751 Main float buoyancy.

(a) Each main float must have—

(1) A buoyancy of 80 percent in excess of the buoyancy required by that float to support its portion of the maximum weight of the seaplane or amphibian in fresh water; and

(2) Enough watertight compartments to provide reasonable assurance that the seaplane or amphibian will stay afloat without capsizing if any two compartments of any main float are flooded.

(b) Each main float must contain at least four watertight compartments approximately equal in volume.

[Doc. No. 4080, 29 FR 17955, Dec. 18, 1964, as amended by Amdt. 23–45, 58 FR 42165, Aug. 6, 1993]

§ 23.753 Main float design.

Each seaplane main float must meet the requirements of § 23.521.

[Doc. No. 26269, 58 FR 42165, Aug. 6, 1993]

§ 23.755 Hulls.

(a) The hull of a hull seaplane or amphibian of 1,500 pounds or more maximum weight must have watertight compartments designed and arranged so that the hull auxiliary floats, and tires (if used), will keep the airplane afloat without capsizing in fresh water when—

(1) For airplanes of 5,000 pounds or more maximum weight, any two adjacent compartments are flooded; and

(2) For airplanes of 1,500 pounds up to, but not including, 5,000 pounds maximum weight, any single compartment is flooded.

(b) Watertight doors in bulkheads may be used for communication between compartments.

[Doc. No. 4080, 29 FR 17955, Dec. 18, 1964, as amended by Amdt. 23–45, 58 FR 42165, Aug. 6, 1993; Amdt. 23–48, 61 FR 5148, Feb. 9, 1996]

§ 23.757 Auxiliary floats.

Auxiliary floats must be arranged so that, when completely submerged in fresh water, they provide a righting moment of at least 1.5 times the upsetting moment caused by the seaplane or amphibian being tilted.

PERSONNEL AND CARGO ACCOMMODATIONS

§ 23.771 Pilot compartment.

For each pilot compartment—

(a) The compartment and its equipment must allow each pilot to perform his duties without unreasonable concentration or fatigue;

(b) Where the flight crew are separated from the passengers by a partition, an opening or openable window or door must be provided to facilitate communication between flight crew and the passengers; and

(c) The aerodynamic controls listed in §23.779, excluding cables and control rods, must be located with respect to the propellers so that no part of the pilot or the controls lies in the region between the plane of rotation of any inboard propeller and the surface generated by a line passing through the center of the propeller hub making an angle of 5 degrees forward or aft of the plane of rotation of the propeller.

[Doc. No. 4080, 29 FR 17955, Dec. 18, 1964, as amended by Amdt. 23–14, 38 FR 31821, Nov. 19, 1973]

§23.773 Pilot compartment view.

(a) Each pilot compartment must be—

(1) Arranged with sufficiently extensive, clear and undistorted view to enable the pilot to safely taxi, takeoff, approach, land, and perform any maneuvers within the operating limitations of the airplane.

(2) Free from glare and reflections that could interfere with the pilot's vision. Compliance must be shown in all operations for which certification is requested; and

(3) Designed so that each pilot is protected from the elements so that moderate rain conditions do not unduly impair the pilot's view of the flight path in normal flight and while landing.

(b) Each pilot compartment must have a means to either remove or prevent the formation of fog or frost on an area of the internal portion of the windshield and side windows sufficiently large to provide the view specified in paragraph (a)(1) of this section. Compliance must be shown under all expected external and internal ambient operating conditions, unless it can be shown that the windshield and side windows can be easily cleared by the pilot without interruption of moral pilot duties.

[Doc. No. 26269, 58 FR 42165, Aug. 6, 1993]

§23.775 Windshields and windows.

(a) The internal panels of windshields and windows must be constructed of a nonsplintering material, such as nonsplintering safety glass.

(b) The design of windshields, windows, and canopies in pressurized airplanes must be based on factors peculiar to high altitude operation, including—

(1) The effects of continuous and cyclic pressurization loadings;

(2) The inherent characteristics of the material used; and

(3) The effects of temperatures and temperature gradients.

(c) On pressurized airplanes, if certification for operation up to and including 25,000 feet is requested, an enclosure canopy including a representative part of the installation must be subjected to special tests to account for the combined effects of continuous and cyclic pressurization loadings and flight loads, or compliance with the fail-safe requirements of paragraph (d) of this section must be shown.

(d) If certification for operation above 25,000 feet is requested the windshields, window panels, and canopies must be strong enough to withstand the maximum cabin pressure differential loads combined with critical aerodynamic pressure and temperature effects, after failure of any load-carrying element of the windshield, window panel, or canopy.

(e) The windshield and side windows forward of the pilot's back when the pilot is seated in the normal flight position must have a luminous transmittance value of not less than 70 percent.

(f) Unless operation in known or forecast icing conditions is prohibited by operating limitations, a means must be provided to prevent or to clear accumulations of ice from the windshield so that the pilot has adequate view for taxi, takeoff, approach, landing, and to perform any maneuvers within the operating limitations of the airplane.

(g) In the event of any probable single failure, a transparency heating system must be incapable of raising the temperature of any windshield or window to a point where there would be—

(1) Structural failure that adversely affects the integrity of the cabin; or

(2) There would be a danger of fire.

(h) In addition, for commuter category airplanes, the following applies:

(1) Windshield panes directly in front of the pilots in the normal conduct of their duties, and the supporting structures for these panes, must withstand, without penetration, the impact of a two-pound bird when the velocity of the airplane (relative to the bird along the airplane's flight path) is equal to the airplane's maximum approach flap speed.

(2) The windshield panels in front of the pilots must be arranged so that, assuming the loss of vision through any one panel, one or more panels remain available for use by a pilot seated at a pilot station to permit continued safe flight and landing.

[Doc. No. 4080, 29 FR 17955, Dec. 18, 1964, as amended by Amdt. 23–7, 34 FR 13092, Aug. 13, 1969; Amdt. 23–45, 58 FR 42165, Aug. 6, 1993; 58 FR 51970, Oct. 5, 1993; Amdt. 23–49, 61 FR 5166, Feb. 9, 1996]

§ 23.777 Cockpit controls.

(a) Each cockpit control must be located and (except where its function is obvious) identified to provide convenient operation and to prevent confusion and inadvertent operation.

(b) The controls must be located and arranged so that the pilot, when seated, has full and unrestricted movement of each control without interference from either his clothing or the cockpit structure.

(c) Powerplant controls must be located—

(1) For multiengine airplanes, on the pedestal or overhead at or near the center of the cockpit;

(2) For single and tandem seated single-engine airplanes, on the left side console or instrument panel;

(3) For other single-engine airplanes at or near the center of the cockpit, on the pedestal, instrument panel, or overhead; and

(4) For airplanes, with side-by-side pilot seats and with two sets of powerplant controls, on left and right consoles.

(d) The control location order from left to right must be power (thrust) lever, propeller (rpm control), and mixture control (condition lever and fuel cutoff for turbine-powered airplanes). Power (thrust) levers must be at least one inch higher or longer to make them more prominent than propeller (rpm control) or mixture controls. Carburetor heat or alternate air control must be to the left of the throttle or at least eight inches from the mixture control when located other than on a pedestal. Carburetor heat or alternate air control, when located on a pedestal must be aft or below the power (thrust) lever. Supercharger controls must be located below or aft of the propeller controls. Airplanes with tandem seating or single-place airplanes may utilize control locations on the left side of the cabin compartment; however, location order from left to right must be power (thrust) lever, propeller (rpm control) and mixture control.

(e) Identical powerplant controls for each engine must be located to prevent confusion as to the engines they control.

(1) Conventional multiengine powerplant controls must be located so that the left control(s) operates the left engines(s) and the right control(s) operates the right engine(s).

(2) On twin-engine airplanes with front and rear engine locations (tandem), the left powerplant controls must operate the front engine and the right powerplant controls must operate the rear engine.

(f) Wing flap and auxiliary lift device controls must be located—

(1) Centrally, or to the right of the pedestal or powerplant throttle control centerline; and

(2) Far enough away from the landing gear control to avoid confusion.

(g) The landing gear control must be located to the left of the throttle centerline or pedestal centerline.

(h) Each fuel feed selector control must comply with § 23.995 and be located and arranged so that the pilot can see and reach it without moving any seat or primary flight control when his seat is at any position in which it can be placed.

(1) For a mechanical fuel selector:

(i) The indication of the selected fuel valve position must be by means of a pointer and must provide positive identification and feel (detent, etc.) of the selected position.

(ii) The position indicator pointer must be located at the part of the handle that is the maximum dimension of the handle measured from the center of rotation.

(2) For electrical or electronic fuel selector:

(i) Digital controls or electrical switches must be properly labelled.

(ii) Means must be provided to indicate to the flight crew the tank or function selected. Selector switch position is not acceptable as a means of indication. The "off" or "closed" position must be indicated in red.

(3) If the fuel valve selector handle or electrical or digital selection is also a fuel shut-off selector, the off position marking must be colored red. If a separate emergency shut-off means is provided, it also must be colored red.

[Doc. No. 4080, 29 FR 17955, Dec. 18, 1964, as amended by Amdt. 23-7, 34 FR 13092, Aug. 13, 1969; Amdt. 23-33, 51 FR 26656, July 24, 1986; Amdt. 23-51, 61 FR 5136, Feb. 9, 1996]

§23.779 Motion and effect of cockpit controls.

Cockpit controls must be designed so that they operate in accordance with the following movement and actuation:

(a) Aerodynamic controls:

Motion and effect

(1) *Primary controls:*

Aileron	Right (clockwise) for right wing down.
Elevator	Rearward for nose up.
Rudder	Right pedal forward for nose right.

(2) *Secondary controls:*

Flaps (or auxiliary lift devices).	Forward or up for flaps up or auxiliary device stowed; rearward or down for flaps down or auxiliary device deployed.

Motion and effect

Trim tabs (or equivalent).	Switch motion or mechanical rotation of control to produce similar rotation of the airplane about an axis parallel to the axis control. Axis of roll trim control may be displaced to accommodate comfortable actuation by the pilot. For single-engine airplanes, direction of pilot's hand movement must be in the same sense as airplane response for rudder trim if only a portion of a rotational element is accessible.

(b) Powerplant and auxiliary controls:

Motion and effect

(1) *Powerplant controls:*

Power (thrust) lever.	Forward to increase forward thrust and rearward to increase rearward thrust.
Propellers ..	Forward to increase rpm.
Mixture	Forward or upward for rich.
Fuel	Forward for open.
Carburetor, air heat or alternate air.	Forward or upward for cold.
Supercharger.	Forward or upward for low blower.
Turbosuperchargers.	Forward, upward, or clockwise to increase pressure.
Rotary controls.	Clockwise from off to full on.

(2) *Auxiliary controls:*

Fuel tank selector.	Right for right tanks, left for left tanks.
Landing gear.	Down to extend.
Speed brakes.	Aft to extend.

[Amdt. 23-33, 51 FR 26656, July 24, 1986, as amended by Amdt. 23-51, 61 FR 5136, Feb. 9, 1996]

§23.781 Cockpit control knob shape.

(a) Flap and landing gear control knobs must conform to the general shapes (but not necessarily the exact sizes or specific proportions) in the following figure:

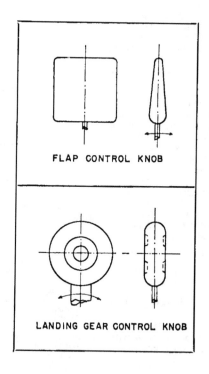

FLAP CONTROL KNOB

LANDING GEAR CONTROL KNOB

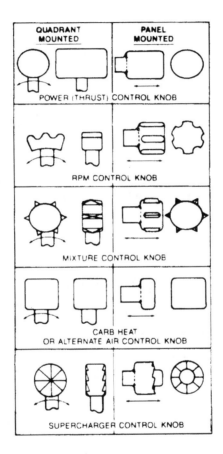

(b) Powerplant control knobs must conform to the general shapes (but not necessarily the exact sizes or specific proportions) in the following figure:

[Doc. No. 4080, 29 FR 17955, Dec. 18, 1964; 30 FR 258, Jan. 9, 1965, as amended by Amdt. 23-33, 51 FR 26657, July 24, 1986]

§ 23.783 Doors.

(a) Each closed cabin with passenger accommodations must have at least one adequate and easily accessible external door.

(b) Passenger doors must not be located with respect to any propeller disk or any other potential hazard so as to endanger persons using the door.

(c) Each external passenger or crew door must comply with the following requirements:

(1) There must be a means to lock and safeguard the door against inadvertent opening during flight by persons, by cargo, or as a result of mechanical failure.

(2) The door must be openable from the inside and the outside when the internal locking mechanism is in the locked position.

(3) There must be a means of opening which is simple and obvious and is arranged and marked inside and outside so that the door can be readily located, unlocked, and opened, even in darkness.

(4) The door must meet the marking requirements of § 23.811 of this part.

(5) The door must be reasonably free from jamming as a result of fuselage deformation in an emergency landing.

(6) Auxiliary locking devices that are actuated externally to the airplane may be used but such devices must be overridden by the normal internal opening means.

(d) In addition, each external passenger or crew door, for a commuter category airplane, must comply with the following requirements:

(1) Each door must be openable from both the inside and outside, even though persons may be crowded against the door on the inside of the airplane.

(2) If inward opening doors are used, there must be a means to prevent occupants from crowding against the door to the extent that would interfere with opening the door.

(3) Auxiliary locking devices may be used.

(e) Each external door on a commuter category airplane, each external door forward of any engine or propeller on a normal, utility, or acrobatic category airplane, and each door of the pressure vessel on a pressurized airplane must comply with the following requirements:

(1) There must be a means to lock and safeguard each external door, including cargo and service type doors, against inadvertent opening in flight, by persons, by cargo, or as a result of mechanical failure or failure of a single structural element, either during or after closure.

(2) There must be a provision for direct visual inspection of the locking mechanism to determine if the external door, for which the initial opening movement is not inward, is fully closed and locked. The provisions must be discernible, under operating lighting conditions, by a crewmember using a flashlight or an equivalent lighting source.

(3) There must be a visual warning means to signal a flight crewmember if the external door is not fully closed and locked. The means must be designed so that any failure, or combination of failures, that would result in an erroneous closed and locked indication is improbable for doors for which the initial opening movement is not inward.

(f) In addition, for commuter category airplanes, the following requirements apply:

(1) Each passenger entry door must qualify as a floor level emergency exit. This exit must have a rectangular opening of not less than 24 inches wide by 48 inches high, with corner radii not greater than one-third the width of the exit.

(2) If an integral stair is installed at a passenger entry door, the stair must be designed so that, when subjected to the inertia loads resulting from the ultimate static load factors in § 23.561(b)(2) and following the collapse of one or more legs of the landing gear, it will not reduce the effectiveness of emergency egress through the passenger entry door.

(g) If lavatory doors are installed, they must be designed to preclude an occupant from becoming trapped inside the lavatory. If a locking mechanism is installed, it must be capable of being unlocked from outside of the lavatory.

[Doc. No. 4080, 29 FR 17955, Dec. 18, 1964; 30 FR 258, Jan. 9, 1965, as amended by Amdt. 23–36, 53 FR 30813, Aug. 15, 1988; Amdt. 23–46, 59 FR 25772, May 17, 1994; Amdt. 23–49, 61 FR 5166, Feb. 9, 1996]

§ 23.785 Seats, berths, litters, safety belts, and shoulder harnesses.

There must be a seat or berth for each occupant that meets the following:

(a) Each seat/restraint system and the supporting structure must be designed to support occupants weighing at least 215 pounds when subjected to the maximum load factors corresponding to the specified flight and ground load conditions, as defined in the approved operating envelope of the airplane. In addition, these loads must be multiplied by a factor of 1.33 in determining the strength of all fittings and the attachment of—

(1) Each seat to the structure; and

(2) Each safety belt and shoulder harness to the seat or structure.

(b) Each forward-facing or aft-facing seat/restraint system in normal, utility, or acrobatic category airplanes must consist of a seat, a safety belt, and a shoulder harness, with a metal-to-metal latching device, that are designed to provide the occupant protection provisions required in § 23.562. Other seat orientations must provide the same level of occupant protection as a forward-facing or aft-facing seat with a safety belt and a shoulder harness, and must provide the protection provisions of § 23.562.

(c) For commuter category airplanes, each seat and the supporting structure must be designed for occupants weighing at least 170 pounds when subjected to the inertia loads resulting from the ultimate static load factors prescribed in § 23.561(b)(2) of this part. Each occupant must be protected from serious head injury when subjected to the inertia loads resulting from these load factors by a safety belt and shoulder harness, with a metal-to-metal latching device, for the front seats and a safety belt, or a safety belt and shoulder harness, with a metal-to-metal latching device, for each seat other than the front seats.

(d) Each restraint system must have a single-point release for occupant evacuation.

(e) The restraint system for each crewmember must allow the crewmember, when seated with the safety belt and shoulder harness fastened, to perform all functions necessary for flight operations.

(f) Each pilot seat must be designed for the reactions resulting from the application of pilot forces to the primary flight controls as prescribed in § 23.395 of this part.

(g) There must be a means to secure each safety belt and shoulder harness, when not in use, to prevent interference with the operation of the airplane and with rapid occupant egress in an emergency.

(h) Unless otherwise placarded, each seat in a utility or acrobatic category airplane must be designed to accommodate an occupant wearing a parachute.

(i) The cabin area surrounding each seat, including the structure, interior walls, instrument panel, control wheel, pedals, and seats within striking distance of the occupant's head or torso (with the restraint system fastened) must be free of potentially injurious objects, sharp edges, protuberances, and hard surfaces. If energy absorbing designs or devices are used to meet this requirement, they must protect the occupant from serious injury when the occupant is subjected to the inertia loads resulting from the ultimate static load factors prescribed in § 23.561(b)(2) of this part, or they must comply with the occupant protection provisions of § 23.562 of this part, as required in paragraphs (b) and (c) of this section.

(j) Each seat track must be fitted with stops to prevent the seat from sliding off the track.

(k) Each seat/restraint system may use design features, such as crushing or separation of certain components, to reduce occupant loads when showing compliance with the requirements of § 23.562 of this part; otherwise, the system must remain intact.

(l) For the purposes of this section, a front seat is a seat located at a flight crewmember station or any seat located alongside such a seat.

(m) Each berth, or provisions for a litter, installed parallel to the longitudinal axis of the airplane, must be designed so that the forward part has a padded end-board, canvas diaphragm, or equivalent means that can withstand the load reactions from a 215-pound occupant when subjected to the inertia loads resulting from the ultimate static load factors of § 23.561(b)(2) of this part. In addition—

(1) Each berth or litter must have an occupant restraint system and may not have corners or other parts likely to cause serious injury to a person occupying it during emergency landing conditions; and

(2) Occupant restraint system attachments for the berth or litter must withstand the inertia loads resulting from the ultimate static load factors of § 23.561(b)(2) of this part.

(n) Proof of compliance with the static strength requirements of this section for seats and berths approved as part of the type design and for seat and berth installations may be shown by—

(1) Structural analysis, if the structure conforms to conventional airplane types for which existing methods of analysis are known to be reliable;

(2) A combination of structural analysis and static load tests to limit load; or

(3) Static load tests to ultimate loads.

[Amdt. 23–36, 53 FR 30813, Aug. 15, 1988; Amdt. 23–36, 54 FR 50737, Dec. 11, 1989; Amdt. 23–49, 61 FR 5167, Feb. 9, 1996]

§ 23.787　Baggage and cargo compartments.

(a) Each baggage and cargo compartment must:

(1) Be designed for its placarded maximum weight of contents and for the critical load distributions at the appropriate maximum load factors corresponding to the flight and ground load conditions of this part.

(2) Have means to prevent the contents of any compartment from becoming a hazard by shifting, and to protect any controls, wiring, lines, equipment or accessories whose damage or failure would affect safe operations.

(3) Have a means to protect occupants from injury by the contents of any compartment, located aft of the occupants and separated by structure, when the ultimate forward inertial load factor is 9g and assuming the maximum allowed baggage or cargo weight for the compartment.

(b) Designs that provide for baggage or cargo to be carried in the same compartment as passengers must have a means to protect the occupants from injury when the baggage or cargo is subjected to the inertial loads resulting from the ultimate static load factors of § 23.561(b)(3), assuming the maximum allowed baggage or cargo weight for the compartment.

(c) For airplanes that are used only for the carriage of cargo, the flightcrew emergency exits must meet the requirements of § 23.807 under any cargo loading conditions.

[Doc. No. 27806, 61 FR 5167, Feb. 9, 1996]

§ 23.791　Passenger information signs.

For those airplanes in which the flightcrew members cannot observe the other occupants' seats or where the flightcrew members' compartment is separated from the passenger compartment, there must be at least one illuminated sign (using either letters or symbols) notifying all passengers when seat belts should be fastened. Signs that notify when seat belts should be fastened must:

(a) When illuminated, be legible to each person seated in the passenger compartment under all probable lighting conditions; and

(b) Be installed so that a flightcrew member can, when seated at the flightcrew member's station, turn the illumination on and off.

[Doc. No. 27806, 61 FR 5167, Feb. 9, 1996]

§ 23.803　Emergency evacuation.

(a) For commuter category airplanes, an evacuation demonstration must be conducted utilizing the maximum number of occupants for which certification is desired. The demonstration must be conducted under simulated night conditions using only the emergency exits on the most critical side of the airplane. The participants must be representative of average airline passengers with no prior practice or rehearsal for the demonstration. Evacuation must be completed within 90 seconds.

(b) In addition, when certification to the emergency exit provisions of § 23.807(d)(4) is requested, only the emergency lighting system required by § 23.812 may be used to provide cabin interior illumination during the evacuation demonstration required in paragraph (a) of this section.

[Amdt. 23–34, 52 FR 1831, Jan. 15, 1987, as amended by Amdt. 23–46, 59 FR 25773, May 17, 1994]

§ 23.805　Flightcrew emergency exits.

For airplanes where the proximity of the passenger emergency exits to the flightcrew area does not offer a convenient and readily accessible means of evacuation for the flightcrew, the following apply:

(a) There must be either one emergency exit on each side of the airplane, or a top hatch emergency exit, in the flightcrew area;

(b) Each emergency exit must be located to allow rapid evacuation of the crew and have a size and shape of at least a 19- by 20-inch unobstructed rectangular opening; and

(c) For each emergency exit that is not less than six feet from the ground, an assisting means must be provided. The assisting means may be a rope or any other means demonstrated to be suitable for the purpose. If the assisting means is a rope, or an approved device equivalent to a rope, it must be—

(1) Attached to the fuselage structure at or above the top of the emergency exit opening or, for a device at a pilot's emergency exit window, at another approved location if the stowed device, or its attachment, would reduce the pilot's view; and

(2) Able (with its attachment) to withstand a 400-pound static load.

[Doc. No. 26324, 59 FR 25773, May 17, 1994]

§ 23.807   Emergency exits.

(a) *Number and location.* Emergency exits must be located to allow escape without crowding in any probable crash attitude. The airplane must have at least the following emergency exits:

(1) For all airplanes with a seating capacity of two or more, excluding airplanes with canopies, at least one emergency exit on the opposite side of the cabin from the main door specified in § 23.783 of this part.

(2) [Reserved]

(3) If the pilot compartment is separated from the cabin by a door that is likely to block the pilot's escape in a minor crash, there must be an exit in the pilot's compartment. The number of exits required by paragraph (a)(1) of this section must then be separately determined for the passenger compartment, using the seating capacity of that compartment.

(4) Emergency exits must not be located with respect to any propeller disk or any other potential hazard so as to endanger persons using that exit.

(b) *Type and operation.* Emergency exits must be movable windows, panels, canopies, or external doors, openable from both inside and outside the airplane, that provide a clear and unobstructed opening large enough to admit a 19-by-26-inch ellipse. Auxiliary locking devices used to secure the airplane

must be designed to be overridden by the normal internal opening means. The inside handles of emergency exits that open outward must be adequately protected against inadvertent operation. In addition, each emergency exit must—

(1) Be readily accessible, requiring no exceptional agility to be used in emergencies;

(2) Have a method of opening that is simple and obvious;

(3) Be arranged and marked for easy location and operation, even in darkness;

(4) Have reasonable provisions against jamming by fuselage deformation; and

(5) In the case of acrobatic category airplanes, allow each occupant to abandon the airplane at any speed between V_{SO} and V_D; and

(6) In the case of utility category airplanes certificated for spinning, allow each occupant to abandon the airplane at the highest speed likely to be achieved in the maneuver for which the airplane is certificated.

(c) *Tests.* The proper functioning of each emergency exit must be shown by tests.

(d) *Doors and exits.* In addition, for commuter category airplanes, the following requirements apply:

(1) In addition to the passenger entry door—

(i) For an airplane with a total passenger seating capacity of 15 or fewer, an emergency exit, as defined in paragraph (b) of this section, is required on each side of the cabin; and

(ii) For an airplane with a total passenger seating capacity of 16 through 19, three emergency exits, as defined in paragraph (b) of this section, are required with one on the same side as the passenger entry door and two on the side opposite the door.

(2) A means must be provided to lock each emergency exit and to safeguard against its opening in flight, either inadvertently by persons or as a result of mechanical failure. In addition, a means for direct visual inspection of the locking mechanism must be provided to determine that each emergency exit for which the initial opening movement is outward is fully locked.

(3) Each required emergency exit, except floor level exits, must be located over the wing or, if not less than six feet from the ground, must be provided with an acceptable means to assist the occupants to descend to the ground. Emergency exits must be distributed as uniformly as practical, taking into account passenger seating configuration.

(4) Unless the applicant has complied with paragraph (d)(1) of this section, there must be an emergency exit on the side of the cabin opposite the passenger entry door, provided that—

(i) For an airplane having a passenger seating configuration of nine or fewer, the emergency exit has a rectangular opening measuring not less than 19 inches by 26 inches high with corner radii not greater than one-third the width of the exit, located over the wing, with a step up inside the airplane of not more than 29 inches and a step down outside the airplane of not more than 36 inches;

(ii) For an airplane having a passenger seating configuration of 10 to 19 passengers, the emergency exit has a rectangular opening measuring not less than 20 inches wide by 36 inches high, with corner radii not greater than one-third the width of the exit, and with a step up inside the airplane of not more than 20 inches. If the exit is located over the wing, the step down outside the airplane may not exceed 27 inches; and

(iii) The airplane complies with the additional requirements of §§ 23.561(b)(2)(iv), 23.803(b), 23.811(c), 23.812, 23.813(b), and 23.815.

(e) For multiengine airplanes, ditching emergency exits must be provided in accordance with the following requirements, unless the emergency exits required by paragraph (a) or (d) of this section already comply with them:

(1) One exit above the waterline on each side of the airplane having the dimensions specified in paragraph (b) or (d) of this section, as applicable; and

(2) If side exits cannot be above the waterline, there must be a readily accessible overhead hatch emergency exit that has a rectangular opening measuring not less than 20 inches wide by 36 inches long, with corner radii not greater than one-third the width of the exit.

[Doc. No. 4080, 29 FR 17955, Dec. 18, 1964, as amended by Amdt. 23–7, 34 FR 13092, Aug. 13, 1969; Amdt. 23–10, 36 FR 2864, Feb. 11, 1971; Amdt. 23–34, 52 FR 1831, Jan. 15, 1987; Amdt. 23–36, 53 FR 30814, Aug. 15, 1988; 53 FR 34194, Sept. 2, 1988; Amdt. 23–46, 59 FR 25773, May 17, 1994; Amdt. 23–49, 61 FR 5167, Feb. 9, 1996]

§ 23.811 Emergency exit marking.

(a) Each emergency exit and external door in the passenger compartment must be externally marked and readily identifiable from outside the airplane by—

(1) A conspicuous visual identification scheme; and

(2) A permanent decal or placard on or adjacent to the emergency exit which shows the means of opening the emergency exit, including any special instructions, if applicable.

(b) In addition, for commuter category airplanes, these exits and doors must be internally marked with the word "exit" by a sign which has white letters 1 inch high on a red background 2 inches high, be self-illuminated or independently, internally electrically illuminated, and have a minimum brightness of at least 160 micro-lamberts. The color may be reversed if the passenger compartment illumination is essentially the same.

(c) In addition, when certification to the emergency exit provisions of § 23.807(d)(4) is requested, the following apply:

(1) Each emergency exit, its means of access, and its means of opening, must be conspicuously marked;

(2) The identity and location of each emergency exit must be recognizable from a distance equal to the width of the cabin;

(3) Means must be provided to assist occupants in locating the emergency exits in conditions of dense smoke;

(4) The location of the operating handle and instructions for opening each emergency exit from inside the airplane must be shown by marking that is readable from a distance of 30 inches;

(5) Each passenger entry door operating handle must—

(i) Be self-illuminated with an initial brightness of at least 160 micro-lamberts; or

(ii) Be conspicuously located and well illuminated by the emergency lighting even in conditions of occupant crowding at the door;

(6) Each passenger entry door with a locking mechanism that is released by rotary motion of the handle must be marked—

(i) With a red arrow, with a shaft of at least three-fourths of an inch wide and a head twice the width of the shaft, extending along at least 70 degrees of arc at a radius approximately equal to three-fourths of the handle length;

(ii) So that the center line of the exit handle is within ± one inch of the projected point of the arrow when the handle has reached full travel and has released the locking mechanism;

(iii) With the word "open" in red letters, one inch high, placed horizontally near the head of the arrow; and

(7) In addition to the requirements of paragraph (a) of this section, the external marking of each emergency exit must—

(i) Include a 2-inch colorband outlining the exit; and

(ii) Have a color contrast that is readily distinguishable from the surrounding fuselage surface. The contrast must be such that if the reflectance of the darker color is 15 percent or less, the reflectance of the lighter color must be at least 45 percent. "Reflectance" is the ratio of the luminous flux reflected by a body to the luminous flux it receives. When the reflectance of the darker color is greater than 15 percent, at least a 30 percent difference between its reflectance and the reflectance of the lighter color must be provided.

[Amdt. 23–36, 53 FR 30814, Aug. 15, 1988; 53 FR 34194, Sept. 2, 1988, as amended by Amdt. 23–46, 59 FR 25773, May 17, 1994]

§ 23.812 Emergency lighting.

When certification to the emergency exit provisions of § 23.807(d)(4) is requested, the following apply:

(a) An emergency lighting system, independent of the main cabin lighting system, must be installed. However, the source of general cabin illumination may be common to both the emergency and main lighting systems if the power supply to the emergency lighting system is independent of the power supply to the main lighting system.

(b) There must be a crew warning light that illuminates in the cockpit when power is on in the airplane and the emergency lighting control device is not armed.

(c) The emergency lights must be operable manually from the flightcrew station and be provided with automatic activation. The cockpit control device must have "on," "off," and "armed" positions so that, when armed in the cockpit, the lights will operate by automatic activation.

(d) There must be a means to safeguard against inadvertent operation of the cockpit control device from the "armed" or "on" positions.

(e) The cockpit control device must have provisions to allow the emergency lighting system to be armed or activated at any time that it may be needed.

(f) When armed, the emergency lighting system must activate and remain lighted when—

(1) The normal electrical power of the airplane is lost; or

(2) The airplane is subjected to an impact that results in a deceleration in excess of 2g and a velocity change in excess of 3.5 feet-per-second, acting along the longitudinal axis of the airplane; or

(3) Any other emergency condition exists where automatic activation of the emergency lighting is necessary to aid with occupant evacuation.

(g) The emergency lighting system must be capable of being turned off and reset by the flightcrew after automatic activation.

(h) The emergency lighting system must provide internal lighting, including—

(1) Illuminated emergency exit marking and locating signs, including those required in § 23.811(b);

(2) Sources of general illumination in the cabin that provide an average illumination of not less than 0.05 foot-candle and an illumination at any point of not less than 0.01 foot-candle when measured along the center line of the main passenger aisle(s) and at the seat armrest height; and

(3) Floor proximity emergency escape path marking that provides emergency

247

evacuation guidance for the airplane occupants when all sources of illumination more than 4 feet above the cabin aisle floor are totally obscured.

(i) The energy supply to each emergency lighting unit must provide the required level of illumination for at least 10 minutes at the critical ambient conditions after activation of the emergency lighting system.

(j) If rechargeable batteries are used as the energy supply for the emergency lighting system, they may be recharged from the main electrical power system of the airplane provided the charging circuit is designed to preclude inadvertent battery discharge into the charging circuit faults. If the emergency lighting system does not include a charging circuit, battery condition monitors are required.

(k) Components of the emergency lighting system, including batteries, wiring, relays, lamps, and switches, must be capable of normal operation after being subjected to the inertia forces resulting from the ultimate load factors prescribed in §23.561(b)(2).

(l) The emergency lighting system must be designed so that after any single transverse vertical separation of the fuselage during a crash landing:

(1) At least 75 percent of all electrically illuminated emergency lights required by this section remain operative; and

(2) Each electrically illuminated exit sign required by §23.811 (b) and (c) remains operative, except those that are directly damaged by the fuselage separation.

[Doc. No. 26324, 59 FR 25774, May 17, 1994]

§23.813   Emergency exit access.

(a) For commuter category airplanes, access to window-type emergency exits may not be obstructed by seats or seat backs.

(b) In addition, when certification to the emergency exit provisions of §23.807(d)(4) is requested, the following emergency exit access must be provided:

(1) The passageway leading from the aisle to the passenger entry door must be unobstructed and at least 20 inches wide.

(2) There must be enough space next to the passenger entry door to allow assistance in evacuation of passengers without reducing the unobstructed width of the passageway below 20 inches.

(3) If it is necessary to pass through a passageway between passenger compartments to reach a required emergency exit from any seat in the passenger cabin, the passageway must be unobstructed; however, curtains may be used if they allow free entry through the passageway.

(4) No door may be installed in any partition between passenger compartments unless that door has a means to latch it in the open position. The latching means must be able to withstand the loads imposed upon it by the door when the door is subjected to the inertia loads resulting from the ultimate static load factors prescribed in §23.561(b)(2).

(5) If it is necessary to pass through a doorway separating the passenger cabin from other areas to reach a required emergency exit from any passenger seat, the door must have a means to latch it in the open position. The latching means must be able to withstand the loads imposed upon it by the door when the door is subjected to the inertia loads resulting from the ultimate static load factors prescribed in §23.561(b)(2).

[Amdt. 23–36, 53 FR 30815, Aug. 15, 1988, as amended by Amdt. 23–46, 59 FR 25774, May 17, 1994]

§23.815   Width of aisle.

(a) Except as provided in paragraph (b) of this section, for commuter category airplanes, the width of the main passenger aisle at any point between seats must equal or exceed the values in the following table:

Number of passenger seats	Minimum main passenger aisle width	
	Less than 25 inches from floor	25 inches and more from floor
10 through 19	9 inches	15 inches.

(b) When certification to the emergency exist provisions of §23.807(d)(4) is requested, the main passenger aisle width at any point between the seats must equal or exceed the following values:

Number of passenger seats	Minimum main passenger aisle width (inches)	
	Less than 25 inches from floor	25 inches and more from floor
10 or fewer	¹12	15
11 through 19	12	20

¹ A narrower width not less than 9 inches may be approved when substantiated by tests found necessary by the Administrator.

[Amdt. 23–34, 52 FR 1831, Jan. 15, 1987, as amended by Amdt. 23–46, 59 FR 25774, May 17, 1994]

§23.831 Ventilation.

(a) Each passenger and crew compartment must be suitably ventilated. Carbon monoxide concentration may not exceed one part in 20,000 parts of air.

(b) For pressurized airplanes, the ventilating air in the flightcrew and passenger compartments must be free of harmful or hazardous concentrations of gases and vapors in normal operations and in the event of reasonably probable failures or malfunctioning of the ventilating, heating, pressurization, or other systems and equipment. If accumulation of hazardous quantities of smoke in the cockpit area is reasonably probable, smoke evacuation must be readily accomplished starting with full pressurization and without depressurizing beyond safe limits.

[Doc. No. 4080, 29 FR 17955, Dec. 18, 1964; 30 FR 258, Jan. 9, 1965, as amended by Amdt. 23–34, 52 FR 1831, Jan. 15, 1987; Amdt. 23–42, 56 FR 354, Jan. 3, 1991]

PRESSURIZATION

§23.841 Pressurized cabins.

(a) If certification for operation over 25,000 feet is requested, the airplane must be able to maintain a cabin pressure altitude of not more than 15,000 feet in event of any probable failure or malfunction in the pressurization system.

(b) Pressurized cabins must have at least the following valves, controls, and indicators, for controlling cabin pressure:

(1) Two pressure relief valves to automatically limit the positive pressure differential to a predetermined value at the maximum rate of flow delivered by the pressure source. The combined capacity of the relief valves must be large enough so that the failure of any one valve would not cause an appreciable rise in the pressure differential. The pressure differential is positive when the internal pressure is greater than the external.

(2) Two reverse pressure differential relief valves (or their equivalent) to automatically prevent a negative pressure differential that would damage the structure. However, one valve is enough if it is of a design that reasonably precludes its malfunctioning.

(3) A means by which the pressure differential can be rapidly equalized.

(4) An automatic or manual regulator for controlling the intake or exhaust airflow, or both, for maintaining the required internal pressures and airflow rates.

(5) Instruments to indicate to the pilot the pressure differential, the cabin pressure altitude, and the rate of change of cabin pressure altitude.

(6) Warning indication at the pilot station to indicate when the safe or preset pressure differential is exceeded and when a cabin pressure altitude of 10,000 feet is exceeded.

(7) A warning placard for the pilot if the structure is not designed for pressure differentials up to the maximum relief valve setting in combination with landing loads.

(8) A means to stop rotation of the compressor or to divert airflow from the cabin if continued rotation of an engine-driven cabin compressor or continued flow of any compressor bleed air will create a hazard if a malfunction occurs.

[Amdt. 23–14, 38 FR 31822, Nov. 19, 1973, as amended by Amdt. 23–17, 41 FR 55464, Dec. 20, 1976; Amdt. 23–49, 61 FR 5167, Feb. 9, 1996]

§23.843 Pressurization tests.

(a) *Strength test.* The complete pressurized cabin, including doors, windows, canopy, and valves, must be tested as a pressure vessel for the pressure differential specified in §23.365(d).

(b) *Functional tests.* The following functional tests must be performed:

(1) Tests of the functioning and capacity of the positive and negative pressure differential valves, and of the emergency release valve, to simulate the effects of closed regulator valves.

(2) Tests of the pressurization system to show proper functioning under each possible condition of pressure, temperature, and moisture, up to the maximum altitude for which certification is requested.

(3) Flight tests, to show the performance of the pressure supply, pressure and flow regulators, indicators, and warning signals, in steady and stepped climbs and descents at rates corresponding to the maximum attainable within the operating limitations of the airplane, up to the maximum altitude for which certification is requested.

(4) Tests of each door and emergency exit, to show that they operate properly after being subjected to the flight tests prescribed in paragraph (b)(3) of this section.

FIRE PROTECTION

§ 23.851 Fire extinguishers.

(a) There must be at least one hand fire extinguisher for use in the pilot compartment that is located within easy access of the pilot while seated.

(b) There must be at least one hand fire extinguisher located conveniently in the passenger compartment—

(1) Of each airplane accommodating more than 6 passengers; and

(2) Of each commuter category airplane.

(c) For hand fire extinguishers, the following apply:

(1) The type and quantity of each extinguishing agent used must be appropriate to the kinds of fire likely to occur where that agent is to be used.

(2) Each extinguisher for use in a personnel compartment must be designed to minimize the hazard of toxic gas concentrations.

[Doc. No. 26269, 58 FR 42165, Aug. 6, 1993]

§ 23.853 Passenger and crew compartment interiors.

For each compartment to be used by the crew or passengers:

(a) The materials must be at least flame-resistant;

(b) [Reserved]

(c) If smoking is to be prohibited, there must be a placard so stating, and if smoking is to be allowed—

(1) There must be an adequate number of self-contained, removable ashtrays; and

(2) Where the crew compartment is separated from the passenger compartment, there must be at least one illuminated sign (using either letters or symbols) notifying all passengers when smoking is prohibited. Signs which notify when smoking is prohibited must—

(i) When illuminated, be legible to each passenger seated in the passenger cabin under all probable lighting conditions; and

(ii) Be so constructed that the crew can turn the illumination on and off; and

(d) In addition, for commuter category airplanes the following requirements apply:

(1) Each disposal receptacle for towels, paper, or waste must be fully enclosed and constructed of at least fire resistant materials and must contain fires likely to occur in it under normal use. The ability of the disposal receptacle to contain those fires under all probable conditions of wear, misalignment, and ventilation expected in service must be demonstrated by test. A placard containing the legible words "No Cigarette Disposal" must be located on or near each disposal receptacle door.

(2) Lavatories must have "No Smoking" or "No Smoking in Lavatory" placards located conspicuously on each side of the entry door and self-contained, removable ashtrays located conspicuously on or near the entry side of each lavatory door, except that one ashtray may serve more than one lavatory door if it can be seen from the cabin side of each lavatory door served. The placards must have red letters at least ½ inch high on a white background at least 1 inch high (a "No Smoking" symbol may be included on the placard).

(3) Materials (including finishes or decorative surfaces applied to the materials) used in each compartment occupied by the crew or passengers must meet the following test criteria as applicable:

(i) Interior ceiling panels, interior wall panels, partitions, galley structure, large cabinet walls, structural flooring, and materials used in the construction of stowage compartments (other than underseat stowage compartments and compartments for stowing small items such as magazines and maps) must be self-extinguishing when tested vertically in accordance with the applicable portions of appendix F of this part or by other equivalent methods. The average burn length may not exceed 6 inches and the average flame time after removal of the flame source may not exceed 15 seconds. Drippings from the test specimen may not continue to flame for more than an average of 3 seconds after falling.

(ii) Floor covering, textiles (including draperies and upholstery), seat cushions, padding, decorative and nondecorative coated fabrics, leather, trays and galley furnishings, electrical conduit, thermal and acoustical insulation and insulation covering, air ducting, joint and edge covering, cargo compartment liners, insulation blankets, cargo covers and transparencies, molded and thermoformed parts, air ducting joints, and trim strips (decorative and chafing), that are constructed of materials not covered in paragraph (d)(3)(iv) of this section must be self extinguishing when tested vertically in accordance with the applicable portions of appendix F of this part or other approved equivalent methods. The average burn length may not exceed 8 inches and the average flame time after removal of the flame source may not exceed 15 seconds. Drippings from the test specimen may not continue to flame for more than an average of 5 seconds after falling.

(iii) Motion picture film must be safety film meeting the Standard Specifications for Safety Photographic Film PH1.25 (available from the American National Standards Institute, 1430 Broadway, New York, N.Y. 10018) or an FAA approved equivalent. If the film travels through ducts, the ducts must meet the requirements of paragraph (d)(3)(ii) of this section.

(iv) Acrylic windows and signs, parts constructed in whole or in part of elastomeric materials, edge-lighted instrument assemblies consisting of two or more instruments in a common housing, seatbelts, shoulder harnesses, and cargo and baggage tiedown equipment, including containers, bins, pallets, etc., used in passenger or crew compartments, may not have an average burn rate greater than 2.5 inches per minute when tested horizontally in accordance with the applicable portions of appendix F of this part or by other approved equivalent methods.

(v) Except for electrical wire cable insulation, and for small parts (such as knobs, handles, rollers, fasteners, clips, grommets, rub strips, pulleys, and small electrical parts) that the Administrator finds would not contribute significantly to the propagation of a fire, materials in items not specified in paragraphs (d)(3)(i), (ii), (iii), or (iv) of this section may not have a burn rate greater than 4.0 inches per minute when tested horizontally in accordance with the applicable portions of appendix F of this part or by other approved equivalent methods.

(e) Lines, tanks, or equipment containing fuel, oil, or other flammable fluids may not be installed in such compartments unless adequately shielded, isolated, or otherwise protected so that any breakage or failure of such an item would not create a hazard.

(f) Airplane materials located on the cabin side of the firewall must be self-extinguishing or be located at such a distance from the firewall, or otherwise protected, so that ignition will not occur if the firewall is subjected to a flame temperature of not less than 2,000 degrees F for 15 minutes. For self-extinguishing materials (except electrical wire and cable insulation and small parts that the Administrator finds would not contribute significantly to the propagation of a fire), a vertifical self-extinguishing test must be conducted in accordance with appendix F of this part or an equivalent method approved by the Administrator. The average burn length of the material may not exceed 6 inches and the average flame time after removal of the flame source may not exceed 15 seconds. Drippings from the material test specimen may not continue to flame for more than an average of 3 seconds after falling.

[Amdt. 23–14, 23 FR 31822, Nov. 19, 1973, as amended by Amdt. 23–23, 43 FR 50593, Oct. 30, 1978; Amdt. 23–25, 45 FR 7755, Feb. 4, 1980; Amdt. 23–34, 52 FR 1831, Jan. 15, 1987]

§ 23.855 Cargo and baggage compartment fire protection.

(a) Sources of heat within each cargo and baggage compartment that are capable of igniting the compartment contents must be shielded and insulated to prevent such ignition.

(b) Each cargo and baggage compartment must be constructed of materials that meet the appropriate provisions of § 23.853(d)(3).

(c) In addition, for commuter category airplanes, each cargo and baggage compartment must:

(1) Be located where the presence of a fire would be easily discovered by the pilots when seated at their duty station, or it must be equipped with a smoke or fire detector system to give a warning at the pilots' station, and provide sufficient access to enable a pilot to effectively reach any part of the compartment with the contents of a hand held fire extinguisher, or

(2) Be equipped with a smoke or fire detector system to give a warning at the pilots' station and have ceiling and sidewall liners and floor panels constructed of materials that have been subjected to and meet the 45 degree angle test of appendix F of this part. The flame may not penetrate (pass through) the material during application of the flame or subsequent to its removal. The average flame time after removal of the flame source may not exceed 15 seconds, and the average glow time may not exceed 10 seconds. The compartment must be constructed to provide fire protection that is not less than that required of its individual panels; or

(3) Be constructed and sealed to contain any fire within the compartment.

[Doc. No. 27806, 61 FR 5167, Feb. 9, 1996]

§ 23.859 Combustion heater fire protection.

(a) *Combustion heater fire regions.* The following combustion heater fire regions must be protected from fire in accordance with the applicable provisions of §§ 23.1182 through 23.1191 and 23.1203:

(1) The region surrounding the heater, if this region contains any flammable fluid system components (excluding the heater fuel system) that could—

(i) Be damaged by heater malfunctioning; or

(ii) Allow flammable fluids or vapors to reach the heater in case of leakage.

(2) The region surrounding the heater, if the heater fuel system has fittings that, if they leaked, would allow fuel vapor to enter this region.

(3) The part of the ventilating air passage that surrounds the combustion chamber.

(b) *Ventilating air ducts.* Each ventilating air duct passing through any fire region must be fireproof. In addition—

(1) Unless isolation is provided by fireproof valves or by equally effective means, the ventilating air duct downstream of each heater must be fireproof for a distance great enough to ensure that any fire originating in the heater can be contained in the duct; and

(2) Each part of any ventilating duct passing through any region having a flammable fluid system must be constructed or isolated from that system so that the malfunctioning of any component of that system cannot introduce flammable fluids or vapors into the ventilating airstream.

(c) *Combustion air ducts.* Each combustion air duct must be fireproof for a distance great enough to prevent damage from backfiring or reverse flame propagation. In addition—

(1) No combustion air duct may have a common opening with the ventilating airstream unless flames from backfires or reverse burning cannot enter the ventilating airstream under any operating condition, including reverse flow or malfunctioning of the heater or its associated components; and

(2) No combustion air duct may restrict the prompt relief of any backfire that, if so restricted, could cause heater failure.

(d) *Heater controls: general.* Provision must be made to prevent the hazardous accumulation of water or ice on or in any heater control component, control system tubing, or safety control.

(e) *Heater safety controls.* (1) Each combustion heater must have the following safety controls:

(i) Means independent of the components for the normal continuous control of air temperature, airflow, and fuel flow must be provided to automatically shut off the ignition and fuel supply to that heater at a point remote from that heater when any of the following occurs:

(A) The heater exchanger temperature exceeds safe limits.

(B) The ventilating air temperature exceeds safe limits.

(C) The combustion airflow becomes inadequate for safe operation.

(D) The ventilating airflow becomes inadequate for safe operation.

(ii) Means to warn the crew when any heater whose heat output is essential for safe operation has been shut off by the automatic means prescribed in paragraph (e)(1)(i) of this section.

(2) The means for complying with paragraph (e)(1)(i) of this section for any individual heater must—

(i) Be independent of components serving any other heater whose heat output is essential for safe operations; and

(ii) Keep the heater off until restarted by the crew.

(f) *Air intakes.* Each combustion and ventilating air intake must be located so that no flammable fluids or vapors can enter the heater system under any operating condition—

(1) During normal operation; or

(2) As a result of the malfunctioning of any other component.

(g) *Heater exhaust.* Heater exhaust systems must meet the provisions of §§ 23.1121 and 23.1123. In addition, there must be provisions in the design of the heater exhaust system to safely expel the products of combustion to prevent the occurrence of—

(1) Fuel leakage from the exhaust to surrounding compartments;

(2) Exhaust gas impingement on surrounding equipment or structure;

(3) Ignition of flammable fluids by the exhaust, if the exhaust is in a compartment containing flammable fluid lines; and

(4) Restrictions in the exhaust system to relieve backfires that, if so restricted, could cause heater failure.

(h) *Heater fuel systems.* Each heater fuel system must meet each powerplant fuel system requirement affecting safe heater operation. Each heater fuel system component within the ventilating airstream must be protected by shrouds so that no leakage from those components can enter the ventilating airstream.

(i) *Drains.* There must be means to safely drain fuel that might accumulate within the combustion chamber or the heater exchanger. In addition—

(1) Each part of any drain that operates at high temperatures must be protected in the same manner as heater exhausts; and

(2) Each drain must be protected from hazardous ice accumulation under any operating condition.

[Amdt. 23–27, 45 FR 70387, Oct. 23, 1980]

§ 23.863 Flammable fluid fire protection.

(a) In each area where flammable fluids or vapors might escape by leakage of a fluid system, there must be means to minimize the probability of ignition of the fluids and vapors, and the resultant hazard if ignition does occur.

(b) Compliance with paragraph (a) of this section must be shown by analysis or tests, and the following factors must be considered:

(1) Possible sources and paths of fluid leakage, and means of detecting leakage.

(2) Flammability characteristics of fluids, including effects of any combustible or absorbing materials.

(3) Possible ignition sources, including electrical faults, overheating of equipment, and malfunctioning of protective devices.

(4) Means available for controlling or extinguishing a fire, such as stopping flow of fluids, shutting down equipment, fireproof containment, or use of extinguishing agents.

(5) Ability of airplane components that are critical to safety of flight to withstand fire and heat.

(c) If action by the flight crew is required to prevent or counteract a fluid fire (e.g. equipment shutdown or actuation of a fire extinguisher), quick acting means must be provided to alert the crew.

(d) Each area where flammable fluids or vapors might escape by leakage of a fluid system must be identified and defined.

[Amdt. 23–23, 43 FR 50593, Oct. 30, 1978]

§ 23.865 Fire protection of flight controls, engine mounts, and other flight structure.

Flight controls, engine mounts, and other flight structure located in designated fire zones, or in adjacent areas that would be subjected to the effects of fire in the designated fire zones, must be constructed of fireproof material or be shielded so that they are capable of withstanding the effects of a fire. Engine vibration isolators must incorporate suitable features to ensure that the engine is retained if the nonfireproof portions of the isolators deteriorate from the effects of a fire.

[Doc. No. 27805, 61 FR 5148, Feb. 9, 1996]

ELECTRICAL BONDING AND LIGHTNING PROTECTION

§ 23.867 Electrical bonding and protection against lightning and static electricity.

(a) The airplane must be protected against catastrophic effects from lightning.

(b) For metallic components, compliance with paragraph (a) of this section may be shown by—

(1) Bonding the components properly to the airframe; or

(2) Designing the components so that a strike will not endanger the airplane.

(c) For nonmetallic components, compliance with paragraph (a) of this section may be shown by—

(1) Designing the components to minimize the effect of a strike; or

(2) Incorporating acceptable means of diverting the resulting electrical current so as not to endanger the airplane.

[Amdt. 23–7, 34 FR 13092, Aug. 13, 1969]

MISCELLANEOUS

§ 23.871 Leveling means.

There must be means for determining when the airplane is in a level position on the ground.

[Amdt. 23–7, 34 FR 13092, Aug. 13, 1969]

Subpart E—Powerplant

GENERAL

§ 23.901 Installation.

(a) For the purpose of this part, the airplane powerplant installation includes each component that—

(1) Is necessary for propulsion; and

(2) Affects the safety of the major propulsive units.

(b) Each powerplant installation must be constructed and arranged to—

(1) Ensure safe operation to the maximum altitude for which approval is requested.

(2) Be accessible for necessary inspections and maintenance.

(c) Engine cowls and nacelles must be easily removable or openable by the pilot to provide adequate access to and exposure of the engine compartment for preflight checks.

(d) Each turbine engine installation must be constructed and arranged to—

(1) Result in carcass vibration characteristics that do not exceed those established during the type certification of the engine.

(2) Ensure that the capability of the installed engine to withstand the ingestion of rain, hail, ice, and birds into the engine inlet is not less than the capability established for the engine itself under § 23.903(a)(2).

(e) The installation must comply with—

(1) The instructions provided under the engine type certificate and the propeller type certificate.

(2) The applicable provisions of this subpart.

(f) Each auxiliary power unit installation must meet the applicable portions of this part.

[Doc. No. 4080, 29 FR 17955, Dec. 18, 1964, as amended by Amdt. 23–7, 34 FR 13092, Aug. 13, 1969; Amdt. 23–18, 42 FR 15041, Mar. 17, 1977; Amdt. 23–29, 49 FR 6846, Feb. 23, 1984; Amdt. 23–34, 52 FR 1832, Jan. 15, 1987; Amdt. 23–34, 52 FR 34745, Sept. 14, 1987; Amdt. 23–43, 58 FR 18970, Apr. 9, 1993; Amdt. 23–51, 61 FR 5136, Feb. 9, 1996; Amdt. 23–53, 63 FR 14797, Mar. 26, 1998]

§ 23.903 Engines.

(a) *Engine type certificate.* (1) Each engine must have a type certificate and must meet the applicable requirements of part 34 of this chapter.

(2) Each turbine engine and its installation must comply with one of the following:

(i) Sections 33.76, 33.77 and 33.78 of this chapter in effect on December 13, 2000.

(ii) Sections 33.77 and 33.78 of this chapter in effect on April 30, 1998, or as subsequently amended before December 13, 2000; or

(iii) Section 33.77 of this chapter in effect on October 31, 1974, or as subsequently amended before April 30, 1998, unless that engine's foreign object ingestion service history has resulted in an unsafe condition; or

(iv) Be shown to have a foreign object ingestion service history in similar installation locations which has not resulted in any unsafe condition.

NOTE: §33.77 of this chapter in effect on October 31, 1974, was published in 14 CFR parts 1 to 59, Revised as of January 1, 1975. See 39 FR 35467, October 1, 1974.

(b) *Turbine engine installations.* For turbine engine installations—

(1) Design precautions must be taken to minimize the hazards to the airplane in the event of an engine rotor failure or of a fire originating inside the engine which burns through the engine case.

(2) The powerplant systems associated with engine control devices, systems, and instrumentation must be designed to give reasonable assurance that those operating limitations that adversely affect turbine rotor structural integrity will not be exceeded in service.

(c) *Engine isolation.* The powerplants must be arranged and isolated from each other to allow operation, in at least one configuration, so that the failure or malfunction of any engine, or the failure or malfunction (including destruction by fire in the engine compartment) of any system that can affect an engine (other than a fuel tank if only one fuel tank is installed), will not:

(1) Prevent the continued safe operation of the remaining engines; or

(2) Require immediate action by any crewmember for continued safe operation of the remaining engines.

(d) *Starting and stopping (piston engine).* (1) The design of the installation must be such that risk of fire or mechanical damage to the engine or airplane, as a result of starting the engine in any conditions in which starting is to be permitted, is reduced to a minimum. Any techniques and associated limitations for engine starting must be established and included in the Airplane Flight Manual, approved manual material, or applicable operating placards. Means must be provided for—

(i) Restarting any engine of a multiengine airplane in flight, and

(ii) Stopping any engine in flight, after engine failure, if continued engine rotation would cause a hazard to the airplane.

(2) In addition, for commuter category airplanes, the following apply:

(i) Each component of the stopping system on the engine side of the firewall that might be exposed to fire must be at least fire resistant.

(ii) If hydraulic propeller feathering systems are used for this purpose, the feathering lines must be at least fire resistant under the operating conditions that may be expected to exist during feathering.

(e) *Starting and stopping (turbine engine).* Turbine engine installations must comply with the following:

(1) The design of the installation must be such that risk of fire or mechanical damage to the engine or the airplane, as a result of starting the engine in any conditions in which starting is to be permitted, is reduced to a minimum. Any techniques and associated limitations must be established and included in the Airplane Flight Manual, approved manual material, or applicable operating placards.

(2) There must be means for stopping combustion within any engine and for stopping the rotation of any engine if continued rotation would cause a hazard to the airplane. Each component of the engine stopping system located in any fire zone must be fire resistant. If hydraulic propeller feathering systems are used for stopping the engine, the hydraulic feathering lines or hoses must be fire resistant.

(3) It must be possible to restart an engine in flight. Any techniques and associated limitations must be established and included in the Airplane Flight Manual, approved manual material, or applicable operating placards.

(4) It must be demonstrated in flight that when restarting engines following a false start, all fuel or vapor is discharged in such a way that it does not constitute a fire hazard.

(f) *Restart envelope.* An altitude and airspeed envelope must be established for the airplane for in-flight engine restarting and each installed engine must have a restart capability within that envelope.

(g) *Restart capability.* For turbine engine powered airplanes, if the minimum windmilling speed of the engines, following the in-flight shutdown of all engines, is insufficient to provide the necessary electrical power for engine ignition, a power source independent of the engine-driven electrical power generating system must be provided to permit in-flight engine ignition for restarting.

[Amdt. 23–14, 38 FR 31822, Nov. 19, 1973, as amended by Amdt. 23–17, 41 FR 55464, Dec. 20, 1976; Amdt. 23–26, 45 FR 60171, Sept. 11, 1980; Amdt. 23–29, 49 FR 6847, Feb. 23, 1984; Amdt. 23–34, 52 FR 1832, Jan. 15, 1987; Amdt. 23–40, 55 FR 32861, Aug. 10, 1990; Amdt. 23–43, 58 FR 18970, Apr. 9, 1993; Amdt. 23–51, 61 FR 5136, Feb. 9, 1996; Amdt. 23–53, 63 FR 14798, Mar. 26, 1998; Amdt. 23–54, 65 FR 55854, Sept. 14, 2000]

§ 23.904 Automatic power reserve system.

If installed, an automatic power reserve (APR) system that automatically advances the power or thrust on the operating engine(s), when any engine fails during takeoff, must comply with appendix H of this part.

[Doc. No. 26344, 58 FR 18970, Apr. 9, 1993]

§ 23.905 Propellers.

(a) Each propeller must have a type certificate.

(b) Engine power and propeller shaft rotational speed may not exceed the limits for which the propeller is certificated.

(c) Each featherable propeller must have a means to unfeather it in flight.

(d) Each component of the propeller blade pitch control system must meet the requirements of § 35.42 of this chapter.

(e) All areas of the airplane forward of the pusher propeller that are likely to accumulate and shed ice into the propeller disc during any operating condition must be suitably protected to prevent ice formation, or it must be shown that any ice shed into the propeller disc will not create a hazardous condition.

(f) Each pusher propeller must be marked so that the disc is conspicuous under normal daylight ground conditions.

(g) If the engine exhaust gases are discharged into the pusher propeller disc, it must be shown by tests, or analysis supported by tests, that the propeller is capable of continuous safe operation.

(h) All engine cowling, access doors, and other removable items must be designed to ensure that they will not separate from the airplane and contact the pusher propeller.

[Doc. No. 4080, 29 FR 17955, Dec. 18, 1964, as amended by Amdt. 23–26, 45 FR 60171, Sept. 11, 1980; Amdt. 23–29, 49 FR 6847, Feb. 23, 1984; Amdt. 23–43, 58 FR 18970, Apr. 9, 1993]

§ 23.907 Propeller vibration.

(a) Each propeller other than a conventional fixed-pitch wooden propeller must be shown to have vibration stresses, in normal operating conditions, that do not exceed values that have been shown by the propeller manufacturer to be safe for continuous operation. This must be shown by—

(1) Measurement of stresses through direct testing of the propeller;

(2) Comparison with similar installations for which these measurements have been made; or

(3) Any other acceptable test method or service experience that proves the safety of the installation.

(b) Proof of safe vibration characteristics for any type of propeller, except for conventional, fixed-pitch, wood propellers must be shown where necessary.

[Doc. No. 4080, 29 FR 17955, Dec. 18, 1964; 30 FR 258, Jan. 9, 1965, as amended by Amdt. 23–51, 61 FR 5136, Feb. 9, 1996]

§ 23.909 Turbocharger systems.

(a) Each turbocharger must be approved under the engine type certificate or it must be shown that the turbocharger system, while in its normal engine installation and operating in the engine environment—

(1) Can withstand, without defect, an endurance test of 150 hours that meets

the applicable requirements of §33.49 of this subchapter; and

(2) Will have no adverse effect upon the engine.

(b) Control system malfunctions, vibrations, and abnormal speeds and temperatures expected in service may not damage the turbocharger compressor or turbine.

(c) Each turbocharger case must be able to contain fragments of a compressor or turbine that fails at the highest speed that is obtainable with normal speed control devices inoperative.

(d) Each intercooler installation, where provided, must comply with the following—

(1) The mounting provisions of the intercooler must be designed to withstand the loads imposed on the system;

(2) It must be shown that, under the installed vibration environment, the intercooler will not fail in a manner allowing portions of the intercooler to be ingested by the engine; and

(3) Airflow through the intercooler must not discharge directly on any airplane component (e.g., windshield) unless such discharge is shown to cause no hazard to the airplane under all operating conditions.

(e) Engine power, cooling characteristics, operating limits, and procedures affected by the turbocharger system installations must be evaluated. Turbocharger operating procedures and limitations must be included in the Airplane Flight Manual in accordance with §23.1581.

[Amdt. 23–7, 34 FR 13092, Aug. 13, 1969, as amended by Amdt. 23–43, 58 FR 18970, Apr. 9, 1993]

§23.925 Propeller clearance.

Unless smaller clearances are substantiated, propeller clearances, with the airplane at the most adverse combination of weight and center of gravity, and with the propeller in the most adverse pitch position, may not be less than the following:

(a) *Ground clearance.* There must be a clearance of at least seven inches (for each airplane with nose wheel landing gear) or nine inches (for each airplane with tail wheel landing gear) between each propeller and the ground with the landing gear statically deflected and in the level, normal takeoff, or taxing attitude, whichever is most critical. In addition, for each airplane with conventional landing gear struts using fluid or mechanical means for absorbing landing shocks, there must be positive clearance between the propeller and the ground in the level takeoff attitude with the critical tire completely deflated and the corresponding landing gear strut bottomed. Positive clearance for airplanes using leaf spring struts is shown with a deflection corresponding to 1.5g.

(b) *Aft-mounted propellers.* In addition to the clearances specified in paragraph (a) of this section, an airplane with an aft mounted propeller must be designed such that the propeller will not contact the runway surface when the airplane is in the maximum pitch attitude attainable during normal takeoffs and landings.

(c) *Water clearance.* There must be a clearance of at least 18 inches between each propeller and the water, unless compliance with §23.239 can be shown with a lesser clearance.

(d) *Structural clearance.* There must be—

(1) At least one inch radial clearance between the blade tips and the airplane structure, plus any additional radial clearance necessary to prevent harmful vibration;

(2) At least one-half inch longitudinal clearance between the propeller blades or cuffs and stationary parts of the airplane; and

(3) Positive clearance between other rotating parts of the propeller or spinner and stationary parts of the airplane.

[Doc. No. 4080, 29 FR 17955, Dec. 18, 1964, as amended by Amdt. 23–43, 58 FR 18971, Apr. 9, 1993; Amdt. 23–51, 61 FR 5136, Feb. 9, 1996; Amdt. 23–48, 61 FR 5148, Feb. 9, 1996]

§23.929 Engine installation ice protection.

Propellers (except wooden propellers) and other components of complete engine installations must be protected against the accumulation of ice as necessary to enable satisfactory functioning without appreciable loss of thrust when operated in the icing conditions for which certification is requested.

[Amdt. 23–14, 33 FR 31822, Nov. 19, 1973, as amended by Amdt. 23–51, 61 FR 5136, Feb. 9, 1996]

§ 23.933 Reversing systems.

(a) *For turbojet and turbofan reversing systems.* (1) Each system intended for ground operation only must be designed so that, during any reversal in flight, the engine will produce no more than flight idle thrust. In addition, it must be shown by analysis or test, or both, that—

(i) Each operable reverser can be restored to the forward thrust position; or

(ii) The airplane is capable of continued safe flight and landing under any possible position of the thrust reverser.

(2) Each system intended for in-flight use must be designed so that no unsafe condition will result during normal operation of the system, or from any failure, or likely combination of failures, of the reversing system under any operating condition including ground operation. Failure of structural elements need not be considered if the probability of this type of failure is extremely remote.

(3) Each system must have a means to prevent the engine from producing more than idle thrust when the reversing system malfunctions; except that it may produce any greater thrust that is shown to allow directional control to be maintained, with aerodynamic means alone, under the most critical reversing condition expected in operation.

(b) *For propeller reversing systems.* (1) Each system must be designed so that no single failure, likely combination of failures or malfunction of the system will result in unwanted reverse thrust under any operating condition. Failure of structural elements need not be considered if the probability of this type of failure is extremely remote.

(2) Compliance with paragraph (b)(1) of this section must be shown by failure analysis, or testing, or both, for propeller systems that allow the propeller blades to move from the flight low-pitch position to a position that is substantially less than the normal flight, low-pitch position. The analysis may include or be supported by the analysis made to show compliance with § 35.21 for the type certification of the propeller and associated installation components. Credit will be given for pertinent analysis and testing completed by the engine and propeller manufacturers.

[Doc. No. 26344, 58 FR 18971, Apr. 9, 1993, as amended by Amdt. 23–51, 61 FR 5136, Feb. 9, 1996]

§ 23.934 Turbojet and turbofan engine thrust reverser systems tests.

Thrust reverser systems of turbojet or turbofan engines must meet the requirements of § 33.97 of this chapter or it must be demonstrated by tests that engine operation and vibratory levels are not affected.

[Doc. No. 26344, 58 FR 18971, Apr. 9, 1993]

§ 23.937 Turbopropeller-drag limiting systems.

(a) Turbopropeller-powered airplane propeller-drag limiting systems must be designed so that no single failure or malfunction of any of the systems during normal or emergency operation results in propeller drag in excess of that for which the airplane was designed under the structural requirements of this part. Failure of structural elements of the drag limiting systems need not be considered if the probability of this kind of failure is extremely remote.

(b) As used in this section, drag limiting systems include manual or automatic devices that, when actuated after engine power loss, can move the propeller blades toward the feather position to reduce windmilling drag to a safe level.

[Amdt. 23–7, 34 FR 13093, Aug. 13, 1969, as amended by Amdt. 23–43, 58 FR 18971, Apr. 9, 1993]

§ 23.939 Powerplant operating characteristics.

(a) Turbine engine powerplant operating characteristics must be investigated in flight to determine that no adverse characteristics (such as stall, surge, or flameout) are present, to a hazardous degree, during normal and emergency operation within the range of operating limitations of the airplane and of the engine.

(b) Turbocharged reciprocating engine operating characteristics must be investigated in flight to assure that no adverse characteristics, as a result of an inadvertent overboost, surge, flooding, or vapor lock, are present during normal or emergency operation of the engine(s) throughout the range of operating limitations of both airplane and engine.

(c) For turbine engines, the air inlet system must not, as a result of airflow distortion during normal operation, cause vibration harmful to the engine.

[Amdt. 23–7, 34 FR 13093 Aug. 13, 1969, as amended by Amdt. 23–14, 38 FR 31823, Nov. 19, 1973; Amdt. 23–18, 42 FR 15041, Mar. 17, 1977; Amdt. 23–42, 56 FR 354, Jan. 3, 1991]

§ 23.943   Negative acceleration.

No hazardous malfunction of an engine, an auxiliary power unit approved for use in flight, or any component or system associated with the powerplant or auxiliary power unit may occur when the airplane is operated at the negative accelerations within the flight envelopes prescribed in § 23.333. This must be shown for the greatest value and duration of the acceleration expected in service.

[Amdt. 23–18, 42 FR 15041, Mar. 17, 1977, as amended by Amdt. 23–43, 58 FR 18971, Apr. 9, 1993]

FUEL SYSTEM

§ 23.951   General.

(a) Each fuel system must be constructed and arranged to ensure fuel flow at a rate and pressure established for proper engine and auxiliary power unit functioning under each likely operating condition, including any maneuver for which certification is requested and during which the engine or auxiliary power unit is permitted to be in operation.

(b) Each fuel system must be arranged so that—

(1) No fuel pump can draw fuel from more than one tank at a time; or

(2) There are means to prevent introducing air into the system.

(c) Each fuel system for a turbine engine must be capable of sustained operation throughout its flow and pressure range with fuel initially saturated with water at 80 °F and having 0.75cc of free water per gallon added and cooled to the most critical condition for icing likely to be encountered in operation.

(d) Each fuel system for a turbine engine powered airplane must meet the applicable fuel venting requirements of part 34 of this chapter.

[Amdt. 23–15, 39 FR 35459, Oct. 1, 1974, as amended by Amdt. 23–40, 55 FR 32861, Aug. 10, 1990; Amdt. 23–43, 58 FR 18971, Apr. 9, 1993]

§ 23.953   Fuel system independence.

(a) Each fuel system for a multiengine airplane must be arranged so that, in at least one system configuration, the failure of any one component (other than a fuel tank) will not result in the loss of power of more than one engine or require immediate action by the pilot to prevent the loss of power of more than one engine.

(b) If a single fuel tank (or series of fuel tanks interconnected to function as a single fuel tank) is used on a multiengine airplane, the following must be provided:

(1) Independent tank outlets for each engine, each incorporating a shut-off valve at the tank. This shutoff valve may also serve as the fire wall shutoff valve required if the line between the valve and the engine compartment does not contain more than one quart of fuel (or any greater amount shown to be safe) that can escape into the engine compartment.

(2) At least two vents arranged to minimize the probability of both vents becoming obstructed simultaneously.

(3) Filler caps designed to minimize the probability of incorrect installation or inflight loss.

(4) A fuel system in which those parts of the system from each tank outlet to any engine are independent of each part of the system supplying fuel to any other engine.

[Doc. No. 4080, 29 FR 17955, Dec. 18, 1964, as amended by Amdt. 23–7, 34 FR 13093 Aug. 13, 1969; Amdt. 23–43, 58 FR 18971, Apr. 9, 1993]

§ 23.954   Fuel system lightning protection.

The fuel system must be designed and arranged to prevent the ignition of fuel vapor within the system by—

(a) Direct lightning strikes to areas having a high probability of stroke attachment;

(b) Swept lightning strokes on areas where swept strokes are highly probable; and

(c) Corona or streamering at fuel vent outlets.

[Amdt. 23-7, 34 FR 13093, Aug. 13, 1969]

§ 23.955 Fuel flow.

(a) *General.* The ability of the fuel system to provide fuel at the rates specified in this section and at a pressure sufficient for proper engine operation must be shown in the attitude that is most critical with respect to fuel feed and quantity of unusable fuel. These conditions may be simulated in a suitable mockup. In addition—

(1) The quantity of fuel in the tank may not exceed the amount established as the unusable fuel supply for that tank under § 23.959(a) plus that quantity necessary to show compliance with this section.

(2) If there is a fuel flowmeter, it must be blocked during the flow test and the fuel must flow through the meter or its bypass.

(3) If there is a flowmeter without a bypass, it must not have any probable failure mode that would restrict fuel flow below the level required for this fuel demonstration.

(4) The fuel flow must include that flow necessary for vapor return flow, jet pump drive flow, and for all other purposes for which fuel is used.

(b) *Gravity systems.* The fuel flow rate for gravity systems (main and reserve supply) must be 150 percent of the takeoff fuel consumption of the engine.

(c) *Pump systems.* The fuel flow rate for each pump system (main and reserve supply) for each reciprocating engine must be 125 percent of the fuel flow required by the engine at the maximum takeoff power approved under this part.

(1) This flow rate is required for each main pump and each emergency pump, and must be available when the pump is operating as it would during takeoff;

(2) For each hand-operated pump, this rate must occur at not more than 60 complete cycles (120 single strokes) per minute.

(3) The fuel pressure, with main and emergency pumps operating simultaneously, must not exceed the fuel inlet pressure limits of the engine unless it can be shown that no adverse effect occurs.

(d) *Auxiliary fuel systems and fuel transfer systems.* Paragraphs (b), (c), and (f) of this section apply to each auxiliary and transfer system, except that—

(1) The required fuel flow rate must be established upon the basis of maximum continuous power and engine rotational speed, instead of takeoff power and fuel consumption; and

(2) If there is a placard providing operating instructions, a lesser flow rate may be used for transferring fuel from any auxiliary tank into a larger main tank. This lesser flow rate must be adequate to maintain engine maximum continuous power but the flow rate must not overfill the main tank at lower engine powers.

(e) *Multiple fuel tanks.* For reciprocating engines that are supplied with fuel from more than one tank, if engine power loss becomes apparent due to fuel depletion from the tank selected, it must be possible after switching to any full tank, in level flight, to obtain 75 percent maximum continuous power on that engine in not more than—

(1) 10 seconds for naturally aspirated single-engine airplanes;

(2) 20 seconds for turbocharged single-engine airplanes, provided that 75 percent maximum continuous naturally aspirated power is regained within 10 seconds; or

(3) 20 seconds for multiengine airplanes.

(f) *Turbine engine fuel systems.* Each turbine engine fuel system must provide at least 100 percent of the fuel flow required by the engine under each intended operation condition and maneuver. The conditions may be simulated in a suitable mockup. This flow must—

(1) Be shown with the airplane in the most adverse fuel feed condition (with respect to altitudes, attitudes, and other conditions) that is expected in operation; and

(2) For multiengine airplanes, notwithstanding the lower flow rate allowed by paragraph (d) of this section, be automatically uninterrupted with respect to any engine until all the fuel

scheduled for use by that engine has been consumed. In addition—

(i) For the purposes of this section, "fuel scheduled for use by that engine" means all fuel in any tank intended for use by a specific engine.

(ii) The fuel system design must clearly indicate the engine for which fuel in any tank is scheduled.

(iii) Compliance with this paragraph must require no pilot action after completion of the engine starting phase of operations.

(3) For single-engine airplanes, require no pilot action after completion of the engine starting phase of operations unless means are provided that unmistakenly alert the pilot to take any needed action at least five minutes prior to the needed action; such pilot action must not cause any change in engine operation; and such pilot action must not distract pilot attention from essential flight duties during any phase of operations for which the airplane is approved.

[Doc. No. 4080, 29 FR 17955, Dec. 18, 1964, as amended by Amdt. 23–7, 34 FR 13093, Aug. 13, 1969; Amdt. 23–43, 58 FR 18971, Apr. 9, 1993; Amdt. 23–51, 61 FR 5136, Feb. 9, 1996]

§ 23.957 Flow between interconnected tanks.

(a) It must be impossible, in a gravity feed system with interconnected tank outlets, for enough fuel to flow between the tanks to cause an overflow of fuel from any tank vent under the conditions in § 23.959, except that full tanks must be used.

(b) If fuel can be pumped from one tank to another in flight, the fuel tank vents and the fuel transfer system must be designed so that no structural damage to any airplane component can occur because of overfilling of any tank.

[Doc. No. 4080, 29 FR 17955, Dec. 18, 1964, as amended by Amdt. 23–43, 58 FR 18972, Apr. 9, 1993]

§ 23.959 Unusable fuel supply.

(a) The unusable fuel supply for each tank must be established as not less than that quantity at which the first evidence of malfunctioning occurs under the most adverse fuel feed condition occurring under each intended operation and flight maneuver involving that tank. Fuel system component failures need not be considered.

(b) The effect on the usable fuel quantity as a result of a failure of any pump shall be determined.

[Amdt. 23–7, 34 FR 13093, Aug. 13, 1969, as amended by Amdt. 23–18, 42 FR 15041, Mar. 17, 1977; Amdt. 23–51, 61 FR 5136, Feb. 9, 1996]

§ 23.961 Fuel system hot weather operation.

Each fuel system must be free from vapor lock when using fuel at its critical temperature, with respect to vapor formation, when operating the airplane in all critical operating and environmental conditions for which approval is requested. For turbine fuel, the initial temperature must be 110 °F, −0 °, +5 °F or the maximum outside air temperature for which approval is requested, whichever is more critical.

[Doc. No. 26344, 58 FR 18972, Apr. 9, 1993; 58 FR 27060, May 6, 1993]

§ 23.963 Fuel tanks: General.

(a) Each fuel tank must be able to withstand, without failure, the vibration, inertia, fluid, and structural loads that it may be subjected to in operation.

(b) Each flexible fuel tank liner must be shown to be suitable for the particular application.

(c) Each integral fuel tank must have adequate facilities for interior inspection and repair.

(d) The total usable capacity of the fuel tanks must be enough for at least one-half hour of operation at maximum continuous power.

(e) Each fuel quantity indicator must be adjusted, as specified in § 23.1337(b), to account for the unusable fuel supply determined under § 23.959(a).

[Doc. No. 4080, 29 FR 17955, Dec. 18, 1964; 30 FR 258, Jan. 9, 1965, as amended by Amdt 23–34, 52 FR 1832, Jan. 15, 1987; Amdt. 23–43, 58 FR 18972, Apr. 9, 1993; Amdt. 23–51, 61 FR 5136, Feb. 9, 1996]

§ 23.965 Fuel tank tests.

(a) Each fuel tank must be able to withstand the following pressures without failure or leakage:

(1) For each conventional metal tank and nonmetallic tank with walls not supported by the airplane structure, a pressure of 3.5 p.s.i., or that pressure

developed during maximum ultimate acceleration with a full tank, whichever is greater.

(2) For each integral tank, the pressure developed during the maximum limit acceleration of the airplane with a full tank, with simultaneous application of the critical limit structural loads.

(3) For each nonmetallic tank with walls supported by the airplane structure and constructed in an acceptable manner using acceptable basic tank material, and with actual or simulated support conditions, a pressure of 2 p.s.i. for the first tank of a specific design. The supporting structure must be designed for the critical loads occurring in the flight or landing strength conditions combined with the fuel pressure loads resulting from the corresponding accelerations.

(b) Each fuel tank with large, unsupported, or unstiffened flat surfaces,whose failure or deformation could cause fuel leakage, must be able to withstand the following test without leakage, failure, or excessive deformation of the tank walls:

(1) Each complete tank assembly and its support must be vibration tested while mounted to simulate the actual installation.

(2) Except as specified in paragraph (b)(4) of this section, the tank assembly must be vibrated for 25 hours at a total displacement of not less than ¹⁄₃₂ of an inch (unless another displacement is substantiated) while ²⁄₃ filled with water or other suitable test fluid.

(3) The test frequency of vibration must be as follows:

(i) If no frequency of vibration resulting from any rpm within the normal operating range of engine or propeller speeds is critical, the test frequency of vibration is:

(A) The number of cycles per minute obtained by multiplying the maximum continuous propeller speed in rpm by 0.9 for propeller-driven airplanes, and

(B) For non-propeller driven airplanes the test frequency of vibration is 2,000 cycles per minute.

(ii) If only one frequency of vibration resulting from any rpm within the normal operating range of engine or propeller speeds is critical, that frequency

of vibration must be the test frequency.

(iii) If more than one frequency of vibration resulting from any rpm within the normal operating range of engine or propeller speeds is critical, the most critical of these frequencies must be the test frequency.

(4) Under paragraph (b)(3) (ii) and (iii) of this section, the time of test must be adjusted to accomplish the same number of vibration cycles that would be accomplished in 25 hours at the frequency specified in paragraph (b)(3)(i) of this section.

(5) During the test, the tank assembly must be rocked at a rate of 16 to 20 complete cycles per minute, through an angle of 15° on either side of the horizontal (30° total), about an axis parallel to the axis of the fuselage, for 25 hours.

(c) Each integral tank using methods of construction and sealing not previously proven to be adequate by test data or service experience must be able to withstand the vibration test specified in paragraphs (b)(1) through (4) of this section.

(d) Each tank with a nonmetallic liner must be subjected to the sloshing test outlined in paragraph (b)(5) of this section, with the fuel at room temperature. In addition, a specimen liner of the same basic construction as that to be used in the airplane must, when installed in a suitable test tank, withstand the sloshing test with fuel at a temperature of 110 °F.

[Doc. No. 4080, 29 FR 17955, Dec. 18, 1964, as amended by Amdt. 23–43, 58 FR 18972, Apr. 9, 1993; Amdt. 23–43, 61 FR 253, Jan. 4, 1996; Amdt. 23–51, 61 FR 5136, Feb. 9, 1996]

§ 23.967 Fuel tank installation.

(a) Each fuel tank must be supported so that tank loads are not concentrated. In addition—

(1) There must be pads, if necessary, to prevent chafing between each tank and its supports;

(2) Padding must be nonabsorbent or treated to prevent the absorption of fuel;

(3) If a flexible tank liner is used, it must be supported so that it is not required to withstand fluid loads;

(4) Interior surfaces adjacent to the liner must be smooth and free from

projections that could cause wear, un-less—

(i) Provisions are made for protection of the liner at those points; or

(ii) The construction of the liner itself provides such protection; and

(5) A positive pressure must be maintained within the vapor space of each bladder cell under any condition of operation, except for a particular condition for which it is shown that a zero or negative pressure will not cause the bladder cell to collapse; and

(6) Syphoning of fuel (other than minor spillage) or collapse of bladder fuel cells may not result from improper securing or loss of the fuel filler cap.

(b) Each tank compartment must be ventilated and drained to prevent the accumulation of flammable fluids or vapors. Each compartment adjacent to a tank that is an integral part of the airplane structure must also be ventilated and drained.

(c) No fuel tank may be on the engine side of the firewall. There must be at least one-half inch of clearance between the fuel tank and the firewall. No part of the engine nacelle skin that lies immediately behind a major air opening from the engine compartment may act as the wall of an integral tank.

(d) Each fuel tank must be isolated from personnel compartments by a fume-proof and fuel-proof enclosure that is vented and drained to the exterior of the airplane. The required enclosure must sustain any personnel compartment pressurization loads without permanent deformation or failure under the conditions of §§ 23.365 and 23.843 of this part. A bladder-type fuel cell, if used, must have a retaining shell at least equivalent to a metal fuel tank in structural integrity.

(e) Fuel tanks must be designed, located, and installed so as to retain fuel:

(1) When subjected to the inertia loads resulting from the ultimate static load factors prescribed in § 23.561(b)(2) of this part; and

(2) Under conditions likely to occur when the airplane lands on a paved runway at a normal landing speed under each of the following conditions:

(i) The airplane in a normal landing attitude and its landing gear retracted.

(ii) The most critical landing gear leg collapsed and the other landing gear legs extended.

In showing compliance with paragraph (e)(2) of this section, the tearing away of an engine mount must be considered unless all the engines are installed above the wing or on the tail or fuselage of the airplane.

[Doc. No. 4080, 29 FR 17955, Dec. 18, 1964, as amended by Amdt. 23–7, 34 FR 13903, Aug. 13, 1969; Amdt. 23–14, 38 FR 31823, Nov. 19, 1973; Amdt. 23–18, 42 FR 15041, Mar. 17, 1977; Amdt. 23–26, 45 FR 60171, Sept. 11, 1980; Amdt. 23–36, 53 FR 30815, Aug. 15, 1988; Amdt. 23–43, 58 FR 18972, Apr. 9, 1993]

§ 23.969 Fuel tank expansion space.

Each fuel tank must have an expansion space of not less than two percent of the tank capacity, unless the tank vent discharges clear of the airplane (in which case no expansion space is required). It must be impossible to fill the expansion space inadvertently with the airplane in the normal ground attitude.

§ 23.971 Fuel tank sump.

(a) Each fuel tank must have a drainable sump with an effective capacity, in the normal ground and flight attitudes, of 0.25 percent of the tank capacity, or 1/16 gallon, whichever is greater.

(b) Each fuel tank must allow drainage of any hazardous quantity of water from any part of the tank to its sump with the airplane in the normal ground attitude.

(c) Each reciprocating engine fuel system must have a sediment bowl or chamber that is accessible for drainage; has a capacity of 1 ounce for every 20 gallons of fuel tank capacity; and each fuel tank outlet is located so that, in the normal flight attitude, water will drain from all parts of the tank except the sump to the sediment bowl or chamber.

(d) Each sump, sediment bowl, and sediment chamber drain required by paragraphs (a), (b), and (c) of this section must comply with the drain provisions of § 23.999(b)(1) and (b)(2).

[Doc. No. 26344, 58 FR 18972, Apr. 9, 1993; 58 FR 27060, May 6, 1993]

§ 23.973 Fuel tank filler connection.

(a) Each fuel tank filler connection must be marked as prescribed in § 23.1557(c).

(b) Spilled fuel must be prevented from entering the fuel tank compartment or any part of the airplane other than the tank itself.

(c) Each filler cap must provide a fuel-tight seal for the main filler opening. However, there may be small openings in the fuel tank cap for venting purposes or for the purpose of allowing passage of a fuel gauge through the cap provided such openings comply with the requirements of § 23.975(a).

(d) Each fuel filling point, except pressure fueling connection points, must have a provision for electrically bonding the airplane to ground fueling equipment.

(e) For airplanes with engines requiring gasoline as the only permissible fuel, the inside diameter of the fuel filler opening must be no larger than 2.36 inches.

(f) For airplanes with turbine engines, the inside diameter of the fuel filler opening must be no smaller than 2.95 inches.

[Doc. No. 4080, 29 FR 17955, Dec. 18, 1964; 30 FR 258, Jan. 9, 1965, as amended by Amdt. 23–18, 42 FR 15041, Mar. 17, 1977; Amdt. 23–43, 58 FR 18972, Apr. 9, 1993; Amdt. 23–51, 61 FR 5136, Feb. 9, 1996]

§ 23.975 Fuel tank vents and carburetor vapor vents.

(a) Each fuel tank must be vented from the top part of the expansion space. In addition—

(1) Each vent outlet must be located and constructed in a manner that minimizes the possibility of its being obstructed by ice or other foreign matter;

(2) Each vent must be constructed to prevent siphoning of fuel during normal operation;

(3) The venting capacity must allow the rapid relief of excessive differences of pressure between the interior and exterior of the tank;

(4) Airspaces of tanks with interconnected outlets must be interconnected;

(5) There may be no point in any vent line where moisture can accumulate with the airplane in either the ground or level flight attitudes, unless drain-

age is provided. Any drain valve installed must be accessible for drainage;

(6) No vent may terminate at a point where the discharge of fuel from the vent outlet will constitute a fire hazard or from which fumes may enter personnel compartments; and

(7) Vents must be arranged to prevent the loss of fuel, except fuel discharged because of thermal expansion, when the airplane is parked in any direction on a ramp having a one-percent slope.

(b) Each carburetor with vapor elimination connections and each fuel injection engine employing vapor return provisions must have a separate vent line to lead vapors back to the top of one of the fuel tanks. If there is more than one tank and it is necessary to use these tanks in a definite sequence for any reason, the vapor vent line must lead back to the fuel tank to be used first, unless the relative capacities of the tanks are such that return to another tank is preferable.

(c) For acrobatic category airplanes, excessive loss of fuel during acrobatic maneuvers, including short periods of inverted flight, must be prevented. It must be impossible for fuel to siphon from the vent when normal flight has been resumed after any acrobatic maneuver for which certification is requested.

[Doc. No. 4080, 29 FR 17955, Dec. 18, 1964; 30 FR 258, Jan. 9, 1965, as amended by Amdt. 23–18, 42 FR 15041, Mar. 17, 1977; Amdt. 23–29, 49 FR 6847, Feb. 23, 1984; Amdt. 23–43, 58 FR 18973, Apr. 9, 1993; Amdt. 23–51, 61 FR 5136, Feb. 9, 1996]

§ 23.977 Fuel tank outlet.

(a) There must be a fuel strainer for the fuel tank outlet or for the booster pump. This strainer must—

(1) For reciprocating engine powered airplanes, have 8 to 16 meshes per inch; and

(2) For turbine engine powered airplanes, prevent the passage of any object that could restrict fuel flow or damage any fuel system component.

(b) The clear area of each fuel tank outlet strainer must be at least five times the area of the outlet line.

(c) The diameter of each strainer must be at least that of the fuel tank outlet.

(d) Each strainer must be accessible for inspection and cleaning.

[Amdt. 23–17, 41 FR 55465, Dec. 20, 1976, as amended by Amdt. 23–43, 58 FR 18973, Apr. 9, 1993]

§ 23.979 Pressure fueling systems.

For pressure fueling systems, the following apply:

(a) Each pressure fueling system fuel manifold connection must have means to prevent the escape of hazardous quantities of fuel from the system if the fuel entry valve fails.

(b) An automatic shutoff means must be provided to prevent the quantity of fuel in each tank from exceeding the maximum quantity approved for that tank. This means must—

(1) Allow checking for proper shutoff operation before each fueling of the tank; and

(2) For commuter category airplanes, indicate at each fueling station, a failure of the shutoff means to stop the fuel flow at the maximum quantity approved for that tank.

(c) A means must be provided to prevent damage to the fuel system in the event of failure of the automatic shutoff means prescribed in paragraph (b) of this section.

(d) All parts of the fuel system up to the tank which are subjected to fueling pressures must have a proof pressure of 1.33 times, and an ultimate pressure of at least 2.0 times, the surge pressure likely to occur during fueling.

[Amdt. 23–14, 38 FR 31823, Nov. 19, 1973, as amended by Amdt. 23–51, 61 FR 5137, Feb. 9, 1996]

FUEL SYSTEM COMPONENTS

§ 23.991 Fuel pumps.

(a) *Main pumps.* For main pumps, the following apply:

(1) For reciprocating engine installations having fuel pumps to supply fuel to the engine, at least one pump for each engine must be directly driven by the engine and must meet § 23.955. This pump is a main pump.

(2) For turbine engine installations, each fuel pump required for proper engine operation, or required to meet the fuel system requirements of this subpart (other than those in paragraph (b) of this section), is a main pump. In addition—

(i) There must be at least one main pump for each turbine engine;

(ii) The power supply for the main pump for each engine must be independent of the power supply for each main pump for any other engine; and

(iii) For each main pump, provision must be made to allow the bypass of each positive displacement fuel pump other than a fuel injection pump approved as part of the engine.

(b) *Emergency pumps.* There must be an emergency pump immediately available to supply fuel to the engine if any main pump (other than a fuel injection pump approved as part of an engine) fails. The power supply for each emergency pump must be independent of the power supply for each corresponding main pump.

(c) *Warning means.* If both the main pump and emergency pump operate continuously, there must be a means to indicate to the appropriate flight crewmembers a malfunction of either pump.

(d) Operation of any fuel pump may not affect engine operation so as to create a hazard, regardless of the engine power or thrust setting or the functional status of any other fuel pump.

[Doc. No. 4080, 29 FR 17955, Dec. 18, 1964, as amended by Amdt. 23–7, 34 FR 13093, Aug. 13, 1969; Amdt. 23–26, 45 FR 60171, Sept. 11, 1980; Amdt. 23–43, 58 FR 18973, Apr. 9, 1993]

§ 23.993 Fuel system lines and fittings.

(a) Each fuel line must be installed and supported to prevent excessive vibration and to withstand loads due to fuel pressure and accelerated flight conditions.

(b) Each fuel line connected to components of the airplane between which relative motion could exist must have provisions for flexibility.

(c) Each flexible connection in fuel lines that may be under pressure and subjected to axial loading must use flexible hose assemblies.

(d) Each flexible hose must be shown to be suitable for the particular application.

(e) No flexible hose that might be adversely affected by exposure to high temperatures may be used where excessive temperatures will exist during operation or after engine shutdown.

[Doc. No. 4080, 29 FR 17955, Dec. 18, 1964, as amended by Amdt. 23–43, 58 FR 18973, Apr. 9, 1993]

§ 23.994 Fuel system components.

Fuel system components in an engine nacelle or in the fuselage must be protected from damage which could result in spillage of enough fuel to constitute a fire hazard as a result of a wheels-up landing on a paved runway.

[Amdt. 23–29, 49 FR 6847, Feb. 23, 1984]

§ 23.995 Fuel valves and controls.

(a) There must be a means to allow appropriate flight crew members to rapidly shut off, in flight, the fuel to each engine individually.

(b) No shutoff valve may be on the engine side of any firewall. In addition, there must be means to—

(1) Guard against inadvertent operation of each shutoff valve; and

(2) Allow appropriate flight crew members to reopen each valve rapidly after it has been closed.

(c) Each valve and fuel system control must be supported so that loads resulting from its operation or from accelerated flight conditions are not transmitted to the lines connected to the valve.

(d) Each valve and fuel system control must be installed so that gravity and vibration will not affect the selected position.

(e) Each fuel valve handle and its connections to the valve mechanism must have design features that minimize the possibility of incorrect installation.

(f) Each check valve must be constructed, or otherwise incorporate provisions, to preclude incorrect assembly or connection of the valve.

(g) Fuel tank selector valves must—

(1) Require a separate and distinct action to place the selector in the "OFF" position; and

(2) Have the tank selector positions located in such a manner that it is impossible for the selector to pass through the "OFF" position when changing from one tank to another.

[Doc. No. 4080, 29 FR 17955, Dec. 18, 1964, as amended by Amdt. 23–14, 38 FR 31823, Nov. 19, 1973; Amdt. 23–17, 41 FR 55465, Dec. 20, 1976; Amdt. 23–18, 42 FR 15041, Mar. 17, 1977; Amdt. 23–29, 49 FR 6847, Feb. 23, 1984]

§ 23.997 Fuel strainer or filter.

There must be a fuel strainer or filter between the fuel tank outlet and the inlet of either the fuel metering device or an engine driven positive displacement pump, whichever is nearer the fuel tank outlet. This fuel strainer or filter must—

(a) Be accessible for draining and cleaning and must incorporate a screen or element which is easily removable;

(b) Have a sediment trap and drain except that it need not have a drain if the strainer or filter is easily removable for drain purposes;

(c) Be mounted so that its weight is not supported by the connecting lines or by the inlet or outlet connections of the strainer or filter itself, unless adequate strength margins under all loading conditions are provided in the lines and connections; and

(d) Have the capacity (with respect to operating limitations established for the engine) to ensure that engine fuel system functioning is not impaired, with the fuel contaminated to a degree (with respect to particle size and density) that is greater than that established for the engine during its type certification.

(e) In addition, for commuter category airplanes, unless means are provided in the fuel system to prevent the accumulation of ice on the filter, a means must be provided to automatically maintain the fuel flow if ice clogging of the filter occurs.

[Amdt. 23–15, 39 FR 35459, Oct. 1, 1974, as amended by Amdt. 23–29, 49 FR 6847, Feb. 23, 1984; Amdt. 23–34, 52 FR 1832, Jan. 15, 1987; Amdt. 23–43, 58 FR 18973, Apr. 9, 1993]

§ 23.999 Fuel system drains.

(a) There must be at least one drain to allow safe drainage of the entire fuel system with the airplane in its normal ground attitude.

(b) Each drain required by paragraph (a) of this section and § 23.971 must—

(1) Discharge clear of all parts of the airplane;

(2) Have a drain valve—

(i) That has manual or automatic means for positive locking in the closed position;

(ii) That is readily accessible;

(iii) That can be easily opened and closed;

(iv) That allows the fuel to be caught for examination;

(v) That can be observed for proper closing; and

(vi) That is either located or protected to prevent fuel spillage in the event of a landing with landing gear retracted.

[Doc. No. 4080, 29 FR 17955, Dec. 18, 1964, as amended by Amdt. 23–17, 41 FR 55465, Dec. 20, 1976; Amdt. 23–43, 58 FR 18973, Apr. 9, 1993]

§ 23.1001 Fuel jettisoning system.

(a) If the design landing weight is less than that permitted under the requirements of § 23.473(b), the airplane must have a fuel jettisoning system installed that is able to jettison enough fuel to bring the maximum weight down to the design landing weight. The average rate of fuel jettisoning must be at least 1 percent of the maximum weight per minute, except that the time required to jettison the fuel need not be less than 10 minutes.

(b) Fuel jettisoning must be demonstrated at maximum weight with flaps and landing gear up and in—

(1) A power-off glide at 1.4 V_{S1};

(2) A climb, at the speed at which the one-engine-inoperative enroute climb data have been established in accordance with § 23.69(b), with the critical engine inoperative and the remaining engines at maximum continuous power; and

(3) Level flight at 1.4 V_S1, if the results of the tests in the conditions specified in paragraphs (b)(1) and (2) of this section show that this condition could be critical.

(c) During the flight tests prescribed in paragraph (b) of this section, it must be shown that—

(1) The fuel jettisoning system and its operation are free from fire hazard;

(2) The fuel discharges clear of any part of the airplane;

(3) Fuel or fumes do not enter any parts of the airplane; and

(4) The jettisoning operation does not adversely affect the controllability of the airplane.

(d) For reciprocating engine powered airplanes, the jettisoning system must be designed so that it is not possible to jettison the fuel in the tanks used for takeoff and landing below the level allowing 45 minutes flight at 75 percent maximum continuous power. However, if there is an auxiliary control independent of the main jettisoning control, the system may be designed to jettison all the fuel.

(e) For turbine engine powered airplanes, the jettisoning system must be designed so that it is not possible to jettison fuel in the tanks used for takeoff and landing below the level allowing climb from sea level to 10,000 feet and thereafter allowing 45 minutes cruise at a speed for maximum range.

(f) The fuel jettisoning valve must be designed to allow flight crewmembers to close the valve during any part of the jettisoning operation.

(g) Unless it is shown that using any means (including flaps, slots, and slats) for changing the airflow across or around the wings does not adversely affect fuel jettisoning, there must be a placard, adjacent to the jettisoning control, to warn flight crewmembers against jettisoning fuel while the means that change the airflow are being used.

(h) The fuel jettisoning system must be designed so that any reasonably probable single malfunction in the system will not result in a hazardous condition due to unsymmetrical jettisoning of, or inability to jettison, fuel.

[Amdt. 23–7, 34 FR 13094, Aug. 13, 1969, as amended by Amdt. 23–43, 58 FR 18973, Apr. 9, 1993; Amdt. 23–51, 61 FR 5137, Feb. 9, 1996]

OIL SYSTEM

§ 23.1011 General.

(a) For oil systems and components that have been approved under the engine airworthiness requirements and where those requirements are equal to or more severe than the corresponding requirements of subpart E of this part, that approval need not be duplicated. Where the requirements of subpart E of

267

this part are more severe, substantiation must be shown to the requirements of subpart E of this part.

(b) Each engine must have an independent oil system that can supply it with an appropriate quantity of oil at a temperature not above that safe for continuous operation.

(c) The usable oil tank capacity may not be less than the product of the endurance of the airplane under critical operating conditions and the maximum oil consumption of the engine under the same conditions, plus a suitable margin to ensure adequate circulation and cooling.

(d) For an oil system without an oil transfer system, only the usable oil tank capacity may be considered. The amount of oil in the engine oil lines, the oil radiator, and the feathering reserve, may not be considered.

(e) If an oil transfer system is used, and the transfer pump can pump some of the oil in the transfer lines into the main engine oil tanks, the amount of oil in these lines that can be pumped by the transfer pump may be included in the oil capacity.

[Doc. No. 4080, 29 FR 17955, Dec. 18, 1964, as amended by Amdt. 23–43, 58 FR 18973, Apr. 9, 1993]

§ 23.1013   Oil tanks.

(a) *Installation.* Each oil tank must be installed to—

(1) Meet the requirements of § 23.967 (a) and (b); and

(2) Withstand any vibration, inertia, and fluid loads expected in operation.

(b) *Expansion space.* Oil tank expansion space must be provided so that—

(1) Each oil tank used with a reciprocating engine has an expansion space of not less than the greater of 10 percent of the tank capacity or 0.5 gallon, and each oil tank used with a turbine engine has an expansion space of not less than 10 percent of the tank capacity; and

(2) It is impossible to fill the expansion space inadvertently with the airplane in the normal ground attitude.

(c) *Filler connection.* Each oil tank filler connection must be marked as specified in § 23.1557(c). Each recessed oil tank filler connection of an oil tank used with a turbine engine, that can retain any appreciable quantity of oil,

must have provisions for fitting a drain.

(d) *Vent.* Oil tanks must be vented as follows:

(1) Each oil tank must be vented to the engine from the top part of the expansion space so that the vent connection is not covered by oil under any normal flight condition.

(2) Oil tank vents must be arranged so that condensed water vapor that might freeze and obstruct the line cannot accumulate at any point.

(3) For acrobatic category airplanes, there must be means to prevent hazardous loss of oil during acrobatic maneuvers, including short periods of inverted flight.

(e) *Outlet.* No oil tank outlet may be enclosed by any screen or guard that would reduce the flow of oil below a safe value at any operating temperature. No oil tank outlet diameter may be less than the diameter of the engine oil pump inlet. Each oil tank used with a turbine engine must have means to prevent entrance into the tank itself, or into the tank outlet, of any object that might obstruct the flow of oil through the system. There must be a shutoff valve at the outlet of each oil tank used with a turbine engine, unless the external portion of the oil system (including oil tank supports) is fireproof.

(f) *Flexible liners.* Each flexible oil tank liner must be of an acceptable kind.

(g) Each oil tank filler cap of an oil tank that is used with an engine must provide an oiltight seal.

[Doc. No. 4080, 29 FR 17955, Dec. 18, 1964, as amended by Amdt. 23–15, 39 FR 35459 Oct. 1, 1974; Amdt. 23–43, 58 FR 18973, Apr. 9, 1993; Amdt. 23–51, 61 FR 5137, Feb. 9, 1996]

§ 23.1015   Oil tank tests.

Each oil tank must be tested under § 23.965, except that—

(a) The applied pressure must be five p.s.i. for the tank construction instead of the pressures specified in § 23.965(a);

(b) For a tank with a nonmetallic liner the test fluid must be oil rather than fuel as specified in § 23.965(d), and the slosh test on a specimen liner must be conducted with the oil at 250 °F.; and

(c) For pressurized tanks used with a turbine engine, the test pressure may not be less than 5 p.s.i. plus the maximum operating pressure of the tank.

[Doc. No. 4080, 29 FR 17955, Dec. 18, 1964, as amended by Amdt. 23–15, 39 FR 35460, Oct. 1, 1974]

§ 23.1017 Oil lines and fittings.

(a) *Oil lines.* Oil lines must meet § 23.993 and must accommodate a flow of oil at a rate and pressure adequate for proper engine functioning under any normal operating condition.

(b) *Breather lines.* Breather lines must be arranged so that—

(1) Condensed water vapor or oil that might freeze and obstruct the line cannot accumulate at any point;

(2) The breather discharge will not constitute a fire hazard if foaming occurs, or cause emitted oil to strike the pilot's windshield;

(3) The breather does not discharge into the engine air induction system; and

(4) For acrobatic category airplanes, there is no excessive loss of oil from the breather during acrobatic maneuvers, including short periods of inverted flight.

(5) The breather outlet is protected against blockage by ice or foreign matter.

[Doc. No. 4080, 29 FR 17955, Dec. 18, 1964, as amended by Amdt. 23–7, 34 FR 13094, Aug. 13, 1969; Amdt. 23–14, 38 FR 31823, Nov. 19, 1973]

§ 23.1019 Oil strainer or filter.

(a) Each turbine engine installation must incorporate an oil strainer or filter through which all of the engine oil flows and which meets the following requirements:

(1) Each oil strainer or filter that has a bypass, must be constructed and installed so that oil will flow at the normal rate through the rest of the system with the strainer or filter completely blocked.

(2) The oil strainer or filter must have the capacity (with respect to operating limitations established for the engine) to ensure that engine oil system functioning is not impaired when the oil is contaminated to a degree (with respect to particle size and density) that is greater than that estab-

lished for the engine for its type certification.

(3) The oil strainer or filter, unless it is installed at an oil tank outlet, must incorporate a means to indicate contamination before it reaches the capacity established in accordance with paragraph (a)(2) of this section.

(4) The bypass of a strainer or filter must be constructed and installed so that the release of collected contaminants is minimized by appropriate location of the bypass to ensure that collected contaminants are not in the bypass flow path.

(5) An oil strainer or filter that has no bypass, except one that is installed at an oil tank outlet, must have a means to connect it to the warning system required in § 23.1305(c)(9).

(b) Each oil strainer or filter in a powerplant installation using reciprocating engines must be constructed and installed so that oil will flow at the normal rate through the rest of the system with the strainer or filter element completely blocked.

[Amdt. 23–15, 39 FR 35460, Oct. 1, 1974, as amended by Amdt. 23–29, 49 FR 6847, Feb. 23, 1984; Amdt. 23–43, 58 FR 18973, Apr. 9, 1993]

§ 23.1021 Oil system drains.

A drain (or drains) must be provided to allow safe drainage of the oil system. Each drain must—

(a) Be accessible;

(b) Have drain valves, or other closures, employing manual or automatic shut-off means for positive locking in the closed position; and

(c) Be located or protected to prevent inadvertent operation.

[Amdt. 23–29, 49 FR 6847, Feb. 23, 1984, as amended by Amdt. 23–43, 58 FR 18973, Apr. 9, 1993]

§ 23.1023 Oil radiators.

Each oil radiator and its supporting structures must be able to withstand the vibration, inertia, and oil pressure loads to which it would be subjected in operation.

§ 23.1027 Propeller feathering system.

(a) If the propeller feathering system uses engine oil and that oil supply can become depleted due to failure of any part of the oil system, a means must be incorporated to reserve enough oil to operate the feathering system.

(b) The amount of reserved oil must be enough to accomplish feathering and must be available only to the feathering pump.

(c) The ability of the system to accomplish feathering with the reserved oil must be shown.

(d) Provision must be made to prevent sludge or other foreign matter from affecting the safe operation of the propeller feathering system.

[Doc. No. 4080, 29 FR 17955, Dec. 18, 1964, as amended by Amdt. 23–14, 38 FR 31823, Nov. 19, 1973; Amdt. 23–43, 58 FR 18973, Apr. 9, 1993]

COOLING

§ 23.1041 General.

The powerplant and auxiliary power unit cooling provisions must maintain the temperatures of powerplant components and engine fluids, and auxiliary power unit components and fluids within the limits established for those components and fluids under the most adverse ground, water, and flight operations to the maximum altitude and maximum ambient atmospheric temperature conditions for which approval is requested, and after normal engine and auxiliary power unit shutdown.

[Doc. No. 26344, 58 FR 18973, Apr. 9, 1993, as amended by Amdt. 23–51, 61 FR 5137, Feb. 9, 1996]

§ 23.1043 Cooling tests.

(a) *General.* Compliance with § 23.1041 must be shown on the basis of tests, for which the following apply:

(1) If the tests are conducted under ambient atmospheric temperature conditions deviating from the maximum for which approval is requested, the recorded powerplant temperatures must be corrected under paragraphs (c) and (d) of this section, unless a more rational correction method is applicable.

(2) No corrected temperature determined under paragraph (a)(1) of this section may exceed established limits.

(3) The fuel used during the cooling tests must be of the minimum grade approved for the engine.

(4) For turbocharged engines, each turbocharger must be operated through that part of the climb profile for which

operation with the turbocharger is requested.

(5) For a reciprocating engine, the mixture settings must be the leanest recommended for climb.

(b) *Maximum ambient atmospheric temperature.* A maximum ambient atmospheric temperature corresponding to sea level conditions of at least 100 degrees F must be established. The assumed temperature lapse rate is 3.6 degrees F per thousand feet of altitude above sea level until a temperature of −69.7 degrees F is reached, above which altitude the temperature is considered constant at −69.7 degrees F. However, for winterization installations, the applicant may select a maximum ambient atmospheric temperature corresponding to sea level conditions of less than 100 degrees F.

(c) *Correction factor (except cylinder barrels).* Temperatures of engine fluids and powerplant components (except cylinder barrels) for which temperature limits are established, must be corrected by adding to them the difference between the maximum ambient atmospheric temperature for the relevant altitude for which approval has been requested and the temperature of the ambient air at the time of the first occurrence of the maximum fluid or component temperature recorded during the cooling test.

(d) *Correction factor for cylinder barrel temperatures.* Cylinder barrel temperatures must be corrected by adding to them 0.7 times the difference between the maximum ambient atmospheric temperature for the relevant altitude for which approval has been requested and the temperature of the ambient air at the time of the first occurrence of the maximum cylinder barrel temperature recorded during the cooling test.

[Doc. No. 4080, 29 FR 17955, Dec. 18, 1964, as amended by Amdt. 23–7, 34 FR 13094, Aug. 13, 1969; Amdt. 23–21, 43 FR 2319, Jan. 16, 1978; Amdt. 23–51, 61 FR 5137, Feb. 9, 1996]

§ 23.1045 Cooling test procedures for turbine engine powered airplanes.

(a) Compliance with § 23.1041 must be shown for all phases of operation. The airplane must be flown in the configurations, at the speeds, and following the procedures recommended in the

Airplane Flight Manual for the relevant stage of flight, that correspond to the applicable performance requirements that are critical to cooling.

(b) Temperatures must be stabilized under the conditions from which entry is made into each stage of flight being investigated, unless the entry condition normally is not one during which component and engine fluid temperatures would stabilize (in which case, operation through the full entry condition must be conducted before entry into the stage of flight being investigated in order to allow temperatures to reach their natural levels at the time of entry). The takeoff cooling test must be preceded by a period during which the powerplant component and engine fluid temperatures are stabilized with the engines at ground idle.

(c) Cooling tests for each stage of flight must be continued until—

(1) The component and engine fluid temperatures stabilize;

(2) The stage of flight is completed; or

(3) An operating limitation is reached.

[Amdt. 23–7, 34 FR 13094, Aug. 13, 1969, as amended by Amdt. 23–51, 61 FR 5137, Feb. 9, 1996]

§23.1047 Cooling test procedures for reciprocating engine powered airplanes.

Compliance with §23.1041 must be shown for the climb (or, for multiengine airplanes with negative one-engine-inoperative rates of climb, the descent) stage of flight. The airplane must be flown in the configurations, at the speeds and following the procedures recommended in the Airplane Flight Manual, that correspond to the applicable performance requirements that are critical to cooling.

[Amdt. 23–51, 61 FR 5137, Feb. 9, 1996]

LIQUID COOLING

§23.1061 Installation.

(a) *General.* Each liquid-cooled engine must have an independent cooling system (including coolant tank) installed so that—

(1) Each coolant tank is supported so that tank loads are distributed over a large part of the tank surface;

(2) There are pads or other isolation means between the tank and its supports to prevent chafing.

(3) Pads or any other isolation means that is used must be nonabsorbent or must be treated to prevent absorption of flammable fluids; and

(4) No air or vapor can be trapped in any part of the system, except the coolant tank expansion space, during filling or during operation.

(b) *Coolant tank.* The tank capacity must be at least one gallon, plus 10 percent of the cooling system capacity. In addition—

(1) Each coolant tank must be able to withstand the vibration, inertia, and fluid loads to which it may be subjected in operation;

(2) Each coolant tank must have an expansion space of at least 10 percent of the total cooling system capacity; and

(3) It must be impossible to fill the expansion space inadvertently with the airplane in the normal ground attitude.

(c) *Filler connection.* Each coolant tank filler connection must be marked as specified in §23.1557(c). In addition—

(1) Spilled coolant must be prevented from entering the coolant tank compartment or any part of the airplane other than the tank itself; and

(2) Each recessed coolant filler connection must have a drain that discharges clear of the entire airplane.

(d) *Lines and fittings.* Each coolant system line and fitting must meet the requirements of §23.993, except that the inside diameter of the engine coolant inlet and outlet lines may not be less than the diameter of the corresponding engine inlet and outlet connections.

(e) *Radiators.* Each coolant radiator must be able to withstand any vibration, inertia, and coolant pressure load to which it may normally be subjected. In addition—

(1) Each radiator must be supported to allow expansion due to operating temperatures and prevent the transmittal of harmful vibration to the radiator; and

(2) If flammable coolant is used, the air intake duct to the coolant radiator must be located so that (in case of fire) flames from the nacelle cannot strike the radiator.

271

(f) *Drains.* There must be an accessible drain that—

(1) Drains the entire cooling system (including the coolant tank, radiator, and the engine) when the airplane is in the normal ground altitude;

(2) Discharges clear of the entire airplane; and

(3) Has means to positively lock it closed.

[Doc. No. 4080, 29 FR 17955, Dec. 18, 1964, as amended by Amdt. 23-43, 58 FR 18973, Apr. 9, 1993]

§ 23.1063 Coolant tank tests.

Each coolant tank must be tested under § 23.965, except that—

(a) The test required by § 23.965(a)(1) must be replaced with a similar test using the sum of the pressure developed during the maximum ultimate acceleration with a full tank or a pressure of 3.5 pounds per square inch, whichever is greater, plus the maximum working pressure of the system; and

(b) For a tank with a nonmetallic liner the test fluid must be coolant rather than fuel as specified in § 23.965(d), and the slosh test on a specimen liner must be conducted with the coolant at operating temperature.

INDUCTION SYSTEM

§ 23.1091 Air induction system.

(a) The air induction system for each engine and auxiliary power unit and their accessories must supply the air required by that engine and auxiliary power unit and their accessories under the operating conditions for which certification is requested.

(b) Each reciprocating engine installation must have at least two separate air intake sources and must meet the following:

(1) Primary air intakes may open within the cowling if that part of the cowling is isolated from the engine accessory section by a fire-resistant diaphragm or if there are means to prevent the emergence of backfire flames.

(2) Each alternate air intake must be located in a sheltered position and may not open within the cowling if the emergence of backfire flames will result in a hazard.

(3) The supplying of air to the engine through the alternate air intake system may not result in a loss of excessive power in addition to the power loss due to the rise in air temperature.

(4) Each automatic alternate air door must have an override means accessible to the flight crew.

(5) Each automatic alternate air door must have a means to indicate to the flight crew when it is not closed.

(c) For turbine engine powered airplanes—

(1) There must be means to prevent hazardous quantities of fuel leakage or overflow from drains, vents, or other components of flammable fluid systems from entering the engine intake system; and

(2) The airplane must be designed to prevent water or slush on the runway, taxiway, or other airport operating surfaces from being directed into the engine or auxiliary power unit air intake ducts in hazardous quantities. The air intake ducts must be located or protected so as to minimize the hazard of ingestion of foreign matter during takeoff, landing, and taxiing.

[Doc. No. 4080, 29 FR 17955, Dec. 18, 1964, as amended by Amdt. 23-7, 34 FR 13095, Aug. 13, 1969; Amdt. 23-43, 58 FR 18973, Apr. 9, 1993; 58 FR 27060, May 6, 1993; Amdt. 23-51, 61 FR 5137, Feb. 9, 1996]

§ 23.1093 Induction system icing protection.

(a) *Reciprocating engines.* Each reciprocating engine air induction system must have means to prevent and eliminate icing. Unless this is done by other means, it must be shown that, in air free of visible moisture at a temperature of 30 °F.—

(1) Each airplane with sea level engines using conventional venturi carburetors has a preheater that can provide a heat rise of 90 °F. with the engines at 75 percent of maximum continuous power;

(2) Each airplane with altitude engines using conventional venturi carburetors has a preheater that can provide a heat rise of 120 °F. with the engines at 75 percent of maximum continuous power;

(3) Each airplane with altitude engines using fuel metering device tending to prevent icing has a preheater

that, with the engines at 60 percent of maximum continuous power, can provide a heat rise of—

(i) 100 °F.; or

(ii) 40 °F., if a fluid deicing system meeting the requirements of §§23.1095 through 23.1099 is installed;

(4) Each airplane with sea level engine(s) using fuel metering device tending to prevent icing has a sheltered alternate source of air with a preheat of not less than 60 °F with the engines at 75 percent of maximum continuous power;

(5) Each airplane with sea level or altitude engine(s) using fuel injection systems having metering components on which impact ice may accumulate has a preheater capable of providing a heat rise of 75 °F when the engine is operating at 75 percent of its maximum continuous power; and

(6) Each airplane with sea level or altitude engine(s) using fuel injection systems not having fuel metering components projecting into the airstream on which ice may form, and introducing fuel into the air induction system downstream of any components or other obstruction on which ice produced by fuel evaporation may form, has a sheltered alternate source of air with a preheat of not less than 60 °F with the engines at 75 percent of its maximum continuous power.

(b) *Turbine engines.* (1) Each turbine engine and its air inlet system must operate throughout the flight power range of the engine (including idling), without the accumulation of ice on engine or inlet system components that would adversely affect engine operation or cause a serious loss of power or thrust—

(i) Under the icing conditions specified in appendix C of part 25 of this chapter; and

(ii) In snow, both falling and blowing, within the limitations established for the airplane for such operation.

(2) Each turbine engine must idle for 30 minutes on the ground, with the air bleed available for engine icing protection at its critical condition, without adverse effect, in an atmosphere that is at a temperature between 15° and 30 °F (between −9° and −1 °C) and has a liquid water content not less than 0.3 grams per cubic meter in the form of

drops having a mean effective diameter not less than 20 microns, followed by momentary operation at takeoff power or thrust. During the 30 minutes of idle operation, the engine may be run up periodically to a moderate power or thrust setting in a manner acceptable to the Administrator.

(c) *Reciprocating engines with Superchargers.* For airplanes with reciprocating engines having superchargers to pressurize the air before it enters the fuel metering device, the heat rise in the air caused by that supercharging at any altitude may be utilized in determining compliance with paragraph (a) of this section if the heat rise utilized is that which will be available, automatically, for the applicable altitudes and operating condition because of supercharging.

[Amdt. 23-7, 34 FR 13095, Aug. 13, 1969, as amended by Amdt. 23–15, 39 FR 35460, Oct. 1, 1974; Amdt. 23–17, 41 FR 55465, Dec. 20, 1976; Amdt. 23–18, 42 FR 15041, Mar. 17, 1977; Amdt. 23–29, 49 FR 6847, Feb. 23, 1984; Amdt. 23–43, 58 FR 18973, Apr. 9, 1993; Amdt. 23–51, 61 FR 5137, Feb. 9, 1996]

§23.1095 Carburetor deicing fluid flow rate.

(a) If a carburetor deicing fluid system is used, it must be able to simultaneously supply each engine with a rate of fluid flow, expressed in pounds per hour, of not less than 2.5 times the square root of the maximum continuous power of the engine.

(b) The fluid must be introduced into the air induction system—

(1) Close to, and upstream of, the carburetor; and

(2) So that it is equally distributed over the entire cross section of the induction system air passages.

§23.1097 Carburetor deicing fluid system capacity.

(a) The capacity of each carburetor deicing fluid system—

(1) May not be less than the greater of—

(i) That required to provide fluid at the rate specified in §23.1095 for a time equal to three percent of the maximum endurance of the airplane; or

(ii) 20 minutes at that flow rate; and

(2) Need not exceed that required for two hours of operation.

(b) If the available preheat exceeds 50 °F. but is less than 100 °F., the capacity of the system may be decreased in proportion to the heat rise available in excess of 50 °F.

§ 23.1099 Carburetor deicing fluid system detail design.

Each carburetor deicing fluid system must meet the applicable requirements for the design of a fuel system, except as specified in §§ 23.1095 and 23.1097.

§ 23.1101 Induction air preheater design.

Each exhaust-heated, induction air preheater must be designed and constructed to—

(a) Ensure ventilation of the preheater when the induction air preheater is not being used during engine operation;

(b) Allow inspection of the exhaust manifold parts that it surrounds; and

(c) Allow inspection of critical parts of the preheater itself.

[Doc. No. 4080, 29 FR 17955, Dec. 18, 1964, as amended by Amdt. 23–43, 58 FR 18974, Apr. 9, 1993]

§ 23.1103 Induction system ducts.

(a) Each induction system duct must have a drain to prevent the accumulation of fuel or moisture in the normal ground and flight attitudes. No drain may discharge where it will cause a fire hazard.

(b) Each duct connected to components between which relative motion could exist must have means for flexibility.

(c) Each flexible induction system duct must be capable of withstanding the effects of temperature extremes, fuel, oil, water, and solvents to which it is expected to be exposed in service and maintenance without hazardous deterioration or delamination.

(d) For reciprocating engine installations, each induction system duct must be—

(1) Strong enough to prevent induction system failures resulting from normal backfire conditions; and

(2) Fire resistant in any compartment for which a fire extinguishing system is required.

(e) Each inlet system duct for an auxiliary power unit must be—

(1) Fireproof within the auxiliary power unit compartment;

(2) Fireproof for a sufficient distance upstream of the auxiliary power unit compartment to prevent hot gas reverse flow from burning through the duct and entering any other compartment of the airplane in which a hazard would be created by the entry of the hot gases;

(3) Constructed of materials suitable to the environmental conditions expected in service, except in those areas requiring fireproof or fire resistant materials; and

(4) Constructed of materials that will not absorb or trap hazardous quantities of flammable fluids that could be ignited by a surge or reverse-flow condition.

(f) Induction system ducts that supply air to a cabin pressurization system must be suitably constructed of material that will not produce hazardous quantities of toxic gases or isolated to prevent hazardous quantities of toxic gases from entering the cabin during a powerplant fire.

[Doc. No. 4080, 29 FR 17955, Dec. 18, 1964, as amended by Amdt. 23–7, 34 FR 13095, Aug. 13, 1969; Amdt. 23–43, 58 FR 18974, Apr. 9, 1993]

§ 23.1105 Induction system screens.

If induction system screens are used—

(a) Each screen must be upstream of the carburetor or fuel injection system.

(b) No screen may be in any part of the induction system that is the only passage through which air can reach the engine, unless—

(1) The available preheat is at least 100 °F.; and

(2) The screen can be deiced by heated air;

(c) No screen may be deiced by alcohol alone; and

(d) It must be impossible for fuel to strike any screen.

[Doc. No. 4080, 29 FR 17955, Dec. 18, 1964; 30 FR 258, Jan. 9, 1996, as amended by Amdt. 23–51, 61 FR 5137, Feb. 9, 1996]

§ 23.1107 Induction system filters.

If an air filter is used to protect the engine against foreign material particles in the induction air supply—

(a) Each air filter must be capable of withstanding the effects of temperature extremes, rain, fuel, oil, and solvents to which it is expected to be exposed in service and maintenance; and

(b) Each air filter shall have a design feature to prevent material separated from the filter media from interfering with proper fuel metering operation.

[Doc. No. 26344, 58 FR 18974, Apr. 9, 1993, as amended by Amdt. 23–51, 61 FR 5137, Feb. 9, 1996]

§23.1109 Turbocharger bleed air system.

The following applies to turbocharged bleed air systems used for cabin pressurization:

(a) The cabin air system may not be subject to hazardous contamination following any probable failure of the turbocharger or its lubrication system.

(b) The turbocharger supply air must be taken from a source where it cannot be contaminated by harmful or hazardous gases or vapors following any probable failure or malfunction of the engine exhaust, hydraulic, fuel, or oil system.

[Amdt. 23–42, 56 FR 354, Jan. 3, 1991]

§23.1111 Turbine engine bleed air system.

For turbine engine bleed air systems, the following apply:

(a) No hazard may result if duct rupture or failure occurs anywhere between the engine port and the airplane unit served by the bleed air.

(b) The effect on airplane and engine performance of using maximum bleed air must be established.

(c) Hazardous contamination of cabin air systems may not result from failures of the engine lubricating system.

[Amdt. 23–7, 34 FR 13095, Aug. 13, 1969, as amended by Amdt. 23–17, 41 FR 55465, Dec. 20, 1976]

EXHAUST SYSTEM

§23.1121 General.

For powerplant and auxiliary power unit installations, the following apply—

(a) Each exhaust system must ensure safe disposal of exhaust gases without fire hazard or carbon monoxide contamination in any personnel compartment.

(b) Each exhaust system part with a surface hot enough to ignite flammable fluids or vapors must be located or shielded so that leakage from any system carrying flammable fluids or vapors will not result in a fire caused by impingement of the fluids or vapors on any part of the exhaust system including shields for the exhaust system.

(c) Each exhaust system must be separated by fireproof shields from adjacent flammable parts of the airplane that are outside of the engine and auxiliary power unit compartments.

(d) No exhaust gases may discharge dangerously near any fuel or oil system drain.

(e) No exhaust gases may be discharged where they will cause a glare seriously affecting pilot vision at night.

(f) Each exhaust system component must be ventilated to prevent points of excessively high temperature.

(g) If significant traps exist, each turbine engine and auxiliary power unit exhaust system must have drains discharging clear of the airplane, in any normal ground and flight attitude, to prevent fuel accumulation after the failure of an attempted engine or auxiliary power unit start.

(h) Each exhaust heat exchanger must incorporate means to prevent blockage of the exhaust port after any internal heat exchanger failure.

(i) For the purpose of compliance with §23.603, the failure of any part of the exhaust system will be considered to adversely affect safety.

[Doc. No. 4080, 29 FR 17955, Dec. 18, 1964, as amended by Amdt. 23–7, 34 FR 13095, Aug. 13, 1969; Amdt. 23–18, 42 FR 15042, Mar. 17, 1977; Amdt. 23–43, 58 FR 18974, Apr. 9, 1993; Amdt. 23–51, 61 FR 5137, Feb. 9, 1996]

§23.1123 Exhaust system.

(a) Each exhaust system must be fireproof and corrosion-resistant, and must have means to prevent failure due to expansion by operating temperatures.

(b) Each exhaust system must be supported to withstand the vibration and inertia loads to which it may be subjected in operation.

(c) Parts of the system connected to components between which relative motion could exist must have means for flexibility.

[Doc. No. 4080, 29 FR 17955, Dec. 18, 1964, as amended by Amdt. 23–43, 58 FR 18974, Apr. 9, 1993]

§ 23.1125 Exhaust heat exchangers.

For reciprocating engine powered airplanes the following apply:

(a) Each exhaust heat exchanger must be constructed and installed to withstand the vibration, inertia, and other loads that it may be subjected to in normal operation. In addition—

(1) Each exchanger must be suitable for continued operation at high temperatures and resistant to corrosion from exhaust gases;

(2) There must be means for inspection of critical parts of each exchanger; and

(3) Each exchanger must have cooling provisions wherever it is subject to contact with exhaust gases.

(b) Each heat exchanger used for heating ventilating air must be constructed so that exhaust gases may not enter the ventilating air.

[Doc. No. 4080, 29 FR 17955, Dec. 18, 1964, as amended by Amdt. 23–17, 41 FR 55465, Dec. 20, 1976]

POWERPLANT CONTROLS AND ACCESSORIES

§ 23.1141 Powerplant controls: General.

(a) Powerplant controls must be located and arranged under § 23.777 and marked under § 23.1555(a).

(b) Each flexible control must be shown to be suitable for the particular application.

(c) Each control must be able to maintain any necessary position without—

(1) Constant attention by flight crew members; or

(2) Tendency to creep due to control loads or vibration.

(d) Each control must be able to withstand operating loads without failure or excessive deflection.

(e) For turbine engine powered airplanes, no single failure or malfunction, or probable combination thereof, in any powerplant control system may cause the failure of any powerplant function necessary for safety.

(f) The portion of each powerplant control located in the engine compartment that is required to be operated in the event of fire must be at least fire resistant.

(g) Powerplant valve controls located in the cockpit must have—

(1) For manual valves, positive stops or in the case of fuel valves suitable index provisions, in the open and closed position; and

(2) For power-assisted valves, a means to indicate to the flight crew when the valve—

(i) Is in the fully open or fully closed position; or

(ii) Is moving between the fully open and fully closed position.

[Doc. No. 4080, 29 FR 17955, Dec. 18, 1964, as amended by Amdt. 23–7, 34 FR 13095, Aug. 13, 1969; Amdt. 23–14, 38 FR 31823, Nov. 19, 1973; Amdt. 23–18, 42 FR 15042, Mar. 17, 1977; Amdt. 23–51, 61 FR 5137, Feb. 9, 1996]

§ 23.1142 Auxiliary power unit controls.

Means must be provided on the flight deck for the starting, stopping, monitoring, and emergency shutdown of each installed auxiliary power unit.

[Doc. No. 26344, 58 FR 18974, Apr. 9, 1993]

§ 23.1143 Engine controls.

(a) There must be a separate power or thrust control for each engine and a separate control for each supercharger that requires a control.

(b) Power, thrust, and supercharger controls must be arranged to allow—

(1) Separate control of each engine and each supercharger; and

(2) Simultaneous control of all engines and all superchargers.

(c) Each power, thrust, or supercharger control must give a positive and immediate responsive means of controlling its engine or supercharger.

(d) The power, thrust, or supercharger controls for each engine or supercharger must be independent of those for every other engine or supercharger.

(e) For each fluid injection (other than fuel) system and its controls not provided and approved as part of the engine, the applicant must show that the flow of the injection fluid is adequately controlled.

(f) If a power, thrust, or a fuel control (other than a mixture control) incorporates a fuel shutoff feature, the control must have a means to prevent the inadvertent movement of the control into the off position. The means must—

(1) Have a positive lock or stop at the idle position; and

(2) Require a separate and distinct operation to place the control in the shutoff position.

(g) For reciprocating single-engine airplanes, each power or thrust control must be designed so that if the control separates at the engine fuel metering device, the airplane is capable of continued safe flight and landing.

[Amdt. 23–7, 34 FR 13095, Aug. 13, 1969, as amended by Amdt. 23–17, 41 FR 55465, Dec. 20, 1976; Amdt. 23–29, 49 FR 6847, Feb. 23, 1984; Amdt. 23–43, 58 FR 18974, Apr. 9, 1993; Amdt. 23–51, 61 FR 5137, Feb. 9, 1996]

§23.1145 Ignition switches.

(a) Ignition switches must control and shut off each ignition circuit on each engine.

(b) There must be means to quickly shut off all ignition on multiengine airplanes by the grouping of switches or by a master ignition control.

(c) Each group of ignition switches, except ignition switches for turbine engines for which continuous ignition is not required, and each master ignition control must have a means to prevent its inadvertent operation.

[Doc. No. 4080, 29 FR 17955, Dec. 18, 1964; 30 FR 258, Jan. 9, 1965, as amended by Amdt. 23–18, 42 FR 15042, Mar. 17, 1977; Amdt. 23–43, 58 FR 18974, Apr. 9, 1993]

§23.1147 Mixture controls.

(a) If there are mixture controls, each engine must have a separate control, and each mixture control must have guards or must be shaped or arranged to prevent confusion by feel with other controls.

(1) The controls must be grouped and arranged to allow—

(i) Separate control of each engine; and

(ii) Simultaneous control of all engines.

(2) The controls must require a separate and distinct operation to move the control toward lean or shut-off position.

(b) For reciprocating single-engine airplanes, each manual engine mixture control must be designed so that, if the control separates at the engine fuel metering device, the airplane is capable of continued safe flight and landing.

[Doc. No. 4080, 29 FR 17955, Dec. 18, 1964, as amended by Amdt. 23–7, 34 FR 13096, Aug. 13, 1969; Amdt. 23–33, 51 FR 26657, July 24, 1986; Amdt. 23–43, 58 FR 18974, Apr. 9, 1993]

§23.1149 Propeller speed and pitch controls.

(a) If there are propeller speed or pitch controls, they must be grouped and arranged to allow—

(1) Separate control of each propeller; and

(2) Simultaneous control of all propellers.

(b) The controls must allow ready synchronization of all propellers on multiengine airplanes.

§23.1153 Propeller feathering controls.

If there are propeller feathering controls installed, it must be possible to feather each propeller separately. Each control must have a means to prevent inadvertent operation.

[Doc. No. 27804, 61 FR 5138, Feb. 9, 1996]

§23.1155 Turbine engine reverse thrust and propeller pitch settings below the flight regime.

For turbine engine installations, each control for reverse thrust and for propeller pitch settings below the flight regime must have means to prevent its inadvertent operation. The means must have a positive lock or stop at the flight idle position and must require a separate and distinct operation by the crew to displace the control from the flight regime (forward thrust regime for turbojet powered airplanes).

[Amdt. 23–7, 34 FR 13096, Aug. 13, 1969]

§23.1157 Carburetor air temperature controls.

There must be a separate carburetor air temperature control for each engine.

§ 23.1163 Powerplant accessories.

(a) Each engine mounted accessory must—

(1) Be approved for mounting on the engine involved and use the provisions on the engines for mounting; or

(2) Have torque limiting means on all accessory drives in order to prevent the torque limits established for those drives from being exceeded; and

(3) In addition to paragraphs (a)(1) or (a)(2) of this section, be sealed to prevent contamination of the engine oil system and the accessory system.

(b) Electrical equipment subject to arcing or sparking must be installed to minimize the probability of contact with any flammable fluids or vapors that might be present in a free state.

(c) Each generator rated at or more than 6 kilowatts must be designed and installed to minimize the probability of a fire hazard in the event it malfunctions.

(d) If the continued rotation of any accessory remotely driven by the engine is hazardous when malfunctioning occurs, a means to prevent rotation without interfering with the continued operation of the engine must be provided.

(e) Each accessory driven by a gearbox that is not approved as part of the powerplant driving the gearbox must—

(1) Have torque limiting means to prevent the torque limits established for the affected drive from being exceeded;

(2) Use the provisions on the gearbox for mounting; and

(3) Be sealed to prevent contamination of the gearbox oil system and the accessory system.

[Doc. No. 4080, 29 FR 17955, Dec. 18, 1964, as amended by Amdt. 23–14, 38 FR 31823, Nov. 19, 1973; Amdt. 23–29, 49 FR 6847, Feb. 23, 1984; Amdt. 23–34, 52 FR 1832, Jan. 15, 1987; Amdt. 23–42, 56 FR 354, Jan. 3, 1991]

§ 23.1165 Engine ignition systems.

(a) Each battery ignition system must be supplemented by a generator that is automatically available as an alternate source of electrical energy to allow continued engine operation if any battery becomes depleted.

(b) The capacity of batteries and generators must be large enough to meet the simultaneous demands of the engine ignition system and the greatest demands of any electrical system components that draw from the same source.

(c) The design of the engine ignition system must account for—

(1) The condition of an inoperative generator;

(2) The condition of a completely depleted battery with the generator running at its normal operating speed; and

(3) The condition of a completely depleted battery with the generator operating at idling speed, if there is only one battery.

(d) There must be means to warn appropriate crewmembers if malfunctioning of any part of the electrical system is causing the continuous discharge of any battery used for engine ignition.

(e) Each turbine engine ignition system must be independent of any electrical circuit that is not used for assisting, controlling, or analyzing the operation of that system.

(f) In addition, for commuter category airplanes, each turbopropeller ignition system must be an essential electrical load.

[Doc. No. 4080, 29 FR 17955, Dec. 18, 1964, as amended by Amdt. 23–17, 41 FR 55465 Dec. 20, 1976; Amdt. 23–34, 52 FR 1833, Jan. 15, 1987]

POWERPLANT FIRE PROTECTION

§ 23.1181 Designated fire zones; regions included.

Designated fire zones are—

(a) For reciprocating engines—

(1) The power section;

(2) The accessory section;

(3) Any complete powerplant compartment in which there is no isolation between the power section and the accessory section.

(b) For turbine engines—

(1) The compressor and accessory sections;

(2) The combustor, turbine and tailpipe sections that contain lines or components carrying flammable fluids or gases.

(3) Any complete powerplant compartment in which there is no isolation between compressor, accessory, combustor, turbine, and tailpipe sections.

(c) Any auxiliary power unit compartment; and

(d) Any fuel-burning heater, and other combustion equipment installation described in § 23.859.

[Doc. No. 26344, 58 FR 18975, Apr. 9, 1993, as amended by Amdt. 23–51, 61 FR 5138, Feb. 9, 1996]

§ 23.1182 Nacelle areas behind fire-walls.

Components, lines, and fittings, except those subject to the provisions of § 23.1351(e), located behind the engine-compartment firewall must be constructed of such materials and located at such distances from the firewall that they will not suffer damage sufficient to endanger the airplane if a portion of the engine side of the firewall is subjected to a flame temperature of not less than 2000 °F for 15 minutes.

[Amdt. 23–14, 38 FR 31816, Nov. 19, 1973]

§ 23.1183 Lines, fittings, and components.

(a) Except as provided in paragraph (b) of this section, each component, line, and fitting carrying flammable fluids, gas, or air in any area subject to engine fire conditions must be at least fire resistant, except that flammable fluid tanks and supports which are part of and attached to the engine must be fireproof or be enclosed by a fireproof shield unless damage by fire to any non-fireproof part will not cause leakage or spillage of flammable fluid. Components must be shielded or located so as to safeguard against the ignition of leaking flammable fluid. Flexible hose assemblies (hose and end fittings) must be shown to be suitable for the particular application. An integral oil sump of less than 25–quart capacity on a reciprocating engine need not be fireproof nor be enclosed by a fireproof shield.

(b) Paragraph (a) of this section does not apply to—

(1) Lines, fittings, and components which are already approved as part of a type certificated engine; and

(2) Vent and drain lines, and their fittings, whose failure will not result in, or add to, a fire hazard.

[Doc. No. 4080, 29 FR 17955, Dec. 18, 1964, as amended by Amdt. 23–5, 32 FR 6912, May 5, 1967; Amdt. 23–15, 39 FR 35460, Oct. 1, 1974; Amdt. 23–29, 49 FR 6847, Feb. 23, 1984; Amdt. 23–51, 61 FR 5138, Feb. 9, 1996]

§ 23.1189 Shutoff means.

(a) For each multiengine airplane the following apply:

(1) Each engine installation must have means to shut off or otherwise prevent hazardous quantities of fuel, oil, deicing fluid, and other flammable liquids from flowing into, within, or through any engine compartment, except in lines, fittings, and components forming an integral part of an engine.

(2) The closing of the fuel shutoff valve for any engine may not make any fuel unavailable to the remaining engines that would be available to those engines with that valve open.

(3) Operation of any shutoff means may not interfere with the later emergency operation of other equipment such as propeller feathering devices.

(4) Each shutoff must be outside of the engine compartment unless an equal degree of safety is provided with the shutoff inside the compartment.

(5) Not more than one quart of flammable fluid may escape into the engine compartment after engine shutoff. For those installations where the flammable fluid that escapes after shutdown cannot be limited to one quart, it must be demonstrated that this greater amount can be safely contained or drained overboard.

(6) There must be means to guard against inadvertent operation of each shutoff means, and to make it possible for the crew to reopen the shutoff means in flight after it has been closed.

(b) Turbine engine installations need not have an engine oil system shutoff if—

(1) The oil tank is integral with, or mounted on, the engine; and

(2) All oil system components external to the engine are fireproof or located in areas not subject to engine fire conditions.

(c) Power operated valves must have means to indicate to the flight crew when the valve has reached the selected position and must be designed so that the valve will not move from the selected position under vibration conditions likely to exist at the valve location.

[Doc. No. 4080, 29 FR 17955, Dec. 18, 1964, as amended by Amdt. 23–7, 34 FR 13096, Aug. 13, 1969; Amdt. 23–14, 38 FR 31823, Nov. 19, 1973; Amdt. 23–29, 49 FR 6847, Feb. 23, 1984; Amdt. 23–43, 58 FR 18975, Apr. 9, 1993]

§ 23.1191 Firewalls.

(a) Each engine, auxiliary power unit, fuel burning heater, and other combustion equipment, must be isolated from the rest of the airplane by firewalls, shrouds, or equivalent means.

(b) Each firewall or shroud must be constructed so that no hazardous quantity of liquid, gas, or flame can pass from the compartment created by the firewall or shroud to other parts of the airplane.

(c) Each opening in the firewall or shroud must be sealed with close fitting, fireproof grommets, bushings, or firewall fittings.

(d) [Reserved]

(e) Each firewall and shroud must be fireproof and protected against corrosion.

(f) Compliance with the criteria for fireproof materials or components must be shown as follows:

(1) The flame to which the materials or components are subjected must be 2,000 ± 150 °F.

(2) Sheet materials approximately 10 inches square must be subjected to the flame from a suitable burner.

(3) The flame must be large enough to maintain the required test temperature over an area approximately five inches square.

(g) Firewall materials and fittings must resist flame penetration for at least 15 minutes.

(h) The following materials may be used in firewalls or shrouds without being tested as required by this section:

(1) Stainless steel sheet, 0.015 inch thick.

(2) Mild steel sheet (coated with aluminum or otherwise protected against corrosion) 0.018 inch thick.

(3) Terne plate, 0.018 inch thick.

(4) Monel metal, 0.018 inch thick.

(5) Steel or copper base alloy firewall fittings.

(6) Titanium sheet, 0.016 inch thick.

[Doc. No. 4080, 29 FR 17955, Dec. 18, 1964, as amended by Amdt. 23–43, 58 FR 18975, Apr. 9, 1993; 58 FR 27060, May 6, 1993; Amdt. 23–51, 61 FR 5138, Feb. 9, 1996]

§ 23.1192 Engine accessory compartment diaphragm.

For aircooled radial engines, the engine power section and all portions of the exhaust sytem must be isolated from the engine accessory compartment by a diaphragm that meets the firewall requirements of § 23.1191.

[Amdt. 23–14, 38 FR 31823, Nov. 19, 1973]

§ 23.1193 Cowling and nacelle.

(a) Each cowling must be constructed and supported so that it can resist any vibration, inertia, and air loads to which it may be subjected in operation.

(b) There must be means for rapid and complete drainage of each part of the cowling in the normal ground and flight attitudes. Drain operation may be shown by test, analysis, or both, to ensure that under normal aerodynamic pressure distribution expected in service each drain will operate as designed. No drain may discharge where it will cause a fire hazard.

(c) Cowling must be at least fire resistant.

(d) Each part behind an opening in the engine compartment cowling must be at least fire resistant for a distance of at least 24 inches aft of the opening.

(e) Each part of the cowling subjected to high temperatures due to its nearness to exhaust sytem ports or exhaust gas impingement, must be fire proof.

(f) Each nacelle of a multiengine airplane with supercharged engines must be designed and constructed so that with the landing gear retracted, a fire in the engine compartment will not burn through a cowling or nacelle and enter a nacelle area other than the engine compartment.

(g) In addition, for commuter category airplanes, the airplane must be designed so that no fire originating in any engine compartment can enter, either through openings or by burn-through, any other region where it would create additional hazards.

[Doc. No. 4080, 29 FR 17955, Dec. 18, 1964; 30 FR 258, Jan. 9, 1965, as amended by Amdt. 23–18, 42 FR 15042, Mar. 17, 1977; Amdt. 23–34, 52 FR 1833, Jan. 15, 1987; 58 FR 18975, Apr. 9, 1993]

§23.1195 Fire extinguishing systems.

(a) For commuter category airplanes, fire extinguishing systems must be installed and compliance shown with the following:

(1) Except for combustor, turbine, and tailpipe sections of turbine-engine installations that contain lines or components carrying flammable fluids or gases for which a fire originating in these sections is shown to be controllable, a fire extinguisher system must serve each engine compartment;

(2) The fire extinguishing system, the quantity of the extinguishing agent, the rate of discharge, and the discharge distribution must be adequate to extinguish fires. An individual "one shot" system may be used.

(3) The fire extinguishing system for a nacelle must be able to simultaneously protect each compartment of the nacelle for which protection is provided.

(b) If an auxiliary power unit is installed in any airplane certificated to this part, that auxiliary power unit compartment must be served by a fire extinguishing system meeting the requirements of paragraph (a)(2) of this section.

[Amdt. 23–34, 52 FR 1833, Jan. 15, 1987, as amended by Amdt. 23–43, 58 FR 18975, Apr. 9, 1993]

§23.1197 Fire extinguishing agents.

For commuter category airplanes, the following applies:

(a) Fire extinguishing agents must—

(1) Be capable of extinguishing flames emanating from any burning of fluids or other combustible materials in the area protected by the fire extinguishing system; and

(2) Have thermal stability over the temperature range likely to be experienced in the compartment in which they are stored.

(b) If any toxic extinguishing agent is used, provisions must be made to prevent harmful concentrations of fluid or fluid vapors (from leakage during normal operation of the airplane or as a result of discharging the fire extinguisher on the ground or in flight) from entering any personnel compartment, even though a defect may exist in the extinguishing system. This must be shown by test except for built-in carbon dioxide fuselage compartment fire extinguishing systems for which—

(1) Five pounds or less of carbon dioxide will be discharged, under established fire control procedures, into any fuselage compartment; or

(2) Protective breathing equipment is available for each flight crewmember on flight deck duty.

[Amdt. 23–34, 52 FR 1833, Jan. 15, 1987]

§23.1199 Extinguishing agent containers.

For commuter category airplanes, the following applies:

(a) Each extinguishing agent container must have a pressure relief to prevent bursting of the container by excessive internal pressures.

(b) The discharge end of each discharge line from a pressure relief connection must be located so that discharge of the fire extinguishing agent would not damage the airplane. The line must also be located or protected to prevent clogging caused by ice or other foreign matter.

(c) A means must be provided for each fire extinguishing agent container to indicate that the container has discharged or that the charging pressure is below the established minimum necessary for proper functioning.

(d) The temperature of each container must be maintained, under intended operating conditions, to prevent the pressure in the container from—

(1) Falling below that necessary to provide an adequate rate of discharge; or

(2) Rising high enough to cause premature discharge.

(e) If a pyrotechnic capsule is used to discharge the extinguishing agent, each container must be installed so that temperature conditions will not cause hazardous deterioration of the pyrotechnic capsule.

[Amdt. 23–34, 52 FR 1833, Jan. 15, 1987; 52 FR 34745, Sept. 14, 1987]

§ 23.1201 Fire extinguishing systems materials.

For commuter category airplanes, the following apply:

(a) No material in any fire extinguishing system may react chemically with any extinguishing agent so as to create a hazard.

(b) Each system component in an engine compartment must be fireproof.

[Amdt. 23–34, 52 FR 1833, Jan. 15, 1987; 52 FR 7262, Mar. 9, 1987]

§ 23.1203 Fire detector system.

(a) There must be means that ensure the prompt detection of a fire in—

(1) An engine compartment of—

(i) Multiengine turbine powered airplanes;

(ii) Multiengine reciprocating engine powered airplanes incorporating turbochargers;

(iii) Airplanes with engine(s) located where they are not readily visible from the cockpit; and

(iv) All commuter category airplanes.

(2) The auxiliary power unit compartment of any airplane incorporating an auxiliary power unit.

(b) Each fire detector must be constructed and installed to withstand the vibration, inertia, and other loads to which it may be subjected in operation.

(c) No fire detector may be affected by any oil, water, other fluids, or fumes that might be present.

(d) There must be means to allow the crew to check, in flight, the functioning of each fire detector electric circuit.

(e) Wiring and other components of each fire detector system in a designated fire zone must be at least fire resistant.

[Amdt. 23–18, 42 FR 15042, Mar. 17, 1977, as amended by Amdt. 23–34, 52 FR 1833, Jan. 15, 1987; Amdt. 23–43, 58 FR 18975, Apr. 9, 1993; Amdt. 23–51, 61 FR 5138, Feb. 9, 1996]

Subpart F—Equipment

GENERAL

§ 23.1301 Function and installation.

Each item of installed equipment must—

(a) Be of a kind and design appropriate to its intended function.

(b) Be labeled as to its identification, function, or operating limitations, or any applicable combination of these factors;

(c) Be installed according to limitations specified for that equipment; and

(d) Function properly when installed.

[Amdt. 23–20, 42 FR 36968, July 18, 1977]

§ 23.1303 Flight and navigation instruments.

The following are the minimum required flight and navigation instruments:

(a) An airspeed indicator.

(b) An altimeter.

(c) A direction indicator (non-stabilized magnetic compass).

(d) For reciprocating engine-powered airplanes of more than 6,000 pounds maximum weight and turbine engine powered airplanes, a free air temperature indicator or an air-temperature indicator which provides indications that are convertible to free-air.

(e) A speed warning device for—

(1) Turbine engine powered airplanes; and

(2) Other airplanes for which V_{MO}/M_{MO} and V_D/M_D are established under §§ 23.335(b)(4) and 23.1505(c) if V_{MO}/M_{MO} is greater than 0.8 V_D/M_D.

The speed warning device must give effective aural warning (differing distinctively from aural warnings used for other purposes) to the pilots whenever the speed exceeds V_{MO} plus 6 knots or $M_{MO}+0.01$. The upper limit of the production tolerance for the warning device may not exceed the prescribed warning speed. The lower limit of the warning device must be set to minimize nuisance warning;

(f) When an attitude display is installed, the instrument design must not provide any means, accessible to the flightcrew, of adjusting the relative positions of the attitude reference symbol and the horizon line beyond that necessary for parallax correction.

(g) In addition, for commuter category airplanes:

(1) If airspeed limitations vary with altitude, the airspeed indicator must have a maximum allowable airspeed indicator showing the variation of V_{MO} with altitude.

(2) The altimeter must be a sensitive type.

(3) Having a passenger seating configuration of 10 or more, excluding the pilot's seats and that are approved for IFR operations, a third attitude instrument must be provided that:

(i) Is powered from a source independent of the electrical generating system;

(ii) Continues reliable operation for a minimum of 30 minutes after total failure of the electrical generating system;

(iii) Operates independently of any other attitude indicating system;

(iv) Is operative without selection after total failure of the electrical generating system;

(v) Is located on the instrument panel in a position acceptable to the Administrator that will make it plainly visible to and usable by any pilot at the pilot's station; and

(vi) Is appropriately lighted during all phases of operation.

[Doc. No. 4080, 29 FR 17955, Dec. 18, 1964, as amended by Amdt. 23–17, 41 FR 55465, Dec. 20, 1976; Amdt. 23–43, 58 FR 18975, Apr. 9, 1993; Amdt. 23–49, 61 FR 5168, Feb. 9, 1996]

§ 23.1305 Powerplant instruments.

The following are required powerplant instruments:

(a) *For all airplanes.* (1) A fuel quantity indicator for each fuel tank, installed in accordance with § 23.1337(b).

(2) An oil pressure indicator for each engine.

(3) An oil temperature indicator for each engine.

(4) An oil quantity measuring device for each oil tank which meets the requirements of § 23.1337(d).

(5) A fire warning means for those airplanes required to comply with § 23.1203.

(b) *For reciprocating engine-powered airplanes.* In addition to the powerplant instruments required by paragraph (a) of this section, the following powerplant instruments are required:

(1) An induction system air temperature indicator for each engine equipped with a preheater and having induction air temperature limitations that can be exceeded with preheat.

(2) A tachometer indicator for each engine.

(3) A cylinder head temperature indicator for—

(i) Each air-cooled engine with cowl flaps;

(ii) [Reserved]

(iii) Each commuter category airplane.

(4) For each pump-fed engine, a means:

(i) That continuously indicates, to the pilot, the fuel pressure or fuel flow; or

(ii) That continuously monitors the fuel system and warns the pilot of any fuel flow trend that could lead to engine failure.

(5) A manifold pressure indicator for each altitude engine and for each engine with a controllable propeller.

(6) For each turbocharger installation:

(i) If limitations are established for either carburetor (or manifold) air inlet temperature or exhaust gas or turbocharger turbine inlet temperature, indicators must be furnished for each temperature for which the limitation is established unless it is shown that the limitation will not be exceeded in all intended operations.

(ii) If its oil system is separate from the engine oil system, oil pressure and oil temperature indicators must be provided.

(7) A coolant temperature indicator for each liquid-cooled engine.

(c) *For turbine engine-powered airplanes.* In addition to the powerplant instruments required by paragraph (a) of this section, the following powerplant instruments are required:

(1) A gas temperature indicator for each engine.

(2) A fuel flowmeter indicator for each engine.

(3) A fuel low pressure warning means for each engine.

(4) A fuel low level warning means for any fuel tank that should not be depleted of fuel in normal operations.

(5) A tachometer indicator (to indicate the speed of the rotors with established limiting speeds) for each engine.

(6) An oil low pressure warning means for each engine.

(7) An indicating means to indicate the functioning of the powerplant ice protection system for each engine.

(8) For each engine, an indicating means for the fuel strainer or filter required by § 23.997 to indicate the occurrence of contamination of the strainer or filter before it reaches the capacity established in accordance with § 23.997(d).

(9) For each engine, a warning means for the oil strainer or filter required by § 23.1019, if it has no bypass, to warn the pilot of the occurrence of contamination of the strainer or filter screen before it reaches the capacity established in accordance with § 23.1019(a)(5).

(10) An indicating means to indicate the functioning of any heater used to prevent ice clogging of fuel system components.

(d) *For turbojet/turbofan engine-powered airplanes.* In addition to the powerplant instruments required by paragraphs (a) and (c) of this section, the following powerplant instruments are required:

(1) For each engine, an indicator to indicate thrust or to indicate a parameter that can be related to thrust, including a free air temperature indicator if needed for this purpose.

(2) For each engine, a position indicating means to indicate to the flight crew when the thrust reverser, if installed, is in the reverse thrust position.

(e) *For turbopropeller-powered airplanes.* In addition to the powerplant instruments required by paragraphs (a) and (c) of this section, the following powerplant instruments are required:

(1) A torque indicator for each engine.

(2) A position indicating means to indicate to the flight crew when the propeller blade angle is below the flight low pitch position, for each propeller, unless it can be shown that such occurrence is highly improbable.

[Doc. No. 26344, 58 FR 18975, Apr. 9, 1993; 58 FR 27060, May 6, 1993; Amdt. 23–51, 61 FR 5138, Feb. 9, 1996; Amdt. 23–52, 61 FR 13644, Mar. 27, 1996]

§ 23.1307 Miscellaneous equipment.

The equipment necessary for an airplane to operate at the maximum operating altitude and in the kinds of operation and meteorological conditions for which certification is requested and is approved in accordance with § 23.1559 must be included in the type design.

[Doc. No. 4080, 29 FR 17955, Dec. 18, 1964; 30 FR 258, Jan. 9, 1965, as amended by Amdt. 23–23, 43 FR 50593, Oct. 30, 1978; Amdt. 23–43, 58 FR 18976, Apr. 9, 1993; Amdt. 23–49, 61 FR 5168, Feb. 9, 1996]

§ 23.1309 Equipment, systems, and installations.

(a) Each item of equipment, each system, and each installation:

(1) When performing its intended function, may not adversely affect the response, operation, or accuracy of any—

(i) Equipment essential to safe operation; or

(ii) Other equipment unless there is a means to inform the pilot of the effect.

(2) In a single-engine airplane, must be designed to minimize hazards to the airplane in the event of a probable malfunction or failure.

(3) In a multiengine airplane, must be designed to prevent hazards to the airplane in the event of a probable malfunction or failure.

(4) In a commuter category airplane, must be designed to safeguard against hazards to the airplane in the event of their malfunction or failure.

(b) The design of each item of equipment, each system, and each installation must be examined separately and in relationship to other airplane systems and installations to determine if the airplane is dependent upon its function for continued safe flight and landing and, for airplanes not limited to VFR conditions, if failure of a system would significantly reduce the capability of the airplane or the ability of the crew to cope with adverse operating conditions. Each item of equipment, each system, and each installation identified by this examination as one upon which the airplane is dependent for proper functioning to ensure continued safe flight and landing, or whose failure would significantly reduce the capability of the airplane or the ability of the crew to cope with adverse operating conditions, must be designed to comply with the following additional requirements:

(1) It must perform its intended function under any foreseeable operating condition.

(2) When systems and associated components are considered separately and in relation to other systems—

(i) The occurrence of any failure condition that would prevent the continued safe flight and landing of the airplane must be extremely improbable; and

(ii) The occurrence of any other failure condition that would significantly reduce the capability of the airplane or the ability of the crew to cope with adverse operating conditions must be improbable.

(3) Warning information must be provided to alert the crew to unsafe system operating conditions and to enable them to take appropriate corrective action. Systems, controls, and associated monitoring and warning means must be designed to minimize crew errors that could create additional hazards.

(4) Compliance with the requirements of paragraph (b)(2) of this section may be shown by analysis and, where necessary, by appropriate ground, flight, or simulator tests. The analysis must consider—

(i) Possible modes of failure, including malfunctions and damage from external sources;

(ii) The probability of multiple failures, and the probability of undetected faults.;

(iii) The resulting effects on the airplane and occupants, considering the stage of flight and operating conditions; and

(iv) The crew warning cues, corrective action required, and the crew's capability of determining faults.

(c) Each item of equipment, each system, and each installation whose functioning is required by this chapter and that requires a power supply is an "essential load" on the power supply. The power sources and the system must be able to supply the following power loads in probable operating combinations and for probable durations:

(1) Loads connected to the power distribution system with the system functioning normally.

(2) Essential loads after failure of—

(i) Any one engine on two-engine airplanes; or

(ii) Any two engines on an airplane with three or more engines; or

(iii) Any power converter or energy storage device.

(3) Essential loads for which an alternate source of power is required, as applicable, by the operating rules of this chapter, after any failure or malfunction in any one power supply system, distribution system, or other utilization system.

(d) In determining compliance with paragraph (c)(2) of this section, the power loads may be assumed to be reduced under a monitoring procedure consistent with safety in the kinds of operations authorized. Loads not required in controlled flight need not be considered for the two-engine-inoperative condition on airplanes with three or more engines.

(e) In showing compliance with this section with regard to the electrical power system and to equipment design and installation, critical environmental and atmospheric conditions, including radio frequency energy and the effects (both direct and indirect) of lightning strikes, must be considered. For electrical generation, distribution, and utilization equipment required by or used in complying with this chapter, the ability to provide continuous, safe service under forseeable environmental conditions may be shown by environmental tests, design analysis, or reference to previous comparable service experience on other airplanes.

(f) As used in this section, "system" refers to all pneumatic systems, fluid systems, electrical systems, mechanical systems, and powerplant systems included in the airplane design, except for the following:

(1) Powerplant systems provided as part of the certificated engine.

(2) The flight structure (such a wing, empennage, control surfaces and their systems, the fuselage, engine mounting, and landing gear and their related

primary attachments) whose requirements are specific in subparts C and D
of this part.

[Amdt. 23–41, 55 FR 43309, Oct. 26, 1990; 55 FR
47028, Nov. 8, 1990, as amended by Amdt. 23–
49, 61 FR 5168, Feb. 9, 1996]

INSTRUMENTS: INSTALLATION

§ 23.1311 Electronic display instrument systems.

(a) Electronic display indicators, including those with features that make
isolation and independence between
powerplant instrument systems impractical, must:

(1) Meet the arrangement and visibility requirements of § 23.1321.

(2) Be easily legible under all lighting
conditions encountered in the cockpit,
including direct sunlight, considering
the expected electronic display brightness level at the end of an electronic
display indictor's useful life. Specific
limitations on display system useful
life must be contained in the Instructions for Continued Airworthiness required by § 23.1529.

(3) Not inhibit the primary display of
attitude, airspeed, altitude, or powerplant parameters needed by any pilot
to set power within established limitations, in any normal mode of operation.

(4) Not inhibit the primary display of
engine parameters needed by any pilot
to properly set or monitor powerplant
limitations during the engine starting
mode of operation.

(5) Have an independent magnetic direction indicator and either an independent secondary mechanical altimeter, airspeed indicator, and attitude
instrument or individual electronic
display indicators for the altitude, airspeed, and attitude that are independent from the airplane's primary
electrical power system. These secondary instruments may be installed in
panel positions that are displaced from
the primary positions specified by
§ 23.1321(d), but must be located where
they meet the pilot's visibility requirements of § 23.1321(a).

(6) Incorporate sensory cues for the
pilot that are equivalent to those in
the instrument being replaced by the
electronic display indicators.

(7) Incorporate visual displays of instrument markings, required by
§§ 23.1541 through 23.1553, or visual displays that alert the pilot to abnormal
operational values or approaches to established limitation values, for each
parameter required to be displayed by
this part.

(b) The electronic display indicators,
including their systems and installations, and considering other airplane
systems, must be designed so that one
display of information essential for
continued safe flight and landing will
remain available to the crew, without
need for immediate action by any pilot
for continued safe operation, after any
single failure or probable combination
of failures.

(c) As used in this section, "instrument" includes devices that are physically contained in one unit, and devices that are composed of two or more
physically separate units or components connected together (such as a remote indicating gyroscopic direction
indicator that includes a magnetic
sensing element, a gyroscopic unit, an
amplifier, and an indicator connected
together). As used in this section,
"primary" display refers to the display
of a parameter that is located in the
instrument panel such that the pilot
looks at it first when wanting to view
that parameter.

[Doc. No. 27806, 61 FR 5168, Feb. 9, 1996]

§ 23.1321 Arrangement and visibility.

(a) Each flight, navigation, and powerplant instrument for use by any required pilot during takeoff, initial
climb, final approach, and landing
must be located so that any pilot seated at the controls can monitor the airplane's flight path and these instruments with minimum head and eye
movement. The powerplant instruments for these flight conditions are
those needed to set power within powerplant limitations.

(b) For each multiengine airplane,
identical powerplant instruments must
be located so as to prevent confusion as
to which engine each instrument relates.

(c) Instrument panel vibration may
not damage, or impair the accuracy of,
any instrument.

(d) For each airplane, the flight instruments required by §23.1303, and, as applicable, by the operating rules of this chapter, must be grouped on the instrument panel and centered as nearly as practicable about the vertical plane of each required pilot's forward vision. In addition:

(1) The instrument that most effectively indicates the attitude must be on the panel in the top center position;

(2) The instrument that most effectively indicates airspeed must be adjacent to and directly to the left of the instrument in the top center position;

(3) The instrument that most effectively indicates altitude must be adjacent to and directly to the right of the instrument in the top center position;

(4) The instrument that most effectively indicates direction of flight, other than the magnetic direction indicator required by §23.1303(c), must be adjacent to and directly below the instrument in the top center position; and

(5) Electronic display indicators may be used for compliance with paragraphs (d)(1) through (d)(4) of this section when such displays comply with requirements in §23.1311.

(e) If a visual indicator is provided to indicate malfunction of an instrument, it must be effective under all probable cockpit lighting conditions.

[Doc. No. 4080, 29 FR 17955, Dec. 18, 1964, as amended by Amdt. 23–14, 38 FR 31824, Nov. 19, 1973; Amdt. 23–20, 42 FR 36968, July 18, 1977; Amdt. 23–41, 55 FR 43310, Oct. 26, 1990; 55 FR 46888, Nov. 7, 1990; Amdt. 23–49, 61 FR 5168, Feb. 9, 1996]

§23.1322 Warning, caution, and advisory lights.

If warning, caution, or advisory lights are installed in the cockpit, they must, unless otherwise approved by the Administrator, be—

(a) Red, for warning lights (lights indicating a hazard which may require immediate corrective action);

(b) Amber, for caution lights (lights indicating the possible need for future corrective action);

(c) Green, for safe operation lights; and

(d) Any other color, including white, for lights not described in paragraphs (a) through (c) of this section, provided the color differs sufficiently from the colors prescribed in paragraphs (a) through (c) of this section to avoid possible confusion.

(e) Effective under all probable cockpit lighting conditions.

[Amdt. 23–17, 41 FR 55465, Dec. 20, 1976, as amended by Amdt. 23–43, 58 FR 18976, Apr. 9, 1993]

§23.1323 Airspeed indicating system.

(a) Each airspeed indicating instrument must be calibrated to indicate true airspeed (at sea level with a standard atmosphere) with a minimum practicable instrument calibration error when the corresponding pitot and static pressures are applied.

(b) Each airspeed system must be calibrated in flight to determine the system error. The system error, including position error, but excluding the airspeed indicator instrument calibration error, may not exceed three percent of the calibrated airspeed or five knots, whichever is greater, throughout the following speed ranges:

(1) $1.3 V_{S1}$ to V_{MO}/M_{MO} or V_{NE}, whichever is appropriate with flaps retracted.

(2) $1.3 V_{S}l$ to V_{FE} with flaps extended.

(c) The design and installation of each airspeed indicating system must provide positive drainage of moisture from the pitot static plumbing.

(d) If certification for instrument flight rules or flight in icing conditions is requested, each airspeed system must have a heated pitot tube or an equivalent means of preventing malfunction due to icing.

(e) In addition, for commuter category airplanes, the airspeed indicating system must be calibrated to determine the system error during the accelerate-takeoff ground run. The ground run calibration must be obtained between 0.8 of the minimum value of V_l, and 1.2 times the maximum value of V_l considering the approved ranges of altitude and weight. The ground run calibration must be determined assuming an engine failure at the minimum value of V_l.

(f) For commuter category airplanes, where duplicate airspeed indicators are required, their respective pitot tubes must be far enough apart to avoid damage to both tubes in a collision with a bird.

[Amdt. 23–20, 42 FR 36968, July 18, 1977, as amended by Amdt. 23–34, 52 FR 1834, Jan. 15, 1987; 52 FR 34745, Sept. 14, 1987; Amdt. 23–42, 56 FR 354, Jan. 3, 1991; Amdt. 23–49, 61 FR 5168, Feb. 9, 1996]

§ 23.1325 Static pressure system.

(a) Each instrument provided with static pressure case connections must be so vented that the influence of airplane speed, the opening and closing of windows, airflow variations, moisture, or other foreign matter will least affect the accuracy of the instruments except as noted in paragraph (b)(3) of this section.

(b) If a static pressure system is necessary for the functioning of instruments, systems, or devices, it must comply with the provisions of paragraphs (b)(1) through (3) of this section.

(1) The design and installation of a static pressure system must be such that—

(i) Positive drainage of moisture is provided;

(ii) Chafing of the tubing, and excessive distortion or restriction at bends in the tubing, is avoided; and

(iii) The materials used are durable, suitable for the purpose intended, and protected against corrosion.

(2) A proof test must be conducted to demonstrate the integrity of the static pressure system in the following manner:

(i) *Unpressurized airplanes.* Evacuate the static pressure system to a pressure differential of approximately 1 inch of mercury or to a reading on the altimeter, 1,000 feet above the aircraft elevation at the time of the test. Without additional pumping for a period of 1 minute, the loss of indicated altitude must not exceed 100 feet on the altimeter.

(ii) *Pressurized airplanes.* Evacuate the static pressure system until a pressure differential equivalent to the maximum cabin pressure differential for which the airplane is type certificated is achieved. Without additional pumping for a period of 1 minute, the loss of indicated altitude must not exceed 2 percent of the equivalent altitude of the maximum cabin differential pressure or 100 feet, whichever is greater.

(3) If a static pressure system is provided for any instrument, device, or system required by the operating rules of this chapter, each static pressure port must be designed or located in such a manner that the correlation between air pressure in the static pressure system and true ambient atmospheric static pressure is not altered when the airplane encounters icing conditions. An antiicing means or an alternate source of static pressure may be used in showing compliance with this requirement. If the reading of the altimeter, when on the alternate static pressure system differs from the reading of the altimeter when on the primary static system by more than 50 feet, a correction card must be provided for the alternate static system.

(c) Except as provided in paragraph (d) of this section, if the static pressure system incorporates both a primary and an alternate static pressure source, the means for selecting one or the other source must be designed so that—

(1) When either source is selected, the other is blocked off; and

(2) Both sources cannot be blocked off simultaneously.

(d) For unpressurized airplanes, paragraph (c)(1) of this section does not apply if it can be demonstrated that the static pressure system calibration, when either static pressure source is selected, is not changed by the other static pressure source being open or blocked.

(e) Each static pressure system must be calibrated in flight to determine the system error. The system error, in indicated pressure altitude, at sea-level, with a standard atmosphere, excluding instrument calibration error, may not exceed ±30 feet per 100 knot speed for the appropriate configuration in the speed range between 1.3 V_{so} with flaps extended, and 1.8 V_{s1} with flaps retracted. However, the error need not be less than 30 feet.

(f) [Reserved]

(g) For airplanes prohibited from flight in instrument meteorological or icing conditions, in accordance with

§23.1559(b) of this part, paragraph (b)(3) of this section does not apply.

[Amdt. 23–1, 30 FR 8261, June 29, 1965, as amended by Amdt. 23–6, 32 FR 7586, May 24, 1967; 32 FR 13505, Sept. 27, 1967; 32 FR 13714, Sept. 30, 1967; Amdt. 23–20, 42 FR 36968, July 18, 1977; Amdt. 23–34, 52 FR 1834, Jan. 15, 1987; Amdt. 23–42, 56 FR 354, Jan. 3, 1991; Amdt. 23–49, 61 FR 5169, Feb. 9, 1996; Amdt. 23–50, 61 FR 5192, Feb. 9, 1996]

§23.1326 Pitot heat indication systems.

If a flight instrument pitot heating system is installed to meet the requirements specified in §23.1323(d), an indication system must be provided to indicate to the flight crew when that pitot heating system is not operating. The indication system must comply with the following requirements:

(a) The indication provided must incorporate an amber light that is in clear view of a flightcrew member.

(b) The indication provided must be designed to alert the flight crew if either of the following conditions exist:

(1) The pitot heating system is switched "off."

(2) The pitot heating system is switched "on" and any pitot tube heating element is inoperative.

[Doc. No. 27806, 61 FR 5169, Feb. 9, 1996]

§23.1327 Magnetic direction indicator.

(a) Except as provided in paragraph (b) of this section—

(1) Each magnetic direction indicator must be installed so that its accuracy is not excessively affected by the airplane's vibration or magnetic fields; and

(2) The compensated installation may not have a deviation in level flight, greater than ten degrees on any heading.

(b) A magnetic nonstabilized direction indicator may deviate more than ten degrees due to the operation of electrically powered systems such as electrically heated windshields if either a magnetic stabilized direction indicator, which does not have a deviation in level flight greater than ten degrees on any heading, or a gyroscopic direction indicator, is installed. Deviations of a magnetic nonstabilized direction indicator of more than 10 de-

grees must be placarded in accordance with §23.1547(e).

[Amdt. 23–20, 42 FR 36969, July 18, 1977]

§23.1329 Automatic pilot system.

If an automatic pilot system is installed, it must meet the following:

(a) Each system must be designed so that the automatic pilot can—

(1) Be quickly and positively disengaged by the pilots to prevent it from interfering with their control of the airplane; or

(2) Be sufficiently overpowered by one pilot to let him control the airplane.

(b) If the provisions of paragraph (a)(1) of this section are applied, the quick release (emergency) control must be located on the control wheel (both control wheels if the airplane can be operated from either pilot seat) on the side opposite the throttles, or on the stick control, (both stick controls, if the airplane can be operated from either pilot seat) such that it can be operated without moving the hand from its normal position on the control.

(c) Unless there is automatic synchronization, each system must have a means to readily indicate to the pilot the alignment of the actuating device in relation to the control system it operates.

(d) Each manually operated control for the system operation must be readily accessible to the pilot. Each control must operate in the same plane and sense of motion as specified in §23.779 for cockpit controls. The direction of motion must be plainly indicated on or near each control.

(e) Each system must be designed and adjusted so that, within the range of adjustment available to the pilot, it cannot produce hazardous loads on the airplane or create hazardous deviations in the flight path, under any flight condition appropriate to its use, either during normal operation or in the event of a malfunction, assuming that corrective action begins within a reasonable period of time.

(f) Each system must be designed so that a single malfunction will not produce a hardover signal in more than one control axis. If the automatic pilot integrates signals from auxiliary controls or furnishes signals for operation of other equipment, positive interlocks and sequencing of engagement to prevent improper operation are required.

(g) There must be protection against adverse interaction of integrated components, resulting from a malfunction.

(h) If the automatic pilot system can be coupled to airborne navigation equipment, means must be provided to indicate to the flight crew the current mode of operation. Selector switch position is not acceptable as a means of indication.

[Doc. No. 4080, 29 FR 17955, Dec. 18, 1964; 30 FR 258, Jan. 9, 1965, as amended by Amdt. 23–23, 43 FR 50593, Oct. 30, 1978; Amdt. 23–43, 58 FR 18976, Apr. 9, 1993; Amdt. 23–49, 61 FR 5169, Feb. 9, 1996]

§ 23.1331 Instruments using a power source.

For each instrument that uses a power source, the following apply:

(a) Each instrument must have an integral visual power annunciator or separate power indicator to indicate when power is not adequate to sustain proper instrument performance. If a separate indicator is used, it must be located so that the pilot using the instruments can monitor the indicator with minimum head and eye movement. The power must be sensed at or near the point where it enters the instrument. For electric and vacuum/pressure instruments, the power is considered to be adequate when the voltage or the vacuum/pressure, respectively, is within approved limits.

(b) The installation and power supply systems must be designed so that—

(1) The failure of one instrument will not interfere with the proper supply of energy to the remaining instrument; and

(2) The failure of the energy supply from one source will not interfere with the proper supply of energy from any other source.

(c) There must be at least two independent sources of power (not driven by the same engine on multiengine airplanes), and a manual or an automatic means to select each power source.

[Doc. No. 26344, 58 FR 18976, Apr. 9, 1993]

§ 23.1335 Flight director systems.

If a flight director system is installed, means must be provided to in-

dicate to the flight crew its current mode of operation. Selector switch position is not acceptable as a means of indication.

[Amdt. 23–20, 42 FR 36969, July 18, 1977]

§ 23.1337 Powerplant instruments installation.

(a) *Instruments and instrument lines.* (1) Each powerplant and auxiliary power unit instrument line must meet the requirements of § 23.993.

(2) Each line carrying flammable fluids under pressure must—

(i) Have restricting orifices or other safety devices at the source of pressure to prevent the escape of excessive fluid if the line fails; and

(ii) Be installed and located so that the escape of fluids would not create a hazard.

(3) Each powerplant and auxiliary power unit instrument that utilizes flammable fluids must be installed and located so that the escape of fluid would not create a hazard.

(b) *Fuel quantity indication.* There must be a means to indicate to the flightcrew members the quantity of usable fuel in each tank during flight. An indicator calibrated in appropriate units and clearly marked to indicate those units must be used. In addition:

(1) Each fuel quantity indicator must be calibrated to read "zero" during level flight when the quantity of fuel remaining in the tank is equal to the unusable fuel supply determined under § 23.959(a);

(2) Each exposed sight gauge used as a fuel quantity indicator must be protected against damage;

(3) Each sight gauge that forms a trap in which water can collect and freeze must have means to allow drainage on the ground;

(4) There must be a means to indicate the amount of usable fuel in each tank when the airplane is on the ground (such as by a stick gauge);

(5) Tanks with interconnected outlets and airspaces may be considered as one tank and need not have separate indicators; and

(6) No fuel quantity indicator is required for an auxiliary tank that is used only to transfer fuel to other tanks if the relative size of the tank,

the rate of fuel transfer, and operating instructions are adequate to—

(i) Guard against overflow; and

(ii) Give the flight crewmembers prompt warning if transfer is not proceeding as planned.

(c) *Fuel flowmeter system.* If a fuel flowmeter system is installed, each metering component must have a means to by-pass the fuel supply if malfunctioning of that component severely restricts fuel flow.

(d) *Oil quantity indicator.* There must be a means to indicate the quantity of oil in each tank—

(1) On the ground (such as by a stick gauge); and

(2) In flight, to the flight crew members, if there is an oil transfer system or a reserve oil supply system.

[Doc. No. 4080, 29 FR 17955, Dec. 18, 1964, as amended by Amdt. 23–7, 34 FR 13096, Aug. 13, 1969; Amdt. 23–18, 42 FR 15042, Mar. 17, 1977; Amdt. 23–43, 58 FR 18976, Apr. 9, 1993; Amdt. 23–51, 61 FR 5138, Feb. 9, 1996; Amdt. 23–49, 61 FR 5169, Feb. 9, 1996]

ELECTRICAL SYSTEMS AND EQUIPMENT

§23.1351 General.

(a) *Electrical system capacity.* Each electrical system must be adequate for the intended use. In addition—

(1) Electric power sources, their transmission cables, and their associated control and protective devices, must be able to furnish the required power at the proper voltage to each load circuit essential for safe operation; and

(2) Compliance with paragraph (a)(1) of this section must be shown as follows—

(i) For normal, utility, and acrobatic category airplanes, by an electrical load analysis or by electrical measurements that account for the electrical loads applied to the electrical system in probable combinations and for probable durations; and

(ii) For commuter category airplanes, by an electrical load analysis that accounts for the electrical loads applied to the electrical system in probable combinations and for probable durations.

(b) *Function.* For each electrical system, the following apply:

(1) Each system, when installed, must be—

(i) Free from hazards in itself, in its method of operation, and in its effects on other parts of the airplane;

(ii) Protected from fuel, oil, water, other detrimental substances, and mechanical damage; and

(iii) So designed that the risk of electrical shock to crew, passengers, and ground personnel is reduced to a minimum.

(2) Electric power sources must function properly when connected in combination or independently.

(3) No failure or malfunction of any electric power source may impair the ability of any remaining source to supply load circuits essential for safe operation.

(4) In addition, for commuter category airplanes, the following apply:

(i) Each system must be designed so that essential load circuits can be supplied in the event of reasonably probable faults or open circuits including faults in heavy current carrying cables;

(ii) A means must be accessible in flight to the flight crewmembers for the individual and collective disconnection of the electrical power sources from the system;

(iii) The system must be designed so that voltage and frequency, if applicable, at the terminals of all essential load equipment can be maintained within the limits for which the equipment is designed during any probable operating conditions;

(iv) If two independent sources of electrical power for particular equipment or systems are required, their electrical energy supply must be ensured by means such as duplicate electrical equipment, throwover switching, or multichannel or loop circuits separately routed; and

(v) For the purpose of complying with paragraph (b)(5) of this section, the distribution system includes the distribution busses, their associated feeders, and each control and protective device.

(c) *Generating system.* There must be at least one generator/alternator if the electrical system supplies power to load circuits essential for safe operation. In addition—

(1) Each generator/alternator must be able to deliver its continuous rated

power, or such power as is limited by its regulation system.

(2) Generator/alternator voltage control equipment must be able to dependably regulate the generator/alternator output within rated limits.

(3) Automatic means must be provided to prevent damage to any generator/alternator and adverse effects on the airplane electrical system due to reverse current. A means must also be provided to disconnect each generator/alternator from the battery and other generators/alternators.

(4) There must be a means to give immediate warning to the flight crew of a failure of any generator/alternator.

(5) Each generator/alternator must have an overvoltage control designed and installed to prevent damage to the electrical system, or to equipment supplied by the electrical system that could result if that generator/alternator were to develop an overvoltage condition.

(d) *Instruments.* A means must exist to indicate to appropriate flight crewmembers the electric power system quantities essential for safe operation.

(1) For normal, utility, and acrobatic category airplanes with direct current systems, an ammeter that can be switched into each generator feeder may be used and, if only one generator exists, the ammeter may be in the battery feeder.

(2) For commuter category airplanes, the essential electric power system quantities include the voltage and current supplied by each generator.

(e) *Fire resistance.* Electrical equipment must be so designed and installed that in the event of a fire in the engine compartment, during which the surface of the firewall adjacent to the fire is heated to 2,000 °F for 5 minutes or to a lesser temperature substantiated by the applicant, the equipment essential to continued safe operation and located behind the firewall will function satisfactorily and will not create an additional fire hazard.

(f) *External power.* If provisions are made for connecting external power to the airplane, and that external power can be electrically connected to equipment other than that used for engine starting, means must be provided to ensure that no external power supply

having a reverse polarity, or a reverse phase sequence, can supply power to the airplane's electrical system. The external power connection must be located so that its use will not result in a hazard to the airplane or ground personnel.

(g) It must be shown by analysis, tests, or both, that the airplane can be operated safely in VFR conditions, for a period of not less than five minutes, with the normal electrical power (electrical power sources excluding the battery and any other standby electrical sources) inoperative, with critical type fuel (from the standpoint of flameout and restart capability), and with the airplane initially at the maximum certificated altitude. Parts of the electrical system may remain on if—

(1) A single malfunction, including a wire bundle or junction box fire, cannot result in loss of the part turned off and the part turned on; and

(2) The parts turned on are electrically and mechanically isolated from the parts turned off.

[Doc. No. 4080, 29 FR 17955, Dec. 18, 1964, as amended by Amdt. 23–7, 34 FR 13096, Aug. 13, 1969; Amdt. 23–14, 38 FR 31824, Nov. 19, 1973; Amdt. 23–17, 41 FR 55465, Dec. 20, 1976; Amdt. 23–20, 42 FR 36969, July 18, 1977; Amdt. 23–34, 52 FR 1834, Jan. 15, 1987; 52 FR 34745, Sept. 14, 1987; Amdt. 23–43, 58 FR 18976, Apr. 9, 1993; Amdt. 23–49, 61 FR 5169, Feb. 9, 1996]

§ 23.1353 Storage battery design and installation.

(a) Each storage battery must be designed and installed as prescribed in this section.

(b) Safe cell temperatures and pressures must be maintained during any probable charging and discharging condition. No uncontrolled increase in cell temperature may result when the battery is recharged (after previous complete discharge)—

(1) At maximum regulated voltage or power;

(2) During a flight of maximum duration; and

(3) Under the most adverse cooling condition likely to occur in service.

(c) Compliance with paragraph (b) of this section must be shown by tests unless experience with similar batteries and installations has shown that maintaining safe cell temperatures and pressures presents no problem.

(d) No explosive or toxic gases emitted by any battery in normal operation, or as the result of any probable malfunction in the charging system or battery installation, may accumulate in hazardous quantities within the airplane.

(e) No corrosive fluids or gases that may escape from the battery may damage surrounding structures or adjacent essential equipment.

(f) Each nickel cadmium battery installation capable of being used to start an engine or auxiliary power unit must have provisions to prevent any hazardous effect on structure or essential systems that may be caused by the maximum amount of heat the battery can generate during a short circuit of the battery or of its individual cells.

(g) Nickel cadmium battery installations capable of being used to start an engine or auxiliary power unit must have—

(1) A system to control the charging rate of the battery automatically so as to prevent battery overheating;

(2) A battery temperature sensing and over-temperature warning system with a means for disconnecting the battery from its charging source in the event of an over-temperature condition; or

(3) A battery failure sensing and warning system with a means for disconnecting the battery from its charging source in the event of battery failure.

(h) In the event of a complete loss of the primary electrical power generating system, the battery must be capable of providing at least 30 minutes of electrical power to those loads that are essential to continued safe flight and landing. The 30 minute time period includes the time needed for the pilots to recognize the loss of generated power and take appropriate load shedding action.

[Doc. No. 4080, 29 FR 17955, Dec. 18, 1964; 30 FR 258, Jan. 9, 1965, as amended by Amdt. 23–20, 42 FR 36969, July 18, 1977; Amdt. 23–21, 43 FR 2319, Jan. 16, 1978; Amdt. 23–49, 61 FR 5169, Feb. 9, 1996]

§23.1357 Circuit protective devices.

(a) Protective devices, such as fuses or circuit breakers, must be installed in all electrical circuits other than—

(1) Main circuits of starter motors used during starting only; and

(2) Circuits in which no hazard is presented by their omission.

(b) A protective device for a circuit essential to flight safety may not be used to protect any other circuit.

(c) Each resettable circuit protective device ("trip free" device in which the tripping mechanism cannot be overridden by the operating control) must be designed so that—

(1) A manual operation is required to restore service after tripping; and

(2) If an overload or circuit fault exists, the device will open the circuit regardless of the position of the operating control.

(d) If the ability to reset a circuit breaker or replace a fuse is essential to safety in flight, that circuit breaker or fuse must be so located and identified that it can be readily reset or replaced in flight.

(e) For fuses identified as replaceable in flight—

(1) There must be one spare of each rating or 50 percent spare fuses of each rating, whichever is greater; and

(2) The spare fuse(s) must be readily accessible to any required pilot.

[Doc. No. 4080, 29 FR 17955, Dec. 18, 1964; 30 FR 258, Jan. 9, 1965, as amended by Amdt. 23–20, 42 FR 36969, July 18, 1977]; Amdt. 23–43, 58 FR 18976, Apr. 9, 1993

§23.1359 Electrical system fire protection.

(a) Each component of the electrical system must meet the applicable fire protection requirements of §§23.863 and 23.1182.

(b) Electrical cables, terminals, and equipment in designated fire zones that are used during emergency procedures must be fire-resistant.

(c) Insulation on electrical wire and electrical cable must be self-extinguishing when tested at an angle of 60 degrees in accordance with the applicable portions of appendix F of this part, or other approved equivalent methods. The average burn length must not exceed 3 inches (76 mm) and the average flame time after removal of the flame source must not exceed 30 seconds. Drippings from the test specimen must not continue to flame for more than an average of 3 seconds after falling.

[Doc. No. 27806, 61 FR 5169, Feb. 9, 1996]

§ 23.1361 Master switch arrangement.

(a) There must be a master switch arrangement to allow ready disconnection of each electric power source from power distribution systems, except as provided in paragraph (b) of this section. The point of disconnection must be adjacent to the sources controlled by the switch arrangement. If separate switches are incorporated into the master switch arrangement, a means must be provided for the switch arrangement to be operated by one hand with a single movement.

(b) Load circuits may be connected so that they remain energized when the master switch is open, if the circuits are isolated, or physically shielded, to prevent their igniting flammable fluids or vapors that might be liberated by the leakage or rupture of any flammable fluid system; and

(1) The circuits are required for continued operation of the engine; or

(2) The circuits are protected by circuit protective devices with a rating of five amperes or less adjacent to the electric power source.

(3) In addition, two or more circuits installed in accordance with the requirements of paragraph (b)(2) of this section must not be used to supply a load of more than five amperes.

(c) The master switch or its controls must be so installed that the switch is easily discernible and accessible to a crewmember.

[Doc. No. 4080, 29 FR 17955, Dec. 18, 1964; 30 FR 258, Jan. 9, 1965, as amended by Amdt. 23–20, 42 FR 36969, July 18, 1977; Amdt. 23–43, 58 FR 18977, Apr. 9, 1993; Amdt. 23–49, 61 FR 5169, Feb. 9, 1996]

§ 23.1365 Electric cables and equipment.

(a) Each electric connecting cable must be of adequate capacity.

(b) Any equipment that is associated with any electrical cable installation and that would overheat in the event of circuit overload or fault must be flame resistant. That equipment and the electrical cables must not emit dangerous quantities of toxic fumes.

(c) Main power cables (including generator cables) in the fuselage must be designed to allow a reasonable degree of deformation and stretching without failure and must—

(1) Be separated from flammable fluid lines; or

(2) Be shrouded by means of electrically insulated flexible conduit, or equivalent, which is in addition to the normal cable insulation.

(d) Means of identification must be provided for electrical cables, terminals, and connectors.

(e) Electrical cables must be installed such that the risk of mechanical damage and/or damage cased by fluids vapors, or sources of heat, is minimized.

(f) Where a cable cannot be protected by a circuit protection device or other overload protection, it must not cause a fire hazard under fault conditions.

[Doc. No. 4080, 29 FR 17955, Dec. 18, 1964, as amended by Amdt. 23–14, 38 FR 31824, Nov. 19, 1973; Amdt. 23–43, 58 FR 18977, Apr. 9, 1993; Amdt. 23–49, 61 FR 5169, Feb. 9, 1996]

§ 23.1367 Switches.

Each switch must be—

(a) Able to carry its rated current;

(b) Constructed with enough distance or insulating material between current carrying parts and the housing so that vibration in flight will not cause shorting;

(c) Accessible to appropriate flight crewmembers; and

(d) Labeled as to operation and the circuit controlled.

LIGHTS

§ 23.1381 Instrument lights.

The instrument lights must—

(a) Make each instrument and control easily readable and discernible;

(b) Be installed so that their direct rays, and rays reflected from the windshield or other surface, are shielded from the pilot's eyes; and

(c) Have enough distance or insulating material between current carrying parts and the housing so that vibration in flight will not cause shorting.

A cabin dome light is not an instrument light.

§ 23.1383 Taxi and landing lights.

Each taxi and landing light must be designed and installed so that:

(a) No dangerous glare is visible to the pilots.

(b) The pilot is not seriously affected by halation.

(c) It provides enough light for night operations.

(d) It does not cause a fire hazard in any configuration.

[Doc. No. 27806, 61 FR 5169, Feb. 9, 1996]

§ 23.1385 Position light system installation.

(a) *General.* Each part of each position light system must meet the applicable requirements of this section and each system as a whole must meet the requirements of §§ 23.1387 through 23.1397.

(b) *Left and right position lights.* Left and right position lights must consist of a red and a green light spaced laterally as far apart as practicable and installed on the airplane such that, with the airplane in the normal flying position, the red light is on the left side and the green light is on the right side.

(c) *Rear position light.* The rear position light must be a white light mounted as far aft as practicable on the tail or on each wing tip.

(d) *Light covers and color filters.* Each light cover or color filter must be at least flame resistant and may not change color or shape or lose any appreciable light transmission during normal use.

[Doc. No. 4080, 29 FR 17955, Dec. 18, 1964, as amended by Amdt. 23–17, 41 FR 55465, Dec. 20, 1976; Amdt. 23–43, 58 FR 18977, Apr. 9, 1993]

§ 23.1387 Position light system dihedral angles.

(a) Except as provided in paragraph (e) of this section, each position light must, as installed, show unbroken light within the dihedral angles described in this section.

(b) Dihedral angle L (left) is formed by two intersecting vertical planes, the first parallel to the longitudinal axis of the airplane, and the other at 110 degrees to the left of the first, as viewed when looking forward along the longitudinal axis.

(c) Dihedral angle R (right) is formed by two intersecting vertical planes, the first parallel to the longitudinal axis of the airplane, and the other at 110 degrees to the right of the first, as viewed when looking forward along the longitudinal axis.

(d) Dihedral angle A (aft) is formed by two intersecting vertical planes making angles of 70 degrees to the right and to the left, respectively, to a vertical plane passing through the longitudinal axis, as viewed when looking aft along the longitudinal axis.

(e) If the rear position light, when mounted as far aft as practicable in accordance with § 23.1385(c), cannot show unbroken light within dihedral angle A (as defined in paragraph (d) of this section), a solid angle or angles of obstructed visibility totaling not more than 0.04 steradians is allowable within that dihedral angle, if such solid angle is within a cone whose apex is at the rear position light and whose elements make an angle of 30° with a vertical line passing through the rear position light.

[Doc. No. 4080, 29 FR 17955, Dec. 18, 1964; 30 FR 258, Jan. 9, 1965, as amended by Amdt. 23–12, 36 FR 21278, Nov. 5, 1971; Amdt. 23–43, 58 FR 18977, Apr. 9, 1993]

§ 23.1389 Position light distribution and intensities.

(a) *General.* The intensities prescribed in this section must be provided by new equipment with each light cover and color filter in place. Intensities must be determined with the light source operating at a steady value equal to the average luminous output of the source at the normal operating voltage of the airplane. The light distribution and intensity of each position light must meet the requirements of paragraph (b) of this section.

(b) *Position lights.* The light distribution and intensities of position lights must be expressed in terms of minimum intensities in the horizontal plane, minimum intensities in any vertical plane, and maximum intensities in overlapping beams, within dihedral angles L, R, and A, and must meet the following requirements:

(1) *Intensities in the horizontal plane.* Each intensity in the horizontal plane (the plane containing the longitudinal

295

axis of the airplane and perpendicular to the plane of symmetry of the airplane) must equal or exceed the values in § 23.1391.

(2) *Intensities in any vertical plane.* Each intensity in any vertical plane (the plane perpendicular to the horizontal plane) must equal or exceed the appropriate value in § 23.1393, where *I* is the minimum intensity prescribed in § 23.1391 for the corresponding angles in the horizontal plane.

(3) *Intensities in overlaps between adjacent signals.* No intensity in any overlap between adjacent signals may exceed the values in § 23.1395, except that higher intensities in overlaps may be used with main beam intensities substantially greater than the minima specified in §§ 23.1391 and 23.1393, if the overlap intensities in relation to the main beam intensities do not adversely affect signal clarity. When the peak intensity of the left and right position lights is more than 100 candles, the maximum overlap intensities between them may exceed the values in § 23.1395 if the overlap intensity in Area A is not more than 10 percent of peak position light intensity and the overlap intensity in Area B is not more than 2.5 percent of peak position light intensity.

(c) *Rear position light installation.* A single rear position light may be installed in a position displaced laterally from the plane of symmetry of an airplane if—

(1) The axis of the maximum cone of illumination is parallel to the flight path in level flight; and

(2) There is no obstruction aft of the light and between planes 70 degrees to the right and left of the axis of maximum illumination.

[Doc. No. 4080, 29 FR 17955, Dec. 18, 1964, as amended by Amdt. 23–43, 58 FR 18977, Apr. 9, 1993]

§ 23.1391 Minimum intensities in the horizontal plane of position lights.

Each position light intensity must equal or exceed the applicable values in the following table:

Dihedral angle (light included)	Angle from right or left of longitudinal axis, measured from dead ahead	Intensity (candles)
L and R (red and green)	0° to 10°	40
	10° to 20°	30
	20° to 110°	5
A (rear white)	110° to 180°	20

[Doc. No. 4080, 29 FR 17955, Dec. 18, 1964, as amended by Amdt. 23–43, 58 FR 18977, Apr. 9, 1993]

§ 23.1393 Minimum intensities in any vertical plane of position lights.

Each position light intensity must equal or exceed the applicable values in the following table:

Angle above or below the horizontal plane	Intensity, *I*
0°	1.00
0° to 5°	0.90
5° to 10°	0.80
10° to 15°	0.70
15° to 20°	0.50
20° to 30°	0.30
30° to 40°	0.10
40° to 90°	0.05

[Doc. No. 4080, 29 FR 17955, Dec. 18, 1964, as amended by Amdt. 23–43, 58 FR 18977, Apr. 9, 1993]

§ 23.1395 Maximum intensities in overlapping beams of position lights.

No position light intensity may exceed the applicable values in the following equal or exceed the applicable values in § 23.1389(b)(3):

Overlaps	Maximum intensity	
	Area A (candles)	Area B (candles)
Green in dihedral angle L	10	1
Red in dihedral angle R	10	1
Green in dihedral angle A	5	1
Red in dihedral angle A	5	1
Rear white in dihedral angle L	5	1
Rear white in dihedral angle R	5	1

Where—

(a) Area A includes all directions in the adjacent dihedral angle that pass through the light source and intersect the common boundary plane at more than 10 degrees but less than 20 degrees; and

(b) Area B includes all directions in the adjacent dihedral angle that pass through the light source and intersect the common boundary plane at more than 20 degrees.

[Doc. No. 4080, 29 FR 17955, Dec. 18, 1964, as amended by Amdt. 23–43, 58 FR 18977, Apr. 9, 1993]

§23.1397 Color specifications.

Each position light color must have the applicable International Commission on Illumination chromaticity coordinates as follows:

(a) *Aviation red—*

y is not greater than 0.335; and
z is not greater than 0.002.

(b) *Aviation green—*

x is not greater than $0.440 - 0.320y$;
x is not greater than $y - 0.170$; and
y is not less than $0.390 - 0.170x$.

(c) *Aviation white—*

x is not less than 0.300 and not greater than 0.540;
y is not less than $x - 0.040$ or $y_0 - 0.010$, whichever is the smaller; and
y is not greater than $x + 0.020$ nor $0.636 - 0.400x$;
Where y_0 is the y coordinate of the Planckian radiator for the value of x considered.

[Doc. No. 4080, 29 FR 17955, Dec. 18, 1964, amended by Amdt. 23–11, 36 FR 12971, July 10, 1971]

§23.1399 Riding light.

(a) Each riding (anchor) light required for a seaplane or amphibian, must be installed so that it can—

(1) Show a white light for at least two miles at night under clear atmospheric conditions; and

(2) Show the maximum unbroken light practicable when the airplane is moored or drifting on the water.

(b) Externally hung lights may be used.

§23.1401 Anticollision light system.

(a) *General.* The airplane must have an anticollision light system that:

(1) Consists of one or more approved anticollision lights located so that their light will not impair the flight crewmembers' vision or detract from the conspicuity of the position lights; and

(2) Meets the requirements of paragraphs (b) through (f) of this section.

(b) *Field of coverage.* The system must consist of enough lights to illuminate the vital areas around the airplane, considering the physical configuration and flight characteristics of the airplane. The field of coverage must extend in each direction within at least 75 degrees above and 75 degrees below the horizontal plane of the airplane, except that there may be solid angles of obstructed visibility totaling not more than 0.5 steradians.

(c) *Flashing characteristics.* The arrangement of the system, that is, the number of light sources, beam width, speed of rotation, and other characteristics, must give an effective flash frequency of not less than 40, nor more than 100, cycles per minute. The effective flash frequency is the frequency at which the airplane's complete anticollision light system is observed from a distance, and applies to each sector of light including any overlaps that exist when the system consists of more than one light source. In overlaps, flash frequencies may exceed 100, but not 180, cycles per minute.

(d) *Color.* Each anticollision light must be either aviation red or aviation white and must meet the applicable requirements of §23.1397.

(e) *Light intensity.* The minimum light intensities in any vertical plane, measured with the red filter (if used) and expressed in terms of "effective" intensities, must meet the requirements of paragraph (f) of this section. The following relation must be assumed:

$$I_e = \frac{\int_{t_1}^{t_2} I(t)dt}{0.2 + \left(t_2 - t_1\right)}$$

where:

I_e=effective intensity (candles).
$I(t)$=instantaneous intensity as a function of time.
$t_2 - t_1$=flash time interval (seconds).

Normally, the maximum value of effective intensity is obtained when t_2 and t_1 are chosen so that the effective intensity is equal to the instantaneous intensity at t_2 and t_1.

(f) *Minimum effective intensities for anticollision lights.* Each anticollision light effective intensity must equal or exceed the applicable values in the following table.

Angle above or below the horizontal plane	Effective intensity (candles)
0° to 5°	400
5° to 10°	240
10° to 20°	80
20° to 30°	40
30° to 75°	20

[Doc. No. 4080, 29 FR 17955, Dec. 18, 1964, as amended by Amdt. 23–11, 36 FR 12972, July 10, 1971; Amdt. 23–20, 42 FR 36969, July 18, 1977; Amdt. 23–49, 61 FR 5169, Feb. 9, 1996]

SAFETY EQUIPMENT

§ 23.1411 General.

(a) Required safety equipment to be used by the flight crew in an emergency, such as automatic liferaft releases, must be readily accessible.

(b) Stowage provisions for required safety equipment must be furnished and must—

(1) Be arranged so that the equipment is directly accessible and its location is obvious; and

(2) Protect the safety equipment from damage caused by being subjected to the inertia loads resulting from the ultimate static load factors specified in § 23.561(b)(3) of this part.

[Amdt. 23–17, 41 FR 55465, Dec. 20, 1976, as amended by Amdt. 23–36, 53 FR 30815, Aug. 15, 1988]

§ 23.1415 Ditching equipment.

(a) Emergency flotation and signaling equipment required by any operating rule in this chapter must be installed so that it is readily available to the crew and passengers.

(b) Each raft and each life preserver must be approved.

(c) Each raft released automatically or by the pilot must be attached to the airplane by a line to keep it alongside the airplane. This line must be weak enough to break before submerging the empty raft to which it is attached.

(d) Each signaling device required by any operating rule in this chapter, must be accessible, function satisfactorily, and must be free of any hazard in its operation.

§ 23.1416 Pneumatic de-icer boot system.

If certification with ice protection provisions is desired and a pneumatic de-icer boot system is installed—

(a) The system must meet the requirements specified in § 23.1419.

(b) The system and its components must be designed to perform their intended function under any normal system operating temperature or pressure, and

(c) Means to indicate to the flight crew that the pneumatic de-icer boot system is receiving adequate pressure and is functioning normally must be provided.

[Amdt. 23–23, 43 FR 50593, Oct. 30, 1978]

§ 23.1419 Ice protection.

If certification with ice protection provisions is desired, compliance with the requirements of this section and other applicable sections of this part must be shown:

(a) An analysis must be performed to establish, on the basis of the airplane's operational needs, the adequacy of the ice protection system for the various components of the airplane. In addition, tests of the ice protection system must be conducted to demonstrate that the airplane is capable of operating safely in continuous maximum and intermittent maximum icing conditions, as described in appendix C of part 25 of this chapter. As used in this section, "Capable of operating safely," means that airplane performance, controllability, maneuverability, and stability must not be less than that required in part 23, subpart B.

(b) Except as provided by paragraph (c) of this section, in addition to the analysis and physical evaluation prescribed in paragraph (a) of this section, the effectiveness of the ice protection system and its components must be shown by flight tests of the airplane or its components in measured natural atmospheric icing conditions and by one or more of the following tests, as found necessary to determine the adequacy of the ice protection system—

(1) Laboratory dry air or simulated icing tests, or a combination of both, of

the components or models of the components.

(2) Flight dry air tests of the ice protection system as a whole, or its individual components.

(3) Flight test of the airplane or its components in measured simulated icing conditions.

(c) If certification with ice protection has been accomplished on prior type certificated airplanes whose designs include components that are thermodynamically and aerodynamically equivalent to those used on a new airplane design, certification of these equivalent components may be accomplished by reference to previously accomplished tests, required in §23.1419 (a) and (b), provided that the applicant accounts for any differences in installation of these components.

(d) A means must be identified or provided for determining the formation of ice on the critical parts of the airplane. Adequate lighting must be provided for the use of this means during night operation. Also, when monitoring of the external surfaces of the airplane by the flight crew is required for operation of the ice protection equipment, external lighting must be provided that is adequate to enable the monitoring to be done at night. Any illumination that is used must be of a type that will not cause glare or reflection that would handicap crewmembers in the performance of their duties. The Airplane Flight Manual or other approved manual material must describe the means of determining ice formation and must contain information for the safe operation of the airplane in icing conditions.

[Doc. No. 26344, 58 FR 18977, Apr. 9, 1993]

MISCELLANEOUS EQUIPMENT

§23.1431 Electronic equipment.

(a) In showing compliance with §23.1309(b)(1) and (2) with respect to radio and electronic equipment and their installations, critical environmental conditions must be considered.

(b) Radio and electronic equipment, controls, and wiring must be installed so that operation of any unit or system of units will not adversely affect the simultaneous operation of any other radio or electronic unit, or system of units, required by this chapter.

(c) For those airplanes required to have more than one flightcrew member, or whose operation will require more than one flightcrew member, the cockpit must be evaluated to determine if the flightcrew members, when seated at their duty station, can converse without difficulty under the actual cockpit noise conditions when the airplane is being operated. If the airplane design includes provision for the use of communication headsets, the evaluation must also consider conditions where headsets are being used. If the evaluation shows conditions under which it will be difficult to converse, an intercommunication system must be provided.

(d) If installed communication equipment includes transmitter "off-on" switching, that switching means must be designed to return from the "transmit" to the "off" position when it is released and ensure that the transmitter will return to the off (non transmitting) state.

(e) If provisions for the use of communication headsets are provided, it must be demonstrated that the flightcrew members will receive all aural warnings under the actual cockpit noise conditions when the airplane is being operated when any headset is being used.

[Doc. No. 26344, 58 FR 18977, Apr. 9, 1993, as amended by Amdt. 23–49, 61 FR 5169, Feb. 9, 1996]

§23.1435 Hydraulic systems.

(a) *Design.* Each hydraulic system must be designed as follows:

(1) Each hydraulic system and its elements must withstand, without yielding, the structural loads expected in addition to hydraulic loads.

(2) A means to indicate the pressure in each hydraulic system which supplies two or more primary functions must be provided to the flight crew.

(3) There must be means to ensure that the pressure, including transient (surge) pressure, in any part of the system will not exceed the safe limit above design operating pressure and to prevent excessive pressure resulting from fluid volumetric changes in all

lines which are likely to remain closed long enough for such changes to occur.

(4) The minimum design burst pressure must be 2.5 times the operating pressure.

(b) *Tests.* Each system must be substantiated by proof pressure tests. When proof tested, no part of any system may fail, malfunction, or experience a permanent set. The proof load of each system must be at least 1.5 times the maximum operating pressure of that system.

(c) *Accumulators.* A hydraulic accumulator or reservoir may be installed on the engine side of any firewall if—

(1) It is an integral part of an engine or propeller system, or

(2) The reservoir is nonpressurized and the total capacity of all such nonpressurized reservoirs is one quart or less.

[Doc. No. 4080, 29 FR 17955, Dec. 18, 1964, as amended by Amdt. 23-7, 34 FR 13096, Aug. 13, 1969; Amdt. 23-14, 38 FR 31824, Nov. 19, 1973; Amdt. 23-43, 58 FR 18977, Apr. 9, 1993; Amdt. 23-49, 61 FR 5170, Feb. 9, 1996]

§ 23.1437 Accessories for multiengine airplanes.

For multiengine airplanes, engine-driven accessories essential to safe operation must be distributed among two or more engines so that the failure of any one engine will not impair safe operation through the malfunctioning of these accessories.

§ 23.1438 Pressurization and pneumatic systems.

(a) Pressurization system elements must be burst pressure tested to 2.0 times, and proof pressure tested to 1.5 times, the maximum normal operating pressure.

(b) Pneumatic system elements must be burst pressure tested to 3.0 times, and proof pressure tested to 1.5 times, the maximum normal operating pressure.

(c) An analysis, or a combination of analysis and test, may be substituted for any test required by paragraph (a) or (b) of this section if the Administrator finds it equivalent to the required test.

[Amdt. 23-20, 42 FR 36969, July 18, 1977]

§ 23.1441 Oxygen equipment and supply.

(a) If certification with supplemental oxygen equipment is requested, or the airplane is approved for operations at or above altitudes where oxygen is required to be used by the operating rules, oxygen equipment must be provided that meets the requirements of this section and §§ 23.1443 through 23.1449. Portable oxygen equipment may be used to meet the requirements of this part if the portable equipment is shown to comply with the applicable requirements, is identified in the airplane type design, and its stowage provisions are found to be in compliance with the requirements of § 23.561.

(b) The oxygen system must be free from hazards in itself, in its method of operation, and its effect upon other components.

(c) There must be a means to allow the crew to readily determine, during the flight, the quantity of oxygen available in each source of supply.

(d) Each required flight crewmember must be provided with—

(1) Demand oxygen equipment if the airplane is to be certificated for operation above 25,000 feet.

(2) Pressure demand oxygen equipment if the airplane is to be certificated for operation above 40,000 feet.

(e) There must be a means, readily available to the crew in flight, to turn on and to shut off the oxygen supply at the high pressure source. This shutoff requirement does not apply to chemical oxygen generators.

[Amdt. 23-9, 35 FR 6386, Apr. 21, 1970, as amended by Amdt. 23-43, 58 FR 18978, Apr. 9, 1993]

§ 23.1443 Minimum mass flow of supplemental oxygen.

(a) If continuous flow oxygen equipment is installed, an applicant must show compliance with the requirements of either paragraphs (a)(1) and (a)(2) or paragraph (a)(3) of this section:

(1) For each passenger, the minimum mass flow of supplemental oxygen required at various cabin pressure altitudes may not be less than the flow required to maintain, during inspiration and while using the oxygen equipment

(including masks) provided, the following mean tracheal oxygen partial pressures:

(i) At cabin pressure altitudes above 10,000 feet up to and including 18,500 feet, a mean tracheal oxygen partial pressure of 100 mm. Hg when breathing 15 liters per minute, Body Temperature, Pressure, Saturated (BTPS) and with a tidal volume of 700 cc. with a constant time interval between respirations.

(ii) At cabin pressure altitudes above 18,500 feet up to and including 40,000 feet, a mean tracheal oxygen partial pressure of 83.8 mm. Hg when breathing 30 liters per minute, BTPS, and with a tidal volume of 1,100 cc. with a con-stant time interval between respirations.

(2) For each flight crewmember, the minimum mass flow may not be less than the flow required to maintain, during inspiration, a mean tracheal oxygen partial pressure of 149 mm. Hg when breathing 15 liters per minute, BTPS, and with a maximum tidal volume of 700 cc. with a constant time interval between respirations.

(3) The minimum mass flow of supplemental oxygen supplied for each user must be at a rate not less than that shown in the following figure for each altitude up to and including the maximum operating altitude of the airplane.

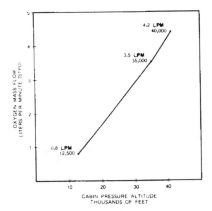

(b) If demand equipment is installed for use by flight crewmembers, the minimum mass flow of supplemental oxygen required for each flight crewmember may not be less than the flow required to maintain, during inspiration, a mean tracheal oxygen partial pressure of 122 mm. Hg up to and including a cabin pressure altitude of 35,000 feet, and 95 percent oxygen between cabin pressure altitudes of 35,000 and 40,000 feet, when breathing 20 liters per minute BTPS. In addition, there must be means to allow the crew to use undiluted oxygen at their discretion.

(c) If first-aid oxygen equipment is installed, the minimum mass flow of oxygen to each user may not be less than 4 liters per minute, STPD. However, there may be a means to decrease this flow to not less than 2 liters per minute, STPD, at any cabin altitude. The quantity of oxygen required is based upon an average flow rate of 3 liters per minute per person for whom first-aid oxygen is required.

(d) As used in this section:

(1) BTPS means Body Temperature, and Pressure, Saturated (which is, 37 °C, and the ambient pressure to which the body is exposed, minus 47 mm. Hg,

which is the tracheal pressure displaced by water vapor pressure when the breathed air becomes saturated with water vapor at 37 °C).

(2) STPD means Standard, Temperature, and Pressure, Dry (which is, 0 °C at 760 mm. Hg with no water vapor).

[Doc. No. 26344, 58 FR 18978, Apr. 9, 1993]

§ 23.1445 Oxygen distribution system.

(a) Except for flexible lines from oxygen outlets to the dispensing units, or where shown to be otherwise suitable to the installation, nonmetallic tubing must not be used for any oxygen line that is normally pressurized during flight.

(b) Nonmetallic oxygen distribution lines must not be routed where they may be subjected to elevated temperatures, electrical arcing, and released flammable fluids that might result from any probable failure.

[Doc. No. 26344, 58 FR 18978, Apr. 9, 1993]

§ 23.1447 Equipment standards for oxygen dispensing units.

If oxygen dispensing units are installed, the following apply:

(a) There must be an individual dispensing unit for each occupant for whom supplemental oxygen is to be supplied. Each dispensing unit must:

(1) Provide for effective utilization of the oxygen being delivered to the unit.

(2) Be capable of being readily placed into position on the face of the user.

(3) Be equipped with a suitable means to retain the unit in position on the face.

(4) If radio equipment is installed, the flightcrew oxygen dispensing units must be designed to allow the use of that equipment and to allow communication with any other required crew member while at their assigned duty station.

(b) If certification for operation up to and including 18,000 feet (MSL) is requested, each oxygen dispensing unit must:

(1) Cover the nose and mouth of the user; or

(2) Be a nasal cannula, in which case one oxygen dispensing unit covering both the nose and mouth of the user must be available. In addition, each

nasal cannula or its connecting tubing must have permanently affixed—

(i) A visible warning against smoking while in use;

(ii) An illustration of the correct method of donning; and

(iii) A visible warning against use with nasal obstructions or head colds with resultant nasal congestion.

(c) If certification for operation above 18,000 feet (MSL) is requested, each oxygen dispensing unit must cover the nose and mouth of the user.

(d) For a pressurized airplane designed to operate at flight altitudes above 25,000 feet (MSL), the dispensing units must meet the following:

(1) The dispensing units for passengers must be connected to an oxygen supply terminal and be immediately available to each occupant wherever seated.

(2) The dispensing units for crewmembers must be automatically presented to each crewmember before the cabin pressure altitude exceeds 15,000 feet, or the units must be of the quick-donning type, connected to an oxygen supply terminal that is immediately available to crewmembers at their station.

(e) If certification for operation above 30,000 feet is requested, the dispensing units for passengers must be automatically presented to each occupant before the cabin pressure altitude exceeds 15,000 feet.

(f) If an automatic dispensing unit (hose and mask, or other unit) system is installed, the crew must be provided with a manual means to make the dispensing units immediately available in the event of failure of the automatic system.

[Amdt. 23-9, 35 FR 6387, Apr. 21, 1970, as amended by Amdt. 23-20, 42 FR 36969, July 18, 1977; Amdt. 23-30, 49 FR 7340, Feb. 28, 1984; Amdt. 23-43, 58 FR 18978, Apr. 9, 1993; Amdt. 23-49, 61 FR 5170, Feb. 9, 1996]

§ 23.1449 Means for determining use of oxygen.

There must be a means to allow the crew to determine whether oxygen is being delivered to the dispensing equipment.

[Amdt. 23-9, 35 FR 6387, Apr. 21, 1970]

§23.1450 Chemical oxygen generators.

(a) For the purpose of this section, a chemical oxygen generator is defined as a device which produces oxygen by chemical reaction.

(b) Each chemical oxygen generator must be designed and installed in accordance with the following requirements:

(1) Surface temperature developed by the generator during operation may not create a hazard to the airplane or to its occupants.

(2) Means must be provided to relieve any internal pressure that may be hazardous.

(c) In addition to meeting the requirements in paragraph (b) of this section, each portable chemical oxygen generator that is capable of sustained operation by successive replacement of a generator element must be placarded to show—

(1) The rate of oxygen flow, in liters per minute;

(2) The duration of oxygen flow, in minutes, for the replaceable generator element; and

(3) A warning that the replaceable generator element may be hot, unless the element construction is such that the surface temperature cannot exceed 100 °F.

[Amdt. 23–20, 42 FR 36969, July 18, 1977]

§23.1451 Fire protection for oxygen equipment.

Oxygen equipment and lines must:

(a) Not be installed in any designed fire zones.

(b) Be protected from heat that may be generated in, or escape from, any designated fire zone.

(c) Be installed so that escaping oxygen cannot come in contact with and cause ignition of grease, fluid, or vapor accumulations that are present in normal operation or that may result from the failure or malfunction of any other system.

[Doc. No. 27806, 61 FR 5170, Feb. 9, 1996]

§23.1453 Protection of oxygen equipment from rupture.

(a) Each element of the oxygen system must have sufficient strength to withstand the maximum pressure and temperature, in combination with any externally applied loads arising from consideration of limit structural loads, that may be acting on that part of the system.

(b) Oxygen pressure sources and the lines between the source and the shut-off means must be:

(1) Protected from unsafe temperatures; and

(2) Located where the probability and hazard of rupture in a crash landing are minimized.

[Doc. No. 27806, 61 FR 5170, Feb. 9, 1996]

§23.1457 Cockpit voice recorders.

(a) Each cockpit voice recorder required by the operating rules of this chapter must be approved and must be installed so that it will record the following:

(1) Voice communications transmitted from or received in the airplane by radio.

(2) Voice communications of flight crewmembers on the flight deck.

(3) Voice communications of flight crewmembers on the flight deck, using the airplane's interphone system.

(4) Voice or audio signals identifying navigation or approach aids introduced into a headset or speaker.

(5) Voice communications of flight crewmembers using the passenger loudspeaker system, if there is such a system and if the fourth channel is available in accordance with the requirements of paragraph (c)(4)(ii) of this section.

(b) The recording requirements of paragraph (a)(2) of this section must be met by installing a cockpit-mounted area microphone, located in the best position for recording voice communications originating at the first and second pilot stations and voice communications of other crewmembers on the flight deck when directed to those stations. The microphone must be so located and, if necessary, the preamplifiers and filters of the recorder must be so adjusted or supplemented, so that the intelligibility of the recorded communications is as high as practicable when recorded under flight cockpit noise conditions and played back. Repeated aural or visual playback of the record may be used in evaluating intelligibility.

(c) Each cockpit voice recorder must be installed so that the part of the communication or audio signals specified in paragraph (a) of this section obtained from each of the following sources is recorded on a separate channel:

(1) For the first channel, from each boom, mask, or handheld microphone, headset, or speaker used at the first pilot station.

(2) For the second channel from each boom, mask, or handheld microphone, headset, or speaker used at the second pilot station.

(3) For the third channel—from the cockpit-mounted area microphone.

(4) For the fourth channel from:

(i) Each boom, mask, or handheld microphone, headset, or speaker used at the station for the third and fourth crewmembers.

(ii) If the stations specified in paragraph (c)(4)(i) of this section are not required or if the signal at such a station is picked up by another channel, each microphone on the flight deck that is used with the passenger loudspeaker system, if its signals are not picked up by another channel.

(5) And that as far as is practicable all sounds received by the microphone listed in paragraphs (c)(1), (2), and (4) of this section must be recorded without interruption irrespective of the position of the interphone-transmitter key switch. The design shall ensure that sidetone for the flight crew is produced only when the interphone, public address system, or radio transmitters are in use.

(d) Each cockpit voice recorder must be installed so that:

(1) It receives its electric power from the bus that provides the maximum reliability for operation of the cockpit voice recorder without jeopardizing service to essential or emergency loads.

(2) There is an automatic means to simultaneously stop the recorder and prevent each erasure feature from functioning, within 10 minutes after crash impact; and

(3) There is an aural or visual means for preflight checking of the recorder for proper operation.

(e) The record container must be located and mounted to minimize the probability of rupture of the container as a result of crash impact and consequent heat damage to the record from fire. In meeting this requirement, the record container must be as far aft as practicable, but may not be where aft mounted engines may crush the container during impact. However, it need not be outside of the pressurized compartment.

(f) If the cockpit voice recorder has a bulk erasure device, the installation must be designed to minimize the probability of inadvertent operation and actuation of the device during crash impact.

(g) Each recorder container must:

(1) Be either bright orange or bright yellow;

(2) Have reflective tape affixed to its external surface to facilitate its location under water; and

(3) Have an underwater locating device, when required by the operating rules of this chapter, on or adjacent to the container which is secured in such manner that they are not likely to be separated during crash impact.

[Amdt. 23–35, 53 FR 26142, July 11, 1988]

§ 23.1459   Flight recorders.

(a) Each flight recorder required by the operating rules of this chapter must be installed so that:

(1) It is supplied with airspeed, altitude, and directional data obtained from sources that meet the accuracy requirements of §§ 23.1323, 23.1325, and 23.1327, as appropriate;

(2) The vertical acceleration sensor is rigidly attached, and located longitudinally either within the approved center of gravity limits of the airplane, or at a distance forward or aft of these limits that does not exceed 25 percent of the airplane's mean aerodynamic chord;

(3) It receives its electrical power power from the bus that provides the maximum reliability for operation of the flight recorder without jeopardizing service to essential or emergency loads;

(4) There is an aural or visual means for preflight checking of the recorder for proper recording of data in the storage medium.

(5) Except for recorders powered solely by the engine-driven electrical generator system, there is an automatic means to simultaneously stop a recorder that has a data erasure feature and prevent each erasure feature from functioning, within 10 minutes after crash impact; and

(b) Each nonejectable record container must be located and mounted so as to minimize the probability of container rupture resulting from crash impact and subsequent damage to the record from fire. In meeting this requirement the record container must be located as far aft as practicable, but need not be aft of the pressurized compartment, and may not be where aft-mounted engines may crush the container upon impact.

(c) A correlation must be established between the flight recorder readings of airspeed, altitude, and heading and the corresponding readings (taking into account correction factors) of the first pilot's instruments. The correlation must cover the airspeed range over which the airplane is to be operated, the range of altitude to which the airplane is limited, and 360 degrees of heading. Correlation may be established on the ground as appropriate.

(d) Each recorder container must:

(1) Be either bright orange or bright yellow;

(2) Have reflective tape affixed to its external surface to facilitate its location under water; and

(3) Have an underwater locating device, when required by the operating rules of this chapter, on or adjacent to the container which is secured in such a manner that they are not likely to be separated during crash impact.

(e) Any novel or unique design or operational characteristics of the aircraft shall be evaluated to determine if any dedicated parameters must be recorded on flight recorders in addition to or in place of existing requirements. CITA≤[Amdt. 23–35, 53 FR 26143, July 11, 1988]

§23.1461 Equipment containing high energy rotors.

(a) Equipment, such as Auxiliary Power Units (APU) and constant speed drive units, containing high energy rotors must meet paragraphs (b), (c), or (d) of this section.

(b) High energy rotors contained in equipment must be able to withstand damage caused by malfunctions, vibration, abnormal speeds, and abnormal temperatures. In addition—

(1) Auxiliary rotor cases must be able to contain damage caused by the failure of high energy rotor blades; and

(2) Equipment control devices, systems, and instrumentation must reasonably ensure that no operating limitations affecting the integrity of high energy rotors will be exceeded in service.

(c) It must be shown by test that equipment containing high energy rotors can contain any failure of a high energy rotor that occurs at the highest speed obtainable with the normal speed control devices inoperative.

(d) Equipment containing high energy rotors must be located where rotor failure will neither endanger the occupants nor adversely affect continued safe flight.

[Amdt. 23–20, 42 FR 36969, July 18, 1977, as amended by Amdt. 23–49, 61 FR 5170, Feb. 9, 1996]

Subpart G—Operating Limitations and Information

§23.1501 General.

(a) Each operating limitation specified in §§23.1505 through 23.1527 and other limitations and information necessary for safe operation must be established.

(b) The operating limitations and other information necessary for safe operation must be made available to the crewmembers as prescribed in §§23.1541 through 23.1589.

[Amdt. 23–21, 43 FR 2319, Jan. 16, 1978]

§23.1505 Airspeed limitations.

(a) The never-exceed speed V_{NE} must be established so that it is—

(1) Not less than 0.9 times the minimum value of V_D allowed under §23.335; and

(2) Not more than the lesser of—

(i) 0.9 V_D established under §23.335; or

(ii) 0.9 times the maximum speed shown under §23.251.

(b) The maximum structural cruising speed V_{NO} must be established so that it is—

(1) Not less than the minimum value of V_C allowed under § 23.335; and

(2) Not more than the lesser of—

(i) V_C established under § 23.335; or

(ii) 0.89 V_{NE} established under paragraph (a) of this section.

(c) Paragraphs (a) and (b) of this section do not apply to turbine airplanes or to airplanes for which a design diving speed V_D/M_D is established under § 23.335(b)(4). For those airplanes, a maximum operating limit speed (V_{MO}/M_{MO}-airspeed or Mach number, whichever is critical at a particular altitude) must be established as a speed that may not be deliberately exceeded in any regime of flight (climb, cruise, or descent) unless a higher speed is authorized for flight test or pilot training operations. V_{MO}/M_{MO} must be established so that it is not greater than the design cruising speed V_C/M_C and so that it is sufficiently below V_D/M_D and the maximum speed shown under § 23.251 to make it highly improbable that the latter speeds will be inadvertently exceeded in operations. The speed margin between V_{MO}/M_{MO} and V_D/M_D or the maximum speed shown under § 23.251 may not be less than the speed margin established between V_C/M_C and V_D/M_D under § 23.335(b), or the speed margin found necessary in the flight test conducted under § 23.253.

[Doc. No. 4080, 29 FR 17955, Dec. 18, 1964, as amended by Amdt. 23–7, 34 FR 13096, Aug. 13, 1969]

§ 23.1507 Operating maneuvering speed.

The maximum operating maneuvering speed, V_O, must be established as an operating limitation. V_O is a selected speed that is not greater than $V_S\sqrt{n}$ established in § 23.335(c).

[Doc. No. 26269, 58 FR 42165, Aug. 6, 1993]

§ 23.1511 Flap extended speed.

(a) The flap extended speed V_{FE} must be established so that it is—

(1) Not less than the minimum value of V_F allowed in § 23.345(b); and

(2) Not more than V_F established under § 23.345(a), (c), and (d).

(i) V_F established under § 23.345; or

(ii) V_F established under § 23.457.

(b) Additional combinations of flap setting, airspeed, and engine power may be established if the structure has been proven for the corresponding design conditions.

[Doc. No. 4080, 29 FR 17955, Dec. 18, 1964; 30 FR 258, Jan. 9, 1965, as amended by Amdt. 23–50, 61 FR 5192, Feb. 9, 1996]

§ 23.1513 Minimum control speed.

The minimum control speed V_{MC}, determined under § 23.149, must be established as an operating limitation.

§ 23.1519 Weight and center of gravity.

The weight and center of gravity limitations determined under § 23.23 must be established as operating limitations.

§ 23.1521 Powerplant limitations.

(a) *General.* The powerplant limitations prescribed in this section must be established so that they do not exceed the corresponding limits for which the engines or propellers are type certificated. In addition, other powerplant limitations used in determining compliance with this part must be established.

(b) *Takeoff operation.* The powerplant takeoff operation must be limited by—

(1) The maximum rotational speed (rpm);

(2) The maximum allowable manifold pressure (for reciprocating engines);

(3) The maximum allowable gas temperature (for turbine engines);

(4) The time limit for the use of the power or thrust corresponding to the limitations established in paragraphs (b)(1) through (3) of this section; and

(5) The maximum allowable cylinder head (as applicable), liquid coolant and oil temperatures.

(c) *Continuous operation.* The continuous operation must be limited by—

(1) The maximum rotational speed;

(2) The maximum allowable manifold pressure (for reciprocating engines);

(3) The maximum allowable gas temperature (for turbine engines); and

(4) The maximum allowable cylinder head, oil, and liquid coolant temperatures.

(d) *Fuel grade or designation.* The minimum fuel grade (for reciprocating engines), or fuel designation (for turbine engines), must be established so that it is not less than that required for the operation of the engines within the limitations in paragraphs (b) and (c) of this section.

(e) *Ambient temperature.* For all airplanes except reciprocating engine-powered airplanes of 6,000 pounds or less maximum weight, ambient temperature limitations (including limitations for winterization installations if applicable) must be established as the maximum ambient atmospheric temperature at which compliance with the cooling provisions of §§23.1041 through 23.1047 is shown.

[Doc. No. 4080, 29 FR 17955, Dec. 18, 1964; 30 FR 258, Jan. 9, 1965, as amended by Amdt. 23–21, 43 FR 2319, Jan. 16, 1978; Amdt. 23–45, 58 FR 42165, Aug. 6, 1993; Amdt. 23–50, 61 FR 5192, Feb. 9, 1996]

§23.1522 Auxiliary power unit limitations.

If an auxiliary power unit is installed, the limitations established for the auxiliary power must be specified in the operating limitations for the airplane.[Doc. No. 26269, 58 FR 42166, Aug. 6, 1993]

§23.1523 Minimum flight crew.

The minimum flight crew must be established so that it is sufficient for safe operation considering—

(a) The workload on individual crewmembers and, in addition for commuter category airplanes, each crewmember workload determination must consider the following:

(1) Flight path control,

(2) Collision avoidance,

(3) Navigation,

(4) Communications,

(5) Operation and monitoring of all essential airplane systems,

(6) Command decisions, and

(7) The accessibility and ease of operation of necessary controls by the appropriate crewmember during all normal and emergency operations when at the crewmember flight station;

(b) The accessibility and ease of operation of necessary controls by the appropriate crewmember; and

(c) The kinds of operation authorized under §23.1525.

[Amdt. 23–21, 43 FR 2319, Jan. 16, 1978, as amended by Amdt. 23–34, 52 FR 1834, Jan. 15, 1987]

§23.1524 Maximum passenger seating configuration.

The maximum passenger seating configuration must be established.

[Amdt. 23–10, 36 FR 2864, Feb. 11, 1971]

§23.1525 Kinds of operation.

The kinds of operation authorized (e.g. VFR, IFR, day or night) and the meteorological conditions (e.g. icing) to which the operation of the airplane is limited or from which it is prohibited, must be established appropriate to the installed equipment.

[Doc. No. 26269, 58 FR 42166, Aug. 6, 1993]

§23.1527 Maximum operating altitude.

(a) The maximum altitude up to which operation is allowed, as limited by flight, structural, powerplant, functional or equipment characteristics, must be established.

(b) A maximum operating altitude limitation of not more than 25,000 feet must be established for pressurized airplanes unless compliance with §23.775(e) is shown.

[Doc. No. 26269, 58 FR 42166, Aug. 6, 1993]

§23.1529 Instructions for Continued Airworthiness.

The applicant must prepare Instructions for Continued Airworthiness in accordance with appendix G to this part that are acceptable to the Administrator. The instructions may be incomplete at type certification if a program exists to ensure their completion prior to delivery of the first airplane or issuance of a standard certificate of airworthiness, whichever occurs later.

[Amdt. 23–26, 45 FR 60171, Sept. 11, 1980]

MARKINGS AND PLACARDS

§23.1541 General.

(a) The airplane must contain—

(1) The markings and placards specified in §§23.1545 through 23.1567; and

(2) Any additional information, instrument markings, and placards required for the safe operation if it has unusual design, operating, or handling characteristics.

(b) Each marking and placard prescribed in paragraph (a) of this section—

(1) Must be displayed in a conspicuous place; and

(2) May not be easily erased, disfigured, or obscured.

(c) For airplanes which are to be certificated in more than one category—

(1) The applicant must select one category upon which the placards and markings are to be based; and

(2) The placards and marking information for all categories in which the airplane is to be certificated must be furnished in the Airplane Flight Manual.

[Doc. No. 4080, 29 FR 17955, Dec. 18, 1964; 30 FR 258, Jan. 9, 1965, as amended by Amdt. 23–21, 43 FR 2319, Jan. 16, 1978]

§ 23.1543 Instrument markings: General.

For each instrument—

(a) When markings are on the cover glass of the instrument, there must be means to maintain the correct alignment of the glass cover with the face of the dial; and

(b) Each arc and line must be wide enough and located to be clearly visible to the pilot.

(c) All related instruments must be calibrated in compatible units.

[Doc. No. 4080, 29 FR 17955, Dec. 18, 1964; 30 FR 258, Jan. 9, 1965, as amended by Amdt. 23–50, 61 FR 5192, Feb. 9, 1996]

§ 23.1545 Airspeed indicator.

(a) Each airspeed indicator must be marked as specified in paragraph (b) of this section, with the marks located at the corresponding indicated airspeeds.

(b) The following markings must be made:

(1) For the never-exceed speed V_{NE}, a radial red line.

(2) For the caution range, a yellow arc extending from the red line specified in paragraph (b)(1) of this section to the upper limit of the green arc specified in paragraph (b)(3) of this section.

(3) For the normal operating range, a green arc with the lower limit at V_{S1} with maximum weight and with landing gear and wing flaps retracted, and the upper limit at the maximum structural cruising speed V_{NO} established under § 23.1505(b).

(4) For the flap operating range, a white arc with the lower limit at V_{S0} at the maximum weight, and the upper limit at the flaps-extended speed V_{FE} established under § 23.1511.

(5) For reciprocating multiengine-powered airplanes of 6,000 pounds or less maximum weight, for the speed at which compliance has been shown with § 23.69(b) relating to rate of climb at maximum weight and at sea level, a blue radial line.

(6) For reciprocating multiengine-powered airplanes of 6,000 pounds or less maximum weight, for the maximum value of minimum control speed, V_{MC}, (one-engine-inoperative) determined under § 23.149(b), a red radial line.

(c) If V_{NE} or V_{NO} vary with altitude, there must be means to indicate to the pilot the appropriate limitations throughout the operating altitude range.

(d) Paragraphs (b)(1) through (b)(3) and paragraph (c) of this section do not apply to aircraft for which a maximum operating speed V_{MO}/M_{MO} is established under § 23.1505(c). For those aircraft there must either be a maximum allowable airspeed indication showing the variation of V_{MO}/M_{MO} with altitude or compressibility limitations (as appropriate), or a radial red line marking for V_{MO}/M_{MO} must be made at lowest value of V_{MO}/M_{MO} established for any altitude up to the maximum operating altitude for the airplane.

[Doc. No. 4080, 29 FR 17955, Dec. 18, 1964, as amended by Amdt. 23–3, 30 FR 14240, Nov. 13, 1965; Amdt. 23–7, 34 FR 13097, Aug. 13, 1969; Amdt. 23–23, 43 FR 50593, Oct. 30, 1978; Amdt. 23–50, 61 FR 5193, Feb. 9, 1996]

§ 23.1547 Magnetic direction indicator.

(a) A placard meeting the requirements of this section must be installed on or near the magnetic direction indicator.

(b) The placard must show the calibration of the instrument in level flight with the engines operating.

(c) The placard must state whether the calibration was made with radio receivers on or off.

(d) Each calibration reading must be in terms of magnetic headings in not more than 30 degree increments.

(e) If a magnetic nonstabilized direction indicator can have a deviation of more than 10 degrees caused by the operation of electrical equipment, the placard must state which electrical loads, or combination of loads, would cause a deviation of more than 10 degrees when turned on.

[Doc. No. 4080, 29 FR 17955, Dec. 18, 1964; 30 FR 258, Jan. 9, 1965, as amended by Amdt. 23–20, 42 FR 36969, July 18, 1977]

§23.1549 Powerplant and auxiliary power unit instruments.

For each required powerplant and auxiliary power unit instrument, as appropriate to the type of instruments—

(a) Each maximum and, if applicable, minimum safe operating limit must be marked with a red radial or a red line;

(b) Each normal operating range must be marked with a green arc or green line, not extending beyond the maximum and minimum safe limits;

(c) Each takeoff and precautionary range must be marked with a yellow arc or a yellow line; and

(d) Each engine, auxiliary power unit, or propeller range that is restricted because of excessive vibration stresses must be marked with red arcs or red lines.

[Amdt. 23–12, 41 FR 55466, Dec. 20, 1976, as amended by Amdt. 23–28, 47 FR 13315, Mar. 29, 1982; Amdt. 23–45, 58 FR 42166, Aug. 6, 1993]

§23.1551 Oil quantity indicator.

Each oil quantity indicator must be marked in sufficient increments to indicate readily and accurately the quantity of oil.

§23.1553 Fuel quantity indicator.

A red radial line must be marked on each indicator at the calibrated zero reading, as specified in §23.1337(b)(1).

[Doc. No. 27807, 61 FR 5193, Feb. 9, 1996]

§23.1555 Control markings.

(a) Each cockpit control, other than primary flight controls and simple push button type starter switches, must be plainly marked as to its function and method of operation.

(b) Each secondary control must be suitably marked.

(c) For powerplant fuel controls—

(1) Each fuel tank selector control must be marked to indicate the posi-

tion corresponding to each tank and to each existing cross feed position;

(2) If safe operation requires the use of any tanks in a specific sequence, that sequence must be marked on or near the selector for those tanks;

(3) The conditions under which the full amount of usable fuel in any restricted usage fuel tank can safely be used must be stated on a placard adjacent to the selector valve for that tank; and

(4) Each valve control for any engine of a multiengine airplane must be marked to indicate the position corresponding to each engine controlled.

(d) Usable fuel capacity must be marked as follows:

(1) For fuel systems having no selector controls, the usable fuel capacity of the system must be indicated at the fuel quantity indicator.

(2) For fuel systems having selector controls, the usable fuel capacity available at each selector control position must be indicated near the selector control.

(e) For accessory, auxiliary, and emergency controls—

(1) If retractable landing gear is used, the indicator required by §23.729 must be marked so that the pilot can, at any time, ascertain that the wheels are secured in the extreme positions; and

(2) Each emergency control must be red and must be marked as to method of operation. No control other than an emergency control, or a control that serves an emergency function in addition to its other functions, shall be this color.

[Doc. No. 4080, 29 FR 17955, Dec. 18, 1964; 30 FR 258, Jan. 9, 1965, as amended by Amdt. 23–21, 43 FR 2319, Jan. 16, 1978; Amdt. 23–50, 61 FR 5193, Feb. 9, 1996]

§23.1557 Miscellaneous markings and placards.

(a) *Baggage and cargo compartments, and ballast location.* Each baggage and cargo compartment, and each ballast location, must have a placard stating any limitations on contents, including weight, that are necessary under the loading requirements.

(b) *Seats.* If the maximum allowable weight to be carried in a seat is less than 170 pounds, a placard stating the lesser weight must be permanently attached to the seat structure.

(c) *Fuel, oil, and coolant filler openings.* The following apply:

(1) Fuel filter openings must be marked at or near the filler cover with—

(i) For reciprocating engine-powered airplanes—

(A) The word "Avgas"; and

(B) The minimum fuel grade.

(ii) For turbine engine-powered airplanes—

(A) The words "Jet Fuel"; and

(B) The permissible fuel designations, or references to the Airplane Flight Manual (AFM) for permissible fuel designations.

(iii) For pressure fueling systems, the maximum permissible fueling supply pressure and the maximum permissible defueling pressure.

(2) Oil filler openings must be marked at or near the filler cover with the word "Oil" and the permissible oil designations, or references to the Airplane Flight Manual (AFM) for permissible oil designations.

(3) Coolant filler openings must be marked at or near the filler cover with the word "Coolant".

(d) *Emergency exit placards.* Each placard and operating control for each emergency exit must be red. A placard must be near each emergency exit control and must clearly indicate the location of that exit and its method of operation.

(e) The system voltage of each direct current installation must be clearly marked adjacent to its external power connection.

[Doc. No. 4080, 29 FR 17955, Dec. 18, 1964; as amended by Amdt. 23–21, 42 FR 15042, Mar. 17, 1977; Amdt. 23–23, 43 FR 50594, Oct. 30, 1978; Amdt. 23–45, 58 FR 42166, Aug. 6, 1993]

§ 23.1559 Operating limitations placard.

(a) There must be a placard in clear view of the pilot stating—

(1) That the airplane must be operated in accordance with the Airplane Flight Manual; and

(2) The certification category of the airplane to which the placards apply.

(b) For airplanes certificated in more than one category, there must be a placard in clear view of the pilot stat-

ing that other limitations are contained in the Airplane Flight Manual.

(c) There must be a placard in clear view of the pilot that specifies the kind of operations to which the operation of the airplane is limited or from which it is prohibited under § 23.1525.

[Doc. No. 27807, 61 FR 5193, Feb. 9, 1996]

§ 23.1561 Safety equipment.

(a) Safety equipment must be plainly marked as to method of operation.

(b) Stowage provisions for required safety equipment must be marked for the benefit of occupants.

§ 23.1563 Airspeed placards.

There must be an airspeed placard in clear view of the pilot and as close as practicable to the airspeed indicator. This placard must list—

(a) The operating maneuvering speed, V_O; and

(b) The maximum landing gear operating speed V_{LO}.

(c) For reciprocating multiengine-powered airplanes of more than 6,000 pounds maximum weight, and turbine engine-powered airplanes, the maximum value of the minimum control speed, V_{MC} (one-engine-inoperative) determined under § 23.149(b).

[Amdt. 23–7, 34 FR 13097, Aug. 13, 1969, as amended by Amdt. 23–45, 58 FR 42166, Aug. 6, 1993; Amdt. 23–50, 61 FR 5193, Feb. 9, 1996]

§ 23.1567 Flight maneuver placard.

(a) For normal category airplanes, there must be a placard in front of and in clear view of the pilot stating: "No acrobatic maneuvers, including spins, approved."

(b) For utility category airplanes, there must be—

(1) A placard in clear view of the pilot stating: "Acrobatic maneuvers are limited to the following ———" (list approved maneuvers and the recommended entry speed for each); and

(2) For those airplanes that do not meet the spin requirements for acrobatic category airplanes, an additional placard in clear view of the pilot stating: "Spins Prohibited."

(c) For acrobatic category airplanes, there must be a placard in clear view of the pilot listing the approved acrobatic maneuvers and the recommended entry airspeed for each. If inverted flight maneuvers are not approved, the placard must bear a notation to this effect.

(d) For acrobatic category airplanes and utility category airplanes approved for spinning, there must be a placard in clear view of the pilot—

(1) Listing the control actions for recovery from spinning maneuvers; and

(2) Stating that recovery must be initiated when spiral characteristics appear, or after not more than six turns or not more than any greater number of turns for which the airplane has been certificated.

[Doc. No. 4080, 29 FR 17955, Dec. 18, 1964; 30 FR 258, Jan. 9, 1965, as amended by Amdt. 23–13, 37 FR 20023, Sept. 23, 1972; Amdt. 23–21, 43 FR 2319, Jan. 16, 1978; Amdt. 23–50, 61 FR 5193, Feb. 9, 1996]

AIRPLANE FLIGHT MANUAL AND
APPROVED MANUAL MATERIAL

§23.1581 General.

(a) *Furnishing information.* An Airplane Flight Manual must be furnished with each airplane, and it must contain the following:

(1) Information required by §§23.1583 through 23.1589.

(2) Other information that is necessary for safe operation because of design, operating, or handling characteristics.

(3) Further information necessary to comply with the relevant operating rules.

(b) *Approved information.* (1) Except as provided in paragraph (b)(2) of this section, each part of the Airplane Flight Manual containing information prescribed in §§23.1583 through 23.1589 must be approved, segregated, identified and clearly distinguished from each unapproved part of that Airplane Flight Manual.

(2) The requirements of paragraph (b)(1) of this section do not apply to reciprocating engine-powered airplanes of 6,000 pounds or less maximum weight, if the following is met:

(i) Each part of the Airplane Flight Manual containing information prescribed in §23.1583 must be limited to such information, and must be approved, identified, and clearly distinguished from each other part of the Airplane Flight Manual.

(ii) The information prescribed in §§23.1585 through 23.1589 must be determined in accordance with the applicable requirements of this part and presented in its entirety in a manner acceptable to the Administrator.

(3) Each page of the Airplane Flight Manual containing information prescribed in this section must be of a type that is not easily erased, disfigured, or misplaced, and is capable of being inserted in a manual provided by the applicant, or in a folder, or in any other permanent binder.

(c) The units used in the Airplane Flight Manual must be the same as those marked on the appropriate instruments and placards.

(d) All Airplane Flight Manual operational airspeeds, unless otherwise specified, must be presented as indicated airspeeds.

(e) Provision must be made for stowing the Airplane Flight Manual in a suitable fixed container which is readily accessible to the pilot.

(f) *Revisions and amendments.* Each Airplane Flight Manual (AFM) must contain a means for recording the incorporation of revisions and amendments.

[Amdt. 23–21, 43 FR 2319, Jan. 16, 1978, as amended by Amdt. 23–34, 52 FR 1834, Jan. 15, 1987; Amdt. 23–45, 58 FR 42166, Aug. 6, 1993; Amdt. 23–50, 61 FR 5193, Feb. 9, 1996]

§23.1583 Operating limitations.

The Airplane Flight Manual must contain operating limitations determined under this part 23, including the following—

(a) *Airspeed limitations.* The following information must be furnished:

(1) Information necessary for the marking of the airspeed limits on the indicator as required in §23.1545, and the significance of each of those limits and of the color coding used on the indicator.

(2) The speeds V_{MC}, V_O, V_{LE}, and V_{LO}, if established, and their significance.

(3) In addition, for turbine powered commuter category airplanes—

(i) The maximum operating limit speed, V_{MO}/M_{MO} and a statement that this speed must not be deliberately exceeded in any regime of flight (climb, cruise or descent) unless a higher speed is authorized for flight test or pilot training;

(ii) If an airspeed limitation is based upon compressibility effects, a statement to this effect and information as to any symptoms, the probable behavior of the airplane, and the recommended recovery procedures; and

(iii) The airspeed limits must be shown in terms of V_{MO}/M_{MO} instead of V_{NO} and V_{NE}.

(b) *Powerplant limitations.* The following information must be furnished:

(1) Limitations required by § 23.1521.

(2) Explanation of the limitations, when appropriate.

(3) Information necessary for marking the instruments required by § 23.1549 through § 23.1553.

(c) *Weight.* The airplane flight manual must include—

(1) The maximum weight; and

(2) The maximum landing weight, if the design landing weight selected by the applicant is less than the maximum weight.

(3) For normal, utility, and acrobatic category reciprocating engine-powered airplanes of more than 6,000 pounds maximum weight and for turbine engine-powered airplanes in the normal, utility, and acrobatic category, performance operating limitations as follows—

(i) The maximum takeoff weight for each airport altitude and ambient temperature within the range selected by the applicant at which the airplane complies with the climb requirements of § 23.63(c)(1).

(ii) The maximum landing weight for each airport altitude and ambient temperature within the range selected by the applicant at which the airplane complies with the climb requirements of § 23.63(c)(2).

(4) For commuter category airplanes, the maximum takeoff weight for each airport altitude and ambient temperature within the range selected by the applicant at which—

(i) The airplane complies with the climb requirements of § 23.63(d)(1); and

(ii) The accelerate-stop distance determined under § 23.55 is equal to the available runway length plus the length of any stopway, if utilized; and either:

(iii) The takeoff distance determined under § 23.59(a) is equal to the available runway length; or

(iv) At the option of the applicant, the takeoff distance determined under § 23.59(a) is equal to the available runway length plus the length of any clearway and the takeoff run determined under § 23.59(b) is equal to the available runway length.

(5) For commuter category airplanes, the maximum landing weight for each airport altitude within the range selected by the applicant at which—

(i) The airplane complies with the climb requirements of § 23.63(d)(2) for ambient temperatures within the range selected by the applicant; and

(ii) The landing distance determined under § 23.75 for standard temperatures is equal to the available runway length.

(6) The maximum zero wing fuel weight, where relevant, as established in accordance with § 23.343.

(d) *Center of gravity.* The established center of gravity limits.

(e) *Maneuvers.* The following authorized maneuvers, appropriate airspeed limitations, and unauthorized maneuvers, as prescribed in this section.

(1) *Normal category airplanes.* No acrobatic maneuvers, including spins, are authorized.

(2) *Utility category airplanes.* A list of authorized maneuvers demonstrated in the type flight tests, together with recommended entry speeds and any other associated limitations. No other maneuver is authorized.

(3) *Acrobatic category airplanes.* A list of approved flight maneuvers demonstrated in the type flight tests, together with recommended entry speeds and any other associated limitations.

(4) *Acrobatic category airplanes and utility category airplanes approved for spinning.* Spin recovery procedure established to show compliance with § 23.221(c).

(5) *Commuter category airplanes.* Maneuvers are limited to any maneuver incident to normal flying, stalls, (except whip stalls) and steep turns in which the angle of bank is not more than 60 degrees.

(f) *Maneuver load factor.* The positive limit load factors in g's, and, in addition, the negative limit load factor for acrobatic category airplanes.

(g) *Minimum flight crew.* The number and functions of the minimum flight crew determined under § 23.1523.

(h) *Kinds of operation.* A list of the kinds of operation to which the airplane is limited or from which it is prohibited under § 23.1525, and also a list of installed equipment that affects any operating limitation and identification as to the equipment's required operational status for the kinds of operation for which approval has been given.

(i) *Maximum operating altitude.* The maximum altitude established under § 23.1527.

(j) *Maximum passenger seating configuration.* The maximum passenger seating configuration.

(k) *Allowable lateral fuel loading.* The maximum allowable lateral fuel loading differential, if less than the maximum possible.

(l) *Baggage and cargo loading.* The following information for each baggage and cargo compartment or zone—

(1) The maximum allowable load; and

(2) The maximum intensity of loading.

(m) *Systems.* Any limitations on the use of airplane systems and equipment.

(n) *Ambient temperatures.* Where appropriate, maximum and minimum ambient air temperatures for operation.

(o) *Smoking.* Any restrictions on smoking in the airplane.

(p) *Types of surface.* A statement of the types of surface on which operations may be conducted. (See § 23.45(g) and § 23.1587 (a)(4), (c)(2), and (d)(4)).

[Doc. No. 4080, 29 FR 17955, Dec. 18, 1964, as amended by Amdt. 23–7, 34 FR 13097, Aug. 13, 1969; Amdt. 23–10, 36 FR 2864, Feb. 11, 1971; Amdt. 23–21, 43 FR 2320, Jan. 16, 1978; Amdt. 23–23, 43 FR 50594, Oct. 30, 1978; Amdt. 23–34, 52 FR 1834, Jan. 15, 1987; Amdt. 23–45, 58 FR 42166, Aug. 6, 1993; Amdt. 23–50, 61 FR 5193, Feb. 9, 1996]

§ 23.1585 Operating procedures.

(a) For all airplanes, information concerning normal, abnormal (if applicable), and emergency procedures and other pertinent information necessary for safe operation and the achievement of the scheduled performance must be furnished, including—

(1) An explanation of significant or unusual flight or ground handling characteristics;

(2) The maximum demonstrated values of crosswind for takeoff and landing, and procedures and information pertinent to operations in crosswinds;

(3) A recommended speed for flight in rough air. This speed must be chosen to protect against the occurrence, as a result of gusts, of structural damage to the airplane and loss of control (for example, stalling);

(4) Procedures for restarting any turbine engine in flight, including the effects of altitude; and

(5) Procedures, speeds, and configuration(s) for making a normal approach and landing, in accordance with §§ 23.73 and 23.75, and a transition to the balked landing condition.

(6) For seaplanes and amphibians, water handling procedures and the demonstrated wave height.

(b) In addition to paragraph (a) of this section, for all single-engine airplanes, the procedures, speeds, and configuration(s) for a glide following engine failure, in accordance with § 23.71 and the subsequent forced landing, must be furnished.

(c) In addition to paragraph (a) of this section, for all multiengine airplanes, the following information must be furnished:

(1) Procedures, speeds, and configuration(s) for making an approach and landing with one engine inoperative;

(2) Procedures, speeds, and configuration(s) for making a balked landing with one engine inoperative and the conditions under which a balked landing can be performed safely, or a warning against attempting a balked landing;

(3) The V_{SSE} determined in § 23.149; and

(4) Procedures for restarting any engine in flight including the effects of altitude.

(d) In addition to paragraphs (a) and either (b) or (c) of this section, as appropriate, for all normal, utility, and acrobatic category airplanes, the following information must be furnished:

(1) Procedures, speeds, and configuration(s) for making a normal takeoff, in

accordance with § 23.51 (a) and (b), and § 23.53 (a) and (b), and the subsequent climb, in accordance with § 23.65 and § 23.69(a).

(2) Procedures for abandoning a takeoff due to engine failure or other cause.

(e) In addition to paragraphs (a), (c), and (d) of this section, for all normal, utility, and acrobatic category multiengine airplanes, the information must include the following:

(1) Procedures and speeds for continuing a takeoff following engine failure and the conditions under which takeoff can safely be continued, or a warning against attempting to continue the takeoff.

(2) Procedures, speeds, and configurations for continuing a climb following engine failure, after takeoff, in accordance with § 23.67, or enroute, in accordance with § 23.69(b).

(f) In addition to paragraphs (a) and (c) of this section, for commuter category airplanes, the information must include the following:

(1) Procedures, speeds, and configuration(s) for making a normal takeoff.

(2) Procedures and speeds for carrying out an accelerate-stop in accordance with § 23.55.

(3) Procedures and speeds for continuing a takeoff following engine failure in accordance with § 23.59(a)(1) and for following the flight path determined under § 23.57 and § 23.61(a).

(g) For multiengine airplanes, information identifying each operating condition in which the fuel system independence prescribed in § 23.953 is necessary for safety must be furnished, together with instructions for placing the fuel system in a configuration used to show compliance with that section.

(h) For each airplane showing compliance with § 23.1353 (g)(2) or (g)(3), the operating procedures for disconnecting the battery from its charging source must be furnished.

(i) Information on the total quantity of usable fuel for each fuel tank, and the effect on the usable fuel quantity, as a result of a failure of any pump, must be furnished.

(j) Procedures for the safe operation of the airplane's systems and equipment, both in normal use and in the event of malfunction, must be furnished.

[Doc. No. 27807, 61 FR 5194, Feb. 9, 1996]

§ 23.1587 Performance information.

Unless otherwise prescribed, performance information must be provided over the altitude and temperature ranges required by § 23.45(b).

(a) For all airplanes, the following information must be furnished—

(1) The stalling speeds V_{SO} and V_{S1} with the landing gear and wing flaps retracted, determined at maximum weight under § 23.49, and the effect on these stalling speeds of angles of bank up to 60 degrees;

(2) The steady rate and gradient of climb with all engines operating, determined under § 23.69(a);

(3) The landing distance, determined under § 23.75 for each airport altitude and standard temperature, and the type of surface for which it is valid;

(4) The effect on landing distances of operation on other than smooth hard surfaces, when dry, determined under § 23.45(g); and

(5) The effect on landing distances of runway slope and 50 percent of the headwind component and 150 percent of the tailwind component.

(b) In addition to paragraph (a) of this section, for all normal, utility, and acrobatic category reciprocating engine-powered airplanes of 6,000 pounds or less maximum weight, the steady angle of climb/descent, determined under § 23.77(a), must be furnished.

(c) In addition to paragraphs (a) and (b) of this section, if appropriate, for normal, utility, and acrobatic category airplanes, the following information must be furnished—

(1) The takeoff distance, determined under § 23.53 and the type of surface for which it is valid.

(2) The effect on takeoff distance of operation on other than smooth hard surfaces, when dry, determined under § 23.45(g);

(3) The effect on takeoff distance of runway slope and 50 percent of the headwind component and 150 percent of the tailwind component;

(4) For multiengine reciprocating engine-powered airplanes of more than 6,000 pounds maximum weight and multiengine turbine powered airplanes, the

one-engine-inoperative takeoff climb/descent gradient, determined under §23.66;

(5) For multiengine airplanes, the enroute rate and gradient of climb/descent with one engine inoperative, determined under §23.69(b); and

(6) For single-engine airplanes, the glide performance determined under §23.71.

(d) In addition to paragraph (a) of this section, for commuter category airplanes, the following information must be furnished—

(1) The accelerate-stop distance determined under §23.55;

(2) The takeoff distance determined under §23.59(a);

(3) At the option of the applicant, the takeoff run determined under §23.59(b);

(4) The effect on accelerate-stop distance, takeoff distance and, if determined, takeoff run, of operation on other than smooth hard surfaces, when dry, determined under §23.45(g);

(5) The effect on accelerate-stop distance, takeoff distance, and if determined, takeoff run, of runway slope and 50 percent of the headwind component and 150 percent of the tailwind component;

(6) The net takeoff flight path determined under §23.61(b);

(7) The enroute gradient of climb/descent with one engine inoperative, determined under §23.69(b);

(8) The effect, on the net takeoff flight path and on the enroute gradient of climb/descent with one engine inoperative, of 50 percent of the headwind component and 150 percent of the tailwind component;

(9) Overweight landing performance information (determined by extrapolation and computed for the range of weights between the maximum landing and maximum takeoff weights) as follows—

(i) The maximum weight for each airport altitude and ambient temperature at which the airplane complies with the climb requirements of §23.63(d)(2); and

(ii) The landing distance determined under §23.75 for each airport altitude and standard temperature.

(10) The relationship between IAS and CAS determined in accordance with §23.1323 (b) and (c).

(11) The altimeter system calibration required by §23.1325(e).

[Doc. No. 27807, 61 FR 5194, Feb. 9, 1996]

§23.1589   Loading information.

The following loading information must be furnished:

(a) The weight and location of each item of equipment that can be easily removed, relocated, or replaced and that is installed when the airplane was weighed under the requirement of §23.25.

(b) Appropriate loading instructions for each possible loading condition between the maximum and minimum weights established under §23.25, to facilitate the center of gravity remaining within the limits established under §23.23.

[Doc. No. 4080, 29 FR 17955, Dec. 18, 1964, as amended by Amdt. 23–45, 58 FR 42167, Aug. 6, 1993; Amdt. 23–50, 61 FR 5195, Feb. 9, 1996]

APPENDIX A TO PART 23—SIMPLIFIED DESIGN LOAD CRITERIA

A23.1   *General.*

(a) The design load criteria in this appendix are an approved equivalent of those in §§23.321 through 23.459 of this subchapter for an airplane having a maximum weight of 6,000 pounds or less and the following configuration:

(1) A single engine excluding turbine powerplants;

(2) A main wing located closer to the airplane's center of gravity than to the aft, fuselage-mounted, empennage;

(3) A main wing that contains a quarter-chord sweep angle of not more than 15 degrees fore or aft;

(4) A main wing that is equipped with trailing-edge controls (ailerons or flaps, or both);

(5) A main wing aspect ratio not greater than 7;

(6) A horizontal tail aspect ratio not greater than 4;

(7) A horizontal tail volume coefficient not less than 0.34;

(8) A vertical tail aspect ratio not greater than 2;

(9) A vertical tail platform area not greater than 10 percent of the wing platform area; and

(10) Symmetrical airfoils must be used in both the horizontal and vertical tail designs.

(b) Appendix A criteria may not be used on any airplane configuration that contains any of the following design features:

(1) Canard, tandem-wing, close-coupled, or tailless arrangements of the lifting surfaces;

(2) Biplane or multiplane wing arrangements;

(3) T-tail, V-tail, or cruciform-tail (+) arrangements;

(4) Highly-swept wing platform (more than 15-degrees of sweep at the quarter-chord), delta planforms, or slatted lifting surfaces; or

(5) Winglets or other wing tip devices, or outboard fins.

A23.3 *Special symbols.*

n_1=Airplane Positive Maneuvering Limit Load Factor.

n_2=Airplane Negative Maneuvering Limit Load Factor.

n_3=Airplane Positive Gust Limit Load Factor at V_C.

n_4=Airplane Negative Gust Limit Load Factor at V_C.

n_{flap}=Airplane Positive Limit Load Factor With Flaps Fully Extended at V_F.

$$* \ V_{F \ min} = \text{Minimum Design Flap Speed} = 11.0\sqrt{n_1 W/S} \quad [\text{kts}]$$

$$* \ V_{A \ min} = \text{Minimum Design Maneuvering Speed} = 15.0\sqrt{n_1 W/S} \quad [\text{kts}]$$

$$* \ V_{C \ min} = \text{Minimum Design Cruising Speed} = 17.0\sqrt{n_1 W/S} \quad [\text{kts}]$$

$$* \ V_{D \ min} = \text{Minimum Design Dive Speed} = 24.0\sqrt{n_1 W/S} \quad [\text{kts}]$$

A23.5 *Certification in more than one category.*

The criteria in this appendix may be used for certification in the normal, utility, and acrobatic categories, or in any combination of these categories. If certification in more than one category is desired, the design category weights must be selected to make the term $n_1 W$ constant for all categories or greater for one desired category than for others. The wings and control surfaces (including wing flaps and tabs) need only be investigated for the maximum value of $n_1 W$, or for the category corresponding to the maximum design weight, where $n_1 W$ is constant. If the acrobatic category is selected, a special unsymmetrical flight load investigation in accordance with paragraphs A23.9(c)(2) and A23.11(c)(2) of this appendix must be completed. The wing, wing carrythrough, and the horizontal tail structures must be checked for this condition. The basic fuselage structure need only be investigated for the highest load factor design category selected. The local supporting structure for dead weight items need only be designed for the highest load factor imposed when the particular items are installed in the airplane. The engine mount, however, must be designed for a higher side load factor, if certification in the acrobatic category is de-

sired, than that required for certification in the normal and utility categories. When designing for landing loads, the landing gear and the airplane as a whole need only be investigated for the category corresponding to the maximum design weight. These simplifications apply to single-engine aircraft of conventional types for which experience is available, and the Administrator may require additional investigations for aircraft with unusual design features.

A23.7 *Flight loads.*

(a) Each flight load may be considered independent of altitude and, except for the local supporting structure for dead weight items, only the maximum design weight conditions must be investigated.

(b) Table 1 and figures 3 and 4 of this appendix must be used to determine values of n_1, n_2, n_3, and n_4, corresponding to the maximum design weights in the desired categories.

(c) Figures 1 and 2 of this appendix must be used to determine values of n_3 and n_4 corresponding to the minimum flying weights in the desired categories, and, if these load factors are greater than the load factors at the design weight, the supporting structure for dead weight items must be substantiated for the resulting higher load factors.

(d) Each specified wing and tail loading is independent of the center of gravity range. The applicant, however, must select a c.g. range, and the basic fuselage structure must be investigated for the most adverse dead weight loading conditions for the c.g. range selected.

(e) The following loads and loading conditions are the minimums for which strength must be provided in the structure:

(1) *Airplane equilibrium.* The aerodynamic wing loads may be considered to act normal to the relative wind, and to have a magnitude of 1.05 times the airplane normal loads (as determined from paragraphs A23.9 (b) and (c) of this appendix) for the positive flight conditions and a magnitude equal to the airplane normal loads for the negative conditions. Each chordwise and normal component of this wing load must be considered.

(2) *Minimum design airspeeds.* The minimum design airspeeds may be chosen by the applicant except that they may not be less than the minimum speeds found by using figure 3 of this appendix. In addition, V_{Cmin} need not exceed values of 0.9 V_H actually obtained at sea level for the lowest design weight category for which certification is desired. In computing these minimum design airspeeds, n_1 may not be less than 3.8.

(3) *Flight load factor.* The limit flight load factors specified in Table 1 of this appendix represent the ratio of the aerodynamic force component (acting normal to the assumed longitudinal axis of the airplane) to the weight of the airplane. A positive flight load

factor is an aerodynamic force acting upward, with respect to the airplane.

A23.9   *Flight conditions.*

(a) *General.* Each design condition in paragraphs (b) and (c) of this section must be used to assure sufficient strength for each condition of speed and load factor on or within the boundary of a $V-n$ diagram for the airplane similar to the diagram in figure 4 of this appendix. This diagram must also be used to determine the airplane structural operating limitations as specified in §§ 23.1501(c) through 23.1513 and § 23.1519.

(b) *Symmetrical flight conditions.* The airplane must be designed for symmetrical flight conditions as follows:

(1) The airplane must be designed for at least the four basic flight conditions, "A", "D", "E", and "G" as noted on the flight envelope of figure 4 of this appendix. In addition, the following requirements apply:

(i) The design limit flight load factors corresponding to conditions "D" and "E" of figure 4 must be at least as great as those specified in Table 1 and figure 4 of this appendix, and the design speed for these conditions must be at least equal to the value of V_D found from figure 3 of this appendix.

(ii) For conditions "A" and "G" of figure 4, the load factors must correspond to those specified in Table 1 of this appendix, and the design speeds must be computed using these load factors with the maximum static lift coefficient C_{NA} determined by the applicant. However, in the absence of more precise computations, these latter conditions may be based on a value of $C_{NA}=\pm1.35$ and the design speed for condition "A" may be less than V_{Amin}.

(iii) Conditions "C" and "F" of figure 4 need only be investigated when n_3 W/S or n_4 W/S are greater than n_1 W/S or n_2 W/S of this appendix, respectively.

(2) If flaps or other high lift devices intended for use at the relatively low airspeed of approach, landing, and takeoff, are installed, the airplane must be designed for the two flight conditions corresponding to the values of limit flap-down factors specified in Table 1 of this appendix with the flaps fully extended at not less than the design flap speed V_{Fmin} from figure 3 of this appendix.

(c) *Unsymmetrical flight conditions.* Each affected structure must be designed for unsymmetrical loadings as follows:

(1) The aft fuselage-to-wing attachment must be designed for the critical vertical surface load determined in accordance with paragraph SA23.11(c)(1) and (2) of this appendix.

(2) The wing and wing carry-through structures must be designed for 100 percent of condition "A" loading on one side of the plane of symmetry and 70 percent on the opposite side for certification in the normal and utility categories, or 60 percent on the opposite

side for certification in the acrobatic category.

(3) The wing and wing carry-through structures must be designed for the loads resulting from a combination of 75 percent of the positive maneuvering wing loading on both sides of the plane of symmetry and the maximum wing torsion resulting from aileron displacement. The effect of aileron displacement on wing torsion at V_C or V_A using the basic airfoil moment coefficient modified over the aileron portion of the span, must be computed as follows:

(i) $Cm=Cm$ $+0.01\delta\mu$ (up aileron side) wing basic airfoil.

(ii) $Cm=Cm$ $-0.01\delta\mu$ (down aileron side) wing basic airfoil, where $\delta\mu$ is the up aileron deflection and δ d is the down aileron deflection.

(4) Δ critical, which is the sum of $\delta\mu+\delta$ d must be computed as follows:

(i) Compute $\Delta\alpha$ and ΔB from the formulas:

$$\Delta_a = \frac{V_A}{V_C}\times\Delta_p \text{ and}$$

$$\Delta_b = 0.5\frac{V_A}{V_D}\times\Delta_p$$

Where $\Delta P=$ the maximum total deflection (sum of both aileron deflections) at V_A with V_A, V_C, and V_D described in subparagraph (2) of § 23.7(e) of this appendix.

(ii) Compute K from the formula:

$$K = \frac{\left(C_m - 0.01\delta_b\right)V_D{}^2}{\left(C_m - 0.01\delta_a\right)V_C{}^2}$$

where $\delta\alpha$ is the down aileron deflection corresponding to $\Delta\alpha$, and δ b is the down aileron deflection corresponding to Δ b as computed in step (i).

(iii) If K is less than 1.0, $\Delta\alpha$ is Δ critical and must be used to determine δU and δd. In this case, V_C is the critical speed which must be used in computing the wing torsion loads over the aileron span.

(iv) If K is equal to or greater than 1.0, ΔB is Δ critical and must be used to determine δU and δD. In this case, V_d is the critical speed which must be used in computing the wing torsion loads over the aileron span.

(d) *Supplementary conditions; rear lift truss; engine torque; side load on engine mount.* Each of the following supplementary conditions must be investigated:

(1) In designing the rear lift truss, the special condition specified in § 23.369 may be investigated instead of condition "G" of figure 4 of this appendix. If this is done, and if certification in more than one category is desired, the value of *W/S* used in the formula

317

appearing in §23.369 must be that for the category corresponding to the maximum gross weight.

(2) Each engine mount and its supporting structures must be designed for the maximum limit torque corresponding to METO power and propeller speed acting simultaneously with the limit loads resulting from the maximum positive maneuvering flight load factor n_1. The limit torque must be obtained by multiplying the mean torque by a factor of 1.33 for engines with five or more cylinders. For 4, 3, and 2 cylinder engines, the factor must be 2, 3, and 4, respectively.

(3) Each engine mount and its supporting structure must be designed for the loads resulting from a lateral limit load factor of not less than 1.47 for the normal and utility categories, or 2.0 for the acrobatic category.

A23.11 *Control surface loads.*

(a) *General.* Each control surface load must be determined using the criteria of paragraph (b) of this section and must lie within the simplified loadings of paragraph (c) of this section.

(b) *Limit pilot forces.* In each control surface loading condition described in paragraphs (c) through (e) of this section, the airloads on the movable surfaces and the corresponding deflections need not exceed those which could be obtained in flight by employing the maximum limit pilot forces specified in the table in §23.397(b). If the surface loads are limited by these maximum limit pilot forces, the tabs must either be considered to be deflected to their maximum travel in the direction which would assist the pilot or the deflection must correspond to the maximum degree of "out of trim" expected at the speed for the condition under consideration. The tab load, however, need not exceed the value specified in Table 2 of this appendix.

(c) *Surface loading conditions.* Each surface loading condition must be investigated as follows:

(1) Simplified limit surface loadings for the horizontal tail, vertical tail, aileron, wing flaps, and trim tabs are specified in figures 5 and 6 of this appendix.

(i) The distribution of load along the span of the surface, irrespective of the chordwise load distribution, must be assumed proportional to the total chord, except on horn balance surfaces.

(ii) The load on the stabilizer and elevator, and the load on fin and rudder, must be distributed chordwise as shown in figure 7 of this appendix.

(iii) In order to ensure adequate torsional strength and to account for maneuvers and gusts, the most severe loads must be considered in association with every center of pressure position between the leading edge and the half chord of the mean chord of the surface (stabilizer and elevator, or fin and rudder).

(iv) To ensure adequate strength under high leading edge loads, the most severe stabilizer and fin loads must be further considered as being increased by 50 percent over the leading 10 percent of the chord with the loads aft of this appropriately decreased to retain the same total load.

(v) The most severe elevator and rudder loads should be further considered as being distributed parabolically from three times the mean loading of the surface (stabilizer and elevator, or fin and rudder) at the leading edge of the elevator and rudder, respectively, to zero at the trailing edge according to the equation:

$$P(x) = 3\,(\overline{w})\,\frac{(c-x)^2}{c_f^{\,2}}$$

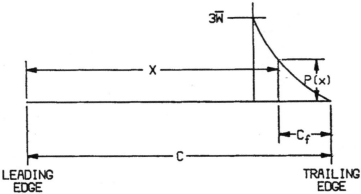

LEADING EDGE OF ELEVATOR
AND RUDDER, RESPECTIVELY

Where—

P(x)=local pressure at the chordwise stations x,

c=chord length of the tail surface,

c_f=chord length of the elevator and rudder respectively, and

$\bar{w}$≤=average surface loading as specified in Figure A5.

(vi) The chordwise loading distribution for ailerons, wing flaps, and trim tabs are specified in Table 2 of this appendix.

(2) If certification in the acrobatic category is desired, the horizontal tail must be investigated for an unsymmetrical load of 100 percent w on one side of the airplane centerline and 50 percent on the other side of the airplane centerline.

(d) *Outboard fins.* Outboard fins must meet the requirements of §23.445.

(e) *Special devices.* Special devices must meet the requirements of §23.459.

A23.13   *Control system loads.*

(a) *Primary flight controls and systems.* Each primary flight control and system must be designed as follows:

(1) The flight control system and its supporting structure must be designed for loads corresponding to 125 percent of the computed hinge moments of the movable control surface in the conditions prescribed in A23.11 of this appendix. In addition—

(i) The system limit loads need not exceed those that could be produced by the pilot and automatic devices operating the controls; and

(ii) The design must provide a rugged system for service use, including jamming, ground gusts, taxiing downwind, control inertia, and friction.

(2) Acceptable maximum and minimum limit pilot forces for elevator, aileron, and rudder controls are shown in the table in §23.397(b). These pilots loads must be assumed to act at the appropriate control grips or pads as they would under flight conditions, and to be reacted at the attachments of the control system to the control surface horn.

(b) *Dual controls.* If there are dual controls, the systems must be designed for pilots operating in opposition, using individual pilot loads equal to 75 percent of those obtained in accordance with paragraph (a) of this section, except that individual pilot loads may not be less than the minimum limit pilot forces shown in the table in §23.397(b).

(c) *Ground gust conditions.* Ground gust conditions must meet the requirements of §23.415.

(d) *Secondary controls and systems.* Secondary controls and systems must meet the requirements of §23.405.

TABLE 1—LIMIT FLIGHT LOAD FACTORS
[Limit flight load factors]

Flight load factors	Normal category	Utility category	Acrobatic category
Flaps up:			
n_1	3.8	4.4	6.0
n_2	$-0.5\, n_1$	....	....
n_3	(1)	....	....
n_4	(2)	....	....
Flaps down:			
n flap	$0.5\, n_1$	....	....
n flap	[3] Zero	....	....

[1] Find n_3 from Fig. 1

319

[2] Find n_4 from Fig. 2

[3] Vertical wing load may be assumed equal to zero and only the flap part of the wing need be checked for this condition.

Table 2 - Average limit control surface loading

AVERAGE LIMIT CONTROL SURFACE LOADING			
SURFACE	DIRECTION OF LOADING	MAGNITUDE OF LOADING	CHORDWISE DISTRIBUTION
Horizontal Tail I	a) Up and Down	Figure A5 Curve [2]	
	b) Unsymmetrical Loading [Up and Down]	100% $\overline{w}$ on one side of airplane ₵ 65% $\overline{w}$ on other side of airplane ₵ for normal and utility categories. For acrobatic category see A23.11[c]	See Figure A7
Vertical Tail II	Right and Left	Figure A5 Curve [1]	Same as above
Aileron III	a) Up and Down	Figure A6 Curve [5]	[C]
Wing Flap IV	a) Up	Figure A6 Curve [4]	[D]
	b) Down	.25 x Up Load [a]	
Trim Tab V	a) Up and Down	Figure A6 Curve [3]	Same as [D] above

NOTE: The surface loading I, II, III, and V above are based on speeds V_A min and V_C min.

The loading of IV is based on V_F min.

If values of speed <u>greater than</u> these minimums are selected for design, the appropriate surface loadings must be multiplied by the ratio $\left(\dfrac{V_{selected}}{V_{minimum}}\right)^2$.

For conditions I, II, III, and V the multiplying factor used must be the higher of $\left(\dfrac{V_A \, sel.}{V_A \, min.}\right)^2$ or $\left(\dfrac{V_C \, sel.}{V_C \, min.}\right)^2$

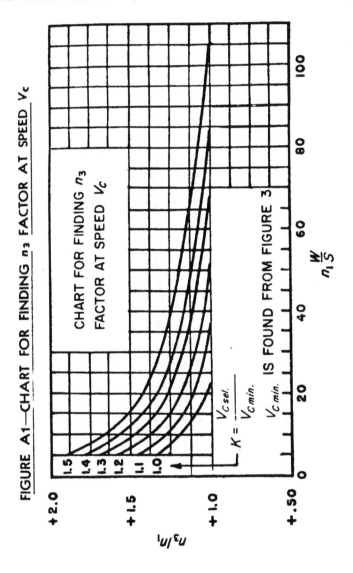

FIGURE A1—CHART FOR FINDING n_3 FACTOR AT SPEED V_c

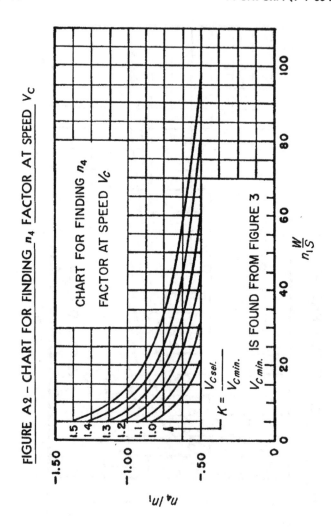

FIGURE A2 – CHART FOR FINDING n_4 FACTOR AT SPEED V_C

FIGURE A3—DETERMINATIONS OF MINIMUM DESIGN SPEEDS—EQUATIONS
SPEEDS ARE IN KNOTS

$V_{D\ min} = 24.0 \sqrt{n_1 \dfrac{W}{S}}$ but need not exceed

$$\dfrac{1.4\sqrt{n_1}}{3.8} V_{C\ min};$$

$V_{C\ min} = 17.0 \sqrt{n_1 \dfrac{W}{S}}$ but need not exceed

$0.9\ V_H;\ V_{A\ min} = 15.0 \sqrt{n_1 \dfrac{W}{S}}$ but need not exceed V_C used

in design. $V_{F\ min} = 11.0 \sqrt{n_1 \dfrac{W}{S}}$

FIGURE A-4—FLIGHT ENVELOPE

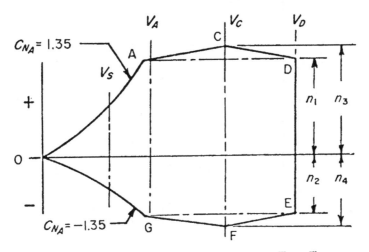

1. Conditions "C" or "F" need only be investigated when $n_3 \dfrac{W}{S}$ or $n_4 \dfrac{W}{S}$ is greater

than $n_1 \dfrac{W}{S}$ $W /_S$, respectively.

2. Condition "G" need not be investigated when the supplementary condition
specified in § 23.369 is investigated.

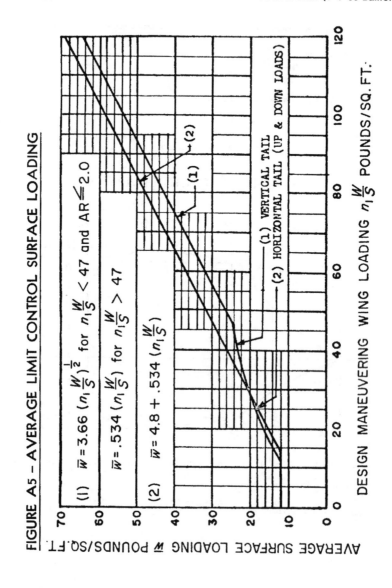

FIGURE A5 – AVERAGE LIMIT CONTROL SURFACE LOADING

(1) $\bar{w} = 3.66 \left(n_1 \frac{W}{S} \right)^{\frac{1}{2}}$ for $n_1 \frac{W}{S} < 47$ and $AR \leq 2.0$

$\bar{w} = .534 \left(n_1 \frac{W}{S} \right)$ for $n_1 \frac{W}{S} > 47$

(2) $\bar{w} = 4.8 + .534 \left(n_1 \frac{W}{S} \right)$

(1) VERTICAL TAIL

(2) HORIZONTAL TAIL (UP & DOWN LOADS)

DESIGN MANEUVERING WING LOADING $n_1 \frac{W}{S}$ POUNDS/SQ. FT.

AVERAGE SURFACE LOADING $\bar{w}$ POUNDS/SQ. FT.

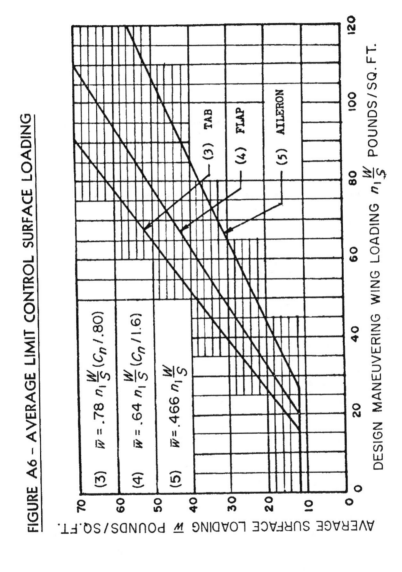

FIGURE A6 – AVERAGE LIMIT CONTROL SURFACE LOADING

(3) $\bar{w} = .78\, n_1 \frac{W}{S}\,(C_n / .80)$

(4) $\bar{w} = .64\, n_1 \frac{W}{S}\,(C_n / 1.6)$

(5) $\bar{w} = .466\, n_1 \frac{W}{S}$

(3) TAB

(4) FLAP

(5) AILERON

AVERAGE SURFACE LOADING $\bar{W}$ POUNDS/SQ. FT.

DESIGN MANEUVERING WING LOADING $n_1 \frac{W}{S}$ POUNDS / SQ. FT.

FIGURE A7.—CHORDWISE LOAD DISTRIBUTION FOR STABILIZER AND ELEVATOR OR FIN AND
RUDDER

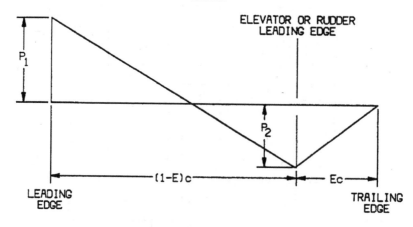

$$P_1 = 2\,(\overline{w})\,\frac{(2 - E - 3d')}{(1 - E)}$$

$$P_2 = 2\,(\overline{w})\,(3d' + E - 1)$$

where:

$\overline{w}$=average surface loading (as specified in figure A.5)

E=ratio of elevator (or rudder) chord to total stabilizer and elevator (or fin and rudder) chord.

d′=ratio of distance of center of pressure of a unit spanwise length of combined stabilizer and elevator (or fin and rudder) measured from stabilizer (or fin) leading edge to the local chord. Sign convention is positive when center of pressure is behind leading edge.

c=local chord.

NOTE: Positive values of $\overline{w}$, P_1 and P_2 are all measured in the same direction.

[Doc. No. 4080, 29 FR 17955, Dec. 18, 1964, as amended by Amdt. 23–7, 34 FR 13097, Aug. 13, 1969; 34 FR 14727, Sept. 24, 1969; Amdt. 23–16, 40 FR 2577, Jan. 14, 1975; Amdt. 23–28, 47 FR 13315, Mar. 29, 1982; Amdt. 23–48, 61 FR 5149, Feb. 9, 1996]

APPENDIX B TO PART 23 [RESERVED]

APPENDIX C TO PART 23—BASIC LANDING CONDITIONS

[C23.1 *Basic landing conditions*]

Condition	Tail wheel type		Nose wheel type		
	Level landing	Tail-down landing	Level landing with inclined reactions	Level landing with nose wheel just clear of ground	Tail-down landing
Reference section	23.479(a)(1)	23.481(a)(1)	23.479(a)(2)(i)	23.479(a)(2)(ii)	23.481(a)(2) and (b).
Vertical component at c. g	nW	nW	nW	nW	nW.
Fore and aft component at c. g	KnW	0	KnW	KnW	0.
Lateral component in either direction at c. g.	0	0	0	0	0.
Shock absorber extension (hydraulic shock absorber).	Note (2)	Note (2)	Note (2)	Note (2)	Note (2).
Shock absorber deflection (rubber or spring shock absorber), percent.	100	100	100	100	100.
Tire deflection	Static	Static	Static	Static	Static.
Main wheel loads (both wheels) (Vr)	(n–L)W	(n–L)W b/d	(n-L)W a′/d′	(n-L)W	(n-L)W.
Main wheel loads (both wheels) (Dr)	KnW	0	KnW a′/d′	KnW	0.
Tail (nose) wheel loads (Vf)	0	(n–L)W a/d	(n–L)W b′/d′	0	0.
Tail (nose) wheel loads (Df)	0	0	KnW b′/d′	0	0.

[C23.1 *Basic landing conditions*]

Condition	Tail wheel type		Nose wheel type		
	Level landing	Tail-down landing	Level landing with inclined reactions	Level landing with nose wheel just clear of ground	Tail-down landing
Notes	(1), (3), and (4).	(4)	(1)	(1), (3), and (4) ..	(3) and (4).

NOTE (1). K may be determined as follows: $K=0.25$ for $W=3,000$ pounds or less; $K=0.33$ for $W=6,000$ pounds or greater, with linear variation of K between these weights.

NOTE (2). For the purpose of design, the maximum load factor is assumed to occur throughout the shock absorber stroke from 25 percent deflection to 100 percent deflection unless otherwise shown and the load factor must be used with whatever shock absorber extension is most critical for each element of the landing gear.

NOTE (3). Unbalanced moments must be balanced by a rational or conservative method.

NOTE (4). L is defined in § 23.735(b).

NOTE (5). n is the limit inertia load factor, at the c.g. of the airplane, selected under § 23.473 (d), (f), and (g).

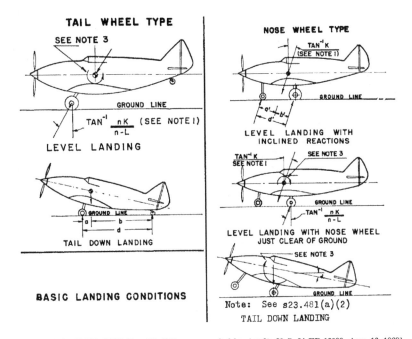

[Doc. No. 4080, 29 FR 17955, Dec. 18, 1964, as amended by Amdt. 23–7, 34 FR 13099, Aug. 13, 1969]

APPENDIX D TO PART 23—WHEEL SPIN-UP AND SPRING-BACK LOADS

D23.1 *Wheel spin-up loads.*

(a) The following method for determining wheel spin-up loads for landing conditions is based on NACA T.N. 863. However, the drag component used for design may not be less than the drag load prescribed in § 23.479(b).

$$F_{Hmax}=1/r_e \sqrt{2I_w(V_H-V_c)nF_{Vmax}/t_S}$$

where—

$F_{Hmax}=$maximum rearward horizontal force acting on the wheel (in pounds);

$r_e=$effective rolling radius of wheel under impact based on recommended operating tire pressure (which may be assumed to be equal to the rolling radius under a static load of n_jW_e) in feet;

$I_w=$rotational mass moment of inertia of rolling assembly (in slug feet);

V_H=linear velocity of airplane parallel to ground at instant of contact (assumed to be 1.2 V_{S0}, in feet per second);

V_c=peripheral speed of tire, if prerotation is used (in feet per second) (there must be a positive means of pre-rotation before pre-rotation may be considered);

n=equals effective coefficient of friction (0.80 may be used);

F_{Vmax}=maximum vertical force on wheel (pounds)=$n_j W_e$, where W_e and n_j are defined in §23.725;

t_s=time interval between ground contact and attainment of maximum vertical force on wheel (seconds). (However, if the value of F_{Vmax}, from the above equation exceeds 0.8 F_{Vmax}, the latter value must be used for F_{Hmax}.)

(b) The equation assumes a linear variation of load factor with time until the peak load is reached and under this assumption, the equation determines the drag force at the time that the wheel peripheral velocity at radius r_e equals the airplane velocity. Most shock absorbers do not exactly follow a linear variation of load factor with time. Therefore, rational or conservative allowances must be made to compensate for these variations. On most landing gears, the time for wheel spin-up will be less than the time required to develop maximum vertical load factor for the specified rate of descent and forward velocity. For exceptionally large wheels, a wheel peripheral velocity equal to the ground speed may not have been attained at the time of maximum vertical gear load. However, as stated above, the drag spin-up load need not exceed 0.8 of the maximum vertical loads.

(c) Dynamic spring-back of the landing gear and adjacent structure at the instant just after the wheels come up to speed may result in dynamic forward acting loads of considerable magnitude. This effect must be determined, in the level landing condition, by assuming that the wheel spin-up loads calculated by the methods of this appendix are reversed. Dynamic spring-back is likely to become critical for landing gear units having wheels of large mass or high landing speeds.

[Doc. No. 4080, 29 FR 17955, Dec. 18, 1964, as amended by Amdt. 23–45, 58 FR 42167, Aug. 6, 1993]

APPENDIX E TO PART 23 [RESERVED]

APPENDIX F TO PART 23—TEST PROCEDURE

Acceptable test procedure for self-extinguishing materials for showing compliance with §§23.853, 23.855 and 23.1359.

(a) *Conditioning.* Specimens must be conditioned to 70 degrees F, plus or minus 5 degrees, and at 50 percent plus or minus 5 per-

cent relative humidity until moisture equilibrium is reached or for 24 hours. Only one specimen at a time may be removed from the conditioning environment immediately before subjecting it to the flame.

(b) *Specimen configuration.* Except as provided for materials used in electrical wire and cable insulation and in small parts, materials must be tested either as a section cut from a fabricated part as installed in the airplane or as a specimen simulating a cut section, such as: a specimen cut from a flat sheet of the material or a model of the fabricated part. The specimen may be cut from any location in a fabricated part; however, fabricated units, such as sandwich panels, may not be separated for a test. The specimen thickness must be no thicker than the minimum thickness to be qualified for use in the airplane, except that: (1) Thick foam parts, such as seat cushions, must be tested in ½ inch thickness; (2) when showing compliance with §23.853(d)(3)(v) for materials used in small parts that must be tested, the materials must be tested in no more than ⅛ inch thickness; (3) when showing compliance with §23.1359(c) for materials used in electrical wire and cable insulation, the wire and cable specimens must be the same size as used in the airplane. In the case of fabrics, both the warp and fill direction of the weave must be tested to determine the most critical flammability conditions. When performing the tests prescribed in paragraphs (d) and (e) of this appendix, the specimen must be mounted in a metal frame so that (1) in the vertical tests of paragraph (d) of this appendix, the two long edges and the upper edge are held securely; (2) in the horizontal test of paragraph (e) of this appendix, the two long edges and the edge away from the flame are held securely; (3) the exposed area of the specimen is at least 2 inches wide and 12 inches long, unless the actual size used in the airplane is smaller; and (4) the edge to which the burner flame is applied must not consist of the finished or protected edge of the specimen but must be representative of the actual cross section of the material or part installed in the airplane. When performing the test prescribed in paragraph (f) of this appendix, the specimen must be mounted in metal frame so that all four edges are held securely and the exposed area of the specimen is at least 8 inches by 8 inches.

(c) *Apparatus.* Except as provided in paragraph (g) of this appendix, tests must be conducted in a draft-free cabinet in accordance with Federal Test Method Standard 191 Method 5903 (revised Method 5902) which is available from the General Services Administration, Business Service Center, Region 3, Seventh and D Streets SW., Washington, D.C. 20407, or with some other approved equivalent method. Specimens which are too large for the cabinet must be tested in similar draft-free conditions.

(d) *Vertical test.* A minimum of three specimens must be tested and the results averaged. For fabrics, the direction of weave corresponding to the most critical flammability conditions must be parallel to the longest dimension. Each specimen must be supported vertically. The specimen must be exposed to a Bunsen or Tirrill burner with a nominal ⅜-inch I.D. tube adjusted to give a flame of 1½ inches in height. The minimum flame temperature measured by a calibrated thermocouple pryometer in the center of the flame must be 1550 °F. The lower edge of the specimen must be three-fourths inch above the top edge of the burner. The flame must be applied to the center line of the lower edge of the specimen. For materials covered by §§ 23.853(d)(3)(i) and 23.853(f), the flame must be applied for 60 seconds and then removed. For materials covered by § 23.853(d)(3)(ii), the flame must be applied for 12 seconds and then removed. Flame time, burn length, and flaming time of drippings, if any, must be recorded. The burn length determined in accordance with paragraph (h) of this appendix must be measured to the nearest one-tenth inch.

(e) *Horizontal test.* A minimum of three specimens must be tested and the results averaged. Each specimen must be supported horizontally. The exposed surface when installed in the airplane must be face down for the test. The specimen must be exposed to a Bunsen burner or Tirrill burner with a nominal ⅜-inch I.D. tube adjusted to give a flame of 1½ inches in height. The minimum flame temperature measured by a calibrated thermocouple pyrometer in the center of the flame must be 1550 °F. The specimen must be positioned so that the edge being tested is three-fourths of an inch above the top of, and on the center line of, the burner. The flame must be applied for 15 seconds and then removed. A minimum of 10 inches of the specimen must be used for timing purposes, approximately 1½ inches must burn before the burning front reaches the timing zone, and the average burn rate must be recorded.

(f) *Forty-five degree test.* A minimum of three specimens must be tested and the results averaged. The specimens must be supported at an angle of 45 degrees to a horizontal surface. The exposed surface when installed in the aircraft must be face down for the test. The specimens must be exposed to a Bunsen or Tirrill burner with a nominal ⅜ inch I.D. tube adjusted to give a flame of 1½ inches in height. The minimum flame temperature measured by a calibrated thermocouple pyrometer in the center of the flame must be 1550 °F. Suitable precautions must be taken to avoid drafts. The flame must be applied for 30 seconds with one-third contacting the material at the center of the specimen and then removed. Flame time,

glow time, and whether the flame penetrates (passes through) the specimen must be recorded.

(g) *Sixty-degree test.* A minimum of three specimens of each wire specification (make and size) must be tested. The specimen of wire or cable (including insulation) must be placed at an angle of 60 degrees with the horizontal in the cabinet specified in paragraph (c) of this appendix, with the cabinet door open during the test or placed within a chamber approximately 2 feet high × 1 foot × 1 foot, open at the top and at one vertical side (front), that allows sufficient flow of air for complete combustion but is free from drafts. The specimen must be parallel to and approximately 6 inches from the front of the chamber. The lower end of the specimen must be held rigidly clamped. The upper end of the specimen must pass over a pulley or rod and must have an appropriate weight attached to it so that the specimen is held tautly throughout the flammability test. The test specimen span between lower clamp and upper pulley or rod must be 24 inches and must be marked 8 inches from the lower end to indicate the central point for flame application. A flame from a Bunsen or Tirrill burner must be applied for 30 seconds at the test mark. The burner must be mounted underneath the test mark on the specimen, perpendicular to the specimen and at an angle of 30 degrees to the vertical plane of the specimen. The burner must have a nominal bore of three-eighths inch, and must be adjusted to provide a three-inch-high flame with an inner cone approximately one-third of the flame height. The minimum temperature of the hottest portion of the flame, as measured with a calibrated thermocouple pyrometer, may not be less than 1,750 °F. The burner must be positioned so that the hottest portion of the flame is applied to the test mark on the wire. Flame time, burn length, and flaming time drippings, if any, must be recorded. The burn length determined in accordance with paragraph (h) of this appendix must be measured to the nearest one-tenth inch. Breaking of the wire specimen is not considered a failure.

(h) *Burn length.* Burn length is the distance from the original edge to the farthest evidence of damage to the test specimen due to flame impingement, including areas of partial or complete consumption, charring, or embrittlement, but not including areas sooted, stained, warped, or discolored, nor areas where material has shrunk or melted away from the heat source.

[Amdt. 23–23, 43 FR 50594, Oct. 30, 1978, as amended by Amdt. 23–34, 52 FR 1835, Jan. 15, 1987; 52 FR 34745, Sept. 14, 1987; Amdt. 23–49, 61 FR 5170, Feb. 9, 1996]

APPENDIX G TO PART 23—INSTRUCTIONS
FOR CONTINUED AIRWORTHINESS

G23.1 *General.* (a) This appendix specifies
requirements for the preparation of Instructions for Continued Airworthiness as required by § 23.1529.

(b) The Instructions for Continued Airworthiness for each airplane must include
the Instructions for Continued Airworthiness
for each engine and propeller (hereinafter
designated 'products'), for each appliance required by this chapter, and any required information relating to the interface of those
appliances and products with the airplane. If
Instructions for Continued Airworthiness are
not supplied by the manufacturer of an appliance or product installed in the airplane,
the Instructions for Continued Airworthiness
for the airplane must include the information essential to the continued airworthiness
of the airplane.

(c) The applicant must submit to the FAA
a program to show how changes to the Instructions for Continued Airworthiness made
by the applicant or by the manufacturers of
products and appliances installed in the airplane will be distributed.

G23.2 *Format.* (a) The Instructions for
Continued Airworthiness must be in the
form of a manual or manuals as appropriate
for the quantity of data to be provided.

(b) The format of the manual or manuals
must provide for a practical arrangement.

G23.3 *Content.* The contents of the manual
or manuals must be prepared in the English
language. The Instructions for Continued
Airworthiness must contain the following
manuals or sections, as appropriate, and information:

(a) *Airplane maintenance manual or section.*
(1) Introduction information that includes an
explanation of the airplane's features and
data to the extent necessary for maintenance or preventive maintenance.

(2) A description of the airplane and its
systems and installations including its engines, propellers, and appliances.

(3) Basic control and operation information
describing how the airplane components and
systems are controlled and how they operate, including any special procedures and
limitations that apply.

(4) Servicing information that covers details regarding servicing points, capacities of
tanks, reservoirs, types of fluids to be used,
pressures applicable to the various systems,
location of access panels for inspection and
servicing, locations of lubrication points, lubricants to be used, equipment required for
servicing, tow instructions and limitations,
mooring, jacking, and leveling information.

(b) *Maintenance instructions.* (1) Scheduling
information for each part of the airplane and
its engines, auxiliary power units, propellers,
accessories, instruments, and equipment
that provides the recommended periods at
which they should be cleaned, inspected, adjusted, tested, and lubricated, and the degree
of inspection, the applicable wear tolerances,
and work recommended at these periods.
However, the applicant may refer to an accessory, instrument, or equipment manufacturer as the source of this information if the
applicant shows that the item has an exceptionally high degree of complexity requiring
specialized maintenance techniques, test
equipment, or expertise. The recommended
overhaul periods and necessary cross reference to the Airworthiness Limitations section of the manual must also be included. In
addition, the applicant must include an inspection program that includes the frequency and extent of the inspections necessary to provide for the continued airworthiness of the airplane.

(2) Troubleshooting information describing
probable malfunctions, how to recognize
those malfunctions, and the remedial action
for those malfunctions.

(3) Information describing the order and
method of removing and replacing products
and parts with any necessary precautions to
be taken.

(4) Other general procedural instructions
including procedures for system testing during ground running, symmetry checks,
weighing and determining the center of gravity, lifting and shoring, and storage limitations.

(c) Diagrams of structural access plates
and information needed to gain access for inspections when access plates are not provided.

(d) Details for the application of special inspection techniques including radiographic
and ultrasonic testing where such processes
are specified.

(e) Information needed to apply protective
treatments to the structure after inspection.

(f) All data relative to structural fasteners
such as identification, discard recommendations, and torque values.

(g) A list of special tools needed.

(h) In addition, for commuter category airplanes, the following information must be
furnished:

(1) Electrical loads applicable to the various systems;

(2) Methods of balancing control surfaces;

(3) Identification of primary and secondary
structures; and

(4) Special repair methods applicable to
the airplane.

G23.4 *Airworthiness Limitations section.* The
Instructions for Continued Airworthiness
must contain a section titled Airworthiness
Limitations that is segregated and clearly

distinguishable from the rest of the document. This section must set forth each mandatory replacement time, structural inspection interval, and related structural inspection procedure required for type certification. If the Instructions for Continued Airworthiness consist of multiple documents, the section required by this paragraph must be included in the principal manual. This section must contain a legible statement in a prominent location that reads: "The Airworthiness Limitations section is FAA approved and specifies maintenance required under §§43.16 and 91.403 of the Federal Aviation Regulations unless an alternative program has been FAA approved."

[Amdt. 23–26, 45 FR 60171, Sept. 11, 1980, as amended by Amdt. 23–34, 52 FR 1835, Jan. 15, 1987; 52 FR 34745, Sept. 14, 1987; Amdt. 23–37, 54 FR 34329, Aug. 18, 1989]

APPENDIX H TO PART 23—INSTALLATION OF AN AUTOMATIC POWER RESERVE (APR) SYSTEM

H23.1, *General.*

(a) This appendix specifies requirements for installation of an APR engine power control system that automatically advances power or thrust on the operating engine(s) in the event any engine fails during takeoff.

(b) With the APR system and associated systems functioning normally, all applicable requirements (except as provided in this appendix) must be met without requiring any action by the crew to increase power or thrust.

H23.2, *Definitions.*

(a) *Automatic power reserve system* means the entire automatic system used only during takeoff, including all devices both mechanical and electrical that sense engine failure, transmit signals, actuate fuel controls or power levers on operating engines, including power sources, to achieve the scheduled power increase and furnish cockpit information on system operation.

(b) *Selected takeoff power*, notwithstanding the definition of "Takeoff Power" in part 1 of the Federal Aviation Regulations, means the power obtained from each initial power setting approved for takeoff.

(c) *Critical Time Interval*, as illustrated in figure H1, means that period starting at V_1 minus one second and ending at the intersection of the engine and APR failure flight path line with the minimum performance all engine flight path line. The engine and APR failure flight path line intersects the one-engine-inoperative flight path line at 400 feet above the takeoff surface. The engine and APR failure flight path is based on the airplane's performance and must have a positive gradient of at least 0.5 percent at 400 feet above the takeoff surface.

FIGURE H1 - CRITICAL TIME INTERVAL ILLUSTRATION.

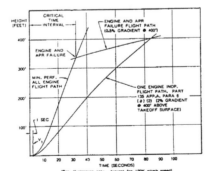

H23.3, *Reliability and performance requirements.*

(a) It must be shown that, during the critical time interval, an APR failure that increases or does not affect power on either engine will not create a hazard to the airplane, or it must be shown that such failures are improbable.

(b) It must be shown that, during the critical time interval, there are no failure modes

331

of the APR system that would result in a failure that will decrease the power on either engine or it must be shown that such failures are extremely improbable.

(c) It must be shown that, during the critical time interval, there will be no failure of the APR system in combination with an engine failure or it must be shown that such failures are extremely improbable.

(d) All applicable performance requirements must be met with an engine failure occurring at the most critical point during takeoff with the APR system functioning normally.

H23.4, *Power setting.*

The selected takeoff power set on each engine at the beginning of the takeoff roll may not be less than—

(a) The power necessary to attain, at V_1, 90 percent of the maximum takeoff power approved for the airplane for the existing conditions;

(b) That required to permit normal operation of all safety-related systems and equipment that are dependent upon engine power or power lever position; and

(c) That shown to be free of hazardous engine response characteristics when power is advanced from the selected takeoff power level to the maximum approved takeoff power.

H23.5, *Powerplant controls—general.*

(a) In addition to the requirements of § 23.1141, no single failure or malfunction (or probable combination thereof) of the APR, including associated systems, may cause the failure of any powerplant function necessary for safety.

(b) The APR must be designed to—

(1) Provide a means to verify to the flight crew before takeoff that the APR is in an operating condition to perform its intended function;

(2) Automatically advance power on the operating engines following an engine failure during takeoff to achieve the maximum attainable takeoff power without exceeding engine operating limits;

(3) Prevent deactivation of the APR by manual adjustment of the power levers following an engine failure;

(4) Provide a means for the flight crew to deactivate the automatic function. This means must be designed to prevent inadvertent deactivation; and

(5) Allow normal manual decrease or increase in power up to the maximum takeoff power approved for the airplane under the existing conditions through the use of power levers, as stated in § 23.1141(c), except as provided under paragraph (c) of H23.5 of this appendix.

(c) For airplanes equipped with limiters that automatically prevent engine operating limits from being exceeded, other means may be used to increase the maximum level of power controlled by the power levers in the event of an APR failure. The means must be located on or forward of the power levers, must be easily identified and operated under all operating conditions by a single action of any pilot with the hand that is normally used to actuate the power levers, and must meet the requirements of § 23.777 (a), (b), and (c).

H23.6, *Powerplant instruments.*

In addition to the requirements of § 23.1305:

(a) A means must be provided to indicate when the APR is in the armed or ready condition.

(b) If the inherent flight characteristics of the airplane do not provide warning that an engine has failed, a warning system independent of the APR must be provided to give the pilot a clear warning of any engine failure during takeoff.

(c) Following an engine failure at V_1 or above, there must be means for the crew to readily and quickly verify that the APR has operated satisfactorily.

[Doc. 26344, 58 FR 18979, Apr. 9, 1993]

APPENDIX I TO PART 23—SEAPLANE LOADS

Appendix I

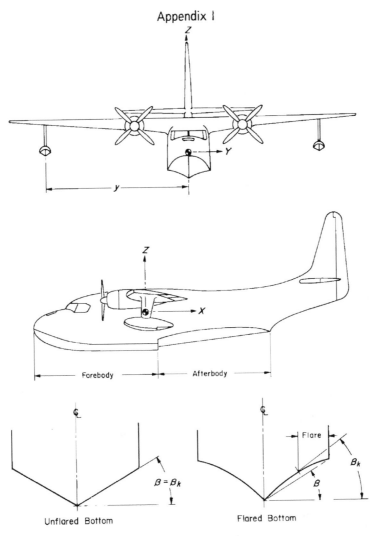

FIGURE 1. Pictorial definition of angles, dimensions, and directions on a seaplane.

Appendix I (continued)

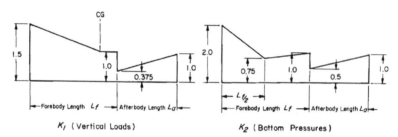

FIGURE 2. Hull station weighing factor.

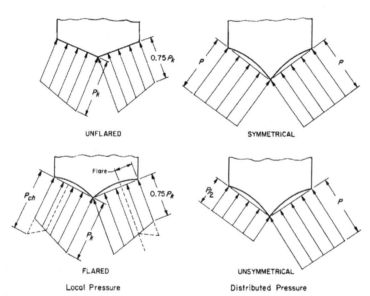

FIGURE 3. Transverse pressure distributions.

[Amdt. 23–45, 58 FR 42167, Aug. 6, 1993; 58 FR 51970, Oct. 5, 1993]

PART 25—AIRWORTHINESS STAND-ARDS: TRANSPORT CATEGORY AIRPLANES

Special Federal Aviation Regulation No. 13

Subpart A—General

Sec.
25.1 Applicability.
25.2 Special retroactive requirements.

AUTHORITY: 49 U.S.C. 106(g), 40113, 44701, 44702 and 44704.

SOURCE: Docket No. 5066, 29 FR 18291, Dec. 24, 1964, unless otherwise noted.

SPECIAL FEDERAL AVIATION REGULATION NO. 13

1. *Applicability.* Contrary provisions of the Civil Air Regulations regarding certification notwithstanding,[1] this regulation shall provide the basis for approval by the Administrator of modifications of individual Douglas DC–3 and Lockheed L–18 airplanes subsequent to the effective date of this regulation.

2. *General modifications.* Except as modified in sections 3 and 4 of this regulation, an applicant for approval of modifications to a DC–3 or L–18 airplane which result in changes in design or in changes to approved limitations shall show that the modifications were accomplished in accordance with the rules of either Part 4a or Part 4b in effect on September 1, 1953, which are applicable to the modification being made: *Provided,* That an applicant may elect to accomplish a modification in accordance with the rules of Part 4b in effect on the date of application

for the modification in lieu of Part 4a or Part 4b as in effect on September 1, 1953: *And provided further,* That each specific modification must be accomplished in accordance with all of the provisions contained in the elected rules relating to the particular modification.

3. *Specific conditions for approval.* An applicant for any approval of the following specific changes shall comply with section 2 of this regulation as modified by the applicable provisions of this section.

(a) *Increase in take-off power limitation— 1,200 to 1,350 horsepower.* The engine take-off power limitation for the airplane may be increased to more than 1,200 horsepower but not to more than 1,350 horsepower per engine if the increase in power does not adversely affect the flight characteristics of the airplane.

(b) *Increase in take-off power limitation to more than 1,350 horsepower.* The engine take-off power limitation for the airplane may be increased to more than 1,350 horsepower per engine if compliance is shown with the flight characteristics and ground handling requirements of Part 4b.

(c) *Installation of engines of not more than 1,830 cubic inches displacement and not having a certificated take-off rating of more than 1,350 horsepower.* Engines of not more than 1,830 cubic inches displacement and not having a certificated take-off rating of more than 1,350 horsepower which necessitate a major modification of redesign of the engine installation may be installed, if the engine fire prevention and fire protection are equivalent to that on the prior engine installation.

(d) *Installation of engines of more than 1,830 cubic inches displacement or having certificated take-off rating of more than 1,350 horsepower.* Engines of more than 1,830 cubic inches displacement or having certificated take-off rating of more than 1,350 horsepower may be installed if compliance is shown with the engine installation requirements of Part 4b: *Provided,* That where literal compliance with the engine installation requirements of Part 4b is extremely difficult to accomplish and would not contribute materially to the objective sought, and the Administrator finds that the experience with the DC–3 or L–18 airplanes justifies it, he is authorized to accept such measures of compliance as he finds will effectively accomplish the basic objective.

4. *Establishment of new maximum certificated weights.* An applicant for approval of new maximum certificated weights shall apply for an amendment of the airworthiness certificate of the airplane and shall show that the weights sought have been established, and the appropriate manual material obtained, as provided in this section.

NOTE: Transport category performance requirements result in the establishment of

---

[1] It is not intended to waive compliance with such airworthiness requirements as are included in the operating parts of the Civil Air Regulations for specific types of operation.

maximum certificated weights for various altitudes.

(a) *Weights–25,200 to 26,900 for the DC–3 and 18,500 to 19,500 for the L–18.* New maximum certificated weights of more than 25,200 but not more than 26,900 pounds for DC–3 and more than 18,500 but not more than 19,500 pounds for L–18 airplanes may be established in accordance with the transport category performance requirements of either Part 4a or Part 4b, if the airplane at the new maximum weights can meet the structural requirements of the elected part.

(b) *Weights of more than 26,900 for the DC–3 and 19,500 for the L–18.* New maximum certificated weights of more than 26,900 pounds for DC–3 and 19,500 pounds for L–18 airplanes shall be established in accordance with the structural performance, flight characteristics, and ground handling requirements of Part 4b: *Provided,* That where literal compliance with the structural requirements of Part 4b is extremely difficult to accomplish and would not contribute materially to the objective sought, and the Administrator finds that the experience with the DC–3 or L–18 airplanes justifies it, he is authorized to accept such measures of compliance as he finds will effectively accomplish the basic objective.

(c) *Airplane flight manual-performance operating information.* An approved airplane flight manual shall be provided for each DC–3 and L–18 airplane which has had new maximum certificated weights established under this section. The airplane flight manual shall contain the applicable performance information prescribed in that part of the regulations under which the new certificated weights were established and such additional information as may be necessary to enable the application of the take-off, en route, and landing limitations prescribed for transport category airplanes in the operating parts of the Civil Air Regulations.

(d) *Performance operating limitations.* Each airplane for which new maximum certificated weights are established in accordance with paragraphs (a) or (b) of this section shall be considered a transport category airplane for the purpose of complying with the performance operating limitations applicable to the operations in which it is utilized.

5. *Reference.* Unless otherwise provided, all references in this regulation to Part 4a and Part 4b are those parts of the Civil Air Regulations in effect on September 1, 1953.

This regulation supersedes Special Civil Air Regulation SR–398 and shall remain effective until superseded or rescinded by the Board.

[19 FR 5039, Aug. 11, 1954. Redesignated at 29 FR 19099, Dec. 30, 1964]

Subpart A—General

§ 25.1 Applicability.

(a) This part prescribes airworthiness standards for the issue of type certificates, and changes to those certificates, for transport category airplanes.

(b) Each person who applies under Part 21 for such a certificate or change must show compliance with the applicable requirements in this part.

§ 25.2 Special retroactive requirements.

The following special retroactive requirements are applicable to an airplane for which the regulations referenced in the type certificate predate the sections specified below—

(a) Irrespective of the date of application, each applicant for a supplemental type certificate (or an amendment to a type certificate) involving an increase in passenger seating capacity to a total greater than that for which the airplane has been type certificated must show that the airplane concerned meets the requirements of:

(1) Sections 25.721(d), 25.783(g), 25.785(c), 25.803(c)(2) through (9), 25.803 (d) and (e), 25.807 (a), (c), and (d), 25.809 (f) and (h), 25.811, 25.812, 25.813 (a), (b), and (c), 25.815, 25.817, 25.853 (a) and (b), 25.855(a), 25.993(f), and 25.1359(c) in effect on October 24, 1967, and

(2) Sections 25.803(b) and 25.803(c)(1) in effect on April 23, 1969.

(b) Irrespective of the date of application, each applicant for a supplemental type certificate (or an amendment to a type certificate) for an airplane manufactured after October 16, 1987, must show that the airplane meets the requirements of § 25.807(c)(7) in effect on July 24, 1989.

(c) Compliance with subsequent revisions to the sections specified in paragraph (a) or (b) of this section may be elected or may be required in accordance with § 21.101(a) of this chapter.

[Amdt. 25–72, 55 FR 29773, July 20, 1990, as amended by Amdt. 25–99, 65 FR 36266, June 7, 2000]

Subpart B—Flight

GENERAL

§ 25.21 Proof of compliance.

(a) Each requirement of this subpart must be met at each appropriate combination of weight and center of gravity within the range of loading conditions for which certification is requested. This must be shown—

(1) By tests upon an airplane of the type for which certification is requested, or by calculations based on, and equal in accuracy to, the results of testing; and

(2) By systematic investigation of each probable combination of weight and center of gravity, if compliance cannot be reasonably inferred from combinations investigated.

(b) [Reserved]

(c) The controllability, stability, trim, and stalling characteristics of the airplane must be shown for each altitude up to the maximum expected in operation.

(d) Parameters critical for the test being conducted, such as weight, loading (center of gravity and inertia), airspeed, power, and wind, must be maintained within acceptable tolerances of the critical values during flight testing.

(e) If compliance with the flight characteristics requirements is dependent upon a stability augmentation system or upon any other automatic or power-operated system, compliance must be shown with §§ 25.671 and 25.672.

(f) In meeting the requirements of §§ 25.105(d), 25.125, 25.233, and 25.237, the wind velocity must be measured at a height of 10 meters above the surface, or corrected for the difference between the height at which the wind velocity is measured and the 10-meter height.

[Doc. No. 5066, 29 FR 18291, Dec. 24, 1964, as amended by Amdt. 25–23, 35 FR 5671, Apr. 8, 1970; Amdt. 25–42, 43 FR 2320, Jan. 16, 1978; Amdt. 25–72, 55 FR 29774, July 20, 1990]

§ 25.23 Load distribution limits.

(a) Ranges of weights and centers of gravity within which the airplane may be safely operated must be established. If a weight and center of gravity combination is allowable only within certain load distribution limits (such as

spanwise) that could be inadvertently exceeded, these limits and the corresponding weight and center of gravity combinations must be established.

(b) The load distribution limits may not exceed—

(1) The selected limits;

(2) The limits at which the structure is proven; or

(3) The limits at which compliance with each applicable flight requirement of this subpart is shown.

§ 25.25 Weight limits.

(a) *Maximum weights.* Maximum weights corresponding to the airplane operating conditions (such as ramp, ground or water taxi, takeoff, en route, and landing), environmental conditions (such as altitude and temperature), and loading conditions (such as zero fuel weight, center of gravity position and weight distribution) must be established so that they are not more than—

(1) The highest weight selected by the applicant for the particular conditions; or

(2) The highest weight at which compliance with each applicable structural loading and flight requirement is shown, except that for airplanes equipped with standby power rocket engines the maximum weight must not be more than the highest weight established in accordance with appendix E of this part; or

(3) The highest weight at which compliance is shown with the certification requirements of Part 36 of this chapter.

(b) *Minimum weight.* The minimum weight (the lowest weight at which compliance with each applicable requirement of this part is shown) must be established so that it is not less than—

(1) The lowest weight selected by the applicant;

(2) The design minimum weight (the lowest weight at which compliance with each structural loading condition of this part is shown); or

(3) The lowest weight at which compliance with each applicable flight requirement is shown.

[Doc. No. 5066, 29 FR 18291, Dec. 24, 1964, as amended by Amdt. 25–23, 35 FR 5671, Apr. 8, 1970; Amdt. 25–63, 53 FR 16365, May 6, 1988]

§ 25.27 Center of gravity limits.

The extreme forward and the extreme aft center of gravity limitations must be established for each practicably separable operating condition. No such limit may lie beyond—

(a) The extremes selected by the applicant;

(b) The extremes within which the structure is proven; or

(c) The extremes within which compliance with each applicable flight requirement is shown.

§ 25.29 Empty weight and corresponding center of gravity.

(a) The empty weight and corresponding center of gravity must be determined by weighing the airplane with—

(1) Fixed ballast;

(2) Unusable fuel determined under § 25.959; and

(3) Full operating fluids, including—

(i) Oil;

(ii) Hydraulic fluid; and

(iii) Other fluids required for normal operation of airplane systems, except potable water, lavatory precharge water, and fluids intended for injection in the engine.

(b) The condition of the airplane at the time of determining empty weight must be one that is well defined and can be easily repeated.

[Doc. No. 5066, 29 FR 18291, Dec. 24, 1964, as amended by Amdt. 25–42, 43 FR 2320, Jan. 16, 1978; Amdt. 25–72, 55 FR 29774, July 20, 1990]

§ 25.31 Removable ballast.

Removable ballast may be used on showing compliance with the flight requirements of this subpart.

§ 25.33 Propeller speed and pitch limits.

(a) The propeller speed and pitch must be limited to values that will ensure—

(1) Safe operation under normal operating conditions; and

(2) Compliance with the performance requirements of §§ 25.101 through 25.125.

(b) There must be a propeller speed limiting means at the governor. It must limit the maximum possible governed engine speed to a value not exceeding the maximum allowable r.p.m.

(c) The means used to limit the low pitch position of the propeller blades must be set so that the engine does not exceed 103 percent of the maximum allowable engine rpm or 99 percent of an approved maximum overspeed, whichever is greater, with—

(1) The propeller blades at the low pitch limit and governor inoperative;

(2) The airplane stationary under standard atmospheric conditions with no wind; and

(3) The engines operating at the takeoff manifold pressure limit for reciprocating engine powered airplanes or the maximum takeoff torque limit for turbopropeller engine-powered airplanes.

[Doc. No. 5066, 29 FR 18291, Dec. 24, 1964, as amended by Amdt. 25–57, 49 FR 6848, Feb. 23, 1984; Amdt. 25–72, 55 FR 29774, July 20, 1990]

PERFORMANCE

§ 25.101 General.

(a) Unless otherwise prescribed, airplanes must meet the applicable performance requirements of this subpart for ambient atmospheric conditions and still air.

(b) The performance, as affected by engine power or thrust, must be based on the following relative humidities;

(1) For turbine engine powered airplanes, a relative humidity of—

(i) 80 percent, at and below standard temperatures; and

(ii) 34 percent, at and above standard temperatures plus 50 °F.

Between these two temperatures, the relative humidity must vary linearly.

(2) For reciprocating engine powered airplanes, a relative humidity of 80 percent in a standard atmosphere. Engine power corrections for vapor pressure must be made in accordance with the following table:

Altitude H (ft.)	Vapor pressure e (In. Hg.)	Specific humidity w (Lb. moisture per lb. dry air)	Density ratio ρ / σ=0.0023769
0	0.403	0.00849	0.99508
1,000	.354	.00773	.96672
2,000	.311	.00703	.93895
3,000	.272	.00638	.91178
4,000	.238	.00578	.88514
5,000	.207	.00523	.85910
6,000	.1805	.00472	.83361
7,000	.1566	.00425	.80870
8,000	.1356	.00382	.78434
9,000	.1172	.00343	.76053
10,000	.1010	.00307	.73722

Altitude *H* (ft.)	Vapor pressure *e* (In. Hg.)	Specific humidity *w* (Lb. moisture per lb. dry air)	Density ratio ρ / σ=0.0023769
15,000	.0463	.001710	.62868
20,000	.01978	.000896	.53263
25,000	.00778	.000436	.44806

(c) The performance must correspond to the propulsive thrust available under the particular ambient atmospheric conditions, the particular flight condition, and the relative humidity specified in paragraph (b) of this section. The available propulsive thrust must correspond to engine power or thrust, not exceeding the approved power or thrust less—

(1) Installation losses; and

(2) The power or equivalent thrust absorbed by the accessories and services appropriate to the particular ambient atmospheric conditions and the particular flight condition.

(d) Unless otherwise prescribed, the applicant must select the takeoff, en route, approach, and landing configurations for the airplane.

(e) The airplane configurations may vary with weight, altitude, and temperature, to the extent they are compatible with the operating procedures required by paragraph (f) of this section.

(f) Unless otherwise prescribed, in determining the accelerate-stop distances, takeoff flight paths, takeoff distances, and landing distances, changes in the airplane's configuration, speed, power, and thrust, must be made in accordance with procedures established by the applicant for operation in service.

(g) Procedures for the execution of balked landings and missed approaches associated with the conditions prescribed in §§ 25.119 and 25.121(d) must be established.

(h) The procedures established under paragraphs (f) and (g) of this section must—

(1) Be able to be consistently executed in service by crews of average skill;

(2) Use methods or devices that are safe and reliable; and

(3) Include allowance for any time delays, in the execution of the procedures, that may reasonably be expected in service.

(i) The accelerate-stop and landing distances prescribed in §§ 25.109 and 25.125, respectively, must be determined with all the airplane wheel brake assemblies at the fully worn limit of their allowable wear range.

[Doc. No. 5066, 29 FR 18291, Dec. 24, 1964, as amended by Amdt. 25–38, 41 FR 55466, Dec. 20, 1976; Amdt. 25–92, 63 FR 8318, Feb. 18, 1998]

§ 25.103 Stall speed.

(a) The reference stall speed, V_{SR}, is a calibrated airspeed defined by the applicant. V_{SR} may not be less than a 1-g stall speed. V_{SR} is expressed as:

$$V_{SR} \geq \frac{V_{CL_{MAX}}}{\sqrt{n_{ZW}}}$$

where:

$V_{CL_{MAX}}$ = Calibrated airspeed obtained when the load factor-corrected lift coefficient

$$\left(\frac{n_{ZW}W}{qS} \right)$$

is first a maximum during the maneuver prescribed in paragraph (c) of this section. In addition, when the maneuver is limited by a device that abruptly pushes the nose down at a selected angle of attack (*e.g.*, a stick pusher), $V_{CL_{MAX}}$ may not be less than the speed existing at the instant the device operates;

n_{ZW} = Load factor normal to the flight path at $V_{CL_{MAX}}$

W = Airplane gross weight;

S = Aerodynamic reference wing area; and

q = Dynamic pressure.

(b) $V_{CL_{MAX}}$ is determined with:

(1) Engines idling, or, if that resultant thrust causes an appreciable decrease in stall speed, not more than zero thrust at the stall speed;

(2) Propeller pitch controls (if applicable) in the takeoff position;

(3) The airplane in other respects (such as flaps and landing gear) in the condition existing in the test or performance standard in which V_{SR} is being used;

(4) The weight used when V_{SR} is being used as a factor to determine compliance with a required performance standard;

(5) The center of gravity position that results in the highest value of reference stall speed; and

(6) The airplane trimmed for straight flight at a speed selected by the applicant, but not less than 1.13V$_{SR}$ and not greater than 1.3V$_{SR}$.

(c) Starting from the stabilized trim condition, apply the longitudinal control to decelerate the airplane so that the speed reduction does not exceed one knot per second.

(d) In addition to the requirements of paragraph (a) of this section, when a device that abruptly pushes the nose down at a selected angle of attack (e.g., a stick pusher) is installed, the reference stall speed, V$_{SR}$, may not be less than 2 knots or 2 percent, whichever is greater, above the speed at which the device operates.

[Doc. No. 28404, 67 FR 70825, Nov. 26, 2002]

§ 25.105 Takeoff.

(a) The takeoff speeds described in § 25.107, the accelerate-stop distance described in § 25.109, the takeoff path described in § 25.111, and the takeoff distance and takeoff run described in § 25.113, must be determined—

(1) At each weight, altitude, and ambient temperature within the operational limits selected by the applicant; and

(2) In the selected configuration for takeoff.

(b) No takeoff made to determine the data required by this section may require exceptional piloting skill or alertness.

(c) The takeoff data must be based on—

(1) In the case of land planes and amphibians:

(i) Smooth, dry and wet, hard-surfaced runways; and

(ii) At the option of the applicant, grooved or porous friction course wet, hard-surfaced runways.

(2) Smooth water, in the case of seaplanes and amphibians; and

(3) Smooth, dry snow, in the case of skiplanes.

(d) The takeoff data must include, within the established operational limits of the airplane, the following operational correction factors:

(1) Not more than 50 percent of nominal wind components along the takeoff path opposite to the direction of takeoff, and not less than 150 percent of nominal wind components along the takeoff path in the direction of takeoff.

(2) Effective runway gradients.

[Doc. No. 5066, 29 FR 18291, Dec. 24, 1964, as amended by Amdt. 25–92, 63 FR 8318, Feb. 18, 1998]

§ 25.107 Takeoff speeds.

(a) V$_1$ must be established in relation to V$_{EF}$ as follows:

(1) V$_{EF}$ is the calibrated airspeed at which the critical engine is assumed to fail. V$_{EF}$ must be selected by the applicant, but may not be less than V$_{MCG}$ determined under § 25.149(e).

(2) V$_1$, in terms of calibrated airspeed, is selected by the applicant; however, V$_1$ may not be less than V$_{EF}$ plus the speed gained with critical engine inoperative during the time interval between the instant at which the critical engine is failed, and the instant at which the pilot recognizes and reacts to the engine failure, as indicated by the pilot's initiation of the first action (e.g., applying brakes, reducing thrust, deploying speed brakes) to stop the airplane during accelerate-stop tests.

(b) V$_{2MIN}$, in terms of calibrated airspeed, may not be less than—

(1) 1.13 V$_{SR}$ for—

(i) Two-engine and three-engine turbopropeller and reciprocating engine powered airplanes; and

(ii) Turbojet powered airplanes without provisions for obtaining a significant reduction in the one-engine-inoperative power-on stall speed;

(2) 1.08 V$_{SR}$ for—

(i) Turbopropeller and reciprocating engine powered airplanes with more than three engines; and

(ii) Turbojet powered airplanes with provisions for obtaining a significant reduction in the one-engine-inoperative power-on stall speed; and

(3) 1.10 times V$_{MC}$ established under § 25.149.

(c) V$_2$, in terms of calibrated airspeed, must be selected by the applicant to provide at least the gradient of climb required by § 25.121(b) but may not be less than—

(1) V$_{2MIN}$;

(2) V$_R$ plus the speed increment attained (in accordance with § 25.111(c)(2)) before reaching a height of 35 feet above the takeoff surface; and

(3) A speed that provides the maneuvering capability specified in §25.143(g).

(d) V_{MU} is the calibrated airspeed at and above which the airplane can safely lift off the ground, and con- tinue the takeoff. V_{MU} speeds must be selected by the applicant throughout the range of thrust-to-weight ratios to be certificated. These speeds may be established from free air data if these data are verified by ground takeoff tests.

(e) V_R, in terms of calibrated airspeed, must be selected in accordance with the conditions of paragraphs (e)(1) through (4) of this section:

(1) V_R may not be less than—

(i) V_1;

(ii) 105 percent of V_{MC};

(iii) The speed (determined in accordance with §25.111(c)(2)) that allows reaching V_2 before reaching a height of 35 feet above the takeoff surface; or

(iv) A speed that, if the airplane is rotated at its maximum practicable rate, will result in a V_{LOF} of not less than 110 percent of V_{MU} in the all-engines-operating condition and not less than 105 percent of V_{MU} determined at the thrust-to-weight ratio corresponding to the one-engine-inoperative condition.

(2) For any given set of conditions (such as weight, configuration, and temperature), a single value of V_R, obtained in accordance with this paragraph, must be used to show compliance with both the one-engine-inoperative and the all-engines-operating takeoff provisions.

(3) It must be shown that the one-engine-inoperative takeoff distance, using a rotation speed of 5 knots less than V_R established in accordance with paragraphs (e)(1) and (2) of this section, does not exceed the corresponding one-engine-inoperative takeoff distance using the established V_R. The takeoff distances must be determined in accordance with §25.113(a)(1).

(4) Reasonably expected variations in service from the established takeoff procedures for the operation of the airplane (such as over-rotation of the airplane and out-of-trim conditions) may not result in unsafe flight characteristics or in marked increases in the scheduled takeoff distances established in accordance with §25.113(a).

(f) V_{LOF} is the calibrated airspeed at which the airplane first becomes airborne.

(g) V_{FTO}, in terms of calibrated airspeed, must be selected by the applicant to provide at least the gradient of climb required by §25.121(c), but may not be less than—

(1) 1.18 V_{SR}; and

(2) A speed that provides the maneuvering capability specified in §25.143(g).

[Doc. No. 5066, 29 FR 18291, Dec. 24, 1964, as amended by Amdt. 25–38, 41 FR 55466, Dec. 20, 1976; Amdt. 25–42, 43 FR 2320, Jan. 16, 1978; Amdt. 25–92, 63 FR 8318, Feb. 18, 1998; Amdt. 25–94, 63 FR 8848, Feb. 23, 1998; Amdt. 25–108, 67 FR 70826, Nov. 26, 2002]

§25.109 Accelerate-stop distance.

(a) The accelerate-stop distance on a dry runway is the greater of the following distances:

(1) The sum of the distances necessary to—

(i) Accelerate the airplane from a standing start with all engines operating to V_{EF} for takeoff from a dry runway;

(ii) Allow the airplane to accelerate from V_{EF} to the highest speed reached during the rejected takeoff, assuming the critical engine fails at V_{EF} and the pilot takes the first action to reject the takeoff at the V_1 for takeoff from a dry runway; and

(iii) Come to a full stop on a dry runway from the speed reached as prescribed in paragraph (a)(1)(ii) of this section; plus

(iv) A distance equivalent to 2 seconds at the V_1 for takeoff from a dry runway.

(2) The sum of the distances necessary to—

(i) Accelerate the airplane from a standing start with all engines operating to the highest speed reached during the rejected takeoff, assuming the pilot takes the first action to reject the takeoff at the V_1 for takeoff from a dry runway; and

(ii) With all engines still operating, come to a full stop on dry runway from the speed reached as prescribed in paragraph (a)(2)(i) of this section; plus

(iii) A distance equivalent to 2 seconds at the V_1 for takeoff from a dry runway.

(b) The accelerate-stop distance on a wet runway is the greater of the following distances:

(1) The accelerate-stop distance on a dry runway determined in accordance with paragraph (a) of this section; or

(2) The accelerate-stop distance determined in accordance with paragraph (a) of this section, except that the runway is wet and the corresponding wet runway values of V_{EF} and V_1 are used. In determining the wet runway accelerate-stop distance, the stopping force from the wheel brakes may never exceed:

(i) The wheel brakes stopping force determined in meeting the requirements of § 25.101(i) and paragraph (a) of this section; and

(ii) The force resulting from the wet runway braking coefficient of friction determined in accordance with paragraphs (c) or (d) of this section, as applicable, taking into account the distribution of the normal load between braked and unbraked wheels at the most adverse center-of-gravity position approved for takeoff.

(c) The wet runway braking coefficient of friction for a smooth wet runway is defined as a curve of friction coefficient versus ground speed and must be computed as follows:

(1) The maximum tire-to-ground wet runway braking coefficient of friction is defined as:

Tire Pressure (psi)	Maximum Braking Coefficient (tire-to-ground)
50	$\mu_{t/g_{MAX}} = -0.0350\left(\dfrac{V}{100}\right)^3 + 0.306\left(\dfrac{V}{100}\right)^2 - 0.851\left(\dfrac{V}{100}\right) + 0.883$
100	$\mu_{t/g_{MAX}} = -0.0437\left(\dfrac{V}{100}\right)^3 + 0.320\left(\dfrac{V}{100}\right)^2 - 0.805\left(\dfrac{V}{100}\right) + 0.804$
200	$\mu_{t/g_{MAX}} = -0.0331\left(\dfrac{V}{100}\right)^3 + 0.252\left(\dfrac{V}{100}\right)^2 - 0.658\left(\dfrac{V}{100}\right) + 0.692$
300	$\mu_{t/g_{MAX}} = -0.0401\left(\dfrac{V}{100}\right)^3 + 0.263\left(\dfrac{V}{100}\right)^2 - 0.611\left(\dfrac{V}{100}\right) + 0.614$

Where—

Tire Pressure=maximum airplane operating tire pressure (psi);

$\mu_{t/g_{MAX}}$=maximum tire-to-ground braking coefficient;

V=airplane true ground speed (knots); and

Linear interpolation may be used for tire pressures other than those listed.

(2) The maximum tire-to-ground wet runway braking coefficient of friction must be adjusted to take into account the efficiency of the anti-skid system on a wet runway. Anti-skid system operation must be demonstrated by flight testing on a smooth wet runway, and its efficiency must be determined. Unless a specific anti-skid system efficiency is determined from a quantitative analysis of the flight testing on a smooth wet runway, the maximum tire-to-ground wet runway braking coefficient of friction determined in paragraph (c)(1) of this section must be multiplied by the efficiency value associated with the type of anti-skid system installed on the airplane:

Type of anti-skid system	Efficiency value
On-Off	0.30
Quasi-Modulating	0.50
Fully Modulating	0.80

(d) At the option of the applicant, a higher wet runway braking coefficient of friction may be used for runway surfaces that have been grooved or treated with a porous friction course material. For grooved and porous friction course runways, the wet runway braking coefficient of friction is defined as either:

(1) 70 percent of the dry runway braking coefficient of friction used to determine the dry runway accelerate-stop distance; or

(2) The wet runway braking coefficient defined in paragraph (c) of this section, except that a specific anti-skid system efficiency, if determined, is appropriate for a grooved or porous friction course wet runway, and the maximum tire-to-ground wet runway braking coefficient of friction is defined as:

Tire Pressure (psi)	Maximum Braking Coefficient (tire-to-ground)
50	$\mu_{t/g_{MAX}} = 0.1470\left(\dfrac{V}{100}\right)^5 - 1.050\left(\dfrac{V}{100}\right)^4 + 2.673\left(\dfrac{V}{100}\right)^3 - 2.683\left(\dfrac{V}{100}\right)^2 + 0.403\left(\dfrac{V}{100}\right) + 0.859$
100	$\mu_{t/g_{MAX}} = 0.1106\left(\dfrac{V}{100}\right)^5 - 0.813\left(\dfrac{V}{100}\right)^4 + 2.130\left(\dfrac{V}{100}\right)^3 - 2.200\left(\dfrac{V}{100}\right)^2 + 0.317\left(\dfrac{V}{100}\right) + 0.807$
200	$\mu_{t/g_{MAX}} = 0.0498\left(\dfrac{V}{100}\right)^5 - 0.398\left(\dfrac{V}{100}\right)^4 + 1.140\left(\dfrac{V}{100}\right)^3 - 1.285\left(\dfrac{V}{100}\right)^2 + 0.140\left(\dfrac{V}{100}\right) + 0.701$
300	$\mu_{t/g_{MAX}} = 0.0314\left(\dfrac{V}{100}\right)^5 - 0.247\left(\dfrac{V}{100}\right)^4 + 0.703\left(\dfrac{V}{100}\right)^3 - 0.779\left(\dfrac{V}{100}\right)^2 - 0.00954\left(\dfrac{V}{100}\right) + 0.614$

Where—

Tire Pressure=maximum airplane operating tire pressure (psi);

$\mu_{t/g_{MAX}}$=maximum tire-to-ground braking coefficient;

V=airplane true ground speed (knots); and

Linear interpolation may be used for tire pressures other than those listed.

(e) Except as provided in paragraph (f)(1) of this section, means other than wheel brakes may be used to determine the accelerate-stop distance if that means—

(1) Is safe and reliable;

(2) Is used so that consistent results can be expected under normal operating conditions; and

(3) Is such that exceptional skill is not required to control the airplane.

(f) The effects of available reverse thrust—

(1) Shall not be included as an additional means of deceleration when determining the accelerate-stop distance on a dry runway; and

(2) May be included as an additional means of deceleration using recommended reverse thrust procedures when determining the accelerate-stop distance on a wet runway, provided the requirements of paragraph (e) of this section are met.

(g) The landing gear must remain extended throughout the accelerate-stop distance.

(h) If the accelerate-stop distance includes a stopway with surface characteristics substantially different from those of the runway, the takeoff data must include operational correction factors for the accelerate-stop distance. The correction factors must account for the particular surface characteristics of the stopway and the variations in these characteristics with seasonal weather conditions (such as temperature, rain, snow, and ice) within the established operational limits.

(i) A flight test demonstration of the maximum brake kinetic energy accelerate-stop distance must be conducted with not more than 10 percent of the allowable brake wear range remaining on each of the airplane wheel brakes.

[Doc. No. 5066, 29 FR 18291, Dec. 24, 1964, as amended by Amdt. 25–42, 43 FR 2321, Jan. 16, 1978; Amdt. 25–92, 63 FR 8318, Feb. 18, 1998]

§25.111 Takeoff path.

(a) The takeoff path extends from a standing start to a point in the takeoff at which the airplane is 1,500 feet above the takeoff surface, or at which the transition from the takeoff to the en route configuration is completed and V_{FTO} is reached, whichever point is higher. In addition—

(1) The takeoff path must be based on the procedures prescribed in §25.101(f);

(2) The airplane must be accelerated on the ground to V_{EF}, at which point the critical engine must be made inoperative and remain inoperative for the rest of the takeoff; and

(3) After reaching V_{EF}, the airplane must be accelerated to V_2.

(b) During the acceleration to speed V_2, the nose gear may be raised off the ground at a speed not less than V_R. However, landing gear retraction may not be begun until the airplane is airborne.

(c) During the takeoff path determination in accordance with paragraphs (a) and (b) of this section—

(1) The slope of the airborne part of the takeoff path must be positive at each point;

(2) The airplane must reach V_2 before it is 35 feet above the takeoff surface and must continue at a speed as close as practical to, but not less than V_2, until it is 400 feet above the takeoff surface;

(3) At each point along the takeoff path, starting at the point at which the airplane reaches 400 feet above the takeoff surface, the available gradient of climb may not be less than—

(i) 1.2 percent for two-engine airplanes;

(ii) 1.5 percent for three-engine airplanes; and

(iii) 1.7 percent for four-engine airplanes; and

(4) Except for gear retraction and propeller feathering, the airplane configuration may not be changed, and no change in power or thrust that requires action by the pilot may be made, until the airplane is 400 feet above the takeoff surface.

(d) The takeoff path must be determined by a continuous demonstrated takeoff or by synthesis from segments. If the takeoff path is determined by the segmental method—

(1) The segments must be clearly defined and must be related to the distinct changes in the configuration, power or thrust, and speed;

(2) The weight of the airplane, the configuration, and the power or thrust must be constant throughout each segment and must correspond to the most critical condition prevailing in the segment;

(3) The flight path must be based on the airplane's performance without ground effect; and

(4) The takeoff path data must be checked by continuous demonstrated takeoffs up to the point at which the airplane is out of ground effect and its speed is stabilized, to ensure that the path is conservative relative to the continous path.

The airplane is considered to be out of the ground effect when it reaches a height equal to its wing span.

(e) For airplanes equipped with standby power rocket engines, the takeoff path may be determined in accordance with section II of appendix E.

[Doc. No. 5066, 29 FR 18291, Dec. 24, 1964, as amended by Amdt. 25–6, 30 FR 8468, July 2, 1965; Amdt. 25–42, 43 FR 2321, Jan. 16, 1978; Amdt. 25–54, 45 FR 60172, Sept. 11, 1980; Amdt. 25–72, 55 FR 29774, July 20, 1990; Amdt. 25–94, 63 FR 8848, Feb. 23, 1998; Amdt. 25–108, 67 FR 70826, Nov. 26, 2002]

§ 25.113 Takeoff distance and takeoff run.

(a) Takeoff distance on a dry runway is the greater of—

(1) The horizontal distance along the takeoff path from the start of the takeoff to the point at which the airplane is 35 feet above the takeoff surface, determined under § 25.111 for a dry runway; or

(2) 115 percent of the horizontal distance along the takeoff path, with all engines operating, from the start of the takeoff to the point at which the airplane is 35 feet above the takeoff surface, as determined by a procedure consistent with § 25.111.

(b) Takeoff distance on a wet runway is the greater of—

(1) The takeoff distance on a dry runway determined in accordance with paragraph (a) of this section; or

(2) The horizontal distance along the takeoff path from the start of the takeoff to the point at which the airplane is 15 feet above the takeoff surface, achieved in a manner consistent with the achievement of V_2 before reaching 35 feet above the takeoff surface, determined under § 25.111 for a wet runway.

(c) If the takeoff distance does not include a clearway, the takeoff run is equal to the takeoff distance. If the takeoff distance includes a clearway—

(1) The takeoff run on a dry runway is the greater of—

(i) The horizontal distance along the takeoff path from the start of the takeoff to a point equidistant between the point at which V_{LOF} is reached and the point at which the airplane is 35 feet above the takeoff surface, as determined under §25.111 for a dry runway; or

(ii) 115 percent of the horizontal distance along the takeoff path, with all engines operating, from the start of the takeoff to a point equidistant between the point at which V_{LOF} is reached and the point at which the airplane is 35 feet above the takeoff surface, determined by a procedure consistent with §25.111.

(2) The takeoff run on a wet runway is the greater of—

(i) The horizontal distance along the takeoff path from the start of the takeoff to the point at which the airplane is 15 feet above the takeoff surface, achieved in a manner consistent with the achievement of V_2 before reaching 35 feet above the takeoff surface, as determined under §25.111 for a wet runway; or

(ii) 115 percent of the horizontal distance along the takeoff path, with all engines operating, from the start of the takeoff to a point equidistant between the point at which V_{LOF} is reached and the point at which the airplane is 35 feet above the takeoff surface, determined by a procedure consistent with §25.111.

[Doc. No. 5066, 29 FR 18291, Dec. 24, 1964, as amended by Amdt. 25–23, 35 FR 5671, Apr. 8, 1970; Amdt. 25–92, 63 FR 8320, Feb. 18, 1998]

§25.115 Takeoff flight path.

(a) The takeoff flight path shall be considered to begin 35 feet above the takeoff surface at the end of the takeoff distance determined in accordance with §25.113(a) or (b), as appropriate for the runway surface condition.

(b) The net takeoff flight path data must be determined so that they represent the actual takeoff flight paths (determined in accordance with §25.111 and with paragraph (a) of this section) reduced at each point by a gradient of climb equal to—

(1) 0.8 percent for two-engine airplanes;

(2) 0.9 percent for three-engine airplanes; and

(3) 1.0 percent for four-engine airplanes.

(c) The prescribed reduction in climb gradient may be applied as an equivalent reduction in acceleration along that part of the takeoff flight path at which the airplane is accelerated in level flight.

[Doc. No. 5066, 29 FR 18291, Dec. 24, 1964, as amended by Amdt. 25–92, 63 FR 8320, Feb. 18, 1998]

§25.117 Climb: general.

Compliance with the requirements of §§25.119 and 25.121 must be shown at each weight, altitude, and ambient temperature within the operational limits established for the airplane and with the most unfavorable center of gravity for each configuration.

§25.119 Landing climb: All-engines-operating.

In the landing configuration, the steady gradient of climb may not be less than 3.2 percent, with—

(a) The engines at the power or thrust that is available eight seconds after initiation of movement of the power or thrust controls from the minimum flight idle to the go-around power or thrust setting; and

(b) A climb speed of not more than V_{REF}.

[Doc. No. 5066, 29 FR 18291, Dec. 24, 1964, as amended by Amdt. 25–84, 60 FR 30749, June 9, 1995; Amdt. 25–108, 67 FR 70826, Nov. 26, 2002]

§25.121 Climb: One-engine-inoperative.

(a) *Takeoff; landing gear extended.* In the critical takeoff configuration existing along the flight path (between the points at which the airplane reaches V_{LOF} and at which the landing gear is fully retracted) and in the configuration used in §25.111 but without ground effect, the steady gradient of climb must be positive for two-engine airplanes, and not less than 0.3 percent for three-engine airplanes or 0.5 percent for four-engine airplanes, at V_{LOF} and with—

(1) The critical engine inoperative and the remaining engines at the power or thrust available when retraction of the landing gear is begun in accordance

with § 25.111 unless there is a more critical power operating condition existing later along the flight path but before the point at which the landing gear is fully retracted; and

(2) The weight equal to the weight existing when retraction of the landing gear is begun, determined under § 25.111.

(b) *Takeoff; landing gear retracted.* In the takeoff configuration existing at the point of the flight path at which the landing gear is fully retracted, and in the configuration used in § 25.111 but without ground effect, the steady gradient of climb may not be less than 2.4 percent for two-engine airplanes, 2.7 percent for three-engine airplanes, and 3.0 percent for four-engine airplanes, at V_2 and with—

(1) The critical engine inoperative, the remaining engines at the takeoff power or thrust available at the time the landing gear is fully retracted, determined under § 25.111, unless there is a more critical power operating condition existing later along the flight path but before the point where the airplane reaches a height of 400 feet above the takeoff surface; and

(2) The weight equal to the weight existing when the airplane's landing gear is fully retracted, determined under § 25.111.

(c) *Final takeoff.* In the en route configuration at the end of the takeoff path determined in accordance with § 25.111, the steady gradient of climb may not be less than 1.2 percent for two-engine airplanes, 1.5 percent for three-engine airplanes and 1.7 percent for four-engine airplanes, at V_{FTO} and with

(1) The critical engine inoperative and the remaining engines at the available maximum continuous power or thrust; and

(2) The weight equal to the weight existing at the end of the takeoff path, determined under § 25.111.

(d) *Approach.* In a configuration corresponding to the normal all-engines-operating procedure in which V_{SR} for this configuration does not exceed 110 percent of the V_{SR} for the related all-engines-operating landing configuration, the steady gradient of climb may not be less than 2.1 percent for two-engine airplanes, 2.4 percent for three-en-

gine airplanes, and 2.7 percent for four engine airplanes, with

(1) The critical engine inoperative, the remaining engines at the go-around power or thrust setting;

(2) The maximum landing weight;

(3) A climb speed established in connection with normal landing procedures, but not more than 1.4 V_{SR}; and

(4) Landing gear retracted.

[Doc. No. 5066, 29 FR 18291, Dec. 24, 1964, as amended by Amdt. 25-84, 60 FR 30749, June 9, 1995; Amdt. 25-108, 67 FR 70826, Nov. 26, 2002]

§ 25.123   En route flight paths.

(a) For the en route configuration, the flight paths prescribed in paragraphs (b) and (c) of this section must be determined at each weight, altitude, and ambient temperature, within the operating limits established for the airplane. The variation of weight along the flight path, accounting for the progressive consumption of fuel and oil by the operating engines, may be included in the computation. The flight paths must be determined at any selected speed, with—

(1) The most unfavorable center of gravity;

(2) The critical engines inoperative;

(3) The remaining engines at the available maximum continuous power or thrust; and

(4) The means for controlling the engine-cooling air supply in the position that provides adequate cooling in the hot-day condition.

(b) The one-engine-inoperative net flight path data must represent the actual climb performance diminished by a gradient of climb of 1.1 percent for two-engine airplanes, 1.4 percent for three-engine airplanes, and 1.6 percent for four-engine airplanes.

(c) For three- or four-engine airplanes, the two-engine-inoperative net flight path data must represent the actual climb performance diminished by a gradient of climb of 0.3 percent for three-engine airplanes and 0.5 percent for four-engine airplanes.

§ 25.125   Landing.

(a) The horizontal distance necessary to land and to come to a complete stop (or to a speed of approximately 3 knots for water landings) from a point 50 feet above the landing surface must be determined (for standard temperatures, at each weight, altitude, and wind within the operational limits established by the applicant for the airplane) as follows:

(1) The airplane must be in the landing configuration.

(2) A stabilized approach, with a calibrated airspeed of V_{REF}, must be maintained down to the 50 foot height. V_{REF} may not be less than

(i) 1.23 V_{SR0};

(ii) V_{MCL} established under §25.149(f); and

(iii) A speed that provides the maneuvering capability specified in §25.143(g).

(3) Changes in configuration, power or thrust, and speed, must be made in accordance with the established procedures for service operation.

(4) The landing must be made without excessive vertical acceleration, tendency to bounce, nose over, ground loop, porpoise, or water loop.

(5) The landings may not require exceptional piloting skill or alertness.

(b) For landplanes and amphibians, the landing distance on land must be determined on a level, smooth, dry, hard-surfaced runway. In addition—

(1) The pressures on the wheel braking systems may not exceed those specified by the brake manufacturer;

(2) The brakes may not be used so as to cause excessive wear of brakes or tires; and

(3) Means other than wheel brakes may be used if that means—

(i) Is safe and reliable;

(ii) Is used so that consistent results can be expected in service; and

(iii) Is such that exceptional skill is not required to control the airplane.

(c) For seaplanes and amphibians, the landing distance on water must be determined on smooth water.

(d) For skiplanes, the landing distance on snow must be determined on smooth, dry, snow.

(e) The landing distance data must include correction factors for not more than 50 percent of the nominal wind components along the landing path opposite to the direction of landing, and not less than 150 percent of the nominal wind components along the landing path in the direction of landing.

(f) If any device is used that depends on the operation of any engine, and if the landing distance would be noticeably increased when a landing is made with that engine inoperative, the landing distance must be determined with that engine inoperative unless the use of compensating means will result in a landing distance not more than that with each engine operating.

[Doc. No. 5066, 29 FR 18291, Dec. 24, 1964, as amended by Amdt. 25–72, 55 FR 29774, July 20, 1990; Amdt. 25–84, 60 FR 30749, June 9, 1995; Amdt. 25–108, 67 FR 70826, Nov. 26, 2002]

CONTROLLABILITY AND
MANEUVERABILITY

§25.143 General.

(a) The airplane must be safely controllable and maneuverable during—

(1) Takeoff;

(2) Climb;

(3) Level flight;

(4) Descent; and

(5) Landing.

(b) It must be possible to make a smooth transition from one flight condition to any other flight condition without exceptional piloting skill, alertness, or strength, and without danger of exceeding the airplane limit-load factor under any probable operating conditions, including—

(1) The sudden failure of the critical engine;

(2) For airplanes with three or more engines, the sudden failure of the second critical engine when the airplane is in the en route, approach, or landing configuration and is trimmed with the critical engine inoperative; and

(3) Configuration changes, including deployment or retraction of deceleration devices.

(c) The following table prescribes, for conventional wheel type controls, the maximum control forces permitted during the testing required by paragraphs (a) and (b) of this section:

Force, in pounds, applied to the control wheel or rudder pedals	Pitch	Roll	Yaw
For short term application for pitch and roll control—two hands available for control	75	50	....
For short term application for pitch and roll control—one hand available for control	50	25	....
For short term application for yaw control	....	....	150

Force, in pounds, applied to the control wheel or rudder pedals	Pitch	Roll	Yaw
For long term application	10	5	20

(d) Approved operating procedures or conventional operating practices must be followed when demonstrating compliance with the control force limitations for short term application that are prescribed in paragraph (c) of this section. The airplane must be in trim, or as near to being in trim as practical, in the immediately preceding steady flight condition. For the takeoff condition, the airplane must be trimmed according to the approved operating procedures.

(e) When demonstrating compliance with the control force limitations for long term application that are prescribed in paragraph (c) of this section, the airplane must be in trim, or as near to being in trim as practical.

(f) When maneuvering at a constant airspeed or Mach number (up to V_{FC}/M_{FC}), the stick forces and the gradient of the stick force versus maneuvering load factor must lie within satisfactory limits. The stick forces must not be so great as to make excessive demands on the pilot's strength when maneuvering the airplane, and must not be so low that the airplane can easily be overstressed inadvertently. Changes of gradient that occur with changes of load factor must not cause undue difficulty in maintaining control of the airplane, and local gradients must not be so low as to result in a danger of overcontrolling.

(g) The maneuvering capabilities in a constant speed coordinated turn at forward center of gravity, as specified in the following table, must be free of stall warning or other characteristics that might interfere with normal maneuvering:

Configuration	Speed	Maneuvering bank angle in a coordinated turn	Thrust power setting
Takeoff	V_2	30°	Asymmetric WAT-Limited.[1]
Takeoff	[2]V_2 + XX	40°	All-engines-operating climb.[3]
En route	V_{FTO}	40°	Asymmetric WAT-Limited.[1]
Landing	V_{REF}	40°	Symmetric for −3° flight path angle.

[1] A combination of weight, altitude, and temperature (WAT) such that the thrust or power setting produces the minimum climb gradient specified in § 25.121 for the flight condition.
[2] Airspeed approved for all-engines-operating initial climb.
[3] That thrust or power setting which, in the event of failure of the critical engine and without any crew action to adjust the thrust or power of the remaining engines, would result in the thrust or power specified for the takeoff condition at V_2, or any lesser thrust or power setting that is used for all-engines-operating initial climb procedures.

[Doc. No. 5066, 29 FR 18291, Dec. 24, 1964, as amended by Amdt. 25–42, 43 FR 2321, Jan. 16, 1978; Amdt. 25–84, 60 FR 30749, June 9, 1995; Amdt. 25–108, 67 FR 70826, Nov. 26, 2002]

§ 25.145 Longitudinal control.

(a) It must be possible, at any point between the trim speed prescribed in § 25.103(b)(6) and stall identification (as defined in § 25.201(d)), to pitch the nose downward so that the acceleration to this selected trim speed is prompt with

(1) The airplane trimmed at the trim speed prescribed in § 25.103(b)(6);

(2) The landing gear extended;

(3) The wing flaps (i) retracted and (ii) extended; and

(4) Power (i) off and (ii) at maximum continuous power on the engines.

(b) With the landing gear extended, no change in trim control, or exertion of more than 50 pounds control force (representative of the maximum short term force that can be applied readily by one hand) may be required for the following maneuvers:

(1) With power off, flaps retracted, and the airplane trimmed at 1.3 V_{SR1}, extend the flaps as rapidly as possible while maintaining the airspeed at approximately 30 percent above the reference stall speed existing at each instant throughout the maneuver.

(2) Repeat paragraph (b)(1) except initially extend the flaps and then retract them as rapidly as possible.

(3) Repeat paragraph (b)(2), except at the go-around power or thrust setting.

(4) With power off, flaps retracted, and the airplane trimmed at 1.3 V_{SR1}, rapidly set go-around power or thrust while maintaining the same airspeed.

(5) Repeat paragraph (b)(4) except with flaps extended.

(6) With power off, flaps extended, and the airplane trimmed at 1.3 V_{SR1}, obtain and maintain airspeeds between V_{SW} and either 1.6 V_{SR1} or V_{FE}, whichever is lower.

(c) It must be possible, without exceptional piloting skill, to prevent loss of altitude when complete retraction of the high lift devices from any position is begun during steady, straight, level flight at 1.08 V_{SR1} for propeller powered airplanes, or 1.13 V_{SR1} for turbojet powered airplanes, with—

(1) Simultaneous movement of the power or thrust controls to the go-around power or thrust setting;

(2) The landing gear extended; and

(3) The critical combinations of landing weights and altitudes.

(d) If gated high-lift device control positions are provided, paragraph (c) of this section applies to retractions of the high-lift devices from any position from the maximum landing position to the first gated position, between gated positions, and from the last gated position to the fully retracted position. The requirements of paragraph (c) of this section also apply to retractions from each approved landing position to the control position(s) associated with the high-lift device configuration(s) used to establish the go-around procedure(s) from that landing position. In addition, the first gated control position from the maximum landing position must correspond with a configuration of the high-lift devices used to establish a go-around procedure from a landing configuration. Each gated control position must require a separate and distinct motion of the control to pass through the gated position and must have features to prevent inadvertent movement of the control through the gated position. It must only be possible to make this separate and distinct motion once the control has reached the gated position.

[Doc. No. 5066, 29 FR 18291, Dec. 24, 1964, as amended by Amdt. 25–23, 35 FR 5671, Apr. 8, 1970; Amdt. 25–72, 55 FR 29774, July 20, 1990; Amdt. 25–84, 60 FR 30749, June 9, 1995; Amdt. 25–98, 64 FR 6164, Feb. 8, 1999; 64 FR 10740, Mar. 5, 1999; Amdt. 25–108, 67 FR 70827, Nov. 26, 2002]

§25.147 Directional and lateral control.

(a) *Directional control; general.* It must be possible, with the wings level, to yaw into the operative engine and to safely make a reasonably sudden change in heading of up to 15 degrees in the direction of the critical inoperative engine. This must be shown at 1.3 V_SR1 for heading changes up to 15 degrees (except that the heading change at which the rudder pedal force is 150 pounds need not be exceeded), and with—

(1) The critical engine inoperative and its propeller in the minimum drag position;

(2) The power required for level flight at 1.3 V_SR1, but not more than maximum continuous power;

(3) The most unfavorable center of gravity;

(4) Landing gear retracted;

(5) Flaps in the approach position; and

(6) Maximum landing weight.

(b) *Directional control; airplanes with four or more engines.* Airplanes with four or more engines must meet the requirements of paragraph (a) of this section except that—

(1) The two critical engines must be inoperative with their propellers (if applicable) in the minimum drag position;

(2) [Reserved]

(3) The flaps must be in the most favorable climb position.

(c) *Lateral control; general.* It must be possible to make 20° banked turns, with and against the inoperative engine, from steady flight at a speed equal to 1.3 V_SR1, with—

(1) The critical engine inoperative and its propeller (if applicable) in the minimum drag position;

(2) The remaining engines at maximum continuous power;

(3) The most unfavorable center of gravity;

(4) Landing gear (i) retracted and (ii) extended;

(5) Flaps in the most favorable climb position; and

(6) Maximum takeoff weight.

(d) *Lateral control; airplanes with four or more engines.* Airplanes with four or more engines must be able to make 20°

banked turns, with and against the inoperative engines, from steady flight at a speed equal to 1.3 V_SR1, with maximum continuous power, and with the airplane in the configuration prescribed by paragraph (b) of this section.

(e) *Lateral control; all engines operating.* With the engines operating, roll response must allow normal maneuvers (such as recovery from upsets produced by gusts and the initiation of evasive maneuvers). There must be enough excess lateral control in sideslips (up to sideslip angles that might be required in normal operation), to allow a limited amount of maneuvering and to correct for gusts. Lateral control must be enough at any speed up to V_{FC}/M_{FC} to provide a peak roll rate necessary for safety, without excessive control forces or travel.

[Doc. No. 5066, 29 FR 18291, Dec. 24, 1964, as amended by Amdt. 25–42, 43 FR 2321, Jan. 16, 1978; Amdt. 25–72, 55 FR 29774, July 20, 1990; Amdt. 25–108, 67 FR 70827, Nov. 26, 2002]

§ 25.149   Minimum control speed.

(a) In establishing the minimum control speeds required by this section, the method used to simulate critical engine failure must represent the most critical mode of powerplant failure with respect to controllability expected in service.

(b) V_{MC} is the calibrated airspeed at which, when the critical engine is suddenly made inoperative, it is possible to maintain control of the airplane with that engine still inoperative and maintain straight flight with an angle of bank of not more than 5 degrees.

(c) V_{MC} may not exceed 1.13 V_{SR} with—

(1) Maximum available takeoff power or thrust on the engines;

(2) The most unfavorable center of gravity;

(3) The airplane trimmed for takeoff;

(4) The maximum sea level takeoff weight (or any lesser weight necessary to show V_{MC});

(5) The airplane in the most critical takeoff configuration existing along the flight path after the airplane becomes airborne, except with the landing gear retracted;

(6) The airplane airborne and the ground effect negligible; and

(7) If applicable, the propeller of the inoperative engine—

(i) Windmilling;

(ii) In the most probable position for the specific design of the propeller control; or

(iii) Feathered, if the airplane has an automatic feathering device acceptable for showing compliance with the climb requirements of § 25.121.

(d) The rudder forces required to maintain control at V_{MC} may not exceed 150 pounds nor may it be necessary to reduce power or thrust of the operative engines. During recovery, the airplane may not assume any dangerous attitude or require exceptional piloting skill, alertness, or strength to prevent a heading change of more than 20 degrees.

(e) V_{MCG}, the minimum control speed on the ground, is the calibrated airspeed during the takeoff run at which, when the critical engine is suddenly made inoperative, it is possible to maintain control of the airplane using the rudder control alone (without the use of nosewheel steering), as limited by 150 pounds of force, and the lateral control to the extent of keeping the wings level to enable the takeoff to be safely continued using normal piloting skill. In the determination of V_{MCG}, assuming that the path of the airplane accelerating with all engines operating is along the centerline of the runway, its path from the point at which the critical engine is made inoperative to the point at which recovery to a direction parallel to the centerline is completed may not deviate more than 30 feet laterally from the centerline at any point. V_{MCG} must be established with—

(1) The airplane in each takeoff configuration or, at the option of the applicant, in the most critical takeoff configuration;

(2) Maximum available takeoff power or thrust on the operating engines;

(3) The most unfavorable center of gravity;

(4) The airplane trimmed for takeoff; and

(5) The most unfavorable weight in the range of takeoff weights.

(f) V_{MCL}, the minimum control speed during approach and landing with all engines operating, is the calibrated airspeed at which, when the critical engine is suddenly made inoperative, it is possible to maintain control of the airplane with that engine still inoperative, and maintain straight flight with an angle of bank of not more than 5 degrees. V_{MCL} must be established with—

(1) The airplane in the most critical configuration (or, at the option of the applicant, each configuration) for approach and landing with all engines operating;

(2) The most unfavorable center of gravity;

(3) The airplane trimmed for approach with all engines operating;

(4) The most favorable weight, or, at the option of the applicant, as a function of weight;

(5) For propeller airplanes, the propeller of the inoperative engine in the position it achieves without pilot action, assuming the engine fails while at the power or thrust necessary to maintain a three degree approach path angle; and

(6) Go-around power or thrust setting on the operating engine(s).

(g) For airplanes with three or more engines, V_{MCL-2}, the minimum control speed during approach and landing with one critical engine inoperative, is the calibrated airspeed at which, when a second critical engine is suddenly made inoperative, it is possible to maintain control of the airplane with both engines still inoperative, and maintain straight flight with an angle of bank of not more than 5 degrees. V_{MCL-2} must be established with—

(1) The airplane in the most critical configuration (or, at the option of the applicant, each configuration) for approach and landing with one critical engine inoperative;

(2) The most unfavorable center of gravity;

(3) The airplane trimmed for approach with one critical engine inoperative;

(4) The most unfavorable weight, or, at the option of the applicant, as a function of weight;

(5) For propeller airplanes, the propeller of the more critical inoperative engine in the position it achieves without pilot action, assuming the engine

fails while at the power or thrust necessary to maintain a three degree approach path angle, and the propeller of the other inoperative engine feathered;

(6) The power or thrust on the operating engine(s) necessary to maintain an approach path angle of three degrees when one critical engine is inoperative; and

(7) The power or thrust on the operating engine(s) rapidly changed, immediately after the second critical engine is made inoperative, from the power or thrust prescribed in paragraph (g)(6) of this section to—

(i) Minimum power or thrust; and

(ii) Go-around power or thrust setting.

(h) In demonstrations of V_{MCL} and V_{MCL-2}—

(1) The rudder force may not exceed 150 pounds;

(2) The airplane may not exhibit hazardous flight characteristics or require exceptional piloting skill, alertness, or strength;

(3) Lateral control must be sufficient to roll the airplane, from an initial condition of steady flight, through an angle of 20 degrees in the direction necessary to initiate a turn away from the inoperative engine(s), in not more than 5 seconds; and

(4) For propeller airplanes, hazardous flight characteristics must not be exhibited due to any propeller position achieved when the engine fails or during any likely subsequent movements of the engine or propeller controls.

[Doc. No. 5066, 29 FR 18291, Dec. 24, 1964, as amended by Amdt. 25–42, 43 FR 2321, Jan. 16, 1978; Amdt. 25–72, 55 FR 29774, July 20, 1990; 55 FR 37607, Sept. 12, 1990; Amdt. 25–84, 60 FR 30749, June 9, 1995; Amdt. 25–108, 67 FR 70827, Nov. 26, 2002]

TRIM

§ 25.161 Trim.

(a) *General.* Each airplane must meet the trim requirements of this section after being trimmed, and without further pressure upon, or movement of, either the primary controls or their corresponding trim controls by the pilot or the automatic pilot.

(b) *Lateral and directional trim.* The airplane must maintain lateral and directional trim with the most adverse lateral displacement of the center of gravity within the relevant operating limitations, during normally expected conditions of operation (including operation at any speed from 1.3 V_{SR1} to V_{MO}/M_{MO}).

(c) *Longitudinal trim.* The airplane must maintain longitudinal trim during—

(1) A climb with maximum continuous power at a speed not more than 1.3 V_{SR1}, with the landing gear retracted, and the flaps (i) retracted and (ii) in the takeoff position;

(2) A glide with power off at a speed not more than 1.3 V_{SR1}, with the landing gear extended, the wing flaps (i) retracted and (ii) extended, the most unfavorable center of gravity position approved for landing with the maximum landing weight, and with the most unfavorable center of gravity position approved for landing regardless of weight; and

(3) Level flight at any speed from 1.3 V_{SR1}, to V_{MO}/M_{MO}, with the landing gear and flaps retracted, and from 1.3 V_{SR1} to V_{LE} with the landing gear extended.

(d) *Longitudinal, directional, and lateral trim.* The airplane must maintain longitudinal, directional, and lateral trim (and for the lateral trim, the angle of bank may not exceed five degrees) at 1.3 V_{SR1} during climbing flight with—

(1) The critical engine inoperative;

(2) The remaining engines at maximum continuous power; and

(3) The landing gear and flaps retracted.

(e) *Airplanes with four or more engines.* Each airplane with four or more engines must maintain trim in rectilinear flight—

(1) At the climb speed, configuration, and power required by § 25.123(a) for the purpose of establishing the rate of climb;

(2) With the most unfavorable center of gravity position; and

(3) At the weight at which the two-engine-inoperative climb is equal to at least 0.013 V_{SR02} at an altitude of 5,000 feet.

[Doc. No. 5066, 29 FR 18291, Dec. 24, 1964, as amended by Amdt. 25–23, 35 FR 5671, Apr. 8, 1970; Amdt. 25–38, 41 FR 55466, Dec. 20, 1976; Amdt. 25–108, 67 FR 70827, Nov. 26, 2002]

STABILITY

§ 25.171 General.

The airplane must be longitudinally, directionally, and laterally stable in accordance with the provisions of §§ 25.173 through 25.177. In addition, suitable stability and control feel (static stability) is required in any condition normally encountered in service, if flight tests show it is necessary for safe operation.

[Doc. No. 5066, 29 FR 18291, Dec. 24, 1964, as amended by Amdt. 25–7, 30 FR 13117, Oct. 15, 1965]

§ 25.173 Static longitudinal stability.

Under the conditions specified in § 25.175, the characteristics of the elevator control forces (including friction) must be as follows:

(a) A pull must be required to obtain and maintain speeds below the specified trim speed, and a push must be required to obtain and maintain speeds above the specified trim speed. This must be shown at any speed that can be obtained except speeds higher than the landing gear or wing flap operating limit speeds or V_{FC}/M_{FC}, whichever is appropriate, or lower than the minimum speed for steady unstalled flight.

(b) The airspeed must return to within 10 percent of the original trim speed for the climb, approach, and landing conditions specified in § 25.175 (a), (c), and (d), and must return to within 7.5 percent of the original trim speed for the cruising condition specified in § 25.175(b), when the control force is slowly released from any speed within the range specified in paragraph (a) of this section.

(c) The average gradient of the stable slope of the stick force versus speed curve may not be less than 1 pound for each 6 knots.

(d) Within the free return speed range specified in paragraph (b) of this section, it is permissible for the airplane, without control forces, to stabilize on speeds above or below the desired trim speeds if exceptional attention on the part of the pilot is not required to return to and maintain the desired trim speed and altitude.

[Amdt. 25–7, 30 FR 13117, Oct. 15, 1965]

§ 25.175 Demonstration of static longitudinal stability.

Static longitudinal stability must be shown as follows:

(a) *Climb.* The stick force curve must have a stable slope at speeds between 85 and 115 percent of the speed at which the airplane—

(1) Is trimmed, with—

(i) Wing flaps retracted;

(ii) Landing gear retracted;

(iii) Maximum takeoff weight; and

(iv) 75 percent of maximum continuous power for reciprocating engines or the maximum power or thrust selected by the applicant as an operating limitation for use during climb for turbine engines; and

(2) Is trimmed at the speed for best rate-of-climb except that the speed need not be less than $1.3\ V_{SR1}$.

(b) *Cruise.* Static longitudinal stability must be shown in the cruise condition as follows:

(1) With the landing gear retracted at high speed, the stick force curve must have a stable slope at all speeds within a range which is the greater of 15 percent of the trim speed plus the resulting free return speed range, or 50 knots plus the resulting free return speed range, above and below the trim speed (except that the speed range need not include speeds less than $1.3\ V_{SR1}$, nor speeds greater than V_{FC}/M_{FC}, nor speeds that require a stick force of more than 50 pounds), with—

(i) The wing flaps retracted;

(ii) The center of gravity in the most adverse position (see § 25.27);

(iii) The most critical weight between the maximum takeoff and maximum landing weights;

(iv) 75 percent of maximum continuous power for reciprocating engines or for turbine engines, the maximum cruising power selected by the applicant as an operating limitation (see § 25.1521), except that the power need not exceed that required at V_{MO}/M_{MO}; and

(v) The airplane trimmed for level flight with the power required in paragraph (b)(1)(iv) of this section.

(2) With the landing gear retracted at low speed, the stick force curve must have a stable slope at all speeds within a range which is the greater of 15 percent of the trim speed plus the resulting free return speed range, or 50 knots plus the resulting free return speed range, above and below the trim speed (except that the speed range need not include speeds less than $1.3\ V_{SR1}$, nor speeds greater than the minimum speed of the applicable speed range prescribed in paragraph (b)(1), nor speeds that require a stick force of more than 50 pounds), with—

(i) Wing flaps, center of gravity position, and weight as specified in paragraph (b)(1) of this section;

(ii) Power required for level flight at a speed equal to $(V_{MO} + 1.3\ V_{SR1})/2$; and

(iii) The airplane trimmed for level flight with the power required in paragraph (b)(2)(ii) of this section.

(3) With the landing gear extended, the stick force curve must have a stable slope at all speeds within a range which is the greater of 15 percent of the trim speed plus the resulting free return speed range, or 50 knots plus the resulting free return speed range, above and below the trim speed (except that the speed range need not include speeds less than $1.3\ V_{SR1}$, nor speeds greater than V_{LE}, nor speeds that require a stick force of more than 50 pounds), with—

(i) Wing flap, center of gravity position, and weight as specified in paragraph (b)(1) of this section;

(ii) 75 percent of maximum continuous power for reciprocating engines or, for turbine engines, the maximum cruising power selected by the applicant as an operating limitation, except that the power need not exceed that required for level flight at V_{LE}; and

(iii) The aircraft trimmed for level flight with the power required in paragraph (b)(3)(ii) of this section.

(c) *Approach.* The stick force curve must have a stable slope at speeds between V_{SW} and $1.7\ V_{SR1}$, with—

(1) Wing flaps in the approach position;

(2) Landing gear retracted;

(3) Maximum landing weight; and

(4) The airplane trimmed at $1.3\ V_{SR1}$ with enough power to maintain level flight at this speed.

(d) *Landing.* The stick force curve must have a stable slope, and the stick force may not exceed 80 pounds, at speeds between V_{SW} and $1.7\ V_{SR0}$ with—

(1) Wing flaps in the landing position;

(2) Landing gear extended;

(3) Maximum landing weight;

(4) Power or thrust off on the engines; and

(5) The airplane trimmed at 1.3 V_{SR0} with power or thrust off.

[Doc. No. 5066, 29 FR 18291, Dec. 24, 1964, as amended by Amdt. 25-7, 30 FR 13117, Oct. 15, 1965; Amdt. 25-108, 67 FR 70827, Nov. 26, 2002]

§ 25.177 Static lateral-directional stability.

(a)-(b) [Reserved]

(c) In straight, steady sideslips, the aileron and rudder control movements and forces must be substantially proportional to the angle of sideslip in a stable sense; and the factor of proportionality must lie between limits found necessary for safe operation throughout the range of sideslip angles appropriate to the operation of the airplane. At greater angles, up to the angle at which full rudder is used or a rudder force of 180 pounds is obtained, the rudder pedal forces may not reverse; and increased rudder deflection must be needed for increased angles of sideslip. Compliance with this paragraph must be demonstrated for all landing gear and flap positions and symmetrical power conditions at speeds from 1.13 V_{SR1} to V_{FE}, V_{LE}, or V_{FC}/M_{FC}, as appropriate.

(d) The rudder gradients must meet the requirements of paragraph (c) at speeds between V_{MO}/M_{MO} and V_{FC}/M_{FC} except that the dihedral effect (aileron deflection opposite the corresponding rudder input) may be negative provided the divergence is gradual, easily recognized, and easily controlled by the pilot.

[Amdt. 25-72, 55 FR 29774, July 20, 1990; 55 FR 37607, Sept. 12, 1990; Amdt. 25-108, 67 FR 70827, Nov. 26, 2002]

§ 25.181 Dynamic stability.

(a) Any short period oscillation, not including combined lateral-directional oscillations, occurring between 1.13 V_{SR} and maximum allowable speed appropriate to the configuration of the airplane must be heavily damped with the primary controls—

(1) Free; and

(2) In a fixed position.

(b) Any combined lateral-directional oscillations ("Dutch roll") occurring

between 1.13 V_{SR} and maximum allowable speed appropriate to the configuration of the airplane must be positively damped with controls free, and must be controllable with normal use of the primary controls without requiring exceptional pilot skill.

[Amdt. 25-42, 43 FR 2322, Jan. 16, 1978, as amended by Amdt. 25-72, 55 FR 29775, July 20, 1990; 55 FR 37607, Sept. 12, 1990; Amdt. 25-108, 67 FR 70827, Nov. 26, 2002]

STALLS

§ 25.201 Stall demonstration.

(a) Stalls must be shown in straight flight and in 30 degree banked turns with—

(1) Power off; and

(2) The power necessary to maintain level flight at 1.5 V_{SR1} (where V_{SR1} corresponds to the reference stall speed at maximum landing weight with flaps in the approach position and the landing gear retracted).

(b) In each condition required by paragraph (a) of this section, it must be possible to meet the applicable requirements of § 25.203 with—

(1) Flaps, landing gear, and deceleration devices in any likely combination of positions approved for operation;

(2) Representative weights within the range for which certification is requested;

(3) The most adverse center of gravity for recovery; and

(4) The airplane trimmed for straight flight at the speed prescribed in § 25.103(b)(6).

(c) The following procedures must be used to show compliance with § 25.203:

(1) Starting at a speed sufficiently above the stalling speed to ensure that a steady rate of speed reduction can be established, apply the longitudinal control so that the speed reduction does not exceed one knot per second until the airplane is stalled.

(2) In addition, for turning flight stalls, apply the longitudinal control to achieve airspeed deceleration rates up to 3 knots per second.

(3) As soon as the airplane is stalled, recover by normal recovery techniques.

(d) The airplane is considered stalled when the behavior of the airplane gives the pilot a clear and distinctive indication of an acceptable nature that the airplane is stalled. Acceptable indications of a stall, occurring either individually or in combination, are—

(1) A nose-down pitch that cannot be readily arrested;

(2) Buffeting, of a magnitude and severity that is a strong and effective deterrent to further speed reduction; or

(3) The pitch control reaches the aft stop and no further increase in pitch attitude occurs when the control is held full aft for a short time before recovery is initiated.

[Doc. No. 5066, 29 FR 18291, Dec. 24, 1964, as amended by Amdt. 25–84, 60 FR 30750, June 9, 1995; Amdt. 25–108, 67 FR 70827, Nov. 26, 2002]

§25.203 Stall characteristics.

(a) It must be possible to produce and to correct roll and yaw by unreversed use of the aileron and rudder controls, up to the time the airplane is stalled. No abnormal nose-up pitching may occur. The longitudinal control force must be positive up to and throughout the stall. In addition, it must be possible to promptly prevent stalling and to recover from a stall by normal use of the controls.

(b) For level wing stalls, the roll occurring between the stall and the completion of the recovery may not exceed approximately 20 degrees.

(c) For turning flight stalls, the action of the airplane after the stall may not be so violent or extreme as to make it difficult, with normal piloting skill, to effect a prompt recovery and to regain control of the airplane. The maximum bank angle that occurs during the recovery may not exceed—

(1) Approximately 60 degrees in the original direction of the turn, or 30 degrees in the opposite direction, for deceleration rates up to 1 knot per second; and

(2) Approximately 90 degrees in the original direction of the turn, or 60 degrees in the opposite direction, for deceleration rates in excess of 1 knot per second.

[Doc. No. 5066, 29 FR 18291, Dec. 24, 1964, as amended by Amdt. 25–84, 60 FR 30750, June 9, 1995]

§25.207 Stall warning.

(a) Stall warning with sufficient margin to prevent inadvertent stalling with the flaps and landing gear in any normal position must be clear and distinctive to the pilot in straight and turning flight.

(b) The warning must be furnished either through the inherent aerodynamic qualities of the airplane or by a device that will give clearly distinguishable indications under expected conditions of flight. However, a visual stall warning device that requires the attention of the crew within the cockpit is not acceptable by itself. If a warning device is used, it must provide a warning in each of the airplane configurations prescribed in paragraph (a) of this section at the speed prescribed in paragraphs (c) and (d) of this section.

(c) When the speed is reduced at rates not exceeding one knot per second, stall warning must begin, in each normal configuration, at a speed, V_{SW}, exceeding the speed at which the stall is identified in accordance with §25.201(d) by not less than five knots or five percent CAS, whichever is greater. Once initiated, stall warning must continue until the angle of attack is reduced to approximately that at which stall warning began.

(d) In addition to the requirement of paragraph (c) of this section, when the speed is reduced at rates not exceeding one knot per second, in straight flight with engines idling and at the center-of-gravity position specified in §25.103(b)(5), V_{SW}, in each normal configuration, must exceed V_{SR} by not less than three knots or three percent CAS, whichever is greater.

(e) The stall warning margin must be sufficient to allow the pilot to prevent stalling (as defined in §25.201(d)) when recovery is initiated not less than one second after the onset of stall warning in slow-down turns with at least 1.5g load factor normal to the flight path and airspeed deceleration rates of at least 2 knots per second, with the flaps and landing gear in any normal position, with the airplane trimmed for straight flight at a speed of 1.3 V_{SR}, and with the power or thrust necessary to maintain level flight at 1.3 V_{SR}.

(f) Stall warning must also be provided in each abnormal configuration of the high lift devices that is likely to be used in flight following system failures (including all configurations covered by Airplane Flight Manual procedures).

[Doc. No. 5066, 29 FR 18291, Dec. 24, 1964, as amended by Amdt. 25–7, 30 FR 13118, Oct. 15, 1965; Amdt. 25–42, 43 FR 2322, Jan. 16, 1978; Amdt. 25–108, 67 FR 70827, Nov. 26, 2002]

GROUND AND WATER HANDLING CHARACTERISTICS

§ 25.231　Longitudinal stability and control.

(a) Landplanes may have no uncontrollable tendency to nose over in any reasonably expected operating condition or when rebound occurs during landing or takeoff. In addition—

(1) Wheel brakes must operate smoothly and may not cause any undue tendency to nose over; and

(2) If a tail-wheel landing gear is used, it must be possible, during the takeoff ground run on concrete, to maintain any attitude up to thrust line level, at 75 percent of V_{SR1}.

(b) For seaplanes and amphibians, the most adverse water conditions safe for takeoff, taxiing, and landing, must be established.

[Docket No. 5066, 29 FR 18291, Dec. 24, 1964, as amended by Amdt. 25–108, 67 FR 70827, Nov. 26, 2002]

§ 25.233　Directional stability and control.

(a) There may be no uncontrollable ground-looping tendency in 90° cross winds, up to a wind velocity of 20 knots or 0.2 V_{SR0}, whichever is greater, except that the wind velocity need not exceed 25 knots at any speed at which the airplane may be expected to be operated on the ground. This may be shown while establishing the 90° cross component of wind velocity required by § 25.237.

(b) Landplanes must be satisfactorily controllable, without exceptional piloting skill or alertness, in power-off landings at normal landing speed, without using brakes or engine power to maintain a straight path. This may be shown during power-off landings made in conjunction with other tests.

(c) The airplane must have adequate directional control during taxiing. This may be shown during taxiing prior to

takeoffs made in conjunction with other tests.

[Doc. No. 5066, 29 FR 18291, Dec. 24, 1964, as amended by Amdt. 25–23, 35 FR 5671, Apr. 8, 1970; Amdt. 25–42, 43 FR 2322, Jan. 16, 1978; Amdt. 25–94, 63 FR 8848, Feb. 23, 1998; Amdt. 25–108, 67 FR 70828, Nov. 26, 2002]

§ 25.235　Taxiing condition.

The shock absorbing mechanism may not damage the structure of the airplane when the airplane is taxied on the roughest ground that may reasonably be expected in normal operation.

§ 25.237　Wind velocities.

(a) For landplanes and amphibians, a 90-degree cross component of wind velocity, demonstrated to be safe for takeoff and landing, must be established for dry runways and must be at least 20 knots or 0.2 V_{SR0}, whichever is greater, except that it need not exceed 25 knots.

(b) For seaplanes and amphibians, the following applies:

(1) A 90-degree cross component of wind velocity, up to which takeoff and landing is safe under all water conditions that may reasonably be expected in normal operation, must be established and must be at least 20 knots or 0.2 V_{SR0}, whichever is greater, except that it need not exceed 25 knots.

(2) A wind velocity, for which taxiing is safe in any direction under all water conditions that may reasonably be expected in normal operation, must be established and must be at least 20 knots or 0.2 V_{SR0}, whichever is greater, except that it need not exceed 25 knots.

[Amdt. 25–42, 43 FR 2322, Jan. 16, 1978, as amended by Amdt. 25–108, 67 FR 70827, Nov. 26, 2002]

§ 25.239　Spray characteristics, control, and stability on water.

(a) For seaplanes and amphibians, during takeoff, taxiing, and landing, and in the conditions set forth in paragraph (b) of this section, there may be no—

(1) Spray characteristics that would impair the pilot's view, cause damage, or result in the taking in of an undue quantity of water;

(2) Dangerously uncontrollable porpoising, bounding, or swinging tendency; or

(3) Immersion of auxiliary floats or sponsons, wing tips, propeller blades, or other parts not designed to withstand the resulting water loads.

(b) Compliance with the requirements of paragraph (a) of this section must be shown—

(1) In water conditions, from smooth to the most adverse condition established in accordance with §25.231;

(2) In wind and cross-wind velocities, water currents, and associated waves and swells that may reasonably be expected in operation on water;

(3) At speeds that may reasonably be expected in operation on water;

(4) With sudden failure of the critical engine at any time while on water; and

(5) At each weight and center of gravity position, relevant to each operating condition, within the range of loading conditions for which certification is requested.

(c) In the water conditions of paragraph (b) of this section, and in the corresponding wind conditions, the seaplane or amphibian must be able to drift for five minutes with engines inoperative, aided, if necessary, by a sea anchor.

MISCELLANEOUS FLIGHT REQUIREMENTS

§25.251 Vibration and buffeting.

(a) The airplane must be demonstrated in flight to be free from any vibration and buffeting that would prevent continued safe flight in any likely operating condition.

(b) Each part of the airplane must be demonstrated in flight to be free from excessive vibration under any appropriate speed and power conditions up to V_{DF}/M_{DF}. The maximum speeds shown must be used in establishing the operating limitations of the airplane in accordance with §25.1505.

(c) Except as provided in paragraph (d) of this section, there may be no buffeting condition, in normal flight, including configuration changes during cruise, severe enough to interfere with the control of the airplane, to cause excessive fatigue to the crew, or to cause structural damage. Stall warning buffeting within these limits is allowable.

(d) There may be no perceptible buffeting condition in the cruise configuration in straight flight at any speed up to V_{MO}/M_{MO}, except that stall warning buffeting is allowable.

(e) For an airplane with M_D greater than .6 or with a maximum operating altitude greater than 25,000 feet, the positive maneuvering load factors at which the onset of perceptible buffeting occurs must be determined with the airplane in the cruise configuration for the ranges of airspeed or Mach number, weight, and altitude for which the airplane is to be certificated. The envelopes of load factor, speed, altitude, and weight must provide a sufficient range of speeds and load factors for normal operations. Probable inadvertent excursions beyond the boundaries of the buffet onset envelopes may not result in unsafe conditions.

[Doc. No. 5066, 29 FR 18291, Dec. 24, 1964, as amended by Amdt. 25–23, 35 FR 5671, Apr. 8, 1970; Amdt. 25–72, 55 FR 29775, July 20, 1990; Amdt. 25–77, 57 FR 28949, June 29, 1992]

§25.253 High-speed characteristics.

(a) *Speed increase and recovery characteristics.* The following speed increase and recovery characteristics must be met:

(1) Operating conditions and characteristics likely to cause inadvertent speed increases (including upsets in pitch and roll) must be simulated with the airplane trimmed at any likely cruise speed up to V_{MO}/M_{MO}. These conditions and characteristics include gust upsets, inadvertent control movements, low stick force gradient in relation to control friction, passenger movement, leveling off from climb, and descent from Mach to airspeed limit altitudes.

(2) Allowing for pilot reaction time after effective inherent or artificial speed warning occurs, it must be shown that the airplane can be recovered to a normal attitude and its speed reduced to V_{MO}/M_{MO}, without–

(i) Exceptional piloting strength or skill;

(ii) Exceeding V_D/M_D, V_{DF}/M_{DF}, or the structural limitations; and

(iii) Buffeting that would impair the pilot's ability to read the instruments or control the airplane for recovery.

(3) With the airplane trimmed at any speed up to V_{MO}/M_{MO}, there must be no reversal of the response to control input about any axis at any speed up to

361

V_{DF}/M_{DF}. Any tendency to pitch, roll, or yaw must be mild and readily controllable, using normal piloting techniques. When the airplane is trimmed at V_{MO}/M_{MO}, the slope of the elevator control force versus speed curve need not be stable at speeds greater than V_{FC}/M_{FC}, but there must be a push force at all speeds up to V_{DF}/M_{DF} and there must be no sudden or excessive reduction of elevator control force as V_{DF}/M_{DF} is reached.

(b) *Maximum speed for stability characteristics, V_{FC}/M_{FC}.* V_{FC}/M_{FC} is the maximum speed at which the requirements of §§ 25.143(f), 25.147(e), 25.175(b)(1), 25.177, and 25.181 must be met with flaps and landing gear retracted. It may not be less than a speed midway between V_{MO}/M_{MO} and V_{DF}/M_{DF}, except that for altitudes where Mach number is the limiting factor, M_{FC} need not exceed the Mach number at which effective speed warning occurs.

[Doc. No. 5066, 29 FR 18291, Dec. 24, 1964, as amended by Amdt. 25–23, 35 FR 5671, Apr. 8, 1970; Amdt. 25–54, 45 FR 60172, Sept. 11, 1980; Amdt. 25–72, 55 FR 29775, July 20, 1990; Amdt. 25–84, 60 FR 30750, June 9, 1995]

§ 25.255 Out-of-trim characteristics.

(a) From an initial condition with the airplane trimmed at cruise speeds up to V_{MO}/M_{MO}, the airplane must have satisfactory maneuvering stability and controllability with the degree of out-of-trim in both the airplane nose-up and nose-down directions, which results from the greater of—

(1) A three-second movement of the longitudinal trim system at its normal rate for the particular flight condition with no aerodynamic load (or an equivalent degree of trim for airplanes that do not have a power-operated trim system), except as limited by stops in the trim system, including those required by § 25.655(b) for adjustable stabilizers; or

(2) The maximum mistrim that can be sustained by the autopilot while maintaining level flight in the high speed cruising condition.

(b) In the out-of-trim condition specified in paragraph (a) of this section, when the normal acceleration is varied from +1 g to the positive and negative values specified in paragraph (c) of this section—

(1) The stick force vs. g curve must have a positive slope at any speed up to and including V_{FC}/M_{FC}; and

(2) At speeds between V_{FC}/M_{FC} and V_{DF}/M_{DF} the direction of the primary longitudinal control force may not reverse.

(c) Except as provided in paragraphs (d) and (e) of this section, compliance with the provisions of paragraph (a) of this section must be demonstrated in flight over the acceleration range—

(1) −1 g to +2.5 g; or

(2) 0 g to 2.0 g, and extrapolating by an acceptable method to −1 g and +2.5 g.

(d) If the procedure set forth in paragraph (c)(2) of this section is used to demonstrate compliance and marginal conditions exist during flight test with regard to reversal of primary longitudinal control force, flight tests must be accomplished from the normal acceleration at which a marginal condition is found to exist to the applicable limit specified in paragraph (b)(1) of this section.

(e) During flight tests required by paragraph (a) of this section, the limit maneuvering load factors prescribed in §§ 25.333(b) and 25.337, and the maneuvering load factors associated with probable inadvertent excursions beyond the boundaries of the buffet onset envelopes determined under § 25.251(e), need not be exceeded. In addition, the entry speeds for flight test demonstrations at normal acceleration values less than 1 g must be limited to the extent necessary to accomplish a recovery without exceeding V_{DF}/M_{DF}.

(f) In the out-of-trim condition specified in paragraph (a) of this section, it must be possible from an overspeed condition at V_{DF}/M_{DF} to produce at least 1.5 g for recovery by applying not more than 125 pounds of longitudinal control force using either the primary longitudinal control alone or the primary longitudinal control and the longitudinal trim system. If the longitudinal trim is used to assist in producing the required load factor, it must be shown at V_{DF}/M_{DF} that the longitudinal trim can be actuated in the airplane nose-up direction with the primary surface loaded to correspond to the least of the following airplane nose-up control forces:

(1) The maximum control forces expected in service as specified in §§ 25.301 and 25.397.

(2) The control force required to produce 1.5 g.

(3) The control force corresponding to buffeting or other phenomena of such intensity that it is a strong deterrent to further application of primary longitudinal control force.

[Amdt. No. 25–42, 43 FR 2322, Jan. 16, 1978]

Subpart C—Structure

GENERAL

§ 25.301 Loads.

(a) Strength requirements are specified in terms of limit loads (the maximum loads to be expected in service) and ultimate loads (limit loads multiplied by prescribed factors of safety). Unless otherwise provided, prescribed loads are limit loads.

(b) Unless otherwise provided, the specified air, ground, and water loads must be placed in equilibrium with inertia forces, considering each item of mass in the airplane. These loads must be distributed to conservatively approximate or closely represent actual conditions. Methods used to determine load intensities and distribution must be validated by flight load measurement unless the methods used for determining those loading conditions are shown to be reliable.

(c) If deflections under load would significantly change the distribution of external or internal loads, this redistribution must be taken into account.

[Doc. No. 5066, 29 FR 18291, Dec. 24, 1964, as amended by Amdt. 25–23, 35 FR 5672, Apr. 8, 1970]

§ 25.303 Factor of safety.

Unless otherwise specified, a factor of safety of 1.5 must be applied to the prescribed limit load which are considered external loads on the structure. When a loading condition is prescribed in terms of ultimate loads, a factor of safety need not be applied unless otherwise specified.

[Amdt. 25–23, 35 FR 5672, Apr. 8, 1970]

§ 25.305 Strength and deformation.

(a) The structure must be able to support limit loads without detrimental permanent deformation. At any load up to limit loads, the deformation may not interfere with safe operation.

(b) The structure must be able to support ultimate loads without failure for at least 3 seconds. However, when proof of strength is shown by dynamic tests simulating actual load conditions, the 3-second limit does not apply. Static tests conducted to ultimate load must include the ultimate deflections and ultimate deformation induced by the loading. When analytical methods are used to show compliance with the ultimate load strength requirements, it must be shown that—

(1) The effects of deformation are not significant;

(2) The deformations involved are fully accounted for in the analysis; or

(3) The methods and assumptions used are sufficient to cover the effects of these deformations.

(c) Where structural flexibility is such that any rate of load application likely to occur in the operating conditions might produce transient stresses appreciably higher than those corresponding to static loads, the effects of this rate of application must be considered.

(d) [Reserved]

(e) The airplane must be designed to withstand any vibration and buffeting that might occur in any likely operating condition up to V_D/M_D, including stall and probable inadvertent excursions beyond the boundaries of the buffet onset envelope. This must be shown by analysis, flight tests, or other tests found necessary by the Administrator.

(f) Unless shown to be extremely improbable, the airplane must be designed to withstand any forced structural vibration resulting from any failure, malfunction or adverse condition in the flight control system. These must be considered limit loads and must be investigated at airspeeds up to V_C/M_C.

[Doc. No. 5066, 29 FR 18291, Dec. 24, 1964, as amended by Amdt. 25–23, 35 FR 5672, Apr. 8, 1970; Amdt. 25–54, 45 FR 60172, Sept. 11, 1980; Amdt. 25–77, 57 FR 28949, June 29, 1992; Amdt. 25–86, 61 FR 5220, Feb. 9, 1996]

§ 25.307   Proof of structure.

(a) Compliance with the strength and deformation requirements of this subpart must be shown for each critical loading condition. Structural analysis may be used only if the structure conforms to that for which experience has shown this method to be reliable. The Administrator may require ultimate load tests in cases where limit load tests may be inadequate.

(b)–(c) [Reserved]

(d) When static or dynamic tests are used to show compliance with the requirements of § 25.305(b) for flight structures, appropriate material correction factors must be applied to the test results, unless the structure, or part thereof, being tested has features such that a number of elements contribute to the total strength of the structure and the failure of one element results in the redistribution of the load through alternate load paths.

[Doc. No. 5066, 29 FR 18291, Dec. 24, 1964, as amended by Amdt. 25–23, 35 FR 5672, Apr. 8, 1970; Amdt. 25–54, 45 FR 60172, Sept. 11, 1980; Amdt. 25–72, 55 FR 29775, July 20, 1990]

FLIGHT LOADS

§ 25.321   General.

(a) Flight load factors represent the ratio of the aerodynamic force component (acting normal to the assumed longitudinal axis of the airplane) to the weight of the airplane. A positive load factor is one in which the aerodynamic force acts upward with respect to the airplane.

(b) Considering compressibility effects at each speed, compliance with the flight load requirements of this subpart must be shown—

(1) At each critical altitude within the range of altitudes selected by the applicant;

(2) At each weight from the design minimum weight to the design maximum weight appropriate to each particular flight load condition; and

(3) For each required altitude and weight, for any practicable distribution of disposable load within the operating limitations recorded in the Airplane Flight Manual.

(c) Enough points on and within the boundaries of the design envelope must be investigated to ensure that the max-

imum load for each part of the airplane structure is obtained.

(d) The significant forces acting on the airplane must be placed in equilibrium in a rational or conservative manner. The linear inertia forces must be considered in equilibrium with the thrust and all aerodynamic loads, while the angular (pitching) inertia forces must be considered in equilibrium with thrust and all aerodynamic moments, including moments due to loads on components such as tail surfaces and nacelles. Critical thrust values in the range from zero to maximum continuous thrust must be considered.

[Doc. No. 5066, 29 FR 18291, Dec. 24, 1964, as amended by Amdt. 25–23, 35 FR 5672, Apr. 8, 1970; Amdt. 25–86, 61 FR 5220, Feb. 9, 1996]

FLIGHT MANEUVER AND GUST
CONDITIONS

§ 25.331   Symmetric maneuvering conditions.

(a) *Procedure.* For the analysis of the maneuvering flight conditions specified in paragraphs (b) and (c) of this section, the following provisions apply:

(1) Where sudden displacement of a control is specified, the assumed rate of control surface displacement may not be less than the rate that could be applied by the pilot through the control system.

(2) In determining elevator angles and chordwise load distribution in the maneuvering conditions of paragraphs (b) and (c) of this section, the effect of corresponding pitching velocities must be taken into account. The in-trim and out-of-trim flight conditions specified in § 25.255 must be considered.

(b) *Maneuvering balanced conditions.* Assuming the airplane to be in equilibrium with zero pitching acceleration, the maneuvering conditions A through I on the maneuvering envelope in § 25.333(b) must be investigated.

(c) *Pitch maneuver conditions.* The conditions specified in paragraphs (c)(1) and (2) of this section must be investigated. The movement of the pitch control surfaces may be adjusted to take into account limitations imposed by the maximum pilot effort specified by § 25.397(b), control system stops and any indirect effect imposed by limitations in the output side of the control system (for example, stalling torque or maximum rate obtainable by a power control system.)

(1) *Maximum pitch control displacement at V_A.* The airplane is assumed to be flying in steady level flight (point A_1, §25.333(b)) and the cockpit pitch control is suddenly moved to obtain extreme nose up pitching acceleration. In defining the tail load, the response of the airplane must be taken into account. Airplane loads that occur subsequent to the time when normal acceleration at the c.g. exceeds the positive limit maneuvering load factor (at point A_2 in §25.333(b)), or the resulting tailplane normal load reaches its maximum, whichever occurs first, need not be considered.

(2) *Specified control displacement.* A checked maneuver, based on a rational pitching control motion vs. time profile, must be established in which the design limit load factor specified in §25.337 will not be exceeded. Unless lesser values cannot be exceeded, the airplane response must result in pitching accelerations not less than the following:

(i) A positive pitching acceleration (nose up) is assumed to be reached concurrently with the airplane load factor of 1.0 (Points A_1 to D_1, §25.333(b)). The positive acceleration must be equal to at least

$$\frac{39n}{v} \, (n-1.5), \; \left(\text{Radians/sec.}^2\right)$$

where—

n is the positive load factor at the speed under consideration, and V is the airplane equivalent speed in knots.

(ii) A negative pitching acceleration (nose down) is assumed to be reached concurrently with the positive maneuvering load factor (points A_2 to D_2, §25.333(b)). This negative pitching acceleration must be equal to at least

$$\frac{-26n}{v} \, (n-1.5), \; \left(\text{Radians/sec.}^2\right)$$

where—

n is the positive load factor at the speed under consideration; and V is the airplane equivalent speed in knots.

[Doc. No. 5066, 29 FR 18291, Dec. 24, 1964, as amended by Amdt. 25–23, 35 FR 5672, Apr. 8, 1970; Amdt. 25–46, 43 FR 50594, Oct. 30, 1978; 43 FR 52495, Nov. 13, 1978; 43 FR 54082, Nov. 20, 1978; Amdt. 25–72, 55 FR 29775, July 20, 1990; 55 FR 37607, Sept. 12, 1990; Amdt. 25–86, 61 FR 5220, Feb. 9, 1996; Amdt. 25–91, 62 FR 40704, July 29, 1997]

§ 25.333 Flight maneuvering envelope.

(a) *General.* The strength requirements must be met at each combination of airspeed and load factor on and within the boundaries of the representative maneuvering envelope (*V-n* diagram) of paragraph (b) of this section. This envelope must also be used in determining the airplane structural operating limitations as specified in §25.1501.

(b) *Maneuvering envelope.*

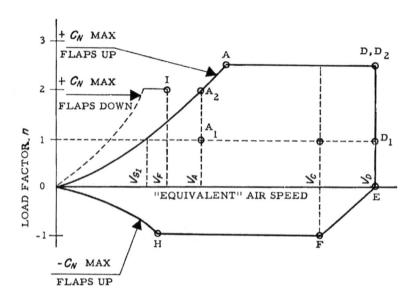

[Doc. No. 5066, 29 FR 18291, Dec. 24, 1964, as amended by Amdt. 25–86, 61 FR 5220, Feb. 9, 1996]

§ 25.335 Design airspeeds.

The selected design airspeeds are equivalent airspeeds (EAS). Estimated values of V_{S0} and V_{S1} must be conservative.

(a) *Design cruising speed, V_C.* For V_C, the following apply:

(1) The minimum value of V_C must be sufficiently greater than V_B to provide for inadvertent speed increases likely to occur as a result of severe atmospheric turbulence.

(2) Except as provided in § 25.335(d)(2), V_C may not be less than $V_B + 1.32\ U_{REF}$ (with U_{REF} as specified in § 25.341(a)(5)(i)). However V_C need not exceed the maximum speed in level flight at maximum continuous power for the corresponding altitude.

(3) At altitudes where V_D is limited by Mach number, V_C may be limited to a selected Mach number.

(b) *Design dive speed, V_D.* V_D must be selected so that V_C/M_C is not greater than $0.8\ V_D/M_D$, or so that the minimum speed margin between V_C/M_C and

V_D/M_D is the greater of the following values:

(1) From an initial condition of stabilized flight at V_C/M_C, the airplane is upset, flown for 20 seconds along a flight path 7.5° below the initial path, and then pulled up at a load factor of $1.5g$ ($0.5g$ acceleration increment). The speed increase occurring in this maneuver may be calculated if reliable or conservative aerodynamic data is used. Power as specified in § 25.175(b)(1)(iv) is assumed until the pullup is initiated, at which time power reduction and the use of pilot controlled drag devices may be assumed;

(2) The minimum speed margin must be enough to provide for atmospheric variations (such as horizontal gusts, and penetration of jet streams and cold fronts) and for instrument errors and airframe production variations. These factors may be considered on a probability basis. The margin at altitude where M_C is limited by compressibility effects must not be less than $0.07M$ unless a lower margin is determined using a rational analysis that includes the effects of any automatic systems. In any

case, the margin may not be reduced to less than 0.05M.

(c) *Design maneuvering speed V_A.* For V_A, the following apply:

(1) V_A may not be less than $V_{S1} \sqrt{n}$ where—

(i) n is the limit positive maneuvering load factor at V_C; and

(ii) V_{S1} is the stalling speed with flaps retracted.

(2) V_A and V_S must be evaluated at the design weight and altitude under consideration.

(3) V_A need not be more than V_C or the speed at which the positive $C_{N\ max}$ curve intersects the positive maneuver load factor line, whichever is less.

(d) *Design speed for maximum gust intensity, V_B.*

(1) V_B may not be less than

$$V_{S1} \left[1 + \frac{K_g U_{ref} V_c a}{498 w} \right]^{1/2}$$

where—

V_{S1}=the 1-g stalling speed based on C_{NAmax} with the flaps retracted at the particular weight under consideration;

V_c=design cruise speed (knots equivalent airspeed);

U_{ref}=the reference gust velocity (feet per second equivalent airspeed) from §25.341(a)(5)(i);

w=average wing loading (pounds per square foot) at the particular weight under consideration.

$$K_g = \frac{.88\mu}{5.3 + \mu}$$

$$\mu = \frac{2w}{\rho c a g}$$

ρ=density of air (slugs/ft³);

c=mean geometric chord of the wing (feet);

g=acceleration due to gravity (ft/sec²);

a=slope of the airplane normal force coefficient curve, C_{NA} per radian;

(2) At altitudes where V_C is limited by Mach number—

(i) V_B may be chosen to provide an optimum margin between low and high speed buffet boundaries; and,

(ii) V_B need not be greater than V_C.

(e) *Design flap speeds, V_F.* For V_F, the following apply:

(1) The design flap speed for each flap position (established in accordance with §25.697(a)) must be sufficiently

greater than the operating speed recommended for the corresponding stage of flight (including balked landings) to allow for probable variations in control of airspeed and for transition from one flap position to another.

(2) If an automatic flap positioning or load limiting device is used, the speeds and corresponding flap positions programmed or allowed by the device may be used.

(3) V_F may not be less than—

(i) 1.6 V_{S1} with the flaps in takeoff position at maximum takeoff weight;

(ii) 1.8 V_{S1} with the flaps in approach position at maximum landing weight, and

(iii) 1.8 V_{S0} with the flaps in landing position at maximum landing weight.

(f) *Design drag device speeds, V_{DD}.* The selected design speed for each drag device must be sufficiently greater than the speed recommended for the operation of the device to allow for probable variations in speed control. For drag devices intended for use in high speed descents, V_{DD} may not be less than V_D. When an automatic drag device positioning or load limiting means is used, the speeds and corresponding drag device positions programmed or allowed by the automatic means must be used for design.

[Doc. No. 5066, 29 FR 18291, Dec. 24, 1964, as amended by Amdt. 25–23, 35 FR 5672, Apr. 8, 1970; Amdt. 25–86, 61 FR 5220, Feb. 9, 1996; Amdt. 25–91, 62 FR 40704, July 29, 1997]

§25.337 Limit maneuvering load factors.

(a) Except where limited by maximum (static) lift coefficients, the airplane is assumed to be subjected to symmetrical maneuvers resulting in the limit maneuvering load factors prescribed in this section. Pitching velocities appropriate to the corresponding pull-up and steady turn maneuvers must be taken into account.

(b) The positive limit maneuvering load factor n for any speed up to V_n may not be less than 2.1+24,000/ (W +10,000) except that n may not be less than 2.5 and need not be greater than 3.8—where W is the design maximum takeoff weight.

(c) The negative limit maneuvering load factor—

(1) May not be less than −1.0 at speeds up to V_C; and

(2) Must vary linearly with speed from the value at V_C to zero at V_D.

(d) Maneuvering load factors lower than those specified in this section may be used if the airplane has design features that make it impossible to exceed these values in flight.

[Doc. No. 5066, 29 FR 18291, Dec. 24, 1964, as amended by Amdt. 25–23, 35 FR 5672, Apr. 8, 1970]

§ 25.341 Gust and turbulence loads.

(a) *Discrete Gust Design Criteria.* The airplane is assumed to be subjected to symmetrical vertical and lateral gusts in level flight. Limit gust loads must be determined in accordance with the provisions:

(1) Loads on each part of the structure must be determined by dynamic analysis. The analysis must take into account unsteady aerodynamic characteristics and all significant structural degrees of freedom including rigid body motions.

(2) The shape of the gust must be:

$$U = \frac{U_{ds}}{2}\left[1 - Cos\left(\frac{\pi s}{H}\right)\right]$$

for $0 \le s \le 2H$

where—

s=distance penetrated into the gust (feet);

U_{ds}=the design gust velocity in equivalent airspeed specified in paragraph (a)(4) of this section; and

H=the gust gradient which is the distance (feet) parallel to the airplane's flight path for the gust to reach its peak velocity.

(3) A sufficient number of gust gradient distances in the range 30 feet to 350 feet must be investigated to find the critical response for each load quantity.

(4) The design gust velocity must be:

$$U_{ds} = U_{ref}F_g\left(H\!\!\Big/\!350\right)^{1/6}$$

where—

U_{ref}=the reference gust velocity in equivalent airspeed defined in paragraph (a)(5) of this section.

F_g=the flight profile alleviation factor defined in paragraph (a)(6) of this section.

(5) The following reference gust velocities apply:

(i) At the airplane design speed $V_{C\le}$ Positive and negative gusts with reference gust velocities of 56.0 ft/sec EAS must be considered at sea level. The reference gust velocity may be reduced linearly from 56.0 ft/sec EAS at sea level to 44.0 ft/sec EAS at 15000 feet. The reference gust velocity may be further reduced linearly from 44.0 ft/sec EAS at 15000 feet to 26.0 ft/sec EAS at 50000 feet.

(ii) At the airplane design speed $V_{D\le}$ The reference gust velocity must be 0.5 times the value obtained under § 25.341(a)(5)(i).

(6) The flight profile alleviation factor, F_g, must be increased linearly from the sea level value to a value of 1.0 at the maximum operating altitude defined in § 25.1527. At sea level, the flight profile alleviation factor is determined by the following equation:

$$F_g = 0.5\left(F_{gz} + F_{gm}\right)$$

Where:

$$F_{gz} = 1 - \frac{Z_{mo}}{250000};$$

$$F_{gm} = \sqrt{R_2 Tan\left(\pi R_1 \Big/ 4\right)};$$

$$R_1 = \frac{Maximum\,Landing\,Weight}{Maximum\,Take\text{-}off\,Weight};$$

$$R_2 = \frac{Maximum\,Zero\,Fuel\,Weight}{Maximum\,Take\text{-}off\,Weight};$$

Z_{mo}=Maximum operating altitude defined in § 25.1527.

(7) When a stability augmentation system is included in the analysis, the effect of any significant system non-linearities should be accounted for when deriving limit loads from limit gust conditions.

(b) *Continuous Gust Design Criteria.* The dynamic response of the airplane to vertical and lateral continuous turbulence must be taken into account. The continuous gust design criteria of appendix G of this part must be used to establish the dynamic response unless more rational criteria are shown.

[Doc. No. 27902, 61 FR 5221, Feb. 9, 1996; 61 FR 9533, Mar. 8, 1996]

§25.343 Design fuel and oil loads.

(a) The disposable load combinations must include each fuel and oil load in the range from zero fuel and oil to the selected maximum fuel and oil load. A structural reserve fuel condition, not exceeding 45 minutes of fuel under the operating conditions in §25.1001(e) and (f), as applicable, may be selected.

(b) If a structural reserve fuel condition is selected, it must be used as the minimum fuel weight condition for showing compliance with the flight load requirements as prescribed in this subpart. In addition—

(1) The structure must be designed for a condition of zero fuel and oil in the wing at limit loads corresponding to—

(i) A maneuvering load factor of +2.25; and

(ii) The gust conditions of §25.341(a) but assuming 85% of the design velocities prescribed in §25.341(a)(4).

(2) Fatigue evaluation of the structure must account for any increase in operating stresses resulting from the design condition of paragraph (b)(1) of this section; and

(3) The flutter, deformation, and vibration requirements must also be met with zero fuel.

[Doc. No. 5066, 29 FR 18291, Dec. 24, 1964, as amended by Amdt. 25–18, 33 FR 12226, Aug. 30, 1968; Amdt. 25–72, 55 FR 37607, Sept. 12, 1990; Amdt. 25–86, 61 FR 5221, Feb. 9, 1996]

§25.345 High lift devices.

(a) If wing flaps are to be used during takeoff, approach, or landing, at the design flap speeds established for these stages of flight under §25.335(e) and with the wing flaps in the corresponding positions, the airplane is assumed to be subjected to symmetrical maneuvers and gusts. The resulting limit loads must correspond to the conditions determined as follows:

(1) Maneuvering to a positive limit load factor of 2.0; and

(2) Positive and negative gusts of 25 ft/sec EAS acting normal to the flight path in level flight. Gust loads resulting on each part of the structure must

be determined by rational analysis. The analysis must take into account the unsteady aerodynamic characteristics and rigid body motions of the aircraft. The shape of the gust must be as described in §25.341(a)(2) except that—

U_{ds}=25 ft/sec EAS;

H=12.5 c; and

c=mean geometric chord of the wing (feet).

(b) The airplane must be designed for the conditions prescribed in paragraph (a) of this section, except that the airplane load factor need not exceed 1.0, taking into account, as separate conditions, the effects of—

(1) Propeller slipstream corresponding to maximum continuous power at the design flap speeds V_F, and with takeoff power at not less than 1.4 times the stalling speed for the particular flap position and associated maximum weight; and

(2) A head-on gust of 25 feet per second velocity (EAS).

(c) If flaps or other high lift devices are to be used in en route conditions, and with flaps in the appropriate position at speeds up to the flap design speed chosen for these conditions, the airplane is assumed to be subjected to symmetrical maneuvers and gusts within the range determined by—

(1) Maneuvering to a positive limit load factor as prescribed in §25.337(b); and

(2) The discrete vertical gust criteria in §25.341(a).

(d) The airplane must be designed for a maneuvering load factor of 1.5 g at the maximum take-off weight with the wing-flaps and similar high lift devices in the landing configurations.

[Doc. No. 5066, 29 FR 18291, Dec. 24, 1964, as amended by Amdt. 25–46, 43 FR 50595, Oct. 30, 1978; Amdt. 25–72, 55 FR 37607, Sept. 17, 1990; Amdt. 25–86, 61 FR 5221, Feb. 9, 1996; Amdt. 25–91, 62 FR 40704, July 29, 1997]

§25.349 Rolling conditions.

The airplane must be designed for loads resulting from the rolling conditions specified in paragraphs (a) and (b) of this section. Unbalanced aerodynamic moments about the center of gravity must be reacted in a rational or conservative manner, considering the principal masses furnishing the reacting inertia forces.

(a) *Maneuvering.* The following conditions, speeds, and aileron deflections (except as the deflections may be limited by pilot effort) must be considered in combination with an airplane load factor of zero and of two-thirds of the positive maneuvering factor used in design. In determining the required aileron deflections, the torsional flexibility of the wing must be considered in accordance with § 25.301(b):

(1) Conditions corresponding to steady rolling velocities must be investigated. In addition, conditions corresponding to maximum angular acceleration must be investigated for airplanes with engines or other weight concentrations outboard of the fuselage. For the angular acceleration conditions, zero rolling velocity may be assumed in the absence of a rational time history investigation of the maneuver.

(2) At V_A, a sudden deflection of the aileron to the stop is assumed.

(3) At V_C, the aileron deflection must be that required to produce a rate of roll not less than that obtained in paragraph (a)(2) of this section.

(4) At V_D, the aileron deflection must be that required to produce a rate of roll not less than one-third of that in paragraph (a)(2) of this section.

(b) *Unsymmetrical gusts.* The airplane is assumed to be subjected to unsymmetrical vertical gusts in level flight. The resulting limit loads must be determined from either the wing maximum airload derived directly from § 25.341(a), or the wing maximum airload derived indirectly from the vertical load factor calculated from § 25.341(a). It must be assumed that 100 percent of the wing air load acts on one side of the airplane and 80 percent of the wing air load acts on the other side.

[Doc. No. 5066, 29 FR 18291, Dec. 24, 1964, as amended by Amdt. 25–23, 35 FR 5672, Apr. 8, 1970; Amdt. 25–86, 61 FR 5222, Feb. 9, 1996; Amdt. 25–94, 63 FR 8848, Feb. 23, 1998]

§ 25.351 Yaw maneuver conditions.

The airplane must be designed for loads resulting from the yaw maneuver conditions specified in paragraphs (a) through (d) of this section at speeds from V_{MC} to V_D. Unbalanced aerodynamic moments about the center of gravity must be reacted in a rational or conservative manner considering the airplane inertia forces. In computing the tail loads the yawing velocity may be assumed to be zero.

(a) With the airplane in unaccelerated flight at zero yaw, it is assumed that the cockpit rudder control is suddenly displaced to achieve the resulting rudder deflection, as limited by:

(1) The control system on control surface stops; or

(2) A limit pilot force of 300 pounds from V_{MC} to V_A and 200 pounds from V_C/M_C to V_D/M_D, with a linear variation between V_A and V_C/M_C.

(b) With the cockpit rudder control deflected so as always to maintain the maximum rudder deflection available within the limitations specified in paragraph (a) of this section, it is assumed that the airplane yaws to the overswing sideslip angle.

(c) With the airplane yawed to the static equilibrium sideslip angle, it is assumed that the cockpit rudder control is held so as to achieve the maximum rudder deflection available within the limitations specified in paragraph (a) of this section.

(d) With the airplane yawed to the static equilibrium sideslip angle of paragraph (c) of this section, it is assumed that the cockpit rudder control is suddenly returned to neutral.

[Amdt. 25–91, 62 FR 40704, July 29, 1997]

SUPPLEMENTARY CONDITIONS

§ 25.361 Engine torque.

(a) Each engine mount and its supporting structure must be designed for the effects of—

(1) A limit engine torque corresponding to takeoff power and propeller speed acting simultaneously with 75 percent of the limit loads from flight condition A of § 25.333(b);

(2) A limit torque corresponding to the maximum continuous power and propeller speed, acting simultaneously with the limit loads from flight condition A of § 25.333(b); and

(3) For turbopropeller installations, in addition to the conditions specified

in paragraphs (a)(1) and (2) of this section, a limit engine torque corresponding to takeoff power and propeller speed, multiplied by a factor accounting for propeller control system malfunction, including quick feathering, acting simultaneously with 1g level flight loads. In the absence of a rational analysis, a factor of 1.6 must be used.

(b) For turbine engine installations, the engine mounts and supporting structure must be designed to withstand each of the following:

(1) A limit engine torque load imposed by sudden engine stoppage due to malfunction or structural failure (such as compressor jamming).

(2) A limit engine torque load imposed by the maximum acceleration of the engine.

(c) The limit engine torque to be considered under paragraph (a) of this section must be obtained by multiplying mean torque for the specified power and speed by a factor of—

(1) 1.25 for turbopropeller installations;

(2) 1.33 for reciprocating engines with five or more cylinders; or

(3) Two, three, or four, for engines with four, three, or two cylinders, respectively.

[Doc. No. 5066, 29 FR 18291, Dec. 24, 1964, as amended by Amdt. 25–23, 35 FR 5672, Apr. 8, 1970; Amdt. 25–46, 43 FR 50595, Oct. 30, 1978; Amdt. 25–72, 55 FR 29776, July 20, 1990]

§ 25.363 Side load on engine and auxiliary power unit mounts.

(a) Each engine and auxiliary power unit mount and its supporting structure must be designed for a limit load factor in lateral direction, for the side load on the engine and auxiliary power unit mount, at least equal to the maximum load factor obtained in the yawing conditions but not less than—

(1) 1.33; or

(2) One-third of the limit load factor for flight condition A as prescribed in § 25.333(b).

(b) The side load prescribed in paragraph (a) of this section may be assumed to be independent of other flight conditions.

[Doc. No. 5066, 29 FR 18291, Dec. 24, 1964, as amended by Amdt. 25–23, 35 FR 5672, Apr. 8, 1970; Amdt. 25–91, 62 FR 40704, July 29, 1997]

§ 25.365 Pressurized compartment loads.

For airplanes with one or more pressurized compartments the following apply:

(a) The airplane structure must be strong enough to withstand the flight loads combined with pressure differential loads from zero up to the maximum relief valve setting.

(b) The external pressure distribution in flight, and stress concentrations and fatigue effects must be accounted for.

(c) If landings may be made with the compartment pressurized, landing loads must be combined with pressure differential loads from zero up to the maximum allowed during landing.

(d) The airplane structure must be designed to be able to withstand the pressure differential loads corresponding to the maximum relief valve setting multiplied by a factor of 1.33 for airplanes to be approved for operation to 45,000 feet or by a factor of 1.67 for airplanes to be approved for operation above 45,000 feet, omitting other loads.

(e) Any structure, component or part, inside or outside a pressurized compartment, the failure of which could interfere with continued safe flight and landing, must be designed to withstand the effects of a sudden release of pressure through an opening in any compartment at any operating altitude resulting from each of the following conditions:

(1) The penetration of the compartment by a portion of an engine following an engine disintegration;

(2) Any opening in any pressurized compartment up to the size H_o in square feet; however, small compartments may be combined with an adjacent pressurized compartment and both considered as a single compartment for openings that cannot reasonably be expected to be confined to the small compartment. The size H_o must be computed by the following formula:

$$H_o = PA_s$$

where,

H_o=Maximum opening in square feet, need not exceed 20 square feet.

$$P = \frac{A_s}{6240} + .024$$

A_s=Maximum cross-sectional area of the pressurized shell normal to the longitudinal axis, in square feet; and

(3) The maximum opening caused by airplane or equipment failures not shown to be extremely improbable.

(f) In complying with paragraph (e) of this section, the fail-safe features of the design may be considered in determining the probability of failure or penetration and probable size of openings, provided that possible improper operation of closure devices and inadvertent door openings are also considered. Furthermore, the resulting differential pressure loads must be combined in a rational and conservative manner with 1–g level flight loads and any loads arising from emergency depressurization conditions. These loads may be considered as ultimate conditions; however, any deformations associated with these conditions must not interfere with continued safe flight and landing. The pressure relief provided by intercompartment venting may also be considered.

(g) Bulkheads, floors, and partitions in pressurized compartments for occupants must be designed to withstand the conditions specified in paragraph (e) of this section. In addition, reasonable design precautions must be taken to minimize the probability of parts becoming detached and injuring occupants while in their seats.

[Doc. No. 5066, 29 FR 18291, Dec. 24, 1964, as amended by Amdt. 25–54, 45 FR 60172, Sept. 11, 1980; Amdt. 25–71, 55 FR 13477, Apr. 10, 1990; Amdt. 25–72, 55 FR 29776, July 20, 1990; Amdt. 25–87, 61 FR 28695, June 5, 1996]

§ 25.367 Unsymmetrical loads due to engine failure.

(a) The airplane must be designed for the unsymmetrical loads resulting from the failure of the critical engine. Turbopropeller airplanes must be designed for the following conditions in combination with a single malfunction of the propeller drag limiting system, considering the probable pilot corrective action on the flight controls:

(1) At speeds between V_{MC} and V_D, the loads resulting from power failure

because of fuel flow interruption are considered to be limit loads.

(2) At speeds between V_{MC} and V_C, the loads resulting from the disconnection of the engine compressor from the turbine or from loss of the turbine blades are considered to be ultimate loads.

(3) The time history of the thrust decay and drag build-up occurring as a result of the prescribed engine failures must be substantiated by test or other data applicable to the particular engine-propeller combination.

(4) The timing and magnitude of the probable pilot corrective action must be conservatively estimated, considering the characteristics of the particular engine-propeller-airplane combination.

(b) Pilot corrective action may be assumed to be initiated at the time maximum yawing velocity is reached, but not earlier than two seconds after the engine failure. The magnitude of the corrective action may be based on the control forces specified in § 25.397(b) except that lower forces may be assumed where it is shown by anaylsis or test that these forces can control the yaw and roll resulting from the prescribed engine failure conditions.

§ 25.371 Gyroscopic loads.

The structure supporting any engine or auxiliary power unit must be designed for the loads including the gyroscopic loads arising from the conditions specified in §§ 25.331, 25.341(a), 25.349, 25.351, 25.473, 25.479, and 25.481, with the engine or auxiliary power unit at the maximum rpm appropriate to the condition. For the purposes of compliance with this section, the pitch maneuver in § 25.331(c)(1) must be carried out until the positive limit maneuvering load factor (point A_2 in § 25.333(b)) is reached.

[Amdt. 25–91, 62 FR 40704, July 29, 1997]

§ 25.373 Speed control devices.

If speed control devices (such as spoilers and drag flaps) are installed for use in en route conditions—

(a) The airplane must be designed for the symmetrical maneuvers prescribed in § 25.333 and § 25.337, the yawing maneuvers prescribed in § 25.351, and the vertical and later gust conditions prescribed in §25.341(a), at each setting and the maximum speed associated with that setting; and

(b) If the device has automatic operating or load limiting features, the airplane must be designed for the maneuver and gust conditions prescribed in paragraph (a) of this section, at the speeds and corresponding device positions that the mechanism allows.

[Doc. No. 5066, 29 FR 18291, Dec. 24, 1964, as amended by Amdt. 25–72, 55 FR 29776, July 20, 1990; Amdt. 25–86, 61 FR 5222, Feb. 9, 1996]

CONTROL SURFACE AND SYSTEM LOADS

§ 25.391 Control surface loads: General.

The control surfaces must be designed for the limit loads resulting from the flight conditions in §§25.331, 25.341(a), 25.349 and 25.351 and the ground gust conditions in §25.415, considering the requirements for—

(a) Loads parallel to hinge line, in §25.393;

(b) Pilot effort effects, in §25.397;

(c) Trim tab effects, in §25.407;

(d) Unsymmetrical loads, in §25.427; and

(e) Auxiliary aerodynamic surfaces, in §25.445.

[Doc. No. 5066, 29 FR 18291, Dec. 24, 1964, as amended by Amdt. 25–86, 61 FR 5222, Feb. 9, 1996]

§ 25.393 Loads parallel to hinge line.

(a) Control surfaces and supporting hinge brackets must be designed for inertia loads acting parallel to the hinge line.

(b) In the absence of more rational data, the inertia loads may be assumed to be equal to KW, where—

(1) $K=24$ for vertical surfaces;

(2) $K=12$ for horizontal surfaces; and

(3) W=weight of the movable surfaces.

§ 25.395 Control system.

(a) Longitudinal, lateral, directional, and drag control system and their supporting structures must be designed for loads corresponding to 125 percent of the computed hinge moments of the movable control surface in the conditions prescribed in §25.391.

(b) The system limit loads, except the loads resulting from ground gusts,

need not exceed the loads that can be produced by the pilot (or pilots) and by automatic or power devices operating the controls.

(c) The loads must not be less than those resulting from application of the minimum forces prescribed in §25.397(c).

[Doc. No. 5066, 29 FR 18291, Dec. 24, 1964, as amended by Amdt. 25–23, 35 FR 5672, Apr. 8, 1970; Amdt. 25–72, 55 FR 29776, July 20, 1990]

§ 25.397 Control system loads.

(a) *General.* The maximum and minimum pilot forces, specified in paragraph (c) of this section, are assumed to act at the appropriate control grips or pads (in a manner simulating flight conditions) and to be reacted at the attachment of the control system to the control surface horn.

(b) *Pilot effort effects.* In the control surface flight loading condition, the air loads on movable surfaces and the corresponding deflections need not exceed those that would result in flight from the application of any pilot force within the ranges specified in paragraph (c) of this section. Two-thirds of the maximum values specified for the aileron and elevator may be used if control surface hinge moments are based on reliable data. In applying this criterion, the effects of servo mechanisms, tabs, and automatic pilot systems, must be considered.

(c) *Limit pilot forces and torques.* The limit pilot forces and torques are as follows:

Control	Maximum forces or torques	Minimum forces or torques
Aileron:		
Stick	100 lbs	40 lbs.
Wheel [1]	80 D in.-lbs [2] ...	40 D in.-lbs.
Elevator:		
Stick	250 lbs	100 lbs.
Wheel (symmetrical)	300 lbs	100 lbs.
Wheel (unsymmetrical) [3]	....	100 lbs.
Rudder	300 lbs	130 lbs.

[1] The critical parts of the aileron control system must be designed for a single tangential force with a limit value equal to 1.25 times the couple force determined from these criteria.

[2] *D*=wheel diameter (inches).

[3] The unsymmetrical forces must be applied at one of the normal handgrip points on the periphery of the control wheel.

[Doc. 5066, 29 FR 18291, Dec. 24, 1964, as amended by Amdt. 25–38, 41 FR 55466, Dec. 20, 1976; Amdt. 25–72, 55 FR 29776, July 20, 1990]

§ 25.399 Dual control system.

(a) Each dual control system must be designed for the pilots operating in opposition, using individual pilot forces not less than—

(1) 0.75 times those obtained under § 25.395; or

(2) The minimum forces specified in § 25.397(c).

(b) The control system must be designed for pilot forces applied in the same direction, using individual pilot forces not less than 0.75 times those obtained under § 25.395.

§ 25.405 Secondary control system.

Secondary controls, such as wheel brake, spoiler, and tab controls, must be designed for the maximum forces that a pilot is likely to apply to those controls. The following values may be used:

PILOT CONTROL FORCE LIMITS (SECONDARY CONTROLS)

Control	Limit pilot forces
Miscellaneous: *Crank, wheel, or lever.	$\dfrac{1+R}{3} \times 50$ lbs., but not less than 50 lbs. nor more than 150 lbs. (R=radius). (Applicable to any angle within 20° of plane of control).
Twist	133 in.-lbs.
Push-pull	To be chosen by applicant.

*Limited to flap, tab, stabilizer, spoiler, and landing gear operation controls.

§ 25.407 Trim tab effects.

The effects of trim tabs on the control surface design conditions must be accounted for only where the surface loads are limited by maximum pilot effort. In these cases, the tabs are considered to be deflected in the direction that would assist the pilot, and the deflections are—

(a) For elevator trim tabs, those required to trim the airplane at any point within the positive portion of the pertinent flight envelope in § 25.333(b), except as limited by the stops; and

(b) For aileron and rudder trim tabs, those required to trim the airplane in the critical unsymmetrical power and loading conditions, with appropriate allowance for rigging tolerances.

§ 25.409 Tabs.

(a) *Trim tabs.* Trim tabs must be designed to withstand loads arising from all likely combinations of tab setting, primary control position, and airplane speed (obtainable without exceeding the flight load conditions prescribed for the airplane as a whole), when the effect of the tab is opposed by pilot effort forces up to those specified in § 25.397(b).

(b) *Balancing tabs.* Balancing tabs must be designed for deflections consistent with the primary control surface loading conditions.

(c) *Servo tabs.* Servo tabs must be designed for deflections consistent with the primary control surface loading conditions obtainable within the pilot maneuvering effort, considering possible opposition from the trim tabs.

§ 25.415 Ground gust conditions.

(a) The control system must be designed as follows for control surface loads due to ground gusts and taxiing downwind:

(1) The control system between the stops nearest the surfaces and the cockpit controls must be designed for loads corresponding to the limit hinge moments H of paragraph (a)(2) of this section. These loads need not exceed—

(i) The loads corresponding to the maximum pilot loads in § 25.397(c) for each pilot alone; or

(ii) 0.75 times these maximum loads for each pilot when the pilot forces are applied in the same direction.

(2) The control system stops nearest the surfaces, the control system locks, and the parts of the systems (if any) between these stops and locks and the control surface horns, must be designed for limit hinge moments H, in foot pounds, obtained from the formula, H=.0034KV²cS, where—

V=65 (wind speed in knots)

K=limit hinge moment factor for ground gusts derived in paragraph (b) of this section.

c=mean chord of the control surface aft of the hinge line (ft);

S=area of the control surface aft of the hinge line (sq ft);

(b) The limit hinge moment factor K for ground gusts must be derived as follows:

Surface	K	Position of controls
(a) Aileron	0.75	Control column locked or lashed in mid-position.
(b) ......do	[1] 1 ±0.50	Ailerons at full throw.
(c) Elevator	[1] 1 ±0.75	(c) Elevator full down.
(d) ......do	[1] 1 ±0.75	(d) Elevator full up.
(e) Rudder	0.75	(e) Rudder in neutral.
(f) ......do	0.75	(f) Rudder at full throw.

[1] A positive value of K indicates a moment tending to depress the surface, while a negative value of K indicates a moment tending to raise the surface.

[Doc. No. 5066, 29 FR 18291, Dec. 24, 1964, as amended by Amdt. 25–72, 55 FR 29776, July 20, 1990; Amdt. 25–91, 62 FR 40705, July 29, 1997]

§25.427 Unsymmetrical loads.

(a) In designing the airplane for lateral gust, yaw maneuver and roll maneuver conditions, account must be taken of unsymmetrical loads on the empennage arising from effects such as slipstream and aerodynamic interference with the wing, vertical fin and other aerodynamic surfaces.

(b) The horizontal tail must be assumed to be subjected to unsymmetrical loading conditions determined as follows:

(1) 100 percent of the maximum loading from the symmetrical maneuver conditions of §25.331 and the vertical gust conditions of §25.341(a) acting separately on the surface on one side of the plane of symmetry; and

(2) 80 percent of these loadings acting on the other side.

(c) For empennage arrangements where the horizontal tail surfaces have dihedral angles greater than plus or minus 10 degrees, or are supported by the vertical tail surfaces, the surfaces and the supporting structure must be designed for gust velocities specified in §25.341(a) acting in any orientation at right angles to the flight path.

(d) Unsymmetrical loading on the empennage arising from buffet conditions of §25.305(e) must be taken into account.

[Doc. No. 27902, 61 FR 5222, Feb. 9, 1996]

§25.445 Auxiliary aerodynamic surfaces.

(a) When significant, the aerodynamic influence between auxiliary aerodynamic surfaces, such as outboard fins and winglets, and their supporting aerodynamic surfaces, must be taken into account for all loading conditions including pitch, roll, and yaw maneuvers, and gusts as specified in §25.341(a) acting at any orientation at right angles to the flight path.

(b) To provide for unsymmetrical loading when outboard fins extend above and below the horizontal surface, the critical vertical surface loading (load per unit area) determined under §25.391 must also be applied as follows:

(1) 100 percent to the area of the vertical surfaces above (or below) the horizontal surface.

(2) 80 percent to the area below (or above) the horizontal surface.

[Doc. No. 5066, 29 FR 18291, Dec. 24, 1964, as amended by Amdt. 25–86, 61 FR 5222, Feb. 9, 1996]

§25.457 Wing flaps.

Wing flaps, their operating mechanisms, and their supporting structures must be designed for critical loads occurring in the conditions prescribed in §25.345, accounting for the loads occurring during transition from one flap position and airspeed to another.

§25.459 Special devices.

The loading for special devices using aerodynamic surfaces (such as slots, slats and spoilers) must be determined from test data.

[Doc. No. 5066, 29 FR 18291, Dec. 24, 1964, as amended by Amdt. 25–72, 55 FR 29776, July 20, 1990]

GROUND LOADS

§25.471 General.

(a) *Loads and equilibrium.* For limit ground loads—

(1) Limit ground loads obtained under this subpart are considered to be external forces applied to the airplane structure; and

(2) In each specified ground load condition, the external loads must be placed in equilibrium with the linear

and angular inertia loads in a rational or conservative manner.

(b) *Critical centers of gravity.* The critical centers of gravity within the range for which certification is requested must be selected so that the maximum design loads are obtained in each landing gear element. Fore and aft, vertical, and lateral airplane centers of gravity must be considered. Lateral displacements of the c.g. from the airplane centerline which would result in main gear loads not greater than 103 percent of the critical design load for symmetrical loading conditions may be selected without considering the effects of these lateral c.g. displacements on the loading of the main gear elements, or on the airplane structure provided—

(1) The lateral displacement of the c.g. results from random passenger or cargo disposition within the fuselage or from random unsymmetrical fuel loading or fuel usage; and

(2) Appropriate loading instructions for random disposable loads are included under the provisions of § 25.1583(c)(1) to ensure that the lateral displacement of the center of gravity is maintained within these limits.

(c) *Landing gear dimension data.* Figure 1 of appendix A contains the basic landing gear dimension data.

[Amdt. 25–23, 35 FR 5673, Apr. 8, 1970]

§ 25.473 Landing load conditions and assumptions.

(a) For the landing conditions specified in § 25.479 to § 25.485 the airplane is assumed to contact the ground—

(1) In the attitudes defined in § 25.479 and § 25.481;

(2) With a limit descent velocity of 10 fps at the design landing weight (the maximum weight for landing conditions at maximum descent velocity); and

(3) With a limit descent velocity of 6 fps at the design take-off weight (the maximum weight for landing conditions at a reduced descent velocity).

(4) The prescribed descent velocities may be modified if it is shown that the airplane has design features that make it impossible to develop these velocities.

(b) Airplane lift, not exceeding airplane weight, may be assumed unless the presence of systems or procedures significantly affects the lift.

(c) The method of analysis of airplane and landing gear loads must take into account at least the following elements:

(1) Landing gear dynamic characteristics.

(2) Spin-up and springback.

(3) Rigid body response.

(4) Structural dynamic response of the airframe, if significant.

(d) The landing gear dynamic characteristics must be validated by tests as defined in § 25.723(a).

(e) The coefficient of friction between the tires and the ground may be established by considering the effects of skidding velocity and tire pressure. However, this coefficient of friction need not be more than 0.8.

[Amdt. 25–91, 62 FR 40705, July 29, 1997; Amdt. 25–91, 62 FR 45481, Aug. 27, 1997; Amdt 25–103, 66 FR 27394, May 16, 2001]

§ 25.477 Landing gear arrangement.

Sections 25.479 through 25.485 apply to airplanes with conventional arrangements of main and nose gears, or main and tail gears, when normal operating techniques are used.

§ 25.479 Level landing conditions.

(a) In the level attitude, the airplane is assumed to contact the ground at forward velocity components, ranging from V_{L1} to 1.25 V_{L2} parallel to the ground under the conditions prescribed in § 25.473 with—

(1) V_{L1} equal to V_{S0} (TAS) at the appropriate landing weight and in standard sea level conditions; and

(2) V_{L2} equal to V_{S0} (TAS) at the appropriate landing weight and altitudes in a hot day temperature of 41 degrees F. above standard.

(3) The effects of increased contact speed must be investigated if approval of downwind landings exceeding 10 knots is requested.

(b) For the level landing attitude for airplanes with tail wheels, the conditions specified in this section must be investigated with the airplane horizontal reference line horizontal in accordance with Figure 2 of Appendix A of this part.

(c) For the level landing attitude for airplanes with nose wheels, shown in

Figure 2 of Appendix A of this part, the conditions specified in this section must be investigated assuming the following attitudes:

(1) An attitude in which the main wheels are assumed to contact the ground with the nose wheel just clear of the ground; and

(2) If reasonably attainable at the specified descent and forward velocities, an attitude in which the nose and main wheels are assumed to contact the ground simultaneously.

(d) In addition to the loading conditions prescribed in paragraph (a) of this section, but with maximum vertical ground reactions calculated from paragraph (a), the following apply:

(1) The landing gear and directly affected attaching structure must be designed for the maximum vertical ground reaction combined with an aft acting drag component of not less than 25% of this maximum vertical ground reaction.

(2) The most severe combination of loads that are likely to arise during a lateral drift landing must be taken into account. In absence of a more rational analysis of this condition, the following must be investigated:

(i) A vertical load equal to 75% of the maximum ground reaction of § 25.473 must be considered in combination with a drag and side load of 40% and 25% respectively of that vertical load.

(ii) The shock absorber and tire deflections must be assumed to be 75% of the deflection corresponding to the maximum ground reaction of § 25.473(a)(2). This load case need not be considered in combination with flat tires.

(3) The combination of vertical and drag components is considered to be acting at the wheel axle centerline.

[Amdt. 25–91, 62 FR 40705, July 29, 1997; Amdt. 25–91, 62 FR 45481, Aug. 27, 1997]

§ 25.481 Tail-down landing conditions.

(a) In the tail-down attitude, the airplane is assumed to contact the ground at forward velocity components, ranging from V_{L1} to V_{L2} parallel to the ground under the conditions prescribed in § 25.473 with—

(1) V_{L1} equal to V_{S0} (TAS) at the appropriate landing weight and in standard sea level conditions; and

(2) V_{L2} equal to V_{S0} (TAS) at the appropriate landing weight and altitudes in a hot day temperature of 41 degrees F. above standard.

(3) The combination of vertical and drag components considered to be acting at the main wheel axle centerline.

(b) For the tail-down landing condition for airplanes with tail wheels, the main and tail wheels are assumed to contact the ground simultaneously, in accordance with figure 3 of appendix A. Ground reaction conditions on the tail wheel are assumed to act—

(1) Vertically; and

(2) Up and aft through the axle at 45 degrees to the ground line.

(c) For the tail-down landing condition for airplanes with nose wheels, the airplane is assumed to be at an attitude corresponding to either the stalling angle or the maximum angle allowing clearance with the ground by each part of the airplane other than the main wheels, in accordance with figure 3 of appendix A, whichever is less.

[Docket No. 5066, 29 FR 18291, Dec. 24, 1964, as amended by Amdt. 25–91, 62 FR 40705, July 29, 1997; Amdt. 25–94, 63 FR 8848, Feb. 23, 1998]

§ 25.483 One-gear landing conditions.

For the one-gear landing conditions, the airplane is assumed to be in the level attitude and to contact the ground on one main landing gear, in accordance with Figure 4 of Appendix A of this part. In this attitude—

(a) The ground reactions must be the same as those obtained on that side under § 25.479(d)(1), and

(b) Each unbalanced external load must be reacted by airplane inertia in a rational or conservative manner.

[Docket No. 5066, 29 FR 18291, Dec. 24, 1964, as amended by Amdt. 25–91, 62 FR 40705, July 29, 1997]

§ 25.485 Side load conditions.

In addition to § 25.479(d)(2) the following conditions must be considered:

(a) For the side load condition, the airplane is assumed to be in the level attitude with only the main wheels contacting the ground, in accordance with figure 5 of appendix A.

(b) Side loads of 0.8 of the vertical reaction (on one side) acting inward and 0.6 of the vertical reaction (on the other side) acting outward must be combined with one-half of the maximum vertical ground reactions obtained in the level landing conditions. These loads are assumed to be applied at the ground contact point and to be resisted by the inertia of the airplane. The drag loads may be assumed to be zero.

[Docket No. 5066, 29 FR 18291, Dec. 24, 1964, as amended by Amdt. 25–91, 62 FR 40705, July 29, 1997]

§ 25.487 Rebound landing condition.

(a) The landing gear and its supporting structure must be investigated for the loads occurring during rebound of the airplane from the landing surface.

(b) With the landing gear fully extended and not in contact with the ground, a load factor of 20.0 must act on the unsprung weights of the landing gear. This load factor must act in the direction of motion of the unsprung weights as they reach their limiting positions in extending with relation to the sprung parts of the landing gear.

§ 25.489 Ground handling conditions.

Unless otherwise prescribed, the landing gear and airplane structure must be investigated for the conditions in §§ 25.491 through 25.509 with the airplane at the design ramp weight (the maximum weight for ground handling conditions). No wing lift may be considered. The shock absorbers and tires may be assumed to be in their static position.

[Doc. No. 5066, 29 FR 18291, Dec. 24, 1964, as amended by Amdt. 25–23, 35 FR 5673, Apr. 8, 1970]

§ 25.491 Taxi, takeoff and landing roll.

Within the range of appropriate ground speeds and approved weights, the airplane structure and landing gear are assumed to be subjected to loads not less than those obtained when the aircraft is operating over the roughest ground that may reasonably be expected in normal operation.

[Amdt. 25–91, 62 FR 40705, July 29, 1997]

§ 25.493 Braked roll conditions.

(a) An airplane with a tail wheel is assumed to be in the level attitude with the load on the main wheels, in accordance with figure 6 of appendix A. The limit vertical load factor is 1.2 at the design landing weight and 1.0 at the design ramp weight. A drag reaction equal to the vertical reaction multiplied by a coefficient of friction of 0.8, must be combined with the vertical ground reaction and applied at the ground contact point.

(b) For an airplane with a nose wheel the limit vertical load factor is 1.2 at the design landing weight, and 1.0 at the design ramp weight. A drag reaction equal to the vertical reaction, multiplied by a coefficient of friction of 0.8, must be combined with the vertical reaction and applied at the ground contact point of each wheel with brakes. The following two attitudes, in accordance with figure 6 of appendix A, must be considered:

(1) The level attitude with the wheels contacting the ground and the loads distributed between the main and nose gear. Zero pitching acceleration is assumed.

(2) The level attitude with only the main gear contacting the ground and with the pitching moment resisted by angular acceleration.

(c) A drag reaction lower than that prescribed in this section may be used if it is substantiated that an effective drag force of 0.8 times the vertical reaction cannot be attained under any likely loading condition.

(d) An airplane equipped with a nose gear must be designed to withstand the loads arising from the dynamic pitching motion of the airplane due to sudden application of maximum braking force. The airplane is considered to be at design takeoff weight with the nose and main gears in contact with the ground, and with a steady-state vertical load factor of 1.0. The steady-state nose gear reaction must be combined with the maximum incremental nose gear vertical reaction caused by the sudden application of maximum braking force as described in paragraphs (b) and (c) of this section.

(e) In the absence of a more rational analysis, the nose gear vertical reaction prescribed in paragraph (d) of this section must be calculated according to the following formula:

$$V_N = \frac{W_T}{A+B}\left[B + \frac{f\mu AE}{A+B+\mu E}\right]$$

Where:

V_N=Nose gear vertical reaction.
W_T=Design takeoff weight.
A=Horizontal distance between the c.g. of the airplane and the nose wheel.
B=Horizontal distance between the c.g. of the airplane and the line joining the centers of the main wheels.
E=Vertical height of the c.g. of the airplane above the ground in the 1.0 g static condition.
μ=Coefficient of friction of 0.80.
f=Dynamic response factor; 2.0 is to be used unless a lower factor is substantiated. In the absence of other information, the dynamic response factor f may be defined by the equation:

$$f = 1 + \exp\left(\frac{-\pi\xi}{\sqrt{1-\xi^2}}\right)$$

Where:

ξ is the effective critical damping ratio of the rigid body pitching mode about the main landing gear effective ground contact point.

[Doc. No. 5066, 29 FR 18291, Dec. 24, 1964, as amended by Amdt. 25–23, 35 FR 5673, Apr. 8, 1970; Amdt. 25–97, 63 FR 29072, May 27, 1998]

§ 25.495 Turning.

In the static position, in accordance with figure 7 of appendix A, the airplane is assumed to execute a steady turn by nose gear steering, or by application of sufficient differential power, so that the limit load factors applied at the center of gravity are 1.0 vertically and 0.5 laterally. The side ground reaction of each wheel must be 0.5 of the vertical reaction.

§ 25.497 Tail-wheel yawing.

(a) A vertical ground reaction equal to the static load on the tail wheel, in combination with a side component of equal magnitude, is assumed.

(b) If there is a swivel, the tail wheel is assumed to be swiveled 90° to the airplane longitudinal axis with the resultant load passing through the axle.

(c) If there is a lock, steering device, or shimmy damper the tail wheel is also assumed to be in the trailing position with the side load acting at the ground contact point.

§ 25.499 Nose-wheel yaw and steering.

(a) A vertical load factor of 1.0 at the airplane center of gravity, and a side component at the nose wheel ground contact equal to 0.8 of the vertical ground reaction at that point are assumed.

(b) With the airplane assumed to be in static equilibrium with the loads resulting from the use of brakes on one side of the main landing gear, the nose gear, its attaching structure, and the fuselage structure forward of the center of gravity must be designed for the following loads:

(1) A vertical load factor at the center of gravity of 1.0.

(2) A forward acting load at the airplane center of gravity of 0.8 times the vertical load on one main gear.

(3) Side and vertical loads at the ground contact point on the nose gear that are required for static equilibrium.

(4) A side load factor at the airplane center of gravity of zero.

(c) If the loads prescribed in paragraph (b) of this section result in a nose gear side load higher than 0.8 times the vertical nose gear load, the design nose gear side load may be limited to 0.8 times the vertical load, with unbalanced yawing moments assumed to be resisted by airplane inertia forces.

(d) For other than the nose gear, its attaching structure, and the forward fuselage structure, the loading conditions are those prescribed in paragraph (b) of this section, except that—

(1) A lower drag reaction may be used if an effective drag force of 0.8 times the vertical reaction cannot be reached under any likely loading condition; and

(2) The forward acting load at the center of gravity need not exceed the maximum drag reaction on one main gear, determined in accordance with § 25.493(b).

(e) With the airplane at design ramp weight, and the nose gear in any steerable position, the combined application of full normal steering torque and vertical force equal to 1.33 times the maximum static reaction on the nose gear must be considered in designing the nose gear, its attaching structure, and the forward fuselage structure.

[Doc. No. 5066, 29 FR 18291, Dec. 24, 1964, as amended by Amdt. 25–23, 35 FR 5673, Apr. 8, 1970; Amdt. 25–46, 43 FR 50595, Oct. 30, 1978; Amdt. 25–91, 62 FR 40705, July 29, 1997]

§ 25.503 Pivoting.

(a) The airplane is assumed to pivot about one side of the main gear with the brakes on that side locked. The limit vertical load factor must be 1.0 and the coefficient of friction 0.8.

(b) The airplane is assumed to be in static equilibrium, with the loads being applied at the ground contact points, in accordance with figure 8 of appendix A.

§ 25.507 Reversed braking.

(a) The airplane must be in a three point static ground attitude. Horizontal reactions parallel to the ground and directed forward must be applied at the ground contact point of each wheel with brakes. The limit loads must be equal to 0.55 times the vertical load at each wheel or to the load developed by 1.2 times the nominal maximum static brake torque, whichever is less.

(b) For airplanes with nose wheels, the pitching moment must be balanced by rotational inertia.

(c) For airplanes with tail wheels, the resultant of the ground reactions must pass through the center of gravity of the airplane.

§ 25.509 Towing loads.

(a) The towing loads specified in paragraph (d) of this section must be considered separately. These loads must be applied at the towing fittings and must act parallel to the ground. In addition—

(1) A vertical load factor equal to 1.0 must be considered acting at the center of gravity;

(2) The shock struts and tires must be in their static positions; and

(3) With W_T as the design ramp weight, the towing load, F_{TOW}, is—

(i) 0.3 W_T for W_T less than 30,000 pounds;

(ii) $(6W_T+450,000)/7$ for W_T between 30,000 and 100,000 pounds; and

(iii) 0.15 W_T for W_T over 100,000 pounds.

(b) For towing points not on the landing gear but near the plane of symmetry of the airplane, the drag and side tow load components specified for the auxiliary gear apply. For towing points located outboard of the main gear, the drag and side tow load components specified for the main gear apply. Where the specified angle of swivel cannot be reached, the maximum obtainable angle must be used.

(c) The towing loads specified in paragraph (d) of this section must be reacted as follows:

(1) The side component of the towing load at the main gear must be reacted by a side force at the static ground line of the wheel to which the load is applied.

(2) The towing loads at the auxiliary gear and the drag components of the towing loads at the main gear must be reacted as follows:

(i) A reaction with a maximum value equal to the vertical reaction must be applied at the axle of the wheel to which the load is applied. Enough airplane inertia to achieve equilibrium must be applied.

(ii) The loads must be reacted by airplane inertia.

(d) The prescribed towing loads are as follows:

Tow point	Position	Load		
		Magnitude	No.	Direction
Main gear	....	0.75 F_{TOW} per main gear unit.	1	Forward, parallel to drag axis.
			2	Forward, at 30° to drag axis.
			3	Aft, parallel to drag axis.
			4	Aft, at 30° to drag axis.
Auxiliary gear	Swiveled forward	1.0 F_{TOW}	5	Forward.
			6	Aft.
	Swiveled aft	......do	7	Forward.
			8	Aft.
	Swiveled 45° from forward	0.5 F_{TOW}	9	Forward, in plane of wheel.
			10	Aft, in plane of wheel.

Tow point	Position	Load		
		Magnitude	No.	Direction
	Swiveled 45° from aft	......do	11	Forward, in plane of wheel.
			12	Aft, in plane of wheel.

[Doc. No. 5066, 29 FR 18291, Dec. 24, 1964, as amended by Amdt. 25-23, 35 FR 5673, Apr. 8, 1970]

§ 25.511 Ground load: unsymmetrical loads on multiple-wheel units.

(a) *General.* Multiple-wheel landing gear units are assumed to be subjected to the limit ground loads prescribed in this subpart under paragraphs (b) through (f) of this section. In addition—

(1) A tandem strut gear arrangement is a multiple-wheel unit; and

(2) In determining the total load on a gear unit with respect to the provisions of paragraphs (b) through (f) of this section, the transverse shift in the load centroid, due to unsymmetrical load distribution on the wheels, may be neglected.

(b) *Distribution of limit loads to wheels; tires inflated.* The distribution of the limit loads among the wheels of the landing gear must be established for each landing, taxiing, and ground handling condition, taking into account the effects of the following factors:

(1) The number of wheels and their physical arrangements. For truck type landing gear units, the effects of any seesaw motion of the truck during the landing impact must be considered in determining the maximum design loads for the fore and aft wheel pairs.

(2) Any differentials in tire diameters resulting from a combination of manufacturing tolerances, tire growth, and tire wear. A maximum tire-diameter differential equal to ⅔ of the most unfavorable combination of diameter variations that is obtained when taking into account manufacturing tolerances, tire growth, and tire wear, may be assumed.

(3) Any unequal tire inflation pressure, assuming the maximum variation to be ±5 percent of the nominal tire inflation pressure.

(4) A runway crown of zero and a runway crown having a convex upward shape that may be approximated by a slope of 1½ percent with the horizontal. Runway crown effects must be considered with the nose gear unit on either slope of the crown.

(5) The airplane attitude.

(6) Any structural deflections.

(c) *Deflated tires.* The effect of deflated tires on the structure must be considered with respect to the loading conditions specified in paragraphs (d) through (f) of this section, taking into account the physical arrangement of the gear components. In addition—

(1) The deflation of any one tire for each multiple wheel landing gear unit, and the deflation of any two critical tires for each landing gear unit using four or more wheels per unit, must be considered; and

(2) The ground reactions must be applied to the wheels with inflated tires except that, for multiple-wheel gear units with more than one shock strut, a rational distribution of the ground reactions between the deflated and inflated tires, accounting for the differences in shock strut extensions resulting from a deflated tire, may be used.

(d) *Landing conditions.* For one and for two deflated tires, the applied load to each gear unit is assumed to be 60 percent and 50 percent, respectively, of the limit load applied to each gear for each of the prescribed landing conditions. However, for the drift landing condition of §25.485, 100 percent of the vertical load must be applied.

(e) *Taxiing and ground handling conditions.* For one and for two deflated tires—

(1) The applied side or drag load factor, or both factors, at the center of gravity must be the most critical value up to 50 percent and 40 percent, respectively, of the limit side or drag load factors, or both factors, corresponding to the most severe condition resulting from consideration of the prescribed taxiing and ground handling conditions;

381

(2) For the braked roll conditions of § 25.493 (a) and (b)(2), the drag loads on each inflated tire may not be less than those at each tire for the symmetrical load distribution with no deflated tires;

(3) The vertical load factor at the center of gravity must be 60 percent and 50 percent, respectively, of the factor with no deflated tires, except that it may not be less than 1g; and

(4) Pivoting need not be considered.

(f) *Towing conditions.* For one and for two deflated tires, the towing load, F_{TOW}, must be 60 percent and 50 percent, respectively, of the load prescribed.

§ 25.519 Jacking and tie-down provisions.

(a) General. The airplane must be designed to withstand the limit load conditions resulting from the static ground load conditions of paragraph (b) of this section and, if applicable, paragraph (c) of this section at the most critical combinations of airplane weight and center of gravity. The maximum allowable load at each jack pad must be specified.

(b) Jacking. The airplane must have provisions for jacking and must withstand the following limit loads when the airplane is supported on jacks—

(1) For jacking by the landing gear at the maximum ramp weight of the airplane, the airplane structure must be designed for a vertical load of 1.33 times the vertical static reaction at each jacking point acting singly and in combination with a horizontal load of 0.33 times the vertical static reaction applied in any direction.

(2) For jacking by other airplane structure at maximum approved jacking weight:

(i) The airplane structure must be designed for a vertical load of 1.33 times the vertical reaction at each jacking point acting singly and in combination with a horizontal load of 0.33 times the vertical static reaction applied in any direction.

(ii) The jacking pads and local structure must be designed for a vertical load of 2.0 times the vertical static reaction at each jacking point, acting singly and in combination with a horizontal load of 0.33 times the vertical

static reaction applied in any direction.

(c) Tie-down. If tie-down points are provided, the main tie-down points and local structure must withstand the limit loads resulting from a 65-knot horizontal wind from any direction.

[Doc. No. 26129, 59 FR 22102, Apr. 28, 1994]

WATER LOADS

§ 25.521 General.

(a) Seaplanes must be designed for the water loads developed during takeoff and landing, with the seaplane in any attitude likely to occur in normal operation, and at the appropriate forward and sinking velocities under the most severe sea conditions likely to be encountered.

(b) Unless a more rational analysis of the water loads is made, or the standards in ANC–3 are used, §§ 25.523 through 25.537 apply.

(c) The requirements of this section and §§ 25.523 through 25.537 apply also to amphibians.

§ 25.523 Design weights and center of gravity positions.

(a) *Design weights.* The water load requirements must be met at each operating weight up to the design landing weight except that, for the takeoff condition prescribed in § 25.531, the design water takeoff weight (the maximum weight for water taxi and takeoff run) must be used.

(b) *Center of gravity positions.* The critical centers of gravity within the limits for which certification is requested must be considered to reach maximum design loads for each part of the seaplane structure.

[Doc. No. 5066, 29 FR 18291, Dec. 24, 1964, as amended by Amdt. 25–23, 35 FR 5673, Apr. 8, 1970]

§ 25.525 Application of loads.

(a) Unless otherwise prescribed, the seaplane as a whole is assumed to be subjected to the loads corresponding to the load factors specified in § 25.527.

(b) In applying the loads resulting from the load factors prescribed in § 25.527, the loads may be distributed over the hull or main float bottom (in order to avoid excessive local shear loads and bending moments at the location of water load application) using pressures not less than those prescribed in §25.533(b).

(c) For twin float seaplanes, each float must be treated as an equivalent hull on a fictitious seaplane with a weight equal to one-half the weight of the twin float seaplane.

(d) Except in the takeoff condition of §25.531, the aerodynamic lift on the seaplane during the impact is assumed to be ⅔ of the weight of the seaplane.

§25.527 Hull and main float load factors.

(a) Water reaction load factors n_W must be computed in the following manner:

(1) For the step landing case

$$n_w = \frac{C_1 V_{S0}^2}{\left(\text{Tan}^{\frac{2}{3}} \beta \right) W^{\frac{1}{3}}}$$

(2) For the bow and stern landing cases

$$n_w = \frac{C_1 V_{S0}^2}{\left(\text{Tan}^{\frac{2}{3}} \beta \right) W^{\frac{1}{3}}} \times \frac{K_1}{\left(1 + r_x^2 \right)^{\frac{2}{3}}}$$

(b) The following values are used:

(1) n_W=water reaction load factor (that is, the water reaction divided by seaplane weight).

(2) C_1=empirical seaplane operations factor equal to 0.012 (except that this factor may not be less than that necessary to obtain the minimum value of step load factor of 2.33).

(3) V_{S0}=seaplane stalling speed in knots with flaps extended in the appropriate landing position and with no slipstream effect.

(4) β=angle of dead rise at the longitudinal station at which the load factor is being determined in accordance with figure 1 of appendix B.

(5) W= seaplane design landing weight in pounds.

(6) K_1=empirical hull station weighing factor, in accordance with figure 2 of appendix B.

(7) r_x=ratio of distance, measured parallel to hull reference axis, from the center of gravity of the seaplane to the hull longitudinal station at which the

load factor is being computed to the radius of gyration in pitch of the seaplane, the hull reference axis being a straight line, in the plane of symmetry, tangential to the keel at the main step.

(c) For a twin float seaplane, because of the effect of flexibility of the attachment of the floats to the seaplane, the factor K_1 may be reduced at the bow and stern to 0.8 of the value shown in figure 2 of appendix B. This reduction applies only to the design of the carry-through and seaplane structure.

[Doc. No. 5066, 29 FR 18291, Dec. 24, 1964, as amended by Amdt. 25–23, 35 FR 5673, Apr. 8, 1970]

§25.529 Hull and main float landing conditions.

(a) *Symmetrical step, bow, and stern landing.* For symmetrical step, bow, and stern landings, the limit water reaction load factors are those computed under §25.527. In addition—

(1) For symmetrical step landings, the resultant water load must be applied at the keel, through the center of gravity, and must be directed perpendicularly to the keel line;

(2) For symmetrical bow landings, the resultant water load must be applied at the keel, one-fifth of the longitudinal distance from the bow to the step, and must be directed perpendicularly to the keel line; and

(3) For symmetrical stern landings, the resultant water load must be applied at the keel, at a point 85 percent of the longitudinal distance from the step to the stern post, and must be directed perpendicularly to the keel line.

(b) *Unsymmetrical landing for hull and single float seaplanes.* Unsymmetrical step, bow, and stern landing conditions must be investigated. In addition—

(1) The loading for each condition consists of an upward component and a side component equal, respectively, to 0.75 and 0.25 tan β times the resultant load in the corresponding symmetrical landing condition; and

(2) The point of application and direction of the upward component of the load is the same as that in the symmetrical condition, and the point of application of the side component is at the same longitudinal station as the

383

upward component but is directed inward perpendicularly to the plane of symmetry at a point midway between the keel and chine lines.

(c) *Unsymmetrical landing; twin float seaplanes.* The unsymmetrical loading consists of an upward load at the step of each float of 0.75 and a side load of 0.25 tan β at one float times the step landing load reached under § 25.527. The side load is directed inboard, perpendicularly to the plane of symmetry midway between the keel and chine lines of the float, at the same longitudinal station as the upward load.

§ 25.531 Hull and main float takeoff condition.

For the wing and its attachment to the hull or main float—

(a) The aerodynamic wing lift is assumed to be zero; and

(b) A downward inertia load, corresponding to a load factor computed from the following formula, must be applied:

$$n = \frac{C_{TO} V_{S1}{}^2}{\left(\tan^{\frac{2}{3}} \beta \right) W^{\frac{1}{3}}}$$

where—

n=inertia load factor;
C_{TO}=empirical seaplane operations factor equal to 0.004;
V_{S1}=seaplane stalling speed (knots) at the design takeoff weight with the flaps extended in the appropriate takeoff position;
β=angle of dead rise at the main step (degrees); and
W=design water takeoff weight in pounds.

[Doc. No. 5066, 29 FR 18291, Dec. 24, 1964, as amended by Amdt. 25–23, 35 FR 5673, Apr. 8, 1970]

§ 25.533 Hull and main float bottom pressures.

(a) *General.* The hull and main float structure, including frames and bulkheads, stringers, and bottom plating, must be designed under this section.

(b) *Local pressures.* For the design of the bottom plating and stringers and their attachments to the supporting structure, the following pressure distributions must be applied:

(1) For an unflared bottom, the pressure at the chine is 0.75 times the pressure at the keel, and the pressures between the keel and chine vary linearly,

in accordance with figure 3 of appendix B. The pressure at the keel (psi) is computed as follows:

$$P_k = C_2 \times \frac{K_2 V_{S1}{}^2}{\tan \beta_k}$$

where—

P_k=pressure (p.s.i.) at the keel;
C_2=0.00213;
K_2=hull station weighing factor, in accordance with figure 2 of appendix B;
V_{S1}=seaplane stalling speed (Knots) at the design water takeoff weight with flaps extended in the appropriate takeoff position; and
βK=angle of dead rise at keel, in accordance with figure 1 of appendix B.

(2) For a flared bottom, the pressure at the beginning of the flare is the same as that for an unflared bottom, and the pressure between the chine and the beginning of the flare varies linearly, in accordance with figure 3 of appendix B. The pressure distribution is the same as that prescribed in paragraph (b)(1) of this section for an unflared bottom except that the pressure at the chine is computed as follows:

$$P_{ch} = C_3 \times \frac{K_2 V_{S1}}{\tan \beta}$$

where—

P_{ch}=pressure (p.s.i.) at the chine;
C_3=0.0016;
K_2=hull station weighing factor, in accordance with figure 2 of appendix B;
V_{S1}=seaplane stalling speed at the design water takeoff weight with flaps extended in the appropriate takeoff position; and
β=angle of dead rise at appropriate station.

The area over which these pressures are applied must simulate pressures occurring during high localized impacts on the hull or float, but need not extend over an area that would induce critical stresses in the frames or in the overall structure.

(c) *Distributed pressures.* For the design of the frames, keel, and chine structure, the following pressure distributions apply:

(1) Symmetrical pressures are computed as follows:

$$P = C_4 \times \frac{K_2 \, V_{S0^2}}{\tan \beta}$$

where—

P=pressure (p.s.i.);

C_4=0.078 C_1 (with C_1 computed under § 25.527);

K_2=hull station weighing factor, determined in accordance with figure 2 of appendix B;

V_{S0}=seaplane stalling speed (Knots) with landing flaps extended in the appropriate position and with no slipstream effect; and

V_{S0}=seaplane stalling speed with landing flaps extended in the appropriate position and with no slipstream effect; and β=angle of dead rise at appropriate station.

(2) The unsymmetrical pressure distribution consists of the pressures prescribed in paragraph (c)(1) of this section on one side of the hull or main float centerline and one-half of that pressure on the other side of the hull or main float centerline, in accordance with figure 3 of appendix B.

These pressures are uniform and must be applied simultaneously over the entire hull or main float bottom. The loads obtained must be carried into the sidewall structure of the hull proper, but need not be transmitted in a fore and aft direction as shear and bending loads.

[Doc. No. 5066, 29 FR 18291, Dec. 24, 1964, as amended by Amdt. 25–23, 35 FR 5673, Apr. 8, 1970]

§ 25.535 Auxiliary float loads.

(a) *General.* Auxiliary floats and their attachments and supporting structures must be designed for the conditions prescribed in this section. In the cases specified in paragraphs (b) through (e) of this section, the prescribed water loads may be distributed over the float bottom to avoid excessive local loads, using bottom pressures not less than those prescribed in paragraph (g) of this section.

(b) *Step loading.* The resultant water load must be applied in the plane of symmetry of the float at a point three-fourths of the distance from the bow to the step and must be perpendicular to the keel. The resultant limit load is computed as follows, except that the value of L need not exceed three times the weight of the displaced water when the float is completely submerged:

$$L = \frac{C_5 \, V_{S0^2} \, W^{\frac{2}{3}}}{\tan^{\frac{2}{3}} \beta_s \left(1 + r_y^2\right)^{\frac{2}{3}}}$$

where—

L=limit load (lbs.);

C_5=0.0053;

V_{S0}=seaplane stalling speed (knots) with landing flaps extended in the appropriate position and with no slipstream effect;

W=seaplane design landing weight in pounds;

β_S=angle of dead rise at a station ¾ of the distance from the bow to the step, but need not be less than 15 degrees; and

r_y=ratio of the lateral distance between the center of gravity and the plane of symmetry of the float to the radius of gyration in roll.

(c) *Bow loading.* The resultant limit load must be applied in the plane of symmetry of the float at a point one-fourth of the distance from the bow to the step and must be perpendicular to the tangent to the keel line at that point. The magnitude of the resultant load is that specified in paragraph (b) of this section.

(d) *Unsymmetrical step loading.* The resultant water load consists of a component equal to 0.75 times the load specified in paragraph (a) of this section and a side component equal to 3.25 tan β times the load specified in paragraph (b) of this section. The side load must be applied perpendicularly to the plane of symmetry of the float at a point midway between the keel and the chine.

(e) *Unsymmetrical bow loading.* The resultant water load consists of a component equal to 0.75 times the load specified in paragraph (b) of this section and a side component equal to 0.25 tan β times the load specified in paragraph (c) of this section. The side load must be applied perpendicularly to the plane of symmetry at a point midway between the keel and the chine.

(f) *Immersed float condition.* The resultant load must be applied at the centroid of the cross section of the float at a point one-third of the distance from the bow to the step. The limit load components are as follows:

$$\text{vertical} = \rho_g V$$

$$\text{aft} = C_{x2} \rho V^{\frac{2}{3}} \left(K V_{s_0} \right)^2$$

$$\text{side} = C_{y2} \rho V^{\frac{2}{3}} \left(K V_{s_0} \right)^2$$

where—

ρ=mass density of water (slugs/ft.²);
V=volume of float (ft.²);
C_x=coefficient of drag force, equal to 0.133;
C_y=coefficient of side force, equal to 0.106;
K=0.8, except that lower values may be used if it is shown that the floats are incapable of submerging at a speed of 0.8 V_{s0} in normal operations;
V_{s0}=seaplane stalling speed (knots) with landing flaps extended in the appropriate position and with no slipstream effect; and
g=acceleration due to gravity (ft./sec.²).

(g) *Float bottom pressures.* The float bottom pressures must be established under §25.533, except that the value of K_2 in the formulae may be taken as 1.0. The angle of dead rise to be used in determining the float bottom pressures is set forth in paragraph (b) of this section.

[Doc. No. 5066, 29 FR 18291, Dec. 24, 1964, as amended by Amdt. 25–23, 35 FR 5673, Apr. 8, 1970]

§ 25.537 Seawing loads.

Seawing design loads must be based on applicable test data.

EMERGENCY LANDING CONDITIONS

§ 25.561 General.

(a) The airplane, although it may be damaged in emergency landing conditions on land or water, must be designed as prescribed in this section to protect each occupant under those conditions.

(b) The structure must be designed to give each occupant every reasonable chance of escaping serious injury in a minor crash landing when—

(1) Proper use is made of seats, belts, and all other safety design provisions;

(2) The wheels are retracted (where applicable); and

(3) The occupant experiences the following ultimate inertia forces acting separately relative to the surrounding structure:

(1) Upward, 3.0g

(ii) Forward, 9.0g

(iii) Sideward, 3.0g on the airframe; and 4.0g on the seats and their attachments.

(iv) Downward, 6.0g

(v) Rearward, 1.5g

(c) For equipment, cargo in the passenger compartments and any other large masses, the following apply:

(1) Except as provided in paragraph (c)(2) of this section, these items must be positioned so that if they break loose they will be unlikely to:

(i) Cause direct injury to occupants;

(ii) Penetrate fuel tanks or lines or cause fire or explosion hazard by damage to adjacent systems; or

(iii) Nullify any of the escape facilities provided for use after an emergency landing.

(2) When such positioning is not practical (e.g. fuselage mounted engines or auxiliary power units) each such item of mass shall be restrained under all loads up to those specified in paragraph (b)(3) of this section. The local attachments for these items should be designed to withstand 1.33 times the specified loads if these items are subject to severe wear and tear through frequent removal (e.g. quick change interior items).

(d) Seats and items of mass (and their supporting structure) must not deform under any loads up to those specified in paragraph (b)(3) of this section in any manner that would impede subsequent rapid evacuation of occupants.

[Doc. No. 5066, 29 FR 18291, Dec. 24, 1964, as amended by Amdt. 25–23, 35 FR 5673, Apr. 8, 1970; Amdt. 25–64, 53 FR 17646, May 17, 1988; Amdt. 25–91, 62 FR 40706, July 29, 1997]

§ 25.562 Emergency landing dynamic conditions.

(a) The seat and restraint system in the airplane must be designed as prescribed in this section to protect each occupant during an emergency landing condition when—

(1) Proper use is made of seats, safety belts, and shoulder harnesses provided for in the design; and

(2) The occupant is exposed to loads resulting from the conditions prescribed in this section.

(b) Each seat type design approved for crew or passenger occupancy during takeoff and landing must successfully complete dynamic tests or be demonstrated by rational analysis based on dynamic tests of a similar type seat, in accordance with each of the following emergency landing conditions. The tests must be conducted with an occupant simulated by a 170-pound anthropomorphic test dummy, as defined by 49 CFR Part 572, Subpart B, or its equivalent, sitting in the normal upright position.

(1) A change in downward vertical velocity (Δ v) of not less than 35 feet per second, with the airplane's longitudinal axis canted downward 30 degrees with respect to the horizontal plane and with the wings level. Peak floor deceleration must occur in not more than 0.08 seconds after impact and must reach a minimum of 14g.

(2) A change in forward longitudinal velocity (Δ v) of not less than 44 feet per second, with the airplane's longitudinal axis horizontal and yawed 10 degrees either right or left, whichever would cause the greatest likelihood of the upper torso restraint system (where installed) moving off the occupant's shoulder, and with the wings level. Peak floor deceleration must occur in not more than 0.09 seconds after impact and must reach a minimum of 16g. Where floor rails or floor fittings are used to attach the seating devices to the test fixture, the rails or fittings must be misaligned with respect to the adjacent set of rails or fittings by at least 10 degrees vertically (i.e., out of Parallel) with one rolled 10 degrees.

(c) The following performance measures must not be exceeded during the dynamic tests conducted in accordance with paragraph (b) of this section:

(1) Where upper torso straps are used for crewmembers, tension loads in individual straps must not exceed 1,750 pounds. If dual straps are used for restraining the upper torso, the total strap tension loads must not exceed 2,000 pounds.

(2) The maximum compressive load measured between the pelvis and the lumbar column of the anthropomorphic dummy must not exceed 1,500 pounds.

(3) The upper torso restraint straps (where installed) must remain on the occupant's shoulder during the impact.

(4) The lap safety belt must remain on the occupant's pelvis during the impact.

(5) Each occupant must be protected from serious head injury under the conditions prescribed in paragraph (b) of this section. Where head contact with seats or other structure can occur, protection must be provided so that the head impact does not exceed a Head Injury Criterion (HIC) of 1,000 units. The level of HIC is defined by the equation:

$$HIC = \left\{ (t_2 - t_1) \left[\frac{1}{(t_2 - t_1)} \int_{t_1}^{t_2} a(t)dt \right]^{2.5} \right\}_{max}$$

Where:

t_1 is the initial integration time,

t_2 is the final integration time, and

a(t) is the total acceleration vs. time curve for the head strike, and where

(t) is in seconds, and (a) is in units of gravity (g).

(6) Where leg injuries may result from contact with seats or other structure, protection must be provided to prevent axially compressive loads exceeding 2,250 pounds in each femur.

(7) The seat must remain attached at all points of attachment, although the structure may have yielded.

(8) Seats must not yield under the tests specified in paragraphs (b)(1) and (b)(2) of this section to the extent they would impede rapid evacuation of the airplane occupants.

[Amdt. 25–64, 53 FR 17646, May 17, 1988]

§ 25.563 Structural ditching provisions.

Structural strength considerations of ditching provisions must be in accordance with § 25.801(e).

FATIGUE EVALUATION

§ 25.571 Damage—tolerance and fatigue evaluation of structure.

(a) *General.* An evaluation of the strength, detail design, and fabrication must show that catastrophic failure due to fatigue, corrosion, manufacturing defects, or accidental damage, will be avoided throughout the operational life of the airplane. This evaluation must be conducted in accordance with the provisions of paragraphs (b) and (e) of this section, except as specified in paragraph (c) of this section, for each part of the structure that could contribute to a catastrophic failure (such as wing, empennage, control surfaces and their systems, the fuselage, engine mounting, landing gear, and their related primary attachments). For turbojet powered airplanes, those parts that could contribute to a catastrophic failure must also be evaluated under paragraph (d) of this section. In addition, the following apply:

(1) Each evaluation required by this section must include—

(i) The typical loading spectra, temperatures, and humidities expected in service;

(ii) The identification of principal structural elements and detail design points, the failure of which could cause catastrophic failure of the airplane; and

(iii) An analysis, supported by test evidence, of the principal structural elements and detail design points identified in paragraph (a)(1)(ii) of this section.

(2) The service history of airplanes of similar structural design, taking due account of differences in operating conditions and procedures, may be used in the evaluations required by this section.

(3) Based on the evaluations required by this section, inspections or other procedures must be established, as necessary, to prevent catastrophic failure, and must be included in the Airworthiness Limitations Section of the Instructions for Continued Airworthiness required by § 25.1529. Inspection thresholds for the following types of structure must be established based on crack growth analyses and/or tests, assuming the structure contains an initial flaw of the maximum probable size that could exist as a result of manufacturing or service-induced damage:

(i) Single load path structure, and

(ii) Multiple load path "fail-safe" structure and crack arrest "fail-safe" structure, where it cannot be demonstrated that load path failure, partial failure, or crack arrest will be detected and repaired during normal maintenance, inspection, or operation of an airplane prior to failure of the remaining structure.

(b) *Damage-tolerance evaluation.* The evaluation must include a determination of the probable locations and modes of damage due to fatigue, corrosion, or accidental damage. Repeated load and static analyses supported by test evidence and (if available) service experience must also be incorporated in the evaluation. Special consideration for widespread fatigue damage must be included where the design is such that this type of damage could occur. It must be demonstrated with sufficient full-scale fatigue test evidence that widespread fatigue damage will not occur within the design service goal of the airplane. The type certificate may be issued prior to completion of full-scale fatigue testing, provided the Administrator has approved a plan for completing the required tests, and the airworthiness limitations section of the instructions for continued airworthiness required by § 25.1529 of this part specifies that no airplane may be operated beyond a number of cycles equal to ½ the number of cycles accumulated on the fatigue test article, until such testing is completed. The extent of damage for residual strength evaluation at any time within the operational life of the airplane must be consistent with the initial detectability and subsequent growth under repeated loads. The residual strength evaluation must show that the remaining structure is able to withstand loads (considered as static ultimate loads) corresponding to the following conditions:

(1) The limit symmetrical maneuvering conditions specified in §25.337 at all speeds up to V_c and in §25.345.

(2) The limit gust conditions specified in §25.341 at the specified speeds up to V_C and in §25.345.

(3) The limit rolling conditions specified in §25.349 and the limit unsymmetrical conditions specified in §§25.367 and 25.427 (a) through (c), at speeds up to V_C.

(4) The limit yaw maneuvering conditions specified in §25.351(a) at the specified speeds up to V_C.

(5) For pressurized cabins, the following conditions:

(i) The normal operating differential pressure combined with the expected external aerodynamic pressures applied simultaneously with the flight loading conditions specified in paragraphs (b)(1) through (4) of this section, if they have a significant effect.

(ii) The maximum value of normal operating differential pressure (including the expected external aerodynamic pressures during 1 g level flight) multiplied by a factor of 1.15, omitting other loads.

(6) For landing gear and directly-affected airframe structure, the limit ground loading conditions specified in §§25.473, 25.491, and 25.493.

If significant changes in structural stiffness or geometry, or both, follow from a structural failure, or partial failure, the effect on damage tolerance must be further investigated.

(c) *Fatigue (safe-life) evaluation.* Compliance with the damage-tolerance requirements of paragraph (b) of this section is not required if the applicant establishes that their application for particular structure is impractical. This structure must be shown by analysis, supported by test evidence, to be able to withstand the repeated loads of variable magnitude expected during its service life without detectable cracks. Appropriate safe-life scatter factors must be applied.

(d) *Sonic fatigue strength.* It must be shown by analysis, supported by test evidence, or by the service history of airplanes of similar structural design and sonic excitation environment, that—

(1) Sonic fatigue cracks are not probable in any part of the flight structure subject to sonic excitation; or

(2) Catastrophic failure caused by sonic cracks is not probable assuming that the loads prescribed in paragraph (b) of this section are applied to all areas affected by those cracks.

(e) *Damage-tolerance (discrete source) evaluation.* The airplane must be capable of successfully completing a flight during which likely structural damage occurs as a result of—

(1) Impact with a 4-pound bird when the velocity of the airplane relative to the bird along the airplane's flight path is equal to V_c at sea level or $0.85V_c$ at 8,000 feet, whichever is more critical;

(2) Uncontained fan blade impact;

(3) Uncontained engine failure; or

(4) Uncontained high energy rotating machinery failure.

The damaged structure must be able to withstand the static loads (considered as ultimate loads) which are reasonably expected to occur on the flight. Dynamic effects on these static loads need not be considered. Corrective action to be taken by the pilot following the incident, such as limiting maneuvers, avoiding turbulence, and reducing speed, must be considered. If significant changes in structural stiffness or geometry, or both, follow from a structural failure or partial failure, the effect on damage tolerance must be further investigated.

[Amdt. 25–45, 43 FR 46242, Oct. 5, 1978, as amended by Amdt. 25–54, 45 FR 60173, Sept. 11, 1980; Amdt. 25–72, 55 FR 29776, July 20, 1990; Amdt. 25–86, 61 FR 5222, Feb. 9, 1996; Amdt. 25–96, 63 FR 15714, Mar. 31, 1998; 63 FR 23338, Apr. 28, 1998]

LIGHTNING PROTECTION

§25.581 Lightning protection.

(a) The airplane must be protected against catastrophic effects from lightning.

(b) For metallic components, compliance with paragraph (a) of this section may be shown by—

(1) Bonding the components properly to the airframe; or

(2) Designing the components so that a strike will not endanger the airplane.

(c) For nonmetallic components, compliance with paragraph (a) of this section may be shown by—

(1) Designing the components to minimize the effect of a strike; or

(2) Incorporating acceptable means of diverting the resulting electrical current so as not to endanger the airplane.

[Amdt. 25–23, 35 FR 5674, Apr. 8, 1970]

Subpart D—Design and Construction

GENERAL

§ 25.601 General.

The airplane may not have design features or details that experience has shown to be hazardous or unreliable. The suitability of each questionable design detail and part must be established by tests.

§ 25.603 Materials.

The suitability and durability of materials used for parts, the failure of which could adversely affect safety, must—

(a) Be established on the basis of experience or tests;

(b) Conform to approved specifications (such as industry or military specifications, or Technical Standard Orders) that ensure their having the strength and other properties assumed in the design data; and

(c) Take into account the effects of environmental conditions, such as temperature and humidity, expected in service.

[Doc. No. 5066, 29 FR 18291, Dec. 24, 1964, as amended by Amdt. 25–38, 41 FR 55466, Dec. 20 1976; Amdt. 25–46, 43 FR 50595, Oct. 30, 1978]

§ 25.605 Fabrication methods.

(a) The methods of fabrication used must produce a consistently sound structure. If a fabrication process (such as gluing, spot welding, or heat treating) requires close control to reach this objective, the process must be performed under an approved process specification.

(b) Each new aircraft fabrication method must be substantiated by a test program.

[Doc. No. 5066, 29 FR 18291, Dec. 24, 1964, as amended by Amdt. 25–46, 43 FR 50595, Oct. 30, 1978]

§ 25.607 Fasteners.

(a) Each removable bolt, screw, nut, pin, or other removable fastener must incorporate two separate locking devices if—

(1) Its loss could preclude continued flight and landing within the design limitations of the airplane using normal pilot skill and strength; or

(2) Its loss could result in reduction in pitch, yaw, or roll control capability or response below that required by Subpart B of this chapter.

(b) The fasteners specified in paragraph (a) of this section and their locking devices may not be adversely affected by the environmental conditions associated with the particular installation.

(c) No self-locking nut may be used on any bolt subject to rotation in operation unless a nonfriction locking device is used in addition to the self-locking device.

[Amdt. 25–23, 35 FR 5674, Apr. 8, 1970]

§ 25.609 Protection of structure.

Each part of the structure must—

(a) Be suitably protected against deterioration or loss of strength in service due to any cause, including—

(1) Weathering;

(2) Corrosion; and

(3) Abrasion; and

(b) Have provisions for ventilation and drainage where necessary for protection.

§ 25.611 Accessibility provisions.

Means must be provided to allow inspection (including inspection of principal structural elements and control systems), replacement of parts normally requiring replacement, adjustment, and lubrication as necessary for continued airworthiness. The inspection means for each item must be practicable for the inspection interval for the item. Nondestructive inspection aids may be used to inspect structural elements where it is impracticable to provide means for direct visual inspection if it is shown that the inspection is effective and the inspection procedures are specified in the maintenance manual required by § 25.1529.

[Amdt. 25–23, 35 FR 5674, Apr. 8, 1970]

§ 25.613 Material strength properties and design values.

(a) Material strength properties must be based on enough tests of material meeting approved specifications to establish design values on a statistical basis.

(b) Design values must be chosen to minimize the probability of structural failures due to material variability. Except as provided in paragraph (e) of this section, compliance with this paragraph must be shown by selecting design values which assure material strength with the following probability:

(1) Where applied loads are eventually distributed through a single member within an assembly, the failure of which would result in loss of structural integrity of the component, 99 percent probability with 95 percent confidence.

(2) For redundant structure, in which the failure of individual elements would result in applied loads being safely distributed to other load carrying members, 90 percent probability with 95 percent confidence.

(c) The effects of temperature on allowable stresses used for design in an essential component or structure must be considered where thermal effects are significant under normal operating conditions.

(d) The strength, detail design, and fabrication of the structure must minimize the probability of disastrous fatigue failure, particularly at points of stress concentration.

(e) Greater design values may be used if a "premium selection" of the material is made in which a specimen of each individual item is tested before use to determine that the actual strength properties of that particular item will equal or exceed those used in design.

[Doc. No. 5066, 29 FR 18291, Dec. 24, 1964, as amended by Amdt. 25–46, 43 FR 50595, Oct. 30, 1978; Amdt. 25–72, 55 FR 29776, July 20, 1990]

§ 25.619 Special factors.

The factor of safety prescribed in § 25.303 must be multiplied by the highest pertinent special factor of safety prescribed in §§ 25.621 through 25.625 for each part of the structure whose strength is—

(a) Uncertain;

(b) Likely to deteriorate in service before normal replacement; or

(c) Subject to appreciable variability because of uncertainties in manufacturing processes or inspection methods.

[Doc. No. 5066, 29 FR 18291, Dec. 24, 1964, as amended by Amdt. 25–23, 35 FR 5674, Apr. 8, 1970]

§ 25.621 Casting factors.

(a) *General.* The factors, tests, and inspections specified in paragraphs (b) through (d) of this section must be applied in addition to those necessary to establish foundry quality control. The inspections must meet approved specifications. Paragraphs (c) and (d) of this section apply to any structural castings except castings that are pressure tested as parts of hydraulic or other fluid systems and do not support structural loads.

(b) *Bearing stresses and surfaces.* The casting factors specified in paragraphs (c) and (d) of this section—

(1) Need not exceed 1.25 with respect to bearing stresses regardless of the method of inspection used; and

(2) Need not be used with respect to the bearing surfaces of a part whose bearing factor is larger than the applicable casting factor.

(c) *Critical castings.* For each casting whose failure would preclude continued safe flight and landing of the airplane or result in serious injury to occupants, the following apply:

(1) Each critical casting must—

(i) Have a casting factor of not less than 1.25; and

(ii) Receive 100 percent inspection by visual, radiographic, and magnetic particle or penetrant inspection methods or approved equivalent nondestructive inspection methods.

(2) For each critical casting with a casting factor less than 1.50, three sample castings must be static tested and shown to meet—

(i) The strength requirements of § 25.305 at an ultimate load corresponding to a casting factor of 1.25; and

(ii) The deformation requirements of § 25.305 at a load of 1.15 times the limit load.

(3) Examples of these castings are structural attachment fittings, parts of flight control systems, control surface hinges and balance weight attachments, seat, berth, safety belt, and fuel and oil tank supports and attachments, and cabin pressure valves.

(d) *Noncritical castings.* For each casting other than those specified in paragraph (c) of this section, the following apply:

(1) Except as provided in paragraphs (d)(2) and (3) of this section, the casting factors and corresponding inspections must meet the following table:

Casting factor	Inspection
2.0 or more	100 percent visual.
Less than 2.0 but more than 1.5.	100 percent visual, and magnetic particle or penetrant or equivalent nondestructive inspection methods.
1.25 through 1.50	100 percent visual, magnetic particle or penetrant, and radiographic, or approved equivalent nondestructive inspection methods.

(2) The percentage of castings inspected by nonvisual methods may be reduced below that specified in paragraph (d)(1) of this section when an approved quality control procedure is established.

(3) For castings procured to a specification that guarantees the mechanical properties of the material in the casting and provides for demonstration of these properties by test of coupons cut from the castings on a sampling basis—

(i) A casting factor of 1.0 may be used; and

(ii) The castings must be inspected as provided in paragraph (d)(1) of this section for casting factors of "1.25 through 1.50" and tested under paragraph (c)(2) of this section.

§ 25.623 Bearing factors.

(a) Except as provided in paragraph (b) of this section, each part that has clearance (free fit), and that is subject to pounding or vibration, must have a bearing factor large enough to provide for the effects of normal relative motion.

(b) No bearing factor need be used for a part for which any larger special factor is prescribed.

§ 25.625 Fitting factors.

For each fitting (a part or terminal used to join one structural member to another), the following apply:

(a) For each fitting whose strength is not proven by limit and ultimate load tests in which actual stress conditions are simulated in the fitting and surrounding structures, a fitting factor of at least 1.15 must be applied to each part of—

(1) The fitting;

(2) The means of attachment; and

(3) The bearing on the joined members.

(b) No fitting factor need be used—

(1) For joints made under approved practices and based on comprehensive test data (such as continuous joints in metal plating, welded joints, and scarf joints in wood); or

(2) With respect to any bearing surface for which a larger special factor is used.

(c) For each integral fitting, the part must be treated as a fitting up to the point at which the section properties become typical of the member.

(d) For each seat, berth, safety belt, and harness, the fitting factor specified in § 25.785(f)(3) applies.

[Doc. No. 5066, 29 FR 18291, Dec. 24, 1964, as amended by Amdt. 25-23, 35 FR 5674, Apr. 8, 1970; Amdt. 25-72, 55 FR 29776, July 20, 1990]

§ 25.629 Aeroelastic stability requirements.

(a) *General.* The aeroelastic stability evaluations required under this section include flutter, divergence, control reversal and any undue loss of stability and control as a result of structural deformation. The aeroelastic evaluation must include whirl modes associated with any propeller or rotating device that contributes significant dynamic forces. Compliance with this section must be shown by analyses, wind tunnel tests, ground vibration tests, flight tests, or other means found necessary by the Administrator.

(b) *Aeroelastic stability envelopes.* The airplane must be designed to be free from aeroelastic instability for all configurations and design conditions within the aeroelastic stability envelopes as follows:

(1) For normal conditions without failures, malfunctions, or adverse conditions, all combinations of altitudes and speeds encompassed by the V_D/M_D versus altitude envelope enlarged at all points by an increase of 15 percent in equivalent airspeed at both constant Mach number and constant altitude. In addition, a proper margin of stability must exist at all speeds up to V_D/M_D and, there must be no large and rapid reduction in stability as V_D/M_D is approached. The enlarged envelope may be limited to Mach 1.0 when M_D is less than 1.0 at all design altitudes, and

(2) For the conditions described in § 25.629(d) below, for all approved altitudes, any airspeed up to the greater airspeed defined by;

(i) The V_D/M_D envelope determined by § 25.335(b); or,

(ii) An altitude-airspeed envelope defined by a 15 percent increase in equivalent airspeed above V_C at constant altitude, from sea level to the altitude of the intersection of 1.15 V_C with the extension of the constant cruise Mach number line, M_C, then a linear variation in equivalent airspeed to $M_C+.05$ at the altitude of the lowest V_C/M_C intersection; then, at higher altitudes, up to the maximum flight altitude, the boundary defined by a .05 Mach increase in M_C at constant altitude.

(c) *Balance weights.* If concentrated balance weights are used, their effectiveness and strength, including supporting structure, must be substantiated.

(d) *Failures, malfunctions, and adverse conditions.* The failures, malfunctions, and adverse conditions which must be considered in showing compliance with this section are:

(1) Any critical fuel loading conditions, not shown to be extremely improbable, which may result from mismanagement of fuel.

(2) Any single failure in any flutter damper system.

(3) For airplanes not approved for operation in icing conditions, the maximum likely ice accumulation expected as a result of an inadvertent encounter.

(4) Failure of any single element of the structure supporting any engine, independently mounted propeller shaft, large auxiliary power unit, or large externally mounted aerodynamic body (such as an external fuel tank).

(5) For airplanes with engines that have propellers or large rotating devices capable of significant dynamic forces, any single failure of the engine structure that would reduce the rigidity of the rotational axis.

(6) The absence of aerodynamic or gyroscopic forces resulting from the most adverse combination of feathered propellers or other rotating devices capable of significant dynamic forces. In addition, the effect of a single feathered propeller or rotating device must be coupled with the failures of paragraphs (d)(4) and (d)(5) of this section.

(7) Any single propeller or rotating device capable of significant dynamic forces rotating at the highest likely overspeed.

(8) Any damage or failure condition, required or selected for investigation by § 25.571. The single structural failures described in paragraphs (d)(4) and (d)(5) of this section need not be considered in showing compliance with this section if;

(i) The structural element could not fail due to discrete source damage resulting from the conditions described in § 25.571(e), and

(ii) A damage tolerance investigation in accordance with § 25.571(b) shows that the maximum extent of damage assumed for the purpose of residual strength evaluation does not involve complete failure of the structural element.

(9) Any damage, failure, or malfunction considered under §§ 25.631, 25.671, 25.672, and 25.1309.

(10) Any other combination of failures, malfunctions, or adverse conditions not shown to be extremely improbable.

(e) *Flight flutter testing.* Full scale flight flutter tests at speeds up to V_{DF}/M_{DF} must be conducted for new type designs and for modifications to a type design unless the modifications have been shown to have an insignificant effect on the aeroelastic stability. These tests must demonstrate that the airplane has a proper margin of damping at all speeds up to V_{DF}/M_{DF}, and that there is no large and rapid reduction in damping as V_{DF}/M_{DF}, is approached. If a failure, malfunction, or adverse condition is simulated during flight test in showing compliance with paragraph (d) of this section, the maximum speed investigated need not exceed V_{FC}/M_{FC} if it is shown, by correlation of the flight test data with other test data or analyses, that the airplane is free from any aeroelastic instability at all speeds within the altitude-airspeed envelope described in paragraph (b)(2) of this section.

[Doc. No. 26007, 57 FR 28949, June 29, 1992]

§ 25.631   Bird strike damage.

The empennage structure must be designed to assure capability of continued safe flight and landing of the airplane after impact with an 8-pound bird when the velocity of the airplane (relative to the bird along the airplane's flight path) is equal to V_C at sea level, selected under § 25.335(a). Compliance with this section by provision of redundant structure and protected location of control system elements or protective devices such as splitter plates or energy absorbing material is acceptable. Where compliance is shown by analysis, tests, or both, use of data on airplanes having similar structural design is acceptable.

[Amdt. 25–23, 35 FR 5674, Apr. 8, 1970]

CONTROL SURFACES

§ 25.651   Proof of strength.

(a) Limit load tests of control surfaces are required. These tests must include the horn or fitting to which the control system is attached.

(b) Compliance with the special factors requirements of §§ 25.619 through 25.625 and 25.657 for control surface hinges must be shown by analysis or individual load tests.

§ 25.655   Installation.

(a) Movable tail surfaces must be installed so that there is no interference between any surfaces when one is held in its extreme position and the others

are operated through their full angular movement.

(b) If an adjustable stabilizer is used, it must have stops that will limit its range of travel to the maximum for which the airplane is shown to meet the trim requirements of § 25.161.

§ 25.657   Hinges.

(a) For control surface hinges, including ball, roller, and self-lubricated bearing hinges, the approved rating of the bearing may not be exceeded. For nonstandard bearing hinge configurations, the rating must be established on the basis of experience or tests and, in the absence of a rational investigation, a factor of safety of not less than 6.67 must be used with respect to the ultimate bearing strength of the softest material used as a bearing.

(b) Hinges must have enough strength and rigidity for loads parallel to the hinge line.

[Amdt. 25–23, 35 FR 5674, Apr. 8, 1970]

CONTROL SYSTEMS

§ 25.671   General.

(a) Each control and control system must operate with the ease, smoothness, and positiveness appropriate to its function.

(b) Each element of each flight control system must be designed, or distinctively and permanently marked, to minimize the probability of incorrect assembly that could result in the malfunctioning of the system.

(c) The airplane must be shown by analysis, tests, or both, to be capable of continued safe flight and landing after any of the following failures or jamming in the flight control system and surfaces (including trim, lift, drag, and feel systems), within the normal flight envelope, without requiring exceptional piloting skill or strength. Probable malfunctions must have only minor effects on control system operation and must be capable of being readily counteracted by the pilot.

(1) Any single failure, excluding jamming (for example, disconnection or failure of mechanical elements, or structural failure of hydraulic components, such as actuators, control spool housing, and valves).

(2) Any combination of failures not shown to be extremely improbable, excluding jamming (for example, dual electrical or hydraulic system failures, or any single failure in combination with any probable hydraulic or electrical failure).

(3) Any jam in a control position normally encountered during takeoff, climb, cruise, normal turns, descent, and landing unless the jam is shown to be extremely improbable, or can be alleviated. A runaway of a flight control to an adverse position and jam must be accounted for if such runaway and subsequent jamming is not extremely improbable.

(d) The airplane must be designed so that it is controllable if all engines fail. Compliance with this requirement may be shown by analysis where that method has been shown to be reliable.

[Doc. No. 5066, 29 FR 18291, Dec. 24, 1964, as amended by Amdt. 25–23, 35 FR 5674, Apr. 8, 1970]

§ 25.672 Stability augmentation and automatic and power-operated systems.

If the functioning of stability augmentation or other automatic or power-operated systems is necessary to show compliance with the flight characteristics requirements of this part, such systems must comply with § 25.671 and the following:

(a) A warning which is clearly distinguishable to the pilot under expected flight conditions without requiring his attention must be provided for any failure in the stability augmentation system or in any other automatic or power-operated system which could result in an unsafe condition if the pilot were not aware of the failure. Warning systems must not activate the control systems.

(b) The design of the stability augmentation system or of any other automatic or power-operated system must permit initial counteraction of failures of the type specified in § 25.671(c) without requiring exceptional pilot skill or strength, by either the deactivation of the system, or a failed portion thereof, or by overriding the failure by movement of the flight controls in the normal sense.

(c) It must be shown that after any single failure of the stability augmentation system or any other automatic or power-operated system—

(1) The airplane is safely controllable when the failure or malfunction occurs at any speed or altitude within the approved operating limitations that is critical for the type of failure being considered;

(2) The controllability and maneuverability requirements of this part are met within a practical operational flight envelope (for example, speed, altitude, normal acceleration, and airplane configurations) which is described in the Airplane Flight Manual; and

(3) The trim, stability, and stall characteristics are not impaired below a level needed to permit continued safe flight and landing.

[Amdt. 25–23, 35 FR 5675 Apr. 8, 1970]

§ 25.675 Stops.

(a) Each control system must have stops that positively limit the range of motion of each movable aerodynamic surface controlled by the system.

(b) Each stop must be located so that wear, slackness, or take-up adjustments will not adversely affect the control characteristics of the airplane because of a change in the range of surface travel.

(c) Each stop must be able to withstand any loads corresponding to the design conditions for the control system.

[Doc. No. 5066, 29 FR 18291, Dec. 24, 1964, as amended by Amdt. 25–38, 41 FR 55466, Dec. 20, 1976]

§ 25.677 Trim systems.

(a) Trim controls must be designed to prevent inadvertent or abrupt operation and to operate in the plane, and with the sense of motion, of the airplane.

(b) There must be means adjacent to the trim control to indicate the direction of the control movement relative to the airplane motion. In addition, there must be clearly visible means to indicate the position of the trim device with respect to the range of adjustment.

(c) Trim control systems must be designed to prevent creeping in flight. Trim tab controls must be irreversible unless the tab is appropriately balanced and shown to be free from flutter.

(d) If an irreversible tab control system is used, the part from the tab to the attachment of the irreversible unit to the airplane structure must consist of a rigid connection.

[Doc. No. 5066, 29 FR 18291, Dec. 24, 1964, as amended by Amdt. 25-23, 35 FR 5675, Apr. 8, 1970]

§ 25.679 Control system gust locks.

(a) There must be a device to prevent damage to the control surfaces (including tabs), and to the control system, from gusts striking the airplane while it is on the ground or water. If the device, when engaged, prevents normal operation of the control surfaces by the pilot, it must—

(1) Automatically disengage when the pilot operates the primary flight controls in a normal manner; or

(2) Limit the operation of the airplane so that the pilot receives unmistakable warning at the start of takeoff.

(b) The device must have means to preclude the possibility of it becoming inadvertently engaged in flight.

§ 25.681 Limit load static tests.

(a) Compliance with the limit load requirements of this Part must be shown by tests in which—

(1) The direction of the test loads produces the most severe loading in the control system; and

(2) Each fitting, pulley, and bracket used in attaching the system to the main structure is included.

(b) Compliance must be shown (by analyses or individual load tests) with the special factor requirements for control system joints subject to angular motion.

§ 25.683 Operation tests.

It must be shown by operation tests that when portions of the control system subject to pilot effort loads are loaded to 80 percent of the limit load specified for the system and the powered portions of the control system are loaded to the maximum load expected in normal operation, the system is free from—

(a) Jamming;

(b) Excessive friction; and

(c) Excessive deflection.

[Doc. No. 5066, 29 FR 18291, Dec. 24, 1964, as amended by Amdt. 25-23, 35 FR 5675, Apr. 8, 1970]

§ 25.685 Control system details.

(a) Each detail of each control system must be designed and installed to prevent jamming, chafing, and interference from cargo, passengers, loose objects, or the freezing of moisture.

(b) There must be means in the cockpit to prevent the entry of foreign objects into places where they would jam the system.

(c) There must be means to prevent the slapping of cables or tubes against other parts.

(d) Sections 25.689 and 25.693 apply to cable systems and joints.

[Doc. No. 5066, 29 FR 18291, Dec. 24, 1964, as amended by Amdt. 25-38, 41 FR 55466, Dec. 20, 1976]

§ 25.689 Cable systems.

(a) Each cable, cable fitting, turnbuckle, splice, and pulley must be approved. In addition—

(1) No cable smaller than 1/8 inch in diameter may be used in the aileron, elevator, or rudder systems; and

(2) Each cable system must be designed so that there will be no hazardous change in cable tension throughout the range of travel under operating conditions and temperature variations.

(b) Each kind and size of pulley must correspond to the cable with which it is used. Pulleys and sprockets must have closely fitted guards to prevent the cables and chains from being displaced or fouled. Each pulley must lie in the plane passing through the cable so that the cable does not rub against the pulley flange.

(c) Fairleads must be installed so that they do not cause a change in cable direction of more than three degrees.

(d) Clevis pins subject to load or motion and retained only by cotter pins may not be used in the control system.

(e) Turnbuckles must be attached to parts having angular motion in a manner that will positively prevent binding throughout the range of travel.

(f) There must be provisions for visual inspection of fairleads, pulleys, terminals, and turnbuckles.

§ 25.693　Joints.

Control system joints (in push-pull systems) that are subject to angular motion, except those in ball and roller bearing systems, must have a special factor of safety of not less than 3.33 with respect to the ultimate bearing strength of the softest material used as a bearing. This factor may be reduced to 2.0 for joints in cable control systems. For ball or roller bearings, the approved ratings may not be exceeded.

[Amdt. 25–72, 55 FR 29777, July 20, 1990]

§ 25.697　Lift and drag devices, controls.

(a) Each lift device control must be designed so that the pilots can place the device in any takeoff, en route, approach, or landing position established under § 25.101(d). Lift and drag devices must maintain the selected positions, except for movement produced by an automatic positioning or load limiting device, without further attention by the pilots.

(b) Each lift and drag device control must be designed and located to make inadvertent operation improbable. Lift and drag devices intended for ground operation only must have means to prevent the inadvertant operation of their controls in flight if that operation could be hazardous.

(c) The rate of motion of the surfaces in response to the operation of the control and the characteristics of the automatic positioning or load limiting device must give satisfactory flight and performance characteristics under steady or changing conditions of airspeed, engine power, and airplane attitude.

(d) The lift device control must be designed to retract the surfaces from the fully extended position, during steady flight at maximum continuous engine power at any speed below V_F +9.0 (knots).

[Amdt. 25–23, 35 FR 5675, Apr. 8, 1970, as amended by Amdt. 25–46, 43 FR 50595, Oct. 30, 1978; Amdt. 25–57, 49 FR 6848, Feb. 23, 1984]

§ 25.699　Lift and drag device indicator.

(a) There must be means to indicate to the pilots the position of each lift or drag device having a separate control in the cockpit to adjust its position. In addition, an indication of unsymmetrical operation or other malfunction in the lift or drag device systems must be provided when such indication is necessary to enable the pilots to prevent or counteract an unsafe flight or ground condition, considering the effects on flight characteristics and performance.

(b) There must be means to indicate to the pilots the takeoff, en route, approach, and landing lift device positions.

(c) If any extension of the lift and drag devices beyond the landing position is possible, the controls must be clearly marked to identify this range of extension.

[Amdt. 25–23, 35 FR 5675, Apr. 8, 1970]

§ 25.701　Flap and slat interconnection.

(a) Unless the airplane has safe flight characteristics with the flaps or slats retracted on one side and extended on the other, the motion of flaps or slats on opposite sides of the plane of symmetry must be synchronized by a mechanical interconnection or approved equivalent means.

(b) If a wing flap or slat interconnection or equivalent means is used, it must be designed to account for the applicable unsymmetrical loads, including those resulting from flight with the engines on one side of the plane of symmetry inoperative and the remaining engines at takeoff power.

(c) For airplanes with flaps or slats that are not subjected to slipstream conditions, the structure must be designed for the loads imposed when the wing flaps or slats on one side are carrying the most severe load occurring in the prescribed symmetrical conditions and those on the other side are carrying not more than 80 percent of that load.

(d) The interconnection must be designed for the loads resulting when interconnected flap or slat surfaces on one side of the plane of symmetry are jammed and immovable while the surfaces on the other side are free to move and the full power of the surface actuating system is applied.

[Amdt. 25–72, 55 FR 29777, July 20, 1990]

§ 25.703 Takeoff warning system.

A takeoff warning system must be installed and must meet the following requirements:

(a) The system must provide to the pilots an aural warning that is automatically activated during the initial portion of the takeoff roll if the airplane is in a configuration, including any of the following, that would not allow a safe takeoff:

(1) The wing flaps or leading edge devices are not within the approved range of takeoff positions.

(2) Wing spoilers (except lateral control spoilers meeting the requirements of § 25.671), speed brakes, or longitudinal trim devices are in a position that would not allow a safe takeoff.

(b) The warning required by paragraph (a) of this section must continue until—

(1) The configuration is changed to allow a safe takeoff;

(2) Action is taken by the pilot to terminate the takeoff roll;

(3) The airplane is rotated for takeoff; or

(4) The warning is manually deactivated by the pilot.

(c) The means used to activate the system must function properly throughout the ranges of takeoff weights, altitudes, and temperatures for which certification is requested.

[Amdt. 25–42, 43 FR 2323, Jan. 16, 1978]

LANDING GEAR

§ 25.721 General.

(a) The main landing gear system must be designed so that if it fails due to overloads during takeoff and landing (assuming the overloads to act in the upward and aft directions), the failure mode is not likely to cause—

(1) For airplanes that have passenger seating configuration, excluding pilots seats, of nine seats or less, the spillage of enough fuel from any fuel system in the fuselage to constitute a fire hazard; and

(2) For airplanes that have a passenger seating configuration, excluding pilots seats, of 10 seats or more, the spillage of enough fuel from any part of the fuel system to constitute a fire hazard.

(b) Each airplane that has a passenger seating configuration excluding pilots seats, of 10 seats or more must be designed so that with the airplane under control it can be landed on a paved runway with any one or more landing gear legs not extended without sustaining a structural component failure that is likely to cause the spillage of enough fuel to constitute a fire hazard.

(c) Compliance with the provisions of this section may be shown by analysis or tests, or both.

[Amdt. 25–32, 37 FR 3969, Feb. 24, 1972]

§ 25.723 Shock absorption tests.

(a) The analytical representation of the landing gear dynamic characteristics that is used in determining the landing loads must be validated by energy absorption tests. A range of tests must be conducted to ensure that the analytical representation is valid for the design conditions specified in § 25.473.

(1) The configurations subjected to energy absorption tests at limit design conditions must include at least the design landing weight or the design takeoff weight, whichever produces the greater value of landing impact energy.

(2) The test attitude of the landing gear unit and the application of appropriate drag loads during the test must simulate the airplane landing conditions in a manner consistent with the development of rational or conservative limit loads.

(b) The landing gear may not fail in a test, demonstrating its reserve energy absorption capacity, simulating a descent velocity of 12 f.p.s. at design landing weight, assuming airplane lift not greater than airplane weight acting during the landing impact.

(c) In lieu of the tests prescribed in this section, changes in previously approved design weights and minor changes in design may be substantiated by analyses based on previous tests conducted on the same basic landing gear system that has similar energy absorption characteristics.

[Doc. No. 1999–5835, 66 FR 27394, May 16, 2001]

§ 25.725 **[Reserved]**

§ 25.727 **[Reserved]**

§ 25.729 **Retracting mechanism.**

(a) *General.* For airplanes with retractable landing gear, the following apply:

(1) The landing gear retracting mechanism, wheel well doors, and supporting structure, must be designed for—

(i) The loads occurring in the flight conditions when the gear is in the retracted position,

(ii) The combination of friction loads, inertia loads, brake torque loads, air loads, and gyroscopic loads resulting from the wheels rotating at a peripheral speed equal to 1.3 V_s (with the flaps in takeoff position at design takeoff weight), occurring during retraction and extension at any airspeed up to 1.6 V_{s1} (with the flaps in the approach position at design landing weight), and

(iii) Any load factor up to those specified in §25.345(a) for the flaps extended condition.

(2) Unless there are other means to decelerate the airplane in flight at this speed, the landing gear, the retracting mechanism, and the airplane structure (including wheel well doors) must be designed to withstand the flight loads occurring with the landing gear in the extended position at any speed up to 0.67 V_C.

(3) Landing gear doors, their operating mechanism, and their supporting structures must be designed for the yawing maneuvers prescribed for the airplane in addition to the conditions of airspeed and load factor prescribed in paragraphs (a)(1) and (2) of this section.

(b) *Landing gear lock.* There must be positive means to keep the landing gear extended, in flight and on the ground.

(c) *Emergency operation.* There must be an emergency means for extending the landing gear in the event of—

(1) Any reasonably probable failure in the normal retraction system; or

(2) The failure of any single source of hydraulic, electric, or equivalent energy supply.

(d) *Operation test.* The proper functioning of the retracting mechanism must be shown by operation tests.

(e) *Position indicator and warning device.* If a retractable landing gear is used, there must be a landing gear position indicator (as well as necessary switches to actuate the indicator) or other means to inform the pilot that the gear is secured in the extended (or retracted) position. This means must be designed as follows:

(1) If switches are used, they must be located and coupled to the landing gear mechanical systems in a manner that prevents an erroneous indication of "down and locked" if the landing gear is not in a fully extended position, or of "up and locked" if the landing gear is not in the fully retracted position. The switches may be located where they are operated by the actual landing gear locking latch or device.

(2) The flightcrew must be given an aural warning that functions continuously, or is periodically repeated, if a landing is attempted when the landing gear is not locked down.

(3) The warning must be given in sufficient time to allow the landing gear to be locked down or a go-around to be made.

(4) There must not be a manual shutoff means readily available to the flightcrew for the warning required by paragraph (e)(2) of this section such that it could be operated instinctively, inadvertently, or by habitual reflexive action.

(5) The system used to generate the aural warning must be designed to eliminate false or inappropriate alerts.

(6) Failures of systems used to inhibit the landing gear aural warning, that would prevent the warning system from operating, must be improbable.

(f) *Protection of equipment in wheel wells.* Equipment that is essential to safe operation of the airplane and that is located in wheel wells must be protected from the damaging effects of—

(1) A bursting tire, unless it is shown that a tire cannot burst from overheat; and

(2) A loose tire tread, unless it is shown that a loose tire tread cannot cause damage.

[Doc. No. 5066, 29 FR 18291, Dec. 24, 1964, as amended by Amdt. 25–23, 35 FR 5676, Apr. 8, 1970; Amdt. 25–42, 43 FR 2323, Jan. 16, 1978; Amdt. 25–72, 55 FR 29777, July 20, 1990; Amdt. 25–75, 56 FR 63762, Dec. 5, 1991]

§ 25.731 Wheels.

(a) Each main and nose wheel must be approved.

(b) The maximum static load rating of each wheel may not be less than the corresponding static ground reaction with—

(1) Design maximum weight; and

(2) Critical center of gravity.

(c) The maximum limit load rating of each wheel must equal or exceed the maximum radial limit load determined under the applicable ground load requirements of this part.

(d) *Overpressure burst prevention.* Means must be provided in each wheel to prevent wheel failure and tire burst that may result from excessive pressurization of the wheel and tire assembly.

(e) *Braked wheels.* Each braked wheel must meet the applicable requirements of § 25.735.

[Doc. No. 5066, 29 FR 18291, Dec. 24, 1964, as amended by Amdt. 25–72, 55 FR 29777, July 20, 1990; Amdt. 25–107, 67 FR 20420, Apr. 24, 2002]

§ 25.733 Tires.

(a) When a landing gear axle is fitted with a single wheel and tire assembly, the wheel must be fitted with a suitable tire of proper fit with a speed rating approved by the Administrator that is not exceeded under critical conditions and with a load rating approved by the Administrator that is not exceeded under—

(1) The loads on the main wheel tire, corresponding to the most critical combination of airplane weight (up to maximum weight) and center of gravity position, and

(2) The loads corresponding to the ground reactions in paragraph (b) of this section, on the nose wheel tire, except as provided in paragraphs (b)(2) and (b)(3) of this section.

(b) The applicable ground reactions for nose wheel tires are as follows:

(1) The static ground reaction for the tire corresponding to the most critical combination of airplane weight (up to maximum ramp weight) and center of gravity position with a force of 1.0g acting downward at the center of gravity. This load may not exceed the load rating of the tire.

(2) The ground reaction of the tire corresponding to the most critical combination of airplane weight (up to maximum landing weight) and center of gravity position combined with forces of 1.0g downward and 0.31g forward acting at the center of gravity. The reactions in this case must be distributed to the nose and main wheels by the principles of statics with a drag reaction equal to 0.31 times the vertical load at each wheel with brakes capable of producing this ground reaction. This nose tire load may not exceed 1.5 times the load rating of the tire.

(3) The ground reaction of the tire corresponding to the most critical combination of airplane weight (up to maximum ramp weight) and center of gravity position combined with forces of 1.0g downward and 0.20g forward acting at the center of gravity. The reactions in this case must be distributed to the nose and main wheels by the principles of statics with a drag reaction equal to 0.20 times the vertical load at each wheel with brakes capable of producing this ground reaction. This nose tire load may not exceed 1.5 times the load rating of the tire.

(c) When a landing gear axle is fitted with more than one wheel and tire assembly, such as dual or dual-tandem, each wheel must be fitted with a suitable tire of proper fit with a speed rating approved by the Administrator that is not exceeded under critical conditions, and with a load rating approved by the Administrator that is not exceeded by—

(1) The loads on each main wheel tire, corresponding to the most critical combination of airplane weight (up to maximum weight) and center of gravity position, when multiplied by a factor of 1.07; and

(2) Loads specified in paragraphs (a)(2), (b)(1), (b)(2), and (b)(3) of this section on each nose wheel tire.

(d) Each tire installed on a retractable landing gear system must, at the maximum size of the tire type expected in service, have a clearance to surrounding structure and systems that is adequate to prevent unintended contact between the tire and any part of the structure or systems.

(e) For an airplane with a maximum certificated takeoff weight of more than 75,000 pounds, tires mounted on braked wheels must be inflated with dry nitrogen or other gases shown to be inert so that the gas mixture in the tire does not contain oxygen in excess of 5 percent by volume, unless it can be shown that the tire liner material will not produce a volatile gas when heated or that means are provided to prevent tire temperatures from reaching unsafe levels.

[Amdt. 25–48, 44 FR 68752, Nov. 29, 1979; Amdt. 25–72, 55 FR 29777, July 20, 1990, as amended by Amdt. 25–78, 58 FR 11781, Feb. 26, 1993]

§25.735 Brakes and braking systems.

(a) *Approval.* Each assembly consisting of a wheel(s) and brake(s) must be approved.

(b) *Brake system capability.* The brake system, associated systems and components must be designed and constructed so that:

(1) If any electrical, pneumatic, hydraulic, or mechanical connecting or transmitting element fails, or if any single source of hydraulic or other brake operating energy supply is lost, it is possible to bring the airplane to rest with a braked roll stopping distance of not more than two times that obtained in determining the landing distance as prescribed in §25.125.

(2) Fluid lost from a brake hydraulic system following a failure in, or in the vicinity of, the brakes is insufficient to cause or support a hazardous fire on the ground or in flight.

(c) *Brake controls.* The brake controls must be designed and constructed so that:

(1) Excessive control force is not required for their operation.

(2) If an automatic braking system is installed, means are provided to:

(i) Arm and disarm the system, and

(ii) Allow the pilot(s) to override the system by use of manual braking.

(d) *Parking brake.* The airplane must have a parking brake control that, when selected on, will, without further attention, prevent the airplane from

rolling on a dry and level paved runway when the most adverse combination of maximum thrust on one engine and up to maximum ground idle thrust on any, or all, other engine(s) is applied. The control must be suitably located or be adequately protected to prevent inadvertent operation. There must be indication in the cockpit when the parking brake is not fully released.

(e) *Antiskid system.* If an antiskid system is installed:

(1) It must operate satisfactorily over the range of expected runway conditions, without external adjustment.

(2) It must, at all times, have priority over the automatic braking system, if installed.

(f) *Kinetic energy capacity*—(1) *Design landing stop.* The design landing stop is an operational landing stop at maximum landing weight. The design landing stop brake kinetic energy absorption requirement of each wheel, brake, and tire assembly must be determined. It must be substantiated by dynamometer testing that the wheel, brake and tire assembly is capable of absorbing not less than this level of kinetic energy throughout the defined wear range of the brake. The energy absorption rate derived from the airplane manufacturer's braking requirements must be achieved. The mean deceleration must not be less than 10 fps^2.

(2) *Maximum kinetic energy accelerate-stop.* The maximum kinetic energy accelerate-stop is a rejected takeoff for the most critical combination of airplane takeoff weight and speed. The accelerate-stop brake kinetic energy absorption requirement of each wheel, brake, and tire assembly must be determined. It must be substantiated by dynamometer testing that the wheel, brake, and tire assembly is capable of absorbing not less than this level of kinetic energy throughout the defined wear range of the brake. The energy absorption rate derived from the airplane manufacturer's braking requirements must be achieved. The mean deceleration must not be less than 6 fps \2\.

(3) *Most severe landing stop.* The most severe landing stop is a stop at the most critical combination of airplane landing weight and speed. The most severe landing stop brake kinetic energy

absorption requirement of each wheel, brake, and tire assembly must be determined. It must be substantiated by dynamometer testing that, at the declared fully worn limit(s) of the brake heat sink, the wheel, brake and tire assembly is capable of absorbing not less than this level of kinetic energy. The most severe landing stop need not be considered for extremely improbable failure conditions or if the maximum kinetic energy accelerate-stop energy is more severe.

(g) *Brake condition after high kinetic energy dynamometer stop(s).* Following the high kinetic energy stop demonstration(s) required by paragraph (f) of this section, with the parking brake promptly and fully applied for at least 3 minutes, it must be demonstrated that for at least 5 minutes from application of the parking brake, no condition occurs (or has occurred during the stop), including fire associated with the tire or wheel and brake assembly, that could prejudice the safe and complete evacuation of the airplane.

(h) *Stored energy systems.* An indication to the flightcrew of the usable stored energy must be provided if a stored energy system is used to show compliance with paragraph (b)(1) of this section. The available stored energy must be sufficient for:

(1) At least 6 full applications of the brakes when an antiskid system is not operating; and

(2) Bringing the airplane to a complete stop when an antiskid system is operating, under all runway surface conditions for which the airplane is certificated.

(i) *Brake wear indicators.* Means must be provided for each brake assembly to indicate when the heat sink is worn to the permissible limit. The means must be reliable and readily visible.

(j) *Overtemperature burst prevention.* Means must be provided in each braked wheel to prevent a wheel failure, a tire burst, or both, that may result from elevated brake temperatures. Additionally, all wheels must meet the requirements of § 25.731(d).

(k) *Compatibility.* Compatibility of the wheel and brake assemblies with

the airplane and its systems must be substantiated.

[Doc. No. FAA–1999–6063, 67 FR 20420, Apr. 24, 2002, as amended by Amdt. 25–108, 67 FR 70827, Nov. 26, 2002; 68 FR 1955, Jan. 15, 2003]

§ 25.737 Skis.

Each ski must be approved. The maximum limit load rating of each ski must equal or exceed the maximum limit load determined under the applicable ground load requirements of this part.

FLOATS AND HULLS

§ 25.751 Main float buoyancy.

Each main float must have—

(a) A buoyancy of 80 percent in excess of that required to support the maximum weight of the seaplane or amphibian in fresh water; and

(b) Not less than five watertight compartments approximately equal in volume.

§ 25.753 Main float design.

Each main float must be approved and must meet the requirements of § 25.521.

§ 25.755 Hulls.

(a) Each hull must have enough watertight compartments so that, with any two adjacent compartments flooded, the buoyancy of the hull and auxiliary floats (and wheel tires, if used) provides a margin of positive stability great enough to minimize the probability of capsizing in rough, fresh water.

(b) Bulkheads with watertight doors may be used for communication between compartments.

PERSONNEL AND CARGO
ACCOMMODATIONS

§ 25.771 Pilot compartment.

(a) Each pilot compartment and its equipment must allow the minimum flight crew (established under § 25.1523) to perform their duties without unreasonable concentration or fatigue.

(b) The primary controls listed in § 25.779(a), excluding cables and control rods, must be located with respect to the propellers so that no member of the minimum flight crew (established under §25.1523), or part of the controls, lies in the region between the plane of rotation of any inboard propeller and the surface generated by a line passing through the center of the propeller hub making an angle of five degrees forward or aft of the plane of rotation of the propeller.

(c) If provision is made for a second pilot, the airplane must be controllable with equal safety from either pilot seat.

(d) The pilot compartment must be constructed so that, when flying in rain or snow, it will not leak in a manner that will distract the crew or harm the structure.

(e) Vibration and noise characteristics of cockpit equipment may not interfere with safe operation of the airplane.

[Doc. No. 5066, 29 FR 18291, Dec. 24, 1964, as amended by Amdt. 25–4, 30 FR 6113, Apr. 30, 1965]

§25.772 Pilot compartment doors.

For an airplane that has a lockable door installed between the pilot compartment and the passenger compartment:

(a) For airplanes with a maximum passenger seating configuration of more than 20 seats, the emergency exit configuration must be designed so that neither crewmembers nor passengers require use of the flightdeck door in order to reach the emergency exits provided for them; and

(b) Means must be provided to enable flight crewmembers to directly enter the passenger compartment from the pilot compartment if the cockpit door becomes jammed.

(c) There must be an emergency means to enable a flight attendant to enter the pilot compartment in the event that the flightcrew becomes incapacitated.

[Doc. No. 24344, 55 FR 29777, July 20, 1990, as amended by Amdt. 25–106, 67 FR 2127, Jan. 15, 2002]

§25.773 Pilot compartment view.

(a) *Nonprecipitation conditions.* For nonprecipitation conditions, the following apply:

(1) Each pilot compartment must be arranged to give the pilots a sufficiently extensive, clear, and undistorted view, to enable them to safely perform any maneuvers within the operating limitations of the airplane, including taxiing takeoff, approach, and landing.

(2) Each pilot compartment must be free of glare and reflection that could interfere with the normal duties of the minimum flight crew (established under §25.1523). This must be shown in day and night flight tests under nonprecipitation conditions.

(b) *Precipitation conditions.* For precipitation conditions, the following apply:

(1) The airplane must have a means to maintain a clear portion of the windshield, during precipitation conditions, sufficient for both pilots to have a sufficiently extensive view along the flight path in normal flight attitudes of the airplane. This means must be designed to function, without continuous attention on the part of the crew, in—

(i) Heavy rain at speeds up to 1.5 V_{SR1} with lift and drag devices retracted; and

(ii) The icing conditions specified in §25.1419 if certification with ice protection provisions is requested.

(2) The first pilot must have—

(i) A window that is openable under the conditions prescribed in paragraph (b)(1) of this section when the cabin is not pressurized, provides the view specified in that paragraph, and gives sufficient protection from the elements against impairment of the pilot's vision; or

(ii) An alternate means to maintain a clear view under the conditions specified in paragraph (b)(1) of this section, considering the probable damage due to a severe hail encounter.

(c) *Internal windshield and window fogging.* The airplane must have a means to prevent fogging of the internal portions of the windshield and window panels over an area which would provide the visibility specified in paragraph (a) of this section under all internal and external ambient conditions, including precipitation conditions, in which the airplane is intended to be operated.

(d) Fixed markers or other guides must be installed at each pilot station to enable the pilots to position themselves in their seats for an optimum combination of outside visibility and instrument scan. If lighted markers or guides are used they must comply with the requirements specified in § 25.1381.

[Doc. No. 5066, 29 FR 18291, Dec. 24, 1964, as amended by Amdt. 25–23, 35 FR 5676, Apr. 8, 1970; Amdt. 25–46, 43 FR 50595, Oct. 30, 1978; Amdt. 25–72, 55 FR 29778, July 20, 1990; Amdt. 25–108, 67 FR 70827, Nov. 26, 2002]

§ 25.775 Windshields and windows.

(a) Internal panes must be made of nonsplintering material.

(b) Windshield panes directly in front of the pilots in the normal conduct of their duties, and the supporting structures for these panes, must withstand, without penetration, the impact of a four-pound bird when the velocity of the airplane (relative to the bird along the airplane's flight path) is equal to the value of V_C, at sea level, selected under § 25.335(a).

(c) Unless it can be shown by analysis or tests that the probability of occurrence of a critical windshield fragmentation condition is of a low order, the airplane must have a means to minimize the danger to the pilots from flying windshield fragments due to bird impact. This must be shown for each transparent pane in the cockpit that—

(1) Appears in the front view of the airplane;

(2) Is inclined 15 degrees or more to the longitudinal axis of the airplane; and

(3) Has any part of the pane located where its fragmentation will constitute a hazard to the pilots.

(d) The design of windshields and windows in pressurized airplanes must be based on factors peculiar to high altitude operation, including the effects of continuous and cyclic pressurization loadings, the inherent characteristics of the material used, and the effects of temperatures and temperature differentials. The windshield and window panels must be capable of withstanding the maximum cabin pressure differential loads combined with critical aerodynamic pressure and temperature effects after any single failure in the installation or associated systems. It may be assumed that, after a single failure that is obvious to the flight crew (established under § 25.1523), the cabin pressure differential is reduced

from the maximum, in accordance with appropriate operating limitations, to allow continued safe flight of the airplane with a cabin pressure altitude of not more than 15,000 feet.

(e) The windshield panels in front of the pilots must be arranged so that, assuming the loss of vision through any one panel, one or more panels remain available for use by a pilot seated at a pilot station to permit continued safe flight and landing.

[Doc. No. 5066, 29 FR 18291, Dec. 24, 1964, as amended by Amdt. 25–23, 35 FR 5676, Apr. 8, 1970; Amdt. 25–38, 41 FR 55466, Dec. 20, 1976]

§ 25.777 Cockpit controls.

(a) Each cockpit control must be located to provide convenient operation and to prevent confusion and inadvertent operation.

(b) The direction of movement of cockpit controls must meet the requirements of § 25.779. Wherever practicable, the sense of motion involved in the operation of other controls must correspond to the sense of the effect of the operation upon the airplane or upon the part operated. Controls of a variable nature using a rotary motion must move clockwise from the off position, through an increasing range, to the full on position.

(c) The controls must be located and arranged, with respect to the pilots' seats, so that there is full and unrestricted movement of each control without interference from the cockpit structure or the clothing of the minimum flight crew (established under § 25.1523) when any member of this flight crew, from 5'2" to 6'3" in height, is seated with the seat belt and shoulder harness (if provided) fastened.

(d) Identical powerplant controls for each engine must be located to prevent confusion as to the engines they control.

(e) Wing flap controls and other auxiliary lift device controls must be located on top of the pedestal, aft of the throttles, centrally or to the right of the pedestal centerline, and not less than 10 inches aft of the landing gear control.

(f) The landing gear control must be located forward of the throttles and must be operable by each pilot when seated with seat belt and shoulder harness (if provided) fastened.

(g) Control knobs must be shaped in accordance with §25.781. In addition, the knobs must be of the same color, and this color must contrast with the color of control knobs for other purposes and the surrounding cockpit.

(h) If a flight engineer is required as part of the minimum flight crew (established under §25.1523), the airplane must have a flight engineer station located and arranged so that the flight crewmembers can perform their functions efficiently and without interfering with each other.

[Doc. No. 5066, 29 FR 18291, Dec. 24, 1964, as amended by Amdt. 25–46, 43 FR 50596, Oct. 30, 1978]

§ 25.779 Motion and effect of cockpit controls.

Cockpit controls must be designed so that they operate in accordance with the following movement and actuation:

(a) Aerodynamic controls:

(1) *Primary.*

Controls	Motion and effect
Aileron	Right (clockwise) for right wing down.
Elevator	Rearward for nose up.
Rudder	Right pedal forward for nose right.

(2) *Secondary.*

Controls	Motion and effect
Flaps (or auxiliary lift devices).	Forward for flaps up; rearward for flaps down.
Trim tabs (or equivalent).	Rotate to produce similar rotation of the airplane about an axis parallel to the axis of the control.

(b) Powerplant and auxiliary controls:

(1) *Powerplant.*

Controls	Motion and effect
Power or thrust	Forward to increase forward thrust and rearward to increase rearward thrust.
Propellers	Forward to increase rpm.
Mixture	Forward or upward for rich.
Carburetor air heat	Forward or upward for cold.
Supercharger	Forward or upward for low blower. For turbosuperchargers, forward, upward, or clockwise, to increase pressure.

(2) *Auxiliary.*

Controls	Motion and effect
Landing gear	Down to extend.

[Doc. No. 5066, 29 FR 18291, Dec. 24, 1964, as amended by Amdt. 25–72, 55 FR 29778, July 20, 1990]

§ 25.781 Cockpit control knob shape.

Cockpit control knobs must conform to the general shapes (but not necessarily the exact sizes or specific proportions) in the following figure:

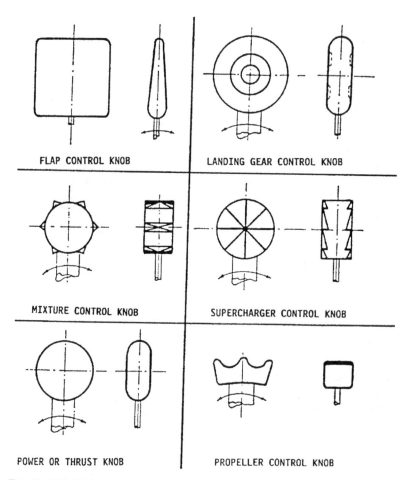

FLAP CONTROL KNOB

LANDING GEAR CONTROL KNOB

MIXTURE CONTROL KNOB

SUPERCHARGER CONTROL KNOB

POWER OR THRUST KNOB

PROPELLER CONTROL KNOB

[Doc. No. 5066, 29 FR 18291, Dec. 24, 1964, as amended by Amdt. 25–72, 55 FR 29779, July 20, 1990]

§ 25.783 Doors.

(a) Each cabin must have at least one easily accessible external door.

(b) There must be a means to lock and safeguard each external door against opening in flight (either inadvertently by persons or as a result of mechanical failure or failure of a single structural element either during or after closure). Each external door must be openable from both the inside and the outside, even though persons may be crowded against the door on the inside of the airplane. Inward opening doors may be used if there are means to prevent occupants from crowding against the door to an extent that would interfere with the opening of the door. The means of opening must be simple and obvious and must be arranged and marked so that it can be readily located and operated, even in darkness. Auxiliary locking devices may be used.

(c) Each external door must be reasonably free from jamming as a result of fuselage deformation in a minor crash.

(d) Each external door must be located where persons using them will not be endangered by the propellers when appropriate operating procedures are used.

(e) There must be a provision for direct visual inspection of the locking mechanism to determine if external doors, for which the initial opening movement is not inward (including passenger, crew, service, and cargo doors), are fully closed and locked. The provision must be discernible under operational lighting conditions by appropriate crewmembers using a flashlight or equivalent lighting source. In addition, there must be a visual warning means to signal the appropriate flight crewmembers if any external door is not fully closed and locked. The means must be designed such that any failure or combination of failures that would result in an erroneous closed and locked indication is improbable for doors for which the initial opening movement is not inward.

(f) External doors must have provisions to prevent the initiation of pressurization of the airplane to an unsafe level if the door is not fully closed and locked. In addition, it must be shown by safety analysis that inadvertent opening is extremely improbable.

(g) Cargo and service doors not suitable for use as emergency exits need only meet paragraphs (e) and (f) of this section and be safeguarded against opening in flight as a result of mechanical failure or failure of a single structural element.

(h) Each passenger entry door in the side of the fuselage must meet the applicable requirements of §§25.807 through 25.813 for a Type II or larger passenger emergency exit.

(i) If an integral stair is installed in a passenger entry door that is qualified as a passenger emergency exit, the stair must be designed so that under the following conditions the effectiveness of passenger emergency egress will not be impaired:

(1) The door, integral stair, and operating mechanism have been subjected to the inertia forces specified in §25.561(b)(3), acting separately relative to the surrounding structure.

(2) The airplane is in the normal ground attitude and in each of the attitudes corresponding to collapse of one or more legs of the landing gear.

(j) All lavatory doors must be designed to preclude anyone from becoming trapped inside the lavatory, and if a locking mechanism is installed, it be capable of being unlocked from the outside without the aid of special tools.

[Doc. No. 5066, 29 FR 18291, Dec. 24, 1964, as amended by Amdt. 25–15, 32 FR 13262, Sept. 20, 1967; Amdt. 25–23, 35 FR 5676, Apr. 8, 1970; Amdt. 25–54, 45 FR 60173, Sept. 11, 1980; Amdt. 25–72, 55 FR 29780, July 20, 1990; Amdt. 25–88, 61 FR 57956, Nov. 8, 1996]

§25.785 Seats, berths, safety belts, and harnesses.

(a) A seat (or berth for a nonambulant person) must be provided for each occupant who has reached his or her second birthday.

(b) Each seat, berth, safety belt, harness, and adjacent part of the airplane at each station designated as occupiable during takeoff and landing must be designed so that a person making proper use of these facilities will not suffer serious injury in an emergency landing as a result of the inertia forces specified in §§25.561 and 25.562.

(c) Each seat or berth must be approved.

(d) Each occupant of a seat that makes more than an 18-degree angle with the vertical plane containing the airplane centerline must be protected from head injury by a safety belt and an energy absorbing rest that will support the arms, shoulders, head, and spine, or by a safety belt and shoulder harness that will prevent the head from contacting any injurious object. Each occupant of any other seat must be protected from head injury by a safety belt and, as appropriate to the type, location, and angle of facing of each seat, by one or more of the following:

(1) A shoulder harness that will prevent the head from contacting any injurious object.

(2) The elimination of any injurious object within striking radius of the head.

(3) An energy absorbing rest that will support the arms, shoulders, head, and spine.

(e) Each berth must be designed so that the forward part has a padded end board, canvas diaphragm, or equivalent means, that can withstand the static load reaction of the occupant when subjected to the forward inertia force specified in § 25.561. Berths must be free from corners and protuberances likely to cause injury to a person occupying the berth during emergency conditions.

(f) Each seat or berth, and its supporting structure, and each safety belt or harness and its anchorage must be designed for an occupant weight of 170 pounds, considering the maximum load factors, inertia forces, and reactions among the occupant, seat, safety belt, and harness for each relevant flight and ground load condition (including the emergency landing conditions prescribed in § 25.561). In addition—

(1) The structural analysis and testing of the seats, berths, and their supporting structures may be determined by assuming that the critical load in the forward, sideward, downward, upward, and rearward directions (as determined from the prescribed flight, ground, and emergency landing conditions) acts separately or using selected combinations of loads if the required strength in each specified direction is substantiated. The forward load factor need not be applied to safety belts for berths.

(2) Each pilot seat must be designed for the reactions resulting from the application of the pilot forces prescribed in § 25.395.

(3) The inertia forces specified in § 25.561 must be multiplied by a factor of 1.33 (instead of the fitting factor prescribed in § 25.625) in determining the strength of the attachment of each seat to the structure and each belt or harness to the seat or structure.

(g) Each seat at a flight deck station must have a restraint system consisting of a combined safety belt and shoulder harness with a single-point release that permits the flight deck occupant, when seated with the restraint system fastened, to perform all of the occupant's necessary flight deck functions. There must be a means to secure each combined restraint system when not in use to prevent interference with the operation of the airplane and with rapid egress in an emergency.

(h) Each seat located in the passenger compartment and designated for use during takeoff and landing by a flight attendant required by the operating rules of this chapter must be:

(1) Near a required floor level emergency exit, except that another location is acceptable if the emergency egress of passengers would be enhanced with that location. A flight attendant seat must be located adjacent to each Type A or B emergency exit. Other flight attendant seats must be evenly distributed among the required floor-level emergency exits to the extent feasible.

(2) To the extent possible, without compromising proximity to a required floor level emergency exit, located to provide a direct view of the cabin area for which the flight attendant is responsible.

(3) Positioned so that the seat will not interfere with the use of a passageway or exit when the seat is not in use.

(4) Located to minimize the probability that occupants would suffer injury by being struck by items dislodged from service areas, stowage compartments, or service equipment.

(5) Either forward or rearward facing with an energy absorbing rest that is designed to support the arms, shoulders, head, and spine.

(6) Equipped with a restraint system consisting of a combined safety belt and shoulder harness unit with a single point release. There must be means to secure each restraint system when not in use to prevent interference with rapid egress in an emergency.

(i) Each safety belt must be equipped with a metal to metal latching device.

(j) If the seat backs do not provide a firm handhold, there must be a handgrip or rail along each aisle to enable persons to steady themselves while using the aisles in moderately rough air.

(k) Each projecting object that would injure persons seated or moving about the airplane in normal flight must be padded.

(l) Each forward observer's seat required by the operating rules must be shown to be suitable for use in conducting the necessary enroute inspection.

[Amdt. 25–72, 55 FR 29780, July 20, 1990, as amended by Amdt. 25–88, 61 FR 57956, Nov. 8, 1996]

§ 25.787 Stowage compartments.

(a) Each compartment for the stowage of cargo, baggage, carry-on articles, and equipment (such as life rafts), and any other stowage compartment must be designed for its placarded maximum weight of contents and for the critical load distribution at the appropriate maximum load factors corresponding to the specified flight and ground load conditions, and to the emergency landing conditions of § 25.561(b), except that the forces specified in the emergency landing conditions need not be applied to compartments located below, or forward, of all occupants in the airplane. If the airplane has a passenger seating configuration, excluding pilots seats, of 10 seats or more, each stowage compartment in the passenger cabin, except for underseat and overhead compartments for passenger convenience, must be completely enclosed.

(b) There must be a means to prevent the contents in the compartments from becoming a hazard by shifting, under the loads specified in paragraph (a) of this section. For stowage compartments in the passenger and crew cabin, if the means used is a latched door, the design must take into consideration the wear and deterioration expected in service.

(c) If cargo compartment lamps are installed, each lamp must be installed so as to prevent contact between lamp bulb and cargo.

[Doc. No. 5066, 29 FR 18291, Dec. 24, 1964, as amended by Amdt. 25–32, 37 FR 3969, Feb. 24, 1972; Amdt. 25–38, 41 FR 55466, Dec. 20, 1976; Amdt. 25–51, 45 FR 7755, Feb. 4, 1980]

§ 25.789 Retention of items of mass in passenger and crew compartments and galleys.

(a) Means must be provided to prevent each item of mass (that is part of the airplane type design) in a passenger or crew compartment or galley from becoming a hazard by shifting under the appropriate maximum load factors corresponding to the specified flight and ground load conditions, and to the emergency landing conditions of § 25.561(b).

(b) Each interphone restraint system must be designed so that when subjected to the load factors specified in § 25.561(b)(3), the interphone will remain in its stowed position.

[Amdt. 25–32, 37 FR 3969, Feb. 24, 1972, as amended by Amdt. 25–46, 43 FR 50596, Oct. 30, 1978]

§ 25.791 Passenger information signs and placards.

(a) If smoking is to be prohibited, there must be at least one placard so stating that is legible to each person seated in the cabin. If smoking is to be allowed, and if the crew compartment is separated from the passenger compartment, there must be at least one sign notifying when smoking is prohibited. Signs which notify when smoking is prohibited must be operable by a member of the flightcrew and, when illuminated, must be legible under all probable conditions of cabin illumination to each person seated in the cabin.

(b) Signs that notify when seat belts should be fastened and that are installed to comply with the operating rules of this chapter must be operable by a member of the flightcrew and, when illuminated, must be legible under all probable conditions of cabin illumination to each person seated in the cabin.

(c) A placard must be located on or adjacent to the door of each receptacle used for the disposal of flammable waste materials to indicate that use of the receptacle for disposal of cigarettes, etc., is prohibited.

(d) Lavatories must have "No Smoking" or "No Smoking in Lavatory" placards conspicuously located on or adjacent to each side of the entry door.

(e) Symbols that clearly express the intent of the sign or placard may be used in lieu of letters.

[Amdt. 25–72, 55 FR 29780, July 20, 1990]

§ 25.793 Floor surfaces.

The floor surface of all areas which are likely to become wet in service must have slip resistant properties.

[Amdt. 25–51, 45 FR 7755, Feb. 4, 1980]

§ 25.795 Security considerations.

(a) *Protection of flightdeck.* If a flightdeck door is required by operating rules, the door installation must be designed to:

(1) Resist forcible intrusion by unauthorized persons and be capable of withstanding impacts of 300 Joules (221.3 foot-pounds) at the critical locations on the door, as well as a 250 pound (1113 Newtons) constant tensile load on the knob or handle, and

(2) Resist penetration by small arms fire and fragmentation devices to a level equivalent to level IIIa of the National Institute of Justice Standard (NIJ) 0101.04.

(b) [Reserved]

[Doc. No. FAA–2001–11032, 67 FR 2127, Jan. 15, 2002]

EMERGENCY PROVISIONS

§ 25.801 Ditching.

(a) If certification with ditching provisions is requested, the airplane must meet the requirements of this section and §§ 25.807(e), 25.1411, and 25.1415(a).

(b) Each practicable design measure, compatible with the general characteristics of the airplane, must be taken to minimize the probability that in an emergency landing on water, the behavior of the airplane would cause immediate injury to the occupants or would make it impossible for them to escape.

(c) The probable behavior of the airplane in a water landing must be investigated by model tests or by comparison with airplanes of similar configuration for which the ditching characteristics are known. Scoops, flaps, projections, and any other factor likely to affect the hydrodynamic characteristics of the airplane, must be considered.

(d) It must be shown that, under reasonably probable water conditions, the flotation time and trim of the airplane will allow the occupants to leave the airplane and enter the liferafts required by § 25.1415. If compliance with this provision is shown by buoyancy and trim computations, appropriate allowances must be made for probable structural damage and leakage. If the airplane has fuel tanks (with fuel jettisoning provisions) that can reasonably be expected to withstand a ditching without leakage, the jettisonable volume of fuel may be considered as buoyancy volume.

(e) Unless the effects of the collapse of external doors and windows are accounted for in the investigation of the probable behavior of the airplane in a water landing (as prescribed in paragraphs (c) and (d) of this section), the external doors and windows must be designed to withstand the probable maximum local pressures.

[Doc. No. 5066, 29 FR 18291, Dec. 24, 1964, as amended by Amdt. 25–72, 55 FR 29781, July 20, 1990]

§ 25.803 Emergency evacuation.

(a) Each crew and passenger area must have emergency means to allow rapid evacuation in crash landings, with the landing gear extended as well as with the landing gear retracted, considering the possibility of the airplane being on fire.

(b) [Reserved]

(c) For airplanes having a seating capacity of more than 44 passengers, it must be shown that the maximum seating capacity, including the number of crewmembers required by the operating rules for which certification is requested, can be evacuated from the airplane to the ground under simulated emergency conditions within 90 seconds. Compliance with this requirement must be shown by actual demonstration using the test criteria outlined in appendix J of this part unless the Administrator finds that a combination of analysis and testing will provide data equivalent to that which would be obtained by actual demonstration.

(d)–(e) [Reserved]

[Doc. No. 24344, 55 FR 29781, July 20, 1990]

§ 25.807 Emergency exits.

(a) *Type.* For the purpose of this part, the types of exits are defined as follows:

(1) *Type I.* This type is a floor-level exit with a rectangular opening of not less than 24 inches wide by 48 inches high, with corner radii not greater than eight inches.

(2) *Type II.* This type is a rectangular opening of not less than 20 inches wide by 44 inches high, with corner radii not greater than seven inches. Type II exits must be floor-level exits unless located over the wing, in which case they must not have a step-up inside the airplane of more than 10 inches nor a step-down outside the airplane of more than 17 inches.

(3) *Type III.* This type is a rectangular opening of not less than 20 inches wide by 36 inches high with corner radii not greater than seven inches, and with a step-up inside the airplane of not more than 20 inches. If the exit is located over the wing, the step-down outside the airplane may not exceed 27 inches.

(4) *Type IV.* This type is a rectangular opening of not less than 19 inches wide by 26 inches high, with corner radii not greater than 6.3 inches, located over the wing, with a step-up inside the airplane of not more than 29 inches and a step-down outside the airplane of not more than 36 inches.

(5) *Ventral.* This type is an exit from the passenger compartment through the pressure shell and the bottom fuselage skin. The dimensions and physical configuration of this type of exit must allow at least the same rate of egress as a Type I exit with the airplane in the normal ground attitude, with landing gear extended.

(6) *Tailcone.* This type is an aft exit from the passenger compartment through the pressure shell and through an openable cone of the fuselage aft of the pressure shell. The means of opening the tailcone must be simple and obvious and must employ a single operation.

(7) *Type A.* This type is a floor-level exit with a rectangular opening of not less than 42 inches wide by 72 inches high, with corner radii not greater than seven inches.

(8) *Type B.* This type is a floor-level exit with a rectangular opening of not less than 32 inches wide by 72 inches high, with corner radii not greater than six inches.

(9) *Type C.* This type is a floor-level exit with a rectangular opening of not less than 30 inches wide by 48 inches high, with corner radii not greater than 10 inches.

(b) *Step down distance.* Step down distance, as used in this section, means the actual distance between the bottom of the required opening and a usable foot hold, extending out from the fuselage, that is large enough to be effective without searching by sight or feel.

(c) *Over-sized exits.* Openings larger than those specified in this section, whether or not of rectangular shape, may be used if the specified rectangular opening can be inscribed within the opening and the base of the inscribed rectangular opening meets the specified step-up and step-down heights.

(d) *Asymmetry.* Exits of an exit pair need not be diametrically opposite each other nor of the same size; however, the number of passenger seats permitted under paragraph (g) of this section is based on the smaller of the two exits.

(e) *Uniformity.* Exits must be distributed as uniformly as practical, taking into account passenger seat distribution.

(f) *Location.* (1) Each required passenger emergency exit must be accessible to the passengers and located where it will afford the most effective means of passenger evacuation.

(2) If only one floor-level exit per side is prescribed, and the airplane does not have a tailcone or ventral emergency exit, the floor-level exits must be in the rearward part of the passenger compartment unless another location affords a more effective means of passenger evacuation.

(3) If more than one floor-level exit per side is prescribed, and the airplane does not have a combination cargo and passenger configuration, at least one floor-level exit must be located in each side near each end of the cabin.

(4) For an airplane that is required to have more than one passenger emergency exit for each side of the fuselage, no passenger emergency exit shall be more than 60 feet from any adjacent passenger emergency exit on the same side of the same deck of the fuselage, as measured parallel to the airplane's longitudinal axis between the nearest exit edges.

(g) *Type and number required.* The maximum number of passenger seats permitted depends on the type and number of exits installed in each side of the fuselage. Except as further restricted in paragraphs (g)(1) through (g)(9) of this section, the maximum number of passenger seats permitted for each exit of a specific type installed in each side of the fuselage is as follows:

Type A	110
Type B	75
Type C	55
Type I	45
Type II	40
Type III	35
Type IV	9

(1) For a passenger seating configuration of 1 to 9 seats, there must be at least one Type IV or larger overwing exit in each side of the fuselage or, if overwing exits are not provided, at least one exit in each side that meets the minimum dimensions of a Type III exit.

(2) For a passenger seating configuration of more than 9 seats, each exit must be a Type III or larger exit.

(3) For a passenger seating configuration of 10 to 19 seats, there must be at least one Type III or larger exit in each side of the fuselage.

(4) For a passenger seating configuration of 20 to 40 seats, there must be at least two exits, one of which must be a Type II or larger exit, in each side of the fuselage.

(5) For a passenger seating configuration of 41 to 110 seats, there must be at least two exits, one of which must be a Type I or larger exit, in each side of the fuselage.

(6) For a passenger seating configuration of more than 110 seats, the emergency exits in each side of the fuselage must include at least two Type I or larger exits.

(7) The combined maximum number of passenger seats permitted for all Type III exits is 70, and the combined maximum number of passenger seats permitted for two Type III exits in each side of the fuselage that are separated by fewer than three passenger seat rows is 65.

(8) If a Type A, Type B, or Type C exit is installed, there must be at least two Type C or larger exits in each side of the fuselage.

(9) If a passenger ventral or tailcone exit is installed and that exit provides at least the same rate of egress as a Type III exit with the airplane in the most adverse exit opening condition that would result from the collapse of one or more legs of the landing gear, an increase in the passenger seating configuration is permitted as follows:

(i) For a ventral exit, 12 additional passenger seats.

(ii) For a tailcone exit incorporating a floor level opening of not less than 20 inches wide by 60 inches high, with corner radii not greater than seven inches, in the pressure shell and incorporating an approved assist means in accordance with §25.810(a), 25 additional passenger seats.

(iii) For a tailcone exit incorporating an opening in the pressure shell which is at least equivalent to a Type III emergency exit with respect to dimensions, step-up and step-down distance, and with the top of the opening not less than 56 inches from the passenger compartment floor, 15 additional passenger seats.

(h) *Excess exits.* Each emergency exit in the passenger compartment in excess of the minimum number of required emergency exits must meet the applicable requirements of §25.809 through §25.812, and must be readily accessible.

(i) *Ditching emergency exits for passengers.* Whether or not ditching certification is requested, ditching emergency exits must be provided in accordance with the following requirements, unless the emergency exits required by paragraph (g) of this section already meet them:

(1) For airplanes that have a passenger seating configuration of nine or fewer seats, excluding pilot seats, one exit above the waterline in each side of

the airplane, meeting at least the dimensions of a Type IV exit.

(2) For airplanes that have a passenger seating configuration of 10 of more seats, excluding pilot seats, one exit above the waterline in a side of the airplane, meeting at least the dimensions of a Type III exit for each unit (or part of a unit) of 35 passenger seats, but no less than two such exits in the passenger cabin, with one on each side of the airplane. The passenger seat/exit ratio may be increased through the use of larger exits, or other means, provided it is shown that the evacuation capability during ditching has been improved accordingly.

(3) If it is impractical to locate side exits above the waterline, the side exits must be replaced by an equal number of readily accessible overhead hatches of not less than the dimensions of a Type III exit, except that for airplanes with a passenger configuration of 35 or fewer seats, excluding pilot seats, the two required Type III side exits need be replaced by only one overhead hatch.

(j) *Flightcrew emergency exits.* For airplanes in which the proximity of passenger emergency exits to the flightcrew area does not offer a convenient and readily accessible means of evacuation of the flightcrew, and for all airplanes having a passenger seating capacity greater than 20, flightcrew exits shall be located in the flightcrew area. Such exits shall be of sufficient size and so located as to permit rapid evacuation by the crew. One exit shall be provided on each side of the airplane; or, alternatively, a top hatch shall be provided. Each exit must encompass an unobstructed rectangular opening of at least 19 by 20 inches unless satisfactory exit utility can be demonstrated by a typical crewmember.

[Amdt. 25–72, 55 FR 29781, July 20, 1990, as amended by Amdt. 25–88, 61 FR 57956, Nov. 8, 1996; 62 FR 1817, Jan. 13, 1997; Amdt. 25–94, 63 FR 8848, Feb. 23, 1998; 63 FR 12862, Mar. 16, 1998]

§25.809 Emergency exit arrangement.

(a) Each emergency exit, including a flight crew emergency exit, must be a movable door or hatch in the external walls of the fuselage, allowing unobstructed opening to the outside.

(b) Each emergency exit must be openable from the inside and the outside except that sliding window emergency exits in the flight crew area need not be openable from the outside if other approved exits are convenient and readily accessible to the flight crew area. Each emergency exit must be capable of being opened, when there is no fuselage deformation—

(1) With the airplane in the normal ground attitude and in each of the attitudes corresponding to collapse of one or more legs of the landing gear; and

(2) Within 10 seconds measured from the time when the opening means is actuated to the time when the exit is fully opened.

(c) The means of opening emergency exits must be simple and obvious and may not require exceptional effort. Internal exit-opening means involving sequence operations (such as operation of two handles or latches or the release of safety catches) may be used for flight crew emergency exits if it can be reasonably established that these means are simple and obvious to crewmembers trained in their use.

(d) If a single power-boost or single power-operated system is the primary system for operating more than one exit in an emergency, each exit must be capable of meeting the requirements of paragraph (b) of this section in the event of failure of the primary system. Manual operation of the exit (after failure of the primary system) is acceptable.

(e) Each emergency exit must be shown by tests, or by a combination of analysis and tests, to meet the requirements of paragraphs (b) and (c) of this section.

(f) There must be a means to lock each emergency exit and to safeguard against its opening in flight, either inadvertently by persons or as a result of mechanical failure. In addition, there must be a means for direct visual inspection of the locking mechanism by crewmembers to determine that each emergency exit, for which the initial opening movement is outward, is fully locked.

(g) There must be provisions to minimize the probability of jamming of the emergency exits resulting from fuselage deformation in a minor crash landing.

(h) When required by the operating rules for any large passenger-carrying turbojet-powered airplane, each ventral exit and tailcone exit must be—

(1) Designed and constructed so that it cannot be opened during flight; and

(2) Marked with a placard readable from a distance of 30 inches and installed at a conspicuous location near the means of opening the exit, stating that the exit has been designed and constructed so that it cannot be opened during flight.

[Doc. No. 5066, 29 FR 18291, Dec. 24, 1964, as amended by Amdt. 25–15, 32 FR 13264, Sept. 20, 1967; Amdt. 25–32, 37 FR 3970, Feb. 24, 1972; Amdt. 25–34, 37 FR 25355, Nov. 30, 1972; Amdt. 25–46, 43 FR 50597, Oct. 30, 1978; Amdt. 25–47, 44 FR 61325, Oct. 25, 1979; Amdt. 25–72, 55 FR 29782, July 20, 1990]

§ 25.810 Emergency egress assist means and escape routes.

(a) Each non over-wing Type A, Type B or Type C exit, and any other non over-wing landplane emergency exit more than 6 feet from the ground with the airplane on the ground and the landing gear extended, must have an approved means to assist the occupants in descending to the ground.

(1) The assisting means for each passenger emergency exit must be a self-supporting slide or equivalent; and, in the case of Type A or Type B exits, it must be capable of carrying simultaneously two parallel lines of evacuees. In addition, the assisting means must be designed to meet the following requirements—

(i) It must be automatically deployed and deployment must begin during the interval between the time the exit opening means is actuated from inside the airplane and the time the exit is fully opened. However, each passenger emergency exit which is also a passenger entrance door or a service door must be provided with means to prevent deployment of the assisting means when it is opened from either the inside or the outside under non-emergency conditions for normal use.

(ii) Except for assisting means installed at Type C exits, it must be automatically erected within 6 seconds after deployment is begun. Assisting means installed at Type C exits must be automatically erected within 10 seconds from the time the opening means of the exit is actuated.

(iii) It must be of such length after full deployment that the lower end is self-supporting on the ground and provides safe evacuation of occupants to the ground after collapse of one or more legs of the landing gear.

(iv) It must have the capability, in 25-knot winds directed from the most critical angle, to deploy and, with the assistance of only one person, to remain usable after full deployment to evacuate occupants safely to the ground.

(v) For each system installation (mockup or airplane installed), five consecutive deployment and inflation tests must be conducted (per exit) without failure, and at least three tests of each such five-test series must be conducted using a single representative sample of the device. The sample devices must be deployed and inflated by the system's primary means after being subjected to the inertia forces specified in § 25.561(b). If any part of the system fails or does not function properly during the required tests, the cause of the failure or malfunction must be corrected by positive means and after that, the full series of five consecutive deployment and inflation tests must be conducted without failure.

(2) The assisting means for flightcrew emergency exits may be a rope or any other means demonstrated to be suitable for the purpose. If the assisting means is a rope, or an approved device equivalent to a rope, it must be—

(i) Attached to the fuselage structure at or above the top of the emergency exit opening, or, for a device at a pilot's emergency exit window, at another approved location if the stowed device, or its attachment, would reduce the pilot's view in flight;

(ii) Able (with its attachment) to withstand a 400-pound static load.

(b) Assist means from the cabin to the wing are required for each type A or Type B exit located above the wing and having a stepdown unless the exit without an assist-means can be shown to have a rate of passenger egress at least equal to that of the same type of non over-wing exit. If an assist means is required, it must be automatically deployed and automatically erected concurrent with the opening of the exit. In the case of assist means installed at Type C exits, it must be self-supporting within 10 seconds from the time the opening means of the exits is actuated. For all other exit types, it must be self-supporting 6 seconds after deployment is begun.

(c) An escape route must be established from each overwing emergency exit, and (except for flap surfaces suitable as slides) covered with a slip resistant surface. Except where a means for channeling the flow of evacuees is provided—

(1) The escape route from each Type A or Type B passenger emergency exit, or any common escape route from two Type III passenger emergency exits, must be at least 42 inches wide; that from any other passenger emergency exit must be at least 24 inches wide; and

(2) The escape route surface must have a reflectance of at least 80 percent, and must be defined by markings with a surface-to-marking contrast ratio of at least 5:1.

(d) Means must be provided to assist evacuees to reach the ground for all Type C exits located over the wing and, if the place on the airplane structure at which the escape route required in paragraph (c) of this section terminates is more than 6 feet from the ground with the airplane on the ground and the landing gear extended, for all other exit types.

(1) If the escape route is over the flap, the height of the terminal edge must be measured with the flap in the takeoff or landing position, whichever is higher from the ground.

(2) The assisting means must be usable and self-supporting with one or more landing gear legs collapsed and under a 25-knot wind directed from the most critical angle.

(3) The assisting means provided for each escape route leading from a Type A or B emergency exit must be capable of carrying simultaneously two parallel lines of evacuees; and, the assisting means leading from any other exit type must be capable of carrying as

many parallel lines of evacuees as there are required escape routes.

(4) The assisting means provided for each escape route leading from a Type C exit must be automatically erected within 10 seconds from the time the opening means of the exit is actuated, and that provided for the escape route leading from any other exit type must be automatically erected within 10 seconds after actuation of the erection system.

[Amdt. 25–72, 55 FR 29782, July 20, 1990, as amended by Amdt. 25–88, 61 FR 57958, Nov. 8, 1996; 62 FR 1817, Jan. 13, 1997]

§ 25.811 Emergency exit marking.

(a) Each passenger emergency exit, its means of access, and its means of opening must be conspicuously marked.

(b) The identity and location of each passenger emergency exit must be recognizable from a distance equal to the width of the cabin.

(c) Means must be provided to assist the occupants in locating the exits in conditions of dense smoke.

(d) The location of each passenger emergency exit must be indicated by a sign visible to occupants approaching along the main passenger aisle (or aisles). There must be—

(1) A passenger emergency exit locator sign above the aisle (or aisles) near each passenger emergency exit, or at another overhead location if it is more practical because of low headroom, except that one sign may serve more than one exit if each exit can be seen readily from the sign;

(2) A passenger emergency exit marking sign next to each passenger emergency exit, except that one sign may serve two such exits if they both can be seen readily from the sign; and

(3) A sign on each bulkhead or divider that prevents fore and aft vision along the passenger cabin to indicate emergency exits beyond and obscured by the bulkhead or divider, except that if this is not possible the sign may be placed at another appropriate location.

(e) The location of the operating handle and instructions for opening exits from the inside of the airplane must be shown in the following manner:

(1) Each passenger emergency exit must have, on or near the exit, a marking that is readable from a distance of 30 inches.

(2) Each Type A, Type B, Type C or Type I passenger emergency exit operating handle must—

(i) Be self-illuminated with an initial brightness of at least 160 microlamberts; or

(ii) Be conspicuously located and well illuminated by the emergency lighting even in conditions of occupant crowding at the exit.

(3) [Reserved]

(4) Each Type A, Type B, Type C, Type I, or Type II passenger emergency exit with a locking mechanism released by rotary motion of the handle must be marked—

(i) With a red arrow, with a shaft at least three-fourths of an inch wide and a head twice the width of the shaft, extending along at least 70 degrees of arc at a radius approximately equal to three-fourths of the handle length.

(ii) So that the centerline of the exit handle is within ±1 inch of the projected point of the arrow when the handle has reached full travel and has released the locking mechanism, and

(iii) With the word "open" in red letters 1 inch high, placed horizontally near the head of the arrow.

(f) Each emergency exit that is required to be openable from the outside, and its means of opening, must be marked on the outside of the airplane. In addition, the following apply:

(1) The outside marking for each passenger emergency exit in the side of the fuselage must include a 2-inch colored band outlining the exit.

(2) Each outside marking including the band, must have color contrast to be readily distinguishable from the surrounding fuselage surface. The contrast must be such that if the reflectance of the darker color is 15 percent or less, the reflectance of the lighter color must be at least 45 percent. "Reflectance" is the ratio of the luminous flux reflected by a body to the luminous flux it receives. When the reflectance of the darker color is greater than 15 percent, at least a 30-percent difference between its reflectance and the reflectance of the lighter color must be provided.

(3) In the case of exists other than those in the side of the fuselage, such as ventral or tailcone exists, the external means of opening, including instructions if applicable, must be conspicuously marked in red, or bright chrome yellow if the background color is such that red is inconspicuous. When the opening means is located on only one side of the fuselage, a conspicuous marking to that effect must be provided on the other side.

(g) Each sign required by paragraph (d) of this section may use the word "exit" in its legend in place of the term "emergency exit".

[Amdt. 25–15, 32 FR 13264, Sept. 20, 1967, as amended by Amdt. 25–32, 37 FR 3970, Feb. 24, 1972; Amdt. 25–46, 43 FR 50597, Oct. 30, 1978; 43 FR 52495, Nov. 13, 1978; Amdt. 25–79, 58 FR 45229, Aug. 26, 1993; Amdt. 25–88, 61 FR 57958, Nov. 8, 1996]

§ 25.812 Emergency lighting.

(a) An emergency lighting system, independent of the main lighting system, must be installed. However, the sources of general cabin illumination may be common to both the emergency and the main lighting systems if the power supply to the emergency lighting system is independent of the power supply to the main lighting system. The emergency lighting system must include:

(1) Illuminated emergency exit marking and locating signs, sources of general cabin illumination, interior lighting in emergency exit areas, and floor proximity escape path marking.

(2) Exterior emergency lighting.

(b) Emergency exit signs—

(1) For airplanes that have a passenger seating configuration, excluding pilot seats, of 10 seats or more must meet the following requirements:

(i) Each passenger emergency exit locator sign required by § 25.811(d)(1) and each passenger emergency exit marking sign required by § 25.811(d)(2) must have red letters at least 1½ inches high on an illuminated white background, and must have an area of at least 21 square inches excluding the letters. The lighted background-to-letter contrast must be at least 10:1. The letter height to stroke-width ratio may not be more than 7:1 nor less than 6:1.

These signs must be internally electrically illuminated with a background brightness of at least 25 foot-lamberts and a high-to-low background contrast no greater than 3:1.

(ii) Each passenger emergency exit sign required by §25.811(d)(3) must have red letters at least 1½ inches high on a white background having an area of at least 21 square inches excluding the letters. These signs must be internally electrically illuminated or self-illuminated by other than electrical means and must have an initial brightness of at least 400 microlamberts. The colors may be reversed in the case of a sign that is self-illuminated by other than electrical means.

(2) For airplanes that have a passenger seating configuration, excluding pilot seats, of nine seats or less, that are required by §25.811(d)(1), (2), and (3) must have red letters at least 1 inch high on a white background at least 2 inches high. These signs may be internally electrically illuminated, or self-illuminated by other than electrical means, with an initial brightness of at least 160 microlamberts. The colors may be reversed in the case of a sign that is self-illuminated by other than electrical means.

(c) General illumination in the passenger cabin must be provided so that when measured along the centerline of main passenger aisle(s), and cross aisle(s) between main aisles, at seat arm-rest height and at 40-inch intervals, the average illumination is not less than 0.05 foot-candle and the illumination at each 40-inch interval is not less than 0.01 foot-candle. A main passenger aisle(s) is considered to extend along the fuselage from the most forward passenger emergency exit or cabin occupant seat, whichever is farther forward, to the most rearward passenger emergency exit or cabin occupant seat, whichever is farther aft.

(d) The floor of the passageway leading to each floor-level passenger emergency exit, between the main aisles and the exit openings, must be provided with illumination that is not less than 0.02 foot-candle measured along a line that is within 6 inches of and parallel to the floor and is centered on the passenger evacuation path.

(e) Floor proximity emergency escape path marking must provide emergency evacuation guidance for passengers when all sources of illumination more than 4 feet above the cabin aisle floor are totally obscured. In the dark of the night, the floor proximity emergency escape path marking must enable each passenger to—

(1) After leaving the passenger seat, visually identify the emergency escape path along the cabin aisle floor to the first exits or pair of exits forward and aft of the seat; and

(2) Readily identify each exit from the emergency escape path by reference only to markings and visual features not more than 4 feet above the cabin floor.

(f) Except for subsystems provided in accordance with paragraph (h) of this section that serve no more than one assist means, are independent of the airplane's main emergency lighting system, and are automatically activated when the assist means is erected, the emergency lighting system must be designed as follows.

(1) The lights must be operable manually from the flight crew station and from a point in the passenger compartment that is readily accessible to a normal flight attendant seat.

(2) There must be a flight crew warning light which illuminates when power is on in the airplane and the emergency lighting control device is not armed.

(3) The cockpit control device must have an "on," "off," and "armed" position so that when armed in the cockpit or turned on at either the cockpit or flight attendant station the lights will either light or remain lighted upon interruption (except an interruption caused by a transverse vertical separation of the fuselage during crash landing) of the airplane's normal electric power. There must be a means to safeguard against inadvertent operation of the control device from the "armed" or "on" positions.

(g) Exterior emergency lighting must be provided as follows:

(1) At each overwing emergency exit the illumination must be—

(i) Not less than 0.03 foot-candle (measured normal to the direction of the incident light) on a 2-square-foot area where an evacuee is likely to make his first step outside the cabin;

(ii) Not less than 0.05 foot-candle (measured normal to the direction of incident light) along the 30 percent of the slip-resistant portion of the escape route required in § 25.810(c) that is farthest from the exit for the minimum required width of the escape route; and

(iii) Not less than 0.03 foot-candle on the ground surface with the landing gear extended (measured normal to the direction of the incident light) where an evacuee using the established escape route would normally make first contact with the ground.

(2) At each non-overwing emergency exit not required by § 25.809(f) to have descent assist means the illumination must be not less than 0.03 foot-candle (measured normal to the direction of the incident light) on the ground surface with the landing gear extended where an evacuee is likely to make his first contact with the ground outside the cabin.

(h) The means required in § 25.809 (f)(1) and (h) to assist the occupants in descending to the ground must be illuminated so that the erected assist means is visible from the airplane.

(1) If the assist means is illuminated by exterior emergency lighting, it must provide illumination of not less than 0.03 foot-candle (measured normal to the direction of the incident light) at the ground end of the erected assist means where an evacuee using the established escape route would normally make first contact with the ground, with the airplane in each of the attitudes corresponding to the collapse of one or more legs of the landing gear.

(2) If the emergency lighting subsystem illuminating the assist means serves no other assist means, is independent of the airplane's main emergency lighting system, and is automatically activated when the assist means is erected, the lighting provisions—

(i) May not be adversely affected by stowage; and

(ii) Must provide illumination of not less than 0.03 foot-candle (measured normal to the direction of incident light) at the ground and of the erected assist means where an evacuee would normally make first contact with the

ground, with the airplane in each of the attitudes corresponding to the collapse of one or more legs of the landing gear.

(i) The energy supply to each emergency lighting unit must provide the required level of illumination for at least 10 minutes at the critical ambient conditions after emergency landing.

(j) If storage batteries are used as the energy supply for the emergency lighting system, they may be recharged from the airplane's main electric power system: *Provided*, That, the charging circuit is designed to preclude inadvertent battery discharge into charging circuit faults.

(k) Components of the emergency lighting system, including batteries, wiring relays, lamps, and switches must be capable of normal operation after having been subjected to the inertia forces listed in § 25.561(b).

(l) The emergency lighting system must be designed so that after any single transverse vertical separation of the fuselage during crash landing—

(1) Not more than 25 percent of all electrically illuminated emergency lights required by this section are rendered inoperative, in addition to the lights that are directly damaged by the separation;

(2) Each electrically illuminated exit sign required under § 25.811(d)(2) remains operative exclusive of those that are directly damaged by the separation; and

(3) At least one required exterior emergency light for each side of the airplane remains operative exclusive of those that are directly damaged by the separation.

[Amdt. 25–15, 32 FR 13265, Sept. 20, 1967, as amended by Amdt. 25–28, 36 FR 16899, Aug. 26, 1971; Amdt. 25–32, 37 FR 3971, Feb. 24, 1972; Amdt. 25–46, 43 FR 50597, Oct. 30, 1978; Amdt. 25–58, 49 FR 43186, Oct. 26, 1984; Amdt. 25–88, 61 FR 57958, Nov. 8, 1996]

§ 25.813 Emergency exit access.

Each required emergency exit must be accessible to the passengers and located where it will afford an effective means of evacuation. Emergency exit distribution must be as uniform as practical, taking passenger distribution into account; however, the size and location of exits on both sides of the cabin need not be symmetrical. If only one floor level exit per side is prescribed, and the airplane does not have a tailcone or ventral emergency exit, the floor level exit must be in the rearward part of the passenger compartment, unless another location affords a more effective means of passenger evacuation. Where more than one floor level exit per side is prescribed, at least one floor level exit per side must be located near each end of the cabin, except that this provision does not apply to combination cargo/passenger configurations. In addition—

(a) There must be a passageway leading from the nearest main aisle to each Type A, Type B, Type C, Type I, or Type II emergency exit and between individual passenger areas. Each passageway leading to a Type A or Type B exit must be unobstructed and at least 36 inches wide. Passageways between individual passenger areas and those leading to Type I, Type II, or Type C emergency exits must be unobstructed and at least 20 inches wide. Unless there are two or more main aisles, each Type A or B exit must be located so that there is passenger flow along the main aisle to that exit from both the forward and aft directions. If two or more main aisles are provided, there must be unobstructed cross-aisles at least 20 inches wide between main aisles. There must be—

(1) A cross-aisle which leads directly to each passageway between the nearest main aisle and a Type A or B exit; and

(2) A cross-aisle which leads to the immediate vicinity of each passageway between the nearest main aisle and a Type 1, Type II, or Type III exit; except that when two Type III exits are located within three passenger rows of each other, a single cross-aisle may be used if it leads to the vicinity between the passageways from the nearest main aisle to each exit.

(b) Adequate space to allow crewmember(s) to assist in the evacuation of passengers must be provided as follows:

(1) The assist space must not reduce the unobstructed width of the passageway below that required for the exit.

(2) For each Type A or Type B exit, assist space must be provided at each

side of the exit regardless of whether a means is required by §25.810(a) to assist passengers in descending to the ground from that exit.

(3) Assist space must be provided at one side of any other type exit required by §25.810(a) to have a means to assist passengers in descending to the ground from that exit.

(c) The following must be provided for each Type III or Type IV exit—(1) There must be access from the nearest aisle to each exit. In addition, for each Type III exit in an airplane that has a passenger seating configuration of 60 or more—

(i) Except as provided in paragraph (c)(1)(ii), the access must be provided by an unobstructed passageway that is at least 10 inches in width for interior arrangements in which the adjacent seat rows on the exit side of the aisle contain no more than two seats, or 20 inches in width for interior arrangements in which those rows contain three seats. The width of the passageway must be measured with adjacent seats adjusted to their most adverse position. The centerline of the required passageway width must not be displaced more than 5 inches horizontally from that of the exit.

(ii) In lieu of one 10- or 20-inch passageway, there may be two passageways, between seat rows only, that must be at least 6 inches in width and lead to an unobstructed space adjacent to each exit. (Adjacent exits must not share a common passageway.) The width of the passageways must be measured with adjacent seats adjusted to their most adverse position. The unobstructed space adjacent to the exit must extend vertically from the floor to the ceiling (or bottom of sidewall stowage bins), inboard from the exit for a distance not less than the width of the narrowest passenger seat installed on the airplane, and from the forward edge of the forward passageway to the aft edge of the aft passageway. The exit opening must be totally within the fore and aft bounds of the unobstructed space.

(2) In addition to the access—

(i) For airplanes that have a passenger seating configuration of 20 or more, the projected opening of the exit provided must not be obstructed and there must be no interference in opening the exit by seats, berths, or other protrusions (including any seatback in the most adverse position) for a distance from that exit not less than the width of the narrowest passenger seat installed on the airplane.

(ii) For airplanes that have a passenger seating configuration of 19 or fewer, there may be minor obstructions in this region, if there are compensating factors to maintain the effectiveness of the exit.

(3) For each Type III exit, regardless of the passenger capacity of the airplane in which it is installed, there must be placards that—

(i) Are readable by all persons seated adjacent to and facing a passageway to the exit;

(ii) Accurately state or illustrate the proper method of opening the exit, including the use of handholds; and

(iii) If the exit is a removable hatch, state the weight of the hatch and indicate an appropriate location to place the hatch after removal.

(d) If it is necessary to pass through a passageway between passenger compartments to reach any required emergency exit from any seat in the passenger cabin, the passageway must be unobstructed. However, curtains may be used if they allow free entry through the passageway.

(e) No door may be installed in any partition between passenger compartments.

(f) If it is necessary to pass through a doorway separating the passenger cabin from other areas to reach any required emergency exit from any passenger seat, the door must have a means to latch it in open position. The latching means must be able to withstand the loads imposed upon it when the door is subjected to the ultimate inertia forces, relative to the surrounding structure, listed in § 25.561(b).

[Amdt. 25–1, 30 FR 3204, Mar. 9, 1965, as amended by Amdt. 25–15, 32 FR 13265, Sept. 20, 1967; Amdt. 25–32, 37 FR 3971, Feb. 24, 1972; Amdt. 25–46, 43 FR 50597, Oct. 30, 1978; Amdt. 25–72, 55 FR 29783, July 20, 1990; Amdt. 25–76, 57 FR 19244, May 4, 1992; Amdt. 25–76, 57 FR 29120, June 30, 1992; Amdt. 25–88, 61 FR 57958, Nov. 8, 1996]

§ 25.815 Width of aisle.

The passenger aisle width at any point between seats must equal or exceed the values in the following table:

Passenger seating capacity	Minimum passenger aisle width (inches)	
	Less than 25 in. from floor	25 in. and more from floor
10 or less	[1] 12	15
11 through 19	12	20
20 or more	15	20

[1] A narrower width not less than 9 inches may be approved when substantiated by tests found necessary by the Administrator.

[Amdt. 25–15, 32 FR 13265, Sept. 20, 1967, as amended by Amdt. 25–38, 41 FR 55466, Dec. 20, 1976]

§ 25.817 Maximum number of seats abreast.

On airplanes having only one passenger aisle, no more than three seats abreast may be placed on each side of the aisle in any one row.

[Amdt. 25–15, 32 FR 13265, Sept. 20, 1967]

§ 25.819 Lower deck service compartments (including galleys).

For airplanes with a service compartment located below the main deck, which may be occupied during taxi or flight but not during takeoff or landing, the following apply:

(a) There must be at least two emergency evacuation routes, one at each end of each lower deck service compartment or two having sufficient separation within each compartment, which could be used by each occupant of the lower deck service compartment to rapidly evacuate to the main deck under normal and emergency lighting conditions. The routes must provide for the evacuation of incapacitated persons, with assistance. The use of the evacuation routes may not be dependent on any powered device. The routes must be designed to minimize the possibility of blockage which might result from fire, mechanical or structural failure, or persons standing on top of or against the escape routes. In the event the airplane's main power system or compartment main lighting system should fail, emergency illumination for each lower deck service compartment must be automatically provided.

(b) There must be a means for two-way voice communication between the flight deck and each lower deck service compartment.

(c) There must be an aural emergency alarm system, audible during normal and emergency conditions, to enable crewmembers on the flight deck and at each required floor level emergency exit to alert occupants of each lower deck service compartment of an emergency situation.

(d) There must be a means, readily detectable by occupants of each lower deck service compartment, that indicates when seat belts should be fastened.

(e) If a public address system is installed in the airplane, speakers must be provided in each lower deck service compartment.

(f) For each occupant permitted in a lower deck service compartment, there must be a forward or aft facing seat which meets the requirements of §25.785(c) and must be able to withstand maximum flight loads when occupied.

(g) For each powered lift system installed between a lower deck service compartment and the main deck for the carriage of persons or equipment, or both, the system must meet the following requirements:

(1) Each lift control switch outside the lift, except emergency stop buttons, must be designed to prevent the activation of the life if the lift door, or the hatch required by paragraph (g)(3) of this section, or both are open.

(2) An emergency stop button, that when activated will immediately stop the lift, must be installed within the lift and at each entrance to the lift.

(3) There must be a hatch capable of being used for evacuating persons from the lift that is openable from inside and outside the lift without tools, with the lift in any position.

[Amdt. 25–53, 45 FR 41593, June 19, 1980; 45 FR 43154, June 26, 1980]

VENTILATION AND HEATING

§25.831 Ventilation.

(a) Under normal operating conditions and in the event of any probable failure conditions of any system which would adversely affect the ventilating air, the ventilation system must be designed to provide a sufficient amount of uncontaminated air to enable the crewmembers to perform their duties without undue discomfort or fatigue and to provide reasonable passenger comfort. For normal operating conditions, the ventilation system must be designed to provide each occupant with an airflow containing at least 0.55 pounds of fresh air per minute.

(b) Crew and passenger compartment air must be free from harmful or hazardous concentrations of gases or vapors. In meeting this requirement, the following apply:

(1) Carbon monoxide concentrations in excess of 1 part in 20,000 parts of air are considered hazardous. For test purposes, any acceptable carbon monoxide detection method may be used.

(2) Carbon dioxide concentration during flight must be shown not to exceed 0.5 percent by volume (sea level equivalent) in compartments normally occupied by passengers or crewmembers.

(c) There must be provisions made to ensure that the conditions prescribed in paragraph (b) of this section are met after reasonably probable failures or malfunctioning of the ventilating, heating, pressurization, or other systems and equipment.

(d) If accumulation of hazardous quantities of smoke in the cockpit area is reasonably probable, smoke evacuation must be readily accomplished, starting with full pressurization and without depressurizing beyond safe limits.

(e) Except as provided in paragraph (f) of this section, means must be provided to enable the occupants of the following compartments and areas to control the temperature and quantity of ventilating air supplied to their compartment or area independently of the temperature and quantity of air supplied to other compartments and areas:

(1) The flight crew compartment.

(2) Crewmember compartments and areas other than the flight crew compartment unless the crewmember compartment or area is ventilated by air interchange with other compartments or areas under all operating conditions.

(f) Means to enable the flight crew to control the temperature and quantity of ventilating air supplied to the flight crew compartment independently of the temperature and quantity of ventilating air supplied to other compartments are not required if all of the following conditions are met:

(1) The total volume of the flight crew and passenger compartments is 800 cubic feet or less.

(2) The air inlets and passages for air to flow between flight crew and passenger compartments are arranged to provide compartment temperatures within 5 degrees F. of each other and adequate ventilation to occupants in both compartments.

(3) The temperature and ventilation controls are accessible to the flight crew.

(g) The exposure time at any given temperature must not exceed the values shown in the following graph after any improbable failure condition.

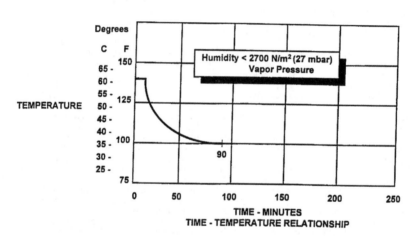

TIME - TEMPERATURE RELATIONSHIP

[Doc. No. 5066, 29 FR 18291, Dec. 24, 1964, as amended by Amdt. 25–41, 42 FR 36970, July 18, 1977; Amdt. 25–87, 61 FR 28695, June 5, 1996; Amdt. 25–89, 61 FR 63956, Dec. 2, 1996]

§ 25.832 Cabin ozone concentration.

(a) The airplane cabin ozone concentration during flight must be shown not to exceed—

(1) 0.25 parts per million by volume, sea level equivalent, at any time above flight level 320; and

(2) 0.1 parts per million by volume, sea level equivalent, time-weighted average during any 3-hour interval above flight level 270.

(b) For the purpose of this section, "sea level equivalent" refers to conditions of 25 °C and 760 millimeters of mercury pressure.

(c) Compliance with this section must be shown by analysis or tests based on airplane operational procedures and performance limitations, that demonstrate that either—

(1) The airplane cannot be operated at an altitude which would result in cabin ozone concentrations exceeding the limits prescribed by paragraph (a) of this section; or

(2) The airplane ventilation system, including any ozone control equipment, will maintain cabin ozone concentrations at or below the limits prescribed by paragraph (a) of this section.

[Amdt. 25–50, 45 FR 3883, Jan. 1, 1980, as amended by Amdt. 25–56, 47 FR 58489, Dec. 30, 1982; Amdt. 25–94, 63 FR 8848, Feb. 23, 1998]

§ 25.833 Combustion heating systems.

Combustion heaters must be approved.

[Amdt. 25–72, 55 FR 29783, July 20, 1990]

PRESSURIZATION

§ 25.841 Pressurized cabins.

(a) Pressurized cabins and compartments to be occupied must be equipped to provide a cabin pressure altitude of not more than 8,000 feet at the maximum operating altitude of the airplane under normal operating conditions.

(1) If certification for operation above 25,000 feet is requested, the airplane must be designed so that occupants will not be exposed to cabin pressure altitudes in excess of 15,000 feet after any probable failure condition in the pressurization system.

(2) The airplane must be designed so that occupants will not be exposed to a cabin pressure altitude that exceeds the following after decompression from any failure condition not shown to be extremely improbable:

(i) Twenty-five thousand (25,000) feet for more than 2 minutes; or

(ii) Forty thousand (40,000) feet for any duration.

(3) Fuselage structure, engine and system failures are to be considered in evaluating the cabin decompression.

(b) Pressurized cabins must have at least the following valves, controls, and indicators for controlling cabin pressure:

(1) Two pressure relief valves to automatically limit the positive pressure differential to a predetermined value at the maximum rate of flow delivered by the pressure source. The combined capacity of the relief valves must be large enough so that the failure of any one valve would not cause an appreciable rise in the pressure differential. The pressure differential is positive when the internal pressure is greater than the external.

(2) Two reverse pressure differential relief valves (or their equivalents) to automatically prevent a negative pressure differential that would damage the structure. One valve is enough, however, if it is of a design that reasonably precludes its malfunctioning.

(3) A means by which the pressure differential can be rapidly equalized.

(4) An automatic or manual regulator for controlling the intake or exhaust airflow, or both, for maintaining the required internal pressures and airflow rates.

(5) Instruments at the pilot or flight engineer station to show the pressure differential, the cabin pressure altitude, and the rate of change of the cabin pressure altitude.

(6) Warning indication at the pilot or flight engineer station to indicate when the safe or preset pressure differential and cabin pressure altitude limits are exceeded. Appropriate warning markings on the cabin pressure differential indicator meet the warning requirement for pressure differential limits and an aural or visual signal (in addition to cabin altitude indicating means) meets the warning requirement for cabin pressure altitude limits if it warns the flight crew when the cabin pressure altitude exceeds 10,000 feet.

(7) A warning placard at the pilot or flight engineer station if the structure is not designed for pressure differentials up to the maximum relief valve setting in combination with landing loads.

(8) The pressure sensors necessary to meet the requirements of paragraphs (b)(5) and (b)(6) of this section and § 25.1447(c), must be located and the sensing system designed so that, in the event of loss of cabin pressure in any passenger or crew compartment (including upper and lower lobe galleys), the warning and automatic presentation devices, required by those provisions, will be actuated without any delay that would significantly increase the hazards resulting from decompression.

[Doc. No. 5066, 29 FR 18291, Dec. 24, 1964, as amended by Amdt. 25–38, 41 FR 55466, Dec. 20, 1976; Amdt. 25–87, 61 FR 28696, June 5, 1996]

§ 25.843 Tests for pressurized cabins.

(a) *Strength test.* The complete pressurized cabin, including doors, windows, and valves, must be tested as a pressure vessel for the pressure differential specified in § 25.365(d).

(b) *Functional tests.* The following functional tests must be performed:

(1) Tests of the functioning and capacity of the positive and negative pressure differential valves, and of the emergency release valve, to stimulate the effects of closed regulator valves.

(2) Tests of the pressurization system to show proper functioning under each possible condition of pressure, temperature, and moisture, up to the maximum altitude for which certification is requested.

(3) Flight tests, to show the performance of the pressure supply, pressure and flow regulators, indicators, and warning signals, in steady and stepped climbs and descents at rates corresponding to the maximum attainable within the operating limitations of the airplane, up to the maximum altitude for which certification is requested.

(4) Tests of each door and emergency exit, to show that they operate properly after being subjected to the flight tests prescribed in paragraph (b)(3) of this section.

FIRE PROTECTION

§ 25.851 Fire extinguishers.

(a) *Hand fire extinguishers.* (1) The following minimum number of hand fire extinguishers must be conveniently located and evenly distributed in passenger compartments:

Passenger capacity	No. of extinguishers
7 through 30	1
31 through 60	2
61 through 200	3
201 through 300	4
301 through 400	5
401 through 500	6
501 through 600	7
601 through 700	8

(2) At least one hand fire extinguisher must be conveniently located in the pilot compartment.

(3) At least one readily accessible hand fire extinguisher must be available for use in each Class A or Class B cargo or baggage compartment and in each Class E cargo or baggage compartment that is accessible to crewmembers in flight.

(4) At least one hand fire extinguisher must be located in, or readily accessible for use in, each galley located above or below the passenger compartment.

(5) Each hand fire extinguisher must be approved.

(6) At least one of the required fire extinguishers located in the passenger compartment of an airplane with a passenger capacity of at least 31 and not more than 60, and at least two of the fire extinguishers located in the passenger compartment of an airplane with a passenger capacity of 61 or more must contain Halon 1211 (bromochlorodifluoromethane $CBrC_1 F_2$), or equivalent, as the extinguishing agent. The type of extinguishing agent used in any other extinguisher required by this section must be appropriate for the kinds of fires likely to occur where used.

(7) The quantity of extinguishing agent used in each extinguisher required by this section must be appropriate for the kinds of fires likely to occur where used.

(8) Each extinguisher intended for use in a personnel compartment must be designed to minimize the hazard of toxic gas concentration.

(b) *Built-in fire extinguishers.* If a built-in fire extinguisher is provided—

(1) Each built-in fire extinguishing system must be installed so that—

(i) No extinguishing agent likely to enter personnel compartments will be hazardous to the occupants; and

(ii) No discharge of the extinguisher can cause structural damage.

(2) The capacity of each required built-in fire extinguishing system must be adequate for any fire likely to occur in the compartment where used, considering the volume of the compartment and the ventilation rate.

[Amdt. 25–74, 56 FR 15456, Apr. 16, 1991]

§ 25.853 Compartment interiors.

For each compartment occupied by the crew or passengers, the following apply:

(a) Materials (including finishes or decorative surfaces applied to the materials) must meet the applicable test criteria prescribed in part I of appendix F of this part, or other approved equivalent methods, regardless of the passenger capacity of the airplane.

(b) [Reserved]

(c) In addition to meeting the requirements of paragraph (a) of this section, seat cushions, except those on flight crewmember seats, must meet the test requirements of part II of appendix F of this part, or other equivalent methods, regardless of the passenger capacity of the airplane.

(d) Except as provided in paragraph (e) of this section, the following interior components of airplanes with passenger capacities of 20 or more must also meet the test requirements of parts IV and V of appendix F of this part, or other approved equivalent method, in addition to the flammability requirements prescribed in paragraph (a) of this section:

(1) Interior ceiling and wall panels, other than lighting lenses and windows;

(2) Partitions, other than transparent panels needed to enhance cabin safety;

(3) Galley structure, including exposed surfaces of stowed carts and standard containers and the cavity walls that are exposed when a full complement of such carts or containers is not carried; and

(4) Large cabinets and cabin stowage compartments, other than underseat stowage compartments for stowing small items such as magazines and maps.

(e) The interiors of compartments, such as pilot compartments, galleys, lavatories, crew rest quarters, cabinets and stowage compartments, need not meet the standards of paragraph (d) of this section, provided the interiors of such compartments are isolated from the main passenger cabin by doors or equivalent means that would normally be closed during an emergency landing condition.

(f) Smoking is not to be allowed in lavatories. If smoking is to be allowed in any other compartment occupied by the crew or passengers, an adequate number of self-contained, removable ashtrays must be provided for all seated occupants.

(g) Regardless of whether smoking is allowed in any other part of the airplane, lavatories must have self-contained, removable ashtrays located conspicuously on or near the entry side of each lavatory door, except that one ashtray may serve more than one lavatory door if the ashtray can be seen readily from the cabin side of each lavatory served.

(h) Each receptacle used for the disposal of flammable waste material must be fully enclosed, constructed of at least fire resistant materials, and must contain fires likely to occur in it

under normal use. The capability of the receptacle to contain those fires under all probable conditions of wear, misalignment, and ventilation expected in service must be demonstrated by test.

[Amdt. 25–83, 60 FR 6623, Feb. 2, 1995]

§ 25.854 Lavatory fire protection.

For airplanes with a passenger capacity of 20 or more:

(a) Each lavatory must be equipped with a smoke detector system or equivalent that provides a warning light in the cockpit, or provides a warning light or audible warning in the passenger cabin that would be readily detected by a flight attendant; and

(b) Each lavatory must be equipped with a built-in fire extinguisher for each disposal receptacle for towels, paper, or waste, located within the lavatory. The extinguisher must be designed to discharge automatically into each disposal receptacle upon occurrence of a fire in that receptacle.

[Amdt. 25–74, 56 FR 15456, Apr. 16, 1991]

§ 25.855 Cargo or baggage compartments.

For each cargo and baggage compartment not occupied by crew or passengers, the following apply:

(a) The compartment must meet one of the class requirements of § 25.857.

(b) Class B through Class E cargo or baggage compartments, as defined in § 25.857, must have a liner, and the liner must be separate from (but may be attached to) the airplane structure.

(c) Ceiling and sidewall liner panels of Class C compartments must meet the test requirements of part III of appendix F of this part or other approved equivalent methods.

(d) All other materials used in the construction of the cargo or baggage compartment must meet the applicable test criteria prescribed in part I of appendix F of this part or other approved equivalent methods.

(e) No compartment may contain any controls, wiring, lines, equipment, or accessories whose damage or failure would affect safe operation, unless those items are protected so that—

(1) They cannot be damaged by the movement of cargo in the compartment, and

(2) Their breakage or failure will not create a fire hazard.

(f) There must be means to prevent cargo or baggage from interfering with the functioning of the fire protective features of the compartment.

(g) Sources of heat within the compartment must be shielded and insulated to prevent igniting the cargo or baggage.

(h) Flight tests must be conducted to show compliance with the provisions of § 25.857 concerning—

(1) Compartment accessibility,

(2) The entries of hazardous quantities of smoke or extinguishing agent into compartments occupied by the crew or passengers, and

(3) The dissipation of the extinguishing agent in Class C compartments.

(i) During the above tests, it must be shown that no inadvertent operation of smoke or fire detectors in any compartment would occur as a result of fire contained in any other compartment, either during or after extinguishment, unless the extinguishing system floods each such compartment simultaneously.

[Amdt. 25–72, 55 FR 29784, July 20, 1990, as amended by Amdt. 25–93, 63 FR 8048, Feb. 17, 1998]

§ 25.857 Cargo compartment classification.

(a) *Class A;* A Class A cargo or baggage compartment is one in which—

(1) The presence of a fire would be easily discovered by a crewmember while at his station; and

(2) Each part of the compartment is easily accessible in flight.

(b) *Class B.* A Class B cargo or baggage compartment is one in which—

(1) There is sufficient access in flight to enable a crewmember to effectively reach any part of the compartment with the contents of a hand fire extinguisher;

(2) When the access provisions are being used, no hazardous quantity of smoke, flames, or extinguishing agent, will enter any compartment occupied by the crew or passengers;

(3) There is a separate approved smoke detector or fire detector system to give warning at the pilot or flight engineer station.

(c) *Class C.* A Class C cargo or baggage compartment is one not meeting the requirements for either a Class A or B compartment but in which—

(1) There is a separate approved smoke detector or fire detector system to give warning at the pilot or flight engineer station;

(2) There is an approved built-in fire extinguishing or suppression system controllable from the cockpit.

(3) There are means to exclude hazardous quantities of smoke, flames, or extinguishing agent, from any compartment occupied by the crew or passengers;

(4) There are means to control ventilation and drafts within the compartment so that the extinguishing agent used can control any fire that may start within the compartment.

(d) [Reserved]

(e) *Class E.* A Class E cargo compartment is one on airplanes used only for the carriage of cargo and in which—

(1) [Reserved]

(2) There is a separate approved smoke or fire detector system to give warning at the pilot or flight engineer station;

(3) There are means to shut off the ventilating airflow to, or within, the compartment, and the controls for these means are accessible to the flight crew in the crew compartment;

(4) There are means to exclude hazardous quantities of smoke, flames, or noxious gases, from the flight crew compartment; and

(5) The required crew emergency exits are accessible under any cargo loading condition.

[Doc. No. 5066, 29 FR 18291, Dec. 24, 1964, as amended by Amdt. 25–32, 37 FR 3972, Feb. 24, 1972; Amdt. 25–60, 51 FR 18243, May 16, 1986; Amdt. 25–93, 63 FR 8048, Feb. 17, 1998]

§ 25.858 Cargo or baggage compartment smoke or fire detection systems.

If certification with cargo or baggage compartment smoke or fire detection provisions is requested, the following must be met for each cargo or baggage compartment with those provisions:

(a) The detection system must provide a visual indication to the flight crew within one minute after the start of a fire.

(b) The system must be capable of detecting a fire at a temperature significantly below that at which the structural integrity of the airplane is substantially decreased.

(c) There must be means to allow the crew to check in flight, the functioning of each fire detector circuit.

(d) The effectiveness of the detection system must be shown for all approved operating configurations and conditions.

[Amdt. 25–54, 45 FR 60173, Sept. 11, 1980, as amended by Amdt. 25–93, 63 FR 8048, Feb. 17, 1998]

§ 25.859 Combustion heater fire protection.

(a) *Combustion heater fire zones.* The following combustion heater fire zones must be protected from fire in accordance with the applicable provisions of §§ 25.1181 through 25.1191 and §§ 25.1195 through 25.1203;

(1) The region surrounding the heater, if this region contains any flammable fluid system components (excluding the heater fuel system), that could—

(i) Be damaged by heater malfunctioning; or

(ii) Allow flammable fluids or vapors to reach the heater in case of leakage.

(2) The region surrounding the heater, if the heater fuel system has fittings that, if they leaked, would allow fuel or vapors to enter this region.

(3) The part of the ventilating air passage that surrounds the combustion chamber. However, no fire extinguishment is required in cabin ventilating air passages.

(b) *Ventilating air ducts.* Each ventilating air duct passing through any fire zone must be fireproof. In addition—

(1) Unless isolation is provided by fireproof valves or by equally effective means, the ventilating air duct downstream of each heater must be fireproof for a distance great enough to ensure that any fire originating in the heater can be contained in the duct; and

(2) Each part of any ventilating duct passing through any region having a flammable fluid system must be constructed or isolated from that system so that the malfunctioning of any component of that system cannot introduce flammable fluids or vapors into the ventilating airstream.

(c) *Combustion air ducts.* Each combustion air duct must be fireproof for a distance great enough to prevent damage from backfiring or reverse flame propagation. In addition—

(1) No combustion air duct may have a common opening with the ventilating airstream unless flames from backfires or reverse burning cannot enter the ventilating airstream under any operating condition, including reverse flow or malfunctioning of the heater or its associated components; and

(2) No combustion air duct may restrict the prompt relief of any backfire that, if so restricted, could cause heater failure.

(d) *Heater controls; general.* Provision must be made to prevent the hazardous accumulation of water or ice on or in any heater control component, control system tubing, or safety control.

(e) *Heater safety controls.* For each combustion heater there must be the following safety control means:

(1) Means independent of the components provided for the normal continuous control of air temperature, airflow, and fuel flow must be provided, for each heater, to automatically shut off the ignition and fuel supply to that heater at a point remote from that heater when any of the following occurs:

(i) The heat exchanger temperature exceeds safe limits.

(ii) The ventilating air temperature exceeds safe limits.

(iii) The combustion airflow becomes inadequate for safe operation.

(iv) The ventilating airflow becomes inadequate for safe operation.

(2) The means of complying with paragraph (e)(1) of this section for any individual heater must—

(i) Be independent of components serving any other heater whose heat output is essential for safe operation; and

(ii) Keep the heater off until restarted by the crew.

(3) There must be means to warn the crew when any heater whose heat output is essential for safe operation has been shut off by the automatic means prescribed in paragraph (e)(1) of this section.

(f) *Air intakes.* Each combustion and ventilating air intake must be located so that no flammable fluids or vapors can enter the heater system under any operating condition—

(1) During normal operation; or

(2) As a result of the malfunctioning of any other component.

(g) *Heater exhaust.* Heater exhaust systems must meet the provisions of §§ 25.1121 and 25.1123. In addition, there must be provisions in the design of the heater exhaust system to safely expel the products of combustion to prevent the occurrence of—

(1) Fuel leakage from the exhaust to surrounding compartments;

(2) Exhaust gas impingement on surrounding equipment or structure;

(3) Ignition of flammable fluids by the exhaust, if the exhaust is in a compartment containing flammable fluid lines; and

(4) Restriction by the exhaust of the prompt relief of backfires that, if so restricted, could cause heater failure.

(h) *Heater fuel systems.* Each heater fuel system must meet each power-plant fuel system requirement affecting safe heater operation. Each heater fuel system component within the ventilating airstream must be protected by shrouds so that no leakage from those components can enter the ventilating airstream.

(i) *Drains.* There must be means to safely drain fuel that might accumulate within the combustion chamber or the heat exchanger. In addition—

(1) Each part of any drain that operates at high temperatures must be protected in the same manner as heater exhausts; and

(2) Each drain must be protected from hazardous ice accumulation under any operating condition.

[Doc. No. 5066, 29 FR 18291, Dec. 24 1964, as amended by Amdt. 25–11, 32 FR 6912, May 5, 1967; Amdt. 25–23, 35 FR 5676, Apr. 8, 1970]

§ 25.863 Flammable fluid fire protection.

(a) In each area where flammable fluids or vapors might escape by leakage of a fluid system, there must be means to minimize the probability of ignition of the fluids and vapors, and the resultant hazards if ignition does occur.

(b) Compliance with paragraph (a) of this section must be shown by analysis or tests, and the following factors must be considered:

(1) Possible sources and paths of fluid leakage, and means of detecting leakage.

(2) Flammability characteristics of fluids, including effects of any combustible or absorbing materials.

(3) Possible ignition sources, including electrical faults, overheating of equipment, and malfunctioning of protective devices.

(4) Means available for controlling or extinguishing a fire, such as stopping flow of fluids, shutting down equipment, fireproof containment, or use of extinguishing agents.

(5) Ability of airplane components that are critical to safety of flight to withstand fire and heat.

(c) If action by the flight crew is required to prevent or counteract a fluid fire (e.g., equipment shutdown or actuation of a fire extinguisher) quick acting means must be provided to alert the crew.

(d) Each area where flammable fluids or vapors might escape by leakage of a fluid system must be identified and defined.

[Amdt. 25–23, 35 FR 5676, Apr. 8, 1970, as amended by Amdt. 25–46, 43 FR 50597, Oct. 30, 1978]

§ 25.865 Fire protection of flight controls, engine mounts, and other flight structure.

Essential flight controls, engine mounts, and other flight structures located in designated fire zones or in adjacent areas which would be subjected to the effects of fire in the fire zone must be constructed of fireproof material or shielded so that they are capable of withstanding the effects of fire.

[Amdt. 25–23, 35 FR 5676, Apr. 8, 1970]

§ 25.867 Fire protection: other components.

(a) Surfaces to the rear of the nacelles, within one nacelle diameter of the nacelle centerline, must be at least fire-resistant.

(b) Paragraph (a) of this section does not apply to tail surfaces to the rear of the nacelles that could not be readily affected by heat, flames, or sparks coming from a designated fire zone or engine compartment of any nacelle.

[Amdt. 25–23, 35 FR 5676, Apr. 8, 1970]

§ 25.869 Fire protection: systems.

(a) Electrical system components:

(1) Components of the electrical system must meet the applicable fire and smoke protection requirements of §§ 25.831(c) and 25.863.

(2) Electrical cables, terminals, and equipment in designated fire zones, that are used during emergency procedures, must be at least fire resistant.

(3) Main power cables (including generator cables) in the fuselage must be designed to allow a reasonable degree of deformation and stretching without failure and must be—

(i) Isolated from flammable fluid lines; or

(ii) Shrouded by means of electrically insulated, flexible conduit, or equivalent, which is in addition to the normal cable insulation.

(4) Insulation on electrical wire and electrical cable installed in any area of the fuselage must be self-extinguishing when tested in accordance with the applicable portions of part I, appendix F of this part.

(b) Each vacuum air system line and fitting on the discharge side of the pump that might contain flammable vapors or fluids must meet the requirements of § 25.1183 if the line or fitting is in a designated fire zone. Other vacuum air systems components in designated fire zones must be at least fire resistant.

(c) Oxygen equipment and lines must—

(1) Not be located in any designated fire zone,

(2) Be protected from heat that may be generated in, or escape from, any designated fire zone, and

(3) Be installed so that escaping oxygen cannot cause ignition of grease, fluid, or vapor accumulations that are present in normal operation or as a result of failure or malfunction of any system.

[Amdt. 25–72, 55 FR 29784, July 20, 1990]

MISCELLANEOUS

§ 25.871 Leveling means.

There must be means for determining when the airplane is in a level position on the ground.

[Amdt. 25–23, 35 FR 5676, Apr. 8, 1970]

§ 25.875 Reinforcement near propellers.

(a) Each part of the airplane near the propeller tips must be strong and stiff enough to withstand the effects of the induced vibration and of ice thrown from the propeller.

(b) No window may be near the propeller tips unless it can withstand the most severe ice impact likely to occur.

Subpart E—Powerplant

GENERAL

§ 25.901 Installation.

(a) For the purpose of this part, the airplane powerplant installation includes each component that—

(1) Is necessary for propulsion;

(2) Affects the control of the major propulsive units; or

(3) Affects the safety of the major propulsive units between normal inspections or overhauls.

(b) For each powerplant—

(1) The installation must comply with—

(i) The installation instructions provided under § 33.5 of this chapter; and

(ii) The applicable provisions of this subpart;

(2) The components of the installation must be constructed, arranged, and installed so as to ensure their continued safe operation between normal inspections or overhauls;

(3) The installation must be accessible for necessary inspections and maintenance; and

(4) The major components of the installation must be electrically bonded to the other parts of the airplane.

(c) For each powerplant and auxiliary power unit installation, it must be established that no single failure or malfunction or probable combination of failures will jeopardize the safe operation of the airplane except that the failure of structural elements need not be considered if the probability of such failure is extremely remote.

(d) Each auxiliary power unit installation must meet the applicable provisions of this subpart.

[Doc. No. 5066, 29 FR 18291, Dec. 24, 1964, as amended by Amdt. 25–23, 35 FR 5676, Apr. 8, 1970; Amdt. 25–40, 42 FR 15042, Mar. 17, 1977; Amdt. 25–46, 43 FR 50597, Oct. 30, 1978]

§ 25.903 Engines.

(a) *Engine type certificate.* (1) Each engine must have a type certificate and must meet the applicable requirements of part 34 of this chapter.

(2) Each turbine engine must comply with one of the following:

(i) Sections 33.76, 33.77 and 33.78 of this chapter in effect on December 13, 2000, or as subsequently amended; or

(ii) Sections 33.77 and 33.78 of this chapter in effect on April 30, 1998, or as subsequently amended before December 13, 2000; or

(iii) Comply with § 33.77 of this chapter in effect on October 31, 1974, or as subsequently amended prior to April 30, 1998, unless that engine's foreign object ingestion service history has resulted in an unsafe condition; or

(iv) Be shown to have a foreign object ingestion service history in similar installation locations which has not resulted in any unsafe condition.

NOTE: § 33.77 of this chapter in effect on October 31, 1974, was published in 14 CFR parts 1 to 59, Revised as of January 1, 1975. See 39 FR 35467, October 1, 1974.

(b) *Engine isolation.* The powerplants must be arranged and isolated from each other to allow operation, in at least one configuration, so that the failure or malfunction of any engine, or of any system that can affect the engine, will not—

(1) Prevent the continued safe operation of the remaining engines; or

(2) Require immediate action by any crewmember for continued safe operation.

(c) *Control of engine rotation.* There must be means for stopping the rotation of any engine individually in flight, except that, for turbine engine installations, the means for stopping the rotation of any engine need be provided only where continued rotation could jeopardize the safety of the airplane. Each component of the stopping system on the engine side of the firewall that might be exposed to fire must be at least fire-resistant. If hydraulic propeller feathering systems are used for this purpose, the feathering lines must be at least fire resistant under the operating conditions that may be expected to exist during feathering.

(d) *Turbine engine installations.* For turbine engine installations—

(1) Design precautions must be taken to minimize the hazards to the airplane in the event of an engine rotor failure or of a fire originating within the engine which burns through the engine case.

(2) The powerplant systems associated with engine control devices, systems, and instrumentation, must be designed to give reasonable assurance that those engine operating limitations that adversely affect turbine rotor structural integrity will not be exceeded in service.

(e) *Restart capability.* (1) Means to restart any engine in flight must be provided.

(2) An altitude and airspeed envelope must be established for in-flight engine restarting, and each engine must have a restart capability within that envelope.

(3) For turbine engine powered airplanes, if the minimum windmilling speed of the engines, following the inflight shutdown of all engines, is insufficient to provide the necessary electrical power for engine ignition, a power source independent of the engine-driven electrical power generating system must be provided to permit inflight engine ignition for restarting.

(f) *Auxiliary Power Unit.* Each auxiliary power unit must be approved or meet the requirements of the category for its intended use.

[Doc. No. 5066, 29 FR 18291, Dec. 24, 1964, as amended by Amdt. 25–23, 35 FR 5676, Apr. 8, 1970; Amdt. 25–40, 42 FR 15042, Mar. 17, 1977; Amdt. 25–57, 49 FR 6848, Feb. 23, 1984; Amdt. 25–72, 55 FR 29784, July 20, 1990; Amdt. 25–73, 55 FR 32861, Aug. 10, 1990; Amdt. 25–94, 63 FR 8848, Feb. 23, 1998; Amdt. 25–95, 63 FR 14798, Mar. 26, 1998; Amdt. 25–100, 65 FR 55854, Sept. 14, 2000]

§ 25.904 Automatic takeoff thrust control system (ATTCS).

Each applicant seeking approval for installation of an engine power control system that automatically resets the power or thrust on the operating engine(s) when any engine fails during the takeoff must comply with the requirements of appendix I of this part.

[Amdt. 25–62, 52 FR 43156, Nov. 9, 1987]

§ 25.905 Propellers.

(a) Each propeller must have a type certificate.

(b) Engine power and propeller shaft rotational speed may not exceed the limits for which the propeller is certificated.

(c) Each component of the propeller blade pitch control system must meet the requirements of § 35.42 of this chapter.

(d) Design precautions must be taken to minimize the hazards to the airplane in the event a propeller blade fails or is released by a hub failure. The hazards which must be considered include damage to structure and vital systems due to impact of a failed or released blade and the unbalance created by such failure or release.

[Doc. No. 5066, 29 FR 18291, Dec. 24, 1964, as amended by Amdt. 25–54, 45 FR 60173, Sept. 11, 1980; Amdt. 25–57, 49 FR 6848, Feb. 23, 1984; Amdt. 25–72, 55 FR 29784, July 20, 1990]

§ 25.907 Propeller vibration.

(a) The magnitude of the propeller blade vibration stresses under any normal condition of operation must be determined by actual measurement or by comparison with similar installations for which these measurements have been made.

(b) The determined vibration stresses may not exceed values that have been shown to be safe for continuous operation.

§ 25.925 Propeller clearance.

Unless smaller clearances are substantiated, propeller clearances with the airplane at maximum weight, with the most adverse center of gravity, and with the propeller in the most adverse pitch position, may not be less than the following:

(a) *Ground clearance.* There must be a clearance of at least seven inches (for each airplane with nose wheel landing gear) or nine inches (for each airplane with tail wheel landing gear) between

each propeller and the ground with the landing gear statically deflected and in the level takeoff, or taxiing attitude, whichever is most critical. In addition, there must be positive clearance between the propeller and the ground when in the level takeoff attitude with the critical tire(s) completely deflated and the corresponding landing gear strut bottomed.

(b) *Water clearance.* There must be a clearance of at least 18 inches between each propeller and the water, unless compliance with § 25.239(a) can be shown with a lesser clearance.

(c) *Structural clearance.* There must be—

(1) At least one inch radial clearance between the blade tips and the airplane structure, plus any additional radial clearance necessary to prevent harmful vibration;

(2) At least one-half inch longitudinal clearance between the propeller blades or cuffs and stationary parts of the airplane; and

(3) Positive clearance between other rotating parts of the propeller or spinner and stationary parts of the airplane.

Doc. No. 5066, 29 FR 18291, Dec. 24, 1964, as amended by Amdt. 25–72, 55 FR 29784, July 20, 1990]

§ 25.929 Propeller deicing.

(a) For airplanes intended for use where icing may be expected, there must be a means to prevent or remove hazardous ice accumulation on propellers or on accessories where ice accumulation would jeopardize engine performance.

(b) If combustible fluid is used for propeller deicing, §§ 25.1181 through 25.1185 and 25.1189 apply.

§ 25.933 Reversing systems.

(a) For turbojet reversing systems—

(1) Each system intended for ground operation only must be designed so that during any reversal in flight the engine will produce no more than flight idle thrust. In addition, it must be shown by analysis or test, or both, that—

(i) Each operable reverser can be restored to the forward thrust position; and

(ii) The airplane is capable of continued safe flight and landing under any possible position of the thrust reverser.

(2) Each system intended for inflight use must be designed so that no unsafe condition will result during normal operation of the system, or from any failure (or reasonably likely combination of failures) of the reversing system, under any anticipated condition of operation of the airplane including ground operation. Failure of structural elements need not be considered if the probability of this kind of failure is extremely remote.

(3) Each system must have means to prevent the engine from producing more than idle thrust when the reversing system malfunctions, except that it may produce any greater forward thrust that is shown to allow directional control to be maintained, with aerodynamic means alone, under the most critical reversing condition expected in operation.

(b) For propeller reversing systems—

(1) Each system intended for ground operation only must be designed so that no single failure (or reasonably likely combination of failures) or malfunction of the system will result in unwanted reverse thrust under any expected operating condition. Failure of structural elements need not be considered if this kind of failure is extremely remote.

(2) Compliance with this section may be shown by failure analysis or testing, or both, for propeller systems that allow propeller blades to move from the flight low-pitch position to a position that is substantially less than that at the normal flight low-pitch position. The analysis may include or be supported by the analysis made to show compliance with the requirements of § 35.21 of this chapter for the propeller and associated installation components.

[Amdt. 25–72, 55 FR 29784, July 20, 1990]

§ 25.934 Turbojet engine thrust reverser system tests.

Thrust reversers installed on turbojet engines must meet the requirements of § 33.97 of this chapter.

[Amdt. 25–23, 35 FR 5677, Apr. 8, 1970]

§ 25.937 Turbopropeller-drag limiting systems.

Turbopropeller power airplane propeller-drag limiting systems must be designed so that no single failure or malfunction of any of the systems during normal or emergency operation results in propeller drag in excess of that for which the airplane was designed under § 25.367. Failure of structural elements of the drag limiting systems need not be considered if the probability of this kind of failure is extremely remote.

§ 25.939 Turbine engine operating characteristics.

(a) Turbine engine operating characteristics must be investigated in flight to determine that no adverse characteristics (such as stall, surge, or flameout) are present, to a hazardous degree, during normal and emergency operation within the range of operating limitations of the airplane and of the engine.

(b) [Reserved]

(c) The turbine engine air inlet system may not, as a result of air flow distortion during normal operation, cause vibration harmful to the engine.

[Amdt. 25–11, 32 FR 6912, May 5, 1967, as amended by Amdt. 25–40, 42 FR 15043, Mar. 17, 1977]

§ 25.941 Inlet, engine, and exhaust compatibility.

For airplanes using variable inlet or exhaust system geometry, or both—

(a) The system comprised of the inlet, engine (including thrust augmentation systems, if incorporated), and exhaust must be shown to function properly under all operating conditions for which approval is sought, including all engine rotating speeds and power settings, and engine inlet and exhaust configurations;

(b) The dynamic effects of the operation of these (including consideration of probable malfunctions) upon the aerodynamic control of the airplane may not result in any condition that would require exceptional skill, alertness, or strength on the part of the pilot to avoid exceeding an operational or structural limitation of the airplane; and

(c) In showing compliance with paragraph (b) of this section, the pilot strength required may not exceed the limits set forth in § 25.143(c), subject to the conditions set forth in paragraphs (d) and (e) of § 25.143.

[Amdt. 25–38, 41 FR 55467, Dec. 20, 1976]

§ 25.943 Negative acceleration.

No hazardous malfunction of an engine, an auxiliary power unit approved for use in flight, or any component or system associated with the powerplant or auxiliary power unit may occur when the airplane is operated at the negative accelerations within the flight envelopes prescribed in § 25.333. This must be shown for the greatest duration expected for the acceleration.

[Amdt. 25–40, 42 FR 15043, Mar. 17, 1977]

§ 25.945 Thrust or power augmentation system.

(a) *General.* Each fluid injection system must provide a flow of fluid at the rate and pressure established for proper engine functioning under each intended operating condition. If the fluid can freeze, fluid freezing may not damage the airplane or adversely affect airplane performance.

(b) *Fluid tanks.* Each augmentation system fluid tank must meet the following requirements:

(1) Each tank must be able to withstand without failure the vibration, inertia, fluid, and structural loads that it may be subject to in operation.

(2) The tanks as mounted in the airplane must be able to withstand without failure or leakage an internal pressure 1.5 times the maximum operating pressure.

(3) If a vent is provided, the venting must be effective under all normal flight conditions.

(4) [Reserved]

(c) Augmentation system drains must be designed and located in accordance with § 25.1455 if—

(1) The augmentation system fluid is subject to freezing; and

(2) The fluid may be drained in flight or during ground operation.

(d) The augmentation liquid tank capacity available for the use of each engine must be large enough to allow operation of the airplane under the ap-

proved procedures for the use of liquid-augmented power. The computation of liquid consumption must be based on the maximum approved rate appropriate for the desired engine output and must include the effect of temperature on engine performance as well as any other factors that might vary the amount of liquid required.

(e) This section does not apply to fuel injection systems.

[Amdt. 25–40, 42 FR 15043, Mar. 17, 1977, as amended by Amdt. 25–72, 55 FR 29785, July 20, 1990]

FUEL SYSTEM

§ 25.951 General.

(a) Each fuel system must be constructed and arranged to ensure a flow of fuel at a rate and pressure established for proper engine and auxiliary power unit functioning under each likely operating condition, including any maneuver for which certification is requested and during which the engine or auxiliary power unit is permitted to be in operation.

(b) Each fuel system must be arranged so that any air which is introduced into the system will not result in—

(1) Power interruption for more than 20 seconds for reciprocating engines; or

(2) Flameout for turbine engines.

(c) Each fuel system for a turbine engine must be capable of sustained operation throughout its flow and pressure range with fuel initially saturated with water at 80 °F and having 0.75cc of free water per gallon added and cooled to the most critical condition for icing likely to be encountered in operation.

(d) Each fuel system for a turbine engine powered airplane must meet the applicable fuel venting requirements of part 34 of this chapter.

[Doc. No. 5066, 29 FR 18291, Dec. 24, 1964, as amended by Amdt. 25–23, 35 FR 5677, Apr. 8, 1970; Amdt. 25–36, 39 FR 35460, Oct. 1, 1974; Amdt. 25–38, 41 FR 55467, Dec. 20, 1976; Amdt. 25–73, 55 FR 32861, Aug. 10, 1990]

§ 25.952 Fuel system analysis and test.

(a) Proper fuel system functioning under all probable operating conditions must be shown by analysis and those tests found necessary by the Administrator. Tests, if required, must be made using the airplane fuel system or a test article that reproduces the operating characteristics of the portion of the fuel system to be tested.

(b) The likely failure of any heat exchanger using fuel as one of its fluids may not result in a hazardous condition.

[Amdt. 25–40, 42 FR 15043, Mar. 17, 1977]

§ 25.953 Fuel system independence.

Each fuel system must meet the requirements of § 25.903(b) by—

(a) Allowing the supply of fuel to each engine through a system independent of each part of the system supplying fuel to any other engine; or

(b) Any other acceptable method.

§ 25.954 Fuel system lightning protection.

The fuel system must be designed and arranged to prevent the ignition of fuel vapor within the system by—

(a) Direct lightning strikes to areas having a high probability of stroke attachment;

(b) Swept lightning strokes to areas where swept strokes are highly probable; and

(c) Corona and streamering at fuel vent outlets.

[Amdt. 25–14, 32 FR 11629, Aug. 11, 1967]

§ 25.955 Fuel flow.

(a) Each fuel system must provide at least 100 percent of the fuel flow required under each intended operating condition and maneuver. Compliance must be shown as follows:

(1) Fuel must be delivered to each engine at a pressure within the limits specified in the engine type certificate.

(2) The quantity of fuel in the tank may not exceed the amount established as the unusable fuel supply for that tank under the requirements of § 25.959 plus that necessary to show compliance with this section.

(3) Each main pump must be used that is necessary for each operating condition and attitude for which compliance with this section is shown, and the appropriate emergency pump must be substituted for each main pump so used.

(4) If there is a fuel flowmeter, it must be blocked and the fuel must flow through the meter or its bypass.

(b) If an engine can be supplied with fuel from more than one tank, the fuel system must—

(1) For each reciprocating engine, supply the full fuel pressure to that engine in not more than 20 seconds after switching to any other fuel tank containing usable fuel when engine malfunctioning becomes apparent due to the depletion of the fuel supply in any tank from which the engine can be fed; and

(2) For each turbine engine, in addition to having appropriate manual switching capability, be designed to prevent interruption of fuel flow to that engine, without attention by the flight crew, when any tank supplying fuel to that engine is depleted of usable fuel during normal operation, and any other tank, that normally supplies fuel to that engine alone, contains usable fuel.

[Doc. No. 5066, 29 FR 18291, Dec. 24, 1964, as amended by Amdt. 25–11, 32 FR 6912, May 5, 1967]

§ 25.957 Flow between interconnected tanks.

If fuel can be pumped from one tank to another in flight, the fuel tank vents and the fuel transfer system must be designed so that no structural damage to the tanks can occur because of overfilling.

§ 25.959 Unusable fuel supply.

The unusable fuel quantity for each fuel tank and its fuel system components must be established at not less than the quantity at which the first evidence of engine malfunction occurs under the most adverse fuel feed condition for all intended operations and flight maneuvers involving fuel feeding from that tank. Fuel system component failures need not be considered.

[Amdt. 25–23, 35 FR 5677, Apr. 8, 1970, as amended by Amdt. 25–40, 42 FR 15043, Mar. 17, 1977]

§ 25.961 Fuel system hot weather operation.

(a) The fuel system must perform satisfactorily in hot weather operation. This must be shown by showing that the fuel system from the tank outlets to each engine is pressurized, under all intended operations, so as to prevent vapor formation, or must be shown by climbing from the altitude of the airport elected by the applicant to the maximum altitude established as an operating limitation under § 25.1527. If a climb test is elected, there may be no evidence of vapor lock or other malfunctioning during the climb test conducted under the following conditions:

(1) For reciprocating engine powered airplanes, the engines must operate at maximum continuous power, except that takeoff power must be used for the altitudes from 1,000 feet below the critical altitude through the critical altitude. The time interval during which takeoff power is used may not be less than the takeoff time limitation.

(2) For turbine engine powered airplanes, the engines must operate at takeoff power for the time interval selected for showing the takeoff flight path, and at maximum continuous power for the rest of the climb.

(3) The weight of the airplane must be the weight with full fuel tanks, minimum crew, and the ballast necessary to maintain the center of gravity within allowable limits.

(4) The climb airspeed may not exceed—

(i) For reciprocating engine powered airplanes, the maximum airspeed established for climbing from takeoff to the maximum operating altitude with the airplane in the following configuration:

(A) Landing gear retracted.

(B) Wing flaps in the most favorable position.

(C) Cowl flaps (or other means of controlling the engine cooling supply) in the position that provides adequate cooling in the hot-day condition.

(D) Engine operating within the maximum continuous power limitations.

(E) Maximum takeoff weight; and

(ii) For turbine engine powered airplanes, the maximum airspeed established for climbing from takeoff to the maximum operating altitude.

(5) The fuel temperature must be at least 110 °F.

(b) The test prescribed in paragraph (a) of this section may be performed in flight or on the ground under closely simulated flight conditions. If a flight test is performed in weather cold enough to interfere with the proper conduct of the test, the fuel tank surfaces, fuel lines, and other fuel system parts subject to cold air must be insulated to simulate, insofar as practicable, flight in hot weather.

[Amdt. 25–11, 32 FR 6912, May 5, 1967, as amended by Amdt. 25–57, 49 FR 6848, Feb. 23, 1984]

§ 25.963 Fuel tanks: general.

(a) Each fuel tank must be able to withstand, without failure, the vibration, inertia, fluid, and structural loads that it may be subjected to in operation.

(b) Flexible fuel tank liners must be approved or must be shown to be suitable for the particular application.

(c) Integral fuel tanks must have facilities for interior inspection and repair.

(d) Fuel tanks within the fuselage contour must be able to resist rupture and to retain fuel, under the inertia forces prescribed for the emergency landing conditions in § 25.561. In addition, these tanks must be in a protected position so that exposure of the tanks to scraping action with the ground is unlikely.

(e) Fuel tank access covers must comply with the following criteria in order to avoid loss of hazardous quantities of fuel:

(1) All covers located in an area where experience or analysis indicates a strike is likely must be shown by analysis or tests to minimize penetration and deformation by tire fragments, low energy engine debris, or other likely debris.

(2) All covers must be fire resistant as defined in part 1 of this chapter.

(f) For pressurized fuel tanks, a means with fail-safe features must be provided to prevent the buildup of an excessive pressure difference between the inside and the outside of the tank.

[Doc. No. 5066, 29 FR 18291, Dec. 24, 1964, as amended by Amdt. 25–40, 42 FR 15043, Mar. 17, 1977; Amdt. 25–69, 54 FR 40354, Sept. 29, 1989]

§ 25.965 Fuel tank tests.

(a) It must be shown by tests that the fuel tanks, as mounted in the airplane, can withstand, without failure or leakage, the more critical of the pressures resulting from the conditions specified in paragraphs (a)(1) and (2) of this section. In addition, it must be shown by either analysis or tests, that tank surfaces subjected to more critical pressures resulting from the condition of paragraphs (a)(3) and (4) of this section, are able to withstand the following pressures:

(1) An internal pressure of 3.5 psi.

(2) 125 percent of the maximum air pressure developed in the tank from ram effect.

(3) Fluid pressures developed during maximum limit accelerations, and deflections, of the airplane with a full tank.

(4) Fluid pressures developed during the most adverse combination of airplane roll and fuel load.

(b) Each metallic tank with large unsupported or unstiffened flat surfaces, whose failure or deformation could cause fuel leakage, must be able to withstand the following test, or its equivalent, without leakage or excessive deformation of the tank walls:

(1) Each complete tank assembly and its supports must be vibration tested while mounted to simulate the actual installation.

(2) Except as specified in paragraph (b)(4) of this section, the tank assembly must be vibrated for 25 hours at an amplitude of not less than 1/32 of an inch (unless another amplitude is substantiated) while 2/3 filled with water or other suitable test fluid.

(3) The test frequency of vibration must be as follows:

(i) If no frequency of vibration resulting from any r.p.m. within the normal operating range of engine speeds is critical, the test frequency of vibration must be 2,000 cycles per minute.

(ii) If only one frequency of vibration resulting from any r.p.m. within the normal operating range of engine speeds is critical, that frequency of vibration must be the test frequency.

(iii) If more than one frequency of vibration resulting from any r.p.m. within the normal operating range of engine speeds is critical, the most critical of these frequencies must be the test frequency.

(4) Under paragraphs (b)(3)(ii) and (iii) of this section, the time of test must be adjusted to accomplish the same number of vibration cycles that would be accomplished in 25 hours at the frequency specified in paragraph (b)(3)(i) of this section.

(5) During the test, the tank assembly must be rocked at the rate of 16 to 20 complete cycles per minute, through an angle of 15° on both sides of the horizontal (30° total), about the most critical axis, for 25 hours. If motion about more than one axis is likely to be critical, the tank must be rocked about each critical axis for 12½ hours.

(c) Except where satisfactory operating experience with a similar tank in a similar installation is shown, nonmetallic tanks must withstand the test specified in paragraph (b)(5) of this section, with fuel at a temperature of 110 °F. During this test, a representative specimen of the tank must be installed in a supporting structure simulating the installation in the airplane.

(d) For pressurized fuel tanks, it must be shown by analysis or tests that the fuel tanks can withstand the maximum pressure likely to occur on the ground or in flight.

[Doc. No. 5066, 29 FR 18291, Dec. 24, 1964, as amended by Amdt. 25–11, 32 FR 6913, May 5, 1967; Amdt. 25–40, 42 FR 15043, Mar. 17, 1977]

§ 25.967 Fuel tank installations.

(a) Each fuel tank must be supported so that tank loads (resulting from the weight of the fuel in the tanks) are not concentrated on unsupported tank surfaces. In addition—

(1) There must be pads, if necessary, to prevent chafing between the tank and its supports;

(2) Padding must be nonabsorbent or treated to prevent the absorption of fluids;

(3) If a flexible tank liner is used, it must be supported so that it is not required to withstand fluid loads; and

(4) Each interior surface of the tank compartment must be smooth and free of projections that could cause wear of the liner unless—

(i) Provisions are made for protection of the liner at these points; or

(ii) The construction of the liner itself provides that protection.

(b) Spaces adjacent to tank surfaces must be ventilated to avoid fume accumulation due to minor leakage. If the tank is in a sealed compartment, ventilation may be limited to drain holes large enough to prevent excessive pressure resulting from altitude changes.

(c) The location of each tank must meet the requirements of § 25.1185(a).

(d) No engine nacelle skin immediately behind a major air outlet from the engine compartment may act as the wall of an integral tank.

(e) Each fuel tank must be isolated from personnel compartments by a fumeproof and fuelproof enclosure.

§ 25.969 Fuel tank expansion space.

Each fuel tank must have an expansion space of not less than 2 percent of the tank capacity. It must be impossible to fill the expansion space inadvertently with the airplane in the normal ground attitude. For pressure fueling systems, compliance with this section may be shown with the means provided to comply with § 25.979(b).

[Amdt. 25–11, 32 FR 6913, May 5, 1967]

§ 25.971 Fuel tank sump.

(a) Each fuel tank must have a sump with an effective capacity, in the normal ground attitude, of not less than the greater of 0.10 percent of the tank capacity or one-sixteenth of a gallon unless operating limitations are established to ensure that the accumulation of water in service will not exceed the sump capacity.

(b) Each fuel tank must allow drainage of any hazardous quantity of water from any part of the tank to its sump with the airplane in the ground attitude.

(c) Each fuel tank sump must have an accessible drain that—

(1) Allows complete drainage of the sump on the ground;

(2) Discharges clear of each part of the airplane; and

(3) Has manual or automatic means for positive locking in the closed position.

§ 25.973 Fuel tank filler connection.

Each fuel tank filler connection must prevent the entrance of fuel into any part of the airplane other than the tank itself. In addition—

(a) [Reserved]

(b) Each recessed filler connection that can retain any appreciable quantity of fuel must have a drain that discharges clear of each part of the airplane;

(c) Each filler cap must provide a fuel-tight seal; and

(d) Each fuel filling point, except pressure fueling connection points, must have a provision for electrically bonding the airplane to ground fueling equipment.

[Doc. No. 5066, 29 FR 18291, Dec. 24, 1964, as amended by Amdt. 25–40, 42 FR 15043, Mar. 17, 1977; Amdt. 25–72, 55 FR 29785, July 20, 1990]

§ 25.975 Fuel tank vents and carburetor vapor vents.

(a) *Fuel tank vents.* Each fuel tank must be vented from the top part of the expansion space so that venting is effective under any normal flight condition. In addition—

(1) Each vent must be arranged to avoid stoppage by dirt or ice formation;

(2) The vent arrangement must prevent siphoning of fuel during normal operation;

(3) The venting capacity and vent pressure levels must maintain acceptable differences of pressure between the interior and exterior of the tank, during—

(i) Normal flight operation;

(ii) Maximum rate of ascent and descent; and

(iii) Refueling and defueling (where applicable);

(4) Airspaces of tanks with interconnected outlets must be interconnected;

(5) There may be no point in any vent line where moisture can accumulate with the airplane in the ground attitude or the level flight attitude, unless drainage is provided; and

(6) No vent or drainage provision may end at any point—

(i) Where the discharge of fuel from the vent outlet would constitute a fire hazard; or

(ii) From which fumes could enter personnel compartments.

(b) *Carburetor vapor vents.* Each carburetor with vapor elimination connections must have a vent line to lead vapors back to one of the fuel tanks. In addition—

(1) Each vent system must have means to avoid stoppage by ice; and

(2) If there is more than one fuel tank, and it is necessary to use the tanks in a definite sequence, each vapor vent return line must lead back to the fuel tank used for takeoff and landing.

§ 25.977 Fuel tank outlet.

(a) There must be a fuel strainer for the fuel tank outlet or for the booster pump. This strainer must—

(1) For reciprocating engine powered airplanes, have 8 to 16 meshes per inch; and

(2) For turbine engine powered airplanes, prevent the passage of any object that could restrict fuel flow or damage any fuel system component.

(b) [Reserved]

(c) The clear area of each fuel tank outlet strainer must be at least five times the area of the outlet line.

(d) The diameter of each strainer must be at least that of the fuel tank outlet.

(e) Each finger strainer must be accessible for inspection and cleaning.

[Amdt. 25–11, 32 FR 6913, May 5, 1967, as amended by Amdt. 25–36, 39 FR 35460, Oct. 1, 1974]

§ 25.979 Pressure fueling system.

For pressure fueling systems, the following apply:

(a) Each pressure fueling system fuel manifold connection must have means to prevent the escape of hazardous quantities of fuel from the system if the fuel entry valve fails.

(b) An automatic shutoff means must be provided to prevent the quantity of fuel in each tank from exceeding the maximum quantity approved for that tank. This means must—

(1) Allow checking for proper shutoff operation before each fueling of the tank; and

(2) Provide indication at each fueling station of failure of the shutoff means to stop the fuel flow at the maximum quantity approved for that tank.

(c) A means must be provided to prevent damage to the fuel system in the event of failure of the automatic shutoff means prescribed in paragraph (b) of this section.

(d) The airplane pressure fueling system (not including fuel tanks and fuel tank vents) must withstand an ultimate load that is 2.0 times the load arising from the maximum pressures, including surge, that is likely to occur during fueling. The maximum surge pressure must be established with any combination of tank valves being either intentionally or inadvertently closed.

(e) The airplane defueling system (not including fuel tanks and fuel tank vents) must withstand an ultimate load that is 2.0 times the load arising from the maximum permissible defueling pressure (positive or negative) at the airplane fueling connection.

[Amdt. 25–11, 32 FR 6913, May 5, 1967, as amended by Amdt. 25–38, 41 FR 55467, Dec. 20, 1976; Amdt. 25–72, 55 FR 29785, July 20, 1990]

§ 25.981 Fuel tank ignition prevention.

(a) No ignition source may be present at each point in the fuel tank or fuel tank system where catastrophic failure could occur due to ignition of fuel or vapors. This must be shown by:

(1) Determining the highest temperature allowing a safe margin below the lowest expected autoignition temperature of the fuel in the fuel tanks.

(2) Demonstrating that no temperature at each place inside each fuel tank where fuel ignition is possible will exceed the temperature determined under paragraph (a)(1) of this section. This must be verified under all probable operating, failure, and malfunction conditions of each component whose operation, failure, or malfunction could increase the temperature inside the tank.

(3) Demonstrating that an ignition source could not result from each single failure, from each single failure in combination with each latent failure condition not shown to be extremely remote, and from all combinations of failures not shown to be extremely improbable. The effects of manufacturing variability, aging, wear, corrosion, and likely damage must be considered.

(b) Based on the evaluations required by this section, critical design configuration control limitations, inspections, or other procedures must be established, as necessary, to prevent development of ignition sources within the fuel tank system and must be included in the Airworthiness Limitations section of the Instructions for Continued Airworthiness required by §25.1529. Visible means to identify critical features of the design must be placed in areas of the airplane where maintenance actions, repairs, or alterations may be apt to violate the critical design configuration limitations (e.g., color-coding of wire to identify separation limitation).

(c) The fuel tank installation must include either—

(1) Means to minimize the development of flammable vapors in the fuel tanks (in the context of this rule, "minimize" means to incorporate practicable design methods to reduce the likelihood of flammable vapors); or

(2) Means to mitigate the effects of an ignition of fuel vapors within fuel tanks such that no damage caused by an ignition will prevent continued safe flight and landing.

[Doc. No. 1999–6411, 66 FR 23129, May 7, 2001]

FUEL SYSTEM COMPONENTS

§25.991 Fuel pumps.

(a) *Main pumps.* Each fuel pump required for proper engine operation, or required to meet the fuel system requirements of this subpart (other than those in paragraph (b) of this section, is a main pump. For each main pump, provision must be made to allow the bypass of each positive displacement fuel pump other than a fuel injection pump (a pump that supplies the proper flow and pressure for fuel injection when the injection is not accomplished in a carburetor) approved as part of the engine.

(b) *Emergency pumps.* There must be emergency pumps or another main pump to feed each engine immediately after failure of any main pump (other than a fuel injection pump approved as part of the engine).

§25.993 Fuel system lines and fittings.

(a) Each fuel line must be installed and supported to prevent excessive vibration and to withstand loads due to fuel pressure and accelerated flight conditions.

(b) Each fuel line connected to components of the airplane between which relative motion could exist must have provisions for flexibility.

(c) Each flexible connection in fuel lines that may be under pressure and subjected to axial loading must use flexible hose assemblies.

(d) Flexible hose must be approved or must be shown to be suitable for the particular application.

(e) No flexible hose that might be adversely affected by exposure to high temperatures may be used where excessive temperatures will exist during operation or after engine shut-down.

(f) Each fuel line within the fuselage must be designed and installed to allow a reasonable degree of deformation and stretching without leakage.

[Doc. No. 5066, 29 FR 18291, Dec. 24, 1964, as amended by Amdt. 25–15, 32 FR 13266, Sept. 20, 1967]

§25.994 Fuel system components.

Fuel system components in an engine nacelle or in the fuselage must be protected from damage which could result in spillage of enough fuel to constitute a fire hazard as a result of a wheels-up landing on a paved runway.

[Amdt. 25–57, 49 FR 6848, Feb. 23, 1984]

§25.995 Fuel valves.

In addition to the requirements of §25.1189 for shutoff means, each fuel valve must—

(a) [Reserved]

(b) Be supported so that no loads resulting from their operation or from accelerated flight conditions are transmitted to the lines attached to the valve.

[Doc. No. 5066, 29 FR 18291, Dec. 24, 1964, as amended by Amdt. 25–40, 42 FR 15043, Mar. 17, 1977]

§25.997 Fuel strainer or filter.

There must be a fuel strainer or filter between the fuel tank outlet and the inlet of either the fuel metering device

or an engine driven positive displacement pump, whichever is nearer the
fuel tank outlet. This fuel strainer or
filter must—

(a) Be accessible for draining and
cleaning and must incorporate a screen
or element which is easily removable;

(b) Have a sediment trap and drain
except that it need not have a drain if
the strainer or filter is easily removable for drain purposes;

(c) Be mounted so that its weight is
not supported by the connecting lines
or by the inlet or outlet connections of
the strainer or filter itself, unless adequate strength margins under all loading conditions are provided in the lines
and connections; and

(d) Have the capacity (with respect to
operating limitations established for
the engine) to ensure that engine fuel
system functioning is not impaired,
with the fuel contaminated to a degree
(with respect to particle size and density) that is greater than that established for the engine in Part 33 of this
chapter.

[Amdt. No. 25–36, 39 FR 35460, Oct. 1, 1974, as
amended by Amdt. 25–57, 49 FR 6848, Feb. 23,
1984]

§ 25.999 Fuel system drains.

(a) Drainage of the fuel system must
be accomplished by the use of fuel
strainer and fuel tank sump drains.

(b) Each drain required by paragraph
(a) of this section must—

(1) Discharge clear of all parts of the
airplane;

(2) Have manual or automatic means
for positive locking in the closed position; and

(3) Have a drain valve—

(i) That is readily accessible and
which can be easily opened and closed;
and

(ii) That is either located or protected to prevent fuel spillage in the
event of a landing with landing gear retracted.

[Doc. No. 5066, 29 FR 18291, Dec. 24, 1964, as
amended by Amdt. 25–38, 41 FR 55467, Dec. 20,
1976]

§ 25.1001 Fuel jettisoning system.

(a) A fuel jettisoning system must be
installed on each airplane unless it is
shown that the airplane meets the
climb requirements of §§ 25.119 and

25.121(d) at maximum takeoff weight,
less the actual or computed weight of
fuel necessary for a 15-minute flight
comprised of a takeoff, go-around, and
landing at the airport of departure
with the airplane configuration, speed,
power, and thrust the same as that
used in meeting the applicable takeoff,
approach, and landing climb performance requirements of this part.

(b) If a fuel jettisoning system is required it must be capable of jettisoning
enough fuel within 15 minutes, starting
with the weight given in paragraph (a)
of this section, to enable the airplane
to meet the climb requirements of
§§ 25.119 and 25.121(d), assuming that the
fuel is jettisoned under the conditions,
except weight, found least favorable
during the flight tests prescribed in
paragraph (c) of this section.

(c) Fuel jettisoning must be demonstrated beginning at maximum takeoff weight with flaps and landing gear
up and in—

(1) A power-off glide at 1.3 V_{SR1};

(2) A climb at the one-engine inoperative best rate-of-climb speed, with the
critical engine inoperative and the remaining engines at maximum continuous power; and

(3) Level flight at 1.3 V_{SR1}; if the results of the tests in the conditions
specified in paragraphs (c)(1) and (2) of
this section show that this condition
could be critical.

(d) During the flight tests prescribed
in paragraph (c) of this section, it must
be shown that—

(1) The fuel jettisoning system and
its operation are free from fire hazard;

(2) The fuel discharges clear of any
part of the airplane;

(3) Fuel or fumes do not enter any
parts of the airplane; and

(4) The jettisoning operation does not
adversely affect the controllability of
the airplane.

(e) For reciprocating engine powered
airplanes, means must be provided to
prevent jettisoning the fuel in the
tanks used for takeoff and landing
below the level allowing 45 minutes
flight at 75 percent maximum continuous power. However, if there is an
auxiliary control independent of the
main jettisoning control, the system

may be designed to jettison the remaining fuel by means of the auxiliary jettisoning control.

(f) For turbine engine powered airplanes, means must be provided to prevent jettisoning the fuel in the tanks used for takeoff and landing below the level allowing climb from sea level to 10,000 feet and thereafter allowing 45 minutes cruise at a speed for maximum range. However, if there is an auxiliary control independent of the main jettisoning control, the system may be designed to jettison the remaining fuel by means of the auxiliary jettisoning control.

(g) The fuel jettisoning valve must be designed to allow flight personnel to close the valve during any part of the jettisoning operation.

(h) Unless it is shown that using any means (including flaps, slots, and slats) for changing the airflow across or around the wings does not adversely affect fuel jettisoning, there must be a placard, adjacent to the jettisoning control, to warn flight crewmembers against jettisoning fuel while the means that change the airflow are being used.

(i) The fuel jettisoning system must be designed so that any reasonably probable single malfunction in the system will not result in a hazardous condition due to unsymmetrical jettisoning of, or inability to jettison, fuel.

[Doc. No. 5066, 29 FR 18291, Dec. 24, 1964, as amended by Amdt. 25–18, 33 FR 12226, Aug. 30, 1968; Amdt. 25–57, 49 FR 6848, Feb. 23, 1984; Amdt. 25–108, 67 FR 70827, Nov. 26, 2002]

OIL SYSTEM

§25.1011 General.

(a) Each engine must have an independent oil system that can supply it with an appropriate quantity of oil at a temperature not above that safe for continuous operation.

(b) The usable oil capacity may not be less than the product of the endurance of the airplane under critical operating conditions and the approved maximum allowable oil consumption of the engine under the same conditions, plus a suitable margin to ensure system circulation. Instead of a rational analysis of airplane range for the purpose of computing oil requirements for reciprocating engine powered airplanes, the following fuel/oil ratios may be used:

(1) For airplanes without a reserve oil or oil transfer system, a fuel/oil ratio of 30:1 by volume.

(2) For airplanes with either a reserve oil or oil transfer system, a fuel/oil ratio of 40:1 by volume.

(c) Fuel/oil ratios higher than those prescribed in paragraphs (b)(1) and (2) of this section may be used if substantiated by data on actual engine oil consumption.

§25.1013 Oil tanks.

(a) *Installation.* Each oil tank installation must meet the requirements of §25.967.

(b) *Expansion space.* Oil tank expansion space must be provided as follows:

(1) Each oil tank used with a reciprocating engine must have an expansion space of not less than the greater of 10 percent of the tank capacity or 0.5 gallon, and each oil tank used with a turbine engine must have an expansion space of not less than 10 percent of the tank capacity.

(2) Each reserve oil tank not directly connected to any engine may have an expansion space of not less than two percent of the tank capacity.

(3) It must be impossible to fill the expansion space inadvertently with the airplane in the normal ground attitude.

(c) *Filler connection.* Each recessed oil tank filler connection that can retain any appreciable quantity of oil must have a drain that discharges clear of each part of the airplane. In addition, each oil tank filler cap must provide an oil-tight seal.

(d) *Vent.* Oil tanks must be vented as follows:

(1) Each oil tank must be vented from the top part of the expansion space so that venting is effective under any normal flight condition.

(2) Oil tank vents must be arranged so that condensed water vapor that might freeze and obstruct the line cannot accumulate at any point.

(e) *Outlet.* There must be means to prevent entrance into the tank itself, or into the tank outlet, of any object that might obstruct the flow of oil through the system. No oil tank outlet may be enclosed by any screen or guard that would reduce the flow of oil below a safe value at any operating temperature. There must be a shutoff valve at the outlet of each oil tank used with a turbine engine, unless the external portion of the oil system (including the oil tank supports) is fireproof.

(f) *Flexible oil tank liners.* Each flexible oil tank liner must be approved or must be shown to be suitable for the particular application.

[Doc. No. 5066, 29 FR 18291, Dec. 24, as amended by Amdt. 25–19, 33 FR 15410, Oct. 17, 1968; Amdt. 25–23, 35 FR 5677, Apr. 8, 1970; Amdt. 25–36, 39 FR 35460, Oct. 1, 1974; Amdt. 25–57, 49 FR 6848, Feb. 23, 1984; Amdt. 25–72, 55 FR 29785, July 20, 1990]

§ 25.1015   Oil tank tests.

Each oil tank must be designed and installed so that—

(a) It can withstand, without failure, each vibration, inertia, and fluid load that it may be subjected to in operation; and

(b) It meets the provisions of § 25.965, except—

(1) The test pressure—

(i) For pressurized tanks used with a turbine engine, may not be less than 5 p.s.i. plus the maximum operating pressure of the tank instead of the pressure specified in § 25.965(a); and

(ii) For all other tanks may not be less than 5 p.s.i. instead of the pressure specified in § 25.965(a); and

(2) The test fluid must be oil at 250 °F. instead of the fluid specified in § 25.965(c).

[Doc. No. 5066, 29 FR 18291, Dec. 24, 1964, as amended by Amdt. 25–36, 39 FR 35461, Oct. 1, 1974]

§ 25.1017   Oil lines and fittings.

(a) Each oil line must meet the requirements of § 25.993 and each oil line and fitting in any designated fire zone must meet the requirements of § 25.1183.

(b) Breather lines must be arranged so that—

(1) Condensed water vapor that might freeze and obstruct the line cannot accumulate at any point;

(2) The breather discharge does not constitute a fire hazard if foaming occurs or causes emitted oil to strike the pilot's windshield; and

(3) The breather does not discharge into the engine air induction system.

§ 25.1019   Oil strainer or filter.

(a) Each turbine engine installation must incorporate an oil strainer or filter through which all of the engine oil flows and which meets the following requirements:

(1) Each oil strainer or filter that has a bypass must be constructed and installed so that oil will flow at the normal rate through the rest of the system with the strainer or filter completely blocked.

(2) The oil strainer or filter must have the capacity (with respect to operating limitations established for the engine) to ensure that engine oil system functioning is not impaired when the oil is contaminated to a degree (with respect to particle size and density) that is greater than that established for the engine under Part 33 of this chapter.

(3) The oil strainer or filter, unless it is installed at an oil tank outlet, must incorporate an indicator that will indicate contamination before it reaches the capacity established in accordance with paragraph (a)(2) of this section.

(4) The bypass of a strainer or filter must be constructed and installed so that the release of collected contaminants is minimized by appropriate location of the bypass to ensure that collected contaminants are not in the bypass flow path.

(5) An oil strainer or filter that has no bypass, except one that is installed at an oil tank outlet, must have a means to connect it to the warning system required in § 25.1305(c)(7).

(b) Each oil strainer or filter in a powerplant installation using reciprocating engines must be constructed and installed so that oil will flow at the normal rate through the rest of the system with the strainer or filter element completely blocked.

[Amdt. 25–36, 39 FR 35461, Oct. 1, 1974, as amended by Amdt. 25–57, 49 FR 6848, Feb. 23, 1984]

§ 25.1021   Oil system drains.

A drain (or drains) must be provided to allow safe drainage of the oil system. Each drain must—

(a) Be accessible; and

(b) Have manual or automatic means for positive locking in the closed position.

[Amdt. 25–57, 49 FR 6848, Feb. 23, 1984]

§ 25.1023   Oil radiators.

(a) Each oil radiator must be able to withstand, without failure, any vibration, inertia, and oil pressure load to which it would be subjected in operation.

(b) Each oil radiator air duct must be located so that, in case of fire, flames coming from normal openings of the engine nacelle cannot impinge directly upon the radiator.

§ 25.1025   Oil valves.

(a) Each oil shutoff must meet the requirements of § 25.1189.

(b) The closing of oil shutoff means may not prevent propeller feathering.

(c) Each oil valve must have positive stops or suitable index provisions in the "on" and "off" positions and must be supported so that no loads resulting from its operation or from accelerated flight conditions are transmitted to the lines attached to the valve.

§ 25.1027   Propeller feathering system.

(a) If the propeller feathering system depends on engine oil, there must be means to trap an amount of oil in the tank if the supply becomes depleted due to failure of any part of the lubricating system other than the tank itself.

(b) The amount of trapped oil must be enough to accomplish the feathering operation and must be available only to the feathering pump.

(c) The ability of the system to accomplish feathering with the trapped oil must be shown. This may be done on the ground using an auxiliary source of oil for lubricating the engine during operation.

(d) Provision must be made to prevent sludge or other foreign matter from affecting the safe operation of the propeller feathering system.

[Doc. No. 5066, 29 FR 18291, Dec. 24, 1964, as amended by Amdt. 25–38, 41 FR 55467, Dec. 20, 1976]

COOLING

§ 25.1041   General.

The powerplant and auxiliary power unit cooling provisions must be able to maintain the temperatures of powerplant components, engine fluids, and auxiliary power unit components and fluids within the temperature limits established for these components and fluids, under ground, water, and flight operating conditions, and after normal engine or auxiliary power unit shutdown, or both.

[Amdt. 25–38, 41 FR 55467, Dec. 20, 1976]

§ 25.1043   Cooling tests.

(a) *General.* Compliance with § 25.1041 must be shown by tests, under critical ground, water, and flight operating conditions. For these tests, the following apply:

(1) If the tests are conducted under conditions deviating from the maximum ambient atmospheric temperature, the recorded powerplant temperatures must be corrected under paragraphs (c) and (d) of this section.

(2) No corrected temperatures determined under paragraph (a)(1) of this section may exceed established limits.

(3) For reciprocating engines, the fuel used during the cooling tests must be the minimum grade approved for the engines, and the mixture settings must be those normally used in the flight stages for which the cooling tests are conducted. The test procedures must be as prescribed in § 25.1045.

(b) *Maximum ambient atmospheric temperature.* A maximum ambient atmospheric temperature corresponding to sea level conditions of at least 100 degrees F must be established. The assumed temperature lapse rate is 3.6 degrees F per thousand feet of altitude above sea level until a temperature of −69.7 degrees F is reached, above which altitude the temperature is considered constant at −69.7 degrees F. However, for winterization installations, the applicant may select a maximum ambient atmospheric temperature corresponding to sea level conditions of less than 100 degrees F.

(c) *Correction factor (except cylinder barrels).* Unless a more rational correction applies, temperatures of engine

443

fluids and powerplant components (except cylinder barrels) for which temperature limits are established, must be corrected by adding to them the difference between the maximum ambient atmospheric temperature and the temperature of the ambient air at the time of the first occurrence of the maximum component or fluid temperature recorded during the cooling test.

(d) *Correction factor for cylinder barrel temperatures.* Unless a more rational correction applies, cylinder barrel temperatures must be corrected by adding to them 0.7 times the difference between the maximum ambient atmospheric temperature and the temperature of the ambient air at the time of the first occurrence of the maximum cylinder barrel temperature recorded during the cooling test.

[Doc. No. 5066, 29 FR 18291, Dec. 24, 1964, as amended by Amdt. 25-42, 43 FR 2323, Jan. 16, 1978]

§ 25.1045 Cooling test procedures.

(a) Compliance with § 25.1041 must be shown for the takeoff, climb, en route, and landing stages of flight that correspond to the applicable performance requirements. The cooling tests must be conducted with the airplane in the configuration, and operating under the conditions, that are critical relative to cooling during each stage of flight. For the cooling tests, a temperature is "stabilized" when its rate of change is less than two degrees F. per minute.

(b) Temperatures must be stabilized under the conditions from which entry is made into each stage of flight being investigated, unless the entry condition normally is not one during which component and the engine fluid temperatures would stabilize (in which case, operation through the full entry condition must be conducted before entry into the stage of flight being investigated in order to allow temperatures to reach their natural levels at the time of entry). The takeoff cooling test must be preceded by a period during which the powerplant component and engine fluid temperatures are stabilized with the engines at ground idle.

(c) Cooling tests for each stage of flight must be continued until—

(1) The component and engine fluid temperatures stabilize;

(2) The stage of flight is completed; or

(3) An operating limitation is reached.

(d) For reciprocating engine powered airplanes, it may be assumed, for cooling test purposes, that the takeoff stage of flight is complete when the airplane reaches an altitude of 1,500 feet above the takeoff surface or reaches a point in the takeoff where the transition from the takeoff to the en route configuration is completed and a speed is reached at which compliance with § 25.121(c) is shown, whichever point is at a higher altitude. The airplane must be in the following configuration:

(1) Landing gear retracted.

(2) Wing flaps in the most favorable position.

(3) Cowl flaps (or other means of controlling the engine cooling supply) in the position that provides adequate cooling in the hot-day condition.

(4) Critical engine inoperative and its propeller stopped.

(5) Remaining engines at the maximum continuous power available for the altitude.

(e) For hull seaplanes and amphibians, cooling must be shown during taxiing downwind for 10 minutes, at five knots above step speed.

[Doc. No. 5066, 29 FR 18291, Dec. 24, 1964, as amended by Amdt. 25-57, 49 FR 6848, Feb. 23, 1984]

INDUCTION SYSTEM

§ 25.1091 Air induction.

(a) The air induction system for each engine and auxiliary power unit must supply—

(1) The air required by that engine and auxiliary power unit under each operating condition for which certification is requested; and

(2) The air for proper fuel metering and mixture distribution with the induction system valves in any position.

(b) Each reciprocating engine must have an alternate air source that prevents the entry of rain, ice, or any other foreign matter.

(c) Air intakes may not open within the cowling, unless—

(1) That part of the cowling is isolated from the engine accessory section by means of a fireproof diaphragm; or

(2) For reciprocating engines, there are means to prevent the emergence of backfire flames.

(d) For turbine engine powered airplanes and airplanes incorporating auxiliary power units—

(1) There must be means to prevent hazardous quantities of fuel leakage or overflow from drains, vents, or other components of flammable fluid systems from entering the engine or auxiliary power unit intake system; and

(2) The airplane must be designed to prevent water or slush on the runway, taxiway, or other airport operating surfaces from being directed into the engine or auxiliary power unit air inlet ducts in hazardous quantities, and the air inlet ducts must be located or protected so as to minimize the ingestion of foreign matter during takeoff, landing, and taxiing.

(e) If the engine induction system contains parts or components that could be damaged by foreign objects entering the air inlet, it must be shown by tests or, if appropriate, by analysis that the induction system design can withstand the foreign object ingestion test conditions of §§33.76, 33.77 and 33.78(a)(1) of this chapter without failure of parts or components that could create a hazard.

[Doc. No. 5066, 29 FR 18291, Dec. 24, 1964, as amended by Amdt. 25–38, 41 FR 55467, Dec. 20, 1976; Amdt. 25–40, 42 FR 15043, Mar. 17, 1977; Amdt. 25–57, 49 FR 6849, Feb. 23, 1984; Amdt. 25–100, 65 FR 55854, Sept. 14, 2000]

§25.1093 Induction system icing protection.

(a) *Reciprocating engines.* Each reciprocating engine air induction system must have means to prevent and eliminate icing. Unless this is done by other means, it must be shown that, in air free of visible moisture at a temperature of 30 F., each airplane with altitude engines using—

(1) Conventional venturi carburetors have a preheater that can provide a heat rise of 120 F. with the engine at 60 percent of maximum continuous power; or

(2) Carburetors tending to reduce the probability of ice formation has a pre-heater that can provide a heat rise of 100 °F. with the engine at 60 percent of maximum continuous power.

(b) *Turbine engines.* (1) Each turbine engine must operate throughout the flight power range of the engine (including idling), without the accumulation of ice on the engine, inlet system components, or airframe components that would adversely affect engine operation or cause a serious loss of power or thrust—

(i) Under the icing conditions specified in appendix C, and

(ii) In falling and blowing snow within the limitations established for the airplane for such operation.

(2) Each turbine engine must idle for 30 minutes on the ground, with the air bleed available for engine icing protection at its critical condition, without adverse effect, in an atmosphere that is at a temperature between 15° and 30 °F (between −9° and −1 °C) and has a liquid water content not less than 0.3 grams per cubic meter in the form of drops having a mean effective diameter not less than 20 microns, followed by momentary operation at takeoff power or thrust. During the 30 minutes of idle operation, the engine may be run up periodically to a moderate power or thrust setting in a manner acceptable to the Administrator.

(c) *Supercharged reciprocating engines.* For each engine having a supercharger to pressurize the air before it enters the carburetor, the heat rise in the air caused by that supercharging at any altitude may be utilized in determining compliance with paragraph (a) of this section if the heat rise utilized is that which will be available, automatically, for the applicable altitude and operating condition because of supercharging.

[Doc. No. 5066, 29 FR 18291, Dec. 24, 1964, as amended by Amdt. 25–38, 41 FR 55467, Dec. 20, 1976; Amdt. 25–40, 42 FR 15043, Mar. 17, 1977; Amdt. 25–57, 49 FR 6849, Feb. 23, 1984; Amdt. 25–72, 55 FR 29785, July 20, 1990]

§25.1101 Carburetor air preheater design.

Each carburetor air preheater must be designed and constructed to—

(a) Ensure ventilation of the preheater when the engine is operated in cold air;

(b) Allow inspection of the exhaust manifold parts that it surrounds; and

(c) Allow inspection of critical parts of the preheater itself.

§ 25.1103 Induction system ducts and air duct systems.

(a) Each induction system duct upstream of the first stage of the engine supercharger and of the auxiliary power unit compressor must have a drain to prevent the hazardous accumulation of fuel and moisture in the ground attitude. No drain may discharge where it might cause a fire hazard.

(b) Each induction system duct must be—

(1) Strong enough to prevent induction system failures resulting from normal backfire conditions; and

(2) Fire-resistant if it is in any fire zone for which a fire-extinguishing system is required, except that ducts for auxiliary power units must be fireproof within the auxiliary power unit fire zone.

(c) Each duct connected to components between which relative motion could exist must have means for flexibility.

(d) For turbine engine and auxiliary power unit bleed air duct systems, no hazard may result if a duct failure occurs at any point between the air duct source and the airplane unit served by the air.

(e) Each auxiliary power unit induction system duct must be fireproof for a sufficient distance upstream of the auxiliary power unit compartment to prevent hot gas reverse flow from burning through auxiliary power unit ducts and entering any other compartment or area of the airplane in which a hazard would be created resulting from the entry of hot gases. The materials used to form the remainder of the induction system duct and plenum chamber of the auxiliary power unit must be capable of resisting the maximum heat conditions likely to occur.

(f) Each auxiliary power unit induction system duct must be constructed of materials that will not absorb or trap hazardous quantities of flammable fluids that could be ignited in the event of a surge or reverse flow condition.

[Doc. No. 5066, 29 FR 18291, Dec. 24, 1964, as amended by Amdt. 25–46, 43 FR 50597, Oct. 30, 1978]

§ 25.1105 Induction system screens.

If induction system screens are used—

(a) Each screen must be upstream of the carburetor;

(b) No screen may be in any part of the induction system that is the only passage through which air can reach the engine, unless it can be deiced by heated air;

(c) No screen may be deiced by alcohol alone; and

(d) It must be impossible for fuel to strike any screen.

§ 25.1107 Inter-coolers and after-coolers.

Each inter-cooler and after-cooler must be able to withstand any vibration, inertia, and air pressure load to which it would be subjected in operation.

EXHAUST SYSTEM

§ 25.1121 General.

For powerplant and auxiliary power unit installations the following apply:

(a) Each exhaust system must ensure safe disposal of exhaust gases without fire hazard or carbon monoxide contamination in any personnel compartment. For test purposes, any acceptable carbon monoxide detection method may be used to show the absence of carbon monoxide.

(b) Each exhaust system part with a surface hot enough to ignite flammable fluids or vapors must be located or shielded so that leakage from any system carrying flammable fluids or vapors will not result in a fire caused by impingement of the fluids or vapors on any part of the exhaust system including shields for the exhaust system.

(c) Each component that hot exhaust gases could strike, or that could be subjected to high temperatures from exhaust system parts, must be fireproof. All exhaust system components must be separated by fireproof shields from adjacent parts of the airplane that are outside the engine and auxiliary power unit compartments.

(d) No exhaust gases may discharge so as to cause a fire hazard with respect to any flammable fluid vent or drain.

(e) No exhaust gases may discharge where they will cause a glare seriously affecting pilot vision at night.

(f) Each exhaust system component must be ventilated to prevent points of excessively high temperature.

(g) Each exhaust shroud must be ventilated or insulated to avoid, during normal operation, a temperature high enough to ignite any flammable fluids or vapors external to the shroud.

[Doc. No. 5066, 29 FR 18291, Dec. 24, 1964, as amended by Amdt. 25–40, 42 FR 15043, Mar. 17, 1977]

§ 25.1123 Exhaust piping.

For powerplant and auxiliary power unit installations, the following apply:

(a) Exhaust piping must be heat and corrosion resistant, and must have provisions to prevent failure due to expansion by operating temperatures.

(b) Piping must be supported to withstand any vibration and inertia loads to which it would be subjected in operation; and

(c) Piping connected to components between which relative motion could exist must have means for flexibility.

[Doc. No. 5066, 29 FR 18291, Dec. 24, 1964, as amended by Amdt. 25–40, 42 FR 15044, Mar. 17, 1977]

§ 25.1125 Exhaust heat exchangers.

For reciprocating engine powered airplanes, the following apply:

(a) Each exhaust heat exchanger must be constructed and installed to withstand each vibration, inertia, and other load to which it would be subjected in operation. In addition—

(1) Each exchanger must be suitable for continued operation at high temperatures and resistant to corrosion from exhaust gases;

(2) There must be means for the inspection of the critical parts of each exchanger;

(3) Each exchanger must have cooling provisions wherever it is subject to contact with exhaust gases; and

(4) No exhaust heat exchanger or muff may have any stagnant areas or liquid traps that would increase the probability of ignition of flammable fluids or vapors that might be present in case of the failure or malfunction of components carrying flammable fluids.

(b) If an exhaust heat exchanger is used for heating ventilating air—

(1) There must be a secondary heat exchanger between the primary exhaust gas heat exchanger and the ventilating air system; or

(2) Other means must be used to preclude the harmful contamination of the ventilating air.

[Doc. No. 5066, 29 FR 18291, Dec. 24, 1964, as amended by Amdt. 25–38, 41 FR 55467, Dec. 20, 1976]

§ 25.1127 Exhaust driven turbo-superchargers.

(a) Each exhaust driven turbo-supercharger must be approved or shown to be suitable for the particular application. It must be installed and supported to ensure safe operation between normal inspections and overhauls. In addition, there must be provisions for expansion and flexibility between exhaust conduits and the turbine.

(b) There must be provisions for lubricating the turbine and for cooling turbine parts where temperatures are critical.

(c) If the normal turbo-supercharger control system malfunctions, the turbine speed may not exceed its maximum allowable value. Except for the waste gate operating components, the components provided for meeting this requirement must be independent of the normal turbo-supercharger controls.

POWERPLANT CONTROLS AND
ACCESSORIES

§ 25.1141 Powerplant controls: general.

Each powerplant control must be located, arranged, and designed under §§ 25.777 through 25.781 and marked under § 25.1555. In addition, it must meet the following requirements:

(a) Each control must be located so that it cannot be inadvertently operated by persons entering, leaving, or moving normally in, the cockpit.

(b) Each flexible control must be approved or must be shown to be suitable for the particular application.

(c) Each control must have sufficient strength and rigidity to withstand operating loads without failure and without excessive deflection.

(d) Each control must be able to maintain any set position without constant attention by flight crewmembers and without creep due to control loads or vibration.

(e) The portion of each powerplant control located in a designated fire zone that is required to be operated in the event of fire must be at least fire resistant.

(f) Powerplant valve controls located in the cockpit must have—

(1) For manual valves, positive stops or in the case of fuel valves suitable index provisions, in the open and closed position; and

(2) For power-assisted valves, a means to indicate to the flight crew when the valve—

(i) Is in the fully open or fully closed position; or

(ii) Is moving between the fully open and fully closed position.

[Doc. No. 5066, 29 FR 18291, Dec. 24, 1964, as amended by Amdt. 25-40, 42 FR 15044, Mar. 17, 1977; Amdt. 25-72, 55 FR 29785, July 20, 1990]

§ 25.1142 Auxiliary power unit controls.

Means must be provided on the flight deck for starting, stopping, and emergency shutdown of each installed auxiliary power unit.

[Amdt. 25-46, 43 FR 50598, Oct. 30, 1978]

§ 25.1143 Engine controls.

(a) There must be a separate power or thrust control for each engine.

(b) Power and thrust controls must be arranged to allow—

(1) Separate control of each engine; and

(2) Simultaneous control of all engines.

(c) Each power and thrust control must provide a positive and immediately responsive means of controlling its engine.

(d) For each fluid injection (other than fuel) system and its controls not provided and approved as part of the engine, the applicant must show that the flow of the injection fluid is adequately controlled.

(e) If a power or thrust control incorporates a fuel shutoff feature, the control must have a means to prevent the inadvertent movement of the control into the shutoff position. The means must—

(1) Have a positive lock or stop at the idle position; and

(2) Require a separate and distinct operation to place the control in the shutoff position.

[Amdt. 25-23, 35 FR 5677, Apr. 8, 1970, as amended by Amdt. 25-38, 41 FR 55467, Dec. 20, 1976; Amdt. 25-57, 49 FR 6849, Feb. 23, 1984]

§ 25.1145 Ignition switches.

(a) Ignition switches must control each engine ignition circuit on each engine.

(b) There must be means to quickly shut off all ignition by the grouping of switches or by a master ignition control.

(c) Each group of ignition switches, except ignition switches for turbine engines for which continuous ignition is not required, and each master ignition control must have a means to prevent its inadvertent operation.

[Doc. No. 5066, 29 FR 18291, Dec. 24, 1964, as amended by Amdt. 25-40, 42 FR 15044 Mar. 17, 1977]

§ 25.1147 Mixture controls.

(a) If there are mixture controls, each engine must have a separate control. The controls must be grouped and arranged to allow—

(1) Separate control of each engine; and

(2) Simultaneous control of all engines.

(b) Each intermediate position of the mixture controls that corresponds to a normal operating setting must be identifiable by feel and sight.

(c) The mixture controls must be accessible to both pilots. However, if there is a separate flight engineer station with a control panel, the controls need be accessible only to the flight engineer.

§25.1149 Propeller speed and pitch controls.

(a) There must be a separate propeller speed and pitch control for each propeller.

(b) The controls must be grouped and arranged to allow—

(1) Separate control of each propeller; and

(2) Simultaneous control of all propellers.

(c) The controls must allow synchronization of all propellers.

(d) The propeller speed and pitch controls must be to the right of, and at least one inch below, the pilot's throttle controls.

§25.1153 Propeller feathering controls.

(a) There must be a separate propeller feathering control for each propeller. The control must have means to prevent its inadvertent operation.

(b) If feathering is accomplished by movement of the propeller pitch or speed control lever, there must be means to prevent the inadvertent movement of this lever to the feathering position during normal operation.

[Doc. No. 5066, 29 FR 18291, Dec. 24, 1964, as amended by Amdt. 25–11, 32 FR 6913, May 5, 1967]

§25.1155 Reverse thrust and propeller pitch settings below the flight regime.

Each control for reverse thrust and for propeller pitch settings below the flight regime must have means to prevent its inadvertent operation. The means must have a positive lock or stop at the flight idle position and must require a separate and distinct operation by the crew to displace the control from the flight regime (forward thrust regime for turbojet powered airplanes).

[Amdt. 25–11, 32 FR 6913, May 5, 1967]

§25.1157 Carburetor air temperature controls.

There must be a separate carburetor air temperature control for each engine.

§25.1159 Supercharger controls.

Each supercharger control must be accessible to the pilots or, if there is a separate flight engineer station with a control panel, to the flight engineer.

§25.1161 Fuel jettisoning system controls.

Each fuel jettisoning system control must have guards to prevent inadvertent operation. No control may be near any fire extinguisher control or other control used to combat fire.

§25.1163 Powerplant accessories.

(a) Each engine mounted accessory must—

(1) Be approved for mounting on the engine involved;

(2) Use the provisions on the engine for mounting; and

(3) Be sealed to prevent contamination of the engine oil system and the accessory system.

(b) Electrical equipment subject to arcing or sparking must be installed to minimize the probability of contact with any flammable fluids or vapors that might be present in a free state.

(c) If continued rotation of an engine-driven cabin supercharger or of any remote accessory driven by the engine is hazardous if malfunctioning occurs, there must be means to prevent rotation without interfering with the continued operation of the engine.

[Doc. No. 5066, 29 FR 18291, Dec. 24, 1964, as amended by Amdt. 25–57, 49 FR 6849, Feb. 23, 1984]

§25.1165 Engine ignition systems.

(a) Each battery ignition system must be supplemented by a generator that is automatically available as an alternate source of electrical energy to allow continued engine operation if any battery becomes depleted.

(b) The capacity of batteries and generators must be large enough to meet the simultaneous demands of the engine ignition system and the greatest demands of any electrical system components that draw electrical energy from the same source.

(c) The design of the engine ignition system must account for—

(1) The condition of an inoperative generator;

(2) The condition of a completely depleted battery with the generator running at its normal operating speed; and

(3) The condition of a completely depleted battery with the generator operating at idling speed, if there is only one battery.

(d) Magneto ground wiring (for separate ignition circuits) that lies on the engine side of the fire wall, must be installed, located, or protected, to minimize the probability of simultaneous failure of two or more wires as a result of mechanical damage, electrical faults, or other cause.

(e) No ground wire for any engine may be routed through a fire zone of another engine unless each part of that wire within that zone is fireproof.

(f) Each ignition system must be independent of any electrical circuit, not used for assisting, controlling, or analyzing the operation of that system.

(g) There must be means to warn appropriate flight crewmembers if the malfunctioning of any part of the electrical system is causing the continuous discharge of any battery necessary for engine ignition.

(h) Each engine ignition system of a turbine powered airplane must be considered an essential electrical load.

[Doc. No. 5066, 29 FR 18291, Dec. 24, 1964, as amended by Amdt. 25-23, 35 FR 5677, Apr. 8, 1970; Amdt. 25-72, 55 FR 29785, July 20, 1990]

§ 25.1167　Accessory gearboxes.

For airplanes equipped with an accessory gearbox that is not certificated as part of an engine—

(a) The engine with gearbox and connecting transmissions and shafts attached must be subjected to the tests specified in § 33.49 or § 33.87 of this chapter, as applicable;

(b) The accessory gearbox must meet the requirements of §§ 33.25 and 33.53 or 33.91 of this chapter, as applicable; and

(c) Possible misalignments and torsional loadings of the gearbox, transmission, and shaft system, expected to result under normal operating conditions must be evaluated.

[Amdt. 25-38, 41 FR 55467, Dec. 20, 1976]

POWERPLANT FIRE PROTECTION

§ 25.1181　Designated fire zones; regions included.

(a) Designated fire zones are—

(1) The engine power section;

(2) The engine accessory section;

(3) Except for reciprocating engines, any complete powerplant compartment in which no isolation is provided between the engine power section and the engine accessory section;

(4) Any auxiliary power unit compartment;

(5) Any fuel-burning heater and other combustion equipment installation described in § 25.859;

(6) The compressor and accessory sections of turbine engines; and

(7) Combustor, turbine, and tailpipe sections of turbine engine installations that contain lines or components carrying flammable fluids or gases.

(b) Each designated fire zone must meet the requirements of §§ 25.867, and 25.1185 through 25.1203.

[Doc. No. 5066, 29 FR 18291, Dec. 24, 1964, as amended by Amdt. 25-11, 32 FR 6913, May 5, 1967; Amdt. 25-23, 35 FR 5677, Apr. 8, 1970; Amdt. 25-72, 55 FR 29785, July 20, 1990]

§ 25.1182　Nacelle areas behind firewalls, and engine pod attaching structures containing flammable fluid lines.

(a) Each nacelle area immediately behind the firewall, and each portion of any engine pod attaching structure containing flammable fluid lines, must meet each requirement of §§ 25.1103(b), 25.1165 (d) and (e), 25.1183, 25.1185(c), 25.1187, 25.1189, and 25.1195 through 25.1203, including those concerning designated fire zones. However, engine pod attaching structures need not contain fire detection or extinguishing means.

(b) For each area covered by paragraph (a) of this section that contains a retractable landing gear, compliance with that paragraph need only be shown with the landing gear retracted.

[Amdt. 25-11, 32 FR 6913, May 5, 1967]

§ 25.1183　Flammable fluid-carrying components.

(a) Except as provided in paragraph (b) of this section, each line, fitting, and other component carrying flammable fluid in any area subject to engine fire conditions, and each component which conveys or contains flammable fluid in a designated fire zone must be fire resistant, except that flammable fluid tanks and supports in a designated fire zone must be fireproof or be enclosed by a fireproof shield unless damage by fire to any non-fireproof part will not cause leakage or spillage of flammable fluid. Components must be shielded or located to safeguard against the ignition of leaking flammable fluid. An integral oil sump of less than 25-quart capacity on a reciprocating engine need not be fireproof nor be enclosed by a fireproof shield.

(b) Paragraph (a) of this section does not apply to—

(1) Lines, fittings, and components which are already approved as part of a type certificated engine; and

(2) Vent and drain lines, and their fittings, whose failure will not result in, or add to, a fire hazard.

(c) All components, including ducts, within a designated fire zone must be fireproof if, when exposed to or damaged by fire, they could—

(1) Result in fire spreading to other regions of the airplane; or

(2) Cause unintentional operation of, or inability to operate, essential services or equipment.

[Doc. No. 5066, 29 FR 18291, Dec. 24, 1964, as amended by Amdt. 25–11, 32 FR 6913, May 5, 1967; Amdt. 25–36, 39 FR 35461, Oct. 1, 1974; Amdt. 25–57, 49 FR 6849, Feb. 23, 1984; Amdt. 25–101, 65 FR 79710, Dec. 19, 2000]

§25.1185 Flammable fluids.

(a) Except for the integral oil sumps specified in §25.1183(a), no tank or reservoir that is a part of a system containing flammable fluids or gases may be in a designated fire zone unless the fluid contained, the design of the system, the materials used in the tank, the shut-off means, and all connections, lines, and control provide a degree of safety equal to that which would exist if the tank or reservoir were outside such a zone.

(b) There must be at least one-half inch of clear airspace between each tank or reservoir and each firewall or shroud isolating a designated fire zone.

(c) Absorbent materials close to flammable fluid system components that might leak must be covered or treated to prevent the absorption of hazardous quantities of fluids.

[Doc. No. 5066, 29 FR 18291, Dec. 24, 1964 as amended by Amdt. 25–19, 33 FR 15410, Oct. 17, 1968; Amdt. 25–94, 63 FR 8848, Feb. 23, 1998]

§25.1187 Drainage and ventilation of fire zones.

(a) There must be complete drainage of each part of each designated fire zone to minimize the hazards resulting from failure or malfunctioning of any component containing flammable fluids. The drainage means must be—

(1) Effective under conditions expected to prevail when drainage is needed; and

(2) Arranged so that no discharged fluid will cause an additional fire hazard.

(b) Each designated fire zone must be ventilated to prevent the accumulation of flammable vapors.

(c) No ventilation opening may be where it would allow the entry of flammable fluids, vapors, or flame from other zones.

(d) Each ventilation means must be arranged so that no discharged vapors will cause an additional fire hazard.

(e) Unless the extinguishing agent capacity and rate of discharge are based on maximum air flow through a zone, there must be means to allow the crew to shut off sources of forced ventilation to any fire zone except the engine power section of the nacelle and the combustion heater ventilating air ducts.

§25.1189 Shutoff means.

(a) Each engine installation and each fire zone specified in §25.1181(a)(4) and (5) must have a means to shut off or otherwise prevent hazardous quantities of fuel, oil, deicer, and other flammable fluids, from flowing into, within, or through any designated fire zone, except that shutoff means are not required for—

(1) Lines, fittings, and components forming an integral part of an engine; and

(2) Oil systems for turbine engine installations in which all components of the system in a designated fire zone,

including oil tanks, are fireproof or located in areas not subject to engine fire conditions.

(b) The closing of any fuel shutoff valve for any engine may not make fuel unavailable to the remaining engines.

(c) Operation of any shutoff may not interfere with the later emergency operation of other equipment, such as the means for feathering the propeller.

(d) Each flammable fluid shutoff means and control must be fireproof or must be located and protected so that any fire in a fire zone will not affect its operation.

(e) No hazardous quantity of flammable fluid may drain into any designated fire zone after shutoff.

(f) There must be means to guard against inadvertent operation of the shutoff means and to make it possible for the crew to reopen the shutoff means in flight after it has been closed.

(g) Each tank-to-engine shutoff valve must be located so that the operation of the valve will not be affected by powerplant or engine mount structural failure.

(h) Each shutoff valve must have a means to relieve excessive pressure accumulation unless a means for pressure relief is otherwise provided in the system.

[Doc. No. 5066, 29 FR 18291, Dec. 24, 1964, as amended by Amdt. 25–23, 35 FR 5677, Apr. 8, 1970; Amdt. 25–57, 49 FR 6849, Feb. 23, 1984]

§ 25.1191 Firewalls.

(a) Each engine, auxiliary power unit, fuel-burning heater, other combustion equipment intended for operation in flight, and the combustion, turbine, and tailpipe sections of turbine engines, must be isolated from the rest of the airplane by firewalls, shrouds, or equivalent means.

(b) Each firewall and shroud must be—

(1) Fireproof;

(2) Constructed so that no hazardous quantity of air, fluid, or flame can pass from the compartment to other parts of the airplane;

(3) Constructed so that each opening is sealed with close fitting fireproof grommets, bushings, or firewall fittings; and

(4) Protected against corrosion.

§ 25.1192 Engine accessory section diaphragm.

For reciprocating engines, the engine power section and all portions of the exhaust system must be isolated from the engine accessory compartment by a diaphragm that complies with the firewall requirements of § 25.1191.

[Amdt. 25–23, 35 FR 5678, Apr. 8, 1970]

§ 25.1193 Cowling and nacelle skin.

(a) Each cowling must be constructed and supported so that it canresist any vibration, inertia, and air load to which it may be subjected in operation.

(b) Cowling must meet the drainage and ventilation requirements of § 25.1187.

(c) On airplanes with a diaphragm isolating the engine power section from the engine accessory section, each part of the accessory section cowling subject to flame in case of fire in the engine power section of the powerplant must—

(1) Be fireproof; and

(2) Meet the requirements of § 25.1191.

(d) Each part of the cowling subject to high temperatures due to its nearness to exhaust system parts or exhaust gas impingement must be fireproof.

(e) Each airplane must—

(1) Be designed and constructed so that no fire originating in any fire zone can enter, either through openings or by burning through external skin, any other zone or region where it would create additional hazards;

(2) Meet paragraph (e)(1) of this section with the landing gear retracted (if applicable); and

(3) Have fireproof skin in areas subject to flame if a fire starts in the engine power or accessory sections.

§ 25.1195 Fire extinguishing systems.

(a) Except for combustor, turbine, and tail pipe sections of turbine engine installations that contain lines or components carrying flammable fluids or gases for which it is shown that a fire originating in these sections can be controlled, there must be a fire extinguisher system serving each designated fire zone.

(b) The fire extinguishing system, the quantity of the extinguishing agent, the rate of discharge, and the discharge distribution must be adequate to extinguish fires. It must be shown by either actual or simulated flights tests that under critical airflow conditions in flight the discharge of the extinguishing agent in each designated fire zone specified in paragraph (a) of this section will provide an agent concentration capable of extinguishing fires in that zone and of minimizing the probability of reignition. An individual "one-shot" system may be used for auxiliary power units, fuel burning heaters, and other combustion equipment. For each other designated fire zone, two discharges must be provided each of which produces adequate agent concentration.

(c) The fire extinguishing system for a nacelle must be able to simultaneously protect each zone of the nacelle for which protection is provided.

[Doc. No. 5066, 29 FR 18291, Dec. 24, 1964, as amended by Amdt. 25–46, 43 FR 50598, Oct. 30, 1978]

§ 25.1197 Fire extinguishing agents.

(a) Fire extinguishing agents must—

(1) Be capable of extinguishing flames emanating from any burning of fluids or other combustible materials in the area protected by the fire extinguishing system; and

(2) Have thermal stability over the temperature range likely to be experienced in the compartment in which they are stored.

(b) If any toxic extinguishing agent is used, provisions must be made to prevent harmful concentrations of fluid or fluid vapors (from leakage during normal operation of the airplane or as a result of discharging the fire extinguisher on the ground or in flight) from entering any personnel compartment, even though a defect may exist in the extinguishing system. This must be shown by test except for built-in carbon dioxide fuselage compartment fire extinguishing systems for which—

(1) Five pounds or less of carbon dioxide will be discharged, under established fire control procedures, into any fuselage compartment; or

(2) There is protective breathing equipment for each flight crewmember on flight deck duty.

[Doc. No. 5066, 29 FR 18291, Dec. 24, 1964, as amended by Amdt. 25–38, 41 FR 55467, Dec. 20, 1976; Amdt. 25–40, 42 FR 15044, Mar. 17, 1977]

§ 25.1199 Extinguishing agent containers.

(a) Each extinguishing agent container must have a pressure relief to prevent bursting of the container by excessive internal pressures.

(b) The discharge end of each discharge line from a pressure relief connection must be located so that discharge of the fire extinguishing agent would not damage the airplane. The line must also be located or protected to prevent clogging caused by ice or other foreign matter.

(c) There must be a means for each fire extinguishing agent container to indicate that the container has discharged or that the charging pressure is below the established minimum necessary for proper functioning.

(d) The temperature of each container must be maintained, under intended operating conditions, to prevent the pressure in the container from—

(1) Falling below that necessary to provide an adequate rate of discharge; or

(2) Rising high enough to cause premature discharge.

(e) If a pyrotechnic capsule is used to discharge the extinguishing agent, each container must be installed so that temperature conditions will not cause hazardous deterioration of the pyrotechnic capsule.

[Doc. No. 5066, 29 FR 18291, Dec. 24, 1964, as amended by Amdt. 25–23, 35 FR 5678, Apr. 8, 1970; Amdt. 25–40, 42 FR 15044, Mar. 17, 1977]

§ 25.1201 Fire extinguishing system materials.

(a) No material in any fire extinguishing system may react chemically with any extinguishing agent so as to create a hazard.

(b) Each system component in an engine compartment must be fireproof.

§ 25.1203 Fire detector system.

(a) There must be approved, quick acting fire or overheat detectors in each designated fire zone, and in the combustion, turbine, and tailpipe sections of turbine engine installations, in numbers and locations ensuring prompt detection of fire in those zones.

(b) Each fire detector system must be constructed and installed so that—

(1) It will withstand the vibration, inertia, and other loads to which it may be subjected in operation;

(2) There is a means to warn the crew in the event that the sensor or associated wiring within a designated fire zone is severed at one point, unless the system continues to function as a satisfactory detection system after the severing; and

(3) There is a means to warn the crew in the event of a short circuit in the sensor or associated wiring within a designated fire zone, unless the system continues to function as a satisfactory detection system after the short circuit.

(c) No fire or overheat detector may be affected by any oil, water, other fluids or fumes that might be present.

(d) There must be means to allow the crew to check, in flight, the functioning of each fire or overheat detector electric circuit.

(e) Wiring and other components of each fire or overheat detector system in a fire zone must be at least fire-resistant.

(f) No fire or overheat detector system component for any fire zone may pass through another fire zone, unless—

(1) It is protected against the possibility of false warnings resulting from fires in zones through which it passes; or

(2) Each zone involved is simultaneously protected by the same detector and extinguishing system.

(g) Each fire detector system must be constructed so that when it is in the configuration for installation it will not exceed the alarm activation time approved for the detectors using the response time criteria specified in the appropriate Technical Standard Order for the detector.

[Doc. No. 5066, 29 FR 18291, Dec. 24, 1964, as amended by Amdt. 25–23, 35 FR 5678, Apr. 8, 1970; Amdt. 25–26, 36 FR 5493, Mar. 24, 1971]

§ 25.1207   Compliance.

Unless otherwise specified, compliance with the requirements of §§ 25.1181 through 25.1203 must be shown by a full scale fire test or by one or more of the following methods:

(a) Tests of similar powerplant configurations;

(b) Tests of components;

(c) Service experience of aircraft with similar powerplant configurations;

(d) Analysis.

[Amdt. 25–46, 43 FR 50598, Oct. 30, 1978]

Subpart F—Equipment

GENERAL

§ 25.1301   Function and installation.

Each item of installed equipment must—

(a) Be of a kind and design appropriate to its intended function;

(b) Be labeled as to its identification, function, or operating limitations, or any applicable combination of these factors;

(c) Be installed according to limitations specified for that equipment; and

(d) Function properly when installed.

§ 25.1303   Flight and navigation instruments.

(a) The following flight and navigation instruments must be installed so that the instrument is visible from each pilot station:

(1) A free air temperature indicator or an air-temperature indicator which provides indications that are convertible to free-air temperature.

(2) A clock displaying hours, minutes, and seconds with a sweep-second pointer or digital presentation.

(3) A direction indicator (non-stabilized magnetic compass).

(b) The following flight and navigation instruments must be installed at each pilot station:

(1) An airspeed indicator. If airspeed limitations vary with altitude, the indicator must have a maximum allowable airspeed indicator showing the variation of V_{MO} with altitude.

(2) An altimeter (sensitive).

(3) A rate-of-climb indicator (vertical speed).

(4) A gyroscopic rate-of-turn indicator combined with an integral slip-skid indicator (turn-and-bank indicator) except that only a slip-skid indicator is required on large airplanes with a third attitude instrument system useable through flight attitudes of 360° of pitch and roll and installed in accordance with §121.305(k) of this title.

(5) A bank and pitch indicator (gyroscopically stabilized).

(6) A direction indicator (gyroscopically stabilized, magnetic or nonmagnetic).

(c) The following flight and navigation instruments are required as prescribed in this paragraph:

(1) A speed warning device is required for turbine engine powered airplanes and for airplanes with V_{MO}/M_{MO} greater than 0.8 V_{DF}/M_{DF} or 0.8 V_D/M_D. The speed warning device must give effective aural warning (differing distinctively from aural warnings used for other purposes) to the pilots, whenever the speed exceeds V_{MO} plus 6 knots or M_{MO} +0.01. The upper limit of the production tolerance for the warning device may not exceed the prescribed warning speed.

(2) A machmeter is required at each pilot station for airplanes with compressibility limitations not otherwise indicated to the pilot by the airspeed indicating system required under paragraph (b)(1) of this section.

[Amdt. 25–23, 35 FR 5678, Apr. 8, 1970, as amended by Amdt. 25–24, 35 FR 7108, May 6, 1970; Amdt. 25–38, 41 FR 55467, Dec. 20, 1976; Amdt. 25–90, 62 FR 13253, Mar. 19, 1997]

§25.1305 Powerplant instruments.

The following are required powerplant instruments:

(a) *For all airplanes.* (1) A fuel pressure warning means for each engine, or a master warning means for all engines with provision for isolating the individual warning means from the master warning means.

(2) A fuel quantity indicator for each fuel tank.

(3) An oil quantity indicator for each oil tank.

(4) An oil pressure indicator for each independent pressure oil system of each engine.

(5) An oil pressure warning means for each engine, or a master warning means for all engines with provision for isolating the individual warning means from the master warning means.

(6) An oil temperature indicator for each engine.

(7) Fire-warning indicators.

(8) An augmentation liquid quantity indicator (appropriate for the manner in which the liquid is to be used in operation) for each tank.

(b) *For reciprocating engine-powered airplanes.* In addition to the powerplant instruments required by paragraph (a) of this section, the following powerplant instruments are required:

(1) A carburetor air temperature indicator for each engine.

(2) A cylinder head temperature indicator for each air-cooled engine.

(3) A manifold pressure indicator for each engine.

(4) A fuel pressure indicator (to indicate the pressure at which the fuel is supplied) for each engine.

(5) A fuel flowmeter, or fuel mixture indicator, for each engine without an automatic altitude mixture control.

(6) A tachometer for each engine.

(7) A device that indicates, to the flight crew (during flight), any change in the power output, for each engine with—

(i) An automatic propeller feathering system, whose operation is initiated by a power output measuring system; or

(ii) A total engine piston displacement of 2,000 cubic inches or more.

(8) A means to indicate to the pilot when the propeller is in reverse pitch, for each reversing propeller.

(c) *For turbine engine-powered airplanes.* In addition to the powerplant instruments required by paragraph (a) of this section, the following powerplant instruments are required:

(1) A gas temperature indicator for each engine.

(2) A fuel flowmeter indicator for each engine.

(3) A tachometer (to indicate the speed of the rotors with established limiting speeds) for each engine.

(4) A means to indicate, to the flight crew, the operation of each engine starter that can be operated continuously but that is neither designed for

continuous operation nor designed to prevent hazard if it failed.

(5) An indicator to indicate the functioning of the powerplant ice protection system for each engine.

(6) An indicator for the fuel strainer or filter required by § 25.997 to indicate the occurrence of contamination of the strainer or filter before it reaches the capacity established in accordance with § 25.997(d).

(7) A warning means for the oil strainer or filter required by § 25.1019, if it has no bypass, to warn the pilot of the occurrence of contamination of the strainer or filter screen before it reaches the capacity established in accordance with § 25.1019(a)(2).

(8) An indicator to indicate the proper functioning of any heater used to prevent ice clogging of fuel system components.

(d) *For turbojet engine powered airplanes.* In addition to the powerplant instruments required by paragraphs (a) and (c) of this section, the following powerplant instruments are required:

(1) An indicator to indicate thrust, or a parameter that is directly related to thrust, to the pilot. The indication must be based on the direct measurement of thrust or of parameters that are directly related to thrust. The indicator must indicate a change in thrust resulting from any engine malfunction, damage, or deterioration.

(2) A position indicating means to indicate to the flight crew when the thrust reversing device is in the reverse thrust position, for each engine using a thrust reversing device.

(3) An indicator to indicate rotor system unbalance.

(e) *For turbopropeller-powered airplanes.* In addition to the powerplant instruments required by paragraphs (a) and (c) of this section, the following powerplant instruments are required:

(1) A torque indicator for each engine.

(2) Position indicating means to indicate to the flight crew when the propeller blade angle is below the flight low pitch position, for each propeller.

(f) For airplanes equipped with fluid systems (other than fuel) for thrust or power augmentation, an approved means must be provided to indicate the proper functioning of that system to the flight crew.

[Amdt. 25-23, 35 FR 5678, Apr. 8, 1970, as amended by Amdt. 25-35, 39 FR 1831, Jan. 15, 1974; Amdt. 25-36, 39 FR 35461, Oct. 1, 1974; Amdt. 25-38, 41 FR 55467, Dec. 20, 1976; Amdt. 25-54, 45 FR 60173, Sept. 11, 1980; Amdt. 25-72, 55 FR 29785, July 20, 1990]

§ 25.1307 Miscellaneous equipment.

The following is required miscellaneous equipment:

(a) [Reserved]

(b) Two or more independent sources of electrical energy.

(c) Electrical protective devices, as prescribed in this part.

(d) Two systems for two-way radio communications, with controls for each accessible from each pilot station, designed and installed so that failure of one system will not preclude operation of the other system. The use of a common antenna system is acceptable if adequate reliability is shown.

(e) Two systems for radio navigation, with controls for each accessible from each pilot station, designed and installed so that failure of one system will not preclude operation of the other system. The use of a common antenna system is acceptable if adequate reliability is shown.

[Amdt. 25-23, 35 FR 5678, Apr. 8, 1970, as amended by Amdt. 25-46, 43 FR 50598, Oct. 30, 1978; Amdt. 25-54, 45 FR 60173, Sept. 11, 1980; Amdt. 25-72, 55 FR 29785, July 20, 1990]

§ 25.1309 Equipment, systems, and installations.

(a) The equipment, systems, and installations whose functioning is required by this subchapter, must be designed to ensure that they perform their intended functions under any foreseeable operating condition.

(b) The airplane systems and associated components, considered separately and in relation to other systems, must be designed so that—

(1) The occurrence of any failure condition which would prevent the continued safe flight and landing of the airplane is extremely improbable, and

(2) The occurrence of any other failure conditions which would reduce the capability of the airplane or the ability of the crew to cope with adverse operating conditions is improbable.

(c) Warning information must be provided to alert the crew to unsafe system operating conditions, and to enable them to take appropriate corrective action. Systems, controls, and associated monitoring and warning means must be designed to minimize crew errors which could create additional hazards.

(d) Compliance with the requirements of paragraph (b) of this section must be shown by analysis, and where necessary, by appropriate ground, flight, or simulator tests. The analysis must consider—

(1) Possible modes of failure, including malfunctions and damage from external sources.

(2) The probability of multiple failures and undetected failures.

(3) The resulting effects on the airplane and occupants, considering the stage of flight and operating conditions, and

(4) The crew warning cues, corrective action required, and the capability of detecting faults.

(e) Each installation whose functioning is required by this subchapter, and that requires a power supply, is an "essential load" on the power supply. The power sources and the system must be able to supply the following power loads in probable operating combinations and for probable durations:

(1) Loads connected to the system with the system functioning normally.

(2) Essential loads, after failure of any one prime mover, power converter, or energy storage device.

(3) Essential loads after failure of—

(i) Any one engine on two-engine airplanes; and

(ii) Any two engines on three-or-more-engine airplanes.

(4) Essential loads for which an alternate source of power is required by this chapter, after any failure or malfunction in any one power supply system, distribution system, or other utilization system.

(f) In determining compliance with paragraphs (e)(2) and (3) of this section, the power loads may be assumed to be reduced under a monitoring procedure consistent with safety in the kinds of operation authorized. Loads not required in controlled flight need not be considered for the two-engine-inoper-

ative condition on airplanes with three or more engines.

(g) In showing compliance with paragraphs (a) and (b) of this section with regard to the electrical system and equipment design and installation, critical environmental conditions must be considered. For electrical generation, distribution, and utilization equipment required by or used in complying with this chapter, except equipment covered by Technical Standard Orders containing environmental test procedures, the ability to provide continuous, safe service under foreseeable environmental conditions may be shown by environmental tests, design analysis, or reference to previous comparable service experience on other aircraft.

[Amdt. 25–23, 35 FR 5679, Apr. 8, 1970, as amended by Amdt. 25–38, 41 FR 55467, Dec. 20, 1976; Amdt. 25–41, 42 FR 36970, July 18, 1977]

§25.1316 **System lightning protection.**

(a) For functions whose failure would contribute to or cause a condition that would prevent the continued safe flight and landing of the airplane, each electrical and electronic system that performs these functions must be designed and installed to ensure that the operation and operational capabilities of the systems to perform these functions are not adversely affected when the airplane is exposed to lightning.

(b) For functions whose failure would contribute to or cause a condition that would reduce the capability of the airplane or the ability of the flightcrew to cope with adverse operating conditions, each electrical and electronic system that performs these functions must be designed and installed to ensure that these functions can be recovered in a timely manner after the airplane is exposed to lightning.

(c) Compliance with the lightning protection criteria prescribed in paragraphs (a) and (b) of this section must be shown for exposure to a severe lightning environment. The applicant must design for and verify that aircraft electrical/electronic systems are protected against the effects of lightning by:

(1) Determining the lightning strike zones for the airplane;

(2) Establishing the external lightning environment for the zones;

(3) Establishing the internal environment;

(4) Identifying all the electrical and electronic systems that are subject to the requirements of this section, and their locations on or within the airplane;

(5) Establishing the susceptibility of the systems to the internal and external lightning environment;

(6) Designing protection; and

(7) Verifying that the protection is adequate.

[Doc. No. 25912, 59 FR 22116, Apr. 28, 1994]

INSTRUMENTS: INSTALLATION

§ 25.1321 Arrangement and visibility.

(a) Each flight, navigation, and powerplant instrument for use by any pilot must be plainly visible to him from his station with the minimum practicable deviation from his normal position and line of vision when he is looking forward along the flight path.

(b) The flight instruments required by § 25.1303 must be grouped on the instrument panel and centered as nearly as practicable about the vertical plane of the pilot's forward vision. In addition—

(1) The instrument that most effectively indicates attitude must be on the panel in the top center position;

(2) The instrument that most effectively indicates airspeed must be adjacent to and directly to the left of the instrument in the top center position;

(3) The instrument that most effectively indicates altitude must be adjacent to and directly to the right of the instrument in the top center position; and

(4) The instrument that most effectively indicates direction of flight must be adjacent to and directly below the instrument in the top center position.

(c) Required powerplant instruments must be closely grouped on the instrument panel. In addition—

(1) The location of identical powerplant instruments for the engines must prevent confusion as to which engine each instrument relates; and

(2) Powerplant instruments vital to the safe operation of the airplane must be plainly visible to the appropriate crewmembers.

(d) Instrument panel vibration may not damage or impair the accuracy of any instrument.

(e) If a visual indicator is provided to indicate malfunction of an instrument, it must be effective under all probable cockpit lighting conditions.

[Amdt. 25–23, 35 FR 5679, Apr. 8, 1970, as amended by Amdt. 25–41, 42 FR 36970, July 18, 1977]

§ 25.1322 Warning, caution, and advisory lights.

If warning, caution or advisory lights are installed in the cockpit, they must, unless otherwise approved by the Administrator, be—

(a) Red, for warning lights (lights indicating a hazard which may require immediate corrective action);

(b) Amber, for caution lights (lights indicating the possible need for future corrective action);

(c) Green, for safe operation lights; and

(d) Any other color, including white, for lights not described in paragraphs (a) through (c) of this section, provided the color differs sufficiently from the colors prescribed in paragraphs (a) through (c) of this section to avoid possible confusion.

[Amdt. 25–38, 41 FR 55467, Dec. 20, 1976]

§ 25.1323 Airspeed indicating system.

For each airspeed indicating system, the following apply:

(a) Each airspeed indicating instrument must be approved and must be calibrated to indicate true airspeed (at sea level with a standard atmosphere) with a minimum practicable instrument calibration error when the corresponding pitot and static pressures are applied.

(b) Each system must be calibrated to determine the system error (that is, the relation between IAS and CAS) in flight and during the accelerated takeoff ground run. The ground run calibration must be determined—

(1) From 0.8 of the minimum value of V_1 to the maximum value of V_2, considering the approved ranges of altitude and weight; and

(2) With the flaps and power settings corresponding to the values determined in the establishment of the takeoff path under § 25.111 assuming that the

critical engine fails at the minimum value of V_1.

(c) The airspeed error of the installation, excluding the airspeed indicator instrument calibration error, may not exceed three percent or five knots, whichever is greater, throughout the speed range, from—

(1) V_{MO} to 1.23 V_{SR1}, with flaps retracted; and

(2) 1.23 V_{SR0} to V_{FE} with flaps in the landing position.

(d) Each system must be arranged, so far as practicable, to prevent malfunction or serious error due to the entry of moisture, dirt, or other substances.

(e) Each system must have a heated pitot tube or an equivalent means of preventing malfunction due to icing.

(f) Where duplicate airspeed indicators are required, their respective pitot tubes must be far enough apart to avoid damage to both tubes in a collision with a bird.

[Doc. No. 5066, 29 FR 18291, Dec. 24, 1964, as amended by Amdt. 25–57, 49 FR 6849, Feb. 23, 1984; Amdt. 25–108, 67 FR 70828, Nov. 26, 2002]

EFFECTIVE DATE NOTE: At 67 FR 76656, Dec. 12, 2002, § 25.1323 was amended by redesignating paragraphs (d) through (f) as paragraphs (h) through (j) and adding new paragraphs (d) through (g), effective Jan. 13, 2003. For the convenience of the user, the added text is set forth as follows:

§ 25.1323 Airspeed indicating system.

*   *   *   *   *

(d) From 1.23 V_{SR} to the speed at which stall warning begins, the IAS must change perceptibly with CAS and in the same sense, and at speeds below stall warning speed the IAS must not change in an incorrect sense.

(e) From V_{MO} to V_{MO} + 2/3 (V_{DF} − V_{MO}), the IAS must change perceptibly with CAS and in the same sense, and at higher speeds up to V_{DF} the IAS must not change in an incorrect sense.

(f) There must be no indication of airspeed that would cause undue difficulty to the pilot during the takeoff between the initiation of rotation and the achievement of a steady climbing condition.

(g) The effects of airspeed indicating system lag may not introduce significant takeoff indicated airspeed bias, or significant errors in takeoff or accelerate-stop distances.

*   *   *   *   *

§ 25.1325 Static pressure systems.

(a) Each instrument with static air case connections must be vented to the outside atmosphere through an appropriate piping system.

(b) Each static port must be designed and located in such manner that the static pressure system performance is least affected by airflow variation, or by moisture or other foreign matter, and that the correlation between air pressure in the static pressure system and true ambient atmospheric static pressure is not changed when the airplane is exposed to the continuous and intermittent maximum icing conditions defined in appendix C of this part.

(c) The design and installation of the static pressure system must be such that—

(1) Positive drainage of moisture is provided; chafing of the tubing and excessive distortion or restriction at bends in the tubing is avoided; and the materials used are durable, suitable for the purpose intended, and protected against corrosion; and

(2) It is airtight except for the port into the atmosphere. A proof test must be conducted to demonstrate the integrity of the static pressure system in the following manner:

(i) *Unpressurized airplanes.* Evacuate the static pressure system to a pressure differential of approximately 1 inch of mercury or to a reading on the altimeter, 1,000 feet above the airplane elevation at the time of the test. Without additional pumping for a period of 1 minute, the loss of indicated altitude must not exceed 100 feet on the altimeter.

(ii) *Pressurized airplanes.* Evacuate the static pressure system until a pressure differential equivalent to the maximum cabin pressure differential for which the airplane is type certificated is achieved. Without additional pumping for a period of 1 minute, the loss of indicated altitude must not exceed 2 percent of the equivalent altitude of the maximum cabin differential pressure or 100 feet, whichever is greater.

(d) Each pressure altimeter must be approved and must be calibrated to indicate pressure altitude in a standard atmosphere, with a minimum practicable calibration error when the corresponding static pressures are applied.

(e) Each system must be designed and installed so that the error in indicated pressure altitude, at sea level, with a standard atmosphere, excluding instrument calibration error, does not result in an error of more than ±30 feet per 100 knots speed for the appropriate configuration in the speed range between 1.23 V_{SR0} with flaps extended and 1.7 V_{SR1} with flaps retracted. However, the error need not be less than ±30 feet.

(f) If an altimeter system is fitted with a device that provides corrections to the altimeter indication, the device must be designed and installed in such manner that it can be bypassed when it malfunctions, unless an alternate altimeter system is provided. Each correction device must be fitted with a means for indicating the occurrence of reasonably probable malfunctions, including power failure, to the flight crew. The indicating means must be effective for any cockpit lighting condition likely to occur.

(g) Except as provided in paragraph (h) of this section, if the static pressure system incorporates both a primary and an alternate static pressure source, the means for selecting one or the other source must be designed so that—

(1) When either source is selected, the other is blocked off; and

(2) Both sources cannot be blocked off simultaneously.

(h) For unpressurized airplanes, paragraph (g)(1) of this section does not apply if it can be demonstrated that the static pressure system calibration, when either static pressure source is selected, is not changed by the other static pressure source being open or blocked.

[Doc. No. 5066, 29 FR 18291, Dec. 24, 1964, as amended by Amdt. 25–5, 30 FR 8261, June 29, 1965; Amdt. 25–12, 32 FR 7587, May 24, 1967; Amdt. 25–41, 42 FR 36970, July 18, 1977; Amdt. 25–108, 67 FR 70828, Nov. 26, 2002]

§ 25.1326 Pitot heat indication systems.

If a flight instrument pitot heating system is installed, an indication system must be provided to indicate to the flight crew when that pitot heating system is not operating. The indication system must comply with the following requirements:

(a) The indication provided must incorporate an amber light that is in clear view of a flight crewmember.

(b) The indication provided must be designed to alert the flight crew if either of the following conditions exist:

(1) The pitot heating system is switched "off".

(2) The pitot heating system is switched "on" and any pitot tube heating element is inoperative.

[Amdt. 25–43, 43 FR 10339, Mar. 13, 1978]

§ 25.1327 Magnetic direction indicator.

(a) Each magnetic direction indicator must be installed so that its accuracy is not excessively affected by the airplane's vibration or magnetic fields.

(b) The compensated installation may not have a deviation, in level flight, greater than 10 degrees on any heading.

§ 25.1329 Automatic pilot system.

(a) Each automatic pilot system must be approved and must be designed so that the automatic pilot can be quickly and positively disengaged by the pilots to prevent it from interfering with their control of the airplane.

(b) Unless there is automatic synchronization, each system must have a means to readily indicate to the pilot the alignment of the actuating device in relation to the control system it operates.

(c) Each manually operated control for the system must be readily accessible to the pilots.

(d) Quick release (emergency) controls must be on both control wheels, on the side of each wheel opposite the throttles.

(e) Attitude controls must operate in the plane and sense of motion specified in §§ 25.777(b) and 25.779(a) for cockpit controls. The direction of motion must be plainly indicated on, or adjacent to, each control.

(f) The system must be designed and adjusted so that, within the range of adjustment available to the human pilot, it cannot produce hazardous loads on the airplane, or create hazardous deviations in the flight path, under any condition of flight appropriate to its use, either during normal operation or in the event of a malfunction, assuming that corrective action begins within a reasonable period of time.

(g) If the automatic pilot integrates signals from auxiliary controls or furnishes signals for operation of other equipment, there must be positive interlocks and sequencing of engagement to prevent improper operation. Protection against adverse interaction of integrated components, resulting from a malfunction, is also required.

(h) If the automatic pilot system can be coupled to airborne navigation equipment, means must be provided to indicate to the flight crew the current mode of operation. Selector switch position is not acceptable as a means of indication.

[Doc. No. 5066, 29 FR 18291, Dec. 24, 1964, as amended by Amdt. 25–46, 43 FR 50598, Oct. 30, 1978]

§ 25.1331 Instruments using a power supply.

(a) For each instrument required by § 25.1303(b) that uses a power supply, the following apply:

(1) Each instrument must have a visual means integral with, the instrument, to indicate when power adequate to sustain proper instrument performance is not being supplied. The power must be measured at or near the point where it enters the instruments. For electric instruments, the power is considered to be adequate when the voltage is within approved limits.

(2) Each instrument must, in the event of the failure of one power source, be supplied by another power source. This may be accomplished automatically or by manual means.

(3) If an instrument presenting navigation data receives information from sources external to that instrument and loss of that information would render the presented data unreliable, the instrument must incorporate a visual means to warn the crew, when such loss of information occurs, that the presented data should not be relied upon.

(b) As used in this section, "instrument" includes devices that are physically contained in one unit, and devices that are composed of two or more physically separate units or compo-

nents connected together (such as a remote indicating gyroscopic direction indicator that includes a magnetic sensing element, a gyroscopic unit, an amplifier and an indicator connected together).

[Doc. No. 5066, 29 FR 18291, Dec. 24, 1964, as amended by Amdt. 25–41, 42 FR 36970, July 18, 1977]

§ 25.1333 Instrument systems.

For systems that operate the instruments required by § 25.1303(b) which are located at each pilot's station—

(a) Means must be provided to connect the required instruments at the first pilot's station to operating systems which are independent of the operating systems at other flight crew stations, or other equipment;

(b) The equipment, systems, and installations must be designed so that one display of the information essential to the safety of flight which is provided by the instruments, including attitude, direction, airspeed, and altitude will remain available to the pilots, without additional crewmember action, after any single failure or combination of failures that is not shown to be extremely improbable; and

(c) Additional instruments, systems, or equipment may not be connected to the operating systems for the required instruments, unless provisions are made to ensure the continued normal functioning of the required instruments in the event of any malfunction of the additional instruments, systems, or equipment which is not shown to be extremely improbable.

[Amdt. 25–23, 35 FR 5679, Apr. 8, 1970, as amended by Amdt. 25–41, 42 FR 36970, July 18, 1977]

§ 25.1335 Flight director systems.

If a flight director system is installed, means must be provided to indicate to the flight crew its current mode of operation. Selector switch position is not acceptable as a means of indication.

[Amdt. 25–41, 42 FR 36970, July 18, 1977]

§ 25.1337 Powerplant instruments.

(a) *Instruments and instrument lines.*
(1) Each powerplant and auxiliary

power unit instrument line must meet the requirements of §§ 25.993 and 25.1183.

(2) Each line carrying flammable fluids under pressure must—

(i) Have restricting orifices or other safety devices at the source of pressure to prevent the escape of excessive fluid if the line fails; and

(ii) Be installed and located so that the escape of fluids would not create a hazard.

(3) Each powerplant and auxiliary power unit instrument that utilizes flammable fluids must be installed and located so that the escape of fluid would not create a hazard.

(b) *Fuel quantity indicator.* There must be means to indicate to the flight crewmembers, the quantity, in gallons or equivalent units, of usable fuel in each tank during flight. In addition—

(1) Each fuel quantity indicator must be calibrated to read "zero" during level flight when the quantity of fuel remaining in the tank is equal to the unusable fuel supply determined under § 25.959;

(2) Tanks with interconnected outlets and airspaces may be treated as one tank and need not have separate indicators; and

(3) Each exposed sight gauge, used as a fuel quantity indicator, must be protected against damage.

(c) *Fuel flowmeter system.* If a fuel flowmeter system is installed, each metering component must have a means for bypassing the fuel supply if malfunction of that component severely restricts fuel flow.

(d) *Oil quantity indicator.* There must be a stick gauge or equivalent means to indicate the quantity of oil in each tank. If an oil transfer or reserve oil supply system is installed, there must be a means to indicate to the flight crew, in flight, the quantity of oil in each tank.

(e) *Turbopropeller blade position indicator.* Required turbopropeller blade position indicators must begin indicating before the blade moves more than eight degrees below the flight low pitch stop. The source of indication must directly sense the blade position.

(f) *Fuel pressure indicator.* There must be means to measure fuel pressure, in each system supplying reciprocating engines, at a point downstream of any fuel pump except fuel injection pumps. In addition—

(1) If necessary for the maintenance of proper fuel delivery pressure, there must be a connection to transmit the carburetor air intake static pressure to the proper pump relief valve connection; and

(2) If a connection is required under paragraph (f)(1) of this section, the gauge balance lines must be independently connected to the carburetor inlet pressure to avoid erroneous readings.

[Doc. No. 5066, 29 FR 18291, Dec. 24, 1964, as amended by Amdt. 25–40, 42 FR 15044, Mar. 17, 1977]

ELECTRICAL SYSTEMS AND EQUIPMENT

§ 25.1351 General.

(a) *Electrical system capacity.* The required generating capacity, and number and kinds of power sources must—

(1) Be determined by an electrical load analysis; and

(2) Meet the requirements of § 25.1309.

(b) *Generating system.* The generating system includes electrical power sources, main power busses, transmission cables, and associated control, regulation, and protective devices. It must be designed so that—

(1) Power sources function properly when independent and when connected in combination;

(2) No failure or malfunction of any power source can create a hazard or impair the ability of remaining sources to supply essential loads;

(3) The system voltage and frequency (as applicable) at the terminals of all essential load equipment can be maintained within the limits for which the equipment is designed, during any probable operating condition; and

(4) System transients due to switching, fault clearing, or other causes do not make essential loads inoperative, and do not cause a smoke or fire hazard.

(5) There are means accessible, in flight, to appropriate crewmembers for the individual and collective disconnection of the electrical power sources from the system.

(6) There are means to indicate to appropriate crewmembers the generating system quantities essential for the safe operation of the system, such as the

voltage and current supplied by each generator.

(c) *External power.* If provisions are made for connecting external power to the airplane, and that external power can be electrically connected to equipment other than that used for engine starting, means must be provided to ensure that no external power supply having a reverse polarity, or a reverse phase sequence, can supply power to the airplane's electrical system.

(d) *Operation without normal electrical power.* It must be shown by analysis, tests, or both, that the airplane can be operated safely in VFR conditions, for a period of not less than five minutes, with the normal electrical power (electrical power sources excluding the battery) inoperative, with critical type fuel (from the standpoint of flameout and restart capability), and with the airplane initially at the maximum certificated altitude. Parts of the electrical system may remain on if—

(1) A single malfunction, including a wire bundle or junction box fire, cannot result in loss of both the part turned off and the part turned on; and

(2) The parts turned on are electrically and mechanically isolated from the parts turned off.

[Doc. No. 5066, 29 FR 18291, Dec. 24, 1964, as amended by Amdt. 25–41, 42 FR 36970, July 18, 1977; Amdt. 25–72, 55 FR 29785, July 20, 1990]

§ 25.1353 Electrical equipment and installations.

(a) Electrical equipment, controls, and wiring must be installed so that operation of any one unit or system of units will not adversely affect the simultaneous operation of any other electrical unit or system essential to the safe operation.

(b) Cables must be grouped, routed, and spaced so that damage to essential circuits will be minimized if there are faults in heavy current-carrying cables.

(c) Storage batteries must be designed and installed as follows:

(1) Safe cell temperatures and pressures must be maintained during any probable charging or discharging condition. No uncontrolled increase in cell temperature may result when the battery is recharged (after previous complete discharge)—

(i) At maximum regulated voltage or power;

(ii) During a flight of maximum duration; and

(iii) Under the most adverse cooling condition likely to occur in service.

(2) Compliance with paragraph (c)(1) of this section must be shown by test unless experience with similar batteries and installations has shown that maintaining safe cell temperatures and pressures presents no problem.

(3) No explosive or toxic gases emitted by any battery in normal operation, or as the result of any probable malfunction in the charging system or battery installation, may accumulate in hazardous quantities within the airplane.

(4) No corrosive fluids or gases that may escape from the battery may damage surrounding airplane structures or adjacent essential equipment.

(5) Each nickel cadmium battery installation capable of being used to start an engine or auxiliary power unit must have provisions to prevent any hazardous effect on structure or essential systems that may be caused by the maximum amount of heat the battery can generate during a short circuit of the battery or of its individual cells.

(6) Nickel cadmium battery installations capable of being used to start an engine or auxiliary power unit must have—

(i) A system to control the charging rate of the battery automatically so as to prevent battery overheating;

(ii) A battery temperature sensing and over-temperature warning system with a means for disconnecting the battery from its charging source in the event of an over-temperature condition; or

(iii) A battery failure sensing and warning system with a means for disconnecting the battery from its charging source in the event of battery failure.

[Doc. No. 5066, 29 FR 18291, Dec. 24, 1964, as amended by Amdt. 25–41, 42 FR 36970, July 18, 1977; Amdt. 25–42, 43 FR 2323, Jan. 16, 1978]

§ 25.1355 Distribution system.

(a) The distribution system includes the distribution busses, their associated feeders, and each control and protective device.

(b) [Reserved]

(c) If two independent sources of electrical power for particular equipment or systems are required by this chapter, in the event of the failure of one power source for such equipment or system, another power source (including its separate feeder) must be automatically provided or be manually selectable to maintain equipment or system operation.

[Doc. No. 5066, 29 FR 18291, Dec. 24, 1964, as amended by Amdt. 25-23, 35 FR 5679, Apr. 8, 1970; Amdt. 25-38, 41 FR 55468, Dec. 20, 1976]

§ 25.1357 Circuit protective devices.

(a) Automatic protective devices must be used to minimize distress to the electrical system and hazard to the airplane in the event of wiring faults or serious malfunction of the system or connected equipment.

(b) The protective and control devices in the generating system must be designed to de-energize and disconnect faulty power sources and power transmission equipment from their associated busses with sufficient rapidity to provide protection from hazardous over-voltage and other malfunctioning.

(c) Each resettable circuit protective device must be designed so that, when an overload or circuit fault exists, it will open the circuit irrespective of the position of the operating control.

(d) If the ability to reset a circuit breaker or replace a fuse is essential to safety in flight, that circuit breaker or fuse must be located and identified so that it can be readily reset or replaced in flight.

(e) Each circuit for essential loads must have individual circuit protection. However, individual protection for each circuit in an essential load system (such as each position light circuit in a system) is not required.

(f) If fuses are used, there must be spare fuses for use in flight equal to at least 50 percent of the number of fuses of each rating required for complete circuit protection.

(g) Automatic reset circuit breakers may be used as integral protectors for electrical equipment (such as thermal cut-outs) if there is circuit protection to protect the cable to the equipment.

§ 25.1363 Electrical system tests.

(a) When laboratory tests of the electrical system are conducted—

(1) The tests must be performed on a mock-up using the same generating equipment used in the airplane;

(2) The equipment must simulate the electrical characteristics of the distribution wiring and connected loads to the extent necessary for valid test results; and

(3) Laboratory generator drives must simulate the actual prime movers on the airplane with respect to their reaction to generator loading, including loading due to faults.

(b) For each flight condition that cannot be simulated adequately in the laboratory or by ground tests on the airplane, flight tests must be made.

LIGHTS

§ 25.1381 Instrument lights.

(a) The instrument lights must—

(1) Provide sufficient illumination to make each instrument, switch and other device necessary for safe operation easily readable unless sufficient illumination is available from another source; and

(2) Be installed so that—

(i) Their direct rays are shielded from the pilot's eyes; and

(ii) No objectionable reflections are visible to the pilot.

(b) Unless undimmed instrument lights are satisfactory under each expected flight condition, there must be a means to control the intensity of illumination.

[Doc. No. 5066, 29 FR 18291, Dec. 24, 1964, as amended by Amdt. 25-72, 55 FR 29785, July 20, 1990]

§ 25.1383 Landing lights.

(a) Each landing light must be approved, and must be installed so that—

(1) No objectionable glare is visible to the pilot;

(2) The pilot is not adversely affected by halation; and

(3) It provides enough light for night landing.

(b) Except when one switch is used for the lights of a multiple light installation at one location, there must be a separate switch for each light.

(c) There must be a means to indicate to the pilots when the landing lights are extended.

§25.1385 Position light system installation.

(a) *General.* Each part of each position light system must meet the applicable requirements of this section and each system as a whole must meet the requirements of §§25.1387 through 25.1397.

(b) *Forward position lights.* Forward position lights must consist of a red and a green light spaced laterally as far apart as practicable and installed forward on the airplane so that, with the airplane in the normal flying position, the red light is on the left side and the green light is on the right side. Each light must be approved.

(c) *Rear position light.* The rear position light must be a white light mounted as far aft as practicable on the tail or on each wing tip, and must be approved.

(d) *Light covers and color filters.* Each light cover or color filter must be at least flame resistant and may not change color or shape or lose any appreciable light transmission during normal use.

[Doc. No. 5066, 29 FR 18291, Dec. 24, 1964, as amended by Amdt. 25–38, 41 FR 55468, Dec. 20, 1976]

§25.1387 Position light system dihedral angles.

(a) Except as provided in paragraph (e) of this section, each forward and rear position light must, as installed, show unbroken light within the dihedral angles described in this section.

(b) Dihedral angle L (left) is formed by two intersecting vertical planes, the first parallel to the longitudinal axis of the airplane, and the other at 110 degrees to the left of the first, as viewed when looking forward along the longitudinal axis.

(c) Dihedral angle R (right) is formed by two intersecting vertical planes, the first parallel to the longitudinal axis of the airplane, and the other at 110 degrees to the right of the first, as viewed when looking forward along the longitudinal axis.

(d) Dihedral angle A (aft) is formed by two intersecting vertical planes making angles of 70 degrees to the right and to the left, respectively, to a vertical plane passing through the longitudinal axis, as viewed when looking aft along the longitudinal axis.

(e) If the rear position light, when mounted as far aft as practicable in accordance with §25.1385(c), cannot show unbroken light within dihedral angle A (as defined in paragraph (d) of this section), a solid angle or angles of obstructed visibility totaling not more than 0.04 steradians is allowable within that dihedral angle, if such solid angle is within a cone whose apex is at the rear position light and whose elements make an angle of 30° with a vertical line passing through the rear position light.

[Doc. No. 5066, 29 FR 18291, Dec. 24, 1964, as amended by Amdt. 25–30, 36 FR 21278, Nov. 5, 1971]

§25.1389 Position light distribution and intensities.

(a) *General.* The intensities prescribed in this section must be provided by new equipment with light covers and color filters in place. Intensities must be determined with the light source operating at a steady value equal to the average luminous output of the source at the normal operating voltage of the airplane. The light distribution and intensity of each position light must meet the requirements of paragraph (b) of this section.

(b) *Forward and rear position lights.* The light distribution and intensities of forward and rear position lights must be expressed in terms of minimum intensities in the horizontal plane, minimum intensities in any vertical plane, and maximum intensities in overlapping beams, within dihedral angles L, R, and A, and must meet the following requirements:

(1) *Intensities in the horizontal plane.* Each intensity in the horizontal plane (the plane containing the longitudinal axis of the airplane and perpendicular to the plane of symmetry of the airplane) must equal or exceed the values in §25.1391.

(2) *Intensities in any vertical plane.* Each intensity in any vertical plane (the plane perpendicular to the horizontal plane) must equal or exceed the appropriate value in §25.1393, where I is

the minimum intensity prescribed in § 25.1391 for the corresponding angles in the horizontal plane.

(3) *Intensities in overlaps between adjacent signals.* No intensity in any overlap between adjacent signals may exceed the values given in § 25.1395, except that higher intensities in overlaps may be used with main beam intensities substantially greater than the minima specified in §§ 25.1391 and 25.1393 if the overlap intensities in relation to the main beam intensities do not adversely affect signal clarity. When the peak intensity of the forward position lights is more than 100 candles, the maximum overlap intensities between them may exceed the values given in § 25.1395 if the overlap intensity in Area A is not more than 10 percent of peak position light intensity and the overlap intensity in Area B is not greater than 2.5 percent of peak position light intensity.

§ 25.1391 Minimum intensities in the horizontal plane of forward and rear position lights.

Each position light intensity must equal or exceed the applicable values in the following table:

Dihedral angle (light included)	Angle from right or left of longitudinal axis, measured from dead ahead	Intensity (candles)
L and R (forward red and green).	0° to 10°	40
	10° to 20°	30
	20° to 110°	5
A (rear white)	110° to 180°	20

§ 25.1393 Minimum intensities in any vertical plane of forward and rear position lights.

Each position light intensity must equal or exceed the applicable values in the following table:

Angle above or below the horizontal plane	Intensity, I
0°	1.00
0° to 5°	0.90
5° to 10°	0.80
10° to 15°	0.70
15° to 20°	0.50
20° to 30°	0.30
30° to 40°	0.10
40° to 90°	0.05

§ 25.1395 Maximum intensities in overlapping beams of forward and rear position lights.

No position light intensity may exceed the applicable values in the following table, except as provided in § 25.1389(b)(3).

Overlaps	Maximum intensity	
	Area A (candles)	Area B (candles)
Green in dihedral angle L	10	1
Red in dihedral angle R	10	1
Green in dihedral angle A	5	1
Red in dihedral angle A	5	1
Rear white in dihedral angle L	5	1
Rear white in dihedral angle R	5	1

Where—

(a) Area A includes all directions in the adjacent dihedral angle that pass through the light source and intersect the common boundary plane at more than 10 degrees but less than 20 degrees; and

(b) Area B includes all directions in the adjacent dihedral angle that pass through the light source and intersect the common boundary plane at more than 20 degrees.

§ 25.1397 Color specifications.

Each position light color must have the applicable International Commission on Illumination chromaticity coordinates as follows:

(a) *Aviation red*—

y is not greater than 0.335; and
z is not greater than 0.002.

(b) *Aviation green*—

x is not greater than $0.440 - 0.320y$;
x is not greater than $y - 0.170$; and
y is not less than $0.390 - 0.170x$.

(c) *Aviation white*—

x is not less than 0.300 and not greater than 0.540;
y is not less than $x - 0.040$; or $y_0 - 0.010$, whichever is the smaller; and
y is not greater than $x + 0.020$ nor $0.636 - 0.400x$;
Where y_0 is the y coordinate of the Planckian radiator for the value of x considered.

[Doc. No. 5066, 29 FR 18291, Dec. 24, 1964, as amended by Amdt. 25-27, 36 FR 12972, July 10, 1971]

§ 25.1399 Riding light.

(a) Each riding (anchor) light required for a seaplane or amphibian must be installed so that it can—

(1) Show a white light for at least 2 nautical miles at night under clear atmospheric conditions; and

(2) Show the maximum unbroken light practicable when the airplane is moored or drifting on the water.

(b) Externally hung lights may be used.

§ 25.1401 Anticollision light system.

(a) *General.* The airplane must have an anticollision light system that—

(1) Consists of one or more approved anticollision lights located so that their light will not impair the crew's vision or detract from the conspicuity of the position lights; and

(2) Meets the requirements of paragraphs (b) through (f) of this section.

(b) *Field of coverage.* The system must consist of enough lights to illuminate the vital areas around the airplane considering the physical configuration and flight characteristics of the airplane. The field of coverage must extend in each direction within at least 75 degrees above and 75 degrees below the horizontal plane of the airplane, except that a solid angle or angles of obstructed visibility totaling not more than 0.03 steradians is allowable within a solid angle equal to 0.15 steradians centered about the longitudinal axis in the rearward direction.

(c) *Flashing characteristics.* The arrangement of the system, that is, the number of light sources, beam width, speed of rotation, and other characteristics, must give an effective flash frequency of not less than 40, nor more than 100 cycles per minute. The effective flash frequency is the frequency at which the airplane's complete anticollision light system is observed from a distance, and applies to each sector of light including any overlaps that exist when the system consists of more than one light source. In overlaps, flash frequencies may exceed 100, but not 180 cycles per minute.

(d) *Color.* Each anticollision light must be either aviation red or aviation white and must meet the applicable requirements of § 25.1397.

(e) *Light intensity.* The minimum light intensities in all vertical planes, measured with the red filter (if used) and expressed in terms of "effective" intensities, must meet the require-

ments of paragraph (f) of this section. The following relation must be assumed:

$$I_e = \frac{\int_{t_1}^{t_2} I(t)dt}{0.2 + (t_2 - t_1)}$$

where:

I_e=effective intensity (candles).

$I(t)$=instantaneous intensity as a function of time.

$t_2 - t_1$=flash time interval (seconds).

Normally, the maximum value of effective intensity is obtained when t_2 and t_1 are chosen so that the effective intensity is equal to the instantaneous intensity at t_2 and t_1.

(f) *Minimum effective intensities for anticollision lights.* Each anticollision light effective intensity must equal or exceed the applicable values in the following table.

Angle above or below the horizontal plane	Effective intensity (candles)
0° to 5°	400
5° to 10°	240
10° to 20°	80
20° to 30°	40
30° to 75°	20

[Doc. No. 5066, 29 FR 18291, Dec. 24, 1964, as amended by Amdt. 25–27, 36 FR 12972, July 10, 1971; Amdt. 25–41, 42 FR 36970, July 18, 1977]

§ 25.1403 Wing icing detection lights.

Unless operations at night in known or forecast icing conditions are prohibited by an operating limitation, a means must be provided for illuminating or otherwise determining the formation of ice on the parts of the wings that are critical from the standpoint of ice accumulation. Any illumination that is used must be of a type that will not cause glare or reflection that would handicap crewmembers in the performance of their duties.

[Amdt. 25–38, 41 FR 55468, Dec. 20, 1976]

SAFETY EQUIPMENT

§ 25.1411 General.

(a) *Accessibility.* Required safety equipment to be used by the crew in an emergency must be readily accessible.

(b) *Stowage provisions.* Stowage provisions for required emergency equipment must be furnished and must—

(1) Be arranged so that the equipment is directly accessible and its location is obvious; and

(2) Protect the safety equipment from inadvertent damage.

(c) *Emergency exit descent device.* The stowage provisions for the emergency exit descent device required by § 25.809(f) must be at the exits for which they are intended.

(d) *Liferafts.* (1) The stowage provisions for the liferafts described in § 25.1415 must accommodate enough rafts for the maximum number of occupants for which certification for ditching is requested.

(2) Liferafts must be stowed near exits through which the rafts can be launched during an unplanned ditching.

(3) Rafts automatically or remotely released outside the airplane must be attached to the airplane by means of the static line prescribed in § 25.1415.

(4) The stowage provisions for each portable liferaft must allow rapid detachment and removal of the raft for use at other than the intended exits.

(e) *Long-range signaling device.* The stowage provisions for the long-range signaling device required by § 25.1415 must be near an exit available during an unplanned ditching.

(f) *Life preserver stowage provisions.* The stowage provisions for life preservers described in § 25.1415 must accommodate one life preserver for each occupant for which certification for ditching is requested. Each life preserver must be within easy reach of each seated occupant.

(g) *Life line stowage provisions.* If certification for ditching under § 25.801 is requested, there must be provisions to store life lines. These provisions must—

(1) Allow one life line to be attached to each side of the fuselage; and

(2) Be arranged to allow the life lines to be used to enable the occupants to stay on the wing after ditching.

[Doc. No. 5066, 29 FR 18291, Dec. 24, 1964, as amended by Amdt. 25-32, 37 FR 3972, Feb. 24, 1972; Amdt. 25-46, 43 FR 50598, Oct. 30, 1978; Amdt. 25-53, 45 FR 41593, June 19, 1980; Amdt. 25-70, 54 FR 43925, Oct. 27, 1989; Amdt. 25-79, 58 FR 45229, Aug. 26, 1993]

§ 25.1415 Ditching equipment.

(a) Ditching equipment used in airplanes to be certificated for ditching under § 25.801, and required by the operating rules of this chapter, must meet the requirements of this section.

(b) Each liferaft and each life preserver must be approved. In addition—

(1) Unless excess rafts of enough capacity are provided, the buoyancy and seating capacity beyond the rated capacity of the rafts must accommodate all occupants of the airplane in the event of a loss of one raft of the largest rated capacity; and

(2) Each raft must have a trailing line, and must have a static line designed to hold the raft near the airplane but to release it if the airplane becomes totally submerged.

(c) Approved survival equipment must be attached to each liferaft.

(d) There must be an approved survival type emergency locator transmitter for use in one life raft.

(e) For airplanes not certificated for ditching under § 25.801 and not having approved life preservers, there must be an approved flotation means for each occupant. This means must be within easy reach of each seated occupant and must be readily removable from the airplane.

[Doc. No. 5066, 29 FR 18291, Dec. 24, 1964, as amended by Amdt. 25-29, 36 FR 18722, Sept. 21, 1971; Amdt 25-50, 45 FR 38348, June 9, 1980; Amdt. 25-72, 55 FR 29785, July 20, 1990; Amdt. 25-82, 59 FR 32057, June 21, 1994]

§ 25.1419 Ice protection.

If certification with ice protection provisions is desired, the airplane must be able to safely operate in the continuous maximum and intermittent maximum icing conditions of appendix C. To establish that the airplane can operate within the continuous maximum and intermittent maximum conditions of appendix C:

(a) An analysis must be performed to establish that the ice protection for the various components of the airplane is adequate, taking into account the various airplane operational configurations; and

(b) To verify the ice protection analysis, to check for icing anomalies, and to demonstrate that the ice protection system and its components are effective, the airplane or its components must be flight tested in the various operational configurations, in measured natural atmospheric icing conditions and, as found necessary, by one or more of the following means:

(1) Laboratory dry air or simulated icing tests, or a combination of both, of the components or models of the components.

(2) Flight dry air tests of the ice protection system as a whole, or of its individual components.

(3) Flight tests of the airplane or its components in measured simulated icing conditions.

(c) Caution information, such as an amber caution light or equivalent, must be provided to alert the flightcrew when the anti-ice or de-ice system is not functioning normally.

(d) For turbine engine powered airplanes, the ice protection provisions of this section are considered to be applicable primarily to the airframe. For the powerplant installation, certain additional provisions of subpart E of this part may be found applicable.

[Amdt. 25–72, 55 FR 29785, July 20, 1990]

§25.1421 Megaphones.

If a megaphone is installed, a restraining means must be provided that is capable of restraining the megaphone when it is subjected to the ultimate inertia forces specified in §25.561(b)(3).

[Amdt. 25–41, 42 FR 36970, July 18, 1977]

§25.1423 Public address system.

A public address system required by this chapter must—

(a) Be powerable when the aircraft is in flight or stopped on the ground, after the shutdown or failure of all engines and auxiliary power units, or the disconnection or failure of all power sources dependent on their continued operation, for—

(1) A time duration of at least 10 minutes, including an aggregate time duration of at least 5 minutes of announcements made by flight and cabin crewmembers, considering all other loads which may remain powered by the same source when all other power sources are inoperative; and

(2) An additional time duration in its standby state appropriate or required for any other loads that are powered by the same source and that are essential to safety of flight or required during emergency conditions.

(b) Be capable of operation within 10 seconds by a flight attendant at those stations in the passenger compartment from which the system is accessible.

(c) Be intelligible at all passenger seats, lavatories, and flight attendant seats and work stations.

(d) Be designed so that no unused, unstowed microphone will render the system inoperative.

(e) Be capable of functioning independently of any required crewmember interphone system.

(f) Be accessible for immediate use from each of two flight crewmember stations in the pilot compartment.

(g) For each required floor-level passenger emergency exit which has an adjacent flight attendant seat, have a microphone which is readily accessible to the seated flight attendant, except that one microphone may serve more than one exit, provided the proximity of the exits allows unassisted verbal communication between seated flight attendants.

[Doc. No. 26003, 58 FR 45229, Aug. 26, 1993]

Miscellaneous Equipment

§25.1431 Electronic equipment.

(a) In showing compliance with §25.1309 (a) and (b) with respect to radio and electronic equipment and their installations, critical environmental conditions must be considered.

(b) Radio and electronic equipment must be supplied with power under the requirements of § 25.1355(c).

(c) Radio and electronic equipment, controls, and wiring must be installed so that operation of any one unit or system of units will not adversely affect the simultaneous operation of any other radio or electronic unit, or system of units, required by this chapter.

§ 25.1433 Vacuum systems.

There must be means, in addition to the normal pressure relief, to automatically relieve the pressure in the discharge lines from the vacuum air pump when the delivery temperature of the air becomes unsafe.

[Doc. No. 5066, 29 FR 18291, Dec. 24, 1964, as amended by Amdt. 25–72, 55 FR 29785, July 20, 1990]

§ 25.1435 Hydraulic systems.

(a) *Element design.* Each element of the hydraulic system must be designed to:

(1) Withstand the proof pressure without permanent deformation that would prevent it from performing its intended functions, and the ultimate pressure without rupture. The proof and ultimate pressures are defined in terms of the design operating pressure (DOP) as follows:

Element	Proof (xDOP)	Ultimate (xDOP)
1. Tubes and fittings.	1.5	3.0
2. Pressure vessels containing gas:		
High pressure (e.g., accumulators)	3.0	4.0
Low pressure (e.g., reservoirs)	1.5	3.0
3. Hoses	2.0	4.0
4. All other elements	1.5	2.0

(2) Withstand, without deformation that would prevent it from performing its intended function, the design operating pressure in combination with limit structural loads that may be imposed;

(3) Withstand, without rupture, the design operating pressure multiplied by a factor of 1.5 in combination with ultimate structural load that can reasonably occur simultaneously;

(4) Withstand the fatigue effects of all cyclic pressures, including transients, and associated externally in-

duced loads, taking into account the consequences of element failure; and

(5) Perform as intended under all environmental conditions for which the airplane is certificated.

(b) *System design.* Each hydraulic system must:

(1) Have means located at a flightcrew station to indicate appropriate system parameters, if

(i) It performs a function necessary for continued safe flight and landing; or

(ii) In the event of hydraulic system malfunction, corrective action by the crew to ensure continued safe flight and landing is necessary;

(2) Have means to ensure that system pressures, including transient pressures and pressures from fluid volumetric changes in elements that are likely to remain closed long enough for such changes to occur, are within the design capabilities of each element, such that they meet the requirements defined in § 25.1435(a)(1) through (a)(5);

(3) Have means to minimize the release of harmful or hazardous concentrations of hydraulic fluid or vapors into the crew and passenger compartments during flight;

(4) Meet the applicable requirements of §§ 25.863, 25.1183, 25.1185, and 25.1189 if a flammable hydraulic fluid is used; and

(5) Be designed to use any suitable hydraulic fluid specified by the airplane manufacturer, which must be identified by appropriate markings as required by § 25.1541.

(c) *Tests.* Tests must be conducted on the hydraulic system(s), and/or subsystem(s) and elements, except that analysis may be used in place of or to supplement testing, where the analysis is shown to be reliable and appropriate. All internal and external influences must be taken into account to an extent necessary to evaluate their effects, and to assure reliable system and element functioning and integration. Failure or unacceptable deficiency of an element or system must be corrected and be sufficiently retested, where necessary.

(1) The system(s), subsystem(s), or element(s) must be subjected to performance, fatigue, and endurance tests

representative of airplane ground and flight operations.

(2) The complete system must be tested to determine proper functional performance and relation to the other systems, including simulation of relevant failure conditions, and to support or validate element design.

(3) The complete hydraulic system(s) must be functionally tested on the airplane in normal operation over the range of motion of all associated user systems. The test must be conducted at the system relief pressure or 1.25 times the DOP if a system pressure relief device is not part of the system design. Clearances between hydraulic system elements and other systems or structural elements must remain adequate and there must be no detrimental effects.

[Doc. No. 28617, 66 FR 27402, May 16, 2001]

§ 25.1438 Pressurization and pneumatic systems.

(a) Pressurization system elements must be burst pressure tested to 2.0 times, and proof pressure tested to 1.5 times, the maximum normal operating pressure.

(b) Pneumatic system elements must be burst pressure tested to 3.0 times, and proof pressure tested to 1.5 times, the maximum normal operating pressure.

(c) An analysis, or a combination of analysis and test, may be substituted for any test required by paragraph (a) or (b) of this section if the Administrator finds it equivalent to the required test.

[Amdt. 25–41, 42 FR 36971, July 18, 1977]

§ 25.1439 Protective breathing equipment.

(a) If there is a class A, B, or E cargo compartment, protective breathing equipment must be installed for the use of appropriate crewmembers. In addition, protective breathing equipment must be installed in each isolated separate compartment in the airplane, including upper and lower lobe galleys, in which crewmember occupancy is permitted during flight for the maximum number of crewmembers expected to be in the area during any operation.

(b) For protective breathing equipment required by paragraph (a) of this section or by any operating rule of this chapter, the following apply:

(1) The equipment must be designed to protect the flight crew from smoke, carbon dioxide, and other harmful gases while on flight deck duty and while combating fires in cargo compartments. The equipment must include—

(i) Masks covering the eyes, nose, and mouth; or

(ii) Masks covering the nose and mouth, plus accessory equipment to cover the eyes.

(3) The equipment, while in use, must allow the flight crew to use the radio equipment and to communicate with each other, while at their assigned duty stations.

(4) The part of the equipment protecting the eyes may not cause any appreciable adverse effect on vision and must allow corrective glasses to be worn.

(5) The equipment must supply protective oxygen of 15 minutes duration per crewmember at a pressure altitude of 8,000 feet with a respiratory minute volume of 30 liters per minute BTPD. If a demand oxygen system is used, a supply of 300 liters of free oxygen at 70 °F. and 760 mm. Hg. pressure is considered to be of 15-minute duration at the prescribed altitude and minute volume. If a continuous flow protective breathing system is used (including a mask with a standard rebreather bag) a flow rate of 60 liters per minute at 8,000 feet (45 liters per minute at sea level) and a supply of 600 liters of free oxygen at 70 °F. and 760 mm. Hg. pressure is considered to be of 15–minute duration at the prescribed altitude and minute volume. BTPD refers to body temperature conditions (that is, 37 °C., at ambient pressure, dry).

(6) The equipment must meet the requirements of paragraphs (b) and (c) of § 25.1441.

[Doc. No. 5066, 29 FR 18291, Dec. 24, 1964, as amended by Amdt. 25–38, 41 FR 55468, Dec. 20, 1976]

§ 25.1441 Oxygen equipment and supply.

(a) If certification with supplemental oxygen equipment is requested, the equipment must meet the requirements of this section and §§ 25.1443 through 25.1453.

(b) The oxygen system must be free from hazards in itself, in its method of operation, and in its effect upon other components.

(c) There must be a means to allow the crew to readily determine, during flight, the quantity of oxygen available in each source of supply.

(d) The oxygen flow rate and the oxygen equipment for airplanes for which certification for operation above 40,000 feet is requested must be approved.

§ 25.1443 Minimum mass flow of supplemental oxygen.

(a) If continuous flow equipment is installed for use by flight crewmembers, the minimum mass flow of supplemental oxygen required for each crewmember may not be less than the flow required to maintain, during inspiration, a mean tracheal oxygen partial pressure of 149 mm. Hg. when breathing 15 liters per minute, BTPS, and with a maximum tidal volume of 700 cc. with a constant time interval between respirations.

(b) If demand equipment is installed for use by flight crewmembers, the minimum mass flow of supplemental oxygen required for each crewmember may not be less than the flow required to maintain, during inspiration, a mean tracheal oxygen partial pressure of 122 mm. Hg., up to and including a cabin pressure altitude of 35,000 feet, and 95 percent oxygen between cabin pressure altitudes of 35,000 and 40,000 feet, when breathing 20 liters per minute BTPS. In addition, there must be means to allow the crew to use undiluted oxygen at their discretion.

(c) For passengers and cabin attendants, the minimum mass flow of supplemental oxygen required for each person at various cabin pressure altitudes may not be less than the flow required to maintain, during inspiration and while using the oxygen equipment (including masks) provided, the following mean tracheal oxygen partial pressures:

(1) At cabin pressure altitudes above 10,000 feet up to and including 18,500 feet, a mean tracheal oxygen partial pressure of 100 mm. Hg. when breathing 15 liters per minute, BTPS, and with a tidal volume of 700 cc. with a constant time interval between respirations.

(2) At cabin pressure altitudes above 18,500 feet up to and including 40,000 feet, a mean tracheal oxygen partial pressure of 83.8 mm. Hg. when breathing 30 liters per minute, BTPS, and with a tidal volume of 1,100 cc. with a constant time interval between respirations.

(d) If first-aid oxygen equipment is installed, the minimum mass flow of oxygen to each user may not be less than four liters per minute, STPD. However, there may be a means to decrease this flow to not less than two liters per minute, STPD, at any cabin altitude. The quantity of oxygen required is based upon an average flow rate of three liters per minute per person for whom first-aid oxygen is required.

(e) If portable oxygen equipment is installed for use by crewmembers, the minimum mass flow of supplemental oxygen is the same as specified in paragraph (a) or (b) of this section, whichever is applicable.

§ 25.1445 Equipment standards for the oxygen distributing system.

(a) When oxygen is supplied to both crew and passengers, the distribution system must be designed for either—

(1) A source of supply for the flight crew on duty and a separate source for the passengers and other crewmembers; or

(2) A common source of supply with means to separately reserve the minimum supply required by the flight crew on duty.

(b) Portable walk-around oxygen units of the continuous flow, diluter-demand, and straight demand kinds may be used to meet the crew or passenger breathing requirements.

§ 25.1447 Equipment standards for oxygen dispensing units.

If oxygen dispensing units are installed, the following apply:

(a) There must be an individual dispensing unit for each occupant for whom supplemental oxygen is to be supplied. Units must be designed to cover the nose and mouth and must be equipped with a suitable means to retain the unit in position on the face. Flight crew masks for supplemental oxygen must have provisions for the use of communication equipment.

(b) If certification for operation up to and including 25,000 feet is requested, an oxygen supply terminal and unit of oxygen dispensing equipment for the immediate use of oxygen by each crewmember must be within easy reach of that crewmember. For any other occupants, the supply terminals and dispensing equipment must be located to allow the use of oxygen as required by the operating rules in this chapter.

(c) If certification for operation above 25,000 feet is requested, there must be oxygen dispensing equipment meeting the following requirements:

(1) There must be an oxygen dispensing unit connected to oxygen supply terminals immediately available to each occupant, wherever seated, and at least two oxygen dispensing units connected to oxygen terminals in each lavatory. The total number of dispensing units and outlets in the cabin must exceed the number of seats by at least 10 percent. The extra units must be as uniformly distributed throughout the cabin as practicable. If certification for operation above 30,000 feet is requested, the dispensing units providing the required oxygen flow must be automatically presented to the occupants before the cabin pressure altitude exceeds 15,000 feet. The crew must be provided with a manual means of making the dispensing units immediately available in the event of failure of the automatic system.

(2) Each flight crewmember on flight deck duty must be provided with a quick-donning type oxygen dispensing unit connected to an oxygen supply terminal. This dispensing unit must be immediately available to the flight crewmember when seated at his station, and installed so that it:

(i) Can be placed on the face from its ready position, properly secured, sealed, and supplying oxygen upon demand, with one hand, within five seconds and without disturbing eyeglasses or causing delay in proceeding with emergency duties; and

(ii) Allows, while in place, the performance of normal communication functions.

(3) The oxygen dispensing equipment for the flight crewmembers must be:

(i) The diluter demand or pressure demand (pressure demand mask with a diluter demand pressure breathing regulator) type, or other approved oxygen equipment shown to provide the same degree of protection, for airplanes to be operated above 25,000 feet.

(ii) The pressure demand (pressure demand mask with a diluter demand pressure breathing regulator) type with mask-mounted regulator, or other approved oxygen equipment shown to provide the same degree of protection, for airplanes operated at altitudes where decompressions that are not extremely improbable may expose the flightcrew to cabin pressure altitudes in excess of 34,000 feet.

(4) Portable oxygen equipment must be immediately available for each cabin attendant.

[Doc. No. 5066, 29 FR 18291, Dec. 24, 1964, as amended by Amdt. 25–41, 42 FR 36971, July 18, 1977; Amdt. 25–87, 61 FR 28696, June 5, 1996]

§25.1449 Means for determining use of oxygen.

There must be a means to allow the crew to determine whether oxygen is being delivered to the dispensing equipment.

§25.1450 Chemical oxygen generators.

(a) For the purpose of this section, a chemical oxygen generator is defined as a device which produces oxygen by chemical reaction.

(b) Each chemical oxygen generator must be designed and installed in accordance with the following requirements:

(1) Surface temperature developed by the generator during operation may not create a hazard to the airplane or to its occupants.

(2) Means must be provided to relieve any internal pressure that may be hazardous.

(c) In addition to meeting the requirements in paragraph (b) of this section, each portable chemical oxygen generator that is capable of sustained operation by successive replacement of a generator element must be placarded to show—

(1) The rate of oxygen flow, in liters per minute;

(2) The duration of oxygen flow, in minutes, for the replaceable generator element; and

(3) A warning that the replaceable generator element may be hot, unless the element construction is such that the surface temperature cannot exceed 100 degrees F.

[Amdt. 25–41, 42 FR 36971, July 18, 1977]

§ 25.1453 Protection of oxygen equipment from rupture.

Oxygen pressure tanks, and lines between tanks and the shutoff means, must be—

(a) Protected from unsafe temperatures; and

(b) Located where the probability and hazards of rupture in a crash landing are minimized.

§ 25.1455 Draining of fluids subject to freezing.

If fluids subject to freezing may be drained overboard in flight or during ground operation, the drains must be designed and located to prevent the formation of hazardous quantities of ice on the airplane as a result of the drainage.

[Amdt. 25–23, 35 FR 5680, Apr. 8, 1970]

§ 25.1457 Cockpit voice recorders.

(a) Each cockpit voice recorder required by the operating rules of this chapter must be approved and must be installed so that it will record the following:

(1) Voice communications transmitted from or received in the airplane by radio.

(2) Voice communications of flight crewmembers on the flight deck.

(3) Voice communications of flight crewmembers on the flight deck, using the airplane's interphone system.

(4) Voice or audio signals identifying navigation or approach aids introduced into a headset or speaker.

(5) Voice communications of flight crewmembers using the passenger loudspeaker system, if there is such a system and if the fourth channel is available in accordance with the requirements of paragraph (c)(4)(ii) of this section.

(b) The recording requirements of paragraph (a)(2) of this section must be met by installing a cockpit-mounted area microphone, located in the best position for recording voice communications originating at the first and second pilot stations and voice communications of other crewmembers on the flight deck when directed to those stations. The microphone must be so located and, if necessary, the preamplifiers and filters of the recorder must be so adjusted or supplemented, that the intelligibility of the recorded communications is as high as practicable when recorded under flight cockpit noise conditions and played back. Repeated aural or visual playback of the record may be used in evaluating intelligibility.

(c) Each cockpit voice recorder must be installed so that the part of the communication or audio signals specified in paragraph (a) of this section obtained from each of the following sources is recorded on a separate channel:

(1) For the first channel, from each boom, mask, or hand-held microphone, headset, or speaker used at the first pilot station.

(2) For the second channel from each boom, mask, or hand-held microphone, headset, or speaker used at the second pilot station.

(3) For the third channel—from the cockpit-mounted area microphone.

(4) For the fourth channel, from—

(i) Each boom, mask, or hand-held microphone, headset, or speaker used at the station for the third and fourth crew members; or

(ii) If the stations specified in paragraph (c)(4)(i) of this section are not required or if the signal at such a station is picked up by another channel, each microphone on the flight deck that is used with the passenger loudspeaker system, if its signals are not picked up by another channel.

(5) As far as is practicable all sounds received by the microphone listed in paragraphs (c)(1), (2), and (4) of this section must be recorded without interruption irrespective of the position of the interphone-transmitter key switch. The design shall ensure that

sidetone for the flight crew is produced only when the interphone, public address system, or radio transmitters are in use.

(d) Each cockpit voice recorder must be installed so that—

(1) It receives its electric power from the bus that provides the maximum reliability for operation of the cockpit voice recorder without jeopardizing service to essential or emergency loads;

(2) There is an automatic means to simultaneously stop the recorder and prevent each erasure feature from functioning, within 10 minutes after crash impact; and

(3) There is an aural or visual means for preflight checking of the recorder for proper operation.

(e) The record container must be located and mounted to minimize the probability of rupture of the container as a result of crash impact and consequent heat damage to the record from fire. In meeting this requirement, the record container must be as far aft as practicable, but may not be where aft mounted engines may crush the container during impact. However, it need not be outside of the pressurized compartment.

(f) If the cockpit voice recorder has a bulk erasure device, the installation must be designed to minimize the probability of inadvertent operation and actuation of the device during crash impact.

(g) Each recorder container must—

(1) Be either bright orange or bright yellow;

(2) Have reflective tape affixed to its external surface to facilitate its location under water; and

(3) Have an underwater locating device, when required by the operating rules of this chapter, on or adjacent to the container which is secured in such manner that they are not likely to be separated during crash impact.

[Doc. No. 5066, 29 FR 18291, Dec. 24, 1964, as amended by Amdt. 25–2, 30 FR 3932, Mar. 26, 1965; Amdt. 25–16, 32 FR 13914, Oct. 6, 1967; Amdt. 25–41, 42 FR 36971, July 18, 1977; Amdt. 25–65, 53 FR 26143, July 11, 1988]

§25.1459 Flight recorders.

(a) Each flight recorder required by the operating rules of this chapter must be installed so that—

(1) It is supplied with airspeed, altitude, and directional data obtained from sources that meet the accuracy requirements of §§25.1323, 25.1325, and 25.1327, as appropriate;

(2) The vertical acceleration sensor is rigidly attached, and located longitudinally either within the approved center of gravity limits of the airplane, or at a distance forward or aft of these limits that does not exceed 25 percent of the airplane's mean aerodynamic chord;

(3) It receives its electrical power from the bus that provides the maximum reliability for operation of the flight recorder without jeopardizing service to essential or emergency loads;

(4) There is an aural or visual means for preflight checking of the recorder for proper recording of data in the storage medium.

(5) Except for recorders powered solely by the engine-driven electrical generator system, there is an automatic means to simultaneously stop a recorder that has a data erasure feature and prevent each erasure feature from functioning, within 10 minutes after crash impact; and

(6) There is a means to record data from which the time of each radio transmission either to or from ATC can be determined.

(b) Each nonejectable record container must be located and mounted so as to minimize the probability of container rupture resulting from crash impact and subsequent damage to the record from fire. In meeting this requirement the record container must be located as far aft as practicable, but need not be aft of the pressurized compartment, and may not be where aft-mounted engines may crush the container upon impact.

(c) A correlation must be established between the flight recorder readings of airspeed, altitude, and heading and the corresponding readings (taking into account correction factors) of the first pilot's instruments. The correlation must cover the airspeed range over which the airplane is to be operated, the range of altitude to which the airplane is limited, and 360 degrees of heading. Correlation may be established on the ground as appropriate.

(d) Each recorder container must—

(1) Be either bright orange or bright yellow;

(2) Have reflective tape affixed to its external surface to facilitate its location under water; and

(3) Have an underwater locating device, when required by the operating rules of this chapter, on or adjacent to the container which is secured in such a manner that they are not likely to be separated during crash impact.

(e) Any novel or unique design or operational characteristics of the aircraft shall be evaluated to determine if any dedicated parameters must be recorded on flight recorders in addition to or in place of existing requirements.

[Amdt. 25–8, 31 FR 127, Jan. 6, 1966, as amended by Amdt. 25–25, 35 FR 13192, Aug. 19, 1970; Amdt. 25–37, 40 FR 2577, Jan. 14, 1975; Amdt. 25–41, 42 FR 36971, July 18, 1977; Amdt. 25–65, 53 FR 26144, July 11, 1988]

§ 25.1461 Equipment containing high energy rotors.

(a) Equipment containing high energy rotors must meet paragraph (b), (c), or (d) of this section.

(b) High energy rotors contained in equipment must be able to withstand damage caused by malfunctions, vibration, abnormal speeds, and abnormal temperatures. In addition—

(1) Auxiliary rotor cases must be able to contain damage caused by the failure of high energy rotor blades; and

(2) Equipment control devices, systems, and instrumentation must reasonably ensure that no operating limitations affecting the integrity of high energy rotors will be exceeded in service.

(c) It must be shown by test that equipment containing high energy rotors can contain any failure of a high energy rotor that occurs at the highest speed obtainable with the normal speed control devices inoperative.

(d) Equipment containing high energy rotors must be located where rotor failure will neither endanger the occupants nor adversely affect continued safe flight.

[Amdt. 25–41, 42 FR 36971, July 18, 1977]

Subpart G—Operating Limitations and Information

§ 25.1501 General.

(a) Each operating limitation specified in §§ 25.1503 through 25.1533 and other limitations and information necessary for safe operation must be established.

(b) The operating limitations and other information necessary for safe operation must be made available to the crewmembers as prescribed in §§ 25.1541 through 25.1587.

[Amdt. 25–42, 43 FR 2323, Jan. 16, 1978]

OPERATING LIMITATIONS

§ 25.1503 Airspeed limitations: general.

When airspeed limitations are a function of weight, weight distribution, altitude, or Mach number, limitations corresponding to each critical combination of these factors must be established.

§ 25.1505 Maximum operating limit speed.

The maximum operating limit speed (V_{MO}/M_{MO} airspeed or Mach Number, whichever is critical at a particular altitude) is a speed that may not be deliberately exceeded in any regime of flight (climb, cruise, or descent), unless a higher speed is authorized for flight test or pilot training operations. V_{MO}/M_{MO} must be established so that it is not greater than the design cruising speed V_C and so that it is sufficiently below V_D/M_D or V_{DF}/M_{DF}, to make it highly improbable that the latter speeds will be inadvertently exceeded in operations. The speed margin between V_{MO}/M_{MO} and V_D/M_D or $V_{DF}M/_{DF}$ may not be less than that determined under § 25.335(b) or found necessary during the flight tests conducted under § 25.253.

[Amdt. 25–23, 35 FR 5680, Apr. 8, 1970]

§ 25.1507 Maneuvering speed.

The maneuvering speed must be established so that it does not exceed the design maneuvering speed V_A determined under § 25.335(c).

§25.1511 Flap extended speed.

The established flap extended speed V_{FE} must be established so that it does not exceed the design flap speed V_F chosen under §§25.335(e) and 25.345, for the corresponding flap positions and engine powers.

§25.1513 Minimum control speed.

The minimum control speed V_{MC} determined under §25.149 must be established as an operating limitation.

§25.1515 Landing gear speeds.

(a) The established landing gear operating speed or speeds, V_{LO}, may not exceed the speed at which it is safe both to extend and to retract the landing gear, as determined under §25.729 or by flight characteristics. If the extension speed is not the same as the retraction speed, the two speeds must be designated as $V_{LO(EXT)}$ and $V_{LO(RET)}$, respectively.

(b) The established landing gear extended speed V_{LE} may not exceed the speed at which it is safe to fly with the landing gear secured in the fully extended position, and that determined under §25.729.

[Doc. No. 5066, 29 FR 18291, Dec. 24, 1964, as amended by Amdt. 25–38, 41 FR 55468, Dec. 20, 1976]

§25.1516 Other speed limitations.

Any other limitation associated with speed must be established.

[Doc. No. 2000–8511, 66 FR 34024, June 26, 2001]

§25.1517 Rough air speed, V_{RA}.

A rough air speed, V_{RA}, for use as the recommended turbulence penetration airspeed in §25.1585(a)(8), must be established, which—

(1) Is not greater than the design airspeed for maximum gust intensity, selected for V_B; and

(2) Is not less than the minimum value of V_B specified in §25.335(d); and

(3) Is sufficiently less than V_{MO} to ensure that likely speed variation during rough air encounters will not cause the overspeed warning to operate too frequently. In the absence of a rational investigation substantiating the use of other values, V_{RA} must be less than V_{MO}—35 knots (TAS).

[Doc. No. 27902, 61 FR 5222, Feb. 9, 1996]

§25.1519 Weight, center of gravity, and weight distribution.

The airplane weight, center of gravity, and weight distribution limitations determined under §§25.23 through 25.27 must be established as operating limitations.

§25.1521 Powerplant limitations.

(a) *General.* The powerplant limitations prescribed in this section must be established so that they do not exceed the corresponding limits for which the engines or propellers are type certificated and do not exceed the values on which compliance with any other requirement of this part is based.

(b) *Reciprocating engine installations.* Operating limitations relating to the following must be established for reciprocating engine installations:

(1) Horsepower or torque, r.p.m., manifold pressure, and time at critical pressure altitude and sea level pressure altitude for—

(i) Maximum continuous power (relating to unsupercharged operation or to operation in each supercharger mode as applicable); and

(ii) Takeoff power (relating to unsupercharged operation or to operation in each supercharger mode as applicable).

(2) Fuel grade or specification.

(3) Cylinder head and oil temperatures.

(4) Any other parameter for which a limitation has been established as part of the engine type certificate except that a limitation need not be established for a parameter that cannot be exceeded during normal operation due to the design of the installation or to another established limitation.

(c) *Turbine engine installations.* Operating limitations relating to the following must be established for turbine engine installations:

(1) Horsepower, torque or thrust, r.p.m., gas temperature, and time for—

(i) Maximum continuous power or thrust (relating to augmented or unaugmented operation as applicable).

(ii) Takeoff power or thrust (relating to augmented or unaugmented operation as applicable).

(2) Fuel designation or specification.

(3) Any other parameter for which a limitation has been established as part of the engine type certificate except that a limitation need not be established for a parameter that cannot be exceeded during normal operation due to the design of the installation or to another established limitation.

(d) *Ambient temperature.* An ambient temperature limitation (including limitations for winterization installations, if applicable) must be established as the maximum ambient atmospheric temperature established in accordance with § 25.1043(b).

[Amdt. 25-72, 55 FR 29786, July 20, 1990]

§ 25.1522 Auxiliary power unit limitations.

If an auxiliary power unit is installed in the airplane, limitations established for the auxiliary power unit, including categories of operation, must be specified as operating limitations for the airplane.

[Amdt. 25-72, 55 FR 29786, July 20, 1990]

§ 25.1523 Minimum flight crew.

The minimum flight crew must be established so that it is sufficient for safe operation, considering—

(a) The workload on individual crewmembers;

(b) The accessibility and ease of operation of necessary controls by the appropriate crewmember; and

(c) The kind of operation authorized under § 25.1525.

The criteria used in making the determinations required by this section are set forth in appendix D.

[Doc. No. 5066, 29 FR 18291, Dec. 24, 1964, as amended by Amdt. 25-3, 30 FR 6067, Apr. 29, 1965]

§ 25.1525 Kinds of operation.

The kinds of operation to which the airplane is limited are established by the category in which it is eligible for certification and by the installed equipment.

§ 25.1527 Ambient air temperature and operating altitude.

The extremes of the ambient air temperature and operating altitude for which operation is allowed, as limited by flight, structural, powerplant, functional, or equipment characteristics, must be established.

[Doc. No. 2000-8511, 66 FR 34024, June 26, 2001]

§ 25.1529 Instructions for Continued Airworthiness.

The applicant must prepare Instructions for Continued Airworthiness in accordance with appendix H to this part that are acceptable to the Administrator. The instructions may be incomplete at type certification if a program exists to ensure their completion prior to delivery of the first airplane or issuance of a standard certificate of airworthiness, whichever occurs later.

[Amdt. 25-54, 45 FR 60173, Sept. 11, 1980]

§ 25.1531 Maneuvering flight load factors.

Load factor limitations, not exceeding the positive limit load factors determined from the maneuvering diagram in § 25.333(b), must be established.

§ 25.1533 Additional operating limitations.

(a) Additional operating limitations must be established as follows:

(1) The maximum takeoff weights must be established as the weights at which compliance is shown with the applicable provisions of this part (including the takeoff climb provisions of § 25.121(a) through (c), for altitudes and ambient temperatures).

(2) The maximum landing weights must be established as the weights at which compliance is shown with the applicable provisions of this part (including the landing and approach climb provisions of §§ 25.119 and 25.121(d) for altitudes and ambient temperatures).

(3) The minimum takeoff distances must be established as the distances at which compliance is shown with the applicable provisions of this part (including the provisions of §§ 25.109 and 25.113, for weights, altitudes, temperatures, wind components, runway surface conditions (dry and wet), and runway gradients) for smooth, hard-surfaced runways. Additionally, at the option of the applicant, wet runway takeoff distances may be established for runway surfaces that have been

grooved or treated with a porous friction course, and may be approved for use on runways where such surfaces have been designed constructed, and maintained in a manner acceptable to the Administrator.

(b) The extremes for variable factors (such as altitude, temperature, wind, and runway gradients) are those at which compliance with the applicable provisions of this part is shown.

[Doc. No. 5066, 29 FR 18291, Dec. 24, 1964, as amended by Amdt. 25–38, 41 FR 55468, Dec. 20, 1976; Amdt. 25–72, 55 FR 29786, July 20, 1990; Amdt. 25–92, 63 FR 8321, Feb. 18, 1998]

MARKINGS AND PLACARDS

§25.1541 General.

(a) The airplane must contain—

(1) The specified markings and placards; and

(2) Any additional information, instrument markings, and placards required for the safe operation if there are unusual design, operating, or handling characteristics.

(b) Each marking and placard prescribed in paragraph (a) of this section—

(1) Must be displayed in a conspicuous place; and

(2) May not be easily erased, disfigured, or obscured.

§25.1543 Instrument markings: general.

For each instrument—

(a) When markings are on the cover glass of the instrument, there must be means to maintain the correct alignment of the glass cover with the face of the dial; and

(b) Each instrument marking must be clearly visible to the appropriate crewmember.

[Doc. No. 5066, 29 FR 18291, Dec. 24, 1964, as amended by Amdt. 25–72, 55 FR 29786, July 20, 1990]

§25.1545 Airspeed limitation information.

The airspeed limitations required by §25.1583 (a) must be easily read and understood by the flight crew.

§25.1547 Magnetic direction indicator.

(a) A placard meeting the requirements of this section must be installed on, or near, the magnetic direction indicator.

(b) The placard must show the calibration of the instrument in level flight with the engines operating.

(c) The placard must state whether the calibration was made with radio receivers on or off.

(d) Each calibration reading must be in terms of magnetic heading in not more than 45 degree increments.

§25.1549 Powerplant and auxiliary power unit instruments.

For each required powerplant and auxiliary power unit instrument, as appropriate to the type of instrument—

(a) Each maximum and, if applicable, minimum safe operating limit must be marked with a red radial or a red line;

(b) Each normal operating range must be marked with a green arc or green line, not extending beyond the maximum and minimum safe limits;

(c) Each takeoff and precautionary range must be marked with a yellow arc or a yellow line; and

(d) Each engine, auxiliary power unit, or propeller speed range that is restricted because of excessive vibration stresses must be marked with red arcs or red lines.

[Amdt. 25–40, 42 FR 15044, Mar. 17, 1977]

§25.1551 Oil quantity indication.

Each oil quantity indicating means must be marked to indicate the quantity of oil readily and accurately.

[Amdt. 25–72, 55 FR 29786, July 20, 1990]

§25.1553 Fuel quantity indicator.

If the unusable fuel supply for any tank exceeds one gallon, or five percent of the tank capacity, whichever is greater, a red arc must be marked on its indicator extending from the calibrated zero reading to the lowest reading obtainable in level flight.

§25.1555 Control markings.

(a) Each cockpit control, other than primary flight controls and controls whose function is obvious, must be plainly marked as to its function and method of operation.

(b) Each aerodynamic control must be marked under the requirements of §§25.677 and 25.699.

(c) For powerplant fuel controls—

(1) Each fuel tank selector control must be marked to indicate the position corresponding to each tank and to each existing cross feed position;

(2) If safe operation requires the use of any tanks in a specific sequence, that sequence must be marked on, or adjacent to, the selector for those tanks; and

(3) Each valve control for each engine must be marked to indicate the position corresponding to each engine controlled.

(d) For accessory, auxiliary, and emergency controls—

(1) Each emergency control (including each fuel jettisoning and fluid shut-off must be colored red; and

(2) Each visual indicator required by § 25.729(e) must be marked so that the pilot can determine at any time when the wheels are locked in either extreme position, if retractable landing gear is used.

§ 25.1557 Miscellaneous markings and placards.

(a) *Baggage and cargo compartments and ballast location.* Each baggage and cargo compartment, and each ballast location must have a placard stating any limitations on contents, including weight, that are necessary under the loading requirements. However, underseat compartments designed for the storage of carry-on articles weighing not more than 20 pounds need not have a loading limitation placard.

(b) *Powerplant fluid filler openings.* The following qpply:

(1) Fuel filler openings must be marked at or near the filler cover with—

(i) The word "fuel";

(ii) For reciprocating engine powered airplanes, the minimum fuel grade;

(iii) For turbine engine powered airplanes, the permissible fuel designations; and

(iv) For pressure fueling systems, the maximum permissible fueling supply pressure and the maximum permissible defueling pressure.

(2) Oil filler openings must be marked at or near the filler cover with the word "oil".

(3) Augmentation fluid filler openings must be marked at or near the filler cover to identify the required fluid.

(c) *Emergency exit placards.* Each emergency exit placard must meet the requirements of § 25.811.

(d) *Doors.* Each door that must be used in order to reach any required emergency exit must have a suitable placard stating that the door is to be latched in the open position during takeoff and landing.

[Doc. No. 5066, 29 FR 18291, Dec. 24, 1964, as amended by Amdt. 25-32, 37 FR 3972, Feb. 24, 1972; Amdt. 25-38, 41 FR 55468, Dec. 20, 1976; Amdt. 25-72, 55 FR 29786, July 20, 1990]

§ 25.1561 Safety equipment.

(a) Each safety equipment control to be operated by the crew in emergency, such as controls for automatic liferaft releases, must be plainly marked as to its method of operation.

(b) Each location, such as a locker or compartment, that carries any fire extinguishing, signaling, or other life saving equipment must be marked accordingly.

(c) Stowage provisions for required emergency equipment must be conspicuously marked to identify the contents and facilitate the easy removal of the equipment.

(d) Each liferaft must have obviously marked operating instructions.

(e) Approved survival equipment must be marked for identification and method of operation.

[Doc. No. 5066, 29 FR 18291, Dec. 24, 1964, as amended by Amdt. 25-46, 43 FR 50598, Oct. 30, 1978]

§ 25.1563 Airspeed placard.

A placard showing the maximum airspeeds for flap extension for the takeoff, approach, and landing positions must be installed in clear view of each pilot.

AIRPLANE FLIGHT MANUAL

§ 25.1581 General.

(a) *Furnishing information.* An Airplane Flight Manual must be furnished with each airplane, and it must contain the following:

(1) Information required by §§ 25.1583 through 25.1587.

(2) Other information that is necessary for safe operation because of design, operating, or handling characteristics.

(3) Any limitation, procedure, or other information established as a condition of compliance with the applicable noise standards of part 36 of this chapter.

(b) *Approved information.* Each part of the manual listed in §§25.1583 through 25.1587, that is appropriate to the airplane, must be furnished, verified, and approved, and must be segregated, identified, and clearly distinguished from each unapproved part of that manual.

(c) [Reserved]

(d) Each Airplane Flight Manual must include a table of contents if the complexity of the manual indicates a need for it.

[Amdt. 25–42, 43 FR 2323, Jan. 16, 1978, as amended by Amdt. 25–72, 55 FR 29786, July 20, 1990]

§25.1583 Operating limitations.

(a) *Airspeed limitations.* The following airspeed limitations and any other airspeed limitations necessary for safe operation must be furnished:

(1) The maximum operating limit speed V_{MO}/M_{MO} and a statement that this speed limit may not be deliberately exceeded in any regime of flight (climb, cruise, or descent) unless a higher speed is authorized for flight test or pilot training.

(2) If an airspeed limitation is based upon compressibility effects, a statement to this effect and information as to any symptoms, the probable behavior of the airplane, and the recommended recovery procedures.

(3) The maneuvering speed V_A and a statement that full application of rudder and aileron controls, as well as maneuvers that involve angles of attack near the stall, should be confined to speeds below this value.

(4) The flap extended speed V_{FE} and the pertinent flap positions and engine powers.

(5) The landing gear operating speed or speeds, and a statement explaining the speeds as defined in §25.1515(a).

(6) The landing gear extended speed V_{LE}, if greater than V_{LO}, and a statement that this is the maximum speed at which the airplane can be safely flown with the landing gear extended.

(b) *Powerplant limitations.* The following information must be furnished:

(1) Limitations required by §25.1521 and §25.1522.

(2) Explanation of the limitations, when appropriate.

(3) Information necessary for marking the instruments required by §§25.1549 through 25.1553.

(c) *Weight and loading distribution.* The weight and center of gravity limitations established under §25.1519 must be furnished in the Airplane Flight Manual. All of the following information, including the weight distribution limitations established under §25.1519, must be presented either in the Airplane Flight Manual or in a separate weight and balance control and loading document that is incorporated by reference in the Airplane Flight Manual:

(1) The condition of the airplane and the items included in the empty weight as defined in accordance with §25.29.

(2) Loading instructions necessary to ensure loading of the airplane within the weight and center of gravity limits, and to maintain the loading within these limits in flight.

(3) If certification for more than one center of gravity range is requested, the appropriate limitations, with regard to weight and loading procedures, for each separate center of gravity range.

(d) *Flight crew.* The number and functions of the minimum flight crew determined under §25.1523 must be furnished.

(e) *Kinds of operation.* The kinds of operation approved under §25.1525 must be furnished.

(f) *Ambient air temperatures and operating altitudes.* The extremes of the ambient air temperatures and operating altitudes established under §25.1527 must be furnished.

(g) [Reserved]

(h) *Additional operating limitations.* The operating limitations established under §25.1533 must be furnished.

(i) *Maneuvering flight load factors.* The positive maneuvering limit load factors for which the structure is proven, described in terms of accelerations, must be furnished.

[Doc. No. 5066, 29 FR 1891, Dec. 24, 1964, as amended by Amdt. 25-38, 41 FR 55468, Dec, 20, 1976; Amdt. 25-42, 43 FR 2323, Jan. 16, 1978; Amdt. 25-46, 43 FR 50598, Oct. 30, 1978; Amdt. 25-72, 55 FR 29787, July 20, 1990; Amdt. 25-105, 66 FR 34024, June 26, 2001]

§ 25.1585 Operating procedures.

(a) Operating procedures must be furnished for—

(1) Normal procedures peculiar to the particular type or model encountered in connection with routine operations;

(2) Non-normal procedures for malfunction cases and failure conditions involving the use of special systems or the alternative use of regular systems; and

(3) Emergency procedures for foreseeable but unusual situations in which immediate and precise action by the crew may be expected to substantially reduce the risk of catastrophe.

(b) Information or procedures not directly related to airworthiness or not under the control of the crew, must not be included, nor must any procedure that is accepted as basic airmanship.

(c) Information identifying each operating condition in which the fuel system independence prescribed in § 25.953 is necessary for safety must be furnished, together with instructions for placing the fuel system in a configuration used to show compliance with that section.

(d) The buffet onset envelopes, determined under § 25.251 must be furnished. The buffet onset envelopes presented may reflect the center of gravity at which the airplane is normally loaded during cruise if corrections for the effect of different center of gravity locations are furnished.

(e) Information must be furnished that indicates that when the fuel quantity indicator reads "zero" in level flight, any fuel remaining in the fuel tank cannot be used safely in flight.

(f) Information on the total quantity of usable fuel for each fuel tank must be furnished.

[Doc. No. 2000-8511, 66 FR 34024, June 26, 2001]

§ 25.1587 Performance information.

(a) Each Airplane Flight Manual must contain information to permit conversion of the indicated temperature to free air temperature if other than a free air temperature indicator is used to comply with the requirements of § 25.1303(a)(1).

(b) Each Airplane Flight Manual must contain the performance information computed under the applicable provisions of this part (including §§ 25.115, 25.123, and 25.125 for the weights, altitudes, temperatures, wind components, and runway gradients, as applicable) within the operational limits of the airplane, and must contain the following:

(1) In each case, the conditions of power, configuration, and speeds, and the procedures for handling the airplane and any system having a significant effect on the performance information.

(2) V_{SR} determined in accordance with § 25.103.

(3) The following performance information (determined by extrapolation and computed for the range of weights between the maximum landing weight and the maximum takeoff weight):

(i) Climb in the landing configuration.

(ii) Climb in the approach configuration.

(iii) Landing distance.

(4) Procedures established under § 25.101(f) and (g) that are related to the limitations and information required by § 25.1533 and by this paragraph (b) in the form of guidance material, including any relevant limitations or information.

(5) An explanation of significant or unusual flight or ground handling characteristics of the airplane.

(6) Corrections to indicated values of airspeed, altitude, and outside air temperature.

(7) An explanation of operational landing runway length factors included in the presentation of the landing distance, if appropriate.

[Doc. No. 2000-8511, 66 FR 34024, June 26, 2001 as amended by Amdt. 25-108, 67 FR 70828, Nov. 26, 2002]

APPENDIX A TO PART 25

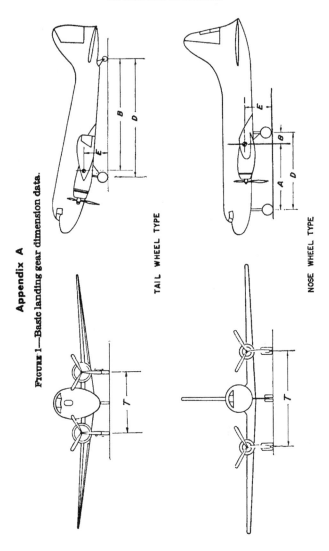

Appendix A

FIGURE 1—Basic landing gear dimension data.

TAIL WHEEL TYPE

NOSE WHEEL TYPE

483

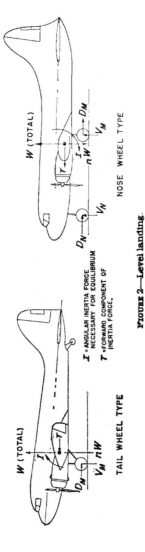

NOSE WHEEL TYPE

TAIL WHEEL TYPE

I = ANGULAR INERTIA FORCE
NECESSARY FOR EQUILIBRIUM

T = FORWARD COMPONENT OF
INERTIA FORCE.

FIGURE 2—Level landing.

FIGURE 3—Tail-down landing.

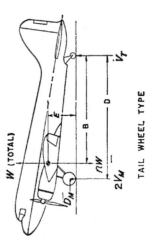

NOSE WHEEL TYPE

TAIL WHEEL TYPE

β = ANGLE FOR MAIN GEAR AND TAIL STRUCTURE
CONTACTING GROUND EXCEPT NEED NOT
EXCEED STALL ANGLE.

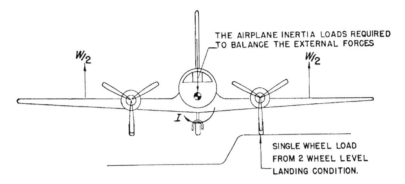

NOSE OR TAIL WHEEL TYPE

FIGURE 5—Lateral drift landing.

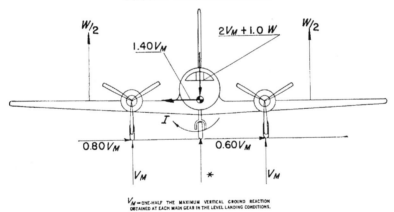

V_M = ONE-HALF THE MAXIMUM VERTICAL GROUND REACTION
OBTAINED AT EACH MAIN GEAR IN THE LEVEL LANDING CONDITIONS.

* NOSE GEAR GROUND REACTION = 0

NOSE OR TAIL WHEEL TYPE AIRPLANE IN LEVEL ALTITUDE

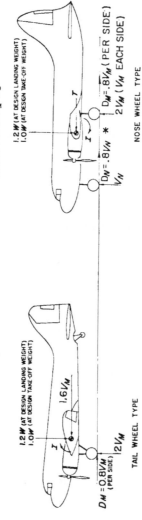

FIGURE 6—Braked roll.

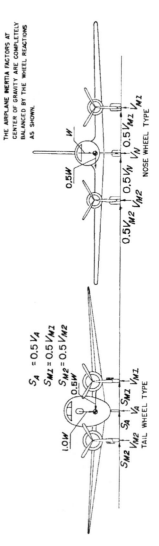

FIGURE 7—Ground turning.

FIGURE 8—Pivoting, nose or tail wheel type.

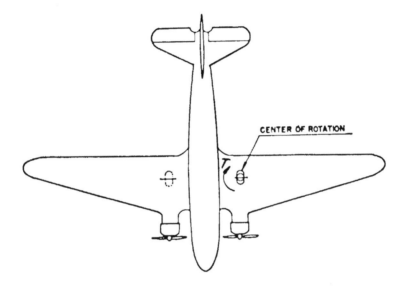

V_N and V_M are static ground reactions. For tail wheel type the airplane is in the three point attitude. Pivoting is assumed to take place about one main landing gear unit.

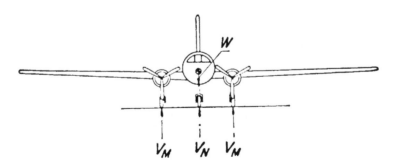

Appendix B to Part 25

Appendix B

Figure 1—Pictorial definition of angles, dimensions, and directions on a seaplane

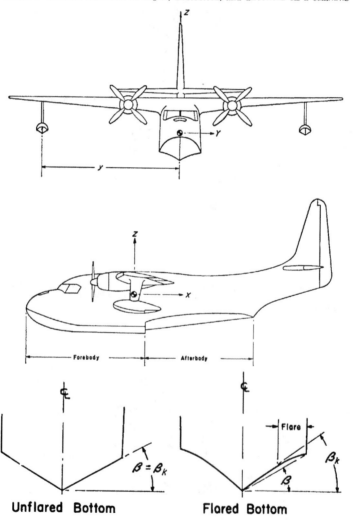

FIGURE 2—Hull station weighing factor.

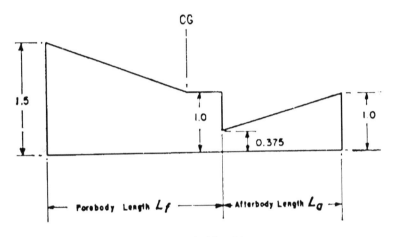

K_1 (Vertical Loads)

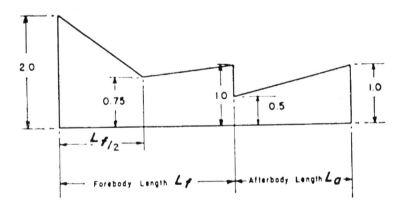

K_2 (Bottom Pressures)

FIGURE 3—Transverse pressure distributions.

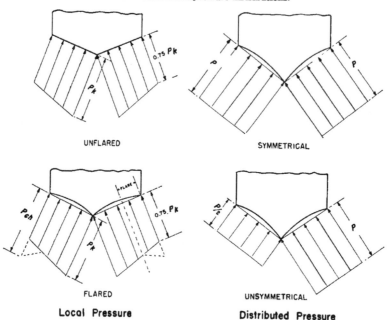

UNFLARED

SYMMETRICAL

FLARED

Local Pressure

UNSYMMETRICAL

Distributed Pressure

APPENDIX C TO PART 25

(a) *Continuous maximum icing.* The maximum continuous intensity of atmospheric icing conditions (continuous maximum icing) is defined by the variables of the cloud liquid water content, the mean effective diameter of the cloud droplets, the ambient air temperature, and the interrelationship of these three variables as shown in figure 1 of this appendix. The limiting icing envelope in terms of altitude and temperature is given in figure 2 of this appendix. The inter-relationship of cloud liquid water content with drop diameter and altitude is determined from figures 1 and 2. The cloud liquid water content for continuous maximum icing conditions of a horizontal extent, other than 17.4 nautical miles, is determined by the value of liquid water content of figure 1, multiplied by the appropriate factor from figure 3 of this appendix.

(b) *Intermittent maximum icing.* The intermittent maximum intensity of atmospheric icing conditions (intermittent maximum icing) is defined by the variables of the cloud liquid water content, the mean effective diameter of the cloud droplets, the ambient air temperature, and the interrelationship of these three variables as shown in figure 4 of this appendix. The limiting icing envelope in terms of altitude and temperature is given in figure 5 of this appendix. The inter-relationship of cloud liquid water content with drop diameter and altitude is determined from figures 4 and 5. The cloud liquid water content for intermittent maximum icing conditions of a horizontal extent, other than 2.6 nautical miles, is determined by the value of cloud liquid water content of figure 4 multiplied by the appropriate factor in figure 6 of this appendix.

FIGURE 1

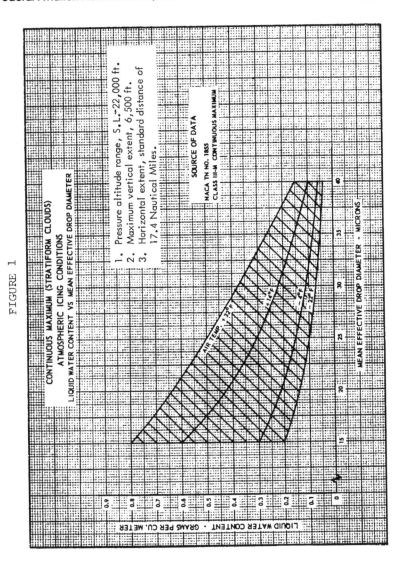

CONTINUOUS MAXIMUM (STRATIFORM CLOUDS)
ATMOSPHERIC ICING CONDITIONS
LIQUID WATER CONTENT VS MEAN EFFECTIVE DROP DIAMETER

1. Pressure altitude range, S. L.-22,000 ft.
2. Maximum vertical extent, 6,500 ft.
3. Horizontal extent, standard distance of 17.4 Nautical Miles.

SOURCE OF DATA
NACA TN NO. 1855
CLASS III-M CONTINUOUS MAXIMUM

FIGURE 2

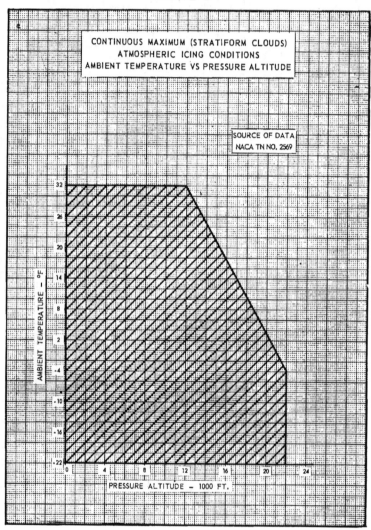

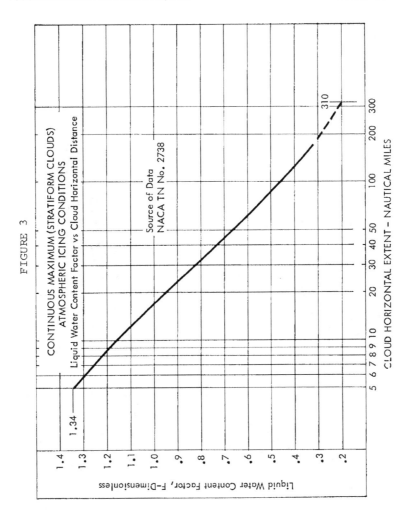

FIGURE 3

CONTINUOUS MAXIMUM (STRATIFORM CLOUDS)
ATMOSPHERIC ICING CONDITIONS
Liquid Water Content Factor vs Cloud Horizontal Distance

Source of Data
NACA TN No. 2738

FIGURE 4

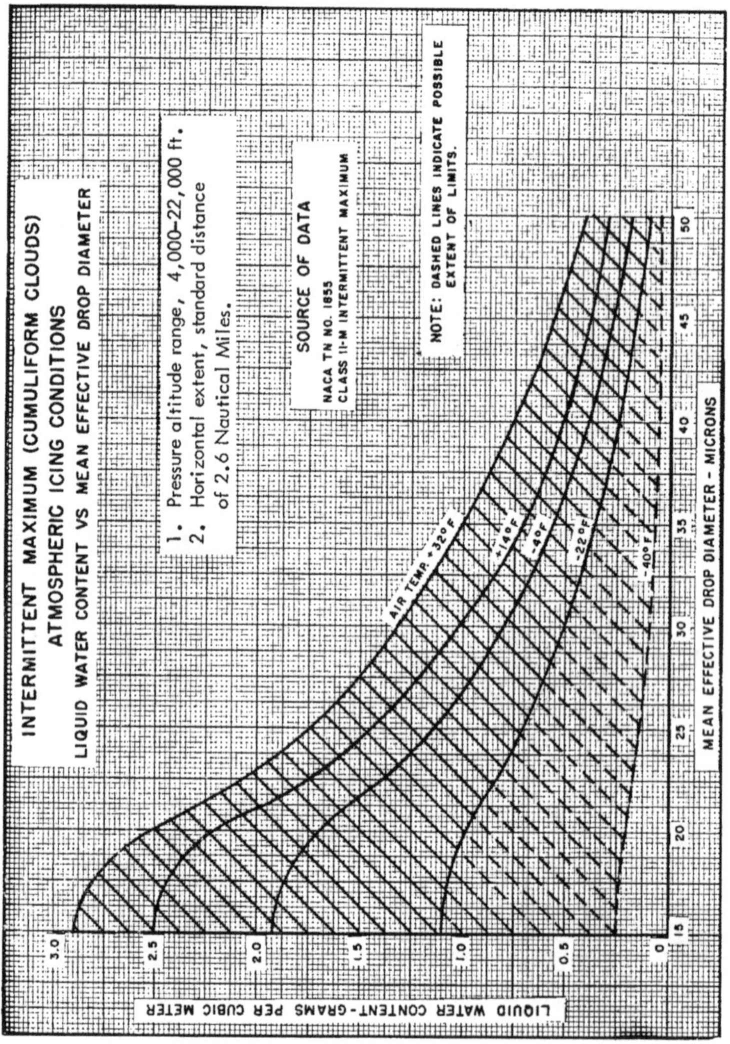

INTERMITTENT MAXIMUM (CUMULIFORM CLOUDS)
ATMOSPHERIC ICING CONDITIONS
LIQUID WATER CONTENT VS MEAN EFFECTIVE DROP DIAMETER

1. Pressure altitude range, 4,000-22,000 ft.
2. Horizontal extent, standard distance
   of 2.6 Nautical Miles.

SOURCE OF DATA

NACA TN NO. 1855
CLASS II-M INTERMITTENT MAXIMUM

NOTE: DASHED LINES INDICATE POSSIBLE
EXTENT OF LIMITS.

AIR TEMP. = 32°F
-4°F
-18°F
-22°F
-40°F

LIQUID WATER CONTENT - GRAMS PER CUBIC METER

MEAN EFFECTIVE DROP DIAMETER - MICRONS

FIGURE 5

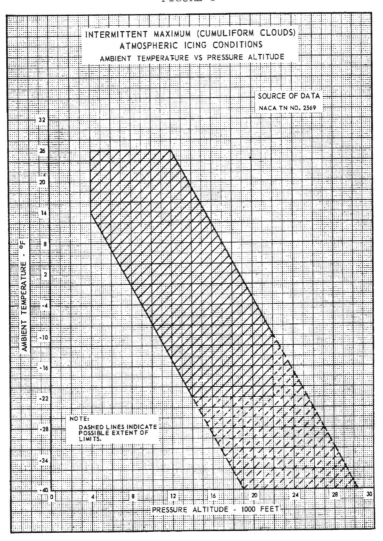

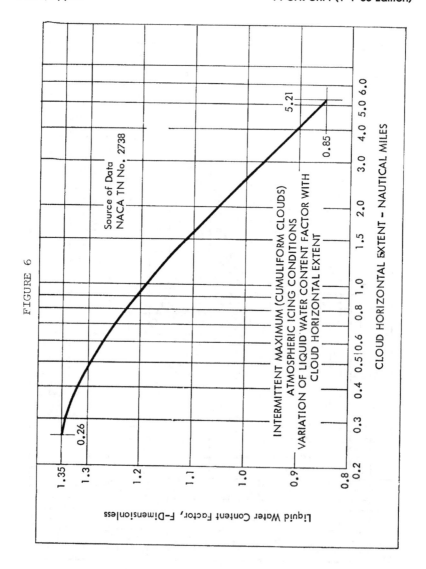

FIGURE 6

Source of Data
NACA TN No. 2738

INTERMITTENT MAXIMUM (CUMULIFORM CLOUDS)
ATMOSPHERIC ICING CONDITIONS
VARIATION OF LIQUID WATER CONTENT FACTOR WITH
CLOUD HORIZONTAL EXTENT

CLOUD HORIZONTAL EXTENT – NAUTICAL MILES

Liquid Water Content Factor, F–Dimensionless

APPENDIX D TO PART 25

Criteria for determining minimum flight crew. The following are considered by the Agency in determining the minimum flight crew under § 25.1523:

(a) *Basic workload functions.* The following basic workload functions are considered:
(1) Flight path control.
(2) Collision avoidance.
(3) Navigation.
(4) Communications.

(5) Operation and monitoring of aircraft engines and systems.

(6) Command decisions.

(b) *Workload factors.* The following workload factors are considered significant when analyzing and demonstrating workload for minimum flight crew determination:

(1) The accessibility, ease, and simplicity of operation of all necessary flight, power, and equipment controls, including emergency fuel shutoff valves, electrical controls, electronic controls, pressurization system controls, and engine controls.

(2) The accessibility and conspicuity of all necessary instruments and failure warning devices such as fire warning, electrical system malfunction, and other failure or caution indicators. The extent to which such instruments or devices direct the proper corrective action is also considered.

(3) The number, urgency, and complexity of operating procedures with particular consideration given to the specific fuel management schedule imposed by center of gravity, structural or other considerations of an airworthiness nature, and to the ability of each engine to operate at all times from a single tank or source which is automatically replenished if fuel is also stored in other tanks.

(4) The degree and duration of concentrated mental and physical effort involved in normal operation and in diagnosing and coping with malfunctions and emergencies.

(5) The extent of required monitoring of the fuel, hydraulic, pressurization, electrical, electronic, deicing, and other systems while en route.

(6) The actions requiring a crewmember to be unavailable at his assigned duty station, including: observation of systems, emergency operation of any control, and emergencies in any compartment.

(7) The degree of automation provided in the aircraft systems to afford (after failures or malfunctions) automatic crossover or isolation of difficulties to minimize the need for flight crew action to guard against loss of hydraulic or electric power to flight controls or to other essential systems.

(8) The communications and navigation workload.

(9) The possibility of increased workload associated with any emergency that may lead to other emergencies.

(10) Incapacitation of a flight crewmember whenever the applicable operating rule requires a minimum flight crew of at least two pilots.

(c) *Kind of operation authorized.* The determination of the kind of operation authorized requires consideration of the operating rules under which the airplane will be operated. Unless an applicant desires approval for a more limited kind of operation. It is assumed that each airplane certificated under this Part will operate under IFR conditions.

[Amdt. 25–3, 30 FR 6067, Apr. 29, 1965]

APPENDIX E TO PART 25

I—Limited Weight Credit For Airplanes Equipped With Standby Power

(a) Each applicant for an increase in the maximum certificated takeoff and landing weights of an airplane equipped with a type-certificated standby power rocket engine may obtain an increase as specified in paragraph (b) if—

(1) The installation of the rocket engine has been approved and it has been established by flight test that the rocket engine and its controls can be operated safely and reliably at the increase in maximum weight; and

(2) The Airplane Flight Manual, or the placard, markings or manuals required in place thereof, set forth in addition to any other operating limitations the Administrator may require, the increased weight approved under this regulation and a prohibition against the operation of the airplane at the approved increased weight when—

(i) The installed standby power rocket engines have been stored or installed in excess of the time limit established by the manufacturer of the rocket engine (usually stenciled on the engine casing); or

(ii) The rocket engine fuel has been expended or discharged.

(b) The currently approved maximum takeoff and landing weights at which an airplane is certificated without a standby power rocket engine installation may be increased by an amount that does not exceed any of the following:

(1) An amount equal in pounds to 0.014 IN, where I is the maximum usable impulse in pounds-seconds available from each standby power rocket engine and N is the number of rocket engines installed.

(2) An amount equal to 5 percent of the maximum certificated weight approved in accordance with the applicable airworthiness regulations without standby power rocket engines installed.

(3) An amount equal to the weight of the rocket engine installation.

(4) An amount that, together with the currently approved maximum weight, would equal the maximum structural weight established for the airplane without standby rocket engines installed.

II—Performance Credit for Transport Category Airplanes Equipped With Standby Power

The Administrator may grant performance credit for the use of standby power on transport category airplanes. However, the performance credit applies only to the maximum certificated takeoff and landing weights, the takeoff distance, and the take-off paths, and may not exceed that found by the Administrator to result in an overall level of safety in the takeoff, approach, and landing regimes of flight equivalent to that prescribed in the regulations under which the airplane was originally certificated without standby power. For the purposes of this appendix, "standby power" is power or thrust, or both, obtained from rocket engines for a relatively short period and actuated only in cases of emergency. The following provisions apply:

(1) *Takeoff; general.* The takeoff data prescribed in paragraphs (2) and (3) of this appendix must be determined at all weights and altitudes, and at ambient temperatures if applicable, at which performance credit is to be applied.

(2) *Takeoff path.*

(a) The one-engine-inoperative takeoff path with standby power in use must be determined in accordance with the performance requirements of the applicable airworthiness regulations.

(b) The one-engine-inoperative takeoff path (excluding that part where the airplane is on or just above the takeoff surface) determined in accordance with paragraph (a) of this section must lie above the one-engine-inoperative takeoff path without standby power at the maximum takeoff weight at which all of the applicable air-worthiness requirements are met. For the purpose of this comparison, the flight path is considered to extend to at least a height of 400 feet above the takeoff surface.

(c) The takeoff path with all engines operating, but without the use of standby power, must reflect a conservatively greater overall level of performance than the one-engine-inoperative takeoff path established in accordance with paragraph (a) of this section. The margin must be established by the Administrator to insure safe day-to-day operations, but in no case may it be less than 15 percent. The all-engines-operating takeoff path must be determined by a procedure consistent with that established in complying with paragraph (a) of this section.

(d) For reciprocating-engine-powered airplanes, the takeoff path to be scheduled in the Airplane Flight Manual must represent the one-engine-operative takeoff path determined in accordance with paragraph (a) of this section and modified to reflect the procedure (see paragraph (6)) established by the applicant for flap retraction and attainment of the en route speed. The scheduled takeoff path must have a positive slope at all points of the airborne portion and at no point must it lie above the takeoff path specified in paragraph (a) of this section.

(3) *Takeoff distance.* The takeoff distance must be the horizontal distance along the one-engine-inoperative take off path determined in accordance with paragraph (2)(a)

from the start of the takeoff to the point where the airplane attains a height of 50 feet above the takeoff surface for reciprocating-engine-powered airplanes and a height of 35 feet above the takeoff surface for turbine-powered airplanes.

(4) *Maximum certificated takeoff weights.* The maximum certificated takeoff weights must be determined at all altitudes, and at ambient temperatures, if applicable, at which performance credit is to be applied and may not exceed the weights established in compliance with paragraphs (a) and (b) of this section.

(a) The conditions of paragraphs (2)(b) through (d) must be met at the maximum certificated takeoff weight.

(b) Without the use of standby power, the airplane must meet all of the en route requirements of the applicable airworthiness regulations under which the airplane was originally certificated. In addition, turbine-powered airplanes without the use of standby power must meet the final takeoff climb requirements prescribed in the applicable airworthiness regulations.

(5) *Maximum certificated landing weights.*

(a) The maximum certificated landing weights (one-engine-inoperative approach and all-engine-operating landing climb) must be determined at all altitudes, and at ambient temperatures if applicable, at which performance credit is to be applied and must not exceed that established in compliance with paragraph (b) of this section.

(b) The flight path, with the engines operating at the power or thrust, or both, appropriate to the airplane configuration and with standby power in use, must lie above the flight path without standby power in use at the maximum weight at which all of the applicable airworthiness requirements are met. In addition, the flight paths must comply with subparagraphs (i) and (ii) of this paragraph.

(i) The flight paths must be established without changing the appropriate airplane configuration.

(ii) The flight paths must be carried out for a minimum height of 400 feet above the point where standby power is actuated.

(6) *Airplane configuration, speed, and power and thrust; general.* Any change in the airplane's configuration, speed, and power or thrust, or both, must be made in accordance with the procedures established by the applicant for the operation of the airplane in service and must comply with paragraphs (a) through (c) of this section. In addition, procedures must be established for the execution of balked landings and missed approaches.

(a) The Administrator must find that the procedure can be consistently executed in service by crews of average skill.

(b) The procedure may not involve methods or the use of devices which have not been proven to be safe and reliable.

(c) Allowances must be made for such time delays in the execution of the procedures as may be reasonably expected to occur during service.

(7) *Installation and operation; standby power.* The standby power unit and its installation must comply with paragraphs (a) and (b) of this section.

(a) The standby power unit and its installation must not adversely affect the safety of the airplane.

(b) The operation of the standby power unit and its control must have proven to be safe and reliable.

[Amdt. 25–6, 30 FR 8468, July 2, 1965]

APPENDIX F TO PART 25

Part I—Test Criteria and Procedures for Showing Compliance with § 25.853, or § 25.855.

(a) *Material test criteria*—(1) *Interior compartments occupied by crew or passengers.* (i) Interior ceiling panels, interior wall panels, partitions, galley structure, large cabinet walls, structural flooring, and materials used in the construction of stowage compartments (other than underseat stowage compartments and compartments for stowing small items such as magazines and maps) must be self-extinguishing when tested vertically in accordance with the applicable portions of part I of this appendix. The average burn length may not exceed 6 inches and the average flame time after removal of the flame source may not exceed 15 seconds. Drippings from the test specimen may not continue to flame for more than an average of 3 seconds after falling.

(ii) Floor covering, textiles (including draperies and upholstery), seat cushions, padding, decorative and nondecorative coated fabrics, leather, trays and galley furnishings, electrical conduit, thermal and acoustical insulation and insulation covering, air ducting, joint and edge covering, liners of Class B and E cargo or baggage compartments, floor panels of Class B, C, D, or E cargo or baggage compartments, insulation blankets, cargo covers and transparencies, molded and thermoformed parts, air ducting joints, and trim strips (decorative and chafing), that are constructed of materials not covered in subparagraph (iv) below, must be self-extinguishing when tested vertically in accordance with the applicable portions of part I of this appendix or other approved equivalent means. The average burn length may not exceed 8 inches, and the average flame time after removal of the flame source may not exceed 15 seconds. Drippings from the test specimen may not continue to flame for more than an average of 5 seconds after falling.

(iii) Motion picture film must be safety film meeting the Standard Specifications for Safety Photographic Film PHI.25 (available from the American National Standards Institute, 1430 Broadway, New York, NY 10018). If the film travels through ducts, the ducts must meet the requirements of subparagraph (ii) of this paragraph.

(iv) Clear plastic windows and signs, parts constructed in whole or in part of elastomeric materials, edge lighted instrument assemblies consisting of two or more instruments in a common housing, seat belts, shoulder harnesses, and cargo and baggage tiedown equipment, including containers, bins, pallets, etc., used in passenger or crew compartments, may not have an average burn rate greater than 2.5 inches per minute when tested horizontally in accordance with the applicable portions of this appendix.

(v) Except for small parts (such as knobs, handles, rollers, fasteners, clips, grommets, rub strips, pulleys, and small electrical parts) that would not contribute significantly to the propagation of a fire and for electrical wire and cable insulation, materials in items not specified in paragraphs (a)(1)(i), (ii), (iii), or (iv) of part I of this appendix may not have a burn rate greater than 4.0 inches per minute when tested horizontally in accordance with the applicable portions of this appendix.

(2) *Cargo and baggage compartments not occupied by crew or passengers.*

(i) Thermal and acoustic insulation (including coverings) used in each cargo and baggage compartment must be constructed of materials that meet the requirements set forth in paragraph (a)(1)(ii) of part I of this appendix.

(ii) A cargo or baggage compartment defined in § 25.857 as Class B or E must have a liner constructed of materials that meet the requirements of paragraph (a)(1)(ii) of part I of this appendix and separated from the airplane structure (except for attachments). In addition, such liners must be subjected to the 45 degree angle test. The flame may not penetrate (pass through) the material during application of the flame or subsequent to its removal. The average flame time after removal of the flame source may not exceed 15 seconds, and the average glow time may not exceed 10 seconds.

(iii) A cargo or baggage compartment defined in § 25.857 as Class B, C, D, or E must have floor panels constructed of materials which meet the requirements of paragraph (a)(1)(ii) of part I of this appendix and which are separated from the airplane structure (except for attachments). Such panels must be subjected to the 45 degree angle test. The flame may not penetrate (pass through) the material during application of the flame or subsequent to its removal. The average flame time after removal of the flame source may not exceed 15 seconds, and the average glow time may not exceed 10 seconds.

(iv) Insulation blankets and covers used to protect cargo must be constructed of materials that meet the requirements of paragraph (a)(1)(ii) of part I of this appendix. Tie-down equipment (including containers, bins, and pallets) used in each cargo and baggage compartment must be constructed of materials that meet the requirements of paragraph (a)(1)(v) of part I of this appendix.

(3) *Electrical system components.* Insulation on electrical wire or cable installed in any area of the fuselage must be self-extinguishing when subjected to the 60 degree test specified in part I of this appendix. The average burn length may not exceed 3 inches, and the average flame time after removal of the flame source may not exceed 30 seconds. Drippings from the test specimen may not continue to flame for more than an average of 3 seconds after falling.

(b) *Test Procedures*—(1) *Conditioning.* Specimens must be conditioned to 70±5 F., and at 50 percent ±5 percent relative humidity until moisture equilibrium is reached or for 24 hours. Each specimen must remain in the conditioning environment until it is subjected to the flame.

(2) *Specimen configuration.* Except for small parts and electrical wire and cable insulation, materials must be tested either as section cut from a fabricated part as installed in the airplane or as a specimen simulating a cut section, such as a specimen cut from a flat sheet of the material or a model of the fabricated part. The specimen may be cut from any location in a fabricated part; however, fabricated units, such as sandwich panels, may not be separated for test. Except as noted below, the specimen thickness must be no thicker than the minimum thickness to be qualified for use in the airplane. Test specimens of thick foam parts, such as seat cushions, must be ½-inch in thickness. Test specimens of materials that must meet the requirements of paragraph (a)(1)(v) of part I of this appendix must be no more than ⅛-inch in thickness. Electrical wire and cable specimens must be the same size as used in the airplane. In the case of fabrics, both the warp and fill direction of the weave must be tested to determine the most critical flammability condition. Specimens must be mounted in a metal frame so that the two long edges and the upper edge are held securely during the vertical test prescribed in subparagraph (4) of this paragraph and the two long edges and the edge away from the flame are held securely during the horizontal test prescribed in subparagraph (5) of this paragraph. The exposed area of the specimen must be at least 2 inches wide and 12 inches long, unless the actual size used in the airplane is smaller. The edge to which the burner flame is applied must not consist of the finished or protected edge of the specimen but must be representative of the actual cross-section of the material or part as in-

stalled in the airplane. The specimen must be mounted in a metal frame so that all four edges are held securely and the exposed area of the specimen is at least 8 inches by 8 inches during the 45° test prescribed in subparagraph (6) of this paragraph.

(3) *Apparatus.* Except as provided in subparagraph (7) of this paragraph, tests must be conducted in a draft-free cabinet in accordance with Federal Test Method Standard 191 Model 5903 (revised Method 5902) for the vertical test, or Method 5906 for horizontal test (available from the General Services Administration, Business Service Center, Region 3, Seventh & D Streets SW., Washington, DC 20407). Specimens which are too large for the cabinet must be tested in similar draft-free conditions.

(4) *Vertical test.* A minimum of three specimens must be tested and results averaged. For fabrics, the direction of weave corresponding to the most critical flammability conditions must be parallel to the longest dimension. Each specimen must be supported vertically. The specimen must be exposed to a Bunsen or Tirrill burner with a nominal ⅜-inch I.D. tube adjusted to give a flame of 1½ inches in height. The minimum flame temperature measured by a calibrated thermocouple pyrometer in the center of the flame must be 1550 °F. The lower edge of the specimen must be ¾-inch above the top edge of the burner. The flame must be applied to the center line of the lower edge of the specimen. For materials covered by paragraph (a)(1)(i) of part I of this appendix, the flame must be applied for 60 seconds and then removed. For materials covered by paragraph (a)(1)(ii) of part I of this appendix, the flame must be applied for 12 seconds and then removed. Flame time, burn length, and flaming time of drippings, if any, may be recorded. The burn length determined in accordance with subparagraph (7) of this paragraph must be measured to the nearest tenth of an inch.

(5) *Horizontal test.* A minimum of three specimens must be tested and the results averaged. Each specimen must be supported horizontally. The exposed surface, when installed in the aircraft, must be face down for the test. The specimen must be exposed to a Bunsen or Tirrill burner with a nominal ⅜-inch I.D. tube adjusted to give a flame of 1½ inches in height. The minimum flame temperature measured by a calibrated thermocouple pyrometer in the center of the flame must be 1550 °F. The specimen must be positioned so that the edge being tested is centered ¾-inch above the top of the burner. The flame must be applied for 15 seconds and then removed. A minimum of 10 inches of specimen must be used for timing purposes, approximately 1½ inches must burn before the burning front reaches the timing zone, and the average burn rate must be recorded.

(6) *Forty-five degree test.* A minimum of three specimens must be tested and the results averaged. The specimens must be supported at an angle of 45° to a horizontal surface. The exposed surface when installed in the aircraft must be face down for the test. The specimens must be exposed to a Bunsen or Tirrill burner with a nominal ⅜-inch I.D. tube adjusted to give a flame of 1½ inches in height. The minimum flame temperature measured by a calibrated thermocouple pyrometer in the center of the flame must be 1550 °F. Suitable precautions must be taken to avoid drafts. The flame must be applied for 30 seconds with one-third contacting the material at the center of the specimen and then removed. Flame time, glow time, and whether the flame penetrates (passes through) the specimen must be recorded.

(7) *Sixty degree test.* A minimum of three specimens of each wire specification (make and size) must be tested. The specimen of wire or cable (including insulation) must be placed at an angle of 60° with the horizontal in the cabinet specified in subparagraph (3) of this paragraph with the cabinet door open during the test, or must be placed within a chamber approximately 2 feet high by 1 foot by 1 foot, open at the top and at one vertical side (front), and which allows sufficient flow of air for complete combustion, but which is free from drafts. The specimen must be parallel to and approximately 6 inches from the front of the chamber. The lower end of the specimen must be held rigidly clamped. The upper end of the specimen must pass over a pulley or rod and must have an appropriate weight attached to it so that the specimen is held tautly throughout the flammability test. The test specimen span between lower clamp and upper pulley or rod must be 24 inches and must be marked 8 inches from the lower end to indicate the central point for flame application. A flame from a Bunsen or Tirrill burner must be applied for 30 seconds at the test mark. The burner must be mounted underneath the test mark on the specimen, perpendicular to the specimen and at an angle of 30° to the vertical plane of the specimen. The burner must have a nominal bore of ⅜-inch and be adjusted to provide a 3-inch high flame with an inner cone approximately one-third of the flame height. The minimum temperature of the hottest portion of the flame, as measured with a calibrated thermocouple pyrometer, may not be less than 1750 °F. The burner must be positioned so that the hottest portion of the flame is applied to the test mark on the wire. Flame time, burn length, and flaming time of drippings, if any, must be recorded. The burn length determined in accordance with paragraph (8) of this paragraph must be measured to the nearest tenth of an inch. Breaking of the wire specimens is not considered a failure.

(8) *Burn length.* Burn length is the distance from the original edge to the farthest evidence of damage to the test specimen due to flame impingement, including areas of partial or complete consumption, charring, or embrittlement, but not including areas sooted, stained, warped, or discolored, nor areas where material has shrunk or melted away from the heat source.

Part II—Flammability of Seat Cushions

(a) *Criteria for Acceptance.* Each seat cushion must meet the following criteria:

(1) At least three sets of seat bottom and seat back cushion specimens must be tested.

(2) If the cushion is constructed with a fire blocking material, the fire blocking material must completely enclose the cushion foam core material.

(3) Each specimen tested must be fabricated using the principal components (i.e., foam core, flotation material, fire blocking material, if used, and dress covering) and assembly processes (representative seams and closures) intended for use in the production articles. If a different material combination is used for the back cushion than for the bottom cushion, both material combinations must be tested as complete specimen sets, each set consisting of a back cushion specimen and a bottom cushion specimen. If a cushion, including outer dress covering, is demonstrated to meet the requirements of this appendix using the oil burner test, the dress covering of that cushion may be replaced with a similar dress covering provided the burn length of the replacement covering, as determined by the test specified in §25.853(c), does not exceed the corresponding burn length of the dress covering used on the cushion subjected to the oil burner test.

(4) For at least two-thirds of the total number of specimen sets tested, the burn length from the burner must not reach the side of the cushion opposite the burner. The burn length must not exceed 17 inches. Burn length is the perpendicular distance from the inside edge of the seat frame closest to the burner to the farthest evidence of damage to the test specimen due to flame impingement, including areas of partial or complete consumption, charring, or embrittlement, but not including areas sooted, stained, warped, or discolored, or areas where material has shrunk or melted away from the heat source.

(5) The average percentage weight loss must not exceed 10 percent. Also, at least two-thirds of the total number of specimen sets tested must not exceed 10 percent weight loss. All droppings falling from the cushions and mounting stand are to be discarded before the after-test weight is determined. The percentage weight loss for a specimen set is the weight of the specimen set before testing less the weight of the specimen set after testing expressed as the percentage of the weight before testing.

(b) *Test Conditions.* Vertical air velocity should average 25 fpm±10 fpm at the top of the back seat cushion. Horizontal air velocity should be below 10 fpm just above the bottom seat cushion. Air velocities should be measured with the ventilation hood operating and the burner motor off.

(c) *Test Specimens.* (1) For each test, one set of cushion specimens representing a seat bottom and seat back cushion must be used.

(2) The seat bottom cushion specimen must be 18±⅛ inches (457±3 mm) wide by 20±⅛ inches (508±3 mm) deep by 4±⅛ inches (102±3 mm) thick, exclusive of fabric closures and seam overlap.

(3) The seat back cushion specimen must be 18±⅛ inches (432±3 mm) wide by 25±⅛ inches (635±3 mm) high by 2±⅛ inches (51±3 mm) thick, exclusive of fabric closures and seam overlap.

(4) The specimens must be conditioned at 70±5 °F (21±2 °C) 55%±10% relative humidity for at least 24 hours before testing.

(d) *Test Apparatus.* The arrangement of the test apparatus is shown in Figures 1 through 5 and must include the components described in this section. Minor details of the apparatus may vary, depending on the model burner used.

(1) *Specimen Mounting Stand.* The mounting stand for the test specimens consists of steel angles, as shown in Figure 1. The length of the mounting stand legs is 12±⅛ inches (305±3 mm). The mounting stand must be used for mounting the test specimen seat bottom and seat back, as shown in Figure 2. The mounting stand should also include a suitable drip pan lined with aluminum foil, dull side up.

(2) *Test Burner.* The burner to be used in testing must—

(i) Be a modified gun type;

(ii) Have an 80-degree spray angle nozzle nominally rated for 2.25 gallons/hour at 100 psi;

(iii) Have a 12-inch (305 mm) burner cone installed at the end of the draft tube, with an opening 6 inches (152 mm) high and 11 inches (280 mm) wide, as shown in Figure 3; and

(iv) Have a burner fuel pressure regulator that is adjusted to deliver a nominal 2.0 gallon/hour of # 2 Grade kerosene or equivalent required for the test.

Burner models which have been used successfully in testing are the Lennox Model OB-32, Carlin Model 200 CRD, and Park Model DPL 3400. FAA published reports pertinent to this type of burner are: (1) Powerplant Enginering Report No. 3A, Standard Fire Test Apparatus and Procedure for Flexible Hose Assemblies, dated March 1978; and (2) Report No. DOT/FAA/RD/76/213, Reevaluation of Burner Characteristics for Fire Resistance Tests, dated January 1977.

(3) *Calorimeter.*

(i) The calorimeter to be used in testing must be a (0–15.0 BTU/ft²-sec. 0–17.0 W/cm²)

calorimeter, accurate ±3%, mounted in a 6-inch by 12-inch (152 by 305 mm) by ¾-inch (19 mm) thick calcium silicate insulating board which is attached to a steel angle bracket for placement in the test stand during burner calibration, as shown in Figure 4.

(ii) Because crumbling of the insulating board with service can result in misalignment of the calorimeter, the calorimeter must be monitored and the mounting shimmed, as necessary, to ensure that the calorimeter face is flush with the exposed plane of the insulating board in a plane parallel to the exit of the test burner cone.

(4) *Thermocouples.* The seven thermocouples to be used for testing must be ¹⁄₁₆- to ⅛-inch metal sheathed, ceramic packed, type K, grounded thermocouples with a nominal 22 to 30 American wire gage (AWG)-size conductor. The seven thermocouples must be attached to a steel angle bracket to form a thermocouple rake for placement in the test stand during burner calibration, as shown in Figure 5.

(5) *Apparatus Arrangement.* The test burner must be mounted on a suitable stand to position the exit of the burner cone a distance of 4±⅛ inches (102±3 mm) from one side of the specimen mounting stand. The burner stand should have the capability of allowing the burner to be swung away from the specimen mounting stand during warmup periods.

(6) *Data Recording.* A recording potentiometer or other suitable calibrated instrument with an appropriate range must be used to measure and record the outputs of the calorimeter and the thermocouples.

(7) *Weight Scale.* Weighing Device—A device must be used that with proper procedures may determine the before and after test weights of each set of seat cushion specimens within 0.02 pound (9 grams). A continuous weighing system is preferred.

(8) *Timing Device.* A stopwatch or other device (calibrated to ±1 second) must be used to measure the time of application of the burner flame and self-extinguishing time or test duration.

(e) *Preparation of Apparatus.* Before calibration, all equipment must be turned on and the burner fuel must be adjusted as specified in paragraph (d)(2).

(f) *Calibration.* To ensure the proper thermal output of the burner, the following test must be made:

(1) Place the calorimeter on the test stand as shown in Figure 4 at a distance of 4±⅛ inches (102±3 mm) from the exit of the burner cone.

(2) Turn on the burner, allow it to run for 2 minutes for warmup, and adjust the burner air intake damper to produce a reading of 10.5±0.5 BTU/ft²-sec. (11.9±0.6 w/cm²) on the calorimeter to ensure steady state conditions have been achieved. Turn off the burner.

(3) Replace the calorimeter with the thermocouple rake (Figure 5).

(4) Turn on the burner and ensure that the thermocouples are reading 1900±100 °F (1038±38 °C) to ensure steady state conditions have been achieved.

(5) If the calorimeter and thermocouples do not read within range, repeat steps in paragraphs 1 through 4 and adjust the burner air intake damper until the proper readings are obtained. The thermocouple rake and the calorimeter should be used frequently to maintain and record calibrated test parameters. Until the specific apparatus has demonstrated consistency, each test should be calibrated. After consistency has been confirmed, several tests may be conducted with the pre-test calibration before and a calibration check after the series.

(g) *Test Procedure.* The flammability of each set of specimens must be tested as follows:

(1) Record the weight of each set of seat bottom and seat back cushion specimens to be tested to the nearest 0.02 pound (9 grams).

(2) Mount the seat bottom and seat back cushion test specimens on the test stand as shown in Figure 2, securing the seat back cushion specimen to the test stand at the top.

(3) Swing the burner into position and ensure that the distance from the exit of the burner cone to the side of the seat bottom cushion specimen is 4±⅛ inches (102±3 mm).

(4) Swing the burner away from the test position. Turn on the burner and allow it to run for 2 minutes to provide adequate warmup of the burner cone and flame stabilization.

(5) To begin the test, swing the burner into the test position and simultaneously start the timing device.

(6) Expose the seat bottom cushion specimen to the burner flame for 2 minutes and then turn off the burner. Immediately swing the burner away from the test position. Terminate test 7 minutes after initiating cushion exposure to the flame by use of a gaseous extinguishing agent (i.e., Halon or CO_2).

(7) Determine the weight of the remains of the seat cushion specimen set left on the mounting stand to the nearest 0.02 pound (9 grams) excluding all droppings.

(h) *Test Report.* With respect to all specimen sets tested for a particular seat cushion for which testing of compliance is performed, the following information must be recorded:

(1) An identification and description of the specimens being tested.

(2) The number of specimen sets tested.

(3) The initial weight and residual weight of each set, the calculated percentage weight loss of each set, and the calculated average percentage weight loss for the total number of sets tested.

(4) The burn length for each set tested.

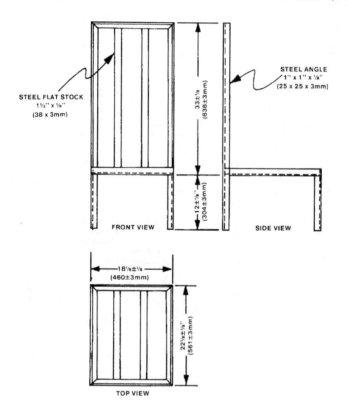

STEEL FLAT STOCK
1 ½'' x ⅛''
(38 x 3mm)

STEEL ANGLE
1'' x 1'' x ⅛''
(25 x 25 x 3mm)

33±⅛
(838±3mm)

12±⅛''
(304±3mm)

FRONT VIEW   SIDE VIEW

18⅛±⅛
(460±3mm)

22⅛±⅛''
(561±3mm)

TOP VIEW

NOTE:
ALL JOINTS WELDED
FLAT STOCK BUTT WELDED
ALL MEASUREMENTS INSIDE

FIGURE 1

504

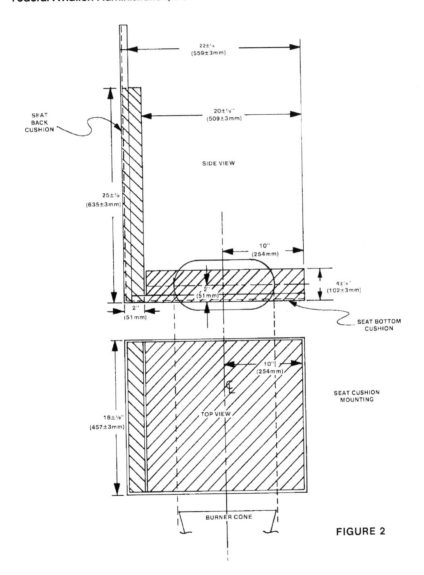

FIGURE 2

505

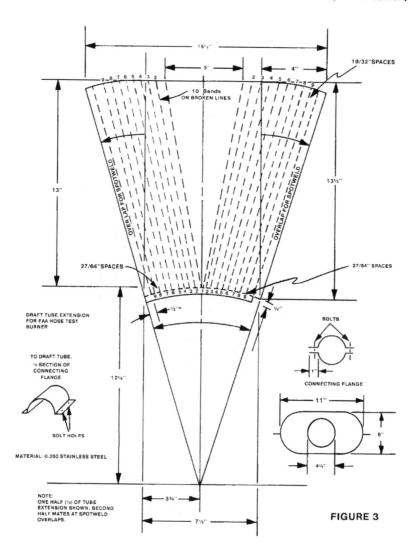

FIGURE 3

506

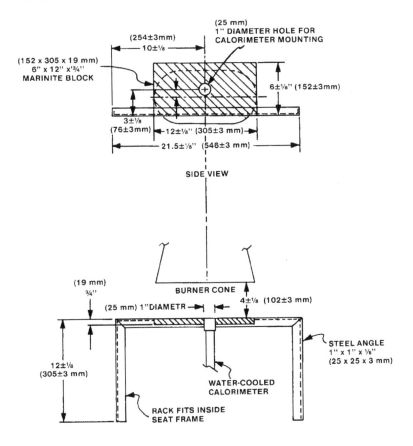

SIDE VIEW

TOP VIEW
CALORIMETER BRACKET

FIGURE 4

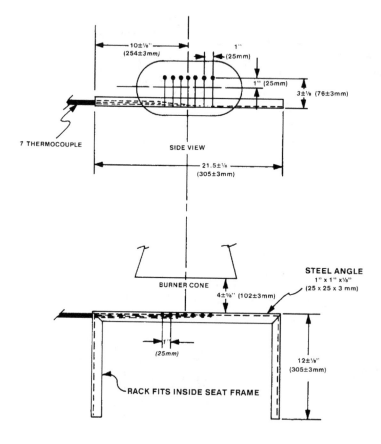

7 THERMOCOUPLE

SIDE VIEW

BURNER CONE

STEEL ANGLE
1" x 1" x⅛"
(25 x 25 x 3 mm)

RACK FITS INSIDE SEAT FRAME

TOP VIEW
THERMOCOUPLE RAKE BRACKET

FIGURE 5

Part III—Test Method to Determine Flame Penetration Resistance of Cargo Compartment Liners.

(a) *Criteria for Acceptance.* (1) At least three specimens of cargo compartment sidewall or ceiling liner panels must be tested.

(2) Each specimen tested must simulate the cargo compartment sidewall or ceiling liner panel, including any design features,

such as joints, lamp assemblies, etc., the failure of which would affect the capability of the liner to safely contain a fire.

(3) There must be no flame penetration of any specimen within 5 minutes after application of the flame source, and the peak temperature measured at 4 inches above the upper surface of the horizontal test sample must not exceed 400 °F.

(b) *Summary of Method.* This method provides a laboratory test procedure for measuring the capability of cargo compartment lining materials to resist flame penetration with a 2 gallon per hour (GPH) #2 Grade kerosene or equivalent burner fire source. Ceiling and sidewall liner panels may be tested individually provided a baffle is used to simulate the missing panel. Any specimen that passes the test as a ceiling liner panel may be used as a sidewall liner panel.

(c) *Test Specimens.* (1) The specimen to be tested must measure 16±⅛ inches (406±3 mm) by 24+⅛ inches (610±3 mm).

(2) The specimens must be conditioned at 70 °F.±5 °F. (21 °C. ±2 °C.) and 55%±5% humidity for at least 24 hours before testing.

(d) *Test Apparatus.* The arrangement of the test apparatus, which is shown in Figure 3 of Part II and Figures 1 through 3 of this part of appendix F, must include the components described in this section. Minor details of the apparatus may vary, depending on the model of the burner used.

(1) *Specimen Mounting Stand.* The mounting stand for the test specimens consists of steel angles as shown in Figure 1.

(2) *Test Burner.* The burner to be used in tesing must—

(i) Be a modified gun type.

(ii) Use a suitable nozzle and maintain fuel pressure to yield a 2 GPH fuel flow. For example: an 80 degree nozzle nominally rated at 2.25 GPH and operated at 85 pounds per square inch (PSI) gage to deliver 2.03 GPH.

(iii) Have a 12 inch (305 mm) burner extension installed at the end of the draft tube with an opening 6 inches (152 mm) high and 11 inches (280 mm) wide as shown in Figure 3 of Part II of this appendix.

(iv) Have a burner fuel pressure regulator that is adjusted to deliver a nominal 2.0 GPH of #2 Grade kerosene or equivalent.

Burner models which have been used successfully in testing are the Lenox Model OB–32, Carlin Model 200 CRD and Park Model DPL. The basic burner is described in FAA Powerplant Engineering Report No. 3A, Standard Fire Test Apparatus and Procedure for Flexible Hose Assemblies, dated March 1978; however, the test settings specified in this appendix differ in some instances from those specified in the report.

(3) *Calorimeter.* (i) The calorimeter to be used in testing must be a total heat flux Foil Type Gardon Gage of an appropriate range (approximately 0 to 15.0 British thermal unit (BTU) per ft.² sec., 0–17.0 watts/cm²). The calorimeter must be mounted in a 6 inch by 12 inch (152 by 305 mm) by ¾ inch (19 mm) thick insulating block which is attached to a steel angle bracket for placement in the test stand during burner calibration as shown in Figure 2 of this part of this appendix.

(ii) The insulating block must be monitored for deterioration and the mounting shimmed as necessary to ensure that the cal-orimeter face is parallel to the exit plane of the test burner cone.

(4) *Thermocouples.* The seven thermocouples to be used for testing must be ⅟₁₆ inch ceramic sheathed, type K, grounded thermocouples with a nominal 30 American wire gage (AWG) size conductor. The seven thermocouples must be attached to a steel angle bracket to form a thermocouple rake for placement in the test stand during burner calibration as shown in Figure 3 of this part of this appendix.

(5) *Apparatus Arrangement.* The test burner must be mounted on a suitable stand to position the exit of the burner cone a distance of 8 inches from the ceiling liner panel and 2 inches from the sidewall liner panel. The burner stand should have the capability of allowing the burner to be swung away from the test specimen during warm-up periods.

(6) *Instrumentation.* A recording potentiometer or other suitable instrument with an appropriate range must be used to measure and record the outputs of the calorimeter and the thermocouples.

(7) *Timing Device.* A stopwatch or other device must be used to measure the time of flame application and the time of flame penetration, if it occurs.

(e) *Preparation of Apparatus.* Before calibration, all equipment must be turned on and allowed to stabilize, and the burner fuel flow must be adjusted as specified in paragraph (d)(2).

(f) *Calibration.* To ensure the proper thermal output of the burner the following test must be made:

(1) Remove the burner extension from the end of the draft tube. Turn on the blower portion of the burner without turning the fuel or igniters on. Measure the air velocity using a hot wire anemometer in the center of the draft tube across the face of the opening. Adjust the damper such that the air velocity is in the range of 1550 to 1800 ft./min. If tabs are being used at the exit of the draft tube, they must be removed prior to this measurement. Reinstall the draft tube extension cone.

(2) Place the calorimeter on the test stand as shown in Figure 2 at a distance of 8 inches (203 mm) from the exit of the burner cone to simulate the position of the horizontal test specimen.

(3) Turn on the burner, allow it to run for 2 minutes for warm-up, and adjust the damper to produce a calorimeter reading of 8.0±0.5 BTU per ft.² sec. (9.1±0.6 Watts/cm²).

(4) Replace the calorimeter with the thermocouple rake (see Figure 3).

(5) Turn on the burner and ensure that each of the seven thermocouples reads 1700 °F. ±100 °F. (927 °C. ±38 °C.) to ensure steady state conditions have been achieved. If the temperature is out of this range, repeat steps 2 through 5 until proper readings are obtained.

(6) Turn off the burner and remove the thermocouple rake.

(7) Repeat (1) to ensure that the burner is in the correct range.

(g) *Test Procedure.* (1) Mount a thermocouple of the same type as that used for calibration at a distance of 4 inches (102 mm) above the horizontal (ceiling) test specimen. The thermocouple should be centered over the burner cone.

(2) Mount the test specimen on the test stand shown in Figure 1 in either the horizontal or vertical position. Mount the insulating material in the other position.

(3) Position the burner so that flames will not impinge on the specimen, turn the burner on, and allow it to run for 2 minutes. Rotate the burner to apply the flame to the specimen and simultaneously start the timing device.

(4) Expose the test specimen to the flame for 5 minutes and then turn off the burner.

The test may be terminated earlier if flame penetration is observed.

(5) When testing ceiling liner panels, record the peak temperature measured 4 inches above the sample.

(6) Record the time at which flame penetration occurs if applicable.

(h) *Test Report.* The test report must include the following:

(1) A complete description of the materials tested including type, manufacturer, thickness, and other appropriate data.

(2) Observations of the behavior of the test specimens during flame exposure such as delamination, resin ignition, smoke, ect., including the time of such occurrence.

(3) The time at which flame penetration occurs, if applicable, for each of the three specimens tested.

(4) Panel orientation (ceiling or sidewall).

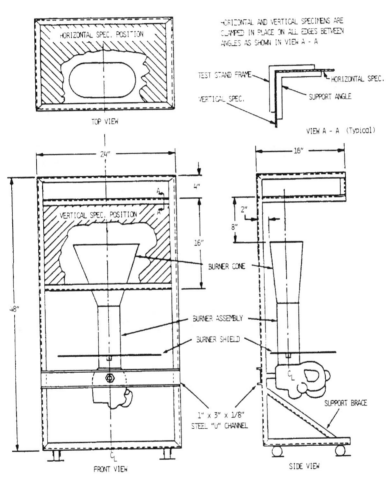

FIGURE 1. TEST APPARATUS FOR HORIZONTAL AND VERTICAL MOUNTING

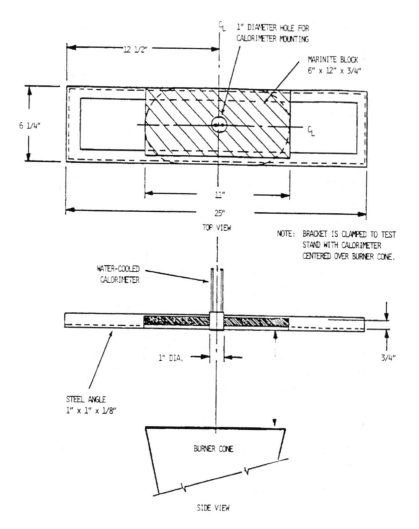

FIGURE 2. CALORIMETER BRACKET

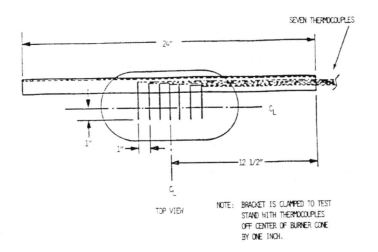

SEVEN THERMOCOUPLES

24"

1"

1"

12 1/2"

C_L

C_L

TOP VIEW

NOTE: BRACKET IS CLAMPED TO TEST
STAND WITH THERMOCOUPLES
OFF CENTER OF BURNER CONE
BY ONE INCH.

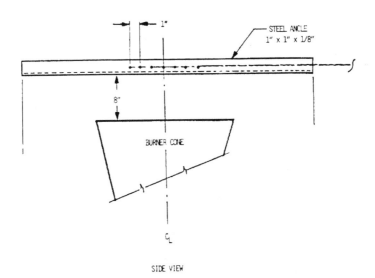

1"

STEEL ANGLE
1" x 1" x 1/8"

8"

BURNER CONE

C_L

SIDE VIEW

FIGURE 3. THERMOCOUPLE RAKE BRACKET

Part IV—Test Method to Determine the Heat Release Rate From Cabin Materials Exposed to Radiant Heat.

(a) *Summary of Method.* Three or more specimens representing the completed aircraft component are tested. Each test specimen is injected into an environmental chamber through which a constant flow of air passes. The specimen's exposure is determined by a radiant heat source adjusted to produce, on the specimen, the desired total heat flux of 3.5 W/cm². The specimen is tested with the exposed surface vertical. Combustion is initiated by piloted ignition. The combustion products leaving the chamber are monitored in order to calculate the release rate of heat.

(b) *Apparatus.* The Ohio State University (OSU) rate of heat release apparatus, as described below, is used. This is a modified version of the rate of heat release apparatus standardized by the American Society of Testing and Materials (ASTM), ASTM E–906.

(1) This apparatus is shown in Figures 1A and 1B of this part IV. All exterior surfaces of the apparatus, except the holding chamber, must be insulated with 1 inch (25 mm) thick, low density, high temperature, fiberglass board insulation. A gasketed door, through which the sample injection rod slides, must be used to form an airtight closure on the specimen hold chamber.

(2) *Thermopile.* The temperature difference between the air entering the environmental chamber and that leaving must be monitored by a thermopile having five hot, and five cold, 24-guage Chromel-Alumel junctions. The hot junctions must be spaced across the top of the exhaust stack, .38 inches (10 mm) below the top of the chimney. The thermocouples must have a .050 ± .010 inch (1.3 ± .3mm) diameter, ball-type, welded tip. One thermocouple must be located in the geometric center, with the other four located 1.18 inch (30 mm) from the center along the diagonal toward each of the corners (Figure 5 of this part IV). The cold junctions must be located in the pan below the lower air distribution plate (see paragraph (b)(4) of this part IV). Thermopile hot junctions must be cleared of soot deposits as needed to maintain the calibrated sensitivity.

(3) *Radiation Source.* A radiant heat source incorporating four Type LL silicon carbide elements, 20 inches (508 mm) long by .63 inch (16 mm) O.D., must be used, as shown in Figures 2A and 2B of this part IV. The heat source must have a nominal resistance of 1.4 ohms and be capable of generating a flux up to 100 kW/m². The silicone carbide elements must be mounted in the stainless steel panel box by inserting them through .63 inch (16 mm) holes in .03 inch (1 mm) thick ceramic fiber or calcium-silicate millboard. Locations of the holes in the pads and stainless steel cover plates are shown in Figure 2B of

this part IV. The truncated diamond-shaped mask of .042±.002 inch (1.07±.05mm) stainless steel must be added to provide uniform heat flux density over the area occupied by the vertical sample.

(4) *Air Distribution System.* The air entering the environmental chamber must be distributed by a .25 inch (6.3 mm) thick aluminum plate having eight No. 4 drill-holes, located 2 inches (51 mm) from sides on 4 inch (102 mm) centers, mounted at the base of the environmental chamber. A second plate of 18 guage stainless steel having 120, evenly spaced, No. 28 drill holes must be mounted 6 inches (152 mm) above the aluminum plate. A well-regulated air supply is required. The air-supply manifold at the base of the pyramidal section must have 48, evenly spaced, No. 26 drill holes located .38 inch (10 mm) from the inner edge of the manifold, resulting in an airflow split of approximately three to one within the apparatus.

(5) *Exhaust Stack.* An exhaust stack, 5.25×2.75 inches (133×70 mm) in cross section, and 10 inches (254 mm) long, fabricated from 28 guage stainless steel must be mounted on the outlet of the pyramidal section. A 1.0×3.0 inch (25×76 mm) baffle plate of .018±.002 inch (.50±.05 mm) stainless steel must be centered inside the stack, perpendicular to the air flow, 3 inches (76 mm) above the base of the stack.

(6) *Specimen Holders.* (i) The specimen must be tested in a vertical orientation. The specimen holder (Figure 3 of this part IV) must incorporate a frame that touches the specimen (which is wrapped with aluminum foil as required by paragraph (d)(3) of this Part) along only the .25 inch (6 mm) perimeter. A "V" shaped spring is used to hold the assembly together. A detachable .50×.50×5.91 inch (12×12×150 mm) drip pan and two .020 inch (.5 mm) stainless steel wires (as shown in Figure 3 of this part IV) must be used for testing materials prone to melting and dripping. The positioning of the spring and frame may be changed to accommodate different specimen thicknesses by inserting the retaining rod in different holes on the specimen holder.

(ii) Since the radiation shield described in ASTM E–906 is not used, a guide pin must be added to the injection mechanism. This fits into a slotted metal plate on the injection mechanism outside of the holding chamber. It can be used to provide accurate positioning of the specimen face after injection. The front surface of the specimen must be 3.9 inches (100 mm) from the closed radiation doors after injection.

(iii) The specimen holder clips onto the mounted bracket (Figure 3 of this part IV). The mounting bracket must be attached to the injection rod by three screws that pass through a wide-area washer welded onto a ½-inch (13 mm) nut. The end of the injection rod must be threaded to screw into the nut, and a .020 inch (5.1 mm) thick wide area washer must be held between two ½-inch (13 mm) nuts that are adjusted to tightly cover the hole in the radiation doors through which the injection rod or calibration calorimeter pass.

(7) *Calorimeter*. A total-flux type calorimeter must be mounted in the center of a ½-inch Kaowool "M" board inserted in the sample holder to measure the total heat flux. The calorimeter must have a view angle of 180 degrees and be calibrated for incident flux. The calorimeter calibration must be acceptable to the Administrator.

(8) *Pilot-Flame Positions*. Pilot ignition of the specimen must be accomplished by simultaneously exposing the specimen to a lower pilot burner and an upper pilot burner, as described in paragraph (b)(8)(i) and (b)(8)(ii) or (b)(8)(iii) of this part IV, respectively. Since intermittent pilot flame extinguishment for more than 3 seconds would invalidate the test results, a spark ignitor may be installed to ensure that the lower pilot burner remains lighted.

(i) *Lower Pilot Burner*. The pilot-flame tubing must be .25 inch (6.3 mm) O.D., .03 inch (0.8mm) wall, stainless steel tubing. A mixture of 120 cm³/min. of methane and 850 cm³/min. of air must be fed to the lower pilot flame burner. The normal position of the end of the pilot burner tubing is .40 inch (10 mm) from and perpendicular to the exposed vertical surface of the specimen. The centerline at the outlet of the burner tubing must intersect the vertical centerline of the sample at a point .20 inch (5 mm) above the lower exposed edge of the specimen.

(ii) *Standard Three-Hole Upper Pilot Burner*. The pilot burner must be a straight length of .25 inch (6.3 mm) O.D., .03 inch (0.8 mm) wall, stainless steel tubing that is 14 inches (360 mm) long. One end of the tubing must be closed, and three No. 40 drill holes must be drilled into the tubing, 2.38 inch (60 mm) apart, for gas ports, all radiating in the same direction. The first hole must be .19 inch (5 mm) from the closed end of the tubing. The tube must be positioned .75 inch (19 mm) above and .75 inch (19 mm) behind the exposed upper edge of the specimen. The middle hole must be in the vertical plane perpendicular to the exposed surface of the specimen which passes through its vertical centerline and must be pointed toward the radiation source. The gas supplied to the burner must be methane and must be adjusted to produce flame lengths of 1 inch (25 mm).

(iii) *Optional Fourteen-Hole Upper Pilot Burner*. This burner may be used in lieu of the standard three-hole burner described in paragraph (b)(8)(ii) of this part IV. The pilot burner must be a straight length of .25 inch (6.3 mm) O.D., .03 inch (0.8 mm) wall, stainless steel tubing that is 15.75 inches (400 mm) long. One end of the tubing must be closed, and 14 No. 59 drill holes must be drilled into the tubing, .50 inch (13 mm) apart, for gas

ports, all radiating in the same direction. The first hole must be .50 inch (13 mm) from the closed end of the tubing. The tube must be positioned above the specimen holder so that the holes are placed above the specimen as shown in Figure 1B of this part IV. The fuel supplied to the burner must be methane mixed with air in a ratio of approximately 50/50 by volume. The total gas flow must be adjusted to produce flame lengths of 1 inch (25 mm). When the gas/air ratio and the flow rate are properly adjusted, approximately .25 inch (6 mm) of the flame length appears yellow in color.

(c) *Calibration of Equipment*. (1) *Heat Release Rate*. A calibration burner, as shown in Figure 4, must be placed over the end of the lower pilot flame tubing using a gas tight connection. The flow of gas to the pilot flame must be at least 99 percent methane and must be accurately metered. Prior to usage, the wet test meter must be properly leveled and filled with distilled water to the tip of the internal pointer while no gas is flowing. Ambient temperature and pressure of the water are based on the internal wet test meter temperature. A baseline flow rate of approximately 1 liter/min. must be set and increased to higher preset flows of 4, 6, 8, 6 and 4 liters/min. Immediately prior to recording methane flow rates, a flow rate of 8 liters/min. must be used for 2 minutes to precondition the chamber. This is not recorded as part of calibration. The rate must be determined by using a stopwatch to time a complete revolution of the wet test meter for both the baseline and higher flow, with the flow returned to baseline before changing to the next higher flow. The thermopile baseline voltage must be measured. The gas flow to the burner must be increased to the higher preset flow and allowed to burn for 2.0 minutes, and the thermopile voltage must be measured. The sequence must be repeated until all five values have been determined. The average of the five values must be used as the calibration factor. The procedure must be repeated if the percent relative standard deviation is greater than 5 percent. Calculations are shown in paragraph (f) of this part IV.

(2) *Flux Uniformity*. Uniformity of flux over the specimen must be checked periodically and after each heating element change to determine if it is within acceptable limits of plus or minus 5 percent.

(3) As noted in paragraph (b)(2) of this part IV, thermopile hot junctions must be cleared of soot deposits as needed to maintain the calibrated sensitivity.

(d) *Preparation of Test Specimens*. (1) The test specimens must be representative of the aircraft component in regard to materials and construction methods. The standard size for the test specimens is 5.91 ± .03 × 5.91 ±.03 inches (149 ±1 × 149 ±1 mm). The thickness of the specimen must be the same as that of the aircraft component it represents up to a maximum thickness of 1.75 inches (45 mm). Test specimens representing thicker components must be 1.75 inches (45 mm).

(2) *Conditioning.* Specimens must be conditioned as described in Part 1 of this appendix.

(3) *Mounting.* Each test specimen must be wrapped tightly on all sides of the specimen, except for the one surface that is exposed with a single layer of .001 inch (.025 mm) aluminum foil.

(e) *Procedure.* (1) The power supply to the radiant panel must be set to produce a radiant flux of 3.5 ±.05 W/cm², as measured at the point the center of the specimen surface will occupy when positioned for the test. The radiant flux must be measured after the air flow through the equipment is adjusted to the desired rate.

(2) After the pilot flames are lighted, their position must be checked as described in paragraph (b)(8) of this part IV.

(3) Air flow through the apparatus must be controlled by a circular plate orifice located in a 1.5 inch (38.1 mm) I.D. pipe with two pressure measuring points, located 1.5 inches (38 mm) upstream and .75 inches (19 mm) downstream of the orifice plate. The pipe must be connected to a manometer set at a pressure differential of 7.87 inches (200 mm) of Hg. (See Figure 1B of this part IV.) The total air flow to the equipment is approximately .04 m³/seconds. The stop on the vertical specimen holder rod must be adjusted so that the exposed surface of the specimen is positioned 3.9 inches (100 mm) from the entrance when injected into the environmental chamber.

(4) The specimen must be placed in the hold chamber with the radiation doors closed. The airtight outer door must be secured, and the recording devices must be started. The specimen must be retained in the hold chamber for 60 seconds, plus or minus 10 seconds, before injection. The thermopile "zero" value must be determined during the last 20 seconds of the hold period. The sample must not be injected before completion of the "zero" value determination.

(5) When the specimen is to be injected, the radiation doors must be opened. After the specimen is injected into the environmental chamber, the radiation doors must be closed behind the specimen.

(6) [Reserved]

(7) Injection of the specimen and closure of the inner door marks time zero. A record of the thermopile output with at least one data point per second must be made during the time the specimen is in the environmental chamber.

(8) The test duration is five minutes. The lower pilot burner and the upper pilot burner must remain lighted for the entire duration of the test, except that there may be intermittent flame extinguishment for periods that do not exceed 3 seconds. Furthermore, if the optional three-hole upper burner is used, at least two flamelets must remain lighted for the entire duration of the test, except that there may be intermittent flame extinguishment of all three flamelets for periods that do not exceed 3 seconds.

(9) A minimum of three specimens must be tested.

(f) *Calculations.* (1) The calibration factor is calculated as follows:

$$K_h = \frac{(F_1 - F_O)}{(V_1 - V_O)} \times \frac{(210.8 - 22)k_{cal}}{mole} \times \frac{273}{T_a} \times \frac{P - P_v}{760} \times \frac{mole\ CH4STP}{22.41} \times \frac{WATT\ min}{.01433kcal} \times \frac{kw}{1000w}$$

F_0=flow of methane at baseline (1pm)
F_1=higher preset flow of methane (1pm)
V_0=thermopile voltage at baseline (mv)
V_1=thermopile voltage at higher flow (mv)
T_a=Ambient temperature (K)
P=Ambient pressure (mm Hg)
P_v=Water vapor pressure (mm Hg)

(2) Heat release rates may be calculated from the reading of the thermopile output voltage at any instant of time as:

$$HRR = \frac{(V_m - V_b)K_n}{.02323m^2}$$

HRR=heat release rate (kw/m²)
V_b=baseline voltage (mv)
V_m=measured thermopile voltage (mv)

K_h=calibration factor (kw/mv)

(3) The integral of the heat release rate is the total heat release as a function of time and is calculated by multiplying the rate by the data sampling frequency in minutes and summing the time from zero to two minutes.

(g) *Criteria.* The total positive heat release over the first two minutes of exposure for each of the three or more samples tested must be averaged, and the peak heat release rate for each of the samples must be averaged. The average total heat release must not exceed 65 kilowatt-minutes per square meter, and the average peak heat release rate must not exceed 65 kilowatts per square meter.

(h) *Report.* The test report must include the following for each specimen tested:

(1) Description of the specimen.

(2) Radiant heat flux to the specimen, expressed in W/cm^2.

(3) Data giving release rates of heat (in kW/m^2) as a function of time, either graphically or tabulated at intervals no greater than 10 seconds. The calibration factor (k_n) must be recorded.

(4) If melting, sagging, delaminating, or other behavior that affects the exposed surface area or the mode of burning occurs, these behaviors must be reported, together with the time at which such behaviors were observed.

(5) The peak heat release and the 2-minute integrated heat release rate must be reported.

FIGURES TO PART IV OF APPENDIX F

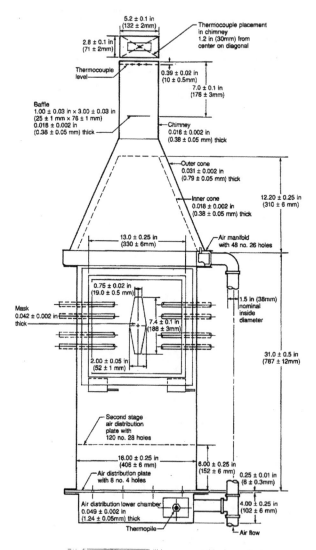

Figure 1A   Rate of Heat Release Apparatus

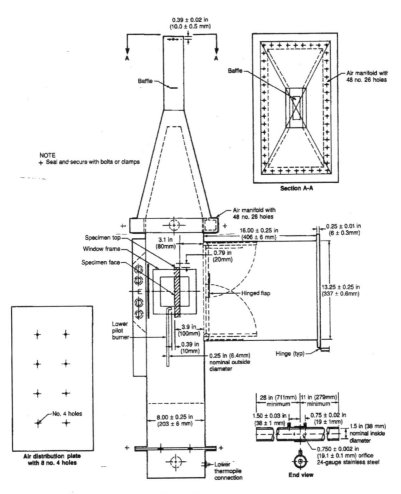

Figure 1B
Rate of Heat Release Apparatus

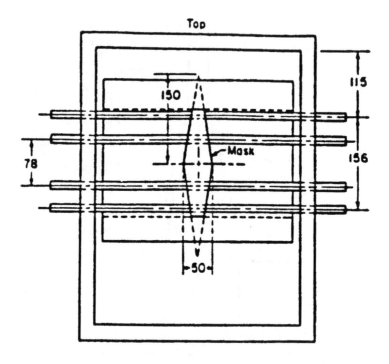

(Unless denoted otherwise all dimensions are in millimeters.)
Figure 2A. "Globar" Radiant Panel

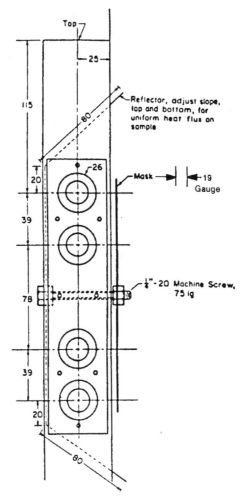

(Unless denoted otherwise all dimensions are in millimeters.)
Figure 2B. "Globar" Radiant Panel

521

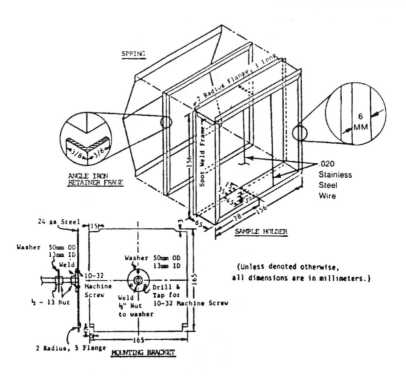

Figure 3.

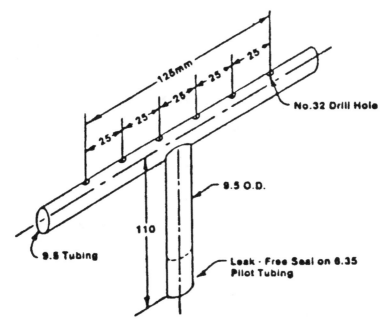

(Unless denoted otherwise, all dimensions are in millimeters.)

Figure 4.

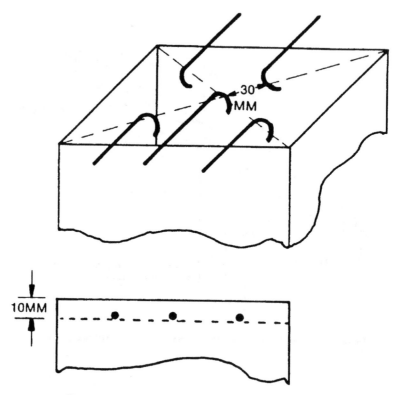

Figure 5. Thermocouple Position

Part V. Test Method to Determine the Smoke Emission Characteristics of Cabin Materials

(a) *Summary of Method.* The specimens must be constructed, conditioned, and tested in the flaming mode in accordance with American Society of Testing and Materials (ASTM) Standard Test Method ASTM F814–83.

(b) *Acceptance Criteria.* The specific optical smoke density (D_s), which is obtained by averaging the reading obtained after 4 minutes with each of the three specimens, shall not exceed 200.

[Amdt. 25–32, 37 FR 3972, Feb. 24, 1972]

EDITORIAL NOTE: For FEDERAL REGISTER citations affecting Appendix F to Part 25, see the List of CFR Sections Affected, which ap-pears in the Finding Aids section of the printed volume and on GPO Access.

APPENDIX G TO PART 25—CONTINUOUS GUST DESIGN CRITERIA

The continuous gust design criteria in this appendix must be used in establishing the dynamic response of the airplane to vertical and lateral continuous turbulence unless a more rational criteria is used. The following gust load requirements apply to mission analysis and design envelope analysis:

(a) The limit gust loads utilizing the continuous turbulence concept must be determined in accordance with the provisions of either paragraph (b) or paragraphs (c) and (d) of this appendix.

(b) *Design envelope analysis.* The limit loads must be determined in accordance with the following:

(1) All critical altitudes, weights, and weight distributions, as specified in §25.321(b), and all critical speeds within the ranges indicated in paragraph (b)(3) of this appendix must be considered.

(2) Values of Ā (ratio of root-mean-square incremental load root-mean-square gust velocity) must be determined by dynamic analysis. The power spectral density of the atmospheric turbulence must be as given by the equation—

$$\phi(\Omega) = \sigma^2 L / \pi \ \frac{1 + \frac{8}{3}(1.339\, L\Omega)^2}{\left[1 + (1.339\, L\Omega)^2\right]^{\frac{11}{6}}}$$

where:

φ=power-spectral density (ft./sec.)^2/rad./ft.
σ=root-mean-square gust velocity, ft./sec.
Ω=reduced frequency, radians per foot.
L=2,500 ft.

(3) The limit loads must be obtained by multiplying the Ā values determined by the dynamic analysis by the following values of the gust velocity Uσ:

(i) At speed V_c: Uσ=85 fps true gust velocity in the interval 0 to 30,000 ft. altitude and is linearly decreased to 30 fps true gust velocity at 80,000 ft. altitude. Where the Administrator finds that a design is comparable to a similar design with extensive satisfactory service experience, it will be acceptable to select Uσ at V_c less than 85 fps, but not less than 75 fps, with linear decrease at that value at 20,000 feet to 30 fps at 80,000 feet. The following factors will be taken into account when assessing comparability to a similar design:

(1) The transfer function of the new design should exhibit no unusual characteristics as compared to the similar design which will significantly affect response to turbulence; e.g., coalescence of modal response in the frequency regime which can result in a significant increase of loads.

(2) The typical mission of the new airplane is substantially equivalent to that of the similar design.

(3) The similar design should demonstrate the adequacy of the Uσ selected.

(ii) At speed V_B: Uσ is equal to 1.32 times the values obtained under paragraph (b)(3)(i) of this appendix.

(iii) At speed V_D: Uσ is equal to ½ the values obtained under paragraph (b)(3)(i) of this appendix.

(iv) At speeds between V_B and V_c and between V_c and V_D: Uσ is equal to a value obtained by linear interpolation.

(4) When a stability augmentation system is included in the analysis, the effect of system nonlinearities on loads at the limit load level must be realistically or conservatively accounted for.

(c) *Mission analysis.* Limit loads must be determined in accordance with the following:

(1) The expected utilization of the airplane must be represented by one or more flight profiles in which the load distribution and the variation with time of speed, altitude, gross weight, and center of gravity position are defined. These profiles must be divided into mission segments or blocks, for analysis, and average or effective values of the pertinent parameters defined for each segment.

(2) For each of the mission segments defined under paragraph (c)(1) of this appendix, values of Ā and N_o must be determined by analysis. Ā is defined as the ratio of root-mean-square incremental load to root-mean-square gust velocity and N_o is the radius of gyration of the load power spectral density function about zero frequency. The power spectral density of the atmospheric turbulence must be given by the equation set forth in paragraph (b)(2) of this appendix.

(3) For each of the load and stress quantities selected, the frequency of exceedance must be determined as a function of load level by means of the equation—

$$N_{(\gamma)} = \sum t\, N_o \left[P_1 \exp\left(-\frac{|y - y_{one-g}|}{b_1 \bar{A}} \right) + P_2 \exp\left(-\frac{|y - y_{one-g}|}{b_2 \bar{A}} \right) \right]$$

where—

t=selected time interval.
y=net value of the load or stress.
Y_{one-g}=value of the load or stress in one-g level flight.

N(y)=average number of exceedances of the indicated value of the load or stress in unit time.
Σ=symbol denoting summation over all mission segments.
N_o, Ā=parameters determined by dynamic analysis as defined in paragraph (c)(2) of this appendix.

P_1, P_2, b_1, b_2=parameters defining the probability distributions of root-mean-square gust velocity, to be read from Figures 1 and 2 of this appendix.

The limit gust loads must be read from the frequency of exceedance curves at a frequency of exceedance of $2 \times 10-5$ exceedances per hour. Both positive and negative load directions must be considered in determining the limit loads.

(4) If a stability augmentation system is utilized to reduce the gust loads, consideration must be given to the fraction of flight time that the system may be inoperative. The flight profiles of paragraph (c)(1) of this appendix must include flight with the system inoperative for this fraction of the flight time. When a stability augmentation system is included in the analysis, the effect of system nonlinearities on loads at the limit load level must be conservatively accounted for.

(d) *Supplementary design envelope analysis.* In addition to the limit loads defined by paragraph (c) of this appendix, limit loads must also be determined in accordance with paragraph (b) of this appendix, except that—

(1) In paragraph (b)(3)(i) of this appendix, the value of Uσ=85 fps true gust velocity is replaced by Uσ=60 fps true gust velocity on the interval 0 to 30,000 ft. altitude, and is linearly decreased to 25 fps true gust velocity at 80,000 ft. altitude; and

(2) In paragraph (b) of this appendix, the reference to paragraphs (b)(3)(i) through (b)(3)(iii) of this appendix is to be understood as referring to the paragraph as modified by paragraph (d)(1).

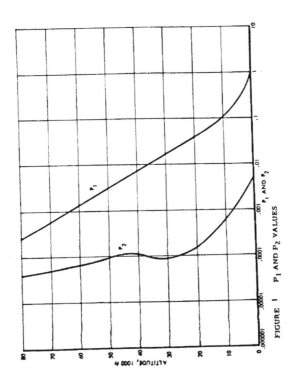

FIGURE 1   P₁ AND P₂ VALUES

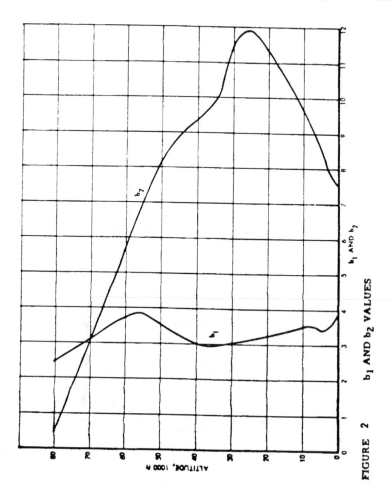

FIGURE 2

[Amdt. 25-54, 45 FR 60173, Sept. 11, 1980]

APPENDIX H TO PART 25—INSTRUCTIONS
FOR CONTINUED AIRWORTHINESS

H25.1 *General.*

(a) This appendix specifies requirements for the preparation of Instructions for Continued Airworthiness as required by §25.1529.

(b) The Instructions for Continued Airworthiness for each airplane must include the Instructions for Continued Airworthiness for each engine and propeller (hereinafter designated "products"), for each appliance required by this chapter, and any required information relating to the interface of those appliances and products with the airplane. If Instructions for Continued Airworthiness are not supplied by the manufacturer of an appliance or product installed in the airplane, the Instructions for Continued Airworthiness for the airplane must include the information essential to the continued airworthiness of the airplane.

(c) The applicant must submit to the FAA a program to show how changes to the Instructions for Continued Airworthiness made by the applicant or by the manufacturers or products and appliances installed in the airplane will be distributed.

H25.2 *Format.*

(a) The Instructions for Continued Airworthiness must be in the form of a manual or manuals as appropriate for the quantity of data to be provided.

(b) The format of the manual or manuals must provide for a practical arrangement.

H25.3 *Content.*

The contents of the manual or manuals must be prepared in the English language. The Instructions for Continued Airworthiness must contain the following manuals or sections, as appropriate, and information:

(a) *Airplane maintenance manual or section.* (1) Introduction information that includes an explanation of the airplane's features and data to the extent necessary for maintenance or preventive maintenance.

(2) A description of the airplane and its systems and installations including its engines, propellers, and appliances.

(3) Basic control and operation information describing how the airplane components and systems are controlled and how they operate, including any special procedures and limitations that apply.

(4) Servicing information that covers details regarding servicing points, capacities of tanks, reservoirs, types of fluids to be used, pressures applicable to the various systems, location of access panels for inspection and servicing, locations of lubrication points, lubricants to be used, equipment required for servicing, tow instructions and limitations, mooring, jacking, and leveling information.

(b) *Maintenance instructions.* (1) Scheduling information for each part of the airplane and its engines, auxiliary power units, propellers, accessories, instruments, and equipment that provides the recommended periods at which they should be cleaned, inspected, adjusted, tested, and lubricated, and the degree of inspection, the applicable wear tolerances, and work recommended at these periods. However, the applicant may refer to an accessory, instrument, or equipment manufacturer as the source of this information if the applicant shows that the item has an exceptionally high degree of complexity requiring specialized maintenance techniques, test equipment, or expertise. The recommended overhaul periods and necessary cross references to the Airworthiness Limitations section of the manual must also be included. In addition, the applicant must include an inspection program that includes the frequency and extent of the inspections necessary to provide for the continued airworthiness of the airplane.

(2) Troubleshooting information describing probable malfunctions, how to recognize those malfunctions, and the remedial action for those malfunctions.

(3) Information describing the order and method of removing and replacing products and parts with any necessary precautions to be taken.

(4) Other general procedural instructions including procedures for system testing during ground running, symmetry checks, weighing and determining the center of gravity, lifting and shoring, and storage limitations.

(c) Diagrams of structural access plates and information needed to gain access for inspections when access plates are not provided.

(d) Details for the application of special inspection techniques including radiographic and ultrasonic testing where such processes are specified.

(e) Information needed to apply protective treatments to the structure after inspection.

(f) All data relative to structural fasteners such as identification, discard recommendations, and torque values.

(g) A list of special tools needed.

H25.4 *Airworthiness Limitations section.*

(a) The Instructions for Continued Airworthiness must contain a section titled Airworthiness Limitations that is segregated and clearly distinguishable from the rest of the document. This section must set forth—

(1) Each mandatory replacement time, structural inspection interval, and related structural inspection procedures approved under §25.571; and

(2) Each mandatory replacement time, inspection interval, related inspection procedure, and all critical design configuration control limitations approved under §25.981 for the fuel tank system.

(b) If the Instructions for Continued Airworthiness consist of multiple documents, the section required by this paragraph must be included in the principal manual. This section must contain a legible statement in a prominent location that reads: "The Airworthiness Limitations section is FAA-approved and specifies maintenance required under §§43.16 and 91.403 of the Federal Aviation Regulations, unless an alternative program has been FAA approved."

[Amdt. 25–54, 45 FR 60177, Sept. 11, 1980, as amended by Amdt. 25–68, 54 FR 34329, Aug. 18, 1989; Amdt. 25–102, 66 FR 23130, May 7, 2001]

APPENDIX I TO PART 25—INSTALLATION OF AN AUTOMATIC TAKEOFF THRUST CONTROL SYSTEM (ATTCS)

I25.1 *General.*

(a) This appendix specifies additional requirements for installation of an engine power control system that automatically resets thrust or power on operating engine(s) in the event of any one engine failure during takeoff.

(b) With the ATTCS and associated systems functioning normally as designed, all applicable requirements of Part 25, except as provided in this appendix, must be met without requiring any action by the crew to increase thrust or power.

I25.2 *Definitions.*

(a) *Automatic Takeoff Thrust Control System (ATTCS).* An ATTCS is defined as the entire automatic system used on takeoff, including all devices, both mechanical and electrical, that sense engine failure, transmit signals,

actuate fuel controls or power levers or increase engine power by other means on operating engines to achieve scheduled thrust or power increases, and furnish cockpit information on system operation.

(b) *Critical Time Interval.* When conducting an ATTCS takeoff, the critical time interval is between V_1 minus 1 second and a point on the minimum performance, all-engine flight path where, assuming a simultaneous occurrence of an engine and ATTCS failure, the resulting minimum flight path thereafter intersects the Part 25 required actual flight path at no less than 400 feet above the takeoff surface. This time interval is shown in the following illustration:

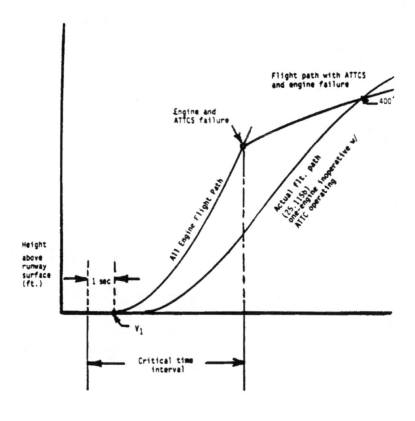

I25.3 *Performance and System Reliability Requirements.*

The applicant must comply with the performance and ATTCS reliability requirements as follows:

(a) An ATTCS failure or a combination of failures in the ATTCS during the critical time interval:

(1) Shall not prevent the insertion of the *maximum approved takeoff* thrust or power, or must be shown to be an improbable event.

(2) Shall not result in a significant loss or reduction in thrust or power, or must be shown to be an extremely improbable event.

(b) The concurrent existence of an ATTCS failure and an engine failure during the critical time interval must be shown to be extremely improbable.

(c) All applicable performance requirements of Part 25 must be met with an engine failure occurring at the most critical point during takeoff with the ATTCS system functioning.

I25.4 *Thrust Setting.*

The initial takeoff thrust or power setting on each engine at the beginning of the takeoff roll may not be less than any of the following:

(a) Ninety (90) percent of the thrust or power set by the ATTCS (the maximum takeoff thrust or power approved for the airplane under existing ambient conditions);

(b) That required to permit normal operation of all safety-related systems and equipment dependent upon engine thrust or power lever position; or

(c) That shown to be free of hazardous engine response characteristics when thrust or power is advanced from the initial takeoff thrust or power to the maximum approved takeoff thrust or power.

I25.5 *Powerplant Controls.*

(a) In addition to the requirements of §25.1141, no single failure or malfunction, or probable combination thereof, of the ATTCS, including associated systems, may cause the failure of any powerplant function necessary for safety.

(b) The ATTCS must be designed to:

(1) Apply thrust or power on the operating engine(s), following any one engine failure during takeoff, to achieve the maximum approved takeoff thrust or power without exceeding engine operating limits;

(2) Permit manual decrease or increase in thrust or power up to the maximum takeoff thrust or power approved for the airplane under existing conditions through the use of the power lever. For airplanes equipped with limiters that automatically prevent engine operating limits from being exceeded under existing ambient conditions, other means may be used to increase the thrust or power in the event of an ATTCS failure provided the means is located on or forward of the power levers; is easily identified and operated under all operating conditions by a single action of either pilot with the hand that is normally used to actuate the power levers; and meets the requirements of §25.777 (a), (b), and (c);

(3) Provide a means to verify to the flightcrew before takeoff that the ATTCS is in a condition to operate; and

(4) Provide a means for the flightcrew to deactivate the automatic function. This means must be designed to prevent inadvertent deactivation.

I25.6 *Powerplant Instruments.*

In addition to the requirements of §25.1305:

(a) A means must be provided to indicate when the ATTCS is in the armed or ready condition; and

(b) If the inherent flight characteristics of the airplane do not provide adequate warning that an engine has failed, a warning system that is independent of the ATTCS must be provided to give the pilot a clear warning of any engine failure during takeoff.

[Amdt. 25–62, 52 FR 43156, Nov. 9, 1987]

APPENDIX J TO PART 25—EMERGENCY EVACUATION

The following test criteria and procedures must be used for showing compliance with §25.803:

(a) The emergency evacuation must be conducted either during the dark of the night or during daylight with the dark of night simulated. If the demonstration is conducted indoors during daylight hours, it must be conducted with each window covered and each door closed to minimize the daylight effect. Illumination on the floor or ground may be used, but it must be kept low and shielded against shining into the airplane's windows or doors.

(b) The airplane must be in a normal attitude with landing gear extended.

(c) Unless the airplane is equipped with an off-wing descent means, stands or ramps may be used for descent from the wing to the ground. Safety equipment such as mats or inverted life rafts may be placed on the floor or ground to protect participants. No other equipment that is not part of the emergency evacuation equipment of the airplane may be used to aid the participants in reaching the ground.

(d) Except as provided in paragraph (a) of this appendix, only the airplane's emergency lighting system may provide illumination.

(e) All emergency equipment required for the planned operation of the airplane must be installed.

(f) Each external door and exit, and each internal door or curtain, must be in the takeoff configuration.

(g) Each crewmember must be seated in the normally assigned seat for takeoff and must remain in the seat until receiving the signal for commencement of the demonstration. Each crewmember must be a person having knowledge of the operation of exits and emergency equipment and, if compliance with § 121.291 is also being demonstrated, each flight attendant must be a member of a regularly scheduled line crew.

(h) A representative passenger load of persons in normal health must be used as follows:

(1) At least 40 percent of the passenger load must be female.

(2) At least 35 percent of the passenger load must be over 50 years of age.

(3) At least 15 percent of the passenger load must be female and over 50 years of age.

(4) Three life-size dolls, not included as part of the total passenger load, must be carried by passengers to simulate live infants 2 years old or younger.

(5) Crewmembers, mechanics, and training personnel, who maintain or operate the airplane in the normal course of their duties, may not be used as passengers.

(i) No passenger may be assigned a specific seat except as the Administrator may require. Except as required by subparagraph (g) of this paragraph, no employee of the applicant may be seated next to an emergency exit.

(j) Seat belts and shoulder harnesses (as required) must be fastened.

(k) Before the start of the demonstration, approximately one-half of the total average amount of carry-on baggage, blankets, pillows, and other similar articles must be distributed at several locations in aisles and emergency exit access ways to create minor obstructions.

(l) No prior indication may be given to any crewmember or passenger of the particular exits to be used in the demonstration.

(m) The applicant may not practice, rehearse, or describe the demonstration for the participants nor may any participant have taken part in this type of demonstration within the preceding 6 months.

(n) The pretakeoff passenger briefing required by § 121.571 may be given. The passengers may also be advised to follow directions of crewmembers but not be instructed on the procedures to be followed in the demonstration.

(o) If safety equipment as allowed by paragraph (c) of this appendix is provided, either all passenger and cockpit windows must be blacked out or all of the emergency exits must have safety equipment in order to prevent disclosure of the available emergency exits.

(p) Not more than 50 percent of the emergency exits in the sides of the fuselage of an airplane that meets all of the requirements applicable to the required emergency exits

for that airplane may be used for the demonstration. Exits that are not to be used in the demonstration must have the exit handle deactivated or must be indicated by red lights, red tape, or other acceptable means placed outside the exits to indicate fire or other reason why they are unusable. The exits to be used must be representative of all of the emergency exits on the airplane and must be designated by the applicant, subject to approval by the Administrator. At least one floor level exit must be used.

(q) Except as provided in paragraph (c) of this section, all evacuees must leave the airplane by a means provided as part of the airplane's equipment.

(r) The applicant's approved procedures must be fully utilized, except the flightcrew must take no active role in assisting others inside the cabin during the demonstration.

(s) The evacuation time period is completed when the last occupant has evacuated the airplane and is on the ground. Provided that the acceptance rate of the stand or ramp is no greater than the acceptance rate of the means available on the airplane for descent from the wing during an actual crash situation, evacuees using stands or ramps allowed by paragraph (c) of this appendix are considered to be on the ground when they are on the stand or ramp.

[Amdt. 25–72, 55 FR 29788, July 20, 1990, as amended by Amdt. 25–79, Aug. 26, 1993]

PART 27—AIRWORTHINESS STANDARDS: NORMAL CATEGORY ROTORCRAFT

Subpart A—General

AUTHORITY: 49 U.S.C. 106(g), 40113, 44701–44702, 44704.

SOURCE: Docket No. 5074, 29 FR 15695, Nov. 24, 1964, unless otherwise noted.

Subpart A—General

§27.1 Applicability.

(a) This part prescribes airworthiness standards for the issue of type certificates, and changes to those certificates, for normal category rotorcraft with maximum weights of 7,000 pounds or less and nine or less passenger seats.

(b) Each person who applies under Part 21 for such a certificate or change must show compliance with the applicable requirements of this part.

(c) Multiengine rotorcraft may be type certified as Category A provided the requirements referenced in appendix C of this part are met.

[Doc. No. 5074, 29 FR 15695, Nov. 24, 1964, as amended by Amdt. 27-33, 61 FR 21906, May 10, 1996; Amdt. 27-37, 64 FR 45094, Aug. 18, 1999]

§ 27.2 Special retroactive requirements.

(a) For each rotorcraft manufactured after September 16, 1992, each applicant must show that each occupant's seat is equipped with a safety belt and shoulder harness that meets the requirements of paragraphs (a), (b), and (c) of this section.

(1) Each occupant's seat must have a combined safety belt and shoulder harness with a single-point release. Each pilot's combined safety belt and shoulder harness must allow each pilot, when seated with safety belt and shoulder harness fastened, to perform all functions necessary for flight operations. There must be a means to secure belts and harnesses, when not in use, to prevent interference with the operation of the rotorcraft and with rapid egress in an emergency.

(2) Each occupant must be protected from serious head injury by a safety belt plus a shoulder harness that will prevent the head from contacting any injurious object.

(3) The safety belt and shoulder harness must meet the static and dynamic strength requirements, if applicable, specified by the rotorcraft type certification basis.

(4) For purposes of this section, the date of manufacture is either—

(i) The date the inspection acceptance records, or equivalent, reflect that the rotorcraft is complete and meets the FAA-Approved Type Design Data; or

(ii) The date the foreign civil airworthiness authority certifies that the rotorcraft is complete and issues an original standard airworthiness certificate, or equivalent, in that country.

(b) For rotorcraft with a certification basis established prior to October 18, 1999—

(1) The maximum passenger seat capacity may be increased to eight or nine provided the applicant shows compliance with all the airworthiness requirements of this part in effect on October 18, 1999.

(2) The maximum weight may be increased to greater than 6,000 pounds provided—

(i) The number of passenger seats is not increased above the maximum

number certificated on October 18, 1999, or

(ii) The applicant shows compliance with all of the airworthiness requirements of this part in effect on October 18, 1999.

[Doc. No. 26078, 56 FR 41051, Aug. 16, 1991, as amended by Amdt. 27–37, 64 FR 45094, Aug. 18, 1999]

Subpart B—Flight

GENERAL

§ 27.21 Proof of compliance.

Each requirement of this subpart must be met at each appropriate combination of weight and center of gravity within the range of loading conditions for which certification is requested. This must be shown—

(a) By tests upon a rotorcraft of the type for which certification is requested, or by calculations based on, and equal in accuracy to, the results of testing; and

(b) By systematic investigation of each required combination of weight and center of gravity if compliance cannot be reasonably inferred from combinations investigated.

[Doc. No. 5074, 29 FR 15695, Nov. 24, 1964, as amended by Amdt. 27–21, 49 FR 44432, Nov. 6, 1984]

§ 27.25 Weight limits.

(a) *Maximum weight.* The maximum weight (the highest weight at which compliance with each applicable requirement of this part is shown) must be established so that it is—

(1) Not more than—

(i) The highest weight selected by the applicant;

(ii) The design maximum (the highest weight at which compliance with each applicable structural loading condition of this part is shown); or

(iii) The highest weight at which compliance with each applicable flight requirement of this part is shown; and

(2) Not less than the sum of—

(i) The empty weight determined under § 27.29; and

(ii) The weight of usable fuel appropriate to the intended operation with full payload;

(iii) The weight of full oil capacity; and

(iv) For each seat, an occupant weight of 170 pounds or any lower weight for which certification is requested.

(b) *Minimum weight.* The minimum weight (the lowest weight at which compliance with each applicable requirement of this part is shown) must be established so that it is—

(1) Not more than the sum of—

(i) The empty weight determined under §27.29; and

(ii) The weight of the minimum crew necessary to operate the rotorcraft, assuming for each crewmember a weight no more than 170 pounds, or any lower weight selected by the applicant or included in the loading instructions; and

(2) Not less than—

(i) The lowest weight selected by the applicant;

(ii) The design minimum weight (the lowest weight at which compliance with each applicable structural loading condition of this part is shown); or

(iii) The lowest weight at which compliance with each applicable flight requirement of this part is shown.

(c) *Total weight with jettisonable external load.* A total weight for the rotorcraft with a jettisonable external load attached that is greater than the maximum weight established under paragraph (a) of this section may be established for any rotorcraft-load combination if—

(1) The rotorcraft-load combination does not include human external cargo,

(2) Structural component approval for external load operations under either §27.865 or under equivalent operational standards is obtained,

(3) The portion of the total weight that is greater than the maximum weight established under paragraph (a) of this section is made up only of the weight of all or part of the jettisonable external load,

(4) Structural components of the rotorcraft are shown to comply with the applicable structural requirements of this part under the increased loads and stresses caused by the weight increase over that established under paragraph (a) of this section, and

(5) Operation of the rotorcraft at a total weight greater than the maximum certificated weight established under paragraph (a) of this section is

limited by appropriate operating limitations under §27.865(a) and (d) of this part.

(Secs. 313(a), 601, 603, 604, and 605 of the Federal Aviation Act of 1958 (49 U.S.C. 1354(a), 1421, 1423, 1424, and 1425); and sec. 6(c) of the Dept. of Transportation Act (49 U.S.C. 1655(c)))

[Doc. No. 5074, 29 FR 15695, Nov. 29, 1964, as amended by Amdt. 27–11, 41 FR 55468, Dec. 20, 1976; Amdt. 25–42, 43 FR 2324, Jan. 16, 1978; Amdt. 27–36, 64 FR 43019, Aug. 6, 1999]

§27.27 Center of gravity limits.

The extreme forward and aft centers of gravity and, where critical, the extreme lateral centers of gravity must be established for each weight established under §27.25. Such an extreme may not lie beyond—

(a) The extremes selected by the applicant;

(b) The extremes within which the structure is proven; or

(c) The extremes within which compliance with the applicable flight requirements is shown.

[Amdt. 27–2, 33 FR 962, Jan. 26, 1968]

§27.29 Empty weight and corresponding center of gravity.

(a) The empty weight and corresponding center of gravity must be determined by weighing the rotorcraft without the crew and payload, but with—

(1) Fixed ballast;

(2) Unusable fuel; and

(3) Full operating fluids, including—

(i) Oil;

(ii) Hydraulic fluid; and

(iii) Other fluids required for normal operation of roto-craft systems, except water intended for injection in the engines.

(b) The condition of the rotorcraft at the time of determining empty weight must be one that is well defined and can be easily repeated, particularly with respect to the weights of fuel, oil, coolant, and installed equipment.

(Secs. 313(a), 601, 603, 604, and 605 of the Federal Aviation Act of 1958 (49 U.S.C. 1354(a), 1421, 1423, 1424, and 1425); and sec. 6(c) of the Dept. of Transportation Act (49 U.S.C. 1655(c)))

[Doc. No. 5074, 29 FR 15695, Nov. 24, 1964, as amended by Amdt. 27–14, 43 FR 2324, Jan. 16, 1978]

§ 27.31   Removable ballast.

Removable ballast may be used in showing compliance with the flight requirements of this subpart.

§ 27.33   Main rotor speed and pitch limits.

(a) *Main rotor speed limits.* A range of main rotor speeds must be established that—

(1) With power on, provides adequate margin to accommodate the variations in rotor speed occurring in any appropriate maneuver, and is consistent with the kind of governor or synchronizer used; and

(2) With power off, allows each appropriate autorotative maneuver to be performed throughout the ranges of airspeed and weight for which certification is requested.

(b) *Normal main rotor high pitch limits (power on).* For rotocraft, except helicopters required to have a main rotor low speed warning under paragraph (e) of this section. It must be shown, with power on and without exceeding approved engine maximum limitations, that main rotor speeds substantially less than the minimum approved main rotor speed will not occur under any sustained flight condition. This must be met by—

(1) Appropriate setting of the main rotor high pitch stop;

(2) Inherent rotorcraft characteristics that make unsafe low main rotor speeds unlikely; or

(3) Adequate means to warn the pilot of unsafe main rotor speeds.

(c) *Normal main rotor low pitch limits (power off).* It must be shown, with power off, that—

(1) The normal main rotor low pitch limit provides sufficient rotor speed, in any autorotative condition, under the most critical combinations of weight and airspeed; and

(2) It is possible to prevent overspeeding of the rotor without exceptional piloting skill.

(d) *Emergency high pitch.* If the main rotor high pitch stop is set to meet paragraph (b)(1) of this section, and if that stop cannot be exceeded inadvertently, additional pitch may be made available for emergency use.

(e) *Main rotor low speed warning for helicopters.* For each single engine

helicopter, and each multiengine helicopter that does not have an approved device that automatically increases power on the operating engines when one engine fails, there must be a main rotor low speed warning which meets the following requirements:

(1) The warning must be furnished to the pilot in all flight conditions, including power-on and power-off flight, when the speed of a main rotor approaches a value that can jeopardize safe flight.

(2) The warning may be furnished either through the inherent aerodynamic qualities of the helicopter or by a device.

(3) The warning must be clear and distinct under all conditons, and must be clearly distinguishable from all other warnings. A visual device that requires the attention of the crew within the cockpit is not acceptable by itself.

(4) If a warning device is used, the device must automatically deactivate and reset when the low-speed condition is corrected. If the device has an audible warning, it must also be equipped with a means for the pilot to manually silence the audible warning before the low-speed condition is corrected.

(Secs. 313(a), 601, 603, 604, and 605 of the Federal Aviation Act of 1958 (49 U.S.C. 1354(a), 1421, 1423, 1424, and 1425); and sec. 6(c) of the Dept. of Transportation Act (49 U.S.C. 1655(c)))

[Doc. No. 5074, 29 FR 15695, Nov. 24, 1964, as amended by Amdt. 27–2, 33 FR 962, Jan. 26, 1968; Amdt. 27–14, 43 FR 2324, Jan. 16, 1978]

PERFORMANCE

§ 27.45   General.

(a) Unless otherwise prescribed, the performance requirements of this subpart must be met for still air and a standard atmosphere.

(b) The performance must correspond to the engine power available under the particular ambient atmospheric conditions, the particular flight condition, and the relative humidity specified in paragraphs (d) or (e) of this section, as appropriate.

(c) The available power must correspond to engine power, not exceeding the approved power, less—

(1) Installation losses; and

(2) The power absorbed by the accessories and services appropriate to the particular ambient atmopheric conditions and the particular flight condition.

(d) For reciprocating engine-powered rotorcraft, the performance, as affected by engine power, must be based on a relative humidity of 80 percent in a standard atmosphere.

(e) For turbine engine-powered rotorcraft, the performance, as affected by engine power, must be based on a relative humidity of—

(1) 80 percent, at and below standard temperature; and

(2) 34 percent, at and above standard temperature plus 50 degrees F. Between these two temperatures, the relative humidity must vary linearly.

(f) For turbine-engine-powered rotorcraft, a means must be provided to permit the pilot to determine prior to takeoff that each engine is capable of developing the power necessary to achieve the applicable rotorcraft performance prescribed in this subpart.

(Secs. 313(a), 601, 603, 604, and 605 of the Federal Aviation Act of 1958 (49 U.S.C. 1354(a), 1421, 1423, 1424, and 1425); and sec. 6(c) of the Dept. of Transportation Act (49 U.S.C. 1655(c)))

[Amdt. 27–14, 43 FR 2324, Jan. 16, 1978, as amended by Amdt. 27–21, 49 FR 44432, Nov. 6, 1984]

§27.51 Takeoff.

(a) The takeoff, with takeoff power and r.p.m., and with the extreme forward center of gravity—

(1) May not require exceptional piloting skill or exceptionally favorable conditions; and

(2) Must be made in such a manner that a landing can be made safely at any point along the flight path if an engine fails.

(b) Paragraph (a) of this section must be met throughout the ranges of—

(1) Altitude, from standard sea level conditions to the maximum altitude capability of the rotorcraft, or 7,000 feet, whichever is less; and

(2) Weight, from the maximum weight (at sea level) to each lesser weight selected by the applicant for each altitude covered by paragraph (b)(1) of this section.

§27.65 Climb: all engines operating.

(a) For rotorcraft other than helicopters—

(1) The steady rate of climb, at V_Y, must be determined—

(i) With maximum continuous power on each engine;

(ii) With the landing gear retracted; and

(iii) For the weights, altitudes, and temperatures for which certification is requested; and

(2) The climb gradient, at the rate of climb determined in accordance with paragraph (a)(1) of this section, must be either—

(i) At least 1:10 if the horizontal distance required to take off and climb over a 50-foot obstacle is determined for each weight, altitude, and temperature within the range for which certification is requested; or

(ii) At least 1:6 under standard sea level conditions.

(b) Each helicopter must meet the following requirements:

(1) V_Y must be determined—

(i) For standard sea level conditions;

(ii) At maximum weight; and

(iii) With maximum continuous power on each engine.

(2) The steady rate of climb must be determined—

(i) At the climb speed selected by the applicant at or below V_{NE};

(ii) Within the range from sea level up to the maximum altitude for which certification is requested;

(iii) For the weights and temperatures that correspond to the altitude range set forth in paragraph (b)(2)(ii) of this section and for which certification is requested; and

(iv) With maximum continuous power on each engine.

(Secs. 313(a), 601, 603, 604, and 605 of the Federal Aviation Act of 1958 (49 U.S.C. 1354(a), 1421, 1423, 1424, and 1425); and sec. 6(c) of the Dept. of Transportation Act (49 U.S.C. 1655(c)))

[Doc. No. 5074, 29 FR 15695, Nov. 24, 1964, as amended by Amdt. 27–14, 43 FR 2324, Jan. 16, 1978; Amdt. 27–33, 61 FR 21907, May 10, 1996]

§27.67 Climb: one engine inoperative.

For multiengine helicopters, the steady rate of climb (or descent), at V_y (or at the speed for minimum rate of descent), must be determined with—

(a) Maximum weight;

(b) The critical engine inoperative and the remaining engines at either—

(1) Maximum continuous power and, for helicopters for which certification for the use of 30-minute OEI power is requested, at 30-minute OEI power; or

(2) Continuous OEI power for helicopters for which certification for the use of continuous OEI power is requested.

(Secs. 313(a), 601, 603, 604, and 605 of the Federal Aviation Act of 1958 (49 U.S.C. 1354(a), 1421, 1423, 1424, and 1425); and sec. 6(c) of the Dept. of Transportation Act (49 U.S.C. 1655(c)))

[Doc. No 5074, 29 FR 15695, Nov. 24, 1964, as amended by Amdt. 27–23, 53 FR 34210, Sept. 2, 1988]

§ 27.71 Glide performance.

For single-engine helicopters and multiengine helicopters that do not meet the Category A engine isolation requirements of Part 29 of this chapter, the minimum rate of descent airspeed and the best angle-of-glide airspeed must be determined in autorotation at—

(a) Maximum weight; and

(b) Rotor speed(s) selected by the applicant.

[Amdt. 27–21, 49 FR 44433, Nov. 6, 1984]

§ 27.73 Performance at minimum operating speed.

(a) For helicopters—

(1) The hovering ceiling must be determined over the ranges of weight, altitude, and temperature for which certification is requested, with—

(i) Takeoff power;

(ii) The landing gear extended; and

(iii) The helicopter in ground effect at a height consistent with normal takeoff procedures; and

(2) The hovering ceiling determined under paragraph (a)(1) of this section must be at least—

(i) For reciprocating engine powered helicopters, 4,000 feet at maximum weight with a standard atmosphere; or

(ii) For turbine engine powered helicopters, 2,500 feet pressure altitude at maximum weight at a temperature of standard +40 degrees F.

(b) For rotorcraft other than helicopters, the steady rate of climb at the minimum operating speed must be determined, over the ranges of weight, altitude, and temperature for which certification is requested, with—

(1) Takeoff power; and

(2) The landing gear extended.

§ 27.75 Landing.

(a) The rotorcraft must be able to be landed with no excessive vertical acceleration, no tendency to bounce, nose over, ground loop, porpoise, or water loop, and without exceptional piloting skill or exceptionally favorable conditions, with—

(1) Approach or glide speeds appropriate to the type of rotorcraft and selected by the applicant;

(2) The approach and landing made with—

(i) Power off, for single-engine rotorcraft; and

(ii) For multiengine rotorcraft, one engine inoperative and with each operating engine within approved operating limitations; and

(3) The approach and landing entered from steady autorotation.

(b) Multiengine rotorcraft must be able to be landed safely after complete power failure under normal operating conditions.

[Doc. No. 5074, 29 FR 15695, Nov. 24, 1964, as amended by Amdt. 27–14, 43 FR 2324, Jan. 16, 1978]

§ 27.79 Limiting height—speed envelope.

(a) If there is any combination of height and forward speed (including hover) under which a safe landing cannot be made under the applicable power failure condition in paragraph (b) of this section, a limiting height-speed envelope must be established (including all pertinent information) for that condition, throughout the ranges of—

(1) Altitude, from standard sea level conditions to the maximum altitude capability of the rotorcraft, or 7,000 feet, whichever is less; and

(2) Weight, from the maximum weight (at sea level) to the lesser weight selected by the applicant for each altitude covered by paragraph (a)(1) of this section. For helicopters, the weight at altitudes above sea level may not be less than the maximum weight or the highest weight allowing

hovering out of ground effect which is lower.

(b) The applicable power failure conditions are—

(1) For single-engine helicopters, full autorotation;

(2) For multiengine helicopters, one engine inoperative (where engine isolation features insure continued operation of the remaining engines), and the remaining engines at the greatest power for which certification is requested, and

(3) For other rotorcraft, conditions appropriate to the type.

(Secs. 313(a), 601, 603, 604, Federal Aviation Act of 1958 (49 U.S.C. 1354(a), 1421, 1423, 1424), sec. 6(c), Dept. of Transportation Act (49 U.S.C. 1655(c)))

[Doc. No. 5074, 29 FR 15695, Nov. 24, 1964, as amended by Amdt. 27–14, 43 FR 2324, Jan. 16, 1978; Amdt. 27–21, 49 FR 44433, Nov. 6, 1984]

FLIGHT CHARACTERISTICS

§27.141 General.

The rotorcraft must—

(a) Except as specifically required in the applicable section, meet the flight characteristics requirements of this subpart—

(1) At the altitudes and temperatures expected in operation;

(2) Under any critical loading condition within the range of weights and centers of gravity for which certification is requested;

(3) For power-on operations, under any condition of speed, power, and rotor r.p.m. for which certification is requested; and

(4) For power-off operations, under any condition of speed and rotor r.p.m. for which certification is requested that is attainable with the controls rigged in accordance with the approved rigging instructions and tolerances;

(b) Be able to maintain any required flight condition and make a smooth transition from any flight condition to any other flight condition without exceptional piloting skill, alertness, or strength, and without danger of exceeding the limit load factor under any operating condition probable for the type, including—

(1) Sudden failure of one engine, for multiengine rotorcraft meeting Trans-

port Category A engine isolation requirements of Part 29 of this chapter;

(2) Sudden, complete power failure for other rotorcraft; and

(3) Sudden, complete control system failures specified in §27.695 of this part; and

(c) Have any additional characteristic required for night or instrument operation, if certification for those kinds of operation is requested. Requirements for helicopter instrument flight are contained in appendix B of this part.

[Doc. No. 5074, 29 FR 15695, Nov. 24, 1964, as amended by Amdt. 27–2, 33 FR 962, Jan. 26, 1968; Amdt. 27–11, 41 FR 55468, Dec. 20, 1976; Amdt. 27–19, 48 FR 4389, Jan. 31, 1983; Amdt. 27–21, 49 FR 44433, Nov. 6, 1984]

§27.143 Controllability and maneuverability.

(a) The rotorcraft must be safely controllable and maneuverable—

(1) During steady flight; and

(2) During any maneuver appropriate to the type, including—

(i) Takeoff;

(ii) Climb;

(iii) Level flight;

(iv) Turning flight;

(v) Glide;

(vi) Landing (power on and power off); and

(vii) Recovery to power-on flight from a balked autorotative approach.

(b) The margin of cyclic control must allow satisfactory roll and pitch control at V_{NE} with—

(1) Critical weight;

(2) Critical center of gravity;

(3) Critical rotor r.p.m.; and

(4) Power off (except for helicopters demonstrating compliance with paragraph (e) of this section) and power on.

(c) A wind velocity of not less than 17 knots must be established in which the rotorcraft can be operated without loss of control on or near the ground in any maneuver appropriate to the type (such as crosswind takeoffs, sideward flight, and rearward flight), with—

(1) Critical weight;

(2) Critical center of gravity;

(3) Critical rotor r.p.m.; and

(4) Altitude, from standard sea level conditions to the maximum altitude capability of the rotorcraft or 7,000 feet, whichever is less.

(d) The rotorcraft, after (1) failure of one engine in the case of multiengine rotorcraft that meet Transport Category A engine isolation requirements, or (2) complete engine failure in the case of other rotorcraft, must be controllable over the range of speeds and altitudes for which certification is requested when such power failure occurs with maximum continuous power and critical weight. No corrective action time delay for any condition following power failure may be less than—

(i) For the cruise condition, one second, or normal pilot reaction time (whichever is greater); and

(ii) For any other condition, normal pilot reaction time.

(e) For helicopters for which a V_{NE} (power-off) is established under § 27.1505(c), compliance must be demonstrated with the following requirements with critical weight, critical center of gravity, and critical rotor r.p.m.:

(1) The helicopter must be safely slowed to V_{NE} (power-off), without exceptional pilot skill, after the last operating engine is made inoperative at power-on V_{NE}.

(2) At a speed of 1.1 V_{NE} (power-off), the margin of cyclic control must allow satisfactory roll and pitch control with power off.

(Secs. 313(a), 601, 603, 604, and 605 of the Federal Aviation Act of 1958 (49 U.S.C. 1354(a), 1421, 1423, 1424, and 1425); and sec. 6(c) of the Dept. of Transportation Act (49 U.S.C. 1655(c)))

[Doc. No. 5074, 29 FR 15695, Nov. 24, 1964, as amended by Amdt. 27–2, 33 FR 963, Jan. 26, 1968; Amdt. 27–14, 43 FR 2325, Jan. 16, 1978; Amdt. 27–21, 49 FR 44433, Nov. 6, 1984]

§ 27.151 Flight controls.

(a) Longitudinal, lateral, directional, and collective controls may not exhibit excessive breakout force, friction, or preload.

(b) Control system forces and free play may not inhibit a smooth, direct rotorcraft response to control system input.

[Amdt. 27–21, 49 FR 44433, Nov. 6, 1984]

§ 27.161 Trim control.

The trim control—

(a) Must trim any steady longitudinal, lateral, and collective control

forces to zero in level flight at any appropriate speed; and

(b) May not introduce any undesirable discontinuities in control force gradients.

[Doc. No. 5074, 29 FR 15695, Nov. 24, 1964, as amended by Amdt. 27–21, 49 FR 44433, Nov. 6, 1984]

§ 27.171 Stability: general.

The rotorcraft must be able to be flown, without undue pilot fatigue or strain, in any normal maneuver for a period of time as long as that expected in normal operation. At least three landings and takeoffs must be made during this demonstration.

§ 27.173 Static longitudinal stability.

(a) The longitudinal control must be designed so that a rearward movement of the control is necessary to obtain a speed less than the trim speed, and a forward movement of the control is necessary to obtain a speed more than the trim speed.

(b) With the throttle and collective pitch held constant during the maneuvers specified in § 27.175 (a) through (c), the slope of the control position versus speed curve must be positive throughout the full range of altitude for which certification is requested.

(c) During the maneuver specified in § 27.175(d), the longitudinal control position versus speed curve may have a negative slope within the specified speed range if the negative motion is not greater than 10 percent of total control travel.

[Amdt. 27–21, 49 FR 44433, Nov. 6, 1984]

§ 27.175 Demonstration of static longitudinal stability.

(a) *Climb.* Static longitudinal stability must be shown in the climb condition at speeds from 0.85 V_Y to 1.2 V_Y, with—

(1) Critical weight;

(2) Critical center of gravity;

(3) Maximum continuous power;

(4) The landing gear retracted; and

(5) The rotorcraft trimmed at V_Y.

(b) *Cruise.* Static longitudinal stability must be shown in the cruise condition at speeds from 0.7 V_H or 0.7 V_{NE}, whichever is less, to 1.1 V_H or 1.1 V_{NE}, whichever is less, with—

(1) Critical weight;

(2) Critical center of gravity;

(3) Power for level flight at 0.9 V_H or 0.9 V_{NE}, whichever is less;

(4) The landing gear retracted; and

(5) The rotorcraft trimmed at 0.9 V_H or 0.9 V_{NE}, whichever is less.

(c) *Autorotation.* Static longitudinal stability must be shown in autorotation at airspeeds from 0.5 times the speed for minimum rate of descent to V_{NE}, or to 1.1 V_{NE} (power-off) if V_{NE} (power-off) is established under §27.1505(c), and with—

(1) Critical weight;

(2) Critical center of gravity;

(3) Power off;

(4) The landing gear—

(i) Retracted; and

(ii) Extended; and

(5) The rotorcraft trimmed at appropriate speeds found necessary by the Administrator to demonstrate stability throughout the prescribed speed range.

(d) *Hovering.* For helicopters, the longitudinal cyclic control must operate with the sense and direction of motion prescribed in §27.173 between the maximum approved rearward speed and a forward speed of 17 knots with—

(1) Critical weight;

(2) Critical center of gravity;

(3) Power required to maintain an approximate constant height in ground effect;

(4) The landing gear extended; and

(5) The helicopter trimmed for hovering.

(Secs. 313(a), 601, 603, 604, and 605 of the Federal Aviation Act of 1958 (49 U.S.C. 1354(a), 1421, 1423, 1424, and 1425); and sec. 6(c) of the Dept. of Transportation Act (49 U.S.C. 1655(c)))

[Doc. No. 5074, 29 FR 15695, Nov. 24, 1964, as amended by Amdt. 27-2, 33 FR 963, Jan. 26, 1968; Amdt. 27-11, 41 FR 55468, Dec. 20, 1976; Amdt. 27-14, 43 FR 2325, Jan. 16, 1978; Amdt. 27-21, 49 FR 44433, Nov. 6, 1984; Amdt. 27-34, 62 FR 46173, Aug. 29, 1997]

§27.177 Static directional stability.

Static directional stability must be positive with throttle and collective controls held constant at the trim conditions specified in §27.175 (a) and (b). This must be shown by steadily increasing directional control deflection for sideslip angles up to ±10° from trim. Sufficient cues must accompany sideslip to alert the pilot when approaching sideslip limits.

[Amdt. 27-21, 49 FR 44433, Nov. 6, 1984]

GROUND AND WATER HANDLING
CHARACTERISTICS

§27.231 General.

The rotorcraft must have satisfactory ground and water handling characteristics, including freedom from uncontrollable tendencies in any condition expected in operation.

§27.235 Taxiing condition.

The rotorcraft must be designed to withstand the loads that would occur when the rotorcraft is taxied over the roughest ground that may reasonably be expected in normal operation.

§27.239 Spray characteristics.

If certification for water operation is requested, no spray characteristics during taxiing, takeoff, or landing may obscure the vision of the pilot or damage the rotors, propellers, or other parts of the rotorcraft.

§27.241 Ground resonance.

The rotorcraft may have no dangerous tendency to oscillate on the ground with the rotor turning.

MISCELLANEOUS FLIGHT REQUIREMENTS

§27.251 Vibration.

Each part of the rotorcraft must be free from excessive vibration under each appropriate speed and power condition.

Subpart C—Strength Requirements

GENERAL

§27.301 Loads.

(a) Strength requirements are specified in terms of limit loads (the maximum loads to be expected in service) and ultimate loads (limit loads multiplied by prescribed factors of safety). Unless otherwise provided, prescribed loads are limit loads.

(b) Unless otherwise provided, the specified air, ground, and water loads must be placed in equilibrium with inertia forces, considering each item of mass in the rotorcraft. These loads must be distributed to closely approximate or conservatively represent actual conditions.

(c) If deflections under load would significantly change the distribution of external or internal loads, this redistribution must be taken into account.

§ 27.303 Factor of safety.

Unless otherwise provided, a factor of safety of 1.5 must be used. This factor applies to external and inertia loads unless its application to the resulting internal stresses is more conservative.

§ 27.305 Strength and deformation.

(a) The structure must be able to support limit loads without detrimental or permanent deformation. At any load up to limit loads, the deformation may not interfere with safe operation.

(b) The structure must be able to support ultimate loads without failure. This must be shown by—

(1) Applying ultimate loads to the structure in a static test for at least three seconds; or

(2) Dynamic tests simulating actual load application.

§ 27.307 Proof of structure.

(a) Compliance with the strength and deformation requirements of this subpart must be shown for each critical loading condition accounting for the environment to which the structure will be exposed in operation. Structural analysis (static or fatigue) may be used only if the structure conforms to those structures for which experience has shown this method to be reliable. In other cases, substantiating load tests must be made.

(b) Proof of compliance with the strength requirements of this subpart must include—

(1) Dynamic and endurance tests of rotors, rotor drives, and rotor controls;

(2) Limit load tests of the control system, including control surfaces;

(3) Operation tests of the control system;

(4) Flight stress measurement tests;

(5) Landing gear drop tests; and

(6) Any additional test required for new or unusual design features.

(Secs. 604, 605, 72 Stat. 778, 49 U.S.C. 1424, 1425)

[Doc. No. 5074, 29 FR 15695, Nov. 24, 1964, as amended by Amdt. 27–3, 33 FR 14105, Sept. 18, 1968; Amdt. 27–26, 55 FR 7999, Mar. 6, 1990]

§ 27.309 Design limitations.

The following values and limitations must be established to show compliance with the structural requirements of this subpart:

(a) The design maximum weight.

(b) The main rotor r.p.m. ranges power on and power off.

(c) The maximum forward speeds for each main rotor r.p.m. within the ranges determined under paragraph (b) of this section.

(d) The maximum rearward and sideward flight speeds.

(e) The center of gravity limits corresponding to the limitations determined under paragraphs (b), (c), and (d) of this section.

(f) The rotational speed ratios between each powerplant and each connected rotating component.

(g) The positive and negative limit maneuvering load factors.

FLIGHT LOADS

§ 27.321 General.

(a) The flight load factor must be assumed to act normal to the longitudinal axis of the rotorcraft, and to be equal in magnitude and opposite in direction to the rotorcraft inertia load factor at the center of gravity.

(b) Compliance with the flight load requirements of this subpart must be shown—

(1) At each weight from the design minimum weight to the design maximum weight; and

(2) With any practical distribution of disposable load within the operating limitations in the Rotorcraft Flight Manual.

[Doc. No. 5074, 29 FR 15695, Nov. 24, 1964, as amended by Amdt. 27–11, 41 FR 55468, Dec. 20, 1976]

§ 27.337 Limit maneuvering load factor.

The rotorcraft must be designed for—

(a) A limit maneuvering load factor ranging from a positive limit of 3.5 to a negative limit of −1.0; or

(b) Any positive limit maneuvering load factor not less than 2.0 and any negative limit maneuvering load factor of not less than −0.5 for which—

(1) The probability of being exceeded is shown by analysis and flight tests to be extremely remote; and

(2) The selected values are appropriate to each weight condition between the design maximum and design minimum weights.

[Amdt. 27–26, 55 FR 7999, Mar. 6, 1990]

§ 27.339 Resultant limit maneuvering loads.

The loads resulting from the application of limit maneuvering load factors are assumed to act at the center of each rotor hub and at each auxiliary lifting surface, and to act in directions, and with distributions of load among the rotors and auxiliary lifting surfaces, so as to represent each critical maneuvering condition, including power-on and power-off flight with the maximum design rotor tip speed ratio. The rotor tip speed ratio is the ratio of the rotorcraft flight velocity component in the plane of the rotor disc to the rotational tip speed of the rotor blades, and is expressed as follows:

$$\mu = \frac{V \cos a}{\Omega R}$$

where—

V = The airspeed along flight path (f.p.s.);

a = The angle between the projection, in the plane of symmetry, of the axis of no feathering and a line perpendicular to the flight path (radians, positive when axis is pointing aft);

$omega$ = The angular velocity of rotor (radians per second); and

R = The rotor radius (ft).

[Doc. No. 5074, 29 FR 15695, Nov. 24, 1964, as amended by Amdt. 27–11, 41 FR 55469, Dec. 20, 1976]

§ 27.341 Gust loads.

The rotorcraft must be designed to withstand, at each critical airspeed including hovering, the loads resulting from a vertical gust of 30 feet per second.

§ 27.351 Yawing conditions.

(a) Each rotorcraft must be designed for the loads resulting from the maneuvers specified in paragraphs (b) and (c) of this section with—

(1) Unbalanced aerodynamic moments about the center of gravity which the aircraft reacts to in a rational or conservative manner considering the principal masses furnishing the reacting inertia forces; and

(2) Maximum main rotor speed.

(b) To produce the load required in paragraph (a) of this section, in unaccelerated flight with zero yaw, at forward speeds from zero up to 0.6 V_{NE}—

(1) Displace the cockpit directional control suddenly to the maximum deflection limited by the control stops or by the maximum pilot force specified in § 27.397(a);

(2) Attain a resulting sideslip angle or 90°, whichever is less; and

(3) Return the directional control suddenly to neutral.

(c) To produce the load required in paragraph (a) of this section, in unaccelerated flight with zero yaw, at forward speeds from 0.6 V_{NE} up to V_{NE} or V_H, whichever is less—

(1) Displace the cockpit directional control suddenly to the maximum deflection limited by the control stops or by the maximum pilot force specified in § 27.397(a);

(2) Attain a resulting sideslip angle or 15°, whichever is less, at the lesser speed of V_{NE} or V_H;

(3) Vary the sideslip angles of paragraphs (b)(2) and (c)(2) of this section directly with speed; and

(4) Return the directional control suddenly to neutral.

[Amdt. 27–26, 55 FR 7999, Mar. 6, 1990, as amended by Amdt. 27–34, 62 FR 46173, Aug. 29, 1997]

§ 27.361 Engine torque.

(a) For turbine engines, the limit torque may not be less than the highest of—

(1) The mean torque for maximum continuous power multiplied by 1.25;

(2) The torque required by § 27.923;

(3) The torque required by § 27.927; or

(4) The torque imposed by sudden engine stoppage due to malfunction or structural failure (such as compressor jamming).

(b) For reciprocating engines, the limit torque may not be less than the mean torque for maximum continuous power multiplied by—

(1) 1.33, for engines with five or more cylinders; and

(2) Two, three, and four, for engines with four, three, and two cylinders, respectively.

[Amdt. 27–23, 53 FR 34210, Sept. 2, 1988]

CONTROL SURFACE AND SYSTEM LOADS

§ 27.391 General.

Each auxiliary rotor, each fixed or movable stabilizing or control surface, and each system operating any flight control must meet the requirements of §§ 27.395, 27.397, 27.399, 27.411, and 27.427.

[Amdt. 27–26, 55 FR 7999, Mar. 6, 1990, as amended by Amdt. 27–34, 62 FR 46173, Aug. 29, 1997]

§ 27.395 Control system.

(a) The part of each control system from the pilot's controls to the control stops must be designed to withstand pilot forces of not less than—

(1) The forces specified in § 27.397; or

(2) If the system prevents the pilot from applying the limit pilot forces to the system, the maximum forces that the system allows the pilot to apply, but not less than 0.60 times the forces specified in § 27.397.

(b) Each primary control system, including its supporting structure, must be designed as follows:

(1) The system must withstand loads resulting from the limit pilot forces prescribed in § 27.397.

(2) Notwithstanding paragraph (b)(3) of this section, when power-operated actuator controls or power boost controls are used, the system must also withstand the loads resulting from the force output of each normally energized power device, including any single power boost or actuator system failure.

(3) If the system design or the normal operating loads are such that a part of the system cannot react to the limit pilot forces prescribed in § 27.397, that part of the system must be designed to withstand the maximum loads that can be obtained in normal operation. The minimum design loads must, in any case, provide a rugged system for service use, including consideration of fatigue, jamming, ground gusts, control inertia, and friction loads. In the absence of rational analysis, the design loads resulting from 0.60 of the specified limit pilot forces are acceptable minimum design loads.

(4) If operational loads may be exceeded through jamming, ground gusts, control inertia, or friction, the system must withstand the limit pilot forces specified in § 27.397, without yielding.

[Doc. No. 5074, 29 FR 15695, Nov. 24, 1964, as amended by Amdt. 27–26, 55 FR 7999, Mar. 6, 1990]

§ 27.397 Limit pilot forces and torques.

(a) Except as provided in paragraph (b) of this section, the limit pilot forces are as follows:

(1) For foot controls, 130 pounds.

(2) For stick controls, 100 pounds fore and aft, and 67 pounds laterally.

(b) For flap, tab, stabilizer, rotor brake, and landing gear operating controls, the follows apply (R=radius in inches):

(1) Crank, wheel, and lever controls, $[1+R]/3 \times 50$ pounds, but not less than 50 pounds nor more than 100 pounds for hand operated controls or 130 pounds for foot operated controls, applied at any angle within 20 degrees of the plane of motion of the control.

(2) Twist controls, 80R inch-pounds.

[Amdt. 27–11, 41 FR 55469, Dec. 20, 1976, as amended by Amdt. 27–40, 66 FR 23538, May 9, 2001]

§ 27.399 Dual control system.

Each dual primary flight control system must be designed to withstand the loads that result when pilot forces of 0.75 times those obtained under § 27.395 are applied—

(a) In opposition; and

(b) In the same direction.

§ 27.411 Ground clearance: tail rotor guard.

(a) It must be impossible for the tail rotor to contact the landing surface during a normal landing.

(b) If a tail rotor guard is required to show compliance with paragraph (a) of this section—

(1) Suitable design loads must be established for the guard; and

(2) The guard and its supporting structure must be designed to withstand those loads.

§27.427 Unsymmetrical loads.

(a) Horizontal tail surfaces and their supporting structure must be designed for unsymmetrical loads arising from yawing and rotor wake effects in combination with the prescribed flight conditions.

(b) To meet the design criteria of paragraph (a) of this section, in the absence of more rational data, both of the following must be met:

(1) One hundred percent of the maximum loading from the symmetrical flight conditions acts on the surface on one side of the plane of symmetry, and no loading acts on the other side.

(2) Fifty percent of the maximum loading from the symmetrical flight conditions acts on the surface on each side of the plane of symmetry but in opposite directions.

(c) For empennage arrangements where the horizontal tail surfaces are supported by the vertical tail surfaces, the vertical tail surfaces and supporting structure must be designed for the combined vertical and horizontal surface loads resulting from each prescribed flight condition, considered separately. The flight conditions must be selected so the maximum design loads are obtained on each surface. In the absence of more rational data, the unsymmetrical horizontal tail surface loading distributions described in this section must be assumed.

[Admt. 27–26, 55 FR 7999, Mar. 6, 1990, as amended by Amdt. 27–27, 55 FR 38966, Sept. 21, 1990]

GROUND LOANS

§27.471 General.

(a) *Loads and equilibrium.* For limit ground loads—

(1) The limit ground loads obtained in the landing conditions in this part must be considered to be external loads that would occur in the rotorcraft structure if it were acting as a rigid body; and

(2) In each specified landing condition, the external loads must be placed in equilibrium with linear and angular

inertia loads in a rational or conservative manner.

(b) *Critical centers of gravity.* The critical centers of gravity within the range for which certification is requested must be selected so that the maximum design loads are obtained in each landing gear element.

§27.473 Ground loading conditions and assumptions.

(a) For specified landing conditions, a design maximum weight must be used that is not less than the maximum weight. A rotor lift may be assumed to act through the center of gravity throughout the landing impact. This lift may not exceed two-thirds of the design maximum weight.

(b) Unless otherwise prescribed, for each specified landing condition, the rotorcraft must be designed for a limit load factor of not less than the limit inertia load factor substantiated under §27.725.

[Amdt. 27–2, 33 FR 963, Jan. 26, 1968]

§27.475 Tires and shock absorbers.

Unless otherwise prescribed, for each specified landing condition, the tires must be assumed to be in their static position and the shock absorbers to be in their most critical position.

§27.477 Landing gear arrangement.

Sections 27.235, 27.479 through 27.485, and 27.493 apply to landing gear with two wheels aft, and one or more wheels forward, of the center of gravity.

§27.479 Level landing conditions.

(a) *Attitudes.* Under each of the loading conditions prescribed in paragraph (b) of this section, the rotorcraft is assumed to be in each of the following level landing attitudes:

(1) An attitude in which all wheels contact the ground simultaneously.

(2) An attitude in which the aft wheels contact the ground with the forward wheels just clear of the ground.

(b) *Loading conditions.* The rotorcraft must be designed for the following landing loading conditions:

(1) Vertical loads applied under §27.471.

(2) The loads resulting from a combination of the loads applied under paragraph (b)(1) of this section with

drag loads at each wheel of not less than 25 percent of the vertical load at that wheel.

(3) If there are two wheels forward, a distribution of the loads applied to those wheels under paragraphs (b)(1) and (2) of this section in a ratio of 40:60.

(c) *Pitching moments.* Pitching moments are assumed to be resisted by—

(1) In the case of the attitude in paragraph (a)(1) of this section, the forward landing gear; and

(2) In the case of the attitude in paragraph (a)(2) of this section, the angular inertia forces.

[Doc. No. 5074, 29 FR 15695, Nov. 24, 1964; 29 FR 17885, Dec. 17, 1964]

§ 27.481 Tail-down landing conditions.

(a) The rotorcraft is assumed to be in the maximum nose-up attitude allowing ground clearance by each part of the rotorcraft.

(b) In this attitude, ground loads are assumed to act perpendicular to the ground.

§ 27.483 One-wheel landing conditions.

For the one-wheel landing condition, the rotorcraft is assumed to be in the level attitude and to contact the ground on one aft wheel. In this attitude—

(a) The vertical load must be the same as that obtained on that side under § 27.479(b)(1); and

(b) The unbalanced external loads must be reacted by rotorcraft inertia.

§ 27.485 Lateral drift landing conditions.

(a) The rotorcraft is assumed to be in the level landing attitude, with—

(1) Side loads combined with one-half of the maximum ground reactions obtained in the level landing conditions of § 27.479 (b)(1); and

(2) The loads obtained under paragraph (a)(1) of this section applied—

(i) At the ground contact point; or

(ii) For full-swiveling gear, at the center of the axle.

(b) The rotorcraft must be designed to withstand, at ground contact—

(1) When only the aft wheels contact the ground, side loads of 0.8 times the vertical reaction acting inward on one side, and 0.6 times the vertical reaction

acting outward on the other side, all combined with the vertical loads specified in paragraph (a) of this section; and

(2) When all wheels contact the ground simultaneously—

(i) For the aft wheels, the side loads specified in paragraph (b)(1) of this section; and

(ii) For the forward wheels, a side load of 0.8 times the vertical reaction combined with the vertical load specified in paragraph (a) of this section.

§ 27.493 Braked roll conditions.

Under braked roll conditions with the shock absorbers in their static positions—

(a) The limit vertical load must be based on a load factor of at least—

(1) 1.33, for the attitude specified in § 27.479(a)(1); and

(2) 1.0 for the attitude specified in § 27.479(a)(2); and

(b) The structure must be designed to withstand at the ground contact point of each wheel with brakes, a drag load at least the lesser of—

(1) The vertical load multiplied by a coefficient of friction of 0.8; and

(2) The maximum value based on limiting brake torque.

§ 27.497 Ground loading conditions: landing gear with tail wheels.

(a) *General.* Rotorcraft with landing gear with two wheels forward, and one wheel aft, of the center of gravity must be designed for loading conditions as prescribed in this section.

(b) *Level landing attitude with only the forward wheels contacting the ground.* In this attitude—

(1) The vertical loads must be applied under §§ 27.471 through 27.475;

(2) The vertical load at each axle must be combined with a drag load at that axle of not less than 25 percent of that vertical load; and

(3) Unbalanced pitching moments are assumed to be resisted by angular inertia forces.

(c) *Level landing attitude with all wheels contacting the ground simultaneously.* In this attitude, the rotorcraft must be designed for landing loading conditions as prescribed in paragraph (b) of this section.

(d) *Maximum nose-up attitude with only the rear wheel contacting the ground.* The attitude for this condition must be the maximum nose-up attitude expected in normal operation, including autorotative landings. In this attitude—

(1) The appropriate ground loads specified in paragraphs (b)(1) and (2) of this section must be determined and applied, using a rational method to account for the moment arm between the rear wheel ground reaction and the rotorcraft center of gravity; or

(2) The probability of landing with initial contact on the rear wheel must be shown to be extremely remote.

(e) *Level landing attitude with only one forward wheel contacting the ground.* In this attitude, the rotorcraft must be designed for ground loads as specified in paragraphs (b)(1) and (3) of this section.

(f) *Side loads in the level landing attitude.* In the attitudes specified in paragraphs (b) and (c) of this section, the following apply:

(1) The side loads must be combined at each wheel with one-half of the maximum vertical ground reactions obtained for that wheel under paragraphs (b) and (c) of this section. In this condition, the side loads must be—

(i) For the forward wheels, 0.8 times the vertical reaction (on one side) acting inward, and 0.6 times the vertical reaction (on the other side) acting outward; and

(ii) For the rear wheel, 0.8 times the vertical reaction.

(2) The loads specified in paragraph (f)(1) of this section must be applied—

(i) At the ground contact point with the wheel in the trailing position (for non-full swiveling landing gear or for full swiveling landing gear with a lock, steering device, or shimmy damper to keep the wheel in the trailing position); or

(ii) At the center of the axle (for full swiveling landing gear without a lock, steering device, or shimmy damper).

(g) *Braked roll conditions in the level landing attitude.* In the attitudes specified in paragraphs (b) and (c) of this section, and with the shock absorbers in their static positions, the rotorcraft must be designed for braked roll loads as follows:

(1) The limit vertical load must be based on a limit vertical load factor of not less than—

(i) 1.0, for the attitude specified in paragraph (b) of this section; and

(ii) 1.33, for the attitude specified in paragraph (c) of this section.

(2) For each wheel with brakes, a drag load must be applied, at the ground contact point, of not less than the lesser of—

(i) 0.8 times the vertical load; and

(ii) The maximum based on limiting brake torque.

(h) *Rear wheel turning loads in the static ground attitude.* In the static ground attitude, and with the shock absorbers and tires in their static positions, the rotorcraft must be designed for rear wheel turning loads as follows:

(1) A vertical ground reaction equal to the static load on the rear wheel must be combined with an equal sideload.

(2) The load specified in paragraph (h)(1) of this section must be applied to the rear landing gear—

(i) Through the axle, if there is a swivel (the rear wheel being assumed to be swiveled 90 degrees to the longitudinal axis of the rotorcraft); or

(ii) At the ground contact point, if there is a lock, steering device or shimmy damper (the rear wheel being assumed to be in the trailing position).

(i) *Taxiing condition.* The rotorcraft and its landing gear must be designed for loads that would occur when the rotorcraft is taxied over the roughest ground that may reasonably be expected in normal operation.

§27.501 Ground loading conditions: landing gear with skids.

(a) *General.* Rotorcraft with landing gear with skids must be designed for the loading conditions specified in this section. In showing compliance with this section, the following apply:

(1) The design maximum weight, center of gravity, and load factor must be determined under §§27.471 through 27.475.

(2) Structural yielding of elastic spring members under limit loads is acceptable.

(3) Design ultimate loads for elastic spring members need not exceed those

obtained in a drop test of the gear
with—

(i) A drop height of 1.5 times that
specified in § 27.725; and

(ii) An assumed rotor lift of not more
than 1.5 times that used in the limit
drop tests prescribed in § 27.725.

(4) Compliance with paragraphs (b)
through (e) of this section must be
shown with—

(i) The gear in its most critically deflected position for the landing condition being considered; and

(ii) The ground reactions rationally
distributed along the bottom of the
skid tube.

(b) *Vertical reactions in the level landing attitude.* In the level attitude, and
with the rotorcraft contacting the
ground along the bottom of both skids,
the vertical reactions must be applied
as prescribed in paragraph (a) of this
section.

(c) *Drag reactions in the level landing
attitude.* In the level attitude, and with
the rotorcraft contacting the ground
along the bottom of both skids, the following apply:

(1) The vertical reactions must be
combined with horizontal drag reactions of 50 percent of the vertical reaction applied at the ground.

(2) The resultant ground loads must
equal the vertical load specified in
paragraph (b) of this section.

(d) *Sideloads in the level landing attitude.* In the level attitude, and with the
rotorcraft contacting the ground along
the bottom of both skids, the following
apply:

(1) The vertical ground reaction must
be—

(i) Equal to the vertical loads obtained in the condition specified in
paragraph (b) of this section; and

(ii) Divided equally among the skids.

(2) The vertical ground reactions
must be combined with a horizontal
sideload of 25 percent of their value.

(3) The total sideload must be applied
equally between the skids and along
the length of the skids.

(4) The unbalanced moments are assumed to be resisted by angular inertia.

(5) The skid gear must be investigated for—

(i) Inward acting sideloads; and

(ii) Outward acting sideloads.

(e) *One-skid landing loads in the level
attitude.* In the level attitude, and with
the rotorcraft contacting the ground
along the bottom of one skid only, the
following apply:

(1) The vertical load on the ground
contact side must be the same as that
obtained on that side in the condition
specified in paragraph (b) of this section.

(2) The unbalanced moments are assumed to be resisted by angular inertia.

(f) *Special conditions.* In addition to
the conditions specified in paragraphs
(b) and (c) of this section, the rotorcraft must be designed for the following ground reactions:

(1) A ground reaction load acting up
and aft at an angle of 45 degrees to the
longitudinal axis of the rotorcraft.
This load must be—

(i) Equal to 1.33 times the maximum
weight;

(ii) Distributed symmetrically among
the skids;

(iii) Concentrated at the forward end
of the straight part of the skid tube;
and

(iv) Applied only to the forward end
of the skid tube and its attachment to
the rotorcraft.

(2) With the rotorcraft in the level
landing attitude, a vertical ground reaction load equal to one-half of the
vertical load determined under paragraph (b) of this section. This load
must be—

(i) Applied only to the skid tube and
its attachment to the rotorcraft; and

(ii) Distributed equally over 33.3 percent of the length between the skid
tube attachments and centrally located
midway between the skid tube attachments.

[Doc. No. 5074, 29 FR 15695, Nov. 24, 1964, as
amended by Amdt. 27–2, 33 FR 963, Jan. 26,
1968; Amdt. 27–26, 55 FR 8000, Mar. 6, 1990]

§ 27.505 Ski landing conditions.

If certification for ski operation is
requested, the rotorcraft, with skis,
must be designed to withstand the following loading conditions (where *P* is
the maximum static weight on each ski
with the rotorcraft at design maximum
weight, and *n* is the limit load factor
determined under § 27.473(b).

(a) Up-load conditions in which—

(1) A vertical load of Pn and a horizontal load of $Pn/4$ are simultaneously applied at the pedestal bearings; and

(2) A vertical load of 1.33 P is applied at the pedestal bearings.

(b) A side-load condition in which a side load of 0.35 Pn is applied at the pedestal bearings in a horizontal plane perpendicular to the centerline of the rotorcraft.

(c) A torque-load condition in which a torque load of 1.33 P (in foot pounds) is applied to the ski about the vertical axis through the centerline of the pedestal bearings.

WATER LOADS

§ 27.521 Float landing conditions.

If certification for float operation is requested, the rotorcraft, with floats, must be designed to withstand the following loading conditions (where the limit load factor is determined under §27.473(b) or assumed to be equal to that determined for wheel landing gear):

(a) Up-load conditions in which—

(1) A load is applied so that, with the rotorcraft in the static level attitude, the resultant water reaction passes vertically through the center of gravity; and

(2) The vertical load prescribed in paragraph (a)(1) of this section is applied simultaneously with an aft component of 0.25 times the vertical component.

(b) A side-load condition in which—

(1) A vertical load of 0.75 times the total vertical load specified in paragraph (a)(1) of this section is divided equally among the floats; and

(2) For each float, the load share determined under paragraph (b)(1) of this section, combined with a total side load of 0.25 times the total vertical load specified in paragraph (b)(1) of this section, is applied to that float only.

MAIN COMPONENT REQUIREMENTS

§ 27.547 Main rotor structure.

(a) Each main rotor assembly (including rotor hubs and blades) must be designed as prescribed in this section.

(b) [Reserved]

(c) The main rotor structure must be designed to withstand the following loads prescribed in §§ 27.337 through 27.341:

(1) Critical flight loads.

(2) Limit loads occurring under normal conditions of autorotation. For this condition, the rotor r.p.m. must be selected to include the effects of altitude.

(d) The main rotor structure must be designed to withstand loads simulating—

(1) For the rotor blades, hubs, and flapping hinges, the impact force of each blade against its stop during ground operation; and

(2) Any other critical condition expected in normal operation.

(e) The main rotor structure must be designed to withstand the limit torque at any rotational speed, including zero. In addition:

(1) The limit torque need not be greater than the torque defined by a torque limiting device (where provided), and may not be less than the greater of—

(i) The maximum torque likely to be transmitted to the rotor structure in either direction; and

(ii) The limit engine torque specified in § 27.361.

(2) The limit torque must be distributed to the rotor blades in a rational manner.

(Secs. 604, 605, 72 Stat. 778, 49 U.S.C. 1424, 1425)

[Doc. No. 5074, 29 FR 15695, Nov. 24, 1964, as amended by Amdt. 27–3, 33 FR 14105, Sept. 18, 1968]

§ 27.549 Fuselage, landing gear, and rotor pylon structures.

(a) Each fuselage, landing gear, and rotor pylon structure must be designed as prescribed in this section. Resultant rotor forces may be represented as a single force applied at the rotor hub attachment point.

(b) Each structure must be designed to withstand—

(1) The critical loads prescribed in §§ 27.337 through 27.341;

(2) The applicable ground loads prescribed in §§ 27.235, 27.471 through 27.485, 27.493, 27.497, 27.501, 27.505, and 27.521; and

(3) The loads prescribed in § 27.547 (d)(2) and (e).

(c) Auxiliary rotor thrust, and the balancing air and inertia loads occurring under accelerated flight conditions, must be considered.

(d) Each engine mount and adjacent fuselage structure must be designed to withstand the loads occurring under accelerated flight and landing conditions, including engine torque.

(Secs. 604, 605, 72 Stat. 778, 49 U.S.C. 1424, 1425)

[Doc. No. 5074, 29 FR 15695, Nov. 24, 1964, as amended by Amdt. 27-3, 33 FR 14105, Sept. 18, 1968]

EMERGENCY LANDING CONDITIONS

§ 27.561 General.

(a) The rotorcraft, although it may be damaged in emergency landing conditions on land or water, must be designed as prescribed in this section to protect the occupants under those conditions.

(b) The structure must be designed to give each occupant every reasonable chance of escaping serious injury in a crash landing when—

(1) Proper use is made of seats, belts, and other safety design provisions;

(2) The wheels are retracted (where applicable); and

(3) Each occupant and each item of mass inside the cabin that could injure an occupant is restrained when subjected to the following ultimate inertial load factors relative to the surrounding structure:

(i) Upward—4g.

(ii) Forward—16g.

(iii) Sideward—8g.

(iv) Downward—20g, after intended displacement of the seat device.

(v) Rearward—1.5g.

(c) The supporting structure must be designed to restrain, under any ultimate inertial load up to those specified in this paragraph, any item of mass above and/or behind the crew and passenger compartment that could injure an occupant if it came loose in an emergency landing. Items of mass to be considered include, but are not limited to, rotors, transmissions, and engines. The items of mass must be restrained for the following ultimate inertial load factors:

(1) Upward—1.5g.

(2) Forward—12g.

(3) Sideward—6g.

(4) Downward—12g.

(5) Rearward—1.5g

(d) Any fuselage structure in the area of internal fuel tanks below the passenger floor level must be designed to resist the following ultimate inertial factors and loads and to protect the fuel tanks from rupture when those loads are applied to that area:

(i) Upward—1.5g.

(ii) Forward—4.0g.

(iii) Sideward—2.0g.

(iv) Downward—4.0g.

[Doc. No. 5074, 29 FR 15695, Nov. 24, 1964, as amended by Amdt. 27-25, 54 FR 47318, Nov. 13, 1989; Amdt. 27-30, 59 FR 50386, Oct. 3, 1994; Amdt. 27-32, 61 FR 10438, Mar. 13, 1996]

§ 27.562 Emergency landing dynamic conditions.

(a) The rotorcraft, although it may be damaged in an emergency crash landing, must be designed to reasonably protect each occupant when—

(1) The occupant properly uses the seats, safety belts, and shoulder harnesses provided in the design; and

(2) The occupant is exposed to the loads resulting from the conditions prescribed in this section.

(b) Each seat type design or other seating device approved for crew or passenger occupancy during takeoff and landing must successfully complete dynamic tests or be demonstrated by rational analysis based on dynamic tests of a similar type seat in accordance with the following criteria. The tests must be conducted with an occupant, simulated by a 170-pound anthropomorphic test dummy (ATD), as defined by 49 CFR 572, subpart B, or its equivalent, sitting in the normal upright position.

(1) A change in downward velocity of not less than 30 feet per second when the seat or other seating device is oriented in its nominal position with respect to the rotorcraft's reference system, the rotorcraft's longitudinal axis is canted upward 60° with respect to the impact velocity vector, and the rotorcraft's lateral axis is perpendicular to a vertical plane containing the impact velocity vector and the rotorcraft's longitudinal axis. Peak floor deceleration must occur in not

more than 0.031 seconds after impact and must reach a minimum of 30g's.

(2) A change in forward velocity of not less than 42 feet per second when the seat or other seating device is oriented in its nominal position with respect to the rotorcraft's reference system, the rotorcraft's longitudinal axis is yawed 10° either right or left of the impact velocity vector (whichever would cause the greatest load on the shoulder harness), the rotorcraft's lateral axis is contained in a horizontal plane containing the impact velocity vector, and the rotorcraft's vertical axis is perpendicular to a horizontal plane containing the impact velocity vector. Peak floor deceleration must occur in not more than 0.071 seconds after impact and must reach a minimum of 18.4g's.

(3) Where floor rails or floor or sidewall attachment devices are used to attach the seating devices to the airframe structure for the conditions of this section, the rails or devices must be misaligned with respect to each other by at least 10° vertically (i.e., pitch out of parallel) and by at least a 10° lateral roll, with the directions optional, to account for possible floor warp.

(c) Compliance with the following must be shown:

(1) The seating device system must remain intact although it may experience separation intended as part of its design.

(2) The attachment between the seating device and the airframe structure must remain intact, although the structure may have exceeded its limit load.

(3) The ATD's shoulder harness strap or straps must remain on or in the immediate vicinity of the ATD's shoulder during the impact.

(4) The safety belt must remain on the ATD's pelvis during the impact.

(5) The ATD's head either does not contact any portion of the crew or passenger compartment, or if contact is made, the head impact does not exceed a head injury criteria (HIC) of 1,000 as determined by this equation.

$$HIC = \left(t_2 - t_1\right)\left[\frac{1}{(t_2 - t_1)}\int_{t_1}^{t_2} a(t)dt\right]^{2.5}$$

Where: $a(t)$ is the resultant acceleration at the center of gravity of the head form expressed as a multiple of g (the acceleration of gravity) and $t_2 - t_1$ is the time duration, in seconds, of major head impact, not to exceed 0.05 seconds.

(6) Loads in individual upper torso harness straps must not exceed 1,750 pounds. If dual straps are used for retaining the upper torso, the total harness strap loads must not exceed 2,000 pounds.

(7) The maximum compressive load measured between the pelvis and the lumbar column of the ATD must not exceed 1,500 pounds.

(d) An alternate approach that achieves an equivalent or greater level of occupant protection, as required by this section, must be substantiated on a rational basis.

[Amdt. 27–25, 54 FR 47318, Nov. 13, 1989]

§27.563 Structural ditching provisions.

If certification with ditching provisions is requested, structural strength for ditching must meet the requirements of this section and §27.801(e).

(a) *Forward speed landing conditions.* The rotorcraft must initially contact the most critical wave for reasonably probable water conditions at forward velocities from zero up to 30 knots in likely pitch, roll, and yaw attitudes. The rotorcraft limit vertical descent velocity may not be less than 5 feet per second relative to the mean water surface. Rotor lift may be used to act through the center of gravity throughout the landing impact. This lift may not exceed two-thirds of the design maximum weight. A maximum forward velocity of less than 30 knots may be used in design if it can be demonstrated that the forward velocity selected would not be exceeded in a normal one-engine-out touchdown.

(b) *Auxiliary or emergency float conditions*—(1) *Floats fixed or deployed before initial water contact.* In addition to the landing loads in paragraph (a) of this section, each auxiliary or emergency float, of its support and attaching structure in the airframe or fuselage, must be designed for the load developed by a fully immersed float unless it can be shown that full immersion is unlikely. If full immersion is unlikely, the highest likely float buoyancy load must be applied. The highest likely buoyancy load must include consideration of a partially immersed float creating restoring moments to compensate the upsetting moments caused by side wind, unsymmetrical rotorcraft loading, water wave action, rotorcraft inertia, and probable structural damage and leakage considered under § 27.801(d). Maximum roll and pitch angles determined from compliance with § 27.801(d) may be used, if significant, to determine the extent of immersion of each float. If the floats are deployed in flight, appropriate air loads derived from the flight limitations with the floats deployed shall be used in substantiation of the floats and their attachment to the rotorcraft. For this purpose, the design airspeed for limit load is the float deployed airspeed operating limit multiplied by 1.11.

(2) *Floats deployed after initial water contact.* Each float must be designed for full or partial immersion perscribed in paragraph (b)(1) of this section. In addition, each float must be designed for combined vertical and drag loads using a relative limit speed of 20 knots between the rotorcraft and the water. The vertical load may not be less than the highest likely buoyancy load determined under paragraph (b)(1) of this section.

[Amdt. 27–26, 55 FR 8000, Mar. 6, 1990]

FATIGUE EVALUATION

§ 27.571 Fatigue evaluation of flight structure.

(a) *General.* Each portion of the flight structure (the flight structure includes rotors, rotor drive systems between the engines and the rotor hubs, controls, fuselage, landing gear, and their related primary attachments), the failure of which could be catastrophic, must be identified and must be evaluated under paragraph (b), (c), (d), or (e) of this section. The following apply to each fatigue evaluation:

(1) The procedure for the evaluation must be approved.

(2) The locations of probable failure must be determined.

(3) Inflight measurement must be included in determining the following:

(i) Loads or stresses in all critical conditions throughout the range of limitations in § 27.309, except that maneuvering load factors need not exceed the maximum values expected in operation.

(ii) The effect of altitude upon these loads or stresses.

(4) The loading spectra must be as severe as those expected in operation including, but not limited to, external cargo operations, if applicable, and ground-air-ground cycles. The loading spectra must be based on loads or stresses determined under paragraph (a)(3) of this section.

(b) *Fatigue tolerance evaluation.* It must be shown that the fatigue tolerance of the structure ensures that the probability of catastrophic fatigue failure is extremely remote without establishing replacement times, inspection intervals or other procedures under section A27.4 of appendix A.

(c) *Replacement time evaluation.* it must be shown that the probability of catastrophic fatigue failure is extremely remote within a replacement time furnished under section A27.4 of appendix A.

(d) *Fail-safe evaluation.* The following apply to fail-safe evaluation:

(1) It must be shown that all partial failures will become readily detectable under inspection procedures furnished under section A27.4 of appendix A.

(2) The interval between the time when any partial failure becomes readily detectable under paragraph (d)(1) of this section, and the time when any such failure is expected to reduce the remaining strength of the structure to limit or maximum attainable loads (whichever is less), must be determined.

(3) It must be shown that the interval determined under paragraph (d)(2) of this section is long enough, in relation to the inspection intervals and related procedures furnished under section

A27.4 of appendix A, to provide a probability of detection great enough to ensure that the probability of catastrophic failure is extremely remote.

(e) *Combination of replacement time and failsafe evaluations.* A component may be evaluated under a combination of paragraphs (c) and (d) of this section. For such component it must be shown that the probability of catastrophic failure is extremely remote with an approved combination of replacement time, inspection intervals, and related procedures furnished under section A27.4 of appendix A.

(Secs. 313(a), 601, 603, 604, and 605, 72 Stat. 752, 775, and 778, (49 U.S.C. 1354(a), 1421, 1423, 1424, and 1425; sec. 6(c), 49 U.S.C. 1655(c)))

[Amdt. 27-3, 33 FR 14106, Sept. 18, 1968, as amended by Amdt. 27-12, 42 FR 15044, Mar. 17, 1977; Amdt. 27-18, 45 FR 60177, Sept. 11 1980; Amdt. 27-26, 55 FR 8000, Mar. 6, 1990]

Subpart D—Design and Construction

GENERAL

§27.601 Design.

(a) The rotorcraft may have no design features or details that experience has shown to be hazardous or unreliable.

(b) The suitability of each questionable design detail and part must be established by tests.

§27.602 Critical parts.

(a) *Critical part.* A critical part is a part, the failure of which could have a catastrophic effect upon the rotorcraft, and for which critical characteristics have been identified which must be controlled to ensure the required level of integrity.

(b) If the type design includes crtical parts, a critical parts list shall be established. Procedures shall be established to define the critical design characteristics, identify processes that affect those characteristics, and identify the design change and process change controls necessary for showing compliance with the quality assurance requirements of part 21 of this chapter.

[Doc. No. 29311, 64 FR 46232, Aug. 24, 1999]

§27.603 Materials.

The suitability and durability of materials used for parts, the failure of which could adversely affect safety, must—

(a) Be established on the basis of experience or tests;

(b) Meet approved specifications that ensure their having the strength and other properties assumed in the design data; and

(c) Take into account the effects of environmental conditions, such as temperature and humidity, expected in service.

(Secs. 313(a), 601, 603, 604, Federal Aviation Act of 1958 (49 U.S.C. 1354(a), 1421, 1423, 1424); and sec. 6(c) of the Dept. of Transportation Act (49 U.S.C. 1655(c)))

[Doc. No. 5074, 29 FR 15695, Nov. 24, 1964, as amended by Amdt. 27-11, 41 FR 55469, Dec. 20, 1976; Amdt. 27-16, 43 FR 50599, Oct. 30, 1978]

§27.605 Fabrication methods.

(a) The methods of fabrication used must produce consistently sound structures. If a fabrication process (such as gluing, spot welding, or heat-treating) requires close control to reach this objective, the process must be performed according to an approved process specification.

(b) Each new aircraft fabrication method must be substantiated by a test program.

(Secs. 313(a), 601, 603, 604, and 605 of the Federal Aviation Act of 1958 (49 U.S.C. 1354(a), 1421, 1423, 1424 and 1425); sec. 6(c) of the Dept. of Transportation Act (49 U.S.C. 1655(c)))

[Doc. No. 5074, 29 FR 15695, Nov. 24, 1964, as amended by Amdt. 27-16, 43 FR 50599, Oct. 30, 1978]

§27.607 Fasteners.

(a) Each removable bolt, screw, nut, pin, or other fastener whose loss could jeopardize the safe operation of the rotorcraft must incorporate two separate locking devices. The fastener and its locking devices may not be adversely affected by the environmental conditions associated with the particular installation.

(b) No self-locking nut may be used on any bolt subject to rotation in operation unless a nonfriction locking device is used in addition to the self-locking device.

[Amdt. 27–4, 33 FR 14533, Sept. 27, 1968]

§ 27.609 Protection of structure.

Each part of the structure must—
(a) Be suitably protected against deterioration or loss of strength in service due to any cause, including—
(1) Weathering;
(2) Corrosion; and
(3) Abrasion; and
(b) Have provisions for ventilation and drainage where necessary to prevent the accumulation of corrosive, flammable, or noxious fluids.

§ 27.610 Lightning and static electricity protection.

(a) The rotorcraft must be protected against catastrophic effects from lightning.
(b) For metallic components, compliance with paragraph (a) of this section may be shown by—
(1) Electrically bonding the components properly to the airframe; or
(2) Designing the components so that a strike will not endanger the rotorcraft.
(c) For nonmetallic components, compliance with paragraph (a) of this section may be shown by—
(1) Designing the components to minimize the effect of a strike; or
(2) Incorporating acceptable means of diverting the resulting electrical current so as not to endanger the rotorcraft.
(d) The electrical bonding and protection against lightning and static electricity must—
(1) Minimize the accumulation of electrostatic charge;
(2) Minimize the risk of electric shock to crew, passengers, and service and maintenance personnel using normal precautions;
(3) Provide an electrical return path, under both normal and fault conditions, on rotorcraft having grounded electrical systems; and
(4) Reduce to an acceptable level the effects of lightning and static elec-

tricity on the functioning of essential electrical and electronic equipment.

[Amdt. 27–21, 49 FR 44433, Nov. 6, 1984, as amended by Amdt. 27–37, 64 FR 45094, Aug. 18, 1999]

§ 27.611 Inspection provisions.

There must be means to allow the close examination of each part that requires—
(a) Recurring inspection;
(b) Adjustment for proper alignment and functioning; or
(c) Lubrication.

§ 27.613 Material strength properties and design values.

(a) Material strength properties must be based on enough tests of material meeting specifications to establish design values on a statistical basis.
(b) Design values must be chosen to minimize the probability of structural failure due to material variability. Except as provided in paragraphs (d) and (e) of this section, compliance with this paragraph must be shown by selecting design values that assure material strength with the following probability—
(1) Where applied loads are eventually distributed through a single member within an assembly, the failure of which would result in loss of structural integrity of the component, 99 percent probability with 95 percent confidence; and
(2) For redundant structure, those in which the failure of individual elements would result in applied loads being safely distributed to other load-carrying members, 90 percent probability with 95 percent confidence.
(c) The strength, detail design, and fabrication of the structure must minimize the probability of disastrous fatigue failure, particularly at points of stress concentration.
(d) Design values may be those contained in the following publications (available from the Naval Publications and Forms Center, 5801 Tabor Avenue, Philadelphia, Pennsylvania 19120) or other values approved by the Administrator:
(1) MIL–HDBK–5, "Metallic Materials and Elements for Flight Vehicle Structure".

(2) MIL–HDBK–17, "Plastics for Flight Vehicles".

(3) ANC–18, "Design of Wood Aircraft Structures".

(4) MIL–HDBK–23, "Composite Construction for Flight Vehicles".

(e) Other design values may be used if a selection of the material is made in which a specimen of each individual item is tested before use and it is determined that the actual strength properties of that particular item will equal or exceed those used in design.

(Secs. 313(a), 601, 603, 604, Federal Aviation Act of 1958 (49 U.S.C. 1354(a), 1421, 1423, 1424), sec. 6(c), Dept. of Transportation Act (49 U.S.C. 1655(c)))

[Doc. No. 5074, 29 FR 15695, Nov. 24, 1964, as amended by Amdt. 27–16, 43 FR 50599, Oct. 30, 1978; Amdt. 27–26, 55 FR 8000, Mar. 6, 1990]

§27.619 Special factors.

(a) The special factors prescribed in §§27.621 through 27.625 apply to each part of the structure whose strength is—

(1) Uncertain;

(2) Likely to deteriorate in service before normal replacement; or

(3) Subject to appreciable variability due to—

(i) Uncertainties in manufacturing processes; or

(ii) Uncertainties in inspection methods.

(b) For each part to which §§27.621 through 27.625 apply, the factor of safety prescribed in §27.303 must be multiplied by a special factor equal to—

(1) The applicable special factors prescribed in §§27.621 through 27.625; or

(2) Any other factor great enough to ensure that the probability of the part being understrength because of the uncertainties specified in paragraph (a) of this section is extremely remote.

§27.621 Casting factors.

(a) *General.* The factors, tests, and inspections specified in paragraphs (b) and (c) of this section must be applied in addition to those necessary to establish foundry quality control. The inspections must meet approved specifications. Paragraphs (c) and (d) of this section apply to structural castings except castings that are pressure tested as parts of hydraulic or other fluid sys-

tems and do not support structural loads.

(b) *Bearing stresses and surfaces.* The casting factors specified in paragraphs (c) and (d) of this section—

(1) Need not exceed 1.25 with respect to bearing stresses regardless of the method of inspection used; and

(2) Need not be used with respect to the bearing surfaces of a part whose bearing factor is larger than the applicable casting factor.

(c) *Critical castings.* For each casting whose failure would preclude continued safe flight and landing of the rotorcraft or result in serious injury to any occupant, the following apply:

(1) Each critical casting must—

(i) Have a casting factor of not less than 1.25; and

(ii) Receive 100 percent inspection by visual, radiographic, and magnetic particle (for ferromagnetic materials) or penetrant (for nonferromagnetic materials) inspection methods or approved equivalent inspection methods.

(2) For each critical casting with a casting factor less than 1.50, three sample castings must be static tested and shown to meet—

(i) The strength requirements of §27.305 at an ultimate load corresponding to a casting factor of 1.25; and

(ii) The deformation requirements of §27.305 at a load of 1.15 times the limit load.

(d) *Noncritical castings.* For each casting other than those specified in paragraph (c) of this section, the following apply:

(1) Except as provided in paragraphs (d)(2) and (3) of this section, the casting factors and corresponding inspections must meet the following table:

Casting factor	Inspection
2.0 or greater	100 percent visual.
Less than 2.0, greater than 1.5.	100 percent visual, and magnetic particle (ferromagnetic materials), penetrant (nonferromagnetic materials), or approved equivalent inspection methods.
1.25 through 1.50	100 percent visual, and magnetic particle (ferromagnetic materials). penetrant (nonferromagnetic materials), and radiographic or approved equivalent inspection methods.

(2) The percentage of castings inspected by nonvisual methods may be

reduced below that specified in paragraph (d)(1) of this section when an approved quality control procedure is established.

(3) For castings procured to a specification that guarantees the mechanical properties of the material in the casting and provides for demonstration of these properties by test of coupons cut from the castings on a sampling basis—

(i) A casting factor of 1.0 may be used; and

(ii) The castings must be inspected as provided in paragraph (d)(1) of this section for casting factors of "1.25 through 1.50" and tested under paragraph (c)(2) of this section.

[Doc. No. 5074, 29 FR 15695, Nov. 24, 1964, as amended by Amdt. 27–34, 62 FR 46173, Aug. 29, 1997]

§ 27.623 Bearing factors.

(a) Except as provided in paragraph (b) of this section, each part that has clearance (free fit), and that is subject to pounding or vibration, must have a bearing factor large enough to provide for the effects of normal relative motion.

(b) No bearing factor need be used on a part for which any larger special factor is prescribed.

§ 27.625 Fitting factors.

For each fitting (part or terminal used to join one structural member to another) the following apply:

(a) For each fitting whose strength is not proven by limit and ultimate load tests in which actual stress conditions are simulated in the fitting and surrounding structures, a fitting factor of at least 1.15 must be applied to each part of—

(1) The fitting;

(2) The means of attachment; and

(3) The bearing on the joined members.

(b) No fitting factor need be used—

(1) For joints made under approved practices and based on comprehensive test data (such as continuous joints in metal plating, welded joints, and scarf joints in wood); and

(2) With respect to any bearing surface for which a larger special factor is used.

(c) For each integral fitting, the part must be treated as a fitting up to the point at which the section properties become typical of the member.

(d) Each seat, berth, litter, safety belt, and harness attachment to the structure must be shown by analysis, tests, or both, to be able to withstand the inertia forces prescribed in § 27.561(b)(3) multiplied by a fitting factor of 1.33.

[Doc. No. 5074, 29 FR 15695, Nov. 24, 1964, as amended by Amdt. 27–35, 63 FR 43285, Aug. 12, 1998]

§ 27.629 Flutter.

Each aerodynamic surface of the rotorcraft must be free from flutter under each appropriate speed and power condition.

[Doc. No. 5074, 29 FR 15695, Nov. 24, 1964, as amended by Amdt. 27–26, 55 FR 8000, Mar. 6, 1990]

ROTORS

§ 27.653 Pressure venting and drainage of rotor blades.

(a) For each rotor blade—

(1) There must be means for venting the internal pressure of the blade;

(2) Drainage holes must be provided for the blade; and

(3) The blade must be designed to prevent water from becoming trapped in it.

(b) Paragraphs (a)(1) and (2) of this section does not apply to sealed rotor blades capable of withstanding the maximum pressure differentials expected in service.

[Amdt. 27–2, 33 FR 963, Jan. 26, 1968]

§ 27.659 Mass balance.

(a) The rotors and blades must be mass balanced as necessary to—

(1) Prevent excessive vibration; and

(2) Prevent flutter at any speed up to the maximum forward speed.

(b) The structural integrity of the mass balance installation must be substantiated.

[Amdt. 27–2, 33 FR 963, Jan. 26, 1968]

§ 27.661 Rotor blade clearance.

There must be enough clearance between the rotor blades and other parts of the structure to prevent the blades from striking any part of the structure during any operating condition.

[Amdt. 27–2, 33 FR 963, Jan. 26, 1968]

§27.663 Ground resonance prevention means.

(a) The reliability of the means for preventing ground resonance must be shown either by analysis and tests, or reliable service experience, or by showing through analysis or tests that malfunction or failure of a single means will not cause ground resonance.

(b) The probable range of variations, during service, of the damping action of the ground resonance prevention means must be established and must be investigated during the test required by §27.241.

[Amdt. 27–2, 33 FR 963, Jan. 26, 1968, as amended by Amdt. 27–26, 55 FR 8000, Mar. 6, 1990]

CONTROL SYSTEMS

§27.671 General.

(a) Each control and control system must operate with the ease, smoothness, and positiveness appropriate to its function.

(b) Each element of each flight control system must be designed, or distinctively and permanently marked, to minimize the probability of any incorrect assembly that could result in the malfunction of the system.

§27.672 Stability augmentation, automatic, and power-operated systems.

If the functioning of stability augmentation or other automatic or power-operated systems is necessary to show compliance with the flight characteristics requirements of this part, such systems must comply with §27.671 of this part and the following:

(a) A warning which is clearly distinguishable to the pilot under expected flight conditions without requiring the pilot's attention must be provided for any failure in the stability augmentation system or in any other automatic or power-operated system which could result in an unsafe condition if the pilot is unaware of the failure. Warning systems must not activate the control systems.

(b) The design of the stability augmentation system or of any other auto-

matic or power-operated system must allow initial counteraction of failures without requiring exceptional pilot skill or strength by overriding the failure by movement of the flight controls in the normal sense and deactivating the failed system.

(c) It must be shown that after any single failure of the stability augmentation system or any other automatic or power-operated system—

(1) The rotorcraft is safely controllable when the failure or malfunction occurs at any speed or altitude within the approved operating limitations;

(2) The controllability and maneuverability requirements of this part are met within a practical operational flight envelope (for example, speed, altitude, normal acceleration, and rotorcraft configurations) which is described in the Rotorcraft Flight Manual; and

(3) The trim and stability characteristics are not impaired below a level needed to permit continued safe flight and landing.

[Amdt. 27–21, 49 FR 44433, Nov. 6, 1984; 49 FR 47594, Dec. 6, 1984]

§27.673 Primary flight control.

Primary flight controls are those used by the pilot for immediate control of pitch, roll, yaw, and vertical motion of the rotorcraft.

[Amdt. 27–21, 49 FR 44434, Nov. 6, 1984]

§27.674 Interconnected controls.

Each primary flight control system must provide for safe flight and landing and operate independently after a malfunction, failure, or jam of any auxiliary interconnected control.

[Amdt. 27–26, 55 FR 8001, Mar. 6, 1990]

§27.675 Stops.

(a) Each control system must have stops that positively limit the range of motion of the pilot's controls.

(b) Each stop must be located in the system so that the range of travel of its control is not appreciably affected by—

(1) Wear;

(2) Slackness; or

(3) Takeup adjustments.

(c) Each stop must be able to withstand the loads corresponding to the design conditions for the system.

(d) For each main rotor blade—

(1) Stops that are appropriate to the blade design must be provided to limit travel of the blade about its hinge points; and

(2) There must be means to keep the blade from hitting the droop stops during any operation other than starting and stopping the rotor.

(Secs. 313(a), 601, 603, 604, Federal Aviation Act of 1958 (49 U.S.C. 1354(a), 1421, 1423, 1424), sec. 6(c), Dept. of Transportation Act (49 U.S.C. 1655(c)))

[Doc. No. 5074, 29 FR 15695, Nov. 24, 1964, as amended by Amdt. 27–16, 43 FR 50599, Oct. 30, 1978]

§ 27.679 Control system locks.

If there is a device to lock the control system with the rotorcraft on the ground or water, there must be means to—

(a) Give unmistakable warning to the pilot when the lock is engaged; and

(b) Prevent the lock from engaging in flight.

§ 27.681 Limit load static tests.

(a) Compliance with the limit load requirements of this part must be shown by tests in which—

(1) The direction of the test loads produces the most severe loading in the control system; and

(2) Each fitting, pulley, and bracket used in attaching the system to the main structure is included.

(b) Compliance must be shown (by analyses or individual load tests) with the special factor requirements for control system joints subject to angular motion.

§ 27.683 Operation tests.

It must be shown by operation tests that, when the controls are operated from the pilot compartment with the control system loaded to correspond with loads specified for the system, the system is free from—

(a) Jamming;

(b) Excessive friction; and

(c) Excessive deflection.

§ 27.685 Control system details.

(a) Each detail of each control system must be designed to prevent jamming, chafing, and interference from cargo, passengers, loose objects or the freezing of moisture.

(b) There must be means in the cockpit to prevent the entry of foreign objects into places where they would jam the system.

(c) There must be means to prevent the slapping of cables or tubes against other parts.

(d) Cable systems must be designed as follows:

(1) Cables, cable fittings, turnbuckles, splices, and pulleys must be of an acceptable kind.

(2) The design of the cable systems must prevent any hazardous change in cable tension throughout the range of travel under any operating conditions and temperature variations.

(3) No cable smaller than three thirty-seconds of an inch diameter may be used in any primary control system.

(4) Pulley kinds and sizes must correspond to the cables with which they are used. The pulley cable combinations and strength values which must be used are specified in Military Handbook MIL–HDBK–5C, Vol. 1 & Vol. 2, Metallic Materials and Elements for Flight Vehicle Structures, (Sept. 15, 1976, as amended through December 15, 1978). This incorporation by reference was approved by the Director of the Federal Register in accordance with 5 U.S.C. section 552(a) and 1 CFR part 51. Copies may be obtained from the Naval Publications and Forms Center, 5801 Tabor Avenue, Philadelphia, Pennsylvania, 19120. Copies may be inspected at the FAA, Rotorcraft Standards Staff, 4400 Blue Mount Road, Fort Worth, Texas, or at the Office of the Federal Register, 800 North Capitol Street, NW., suite 700, Washington, DC.

(5) Pulleys must have close fitting guards to prevent the cables from being displaced or fouled.

(6) Pulleys must lie close enough to the plane passing through the cable to prevent the cable from rubbing against the pulley flange.

(7) No fairlead may cause a change in cable direction of more than 3°.

(8) No clevis pin subject to load or motion and retained only by cotter pins may be used in the control system.

(9) Turnbuckles attached to parts having angular motion must be installed to prevent binding throughout the range of travel.

(10) There must be means for visual inspection at each fairlead, pulley, terminal, and turnbuckle.

(e) Control system joints subject to angular motion must incorporate the following special factors with respect to the ultimate bearing strength of the softest material used as a bearing:

(1) 3.33 for push-pull systems other than ball and roller bearing systems.

(2) 2.0 for cable systems.

(f) For control system joints, the manufacturer's static, non-Brinell rating of ball and roller bearings must not be exceeded.

[Doc. No. 5074, 29 FR 15695, Nov. 24, 1964, as amended by Amdt. 27–11, 41 FR 55469, Dec. 20, 1976; Amdt. 27–26, 55 FR 8001, Mar. 6, 1990]

§27.687 Spring devices.

(a) Each control system spring device whose failure could cause flutter or other unsafe characteristics must be reliable.

(b) Compliance with paragraph (a) of this section must be shown by tests simulating service conditions.

§27.691 Autorotation control mechanism.

Each main rotor blade pitch control mechanism must allow rapid entry into autorotation after power failure.

§27.695 Power boost and power-operated control system.

(a) If a power boost or power-operated control system is used, an alternate system must be immediately available that allows continued safe flight and landing in the event of—

(1) Any single failure in the power portion of the system; or

(2) The failure of all engines.

(b) Each alternate system may be a duplicate power portion or a manually operated mechanical system. The power portion includes the power source (such as hydraulic pumps), and such items as valves, lines, and actuators.

(c) The failure of mechanical parts (such as piston rods and links), and the jamming of power cylinders, must be

considered unless they are extremely improbable.

LANDING GEAR

§27.723 Shock absorption tests.

The landing inertia load factor and the reserve energy absorption capacity of the landing gear must be substantiated by the tests prescribed in §§27.725 and 27.727, respectively. These tests must be conducted on the complete rotorcraft or on units consisting of wheel, tire, and shock absorber in their proper relation.

§27.725 Limit drop test.

The limit drop test must be conducted as follows:

(a) The drop height must be—

(1) 13 inches from the lowest point of the landing gear to the ground; or

(2) Any lesser height, not less than eight inches, resulting in a drop contact velocity equal to the greatest probable sinking speed likely to occur at ground contact in normal power-off landings.

(b) If considered, the rotor lift specified in §27.473(a) must be introduced into the drop test by appropriate energy absorbing devices or by the use of an effective mass.

(c) Each landing gear unit must be tested in the attitude simulating the landing condition that is most critical from the standpoint of the energy to be absorbed by it.

(d) When an effective mass is used in showing compliance with paragraph (b) of this section, the following formula may be used instead of more rational computations:

$$W_e = W \times \frac{h + (1-L)d}{h+d}; \text{ and}$$

$$n = n_j \frac{W_e}{W} + L$$

where:

W_e=the effective weight to be used in the drop test (lbs.);

$W=W_M$ for main gear units (lbs.), equal to the static reaction on the particular unit with the rotorcraft in the most critical attitude. A rational method may be used in computing a main gear static reaction, taking into consideration the moment arm between the main wheel reaction and the rotorcraft center of gravity.

$W=W_N$ for nose gear units (lbs.), equal to the vertical component of the static reaction that would exist at the nose wheel, assuming that the mass of the rotorcraft acts at the center of gravity and exerts a force of $1.0g$ downward and $0.25g$ forward.

$W=W_T$ for tailwheel units (lbs.), equal to whichever of the following is critical:

(1) The static weight on the tailwheel with the rotorcraft resting on all wheels; or

(2) The vertical component of the ground reaction that would occur at the tailwheel, assuming that the mass of the rotorcraft acts at the center of gravity and exerts a force of $1g$ downward with the rotorcraft in the maximum nose-up attitude considered in the nose-up landing conditions.

h=specified free drop height (inches).

L=ration of assumed rotor lift to the rotorcraft weight.

d=deflection under impact of the tire (at the proper inflation pressure) plus the vertical component of the axle travels (inches) relative to the drop mass.

n=limit inertia load factor.

n_j=the load factor developed, during impact, on the mass used in the drop test (i.e., the acceleration dv/dt in g 's recorded in the drop test plus 1.0).

§ 27.727 Reserve energy absorption drop test.

The reserve energy absorption drop test must be conducted as follows:

(a) The drop height must be 1.5 times that specified in § 27.725(a).

(b) Rotor lift, where considered in a manner similar to that prescribed in § 27.725(b), may not exceed 1.5 times the lift allowed under that paragraph.

(c) The landing gear must withstand this test without collapsing. Collapse of the landing gear occurs when a member of the nose, tail, or main gear will not support the rotorcraft in the proper attitude or allows the rotorcraft structure, other than the landing gear and external accessories, to impact the landing surface.

[Doc. No. 5074, 29 FR 15695, Nov. 24, 1964, as amended by Amdt. 27–26, 55 FR 8001, Mar. 6, 1990]

§ 27.729 Retracting mechanism.

For rotorcraft with retractable landing gear, the following apply:

(a) *Loads.* The landing gear, retracting mechansim, wheel-well doors, and supporting structure must be designed for—

(1) The loads occurring in any maneuvering condition with the gear retracted;

(2) The combined friction, inertia, and air loads occurring during retraction and extension at any airspeed up to the design maximum landing gear operating speed; and

(3) The flight loads, including those in yawed flight, occurring with the gear extended at any airspeed up to the design maximum landing gear extended speed.

(b) *Landing gear lock.* A positive means must be provided to keep the gear extended.

(c) *Emergency operation.* When other than manual power is used to operate the gear, emergency means must be provided for extending the gear in the event of—

(1) Any reasonably probable failure in the normal retraction system; or

(2) The failure of any single source of hydraulic, electric, or equivalent energy.

(d) *Operation tests.* The proper functioning of the retracting mechanism must be shown by operation tests.

(e) *Position indicator.* There must be a means to indicate to the pilot when the gear is secured in the extreme positions.

(f) *Control.* The location and operation of the retraction control must meet the requirements of §§ 27.777 and 27.779.

(g) *Landing gear warning.* An aural or equally effective landing gear warning device must be provided that functions continuously when the rotorcraft is in a normal landing mode and the landing gear is not fully extended and locked. A manual shutoff capability must be provided for the warning device and the warning system must automatically reset when the rotorcraft is no longer in the landing mode.

[Amdt. 27–21, 49 FR 44434, Nov. 6, 1984]

§ 27.731 Wheels.

(a) Each landing gear wheel must be approved.

(b) The maximum static load rating of each wheel may not be less than the corresponding static ground reaction with—

(1) Maximum weight; and

(2) Critical center of gravity.

(c) The maximum limit load rating of each wheel must equal or exceed the maximum radial limit load determined under the applicable ground load requirements of this part.

§27.733 Tires.

(a) Each landing gear wheel must have a tire—

(1) That is a proper fit on the rim of the wheel; and

(2) Of the proper rating.

(b) The maximum static load rating of each tire must equal or exceed the static ground reaction obtained at its wheel, assuming—

(1) The design maximum weight; and

(2) The most unfavorable center of gravity.

(c) Each tire installed on a retractable landing gear system must, at the maximum size of the tire type expected in service, have a clearance to surrounding structure and systems that is adequate to prevent contact between the tire and any part of the structure or systems.

[Doc. No. 5074, 29 FR 15695, Nov. 24, 1964, as amended by Amdt. 27–11, 41 FR 55469, Dec. 20, 1976]

§27.735 Brakes.

For rotorcraft with wheel-type landing gear, a braking device must be installed that is—

(a) Controllable by the pilot;

(b) Usable during power-off landings; and

(c) Adequate to—

(1) Counteract any normal unbalanced torque when starting or stopping the rotor; and

(2) Hold the rotorcraft parked on a 10-degree slope on a dry, smooth pavement.

[Doc. No. 5074, 29 FR 15695, Nov. 24, 1964, as amended by Amdt. 27–21, 49 FR 44434, Nov. 6, 1984]

§27.737 Skis.

The maximum limit load rating of each ski must equal or exceed the maximum limit load determined under the applicable ground load requirements of this part.

FLOATS AND HULLS

§27.751 Main float buoyancy.

(a) For main floats, the buoyancy necessary to support the maximum weight of the rotorcraft in fresh water must be exceeded by—

(1) 50 percent, for single floats; and

(2) 60 percent, for multiple floats.

(b) Each main float must have enough water-tight compartments so that, with any single main float compartment flooded, the main floats will provide a margin of positive stability great enough to minimize the probability of capsizing.

[Doc. No. 5074, 29 FR 15695, Nov. 24, 1964, as amended by Amdt. 27–2, 33 FR 963, Jan. 26, 1968]

§27.753 Main float design.

(a) *Bag floats.* Each bag float must be designed to withstand—

(1) The maximum pressure differential that might be developed at the maximum altitude for which certification with that float is requested; and

(2) The vertical loads prescribed in §27.521(a), distributed along the length of the bag over three-quarters of its projected area.

(b) *Rigid floats.* Each rigid float must be able to withstand the vertical, horizontal, and side loads prescribed in §27.521. These loads may be distributed along the length of the float.

§27.755 Hulls.

For each rotorcraft, with a hull and auxiliary floats, that is to be approved for both taking off from and landing on water, the hull and auxiliary floats must have enough watertight compartments so that, with any single compartment flooded, the buoyancy of the hull and auxiliary floats (and wheel tires if used) provides a margin of positive stability great enough to minimize the probability of capsizing.

PERSONNEL AND CARGO ACCOMMODATIONS

§27.771 Pilot compartment.

For each pilot compartment—

(a) The compartment and its equipment must allow each pilot to perform his duties without unreasonable concentration or fatigue;

(b) If there is provision for a second pilot, the rotorcraft must be controllable with equal safety from either pilot seat; and

(c) The vibration and noise characteristics of cockpit appurtenances may not interfere with safe operation.

§ 27.773 Pilot compartment view.

(a) Each pilot compartment must be free from glare and reflections that could interfere with the pilot's view, and designed so that—

(1) Each pilot's view is sufficiently extensive, clear, and undistorted for safe operation; and

(2) Each pilot is protected from the elements so that moderate rain conditions do not unduly impair his view of the flight path in normal flight and while landing.

(b) If certification for night operation is requested, compliance with paragraph (a) of this section must be shown in night flight tests.

§ 27.775 Windshields and windows.

Windshields and windows must be made of material that will not break into dangerous fragments.

[Amdt. 27–27, 55 FR 38966, Sept. 21, 1990]

§ 27.777 Cockpit controls.

Cockpit controls must be—

(a) Located to provide convenient operation and to prevent confusion and inadvertent operation; and

(b) Located and arranged with respect to the pilots' seats so that there is full and unrestricted movement of each control without interference from the cockpit structure or the pilot's clothing when pilots from 5'2" to 6'0" in height are seated.

§ 27.779 Motion and effect of cockpit controls.

Cockpit controls must be designed so that they operate in accordance with the following movements and actuation:

(a) Flight controls, including the collective pitch control, must operate with a sense of motion which corresponds to the effect on the rotorcraft.

(b) Twist-grip engine power controls must be designed so that, for lefthand operation, the motion of the pilot's

hand is clockwise to increase power when the hand is viewed from the edge containing the index finger. Other engine power controls, excluding the collective control, must operate with a forward motion to increase power.

(c) Normal landing gear controls must operate downward to extend the landing gear.

[Amdt. 27–21, 49 FR 44434, Nov. 6, 1984]

§ 27.783 Doors.

(a) Each closed cabin must have at least one adequate and easily accessible external door.

(b) Each external door must be located where persons using it will not be endangered by the rotors, propellers, engine intakes, and exhausts when appropriate operating procedures are used. If opening procedures are required, they must be marked inside, on or adjacent to the door opening device.

[Doc. No. 5074, 29 FR 15695, Nov. 24, 1964, as amended by Amdt. 27–26, 55 FR 8001, Mar. 6, 1990]

§ 27.785 Seats, berths, litters, safety belts, and harnesses.

(a) Each seat, safety belt, harness, and adjacent part of the rotorcraft at each station designated for occupancy during takeoff and landing must be free of potentially injurious objects, sharp edges, protuberances, and hard surfaces and must be designed so that a person making proper use of these facilities will not suffer serious injury in an emergency landing as a result of the static inertial load factors specified in § 27.561(b) and dynamic conditions specified in § 27.562.

(b) Each occupant must be protected from serious head injury by a safety belt plus a shoulder harness that will prevent the head from contacting any injurious object except as provided for in § 27.562(c)(5). A shoulder harness (upper torso restraint), in combination with the safety belt, constitutes a torso restraint system as described in TSO–C114.

(c) Each occupant's seat must have a combined safety belt and shoulder harness with a single-point release. Each pilot's combined safety belt and shoulder harness must allow each pilot when seated with safety belt and shoulder harness fastened to perform all functions necessary for flight operations. There must be a means to secure belts and harnesses, when not in use, to prevent interference with the operation of the rotorcraft and with rapid egress in an emergency.

(d) If seat backs do not have a firm handhold, there must be hand grips or rails along each aisle to enable the occupants to steady themselves while using the aisle in moderately rough air.

(e) Each projecting object that could injure persons seated or moving about in the rotorcraft in normal flight must be padded.

(f) Each seat and its supporting structure must be designed for an occupant weight of at least 170 pounds considering the maximum load factors, inertial forces, and reactions between occupant, seat, and safety belt or harness corresponding with the applicable flight and ground load conditions, including the emergency landing conditions of §27.561(b). In addition—

(1) Each pilot seat must be designed for the reactions resulting from the application of the pilot forces prescribed in §27.397; and

(2) The inertial forces prescribed in §27.561(b) must be multiplied by a factor of 1.33 in determining the strength of the attachment of—

(i) Each seat to the structure; and

(ii) Each safety belt or harness to the seat or structure.

(g) When the safety belt and shoulder harness are combined, the rated strength of the safety belt and shoulder harness may not be less than that corresponding to the inertial forces specified in §27.561(b), considering the occupant weight of at least 170 pounds, considering the dimensional characteristics of the restraint system installation, and using a distribution of at least a 60-percent load to the safety belt and at least a 40-percent load to the shoulder harness. If the safety belt is capable of being used without the shoulder harness, the inertial forces specified must be met by the safety belt alone.

(h) When a headrest is used, the headrest and its supporting structure must be designed to resist the inertia forces specified in §27.561, with a 1.33 fitting factor and a head weight of at least 13 pounds.

(i) Each seating device system includes the device such as the seat, the cushions, the occupant restraint system, and attachment devices.

(j) Each seating device system may use design features such as crushing or separation of certain parts of the seats to reduce occupant loads for the emergency landing dynamic conditions of §27.562; otherwise, the system must remain intact and must not interfere with rapid evacuation of the rotorcraft.

(k) For the purposes of this section, a litter is defined as a device designed to carry a nonambulatory person, primarily in a recumbent position, into and on the rotorcraft. Each berth or litter must be designed to withstand the load reaction of an occupant weight of at least 170 pounds when the occupant is subjected to the forward inertial factors specified in §27.561(b). A berth or litter installed within 15° or less of the longitudinal axis of the rotorcraft must be provided with a padded end-board, cloth diaphram, or equivalent means that can withstand the forward load reaction. A berth or litter oriented greater than 15° with the longitudinal axis of the rotorcraft must be equipped with appropriate restraints, such as straps or safety belts, to withstand the forward load reaction. In addition—

(1) The berth or litter must have a restraint system and must not have corners or other protuberances likely to cause serious injury to a person occupying it during emergency landing conditions; and

(2) The berth or litter attachment and the occupant restraint system attachments to the structure must be designed to withstand the critical loads resulting from flight and ground load conditions and from the conditions prescribed in §27.561(b). The fitting factor required by §27.625(d) shall be applied.

[Amdt. 27–21, 49 FR 44434, Nov. 6, 1984, as amended by Amdt. 27–25, 54 FR 47319, Nov. 13, 1989; Amdt. 27–35, 63 FR 43285, Aug. 12, 1998]

§27.787 Cargo and baggage compartments.

(a) Each cargo and baggage compartment must be designed for its placarded maximum weight of contents and for the critical load distributions at the appropriate maximum load factors corresponding to the specified flight and ground load conditions, except the emergency landing conditions of § 27.561.

(b) There must be means to prevent the contents of any compartment from becoming a hazard by shifting under the loads specified in paragraph (a) of this section.

(c) Under the emergency landing conditions of § 27.561, cargo and baggage compartments must—

(1) Be positioned so that if the contents break loose they are unlikely to cause injury to the occupants or restrict any of the escape facilities provided for use after an emergency landing; or

(2) Have sufficient strength to withstand the conditions specified in § 27.561 including the means of restraint, and their attachments, required by paragraph (b) of this section. Sufficient strength must be provided for the maximum authorized weight of cargo and baggage at the critical loading distribution.

(d) If cargo compartment lamps are installed, each lamp must be installed so as to prevent contact between lamp bulb and cargo.

[Doc. No. 5074, 29 FR 15695, Nov. 24, 1964, as amended by Amdt. 27–11, 41 FR 55469, Dec. 20, 1976; Amdt. 27–27, 55 FR 38966, Sept. 21, 1990]

§ 27.801 Ditching.

(a) If certification with ditching provisions is requested, the rotorcraft must meet the requirements of this section and §§ 27.807(d), 27.1411 and 27.1415.

(b) Each practicable design measure, compatible with the general characteristics of the rotorcraft, must be taken to minimize the probability that in an emergency landing on water, the behavior of the rotorcraft would cause immediate injury to the occupants or would make it impossible for them to escape.

(c) The probable behavior of the rotorcraft in a water landing must be investigated by model tests or by comparison with rotorcraft of similar configuration for which the ditching characteristics are known. Scoops, flaps, projections, and any other factor likely to affect the hydrodynamic characteristics of the rotorcraft must be considered.

(d) It must be shown that, under reasonably probable water conditions, the flotation time and trim of the rotorcraft will allow the occupants to leave the rotorcraft and enter the life rafts required by § 27.1415. If compliance with this provision is shown by buoyancy and trim computations, appropriate allowances must be made for probable structural damage and leakage. If the rotorcraft has fuel tanks (with fuel jettisoning provisions) that can reasonably be expected to withstand a ditching without leakage, the jettisonable volume of fuel may be considered as buoyancy volume.

(e) Unless the effects of the collapse of external doors and windows are accounted for in the investigation of the probable behavior of the rotorcraft in a water landing (as prescribed in paragraphs (c) and (d) of this section), the external doors and windows must be designed to withstand the probable maximum local pressures.

[Amdt. 27–11, 41 FR 55469, Dec. 20, 1976]

§ 27.805 Flight crew emergency exits.

(a) For rotorcraft with passenger emergency exits that are not convenient to the flight crew, there must be flight crew emergency exits, on both sides of the rotorcraft or as a top hatch in the flight crew area.

(b) Each flight crew emergency exit must be of sufficient size and must be located so as to allow rapid evacuation of the flight crew. This must be shown by test.

(c) Each flight crew emergency exit must not be obstructed by water or flotation devices after an emergency landing on water. This must be shown by test, demonstration, or analysis.

[Doc. No. 29247, 64 FR 45094, Aug. 18, 1999]

§ 27.807 Emergency exits.

(a) *Number and location.* (1) There must be at least one emergency exit on each side of the cabin readily accessible to each passenger. One of these exits must be usable in any probable attitude that may result from a crash;

(2) Doors intended for normal use may also serve as emergency exits, provided that they meet the requirements of this section; and

(3) If emergency flotation devices are installed, there must be an emergency exit accessible to each passenger on each side of the cabin that is shown by test, demonstration, or analysis to;

(i) Be above the waterline; and

(ii) Open without interference from flotation devices, whether stowed or deployed.

(b) *Type and operation.* Each emergency exit prescribed by paragraph (a) of this section must—

(1) Consist of a movable window or panel, or additional external door, providing an unobstructed opening that will admit a 19-by 26-inch ellipse;

(2) Have simple and obvious methods of opening, from the inside and from the outside, which do not require exceptional effort;

(3) Be arranged and marked so as to be readily located and opened even in darkness; and

(4) Be reasonably protected from jamming by fuselage deformation.

(c) *Tests.* The proper functioning of each emergency exit must be shown by test.

(d) *Ditching emergency exits for passengers.* If certification with ditching provisions is requested, the markings required by paragraph (b)(3) of this section must be designed to remain visible if the rotorcraft is capsized and the cabin is submerged.

[Doc. No. 29247, 64 FR 45094, Aug. 18, 1999]

§27.831 Ventilation.

(a) The ventilating system for the pilot and passenger compartments must be designed to prevent the presence of excessive quantities of fuel fumes and carbon monoxide.

(b) The concentration of carbon monoxide may not exceed one part in 20,000 parts of air during forward flight or hovering in still air. If the concentration exceeds this value under other conditions, there must be suitable operating restrictions.

§27.833 Heaters.

Each combustion heater must be approved.

[Amdt. 27–23, 53 FR 34210, Sept. 2, 1988]

FIRE PROTECTION

§27.853 Compartment interiors.

For each compartment to be used by the crew or passengers—

(a) The materials must be at least flame-resistant;

(b) [Reserved]

(c) If smoking is to be prohibited, there must be a placard so stating, and if smoking is to be allowed—

(1) There must be an adequate number of self-contained, removable ashtrays; and

(2) Where the crew compartment is separated from the passenger compartment, there must be at least one illuminated sign (using either letters or symbols) notifying all passengers when smoking is prohibited. Signs which notify when smoking is prohibited must—

(i) When illuminated, be legible to each passenger seated in the passenger cabin under all probable lighting conditions; and

(ii) Be so constructed that the crew can turn the illumination on and off.

[Amdt. 27–17, 45 FR 7755, Feb. 4, 1980, as amended by Amdt. 27–37, 64 FR 45095, Aug. 18, 1999]

§27.855 Cargo and baggage compartments.

(a) Each cargo and baggage compartment must be constructed of, or lined with, materials that are at least—

(1) Flame resistant, in the case of compartments that are readily accessible to a crewmember in flight; and

(2) Fire resistant, in the case of other compartments.

(b) No compartment may contain any controls, wiring, lines, equipment, or accessories whose damage or failure would affect safe operation, unless those items are protected so that—

(1) They cannot be damaged by the movement of cargo in the compartment; and

(2) Their breakage or failure will not create a fire hazard.

§ 27.859 Heating systems.

(a) *General.* For each heating system that involves the passage of cabin air over, or close to, the exhaust manifold, there must be means to prevent carbon monoxide from entering any cabin or pilot compartment.

(b) *Heat exchangers.* Each heat exchanger must be—

(1) Of suitable materials;

(2) Adequately cooled under all conditions; and

(3) Easily disassembled for inspection.

(c) *Combustion heater fire protection.* Except for heaters which incorporate designs to prevent hazards in the event of fuel leakage in the heater fuel system, fire within the ventilating air passage, or any other heater malfunction, each heater zone must incorporate the fire protection features of the applicable requirements of §§ 27.1183, 27.1185, 27.1189, 27.1191, and be provided with—

(1) Approved, quick-acting fire detectors in numbers and locations ensuring prompt detection of fire in the heater region.

(2) Fire extinguisher systems that provide at least one adequate discharge to all areas of the heater region.

(3) Complete drainage of each part of each zone to minimize the hazards resulting from failure or malfunction of any component containing flammable fluids. The drainage means must be—

(i) Effective under conditions expected to prevail when drainage is needed; and

(ii) Arranged so that no discharged fluid will cause an additional fire hazard.

(4) Ventilation, arranged so that no discharged vapors will cause an additional fire hazard.

(d) *Ventilating air ducts.* Each ventilating air duct passing through any heater region must be fireproof.

(1) Unless isolation is provided by fireproof valves or by equally effective means, the ventilating air duct downstream of each heater must be fireproof for a distance great enough to ensure that any fire originating in the heater can be contained in the duct.

(2) Each part of any ventilating duct passing through any region having a flammable fluid system must be so constructed or isolated from that system that the malfunctioning of any component of that system cannot introduce flammable fluids or vapors into the ventilating airstream.

(e) *Combustion air ducts.* Each combustion air duct must be fireproof for a distance great enough to prevent damage from backfiring or reverse flame propagation.

(1) No combustion air duct may connect with the ventilating airstream unless flames from backfires or reverse burning cannot enter the ventilating airstream under any operating condition, including reverse flow or malfunction of the heater or its associated components.

(2) No combustion air duct may restrict the prompt relief of any backfire that, if so restricted, could cause heater failure.

(f) *Heater control: General.* There must be means to prevent the hazardous accumulation of water or ice on or in any heater control component, control system tubing, or safety control.

(g) *Heater safety controls.* For each combustion heater, safety control means must be provided as follows:

(1) Means independent of the components provided for the normal continuous control of air temperature, airflow, and fuel flow must be provided for each heater to automatically shut off the ignition and fuel supply of that heater at a point remote from that heater when any of the following occurs:

(i) The heat exchanger temperature exceeds safe limits.

(ii) The ventilating air temperature exceeds safe limits.

(iii) The combustion airflow becomes inadequate for safe operation.

(iv) The ventilating airflow becomes inadequate for safe operation.

(2) The means of complying with paragraph (g)(1) of this section for any individual heater must—

(i) Be independent of components serving any other heater, the heat output of which is essential for safe operation; and

(ii) Keep the heater off until restarted by the crew.

(3) There must be means to warn the crew when any heater, the heat output of which is essential for safe operation, has been shut off by the automatic

means prescribed in paragraph (g)(1) of this section.

(h) *Air intakes.* Each combustion and ventilating air intake must be located so that no flammable fluids or vapors can enter the heater system—

(1) During normal operation; or

(2) As a result of the malfunction of any other component.

(i) *Heater exhaust.* Each heater exhaust system must meet the requirements of §§27.1121 and 27.1123.

(1) Each exhaust shroud must be sealed so that no flammable fluids or hazardous quantities of vapors can reach the exhaust system through joints.

(2) No exhaust system may restrict the prompt relief of any backfire that, if so restricted, could cause heater failure.

(j) *Heater fuel systems.* Each heater fuel system must meet the powerplant fuel system requirements affecting safe heater operation. Each heater fuel system component in the ventilating airstream must be protected by shrouds so that no leakage from those components can enter the ventilating airstream.

(k) *Drains.* There must be means for safe drainage of any fuel that might accumulate in the combustion chamber or the heat exchanger.

(1) Each part of any drain that operates at high temperatures must be protected in the same manner as heater exhausts.

(2) Each drain must be protected against hazardous ice accumulation under any operating condition.

[Doc. No. 5074, 29 FR 15695, Nov. 24, 1964, as amended by Amdt. 27–23, 53 FR 34211, Sept. 2, 1988]

§27.861 Fire protection of structure, controls, and other parts.

Each part of the structure, controls, rotor mechanism, and other parts essential to a controlled landing that would be affected by powerplant fires must be fireproof or protected so they can perform their essential functions for at least 5 minutes under any foreseeable powerplant fire conditions.

[Amdt. 27–26, 55 FR 8001, Mar. 6, 1990]

§27.863 Flammable fluid fire protection.

(a) In each area where flammable fluids or vapors might escape by leakage of a fluid system, there must be means to minimize the probability of ignition of the fluids and vapors, and the resultant hazards if ignition does occur.

(b) Compliance with paragraph (a) of this section must be shown by analysis or tests, and the following factors must be considered:

(1) Possible sources and paths of fluid leakage, and means of detecting leakage.

(2) Flammability characteristics of fluids, including effects of any combustible or absorbing materials.

(3) Possible ignition sources, including electrical faults, overheating of equipment, and malfunctioning of protective devices.

(4) Means available for controlling or extinguishing a fire, such as stopping flow of fluids, shutting down equipment, fireproof containment, or use of extinguishing agents.

(5) Ability of rotorcraft components that are critical to safety of flight to withstand fire and heat.

(c) If action by the flight crew is required to prevent or counteract a fluid fire (e.g. equipment shutdown or actuation of a fire extinguisher) quick acting means must be provided to alert the crew.

(d) Each area where flammable fluids or vapors might escape by leakage of a fluid system must be identified and defined.

(Secs. 313(a), 601, 603, 604, Federal Aviation Act of 1958 (49 U.S.C. 1354(a), 1421, 1423, 1424), sec. 6(c), Dept. of Transportation Act (49 U.S.C. 1655(c)))

[Amdt. 27–16, 43 FR 50599, Oct. 30, 1978]

EXTERNAL LOADS

§27.865 External loads.

(a) It must be shown by analysis, test, or both, that the rotorcraft external load attaching means for rotorcraft-load combinations to be used for nonhuman external cargo applications can withstand a limit static load equal to 2.5, or some lower load factor approved under §§27.337 through 27.341, multiplied by the maximum external load for which authorization is requested. It must be shown by analysis, test, or both that the rotorcraft external load attaching means and corresponding personnel carrying device system for rotorcraft-load combinations to be used for human external cargo applications can withstand a limit static load equal to 3.5 or some lower load factor, not less than 2.5, approved under §§ 27.337 through 27.341, multiplied by the maximum external load for which authorization is requested. The load for any rotorcraft-load combination class, for any external cargo type, must be applied in the vertical direction. For jettisonable external loads of any applicable external cargo type, the load must also be applied in any direction making the maximum angle with the vertical that can be achieved in service but not less than 30°. However, the 30° angle may be reduced to a lesser angle if—

(1) An operating limitation is established limiting external load operations to such angles for which compliance with this paragraph has been shown; or

(2) It is shown that the lesser angle can not be exceeded in service.

(b) The external load attaching means, for jettisonable rotorcraft-load combinations, must include a quick-release system to enable the pilot to release the external load quickly during flight. The quick-release system must consist of a primary quick release subsystem and a backup quick release subsystem that are isolated from one another. The quick-release system, and the means by which it is controlled, must comply with the following:

(1) A control for the primary quick release subsystem must be installed either on one of the pilot's primary controls or in an equivalently accessible location and must be designed and located so that it may be operated by either the pilot or a crewmember without hazardously limiting the ability to control the rotorcraft during an emergency situation.

(2) A control for the backup quick release subsystem, readily accessible to either the pilot or another crewmember, must be provided.

(3) Both the primary and backup quick release subsystems must—

(i) Be reliable, durable, and function properly with all external loads up to and including the maximum external limit load for which authorization is requested.

(ii) Be protected against electromagnetic interference (EMI) from external and internal sources and against lightning to prevent inadvertent load release.

(A) The minimum level of protection required for jettisonable rotorcraft-load combinations used for nonhuman external cargo is a radio frequency field strength of 20 volts per meter.

(B) The minimum level of protection required for jettisonable rotorcraft-load combinations used for human external cargo is a radio frequency field strength of 200 volts per meter.

(iii) Be protected against any failure that could be induced by a failure mode of any other electrical or mechanical rotorcraft system.

(c) For rotorcraft-load combinations to be used for human external cargo applications, the rotorcraft must—

(1) For jettisonable external loads, have a quick-release system that meets the requirements of paragraph (b) of this section and that—

(i) Provides a dual actuation device for the primary quick release subsystem, and

(ii) Provides a separate dual actuation device for the backup quick release subsystem;

(2) Have a reliable, approved personnel carrying device system that has the structural capability and personnel safety features essential for external occupant safety;

(3) Have placards and markings at all appropriate locations that clearly state the essential system operating instructions and, for the personnel carrying device system, the ingress and egress instructions;

(4) Have equipment to allow direct intercommunication among required crewmembers and external occupants; and

(5) Have the appropriate limitations and procedures incorporated in the flight manual for conducting human external cargo operations.

(d) The critically configured jettisonable external loads must be shown by a combination of analysis, ground tests, and flight tests to be both transportable and releasable throughout the approved operational envelope without hazard to the rotorcraft during normal flight conditions. In addition, these external loads must be shown to be releasable without hazard to the rotorcraft during emergency flight conditions.

(e) A placard or marking must be installed next to the external-load attaching means clearly stating any operational limitations and the maximum authorized external load as demonstrated under §27.25 and this section.

(f) The fatigue evaluation of §27.571 of this part does not apply to rotorcraft-load combinations to be used for nonhuman external cargo except for the failure of critical structural elements that would result in a hazard to the rotorcraft. For rotorcraft-load combinations to be used for human external cargo, the fatigue evaluation of §27.571 of this part applies to the entire quick release and personnel carrying device structural systems and their attachments.

[Amdt. 27–11, 41 FR 55469, Dec. 20, 1976; as amended by Amdt. 27–26, 55 FR 8001, Mar. 6, 1990; Amdt. 27–36, 64 FR 43019, Aug. 6, 1999]

MISCELLANEOUS

§27.871 Leveling marks.

There must be reference marks for leveling the rotorcraft on the ground.

§27.873 Ballast provisions.

Ballast provisions must be designed and constructed to prevent inadvertent shifting of ballast in flight.

Subpart E—Powerplant

GENERAL

§27.901 Installation.

(a) For the purpose of this part, the powerplant installation includes each part of the rotorcraft (other than the main and auxiliary rotor structures) that—

(1) Is necessary for propulsion;

(2) Affects the control of the major propulsive units; or

(3) Affects the safety of the major propulsive units between normal inspections or overhauls.

(b) For each powerplant installation—

(1) Each component of the installation must be constructed, arranged, and installed to ensure its continued safe operation between normal inspections or overhauls for the range of temperature and altitude for which approval is requested;

(2) Accessibility must be provided to allow any inspection and maintenance necessary for continued airworthiness;

(3) Electrical interconnections must be provided to prevent differences of potential between major components of the installation and the rest of the rotorcraft;

(4) Axial and radial expansion of turbine engines may not affect the safety of the installation; and

(5) Design precautions must be taken to minimize the possibility of incorrect assembly of components and equipment essential to safe operation of the rotorcraft, except where operation with the incorrect assembly can be shown to be extremely improbable.

(c) The installation must comply with—

(1) The installation instructions provided under §33.5 of this chapter; and

(2) The applicable provisions of this subpart.

(Secs. 313(a), 601, and 603, 72 Stat. 752, 775, 49 U.S.C. 1354(a), 1421, and 1423; sec. 6(c), 49 U.S.C. 1655(c))

[Doc. No. 5074, 29 FR 15695, Nov. 24, 1964, as amended by Amdt. 27–2, 33 FR 963, Jan. 26, 1968; Amdt. 27–12, 42 FR 15044, Mar. 17, 1977; Amdt. 27–23, 53 FR 34211, Sept. 2, 1988]

§27.903 Engines.

(a) *Engine type certification.* Each engine must have an approved type certificate. Reciprocating engines for use in helicopters must be qualified in accordance with §33.49(d) of this chapter or be otherwise approved for the intended usage.

(b) *Engine or drive system cooling fan blade protection.* (1) If an engine or rotor drive system cooling fan is installed, there must be a means to protect the rotorcraft and allow a safe landing if a fan blade fails. This must be shown by showing that—

(i) The fan blades are contained in case of failure;

(ii) Each fan is located so that a failure will not jeopardize safety; or

(iii) Each fan blade can withstand an ultimate load of 1.5 times the centrifugal force resulting from operation limited by the following:

(A) For fans driven directly by the engine—

(1) The terminal engine r.p.m. under uncontrolled conditions; or

(2) An overspeed limiting device.

(B) For fans driven by the rotor drive system, the maximum rotor drive system rotational speed to be expected in service, including transients.

(2) Unless a fatigue evaluation under § 27.571 is conducted, it must be shown that cooling fan blades are not operating at resonant conditions within the operating limits of the rotorcraft.

(c) *Turbine engine installation.* For turbine engine installations, the powerplant systems associated with engine control devices, systems, and instrumentation must be designed to give reasonable assurance that those engine operating limitations that adversely affect turbine rotor structural integrity will not be exceeded in service.

[Doc. No. 5074, 29 FR 15695, Nov. 24, 1964, as amended by Amdt. 27–11, 41 FR 55469, Dec. 20, 1976; Amdt. 27–23, 53 FR 34211, Sept. 2, 1988]

§ 27.907   Engine vibration.

(a) Each engine must be installed to prevent the harmful vibration of any part of the engine or rotorcraft.

(b) The addition of the rotor and the rotor drive system to the engine may not subject the principal rotating parts of the engine to excessive vibration stresses. This must be shown by a vibration investigation.

(c) No part of the rotor drive system may be subjected to excessive vibration stresses.

ROTOR DRIVE SYSTEM

§ 27.917   Design.

(a) Each rotor drive system must incorporate a unit for each engine to automatically disengage that engine from the main and auxiliary rotors if that engine fails.

(b) Each rotor drive system must be arranged so that each rotor necessary for control in autorotation will continue to be driven by the main rotors

after disengagement of the engine from the main and auxiliary rotors.

(c) If a torque limiting device is used in the rotor drive system, it must be located so as to allow continued control of the rotorcraft when the device is operating.

(d) The rotor drive system includes any part necessary to transmit power from the engines to the rotor hubs. This includes gear boxes, shafting, universal joints, couplings, rotor brake assemblies, clutches, supporting bearings for shafting, any attendant accessory pads or drives, and any cooling fans that are a part of, attached to, or mounted on the rotor drive system.

[Doc. No. 5074, 29 FR 15695, Nov. 24, 1964, as amended by Amdt. 27–11, 41 FR 55469, Dec. 20, 1976]

§ 27.921   Rotor brake.

If there is a means to control the rotation of the rotor drive system independently of the engine, any limitations on the use of that means must be specified, and the control for that means must be guarded to prevent inadvertent operation.

§ 27.923   Rotor drive system and control mechanism tests.

(a) Each part tested as prescribed in this section must be in a serviceable condition at the end of the tests. No intervening disassembly which might affect test results may be conducted.

(b) Each rotor drive system and control mechanism must be tested for not less than 100 hours. The test must be conducted on the rotorcraft, and the torque must be absorbed by the rotors to be installed, except that other ground or flight test facilities with other appropriate methods of torque absorption may be used if the conditions of support and vibration closely simulate the conditions that would exist during a test on the rotorcraft.

(c) A 60-hour part of the test prescribed in paragraph (b) of this section must be run at not less than maximum continuous torque and the maximum speed for use with maximum continuous torque. In this test, the main rotor controls must be set in the position that will give maximum longitudinal cyclic pitch change to simulate forward flight. The auxiliary rotor controls must be in the position for normal operation under the conditions of the test.

(d) A 30-hour or, for rotorcraft for which the use of either 30-minute OEI power or continuous OEI power is requested, a 25-hour part of the test prescribed in paragraph (b) of this section must be run at not less than 75 percent of maximum continuous torque and the minimum speed for use with 75 percent of maximum continuous torque. The main and auxiliary rotor controls must be in the position for normal operation under the conditions of the test.

(e) A 10-hour part of the test prescribed in paragraph (b) of this section must be run at not less than takeoff torque and the maximum speed for use with takeoff torque. The main and auxiliary rotor controls must be in the normal position for vertical ascent.

(1) For multiengine rotorcraft for which the use of 2½ minute OEI power is requested, 12 runs during the 10-hour test must be conducted as follows:

(i) Each run must consist of at least one period of 2½ minutes with takeoff torque and the maximum speed for use with takeoff torque on all engines.

(ii) Each run must consist of at least one period for each engine in sequence, during which that engine simulates a power failure and the remaining engines are run at 2½ minute OEI torque and the maximum speed for use with 2½ minute OEI torque for 2½ minutes.

(2) For multiengine turbine-powered rotorcraft for which the use of 30-second and 2-minute OEI power is requested, 10 runs must be conducted as follows:

(i) Immediately following a takeoff run of at least 5 minutes, each power source must simulate a failure, in turn, and apply the maximum torque and the maximum speed for use with 30-second OEI power to the remaining affected drive system power inputs for not less than 30 seconds, followed by application of the maximum torque and the maximum speed for use with 2-minute OEI power for not less than 2 minutes. At least one run sequence must be conducted from a simulated "flight idle" condition. When conducted on a bench test, the test sequence must be con-

ducted following stabilization at takeoff power.

(ii) For the purpose of this paragraph, an affected power input includes all parts of the rotor drive system which can be adversely affected by the application of higher or asymmetric torque and speed prescribed by the test.

(iii) This test may be conducted on a representative bench test facility when engine limitations either preclude repeated use of this power or would result in premature engine removal during the test. The loads, the vibration frequency, and the methods of application to the affected rotor drive system components must be representative of rotorcraft conditions. Test components must be those used to show compliance with the remainder of this section.

(f) The parts of the test prescribed in paragraphs (c) and (d) of this section must be conducted in intervals of not less than 30 minutes and may be accomplished either on the ground or in flight. The part of the test prescribed in paragraph (e) of this section must be conducted in intervals of not less than five minutes.

(g) At intervals of not more than five hours during the tests prescribed in paragraphs (c), (d), and (e) of this section, the engine must be stopped rapidly enough to allow the engine and rotor drive to be automatically disengaged from the rotors.

(h) Under the operating conditions specified in paragraph (c) of this section, 500 complete cycles of lateral control, 500 complete cycles of longitudinal control of the main rotors, and 500 complete cycles of control of each auxiliary rotor must be accomplished. A "complete cycle" involves movement of the controls from the neutral position, through both extreme positions, and back to the neutral position, except that control movements need not produce loads or flapping motions exceeding the maximum loads or motions encountered in flight. The cycling may be accomplished during the testing prescribed in paragraph (c) of this section.

(i) At least 200 start-up clutch engagements must be accomplished—

(1) So that the shaft on the driven side of the clutch is accelerated; and

(2) Using a speed and method selected by the applicant.

(j) For multiengine rotorcraft for which the use of 30-minute OEI power is requested, five runs must be made at 30-minute OEI torque and the maximum speed for use with 30-minute OEI torque, in which each engine, in sequence, is made inoperative and the remaining engine(s) is run for a 30-minute period.

(k) For multiengine rotorcraft for which the use of continuous OEI power is requested, five runs must be made at continuous OEI torque and the maximum speed for use with continuous OEI torque, in which each engine, in sequence, is made inoperative and the remaining engine(s) is run for a 1-hour period.

(Secs. 313(a), 601, and 603, 72 Stat. 752, 775, 49 U.S.C. 1354(a), 1421, and 1423; sec. 6(c), 49 U.S.C. 1655(c))

[Doc. No. 5074, 29 FR 15695, Nov. 24, 1964, as amended by Amdt. 27–2, 33 FR 963, Jan. 26, 1968; Amdt. 27–12, 42 FR 15044, Mar. 17, 1977; Amdt. 27–23, 53 FR 34212, Sept. 2, 1988; Amdt. 27–29, 59 FR 47767, Sept. 16, 1994]

§ 27.927 Additional tests.

(a) Any additional dynamic, endurance, and operational tests, and vibratory investigations necessary to determine that the rotor drive mechanism is safe, must be performed.

(b) If turbine engine torque output to the transmission can exceed the highest engine or transmission torque rating limit, and that output is not directly controlled by the pilot under normal operating conditions (such as where the primary engine power control is accomplished through the flight control), the following test must be made:

(1) Under conditions associated with all engines operating, make 200 applications, for 10 seconds each, or torque that is at least equal to the lesser of—

(i) The maximum torque used in meeting § 27.923 plus 10 percent; or

(ii) The maximum attainable torque output of the engines, assuming that torque limiting devices, if any, function properly.

(2) For multiengine rotorcraft under conditions associated with each engine, in turn, becoming inoperative, apply to the remaining transmission torque inputs the maximum torque attainable under probable operating conditions, assuming that torque limiting devices, if any, function properly. Each transmission input must be tested at this maximum torque for at least 15 minutes.

(3) The tests prescribed in this paragraph must be conducted on the rotorcraft at the maximum rotational speed intended for the power condition of the test and the torque must be absorbed by the rotors to be installed, except that other ground or flight test facilities with other appropriate methods of torque absorption may be used if the conditions of support and vibration closely simulate the conditions that would exist during a test on the rotorcraft.

(c) It must be shown by tests that the rotor drive system is capable of operating under autorotative conditions for 15 minutes after the loss of pressure in the rotor drive primary oil system.

(Secs. 313(a), 601, and 603, 72 Stat. 752, 775, 49 U.S.C. 1354(a), 1421, and 1423; sec. 6(c), 49 U.S.C. 1655(c))

[Amdt. 27–2, 33 FR 963, Jan. 26, 1968, as amended by Amdt. 27–12, 42 FR 15045, Mar. 17, 1977; Amdt. 27–23, 53 FR 34212, Sept. 2, 1988]

§ 27.931 Shafting critical speed.

(a) The critical speeds of any shafting must be determined by demonstration except that analytical methods may be used if reliable methods of analysis are available for the particular design.

(b) If any critical speed lies within, or close to, the operating ranges for idling, power on, and autorotative conditions, the stresses occurring at that speed must be within safe limits. This must be shown by tests.

(c) If analytical methods are used and show that no critical speed lies within the permissible operating ranges, the margins between the calculated critical speeds and the limits of the allowable operating ranges must be adequate to allow for possible variations between the computed and actual values.

§ 27.935 Shafting joints.

Each universal joint, slip joint, and other shafting joints whose lubrication is necessary for operation must have provision for lubrication.

§27.939 Turbine engine operating characteristics.

(a) Turbine engine operating characteristics must be investigated in flight to determine that no adverse characteristics (such as stall, surge, or flameout) are present, to a hazardous degree, during normal and emergency operation within the range of operating limitations of the rotorcraft and of the engine.

(b) The turbine engine air inlet system may not, as a result of airflow distortion during normal operation, cause vibration harmful to the engine.

(c) For governor-controlled engines, it must be shown that there exists no hazardous torsional instability of the drive system associated with critical combinations of power, rotational speed, and control displacement.

[Amdt. 27–1, 32 FR 6914, May 5, 1967, as amended by Amdt. 27–11, 41 FR 55469, Dec. 20, 1976]

FUEL SYSTEM

§27.951 General.

(a) Each fuel system must be constructed and arranged to ensure a flow of fuel at a rate and pressure established for proper engine functioning under any likely operating condition, including the maneuvers for which certification is requested.

(b) Each fuel system must be arranged so that—

(1) No fuel pump can draw fuel from more than one tank at a time; or

(2) There are means to prevent introducing air into the system.

(c) Each fuel system for a turbine engine must be capable of sustained operation throughout its flow and pressure range with fuel initially saturated with water at 80 °F. and having 0.75cc of free water per gallon added and cooled to the most critical condition for icing likely to be encountered in operation.

[Doc. No. 5074, 29 FR 15695, Nov. 24, 1964, as amended by Amdt. 27–9, 39 FR 35461, Oct. 1, 1974]

§27.952 Fuel system crash resistance.

Unless other means acceptable to the Administrator are employed to minimize the hazard of fuel fires to occupants following an otherwise surviv- able impact (crash landing), the fuel systems must incorporate the design features of this section. These systems must be shown to be capable of sustaining the static and dynamic deceleration loads of this section, considered as ultimate loads acting alone, measured at the system component's center of gravity, without structural damage to system components, fuel tanks, or their attachments that would leak fuel to an ignition source.

(a) *Drop test requirements.* Each tank, or the most critical tank, must be drop-tested as follows:

(1) The drop height must be at least 50 feet.

(2) The drop impact surface must be nondeforming.

(3) The tank must be filled with water to 80 percent of the normal, full capacity.

(4) The tank must be enclosed in a surrounding structure representative of the installation unless it can be established that the surrounding structure is free of projections or other design features likely to contribute to rupture of the tank.

(5) The tank must drop freely and impact in a horizontal position ±10°.

(6) After the drop test, there must be no leakage.

(b) *Fuel tank load factors.* Except for fuel tanks located so that tank rupture with fuel release to either significant ignition sources, such as engines, heaters, and auxiliary power units, or occupants is extremely remote, each fuel tank must be designed and installed to retain its contents under the following ultimate inertial load factors, acting alone.

(1) For fuel tanks in the cabin:

(i) Upward—4g.

(ii) Forward—16g.

(iii) Sideward—8g.

(iv) Downward—20g.

(2) For fuel tanks located above or behind the crew or passenger compartment that, if loosened, could injure an occupant in an emergency landing:

(i) Upward—1.5g.

(ii) Forward—8g.

(iii) Sideward—2g.

(iv) Downward—4g.

(3) For fuel tanks in other areas:

(i) Upward—1.5g.

(ii) Forward—4g.

(iii) Sideward—2g.

(iv) Downward—4g.

(c) *Fuel line self-sealing breakaway couplings.* Self-sealing breakaway couplings must be installed unless hazardous relative motion of fuel system components to each other or to local rotorcraft structure is demonstrated to be extremely improbable or unless other means are provided. The couplings or equivalent devices must be installed at all fuel tank-to-fuel line connections, tank-to-tank interconnects, and at other points in the fuel system where local structural deformation could lead to the release of fuel.

(1) The design and construction of self-sealing breakaway couplings must incorporate the following design features:

(i) The load necessary to separate a breakaway coupling must be between 25 to 50 percent of the minimum ultimate failure load (ultimate strength) of the weakest component in the fluid-carrying line. The separation load must in no case be less than 300 pounds, regardless of the size of the fluid line.

(ii) A breakaway coupling must separate whenever its ultimate load (as defined in paragraph (c)(1)(i) of this section) is applied in the failure modes most likely to occur.

(iii) All breakaway couplings must incorporate design provisions to visually ascertain that the coupling is locked together (leak-free) and is open during normal installation and service.

(iv) All breakaway couplings must incorporate design provisions to prevent uncoupling or unintended closing due to operational shocks, vibrations, or accelerations.

(v) No breakaway coupling design may allow the release of fuel once the coupling has performed its intended function.

(2) All individual breakaway couplings, coupling fuel feed systems, or equivalent means must be designed, tested, installed, and maintained so that inadvertent fuel shutoff in flight is improbable in accordance with § 27.955(a) and must comply with the fatigue evaluation requirements of § 27.571 without leaking.

(3) Alternate, equivalent means to the use of breakaway couplings must not create a survivable impact-induced load on the fuel line to which it is installed greater than 25 to 50 percent of the ultimate load (strength) of the weakest component in the line and must comply with the fatigue requirements of § 27.571 without leaking.

(d) *Frangible or deformable structural attachments.* Unless hazardous relative motion of fuel tanks and fuel system components to local rotorcraft structure is demonstrated to be extremely improbable in an otherwise survivable impact, frangible or locally deformable attachments of fuel tanks and fuel system components to local rotorcraft structure must be used. The attachment of fuel tanks and fuel system components to local rotorcraft structure, whether frangible or locally deformable, must be designed such that its separation or relative local deformation will occur without rupture or local tear-out of the fuel tank or fuel system components that will cause fuel leakage. The ultimate strength of frangible or deformable attachments must be as follows:

(1) The load required to separate a frangible attachment from its support structure, or deform a locally deformable attachment relative to its support structure, must be between 25 and 50 percent of the minimum ultimate load (ultimate strength) of the weakest component in the attached system. In no case may the load be less than 300 pounds.

(2) A frangible or locally deformable attachment must separate or locally deform as intended whenever its ultimate load (as defined in paragraph (d)(1) of this section) is applied in the modes most likely to occur.

(3) All frangible or locally deformable attachments must comply with the fatigue requirements of § 27.571.

(e) *Separation of fuel and ignition sources.* To provide maximum crash resistance, fuel must be located as far as practicable from all occupiable areas and from all potential ignition sources.

(f) *Other basic mechanical design criteria.* Fuel tanks, fuel lines, electrical wires, and electrical devices must be designed, constructed, and installed, as far as practicable, to be crash resistant.

(g) *Rigid or semirigid fuel tanks.* Rigid or semirigid fuel tank or bladder walls must be impact and tear resistant.

[Doc. No. 26352, 59 FR 50386, Oct. 3, 1994]

§27.953   Fuel system independence.

(a) Each fuel system for multiengine rotorcraft must allow fuel to be supplied to each engine through a system independent of those parts of each system supplying fuel to other engines. However, separate fuel tanks need not be provided for each engine.

(b) If a single fuel tank is used on a multiengine rotorcraft, the following must be provided:

(1) Independent tank outlets for each engine, each incorporating a shutoff valve at the tank. This shutoff valve may also serve as the firewall shutoff valve required by §27.995 if the line between the valve and the engine compartment does not contain a hazardous amount of fuel that can drain into the engine compartment.

(2) At least two vents arranged to minimize the probability of both vents becoming obstructed simultaneously.

(3) Filler caps designed to minimize the probability of incorrect installation or inflight loss.

(4) A fuel system in which those parts of the system from each tank outlet to any engine are independent of each part of each system supplying fuel to other engines.

§27.954   Fuel system lightning protection.

The fuel system must be designed and arranged to prevent the ignition of fuel vapor within the system by—

(a) Direct lightning strikes to areas having a high probability of stroke attachment;

(b) Swept lightning strokes to areas where swept strokes are highly probable; or

(c) Corona and streamering at fuel vent outlets.

[Amdt. 27-23, 53 FR 34212, Sept. 2, 1988]

§27.955   Fuel flow.

(a) *General.* The fuel system for each engine must be shown to provide the engine with at least 100 percent of the fuel required under each operating and maneuvering condition to be approved for the rotorcraft including, as applicable, the fuel required to operate the engine(s) under the test conditions required by §27.927. Unless equivalent methods are used, compliance must be shown by test during which the following provisions are met except that combinations of conditions which are shown to be improbable need not be considered.

(1) The fuel pressure, corrected for critical accelerations, must be within the limits specified by the engine type certificate data sheet.

(2) The fuel level in the tank may not exceed that established as the unusable fuel supply for that tank under §27.959, plus the minimum additional fuel necessary to conduct the test.

(3) The fuel head between the tank outlet and the engine inlet must be critical with respect to rotorcraft flight attitudes.

(4) The critical fuel pump (for pump-fed systems) is installed to produce (by actual or simulated failure) the critical restriction to fuel flow to be expected from pump failure.

(5) Critical values of engine rotation speed, electrical power, or other sources of fuel pump motive power must be applied.

(6) Critical values of fuel properties which adversely affect fuel flow must be applied.

(7) The fuel filter required by §27.997 must be blocked to the degree necessary to simulate the accumulation of fuel contamination required to activate the indicator required by §27.1305(q).

(b) *Fuel transfer systems.* If normal operation of the fuel system requires fuel to be transferred to an engine feed tank, the transfer must occur automatically via a system which has been shown to maintain the fuel level in the engine feed tank within acceptable limits during flight or surface operation of the rotorcraft.

(c) *Multiple fuel tanks.* If an engine can be supplied with fuel from more than one tank, the fuel systems must, in addition to having appropriate manual switching capability, be designed to prevent interruption of fuel flow to that engine, without attention by the flightcrew, when any tank supplying fuel to that engine is depleted of usable fuel during normal operation, and any other tank that normally supplies fuel to the engine alone contains usable fuel.

[Amdt. 27–23, 53 FR 34212, Sept. 2, 1988]

§ 27.959 Unusable fuel supply.

The unusable fuel supply for each tank must be established as not less than the quantity at which the first evidence of malfunction occurs under the most adverse fuel feed condition occurring under any intended operations and flight maneuvers involving that tank.

§ 27.961 Fuel system hot weather operation.

Each suction lift fuel system and other fuel systems with features conducive to vapor formation must be shown by test to operate satisfactorily (within certification limits) when using fuel at a temperature of 110 °F under critical operating conditions including, if applicable, the engine operating conditions defined by § 27.927 (b)(1) and (b)(2).

[Amdt. 27–23, 53 FR 34212, Sept. 2, 1988]

§ 27.963 Fuel tanks: general.

(a) Each fuel tank must be able to withstand, without failure, the vibration, inertia, fluid, and structural loads to which it may be subjected in operation.

(b) Each fuel tank of 10 gallons or greater capacity must have internal baffles, or must have external support to resist surging.

(c) Each fuel tank must be separated from the engine compartment by a firewall. At least one-half inch of clear airspace must be provided between the tank and the firewall.

(d) Spaces adjacent to the surfaces of fuel tanks must be ventilated so that fumes cannot accumulate in the tank compartment in case of leakage. If two or more tanks have interconnected outlets, they must be considered as one tank, and the airspaces in those tanks must be interconnected to prevent the flow of fuel from one tank to another as a result of a difference in pressure between those airspaces.

(e) The maximum exposed surface temperature of any component in the fuel tank must be less, by a safe margin as determined by the Administrator, than the lowest expected autoignition temperature of the fuel or fuel vapor in the tank. Compliance with this requirement must be shown under all operating conditions and under all failure or malfunction conditions of all components inside the tank.

(f) Each fuel tank installed in personnel compartments must be isolated by fume-proof and fuel-proof enclosures that are drained and vented to the exterior of the rotorcraft. The design and construction of the enclosures must provide necessary protection for the tank, must be crash resistant during a survivable impact in accordance with § 27.952, and must be adequate to withstand loads and abrasions to be expected in personnel compartments.

(g) Each flexible fuel tank bladder or liner must be approved or shown to be suitable for the particular application and must be puncture resistant. Puncture resistance must be shown by meeting the TSO–C80, paragraph 16.0, requirements using a minimum puncture force of 370 pounds.

(h) Each integral fuel tank must have provisions for inspection and repair of its interior.

[Doc. No. 5074, 29 FR 15695, Nov. 24, 1964, as amended by Amdt. 27–23, 53 FR 34213, Sept. 2, 1988; Amdt. 27–30, 59 FR 50387, Oct. 3, 1994]

§ 27.965 Fuel tank tests.

(a) Each fuel tank must be able to withstand the applicable pressure tests in this section without failure or leakage. If practicable, test pressures may be applied in a manner simulating the pressure distribution in service.

(b) Each conventional metal tank, nonmetallic tank with walls that are not supported by the rotorcraft structure, and integral tank must be subjected to a pressure of 3.5 p.s.i. unless the pressure developed during maximum limit acceleration or emergency deceleration with a full tank exceeds this value, in which case a hydrostatic head, or equivalent test, must be applied to duplicate the acceleration loads as far as possible. However, the pressure need not exceed 3.5 p.s.i. on surfaces not exposed to the acceleration loading.

(c) Each nonmetallic tank with walls supported by the rotorcraft structure must be subjected to the following tests:

(1) A pressure test of at least 2.0 p.s.i. This test may be conducted on the tank alone in conjunction with the test specified in paragraph (c)(2) of this section.

(2) A pressure test, with the tank mounted in the rotorcraft structure, equal to the load developed by the reaction of the contents, with the tank full, during maximum limit acceleration or emergency deceleration. However, the pressure need not exceed 2.0 p.s.i. on surfaces not exposed to the acceleration loading.

(d) Each tank with large unsupported or unstiffened flat areas, or with other features whose failure or deformation could cause leakage, must be subjected to the following test or its equivalent:

(1) Each complete tank assembly and its support must be vibration tested while mounted to simulate the actual installation.

(2) The tank assembly must be vibrated for 25 hours while two-thirds full of any suitable fluid. The amplitude of vibration may not be less than one thirty-second of an inch, unless otherwise substantiated.

(3) The test frequency of vibration must be as follows:

(i) If no frequency of vibration resulting from any r.p.m. within the normal operating range of engine or rotor system speeds is critical, the test frequency of vibration, in number of cycles per minute must, unless a frequency based on a more rational calculation is used, be the number obtained by averaging the maximum and minimum power-on engine speeds (r.p.m.) for reciprocating engine powered rotorcraft or 2,000 c.p.m. for turbine engine powered rotorcraft.

(ii) If only one frequency of vibration resulting from any r.p.m. within the normal operating range of engine or rotor system speeds is critical, that frequency of vibration must be the test frequency.

(iii) If more than one frequency of vibration resulting from any r.p.m. within the normal operating range of engine or rotor system speeds is critical, the most critical of these frequencies must be the test frequency.

(4) Under paragraphs (d)(3)(ii) and (iii) of this section, the time of test must be adjusted to accomplish the same number of vibration cycles as would be accomplished in 25 hours at the frequency specified in paragraph (d)(3)(i) of this section.

(5) During the test, the tank assembly must be rocked at the rate of 16 to 20 complete cycles per minute through an angle of 15 degrees on both sides of the horizontal (30 degrees total), about the most critical axis, for 25 hours. If motion about more than one axis is likely to be critical, the tank must be rocked about each critical axis for 12½ hours.

(Secs. 313(a), 601, and 603, 72 Stat. 752, 775, 49 U.S.C. 1354(a), 1421, and 1423; sec. 6(c), 49 U.S.C. 1655(c))

[Amdt. 27–12, 42 FR 15045, Mar. 17, 1977]

§27.967 Fuel tank installation.

(a) Each fuel tank must be supported so that tank loads are not concentrated on unsupported tank surfaces. In addition—

(1) There must be pads, if necessary, to prevent chafing between each tank and its supports;

(2) The padding must be nonabsorbent or treated to prevent the absorption of fuel;

(3) If flexible tank liners are used, they must be supported so that it is not necessary for them to withstand fluid loads; and

(4) Each interior surface of tank compartments must be smooth and free of projections that could cause wear of the liner unless—

(i) There are means for protection of the liner at those points; or

(ii) The construction of the liner itself provides such protection.

(b) Any spaces adjacent to tank surfaces must be adequately ventilated to avoid accumulation of fuel or fumes in those spaces due to minor leakage. If the tank is in a sealed compartment, ventilation may be limited to drain holes that prevent clogging and excessive pressure resulting from altitude changes. If flexible tank liners are installed, the venting arrangement for the spaces between the liner and its container must maintain the proper relationship to tank vent pressures for any expected flight condition.

(c) The location of each tank must meet the requirements of § 27.1185 (a) and (c).

(d) No rotorcraft skin immediately adjacent to a major air outlet from the engine compartment may act as the wall of the integral tank.

[Doc. No. 26352, 59 FR 50387, Oct. 3, 1994]

§ 27.969 Fuel tank expansion space.

Each fuel tank or each group of fuel tanks with interconnected vent systems must have an expansion space of not less than 2 percent of the tank capacity. It must be impossible to fill the fuel tank expansion space inadvertently with the rotorcraft in the normal ground attitude.

[Amdt. 27–23, 53 FR 34213, Sept. 2, 1988]

§ 27.971 Fuel tank sump.

(a) Each fuel tank must have a drainable sump with an effective capacity in any ground attitude to be expected in service of 0.25 percent of the tank capacity or 1/16 gallon, whichever is greater, unless—

(1) The fuel system has a sediment bowl or chamber that is accessible for preflight drainage and has a minimum capacity of 1 ounce for every 20 gallons of fuel tank capacity; and

(2) Each fuel tank drain is located so that in any ground attitude to be expected in service, water will drain from all parts of the tank to the sediment bowl or chamber.

(b) Each sump, sediment bowl, and sediment chamber drain required by this section must comply with the drain provisions of § 27.999(b).

[Amdt. 27–23, 53 FR 34213, Sept. 2, 1988]

§ 27.973 Fuel tank filler connection.

(a) Each fuel tank filler connection must prevent the entrance of fuel into any part of the rotorcraft other than the tank itself during normal operations and must be crash resistant during a survivable impact in accordance with § 27.952(c). In addition—

(1) Each filler must be marked as prescribed in § 27.1557(c)(1);

(2) Each recessed filler connection that can retain any appreciable quan-

tity of fuel must have a drain that discharges clear of the entire rotorcraft; and

(3) Each filler cap must provide a fuel-tight seal under the fluid pressure expected in normal operation and in a survivable impact.

(b) Each filler cap or filler cap cover must warn when the cap is not fully locked or seated on the filler connection.

[Doc. No. 26352, 59 FR 50387, Oct. 3, 1994]

§ 27.975 Fuel tank vents.

(a) Each fuel tank must be vented from the top part of the expansion space so that venting is effective under all normal flight conditions. Each vent must minimize the probability of stoppage by dirt or ice.

(b) The venting system must be designed to minimize spillage of fuel through the vents to an ignition source in the event of a rollover during landing, ground operation, or a survivable impact.

[Doc. No. 5074, 29 FR 15695, Nov. 24, 1964, as amended by Amdt. 27–23, 53 FR 34213, Sept. 2, 1988; Amdt. 27–30, 59 FR 50387, Oct. 3, 1994; Amdt. 27–35, 63 FR 43285, Aug. 12, 1998]

§ 27.977 Fuel tank outlet.

(a) There must be a fuel stainer for the fuel tank outlet or for the booster pump. This strainer must—

(1) For reciprocating engine powered rotorcraft, have 8 to 16 meshes per inch; and

(2) For turbine engine powered rotorcraft, prevent the passage of any object that could restrict fuel flow or damage any fuel system component.

(b) The clear area of each fuel tank outlet strainer must be at least five times the area of the outlet line.

(c) The diameter of each strainer must be at least that of the fuel tank outlet.

(d) Each finger strainer must be accessible for inspection and cleaning.

[Amdt. 27–11, 41 FR 55470, Dec. 20, 1976]

FUEL SYSTEM COMPONENTS

§ 27.991 Fuel pumps.

Compliance with § 27.955 may not be jeopardized by failure of—

(a) Any one pump except pumps that are approved and installed as parts of a type certificated engine; or

(b) Any component required for pump operation except, for engine driven pumps, the engine served by that pump.

[Amdt. 27-23, 53 FR 34213, Sept. 2, 1988]

§ 27.993 Fuel system lines and fittings.

(a) Each fuel line must be installed and supported to prevent excessive vibration and to withstand loads due to fuel pressure and accelerated flight conditions.

(b) Each fuel line connected to components of the rotorcraft between which relative motion could exist must have provisions for flexibility.

(c) Flexible hose must be approved.

(d) Each flexible connection in fuel lines that may be under pressure or subjected to axial loading must use flexible hose assemblies.

(e) No flexible hose that might be adversely affected by high temperatures may be used where excessive temperatures will exist during operation or after engine shutdown.

[Doc. No. 5074, 29 FR 15695, Nov. 24, 1964, as amended by Amdt. 27-2, 33 FR 964, Jan. 26, 1968]

§ 27.995 Fuel valves.

(a) There must be a positive, quick-acting valve to shut off fuel to each engine individually.

(b) The control for this valve must be within easy reach of appropriate crewmembers.

(c) Where there is more than one source of fuel supply there must be means for independent feeding from each source.

(d) No shutoff valve may be on the engine side of any firewall.

§ 27.997 Fuel strainer or filter.

There must be a fuel strainer or filter between the fuel tank outlet and the inlet of the first fuel system component which is susceptible to fuel contamination, including but not limited to the fuel metering device or an engine positive displacement pump, whichever is nearer the fuel tank outlet. This fuel strainer or filter must—

(a) Be accessible for draining and cleaning and must incorporate a screen or element which is easily removable;

(b) Have a sediment trap and drain except that it need not have a drain if the strainer or filter is easily removable for drain purposes;

(c) Be mounted so that its weight is not supported by the connecting lines or by the inlet or outlet connections of the strainer or filter itself, unless adequate strength margins under all loading conditions are provided in the lines and connections; and

(d) Provide a means to remove from the fuel any contaminant which would jeopardize the flow of fuel through rotorcraft or engine fuel system components required for proper rotorcraft fuel system or engine fuel system operation.

[Amdt. No. 27-9, 39 FR 35461, Oct. 1, 1974, as amended by Amdt. 27-20, 49 FR 6849, Feb. 23, 1984; Amdt. 27-23, 53 FR 34213, Sept. 2, 1988]

§ 27.999 Fuel system drains.

(a) There must be at least one accessible drain at the lowest point in each fuel system to completely drain the system with the rotorcraft in any ground attitude to be expected in service.

(b) Each drain required by paragraph (a) of this section must—

(1) Discharge clear of all parts of the rotorcraft;

(2) Have manual or automatic means to assure positive closure in the off position; and

(3) Have a drain valve—

(i) That is readily accessible and which can be easily opened and closed; and

(ii) That is either located or protected to prevent fuel spillage in the event of a landing with landing gear retracted.

[Doc. No. 574, 29 FR 15695, Nov. 24, 1964, as amended by Amdt. 27-11, 41 FR 55470, Dec. 20, 1976; Amdt. 27-23, 53 FR 34213, Sept. 2, 1988]

OIL SYSTEM

§ 27.1011 Engines: General.

(a) Each engine must have an independent oil system that can supply it with an appropriate quantity of oil at a temperature not above that safe for continuous operation.

(b) The usable oil capacity of each system may not be less than the product of the endurance of the rotorcraft under critical operating conditions and the maximum oil consumption of the engine under the same conditions, plus a suitable margin to ensure adequate circulation and cooling. Instead of a rational analysis of endurance and consumption, a usable oil capacity of one gallon for each 40 gallons of usable fuel may be used.

(c) The oil cooling provisions for each engine must be able to maintain the oil inlet temperature to that engine at or below the maximum established value. This must be shown by flight tests.

[Doc. No. 5074, 29 FR 15695, Nov. 24, 1964, as amended by Amdt. 27–23, 53 FR 34213, Sept. 2, 1988]

§ 27.1013 Oil tanks.

Each oil tank must be designed and installed so that—

(a) It can withstand, without failure, each vibration, inertia, fluid, and structural load expected in operation;

(b) [Reserved]

(c) Where used with a reciprocating engine, it has an expansion space of not less than the greater of 10 percent of the tank capacity or 0.5 gallon, and where used with a turbine engine, it has an expansion space of not less than 10 percent of the tank capacity.

(d) It is impossible to fill the tank expansion space inadvertently with the rotorcraft in the normal ground attitude;

(e) Adequate venting is provided; and

(f) There are means in the filler opening to prevent oil overflow from entering the oil tank compartment.

[Doc. No. 5074, 29 FR 15695, Nov. 24, 1964, as amended by Amdt. 27–9, 39 FR 35461, Oct. 1, 1974]

§ 27.1015 Oil tank tests.

Each oil tank must be designed and installed so that it can withstand, without leakage, an internal pressure of 5 p.s.i., except that each pressurized oil tank used with a turbine engine must be designed and installed so that it can withstand, without leakage, an internal pressure of 5 p.s.i., plus the maximum operating pressure of the tank.

[Amdt. 27–9, 39 FR 35462, Oct. 1, 1974]

§ 27.1017 Oil lines and fittings.

(a) Each oil line must be supported to prevent excessive vibration.

(b) Each oil line connected to components of the rotorcraft between which relative motion could exist must have provisions for flexibility.

(c) Flexible hose must be approved.

(d) Each oil line must have an inside diameter of not less than the inside diameter of the engine inlet or outlet. No line may have splices between connections.

§ 27.1019 Oil strainer or filter.

(a) Each turbine engine installation must incorporate an oil strainer or filter through which all of the engine oil flows and which meets the following requirements:

(1) Each oil strainer or filter that has a bypass must be constructed and installed so that oil will flow at the normal rate through the rest of the system with the strainer or filter completely blocked.

(2) The oil strainer or filter must have the capacity (with respect to operating limitations established for the engine) to ensure that engine oil system functioning is not impaired when the oil is contaminated to a degree (with respect to particle size and density) that is greater than that established for the engine under Part 33 of this chapter.

(3) The oil strainer or filter, unless it is installed at an oil tank outlet, must incorporate a means to indicate contamination before it reaches the capacity established in accordance with paragraph (a)(2) of this section.

(4) The bypass of a strainer or filter must be constructed and installed so that the release of collected contaminants is minimized by appropriate location of the bypass to ensure that collected contaminants are not in the bypass flow path.

(5) An oil strainer or filter that has no bypass, except one that is installed at an oil tank outlet, must have a means to connect it to the warning system required in § 27.1305(r).

(b) Each oil strainer or filter in a powerplant installation using reciprocating engines must be constructed and installed so that oil will flow at the normal rate through the rest of the system with the strainer or filter element completely blocked.

[Amdt. 27–9, 39 FR 35462, Oct. 1, 1974, as amended by Amdt. 27–20, 49 FR 6849, Feb. 23, 1984; Amdt. 27–23, 53 FR 34213, Sept. 2, 1988]

§27.1021 Oil system drains.

A drain (or drains) must be provided to allow safe drainage of the oil system. Each drain must—

(a) Be accessible; and

(b) Have manual or automatic means for positive locking in the closed position.

[Amdt. 27–20, 49 FR 6849, Feb. 23, 1984]

§27.1027 Transmissions and gearboxes: General.

(a) The lubrication system for components of the rotor drive system that require continuous lubrication must be sufficiently independent of the lubrication systems of the engine(s) to ensure lubrication during autorotation.

(b) Pressure lubrication systems for transmissions and gearboxes must comply with the engine oil system requirements of §§27.1013 (except paragraph (c)), 27.1015, 27.1017, 27.1021, and 27.1337(d).

(c) Each pressure lubrication system must have an oil strainer or filter through which all of the lubricant flows and must—

(1) Be designed to remove from the lubricant any contaminant which may damage transmission and drive system components or impede the flow of lubricant to a hazardous degree;

(2) Be equipped with a means to indicate collection of contaminants on the filter or strainer at or before opening of the bypass required by paragraph (c)(3) of this section; and

(3) Be equipped with a bypass constructed and installed so that—

(i) The lubricant will flow at the normal rate through the rest of the system with the strainer or filter completely blocked; and

(ii) The release of collected contaminants is minimized by appropriate location of the bypass to ensure that collected contaminants are not in the bypass flowpath.

(d) For each lubricant tank or sump outlet supplying lubrication to rotor drive systems and rotor drive system components, a screen must be provided to prevent entrance into the lubrication system of any object that might obstruct the flow of lubricant from the outlet to the filter required by paragraph (c) of this section. The requirements of paragraph (c) do not apply to screens installed at lubricant tank or sump outlets.

(e) Splash-type lubrication systems for rotor drive system gearboxes must comply with §§27.1021 and 27.1337(d).

[Amdt. 27–23, 53 FR 34213, Sept. 2, 1988, as amended by Amdt. 27–37, 64 FR 45095, Aug. 18, 1999]

COOLING

§27.1041 General.

(a) Each powerplant cooling system must be able to maintain the temperatures of powerplant components within the limits established for these components under critical surface (ground or water) and flight operating conditions for which certification is required and after normal shutdown. Powerplant components to be considered include but may not be limited to engines, rotor drive system components, auxiliary power units, and the cooling or lubricating fluids used with these components.

(b) Compliance with paragraph (a) of this section must be shown in tests conducted under the conditions prescribed in that paragraph.

[Doc. No. 5074, 29 FR 15695, Nov. 24, 1964, as amended by Amdt. 27–23, 53 FR 34213, Sept. 2, 1988]

§27.1043 Cooling tests.

(a) *General.* For the tests prescribed in §27.1041(b), the following apply:

(1) If the tests are conducted under conditions deviating from the maximum ambient atmospheric temperature specified in paragraph (b) of this section, the recorded powerplant temperatures must be corrected under paragraphs (c) and (d) of this section unless a more rational correction method is applicable.

(2) No corrected temperature determined under paragraph (a)(1) of this section may exceed established limits.

(3) For reciprocating engines, the fuel used during the cooling tests must be of the minimum grade approved for the engines, and the mixture settings must be those normally used in the flight stages for which the cooling tests are conducted.

(4) The test procedures must be as prescribed in § 27.1045.

(b) *Maximum ambient atmospheric temperature.* A maximum ambient atmospheric temperature corresponding to sea level conditions of at least 100 degrees F. must be established. The assumed temperature lapse rate is 3.6 degrees F. per thousand feet of altitude above sea level until a temperature of −69.7 degrees F. is reached, above which altitude the temperature is considered constant at −69.7 degrees F. However, for winterization installations, the applicant may select a maximum ambient atmospheric temperature corresponding to sea level conditions of less than 100 degrees F.

(c) *Correction factor (except cylinder barrels).* Unless a more rational correction applies, temperatures of engine fluids and power-plant components (except cylinder barrels) for which temperature limits are established, must be corrected by adding to them the difference between the maximum ambient atmospheric temperature and the temperature of the ambient air at the time of the first occurrence of the maximum component or fluid temperature recorded during the cooling test.

(d) *Correction factor for cylinder barrel temperatures.* Cylinder barrel temperatures must be corrected by adding to them 0.7 times the difference between the maximum ambient atmospheric temperature and the temperature of the ambient air at the time of the first occurrence of the maximum cylinder barrel temperature recorded during the cooling test.

(Secs. 313(a), 601, 603, 604, and 605 of the Federal Aviation Act of 1958 (49 U.S.C. 1354(a), 1421, 1423, 1424, and 1425); and sec. 6(c) of the Dept. of Transportation Act (49 U.S.C. 1655(c)))

[Doc. No. 5074, 29 FR 15695, Nov. 24, 1964, as amended by Amdt. 27–11, 41 FR 55470, Dec. 20, 1976; Amdt. 27–14, 43 FR 2325, Jan. 16, 1978]

§ 27.1045　Cooling test procedures.

(a) *General.* For each stage of flight, the cooling tests must be conducted with the rotorcraft—

(1) In the configuration most critical for cooling; and

(2) Under the conditions most critical for cooling.

(b) *Temperature stabilization.* For the purpose of the cooling tests, a temperature is "stabilized" when its rate of change is less than two degrees F. per minute. The following component and engine fluid temperature stabilization rules apply:

(1) For each rotorcraft, and for each stage of flight—

(i) The temperatures must be stabilized under the conditions from which entry is made into the stage of flight being investigated; or

(ii) If the entry condition normally does not allow temperatures to stabilize, operation through the full entry condition must be conducted before entry into the stage of flight being investigated in order to allow the temperatures to attain their natural levels at the time of entry.

(2) For each helicopter during the takeoff stage of flight, the climb at takeoff power must be preceded by a period of hover during which the temperatures are stabilized.

(c) *Duration of test.* For each stage of flight the tests must be continued until—

(1) The temperatures stabilize or 5 minutes after the occurrence of the highest temperature recorded, as appropriate to the test condition;

(2) That stage of flight is completed; or

(3) An operating limitation is reached.

[Doc. No. 5074, 29 FR 15695, Nov. 24, 1964, as amended by Amdt. 27–23, 53 FR 34214, Sept. 2, 1988]

INDUCTION SYSTEM

§ 27.1091　Air induction.

(a) The air induction system for each engine must supply the air required by that engine under the operating conditions and maneuvers for which certification is requested.

(b) Each cold air induction system opening must be outside the cowling if backfire flames can emerge.

(c) If fuel can accumulate in any air induction system, that system must have drains that discharge fuel—

(1) Clear of the rotorcraft; and

(2) Out of the path of exhaust flames.

(d) For turbine engine powered rotorcraft—

(1) There must be means to prevent hazardous quantities of fuel leakage or overflow from drains, vents, or other components of flammable fluid systems from entering the engine intake system; and

(2) The air inlet ducts must be located or protected so as to minimize the ingestion of foreign matter during takeoff, landing, and taxiing.

[Doc. No. 5074, 29 FR 15695, Nov. 24, 1964, as amended by Amdt. 27–2, 33 FR 964, Jan. 26, 1968; Amdt. 27–23, 53 FR 34214, Sept. 2, 1988]

§27.1093 Induction system icing protection.

(a) *Reciprocating engines.* Each reciprocating engine air induction system must have means to prevent and eliminate icing. Unless this is done by other means, it must be shown that, in air free of visible moisture at a temperature of 30 degrees F., and with the engines at 75 percent of maximum continuous power—

(1) Each rotorcraft with sea level engines using conventional venturi carburetors has a preheater that can provide a heat rise of 90 degrees F.;

(2) Each rotorcraft with sea level engines using carburetors tending to prevent icing has a sheltered alternate source of air, and that the preheat supplied to the alternate air intake is not less than that provided by the engine cooling air downstream of the cylinders;

(3) Each rotorcraft with altitude engines using conventional venturi carburetors has a preheater capable of providing a heat rise of 120 degrees F.; and

(4) Each rotorcraft with altitude engines using carburetors tending to prevent icing has a preheater that can provide a heat rise of—

(i) 100 degrees F.; or

(ii) If a fluid deicing system is used, at least 40 degrees F.

(b) *Turbine engine.* (1) It must be shown that each turbine engine and its air inlet system can operate throughout the flight power range of the engine (including idling)—

(i) Without accumulating ice on engine or inlet system components that would adversely affect engine operation or cause a serious loss of power under the icing conditions specified in appendix C of Part 29 of this chapter; and

(ii) In snow, both falling and blowing, without adverse effect on engine operation, within the limitations established for the rotorcraft.

(2) Each turbine engine must idle for 30 minutes on the ground, with the air bleed available for engine icing protection at its critical condition, without adverse effect, in an atmosphere that is at a temperature between 15° and 30 °F (between −9° and −1 °C) and has a liquid water content not less than 0.3 gram per cubic meter in the form of drops having a mean effective diameter not less than 20 microns, followed by momentary operation at takeoff power or thrust. During the 30 minutes of idle operation, the engine may be run up periodically to a moderate power or thrust setting in a manner acceptable to the Administrator.

(c) *Supercharged reciprocating engines.* For each engine having superchargers to pressurize the air before it enters the carburetor, the heat rise in the air caused by that supercharging at any altitude may be utilized in determining compliance with paragraph (a) of this section if the heat rise utilized is that which will be available, automatically, for the applicable altitude and operating condition because of supercharging.

(Secs. 313(a), 601, and 603, 72 Stat. 752, 775, 49 U.S.C. 1354(a), 1421, and 1423; sec. 6(c), 49 U.S.C. 1655(c))

[Doc. No. 5074, 29 FR 15695, Nov. 24, 1964, as amended by Amdt. 27–11, 41 FR 55470, Dec. 20, 1976; Amdt. 27–12, 42 FR 15045, Mar. 17, 1977; Amdt. 27–20, 49 FR 6849, Feb. 23, 1984; Amdt. 27–23, 53 FR 34214, Sept. 2, 1988]

EXHAUST SYSTEM

§27.1121 General.

For each exhaust system—

(a) There must be means for thermal expansion of manifolds and pipes;

(b) There must be means to prevent local hot spots;

(c) Exhaust gases must discharge clear of the engine air intake, fuel system components, and drains;

(d) Each exhaust system part with a surface hot enough to ignite flammable fluids or vapors must be located or shielded so that leakage from any system carrying flammable fluids or vapors will not result in a fire caused by impingement of the fluids or vapors on any part of the exhaust system including shields for the exhaust system;

(e) Exhaust gases may not impair pilot vision at night due to glare;

(f) If significant traps exist, each turbine engine exhaust system must have drains discharging clear of the rotorcraft, in any normal ground and flight attitudes, to prevent fuel accumulation after the failure of an attempted engine start;

(g) Each exhaust heat exchanger must incorporate means to prevent blockage of the exhaust port after any internal heat exchanger failure.

(Secs. 313(a), 601, and 603, 72 Stat. 752, 775, 49 U.S.C. 1354(a), 1421, and 1423; sec. 6(c), 49 U.S.C. 1655(c))

[Doc. No. 5074, 29 FR 15695, Nov. 24, 1964 as amended by Amdt. 27–12, 42 FR 15045, Mar. 17, 1977]

§ 27.1123 Exhaust piping.

(a) Exhaust piping must be heat and corrosion resistant, and must have provisions to prevent failure due to expansion by operating temperatures.

(b) Exhaust piping must be supported to withstand any vibration and inertia loads to which it would be subjected in operations.

(c) Exhaust piping connected to components between which relative motion could exist must have provisions for flexibility.

[Amdt. 27–11, 41 FR 55470, Dec. 20, 1976]

POWERPLANT CONTROLS AND
ACCESSORIES

§ 27.1141 Powerplant controls: general.

(a) Powerplant controls must be located and arranged under § 27.777 and marked under § 27.1555.

(b) Each flexible powerplant control must be approved.

(c) Each control must be able to maintain any set position without—

(1) Constant attention; or

(2) Tendency to creep due to control loads or vibration.

(d) Controls of powerplant valves required for safety must have—

(1) For manual valves, positive stops or in the case of fuel valves suitable index provisions, in the open and closed position; and

(2) For power-assisted valves, a means to indicate to the flight crew when the valve—

(i) Is in the fully open or fully closed position; or

(ii) Is moving between the fully open and fully closed position.

(e) For turbine engine powered rotorcraft, no single failure or malfunction, or probable combination thereof, in any powerplant control system may cause the failure of any powerplant function necessary for safety.

(Secs. 313(a), 601, and 603, 72 Stat. 752, 775, 49 U.S.C. 1354(a), 1421, and 1423; sec. 6(c), 49 U.S.C. 1655(c))

[Doc. No. 5074, 29 FR 15695, Nov. 24, 1964, as amended by Amdt. 27–12, 42 FR 15045, Mar. 17, 1977; Amdt. 27–23, 53 FR 34214, Sept. 2, 1988; Amdt. 27–33, 61 FR 21907, May 10, 1996]

§ 27.1143 Engine controls.

(a) There must be a separate power control for each engine.

(b) Power controls must be grouped and arranged to allow—

(1) Separate control of each engine; and

(2) Simultaneous control of all engines.

(c) Each power control must provide a positive and immediately responsive means of controlling its engine.

(d) If a power control incorporates a fuel shutoff feature, the control must have a means to prevent the inadvertent movement of the control into the shutoff position. The means must—

(1) Have a positive lock or stop at the idle position; and

(2) Require a separate and distinct operation to place the control in the shutoff position.

(e) For rotorcraft to be certificated for a 30-second OEI power rating, a means must be provided to automatically activate and control the 30-second OEI power and prevent any engine from exceeding the installed engine limits associated with the 30-second OEI power rating approved for the rotorcraft.

[Doc. No. 5074, 29 FR 15695, Nov. 24, 1964, as amended by Amdt. 27–11, 41 FR 55470, Dec. 20, 1976; Amdt. 27–23, 53 FR 34214, Sept. 2, 1988; Amdt. 27–29, 59 FR 47767, Sept. 16, 1994]

§27.1145 Ignition switches.

(a) There must be means to quickly shut off all ignition by the grouping of switches or by a master ignition control.

(b) Each group of ignition switches, except ignition switches for turbine engines for which continuous ignition is not required, and each master ignition control must have a means to prevent its inadvertent operation.

(Secs. 313(a), 601, and 603, 72 Stat. 752, 775, 49 U.S.C. 1354(a), 1421, and 1423; sec. 6(c), 49 U.S.C. 1655(c))

[Doc. No. 5074, 29 FR 15695, Nov. 24, 1964, as amended by Amdt. 27–12, 42 FR 15045, Mar. 17, 1977]

§27.1147 Mixture controls.

If there are mixture controls, each engine must have a separate control and the controls must be arranged to allow—

(a) Separate control of each engine; and

(b) Simultaneous control of all engines.

§27.1151 Rotor brake controls.

(a) It must be impossible to apply the rotor brake inadvertently in flight.

(b) There must be means to warn the crew if the rotor brake has not been completely released before takeoff.

[Doc. No. 28008, 61 FR 21907, May 10, 1996]

§27.1163 Powerplant accessories.

(a) Each engine-mounted accessory must—

(1) Be approved for mounting on the engine involved;

(2) Use the provisions on the engine for mounting; and

(3) Be sealed in such a way as to prevent contamination of the engine oil system and the accessory system.

(b) Unless other means are provided, torque limiting means must be provided for accessory drives located on any component of the transmission and rotor drive system to prevent damage to these components from excessive accessory load.

[Amdt. 27–2, 33 FR 964, Jan. 26, 1968, as amended by Amdt. 27–20, 49 FR 6849, Feb. 23, 1984; Amdt. 27–23, 53 FR 34214, Sept. 2, 1988]

POWERPLANT FIRE PROTECTION

§27.1183 Lines, fittings, and components.

(a) Except as provided in paragraph (b) of this section, each line, fitting, and other component carrying flammable fluid in any area subject to engine fire conditions must be fire resistant, except that flammable fluid tanks and supports which are part of and attached to the engine must be fireproof or be enclosed by a fireproof shield unless damage by fire to any non-fireproof part will not cause leakage or spillage of flammable fluid. Components must be shielded or located so as to safeguard against the ignition of leaking flammable fluid. An integral oil sump of less than 25-quart capacity on a reciprocating engine need not be fireproof nor be enclosed by a fireproof shield.

(b) Paragraph (a) does not apply to—

(1) Lines, fittings, and components which are already approved as part of a type certificated engine; and

(2) Vent and drain lines, and their fittings, whose failure will not result in, or add to, a fire hazard.

(c) Each flammable fluid drain and vent must discharge clear of the induction system air inlet.

[Doc. No. 5074, 29 FR 15695, Nov. 24, 1964, as amended by Amdt. 27–1, 32 FR 6914, May 5, 1967; Amdt. 27–9, 39 FR 35462, Oct. 1, 1974; Amdt. 27–20, 49 FR 6849, Feb. 23, 1984]

§27.1185 Flammable fluids.

(a) Each fuel tank must be isolated from the engines by a firewall or shroud.

(b) Each tank or reservoir, other than a fuel tank, that is part of a system containing flammable fluids or gases must be isolated from the engine by a firewall or shroud, unless the design of the system, the materials used in the tank and its supports, the shut-off means, and the connections, lines and controls provide a degree of safety equal to that which would exist if the tank or reservoir were isolated from the engines.

(c) There must be at least one-half inch of clear airspace between each tank and each firewall or shroud isolating that tank, unless equivalent means are used to prevent heat transfer from each engine compartment to the flammable fluid.

(d) Absorbent materials close to flammable fluid system components that might leak must be covered or treated to prevent the absorption of hazardous quantities of fluids.

[Doc. No. 5074, 29 FR 15695, Nov. 24, 1964, as amended by Amdt. 27–2, 33 FR 964, Jan. 26, 1968; Amdt. 27–11, 41 FR 55470, Dec. 20, 1976; Amdt. 27–37, 64 FR 45095, Aug. 18, 1999]

§ 27.1187 Ventilation and drainage.

Each compartment containing any part of the powerplant installation must have provision for ventilation and drainage of flammable fluids. The drainage means must be—

(a) Effective under conditions expected to prevail when drainage is needed, and

(b) Arranged so that no discharged fluid will cause an additional fire hazard.

[Doc. No. 29247, 64 FR 45095, Aug. 18, 1999]

§ 27.1189 Shutoff means.

(a) There must be means to shut off each line carrying flammable fluids into the engine compartment, except—

(1) Lines, fittings, and components forming an intergral part of an engine;

(2) For oil systems for which all components of the system, including oil tanks, are fireproof or located in areas not subject to engine fire conditions; and

(3) For reciprocating engine installations only, engine oil system lines in installation using engines of less than 500 cu. in. displacement.

(b) There must be means to guard against inadvertent operation of each shutoff, and to make it possible for the crew to reopen it in flight after it has been closed.

(c) Each shutoff valve and its control must be designed, located, and pro-

tected to function properly under any condition likely to result from an engine fire.

[Doc. No. 5074, 29 FR 15695, Nov. 24, 1964, as amended by Amdt. 27–2, 33 FR 964, Jan. 26, 1968; Amdt. 27–20, 49 FR 6850, Feb. 23, 1984; Amdt. 27–23, 53 FR 34214, Sept. 2, 1988]

§ 27.1191 Firewalls.

(a) Each engine, including the combustor, turbine, and tailpipe sections of turbine engines must be isolated by a firewall, shroud, or equivalent means, from personnel compartments, structures, controls, rotor mechanisms, and other parts that are—

(1) Essential to a controlled landing: and

(2) Not protected under § 27.861.

(b) Each auxiliary power unit and combustion heater, and any other combustion equipment to be used in flight, must be isolated from the rest of the rotorcraft by firewalls, shrouds, or equivalent means.

(c) In meeting paragraphs (a) and (b) of this section, account must be taken of the probable path of a fire as affected by the airflow in normal flight and in autorotation.

(d) Each firewall and shroud must be constructed so that no hazardous quantity of air, fluids, or flame can pass from any engine compartment to other parts of the rotorcraft.

(e) Each opening in the firewall or shroud must be sealed with close-fitting, fireproof grommets, bushings, or firewall fittings.

(f) Each firewall and shroud must be fireproof and protected against corrosion.

[Doc. No. 5074, 29 FR 15695, Nov. 24, 1964, as amended by Amdt. 27–2, 22 FR 964, Jan. 26, 1968]

§ 27.1193 Cowling and engine compartment covering.

(a) Each cowling and engine compartment covering must be constructed and supported so that it can resist the vibration, inertia, and air loads to which it may be subjected in operation.

(b) There must be means for rapid and complete drainage of each part of the cowling or engine compartment in the normal ground and flight attitudes.

(c) No drain may discharge where it might cause a fire hazard.

(d) Each cowling and engine compartment covering must be at least fire resistant.

(e) Each part of the cowling or engine compartment covering subject to high temperatures due to its nearness to exhaust system parts or exhaust gas impingement must be fireproof.

(f) A means of retaining each openable or readily removable panel, cowling, or engine or rotor drive system covering must be provided to preclude hazardous damage to rotors or critical control components in the event of structural or mechanical failure of the normal retention means, unless such failure is extremely improbable.

[Doc. No. 5074, 29 FR 15695, Nov. 24, 1964, as amended by Amdt. 27–23, 53 FR 34214, Sept. 2, 1988]

§27.1194 Other surfaces.

All surfaces aft of, and near, powerplant compartments, other than tail surfaces not subject to heat, flames, or sparks emanating from a powerplant compartment, must be at least fire resistant.

[Amdt. 27–2, 33 FR 964, Jan. 26, 1968]

§27.1195 Fire detector systems.

Each turbine engine powered rotorcraft must have approved quick-acting fire detectors in numbers and locations insuring prompt detection of fire in the engine compartment which cannot be readily observed in flight by the pilot in the cockpit.

[Amdt. 27–5, 36 FR 5493, Mar. 24, 1971]

Subpart F—Equipment

GENERAL

§27.1301 Function and installation.

Each item of installed equipment must—

(a) Be of a kind and design appropriate to its intended function;

(b) Be labeled as to its identification, function, or operating limitations, or any applicable combination of these factors;

(c) Be installed according to limitations specified for that equipment; and

(d) Function properly when installed.

§27.1303 Flight and navigation instruments.

The following are the required flight and navigation instruments:

(a) An airspeed indicator.

(b) An altimeter.

(c) A magnetic direction indicator.

§27.1305 Powerplant instruments.

The following are the required powerplant instruments:

(a) A carburetor air temperature indicator, for each engine having a preheater that can provide a heat rise in excess of 60 °F.

(b) A cylinder head temperature indicator, for each—

(1) Air cooled engine;

(2) Rotorcraft with cooling shutters; and

(3) Rotorcraft for which compliance with §27.1043 is shown in any condition other than the most critical flight condition with respect to cooling.

(c) A fuel pressure indicator, for each pump-fed engine.

(d) A fuel quantity indicator, for each fuel tank.

(e) A manifold pressure indicator, for each altitude engine.

(f) An oil temperature warning device to indicate when the temperature exceeds a safe value in each main rotor drive gearbox (including any gearboxes essential to rotor phasing) having an oil system independent of the engine oil system.

(g) An oil pressure warning device to indicate when the pressure falls below a safe value in each pressure-lubricated main rotor drive gearbox (including any gearboxes essential to rotor phasing) having an oil system independent of the engine oil system.

(h) An oil pressure indicator for each engine.

(i) An oil quantity indicator for each oil tank.

(j) An oil temperature indicator for each engine.

(k) At least one tachometer to indicate the r.p.m. of each engine and, as applicable—

(1) The r.p.m. of the single main rotor;

(2) The common r.p.m. of any main rotors whose speeds cannot vary appreciably with respect to each other; or

(3) The r.p.m. of each main rotor whose speed can vary appreciably with respect to that of another main rotor.

(l) A low fuel warning device for each fuel tank which feeds an engine. This device must—

(1) Provide a warning to the flightcrew when approximately 10 minutes of usable fuel remains in the tank; and

(2) Be independent of the normal fuel quantity indicating system.

(m) Means to indicate to the flightcrew the failure of any fuel pump installed to show compliance with § 27.955.

(n) A gas temperature indicator for each turbine engine.

(o) Means to enable the pilot to determine the torque of each turboshaft engine, if a torque limitation is established for that engine under § 27.1521(e).

(p) For each turbine engine, an indicator to indicate the functioning of the powerplant ice protection system.

(q) An indicator for the fuel filter required by § 27.997 to indicate the occurrence of contamination of the filter at the degree established by the applicant in compliance with § 27.955.

(r) For each turbine engine, a warning means for the oil strainer or filter required by § 27.1019, if it has no bypass, to warn the pilot of the occurrence of contamination of the strainer or filter before it reaches the capacity established in accordance with § 27.1019(a)(2).

(s) An indicator to indicate the functioning of any selectable or controllable heater used to prevent ice clogging of fuel system components.

(t) For rotorcraft for which a 30-second/2-minute OEI power rating is requested, a means must be provided to alert the pilot when the engine is at the 30-second and the 2-minute OEI power levels, when the event begins, and when the time interval expires.

(u) For each turbine engine utilizing 30-second/2-minute OEI power, a device or system must be provided for use by ground personnel which—

(1) Automatically records each usage and duration of power at the 30-second and 2-minute OEI levels;

(2) Permits retrieval of the recorded data;

(3) Can be reset only by ground maintenance personnel; and

(4) Has a means to verify proper operation of the system or device.

(v) Warning or caution devices to signal to the flight crew when ferromagnetic particles are detected by the chip detector required by § 27.1337(e).

[Doc. No. 5074, 29 FR 15695, Nov. 24, 1964, as amended by Amdt. 27–9, 39 FR 35462, Oct. 1, 1974; Amdt. 27–23, 53 FR 34214, Sept. 2, 1988; Amdt. 27–29, 59 FR 47767, Sept. 16, 1994; Amdt. 27–37, 64 FR 45095, Aug. 18, 1999; 64 FR 47563, Aug. 31, 1999]

§ 27.1307 Miscellaneous equipment.

The following is the required miscellaneous equipment:

(a) An approved seat for each occupant.

(b) An approved safety belt for each occupant.

(c) A master switch arrangement.

(d) An adequate source of electrical energy, where electrical energy is necessary for operation of the rotorcraft.

(e) Electrical protective devices.

§ 27.1309 Equipment, systems, and installations.

(a) The equipment, systems, and installations whose functioning is required by this subchapter must be designed and installed to ensure that they perform their intended functions under any foreseeable operating condition.

(b) The equipment, systems, and installations of a multiengine rotorcraft must be designed to prevent hazards to the rotorcraft in the event of a probable malfunction or failure.

(c) The equipment, systems, and installations of single-engine rotorcraft must be designed to minimize hazards to the rotorcraft in the event of a probable malfunction or failure.

(d) In showing compliance with paragraph (a), (b), or (c) of this section, the effects of lightning strikes on the rotorcraft must be considered in accordance with § 27.610.

[Doc. No. 5074, 29 FR 15695, Nov. 24, 1964, as amended by Amdt. 27–21, 49 FR 44435, Nov. 6, 1984]

INSTRUMENTS: INSTALLATION

§27.1321 Arrangement and visibility.

(a) Each flight, navigation, and powerplant instrument for use by any pilot must be easily visible to him.

(b) For each multiengine rotorcraft, identical powerplant instruments must be located so as to prevent confusion as to which engine each instrument relates.

(c) Instrument panel vibration may not damage, or impair the readability or accuracy of, any instrument.

(d) If a visual indicator is provided to indicate malfunction of an instrument, it must be effective under all probable cockpit lighting conditions.

(Secs. 313(a), 601, 603, 604, and 605 of the Federal Aviation Act of 1958 (49 U.S.C. 1354(a), 1421, 1423, 1424, and 1425); and sec. 6(c) of the Dept. of Transportation Act (49 U.S.C. 1655(c)))

[Doc. No. 5074, 29 FR 15695, Nov. 24, 1964; 29 FR 17885, Dec. 17, 1964, as amended by Amdt. 27-13, 42 FR 36971, July 18, 1977]

§27.1322 Warning, caution, and advisory lights.

If warning, caution or advisory lights are installed in the cockpit, they must, unless otherwise approved by the Administrator, be—

(a) Red, for warning lights (lights indicating a hazard which may require immediate corrective action);

(b) Amber, for caution lights (lights indicating the possible need for future corrective action);

(c) Green, for safe operation lights; and

(d) Any other color, including white, for lights not described in paragraphs (a) through (c) of this section, provided the color differs sufficiently from the colors prescribed in paragraphs (a) through (c) of this section to avoid possible confusion.

[Amdt. 27-11, 41 FR 55470, Dec. 20, 1976]

§27.1323 Airspeed indicating system.

(a) Each airspeed indicating instrument must be calibrated to indicate true airspeed (at sea level with a standard atmosphere) with a minimum practicable instrument calibration error when the corresponding pitot and static pressures are applied.

(b) The airspeed indicating system must be calibrated in flight at forward speeds of 20 knots and over.

(c) At each forward speed above 80 percent of the climbout speed, the airspeed indicator must indicate true airspeed, at sea level with a standard atmosphere, to within an allowable installation error of not more than the greater of—

(1) ±3 percent of the calibrated airspeed; or

(2) Five knots.

(Secs. 313(a), 601, 603, 604, and 605 of the Federal Aviation Act of 1958 (49 U.S.C. 1354(a), 1421, 1423, 1424, and 1425); and sec. 6(c) of the Dept. of Transportation Act (49 U.S.C. 1655(c)))

[Doc. No. 5074, 29 FR 15695, Nov. 24, 1964, as amended by Amdt. 27-13, 42 FR 36972, July 18, 1977]

§27.1325 Static pressure systems.

(a) Each instrument with static air case connections must be vented so that the influence of rotorcraft speed, the opening and closing of windows, airflow variation, and moisture or other foreign matter does not seriously affect its accuracy.

(b) Each static pressure port must be designed and located in such manner that the correlation between air pressure in the static pressure system and true ambient atmospheric static pressure is not altered when the rotorcraft encounters icing conditions. An anti-icing means or an alternate source of static pressure may be used in showing compliance with this requirement. If the reading of the altimeter, when on the alternate static pressure system, differs from the reading of the altimeter when on the primary static system by more than 50 feet, a correction card must be provided for the alternate static system.

(c) Except as provided in paragraph (d) of this section, if the static pressure system incorporates both a primary and an alternate static pressure source, the means for selecting one or the other source must be designed so that—

(1) When either source is selected, the other is blocked off; and

(2) Both sources cannot be blocked off simultaneously.

(d) For unpressurized rotorcraft, paragraph (c)(1) of this section does not apply if it can be demonstrated that the static pressure system calibration, when either static pressure source is selected is not changed by the other static pressure source being open or blocked.

(Secs. 313(a), 601, 603, 604, and 605 of the Federal Aviation Act of 1958 (49 U.S.C. 1354(a), 1421, 1423, 1424, and 1425); and sec. 6(c) of the Dept. of Transportation Act (49 U.S.C. 1655(c)))

[Doc. No. 5074, 29 FR 15695, Nov. 24, 1964, as amended by Amdt. 27–13, 42 FR 36972, July 18, 1977]

§ 27.1327 Magnetic direction indicator.

(a) Except as provided in paragraph (b) of this section—

(1) Each magnetic direction indicator must be installed so that its accuracy is not excessively affected by the rotorcraft's vibration or magnetic fields; and

(2) The compensated installation may not have a deviation, in level flight, greater than 10 degrees on any heading.

(b) A magnetic nonstabilized direction indicator may deviate more than 10 degrees due to the operation of electrically powered systems such as electrically heated windshields if either a magnetic stabilized direction indicator, which does not have a deviation in level flight greater than 10 degrees on any heading, or a gyroscopic direction indicator, is installed. Deviations of a magnetic nonstabilized direction indicator of more than 10 degrees must be placarded in accordance with § 27.1547(e).

(Secs. 313(a), 601, 603, 604, and 605 of the Federal Aviation Act of 1958 (49 U.S.C. 1354(a), 1421, 1423, 1424, and 1425); and sec. 6(c) of the Dept. of Transportation Act (49 U.S.C. 1655(c)))

[Amdt. 27–13, 42 FR 36972, July 18, 1977]

§ 27.1329 Automatic pilot system.

(a) Each automatic pilot system must be designed so that the automatic pilot can—

(1) Be sufficiently overpowered by one pilot to allow control of the rotorcraft; and

(2) Be readily and positively disengaged by each pilot to prevent it from interfering with control of the rotorcraft.

(b) Unless there is automatic synchronization, each system must have a means to readily indicate to the pilot the alignment of the actuating device in relation to the control system it operates.

(c) Each manually operated control for the system's operation must be readily accessible to the pilots.

(d) The system must be designed and adjusted so that, within the range of adjustment available to the pilot, it cannot produce hazardous loads on the rotorcraft or create hazardous deviations in the flight path under any flight condition appropriate to its use, either during normal operation or in the event of a malfunction, assuming that corrective action begins within a reasonable period of time.

(e) If the automatic pilot integrates signals from auxiliary controls or furnishes signals for operation of other equipment, there must be positive interlocks and sequencing of engagement to prevent improper operation.

(f) If the automatic pilot system can be coupled to airborne navigation equipment, means must be provided to indicate to the pilots the current mode of operation. Selector switch position is not acceptable as a means of indication.

[Amdt. 27–21, 49 FR 44435, Nov. 6, 1984, as amended by Amdt. 27–35, 63 FR 43285, Aug. 12, 1998]

§ 27.1335 Flight director systems.

If a flight director system is installed, means must be provided to indicate to the flight crew its current mode of operation. Selector switch position is not acceptable as a means of indication.

(Secs. 313(a), 601, 603, 604, and 605 of the Federal Aviation Act of 1958 (49 U.S.C. 1354(a), 1421, 1423, 1424, and 1425); and sec. 6(c) of the Dept. of Transportation Act (49 U.S.C. 1655(c)))

[Amdt. 27–13, 42 FR 36972, July 18, 1977]

§ 27.1337 Powerplant instruments.

(a) *Instruments and instrument lines.*

(1) Each powerplant instrument line must meet the requirements of §§ 27.961 and 27.993.

(2) Each line carrying flammable fluids under pressure must—

(i) Have restricting orifices or other safety devices at the source of pressure to prevent the escape of excessive fluid if the line fails; and

(ii) Be installed and located so that the escape of fluids would not create a hazard.

(3) Each powerplant instrument that utilizes flammable fluids must be installed and located so that the escape of fluid would not create a hazard.

(b) *Fuel quantity indicator.* Each fuel quantity indicator must be installed to clearly indicate to the flight crew the quantity of fuel in each tank in flight. In addition—

(1) Each fuel quantity indicator must be calibrated to read "zero" during level flight when the quantity of fuel remaining in the tank is equal to the unusable fuel supply determined under §27.959;

(2) When two or more tanks are closely interconnected by a gravity feed system and vented, and when it is impossible to feed from each tank separately, at least one fuel quantity indicator must be installed; and

(3) Each exposed sight gauge used as a fuel quantity indicator must be protected against damage.

(c) *Fuel flowmeter system.* If a fuel flowmeter system is installed, each metering component must have a means for bypassing the fuel supply if malfunction of that component severely restricts fuel flow.

(d) *Oil quantity indicator.* There must be means to indicate the quantity of oil in each tank—

(1) On the ground (including during the filling of each tank); and

(2) In flight, if there is an oil transfer system or reserve oil supply system.

(e) Rotor drive system transmissions and gearboxes utilizing ferromagnetic materials must be equipped with chip detectors designed to indicate the presence of ferromagnetic particles resulting from damage or excessive wear. Chip detectors must—

(1) Be designed to provide a signal to the device required by §27.1305(v) and be provided with a means to allow crewmembers to check, in flight, the function of each detector electrical circuit and signal.

(2) [Reserved]

(Secs. 313(a), 601, and 603, 72 Stat. 752, 775, 49 U.S.C. 1354(a), 1421, and 1423; sec. 6(c) 49 U.S.C. 1655(c))

[Doc. No. 5074, 29 FR 15695, Nov. 24, 1964, as amended by Amdt. 27–12, 42 FR 15046, Mar. 17, 1977; Amdt. 27–23, 53 FR 34214, Sept. 2, 1988; Amdt. 27–37, 64 FR 45095, Aug. 18, 1999]

ELECTRICAL SYSTEMS AND EQUIPMENT

§27.1351 General.

(a) *Electrical system capacity.* Electrical equipment must be adequate for its intended use. In addition—

(1) Electric power sources, their transmission cables, and their associated control and protective devices must be able to furnish the required power at the proper voltage to each load circuit essential for safe operation; and

(2) Compliance with paragraph (a)(1) of this section must be shown by an electrical load analysis, or by electrical measurements that take into account the electrical loads applied to the electrical system, in probable combinations and for probable durations.

(b) *Function.* For each electrical system, the following apply:

(1) Each system, when installed, must be—

(i) Free from hazards in itself, in its method of operation, and in its effects on other parts of the rotorcraft; and

(ii) Protected from fuel, oil, water, other detrimental substances, and mechanical damage.

(2) Electric power sources must function properly when connected in combination or independently.

(3) No failure or malfunction of any source may impair the ability of any remaining source to supply load circuits essential for safe operation.

(4) Each electric power source control must allow the independent operation of each source.

(c) *Generating system.* There must be at least one generator if the system supplies power to load circuits essential for safe operation. In addition—

(1) Each generator must be able to deliver its continuous rated power;

(2) Generator voltage control equipment must be able to dependably regulate each generator output within rated limits;

(3) Each generator must have a reverse current cutout designed to disconnect the generator from the battery and from the other generators when enough reverse current exists to damage that generator; and

(4) Each generator must have an overvoltage control designed and installed to prevent damage to the electrical system, or to equipment supplied by the electrical system, that could result if that generator were to develop an overvoltage condition.

(d) *Instruments.* There must be means to indicate to appropriate crewmembers the electric power system quantities essential for safe operation of the system. In addition—

(1) For direct current systems, an ammeter that can be switched into each generator feeder may be used; and

(2) If there is only one generator, the ammeter may be in the battery feeder.

(e) *External power.* If provisions are made for connecting external power to the rotorcraft, and that external power can be electrically connected to equipment other than that used for engine starting, means must be provided to ensure that no external power supply having a reverse polarity, or a reverse phase sequence, can supply power to the rotorcraft's electrical system.

(Secs. 313(a), 601, 603, 604, and 605 of the Federal Aviation Act of 1958 (49 U.S.C. 1354(a), 1421, 1423, 1424, and 1425); and sec. 6(c) of the Dept. of Transportation Act (49 U.S.C. 1655(c)))

[Doc. No. 5074, 29 FR 15695, Nov. 24, 1964, as amended by Amdt. 27–11, 41 FR 55470, Dec. 20, 1976; Amdt. 27–13, 42 FR 36972, July 18, 1977]

§ 27.1353 Storage battery design and installation.

(a) Each storage battery must be designed and installed as prescribed in this section.

(b) Safe cell temperatures and pressures must be maintained during any probable charging and discharging condition. No uncontrolled increase in cell temperature may result when the battery is recharged (after previous complete discharge)—

(1) At maximum regulated voltage or power;

(2) During a flight of maximum duration; and

(3) Under the most adverse cooling condition likely to occur in service.

(c) Compliance with paragraph (b) of this section must be shown by test unless experience with similar batteries and installations has shown that maintaining safe cell temperatures and pressures presents no problem.

(d) No explosive or toxic gases emitted by any battery in normal operation, or as the result of any probable malfunction in the charging system or battery installation, may accumulate in hazardous quantities within the rotorcraft.

(e) No corrosive fluids or gases that may escape from the battery may damage surrounding structures or adjacent essential equipment.

(f) Each nickel cadmium battery installation capable of being used to start an engine or auxiliary power unit must have provisions to prevent any hazardous effect on structure or essential systems that may be caused by the maximum amount of heat the battery can generate during a short circuit of the battery or of its individual cells.

(g) Nickel cadmium battery installations capable of being used to start an engine or auxiliary power unit must have—

(1) A system to control the charging rate of the battery automatically so as to prevent battery overheating;

(2) A battery temperature sensing and over-temperature warning system with a means for disconnecting the battery from its charging source in the event of an over-temperature condition; or

(3) A battery failure sensing and warning system with a means for disconnecting the battery from its charging source in the event of battery failure.

(Secs. 313(a), 601, 603, 604, and 605 of the Federal Aviation Act of 1958 (49 U.S.C. 1354(a), 1421, 1423, 1424, and 1425); and sec. 6(c) of the Dept. of Transportation Act (49 U.S.C. 1655(c)))

[Doc. No. 5074, 29 FR 15695, Nov. 24, 1964, as amended by Amdt. 27–13, 42 FR 36972, July 18, 1977; Amdt. 27–14, 43 FR 2325, Jan. 16, 1978]

§ 27.1357 Circuit protective devices.

(a) Protective devices, such as fuses or circuit breakers, must be installed in each electrical circuit other than—

(1) The main circuits of starter motors; and

(2) Circuits in which no hazard is presented by their omission.

(b) A protective device for a circuit essential to flight safety may not be used to protect any other circuit.

(c) Each resettable circuit protective device ("trip free" device in which the tripping mechanism cannot be overridden by the operating control) must be designed so that—

(1) A manual operation is required to restore service after trippling; and

(2) If an overload or circuit fault exists, the device will open the circuit regardless of the position of the operating control.

(d) If the ability to reset a circuit breaker or replace a fuse is essential to safety in flight, that circuit breaker or fuse must be located and identified so that it can be readily reset or replaced in flight.

(e) If fuses are used, there must be one spare of each rating, or 50 percent spare fuses of each rating, whichever is greater.

(Secs. 313(a), 601, 603, 604, and 605 of the Federal Aviation Act of 1958 (49 U.S.C. 1354(a), 1421, 1423, 1424, and 1425); and sec. 6(c) of the Dept. of Transportation Act (49 U.S.C. 1655(c)))

[Doc. No. 5074, 29 FR 15695, Nov. 24, 1964; 29 FR 17885, Dec. 17, 1964, as amended by Amdt. 27–13, 42 FR 36972, July 18, 1977]

§ 27.1361 Master switch.

(a) There must be a master switch arrangement to allow ready disconnection of each electric power source from the main bus. The point of disconnection must be adjacent to the sources controlled by the switch.

(b) Load circuits may be connected so that they remain energized after the switch is opened, if they are protected by circuit protective devices, rated at five amperes or less, adjacent to the electric power source.

(c) The master switch or its controls must be installed so that the switch is easily discernible and accessible to a crewmember in flight.

§ 27.1365 Electric cables.

(a) Each electric connecting cable must be of adequate capacity.

(b) Each cable that would overheat in the event of circuit overload or fault must be at least flame resistant and may not emit dangerous quantities of toxic fumes.

(c) Insulation on electrical wire and cable installed in the rotorcraft must be self-extinguishing when tested in accordance with Appendix F, Part I(a)(3), of part 25 of this chapter.

[Doc. No. 5074, 29 FR 15695, Nov. 24, 1964, as amended by Amdt. 27–35, 63 FR 43285, Aug. 12, 1998]

§ 27.1367 Switches.

Each switch must be—

(a) Able to carry its rated current;

(b) Accessible to the crew; and

(c) Labeled as to operation and the circuit controlled.

LIGHTS

§ 27.1381 Instrument lights.

The instrument lights must—

(a) Make each instrument, switch, and other devices for which they are provided easily readable; and

(b) Be installed so that—

(1) Their direct rays are shielded from the pilot's eyes; and

(2) No objectionable reflections are visible to the pilot.

§ 27.1383 Landing lights.

(a) Each required landing or hovering light must be approved.

(b) Each landing light must be installed so that—

(1) No objectionable glare is visible to the pilot;

(2) The pilot is not adversely affected by halation; and

(3) It provides enough light for night operation, including hovering and landing.

(c) At least one separate switch must be provided, as applicable—

(1) For each separately installed landing light; and

(2) For each group of landing lights installed at a common location.

§ 27.1385 Position light system installation.

(a) *General.* Each part of each position light system must meet the applicable requirements of this section, and each system as a whole must meet the requirements of §§ 27.1387 through 27.1397.

(b) *Forward position lights.* Forward position lights must consist of a red and a green light spaced laterally as far apart as practicable and installed forward on the rotorcraft so that, with the rotorcraft in the normal flying position, the red light is on the left side and the green light is on the right side. Each light must be approved.

(c) *Rear position light.* The rear position light must be a white light mounted as far aft as practicable, and must be approved.

(d) *Circuit.* The two forward position lights and the rear position light must make a single circuit.

(e) *Light covers and color filters.* Each light cover or color filter must be at least flame resistant and may not change color or shape or lose any appreciable light transmission during normal use.

§ 27.1387 Position light system dihedral angles.

(a) Except as provided in paragraph (e) of this section, each forward and rear position light must, as installed, show unbroken light within the dihedral angles described in this section.

(b) Dihedral angle L (left) is formed by two intersecting vertical planes, the first parallel to the longitudinal axis of the rotorcraft, and the other at 110 degrees to the left of the first, as viewed when looking forward along the longitudinal axis.

(c) Dihedral angle R (right) is formed by two intersecting vertical planes, the first parallel to the longitudinal axis of the rotorcraft, and the other at 110 degrees to the right of the first, as viewed when looking forward along the longitudinal axis.

(d) Dihedral angle A (aft) is formed by two intersecting vertical planes making angles of 70 degrees to the right and to the left, respectively, to a vertical plane passing through the longitudinal axis, as viewed when looking aft along the longitudinal axis.

(e) If the rear position light, when mounted as far aft as practicable in accordance with § 25.1385(c), cannot show unbroken light within dihedral angle A (as defined in paragraph (d) of this section), a solid angle or angles of obstructed visibility totaling not more than 0.04 steradians is allowable within that dihedral angle, if such solid angle is within a cone whose apex is at the rear position light and whose elements make an angle of 30° with a vertical line passing through the rear position light.

(49 U.S.C. 1655(c))

[Doc. No. 5074, 29 FR 15695, Nov. 24, 1964, as amended by Amdt. 27-7, 36 FR 21278, Nov. 5, 1971]

§ 27.1389 Position light distribution and intensities.

(a) *General.* the intensities prescribed in this section must be provided by new equipment with light covers and color filters in place. Intensities must be determined with the light source operating at a steady value equal to the average luminous output of the source at the normal operating voltage of the rotorcraft. The light distribution and intensity of each position light must meet the requirements of paragraph (b) of this section.

(b) *Forward and rear position lights.* The light distribution and intensities of forward and rear position lights must be expressed in terms of minimum intensities in the horizontal plane, minimum intensities in any vertical plane, and maximum intensities in overlapping beams, within dihedral angles L, R, and A, and must meet the following requirements:

(1) *Intensities in the horizontal plane.* Each intensity in the horizontal plane (the plane containing the longitudinal axis of the rotorcraft and perpendicular to the plane of symmetry of the rotorcraft) must equal or exceed the values in § 27.1391.

(2) *Intensities in any vertical plane.* Each intensity in any vertical plane (the plane perpendicular to the horizontal plane) must equal or exceed the appropriate value in § 27.1393, where I is the minimum intensity prescribed in § 27.1391 for the corresponding angles in the horizontal plane.

(3) *Intensities in overlaps between adjacent signals.* No intensity in any overlap between adjacent signals may exceed the values in § 27.1395, except that higher intensities in overlaps may be used with main beam intensities substantially greater than the minima

specified in §§27.1391 and 27.1393, if the overlap intensities in relation to the main beam intensities do not adversely affect signal clarity. When the peak intensity of the forward position lights is greater than 100 candles, the maximum overlap intensities between them may exceed the values in §27.1395 if the overlap intensity in Area A is not more than 10 percent of peak position light intensity and the overlap intensity in Area B is not more than 2.5 percent of peak position light intensity.

§27.1391 Minimum intensities in the horizontal plane of forward and rear position lights.

Each position light intensity must equal or exceed the applicable values in the following table:

Dihedral angle (light included)	Angle from right or left of longitudinal axis, measured from dead ahead	Intensity (candles)
L and R (forward red and green).	10° to 10°	40
	10° to 20°	30
	20° to 110°	5
A (rear white)	110° to 180°	20

§27.1393 Minimum intensities in any vertical plane of forward and rear position lights.

Each position light intensity must equal or exceed the applicable values in the following table:

Angle above or below the horizontal plane	Intensity, I
0°	1.00
0° to 5°	0.90
5° to 10°	0.80
10° to 15°	0.70
15° to 20°	0.50
20° to 30°	0.30
30° to 40°	0.10
40° to 90°	0.05

§27.1395 Maximum intensities in overlapping beams of forward and rear position lights.

No position light intensity may exceed the applicable values in the following table, except as provided in §27.1389(b)(3).

Overlaps	Maximum Intensity	
	Area A (candles)	Area B (candles)
Green in dihedral angle L	10	1
Red in dihedral angle R	10	1
Green in dihedral angle A	5	1
Red in dihedral angle A	5	1
Rear white in dihedral angle L	5	1

Overlaps	Maximum Intensity	
	Area A (candles)	Area B (candles)
Rear white in dihedral angle R	5	1

Where—

(a) Area A includes all directions in the adjacent dihedral angle that pass through the light source and intersect the common boundary plane at more than 10 degrees but less than 20 degrees, and

(b) Area B includes all directions in the adjacent dihedral angle that pass through the light source and intersect the common boundary plane at more than 20 degrees.

§27.1397 Color specifications.

Each position light color must have the applicable International Commission on Illumination chromaticity coordinates as follows:

(a) *Aviation red*—

y is not greater than 0.335; and
z is not greater than 0.002.

(b) *Aviation green*—

x is not greater than $0.440 - 0.320y$;
x is not greater than $y - 0.170$; and
y is not less than $0.390 - 0.170x$.

(c) *Aviation white*—

x is not less than 0.300 and not greater than 0.540;

y is not less than $x - 0.040$'' or $y_c - 0.010$, whichever is the smaller; and

y is not greater than $x + 0.020$ nor $0.636 - 0.400x$;

Where y_c is the y coordinate of the Planckian radiator for the value of x considered.

[Doc. No. 5074, 29 FR 15695, Nov. 24, 1964, as amended by Amdt. 27–6, 36 FR 12972, July 10, 1971]

§27.1399 Riding light.

(a) Each riding light required for water operation must be installed so that it can—

(1) Show a white light for at least two nautical miles at night under clear atmospheric conditions; and

(2) Show a maximum practicable unbroken light with the rotorcraft on the water.

(b) Externally hung lights may be used.

[Doc. No. 5074, 29 FR 15695, Nov. 24, 1964, as amended by Amdt. 27–2, 33 FR 964, Jan. 26, 1968]

§ 27.1401 Anticollision light system.

(a) *General.* If certification for night operation is requested, the rotorcraft must have an anticollision light system that—

(1) Consists of one or more approved anticollision lights located so that their emitted light will not impair the crew's vision or detract from the conspicuity of the position lights; and

(2) Meets the requirements of paragraphs (b) through (f) of this section.

(b) *Field of coverage.* The system must consist of enough lights to illuminate the vital areas around the rotorcraft, considering the physical configuration and flight characteristics of the rotorcraft. The field of coverage must extend in each direction within at least 30 degrees below the horizontal plane of the rotorcraft, except that there may be solid angles of obstructed visibility totaling not more than 0.5 steradians.

(c) *Flashing characteristics.* The arrangement of the system, that is, the number of light sources, beam width, speed of rotation, and other characteristics, must give an effective flash frequency of not less than 40, nor more than 100, cycles per minute. The effective flash frequency is the frequency at which the rotorcraft's complete anticollision light system is observed from a distance, and applies to each sector of light including any overlaps that exist when the system consists of more than one light source. In overlaps, flash frequencies may exceed 100, but not 180, cycles per minute.

(d) *Color.* Each anticollision light must be aviation red and must meet the applicable requirements of § 27.1397.

(e) *Light intensity.* The minimum light intensities in any vertical plane, measured with the red filter (if used) and expressed in terms of "effective" intensities, must meet the requirements of paragraph (f) of this section.

The following relation must be assumed:

$$I_e = \frac{\int_{t_1}^{t_2} I(t)\,dt}{0.2 + \left(t_2 - t_1\right)}$$

where:

I_e=effective intensity (candles).
$I(t)$=instantaneous intensity as a function of time.
$t_2 - t_1$=flash time interval (seconds).
Normally, the maximum value of effective intensity is obtained when t_2 and t_1 are chosen so that the effective intensity is equal to the instantaneous intensity at t_2 and t_1.

(f) *Minimum effective intensities for anticollision light.* Each anticollision light effective intensity must equal or exceed the applicable values in the following table:

Angle above or below the horizontal plane	Effective intensity (candles)
0° to 5°	150
5° to 10°	90
10° to 20°	30
20° to 30°	15

[Doc. No. 5074, 29 FR 15695, Nov. 24, 1964, as amended by Amdt. 27–6, 36 FR 12972, July 10, 1971; Amdt. 27–10, 41 FR 5290, Feb. 5, 1976]

SAFETY EQUIPMENT

§ 27.1411 General.

(a) Required safety equipment to be used by the crew in an emergency, such as flares and automatic liferaft releases, must be readily accessible.

(b) Stowage provisions for required safety equipment must be furnished and must—

(1) Be arranged so that the equipment is directly accessible and its location is obvious; and

(2) Protect the safety equipment from damage caused by being subjected to the inertia loads specified in § 27.561.

[Doc. No. 5074, 29 FR 15695, Nov. 24, 1964, as amended by Amdt. 27–11, 41 FR 55470, Dec. 20, 1976]

§27.1413 Safety belts.

Each safety belt must be equipped with a metal to metal latching device.

(Secs. 313, 314, and 601 through 610 of the Federal Aviation Act of 1958 (49 U.S.C. 1354, 1355, and 1421 through 1430) and sec. 6(c), Dept. of Transportation Act (49 U.S.C. 1655(c)))

[Doc. No. 5074, 29 FR 15695, Nov. 24, 1964, as amended by Amdt. 27–15, 43 FR 46233, Oct. 5, 1978; Amdt. 27–21, 49 FR 44435, Nov. 6, 1984]

§27.1415 Ditching equipment.

(a) Emergency flotation and signaling equipment required by any operating rule in this chapter must meet the requirements of this section.

(b) Each raft and each life preserver must be approved and must be installed so that it is readily available to the crew and passengers. The storage provisions for life preservers must accommodate one life preserver for each occupant for which certification for ditching is requested.

(c) Each raft released automatically or by the pilot must be attached to the rotorcraft by a line to keep it alongside the rotorcraft. This line must be weak enough to break before submerging the empty raft to which it is attached.

(d) Each signaling device must be free from hazard in its operation and must be installed in an accessible location.

[Doc. No. 5074, 29 FR 15695, Nov. 24, 1964, as amended by Amdt. 27–11, 41 FR 55470, Dec. 20, 1976]

§27.1419 Ice protection.

(a) To obtain certification for flight into icing conditions, compliance with this section must be shown.

(b) It must be demonstrated that the rotorcraft can be safely operated in the continuous maximum and intermittent maximum icing conditions determined under appendix C of Part 29 of this chapter within the rotorcraft altitude envelope. An analysis must be performed to establish, on the basis of the rotorcraft's operational needs, the adequacy of the ice protection system for the various components of the rotorcraft.

(c) In addition to the analysis and physical evaluation prescribed in paragraph (b) of this section, the effectiveness of the ice protection system and its components must be shown by flight tests of the rotorcraft or its components in measured natural atmospheric icing conditions and by one or more of the following tests as found necessary to determine the adequacy of the ice protection system:

(1) Laboratory dry air or simulated icing tests, or a combination of both, of the components or models of the components.

(2) Flight dry air tests of the ice protection system as a whole, or its individual components.

(3) Flight tests of the rotorcraft or its components in measured simulated icing conditions.

(d) The ice protection provisions of this section are considered to be applicable primarily to the airframe. Powerplant installation requirements are contained in Subpart E of this part.

(e) A means must be indentified or provided for determining the formation of ice on critical parts of the rotorcraft. Unless otherwise restricted, the means must be available for nighttime as well as daytime operation. The rotorcraft flight manual must describe the means of determining ice formation and must contain information necessary for safe operation of the rotorcraft in icing conditions.

[Amdt. 27–19, 48 FR 4389, Jan. 31, 1983]

§27.1435 Hydraulic systems.

(a) *Design.* Each hydraulic system and its elements must withstand, without yielding, any structural loads expected in addition to hydraulic loads.

(b) *Tests.* Each system must be substantiated by proof pressure tests. When proof tested, no part of any system may fail, malfunction, or experience a permanent set. The proof load of each system must be at least 1.5 times the maximum operating pressure of that system.

(c) *Accumulators.* No hydraulic accumulator or pressurized reservoir may be installed on the engine side of any firewall unless it is an integral part of an engine.

§27.1457 Cockpit voice recorders.

(a) Each cockpit voice recorder required by the operating rules of this chapter must be approved, and must be installed so that it will record the following:

(1) Voice communications transmitted from or received in the rotorcraft by radio.

(2) Voice communications of flight crewmembers on the flight deck.

(3) Voice communications of flight crewmembers on the flight deck, using the rotorcraft's interphone system.

(4) Voice or audio signals identifying navigation or approach aids introduced into a headset or speaker.

(5) Voice communications of flight crewmembers using the passenger loudspeaker system, if there is such a system, and if the fourth channel is available in accordance with the requirements of paragraph (c)(4)(ii) of this section.

(b) The recording requirements of paragraph (a)(2) of this section may be met:

(1) By installing a cockpit-mounted area microphone located in the best position for recording voice communications originating at the first and second pilot stations and voice communications of other crewmembers on the flight deck when directed to those stations; or

(2) By installing a continually energized or voice-actuated lip microphone at the first and second pilot stations.

The microphone specified in this paragraph must be so located and, if necessary, the preamplifiers and filters of the recorder must be adjusted or supplemented so that the recorded communications are intelligible when recorded under flight cockpit noise conditions and played back. The level of intelligibility must be approved by the Administrator. Repeated aural or visual playback of the record may be used in evaluating intelligibility.

(c) Each cockpit voice recorder must be installed so that the part of the communication or audio signals specified in paragraph (a) of this section obtained from each of the following sources is recorded on a separate channel:

(1) For the first channel, from each microphone, headset, or speaker used at the first pilot station.

(2) For the second channel, from each microphone, headset, or speaker used at the second pilot station.

(3) For the third channel, from the cockpit-mounted area microphone, or the continually energized or voice-actuated lip microphone at the first and second pilot stations.

(4) For the fourth channel, from:

(i) Each microphone, headset, or speaker used at the stations for the third and fourth crewmembers; or

(ii) If the stations specified in paragraph (c)(4)(i) of this section are not required or if the signal at such a station is picked up by another channel, each microphone on the flight deck that is used with the passenger loudspeaker system if its signals are not picked up by another channel.

(iii) Each microphone on the flight deck that is used with the rotorcraft's loudspeaker system if its signals are not picked up by another channel.

(d) Each cockpit voice recorder must be installed so that:

(1) It receives its electric power from the bus that provides the maximum reliability for operation of the cockpit voice recorder without jeopardizing service to essential or emergency loads;

(2) There is an automatic means to simultaneously stop the recorder and prevent each erasure feature from functioning, within 10 minutes after crash impact; and

(3) There is an aural or visual means for preflight checking of the recorder for proper operation.

(e) The record container must be located and mounted to minimize the probability of rupture of the container as a result of crash impact and consequent heat damage to the record from fire.

(f) If the cockpit voice recorder has a bulk erasure device, the installation must be designed to minimize the probability of inadvertent operation and actuation of the device during crash impact.

(g) Each recorder container must be either bright orange or bright yellow.

[Amdt. 27–22, 53 FR 26144, July 11, 1988]

§ 27.1459 Flight recorders.

(a) Each flight recorder required by the operating rules of Subchapter G of this chapter must be installed so that:

(1) It is supplied with airspeed, altitude, and directional data obtained

from sources that meet the accuracy requirements of §§27.1323, 27.1325, and 27.1327 of this part, as applicable;

(2) The vertical acceleration sensor is rigidly attached, and located longitudinally within the approved center of gravity limits of the rotorcraft;

(3) It receives its electrical power from the bus that provides the maximum reliability for operation of the flight recorder without jeopardizing service to essential or emergency loads;

(4) There is an aural or visual means for preflight checking of the recorder for proper recording of data in the storage medium;

(5) Except for recorders powered solely by the engine-driven electrical generator system, there is an automatic means to simultaneously stop a recorder that has a data erasure feature and prevent each erasure feature from functioning, within 10 minutes after any crash impact; and

(b) Each nonejectable recorder container must be located and mounted so as to minimize the probability of container rupture resulting from crash impact and subsequent damage to the record from fire.

(c) A correlation must be established between the flight recorder readings of airspeed, altitude, and heading and the corresponding readings (taking into account correction factors) of the first pilot's instruments. This correlation must cover the airspeed range over which the aircraft is to be operated, the range of altitude to which the aircraft is limited, and 360 degrees of heading. Correlation may be established on the ground as appropriate.

(d) Each recorder container must:

(1) Be either bright orange or bright yellow;

(2) Have a reflective tape affixed to its external surface to facilitate its location under water; and

(3) Have an underwater locating device, when required by the operating rules of this chapter, on or adjacent to the container which is secured in such a manner that they are not likely to be separated during crash impact.

[Amdt. 27–22, 53 FR 26144, July 11, 1988]

§27.1461 Equipment containing high energy rotors.

(a) Equipment containing high energy rotors must meet paragraph (b), (c), or (d) of this section.

(b) High energy rotors contained in equipment must be able to withstand damage caused by malfunctions, vibration, abnormal speeds, and abnormal temperatures. In addition—

(1) Auxiliary rotor cases must be able to contain damage caused by the failure of high energy rotor blades; and

(2) Equipment control devices, systems, and instrumentation must reasonably ensure that no operating limitations affecting the integrity of high energy rotors will be exceeded in service.

(c) It must be shown by test that equipment containing high energy rotors can contain any failure of a high energy rotor that occurs at the highest speed obtainable with the normal speed control devices inoperative.

(d) Equipment containing high energy rotors must be located where rotor failure will neither endanger the occupants nor adversely affect continued safe flight.

[Amdt. 27–2, 33 FR 964, Jan. 26, 1968]

Subpart G—Operating Limitations and Information

§27.1501 General.

(a) Each operating limitation specified in §§27.1503 through 27.1525 and other limitations and information necessary for safe operation must be established.

(b) The operating limitations and other information necessary for safe operation must be made available to the crewmembers as prescribed in §§27.1541 through 27.1589.

(Secs. 313(a), 601, 603, 604, and 605 of the Federal Aviation Act of 1958 (49 U.S.C. 1354(a), 1421, 1423, 1424, and 1425); and sec. 6(c) of the Dept. of Transportation Act (49 U.S.C. 1655(c)))

[Amdt. 27–14, 43 FR 2325, Jan. 16, 1978]

OPERATING LIMITATIONS

§27.1503 Airspeed limitations: general.

(a) An operating speed range must be established.

(b) When airspeed limitations are a function of weight, weight distribution, altitude, rotor speed, power, or other factors, airspeed limitations corresponding with the critical combinations of these factors must be established.

§ 27.1505 Never-exceed speed.

(a) The never-exceed speed, V_{NE}, must be established so that it is—

(1) Not less than 40 knots (CAS); and

(2) Not more than the lesser of—

(i) 0.9 times the maximum forward speeds established under § 27.309;

(ii) 0.9 times the maximum speed shown under §§ 27.251 and 27.629; or

(iii) 0.9 times the maximum speed substantiated for advancing blade tip mach number effects.

(b) V_{NE} may vary with altitude, r.p.m., temperature, and weight, if—

(1) No more than two of these variables (or no more than two instruments integrating more than one of these variables) are used at one time; and

(2) The ranges of these variables (or of the indications on instruments integrating more than one of these variables) are large enough to allow an operationally practical and safe variation of V_{NE}.

(c) For helicopters, a stabilized power-off V_{NE} denoted as V_{NE} (power-off) may be established at a speed less than V_{NE} established pursuant to paragraph (a) of this section, if the following conditions are met:

(1) V_{NE} (power-off) is not less than a speed midway between the power-on V_{NE} and the speed used in meeting the requirements of—

(i) § 27.65(b) for single engine helicopters; and

(ii) § 27.67 for multiengine helicopters.

(2) V_{NE} (power-off) is—

(i) A constant airspeed;

(ii) A constant amount less than power-on V_{NE}; or

(iii) A constant airspeed for a portion of the altitude range for which certification is requested, and a constant

amount less than power-on V_{NE} for the remainder of the altitude range.

(Secs. 313(a), 601, 603, 604, and 605 of the Federal Aviation Act of 1958 (49 U.S.C. 1354(a), 1421, 1423, 1424, and 1425); and sec. 6(c) of the Dept. of Transportation Act (49 U.S.C. 1655(c)))

[Amdt. 27–2, 33 FR 964, Jan. 26, 1968, and Amdt. 27–14, 43 FR 2325, Jan. 16, 1978; Amdt. 27–21, 49 FR 44435, Nov. 6, 1984]

§ 27.1509 Rotor speed.

(a) Maximum power-off (autorotation). The maximum power-off rotor speed must be established so that it does not exceed 95 percent of the lesser of—

(1) The maximum design r.p.m. determined under § 27.309(b); and

(2) The maximum r.p.m. shown during the type tests.

(b) Minimum power off. The minimum power-off rotor speed must be established so that it is not less than 105 percent of the greater of—

(1) The minimum shown during the type tests; and

(2) The minimum determined by design substantiation.

(c) Minimum power on. The minimum power-on rotor speed must be established so that it is—

(1) Not less than the greater of—

(i) The minimum shown during the type tests; and

(ii) The minimum determined by design substantiation; and

(2) Not more than a value determined under § 27.33(a)(1) and (b)(1).

§ 27.1519 Weight and center of gravity.

The weight and center of gravity limitations determined under §§ 27.25 and 27.27, respectively, must be established as operating limitations.

[Amdt. 27–2, 33 FR 965, Jan. 26, 1968, as amended by Amdt. 27–21, 49 FR 44435, Nov. 6, 1984]

§ 27.1521 Powerplant limitations.

(a) General. The powerplant limitations prescribed in this section must be established so that they do not exceed the corresponding limits for which the engines are type certificated.

(b) Takeoff operation. The powerplant takeoff operation must be limited by—

(1) The maximum rotational speed, which may not be greater than—

(i) The maximum value determined by the rotor design; or

(ii) The maximum value shown during the type tests;

(2) The maximum allowable manifold pressure (for reciprocating engines);

(3) The time limit for the use of the power corresponding to the limitations established in paragraphs (b)(1) and (2) of this section;

(4) If the time limit in paragraph (b)(3) of this section exceeds two minutes, the maximum allowable cylinder head, coolant outlet, or oil temperatures;

(5) The gas temperature limits for turbine engines over the range of operating and atmospheric conditions for which certification is requested.

(c) *Continuous operation.* The continuous operation must be limited by—

(1) The maximum rotational speed which may not be greater than—

(i) The maximum value determined by the rotor design; or

(ii) The maximum value shown during the type tests;

(2) The minimum rotational speed shown under the rotor speed requirements in §27.1509(c); and

(3) The gas temperature limits for turbine engines over the range of operating and atmospheric conditions for which certification is requested.

(d) *Fuel grade or designation.* The minimum fuel grade (for reciprocating engines), or fuel designation (for turbine engines), must be established so that it is not less than that required for the operation of the engines within the limitations in paragraphs (b) and (c) of this section.

(e) *Turboshaft engine torque.* For rotorcraft with main rotors driven by turboshaft engines, and that do not have a torque limiting device in the transmission system, the following apply:

(1) A limit engine torque must be established if the maximum torque that the engine can exert is greater than—

(i) The torque that the rotor drive system is designed to transmit; or

(ii) The torque that the main rotor assembly is designed to withstand in showing compliance with §27.547(e).

(2) The limit engine torque established under paragraph (e)(1) of this section may not exceed either torque specified in paragraph (e)(1)(i) or (ii) of this section.

(f) *Ambient temperature.* For turbine engines, ambient temperature limitations (including limitations for winterization installations, if applicable) must be established as the maximum ambient atmospheric temperature at which compliance with the cooling provisions of §§27.1041 through 27.1045 is shown.

(g) *Two and one-half-minute OEI power operation.* Unless otherwise authorized, the use of 2½-minute OEI power must be limited to engine failure operation of multiengine, turbine-powered rotorcraft for not longer than 2½ minutes after failure of an engine. The use of 2½-minute OEI power must also be limited by—

(1) The maximum rotational speed, which may not be greater than—

(i) The maximum value determined by the rotor design; or

(ii) The maximum demonstrated during the type tests;

(2) The maximum allowable gas temperature; and

(3) The maximum allowable torque.

(h) *Thirty-minute OEI power operation.* Unless otherwise authorized, the use of 30-minute OEI power must be limited to multiengine, turbine-powered rotorcraft for not longer than 30 minutes after failure of an engine. The use of 30-minute OEI power must also be limited by—

(1) The maximum rotational speed, which may not be greater than—

(i) The maximum value determined by the rotor design; or

(ii) The maximum value demonstrated during the type tests;

(2) The maximum allowable gas temperature; and

(3) The maximum allowable torque.

(i) *Continuous OEI power operation.* Unless otherwise authorized, the use of continuous OEI power must be limited to multiengine, turbine-powered rotorcraft for continued flight after failure of an engine. The use of continuous OEI power must also be limited by—

(1) The maximum rotational speed, which may not be greater than—

(i) The maximum value determined by the rotor design; or

(ii) The maximum value demonstrated during the type tests;

(2) The maximum allowable gas temperature; and

(3) The maximum allowable torque.

(j) *Rated 30-second OEI power operation.* Rated 30-second OEI power is permitted only on multiengine, turbine-powered rotorcraft, also certificated for the use of rated 2-minute OEI power, and can only be used for continued operation of the remaining engine(s) after a failure or precautionary shutdown of an engine. It must be shown that following application of 30-second OEI power, any damage will be readily detectable by the applicable inspections and other related procedures furnished in accordance with Section A27.4 of appendix A of this part and Section A33.4 of appendix A of part 33. The use of 30-second OEI power must be limited to not more than 30 seconds for any period in which that power is used, and by—

(1) The maximum rotational speed, which may not be greater than—

(i) The maximum value determined by the rotor design; or

(ii) The maximum value demonstrated during the type tests;

(2) The maximum allowable gas temperature; and

(3) The maximum allowable torque.

(k) *Rated 2-minute OEI power operation.* Rated 2-minute OEI power is permitted only on multiengine, turbine-powered rotorcraft, also certificated for the use of rated 30-second OEI power, and can only be used for continued operation of the remaining engine(s) after a failure or precautionary shutdown of an engine. It must be shown that following application of 2-minute OEI power, any damage will be readily detectable by the applicable inspections and other related procedures furnished in accordance with Section A27.4 of appendix A of this part and Section A33.4 of appendix A of part 33. The use of 2-minute OEI power must be limited to not more than 2 minutes for any period in which that power is used, and by—

(1) The maximum rotational speed, which may not be greater than—

(i) The maximum value determined by the rotor design; or

(ii) The maximum value demonstrated during the type tests;

(2) The maximum allowable gas temperature; and

(3) The maximum allowable torque.

(Secs. 313(a), 601, 603, 604, and 605 of the Federal Aviation Act of 1958 (49 U.S.C. 1354(a), 1421, 1423, 1424, and 1425); and sec. 6(c) of the Dept. of Transportation Act (49 U.S.C. 1655(c)))

[Doc. No. 5074, 29 FR 15695, Nov. 24, 1964, as amended by Amdt. 27–14, 43 FR 2325, Jan. 16, 1978; Amdt. 27–23, 53 FR 34214, Sept. 2, 1988; Amdt. 27–29, 59 FR 47767, Sept. 16, 1994]

§ 27.1523   Minimum flight crew.

The minimum flight crew must be established so that it is sufficient for safe operation, considering—

(a) The workload on individual crewmembers;

(b) The accessibility and ease of operation of necessary controls by the appropriate crewmember; and

(c) The kinds of operation authorized under § 27.1525.

§ 27.1525   Kinds of operations.

The kinds of operations (such as VFR, IFR, day, night, or icing) for which the rotorcraft is approved are established by demonstrated compliance with the applicable certification requirements and by the installed equipment.

[Amdt. 27–21, 49 FR 44435, Nov. 6, 1984]

§ 27.1527   Maximum operating altitude.

The maximum altitude up to which operation is allowed, as limited by flight, structural, powerplant, functional, or equipment characteristics, must be established.

(Secs. 313(a), 601, 603, 604, and 605 of the Federal Aviation Act of 1958 (49 U.S.C. 1354(a), 1421, 1423, 1424, and 1425); and sec. 6(c) of the Dept. of Transportation Act (49 U.S.C. 1655(c)))

[Amdt. 27–14, 43 FR 2325, Jan. 16, 1978]

§ 27.1529   Instructions for Continued Airworthiness.

The applicant must prepare Instructions for Continued Airworthiness in accordance with appendix A to this part that are acceptable to the Administrator. The instructions may be incomplete at type certification if a program exists to ensure their completion prior to delivery of the first rotorcraft or issuance of a standard certificate of airworthiness, whichever occurs later.

[Amdt. 27–18, 45 FR 60177, Sept. 11, 1980]

MARKINGS AND PLACARDS

§ 27.1541 General.

(a) The rotorcraft must contain—

(1) The markings and placards specified in §§ 27.1545 through 27.1565, and

(2) Any additional information, instrument markings, and placards required for the safe operation of rotorcraft with unusual design, operating or handling characteristics.

(b) Each marking and placard prescribed in paragraph (a) of this section—

(1) Must be displayed in a conspicuous place; and

(2) May not be easily erased, disfigured, or obscured.

§ 27.1543 Instrument markings: general.

For each instrument—

(a) When markings are on the cover glass of the instrument, there must be means to maintain the correct alignment of the glass cover with the face of the dial; and

(b) Each arc and line must be wide enough, and located, to be clearly visible to the pilot.

§ 27.1545 Airspeed indicator.

(a) Each airspeed indicator must be marked as specified in paragraph (b) of this section, with the marks located at the corresponding indicated airspeeds.

(b) The following markings must be made:

(1) A red radial line—

(i) For rotorcraft other than helicopters, at V_{NE}; and

(ii) For helicopters at V_{NE} (power-on).

(2) A red cross–hatched radial line at V_{NE} (power-off) for helicopters, if V_{NE} (power-off) is less than V_{NE} (power-on).

(3) For the caution range, a yellow arc.

(4) For the safe operating range, a green arc.

(Secs. 313(a), 601, 603, 604, and 605 of the Federal Aviation Act of 1958 (49 U.S.C. 1354(a), 1421, 1423, 1424, and 1425); and sec. 6(c) of the Dept. of Transportation Act (49 U.S.C. 1655(c)))

[Doc. No. 5074, 29 FR 15695, Nov. 24, 1964, as amended by Amdt. 27–14, 43 FR 2325, Jan. 16, 1978; 43 FR 3900, Jan. 30, 1978; Amdt. 27–16, 43 FR 50599, Oct. 30, 1978]

§ 27.1547 Magnetic direction indicator.

(a) A placard meeting the requirements of this section must be installed on or near the the magnetic direction indicator.

(b) The placard must show the calibration of the instrument in level flight with the engines operating.

(c) The placard must state whether the calibration was made with radio receivers on or off.

(d) Each calibration reading must be in terms of magnetic heading in not more than 45 degree increments.

(e) If a magnetic nonstabilized direction indicator can have a deviation of more than 10 degrees caused by the operation of electrical equipment, the placard must state which electrical loads, or combination of loads, would cause a deviation of more than 10 degrees when turned on.

(Secs. 313(a), 601, 603, 604, and 605 of the Federal Aviation Act of 1958 (49 U.S.C. 1354(a), 1421, 1423, 1424, and 1425); and sec. 6(c) of the Dept. of Transportation Act (49 U.S.C. 1655(c)))

[Doc. No. 5074, 29 FR 15695, Nov. 24, 1964, as amended by Amdt. 27–13, 42 FR 36972, July 18, 1977]

§ 27.1549 Powerplant instruments.

For each required powerplant instrument, as appropriate to the type of instrument—

(a) Each maximum and, if applicable, minimum safe operating limit must be marked with a red radial or a red line;

(b) Each normal operating range must be marked with a green arc or green line, not extending beyond the maximum and minimum safe limits;

(c) Each takeoff and precautionary range must be marked with a yellow arc or yellow line;

(d) Each engine or propeller range that is restricted because of excessive vibration stresses must be marked with red arcs or red lines; and

(e) Each OEI limit or approved operating range must be marked to be clearly differentiated from the markings of paragraphs (a) through (d) of this section except that no marking is normally required for the 30-second OEI limit.

[Amdt. 27–11, 41 FR 55470, Dec. 20, 1976, as amended by Amdt. 27–23, 53 FR 34215, Sept. 2, 1988; Amdt. 27–29, 59 FR 47768, Sept. 16, 1994]

§ 27.1551 Oil quantity indicator.

Each oil quantity indicator must be marked with enough increments to indicate readily and accurately the quantity of oil.

§ 27.1553 Fuel quantity indicator.

If the unusable fuel supply for any tank exceeds one gallon, or five percent of the tank capacity, whichever is greater, a red arc must be marked on its indicator extending from the calibrated zero reading to the lowest reading obtainable in level flight.

§ 27.1555 Control markings.

(a) Each cockpit control, other than primary flight controls or control whose function is obvious, must be plainly marked as to its function and method of operation.

(b) For powerplant fuel controls—

(1) Each fuel tank selector control must be marked to indicate the position corresponding to each tank and to each existing cross feed position;

(2) If safe operation requires the use of any tanks in a specific sequence, that sequence must be marked on, or adjacent to, the selector for those tanks; and

(3) Each valve control for any engine of a multiengine rotorcraft must be marked to indicate the position corresponding to each engine controlled.

(c) Usable fuel capacity must be marked as follows:

(1) For fuel systems having no selector controls, the usable fuel capacity of the system must be indicated at the fuel quantity indicator.

(2) For fuel systems having selector controls, the usable fuel capacity available at each selector control position must be indicated near the selector control.

(d) For accessory, auxiliary, and emergency controls—

(1) Each essential visual position indicator, such as those showing rotor pitch or landing gear position, must be marked so that each crewmember can determine at any time the position of the unit to which it relates; and

(2) Each emergency control must be red and must be marked as to method of operation.

(e) For rotorcraft incorporating retractable landing gear, the maximum landing gear operating speed must be displayed in clear view of the pilot.

[Doc. No. 5074, 29 FR 15695, Nov. 24, 1964, as amended by Amdt. 27–11, 41 FR 55470, Dec. 20, 1976; Amdt. 27–21, 49 FR 44435, Nov. 6, 1984]

§ 27.1557 Miscellaneous markings and placards.

(a) *Baggage and cargo compartments, and ballast location.* Each baggage and cargo compartment, and each ballast location must have a placard stating any limitations on contents, including weight, that are necessary under the loading requirements.

(b) *Seats.* If the maximum allowable weight to be carried in a seat is less than 170 pounds, a placard stating the lesser weight must be permanently attached to the seat structure.

(c) *Fuel and oil filler openings.* The following apply:

(1) Fuel filler openings must be marked at or near the filler cover with—

(i) The word "fuel";

(ii) For reciprocating engine powered rotorcraft, the minimum fuel grade;

(iii) For turbine engine powered rotorcraft, the permissible fuel designations; and

(iv) For pressure fueling systems, the maximum permissible fueling supply pressure and the maximum permissible defueling pressure.

(2) Oil filler openings must be marked at or near the filler cover with the word "oil".

(d) *Emergency exit placards.* Each placard and operating control for each emergency exit must be red. A placard must be near each emergency exit control and must clearly indicate the location of that exit and its method of operation.

[Doc. No. 5074, 29 FR 15695, Nov. 24, 1964, as amended by Amdt. 27–11, 41 FR 55471, Dec. 20, 1976]

§ 27.1559 Limitations placard.

There must be a placard in clear view of the pilot that specifies the kinds of operations (such as VFR, IFR, day, night, or icing) for which the rotorcraft is approved.

[Amdt. 27–21, 49 FR 44435, Nov. 6, 1984]

§ 27.1561 Safety equipment.

(a) Each safety equipment control to be operated by the crew in emergency, such as controls for automatic liferaft releases, must be plainly marked as to its method of operation.

(b) Each location, such as a locker or compartment, that carries any fire extinguishing, signaling, or other life saving equipment, must be so marked.

§ 27.1565 Tail rotor.

Each tail rotor must be marked so that its disc is conspicuous under normal daylight ground conditions.

[Amdt. 27–2, 33 FR 965, Jan. 26, 1968]

ROTORCRAFT FLIGHT MANUAL AND
APPROVED MANUAL MATERIAL

§ 27.1581 General.

(a) *Furnishing information.* A Rotorcraft Flight Manual must be furnished with each rotorcraft, and it must contain the following:

(1) Information required by §§ 27.1583 through 27.1589.

(2) Other information that is necessary for safe operation because of design, operating, or handling characteristics.

(b) *Approved information.* Each part of the manual listed in §§ 27.1583 through 27.1589, that is appropriate to the rotorcraft, must be furnished, verified, and approved, and must be segregated, identified, and clearly distinguished from each unapproved part of that manual.

(c) [Reserved]

(d) *Table of contents.* Each Rotorcraft Flight Manual must include a table of contents if the complexity of the manual indicates a need for it.

(Secs. 313(a), 601, 603, 604, and 605 of the Federal Aviation Act of 1958 (49 U.S.C. 1354(a), 1421, 1423, 1424, and 1425); and sec. 6(c) of the Dept. of Transportation Act (49 U.S.C. 1655(c)))

[Amdt. 27–14, 43 FR 2325, Jan. 16, 1978]

§ 27.1583 Operating limitations.

(a) *Airspeed and rotor limitations.* Information necessary for the marking of airspeed and rotor limitations on, or near, their respective indicators must be furnished. The significance of each limitation and of the color coding must be explained.

(b) *Powerplant limitations.* The following information must be furnished:

(1) Limitations required by § 27.1521.

(2) Explanation of the limitations, when appropriate.

(3) Information necessary for marking the instruments required by §§ 27.1549 through 27.1553.

(c) *Weight and loading distribution.* The weight and center of gravity limits required by §§ 27.25 and 27.27, respectively, must be furnished. If the variety of possible loading conditions warrants, instructions must be included to allow ready observance of the limitations.

(d) *Flight crew.* When a flight crew of more than one is required, the number and functions of the minimum flight crew determined under § 27.1523 must be furnished.

(e) *Kinds of operation.* Each kind of operation for which the rotorcraft and its equipment installations are approved must be listed.

(f) [Reserved]

(g) *Altitude.* The altitude established under § 27.1527 and an explanation of the limiting factors must be furnished.

(Secs. 313(a), 601, 603, 604, and 605 of the Federal Aviation Act of 1958 (49 U.S.C. 1354(a), 1421, 1423, 1424, and 1425); and sec. 6(c) of the Dept. of Transportation Act (49 U.S.C. 1655(c)))

[Doc. No. 5074, 29 FR 15695, Nov. 24, 1964, as amended by Amdt. 27–2, 33 FR 965, Jan. 26, 1968; Amdt. 27–14, 43 FR 2325, Jan. 16, 1978; Amdt. 27–16, 43 FR 50599, Oct. 30, 1978]

§ 27.1585 Operating procedures.

(a) Parts of the manual containing operating procedures must have information concerning any normal and emergency procedures and other information necessary for safe operation, including takeoff and landing procedures and associated airspeeds. The manual must contain any pertinent information including—

(1) The kind of takeoff surface used in the tests and each appropriate climbout speed; and

(2) The kind of landing surface used in the tests and appropriate approach and glide airspeeds.

(b) For multiengine rotorcraft, information identifying each operating condition in which the fuel system independence prescribed in § 27.953 is necessary for safety must be furnished, together with instructions for placing the fuel system in a configuration used to show compliance with that section.

(c) For helicopters for which a V_{NE} (power-off) is established under § 27.1505(c), information must be furnished to explain the V_{NE} (power-off) and the procedures for reducing airspeed to not more than the V_{NE} (power-off) following failure of all engines.

(d) For each rotorcraft showing compliance with § 27.1353 (g)(2) or (g)(3), the operating procedures for disconnecting the battery from its charging source must be furnished.

(e) If the unusable fuel supply in any tank exceeds five percent of the tank capacity, or one gallon, whichever is greater, information must be furnished which indicates that when the fuel quantity indicator reads "zero" in level flight, any fuel remaining in the fuel tank cannot be used safely in flight.

(f) Information on the total quantity of usable fuel for each fuel tank must be furnished.

(g) The airspeeds and rotor speeds for minimum rate of descent and best glide angle as prescribed in § 27.71 must be provided.

(Secs. 313(a), 601, 603, 604, and 605 of the Federal Aviation Act of 1958 (49 U.S.C. 1354(a), 1421, 1423, 1424, and 1425); and sec. 6(c) of the Dept. of Transportation Act (49 U.S.C. 1655(c)))

[Amdt. 27-1, 32 FR 6914, May 5, 1967, as amended by Amdt. 27-14, 43 FR 2326, Jan. 16, 1978; Amdt. 27-16, 43 FR 50599, Oct. 30, 1978; Amdt. 27-21, 49 FR 44435, Nov. 6, 1984]

§ 27.1587 Performance information.

(a) The rotorcraft must be furnished with the following information, determined in accordance with §§ 27.51 through 27.79 and 27.143(c):

(1) Enough information to determine the limiting height-speed envelope.

(2) Information relative to—

(i) The hovering ceilings and the steady rates of climb and descent, as affected by any pertinent factors such as airspeed, temperature, and altitude;

(ii) The maximum safe wind for operation near the ground. If there are combinations of weight, altitude, and temperature for which performance information is provided and at which the rotorcraft cannot land and takeoff safely with the maximum wind value, those portions of the operating envelope and the appropriate safe wind conditions shall be identified in the flight manual;

(iii) For reciprocating engine-powered rotorcraft, the maximum atmospheric temperature at which compliance with the cooling provisions of §§ 27.1041 through 27.1045 is shown; and

(iv) Glide distance as a function of altitude when autorotating at the speeds and conditions for minimum rate of descent and best glide as determined in § 27.71.

(b) The Rotorcraft Flight Manual must contain—

(1) In its performance information section any pertinent information concerning the takeoff weights and altitudes used in compliance with § 27.51; and

(i) Any pertinent information concerning the takeoff procedure, including the kind of takeoff surface used in the tests and each appropriate climb-out speed; and

(ii) Any pertinent landing procedures, including the kind of landing surface used in the tests and appropriate approach and glide airspeeds; and

(2) The horizontal takeoff distance determined in accordance with § 27.65(a)(2)(i).

(Secs. 313(a), 601, 603, 604, and 605 of the Federal Aviation Act of 1958 (49 U.S.C. 1354(a), 1421, 1423, 1424, and 1425); and sec. 6(c) of the Dept. of Transportation Act (49 U.S.C. 1655(c)))

[Doc. No. 5074, 29 FR 15695, Nov. 24, 1964, as amended by Amdt. 27–14, 43 FR 2326, Jan. 16, 1978; Amdt. 27–21, 49 FR 44435, Nov. 6, 1984]

§ 27.1589 Loading information.

There must be loading instructions for each possible loading condition between the maximum and minimum weights determined under § 27.25 that can result in a center of gravity beyond any extreme prescribed in § 27.27, assuming any probable occupant weights.

APPENDIX A TO PART 27—INSTRUCTIONS FOR CONTINUED AIRWORTHINESS

A27.1 *General.*

(a) This appendix specifies requirements for the preparation of Instructions for Continued Airworthiness as required by § 27.1529.

(b) The Instructions for Continued Airworthiness for each rotorcraft must include the Instructions for Continued Airworthiness for each engine and rotor (hereinafter designated 'products'), for each appliance required by this chapter, and any required information relating to the interface of those appliances and products with the rotorcraft. If Instructions for Continued Airworthiness are not supplied by the manufacturer of an appliance or product installed in the rotorcraft, the Instructions for Continued Airworthiness for the rotorcraft must include the information essential to the continued airworthiness of the rotorcraft.

(c) The applicant must submit to the FAA a program to show how changes to the Instructions for Continued Airworthiness made by the applicant or by the manufacturers of products and appliances installed in the rotorcraft will be distributed.

A27.2 *Format.*

(a) The Instructions for Continued Airworthiness must be in the form of a manual or manuals as appropriate for the quantity of data to be provided.

(b) The format of the manual or manuals must provide for a practical arrangement.≤

A27.3 *Content.*

The contents of the manual or manuals must be prepared in the English language. The Instructions for Continued Airworthiness must contain the following manuals or sections, as appropriate, and information:

(a) *Rotorcraft maintenance manual or section.* (1) Introduction information that includes an explanation of the rotorcraft's features and data to the extent necessary for maintenance or preventive maintenance.

(2) A description of the rotorcraft and its systems and installations including its engines, rotors, and appliances.

(3) Basic control and operation information describing how the rotorcraft components and systems are controlled and how they operate, including any special procedures and limitations that apply.

(4) Servicing information that covers details regarding servicing points, capacities of tanks, reservoirs, types of fluids to be used, pressures applicable to the various systems, location of access panels for inspection and servicing, locations of lubrication points, the lubricants to be used, equipment required for servicing, tow instructions and limitations, mooring, jacking, and leveling information.

(b) *Maintenance instructions.* (1) Scheduling information for each part of the rotorcraft and its engines, auxiliary power units, rotors, accessories, instruments and equipment that provides the recommended periods at which they should be cleaned, inspected, adjusted, tested, and lubricated, and the degree of inspection, the applicable wear tolerances, and work recommended at these periods. However, the applicant may refer to an accessory, instrument, or equipment manufacturer as the source of this information if the applicant shows the item has an exceptionally high degree of complexity requiring specialized maintenance techniques, test equipment, or expertise. The recommended overhaul periods and necessary cross references to the Airworthiness Limitations section of the manual must also be included. In addition, the applicant must include an inspection program that includes the frequency and extent of the inspections necessary to provide for the continued airworthiness of the rotorcraft.

(2) Troubleshooting information describing problem malfunctions, how to recognize those malfunctions, and the remedial action for those malfunctions.

(3) Information describing the order and method of removing and replacing products and parts with any necessary precautions to be taken.

(4) Other general procedural instructions including procedures for system testing during ground running, symmetry checks,

weighing and determining the center of gravity, lifting and shoring, and storage limitations.

(c) Diagrams of structural access plates and information needed to gain access for inspections when access plates are not provided.

(d) Details for the application of special inspection techniques including radiographic and ultrasonic testing where such processes are specified.

(e) Information needed to apply protective treatments to the structure after inspection.

(f) All data relative to structural fasteners such as identification, discarded recommendations, and torque values.

(g) A list of special tools needed.

A27.4 *Airworthiness Limitations section.*

The Instructions for Continued Airworthiness must contain a section, titled Airworthiness Limitations that is segregated and clearly distinguishable from the rest of the document. This section must set forth each mandatory replacement time, structural inspection interval, and related structural inspection procedure approved under §27.571. If the Instructions for Continued Airworthiness consist of multiple documents, the section required by this paragraph must be included in the principal manual. This section must contain a legible statement in a prominent location that reads: "The Airworthiness Limitations section is FAA approved and specifies inspections and other maintenance required under §§43.16 and 91.403 of the Federal Aviation Regulations unless an alternative program has been FAA approved."

[Amdt. 27–17, 45 FR 60178, Sept. 11, 1980, as amended by Amdt. 27–24, 54 FR 34329, Aug. 18, 1989]

APPENDIX B TO PART 27—AIRWORTHI-
NESS CRITERIA FOR HELICOPTER IN-
STRUMENT FLIGHT

I. *General.* A normal category helicopter may not be type certificated for operation under the instrument flight rules (IFR) of this chapter unless it meets the design and installation requirements contained in this appendix.

II. *Definitions.* (a) V_{YI} means instrument climb speed, utilized instead of V_Y for compliance with the climb requirements for instrument flight.

(b) V_{NEI} means instrument flight never exceed speed, utilized instead of V_{NE} for compliance with maximum limit speed requirements for instrument flight.

(c) V_{MINI} means instrument flight minimum speed, utilized in complying with minimum limit speed requirements for instrument flight.

III. *Trim.* It must be possible to trim the cyclic, collective, and directional control

forces to zero at all approved IFR airspeeds, power settings, and configurations appropriate to the type.

IV. *Static longitudinal stability.* (a) *General.* The helicopter must possess positive static longitudinal control force stability at critical combinations of weight and center of gravity at the conditions specified in paragraph IV (b) or (c) of this appendix, as appropriate. The stick force must vary with speed so that any substantial speed change results in a stick force clearly perceptible to the pilot. For single-pilot approval, the airspeed must return to within 10 percent of the trim speed when the control force is slowly released for each trim condition specified in paragraph IV(b) of the this appendix.

(b) *For single-pilot approval:*

(1) *Climb.* Stability must be shown in climb throughout the speed range 20 knots either side of trim with—

(i) The helicopter trimmed at V_{YI};

(ii) Landing gear retracted (if retractable); and

(iii) Power required for limit climb rate (at least 1,000 fpm) at V_{YI} or maximum continuous power, whichever is less.

(2) *Cruise.* Stability must be shown throughout the speed range from 0.7 to 1.1 V_H or V_{NEI}, whichever is lower, not to exceed ±20 knots from trim with—

(i) The helicopter trimmed and power adjusted for level flight at 0.9 V_H or 0.9 V_{NEI}, whichever is lower; and

(ii) Landing gear retracted (if retractable).

(3) *Slow cruise.* Stability must be shown throughout the speed range from 0.9 V_{MINI} to 1.3 V_{MINI} or 20 knots above trim speed, whichever is greater, with—

(i) the helicopter trimmed and power adjusted for level flight at 1.1 V_{MINI}; and

(ii) Landing gear retracted (if retractable).

(4) *Descent.* Stability must be shown throughout the speed range 20 knots either side of trim with—

(i) The helicopter trimmed at 0.8 V_H or 0.8 V_{NEI} (or 0.8 V_{LE} for the landing gear extended case), whichever is lower;

(ii) Power required for 1,000 fpm descent at trim speed; and

(iii) Landing gear extended and retracted, if applicable.

(5) *Approach.* Stability must be shown throughout the speed range from 0.7 times the minimum recommended approach speed to 20 knots above the maximum recommended approach speed with—

(i) The helicopter trimmed at the recommended approach speed or speeds;

(ii) Landing gear extended and retracted, if applicable; and

(iii) Power required to maintain a 3° glide path and power required to maintain the steepest approach gradient for which approval is requested.

(c) Helicopters approved for a minimum crew of two pilots must comply with the provisions of paragraphs IV(b)(2) and IV(b)(5) of this appendix.

V. *Static lateral-directional stability.* (a) Static directional stability must be positive throughout the approved ranges of airspeed, power, and vertical speed. In straight, steady sideslips up to ±10° from trim, directional control position must increase in approximately constant proportion to angle of sideslip. At greater angles up to the maximum sideslip angle appropriate to the type, increased directional control position must produce increased angle of sideslip.

(b) During sideslips up to ±10° from trim throughout the approved ranges of airspeed, power, and vertical speed, there must be no negative dihedral stability perceptible to the pilot through lateral control motion or force. Longitudinal cyclic movement with sideslip must not be excessive.

VI. *Dynamic stability.* (a) For single-pilot approval—

(1) Any oscillation having a period of less than 5 seconds must damp to ½ amplitude in not more than one cycle.

(2) Any oscillation having a period of 5 seconds or more but less than 10 seconds must damp to ½ amplitude in not more than two cycles.

(3) Any oscillation having a period of 10 seconds or more but less than 20 seconds must be damped.

(4) Any oscillation having a period of 20 seconds or more may not achieve double amplitude in less than 20 seconds.

(5) Any aperiodic response may not achieve double amplitude in less than 6 seconds.

(b) For helicopters approved with a minimum crew of two pilots—

(1) Any oscillation having a period of less than 5 seconds must damp to ½ amplitude in not more than two cycles.

(2) Any oscillation having a period of 5 seconds or more but less than 10 seconds must be damped.

(3) Any oscillation having a period of 10 seconds or more may not achieve double amplitude in less than 10 seconds.

VII. *Stability augmentation system (SAS).* (a) If a SAS is used, the reliability of the SAS must be related to the effects of its failure. The occurrence of any failure condition which would prevent continued safe flight and landing must be extremely improbable. For any failure condition of the SAS which is not shown to be extremely improbable—

(1) The helicopter must be safely controllable and capable of prolonged instrument flight without undue pilot effort. Additional unrelated probable failures affecting the control system must be considered; and

(2) The flight characteristics requirements in Subpart B of Part 27 must be met throughout a practical flight envelope.

(b) The SAS must be designed so that it cannot create a hazardous deviation in flight path or produce hazardous loads on the helicopter during normal operation or in the event of malfunction or failure, assuming corrective action begins within an appropriate period of time. Where multiple systems are installed, subsequent malfunction conditions must be considered in sequence unless their occurrence is shown to be improbable.

VIII. *Equipment, systems, and installation.* The basic equipment and installation must comply with §§ 29.1303, 29.1431, and 29.1433 through Amendment 29–14, with the following exceptions and additions:

(a) *Flight and Navigation Instruments.* (1) A magnetic gyro-stablized direction indicator instead of a gyroscopic direction indicator required by § 29.1303(h); and

(2) A standby attitude indicator which meets the requirements of §§ 29.1303(g)(1) through (7) instead of a rate-of-turn indicator required by § 29.1303(g). For two-pilot configurations, one pilot's primary indicator may be designated for this purpose. If standby batteries are provided, they may be charged from the aircraft electrical system if adequate isolation is incorporated.

(b) *Miscellaneous requirements.* (1) Instrument systems and other systems essential for IFR flight that could be adversely affected by icing must be adequately protected when exposed to the continuous and intermittent maximum icing conditions defined in appendix C of Part 29 of this chapter, whether or not the rotorcraft is certificated for operation in icing conditions.

(2) There must be means in the generating system to automatically de-energize and disconnect from the main bus any power source developing hazardous overvoltage.

(3) Each required flight instrument using a power supply (electric, vacuum, etc.) must have a visual means integral with the instrument to indicate the adequacy of the power being supplied.

(4) When multiple systems performing like functions are required, each system must be grouped, routed, and spaced so that physical separation between systems is provided to ensure that a single malfunction will not adversely affect more than one system.

(5) For systems that operate the required flight instruments at each pilot's station—

(i) Only the required flight instruments for the first pilot may be connected to that operating system;

(ii) Additional instruments, systems, or equipment may not be connected to an operating system for a second pilot unless provisions are made to ensure the continued normal functioning of the required instruments in the event of any malfunction of the additional instruments, systems, or equipment which is not shown to be extremely improbable;

(iii) The equipment, systems, and installations must be designed so that one display of the information essential to the safety of flight which is provided by the instruments will remain available to a pilot, without additional crewmember action, after any single failure or combination of failures that is not shown to be extremely improbable; and

(iv) For single-pilot configurations, instruments which require a static source must be provided with a means of selecting an alternate source and that source must be calibrated.

IX. *Rotorcraft Flight Manual.* A Rotorcraft Flight Manual or Rotorcraft Flight Manual IFR Supplement must be provided and must contain—

(a) *Limitations.* The approved IFR flight envelope, the IFR flightcrew composition, the revised kinds of operation, and the steepest IFR precision approach gradient for which the helicopter is approved;

(b) *Procedures.* Required information for proper operation of IFR systems and the recommended procedures in the event of stability augmentation or electrical system failures; and

(c) *Performance.* If V_{YI} differs from V_Y, climb performance at V_{YI} and with maximum continuous power throughout the ranges of weight, altitude, and temperature for which approval is requested.

[Amdt. 27–19, 48 FR 4389, Jan. 31, 1983]

APPENDIX C TO PART 27—CRITERIA FOR CATEGORY A

C27.1 General.

A small multiengine rotorcraft may not be type certificated for Category A operation unless it meets the design installation and performance requirements contained in this appendix in addition to the requirements of this part.

C27.2 Applicable part 29 sections. The following sections of part 29 of this chapter must be met in addition to the requirements of this part:

29.45(a) and (b)(2)—General.
29.49(a)—Performance at minimum operating speed.
29.51—Takeoff data: General.
29.53—Takeoff: Category A.
29.55—Takeoff decision point: Category A.
29.59—Takeoff Path: Category A.
29.60—Elevated heliport takeoff path: Category A.
29.61—Takeoff distance: Category A.
29.62—Rejected takeoff: Category A.
29.64—Climb: General.
29.65(a)—Climb: AEO.
29.67(a)—Climb: OEI.
29.75—Landing: General.
29.77—Landing decision point: Category A.
29.79—Landing: Category A.

29.81—Landing distance (Ground level sites): Category A.
29.85—Balked landing: Category A.
29.87(a)—Height-velocity envelope.
29.547(a) and (b)—Main and tail rotor structure.
29.861(a)—Fire protection of structure, controls, and other parts.
29.901(c)—Powerplant: Installation.
29.903(b) (c) and (e)—Engines.
29.908(a)—Cooling fans.
29.917(b) and (c)(1)—Rotor drive system: Design.
29.927(c)(1)—Additional tests.
29.953(a)—Fuel system independence.
29.1027(a)—Transmission and gearboxes: General.
29.1045(a)(1), (b), (c), (d), and (f)—Climb cooling test procedures.
29.1047(a)—Takeoff cooling test procedures.
29.1181(a)—Designated fire zones: Regions included.
29.1187(e)—Drainage and ventilation of fire zones.
29.1189(c)—Shutoff means.
29.1191(a)(1)—Firewalls.
29.1193(e)—Cowling and engine compartment covering.
29.1195(a) and (d)—Fire extinguishing systems (one shot).
29.1197—Fire extinguishing agents.
29.1199—Extinguishing agent containers.
29.1201—Fire extinguishing system materials.
29.1305(a) (6) and (b)—Powerplant instruments.
29.1309(b)(2) (i) and (d)—Equipment, systems, and installations.
29.1323(c)(1)—Airspeed indicating system.
29.1331(b)—Instruments using a power supply.
29.1351(d)(2)—Electrical systems and equipment: General (operation without normal electrical power).
29.1587(a)—Performance information.

NOTE: In complying with the paragraphs listed in paragraph C27.2 above, relevant material in the AC "Certification of Transport Category Rotorcraft" should be used.

[Doc. No. 28008, 61 FR 21907, May 10, 1996]

PART 29—AIRWORTHINESS STANDARDS: TRANSPORT CATEGORY ROTORCRAFT

Subpart A—General

Sec.
29.1   Applicability.
29.2   Special retroactive requirements.

Subpart B—Flight

GENERAL

29.21   Proof of compliance.
29.25   Weight limits.
29.27   Center of gravity limits.

AUTHORITY: 49 U.S.C. 106(g), 40113, 44701–44702, 44704.

SOURCE: Docket No. 5084, 29 FR 16150, Dec. 3, 1964, unless otherwise noted.

Subpart A—General

§ 29.1 Applicability.

(a) This part prescribes airworthiness standards for the issue of type certificates, and changes to those certificates, for transport category rotorcraft.

(b) Transport category rotorcraft must be certificated in accordance with either the Category A or Category B requirements of this part. A multiengine rotorcraft may be type certificated as both Category A and Category B with appropriate and different operating limitations for each category.

(c) Rotorcraft with a maximum weight greater than 20,000 pounds and 10 or more passenger seats must be type certificated as Category A rotorcraft.

(d) Rotorcraft with a maximum weight greater than 20,000 pounds and nine or less passenger seats may be type certificated as Category B rotorcraft provided the Category A requirements of Subparts C, D, E, and F of this part are met.

(e) Rotorcraft with a maximum weight of 20,000 pounds or less but with 10 or more passenger seats may be type certificated as Category B rotorcraft provided the Category A requirements of §§ 29.67(a)(2), 29.87, 29.1517, and subparts C, D, E, and F of this part are met.

(f) Rotorcraft with a maximum weight of 20,000 pounds or less and nine or less passenger seats may be type certificated as Category B rotorcraft.

(g) Each person who applies under Part 21 for a certificate or change described in paragraphs (a) through (f) of this section must show compliance with the applicable requirements of this part.

[Amdt. 29–21, 48 FR 4391, Jan. 31, 1983, as amended by Amdt. 29–39, 61 FR 21898, May 10, 1996; 61 FR 33963, July 1, 1996]

§ 29.2 Special retroactive requirements.

For each rotorcraft manufactured after September 16, 1992, each applicant must show that each occupant's seat is equipped with a safety belt and shoulder harness that meets the requirements of paragraphs (a), (b), and (c) of this section.

(a) Each occupant's seat must have a combined safety belt and shoulder harness with a single-point release. Each pilot's combined safety belt and shoulder harness must allow each pilot, when seated with safety belt and shoulder harness fastened, to perform all functions necessary for flight operations. There must be a means to secure belts and harnesses, when not in use, to prevent interference with the operation of the rotorcraft and with rapid egress in an emergency.

(b) Each occupant must be protected from serious head injury by a safety belt plus a shoulder harness that will prevent the head from contacting any injurious object.

(c) The safety belt and shoulder harness must meet the static and dynamic strength requirements, if applicable, specified by the rotorcraft type certification basis.

(d) For purposes of this section, the date of manufacture is either—

(1) The date the inspection acceptance records, or equivalent, reflect that the rotorcraft is complete and meets the FAA-Approved Type Design Data; or

(2) The date that the foreign civil airworthiness authority certifies the rotorcraft is complete and issues an original standard airworthiness certificate, or equivalent, in that country.

[Doc. No. 26078, 56 FR 41052, Aug. 16, 1991]

Subpart B—Flight

GENERAL

§ 29.21 Proof of compliance.

Each requirement of this subpart must be met at each appropriate combination of weight and center of gravity within the range of loading conditions for which certification is requested. This must be shown—

(a) By tests upon a rotorcraft of the type for which certification is requested, or by calculations based on, and equal in accuracy to, the results of testing; and

(b) By systematic investigation of each required combination of weight and center of gravity, if compliance cannot be reasonably inferred from combinations investigated.

[Doc. No. 5084, 29 FR 16150, Dec. 3, 1964, as amended by Amdt. 29–24, 49 FR 44435, Nov. 6, 1984]

§ 29.25 Weight limits.

(a) *Maximum weight.* The maximum weight (the highest weight at which compliance with each applicable requirement of this part is shown) or, at the option of the applicant, the highest weight for each altitude and for each practicably separable operating condition, such as takeoff, enroute operation, and landing, must be established so that it is not more than—

(1) The highest weight selected by the applicant;

(2) The design maximum weight (the highest weight at which compliance with each applicable structural loading condition of this part is shown); or

(3) The highest weight at which compliance with each applicable flight requirement of this part is shown.

(b) *Minimum weight.* The minimum weight (the lowest weight at which compliance with each applicable requirement of this part is shown) must be established so that it is not less than—

(1) The lowest weight selected by the applicant;

(2) The design minimum weight (the lowest weight at which compliance with each structural loading condition of this part is shown); or

(3) The lowest weight at which compliance with each applicable flight requirement of this part is shown.

(c) *Total weight with jettisonable external load.* A total weight for the rotorcraft with a jettisonable external load attached that is greater than the maximum weight established under paragraph (a) of this section may be established for any rotorcraft-load combination if—

(1) The rotorcraft-load combination does not include human external cargo,

(2) Structural component approval for external load operations under either § 29.865 or under equivalent operational standards is obtained,

(3) The portion of the total weight that is greater than the maximum weight established under paragraph (a) of this section is made up only of the

weight of all or part of the jettisonable external load,

(4) Structural components of the rotorcraft are shown to comply with the applicable structural requirements of this part under the increased loads and stresses caused by the weight increase over that established under paragraph (a) of this section, and

(5) Operation of the rotorcraft at a total weight greater than the maximum certificated weight established under paragraph (a) of this section is limited by appropriate operating limitations under § 29.865 (a) and (d) of this part.

[Doc. No. 5084, 29 FR 16150, Dec. 3, 1964, as amended by Amdt. 29–12, 41 FR 55471, Dec. 20, 1976; Amdt. 29–43, 64 FR 43020, Aug. 6, 1999]

§ 29.27 Center of gravity limits.

The extreme forward and aft centers of gravity and, where critical, the extreme lateral centers of gravity must be established for each weight established under § 29.25. Such an extreme may not lie beyond—

(a) The extremes selected by the applicant;

(b) The extremes within which the structure is proven; or

(c) The extremes within which compliance with the applicable flight requirements is shown.

[Amdt. 29–3, 33 FR 965, Jan. 26, 1968]

§ 29.29 Empty weight and corresponding center of gravity.

(a) The empty weight and corresponding center of gravity must be determined by weighing the rotorcraft without the crew and payload, but with—

(1) Fixed ballast;

(2) Unusable fuel; and

(3) Full operating fluids, including—

(i) Oil;

(ii) Hydraulic fluid; and

(iii) Other fluids required for normal operation of rotorcraft systems, except water intended for injection in the engines.

(b) The condition of the rotorcraft at the time of determining empty weight must be one that is well defined and can be easily repeated, particularly with respect to the weights of fuel, oil, coolant, and installed equipment.

(Secs. 313(a), 601, 603, 604, and 605 of the Federal Aviation Act of 1958 (49 U.S.C. 1354(a), 1421, 1423, 1424, and 1425); and sec. 6(c) of the Dept. of Transportation Act (49 U.S.C. 1655(c)))

[Doc. No. 5084, 29 FR 16150. Dec. 3, 1964, as amended by Amdt. 29–15, 43 FR 2326, Jan. 16, 1978]

§ 29.31 Removable ballast.

Removable ballast may be used in showing compliance with the flight requirements of this subpart.

§ 29.33 Main rotor speed and pitch limits.

(a) *Main rotor speed limits.* A range of main rotor speeds must be established that—

(1) With power on, provides adequate margin to accommodate the variations in rotor speed occurring in any appropriate maneuver, and is consistent with the kind of governor or synchronizer used; and

(2) With power off, allows each appropriate autorotative maneuver to be performed throughout the ranges of airspeed and weight for which certification is requested.

(b) *Normal main rotor high pitch limit (power on).* For rotorcraft, except helicopters required to have a main rotor low speed warning under paragraph (e) of this section, it must be shown, with power on and without exceeding approved engine maximum limitations, that main rotor speeds substantially less than the minimum approved main rotor speed will not occur under any sustained flight condition. This must be met by—

(1) Appropriate setting of the main rotor high pitch stop;

(2) Inherent rotorcraft characteristics that make unsafe low main rotor speeds unlikely; or

(3) Adequate means to warn the pilot of unsafe main rotor speeds.

(c) *Normal main rotor low pitch limit (power off).* It must be shown, with power off, that—

(1) The normal main rotor low pitch limit provides sufficient rotor speed, in any autorotative condition, under the most critical combinations of weight and airspeed; and

(2) It is possible to prevent over-speeding of the rotor without exceptional piloting skill.

(d) *Emergency high pitch.* If the main rotor high pitch stop is set to meet paragraph (b)(1) of this section, and if that stop cannot be exceeded inadvertently, additional pitch may be made available for emergency use.

(e) *Main rotor low speed warning for helicopters.* For each single engine helicopter, and each multiengine helicopter that does not have an approved device that automatically increases power on the operating engines when one engine fails, there must be a main rotor low speed warning which meets the following requirements:

(1) The warning must be furnished to the pilot in all flight conditions, including power-on and power-off flight, when the speed of a main rotor approaches a value that can jeopardize safe flight.

(2) The warning may be furnished either through the inherent aerodynamic qualities of the helicopter or by a device.

(3) The warning must be clear and distinct under all conditions, and must be clearly distinguishable from all other warnings. A visual device that requires the attention of the crew within the cockpit is not acceptable by itself.

(4) If a warning device is used, the device must automatically deactivate and reset when the low-speed condition is corrected. If the device has an audible warning, it must also be equipped with a means for the pilot to manually silence the audible warning before the low-speed condition is corrected.

(Secs. 313(a), 601, 603, 604, and 605 of the Federal Aviation Act of 1958 (49 U.S.C. 1354(a), 1421, 1423, 1424, and 1425); and sec. 6(c) of the Dept. of Transportation Act (49 U.S.C. 1655(c)))

[Doc. No. 5084, 29 FR 16150, Dec. 3, 1964, as amended by Amdt. 29-3, 33 FR 965, Jan. 26, 1968; Amdt. 29-15, 43 FR 2326, Jan. 16, 1978]

PERFORMANCE

§ 29.45 General.

(a) The performance prescribed in this subpart must be determined—

(1) With normal piloting skill and;

(2) Without exceptionally favorable conditions.

(b) Compliance with the performance requirements of this subpart must be shown—

(1) For still air at sea level with a standard atmosphere and;

(2) For the approved range of atmospheric variables.

(c) The available power must correspond to engine power, not exceeding the approved power, less—

(1) Installation losses; and

(2) The power absorbed by the accessories and services at the values for which certification is requested and approved.

(d) For reciprocating engine-powered rotorcraft, the performance, as affected by engine power, must be based on a relative humidity of 80 percent in a standard atmosphere.

(e) For turbine engine-powered rotorcraft, the performance, as affected by engine power, must be based on a relative humidity of—

(1) 80 percent, at and below standard temperature; and

(2) 34 percent, at and above standard temperature plus 50 °F.

Between these two temperatures, the relative humidity must vary linearly.

(f) For turbine-engine-power rotorcraft, a means must be provided to permit the pilot to detemine prior to takeoff that each engine is capable of developing the power necessary to achieve the applicable rotorcraft performance prescribed in this subpart.

(Secs. 313(a), 601, 603, 604, and 605 of the Federal Aviation Act of 1958 (49 U.S.C. 1354(a), 1421, 1423, 1424, and 1425); and sec. 6(c), Dept. of Transportation Act (49 U.S.C. 1655(c)))

[Doc. No. 5084, 29 FR 16150, Dec. 3, 1964, as amended by Amdt. 29-15, 43 FR 2326, Jan. 16, 1978; Amdt. 29-24, 49 FR 44436, Nov. 6, 1984]

§ 29.49 Performance at minimum operating speed.

(a) For each Category A helicopter, the hovering performance must be determined over the ranges of weight, altitude, and temperature for which takeoff data are scheduled—

(1) With not more than takeoff power;

(2) With the landing gear extended; and

619

(3) At a height consistent with the procedure used in establishing the takeoff, climbout, and rejected takeoff paths.

(b) For each Category B helicopter, the hovering performance must be determined over the ranges of weight, altitude, and temperature for which certification is requested, with—

(1) Takeoff power;

(2) The landing gear extended; and

(3) The helicopter in ground effect at a height consistent with normal takeoff procedures.

(c) For each helicopter, the out-of-ground effect hovering performance must be determined over the ranges of weight, altitude, and temperature for which certification is requested with takeoff power.

(d) For rotorcraft other than helicopters, the steady rate of climb at the minimum operating speed must be determined over the ranges of weight, altitude, and temperature for which certification is requested with—

(1) Takeoff power; and

(2) The landing gear extended.

[Doc. No. 24802, 61 FR 21898, May 10, 1996; 61 FR 33963, July 1, 1996]

§ 29.51 Takeoff data: general.

(a) The takeoff data required by §§ 29.53, 29.55, 29.59, 29.60, 29.61, 29.62, 29.63, and 29.67 must be determined—

(1) At each weight, altitude, and temperature selected by the applicant; and

(2) With the operating engines within approved operating limitations.

(b) Takeoff data must—

(1) Be determined on a smooth, dry, hard surface; and

(2) Be corrected to assume a level takeoff surface.

(c) No takeoff made to determine the data required by this section may require exceptional piloting skill or alertness, or exceptionally favorable conditions.

[Doc. No. 5084, 29 FR 16150, Dec. 3, 1964, as amended by Amdt. 29–39, 61 FR 21899, May 10, 1996]

§ 29.53 Takeoff: Category A.

The takeoff performance must be determined and scheduled so that, if one engine fails at any time after the start of takeoff, the rotorcraft can—

(a) Return to, and stop safely on, the takeoff area; or

(b) Continue the takeoff and climbout, and attain a configuration and airspeed allowing compliance with § 29.67(a)(2).

[Doc. No. 24802, 61 FR 21899, May 10, 1996; 61 FR 33963, July 1, 1996]

§ 29.55 Takeoff decision point (TDP): Category A.

(a) The TDP is the first point from which a continued takeoff capability is assured under § 29.59 and is the last point in the takeoff path from which a rejected takeoff is assured within the distance determined under § 29.62.

(b) The TDP must be established in relation to the takeoff path using no more than two parameters; e.g., airspeed and height, to designate the TDP.

(c) Determination of the TDP must include the pilot recognition time interval following failure of the critical engine.

[Doc. No. 24802, 61 FR 21899, May 10, 1996]

§ 29.59 Takeoff path: Category A.

(a) The takeoff path extends from the point of commencement of the takeoff procedure to a point at which the rotorcraft is 1,000 feet above the takeoff surface and compliance with § 29.67(a)(2) is shown. In addition—

(1) The takeoff path must remain clear of the height-velocity envelope established in accordance with § 29.87;

(2) The rotorcraft must be flown to the engine failure point; at which point, the critical engine must be made inoperative and remain inoperative for the rest of the takeoff;

(3) After the critical engine is made inoperative, the rotorcraft must continue to the takeoff decision point, and then attain V_{TOSS};

(4) Only primary controls may be used while attaining V_{TOSS} and while establishing a positive rate of climb. Secondary controls that are located on the primary controls may be used after a positive rate of climb and V_{TOSS} are established but in no case less than 3 seconds after the critical engine is made inoperative; and

(5) After attaining V_{TOSS} and a positive rate of a climb, the landing gear may be retracted.

(b) During the takeoff path determination made in accordance with paragraph (a) of this section and after attaining V_{TOSS} and a positive rate of climb, the climb must be continued at a speed as close as practicable to, but not less than, V_{TOSS} until the rotorcraft is 200 feet above the takeoff surface. During this interval, the climb performance must meet or exceed that required by §29.67(a)(1).

(c) During the continued takeoff, the rotorcraft shall not descend below 15 feet above the takeoff surface when the takeoff decision point is above 15 feet.

(d) From 200 feet above the takeoff surface, the rotorcraft takeoff path must be level or positive until a height 1,000 feet above the takeoff surface is attained with not less than the rate of climb required by §29.67(a)(2). Any secondary or auxiliary control may be used after attaining 200 feet above the takeoff surface.

(e) Takeoff distance will be determined in accordance with §29.61.

[Doc. No. 24802, 61 FR 21899, May 10, 1996; 61 FR 33963, July 1, 1996, as amended by Amdt. 29–44, 64 FR 45337, Aug. 19, 1999]

§29.60 Elevated heliport takeoff path: Category A.

(a) The elevated heliport takeoff path extends from the point of commencement of the takeoff procedure to a point in the takeoff path at which the rotorcraft is 1,000 feet above the takeoff surface and compliance with §29.67(a)(2) is shown. In addition—

(1) The requirements of §29.59(a) must be met;

(2) While attaining V_{TOSS} and a positive rate of climb, the rotorcraft may descend below the level of the takeoff surface if, in so doing and when clearing the elevated heliport edge, every part of the rotorcraft clears all obstacles by at least 15 feet;

(3) The vertical magnitude of any descent below the takeoff surface must be determined; and

(4) After attaining V_{TOSS} and a positive rate of climb, the landing gear may be retracted.

(b) The scheduled takeoff weight must be such that the climb requirements of §29.67 (a)(1) and (a)(2) will be met.

(c) Takeoff distance will be determined in accordance with §29.61.

[Doc. No. 24802, 61 FR 21899, May 10, 1996; 61 FR 33963, July 1, 1996]

§29.61 Takeoff distance: Category A.

(a) The normal takeoff distance is the horizontal distance along the takeoff path from the start of the takeoff to the point at which the rotorcraft attains and remains at least 35 feet above the takeoff surface, attains and maintains a speed of at least V_{TOSS}, and establishes a positive rate of climb, assuming the critical engine failure occurs at the engine failure point prior to the takeoff decision point.

(b) For elevated heliports, the takeoff distance is the horizontal distance along the takeoff path from the start of the takeoff to the point at which the rotorcraft attains and maintains a speed of at least V_{TOSS} and establishes a positive rate of climb, assuming the critical engine failure occurs at the engine failure point prior to the takeoff decision point.

[Doc. No. 24802, 61 FR 21899, May 10, 1996]

§29.62 Rejected takeoff: Category A.

The rejected takeoff distance and procedures for each condition where takeoff is approved will be established with—

(a) The takeoff path requirements of §§29.59 and 29.60 being used up to the TDP where the critical engine failure is recognized and the rotorcraft is landed and brought to a complete stop on the takeoff surface;

(b) The remaining engines operating within approved limits;

(c) The landing gear remaining extended throughout the entire rejected takeoff; and

(d) The use of only the primary controls until the rotorcraft is on the ground. Secondary controls located on the primary control may not be used until the rotorcraft is on the ground. Means other than wheel brakes may be used to stop the rotorcraft if the means are safe and reliable and consistent results can be expected under normal operating conditions.

[Doc. No. 24802, 61 FR 21899, May 10, 1996, as amended by Amdt. 29–44, 64 FR 45337, Aug. 19, 1999]

§ 29.63 Takeoff: Category B.

The horizontal distance required to take off and climb over a 50-foot obstacle must be established with the most unfavorable center of gravity. The takeoff may be begun in any manner if—

(a) The takeoff surface is defined;

(b) Adequate safeguards are maintained to ensure proper center of gravity and control positions; and

(c) A landing can be made safely at any point along the flight path if an engine fails.

[Doc. No. 5084, 29 FR 16150, Dec. 3, 1964, as amended by Amdt. 29–12, 41 FR 55471, Dec. 20, 1976]

§ 29.64 Climb: General.

Compliance with the requirements of §§ 29.65 and 29.67 must be shown at each weight, altitude, and temperature within the operational limits established for the rotorcraft and with the most unfavorable center of gravity for each configuration. Cowl flaps, or other means of controlling the engine-cooling air supply, will be in the position that provides adequate cooling at the temperatures and altitudes for which certification is requested.

[Doc. No. 24802, 61 FR 21900, May 10, 1996]

§ 29.65 Climb: All engines operating.

(a) The steady rate of climb must be determined—

(1) With maximum continuous power;

(2) With the landing gear retracted; and

(3) At V_y for standard sea level conditions and at speeds selected by the applicant for other conditions.

(b) For each Category B rotorcraft except helicopters, the rate of climb determined under paragraph (a) of this section must provide a steady climb gradient of at least 1:6 under standard sea level conditions.

(Secs. 313(a), 601, 603, 604, and 605 of the Federal Aviation Act of 1958 (49 U.S.C. 1354(a), 1421, 1423, 1424, and 1425); and sec. 6(c), Dept. of Transportation Act (49 U.S.C. 1655(c)))

[Doc. No. 5084, 29 FR 16150. Dec. 3, 1964, as amended by Amdt. 29–15, 43 FR 2326, Jan. 16, 1978; Amdt. 29–39, 61 FR 21900, May 10, 1996; 61 FR 33963, July 1, 1996]

§ 29.67 Climb: One engine inoperative (OEI).

(a) For Category A rotorcraft, in the critical takeoff configuration existing along the takeoff path, the following apply:

(1) The steady rate of climb without ground effect, 200 feet above the takeoff surface, must be at least 100 feet per minute for each weight, altitude, and temperature for which takeoff data are to be scheduled with—

(i) The critical engine inoperative and the remaining engines within approved operating limitations, except that for rotorcraft for which the use of 30-second/2-minute OEI power is requested, only the 2-minute OEI power may be used in showing compliance with this paragraph;

(ii) The landing gear extended; and

(iii) The takeoff safety speed selected by the applicant.

(2) The steady rate of climb without ground effect, 1000 feet above the takeoff surface, must be at least 150 feet per minute, for each weight, altitude, and temperature for which takeoff data are to be scheduled with—

(i) The critical engine inoperative and the remaining engines at maximum continuous power including continuous OEI power, if approved, or at 30-minute OEI power for rotorcraft for which certification for use of 30-minute OEI power is requested;

(ii) The landing gear retracted; and

(iii) The speed selected by the applicant.

(3) The steady rate of climb (or descent) in feet per minute, at each altitude and temperature at which the rotorcraft is expected to operate and at any weight within the range of weights for which certification is requested, must be determined with—

(i) The critical engine inoperative and the remaining engines at maximum continuous power including continuous OEI power, if approved, and at 30-minute OEI power for rotorcraft for which certification for the use of 30-minute OEI power is requested;

(ii) The landing gear retracted; and

(iii) The speed selected by the applicant.

(b) For multiengine Category B rotorcraft meeting the Category A engine isolation requirements, the steady rate of climb (or descent) must be determined at the speed for best rate of climb (or minimum rate of descent) at each altitude, temperature, and weight at which the rotorcraft is expected to operate, with the critical engine inoperative and the remaining engines at maximum continuous power including continuous OEI power, if approved, and at 30-minute OEI power for rotorcraft for which certification for the use of 30-minute OEI power is requested.

[Doc. No. 24802, 61 FR 21900, May 10, 1996; 61 FR 33963, July 1, 1996, as amended by Amdt. 29–44, 64 FR 45337, Aug. 19, 1999; 64 FR 47563, Aug. 31, 1999]

§29.71 Helicopter angle of glide: Category B.

For each category B helicopter, except multiengine helicopters meeting the requirements of §29.67(b) and the powerplant installation requirements of category A, the steady angle of glide must be determined in autorotation—

(a) At the forward speed for minimum rate of descent as selected by the applicant;

(b) At the forward speed for best glide angle;

(c) At maximum weight; and

(d) At the rotor speed or speeds selected by the applicant.

[Amdt. 29–12, 41 FR 55471, Dec. 20, 1976]

§29.75 Landing: General.

(a) For each rotorcraft—

(1) The corrected landing data must be determined for a smooth, dry, hard, and level surface;

(2) The approach and landing must not require exceptional piloting skill or exceptionally favorable conditions; and

(3) The landing must be made without excessive vertical acceleration or tendency to bounce, nose over, ground loop, porpoise, or water loop.

(b) The landing data required by §§29.77, 29.79, 29.81, 29.83, and 29.85 must be determined—

(1) At each weight, altitude, and temperature for which landing data are approved;

(2) With each operating engine within approved operating limitations; and

(3) With the most unfavorable center of gravity.

[Doc. No. 24802, 61 FR 21900, May 10, 1996]

§29.77 Landing Decision Point (LDP): Category A.

(a) The LDP is the last point in the approach and landing path from which a balked landing can be accomplished in accordance with §29.85.

(b) Determination of the LDP must include the pilot recognition time interval following failure of the critical engine.

[Doc. No. 24802, 64 FR 45338, Aug. 19, 1999]

§29.79 Landing: Category A.

(a) For Category A rotorcraft—

(1) The landing performance must be determined and scheduled so that if the critical engine fails at any point in the approach path, the rotorcraft can either land and stop safely or climb out and attain a rotorcraft configuration and speed allowing compliance with the climb requirement of §29.67(a)(2);

(2) The approach and landing paths must be established with the critical engine inoperative so that the transition between each stage can be made smoothly and safely;

(3) The approach and landing speeds must be selected by the applicant and must be appropriate to the type of rotorcraft; and

(4) The approach and landing path must be established to avoid the critical areas of the height-velocity envelope determined in accordance with §29.87.

(b) It must be possible to make a safe landing on a prepared landing surface after complete power failure occurring during normal cruise.

[Doc. No. 24802, 61 FR 21900, May 10, 1996]

§ 29.81 Landing distance: Category A.

The horizontal distance required to land and come to a complete stop (or to a speed of approximately 3 knots for water landings) from a point 50 ft above the landing surface must be determined from the approach and landing paths established in accordance with § 29.79.

[Doc. No. 24802, 64 FR 45338, Aug. 19, 1999]

§ 29.83 Landing: Category B.

(a) For each Category B rotorcraft, the horizontal distance required to land and come to a complete stop (or to a speed of approximately 3 knots for water landings) from a point 50 feet above the landing surface must be determined with—

(1) Speeds appropriate to the type of rotorcraft and chosen by the applicant to avoid the critical areas of the height-velocity envelope established under § 29.87; and

(2) The approach and landing made with power on and within approved limits.

(b) Each multiengined Category B rotorcraft that meets the powerplant installation requirements for Category A must meet the requirements of—

(1) Sections 29.79 and 29.81; or

(2) Paragraph (a) of this section.

(c) It must be possible to make a safe landing on a prepared landing surface if complete power failure occurs during normal cruise.

[Doc. No. 24802, 61 FR 21900, May 10, 1996; 61 FR 33963, July 1, 1996]

§ 29.85 Balked landing: Category A.

For Category A rotorcraft, the balked landing path with the critical engine inoperative must be established so that—

(a) The transition from each stage of the maneuver to the next stage can be made smoothly and safely;

(b) From the LDP on the approach path selected by the applicant, a safe climbout can be made at speeds allowing compliance with the climb requirements of § 29.67(a)(1) and (2); and

(c) The rotorcraft does not descend below 15 feet above the landing surface. For elevated heliport operations, descent may be below the level of the landing surface provided the deck edge clearance of § 29.60 is maintained and the descent (loss of height) below the landing surface is determined.

[Doc. No. 24802, 64 FR 45338, Aug. 19, 1999]

§ 29.87 Height-velocity envelope.

(a) If there is any combination of height and forward velocity (including hover) under which a safe landing cannot be made after failure of the critical engine and with the remaining engines (where applicable) operating within approved limits, a height-velocity envelope must be established for—

(1) All combinations of pressure altitude and ambient temperature for which takeoff and landing are approved; and

(2) Weight from the maximum weight (at sea level) to the highest weight approved for takeoff and landing at each altitude. For helicopters, this weight need not exceed the highest weight allowing hovering out-of-ground effect at each altitude.

(b) For single-engine or multiengine rotorcraft that do not meet the Category A engine isolation requirements, the height-velocity envelope for complete power failure must be established.

[Doc. No. 24802, 61 FR 21901, May 10, 1996; 61 FR 33963, July 1, 1996]

FLIGHT CHARACTERISTICS

§ 29.141 General.

The rotorcraft must—

(a) Except as specifically required in the applicable section, meet the flight characteristics requirements of this subpart—

(1) At the approved operating altitudes and temperatures;

(2) Under any critical loading condition within the range of weights and centers of gravity for which certification is requested; and

(3) For power-on operations, under any condition of speed, power, and rotor r.p.m. for which certification is requested; and

(4) For power-off operations, under any condition of speed, and rotor r.p.m. for which certification is requested that is attainable with the controls rigged in accordance with the approved rigging instructions and tolerances;

(b) Be able to maintain any required flight condition and make a smooth transition from any flight condition to any other flight condition without exceptional piloting skill, alertness, or strength, and without danger of exceeding the limit load factor under any operating condition probable for the type, including—

(1) Sudden failure of one engine, for multiengine rotorcraft meeting Transport Category A engine isolation requirements;

(2) Sudden, complete power failure, for other rotorcraft; and

(3) Sudden, complete control system failures specified in §29.695 of this part; and

(c) Have any additional characteristics required for night or instrument operation, if certification for those kinds of operation is requested. Requirements for helicopter instrument flight are contained in appendix B of this part.

[Doc. No. 5084, 29 FR 16150, Dec. 8, 1964, as amended by Amdt. 29–3, 33 FR 905, Jan. 26, 1968; Amdt. 29–12, 41 FR 55471, Dec. 20, 1976; Amdt. 29–21, 48 FR 4391, Jan. 31, 1983; Amdt. 29–24, 49 FR 44436, Nov. 6, 1984]

§29.143 Controllability and maneuverability.

(a) The rotorcraft must be safely controllable and maneuverable—

(1) During steady flight; and

(2) During any maneuver appropriate to the type, including—

(i) Takeoff;

(ii) Climb;

(iii) Level flight;

(iv) Turning flight;

(v) Glide; and

(vi) Landing (power on and power off).

(b) The margin of cyclic control must allow satisfactory roll and pitch control at V_{NE} with—

(1) Critical weight;

(2) Critical center of gravity;

(3) Critical rotor r.p.m.; and

(4) Power off (except for helicopters demonstrating compliance with paragraph (e) of this section) and power on.

(c) A wind velocity of not less than 17 knots must be established in which the rotorcraft can be operated without loss of control on or near the ground in any maneuver appropriate to the type (such as crosswind takeoffs, sideward flight, and rearward flight), with—

(1) Critical weight;

(2) Critical center of gravity; and

(3) Critical rotor r.p.m.

(d) The rotorcraft, after (1) failure of one engine, in the case of multiengine rotorcraft that meet Transport Category A engine isolation requirements, or (2) complete power failure in the case of other rotorcraft, must be controllable over the range of speeds and altitudes for which certification is requested when such power failure occurs with maximum continuous power and critical weight. No corrective action time delay for any condition following power failure may be less than—

(i) For the cruise condition, one second, or normal pilot reaction time (whichever is greater); and

(ii) For any other condition, normal pilot reaction time.

(e) For helicopters for which a V_{NE} (power-off) is established under §29.1505(c), compliance must be demonstrated with the following requirements with critical weight, critical center of gravity, and critical rotor r.p.m.:

(1) The helicopter must be safely slowed to V_{NE} (power-off), without exceptional pilot skill after the last operating engine is made inoperative at power-on V_{NE}.

(2) At a speed of 1.1 V_{NE} (power-off), the margin of cyclic control must allow satisfactory roll and pitch control with power off.

(Secs. 313(a), 601, 603, 604, and 605 of the Federal Aviation Act of 1958 (49 U.S.C. 1354(a), 1421, 1423, 1424, and 1425); and sec. 6(c) of the Dept. of Transportation Act (49 U.S.C. 1655(c)))

[Doc. No. 5084, 29 FR 16150, Dec. 3, 1964, as amended by Amdt. 29–3, 33 FR 965, Jan. 26, 1968; Amdt. 29–15, 43 FR 2326, Jan. 16, 1978; Amdt. 29–24, 49 FR 44436, Nov. 6, 1984]

§29.151 Flight controls.

(a) Longitudinal, lateral, directional, and collective controls may not exhibit excessive breakout force, friction, or preload.

(b) Control system forces and free play may not inhibit a smooth, direct rotorcraft response to control system input.

[Amdt. 29–24, 49 FR 44436, Nov. 6, 1984]

§ 29.161 Trim control.

The trim control—

(a) Must trim any steady longitudinal, lateral, and collective control forces to zero in level flight at any appropriate speed; and

(b) May not introduce any undesirable discontinuities in control force gradients.

[Doc. No. 5084, 29 FR 16150, Dec. 3, 1964, as amended by Amdt. 29–24, 49 FR 44436, Nov. 6, 1984]

§ 29.171 Stability: general.

The rotorcraft must be able to be flown, without undue pilot fatigue or strain, in any normal maneuver for a period of time as long as that expected in normal operation. At least three landings and takeoffs must be made during this demonstration.

§ 29.173 Static longitudinal stability.

(a) The longitudinal control must be designed so that a rearward movement of the control is necessary to obtain a speed less than the trim speed, and a forward movement of the control is necessary to obtain a speed more than the trim speed.

(b) With the throttle and collective pitch held constant during the maneuvers specified in § 29.175 (a) through (c), the slope of the control position versus speed curve must be positive throughout the full range of altitude for which certification is requested.

(c) During the maneuver specified in § 29.175(d), the longitudinal control position versus speed curve may have a negative slope within the specified speed range if the negative motion is not greater than 10 percent of total control travel.

[Amdt. 29–24, 49 FR 44436, Nov. 6, 1984]

§ 29.175 Demonstration of static longitudinal stability.

(a) *Climb.* Static longitudinal stability must be shown in the climb condition at speeds from 0.85 V_Y, or 15 knots below V_Y, whichever is less, to 1.2 V_Y or 15 knots above V_Y, whichever is greater, with—

(1) Critical weight;

(2) Critical center of gravity;

(3) Maximum continuous power;

(4) The landing gear retracted; and

(5) The rotorcraft trimmed at V_Y.

(b) *Cruise.* Static longitudinal stability must be shown in the cruise condition at speeds from 0.7 V_H or 0.7 V_{NE}, whichever is less, to 1.1 V_H or 1.1 V_{NE}, whichever is less, with—

(1) Critical weight;

(2) Critical center of gravity;

(3) Power for level flight at 0.9 V_H or 0.9 V_{NE}, whichever is less;

(4) The landing gear retracted, and

(5) The rotorcraft trimmed at 0.9 V_H or 0.9 V_{NE}, whichever is less.

(c) *Autorotation.* Static longitudinal stability must be shown in autorotation at airspeeds from 0.5 times the speed for minimum rate of descent, or 0.5 times the maximum range glide speed for Category A rotorcraft, to V_{NE} or to 1.1 V_{NE} (power-off) if V_{NE} (power-off) is established under § 29.1505(c), and with—

(1) Critical weight;

(2) Critical center of gravity;

(3) Power off;

(4) The landing gear——

(i) Retracted; and

(ii) Extended; and

(5) The rotorcraft trimmed at appropriate speeds found necessary by the Administrator to demonstrate stability throughout the prescribed speed range.

(d) *Hovering.* For helicopters, the longitudinal cyclic control must operate with the sense, direction of motion, and position as prescribed in § 29.173 between the maximum approved rearward speed and a forward speed of 17 knots with—

(1) Critical weight;

(2) Critical center of gravity;

(3) Power required to maintain an approximate constant height in ground effect;

(4) The landing gear extended; and

(5) The helicopter trimmed for hovering.

(Secs. 313(a), 601, 603, 604, and 605 of the Federal Aviation Act of 1958 (49 U.S.C. 1354(a), 1421, 1423, 1424, and 1425); and sec. 6(c), Dept. of Transportation Act (49 U.S.C. 1655(c)))

[Doc. No. 5084, 29 FR 16150, Dec. 3, 1964, as amended by Amdt. 29–3, 33 FR 966, Jan. 26, 1968; Amdt. 29–12, 41 FR 55471, Dec. 20, 1976; Amdt. 29–15, 43 FR 2327, Jan. 16, 1978; Amdt. 29–24, 49 FR 44436, Nov. 6, 1984]

§29.177 Static directional stability.

Static directional stability must be positive with throttle and collective controls held constant at the trim conditions specified in §29.175 (a), (b), and (c). Sideslip angle must increase steadily with directional control deflection for sideslip angles up to ±10° from trim. Sufficient cues must accompany sideslip to alert the pilot when approaching sideslip limits.

[Amdt. 29–24, 49 FR 44436, Nov. 6, 1984]

§29.181 Dynamic stability: Category A rotorcraft.

Any short-period oscillation occurring at any speed from V_Y to V_{NE} must be positively damped with the primary flight controls free and in a fixed position.

[Amdt. 29–24, 49 FR 44437, Nov. 6, 1984]

GROUND AND WATER HANDLING CHARACTERISTICS

§29.231 General.

The rotorcraft must have satisfactory ground and water handling characteristics, including freedom from uncontrollable tendencies in any condition expected in operation.

§29.235 Taxiing condition.

The rotorcraft must be designed to withstand the loads that would occur when the rotorcraft is taxied over the roughest ground that may reasonably be expected in normal operation.

§29.239 Spray characteristics.

If certification for water operation is requested, no spray characteristics during taxiing, takeoff, or landing may obscure the vision of the pilot or damage the rotors, propellers, or other parts of the rotorcraft.

§29.241 Ground resonance.

The rotorcraft may have no dangerous tendency to oscillate on the ground with the rotor turning.

MISCELLANEOUS FLIGHT REQUIREMENTS

§29.251 Vibration.

Each part of the rotorcraft must be free from excessive vibration under each appropriate speed and power condition.

Subpart C—Strength Requirements

GENERAL

§29.301 Loads.

(a) Strength requirements are specified in terms of limit loads (the maximum loads to be expected in service) and ultimate loads (limit loads multiplied by prescribed factors of safety). Unless otherwise provided, prescribed loads are limit loads.

(b) Unless otherwise provided, the specified air, ground, and water loads must be placed in equilibrium with inertia forces, considering each item of mass in the rotorcraft. These loads must be distributed to closely approximate or conservatively represent actual conditions.

(c) If deflections under load would significantly change the distribution of external or internal loads, this redistribution must be taken into account.

§29.303 Factor of safety.

Unless otherwise provided, a factor of safety of 1.5 must be used. This factor applies to external and inertia loads unless its application to the resulting internal stresses is more conservative.

§29.305 Strength and deformation.

(a) The structure must be able to support limit loads without detrimental or permanent deformation. At any load up to limit loads, the deformation may not interfere with safe operation.

(b) The structure must be able to support ultimate loads without failure. This must be shown by—

(1) Applying ultimate loads to the structure in a static test for at least three seconds; or

(2) Dynamic tests simulating actual load application.

§29.307 Proof of structure.

(a) Compliance with the strength and deformation requirements of this subpart must be shown for each critical loading condition accounting for the environment to which the structure will be exposed in operation. Structural analysis (static or fatigue) may be used only if the structure conforms to those structures for which experience has shown this method to be reliable. In other cases, substantiating load tests must be made.

(b) Proof of compliance with the strength requirements of this subpart must include—

(1) Dynamic and endurance tests of rotors, rotor drives, and rotor controls;

(2) Limit load tests of the control system, including control surfaces;

(3) Operation tests of the control system;

(4) Flight stress measurement tests;

(5) Landing gear drop tests; and

(6) Any additional tests required for new or unusual design features.

(Secs. 604, 605, 72 Stat. 778, 49 U.S.C. 1424, 1425)

[Doc. No. 5084, 29 FR 16150, Dec. 3, 1964, as amended by Amdt. 29–4, 33 FR 14106, Sept. 18, 1968; Amdt. 27–26, 55 FR 8001, Mar. 6, 1990]

§ 29.309 Design limitations.

The following values and limitations must be established to show compliance with the structural requirements of this subpart:

(a) The design maximum and design minimum weights.

(b) The main rotor r.p.m. ranges, power on and power off.

(c) The maximum forward speeds for each main rotor r.p.m. within the ranges determined under paragraph (b) of this section.

(d) The maximum rearward and sideward flight speeds.

(e) The center of gravity limits corresponding to the limitations determined under paragraphs (b), (c), and (d) of this section.

(f) The rotational speed ratios between each powerplant and each connected rotating component.

(g) The positive and negative limit maneuvering load factors.

FLIGHT LOADS

§ 29.321 General.

(a) The flight load factor must be assumed to act normal to the longitudinal axis of the rotorcraft, and to be equal in magnitude and opposite in direction to the rotorcraft inertia load factor at the center of gravity.

(b) Compliance with the flight load requirements of this subpart must be shown—

(1) At each weight from the design minimum weight to the design maximum weight; and

(2) With any practical distribution of disposable load within the operating limitations in the Rotorcraft Flight Manual.

§ 29.337 Limit maneuvering load factor.

The rotorcraft must be designed for—

(a) A limit maneuvering load factor ranging from a positive limit of 3.5 to a negative limit of −1.0; or

(b) Any positive limit maneuvering load factor not less than 2.0 and any negative limit maneuvering load factor of not less than −0.5 for which—

(1) The probability of being exceeded is shown by analysis and flight tests to be extremely remote; and

(2) The selected values are appropriate to each weight condition between the design maximum and design minimum weights.

[Doc. No. 5084, 29 FR 16150, Dec. 3, 1964, as amended by Amdt. 27–26, 55 FR 8002, Mar. 6, 1990]

§ 29.339 Resultant limit maneuvering loads.

The loads resulting from the application of limit maneuvering load factors are assumed to act at the center of each rotor hub and at each auxiliary lifting surface, and to act in directions and with distributions of load among the rotors and auxiliary lifting surfaces, so as to represent each critical maneuvering condition, including power-on and power-off flight with the maximum design rotor tip speed ratio. The rotor tip speed ratio is the ratio of the rotorcraft flight velocity component in the plane of the rotor disc to the rotational tip speed of the rotor blades, and is expressed as follows:

$$\mu = \frac{V \cos a}{\Omega R}$$

where—

V=The airspeed along the flight path (f.p.s.);

a=The angle between the projection, in the plane of symmetry, of the axis of no feathering and a line perpendicular to the flight path (radians, positive when axis is pointing aft);

Ω=The angular velocity of rotor (radians per second); and

R=The rotor radius (ft.).

§29.341 Gust loads.

Each rotorcraft must be designed to withstand, at each critical airspeed including hovering, the loads resulting from vertical and horizontal gusts of 30 feet per second.

§29.351 Yawing conditions.

(a) Each rotorcraft must be designed for the loads resulting from the maneuvers specified in paragraphs (b) and (c) of this section, with—

(1) Unbalanced aerodynamic moments about the center of gravity which the aircraft reacts to in a rational or conservative manner considering the principal masses furnishing the reacting inertia forces; and

(2) Maximum main rotor speed.

(b) To produce the load required in paragraph (a) of this section, in unaccelerated flight with zero yaw, at forward speeds from zero up to 0.6 V_{NE}—

(1) Displace the cockpit directional control suddenly to the maximum deflection limited by the control stops or by the maximum pilot force specified in §29.397(a);

(2) Attain a resulting sideslip angle or 90°, whichever is less; and

(3) Return the directional control suddenly to neutral.

(c) To produce the load required in paragraph (a) of the section, in unaccelerated flight with zero yaw, at forward speeds from 0.6 V_{NE} up to V_{NE} or V_H, whichever is less—

(1) Displace the cockpit directional control suddenly to the maximum deflection limited by the control stops or by the maximum pilot force specified in §29.397(a);

(2) Attain a resulting sideslip angle or 15°, whichever is less, at the lesser speed of V_{NE} or V_H;

(3) Vary the sideslip angles of paragraphs (b)(2) and (c)(2) of this section directly with speed; and

(4) Return the directional control suddenly to neutral.

[Amdt. 29–26, 55 FR 8002, Mar. 6, 1990, as amended by Amdt. 29–41, 62 FR 46173, Aug. 29, 1997]

§29.361 Engine torque.

The limit engine torque may not be less than the following:

(a) For turbine engines, the highest of—

(1) The mean torque for maximum continuous power multiplied by 1.25;

(2) The torque required by §29.923;

(3) The torque required by §29.927; or

(4) The torque imposed by sudden engine stoppage due to malfunction or structural failure (such as compressor jamming).

(b) For reciprocating engines, the mean torque for maximum continuous power multiplied by—

(1) 1.33, for engines with five or more cylinders; and

(2) Two, three, and four, for engines with four, three, and two cylinders, respectively.

[Amdt. 29–26, 53 FR 34215, Sept. 2, 1988]

CONTROL SURFACE AND SYSTEM LOADS

§29.391 General.

Each auxiliary rotor, each fixed or movable stabilizing or control surface, and each system operating any flight control must meet the requirements of §§29.395 through 29.399, 29.411, and 29.427.

[Amdt. 29–26, 55 FR 8002, Mar. 6, 1990, as amended by Amdt. 29–41, 62 FR 46173, Aug. 29, 1997]

§29.395 Control system.

(a) The reaction to the loads prescribed in §29.397 must be provided by—

(1) The control stops only;

(2) The control locks only;

(3) The irreversible mechanism only (with the mechanism locked and with the control surface in the critical positions for the effective parts of the system within its limit of motion);

(4) The attachment of the control system to the rotor blade pitch control horn only (with the control in the critical positions for the affected parts of the system within the limits of its motion); and

(5) The attachment of the control system to the control surface horn (with the control in the critical positions for the affected parts of the system within the limits of its motion).

(b) Each primary control system, including its supporting structure, must be designed as follows:

(1) The system must withstand loads resulting from the limit pilot forces prescribed in § 29.397;

(2) Notwithstanding paragraph (b)(3) of this section, when power-operated actuator controls or power boost controls are used, the system must also withstand the loads resulting from the limit pilot forces prescribed in § 29.397 in conjunction with the forces output of each normally energized power device, including any single power boost or actuator system failure;

(3) If the system design or the normal operating loads are such that a part of the system cannot react to the limit pilot forces prescribed in § 29.397, that part of the system must be designed to withstand the maximum loads that can be obtained in normal operation. The minimum design loads must, in any case, provide a rugged system for service use, including consideration of fatigue, jamming, ground gusts, control inertia, and friction loads. In the absence of a rational analysis, the design loads resulting from 0.60 of the specified limit pilot forces are acceptable minimum design loads; and

(4) If operational loads may be exceeded through jamming, ground gusts, control inertia, or friction, the system must withstand the limit pilot forces specified in § 29.397, without yielding.

[Doc. No. 5084, 29 FR 16150, Dec. 3, 1964, as amended by Amdt. 29–26, 55 FR 8002, Mar. 6, 1990]

§ 29.397 Limit pilot forces and torques.

(a) Except as provided in paragraph (b) of this section, the limit pilot forces are as follows:

(1) For foot controls, 130 pounds.

(2) For stick controls, 100 pounds fore and aft, and 67 pounds laterally.

(b) For flap, tab, stabilizer, rotor brake, and landing gear operating controls, the following apply (R=radius in inches):

(1) Crank wheel, and lever controls, [1 + R]/3 × 50 pounds, but not less than 50 pounds nor more than 100 pounds for hand operated controls or 130 pounds for foot operated controls, applied at any angle within 20 degrees of the plane of motion of the control.

(2) Twist controls, 80R inch-pounds.

[Amdt. 29–12, 41 FR 55471, Dec. 20, 1976, as amended by Amdt. 29–47, 66 FR 23538, May 9, 2001]

§ 29.399 Dual control system.

Each dual primary flight control system must be able to withstand the loads that result when pilot forces not less than 0.75 times those obtained under § 29.395 are applied—

(a) In opposition; and

(b) In the same direction.

§ 29.411 Ground clearance: tail rotor guard.

(a) It must be impossible for the tail rotor to contact the landing surface during a normal landing.

(b) If a tail rotor guard is required to show compliance with paragraph (a) of this section—

(1) Suitable design loads must be established for the guard: and

(2) The guard and its supporting structure must be designed to withstand those loads.

§ 29.427 Unsymmetrical loads.

(a) Horizontal tail surfaces and their supporting structure must be designed for unsymmetrical loads arising from yawing and rotor wake effects in combination with the prescribed flight conditions.

(b) To meet the design criteria of paragraph (a) of this section, in the absence of more rational data, both of the following must be met:

(1) One hundred percent of the maximum loading from the symmetrical flight conditions acts on the surface on one side of the plane of symmetry, and no loading acts on the other side.

(2) Fifty percent of the maximum loading from the symmetrical flight conditions acts on the surface on each side of the plane of symmetry, in opposite directions.

(c) For empennage arrangements where the horizontal tail surfaces are supported by the vertical tail surfaces, the vertical tail surfaces and supporting structure must be designed for the combined vertical and horizontal surface loads resulting from each prescribed flight condition, considered separately. The flight conditions must be selected so that the maximum design loads are obtained on each surface. In the absence of more rational data, the unsymmetrical horizontal tail surface loading distributions described in this section must be assumed.

[Amdt. 27–26, 55 FR 8002, Mar. 6, 1990, as amended by Amdt. 29–31, 55 FR 38966, Sept. 21, 1990]

GROUND LOADS

§29.471 General.

(a) *Loads and equilibrium.* For limit ground loads—

(1) The limit ground loads obtained in the landing conditions in this part must be considered to be external loads that would occur in the rotorcraft structure if it were acting as a rigid body; and

(2) In each specified landing condition, the external loads must be placed in equilibrium with linear and angular inertia loads in a rational or conservative manner.

(b) *Critical centers of gravity.* The critical centers of gravity within the range for which certification is requested must be selected so that the maximum design loads are obtained in each landing gear element.

§29.473 Ground loading conditions and assumptions.

(a) For specified landing conditions, a design maximum weight must be used that is not less than the maximum weight. A rotor lift may be assumed to act through the center of gravity throughout the landing impact. This lift may not exceed two-thirds of the design maximum weight.

(b) Unless otherwise prescribed, for each specified landing condition, the rotorcraft must be designed for a limit load factor of not less than the limit inertia load factor substantiated under §29.725.

(c) Triggering or actuating devices for additional or supplementary energy absorption may not fail under loads established in the tests prescribed in §§29.725 and 29.727, but the factor of safety prescribed in §29.303 need not be used.

[Amdt. 29–3, 33 FR 966, Jan. 26, 1968]

§29.475 Tires and shock absorbers.

Unless otherwise prescribed, for each specified landing condition, the tires must be assumed to be in their static position and the shock absorbers to be in their most critical position.

§29.477 Landing gear arrangement.

Sections 29.235, 29.479 through 29.485, and 29.493 apply to landing gear with two wheels aft, and one or more wheels forward, of the center of gravity.

§29.479 Level landing conditions.

(a) *Attitudes.* Under each of the loading conditions prescribed in paragraph (b) of this section, the rotorcraft is assumed to be in each of the following level landing attitudes:

(1) An attitude in which each wheel contacts the ground simultaneously.

(2) An attitude in which the aft wheels contact the ground with the forward wheels just clear of the ground.

(b) *Loading conditions.* The rotorcraft must be designed for the following landing loading conditions:

(1) Vertical loads applied under §29.471.

(2) The loads resulting from a combination of the loads applied under paragraph (b)(1) of this section with drag loads at each wheel of not less than 25 percent of the vertical load at that wheel.

(3) The vertical load at the instant of peak drag load combined with a drag component simulating the forces required to accelerate the wheel rolling assembly up to the specified ground speed, with—

(i) The ground speed for determination of the spin-up loads being at least 75 percent of the optimum forward flight speed for minimum rate of descent in autorotation; and

(ii) The loading conditions of paragraph (b) applied to the landing gear and its attaching structure only.

(4) If there are two wheels forward, a distribution of the loads applied to those wheels under paragraphs (b)(1) and (2) of this section in a ratio of 40:60.

(c) *Pitching moments.* Pitching moments are assumed to be resisted by—

(1) In the case of the attitude in paragraph (a)(1) of this section, the forward landing gear; and

(2) In the case of the attitude in paragraph (a)(2) of this section, the angular inertia forces.

§ 29.481 Tail-down landing conditions.

(a) The rotorcraft is assumed to be in the maximum nose-up attitude allowing ground clearance by each part of the rotorcraft.

(b) In this attitude, ground loads are assumed to act perpendicular to the ground.

§ 29.483 One-wheel landing conditions.

For the one-wheel landing condition, the rotorcraft is assumed to be in the level attitude and to contact the ground on one aft wheel. In this attitude—

(a) The vertical load must be the same as that obtained on that side under § 29.479(b)(1); and

(b) The unbalanced external loads must be reacted by rotorcraft inertia.

§ 29.485 Lateral drift landing conditions.

(a) The rotorcraft is assumed to be in the level landing attitude, with—

(1) Side loads combined with one-half of the maximum ground reactions obtained in the level landing conditions of § 29.479(b)(1); and

(2) The loads obtained under paragraph (a)(1) of this section applied—

(i) At the ground contact point; or

(ii) For full-swiveling gear, at the center of the axle.

(b) The rotorcraft must be designed to withstand, at ground contact—

(1) When only the aft wheels contact the ground, side loads of 0.8 times the vertical reaction acting inward on one side and 0.6 times the vertical reaction acting outward on the other side, all combined with the vertical loads specified in paragraph (a) of this section; and

(2) When the wheels contact the ground simultaneously—

(i) For the aft wheels, the side loads specified in paragraph (b)(1) of this section; and

(ii) For the forward wheels, a side load of 0.8 times the vertical reaction combined with the vertical load specified in paragraph (a) of this section.

§ 29.493 Braked roll conditions.

Under braked roll conditions with the shock absorbers in their static positions—

(a) The limit vertical load must be based on a load factor of at least—

(1) 1.33, for the attitude specified in § 29.479(a)(1); and

(2) 1.0, for the attitude specified in § 29.479(a)(2); and

(b) The structure must be designed to withstand, at the ground contact point of each wheel with brakes, a drag load of at least the lesser of—

(1) The vertical load multiplied by a coefficient of friction of 0.8; and

(2) The maximum value based on limiting brake torque.

§ 29.497 Ground loading conditions: landing gear with tail wheels.

(a) *General.* Rotorcraft with landing gear with two wheels forward and one wheel aft of the center of gravity must be designed for loading conditions as prescribed in this section.

(b) *Level landing attitude with only the forward wheels contacting the ground.* In this attitude—

(1) The vertical loads must be applied under §§ 29.471 through 29.475;

(2) The vertical load at each axle must be combined with a drag load at that axle of not less than 25 percent of that vertical load; and

(3) Unbalanced pitching moments are assumed to be resisted by angular inertia forces.

(c) *Level landing attitude with all wheels contacting the ground simultaneously.* In this attitude, the rotorcraft must be designed for landing loading conditions as prescribed in paragraph (b) of this section.

(d) *Maximum nose-up attitude with only the rear wheel contacting the ground.* The attitude for this condition must be the maximum nose-up attitude expected in normal operation, including autorotative landings. In this attitude—

(1) The appropriate ground loads specified in paragraph (b)(1) and (2) of this section must be determined and applied, using a rational method to account for the moment arm between the rear wheel ground reaction and the rotorcraft center of gravity; or

(2) The probability of landing with initial contact on the rear wheel must be shown to be extremely remote.

(e) *Level landing attitude with only one forward wheel contacting the ground.* In this attitude, the rotorcraft must be designed for ground loads as specified in paragraph (b)(1) and (3) of this section.

(f) *Side loads in the level landing attitude.* In the attitudes specified in paragraphs (b) and (c) of this section, the following apply:

(1) The side loads must be combined at each wheel with one-half of the maximum vertical ground reactions obtained for that wheel under paragraphs (b) and (c) of this section. In this condition, the side loads must be—

(i) For the forward wheels, 0.8 times the the vertical reaction (on one side) acting inward, and 0.6 times the vertical reaction (on the other side) acting outward; and

(ii) For the rear wheel, 0.8 times the vertical reaction.

(2) The loads specified in paragraph (f)(1) of this section must be applied—

(i) At the ground contact point with the wheel in the trailing position (for non-full swiveling landing gear or for full swiveling landing gear with a lock, steering device, or shimmy damper to keep the wheel in the trailing position); or

(ii) At the center of the axle (for full swiveling landing gear without a lock, steering device, or shimmy damper).

(g) *Braked roll conditions in the level landing attitude.* In the attitudes specified in paragraphs (b) and (c) of this section, and with the shock absorbers in their static positions, the rotorcraft must be designed for braked roll loads as follows:

(1) The limit vertical load must be based on a limit vertical load factor of not less than—

(i) 1.0, for the attitude specified in paragraph (b) of this section; and

(ii) 1.33, for the attitude specified in paragraph (c) of this section.

(2) For each wheel with brakes, a drag load must be applied, at the ground contact point, of not less than the lesser of—

(i) 0.8 times the vertical load; and

(ii) The maximum based on limiting brake torque.

(h) *Rear wheel turning loads in the static ground attitude.* In the static ground attitude, and with the shock absorbers and tires in their static positions, the rotorcraft must be designed for rear wheel turning loads as follows:

(1) A vertical ground reaction equal to the static load on the rear wheel must be combined with an equal side load.

(2) The load specified in paragraph (h)(1) of this section must be applied to the rear landing gear—

(i) Through the axle, if there is a swivel (the rear wheel being assumed to be swiveled 90 degrees to the longitudinal axis of the rotorcraft); or

(ii) At the ground contact point if there is a lock, steering device or shimmy damper (the rear wheel being assumed to be in the trailing position).

(i) *Taxiing condition.* The rotorcraft and its landing gear must be designed for the loads that would occur when the rotorcraft is taxied over the roughest ground that may reasonably be expected in normal operation.

§29.501 Ground loading conditions: landing gear with skids.

(a) *General.* Rotorcraft with landing gear with skids must be designed for the loading conditions specified in this section. In showing compliance with this section, the following apply:

(1) The design maximum weight, center of gravity, and load factor must be determined under §§29.471 through 29.475.

(2) Structural yielding of elastic spring members under limit loads is acceptable.

(3) Design ultimate loads for elastic spring members need not exceed those obtained in a drop test of the gear with—

(i) A drop height of 1.5 times that specified in §29.725; and

(ii) An assumed rotor lift of not more than 1.5 times that used in the limit drop tests prescribed in §29.725.

(4) Compliance with paragraph (b) through (e) of this section must be shown with—

(i) The gear in its most critically deflected position for the landing condition being considered; and

(ii) The ground reactions rationally distributed along the bottom of the skid tube.

(b) *Vertical reactions in the level landing attitude.* In the level attitude, and with the rotorcraft contacting the ground along the bottom of both skids, the vertical reactions must be applied as prescribed in paragraph (a) of this section.

(c) *Drag reactions in the level landing attitude.* In the level attitude, and with the rotorcraft contacting the ground along the bottom of both skids, the following apply:

(1) The vertical reactions must be combined with horizontal drag reactions of 50 percent of the vertical reaction applied at the ground.

(2) The resultant ground loads must equal the vertical load specified in paragraph (b) of this section.

(d) *Sideloads in the level landing attitude.* In the level attitude, and with the rotorcraft contacting the ground along the bottom of both skids, the following apply:

(1) The vertical ground reaction must be—

(i) Equal to the vertical loads obtained in the condition specified in paragraph (b) of this section; and

(ii) Divided equally among the skids.

(2) The vertical ground reactions must be combined with a horizontal sideload of 25 percent of their value.

(3) The total sideload must be applied equally between skids and along the length of the skids.

(4) The unbalanced moments are assumed to be resisted by angular inertia.

(5) The skid gear must be investigated for—

(i) Inward acting sideloads; and

(ii) Outward acting sideloads.

(e) *One-skid landing loads in the level attitude.* In the level attitude, and with the rotorcraft contacting the ground along the bottom of one skid only, the following apply:

(1) The vertical load on the ground contact side must be the same as that obtained on that side in the condition specified in paragraph (b) of this section.

(2) The unbalanced moments are assumed to be resisted by angular inertia.

(f) *Special conditions.* In addition to the conditions specified in paragraphs (b) and (c) of this section, the rotorcraft must be designed for the following ground reactions:

(1) A ground reaction load acting up and aft at an angle of 45 degrees to the longitudinal axis of the rotorcraft. This load must be—

(i) Equal to 1.33 times the maximum weight;

(ii) Distributed symmetrically among the skids;

(iii) Concentrated at the forward end of the straight part of the skid tube; and

(iv) Applied only to the forward end of the skid tube and its attachment to the rotorcraft.

(2) With the rotorcraft in the level landing attitude, a vertical ground reaction load equal to one-half of the vertical load determined under paragraph (b) of this section. This load must be—

(i) Applied only to the skid tube and its attachment to the rotorcraft; and

(ii) Distributed equally over 33.3 percent of the length between the skid tube attachments and centrally located midway between the skid tube attachments.

[Amdt. 29–3, 33 FR 966, Jan. 26, 1968; as amended by Amdt. 27–26, 55 FR 8002, Mar. 6, 1990]

§ 29.505   Ski landing conditions.

If certification for ski operation is requested, the rotorcraft, with skis, must be designed to withstand the following loading conditions (where P is the maximum static weight on each ski with the rotorcraft at design maximum weight, and n is the limit load factor determined under § 29.473(b)):

(a) Up-load conditions in which—

(1) A vertical load of Pn and a horizontal load of $Pn/4$ are simultaneously applied at the pedestal bearings; and

(2) A vertical load of 1.33 P is applied at the pedestal bearings.

(b) A side load condition in which a side load of 0.35 Pn is applied at the pedestal bearings in a horizontal plane perpendicular to the centerline of the rotorcraft.

(c) A torque-load condition in which a torque load of 1.33 P (in foot-pounds) is applied to the ski about the vertical axis through the centerline of the pedestal bearings.

§29.511 Ground load: unsymmetrical loads on multiple-wheel units.

(a) In dual-wheel gear units, 60 percent of the total ground reaction for the gear unit must be applied to one wheel and 40 percent to the other.

(b) To provide for the case of one deflated tire, 60 percent of the specified load for the gear unit must be applied to either wheel except that the vertical ground reaction may not be less than the full static value.

(c) In determining the total load on a gear unit, the transverse shift in the load centroid, due to unsymmetrical load distribution on the wheels, may be neglected.

[Amdt. 29–3, 33 FR 966, Jan. 26, 1968]

WATER LOADS

§29.519 Hull type rotorcraft: Water-based and amphibian.

(a) *General.* For hull type rotorcraft, the structure must be designed to withstand the water loading set forth in paragraphs (b), (c), and (d) of this section considering the most severe wave heights and profiles for which approval is desired. The loads for the landing conditions of paragraphs (b) and (c) of this section must be developed and distributed along and among the hull and auxiliary floats, if used, in a rational and conservative manner, assuming a rotor lift not exceeding two-thirds of the rotorcraft weight to act throughout the landing impact.

(b) *Vertical landing conditions.* The rotorcraft must initially contact the most critical wave surface at zero forward speed in likely pitch and roll attitudes which result in critical design loadings. The vertical descent velocity may not be less than 6.5 feet per second relative to the mean water surface.

(c) *Forward speed landing conditions.* The rotorcraft must contact the most critical wave at forward velocities from zero up to 30 knots in likely pitch, roll, and yaw attitudes and with a vertical descent velocity of not less than 6.5 feet per second relative to the mean water surface. A maximum forward velocity of less than 30 knots may be used in design if it can be dem-

onstrated that the forward velocity selected would not be exceeded in a normal one-engine-out landing.

(d) *Auxiliary float immersion condition.* In addition to the loads from the landing conditions, the auxiliary float, and its support and attaching structure in the hull, must be designed for the load developed by a fully immersed float unless it can be shown that full immersion of the float is unlikely, in which case the highest likely float buoyancy load must be applied that considers loading of the float immersed to create restoring moments compensating for upsetting moments caused by side wind, asymmetrical rotorcraft loading, water wave action, and rotorcraft inertia.

[Amdt. 29–3, 33 FR 966, Jan. 26, 196; as amended by Amdt. 27–26, 55 FR 8002, Mar. 6, 1990]

§29.521 Float landing conditions.

If certification for float operation (including float amphibian operation) is requested, the rotorcraft, with floats, must be designed to withstand the following loading conditions (where the limit load factor is determined under §29.473(b) or assumed to be equal to that determined for wheel landing gear):

(a) Up-load conditions in which—

(1) A load is applied so that, with the rotorcraft in the static level attitude, the resultant water reaction passes vertically through the center of gravity; and

(2) The vertical load prescribed in paragraph (a)(1) of this section is applied simultaneously with an aft component of 0.25 times the vertical component

(b) A side load condition in which—

(1) A vertical load of 0.75 times the total vertical load specified in paragraph (a)(1) of this section is divided equally among the floats; and

(2) For each float, the load share determined under paragraph (b)(1) of this section, combined with a total side load of 0.25 times the total vertical load specified in paragraph (b)(1) of this section, is applied to that float only.

[Amdt. 29–3, 33 FR 967, Jan. 26, 1968]

MAIN COMPONENT REQUIREMENTS

§ 29.547 Main and tail rotor structure.

(a) A rotor is an assembly of rotating components, which includes the rotor hub, blades, blade dampers, the pitch control mechanisms, and all other parts that rotate with the assembly.

(b) Each rotor assembly must be designed as prescribed in this section and must function safely for the critical flight load and operating conditions. A design assessment must be performed, including a detailed failure analysis to identify all failures that will prevent continued safe flight or safe landing, and must identify the means to minimize the likelihood of their occurrence.

(c) The rotor structure must be designed to withstand the following loads prescribed in §§ 29.337 through 29.341 and 29.351:

(1) Critical flight loads.

(2) Limit loads occurring under normal conditions of autorotation.

(d) The rotor structure must be designed to withstand loads simulating—

(1) For the rotor blades, hubs, and flapping hinges, the impact force of each blade against its stop during ground operation; and

(2) Any other critical condition expected in normal operation.

(e) The rotor structure must be designed to withstand the limit torque at any rotational speed, including zero. In addition:

(1) The limit torque need not be greater than the torque defined by a torque limiting device (where provided), and may not be less than the greater of—

(i) The maximum torque likely to be transmitted to the rotor structure, in either direction, by the rotor drive or by sudden application of the rotor brake; and

(ii) For the main rotor, the limit engine torque specified in § 29.361.

(2) The limit torque must be equally and rationally distributed to the rotor blades.

(Secs. 604, 605, 72 Stat. 778, 49 U.S.C. 1424, 1425)

[Doc. No. 5084, 29 FR 16150, Dec. 3, 1964, as amended by Amdt. 29–4, 33 FR 14106, Sept. 18, 1968; Amdt. 29–40, 61 FR 21907, May 10, 1996]

§ 29.549 Fuselage and rotor pylon structures.

(a) Each fuselage and rotor pylon structure must be designed to withstand—

(1) The critical loads prescribed in §§ 29.337 through 29.341, and 29.351;

(2) The applicable ground loads prescribed in §§ 29.235, 29.471 through 29.485, 29.493, 29.497, 29.505, and 29.521; and

(3) The loads prescribed in § 29.547 (d)(1) and (e)(1)(i).

(b) Auxiliary rotor thrust, the torque reaction of each rotor drive system, and the balancing air and inertia loads occurring under accelerated flight conditions, must be considered.

(c) Each engine mount and adjacent fuselage structure must be designed to withstand the loads occurring under accelerated flight and landing conditions, including engine torque.

(d) [Reserved]

(e) If approval for the use of 2½-minute OEI power is requested, each engine mount and adjacent structure must be designed to withstand the loads resulting from a limit torque equal to 1.25 times the mean torque for 2½-minute OEI power combined with 1g flight loads.

(Secs. 604, 605, 72 Stat. 778, 49 U.S.C. 1424, 1425)

[Doc. No. 5084, 29 FR 16150, Dec. 3, 1964, as amended by Amdt. 29–4, 33 FR 14106, Sept. 18, 1968; Amdt. 29–26, 53 FR 34215, Sept. 2, 1988]

§ 29.551 Auxiliary lifting surfaces.

Each auxiliary lifting surface must be designed to withstand—

(a) The critical flight loads in §§ 29.337 through 29.341, and 29.351;

(b) the applicable ground loads in §§ 29.235, 29.471 through 29.485, 29.493, 29.505, and 29.521; and

(c) Any other critical condition expected in normal operation.

EMERGENCY LANDING CONDITIONS

§ 29.561 General.

(a) The rotorcraft, although it may be damaged in emergency landing conditions on land or water, must be designed as prescribed in this section to protect the occupants under those conditions.

(b) The structure must be designed to give each occupant every reasonable chance of escaping serious injury in a crash landing when—

(1) Proper use is made of seats, belts, and other safety design provisions;

(2) The wheels are retracted (where applicable); and

(3) Each occupant and each item of mass inside the cabin that could injure an occupant is restrained when subjected to the following ultimate inertial load factors relative to the surrounding structure:

(i) Upward—4g.

(ii) Forward—16g.

(iii) Sideward—8g.

(iv) Downward—20g, after the intended displacement of the seat device.

(v) Rearward—1.5g.

(c) The supporting structure must be designed to restrain under any ultimate inertial load factor up to those specified in this paragraph, any item of mass above and/or behind the crew and passenger compartment that could injure an occupant if it came loose in an emergency landing. Items of mass to be considered include, but are not limited to, rotors, transmission, and engines. The items of mass must be restrained for the following ultimate inertial load factors:

(1) Upward—1.5g.

(2) Forward—12g.

(3) Sideward—6g.

(4) Downward—12g.

(5) Rearward—1.5g.

(d) Any fuselage structure in the area of internal fuel tanks below the passenger floor level must be designed to resist the following ultimate inertial factors and loads, and to protect the fuel tanks from rupture, if rupture is likely when those loads are applied to that area:

(1) Upward—1.5g.

(2) Forward—4.0g.

(3) Sideward—2.0g.

(4) Downward—4.0g.

[Doc. No. 5084, 29 FR 16150, Dec. 3, 1964, as amended by Amdt. 29–29, 54 FR 47319, Nov. 13, 1989; Amdt. 29–38, 61 FR 10438, Mar. 13, 1996]

§29.562 Emergency landing dynamic conditions.

(a) The rotorcraft, although it may be damaged in a crash landing, must be designed to reasonably protect each occupant when—

(1) The occupant properly uses the seats, safety belts, and shoulder harnesses provided in the design; and

(2) The occupant is exposed to loads equivalent to those resulting from the conditions prescribed in this section.

(b) Each seat type design or other seating device approved for crew or passenger occupancy during takeoff and landing must successfully complete dynamic tests or be demonstrated by rational analysis based on dynamic tests of a similar type seat in accordance with the following criteria. The tests must be conducted with an occupant simulated by a 170-pound anthropomorphic test dummy (ATD), as defined by 49 CFR 572, Subpart B, or its equivalent, sitting in the normal upright position.

(1) A change in downward velocity of not less than 30 feet per second when the seat or other seating device is oriented in its nominal position with respect to the rotorcraft's reference system, the rotorcraft's longitudinal axis is canted upward 60° with respect to the impact velocity vector, and the rotorcraft's lateral axis is perpendicular to a vertical plane containing the impact velocity vector and the rotorcraft's longitudinal axis. Peak floor deceleration must occur in not more than 0.031 seconds after impact and must reach a minimum of 30g's.

(2) A change in forward velocity of not less than 42 feet per second when the seat or other seating device is oriented in its nominal position with respect to the rotorcraft's reference system, the rotorcraft's longitudinal axis is yawed 10° either right or left of the impact velocity vector (whichever would cause the greatest load on the shoulder harness), the rotorcraft's lateral axis is contained in a horizontal plane containing the impact velocity vector, and the rotorcraft's vertical axis is perpendicular to a horizontal plane containing the impact velocity vector. Peak floor deceleration must occur in not more than 0.071 seconds after impact and must reach a minimum of 18.4g's.

(3) Where floor rails or floor or sidewall attachment devices are used to attach the seating devices to the airframe structure for the conditions of this section, the rails or devices must

be misaligned with respect to each other by at least 10° vertically (i.e., pitch out of parallel) and by at least a 10° lateral roll, with the directions optional, to account for possible floor warp.

(c) Compliance with the following must be shown:

(1) The seating device system must remain intact although it may experience separation intended as part of its design.

(2) The attachment between the seating device and the airframe structure must remain intact although the structure may have exceeded its limit load.

(3) The ATD's shoulder harness strap or straps must remain on or in the immediate vicinity of the ATD's shoulder during the impact.

(4) The safety belt must remain on the ATD's pelvis during the impact.

(5) The ATD's head either does not contact any portion of the crew or passenger compartment or, if contact is made, the head impact does not exceed a head injury criteria (HIC) of 1,000 as determined by this equation.

$$HIC = (t_2 - t_1) \left[\frac{1}{(t_2 - t_1)} \int_{t_1}^{t_2} a(t)dt \right]^{2.5}$$

Where: a(t) is the resultant acceleration at the center of gravity of the head form expressed as a multiple of g (the acceleration of gravity) and $t_2 - t_1$ is the time duration, in seconds, of major head impact, not to exceed 0.05 seconds.

(6) Loads in individual shoulder harness straps must not exceed 1,750 pounds. If dual straps are used for retaining the upper torso, the total harness strap loads must not exceed 2,000 pounds.

(7) The maximum compressive load measured between the pelvis and the lumbar column of the ATD must not exceed 1,500 pounds.

(d) An alternate approach that achieves an equivalent or greater level of occupant protection, as required by this section, must be substantiated on a rational basis.

[Amdt. 29–29, 54 FR 47320, Nov. 13, 1989, as amended by Amdt. 29–41, 62 FR 46173, Aug. 29, 1997]

§ 29.563 Structural ditching provisions.

If certification with ditching provisions is requested, structural strength for ditching must meet the requirements of this section and § 29.801(e).

(a) *Forward speed landing conditions.* The rotorcraft must initially contact the most critical wave for reasonably probable water conditions at forward velocities from zero up to 30 knots in likely pitch, roll, and yaw attitudes. The rotorcraft limit vertical descent velocity may not be less than 5 feet per second relative to the mean water surface. Rotor lift may be used to act through the center of gravity throughout the landing impact. This lift may not exceed two-thirds of the design maximum weight. A maximum forward velocity of less than 30 knots may be used in design if it can be demonstrated that the forward velocity selected would not be exceeded in a normal one-engine-out touchdown.

(b) *Auxiliary or emergency float conditions—*(1) *Floats fixed or deployed before initial water contact.* In addition to the landing loads in paragraph (a) of this section, each auxiliary or emergency float, or its support and attaching structure in the airframe or fuselage, must be designed for the load developed by a fully immersed float unless it can be shown that full immersion is unlikely. If full immersion is unlikely, the highest likely float buoyancy load must be applied. The highest likely buoyancy load must include consideration of a partially immersed float creating restoring moments to compensate the upsetting moments caused by side wind, unsymmetrical rotorcraft loading, water wave action, rotorcraft inertia, and probable structural damage and leakage considered under § 29.801(d). Maximum roll and pitch angles determined from compliance with § 29.801(d) may be used, if significant, to determine the extent of immersion of each float. If the floats are deployed in flight, appropriate air loads derived from the flight limitations with the floats deployed shall be used in substantiation of the floats and their attachment to the rotorcraft. For this purpose, the design airspeed for limit load is the float deployed airspeed operating limit multiplied by 1.11.

(2) *Floats deployed after initial water contact.* Each float must be designed for full or partial immersion prescribed in paragraph (b)(1) of this section. In addition, each float must be designed for combined vertical and drag loads using a relative limit speed of 20 knots between the rotorcraft and the water. The vertical load may not be less than the highest likely buoyancy load determined under paragraph (b)(1) of this section.

[Amdt. 27–26, 55 FR 8003, Mar. 6, 1990]

FATIGUE EVALUATION

§ 29.571 Fatigue evaluation of structure.

(a) *General.* An evaluation of the strength of principal elements, detail design points, and fabrication techniques must show that catastrophic failure due to fatigue, considering the effects of environment, intrinsic/discrete flaws, or accidental damage will be avoided. Parts to be evaluated include, but are not limited to, rotors, rotor drive systems between the engines and rotor hubs, controls, fuselage, fixed and movable control surfaces, engine and transmission mountings, landing gear, and their related primary attachments. In addition, the following apply:

(1) Each evaluation required by this section must include—

(i) The identification of principal structural elements, the failure of which could result in catastrophic failure of the rotorcraft;

(ii) In-flight measurement in determining the loads or stresses for items in paragraph (a)(1)(i) of this section in all critical conditions throughout the range of limitations in § 29.309 (including altitude effects), except that maneuvering load factors need not exceed the maximum values expected in operations; and

(iii) Loading spectra as severe as those expected in operation based on loads or stresses determined under paragraph (a)(1)(ii) of this section, including external load operations, if applicable, and other high frequency power cycle operations.

(2) Based on the evaluations required by this section, inspections, replacement times, combinations thereof, or other procedures must be established as necessary to avoid catastrophic failure. These inspections, replacement times, combinations thereof, or other procedures must be included in the airworthiness limitations section of the Instructions for Continued Airworthiness required by § 29.1529 and section A29.4 of appendix A of this part.

(b) *Fatigue tolerance evaluation (including tolerance to flaws).* The structure must be shown by analysis supported by test evidence and, if available, service experience to be of fatigue tolerant design. The fatigue tolerance evaluation must include the requirements of either paragraph (b)(1), (2), or (3) of this section, or a combination thereof, and also must include a determination of the probable locations and modes of damage caused by fatigue, considering environmental effects, intrinsic/discrete flaws, or accidental damage. Compliance with the flaw tolerance requirements of paragraph (b)(1) or (2) of this section is required unless the applicant establishes that these fatigue flaw tolerant methods for a particular structure cannot be achieved within the limitations of geometry, inspectability, or good design practice. Under these circumstances, the safe-life evaluation of paragraph (b)(3) of this section is required.

(1) *Flaw tolerant safe-life evaluation.* It must be shown that the structure, with flaws present, is able to withstand repeated loads of variable magnitude without detectable flaw growth for the following time intervals—

(i) Life of the rotorcraft; or

(ii) Within a replacement time furnished under section A29.4 of appendix A to this part.

(2) *Fail-safe (residual strength after flaw growth) evaluation.* It must be shown that the structure remaining after a partial failure is able to withstand design limit loads without failure within an inspection period furnished under section A29.4 of appendix A to this part. Limit loads are defined in § 29.301(a).

(i) The residual strength evaluation must show that the remaining structure after flaw growth is able to withstand design limit loads without failure within its operational life.

639

(ii) Inspection intervals and methods must be established as necessary to ensure that failures are detected prior to residual strength conditions being reached.

(iii) If significant changes in structural stiffness or geometry, or both, follow from a structural failure or partial failure, the effect on flaw tolerance must be further investigated.

(3) *Safe-life evaluation.* It must be shown that the structure is able to withstand repeated loads of variable magnitude without detectable cracks for the following time intervals—

(i) Life of the rotorcraft; or

(ii) Within a replacement time furnished under section A29.4 of appendix A to this part.

[Amdt. 29–28, 54 FR 43930, Oct. 27, 1989]

Subpart D—Design and Construction

GENERAL

§ 29.601 Design.

(a) The rotorcraft may have no design features or details that experience has shown to be hazardous or unreliable.

(b) The suitability of each questionable design detail and part must be established by tests.

§ 29.602 Critical parts.

(a) *Critical part.* A critical part is a part, the failure of which could have a catastrophic effect upon the rotorcraft, and for which critical characterists have been identified which must be controlled to ensure the required level of integrity.

(b) If the type design includes critical parts, a critical parts list shall be established. Procedures shall be established to define the critical design characteristics, identify processes that affect those characteristics, and identify the design change and process change controls necessary for showing compliance with the quality assurance requirements of part 21 of this chapter.

[Doc. No. 29311, 64 FR 46232, Aug. 24, 1999]

§ 29.603 Materials.

The suitability and durability of materials used for parts, the failure of which could adversely affect safety, must—

(a) Be established on the basis of experience or tests;

(b) Meet approved specifications that ensure their having the strength and other properties assumed in the design data; and

(c) Take into account the effects of environmental conditions, such as temperature and humidity, expected in service.

(Secs. 313(a), 601, 603, 604, and 605 of the Federal Aviation Act of 1958 (49 U.S.C. 1354(a), 1421, 1423, 1424), and sec. 6(c), Dept. of Transportation Act (49 U.S.C. 1655(c)))

[Doc. No. 5084, 29 FR 16150, Dec. 3, 1964, as amended by Amdt. 29–12, 41 FR 55471, Dec. 20, 1976; Amdt. 29–17, 43 FR 50599, Oct. 30, 1978]

§ 29.605 Fabrication methods.

(a) The methods of fabrication used must produce consistently sound structures. If a fabrication process (such as gluing, spot welding, or heat-treating) requires close control to reach this objective, the process must be performed according to an approved process specification.

(b) Each new aircraft fabrication method must be substantiated by a test program.

(Secs. 313(a), 601, 603, 604, Federal Aviation Act of 1958 (49 U.S.C. 1354(a), 1421, 1423, 1424), sec. 6(c), Dept. of Transportation Act (49 U.S.C. 1655(c)))

[Doc. No. 5084, 29 FR 16150. Dec. 3, 1964, as amended by Amdt. 29–17, 43 FR 50599, Oct. 30, 1978]

§ 29.607 Fasteners.

(a) Each removable bolt, screw, nut, pin, or other fastener whose loss could jeopardize the safe operation of the rotorcraft must incorporate two separate locking devices. The fastener and its locking devices may not be adversely affected by the environmental conditions associated with the particular installation.

(b) No self-locking nut may be used on any bolt subject to rotation in operation unless a nonfriction locking device is used in addition to the self-locking device.

[Amdt. 29–5, 33 FR 14533, Sept. 27, 1968]

§29.609 Protection of structure.

Each part of the structure must—

(a) Be suitably protected against deterioration or loss of strength in service due to any cause, including—

(1) Weathering;

(2) Corrosion; and

(3) Abrasion; and

(b) Have provisions for ventilation and drainage where necessary to prevent the accumulation of corrosive, flammable, or noxious fluids.

§29.610 Lightning and static electricity protection.

(a) The rotorcraft structure must be protected against catastrophic effects from lightning.

(b) For metallic components, compliance with paragraph (a) of this section may be shown by—

(1) Electrically bonding the components properly to the airframe; or

(2) Designing the components so that a strike will not endanger the rotorcraft.

(c) For nonmetallic components, compliance with paragraph (a) of this section may be shown by—

(1) Designing the components to minmize the effect of a strike; or

(2) Incorporating acceptable means of diverting the resulting electrical current to not endanger the rotorcraft.

(d) The electric bonding and protection against lightning and static electricity must—

(1) Minimize the accumulation of electrostatic charge;

(2) Minimize the risk of electric shock to crew, passengers, and service and maintenance personnel using normal precautions;

(3) Provide and electrical return path, under both normal and fault conditions, on rotorcraft having grounded electrical systems; and

(4) Reduce to an acceptable level the effects of lightning and static electricity on the functioning of essential electrical and electronic equipment.

[Amdt. 29–24, 49 FR 44437, Nov. 6, 1984; Amdt. 29–40, 61 FR 21907, May 10, 1996; 61 FR 33963, July 1, 1996]

§29.611 Inspection provisions.

There must be means to allow close examination of each part that requires—

(a) Recurring inspection;

(b) Adjustment for proper alignment and functioning; or

(c) Lubrication.

§29.613 Material strength properties and design values.

(a) Material strength properties must be based on enough tests of material meeting specifications to establish design values on a statistical basis.

(b) Design values must be chosen to minimize the probability of structural failure due to material variability. Except as provided in paragraphs (d) and (e) of this section, compliance with this paragraph must be shown by selecting design values that assure material strength with the following probability—

(1) Where applied loads are eventually distributed through a single member within an assembly, the failure of which would result in loss of structural integrity of the component, 99 percent probability with 95 percent confidence; and

(2) For redundant structures, those in which the failure of individual elements would result in applied loads being safely distributed to other load-carrying members, 90 percent probability with 95 percent confidence.

(c) The strength, detail design, and fabrication of the structure must minimize the probability of disastrous fatigue failure, particularly at points of stress concentration.

(d) Design values may be those contained in the following publications (available from the Naval Publications and Forms Center, 5801 Tabor Avenue, Philadelphia, PA 19120) or other values approved by the Administrator:

(1) MIL—HDBK–5, "Metallic Materials and Elements for Flight Vehicle Structure".

(2) MIL—HDBK–17, "Plastics for Flight Vehicles".

(3) ANC–18, "Design of Wood Aircraft Structures".

(4) MIL—HDBK–23, "Composite Construction for Flight Vehicles".

(e) Other design values may be used if a selection of the material is made in which a specimen of each individual item is tested before use and it is determined that the actual strength properties of that particular item will equal or exceed those used in design.

(Secs. 313(a), 601, 603, 604, Federal Aviation Act of 1958 (49 U.S.C. 1354(a), 1421, 1423, 1424), sec. 6(c), Dept. of Transportation Act (49 U.S.C. 1655(c)))

[Doc. No. 5084, 29 FR 16150, Dec. 3, 1964, as amended by Amdt. 29–17, 43 FR 50599, Oct. 30, 1978; Amdt. 27–26, 55 FR 8003, Mar. 6, 1990]

§ 29.619 Special factors.

(a) The special factors prescribed in §§ 29.621 through 29.625 apply to each part of the structure whose strength is—

(1) Uncertain;

(2) Likely to deteriorate in service before normal replacement; or

(3) Subject to appreciable variability due to—

(i) Uncertainties in manufacturing processes; or

(ii) Uncertainties in inspection methods.

(b) For each part of the rotorcraft to which §§ 29.621 through 29.625 apply, the factor of safety prescribed in § 29.303 must be multiplied by a special factor equal to—

(1) The applicable special factors prescribed in §§ 29.621 through 29.625; or

(2) Any other factor great enough to ensure that the probability of the part being understrength because of the uncertainties specified in paragraph (a) of this section is extremely remote.

§ 29.621 Casting factors.

(a) *General.* The factors, tests, and inspections specified in paragraphs (b) and (c) of this section must be applied in addition to those necessary to establish foundry quality control. The inspections must meet approved specifications. Paragraphs (c) and (d) of this section apply to structural castings except castings that are pressure tested as parts of hydraulic or other fluid systems and do not support structural loads.

(b) *Bearing stresses and surfaces.* The casting factors specified in paragraphs (c) and (d) of this section—

(1) Need not exceed 1.25 with respect to bearing stresses regardless of the method of inspection used; and

(2) Need not be used with respect to the bearing surfaces of a part whose

bearing factor is larger than the applicable casting factor.

(c) *Critical castings.* For each casting whose failure would preclude continued safe flight and landing of the rotorcraft or result in serious injury to any occupant, the following apply:

(1) Each critical casting must—

(i) Have a casting factor of not less than 1.25; and

(ii) Receive 100 percent inspection by visual, radiographic, and magnetic particle (for ferromagnetic materials) or penetrant (for nonferromagnetic materials) inspection methods or approved equivalent inspection methods.

(2) For each critical casting with a casting factor less than 1.50, three sample castings must be static tested and shown to meet—

(i) The strength requirements of § 29.305 at an ultimate load corresponding to a casting factor of 1.25; and

(ii) The deformation requirements of § 29.305 at a load of 1.15 times the limit load.

(d) *Noncritical castings.* For each casting other than those specified in paragraph (c) of this section, the following apply:

(1) Except as provided in paragraphs (d)(2) and (3) of this section, the casting factors and corresponding inspections must meet the following table:

Casting factor	Inspection
2.0 or greater	100 percent visual.
Less than 2.0, greater than 1.5.	100 percent visual, and magnetic particle (ferromagnetic materials), penetrant (nonferromagnetic materials), or approved equivalent inspection methods.
1.25 through 1.50	100 percent visual, and magnetic particle (ferromagnetic materials), penetrant (nonferromagnetic materials), and radiographic or approved equivalent inspection methods.

(2) The percentage of castings inspected by nonvisual methods may be reduced below that specified in paragraph (d)(1) of this section when an approved quality control procedure is established.

(3) For castings procured to a specification that guarantees the mechanical properties of the material in the casting and provides for demonstration of these properties by test of coupons

cut from the castings on a sampling basis—

(i) A casting factor of 1.0 may be used; and

(ii) The castings must be inspected as provided in paragraph (d)(1) of this section for casting factors of "1.25 through 1.50" and tested under paragraph (c)(2) of this section.

[Doc. No. 5084, 29 FR 16150, Dec. 3, 1964, as amended by Amdt. 29–41, 62 FR 46173, Aug. 29, 1997]

§29.623 Bearing factors.

(a) Except as provided in paragraph (b) of this section, each part that has clearance (free fit), and that is subject to pounding or vibration, must have a bearing factor large enough to provide for the effects of normal relative motion.

(b) No bearing factor need be used on a part for which any larger special factor is prescribed.

§29.625 Fitting factors.

For each fitting (part or terminal used to join one structural member to another) the following apply:

(a) For each fitting whose strength is not proven by limit and ultimate load tests in which actual stress conditions are simulated in the fitting and surrounding structures, a fitting factor of at least 1.15 must be applied to each part of—

(1) The fitting;

(2) The means of attachment; and

(3) The bearing on the joined members.

(b) No fitting factor need be used—

(1) For joints made under approved practices and based on comprehensive test data (such as continuous joints in metal plating, welded joints, and scarf joints in wood); and

(2) With respect to any bearing surface for which a larger special factor is used.

(c) For each integral fitting, the part must be treated as a fitting up to the point at which the section properties become typical of the member.

(d) Each seat, berth, litter, safety belt, and harness attachment to the structure must be shown by analysis, tests, or both, to be able to withstand the inertia forces prescribed in §29.561(b)(3) multiplied by a fitting factor of 1.33.

[Doc. No. 5084, 29 FR 16150, Dec. 3, 1964, as amended by Amdt. 29–42, 63 FR 43285, Aug. 12, 1998]

§29.629 Flutter and divergence.

Each aerodynamic surface of the rotorcraft must be free from flutter and divergence under each appropriate speed and power condition.

[Doc. No. 28008, 61 FR 21907, May 10, 1996]

§29.631 Bird strike.

The rotorcraft must be designed to ensure capability of continued safe flight and landing (for Category A) or safe landing (for Category B) after impact with a 2.2-lb (1.0 kg) bird when the velocity of the rotorcraft (relative to the bird along the flight path of the rotorcraft) is equal to V_{NE} or V_H (whichever is the lesser) at altitudes up to 8,000 feet. Compliance must be shown by tests or by analysis based on tests carried out on sufficiently representative structures of similar design.

[Doc. No. 28008, 61 FR 21907, May 10, 1996; 61 FR 33963, July 1, 1996]

ROTORS

§29.653 Pressure venting and drainage of rotor blades.

(a) For each rotor blade—

(1) There must be means for venting the internal pressure of the blade;

(2) Drainage holes must be provided for the blade; and

(3) The blade must be designed to prevent water from becoming trapped in it.

(b) Paragraphs (a)(1) and (2) of this section does not apply to sealed rotor blades capable of withstanding the maximum pressure differentials expected in service.

[Amdt. 29–3, 33 FR 967, Jan. 26, 1968]

§29.659 Mass balance.

(a) The rotor and blades must be mass balanced as necessary to—

(1) Prevent excessive vibration; and

(2) Prevent flutter at any speed up to the maximum forward speed.

(b) The structural integrity of the mass balance installation must be substantiated.

[Amdt. 29-3, 33 FR 967, Jan. 26, 1968]

§ 29.661 Rotor blade clearance.

There must be enough clearance between the rotor blades and other parts of the structure to prevent the blades from striking any part of the structure during any operating condition.

[Amdt. 29-3, 33 FR 967, Jan. 26, 1968]

§ 29.663 Ground resonance prevention means.

(a) The reliability of the means for preventing ground resonance must be shown either by analysis and tests, or reliable service experience, or by showing through analysis or tests that malfunction or failure of a single means will not cause ground resonance.

(b) The probable range of variations, during service, of the damping action of the ground resonance prevention means must be established and must be investigated during the test required by § 29.241.

[Amdt. 27-26, 55 FR 8003, Mar. 6, 1990]

CONTROL SYSTEMS

§ 29.671 General.

(a) Each control and control system must operate with the ease, smoothness, and positiveness appropriate to its function.

(b) Each element of each flight control system must be designed, or distinctively and permanently marked, to minimize the probability of any incorrect assembly that could result in the malfunction of the system.

(c) A means must be provided to allow full control movement of all primary flight controls prior to flight, or a means must be provided that will allow the pilot to determine that full control authority is available prior to flight.

[Doc. No. 5084, 29 FR 16150, Dec. 3, 1964, as amended by Amdt. 29-24, 49 FR 44437, Nov. 6, 1984]

§ 29.672 Stability augmentation, automatic, and power-operated systems.

If the functioning of stability augmentation or other automatic or power-operated system is necessary to show compliance with the flight characteristics requirements of this part, the system must comply with § 29.671 of this part and the following:

(a) A warning which is clearly distinguishable to the pilot under expected flight conditions without requiring the pilot's attention must be provided for any failure in the stability augmentation system or in any other automatic or power-operated system which could result in an unsafe condition if the pilot is unaware of the failure. Warning systems must not activate the control systems.

(b) The design of the stability augmentation system or of any other automatic or power-operated system must allow initial counteraction of failures without requiring exceptional pilot skill or strength, by overriding the failure by moving the flight controls in the normal sense, and by deactivating the failed system.

(c) It must be show that after any single failure of the stability augmentation system or any other automatic or power-operated system—

(1) The rotorcraft is safely controllable when the failure or malfunction occurs at any speed or altitude within the approved operating limitations;

(2) The controllability and maneuverability requirements of this part are met within a practical operational flight envelope (for example, speed, altitude, normal acceleration, and rotorcraft configurations) which is described in the Rotorcraft Flight Manual; and

(3) The trim and stability characteristics are not impaired below a level needed to allow continued safe flight and landing.

[Amdt. 29-24, 49 FR 44437, Nov. 6, 1984]

§ 29.673 Primary flight controls.

Primary flight controls are those used by the pilot for immediate control of pitch, roll, yaw, and vertical motion of the rotorcraft.

[Amdt. 29-24, 49 FR 44437, Nov. 6, 1984]

§ 29.674 Interconnected controls.

Each primary flight control system must provide for safe flight and landing and operate independently after a malfunction, failure, or jam of any auxiliary interconnected control.

[Amdt. 27–26, 55 FR 8003, Mar. 6, 1990]

§29.675 Stops.

(a) Each control system must have stops that positively limit the range of motionof the pilot's controls.

(b) Each stop must be located in the system so that the range of travel of its control is not appreciably affected by—

(1) Wear;

(2) Slackness; or

(3) Takeup adjustments.

(c) Each stop must be able to withstand the loads corresponding to the design conditions for the system.

(d) For each main rotor blade—

(1) Stops that are appropriate to the blade design must be provided to limit travel of the blade about its hinge points; and

(2) There must be means to keep the blade from hitting the droop stops during any operation other than starting and stopping the rotor.

(Secs. 313(a), 601, 603, 604, Federal Aviation Act of 1958 (49 U.S.C. 1354(a), 1421, 1423, 1424), sec. 6(c), Dept. of Transportation Act (49 U.S.C. 1655(c)))

[Doc. No. 5084, 29 FR 16150. Dec. 3, 1964, as amended by Amdt. 29–17, 43 FR 50599, Oct. 30, 1978]

§29.679 Control system locks.

If there is a device to lock the control system with the rotorcraft on the ground or water, there must be means to—

(a) Automatically disengage the lock when the pilot operates the controls in a normal manner, or limit the operation of the rotorcraft so as to give unmistakable warning to the pilot before takeoff; and

(b) Prevent the lock from engaging in flight.

§29.681 Limit load static tests.

(a) Compliance with the limit load requirements of this part must be shown by tests in which—

(1) The direction of the test loads produces the most severe loading in the control system; and

(2) Each fitting, pulley, and bracket used in attaching the system to the main structure is included;

(b) Compliance must be shown (by analyses or individual load tests) with the special factor requirements for control system joints subject to angular motion.

§29.683 Operation tests.

It must be shown by operation tests that, when the controls are operated from the pilot compartment with the control system loaded to correspond with loads specified for the system, the system is free from—

(a) Jamming;

(b) Excessive friction; and

(c) Excessive deflection.

§29.685 Control system details.

(a) Each detail of each control system must be designed to prevent jamming, chafing, and interference from cargo, passengers, loose objects, or the freezing of moisture.

(b) There must be means in the cockpit to prevent the entry of foreign objects into places where they would jam the system.

(c) There must be means to prevent the slapping of cables or tubes against other parts.

(d) Cable systems must be designed as follows:

(1) Cables, cable fittings, turnbuckles, splices, and pulleys must be of an acceptable kind.

(2) The design of cable systems must prevent any hazardous change in cable tension throughout the range of travel under any operating conditions and temperature variations.

(3) No cable smaller than ⅛ inch diameter may be used in any primary control system.

(4) Pulley kinds and sizes must correspond to the cables with which they are used. The pulley-cable combinations and strength values specified in MIL–HDBK–5 must be used unless they are inapplicable.

(5) Pulleys must have close fitting guards to prevent the cables from being displaced or fouled.

(6) Pulleys must lie close enough to the plane passing through the cable to prevent the cable from rubbing against the pulley flange.

(7) No fairlead may cause a change in cable direction of more than three degrees.

(8) No clevis pin subject to load or motion and retained only by cotter pins may be used in the control system.

(9) Turnbuckles attached to parts having angular motion must be installed to prevent binding throughout the range of travel.

(10) There must be means for visual inspection at each fairlead, pulley, terminal, and turnbuckle.

(e) Control system joints subject to angular motion must incorporate the following special factors with respect to the ultimate bearing strength of the softest material used as a bearing:

(1) 3.33 for push-pull systems other than ball and roller bearing systems.

(2) 2.0 for cable systems.

(f) For control system joints, the manufacturer's static, non-Brinell rating of ball and roller bearings may not be exceeded.

[Doc. No. 5084, 29 FR 16150, Dec. 3, 1964, as amended by Amdt. 29–12, 41 FR 55471, Dec. 20, 1976]

§ 29.687 Spring devices.

(a) Each control system spring device whose failure could cause flutter or other unsafe characteristics must be reliable.

(b) Compliance with paragraph (a) of this section must be shown by tests simulating service conditions.

§ 29.691 Autorotation control mechanism.

Each main rotor blade pitch control mechanism must allow rapid entry into autorotation after power failure.

§ 29.695 Power boost and power-operated control system.

(a) If a power boost or power-operated control system is used, an alternate system must be immediately available that allows continued safe flight and landing in the event of—

(1) Any single failure in the power portion of the system; or

(2) The failure of all engines.

(b) Each alternate system may be a duplicate power portion or a manually operated mechanical system. The power portion includes the power

source (such as hydraulic pumps), and such items as valves, lines, and actuators.

(c) The failure of mechanical parts (such as piston rods and links), and the jamming of power cylinders, must be considered unless they are extremely improbable.

Landing Gear

§ 29.723 Shock absorption tests.

The landing inertia load factor and the reserve energy absorption capacity of the landing gear must be substantiated by the tests prescribed in §§ 29.725 and 29.727, respectively. These tests must be conducted on the complete rotorcraft or on units consisting of wheel, tire, and shock absorber in their proper relation.

§ 29.725 Limit drop test.

The limit drop test must be conducted as follows:

(a) The drop height must be at least 8 inches.

(b) If considered, the rotor lift specified in § 29.473(a) must be introduced into the drop test by appropriate energy absorbing devices or by the use of an effective mass.

(c) Each landing gear unit must be tested in the attitude simulating the landing condition that is most critical from the standpoint of the energy to be absorbed by it.

(d) When an effective mass is used in showing compliance with paragraph (b) of this section, the following formulae may be used instead of more rational computations.

$$W_e = W \times \frac{h + (1 - L)d}{h + d}; \text{ and}$$

$$n = n_j \frac{W_e}{W} + L$$

where:

W_e=the effective weight to be used in the drop test (lbs.).

$W=W_M$ for main gear units (lbs.), equal to the static reaction on the particular unit with the rotorcraft in the most critical attitude. A rational method may be used in computing a main gear static reaction, taking into consideration the moment arm between the main wheel reaction and the rotorcraft center of gravity.

$W=W_N$ for nose gear units (lbs.), equal to the vertical component of the static reaction that would exist at the nose wheel, assuming that the mass of the rotorcraft acts at the center of gravity and exerts a force of $1.0g$ downward and $0.25g$ forward.

$W=W_t$ for tailwheel units (lbs.) equal to whichever of the following is critical—

(1) The static weight on the tailwheel with the rotorcraft resting on all wheels; or

(2) The vertical component of the ground reaction that would occur at the tailwheel assuming that the mass of the rotorcraft acts at the center of gravity and exerts a force of $1g$ downward with the rotorcraft in the maximum nose-up attitude considered in the nose-up landing conditions.

h=specified free drop height (inches).

L=ratio of assumed rotor lift to the rotorcraft weight.

d=deflection under impact of the tire (at the proper inflation pressure) plus the vertical component of the axle travel (inches) relative to the drop mass.

n=limit inertia load factor.

n_j=the load factor developed, during impact, on the mass used in the drop test (i.e., the acceleration dv/dt in g's recorded in the drop test plus 1.0).

[Doc. No. 5084, 29 FR 16150, Dec. 3, 1964, as amended by Amdt. 29-3, 33 FR 967, Jan. 26. 1968]

§29.727 Reserve energy absorption drop test.

The reserve energy absorption drop test must be conducted as follows:

(a) The drop height must be 1.5 times that specified in §29.725(a).

(b) Rotor lift, where considered in a manner similar to that prescribed in §29.725(b), may not exceed 1.5 times the lift allowed under that paragraph.

(c) The landing gear must withstand this test without collapsing. Collapse of the landing gear occurs when a member of the nose, tail, or main gear will not support the rotorcraft in the proper attitude or allows the rotorcraft structure, other than landing gear and external accessories, to impact the landing surface.

[Doc. No. 5084, 29 FR 16150, Dec. 3, 1964, as amended by Amdt. 27-26, 55 FR 8003, Mar. 6, 1990]

§29.729 Retracting mechanism.

For rotorcraft with retractable landing gear, the following apply:

(a) *Loads.* The landing gear, retracting mechanism, wheel well doors, and supporting structure must be designed for—

(1) The loads occurring in any maneuvering condition with the gear retracted;

(2) The combined friction, inertia, and air loads occurring during retraction and extension at any airspeed up to the design maximum landing gear operating speed; and

(3) The flight loads, including those in yawed flight, occurring with the gear extended at any airspeed up to the design maximum landing gear extended speed.

(b) *Landing gear lock.* A positive means must be provided to keep the gear extended.

(c) *Emergency operation.* When other than manual power is used to operate the gear, emergency means must be provided for extending the gear in the event of—

(1) Any reasonably probable failure in the normal retraction system; or

(2) The failure of any single source of hydraulic, electric, or equivalent energy.

(d) *Operation tests.* The proper functioning of the retracting mechanism must be shown by operation tests.

(e) *Position indicator.* There must be means to indicate to the pilot when the gear is secured in the extreme positions.

(f) *Control.* The location and operation of the retraction control must meet the requirements of §§29.777 and 29.779.

(g) *Landing gear warning.* An aural or equally effective landing gear warning device must be provided that functions continuously when the rotorcraft is in a normal landing mode and the landing gear is not fully extended and locked. A manual shutoff capability must be provided for the warning device and the warning system must automatically reset when the rotorcraft is no longer in the landing mode.

[Doc. No. 5084, 29 FR 16150, Dec. 3, 1964, as amended by Amdt. 29-24, 49 FR 44437, Nov. 6, 1984]

§29.731 Wheels.

(a) Each landing gear wheel must be approved.

(b) The maximum static load rating of each wheel may not be less than the corresponding static ground reaction with—

(1) Maximum weight; and

(2) Critical center of gravity.

(c) The maximum limit load rating of each wheel must equal or exceed the maximum radial limit load determined under the applicable ground load requirements of this part.

§ 29.733 Tires.

Each landing gear wheel must have a tire—

(a) That is a proper fit on the rim of the wheel; and

(b) Of a rating that is not exceeded under—

(1) The design maximum weight;

(2) A load on each main wheel tire equal to the static ground reaction corresponding to the critical center of gravity; and

(3) A load on nose wheel tires (to be compared with the dynamic rating established for those tires) equal to the reaction obtained at the nose wheel, assuming that the mass of the rotorcraft acts as the most critical center of gravity and exerts a force of 1.0 g downward and 0.25 g forward, the reactions being distributed to the nose and main wheels according to the principles of statics with the drag reaction at the ground applied only at wheels with brakes.

(c) Each tire installed on a retractable landing gear system must, at the maximum size of the tire type expected in service, have a clearance to surrounding structure and systems that is adequate to prevent contact between the tire and any part of the structure or systems.

[Doc. No. 5084, 29 FR 16150, Dec. 3, 1964, as amended by Amdt. 29–12, 41 FR 55471, Dec. 20, 1976]

§ 29.735 Brakes.

For rotorcraft with wheel-type landing gear, a braking device must be installed that is—

(a) Controllable by the pilot;

(b) Usable during power-off landings; and

(c) Adequate to—

(1) Counteract any normal unbalanced torque when starting or stopping the rotor; and

(2) Hold the rotorcraft parked on a 10-degree slope on a dry, smooth pavement.

[Doc. No. 5084, 29 FR 16150, Dec. 3, 1964, as amended by Amdt. 29–24, 49 FR 44437, Nov. 6, 1984]

§ 29.737 Skis.

(a) The maximum limit load rating of each ski must equal or exceed the maximum limit load determined under the applicable ground load requirements of this part.

(b) There must be a stabilizing means to maintain the ski in an appropriate position during flight. This means must have enough strength to withstand the maximum aerodynamic and inertia loads on the ski.

FLOATS AND HULLS

§ 29.751 Main float buoyancy.

(a) For main floats, the buoyancy necessary to support the maximum weight of the rotorcraft in fresh water must be exceeded by—

(1) 50 percent, for single floats; and

(2) 60 percent, for multiple floats.

(b) Each main float must have enough water-tight compartments so that, with any single main float compartment flooded, the mainfloats will provide a margin of positive stability great enough to minimize the probability of capsizing.

[Doc. No. 5084, 29 FR 16150, Dec. 3, 1964, as amended by Amdt. 29–3, 33 FR 967, Jan. 26, 1968]

§ 29.753 Main float design.

(a) *Bag floats.* Each bag float must be designed to withstand—

(1) The maximum pressure differential that might be developed at the maximum altitude for which certification with that float is requested; and

(2) The vertical loads prescribed in § 29.521(a), distributed along the length of the bag over three-quarters of its projected area.

(b) *Rigid floats.* Each rigid float must be able to withstand the vertical, horizontal, and side loads prescribed in § 29.521. An appropriate load distribution under critical conditions must be used.

§ 29.755 Hull buoyancy.

Water-based and amphibian rotorcraft. The hull and auxiliary floats, if used, must have enough watertight compartments so that, with any single compartment of the hull or auxiliary floats flooded, the buoyancy of the hull and auxiliary floats, and wheel tires if used, provides a margin of positive water stability great enough to minimize the probability of capsizing the rotorcraft for the worst combination of wave heights and surface winds for which approval is desired.

[Amdt. 29–3, 33 FR 967, Jan. 26, 1968; as amended by Amdt. 27–26, 55 FR 8003, Mar. 6, 1990]

§ 29.757 Hull and auxiliary float strength.

The hull, and auxiliary floats if used, must withstand the water loads prescribed by § 29.519 with a rational and conservative distribution of local and distributed water pressures over the hull and float bottom.

[Amdt. 29–3, 33 FR 967, Jan. 26, 1968]

PERSONNEL AND CARGO
ACCOMMODATIONS

§ 29.771 Pilot compartment.

For each pilot compartment—

(a) The compartment and its equipment must allow each pilot to perform his duties without unreasonable concentration or fatigue;

(b) If there is provision for a second pilot, the rotorcraft must be controllable with equal safety from either pilot position. Flight and powerplant controls must be designed to prevent confusion or inadvertent operation when the rotorcraft is piloted from either position;

(c) The vibration and noise characteristics of cockpit appurtenances may not interfere with safe operation; and

(d) Inflight leakage of rain or snow that could distract the crew or harm the structure must be prevented.

[Doc. No. 5084, 29 FR 16150, Dec. 3, 1964, as amended by Amdt. 29–3, 33 FR 967, Jan. 26, 1968; Amdt. 29–24, 49 FR 44437, Nov. 6, 1984]

§ 29.773 Pilot compartment view.

(a) *Nonprecipitation conditions.* For nonprecipitation conditions, the following apply:

(1) Each pilot compartment must be arranged to give the pilots a sufficiently extensive, clear, and undistorted view for safe operation.

(2) Each pilot compartment must be free of glare and reflection that could interfere with the pilot's view. If certification for night operation is requested, this must be shown by night flight tests.

(b) *Precipitation conditions.* For precipitation conditions, the following apply:

(1) Each pilot must have a sufficiently extensive view for safe operation—

(i) In heavy rain at forward speeds up to V_H; and

(ii) In the most severe icing condition for which certification is requested.

(2) The first pilot must have a window that—

(i) Is openable under the conditions prescribed in paragraph (b)(1) of this section; and

(ii) Provides the view prescribed in that paragraph.

[Doc. No. 5084, 29 FR 16150, Dec. 3, 1964, as amended by Amdt. 29–3, 33 FR 967, Jan. 26, 1968]

§ 29.775 Windshields and windows.

Windshields and windows must be made of material that will not break into dangerous fragments.

[Amdt. 29–31, 55 FR 38966, Sept. 21, 1990]

§ 29.777 Cockpit controls.

Cockpit controls must be—

(a) Located to provide convenient operation and to prevent confusion and inadvertent operation; and

(b) Located and arranged with respect to the pilot's seats so that there is full and unrestricted movement of each control without interference from the cockpit structure or the pilot's clothing when pilots from 5′2″ to 6′0″ in height are seated.

§ 29.779 Motion and effect of cockpit controls.

Cockpit controls must be designed so that they operate in accordance with the following movements and actuation:

(a) Flight controls, including the collective pitch control, must operate with a sense of motion which corresponds to the effect on the rotorcraft.

(b) Twist-grip engine power controls must be designed so that, for lefthand operation, the motion of the pilot's hand is clockwise to increase power when the hand is viewed from the edge containing the index finger. Other engine power controls, excluding the collective control, must operate with a forward motion to increase power.

(c) Normal landing gear controls must operate downward to extend the landing gear.

[Amdt. 29–24, 49 FR 44437, Nov. 6, 1984]

§ 29.783 Doors.

(a) Each closed cabin must have at least one adequate and easily accessible external door.

(b) Each external door must be located, and appropriate operating procedures must be established, to ensure that persons using the door will not be endangered by the rotors, propellers, engine intakes, and exhausts when the operating procedures are used.

(c) There must be means for locking crew and external passenger doors and for preventing their opening in flight inadvertently or as a result of mechanical failure. It must be possible to open external doors from inside and outside the cabin with the rotorcraft on the ground even though persons may be crowded against the door on the inside of the rotorcraft. The means of opening must be simple and obvious and so arranged and marked that it can be readily located and operated.

(d) There must be reasonable provisions to prevent the jamming of any external doors in a minor crash as a result of fuselage deformation under the following ultimate inertial forces except for cargo or service doors not suitable for use as an exit in an emergency:

(1) Upward—1.5g.
(2) Forward—4.0g.

(3) Sideward—2.0g.
(4) Downward—4.0g.

(e) There must be means for direct visual inspection of the locking mechanism by crewmembers to determine whether the external doors (including passenger, crew, service, and cargo doors) are fully locked. There must be visual means to signal to appropriate crewmembers when normally used external doors are closed and fully locked.

(f) For outward opening external doors usable for entrance or egress, there must be an auxiliary safety latching device to prevent the door from opening when the primary latching mechanism fails. If the door does not meet the requirements of paragraph (c) of this section with this device in place, suitable operating procedures must be established to prevent the use of the device during takeoff and landing.

(g) If an integral stair is installed in a passenger entry door that is qualified as a passenger emergency exit, the stair must be designed so that under the following conditions the effectiveness of passenger emergency egress will not be impaired:

(1) The door, integral stair, and operating mechanism have been subjected to the inertial forces specified in paragraph (d) of this section, acting separately relative to the surrounding structure.

(2) The rotorcraft is in the normal ground attitude and in each of the attitudes corresponding to collapse of one or more legs, or primary members, as applicable, of the landing gear.

(h) Nonjettisonable doors used as ditching emergency exits must have means to enable them to be secured in the open position and remain secure for emergency egress in sea state conditions prescribed for ditching.

[Doc. No. 5084, 29 FR 16150, Dec. 3, 1964, as amended by Amdt. 29–20, 45 FR 60178, Sept. 11, 1980; Amdt. 29–29, 54 FR 47320, Nov. 13, 1989; Amdt. 27–26, 55 FR 8003, Mar. 6, 1990; Amdt. 29–31, 55 FR 38966, Sept. 21, 1990]

§ 29.785 Seats, berths, litters, safety belts, and harnesses.

(a) Each seat, safety belt, harness, and adjacent part of the rotorcraft at each station designated for occupancy during takeoff and landing must be free of potentially injurious objects, sharp edges, protuberances, and hard surfaces and must be designed so that a person making proper use of these facilities will not suffer serious injury in an emergency landing as a result of the inertial factors specified in §29.561(b) and dynamic conditions specified in §29.562.

(b) Each occupant must be protected from serious head injury by a safety belt plus a shoulder harness that will prevent the head from contacting any injurious object, except as provided for in §29.562(c)(5). A shoulder harness (upper torso restraint), in combination with the safety belt, constitutes a torso restraint system as described in TSO–C114.

(c) Each occupant's seat must have a combined safety belt and shoulder harness with a single-point release. Each pilot's combined safety belt and shoulder harness must allow each pilot when seated with safety belt and shoulder harness fastened to perform all functions necessary for flight operations. There must be a means to secure belt and harness when not in use to prevent interference with the operation of the rotorcraft and with rapid egress in an emergency.

(d) If seat backs do not have a firm handhold, there must be hand grips or rails along each aisle to let the occupants steady themselves while using the aisle in moderately rough air.

(e) Each projecting object that would injure persons seated or moving about in the rotorcraft in normal flight must be padded.

(f) Each seat and its supporting structure must be designed for an occupant weight of at least 170 pounds, considering the maximum load factors, inertial forces, and reactions between the occupant, seat, and safety belt or harness corresponding with the applicable flight and ground-load conditions, including the emergency landing conditions of §29.561(b). In addition—

(1) Each pilot seat must be designed for the reactions resulting from the application of the pilot forces prescribed in §29.397; and

(2) The inertial forces prescribed in §29.561(b) must be multiplied by a factor of 1.33 in determining the strength of the attachment of—

(i) Each seat to the structure; and

(ii) Each safety belt or harness to the seat or structure.

(g) When the safety belt and shoulder harness are combined, the rated strength of the safety belt and shoulder harness may not be less than that corresponding to the inertial forces specified in §29.561(b), considering the occupant weight of at least 170 pounds, considering the dimensional characteristics of the restraint system installation, and using a distribution of at least a 60-percent load to the safety belt and at least a 40-percent load to the shoulder harness. If the safety belt is capable of being used without the shoulder harness, the inertial forces specified must be met by the safety belt alone.

(h) When a headrest is used, the headrest and its supporting structure must be designed to resist the inertia forces specified in §29.561, with a 1.33 fitting factor and a head weight of at least 13 pounds.

(i) Each seating device system includes the device such as the seat, the cushions, the occupant restraint system and attachment devices.

(j) Each seating device system may use design features such as crushing or separation of certain parts of the seat in the design to reduce occupant loads for the emergency landing dynamic conditions of §29.562; otherwise, the system must remain intact and must not interfere with rapid evacuation of the rotorcraft.

(k) For purposes of this section, a litter is defined as a device designed to carry a nonambulatory person, primarily in a recumbent position, into and on the rotorcraft. Each berth or litter must be designed to withstand the load reaction of an occupant weight of at least 170 pounds when the occupant is subjected to the forward inertial factors specified in §29.561(b). A berth or litter installed within 15° or less of the longitudinal axis of the rotorcraft must be provided with a padded end-board, cloth diaphragm, or equivalent means that can withstand the forward load reaction. A berth or litter oriented greater than 15° with the longitudinal axis of the rotorcraft must be equipped with appropriate restraints, such as straps or safety belts, to withstand the forward reaction. In addition—

(1) The berth or litter must have a restraint system and must not have corners or other protuberances likely to cause serious injury to a person occupying it during emergency landing conditions; and

(2) The berth or litter attachment and the occupant restraint system attachments to the structure must be designed to withstand the critical loads resulting from flight and ground load conditions and from the conditions prescribed in § 29.561(b). The fitting factor required by § 29.625(d) shall be applied.

[Doc. No. 5084, 29 FR 16150, Dec. 3, 1964, as amended by Amdt. 29–24, 49 FR 44437, Nov. 6, 1984; Amdt. 29–29, 54 FR 47320, Nov. 13, 1989; Amdt. 29–42, 63 FR 43285, Aug. 12, 1998]

§ 29.787 Cargo and baggage compartments.

(a) Each cargo and baggage compartment must be designed for its placarded maximum weight of contents and for the critical load distributions at the appropriate maximum load factors corresponding to the specified flight and ground load conditions, except the emergency landing conditions of § 29.561.

(b) There must be means to prevent the contents of any compartment from becoming a hazard by shifting under the loads specified in paragraph (a) of this section.

(c) Under the emergency landing conditions of § 29.561, cargo and baggage compartments must—

(1) Be positioned so that if the contents break loose they are unlikely to cause injury to the occupants or restrict any of the escape facilities provided for use after an emergency landing; or

(2) Have sufficient strength to withstand the conditions specified in § 29.561, including the means of restraint and their attachments required by paragraph (b) of this section. Sufficient strength must be provided for the maximum authorized weight of cargo and baggage at the critical loading distribution.

(d) If cargo compartment lamps are installed, each lamp must be installed so as to prevent contact between lamp bulb and cargo.

[Doc. No. 5084, 29 FR 16150, Dec. 3, 1964, as amended by Amdt. 29–12, 41 FR 55472, Dec. 20, 1976; Amdt. 29–31, 55 FR 38966, Sept. 21, 1990]

§ 29.801 Ditching.

(a) If certification with ditching provisions is requested, the rotorcraft must meet the requirements of this section and §§ 29.807(d), 29.1411 and 29.1415.

(b) Each practicable design measure, compatible with the general characteristics of the rotorcraft, must be taken to minimize the probability that in an emergency landing on water, the behavior of the rotorcraft would cause immediate injury to the occupants or would make it impossible for them to escape.

(c) The probable behavior of the rotorcraft in a water landing must be investigated by model tests or by comparison with rotorcraft of similar configuration for which the ditching characteristics are known. Scoops, flaps, projections, and any other factors likely to affect the hydrodynamic characteristics of the rotorcraft must be considered.

(d) It must be shown that, under reasonably probable water conditions, the flotation time and trim of the rotorcraft will allow the occupants to leave the rotorcraft and enter the liferafts required by § 29.1415. If compliance with this provision is shown by bouyancy and trim computations, appropriate allowances must be made for probable structural damage and leakage. If the rotorcraft has fuel tanks (with fuel jettisoning provisions) that can reasonably be expected to withstand a ditching without leakage, the jettisonable volume of fuel may be considered as bouyancy volume.

(e) Unless the effects of the collapse of external doors and windows are accounted for in the investigation of the probable behavior of the rotorcraft in a water landing (as prescribed in paragraphs (c) and (d) of this section), the external doors and windows must be designed to withstand the probable maximum local pressures.

[Amdt. 29–12, 41 FR 55472, Dec. 20, 1976]

§ 29.803 Emergency evacuation.

(a) Each crew and passenger area must have means for rapid evacuation in a crash landing, with the landing gear (1) extended and (2) retracted, considering the possibility of fire.

(b) Passenger entrance, crew, and service doors may be considered as emergency exits if they meet the requirements of this section and of §§ 29.805 through 29.815.

(c) [Reserved]

(d) Except as provided in paragraph (e) of this section, the following categories of rotorcraft must be tested in accordance with the requirements of appendix D of this part to demonstrate that the maximum seating capacity, including the crewmembers required by the operating rules, can be evacuated from the rotorcraft to the ground within 90 seconds:

(1) Rotorcraft with a seating capacity of more than 44 passengers.

(2) Rotorcraft with all of the following:

(i) Ten or more passengers per passenger exit as determined under § 29.807(b).

(ii) No main aisle, as described in § 29.815, for each row of passenger seats.

(iii) Access to each passenger exit for each passenger by virtue of design features of seats, such as folding or breakover seat backs or folding seats.

(e) A combination of analysis and tests may be used to show that the rotorcraft is capable of being evacuated within 90 seconds under the conditions specified in § 29.803(d) if the Administrator finds that the combination of analysis and tests will provide data, with respect to the emergency evacuation capability of the rotorcraft, equivalent to that which would be obtained by actual demonstration.

[Doc. No. 5084, 29 FR 16150, Dec. 3, 1964, as amended by Amdt. 29-3, 33 FR 967, Jan. 26, 1968; Amdt. 27-26, 55 FR 8004, Mar. 6, 1990]

§ 29.805 Flight crew emergency exits.

(a) For rotorcraft with passenger emergency exits that are not convenient to the flight crew, there must be flight crew emergency exits, on both sides of the rotorcraft or as a top hatch, in the flight crew area.

(b) Each flight crew emergency exit must be of sufficient size and must be located so as to allow rapid evacuation of the flight crew. This must be shown by test.

(c) Each exit must not be obstructed by water or flotation devices after a ditching. This must be shown by test, demonstration, or analysis.

[Amdt. 29-3, 33 FR 968, Jan. 26, 1968; as amended by Amdt. 27-26, 55 FR 8004, Mar. 6, 1990]

§ 29.807 Passenger emergency exits.

(a) *Type.* For the purpose of this part, the types of passenger emergency exit are as follows:

(1) *Type I.* This type must have a rectangular opening of not less than 24 inches wide by 48 inches high, with corner radii not greater than one-third the width of the exit, in the passenger area in the side of the fuselage at floor level and as far away as practicable from areas that might become potential fire hazards in a crash.

(2) *Type II.* This type is the same as Type I, except that the opening must be at least 20 inches wide by 44 inches high.

(3) *Type III.* This type is the same as Type I, except that—

(i) The opening must be at least 20 inches wide by 36 inches high; and

(ii) The exits need not be at floor level.

(4) *Type IV.* This type must have a rectangular opening of not less than 19 inches wide by 26 inches high, with corner radii not greater than one-third the width of the exit, in the side of the fuselage with a step-up inside the rotorcraft of not more than 29 inches.

Openings with dimensions larger than those specified in this section may be used, regardless of shape, if the base of the opening has a flat surface of not less than the specified width.

(b) *Passenger emergency exits; side-of-fuselage.* Emergency exits must be accessible to the passengers and, except as provided in paragraph (d) of this section, must be provided in accordance with the following table:

Passenger seating capacity	Emergency exits for each side of the fuselage			
	Type I	Type II	Type III	Type IV
1 through 10	....	....	....	1
11 through 19	....	....	1 or	2

Passenger seating capacity	Emergency exits for each side of the fuselage			
	Type I	Type II	Type III	Type IV
20 through 39	....	1	....	1
40 through 59	1	....	....	1
60 through 79	1	....	1 or	2

(c) *Passenger emergency exits; other than side-of-fuselage.* In addition to the requirements of paragraph (b) of this section—

(1) There must be enough openings in the top, bottom, or ends of the fuselage to allow evacuation with the rotorcraft on its side; or

(2) The probability of the rotorcraft coming to rest on its side in a crash landing must be extremely remote.

(d) *Ditching emergency exits for passengers.* If certification with ditching provisions is requested, ditching emergency exits must be provided in accordance with the following requirements and must be proven by test, demonstration, or analysis unless the emergency exits required by paragraph (b) of this section already meet these requirements.

(1) For rotorcraft that have a passenger seating configuration, excluding pilots seats, of nine seats or less, one exit above the waterline in each side of the rotorcraft, meeting at least the dimensions of a Type IV exit.

(2) For rotorcraft that have a passenger seating configuration, excluding pilots seats, of 10 seats or more, one exit above the waterline in a side of the rotorcraft meeting at least the dimensions of a Type III exit, for each unit (or part of a unit) of 35 passenger seats, but no less than two such exits in the passenger cabin, with one on each side of the rotorcraft. However, where it has been shown through analysis, ditching demonstrations, or any other tests found necessary by the Administrator, that the evacuation capability of the rotorcraft during ditching is improved by the use of larger exits, or by other means, the passenger seat to exit ratio may be increased.

(3) Flotation devices, whether stowed or deployed, may not interfere with or obstruct the exits.

(e) *Ramp exits.* One Type I exit only, or one Type II exit only, that is required in the side of the fuselage under paragraph (b) of this section, may be installed instead in the ramp of floor ramp rotorcraft if—

(1) Its installation in the side of the fuselage is impractical; and

(2) Its installation in the ramp meets § 29.813.

(f) *Tests.* The proper functioning of each emergency exit must be shown by test.

[Amdt. 29–3, 33 FR 968, Jan. 26, 1968, as amended by Amdt. 29–12, 41 FR 55472, Dec. 20, 1976; Amdt. 27–26, 55 FR 8004, Mar. 6, 1990]

§ 29.809 Emergency exit arrangement.

(a) Each emergency exit must consist of a movable door or hatch in the external walls of the fuselage and must provide an unobstructed opening to the outside.

(b) Each emergency exit must be openable from the inside and from the outside.

(c) The means of opening each emergency exit must be simple and obvious and may not require exceptional effort.

(d) There must be means for locking each emergency exit and for preventing opening in flight inadvertently or as a result of mechanical failure.

(e) There must be means to minimize the probability of the jamming of any emergency exit in a minor crash landing as a result of fuselage deformation under the ultimate inertial forces in § 29.783(d).

(f) Except as provided in paragraph (h) of this section, each land-based rotorcraft emergency exit must have an approved slide as stated in paragraph (g) of this section, or its equivalent, to assist occupants in descending to the ground from each floor level exit and an approved rope, or its equivalent, for all other exits, if the exit threshold is more that 6 feet above the ground—

(1) With the rotorcraft on the ground and with the landing gear extended;

(2) With one or more legs or part of the landing gear collapsed, broken, or not extended; and

(3) With the rotorcraft resting on its side, if required by § 29.803(d).

(g) The slide for each passenger emergency exit must be a self-supporting slide or equivalent, and must be designed to meet the following requirements:

(1) It must be automatically deployed, and deployment must begin

during the interval between the time the exit opening means is actuated from inside the rotorcraft and the time the exit is fully opened. However, each passenger emergency exit which is also a passenger entrance door or a service door must be provided with means to prevent deployment of the slide when the exit is opened from either the inside or the outside under non-emergency conditions for normal use.

(2) It must be automatically erected within 10 seconds after deployment is begun.

(3) It must be of such length after full deployment that the lower end is self-supporting on the ground and provides safe evacuation of occupants to the ground after collapse of one or more legs or part of the landing gear.

(4) It must have the capability, in 25-knot winds directed from the most critical angle, to deploy and, with the assistance of only one person, to remain usable after full deployment to evacuate occupants safely to the ground.

(5) Each slide installation must be qualified by five consecutive deployment and inflation tests conducted (per exit) without failure, and at least three tests of each such five-test series must be conducted using a single representative sample of the device. The sample devices must be deployed and inflated by the system's primary means after being subjected to the inertia forces specified in §29.561(b). If any part of the system fails or does not function properly during the required tests, the cause of the failure or malfunction must be corrected by positive means and after that, the full series of five consecutive deployment and inflation tests must be conducted without failure.

(h) For rotorcraft having 30 or fewer passenger seats and having an exit threshold more than 6 feet above the ground, a rope or other assist means may be used in place of the slide specified in paragraph (f) of this section, provided an evacuation demonstration is accomplished as prescribed in §29.803(d) or (e).

(i) If a rope, with its attachment, is used for compliance with paragraph (f), (g), or (h) of this section, it must—

(1) Withstand a 400-pound static load; and

(2) Attach to the fuselage structure at or above the top of the emergency exit opening, or at another approved location if the stowed rope would reduce the pilot's view in flight.

[Amdt. 29–3, 33 FR 968, Jan. 26, 1968, as amended by Amdt. 29–29, 54 FR 47321, Nov. 13, 1989; Amdt. 27–26, 55 FR 8004, Mar. 6, 1990]

§29.811 Emergency exit marking.

(a) Each passenger emergency exit, its means of access, and its means of opening must be conspicuously marked for the guidance of occupants using the exits in daylight or in the dark. Such markings must be designed to remain visible for rotorcraft equipped for overwater flights if the rotorcraft is capsized and the cabin is submerged.

(b) The identity and location of each passenger emergency exit must be recognizable from a distance equal to the width of the cabin.

(c) The location of each passenger emergency exit must be indicated by a sign visible to occupants approaching along the main passenger aisle. There must be a locating sign—

(1) Next to or above the aisle near each floor emergency exit, except that one sign may serve two exits if both exists can be seen readily from that sign; and

(2) On each bulkhead or divider that prevents fore and aft vision along the passenger cabin, to indicate emergency exits beyond and obscured by it, except that if this is not possible the sign may be placed at another appropriate location.

(d) Each passenger emergency exit marking and each locating sign must have white letters 1 inch high on a red background 2 inches high, be self or electrically illuminated, and have a minimum luminescence (brightness) of at least 160 microlamberts. The colors may be reversed if this will increase the emergency illumination of the passenger compartment.

(e) The location of each passenger emergency exit operating handle and instructions for opening must be shown—

(1) For each emergency exit, by a marking on or near the exit that is

readable from a distance of 30 inches; and

(2) For each Type I or Type II emergency exit with a locking mechanism released by rotary motion of the handle, by—

(i) A red arrow, with a shaft at least three-fourths inch wide and a head twice the width of the shaft, extending along at least 70 degrees of arc at a radius approximately equal to three-fourths of the handle length; and

(ii) The word "open" in red letters 1 inch high, placed horizontally near the head of the arrow.

(f) Each emergency exit, and its means of opening, must be marked on the outside of the rotorcraft. In addition, the following apply:

(1) There must be a 2-inch colored band outlining each passenger emergency exit, except small rotorcraft with a maximum weight of 12,500 pounds or less may have a 2-inch colored band outlining each exit release lever or device of passenger emergency exits which are normally used doors.

(2) Each outside marking, including the band, must have color contrast to be readily distinguishable from the surrounding fuselage surface. The contrast must be such that, if the reflectance of the darker color is 15 percent or less, the reflectance of the lighter color must be at least 45 percent. "Reflectance" is the ratio of the luminous flux reflected by a body to the luminous flux it receives. When the reflectance of the darker color is greater than 15 percent, at least a 30 percent difference between its reflectance and the reflectance of the lighter color must be provided.

(g) Exits marked as such, though in excess of the required number of exits, must meet the requirements for emergency exits of the particular type. Emergency exits need only be marked with the word "Exit."

[Amdt. 29-3, 33 FR 968, Jan. 26, 1968, as amended by Amdt. 29-24, 49 FR 44438, Nov. 6, 1984; Amdt. 27-26, 55 FR 8004, Mar. 6, 1990; Amdt. 29-31, 55 FR 38967, Sept. 21, 1990]

§ 29.812 Emergency lighting.

For transport Category A rotorcraft, the following apply:

(a) A source of light with its power supply independent of the main lighting system must be installed to—

(1) Illuminate each passenger emergency exit marking and locating sign; and

(2) Provide enough general lighting in the passenger cabin so that the average illumination, when measured at 40-inch intervals at seat armrest height on the center line of the main passenger aisle, is at least 0.05 foot-candle.

(b) Exterior emergency lighting must be provided at each emergency exit. The illumination may not be less than 0.05 foot-candle (measured normal to the direction of incident light) for minimum width on the ground surface, with landing gear extended, equal to the width of the emergency exit where an evacuee is likely to make first contact with the ground outside the cabin. The exterior emergency lighting may be provided by either interior or exterior sources with light intensity measurements made with the emergency exits open.

(c) Each light required by paragraph (a) or (b) of this section must be operable manually from the cockpit station and from a point in the passenger compartment that is readily accessible. The cockpit control device must have an "on," "off," and "armed" position so that when turned on at the cockpit or passenger compartment station or when armed at the cockpit station, the emergency lights will either illuminate or remain illuminated upon interruption of the rotorcraft's normal electric power.

(d) Any means required to assist the occupants in descending to the ground must be illuminated so that the erected assist means is visible from the rotorcraft.

(1) The assist means must be provided with an illumination of not less than 0.03 foot-candle (measured normal to the direction of the incident light) at the ground end of the erected assist means where an evacuee using the established escape route would normally make first contact with the ground, with the rotorcraft in each of the attitudes corresponding to the collapse of one or more legs of the landing gear.

(2) If the emergency lighting subsystem illuminating the assist means

is independent of the rotorcraft's main emergency lighting system, it—

(i) Must automatically be activated when the assist means is erected;

(ii) Must provide the illumination required by paragraph (d)(1); and

(iii) May not be adversely affected by stowage.

(e) The energy supply to each emergency lighting unit must provide the required level of illumination for at least 10 minutes at the critical ambient conditions after an emergency landing.

(f) If storage batteries are used as the energy supply for the emergency lighting system, they may be recharged from the rotorcraft's main electrical power system provided the charging circuit is designed to preclude inadvertent battery discharge into charging circuit faults.

[Amdt. 29–24, 49 FR 44438, Nov. 6, 1984]

§ 29.813 Emergency exit access.

(a) Each passageway between passenger compartments, and each passageway leading to Type I and Type II emergency exits, must be—

(1) Unobstructed; and

(2) At least 20 inches wide.

(b) For each emergency exit covered by § 29.809(f), there must be enough space adjacent to that exit to allow a crewmember to assist in the evacuation of passengers without reducing the unobstructed width of the passageway below that required for that exit.

(c) There must be access from each aisle to each Type III and Type IV exit, and

(1) For rotorcraft that have a passenger seating configuration, excluding pilot seats, of 20 or more, the projected opening of the exit provided must not be obstructed by seats, berths, or other protrusions (including seatbacks in any position) for a distance from that exit of not less than the width of the narrowest passenger seat installed on the rotorcraft;

(2) For rotorcraft that have a passenger seating configuration, excluding pilot seats, of 19 or less, there may be minor obstructions in the region described in paragraph (c)(1) of this section, if there are compensating factors to maintain the effectiveness of the exit.

[Doc. No. 5084, 29 FR 16150, Dec. 3, 1964, as amended by Amdt. 29–12, 41 FR 55472, Dec. 20, 1976]

§ 29.815 Main aisle width.

The main passenger aisle width between seats must equal or exceed the values in the following table:

Passenger seating capacity	Minimum main passenger aisle width	
	Less than 25 inches from floor (inches)	25 Inches and more from floor (inches)
10 or less	12	15
11 through 19	12	20
20 or more	15	20

[1] A narrower width not less than 9 inches may be approved when substantiated by tests found necessary by the Administrator.

[Doc. No. 5084, 29 FR 16150, Dec. 3, 1964, as amended by Amdt. 29–12, 41 FR 55472, Dec. 20, 1976]

§ 29.831 Ventilation.

(a) Each passenger and crew compartment must be ventilated, and each crew compartment must have enough fresh air (but not less than 10 cu. ft. per minute per crewmember) to let crewmembers perform their duties without undue discomfort or fatigue.

(b) Crew and passenger compartment air must be free from harmful or hazardous concentrations of gases or vapors.

(c) The concentration of carbon monoxide may not exceed one part in 20,000 parts of air during forward flight. If the concentration exceeds this value under other conditions, there must be suitable operating restrictions.

(d) There must be means to ensure compliance with paragraphs (b) and (c) of this section under any reasonably probable failure of any ventilating, heating, or other system or equipment.

§ 29.833 Heaters.

Each combustion heater must be approved.

FIRE PROTECTION

§ 29.851 Fire extinguishers.

(a) *Hand fire extinguishers.* For hand fire extinguishers the following apply:

(1) Each hand fire extinguisher must be approved.

(2) The kinds and quantities of each extinguishing agent used must be appropriate to the kinds of fires likely to occur where that agent is used.

(3) Each extinguisher for use in a personnel compartment must be designed to minimize the hazard of toxic gas concentrations.

(b) *Built-in fire extinguishers.* If a built-in fire extinguishing system is required—

(1) The capacity of each system, in relation to the volume of the compartment where used and the ventilation rate, must be adequate for any fire likely to occur in that compartment.

(2) Each system must be installed so that—

(i) No extinguishing agent likely to enter personnel compartments will be present in a quantity that is hazardous to the occupants; and

(ii) No discharge of the extinguisher can cause structural damage.

§ 29.853 Compartment interiors.

For each compartment to be used by the crew or passengers—

(a) The materials (including finishes or decorative surfaces applied to the materials) must meet the following test criteria as applicable:

(1) Interior ceiling panels, interior wall panels, partitions, galley structure, large cabinet walls, structural flooring, and materials used in the construction of stowage compartments (other than underseat stowage compartments and compartments for stowing small items such as magazines and maps) must be self-extinguishing when tested vertically in accordance with the applicable portions of appendix F of Part 25 of this chapter, or other approved equivalent methods. The average burn length may not exceed 6 inches and the average flame time after removal of the flame source may not exceed 15 seconds. Drippings from the test specimen may not continue to flame for more than an average of 3 seconds after falling.

(2) Floor covering, textiles (including draperies and upholstery), seat cushions, padding, decorative and non-decorative coated fabrics, leather, trays and galley furnishings, electrical

conduit, thermal and acoustical insulation and insulation covering, air ducting, joint and edge covering, cargo compartment liners, insulation blankets, cargo covers, and transparencies, molded and thermoformed parts, air ducting joints, and trim strips (decorative and chafing) that are constructed of materials not covered in paragraph (a)(3) of this section, must be self extinguishing when tested vertically in accordance with the applicable portion of appendix F of Part 25 of this chapter, or other approved equivalent methods. The average burn length may not exceed 8 inches and the average flame time after removal of the flame source may not exceed 15 seconds. Drippings from the test specimen may not continue to flame for more than an average of 5 seconds after falling.

(3) Acrylic windows and signs, parts constructed in whole or in part of elastometric materials, edge lighted instrument assemblies consisting of two or more instruments in a common housing, seat belts, shoulder harnesses, and cargo and baggage tiedown equipment, including containers, bins, pallets, etc., used in passenger or crew compartments, may not have an average burn rate greater than 2.5 inches per minute when tested horizontally in accordance with the applicable portions of appendix F of Part 25 of this chapter, or other approved equivalent methods.

(4) Except for electrical wire and cable insulation, and for small parts (such as knobs, handles, rollers, fasteners, clips, grommets, rub strips, pulleys, and small electrical parts) that the Administrator finds would not contribute significantly to the propagation of a fire, materials in items not specified in paragraphs (a)(1), (a)(2), or (a)(3) of this section may not have a burn rate greater than 4 inches per minute when tested horizontally in accordance with the applicable portions of appendix F of Part 25 of this chapter, or other approved equivalent methods.

(b) In addition to meeting the requirements of paragraph (a)(2), seat cushions, except those on flight crewmember seats, must meet the test requirements of Part II of appendix F of Part 25 of this chapter, or equivalent.

(c) If smoking is to be prohibited, there must be a placard so stating, and if smoking is to be allowed—

(1) There must be an adequate number of self-contained, removable ashtrays; and

(2) Where the crew compartment is separated from the passenger compartment, there must be at least one illuminated sign (using either letters or symbols) notifying all passengers when smoking is prohibited. Signs which notify when smoking is prohibited must—

(i) When illuminated, be legible to each passenger seated in the passenger cabin under all probable lighting conditions; and

(ii) Be so constructed that the crew can turn the illumination on and off.

(d) Each receptacle for towels, paper, or waste must be at least fire-resistant and must have means for containing possible fires;

(e) There must be a hand fire extinguisher for the flight crewmembers; and

(f) At least the following number of hand fire extinguishers must be conveniently located in passenger compartments:

Passenger capacity	Fire extinguishers
7 through 30	1
31 through 60	2
61 or more	3

(Secs. 313(a), 601, 603, 604, Federal Aviation Act of 1958 (49 U.S.C. 1354(a), 1421, 1423, 1424), sec. 6(c), Dept. of Transportation Act (49 U.S.C. 1655(c)))

[Doc. No. 5084, 29 FR 16150, Dec. 3, 1964, as amended by Amdt. 29–3, 33 FR 969, Jan. 26, 1968; Amdt. 29–17, 43 FR 50600, Oct. 30, 1978; Amdt 29–18, 45 FR 7756, Feb. 4, 1980; Amdt. 29–23, 49 FR 43200, Oct. 26, 1984]

§29.855 Cargo and baggage compartments.

(a) Each cargo and baggage compartment must be construced of or lined with materials in accordance with the following:

(1) For accessible and inaccessible compartments not occupied by passengers or crew, the material must be at least fire resistant.

(2) Materials must meet the requirements in §29.853(a)(1), (a)(2), and (a)(3)

for cargo or baggage compartments in which—

(i) The presence of a compartment fire would be easily discovered by a crewmember while at the crewmember's station;

(ii) Each part of the compartment is easily accessible in flight;

(iii) The compartment has a volume of 200 cubic feet or less; and

(iv) Notwithstanding §29.1439(a), protective breathing equipment is not required.

(b) No compartment may contain any controls, wiring, lines, equipment, or accessories whose damage or failure would affect safe operation, unless those items are protected so that—

(1) They cannot be damaged by the movement of cargo in the compartment; and

(2) Their breakage or failure will not create a fire hazard.

(c) The design and sealing of inaccessible compartments must be adequate to contain compartment fires until a landing and safe evacuation can be made.

(d) Each cargo and baggage compartment that is not sealed so as to contain cargo compartment fires completely without endangering the safety of a rotorcraft or its occupants must be designed, or must have a device, to ensure detection of fires or smoke by a crewmember while at his station and to prevent the accumulation of harmful quantities of smoke, flame, extinguishing agents, and other noxious gases in any crew or passenger compartment. This must be shown in flight.

(e) For rotorcraft used for the carriage of cargo only, the cabin area may be considered a cargo compartment and, in addition to paragraphs (a) through (d) of this section, the following apply:

(1) There must be means to shut off the ventilating airflow to or within the compartment. Controls for this purpose must be accessible to the flight crew in the crew compartment.

(2) Required crew emergency exits must be accessible under all cargo loading conditions.

(3) Sources of heat within each compartment must be shielded and insulated to prevent igniting the cargo.

[Doc. No. 5084, 29 FR 16150, Dec. 3, 1964, as amended by Amdt. 29–3, 33 FR 969, Jan 26, 1968; Amdt. 29–24, 49 FR 44438, Nov. 6, 1984; Amdt. 27–26, 55 FR 8004, Mar. 6, 1990]

§ 29.859 Combustion heater fire protection.

(a) *Combustion heater fire zones.* The following combustion heater fire zones must be protected against fire under the applicable provisions of §§ 29.1181 through 29.1191, and 29.1195 through 29.1203:

(1) The region surrounding any heater, if that region contains any flammable fluid system components (including the heater fuel system), that could—

(i) Be damaged by heater malfunctioning; or

(ii) Allow flammable fluids or vapors to reach the heater in case of leakage.

(2) Each part of any ventilating air passage that—

(i) Surrounds the combustion chamber; and

(ii) Would not contain (without damage to other rotorcraft components) any fire that may occur within the passage.

(b) *Ventilating air ducts.* Each ventilating air duct passing through any fire zone must be fireproof. In addition—

(1) Unless isolation is provided by fireproof valves or by equally effective means, the ventilating air duct downstream of each heater must be fireproof for a distance great enough to ensure that any fire originating in the heater can be contained in the duct; and

(2) Each part of any ventilating duct passing through any region having a flammable fluid system must be so constructed or isolated from that system that the malfunctioning of any component of that system cannot introduce flammable fluids or vapors into the ventilating airstream.

(c) *Combustion air ducts.* Each combustion air duct must be fireproof for a distance great enough to prevent damage from backfiring or reverse flame propagation. In addition—

(1) No combustion air duct may communicate with the ventilating airstream unless flames from backfires or reverse burning cannot enter the ventilating airstream under any operating condition, including reverse flow or malfunction of the heater or its associated components; and

(2) No combustion air duct may restrict the prompt relief of any backfire that, if so restricted, could cause heater failure.

(d) *Heater controls; general.* There must be means to prevent the hazardous accumulation of water or ice on or in any heater control component, control system tubing, or safety control.

(e) *Heater safety controls.* For each combustion heater, safety control means must be provided as follows:

(1) Means independent of the components provided for the normal continuous control of air temperature, airflow, and fuel flow must be provided, for each heater, to automatically shut off the ignition and fuel supply of that heater at a point remote from that heater when any of the following occurs:

(i) The heat exchanger temperature exceeds safe limits.

(ii) The ventilating air temperature exceeds safe limits.

(iii) The combustion airflow becomes inadequate for safe operation.

(iv) The ventilating airflow becomes inadequate for safe operation.

(2) The means of complying with paragraph (e)(1) of this section for any individual heater must—

(i) Be independent of components serving any other heater whose heat output is essential for safe operation; and

(ii) Keep the heater off until restarted by the crew.

(3) There must be means to warn the crew when any heater whose heat output is essential for safe operation has been shut off by the automatic means prescribed in paragraph (e)(1) of this section.

(f) *Air intakes.* Each combustion and ventilating air intake must be where no flammable fluids or vapors can enter the heater system under any operating condition—

(1) During normal operation; or

(2) As a result of the malfunction of any other component.

(g) *Heater exhaust.* Each heater exhaust system must meet the requirements of §§29.1121 and 29.1123. In addition—

(1) Each exhaust shroud must be sealed so that no flammable fluids or hazardous quantities of vapors can reach the exhaust systems through joints; and

(2) No exhaust system may restrict the prompt relief of any backfire that, if so restricted, could cause heater failure.

(h) *Heater fuel systems.* Each heater fuel system must meet the powerplant fuel system requirements affecting safe heater operation. Each heater fuel system component in the ventilating airstream must be protected by shrouds so that no leakage from those components can enter the ventilating airstream.

(i) *Drains.* There must be means for safe drainage of any fuel that might accumulate in the combustion chamber or the heat exchanger. In addition—

(1) Each part of any drain that operates at high temperatures must be protected in the same manner as heater exhausts; and

(2) Each drain must be protected against hazardous ice accumulation under any operating condition.

[Doc. No. 5084, 29 FR 16150, Dec. 3, 1964, as amended by Amdt. 29–2, 32 FR 6914, May 5, 1967]

§29.861 Fire protection of structure, controls, and other parts.

Each part of the structure, controls, and the rotor mechanism, and other parts essential to controlled landing and (for category A) flight that would be affected by powerplant fires must be isolated under §29.1191, or must be—

(a) For category A rotorcraft, fireproof; and

(b) For Category B rotorcraft, fireproof or protected so that they can perform their essential functions for at least 5 minutes under any foreseeable powerplant fire conditions.

[Doc. No. 5084, 29 FR 16150, Dec. 3, 1964, as amended by Amdt. 27–26, 55 FR 8005, Mar. 6, 1990]

§29.863 Flammable fluid fire protection.

(a) In each area where flammable fluids or vapors might escape by leakage of a fluid system, there must be means to minimize the probability of ignition of the fluids and vapors, and the resultant hazards if ignition does occur.

(b) Compliance with paragraph (a) of this section must be shown by analysis or tests, and the following factors must be considered:

(1) Possible sources and paths of fluid leakage, and means of detecting leakage.

(2) Flammability characteristics of fluids, including effects of any combustible or absorbing materials.

(3) Possible ignition sources, including electrical faults, overheating of equipment, and malfunctioning of protective devices.

(4) Means available for controlling or extinguishing a fire, such as stopping flow of fluids, shutting down equipment, fireproof containment, or use of extinguishing agents.

(5) Ability of rotorcraft components that are critical to safety of flight to withstand fire and heat.

(c) If action by the flight crew is required to prevent or counteract a fluid fire (e.g. equipment shutdown or actuation of a fire extinguisher), quick acting means must be provided to alert the crew.

(d) Each area where flammable fluids or vapors might escape by leakage of a fluid system must be identified and defined.

(Secs. 313(a), 601, 603, 604, Federal Aviation Act of 1958 (49 U.S.C. 1354(a), 1421, 1423, 1424), sec. 6(c), Dept. of Transportation Act (49 U.S.C. 1655(c)))

[Amdt. 29–17, 43 FR 50600, Oct. 30, 1978]

EXTERNAL LOADS

§29.865 External loads.

(a) It must be shown by analysis, test, or both, that the rotorcraft external load attaching means for rotorcraft-load combinations to be used for nonhuman external cargo applications can withstand a limit static load equal to 2.5, or some lower load factor approved under §§29.337 through 29.341, multiplied by the maximum external load for which authorization is requested. It must be shown by analysis, test, or both that the rotorcraft external load attaching means and corresponding personnel carrying device system for rotorcraft-load combinations to be used for human external cargo applications can withstand a limit static load equal to 3.5 or some lower load factor, not less than 2.5, approved under §§ 29.337 through 29.341, multiplied by the maximum external load for which authorization is requested. The load for any rotorcraft-load combination class, for any external cargo type, must be applied in the vertical direction. For jettisonable external loads of any applicable external cargo type, the load must also be applied in any direction making the maximum angle with the vertical that can be achieved in service but not less than 30°. However, the 30° angle may be reduced to a lesser angle if—

(1) An operating limitation is established limiting external load operations to such angles for which compliance with this paragraph has been shown; or

(2) It is shown that the lesser angle can not be exceeded in service.

(b) The external load attaching means, for jettisonable rotorcraft-load combinations, must include a quick-release system to enable the pilot to release the external load quickly during flight. The quick-release system must consist of a primary quick release subsystem and a backup quick release subsystem that are isolated from one another. The quick release system, and the means by which it is controlled, must comply with the following:

(1) A control for the primary quick release subsystem must be installed either on one of the pilot's primary controls or in an equivalently accessible location and must be designed and located so that it may be operated by either the pilot or a crewmember without hazardously limiting the ability to control the rotorcraft during an emergency situation.

(2) A control for the backup quick release subsystem, readily accessible to either the pilot or another crewmember, must be provided.

(3) Both the primary and backup quick release subsystems must—

(i) Be reliable, durable, and function properly with all external loads up to and including the maximum external limit load for which authorization is requested.

(ii) Be protected against electromagnetic interference (EMI) from external and internal sources and against lightning to prevent inadvertent load release.

(A) The minimum level of protection required for jettisonable rotorcraft-load combinations used for nonhuman external cargo is a radio frequency field strength of 20 volts per meter.

(B) The minimum level of protection required for jettisonable rotorcraft-load combinations used for human external cargo is a radio frequency field strength of 200 volts per meter.

(iii) Be protected against any failure that could be induced by a failure mode of any other electrical or mechanical rotorcraft system.

(c) For rotorcraft-load combinations to be used for human external cargo applications, the rotorcraft must—

(1) For jettisonable external loads, have a quick-release system that meets the requirements of paragraph (b) of this section and that—

(i) Provides a dual actuation device for the primary quick release subsystem, and

(ii) Provides a separate dual actuation device for the backup quick release subsystem;

(2) Have a reliable, approved personnel carrying device system that has the structural capability and personnel safety features essential for external occupant safety;

(3) Have placards and markings at all appropriate locations that clearly state the essential system operating instructions and, for the personnel carrying device system, ingress and egress instructions;

(4) Have equipment to allow direct intercommunication among required crewmembers and external occupants;

(5) Have the appropriate limitations and procedures incorporated in the flight manual for conducting human external cargo operations; and

(6) For human external cargo applications requiring use of Category A rotorcraft, have one-engine-inoperative hover performance data and procedures

in the flight manual for the weights, altitudes, and temperatures for which external load approval is requested.

(d) The critically configured jettisonable external loads must be shown by a combination of analysis, ground tests, and flight tests to be both transportable and releasable throughout the approved operational envelope without hazard to the rotorcraft during normal flight conditions. In addition, these external loads—must be shown to be releasable without hazard to the rotorcraft during emergency flight conditions.

(e) A placard or marking must be installed next to the external-load attaching means clearly stating any operational limitations and the maximum authorized external load as demonstrated under §29.25 and this section.

(f) The fatigue evaluation of §29.571 of this part does not apply to rotorcraft-load combinations to be used for nonhuman external cargo except for the failure of critical structural elements that would result in a hazard to the rotorcraft. For rotorcraft-load combinations to be used for human external cargo, the fatigue evaluation of §29.571 of this part applies to the entire quick release and personnel carrying device structural systems and their attachments.

[Amdt. 29–12, 41 FR 55472, Dec. 20, 1976, as amended by Amdt. 27–26, 55 FR 8005, Mar. 6, 1990; Amdt. 29–43, 64 FR 43020, Aug. 6, 1999]

MISCELLANEOUS

§29.871 Leveling marks.

There must be reference marks for leveling the rotorcraft on the ground.

§29.873 Ballast provisions.

Ballast provisions must be designed and constructed to prevent inadvertent shifting of ballast in flight.

Subpart E—Powerplant

GENERAL

§29.901 Installation.

(a) For the purpose of this part, the powerplant installation includes each part of the rotorcraft (other than the main and auxiliary rotor structures) that—

(1) Is necessary for propulsion;

(2) Affects the control of the major propulsive units; or

(3) Affects the safety of the major propulsive units between normal inspections or overhauls.

(b) For each powerplant installation—

(1) The installation must comply with—

(i) The installation instructions provided under §33.5 of this chapter; and

(ii) The applicable provisions of this subpart.

(2) Each component of the installation must be constructed, arranged, and installed to ensure its continued safe operation between normal inspections or overhauls for the range of temperature and altitude for which approval is requested.

(3) Accessibility must be provided to allow any inspection and maintenance necessary for continued airworthiness; and

(4) Electrical interconnections must be provided to prevent differences of potential between major components of the installation and the rest of the rotorcraft.

(5) Axial and radial expansion of turbine engines may not affect the safety of the installation.

(6) Design precautions must be taken to minimize the possibility of incorrect assembly of components and equipment essential to safe operation of the rotorcraft, except where operation with the incorrect assembly can be shown to be extremely improbable.

(c) For each powerplant and auxiliary power unit installation, it must be established that no single failure or malfunction or probable combination of failures will jeopardize the safe operation of the rotorcraft except that the failure of structural elements need not be considered if the probability of any such failure is extremely remote.

(d) Each auxiliary power unit installation must meet the applicable provisions of this subpart.

(Secs. 313(a), 601, 603, 604, Federal Aviation Act of 1958 (49 U.S.C. 1354(a), 1421, 1423, 1424), sec. 6(c), Dept. of Transportation Act (49 U.S.C. 1655(c)))

[Doc. No. 5084, 29 FR 16150, Dec. 3, 1964, as amended by Amdt. 29–3, 33 FR 969, Jan. 26, 1968; Amdt. 29–13, 42 FR 15046, Mar. 17, 1977; Amdt. 29–17, 43 FR 50600, Oct. 30, 1978; Amdt. 29–26, 53 FR 34215, Sept. 2, 1988; Amdt. 29–36, 60 FR 55776, Nov. 2, 1995]

§ 29.903 Engines.

(a) *Engine type certification.* Each engine must have an approved type certificate. Reciprocating engines for use in helicopters must be qualified in accordance with § 33.49(d) of this chapter or be otherwise approved for the intended usage.

(b) *Category A; engine isolation.* For each category A rotorcraft, the powerplants must be arranged and isolated from each other to allow operation, in at least one configuration, so that the failure or malfunction of any engine, or the failure of any system that can affect any engine, will not—

(1) Prevent the continued safe operation of the remaining engines; or

(2) Require immediate action, other than normal pilot action with primary flight controls, by any crewmember to maintain safe operation.

(c) *Category A; control of engine rotation.* For each Category A rotorcraft, there must be a means for stopping the rotation of any engine individually in flight, except that, for turbine engine installations, the means for stopping the engine need be provided only where necessary for safety. In addition—

(1) Each component of the engine stopping system that is located on the engine side of the firewall, and that might be exposed to fire, must be at least fire resistant; or

(2) Duplicate means must be available for stopping the engine and the controls must be where all are not likely to be damaged at the same time in case of fire.

(d) *Turbine engine installation.* For turbine engine installations—

(1) Design precautions must be taken to minimize the hazards to the rotorcraft in the event of an engine rotor failure; and

(2) The powerplant systems associated with engine control devices, systems, and instrumentation must be designed to give reasonable assurance that those engine operating limitations that adversely affect engine rotor structural integrity will not be exceeded in service.

(e) *Restart capability.* (1) A means to restart any engine in flight must be provided.

(2) Except for the in-flight shutdown of all engines, engine restart capability must be demonstrated throughout a flight envelope for the rotorcraft.

(3) Following the in-flight shutdown of all engines, in-flight engine restart capability must be provided.

(Secs. 313(a), 601, and 603, 72 Stat. 752, 775, 49 U.S.C. 1354(a), 1421, and 1423; sec. 6(c), 49 U.S.C. 1655(c))

[Doc. No. 5084, 29 FR 16150, Dec. 3, 1964, as amended by Amdt. 29–12, 41 FR 55472, Dec. 20, 1976; Amdt. 29–26, 53 FR 34215, Sept. 2, 1988; Amdt. 29–31, 55 FR 38967, Sept. 21, 1990; 55 FR 41309, Oct. 10, 1990; Amdt. 29–36, 60 FR 55776, Nov. 2, 1995]

§ 29.907 Engine vibration.

(a) Each engine must be installed to prevent the harmful vibration of any part of the engine or rotorcraft.

(b) The addition of the rotor and the rotor drive system to the engine may not subject the principal rotating parts of the engine to excessive vibration stresses. This must be shown by a vibration investigation.

§ 29.908 Cooling fans.

For cooling fans that are a part of a powerplant installation the following apply:

(a) *Category A.* For cooling fans installed in Category A rotorcraft, it must be shown that a fan blade failure will not prevent continued safe flight either because of damage caused by the failed blade or loss of cooling air.

(b) *Category B.* For cooling fans installed in category B rotorcraft, there must be means to protect the rotorcraft and allow a safe landing if a fan blade fails. It must be shown that—

(1) The fan blade would be contained in the case of a failure;

(2) Each fan is located so that a fan blade failure will not jeopardize safety; or

(3) Each fan blade can withstand an ultimate load of 1.5 times the centrifugal force expected in service, limited by either—

(i) The highest rotational speeds achievable under uncontrolled conditions; or

(ii) An overspeed limiting device.

(c) *Fatigue evaluation.* Unless a fatigue evaluation under § 29.571 is conducted, it must be shown that cooling fan blades are not operating at resonant conditions within the operating limits of the rotorcraft.

(Secs. 313(a), 601, and 603, 72 Stat. 752, 775, 49 U.S.C. 1354(a), 1421, and 1423; sec. 6(c), 49 U.S.C. 1655 (c))

[Amdt. 29–13, 42 FR 15046, Mar. 17, 1977, as amended by Amdt. 29–26, 53 FR 34215, Sept. 2, 1988]

ROTOR DRIVE SYSTEM

§ 29.917 Design.

(a) *General.* The rotor drive system includes any part necessary to transmit power from the engines to the rotor hubs. This includes gear boxes, shafting, universal joints, couplings, rotor brake assemblies, clutches, supporting bearings for shafting, any attendant accessory pads or drives, and any cooling fans that are a part of, attached to, or mounted on the rotor drive system.

(b) *Design assessment.* A design assessment must be performed to ensure that the rotor drive system functions safely over the full range of conditions for which certification is sought. The design assessment must include a detailed failure analysis to identify all failures that will prevent continued safe flight or safe landing and must identify the means to minimize the likelihood of their occurrence.

(c) *Arrangement.* Rotor drive systems must be arranged as follows:

(1) Each rotor drive system of multiengine rotorcraft must be arranged so that each rotor necessary for operation and control will continue to be driven by the remaining engines if any engine fails.

(2) For single-engine rotorcraft, each rotor drive system must be so arranged that each rotor necessary for control in autorotation will continue to be driven by the main rotors after disengagement of the engine from the main and auxiliary rotors.

(3) Each rotor drive system must incorporate a unit for each engine to automatically disengage that engine from the main and auxiliary rotors if that engine fails.

(4) If a torque limiting device is used in the rotor drive system, it must be located so as to allow continued control of the rotorcraft when the device is operating.

(5) If the rotors must be phased for intermeshing, each system must provide constant and positive phase relationship under any operating condition.

(6) If a rotor dephasing device is incorporated, there must be means to keep the rotors locked in proper phase before operation.

[Doc. No. 5084, 29 FR 16150, Dec. 3, 1964, as amended by Amdt. 29–12, 41 FR 55472, Dec. 20, 1976; Amdt. 29–40, 61 FR 21908, May 10, 1996]

§ 29.921 Rotor brake.

If there is a means to control the rotation of the rotor drive system independently of the use of the engine, any limitations on the use of that means must be specified, and the control for that means must be guarded to prevent inadvertent operation.

§ 29.923 Rotor drive system and control mechanism tests.

(a) *Endurance tests, general.* Each rotor drive system and rotor control mechanism must be tested, as prescribed in paragraphs (b) through (n) and (p) of this section, for at least 200 hours plus the time required to meet the requirements of paragraphs (b)(2), (b)(3), and (k) of this section. These tests must be conducted as follows:

(1) Ten-hour test cycles must be used, except that the test cycle must be extended to include the OEI test of paragraphs (b)(2) and (k), of this section if OEI ratings are requested.

(2) The tests must be conducted on the rotorcraft.

(3) The test torque and rotational speed must be—

(i) Determined by the powerplant limitations; and

(ii) Absorbed by the rotors to be approved for the rotorcraft.

(b) *Endurance tests; takeoff run.* The takeoff run must be conducted as follows:

(1) Except as prescribed in paragraphs (b)(2) and (b)(3) of this section, the takeoff torque run must consist of 1 hour of alternate runs of 5 minutes at takeoff torque and the maximum speed for use with takeoff torque, and 5 minutes at as low an engine idle speed as practicable. The engine must be declutched from the rotor drive system, and the rotor brake, if furnished and so intended, must be applied during the first minute of the idle run. During the remaining 4 minutes of the idle run, the clutch must be engaged so that the engine drives the rotors at the minimum practical r.p.m. The engine and the rotor drive system must be accelerated at the maximum rate. When declutching the engine, it must be decelerated rapidly enough to allow the operation of the overrunning clutch.

(2) For helicopters for which the use of a 2½-minute OEI rating is requested, the takeoff run must be conducted as prescribed in paragraph (b)(1) of this section, except for the third and sixth runs for which the takeoff torque and the maximum speed for use with takeoff torque are prescribed in that paragraph. For these runs, the following apply:

(i) Each run must consist of at least one period of 2½ minutes with takeoff torque and the maximum speed for use with takeoff torque on all engines.

(ii) Each run must consist of at least one period, for each engine in sequence, during which that engine simulates a power failure and the remaining engines are run at the 2½-minute OEI torque and the maximum speed for use with 2½-minute OEI torque for 2½ minutes.

(3) For multiengine, turbine-powered rotorcraft for which the use of 30-second/2-minute OEI power is requested, the takeoff run must be conducted as prescribed in paragraph (b)(1) of this section except for the following:

(i) Immediately following any one 5-minute power-on run required by paragraph (b)(1) of this section, simulate a failure for each power source in turn, and apply the maximum torque and the maximum speed for use with 30-second OEI power to the remaining affected drive system power inputs for not less than 30 seconds. Each application of 30-second OEI power must be followed by two applications of the maximum torque and the maximum speed for use with the 2 minute OEI power for not less than 2 minutes each; the second application must follow a period at stabilized continuous or 30 minute OEI power (whichever is requested by the applicant). At least one run sequence must be conducted from a simulated "flight idle" condition. When conducted on a bench test, the test sequence must be conducted following stabilization at take-off power.

(ii) For the purpose of this paragraph, an affected power input includes all parts of the rotor drive system which can be adversely affected by the application of higher or asymmetric torque and speed prescribed by the test.

(iii) This test may be conducted on a representative bench test facility when engine limitations either preclude repeated use of this power or would result in premature engine removals during the test. The loads, the vibration frequency, and the methods of application to the affected rotor drive system components must be representative of rotorcraft conditions. Test components must be those used to show compliance with the remainder of this section.

(c) *Endurance tests; maximum continuous run.* Three hours of continuous operation at maximum continuous torque and the maximum speed for use with maximum continuous torque must be conducted as follows:

(1) The main rotor controls must be operated at a minimum of 15 times each hour through the main rotor pitch positions of maximum vertical thrust, maximum forward thrust component,

maximum aft thrust component, maximum left thrust component, and maximum right thrust component, except that the control movements need not produce loads or blade flapping motion exceeding the maximum loads of motions encountered in flight.

(2) The directional controls must be operated at a minimum of 15 times each hour through the control extremes of maximum right turning torque, neutral torque as required by the power applied to the main rotor, and maximum left turning torque.

(3) Each maximum control position must be held for at least 10 seconds, and the rate of change of control position must be at least as rapid as that for normal operation.

(d) *Endurance tests; 90 percent of maximum continuous run.* One hour of continuous operation at 90 percent of maximum continuous torque and the maximum speed for use with 90 percent of maximum continuous torque must be conducted.

(e) *Endurance tests; 80 percent of maximum continuous run.* One hour of continuous operation at 80 percent of maximum continuous torque and the minimum speed for use with 80 percent of maximum continuous torque must be conducted.

(f) *Endurance tests; 60 percent of maximum continuous run.* Two hours or, for helicopters for which the use of either 30-minute OEI power or continuous OEI power is requested, 1 hour of continuous operation at 60 percent of maximum continuous torque and the minimum speed for use with 60 percent of maximum continuous torque must be conducted.

(g) *Endurance tests; engine malfunctioning run.* It must be determined whether malfunctioning of components, such as the engine fuel or ignition systems, or whether unequal engine power can cause dynamic conditions detrimental to the drive system. If so, a suitable number of hours of operation must be accomplished under those conditions, 1 hour of which must be included in each cycle, and the remaining hours of which must be accomplished at the end of the 20 cycles. If no detrimental condition results, an additional hour of operation in compliance with paragraph (b) of this section

must be conducted in accordance with the run schedule of paragraph (b)(1) of this section without consideration of paragraph (b)(2) of this section.

(h) *Endurance tests; overspeed run.* One hour of continuous operation must be conducted at maximum continuous torque and the maximum power-on overspeed expected in service, assuming that speed and torque limiting devices, if any, function properly.

(i) *Endurance tests; rotor control positions.* When the rotor controls are not being cycled during the tie-down tests, the rotor must be operated, using the procedures prescribed in paragraph (c) of this section, to produce each of the maximum thrust positions for the following percentages of test time (except that the control positions need not produce loads or blade flapping motion exceeding the maximum loads or motions encountered in flight):

(1) For full vertical thrust, 20 percent.

(2) For the forward thrust component, 50 percent.

(3) For the right thrust component, 10 percent.

(4) For the left thrust component, 10 percent.

(5) For the aft thrust component, 10 percent.

(j) *Endurance tests, clutch and brake engagements.* A total of at least 400 clutch and brake engagements, including the engagements of paragraph (b) of this section, must be made during the takeoff torque runs and, if necessary, at each change of torque and speed throughout the test. In each clutch engagement, the shaft on the driven side of the clutch must be accelerated from rest. The clutch engagements must be accomplished at the speed and by the method prescribed by the applicant. During deceleration after each clutch engagement, the engines must be stopped rapidly enough to allow the engines to be automatically disengaged from the rotors and rotor drives. If a rotor brake is installed for stopping the rotor, the clutch, during brake engagements, must be disengaged above 40 percent of maximum continuous rotor speed and the rotors allowed to decelerate to 40 percent of maximum continuous rotor speed, at which time the rotor brake

667

must be applied. If the clutch design does not allow stopping the rotors with the engine running, or if no clutch is provided, the engine must be stopped before each application of the rotor brake, and then immediately be started after the rotors stop.

(k) *Endurance tests; OEI power run.* (1) *30-minute OEI power run.* For rotorcraft for which the use of 30-minute OEI power is requested, a run at 30-minute OEI torque and the maximum speed for use with 30-minute OEI torque must be conducted as follows: For each engine, in sequence, that engine must be inoperative and the remaining engines must be run for a 30-minute period.

(2) *Continuous OEI power run.* For rotorcraft for which the use of continuous OEI power is requested, a run at continuous OEI torque and the maximum speed for use with continuous OEI torque must be conducted as follows: For each engine, in sequence, that engine must be inoperative and the remaining engines must be run for 1 hour.

(3) The number of periods prescribed in paragraph (k)(1) or (k)(2) of this section may not be less than the number of engines, nor may it be less than two.

(l) [Reserved]

(m) Any components that are affected by maneuvering and gust loads must be investigated for the same flight conditions as are the main rotors, and their service lives must be determined by fatigue tests or by other acceptable methods. In addition, a level of safety equal to that of the main rotors must be provided for—

(1) Each component in the rotor drive system whose failure would cause an uncontrolled landing;

(2) Each component essential to the phasing of rotors on multirotor rotorcraft, or that furnishes a driving link for the essential control of rotors in autorotation; and

(3) Each component common to two or more engines on multiengine rotorcraft.

(n) *Special tests.* Each rotor drive system designed to operate at two or more gear ratios must be subjected to special testing for durations necessary to substantiate the safety of the rotor drive system.

(o) Each part tested as prescribed in this section must be in a serviceable condition at the end of the tests. No intervening disassembly which might affect test results may be conducted.

(p) *Endurance tests; operating lubricants.* To be approved for use in rotor drive and control systems, lubricants must meet the specifications of lubricants used during the tests prescribed by this section. Additional or alternate lubricants may be qualified by equivalent testing or by comparative analysis of lubricant specifications and rotor drive and control system characteristics. In addition—

(1) At least three 10-hour cycles required by this section must be conducted with transmission and gearbox lubricant temperatures, at the location prescribed for measurement, not lower than the maximum operating temperature for which approval is requested;

(2) For pressure lubricated systems, at least three 10-hour cycles required by this section must be conducted with the lubricant pressure, at the location prescribed for measurement, not higher than the minimum operating pressure for which approval is requested; and

(3) The test conditions of paragraphs (p)(1) and (p)(2) of this section must be applied simultaneously and must be extended to include operation at any one-engine-inoperative rating for which approval is requested.

(Secs. 313(a), 601, 603, 604, Federal Aviation Act of 1958 (49 U.S.C. 1354(a), 1421, 1423, 1424), sec. 6(c), Dept. of Transportation Act (49 U.S.C. 1655(c)))

[Doc. No. 5084, 29 FR 16150, Dec. 3, 1964, as amended by Amdt. 29–1, 30 FR 8778, July 13, 1965; Amdt. 29–17, 43 FR 50600, Oct. 30, 1978; Amdt. 29–26, 53 FR 34215, Sept. 2, 1988; Amdt. 29–31, 55 FR 38967, Sept. 21, 1990; Amdt. 29–34, 59 FR 47768, Sept. 16, 1994; Amdt. 29–40, 61 FR 21908, May 10, 1996; Amdt. 29–42, 63 FR 43285, Aug. 12, 1998]

§ 29.927 Additional tests.

(a) Any additional dynamic, endurance, and operational tests, and vibratory investigations necessary to determine that the rotor drive mechanism is safe, must be performed.

(b) If turbine engine torque output to the transmission can exceed the highest engine or transmission torque limit, and that output is not directly controlled by the pilot under normal operating conditions (such as where the primary engine power control is accomplished through the flight control), the following test must be made:

(1) Under conditions associated with all engines operating, make 200 applications, for 10 seconds each, of torque that is at least equal to the lesser of—

(i) The maximum torque used in meeting §29.923 plus 10 percent; or

(ii) The maximum torque attainable under probable operating conditions, assuming that torque limiting devices, if any, function properly.

(2) For multiengine rotorcraft under conditions associated with each engine, in turn, becoming inoperative, apply to the remaining transmission torque inputs the maximum torque attainable under probable operating conditions, assuming that torque limiting devices, if any, function properly. Each transmission input must be tested at this maximum torque for at least fifteen minutes.

(c) *Lubrication system failure.* For lubrication systems required for proper operation of rotor drive systems, the following apply:

(1) *Category A.* Unless such failures are extremely remote, it must be shown by test that any failure which results in loss of lubricant in any normal use lubrication system will not prevent continued safe operation, although not necessarily without damage, at a torque and rotational speed prescribed by the applicant for continued flight, for at least 30 minutes after perception by the flightcrew of the lubrication system failure or loss of lubricant.

(2) *Category B.* The requirements of Category A apply except that the rotor drive system need only be capable of operating under autorotative conditions for at least 15 minutes.

(d) *Overspeed test.* The rotor drive system must be subjected to 50 overspeed runs, each 30±3 seconds in duration, at not less than either the higher of the rotational speed to be expected from an engine control device failure or 105 percent of the maximum rotational speed, including transients, to be expected in service. If speed and torque limiting devices are installed, are independent of the normal engine control, and are

shown to be reliable, their rotational speed limits need not be exceeded. These runs must be conducted as follows:

(1) Overspeed runs must be alternated with stabilizing runs of from 1 to 5 minutes duration each at 60 to 80 percent of maximum continuous speed.

(2) Acceleration and deceleration must be accomplished in a period not longer than 10 seconds (except where maximum engine acceleration rate will require more than 10 seconds), and the time for changing speeds may not be deducted from the specified time for the overspeed runs.

(3) Overspeed runs must be made with the rotors in the flattest pitch for smooth operation.

(e) The tests prescribed in paragraphs (b) and (d) of this section must be conducted on the rotorcraft and the torque must be absorbed by the rotors to be installed, except that other ground or flight test facilities with other appropriate methods of torque absorption may be used if the conditions of support and vibration closely simulate the conditions that would exist during a test on the rotorcraft.

(f) Each test prescribed by this section must be conducted without intervening disassembly and, except for the lubrication system failure test required by paragraph (c) of this section, each part tested must be in a serviceable condition at the conclusion of the test.

(Secs. 313(a), 601, 603, 604, Federal Aviation Act of 1958 (49 U.S.C. 1354(a), 1421, 1423 1424), sec. 6(c), Dept. of Transportation Act (49 U.S.C. 1655(c)))

[Amdt. 29–3, 33 FR 969, Jan. 26, 1968, as amended by Amdt. 29–17, 43 FR 50601, Oct. 30, 1978; Amdt. 29–26, 53 FR 34216, Sept. 2, 1988]

§29.931 Shafting critical speed.

(a) The critical speeds of any shafting must be determined by demonstration except that analytical methods may be used if reliable methods of analysis are available for the particular design.

(b) If any critical speed lies within, or close to, the operating ranges for idling, power-on, and autorotative conditions, the stresses occurring at that speed must be within safe limits. This must be shown by tests.

(c) If analytical methods are used and show that no critical speed lies within the permissible operating ranges, the margins between the calculated critical speeds and the limits of the allowable operating ranges must be adequate to allow for possible variations between the computed and actual values.

[Amdt. 29–12, 41 FR 55472, Dec. 20, 1976]

§ 29.935 Shafting joints.

Each universal joint, slip joint, and other shafting joints whose lubrication is necessary for operation must have provision for lubrication.

§ 29.939 Turbine engine operating characteristics.

(a) Turbine engine operating characteristics must be investigated in flight to determine that no adverse characteristics (such as stall, surge, of flameout) are present, to a hazardous degree, during normal and emergency operation within the range of operating limitations of the rotorcraft and of the engine.

(b) The turbine engine air inlet system may not, as a result of airflow distortion during normal operation, cause vibration harmful to the engine.

(c) For governor-controlled engines, it must be shown that there exists no hazardous torsional instability of the drive system associated with critical combinations of power, rotational speed, and control displacement.

[Amdt. 29–2, 32 FR 6914, May 5, 1967, as amended by Amdt. 29–12, 41 FR 55473, Dec. 20, 1976]

FUEL SYSTEM

§ 29.951 General.

(a) Each fuel system must be constructed and arranged to ensure a flow of fuel at a rate and pressure established for proper engine and auxiliary power unit functioning under any likely operating conditions, including the maneuvers for which certification is requested and during which the engine or auxiliary power unit is permitted to be in operation.

(b) Each fuel system must be arranged so that—

(1) No engine or fuel pump can draw fuel from more than one tank at a time; or

(2) There are means to prevent introducing air into the system.

(c) Each fuel system for a turbine engine must be capable of sustained operation throughout its flow and pressure range with fuel initially saturated with water at 80 degrees F. and having 0.75cc of free water per gallon added and cooled to the most critical condition for icing likely to be encountered in operation.

[Doc. No. 5084, 29 FR 16150, Dec. 3, 1964, as amended by Amdt. 29–10, 39 FR 35462, Oct. 1, 1974; Amdt. 29–12, 41 FR 55473, Dec. 20, 1976]

§ 29.952 Fuel system crash resistance.

Unless other means acceptable to the Administrator are employed to minimize the hazard of fuel fires to occupants following an otherwise survivable impact (crash landing), the fuel systems must incorporate the design features of this section. These systems must be shown to be capable of sustaining the static and dynamic deceleration loads of this section, considered as ultimate loads acting alone, measured at the system component's center of gravity without structural damage to the system components, fuel tanks, or their attachments that would leak fuel to an ignition source.

(a) *Drop test requirements.* Each tank, or the most critical tank, must be drop-tested as follows:

(1) The drop height must be at least 50 feet.

(2) The drop impact surface must be nondeforming.

(3) The tanks must be filled with water to 80 percent of the normal, full capacity.

(4) The tank must be enclosed in a surrounding structure representative of the installation unless it can be established that the surrounding structure is free of projections or other design features likely to contribute to upture of the tank.

(5) The tank must drop freely and impact in a horizontal position ±10°.

(6) After the drop test, there must be no leakage.

(b) *Fuel tank load factors.* Except for fuel tanks located so that tank rupture with fuel release to either significant ignition sources, such as engines, heaters, and auxiliary power units, or occupants is extremely remote, each fuel tank must be designed and installed to retain its contents under the following ultimate inertial load factors, acting alone.

(1) For fuel tanks in the cabin:

(i) Upward—4g.

(ii) Forward—16g.

(iii) Sideward—8g.

(iv) Downward—20g.

(2) For fuel tanks located above or behind the crew or passenger compartment that, if loosened, could injure an occupant in an emergency landing:

(i) Upward—1.5g.

(ii) Forward—8g.

(iii) Sideward—2g.

(iv) Downward—4g.

(3) For fuel tanks in other areas:

(i) Upward—1.5g.

(ii) Forward—4g.

(iii) Sideward—2g.

(iv) Downward—4g.

(c) *Fuel line self-sealing breakaway couplings.* Self-sealing breakaway couplings must be installed unless hazardous relative motion of fuel system components to each other or to local rotorcraft structure is demonstrated to be extremely improbable or unless other means are provided. The couplings or equivalent devices must be installed at all fuel tank-to-fuel line connections, tank-to-tank interconnects, and at other points in the fuel system where local structural deformation could lead to the release of fuel.

(1) The design and construction of self-sealing breakaway couplings must incorporate the following design features:

(i) The load necessary to separate a breakaway coupling must be between 25 to 50 percent of the minimum ultimate failure load (ultimate strength) of the weakest component in the fluid-carrying line. The separation load must in no case be less than 300 pounds, regardless of the size of the fluid line.

(ii) A breakaway coupling must separate whenever its ultimate load (as defined in paragraph (c)(1)(i) of this section) is applied in the failure modes most likely to occur.

(iii) All breakaway couplings must incorporate design provisions to visually ascertain that the coupling is locked together (leak-free) and is open during normal installation and service.

(iv) All breakaway couplings must incorporate design provisions to prevent uncoupling or unintended closing due to operational shocks, vibrations, or accelerations.

(v) No breakaway coupling design may allow the release of fuel once the coupling has performed its intended function.

(2) All individual breakaway couplings, coupling fuel feed systems, or equivalent means must be designed, tested, installed, and maintained so inadvertent fuel shutoff in flight is improbable in accordance with §29.955(a) and must comply with the fatigue evaluation requirements of §29.571 without leaking.

(3) Alternate, equivalent means to the use of breakaway couplings must not create a survivable impact-induced load on the fuel line to which it is installed greater than 25 to 50 percent of the ultimate load (strength) of the weakest component in the line and must comply with the fatigue requirements of §29.571 without leaking.

(d) *Frangible or deformable structural attachments.* Unless hazardous relative motion of fuel tanks and fuel system components to local rotorcraft structure is demonstrated to be extremely improbable in an otherwise survivable impact, frangible or locally deformable attachments of fuel tanks and fuel system components to local rotorcraft structure must be used. The attachment of fuel tanks and fuel system components to local rotorcraft structure, whether frangible or locally deformable, must be designed such that its separation or relative local deformation will occur without rupture or local tear-out of the fuel tank or fuel system component that will cause fuel leakage. The ultimate strength of frangible or deformable attachments must be as follows:

(1) The load required to separate a frangible attachment from its support structure, or deform a locally deformable attachment relative to its support structure, must be between 25 and 50 percent of the minimum ultimate load (ultimate strength) of the weakest component in the attached system. In no case may the load be less than 300 pounds.

(2) A frangible or locally deformable attachment must separate or locally deform as intended whenever its ultimate load (as defined in paragraph (d)(1) of this section) is applied in the modes most likely to occur.

(3) All frangible or locally deformable attachments must comply with the fatigue requirements of § 29.571.

(e) *Separation of fuel and ignition sources.* To provide maximum crash resistance, fuel must be located as far as practicable from all occupiable areas and from all potential ignition sources.

(f) *Other basic mechanical design criteria.* Fuel tanks, fuel lines, electrical wires, and electrical devices must be designed, constructed, and installed, as far as practicable, to be crash resistant.

(g) *Rigid or semirigid fuel tanks.* Rigid or semirigid fuel tank or bladder walls must be impact and tear resistant.

[Doc. No. 26352, 59 FR 50387, Oct. 3, 1994]

§ 29.953 Fuel system independence.

(a) For category A rotorcraft—

(1) The fuel system must meet the requirements of § 29.903(b); and

(2) Unless other provisions are made to meet paragraph (a)(1) of this section, the fuel system must allow fuel to be supplied to each engine through a system independent of those parts of each system supplying fuel to other engines.

(b) Each fuel system for a multiengine category B rotorcraft must meet the requirements of paragraph (a)(2) of this section. However, separate fuel tanks need not be provided for each engine.

§ 29.954 Fuel system lightning protection.

The fuel system must be designed and arranged to prevent the ignition of fuel vapor within the system by—

(a) Direct lightning strikes to areas having a high probability of stroke attachment;

(b) Swept lightning strokes to areas where swept strokes are highly probable; and

(c) Corona and streamering at fuel vent outlets.

[Amdt. 29–26, 53 FR 34217, Sept. 2, 1988]

§ 29.955 Fuel flow.

(a) *General.* The fuel system for each engine must provide the engine with at least 100 percent of the fuel required under all operating and maneuvering conditions to be approved for the rotorcraft, including, as applicable, the fuel required to operate the engines under the test conditions required by § 29.927. Unless equivalent methods are used, compliance must be shown by test during which the following provisions are met, except that combinations of conditions which are shown to be improbable need not be considered.

(1) The fuel pressure, corrected for accelerations (load factors), must be within the limits specified by the engine type certificate data sheet.

(2) The fuel level in the tank may not exceed that established as the unusable fuel supply for that tank under § 29.959, plus that necessary to conduct the test.

(3) The fuel head between the tank and the engine must be critical with respect to rotorcraft flight attitudes.

(4) The fuel flow transmitter, if installed, and the critical fuel pump (for pump-fed systems) must be installed to produce (by actual or simulated failure) the critical restriction to fuel flow to be expected from component failure.

(5) Critical values of engine rotational speed, electrical power, or other sources of fuel pump motive power must be applied.

(6) Critical values of fuel properties which adversely affect fuel flow are applied during demonstrations of fuel flow capability.

(7) The fuel filter required by § 29.997 is blocked to the degree necessary to simulate the accumulation of fuel contamination required to activate the indicator required by § 29.1305(a)(17).

(b) *Fuel transfer system.* If normal operation of the fuel system requires fuel to be transferred to another tank, the transfer must occur automatically via a system which has been shown to maintain the fuel level in the receiving tank within acceptable limits during flight or surface operation of the rotorcraft.

(c) *Multiple fuel tanks.* If an engine can be supplied with fuel from more than one tank, the fuel system, in addition to having appropriate manual switching capability, must be designed to prevent interruption of fuel flow to that engine, without attention by the flightcrew, when any tank supplying fuel to that engine is depleted of usable fuel during normal operation and any other tank that normally supplies fuel to that engine alone contains usable fuel.

[Amdt. 29–26, 53 FR 34217, Sept. 2, 1988]

§29.957 Flow between interconnected tanks.

(a) Where tank outlets are interconnected and allow fuel to flow between them due to gravity or flight accelerations, it must be impossible for fuel to flow between tanks in quantities great enough to cause overflow from the tank vent in any sustained flight condition.

(b) If fuel can be pumped from one tank to another in flight—

(1) The design of the vents and the fuel transfer system must prevent structural damage to tanks from overfilling; and

(2) There must be means to warn the crew before overflow through the vents occurs.

§29.959 Unusable fuel supply.

The unusable fuel supply for each tank must be established as not less than the quantity at which the first evidence of malfunction occurs under the most adverse fuel feed condition occurring under any intended operations and flight maneuvers involving that tank.

§29.961 Fuel system hot weather operation.

Each suction lift fuel system and other fuel systems conducive to vapor formation must be shown to operate satisfactorily (within certification limits) when using fuel at the most critical temperature for vapor formation under critical operating conditions including, if applicable, the engine operating conditions defined by §29.927(b)(1) and (b)(2).

[Amdt. 29–26, 53 FR 34217, Sept. 2, 1988]

§29.963 Fuel tanks: general.

(a) Each fuel tank must be able to withstand, without failure, the vibra-

tion, inertia, fluid, and structural loads to which it may be subjected in operation.

(b) Each flexible fuel tank bladder or liner must be approved or shown to be suitable for the particular application and must be puncture resistant. Puncture resistance must be shown by meeting the TSO–C80, paragraph 16.0, requirements using a minimum puncture force of 370 pounds.

(c) Each integral fuel tank must have facilities for inspection and repair of its interior.

(d) The maximum exposed surface temperature of all components in the fuel tank must be less by a safe margin than the lowest expected autoignition temperature of the fuel or fuel vapor in the tank. Compliance with this requirement must be shown under all operating conditions and under all normal or malfunction conditions of all components inside the tank.

(e) Each fuel tank installed in personnel compartments must be isolated by fume-proof and fuel-proof enclosures that are drained and vented to the exterior of the rotorcraft. The design and construction of the enclosures must provide necessary protection for the tank, must be crash resistant during a survivable impact in accordance with §29.952, and must be adequate to withstand loads and abrasions to be expected in personnel compartments.

[Doc. No. 5084, 29 FR 16150, Dec. 3, 1964, as amended by Amdt. 29–26, 53 FR 34217, Sept. 2, 1988; Amdt. 29–35, 59 FR 50388, Oct. 3, 1994]

§29.965 Fuel tank tests.

(a) Each fuel tank must be able to withstand the applicable pressure tests in this section without failure or leakage. If practicable, test pressures may be applied in a manner simulating the pressure distribution in service.

(b) Each conventional metal tank, each nonmetallic tank with walls that are not supported by the rotorcraft structure, and each integral tank must be subjected to a pressure of 3.5 p.s.i. unless the pressure developed during maximum limit acceleration or emergency deceleration with a full tank exceeds this value, in which case a hydrostatic head, or equivalent test, must be applied to duplicate the acceleration loads as far as possible. However, the pressure need not exceed 3.5 p.s.i. on surfaces not exposed to the acceleration loading.

(c) Each nonmetallic tank with walls supported by the rotorcraft structure must be subjected to the following tests:

(1) A pressure test of at least 2.0 p.s.i. This test may be conducted on the tank alone in conjunction with the test specified in paragraph (c)(2) of this section.

(2) A pressure test, with the tank mounted in the rotorcraft structure, equal to the load developed by the reaction of the contents, with the tank full, during maximum limit acceleration or emergency deceleration. However, the pressure need not exceed 2.0 p.s.i. on surfaces faces not exposed to the acceleration loading.

(d) Each tank with large unsupported or unstiffened flat areas, or with other features whose failure or deformation could cause leakage, must be subjected to the following test or its equivalent:

(1) Each complete tank assembly and its supports must be vibration tested while mounted to simulate the actual installation.

(2) The tank assembly must be vibrated for 25 hours while two-thirds full of any suitable fluid. The amplitude of vibration may not be less than one thirty-second of an inch, unless otherwise substantiated.

(3) The test frequency of vibration must be as follows:

(i) If no frequency of vibration resulting from any r.p.m. within the normal operating range of engine or rotor system speeds is critical, the test frequency of vibration, in number of cycles per minute, must, unless a frequency based on a more rational analysis is used, be the number obtained by averaging the maximum and minimum power-on engine speeds (r.p.m.) for reciprocating engine powered rotorcraft or 2,000 c.p.m. for turbine engine powered rotorcraft.

(ii) If only one frequency of vibration resulting from any r.p.m. within the normal operating range of engine or rotor system speeds is critical, that frequency of vibration must be the test frequency.

(iii) If more than one frequency of vibration resulting from any r.p.m. with-

in the normal operating range of engine or rotor system speeds is critical, the most critical of these frequencies must be the test frequency.

(4) Under paragraph (d)(3)(ii) and (iii), the time of test must be adjusted to accomplish the same number of vibration cycles as would be accomplished in 25 hours at the frequency specified in paragraph (d)(3)(i) of this section.

(5) During the test, the tank assembly must be rocked at the rate of 16 to 20 complete cycles per minute through an angle of 15 degrees on both sides of the horizontal (30 degrees total), about the most critical axis, for 25 hours. If motion about more than one axis is likely to be critical, the tank must be rocked about each critical axis for 12½ hours.

(Secs. 313(a), 601, and 603, 72 Stat. 752, 775, 49 U.S.C. 1354(a), 1421, and 1423; sec. 6(c), 49 U.S.C. 1655 (c))

[Doc. No. 5084, 29 FR 16150, Dec. 3, 1964, as amended by Amdt. 29–13, 42 FR 15046, Mar. 17, 1977]

§ 29.967 Fuel tank installation.

(a) Each fuel tank must be supported so that tank loads are not concentrated on unsupported tank surfaces. In addition—

(1) There must be pads, if necessary, to prevent chafing between each tank and its supports;

(2) The padding must be nonabsorbent or treated to prevent the absorption of fuel;

(3) If flexible tank liners are used, they must be supported so that they are not required to withstand fluid loads; and

(4) Each interior surface of tank compartments must be smooth and free of projections that could cause wear of the liner, unless—

(i) There are means for protection of the liner at those points; or

(ii) The construction of the liner itself provides such protection.

(b) Any spaces adjacent to tank surfaces must be adequately ventilated to avoid accumulation of fuel or fumes in those spaces due to minor leakage. If the tank is in a sealed compartment, ventilation may be limited to drain holes that prevent clogging and that prevent excessive pressure resulting from altitude changes. If flexible tank liners are installed, the venting arrangement for the spaces between the liner and its container must maintain the proper relationship to tank vent pressures for any expected flight condition.

(c) The location of each tank must meet the requirements of §29.1185(b) and (c).

(d) No rotorcraft skin immediately adjacent to a major air outlet from the engine compartment may act as the wall of an integral tank.

[Doc. No. 5084, 29 FR 16150, Dec. 3, 1964, as amended by Amdt. 29–26, 53 FR 34217, Sept. 2, 1988; Amdt. 29–35, 59 FR 50388, Oct. 3, 1994]

§ 29.969   Fuel tank expansion space.

Each fuel tank or each group of fuel tanks with interconnected vent systems must have an expansion space of not less than 2 percent of the combined tank capacity. It must be impossible to fill the fuel tank expansion space inadvertently with the rotorcraft in the normal ground attitude.

[Amdt. 29–26, 53 FR 34217, Sept. 2, 1988]

§ 29.971   Fuel tank sump.

(a) Each fuel tank must have a sump with a capacity of not less than the greater of—

(1) 0.10 per cent of the tank capacity; or

(2) 1/16 gallon.

(b) The capacity prescribed in paragraph (a) of this section must be effective with the rotorcraft in any normal attitude, and must be located so that the sump contents cannot escape through the tank outlet opening.

(c) Each fuel tank must allow drainage of hazardous quantities of water from each part of the tank to the sump with the rotorcraft in any ground attitude to be expected in service.

(d) Each fuel tank sump must have a drain that allows complete drainage of the sump on the ground.

[Doc. No. 5084, 29 FR 16150, Dec. 3, 1964, as amended by Amdt. 29–12, 41 FR 55473, Dec. 20, 1976; Amdt. 29–26, 53 FR 34217, Sept. 2, 1988]

§ 29.973   Fuel tank filler connection.

(a) Each fuel tank filler connection must prevent the entrance of fuel into any part of the rotorcraft other than the tank itself during normal operations and must be crash resistant during a survivable impact in accordance with §29.952(c). In addition—

(1) Each filler must be marked as prescribed in §29.1557(c)(1);

(2) Each recessed filler connection that can retain any appreciable quantity of fuel must have a drain that discharges clear of the entire rotorcraft; and

(3) Each filler cap must provide a fuel-tight seal under the fluid pressure expected in normal operation and in a survivable impact.

(b) Each filler cap or filler cap cover must warn when the cap is not fully locked or seated on the filler connection.

[Doc. No. 26352, 59 FR 50388, Oct. 3, 1994]

§ 29.975   Fuel tank vents and carburetor vapor vents.

(a) *Fuel tank vents.* Each fuel tank must be vented from the top part of the expansion space so that venting is effective under normal flight conditions. In addition—

(1) The vents must be arranged to avoid stoppage by dirt or ice formation;

(2) The vent arrangement must prevent siphoning of fuel during normal operation;

(3) The venting capacity and vent pressure levels must maintain acceptable differences of pressure between the interior and exterior of the tank, during—

(i) Normal flight operation;

(ii) Maximum rate of ascent and descent; and

(iii) Refueling and defueling (where applicable);

(4) Airspaces of tanks with interconnected outlets must be interconnected;

(5) There may be no point in any vent line where moisture can accumulate with the rotorcraft in the ground attitude or the level flight attitude, unless drainage is provided;

(6) No vent or drainage provision may end at any point—

(i) Where the discharge of fuel from the vent outlet would constitute a fire hazard; or

(ii) From which fumes could enter personnel compartments; and

(7) The venting system must be designed to minimize spillage of fuel through the vents to an ignition source in the event of a rollover during landing, ground operations, or a survivable impact.

(b) *Carburetor vapor vents.* Each carburetor with vapor elimination connections must have a vent line to lead vapors back to one of the fuel tanks. In addition—

(1) Each vent system must have means to avoid stoppage by ice; and

(2) If there is more than one fuel tank, and it is necessary to use the tanks in a definite sequence, each vapor vent return line must lead back to the fuel tank used for takeoff and landing.

[Doc. No. 5084, 29 FR 16150, Dec. 3, 1964, as amended by Amdt. 29–26, 53 FR 34217, Sept. 2, 1988; Amdt. 29–35, 59 FR 50388, Oct. 3, 1994; Amdt. 29–42, 63 FR 43285, Aug. 12, 1998]

§ 29.977 Fuel tank outlet.

(a) There must be a fuel strainer for the fuel tank outlet or for the booster pump. This strainer must—

(1) For reciprocating engine powered airplanes, have 8 to 16 meshes per inch; and

(2) For turbine engine powered airplanes, prevent the passage of any object that could restrict fuel flow or damage any fuel system component.

(b) The clear area of each fuel tank outlet strainer must be at least five times the area of the outlet line.

(c) The diameter of each strainer must be at least that of the fuel tank outlet.

(d) Each finger strainer must be accessible for inspection and cleaning.

[Amdt. 29–12, 41 FR 55473, Dec. 20, 1976]

§ 29.979 Pressure refueling and fueling provisions below fuel level.

(a) Each fueling connection below the fuel level in each tank must have means to prevent the escape of hazardous quantities of fuel from that tank in case of malfunction of the fuel entry valve.

(b) For systems intended for pressure refueling, a means in addition to the normal means for limiting the tank content must be installed to prevent damage to the tank in case of failure of the normal means.

(c) The rotorcraft pressure fueling system (not fuel tanks and fuel tank vents) must withstand an ultimate load that is 2.0 times the load arising from the maximum pressure, including surge, that is likely to occur during fueling. The maximum surge pressure must be established with any combination of tank valves being either intentionally or inadvertently closed.

(d) The rotorcraft defueling system (not including fuel tanks and fuel tank vents) must withstand an ultimate load that is 2.0 times the load arising from the maximum permissible defueling pressure (positive or negative) at the rotorcraft fueling connection.

[Doc. No. 5084, 29 FR 16150, Dec. 3, 1964, as amended by Amdt. 29–12, 41 FR 55473, Dec. 20, 1976]

FUEL SYSTEM COMPONENTS

§ 29.991 Fuel pumps.

(a) Compliance with § 29.955 must not be jeopardized by failure of—

(1) Any one pump except pumps that are approved and installed as parts of a type certificated engine; or

(2) Any component required for pump operation except the engine served by that pump.

(b) The following fuel pump installation requirements apply:

(1) When necessary to maintain the proper fuel pressure—

(i) A connection must be provided to transmit the carburetor air intake static pressure to the proper fuel pump relief valve connection; and

(ii) The gauge balance lines must be independently connected to the carburetor inlet pressure to avoid incorrect fuel pressure readings.

(2) The installation of fuel pumps having seals or diaphragms that may leak must have means for draining leaking fuel.

(3) Each drain line must discharge where it will not create a fire hazard.

[Amdt. 29–26, 53 FR 34217, Sept. 2, 1988]

§ 29.993 Fuel system lines and fittings.

(a) Each fuel line must be installed and supported to prevent excessive vibration and to withstand loads due to fuel pressure, valve actuation, and accelerated flight conditions.

(b) Each fuel line connected to components of the rotorcraft between which relative motion could exist must have provisions for flexibility.

(c) Each flexible connection in fuel lines that may be under pressure or subjected to axial loading must use flexible hose assemblies.

(d) Flexible hose must be approved.

(e) No flexible hose that might be adversely affected by high temperatures may be used where excessive temperatures will exist during operation or after engine shutdown.

§ 29.995 Fuel valves.

In addition to meeting the requirements of § 29.1189, each fuel valve must—

(a) [Reserved]

(b) Be supported so that no loads resulting from their operation or from accelerated flight conditions are transmitted to the lines attached to the valve.

(Secs. 313(a), 601, and 603, 72 Stat. 759, 775, 49 U.S.C. 1354(a), 1421, and 1423; sec. 6(c), 49 U.S.C. 1655 (c))

[Doc. No. 5084, 29 FR 16150, Dec. 3, 1964, as amended by Amdt. 29-13, 42 FR 15046, Mar. 17, 1977]

§ 29.997 Fuel strainer or filter.

There must be a fuel strainer or filter between the fuel tank outlet and the inlet of the first fuel system component which is susceptible to fuel contamination, including but not limited to the fuel metering device or an engine positive displacement pump, whichever is nearer the fuel tank outlet. This fuel strainer or filter must—

(a) Be accessible for draining and cleaning and must incorporate a screen or element which is easily removable;

(b) Have a sediment trap and drain, except that it need not have a drain if the strainer or filter is easily removable for drain purposes;

(c) Be mounted so that its weight is not supported by the connecting lines or by the inlet or outlet connections of the strainer or filter inself, unless adequate strengh margins under all loading conditions are provided in the lines and connections; and

(d) Provide a means to remove from the fuel any contaminant which would jeopardize the flow of fuel through rotorcraft or engine fuel system components required for proper rotorcraft or engine fuel system operation.

[Amdt. No. 29-10, 39 FR 35462, Oct. 1, 1974, as amended by Amdt. 29-22, 49 FR 6850, Feb. 23, 1984; Amdt. 29-26, 53 FR 34217, Sept. 2, 1988]

§ 29.999 Fuel system drains.

(a) There must be at least one accessible drain at the lowest point in each fuel system to completely drain the system with the rotorcraft in any ground attitude to be expected in service.

(b) Each drain required by paragraph (a) of this section including the drains prescribed in § 29.971 must—

(1) Discharge clear of all parts of the rotorcraft;

(2) Have manual or automatic means to ensure positive closure in the off position; and

(3) Have a drain valve—

(i) That is readily accessible and which can be easily opened and closed; and

(ii) That is either located or protected to prevent fuel spillage in the event of a landing with landing gear retracted.

[Doc. No. 5084, 29 FR 16150, Dec. 3, 1964, as amended by Amdt. 29-12, 41 FR 55473, Dec. 20, 1976; Amdt. 29-26, 53 FR 34218, Sept. 2, 1988]

§ 29.1001 Fuel jettisoning.

If a fuel jettisoning system is installed, the following apply:

(a) Fuel jettisoning must be safe during all flight regimes for which jettisoning is to be authorized.

(b) In showing compliance with paragraph (a) of this section, it must be shown that—

(1) The fuel jettisoning system and its operation are free from fire hazard;

(2) No hazard results from fuel or fuel vapors which impinge on any part of the rotorcraft during fuel jettisoning; and

(3) Controllability of the rotorcraft remains satisfactory throughout the fuel jettisoning operation.

(c) Means must be provided to automatically prevent jettisoning fuel below the level required for an all-engine climb at maximum continuous power from sea level to 5,000 feet altitude and cruise thereafter for 30 minutes at maximum range engine power.

(d) The controls for any fuel jettisoning system must be designed to allow flight personnel (minimum crew) to safely interrupt fuel jettisoning during any part of the jettisoning operation.

(e) The fuel jettisoning system must be designed to comply with the powerplant installation requirements of § 29.901(c).

(f) An auxiliary fuel jettisoning system which meets the requirements of paragraphs (a), (b), (d), and (e) of this section may be installed to jettison additional fuel provided it has separate and independent controls.

[Amdt. 29–26, 53 FR 34218, Sept. 2, 1988]

OIL SYSTEM

§ 29.1011 Engines: general.

(a) Each engine must have an independent oil system that can supply it with an appropriate quantity of oil at a temperature not above that safe for continuous operation.

(b) The usable oil capacity of each system may not be less than the product of the endurance of the rotorcraft under critical operating conditions and the maximum allowable oil consumption of the engine under the same conditions, plus a suitable margin to ensure adequate circulation and cooling. Instead of a rational analysis of endurance and consumption, a usable oil capacity of one gallon for each 40 gallons of usable fuel may be used for reciprocating engine installations.

(c) Oil-fuel ratios lower than those prescribed in paragraph (c) of this section may be used if they are substantiated by data on the oil consumption of the engine.

(d) The ability of the engine and oil cooling provisions to maintain the oil temperature at or below the maximum established value must be shown under the applicable requirements of §§ 29.1041 through 29.1049.

[Doc. No. 5084, 29 FR 16150, Dec. 3, 1964, as amended by Amdt. 29–26, 53 FR 34218, Sept. 2, 1988]

§ 29.1013 Oil tanks.

(a) *Installation.* Each oil tank installation must meet the requirements of § 29.967.

(b) *Expansion space.* Oil tank expansion space must be provided so that—

(1) Each oil tank used with a reciprocating engine has an expansion space of not less than the greater of 10 percent of the tank capacity or 0.5 gallon, and each oil tank used with a turbine engine has an expansion space of not less than 10 percent of the tank capacity;

(2) Each reserve oil tank not directly connected to any engine has an expansion space of not less than two percent of the tank capacity; and

(3) It is impossible to fill the expansion space inadvertently with the rotorcraft in the normal ground attitude.

(c) *Filler connections.* Each recessed oil tank filler connection that can retain any appreciable quantity of oil must have a drain that discharges clear of the entire rotorcraft. In addition—

(1) Each oil tank filler cap must provide an oil-tight seal under the pressure expected in operation;

(2) For category A rotorcraft, each oil tank filler cap or filler cap cover must incorporate features that provide a warning when caps are not fully locked or seated on the filler connection; and

(3) Each oil filler must be marked under § 29.1557(c)(2).

(d) *Vent.* Oil tanks must be vented as follows:

(1) Each oil tank must be vented from the top part of the expansion space to that venting is effective under all normal flight conditions.

(2) Oil tank vents must be arranged so that condensed water vapor that might freeze and obstruct the line cannot accumulate at any point;

(e) *Outlet.* There must be means to prevent entrance into the tank itself, or into the tank outlet, of any object that might obstruct the flow of oil through the system. No oil tank outlet may be enclosed by a screen or guard that would reduce the flow of oil below a safe value at any operating temperature. There must be a shutoff valve at the outlet of each oil tank used with a turbine engine unless the external portion of the oil system (including oil tank supports) is fireproof.

(f) *Flexible liners.* Each flexible oil tank liner must be approved or shown to be suitable for the particular installation.

[Doc. No. 5084, 29 FR 16150, Dec. 3, 1964, as amended by Amdt. 29–10, 39 FR 35462, Oct. 1, 1974]

§ 29.1015 Oil tank tests.

Each oil tank must be designed and installed so that—

(a) It can withstand, without failure, any vibration, inertia, and fluid loads to which it may be subjected in operation; and

(b) It meets the requirements of § 29.965, except that instead of the pressure specified in § 29.965(b)—

(1) For pressurized tanks used with a turbine engine, the test pressure may not be less than 5 p.s.i. plus the maximum operating pressure of the tank; and

(2) For all other tanks, the test pressure may not be less than 5 p.s.i.

[Doc. No. 5084, 29 FR 16150, Dec. 3, 1964, as amended by Amdt. 29–10, 39 FR 35462, Oct. 1, 1974]

§ 29.1017 Oil lines and fittings.

(a) Each oil line must meet the requirements of § 29.993.

(b) Breather lines must be arranged so that—

(1) Condensed water vapor that might freeze and obstruct the line cannot accumulate at any point;

(2) The breather discharge will not constitute a fire hazard if foaming occurs, or cause emitted oil to strike the pilot's windshield; and

(3) The breather does not discharge into the engine air induction system.

§ 29.1019 Oil strainer or filter.

(a) Each turbine engine installation must incorporate an oil strainer or filter through which all of the engine oil flows and which meets the following requirements:

(1) Each oil strainer or filter that has a bypass must be constructed and installed so that oil will flow at the normal rate through the rest of the system with the strainer or filter completely blocked.

(2) The oil strainer or filter must have the capacity (with respect to operating limitations established for the engine) to ensure that engine oil system functioning is not impaired when

the oil is contaminated to a degree (with respect to particle size and density) that is greater than that established for the engine under Part 33 of this chapter.

(3) The oil strainer or filter, unless it is installed at an oil tank outlet, must incorporate a means to indicate contamination before it reaches the capacity established in accordance with paragraph (a)(2) of this section.

(4) The bypass of a strainer or filter must be constructed and installed so that the release of collected contaminants is minimized by appropriate location of the bypass to ensure that collected contaminants are not in the bypass flow path.

(5) An oil strainer or filter that has no bypass, except one that is installed at an oil tank outlet, must have a means to connect it to the warning system required in § 29.1305(a)(18).

(b) Each oil strainer or filter in a powerplant installation using reciprocating engines must be constructed and installed so that oil will flow at the normal rate through the rest of the system with the strainer or filter element completely blocked.

[Amdt. 29–10, 39 FR 35463, Oct. 1, 1974, as amended by Amdt. 29–22, 49 FR 6850, Feb. 23, 1984; Amdt. 29–26, 53 FR 34218, Sept. 2, 1988]

§ 29.1021 Oil system drains.

A drain (or drains) must be provided to allow safe drainage of the oil system. Each drain must—

(a) Be accessible; and

(b) Have manual or automatic means for positive locking in the closed position.

[Amdt. 29–22, 49 FR 6850, Feb. 23, 1984]

§ 29.1023 Oil radiators.

(a) Each oil radiator must be able to withstand any vibration, inertia, and oil pressure loads to which it would be subjected in operation.

(b) Each oil radiator air duct must be located, or equipped, so that, in case of fire, and with the airflow as it would be with and without the engine operating, flames cannot directly strike the radiator.

679

§ 29.1025   Oil valves.

(a) Each oil shutoff must meet the requirements of § 29.1189.

(b) The closing of oil shutoffs may not prevent autorotation.

(c) Each oil valve must have positive stops or suitable index provisions in the "on" and "off" positions and must be supported so that no loads resulting from its operation or from accelerated flight conditions are transmitted to the lines attached to the valve.

§ 29.1027   Transmission and gearboxes: general.

(a) The oil system for components of the rotor drive system that require continuous lubrication must be sufficiently independent of the lubrication systems of the engine(s) to ensure—

(1) Operation with any engine inoperative; and

(2) Safe autorotation.

(b) Pressure lubrication systems for transmissions and gearboxes must comply with the requirements of §§ 29.1013, paragraphs (c), (d), and (f) only, 29.1015, 29.1017, 29.1021, 29.1023, and 29.1337(d). In addition, the system must have—

(1) An oil strainer or filter through which all the lubricant flows, and must—

(i) Be designed to remove from the lubricant any contaminant which may damage transmission and drive system components or impede the flow of lubricant to a hazardous degree; and

(ii) Be equipped with a bypass constructed and installed so that—

(A) The lubricant will flow at the normal rate through the rest of the system with the strainer or filter completely blocked; and

(B) The release of collected contaminants is minimized by appropriate location of the bypass to ensure that collected contaminants are not in the bypass flowpath;

(iii) Be equipped with a means to indicate collection of contaminants on the filter or strainer at or before opening of the bypass;

(2) For each lubricant tank or sump outlet supplying lubrication to rotor drive systems and rotor drive system components, a screen to prevent entrance into the lubrication system of any object that might obstruct the flow of lubricant from the outlet to the filter required by paragraph (b)(1) of this section. The requirements of paragraph (b)(1) of this section do not apply to screens installed at lubricant tank or sump outlets.

(c) Splash type lubrication systems for rotor drive system gearboxes must comply with §§ 29.1021 and 29.1337(d).

[Amdt. 29–26, 53 FR 34218, Sept. 2, 1988]

COOLING

§ 29.1041   General.

(a) The powerplant and auxiliary power unit cooling provisions must be able to maintain the temperatures of powerplant components, engine fluids, and auxiliary power unit components and fluids within the temperature limits established for these components and fluids, under ground, water, and flight operating conditions for which certification is requested, and after normal engine or auxiliary power unit shutdown, or both.

(b) There must be cooling provisions to maintain the fluid temperatures in any power transmission within safe values under any critical surface (ground or water) and flight operating conditions.

(c) Except for ground-use-only auxiliary power units, compliance with paragraphs (a) and (b) of this section must be shown by flight tests in which the temperatures of selected powerplant component and auxiliary power unit component, engine, and transmission fluids are obtained under the conditions prescribed in those paragraphs.

[Doc. No. 5084, 29 FR 16150, Dec. 3, 1964, as amended by Amdt. 29–26, 53 FR 34218, Sept. 2, 1988]

§ 29.1043   Cooling tests.

(a) *General.* For the tests prescribed in § 29.1041(c), the following apply:

(1) If the tests are conducted under conditions deviating from the maximum ambient atmospheric temperature specified in paragraph (b) of this section, the recorded powerplant temperatures must be corrected under paragraphs (c) and (d) of this section, unless a more rational correction method is applicable.

(2) No corrected temperature determined under paragraph (a)(1) of this section may exceed established limits.

(3) The fuel used during the cooling tests must be of the minimum grade approved for the engines, and the mixture settings must be those used in normal operation.

(4) The test procedures must be as prescribed in §§ 29.1045 through 29.1049.

(5) For the purposes of the cooling tests, a temperature is "stabilized" when its rate of change is less than 2 °F per minute.

(b) *Maximum ambient atmospheric temperature.* A maximum ambient atmospheric temperature corresponding to sea level conditions of at least 100 degrees F. must be established. The assumed temperature lapse rate is 3.6 degrees F. per thousand feet of altitude above sea level until a temperature of −69.7 degrees F. is reached, above which altitude the temperature is considered constant at −69.7 degrees F. However, for winterization installations, the applicant may select a maximum ambient atmospheric temperature corresponding to sea level conditions of less than 100 degrees F.

(c) *Correction factor (except cylinder barrels).* Unless a more rational correction applies, temperatures of engine fluids and powerplant components (except cylinder barrels) for which temperature limits are established, must be corrected by adding to them the difference between the maximum ambient atmospheric temperature and the temperature of the ambient air at the time of the first occurrence of the maximum component or fluid temperature recorded during the cooling test.

(d) *Correction factor for cylinder barrel temperatures.* Cylinder barrel temperatures must be corrected by adding to them 0.7 times the difference between the maximum ambient atmospheric temperature and the temperature of the ambient air at the time of the first occurrence of the maximum cylinder

barrel temperature recorded during the cooling test.

(Secs. 313(a), 601, 603, 604, and 605 of the Federal Aviation Act of 1958 (49 U.S.C. 1354(a), 1421, 1423, 1424, and 1425); and sec. 6(c) of the Dept. of Transportation Act (49 U.S.C. 1655(c)))

[Doc. No. 5084, 29 FR 16150, Dec. 3, 1964, as amended by Amdt. 29–12, 41 FR 55473, Dec. 20, 1976; Amdt. 29–15, 43 FR 2327, Jan. 16, 1978; Amdt. 29–26, 53 FR 34218, Sept. 2, 1988]

§ 29.1045 Climb cooling test procedures.

(a) Climb cooling tests must be conducted under this section for—

(1) Category A rotorcraft; and

(2) Multiengine category B rotorcraft for which certification is requested under the category A powerplant installation requirements, and under the requirements of § 29.861(a) at the steady rate of climb or descent established under § 29.67(b).

(b) The climb or descent cooling tests must be conducted with the engine inoperative that produces the most adverse cooling conditions for the remaining engines and powerplant components.

(c) Each operating engine must—

(1) For helicopters for which the use of 30-minute OEI power is requested, be at 30-minute OEI power for 30 minutes, and then at maximum continuous power (or at full throttle when above the critical altitude);

(2) For helicopters for which the use of continuous OEI power is requested, be at continuous OEI power (or at full throttle when above the critical altitude); and

(3) For other rotorcraft, be at maximum continuous power (or at full throttle when above the critical altitude).

(d) After temperatures have stabilized in flight, the climb must be—

(1) Begun from an altitude not greater than the lower of—

(i) 1,000 feet below the engine critcal altitude; and

681

(ii) 1,000 feet below the maximum altitude at which the rate of climb is 150 f.p.m; and

(2) Continued for at least five minutes after the occurrence of the highest temperature recorded, or until the rotorcraft reaches the maximum altitude for which certification is requested.

(e) For category B rotorcraft without a positive rate of climb, the descent must begin at the all-engine-critical altitude and end at the higher of—

(1) The maximum altitude at which level flight can be maintained with one engine operative; and

(2) Sea level.

(f) The climb or descent must be conducted at an airspeed representing a normal operational practice for the configuration being tested. However, if the cooling provisions are sensitive to rotorcraft speed, the most critical airspeed must be used, but need not exceed the speeds established under § 29.67(a)(2) or § 29.67(b). The climb cooling test may be conducted in conjunction with the takeoff cooling test of § 29.1047.

[Doc. No. 5084, 29 FR 16150, Dec. 3, 1964, as amended by Amdt. 29–26, 53 FR 34218, Sept. 2, 1988]

§ 29.1047 Takeoff cooling test procedures.

(a) *Category A.* For each category A rotorcraft, cooling must be shown during takeoff and subsequent climb as follows:

(1) Each temperature must be stabilized while hovering in ground effect with—

(i) The power necessary for hovering;

(ii) The appropriate cowl flap and shutter settings; and

(iii) The maximum weight.

(2) After the temperatures have stabilized, a climb must be started at the lowest practicable altitude and must be conducted with one engine inoperative.

(3) The operating engines must be at the greatest power for which approval is sought (or at full throttle when above the critical altitude) for the same period as this power is used in determining the takeoff climbout path under § 29.59.

(4) At the end of the time interval prescribed in paragraph (b)(3) of this section, the power must be changed to that used in meeting § 29.67(a)(2) and the climb must be continued for—

(i) Thirty minutes, if 30-minute OEI power is used; or

(ii) At least 5 minutes after the occurrence of the highest temperature recorded, if continuous OEI power or maximum continuous power is used.

(5) The speeds must be those used in determining the takeoff flight path under § 29.59.

(b) *Category B.* For each category B rotorcraft, cooling must be shown during takeoff and subsequent climb as follows:

(1) Each temperature must be stabilized while hovering in ground effect with—

(i) The power necessary for hovering;

(ii) The appropriate cowl flap and shutter settings; and

(iii) The maximum weight.

(2) After the temperatures have stabilized, a climb must be started at the lowest practicable altitude with takeoff power.

(3) Takeoff power must be used for the same time interval as takeoff power is used in determining the takeoff flight path under § 29.63.

(4) At the end of the time interval prescribed in paragraph (a)(3) of this section, the power must be reduced to maximum continuous power and the climb must be continued for at least five minutes after the occurence of the highest temperature recorded.

(5) The cooling test must be conducted at an airspeed corresponding to normal operating practice for the configuration being tested. However, if the cooling provisions are sensitive to rotorcraft speed, the most critical airspeed must be used, but need not exceed the speed for best rate of climb with maximum continuous power.

[Doc. No. 5084, 29 FR 16150, Dec. 3, 1964, as amended by Amdt. 29–1, 30 FR 8778, July 13, 1965; Amdt. 29–26, 53 FR 34219, Sept. 2, 1988]

§ 29.1049 Hovering cooling test procedures.

The hovering cooling provisions must be shown—

(a) At maximum weight or at the greatest weight at which the rotorcraft can hover (if less), at sea level, with the power required to hover but not more than maximum continuous power, in the ground effect in still air, until at least five minutes after the occurrence of the highest temperature recorded; and

(b) With maximum continuous power, maximum weight, and at the altitude resulting in zero rate of climb for this configuration, until at least five minutes after the occurrence of the highest temperature recorded.

INDUCTION SYSTEM

§29.1091 Air induction.

(a) The air induction system for each engine and auxiliary power unit must supply the air required by that engine and auxiliary power unit under the operating conditions for which certification is requested.

(b) Each engine and auxiliary power unit air induction system must provide air for proper fuel metering and mixture distribution with the induction system valves in any position.

(c) No air intake may open within the engine accessory section or within other areas of any powerplant compartment where emergence of backfire flame would constitute a fire hazard.

(d) Each reciprocating engine must have an alternate air source.

(e) Each alternate air intake must be located to prevent the entrance of rain, ice, or other foreign matter.

(f) For turbine engine powered rotorcraft and rotorcraft incorporating auxiliary power units—

(1) There must be means to prevent hazardous quantities of fuel leakage or overflow from drains, vents, or other components of flammable fluid systems from entering the engine or auxiliary power unit intake system; and

(2) The air inlet ducts must be located or protected so as to minimize the ingestion of foreign matter during takeoff, landing, and taxiing.

(Secs. 313(a), 601, 603, 604, Federal Aviation Act of 1958 (49 U.S.C. 1354(a), 1421, 1423, 1424), sec. 6(c), Dept. of Transportation Act (49 U.S.C. 1655(c)))

[Doc. No. 5084, 29 FR 16150, Dec. 3, 1964, as amended by Amdt. 29–3, 33 FR 969, Jan. 26, 1968; Amdt. 29–17, 43 FR 50601, Oct. 30, 1978]

§29.1093 Induction system icing protection.

(a) *Reciprocating engines.* Each reciprocating engine air induction system must have means to prevent and eliminate icing. Unless this is done by other means, it must be shown that, in air free of visible moisture at a temperature of 30 °F., and with the engines at 60 percent of maximum continuous power—

(1) Each rotorcraft with sea level engines using conventional venturi carburetors has a preheater that can provide a heat rise of 90 °F.;

(2) Each rotorcraft with sea level engines using carburetors tending to prevent icing has a preheater that can provide a heat rise of 70 °F.;

(3) Each rotorcraft with altitude engines using conventional venturi carburetors has a preheater that can provide a heat rise of 120 °F.; and

(4) Each rotorcraft with altitude engines using carburetors tending to prevent icing has a preheater that can provide a heat rise of 100 °F.

(b) *Turbine engines.* (1) It must be shown that each turbine engine and its air inlet system can operate throughout the flight power range of the engine (including idling)—

(i) Without accumulating ice on engine or inlet system components that would adversely affect engine operation or cause a serious loss of power under the icing conditions specified in appendix C of this Part; and

(ii) In snow, both falling and blowing, without adverse effect on engine operation, within the limitations established for the rotorcraft.

(2) Each turbine engine must idle for 30 minutes on the ground, with the air bleed available for engine icing protection at its critical condition, without adverse effect, in an atmosphere that is at a temperature between 15° and 30 °F (between −9° and −1 °C) and has a liquid water content not less than 0.3 grams per cubic meter in the form of drops having a mean effective diameter not less than 20 microns, followed by momentary operation at takeoff power or thrust. During the 30 minutes of idle operation, the engine may be run up periodically to a moderate power or thrust setting in a manner acceptable to the Administrator.

(c) *Supercharged reciprocating engines.* For each engine having a supercharger to pressurize the air before it enters the carburetor, the heat rise in the air caused by that supercharging at any altitude may be utilized in determining compliance with paragraph (a) of this section if the heat rise utilized is that which will be available, automatically, for the applicable altitude and operation condition because of supercharging.

(Secs. 313(a), 601, and 603, 72 Stat. 752, 775, 49 U.S.C. 1354(a), 1421, and 1423; sec. 6(c), 49 U.S.C. 1655 (c))

[Amdt. No. 29-3, 33 FR 969, Jan. 26, 1968, as amended by Amdt. 29-12, 41 FR 55473, Dec. 20, 1976; Amdt. 29-13, 42 FR 15046, Mar. 17, 1977; Amdt. 29-22, 49 FR 6850, Feb. 23, 1984; Amdt. 29-26, 53 FR 34219, Sept. 2, 1988]

§ 29.1101 Carburetor air preheater design.

Each carburetor air preheater must be designed and constructed to—

(a) Ensure ventilation of the preheater when the engine is operated in cold air;

(b) Allow inspection of the exhaust manifold parts that it surrounds; and

(c) Allow inspection of critical parts of the preheater itself.

§ 29.1103 Induction systems ducts and air duct systems.

(a) Each induction system duct upstream of the first stage of the engine supercharger and of the auxiliary power unit compressor must have a drain to prevent the hazardous accumulation of fuel and moisture in the ground attitude. No drain may discharge where it might cause a fire hazard.

(b) Each duct must be strong enough to prevent induction system failure from normal backfire conditions.

(c) Each duct connected to components between which relative motion could exist must have means for flexibility.

(d) Each duct within any fire zone for which a fire-extinguishing system is required must be at least—

(1) Fireproof, if it passes through any firewall; or

(2) Fire resistant, for other ducts, except that ducts for auxiliary power units must be fireproof within the auxiliary power unit fire zone.

(e) Each auxiliary power unit induction system duct must be fireproof for a sufficient distance upstream of the auxiliary power unit compartment to prevent hot gas reverse flow from burning through auxiliary power unit ducts and entering any other compartment or area of the rotorcraft in which a hazard would be created resulting from the entry of hot gases. The materials used to form the remainder of the induction system duct and plenum chamber of the auxiliary power unit must be capable of resisting the maximum heat conditions likely to occur.

(f) Each auxiliary power unit induction system duct must be constructed of materials that will not absorb or trap hazardous quantities of flammable fluids that could be ignited in the event of a surge or reverse flow condition.

(Secs. 313(a), 601, 603, 604, Federal Aviation Act of 1958 (49 U.S.C. 1354(a), 1421, 1423, 1424), sec. 6(c), Dept. of Transportation Act (49 U.S.C. 1655(c)))

[Doc. No. 5084, 29 FR 16150, Dec. 3, 1964, as amended by Amdt. 29-17, 43 FR 50602, Oct. 30, 1978]

§ 29.1105 Induction system screens.

If induction system screens are used—

(a) Each screen must be upstream of the carburetor;

(b) No screen may be in any part of the induction system that is the only passage through which air can reach the engine, unless it can be deiced by heated air;

(c) No screen may be deiced by alcohol alone; and

(d) It must be impossible for fuel to strike any screen.

§ 29.1107 Inter-coolers and after-coolers.

Each inter-cooler and after-cooler must be able to withstand the vibration, inertia, and air pressure loads to which it would be subjected in operation.

§ 29.1109 Carburetor air cooling.

It must be shown under § 29.1043 that each installation using two-stage superchargers has means to maintain the air temperature, at the carburetor inlet, at or below the maximum established value.

EXHAUST SYSTEM

§29.1121 General.

For powerplant and auxiliary power unit installations the following apply:

(a) Each exhaust system must ensure safe disposal of exhaust gases without fire hazard or carbon monoxide contamination in any personnel compartment.

(b) Each exhaust system part with a surface hot enough to ignite flammable fluids or vapors must be located or shielded so that leakage from any system carrying flammable fluids or vapors will not result in a fire caused by impingement of the fluids or vapors on any part of the exhaust system including shields for the exhaust system.

(c) Each component upon which hot exhaust gases could impinge, or that could be subjected to high temperatures from exhaust system parts, must be fireproof. Each exhaust system component must be separated by a fireproof shield from adjacent parts of the rotorcraft that are outside the engine and auxiliary power unit compartments.

(d) No exhaust gases may discharge so as to cause a fire hazard with respect to any flammable fluid vent or drain.

(e) No exhaust gases may discharge where they will cause a glare seriously affecting pilot vision at night.

(f) Each exhaust system component must be ventilated to prevent points of excessively high temperature.

(g) Each exhaust shroud must be ventilated or insulated to avoid, during normal operation, a temperature high enough to ignite any flammable fluids or vapors outside the shroud.

(h) If significant traps exist, each turbine engine exhaust system must have drains discharging clear of the rotorcraft, in any normal ground and flight attitudes, to prevent fuel accumulation after the failure of an attempted engine start.

(Secs. 313(a), 601, and 603, 72 Stat. 752, 755, 49 U.S.C. 1354(a), 1421, and 1423; sec. 6(c), 49 U.S.C. 1655 (c))

[Doc. No. 5084, 29 FR 16150, Dec. 3, 1964, as amended by Amdt. 29–3, 33 FR 970, Jan. 26, 1968; Amdt. 29–13, 42 FR 15046, Mar. 17, 1977]

§29.1123 Exhaust piping.

(a) Exhaust piping must be heat and corrosion resistant, and must have provisions to prevent failure due to expansion by operating temperatures.

(b) Exhaust piping must be supported to withstand any vibration and inertia loads to which it would be subjected in operation.

(c) Exhaust piping connected to components between which relative motion could exist must have provisions for flexibility.

§29.1125 Exhaust heat exchangers.

For reciprocating engine powered rotorcraft the following apply:

(a) Each exhaust heat exchanger must be constructed and installed to withstand the vibration, inertia, and other loads to which it would be subjected in operation. In addition—

(1) Each exchanger must be suitable for continued operation at high temperatures and resistant to corrosion from exhaust gases;

(2) There must be means for inspecting the critical parts of each exchanger;

(3) Each exchanger must have cooling provisions wherever it is subject to contact with exhaust gases; and

(4) No exhaust heat exchanger or muff may have stagnant areas or liquid traps that would increase the probability of ignition of flammable fluids or vapors that might be present in case of the failure or malfunction of components carrying flammable fluids.

(b) If an exhaust heat exchanger is used for heating ventilating air used by personnel—

(1) There must be a secondary heat exchanger between the primary exhaust gas heat exchanger and the ventilating air system; or

(2) Other means must be used to prevent harmful contamination of the ventilating air.

[Doc. No. 5084, 29 FR 16150, Dec. 3, 1964, as amended by Amdt. 29–12, 41 FR 55473, Dec. 20, 1976; Amdt. 29–41, 62 FR 46173, Aug. 29, 1997]

POWERPLANT CONTROLS AND ACCESSORIES

§ 29.1141 Powerplant controls: general.

(a) Powerplant controls must be located and arranged under § 29.777 and marked under § 29.1555.

(b) Each control must be located so that it cannot be inadvertently operated by persons entering, leaving, or moving normally in the cockpit.

(c) Each flexible powerplant control must be approved.

(d) Each control must be able to maintain any set position without—

(1) Constant attention; or

(2) Tendency to creep due to control loads or vibration.

(e) Each control must be able to withstand operating loads without excessive deflection.

(f) Controls of powerplant valves required for safety must have—

(1) For manual valves, positive stops or in the case of fuel valves suitable index provisions, in the open and closed position; and

(2) For power-assisted valves, a means to indicate to the flight crew when the valve—

(i) Is in the fully open or fully closed position; or

(ii) Is moving between the fully open and fully closed position.

(Secs. 313(a), 601, and 603, 72 Stat. 752, 775, 49 U.S.C. 1354(a), 1421, and 1423; sec. 6(c), 49 U.S.C. 1655(c))

[Doc. No. 5084, 29 FR 16150, Dec. 3, 1964, as amended by Amdt. 29–13, 42 FR 15046, Mar. 17, 1977; Amdt. 29–26, 53 FR 34219, Sept. 2, 1988]

§ 29.1142 Auxiliary power unit controls.

Means must be provided on the flight deck for starting, stopping, and emergency shutdown of each installed auxiliary power unit.

(Secs. 313(a), 601, 603, 604, Federal Aviation Act of 1958 (49 U.S.C. 1354(a), 1421, 1423, 1424), sec. 6(c), Dept. of Transportation Act (49 U.S.C. 1655(c)))

[Amdt. 29–17, 43 FR 50602, Oct. 30, 1978]

§ 29.1143 Engine controls.

(a) There must be a separate power control for each engine.

(b) Power controls must be arranged to allow ready synchronization of all engines by—

(1) Separate control of each engine; and

(2) Simultaneous control of all engines.

(c) Each power control must provide a positive and immediately responsive means of controlling its engine.

(d) Each fluid injection control other than fuel system control must be in the corresponding power control. However, the injection system pump may have a separate control.

(e) If a power control incorporates a fuel shutoff feature, the control must have a means to prevent the inadvertent movement of the control into the shutoff position. The means must—

(1) Have a positive lock or stop at the idle position; and

(2) Require a separate and distinct operation to place the control in the shutoff position.

(f) For rotorcraft to be certificated for a 30-second OEI power rating, a means must be provided to automatically activate and control the 30-second OEI power and prevent any engine from exceeding the installed engine limits associated with the 30-second OEI power rating approved for the rotorcraft.

[Amdt. 29–26, 53 FR 34219, Sept. 2, 1988, as amended by Amdt. 29–34, 59 FR 47768, Sept. 16, 1994]

§ 29.1145 Ignition switches.

(a) Ignition switches must control each ignition circuit on each engine.

(b) There must be means to quickly shut off all ignition by the grouping of switches or by a master ignition control.

(c) Each group of ignition switches, except ignition switches for turbine engines for which continuous ignition is not required, and each master ignition control must have a means to prevent its inadvertent operation.

(Secs. 313(a), 601, and 603, 72 Stat. 759, 775, 49 U.S.C. 1354(a), 1421, and 1423; sec. 6(c), 49 U.S.C. 1655 (c))

[Doc. No. 5084, 29 FR 16150, Dec. 3, 1964, as amended by Amdt. 29–13, 42 FR 15046, Mar. 17, 1977]

§29.1147 Mixture controls.

(a) If there are mixture controls, each engine must have a separate control, and the controls must be arranged to allow—

(1) Separate control of each engine; and

(2) Simultaneous control of all engines.

(b) Each intermediate position of the mixture controls that corresponds to a normal operating setting must be identifiable by feel and sight.

§29.1151 Rotor brake controls.

(a) It must be impossible to apply the rotor brake inadvertently in flight.

(b) There must be means to warn the crew if the rotor brake has not been completely released before takeoff.

§29.1157 Carburetor air temperature controls.

There must be a separate carburetor air temperature control for each engine.

§29.1159 Supercharger controls.

Each supercharger control must be accessible to—

(a) The pilots; or

(b) (If there is a separate flight engineer station with a control panel) the flight engineer.

§29.1163 Powerplant accessories.

(a) Each engine mounted accessory must—

(1) Be approved for mounting on the engine involved;

(2) Use the provisions on the engine for mounting; and

(3) Be sealed in such a way as to prevent contamination of the engine oil system and the accessory system.

(b) Electrical equipment subject to arcing or sparking must be installed, to minimize the probability of igniting flammable fluids or vapors.

(c) If continued rotation of an engine-driven cabin supercharger or any remote accessory driven by the engine will be a hazard if they malfunction, there must be means to prevent their hazardous rotation without interfering with the continued operation of the engine.

(d) Unless other means are provided, torque limiting means must be provided for accessory drives located on any component of the transmission and rotor drive system to prevent damage to these components from excessive accessory load.

[Doc. No. 5084, 29 FR 16150, Dec. 3, 1964, as amended by Amdt. 29–22, 49 FR 6850, Feb. 23, 1984; Amdt. 29–26, 53 FR 34219, Sept. 2, 1988]

§29.1165 Engine ignition systems.

(a) Each battery ignition system must be supplemented with a generator that is automatically available as an alternate source of electrical energy to allow continued engine operation if any battery becomes depleted.

(b) The capacity of batteries and generators must be large enough to meet the simultaneous demands of the engine ignition system and the greatest demands of any electrical system components that draw from the same source.

(c) The design of the engine ignition system must account for—

(1) The condition of an inoperative generator;

(2) The condition of a completely depleted battery with the generator running at its normal operating speed; and

(3) The condition of a completely depleted battery with the generator operating at idling speed, if there is only one battery.

(d) Magneto ground wiring (for separate ignition circuits) that lies on the engine side of any firewall must be installed, located, or protected, to minimize the probability of the simultaneous failure of two or more wires as a result of mechanical damage, electrical fault, or other cause.

(e) No ground wire for any engine may be routed through a fire zone of another engine unless each part of that wire within that zone is fireproof.

(f) Each ignition system must be independent of any electrical circuit that is not used for assisting, controlling, or analyzing the operation of that system.

(g) There must be means to warn appropriate crewmembers if the malfunctioning of any part of the electrical system is causing the continuous discharge of any battery necessary for engine ignition.

[Doc. No. 5084, 29 FR 16150, Dec. 3, 1964, as amended by Amdt. 29–12, 41 FR 55473, Dec. 20, 1976]

POWERPLANT FIRE PROTECTION

§ 29.1181 Designated fire zones: regions included.

(a) Designated fire zones are—

(1) The engine power section of reciprocating engines;

(2) The engine accessory section of reciprocating engines;

(3) Any complete powerplant compartment in which there is no isolation between the engine power section and the engine accessory section, for reciprocating engines;

(4) Any auxiliary power unit compartment;

(5) Any fuel-burning heater and other combustion equipment installation described in § 29.859;

(6) The compressor and accessory sections of turbine engines; and

(7) The combustor, turbine, and tailpipe sections of turbine engine installations except sections that do not contain lines and components carrying flammable fluids or gases and are isolated from the designated fire zone prescribed in paragraph (a)(6) of this section by a firewall that meets § 29.1191.

(b) Each designated fire zone must meet the requirements of §§ 29.1183 through 29.1203.

[Amdt. 29–3, 33 FR 970, Jan. 26, 1968, as amended by Amdt. 29–26, 53 FR 34219, Sept. 2, 1988]

§ 29.1183 Lines, fittings, and components.

(a) Except as provided in paragraph (b) of this section, each line, fitting, and other component carrying flammable fluid in any area subject to en-

gine fire conditions and each component which conveys or contains flammable fluid in a designated fire zone must be fire resistant, except that flammable fluid tanks and supports in a designated fire zone must be fireproof or be enclosed by a fireproof shield unless damage by fire to any non-fireproof part will not cause leakage or spillage of flammable fluid. Components must be shielded or located so as to safeguard against the ignition of leaking flammable fluid. An integral oil sump of less than 25-quart capacity on a reciprocating engine need not be fireproof nor be enclosed by a fireproof shield.

(b) Paragraph (a) of this section does not apply to—

(1) Lines, fittings, and components which are already approved as part of a type certificated engine; and

(2) Vent and drain lines, and their fittings, whose failure will not result in or add to, a fire hazard.

[Doc. No. 5084, 29 FR 16150, Dec. 3, 1964, as amended by Amdt. 29–2, 32 FR 6914, May 5, 1967; Amdt. 29–10, 39 FR 35463, Oct. 1, 1974; Amdt. 29–22, 49 FR 6850, Feb. 23, 1984]

§ 29.1185 Flammable fluids.

(a) No tank or reservoir that is part of a system containing flammable fluids or gases may be in a designated fire zone unless the fluid contained, the design of the system, the materials used in the tank and its supports, the shutoff means, and the connections, lines, and controls provide a degree of safety equal to that which would exist if the tank or reservoir were outside such a zone.

(b) Each fuel tank must be isolated from the engines by a firewall or shroud.

(c) There must be at least one-half inch of clear airspace between each tank or reservoir and each firewall or shroud isolating a designated fire zone, unless equivalent means are used to prevent heat transfer from the fire zone to the flammable fluid.

(d) Absorbent material close to flammable fluid system components that might leak must be covered or treated to prevent the absorption of hazardous quantities of fluids.

§29.1187 Drainage and ventilation of fire zones.

(a) There must be complete drainage of each part of each designated fire zone to minimize the hazards resulting from failure or malfunction of any component containing flammable fluids. The drainage means must be—

(1) Effective under conditions expected to prevail when drainage is needed; and

(2) Arranged so that no discharged fluid will cause an additional fire hazard.

(b) Each designated fire zone must be ventilated to prevent the accumulation of flammable vapors.

(c) No ventilation opening may be where it would allow the entry of flammable fluids, vapors, or flame from other zones.

(d) Ventilation means must be arranged so that no discharged vapors will cause an additional fire hazard.

(e) For category A rotorcraft, there must be means to allow the crew to shut off the sources of forced ventilation in any fire zone (other than the engine power section of the powerplant compartment) unless the amount of extinguishing agent and the rate of discharge are based on the maximum airflow through that zone.

§29.1189 Shutoff means.

(a) There must be means to shut off or otherwise prevent hazardous quantities of fuel, oil, de-icing fluid, and other flammable fluids from flowing into, within, or through any designated fire zone, except that this means need not be provided—

(1) For lines, fittings, and components forming an integral part of an engine;

(2) For oil systems for turbine engine installations in which all components of the system, including oil tanks, are fireproof or located in areas not subject to engine fire conditions; or

(3) For engine oil systems in category B rotorcraft using reciprocating engines of less than 500 cubic inches displacement.

(b) The closing of any fuel shutoff valve for any engine may not make fuel unavailable to the remaining engines.

(c) For category A rotorcraft, no hazardous quantity of flammable fluid may drain into any designated fire zone after shutoff has been accomplished, nor may the closing of any fuel shutoff valve for an engine make fuel unavailable to the remaining engines.

(d) The operation of any shutoff may not interfere with the later emergency operation of any other equipment, such as the means for declutching the engine from the rotor drive.

(e) Each shutoff valve and its control must be designed, located, and protected to function properly under any condition likely to result from fire in a designated fire zone.

(f) Except for ground-use-only auxiliary power unit installations, there must be means to prevent inadvertent operation of each shutoff and to make it possible to reopen it in flight after it has been closed.

[Doc. No. 5084, 29 FR 16150, Dec. 3, 1964, as amended by Amdt. 29–12, 41 FR 55473, Dec. 20, 1976; Amdt. 29–22, 49 FR 6850, Feb. 23, 1984; Amdt. 29–26, 53 FR 34219, Sept. 2, 1988]

§29.1191 Firewalls.

(a) Each engine, including the combustor, turbine, and tailpipe sections of turbine engine installations, must be isolated by a firewall, shroud, or equivalent means, from personnel compartments, structures, controls, rotor mechanisms, and other parts that are—

(1) Essential to controlled flight and landing; and

(2) Not protected under §29.861.

(b) Each auxiliary power unit, combustion heater, and other combustion equipment to be used in flight, must be isolated from the rest of the rotorcraft by firewalls, shrouds, or equivalent means.

(c) Each firewall or shroud must be constructed so that no hazardous quantity of air, fluid, or flame can pass from any engine compartment to other parts of the rotorcraft.

(d) Each opening in the firewall or shroud must be sealed with close-fitting fireproof grommets, bushings, or firewall fittings.

(e) Each firewall and shroud must be fireproof and protected against corrosion.

(f) In meeting this section, account must be taken of the probable path of a fire as affected by the airflow in normal flight and in autorotation.

[Doc. No. 5084, 29 FR 16150, Dec. 3, 1964, as amended by Amdt. 29–3, 33 FR 970, Jan. 26, 1968]

§ 29.1193 Cowling and engine compartment covering.

(a) Each cowling and engine compartment covering must be constructed and supported so that it can resist the vibration, inertia, and air loads to which it may be subjected in operation.

(b) Cowling must meet the drainage and ventilation requirements of § 29.1187.

(c) On rotorcraft with a diaphragm isolating the engine power section from the engine accessory section, each part of the accessory section cowling subject to flame in case of fire in the engine power section of the powerplant must—

(1) Be fireproof; and

(2) Meet the requirements of § 29.1191.

(d) Each part of the cowling or engine compartment covering subject to high temperatures due to its nearness to exhaust system parts or exhaust gas impingement must be fireproof.

(e) Each rotorcraft must—

(1) Be designated and constructed so that no fire originating in any fire zone can enter, either through openings or by burning through external skin, any other zone or region where it would create additional hazards;

(2) Meet the requirements of paragraph (e)(1) of this section with the landing gear retracted (if applicable); and

(3) Have fireproof skin in areas subject to flame if a fire starts in or burns out of any designated fire zone.

(f) A means of retention for each openable or readily removable panel, cowling, or engine or rotor drive system covering must be provided to preclude hazardous damage to rotors or critical control components in the event of—

(1) Structural or mechanical failure of the normal retention means, unless such failure is extremely improbable; or

(2) Fire in a fire zone, if such fire could adversely affect the normal means of retention.

(Secs. 313(a), 601, and 603, 72 Stat. 759, 775, 49 U.S.C. 1354(a), 1421, and 1423; sec. 6(c), 49 U.S.C. 1655(c))

[Doc. No. 5084, 29 FR 16150, Dec. 3, 1964, as amended by Amdt. 29–3, 33 FR 970, Jan. 26, 1968; Amdt. 29–13, 42 FR 15046, Mar. 17, 1977; Amdt. 29–26, 53 FR 34219, Sept. 2, 1988]

§ 29.1194 Other surfaces.

All surfaces aft of, and near, engine compartments and designated fire zones, other than tail surfaces not subject to heat, flames, or sparks emanating from a designated fire zone or engine compartment, must be at least fire resistant.

[Amdt. 29–3, 33 FR 970, Jan. 26, 1968]

§ 29.1195 Fire extinguishing systems.

(a) Each turbine engine powered rotorcraft and Category A reciprocating engine powered rotorcraft, and each Category B reciprocating engine powered rotorcraft with engines of more than 1,500 cubic inches must have a fire extinguishing system for the designated fire zones. The fire extinguishing system for a powerplant must be able to simultaneously protect all zones of the powerplant compartment for which protection is provided.

(b) For multiengine powered rotorcraft, the fire extinguishing system, the quantity of extinguishing agent, and the rate of discharge must—

(1) For each auxiliary power unit and combustion equipment, provide at least one adequate discharge; and

(2) For each other designated fire zone, provide two adequate discharges.

(c) For single engine rotorcraft, the quantity of extinguishing agent and the rate of discharge must provide at least one adequate discharge for the engine compartment.

(d) It must be shown by either actual or simulated flight tests that under critical airflow conditions in flight the discharge of the extinguishing agent in each designated fire zone will provide an agent concentration capable of extinguishing fires in that zone and of minimizing the probability of reignition.

(Secs. 313(a), 601, 603, 604, Federal Aviation Act of 1958 (49 U.S.C. 1354(a), 1421, 1423, 1424), sec. 6(c), Dept. of Transportation Act (49 U.S.C. 1655(c)))

[Doc. No. 5084, 29 FR 16150, Dec. 3, 1964, as amended by Amdt. 29–3, 33 FR 970, Jan. 26, 1968; Amdt. 29–13, 42 FR 15047, Mar. 17, 1977; Amdt. 29–17, 43 FR 50602, Oct. 30, 1978]

§ 29.1197 Fire extinguishing agents.

(a) Fire extinguishing agents must—
(1) Be capable of extinguishing flames emanating from any burning of fluids or other combustible materials in the area protected by the fire extinguishing system; and
(2) Have thermal stability over the temperature range likely to be experienced in the compartment in which they are stored.
(b) If any toxic extinguishing agent is used, it must be shown by test that entry of harmful concentrations of fluid or fluid vapors into any personnel compartment (due to leakage during normal operation of the rotorcraft, or discharge on the ground or in flight) is prevented, even though a defect may exist in the extinguishing system.

(Secs. 313(a), 601, and 603, 72 Stat. 759, 775, 49 U.S.C. 1354(a), 1421, and 1423; sec. 6(c), 49 U.S.C. 1655(c))

[Doc. No. 5084, 29 FR 16150, Dec. 3, 1964, as amended by Amdt. 29–12, 41 FR 55473, Dec. 20, 1976; Amdt. 29–13, 42 FR 15047, Mar. 17, 1977]

§ 29.1199 Extinguishing agent containers.

(a) Each extinguishing agent container must have a pressure relief to prevent bursting of the container by excessive internal pressures.
(b) The discharge end of each discharge line from a pressure relief connection must be located so that discharge of the fire extinguishing agent would not damage the rotorcraft. The line must also be located or protected to prevent clogging caused by ice or other foreign matter.
(c) There must be a means for each fire extinguishing agent container to indicate that the container has discharged or that the charging pressure is below the established minimum necessary for proper functioning.

(d) The temperature of each container must be maintained, under intended operating conditions, to prevent the pressure in the container from—
(1) Falling below that necessary to provide an adequate rate of discharge; or
(2) Rising high enough to cause premature discharge.

(Secs. 313(a), 601, and 603, 72 Stat. 759, 775, 49 U.S.C. 1354(a), 1421, and 1423; sec. 6(c), 49 U.S.C. 1655 (c))

[Doc. No. 5084, 29 FR 16150, Dec. 3, 1964, as amended by Amdt. 29–13, 42 FR 15047, Mar. 17, 1977]

§ 29.1201 Fire extinguishing system materials.

(a) No materials in any fire extinguishing system may react chemically with any extinguishing agent so as to create a hazard.
(b) Each system component in an engine compartment must be fireproof.

§ 29.1203 Fire detector systems.

(a) For each turbine engine powered rotorcraft and Category A reciprocating engine powered rotorcraft, and for each Category B reciprocating engine powered rotorcraft with engines of more than 900 cubic inches displacement, there must be approved, quick-acting fire detectors in designated fire zones and in the combustor, turbine, and tailpipe sections of turbine installations (whether or not such sections are designated fire zones) in numbers and locations ensuring prompt detection of fire in those zones.
(b) Each fire detector must be constructed and installed to withstand any vibration, inertia, and other loads to which it would be subjected in operation.
(c) No fire detector may be affected by any oil, water, other fluids, or fumes that might be present.
(d) There must be means to allow crewmembers to check, in flight, the functioning of each fire detector system electrical circuit.
(e) The writing and other components of each fire detector system in an engine compartment must be at least fire resistant.
(f) No fire detector system component for any fire zone may pass through another fire zone, unless—

(1) It is protected against the possibility of false warnings resulting from fires in zones through which it passes; or

(2) The zones involved are simultaneously protected by the same detector and extinguishing systems.

[Doc. No. 5084, 29 FR 16150, Dec. 3, 1964, as amended by Amdt. 29–3, 33 FR 970, Jan. 26, 1968]

Subpart F—Equipment

General

§ 29.1301 Function and installation.

Each item of installed equipment must—

(a) Be of a kind and design appropriate to its intended function;

(b) Be labeled as to its identification, function, or operating limitations, or any applicable combination of these factors;

(c) Be installed according to limitations specified for that equipment; and

(d) Function properly when installed.

§ 29.1303 Flight and navigation instruments.

The following are required flight and navigational instruments:

(a) An airspeed indicator. For Category A rotorcraft with V_{NE} less than a speed at which unmistakable pilot cues provide overspeed warning, a maximum allowable airspeed indicator must be provided. If maximum allowable airspeed varies with weight, altitude, temperature, or r.p.m., the indicator must show that variation.

(b) A sensitive altimeter.

(c) A magnetic direction indicator.

(d) A clock displaying hours, minutes, and seconds with a sweep-second pointer or digital presentation.

(e) A free-air temperature indicator.

(f) A non-tumbling gyroscopic bank and pitch indicator.

(g) A gyroscopic rate-of-turn indicator combined with an integral slip-skid indicator (turn-and-bank indicator) except that only a slip-skid indicator is required on rotorcraft with a third altitude instrument system that—

(1) Is useable through flight altitudes of ± 80 degrees of pitch and ± 120 degrees of roll;

(2) Is powered from a source independent of the electrical generating system;

(3) Continues reliable operation for a minimum of 30 minutes after total failure of the electrical generating system;

(4) Operates independently of any other altitude indicating system;

(5) Is operative without selection after total failure of the electrical generating system;

(6) Is located on the instrument panel in a position acceptable to the Administrator that will make it plainly visible to and useable by any pilot at his station; and

(7) Is appropriately lighted during all phases of operation.

(h) A gyroscopic direction indicator.

(i) A rate-of-climb (vertical speed) indicator.

(j) For Category A rotorcraft, a speed warning device when V_{NE} is less than the speed at which unmistakable overspeed warning is provided by other pilot cues. The speed warning device must give effective aural warning (differing distinctively from aural warnings used for other purposes) to the pilots whenever the indicated speed exceeds V_{NE} plus 3 knots and must operate satisfactorily throughout the approved range of altitudes and temperatures.

(Secs. 313(a), 601, 603, 604, and 605 of the Federal Aviation Act of 1958 (49 U.S.C. 1354(a), 1421, 1423, 1424, and 1425); and sec. 6(c), Dept. of Transportation Act (49 U.S.C. 1655(c)))

[Doc. No. 5084, 29 FR 16150, Dec. 3, 1964, as amended by Amdt. 29–12, 41 FR 55474, Dec. 20, 1976; Amdt. 29–14, 42 FR 36972, July 18, 1977; Amdt. 29–24, 49 FR 44438, Nov. 6, 1984]

§ 29.1305 Powerplant instruments.

The following are required powerplant instruments:

(a) For each rotorcraft—

(1) A carburetor air temperature indicator for each reciprocating engine;

(2) A cylinder head temperature indicator for each air-cooled reciprocating engine, and a coolant temperature indicator for each liquid-cooled reciprocating engine;

(3) A fuel quantity indicator for each fuel tank;

(4) A low fuel warning device for each fuel tank which feeds an engine. This device must—

(i) Provide a warning to the crew when approximately 10 minutes of usable fuel remains in the tank; and

(ii) Be independent of the normal fuel quantity indicating system.

(5) A manifold pressure indicator, for each reciprocating engine of the altitude type;

(6) An oil pressure indicator for each pressure-lubricated gearbox.

(7) An oil pressure warning device for each pressure-lubricated gearbox to indicate when the oil pressure falls below a safe value;

(8) An oil quantity indicator for each oil tank and each rotor drive gearbox, if lubricant is self-contained;

(9) An oil temperature indicator for each engine;

(10) An oil temperature warning device to indicate unsafe oil temperatures in each main rotor drive gearbox, including gearboxes necessary for rotor phasing;

(11) A gas temperature indicator for each turbine engine;

(12) A gas producer rotor tachometer for each turbine engine;

(13) A tachometer for each engine that, if combined with the applicable instrument required by paragraph (a)(14) of this section, indicates rotor r.p.m. during autorotation.

(14) At least one tachometer to indicate, as applicable—

(i) The r.p.m. of the single main rotor;

(ii) The common r.p.m. of any main rotors whose speeds cannot vary appreciably with respect to each other; and

(iii) The r.p.m. of each main rotor whose speed can vary appreciably with respect to that of another main rotor;

(15) A free power turbine tachometer for each turbine engine;

(16) A means, for each turbine engine, to indicate power for that engine;

(17) For each turbine engine, an indicator to indicate the functioning of the powerplant ice protection system;

(18) An indicator for the filter required by §29.997 to indicate the occurrence of contamination of the filter to the degree established in compliance with §29.955;

(19) For each turbine engine, a warning means for the oil strainer or filter required by §29.1019, if it has no bypass, to warn the pilot of the occurrence of contamination of the strainer or filter before it reaches the capacity established in accordance with §29.1019(a)(2);

(20) An indicator to indicate the functioning of any selectable or controllable heater used to prevent ice clogging of fuel system components;

(21) An individual fuel pressure indicator for each engine, unless the fuel system which supplies that engine does not employ any pumps, filters, or other components subject to degradation or failure which may adversely affect fuel pressure at the engine;

(22) A means to indicate to the flightcrew the failure of any fuel pump installed to show compliance with §29.955;

(23) Warning or caution devices to signal to the flightcrew when ferromagnetic particles are detected by the chip detector required by §29.1337(e); and

(24) For auxiliary power units, an individual indicator, warning or caution device, or other means to advise the flightcrew that limits are being exceeded, if exceeding these limits can be hazardous, for—

(i) Gas temperature;

(ii) Oil pressure; and

(iii) Rotor speed.

(25) For rotorcraft for which a 30-second/2-minute OEI power rating is requested, a means must be provided to alert the pilot when the engine is at the 30-second and 2-minute OEI power levels, when the event begins, and when the time interval expires.

(26) For each turbine engine utilizing 30-second/2-minute OEI power, a device or system must be provided for use by ground personnel which—

(i) Automatically records each usage and duration of power at the 30-second and 2-minute OEI levels;

(ii) Permits retrieval of the recorded data;

(iii) Can be reset only by ground maintenance personnel; and

(iv) Has a means to verify proper operation of the system or device.

(b) For category A rotorcraft—

(1) An individual oil pressure indicator for each engine, and either an independent warning device for each engine or a master warning device for the engines with means for isolating

the individual warning circuit from the master warning device;

(2) An independent fuel pressure warning device for each engine or a master warning device for all engines with provision for isolating the individual warning device from the master warning device; and

(3) Fire warning indicators.

(c) For category B rotorcraft—

(1) An individual oil pressure indicator for each engine; and

(2) Fire warning indicators, when fire detection is required.

[Doc. No. 5084, 29 FR 16150, Dec. 3, 1964, as amended by Amdt. 29–3, 33 FR 970, Jan. 26, 1968; Amdt. 29–10, 39 FR 35463, Oct. 1, 1974; Amdt. 29–26, 53 FR 34219, Sept. 2, 1988; Amdt. 29–34, 59 FR 47768, Sept. 16, 1994; Amdt. 29–40, 61 FR 21908, May 10, 1996; 61 FR 43952, Aug. 27, 1996]

§ 29.1307 Miscellaneous equipment.

The following is required miscellaneous equipment:

(a) An approved seat for each occupant.

(b) A master switch arrangement for electrical circuits other than ignition.

(c) Hand fire extinguishers.

(d) A windshield wiper or equivalent device for each pilot station.

(e) A two-way radio communication system.

[Amdt. 29–12, 41 FR 55473, Dec. 20, 1976]

§ 29.1309 Equipment, systems, and installations.

(a) The equipment, systems, and installations whose functioning is required by this subchapter must be designed and installed to ensure that they perform their intended functions under any foreseeable operating condition.

(b) The rotorcraft systems and associated components, considered separately and in relation to other systems, must be designed so that—

(1) For Category B rotorcraft, the equipment, systems, and installations must be designed to prevent hazards to the rotorcraft if they malfunction or fail; or

(2) For Category A rotorcraft—

(i) The occurrence of any failure condition which would prevent the continued safe flight and landing of the rotorcraft is extremely improbable; and

(ii) The occurrence of any other failure conditions which would reduce the capability of the rotorcraft or the ability of the crew to cope with adverse operating conditions is improbable.

(c) Warning information must be provided to alert the crew to unsafe system operating conditions and to enable them to take appropriate corrective action. Systems, controls, and associated monitoring and warning means must be designed to minimize crew errors which could create additional hazards.

(d) Compliance with the requirements of paragraph (b)(2) of this section must be shown by analysis and, where necessary, by appropriate ground, flight, or simulator tests. The analysis must consider—

(1) Possible modes of failure, including malfunctions and damage from external sources;

(2) The probability of multiple failures and undetected failures;

(3) The resulting effects on the rotorcraft and occupants, considering the stage of flight and operating conditions; and

(4) The crew warning cues, corrective action required, and the capability of detecting faults.

(e) For Category A rotorcraft, each installation whose functioning is required by this subchapter and which requires a power supply is an "essential load" on the power supply. The power sources and the system must be able to supply the following power loads in probable operating combinations and for probable durations:

(1) Loads connected to the system with the system functioning normally.

(2) Essential loads, after failure of any one prime mover, power converter, or energy storage device.

(3) Essential loads, after failure of—

(i) Any one engine, on rotorcraft with two engines; and

(ii) Any two engines, on rotorcraft with three or more engines.

(f) In determining compliance with paragraphs (e)(2) and (3) of this section, the power loads may be assumed to be reduced under a monitoring procedure consistent with safety in the kinds of operations authorized. Loads not required for controlled flight need not be considered for the two-engine-inoperative condition on rotorcraft with three or more engines.

(g) In showing compliance with paragraphs (a) and (b) of this section with regard to the electrical system and to equipment design and installation, critical environmental conditions must be considered. For electrical generation, distribution, and utilization equipment required by or used in complying with this subchapter, except equipment covered by Technical Standard Orders containing environmental test procedures, the ability to provide continuous, safe service under foreseeable environmental conditions may be shown by environmental tests, design analysis, or reference to previous comparable service experience on other aircraft.

(h) In showing compliance with paragraphs (a) and (b) of this section, the effects of lightning strikes on the rotorcraft must be considered.

(Secs. 313(a), 601, 603, 604, and 605 of the Federal Aviation Act of 1958 (49 U.S.C. 1354(a), 1421, 1423, 1424, and 1425); and sec. 6(c), Dept. of Transportation Act (49 U.S.C. 1655(c)))

[Doc. No. 5084, 29 FR 16150, Dec. 3, 1964, as amended by Amdt. 29–14, 42 FR 36972, July 18, 1977; Amdt. 29–24, 49 FR 44438, Nov. 6, 1984; Amdt. 29–40, 61 FR 21908, May 10, 1996]

INSTRUMENTS: INSTALLATION

§29.1321 Arrangement and visibility.

(a) Each flight, navigation, and powerplant instrument for use by any pilot must be easily visible to him from his station with the minimum practicable deviation from his normal position and line of vision when he is looking forward along the flight path.

(b) Each instrument necessary for safe operation, including the airspeed indicator, gyroscopic direction indicator, gyroscopic bank-and-pitch indicator, slip-skid indicator, altimeter, rate-of-climb indicator, rotor tachometers, and the indicator most representative of engine power, must be grouped and centered as nearly as practicable about the vertical plane of the pilot's forward vision. In addition, for rotorcraft approved for IFR flight—

(1) The instrument that most effectively indicates attitude must be on the panel in the top center position;

(2) The instrument that most effectively indicates direction of flight must be adjacent to and directly below the attitude instrument;

(3) The instrument that most effectively indicates airspeed must be adjacent to and to the left of the attitude instrument; and

(4) The instrument that most effectively indicates altitude or is most frequently utilized in control of altitude must be adjacent to and to the right of the attitude instrument.

(c) Other required powerplant instruments must be closely grouped on the instrument panel.

(d) Identical powerplant instruments for the engines must be located so as to prevent any confusion as to which engine each instrument relates.

(e) Each powerplant instrument vital to safe operation must be plainly visible to appropriate crewmembers.

(f) Instrument panel vibration may not damage, or impair the readability or accuracy of, any instrument.

(g) If a visual indicator is provided to indicate malfunction of an instrument, it must be effective under all probable cockpit lighting conditions.

(Secs. 313(a), 601, 603, 604, and 605 of the Federal Aviation Act of 1958 (49 U.S.C. 1354(a), 1421, 1423, 1424, and 1425); and sec. 6(c), Dept. of Transportation Act (49 U.S.C. 1655(c)))

[Doc. No. 5084, 29 FR 16150, Dec. 3, 1964, as amended by Amdt. 29–14, 42 FR 36972, July 18, 1977; Amdt. 29–21, 48 FR 4391, Jan. 31, 1983]

§29.1322 Warning, caution, and advisory lights.

If warning, caution or advisory lights are installed in the cockpit they must, unless otherwise approved by the Administrator, be—

(a) Red, for warning lights (lights indicating a hazard which may require immediate corrective action);

(b) Amber, for caution lights (lights indicating the possible need for future corrective action);

(c) Green, for safe operation lights; and

(d) Any other color, including white, for lights not described in paragraphs (a) through (c) of this section, provided the color differs sufficiently from the colors prescribed in paragraphs (a) through (c) of this section to avoid possible confusion.

[Amdt. 29–12, 41 FR 55474, Dec. 20, 1976]

§ 29.1323 Airspeed indicating system.

For each airspeed indicating system, the following apply:

(a) Each airspeed indicating instrument must be calibrated to indicate true airspeed (at sea level with a standard atmosphere) with a minimum practicable instrument calibration error when the corresponding pitot and static pressures are applied.

(b) Each system must be calibrated to determine system error excluding airspeed instrument error. This calibration must be determined—

(1) In level flight at speeds of 20 knots and greater, and over an appropriate range of speeds for flight conditions of climb and autorotation; and

(2) During takeoff, with repeatable and readable indications that ensure—

(i) Consistent realization of the field lengths specified in the Rotorcraft Flight Manual; and

(ii) Avoidance of the critical areas of the height-velocity envelope as established under § 29.87.

(c) For Category A rotorcraft—

(1) The indication must allow consistent definition of the takeoff decision point; and

(2) The system error, excluding the airspeed instrument calibration error, may not exceed—

(i) Three percent or 5 knots, whichever is greater, in level flight at speeds above 80 percent of takeoff safety speed; and

(ii) Ten knots in climb at speeds from 10 knots below takeoff safety speed to 10 knots above V_Y.

(d) For Category B rotorcraft, the system error, excluding the airspeed instrument calibration error, may not exceed 3 percent or 5 knots, whichever is greater, in level flight at speeds above 80 percent of the climbout speed attained at 50 feet when complying with § 29.63.

(e) Each system must be arranged, so far as practicable, to prevent malfunction or serious error due to the entry of moisture, dirt, or other substances.

(f) Each system must have a heated pitot tube or an equivalent means of preventing malfunction due to icing.

[Doc. No. 5084, 29 FR 16150, Dec. 3, 1964 as amended by Amdt. 29–3, 33 FR 970, Jan. 26, 1968; Amdt. 29–24, 49 FR 44439, Nov. 6, 1984; Amdt. 29–39, 61 FR 21901, May 10, 1996; Amdt. 29–44, 64 FR 45338, Aug. 19, 1999]

§ 29.1325 Static pressure and pressure altimeter systems.

(a) Each instrument with static air case connections must be vented to the outside atmosphere through an appropriate piping system.

(b) Each vent must be located where its orifices are least affected by airflow variation, moisture, or foreign matter.

(c) Each static pressure port must be designed and located in such manner that the correlation between air pressure in the static pressure system and true ambient atmospheric static pressure is not altered when the rotorcraft encounters icing conditions. An anti-icing means or an alternate source of static pressure may be used in showing compliance with this requirement. If the reading of the altimeter, when on the alternate static pressure system, differs from the reading of altimeter when on the primary static system by more than 50 feet, a correction card must be provided for the alternate static system.

(d) Except for the vent into the atmosphere, each system must be airtight.

(e) Each pressure altimeter must be approved and calibrated to indicate pressure altitude in a standard atmosphere with a minimum practicable calibration error when the corresponding static pressures are applied.

(f) Each system must be designed and installed so that an error in indicated pressure altitude, at sea level, with a standard atmosphere, excluding instrument calibration error, does not result in an error of more than ±30 feet per 100 knots speed. However, the error need not be less than ±30 feet.

(g) Except as provided in paragraph (h) of this section, if the static pressure system incorporates both a primary and an alternate static pressure source, the means for selecting one or the other source must be designed so that—

(1) When either source is selected, the other is blocked off; and

(2) Both sources cannot be blocked off simultaneously.

(h) For unpressurized rotorcraft, paragraph (g)(1) of this section does not apply if it can be demonstrated that the static pressure system calibration, when either static pressure source is selected, is not changed by the other static pressure source being open or blocked.

(Secs. 313(a), 601, 603, 604, and 605 of the Federal Aviation Act of 1958 (49 U.S.C. 1354(a), 1421, 1423, 1424, and 1425); and sec. 6(c), Dept. of Transportation Act (49 U.S.C. 1655(c)))

[Doc. No. 5084, 29 FR 16150, Dec. 3, 1964, as amended by Amdt. 29–14, 42 FR 36972, July 18, 1977; Amdt. 29–24, 49 FR 44439, Nov. 6, 1984]

§29.1327 Magnetic direction indicator.

(a) Each magnetic direction indicator must be installed so that its accuracy is not excessively affected by the rotorcraft's vibration or magnetic fields.

(b) The compensated installation may not have a deviation, in level flight, greater than 10 degrees on any heading.

§29.1329 Automatic pilot system.

(a) Each automatic pilot system must be designed so that the automatic pilot can—

(1) Be sufficiently overpowered by one pilot to allow control of the rotorcraft; and

(2) Be readily and positively disengaged by each pilot to prevent it from interfering with the control of the rotorcraft.

(b) Unless there is automatic synchronization, each system must have a means to readily indicate to the pilot the alignment of the actuating device in relation to the control system it operates.

(c) Each manually operated control for the system's operation must be readily accessible to the pilots.

(d) The system must be designed and adjusted so that, within the range of adjustment available to the pilot, it cannot produce hazardous loads on the rotorcraft, or create hazardous deviations in the flight path, under any flight condition appropriate to its use, either during normal operation or in the event of a malfunction, assuming that corrective action begins within a reasonable period of time.

(e) If the automatic pilot integrates signals from auxiliary controls or furnishes signals for operation of other equipment, there must be positive interlocks and sequencing of engagement to prevent improper operation.

(f) If the automatic pilot system can be coupled to airborne navigation equipment, means must be provided to indicate to the pilots the current mode of operation. Selector switch position is not acceptable as a means of indication.

[Doc. No. 5084, 29 FR 16150, Dec. 3, 1964, as amended by Amdt. 29–24, 49 FR 44439, Nov. 6, 1984; Amdt. 29–24, 49 FR 47594, Dec. 6, 1984; Amdt. 29–42, 63 FR 43285, Aug. 12, 1998]

§29.1331 Instruments using a power supply.

For category A rotorcraft—

(a) Each required flight instrument using a power supply must have—

(1) Two independent sources of power;

(2) A means of selecting either power source; and

(3) A visual means integral with each instrument to indicate when the power adequate to sustain proper instrument performance is not being supplied. The power must be measured at or near the point where it enters the instrument. For electrical instruments, the power is considered to be adequate when the voltage is within the approved limits; and

(b) The installation and power supply system must be such that failure of any flight instrument connected to one source, or of the energy supply from one source, or a fault in any part of the power distribution system does not interfere with the proper supply of energy from any other source.

[Doc. No. 5084, 29 FR 16150, Dec. 3, 1964, as amended by Amdt. 29–24, 49 FR 44439, Nov. 6, 1984]

§29.1333 Instrument systems.

For systems that operate the required flight instruments which are located at each pilot's station, the following apply:

(a) Only the required flight instruments for the first pilot may be connected to that operating system.

(b) The equipment, systems, and installations must be designed so that one display of the information essential to the safety of flight which is provided by the flight instruments remains available to a pilot, without additional crewmember action, after any single failure or combination of failures that are not shown to be extremely improbable.

(c) Additional instruments, systems, or equipment may not be connected to the operating system for a second pilot unless provisions are made to ensure the continued normal functioning of the required flight instruments in the event of any malfunction of the additional instruments, systems, or equipment which is not shown to be extremely improbable.

[Amdt. 29–24, 49 FR 44439, Nov. 6, 1984]

§ 29.1335 Flight director systems.

If a flight director system is installed, means must be provided to indicate to the flight crew its current mode of operation. Selector switch position is not acceptable as a means of indication.

(Secs. 313(a), 601, 603, 604, and 605 of the Federal Aviation Act of 1958 (49 U.S.C. 1354(a), 1421, 1423, 1424, and 1425); and sec. 6(c), Dept. of Transportation Act (49 U.S.C. 1655(c)))

[Amdt. 29–14, 42 FR 36973, July 18, 1977]

§ 29.1337 Powerplant instruments.

(a) *Instruments and instrument lines.* (1) Each powerplant and auxiliary power unit instrument line must meet the requirements of §§ 29.993 and 29.1183.

(2) Each line carrying flammable fluids under pressure must—

(i) Have restricting orifices or other safety devices at the source of pressure to prevent the escape of excessive fluid if the line fails; and

(ii) Be installed and located so that the escape of fluids would not create a hazard.

(3) Each powerplant and auxiliary power unit instrument that utilizes flammable fluids must be installed and located so that the escape of fluid would not create a hazard.

(b) *Fuel quantity indicator.* There must be means to indicate to the flight crew members the quantity, in gallons or equivalent units, of usable fuel in each tank during flight. In addition—

(1) Each fuel quantity indicator must be calibrated to read "zero" during level flight when the quantity of fuel remaining in the tank is equal to the unusable fuel supply determined under § 29.959;

(2) When two or more tanks are closely interconnected by a gravity feed system and vented, and when it is impossible to feed from each tank separately, at least one fuel quantity indicator must be installed;

(3) Tanks with interconnected outlets and airspaces may be treated as one tank and need not have separate indicators; and

(4) Each exposed sight gauge used as a fuel quantity indicator must be protected against damage.

(c) *Fuel flowmeter system.* If a fuel flowmeter system is installed, each metering component must have a means for bypassing the fuel supply if malfunction of that component severely restricts fuel flow.

(d) *Oil quantity indicator.* There must be a stick gauge or equivalent means to indicate the quantity of oil—

(1) In each tank; and

(2) In each transmission gearbox.

(e) Rotor drive system transmissions and gearboxes utilizing ferromagnetic materials must be equipped with chip detectors designed to indicate the presence of ferromagnetic particles resulting from damage or excessive wear within the transmission or gearbox. Each chip detector must—

(1) Be designed to provide a signal to the indicator required by § 29.1305(a)(22); and

(2) Be provided with a means to allow crewmembers to check, in flight, the function of each detector electrical circuit and signal.

(Secs. 313(a), 601, and 603, 72 Stat. 759, 775, 49 U.S.C. 1354(a), 1421, and 1423; sec. 6(c), 49 U.S.C. 1655(c))

[Doc. No. 5084, 29 FR 16150, Dec. 3, 1964, as amended by Amdt. 29–13, 42 FR 15047, Mar. 17, 1977; Amdt. 29–26, 53 FR 34219, Sept. 2, 1988]

ELECTRICAL SYSTEMS AND EQUIPMENT

§ 29.1351 General.

(a) *Electrical system capacity.* The required generating capacity and the number and kind of power sources must—

(1) Be determined by an electrical load analysis; and

(2) Meet the requirements of §29.1309.

(b) *Generating system.* The generating system includes electrical power sources, main power busses, transmission cables, and associated control, regulation, and protective devices. It must be designed so that—

(1) Power sources function properly when independent and when connected in combination;

(2) No failure or malfunction of any power source can create a hazard or impair the ability of remaining sources to supply essential loads;

(3) The system voltage and frequency (as applicable) at the terminals of essential load equipment can be maintained within the limits for which the equipment is designed, during any probable operating condition;

(4) System transients due to switching, fault clearing, or other causes do not make essential loads inoperative, and do not cause a smoke or fire hazard;

(5) There are means accessible in flight to appropriate crewmembers for the individual and collective disconnection of the electrical power sources from the main bus; and

(6) There are means to indicate to appropriate crewmembers the generating system quantities essential for the safe operation of the system, such as the voltage and current supplied by each generator.

(c) *External power.* If provisions are made for connecting external power to the rotorcraft, and that external power can be electrically connected to equipment other than that used for engine starting, means must be provided to ensure that no external power supply having a reverse polarity, or a reverse phase sequence, can supply power to the rotorcraft's electrical system.

(d) Operation with the normal electrical power generating system inoperative.

(1) It must be shown by analysis, tests, or both, that the rotorcraft can be operated safely in VFR conditions for a period of not less than 5 minutes, with the normal electrical power generating system (electrical power sources excluding the battery) inoperative, with critical type fuel (from the standpoint of flameout and restart capability), and with the rotorcraft initially at the maximum certificated altitude. Parts of the electrical system may remain on if—

(i) A single malfunction, including a wire bundle or junction box fire, cannot result in loss of the part turned off and the part turned on;

(ii) The parts turned on are electrically and mechanically isolated from the parts turned off; and

(2) Additional requirements for Category A Rotorcraft.

(i) Unless it can be shown that the loss of the normal electrical power generating system is extremely improbable, an emergency electrical power system, independent of the normal electrical power generating system, must be provided, with sufficient capacity to power all systems necessary for continued safe flight and landing.

(ii) Failures, including junction box, control panel, or wire bundle fires, which would result in the loss of the normal and emergency systems, must be shown to be extremely improbable.

(iii) Systems necessary for immediate safety must continue to operate following the loss of the normal electrical power generating system, without the need for flight crew action.

(Secs. 313(a), 601, 603, 604, and 605 of the Federal Aviation Act of 1958 (49 U.S.C. 1354(a), 1421, 1423, 1424, and 1425); and sec. 6(c), Dept. of Transportation Act (49 U.S.C. 1655(c)))

[Doc. No. 5084, 29 FR 16150, Dec. 3, 1964, as amended by Amdt. 29–14, 42 FR 36973, July 18, 1977; Amdt. 29–40, 61 FR 21908, May 10, 1996; Amdt. 29–42, 63 FR 43285, Aug. 12, 1998]

§29.1353 Electrical equipment and installations.

(a) Electrical equipment, controls, and wiring must be installed so that operation of any one unit or system of units will not adversely affect the simultaneous operation of any other electrical unit or system essential to safe operation.

(b) Cables must be grouped, routed, and spaced so that damage to essential circuits will be minimized if there are faults in heavy current-carrying cables.

(c) Storage batteries must be designed and installed as follows:

(1) Safe cell temperatures and pressures must be maintained during any probable charging and discharging condition. No uncontrolled increase in cell temperature may result when the battery is recharged (after previous complete discharge)—

(i) At maximum regulated voltage or power;

(ii) During a flight of maximum duration; and

(iii) Under the most adverse cooling condition likely in service.

(2) Compliance with paragraph (a)(1) of this section must be shown by test unless experience with similar batteries and installations has shown that maintaining safe cell temperatures and pressures presents no problem.

(3) No explosive or toxic gases emitted by any battery in normal operation, or as the result of any probable malfunction in the charging system or battery installation, may accumulate in hazardous quantities within the rotorcraft.

(4) No corrosive fluids or gases that may escape from the battery may damage surrounding structures or adjacent essential equipment.

(5) Each nickel cadmium battery installation capable of being used to start an engine or auxiliary power unit must have provisions to prevent any hazardous effect on structure or essential systems that may be caused by the maximum amount of heat the battery can generate during a short circuit of the battery or of its individual cells.

(6) Nickel cadmium battery installations capable of being used to start an engine or auxiliary power unit must have—

(i) A system to control the charging rate of the battery automatically so as to prevent battery overheating;

(ii) A battery temperature sensing and over-temperature warning system with a means for disconnecting the battery from its charging source in the event of an over-temperature condition; or

(iii) A battery failure sensing and warning system with a means for disconnecting the battery from its charg-

ing source in the event of battery failure.

(Secs. 313(a), 601, 603, 604, and 605 of the Federal Aviation Act of 1958 (49 U.S.C. 1354(a), 1421, 1423, 1424, and 1425); and sec. 6(c), Dept. of Transportation Act (49 U.S.C. 1655(c)))

[Doc. No. 5084, 29 FR 16150, Dec. 3, 1964, as amended by Amdt. 29–14, 42 FR 36973, July 18, 1977; Amdt. 29–15, 43 FR 2327, Jan. 16, 1978]

§ 29.1355　Distribution system.

(a) The distribution system includes the distribution busses, their associated feeders, and each control and protective device.

(b) If two independent sources of electrical power for particular equipment or systems are required by this chapter, in the event of the failure of one power source for such equipment or system, another power source (including its separate feeder) must be provided automatically or be manually selectable to maintain equipment or system operation.

(Secs. 313(a), 601, 603, 604, and 605 of the Federal Aviation Act of 1958 (49 U.S.C. 1354(a), 1421, 1423, 1424, and 1425); and sec. 6(c), Dept. of Transportation Act (49 U.S.C. 1655(c)))

[Doc. No. 5084, 29 FR 16150, Dec. 3, 1964, as amended by Amdt. 29–14, 42 FR 36973, July 18, 1977; Amdt. 29–24, 49 FR 44439, Nov. 6, 1984]

§ 29.1357　Circuit protective devices.

(a) Automatic protective devices must be used to minimize distress to the electrical system and hazard to the rotorcraft system and hazard to the rotorcraft in the event of wiring faults or serious malfunction of the system or connected equipment.

(b) The protective and control devices in the generating system must be designed to de-energize and disconnect faulty power sources and power transmission equipment from their associated buses with sufficient rapidity to provide protection from hazardous overvoltage and other malfunctioning.

(c) Each resettable circuit protective device must be designed so that, when an overload or circuit fault exists, it will open the circuit regardless of the position of the operating control.

(d) If the ability to reset a circuit breaker or replace a fuse is essential to safety in flight, that circuit breaker or fuse must be located and identified so that it can be readily reset or replaced in flight.

(e) Each essential load must have individual circuit protection. However, individual protection for each circuit in an essential load system (such as each position light circuit in a system) is not required.

(f) If fuses are used, there must be spare fuses for use in flight equal to at least 50 percent of the number of fuses of each rating required for complete circuit protection.

(g) Automatic reset circuit breakers may be used as integral protectors for electrical equipment provided there is circuit protection for the cable supplying power to the equipment.

[Doc. No. 5084, 29 FR 16150, Dec. 3, 1964, as amended by Amdt. 29–24, 49 FR 44440, Nov. 6, 1984]

§29.1359 Electrical system fire and smoke protection.

(a) Components of the electrical system must meet the applicable fire and smoke protection provisions of §§29.831 and 29.863.

(b) Electrical cables, terminals, and equipment, in designated fire zones, and that are used in emergency procedures, must be at least fire resistant.

(c) Insulation on electrical wire and cable installed in the rotorcraft must be self-extinguishing when tested in accordance with Appendix F, Part I(a)(3), of part 25 of this chapter.

[Doc. No. 5084, 29 FR 16150, Dec. 3, 1964, as amended by Amdt. 29–42, 63 FR 43285, Aug. 12, 1998]

§29.1363 Electrical system tests.

(a) When laboratory tests of the electrical system are conducted—

(1) The tests must be performed on a mock-up using the same generating equipment used in the rotorcraft;

(2) The equipment must simulate the electrical characteristics of the distribution wiring and connected loads to the extent necessary for valid test results; and

(3) Laboratory generator drives must simulate the prime movers on the rotorcraft with respect to their reaction to generator loading, including loading due to faults.

(b) For each flight condition that cannot be simulated adequately in the laboratory or by ground tests on the rotorcraft, flight tests must be made.

LIGHTS

§29.1381 Instrument lights.

The instrument lights must—

(a) Make each instrument, switch, and other device for which they are provided easily readable; and

(b) Be installed so that—

(1) Their direct rays are shielded from the pilot's eyes; and

(2) No objectionable reflections are visible to the pilot.

§29.1383 Landing lights.

(a) Each required landing or hovering light must be approved.

(b) Each landing light must be installed so that—

(1) No objectionable glare is visible to the pilot;

(2) The pilot is not adversely affected by halation; and

(3) It provides enough light for night operation, including hovering and landing.

(c) At least one separate switch must be provided, as applicable—

(1) For each separately installed landing light; and

(2) For each group of landing lights installed at a common location.

§29.1385 Position light system installation.

(a) *General.* Each part of each position light system must meet the applicable requirements of this section and each system as a whole must meet the requirements of §§29.1387 through 29.1397.

(b) *Forward position lights.* Forward position lights must consist of a red and a green light spaced laterally as far apart as practicable and installed forward on the rotorcraft so that, with the rotorcraft in the normal flying position, the red light is on the left side, and the green light is on the right side. Each light must be approved.

(c) *Rear position light.* The rear position light must be a white light mounted as far aft as practicable, and must be approved.

(d) *Circuit.* The two forward position lights and the rear position light must make a single circuit.

(e) *Light covers and color filters.* Each light cover or color filter must be at least flame resistant and may not change color or shape or lose any appreciable light transmission during normal use.

§ 29.1387 Position light system dihedral angles.

(a) Except as provided in paragraph (e) of this section, each forward and rear position light must, as installed, show unbroken light within the dihedral angles described in this section.

(b) Dihedral angle L (left) is formed by two intersecting vertical planes, the first parallel to the longitudinal axis of the rotorcraft, and the other at 110 degrees to the left of the first, as viewed when looking forward along the longitudinal axis.

(c) Dihedral angle R (right) is formed by two intersecting vertical planes, the first parallel to the longitudinal axis of the rotorcraft, and the other at 110 degrees to the right of the first, as viewed when looking forward along the longitudinal axis.

(d) Dihedral angle A (aft) is formed by two intersecting vertical planes making angles of 70 degrees to the right and to the left, respectively, to a vertical plane passing through the longitudinal axis, as viewed when looking aft along the longitudinal axis.

(e) If the rear position light, when mounted as far aft as practicable in accordance with § 29.1385(c), cannot show unbroken light within dihedral angle A (as defined in paragraph (d) of this section), a solid angle or angles of obstructed visibility totaling not more than 0.04 steradians is allowable within that dihedral angle, if such solid angle is within a cone whose apex is at the rear position light and whose elements make an angle of 30° with a vertical line passing through the rear position light.

(49 U.S.C. 1655(c))

[Doc. No. 5084, 29 FR 16150, Dec. 3, 1964, as amended by Amdt. 29–9, 36 FR 21279, Nov. 5, 1971]

§ 29.1389 Position light distribution and intensities.

(a) *General.* The intensities prescribed in this section must be provided by new equipment with light covers and color

filters in place. Intensities must be determined with the light source operating at a steady value equal to the average luminous output of the source at the normal operating voltage of the rotorcraft. The light distribution and intensity of each position light must meet the requirements of paragraph (b) of this section.

(b) *Forward and rear position lights.* The light distribution and intensities of forward and rear position lights must be expressed in terms of minimum intensities in the horizontal plane, minimum intensities in any vertical plane, and maximum intensities in overlapping beams, within dihedral angles, L, R, and A, and must meet the following requirements:

(1) *Intensities in the horizontal plane.* Each intensity in the horizontal plane (the plane containing the longitudinal axis of the rotorcraft and perpendicular to the plane of symmetry of the rotorcraft), must equal or exceed the values in § 29.1391.

(2) *Intensities in any vertical plane.* Each intensity in any vertical plane (the plane perpendicular to the horizontal plane) must equal or exceed the appropriate value in § 29.1393 where I is the minimum intensity prescribed in § 29.1391 for the corresponding angles in the horizontal plane.

(3) *Intensities in overlaps between adjacent signals.* No intensity in any overlap between adjacent signals may exceed the values in § 29.1395, except that higher intensities in overlaps may be used with the use of main beam intensities substantially greater than the minima specified in §§ 29.1391 and 29.1393 if the overlap intensities in relation to the main beam intensities do not adversely affect signal clarity.

§ 29.1391 Minimum intensities in the horizontal plane of forward and rear position lights.

Each position light intensity must equal or exceed the applicable values in the following table:

Dihedral angle (light included)	Angle from right or left of longitudinal axis, measured from dead ahead	Intensity (candles)
L and R (forward red and green).	0° to 10°	40
	10° to 20°	30
	20° to 110°	5

Dihedral angle (light included)	Angle from right or left of longitudinal axis, measured from dead ahead	Intensity (candles)
A (rear white)	110° to 180°	20

§29.1393 Minimum intensities in any vertical plane of forward and rear position lights.

Each position light intensity must equal or exceed the applicable values in the following table:

Angle above or below the horizontal plane	Intensity, I
0°	1.00
0° to 5°	.90
5° to 10°	.80
10° to 15°	.70
15° to 20°	.50
20° to 30°	.30
30° to 40°	.10
40° to 90°	.05

§29.1395 Maximum intensities in overlapping beams of forward and rear position lights.

No position light intensity may exceed the applicable values in the following table, except as provided in §29.1389(b)(3).

Overlaps	Maximum intensity	
	Area A (candles)	Area B (candles)
Green in dihedral angle L	10	1
Red in dihedral angle R	10	1
Green in dihedral angle A	5	1
Red in dihedral angle A	5	1
Rear white in dihedral angle L	5	1
Rear white in dihedral angle R	5	1

Where—

(a) Area A includes all directions in the adjacent dihedral angle that pass through the light source and intersect the common boundary plane at more than 10 degrees but less than 20 degrees; and

(b) Area B includes all directions in the adjacent dihedral angle that pass through the light source and intersect the common boundary plane at more than 20 degrees.

§29.1397 Color specifications.

Each position light color must have the applicable International Commission on Illumination chromaticity coordinates as follows:

(a) *Aviation red*—

y is not greater than 0.335; and

z is not greater than 0.002.

(b) *Aviation green*—

x is not greater than $0.440 - 0.320y$;
x is not greater than $y - 0.170$; and
y is not less than $0.390 - 0.170x$.

(c) *Aviation white*—

x is not less than 0.300 and not greater than 0.540;

y is not less than $x - 0.040$ or $y_c - 0.010$, whichever is the smaller; and

y is not greater than $x + 0.020$ nor $0.636 - 0.400x$;

Where Y_e is the y coordinate of the Planckian radiator for the value of x considered.

[Doc. No. 5084, 29 FR 16150, Dec. 3, 1964, as amended by Amdt. 29-7, 36 FR 12972, July 10, 1971]

§29.1399 Riding light.

(a) Each riding light required for water operation must be installed so that it can—

(1) Show a white light for at least two miles at night under clear atmospheric conditions; and

(2) Show a maximum practicable unbroken light with the rotorcraft on the water.

(b) Externally hung lights may be used.

§29.1401 Anticollision light system.

(a) *General.* If certification for night operation is requested, the rotorcraft must have an anticollision light system that—

(1) Consists of one or more approved anticollision lights located so that their emitted light will not impair the crew's vision or detract from the conspicuity of the position lights; and

(2) Meets the requirements of paragraphs (b) through (f) of this section.

(b) *Field of coverage.* The system must consist of enough lights to illuminate the vital areas around the rotorcraft, considering the physical configuration and flight characteristics of the rotorcraft. The field of coverage must extend in each direction within at least 30 degrees above and 30 degrees below the horizontal plane of the rotorcraft, except that there may be solid angles of obstructed visibility totaling not more than 0.5 steradians.

(c) *Flashing characteristics.* The arrangement of the system, that is, the number of light sources, beam width, speed of rotation, and other characteristics, must give an effective flash frequency of not less than 40, nor more than 100, cycles per minute. The effective flash frequency is the frequency at which the rotorcraft's complete anticollision light system is observed from a distance, and applies to each sector of light including any overlaps that exist when the system consists of more than one light source. In overlaps, flash frequencies may exceed 100, but not 180, cycles per minute.

(d) *Color.* Each anticollision light must be aviation red and must meet the applicable requirements of § 29.1397.

(e) *Light intensity.* The minimum light intensities in any vertical plane, measured with the red filter (if used) and expressed in terms of "effective" intensities must meet the requirements of paragraph (f) of this section. The following relation must be assumed:

$$I_e = \frac{\int_{t_1}^{t_2} I(t)dt}{0.2 + (t_2 - t_1)}$$

where:

I_e=effective intensity (candles).
$I(t)$=instantaneous intensity as a function of time.
$t_2 - t_1$=flash time interval (seconds).

Normally, the maximum value of effective intensity is obtained when t_2 and t_1 are chosen so that the effective intensity is equal to the instantaneous intensity at t_2 and t_1.

(f) *Minimum effective intensities for anticollision light.* Each anticollision light effective intensity must equal or exceed the applicable values in the following table:

Angle above or below the horizontal plane	Effective intensity (candles)
0° to 5°	150
5° to 10°	90
10° to 20°	30
20° to 30°	15

[Doc. No. 5084, 29 FR 16150, Dec. 3, 1964, as amended by Amdt. 29–7, 36 FR 12972, July 10, 1971; Amdt. 29–11, 41 FR 5290, Feb. 5, 1976]

SAFETY EQUIPMENT

§ 29.1411 General.

(a) *Accessibility.* Required safety equipment to be used by the crew in an emergency, such as automatic liferaft releases, must be readily accessible.

(b) *Stowage provisions.* Stowage provisions for required emergency equipment must be furnished and must—

(1) Be arranged so that the equipment is directly accessible and its location is obvious; and

(2) Protect the safety equipment from inadvertent damage.

(c) *Emergency exit descent device.* The stowage provisions for the emergency exit descent device required by § 29.809(f) must be at the exits for which they are intended.

(d) *Liferafts.* Liferafts must be stowed near exits through which the rafts can be launched during an unplanned ditching. Rafts automatically or remotely released outside the rotorcraft must be attached to the rotorcraft by the static line prescribed in § 29.1415.

(e) *Long-range signaling device.* The stowage provisions for the long-range signaling device required by § 29.1415 must be near an exit available during an unplanned ditching.

(f) *Life preservers.* Each life preserver must be within easy reach of each occupant while seated.

§ 29.1413 Safety belts: passenger warning device.

(a) If there are means to indicate to the passengers when safety belts should be fastened, they must be installed to be operated from either pilot seat.

(b) Each safety belt must be equipped with a metal to metal latching device.

(Secs. 313, 314, and 601 through 610 of the Federal Aviation Act of 1958 (49 U.S.C. 1354, 1355, and 1421 through 1430) and sec. 6(c), Dept. of Transportation Act (49 U.S.C. 1655(c)))

[Doc. No. 5084, 29 FR 16150, Dec. 3, 1964, as amended by Amdt. 29–16 43 FR 46233, Oct. 5, 1978]

§ 29.1415 Ditching equipment.

(a) Emergency flotation and signaling equipment required by any operating rule of this chapter must meet the requirements of this section.

(b) Each liferaft and each life preserver must be approved. In addition—

(1) Provide not less than two rafts, of an approximately equal rated capacity and buoyancy to accommodate the occupants of the rotorcraft; and

(2) Each raft must have a trailing line, and must have a static line designed to hold the raft near the rotorcraft but to release it if the rotorcraft becomes totally submerged.

(c) Approved survival equipment must be attached to each liferaft.

(d) There must be an approved survival type emergency locator transmitter for use in one life raft.

[Doc. No. 5084, 29 FR 16150, Dec. 3, 1964, as amended by Amdt. 29–8, 36 FR 18722, Sept. 21, 1971; Amdt. 29–19, 45 FR 38348, June 9, 1980; Amdt. 27–26, 55 FR 8005, Mar. 6, 1990; Amdt. 29–33, 59 FR 32057, June 21, 1994]

§29.1419 Ice protection.

(a) To obtain certification for flight into icing conditions, compliance with this section must be shown.

(b) It must be demonstrated that the rotorcraft can be safely operated in the continuous maximum and intermittent maximum icing conditions determined under appendix C of this part within the rotorcraft altitude envelope. An analysis must be performed to establish, on the basis of the rotorcraft's operational needs, the adequacy of the ice protection system for the various components of the rotorcraft.

(c) In addition to the analysis and physical evaluation prescribed in paragraph (b) of this section, the effectiveness of the ice protection system and its components must be shown by flight tests of the rotorcraft or its components in measured natural atmospheric icing conditions and by one or more of the following tests as found necessary to determine the adequacy of the ice protection system:

(1) Laboratory dry air or simulated icing tests, or a combination of both, of the components or models of the components.

(2) Flight dry air tests of the ice protection system as a whole, or its individual components.

(3) Flight tests of the rotorcraft or its components in measured simulated icing conditions.

(d) The ice protection provisions of this section are considered to be applicable primarily to the airframe. Powerplant installation requirements are contained in Subpart E of this part.

(e) A means must be identified or provided for determining the formation of ice on critical parts of the rotorcraft. Unless otherwise restricted, the means must be available for nighttime as well as daytime operation. The rotorcraft flight manual must describe the means of determining ice formation and must contain information necessary for safe operation of the rotorcraft in icing conditions.

[Amdt. 29–21, 48 FR 4391, Jan. 31, 1983]

MISCELLANEOUS EQUIPMENT

§29.1431 Electronic equipment.

(a) Radio communication and navigation equipment installations must be free from hazards in themselves, in their method of operation, and in their effects on other components, under any critical environmental conditions.

(b) Radio communication and navigation equipment, controls, and wiring must be installed so that operation of any one unit or system of units will not adversely affect the simultaneous operation of any other radio or electronic unit, or system of units, required by this chapter.

§29.1433 Vacuum systems.

(a) There must be means, in addition to the normal pressure relief, to automatically relieve the pressure in the discharge lines from the vacuum air pump when the delivery temperature of the air becomes unsafe.

(b) Each vacuum air system line and fitting on the discharge side of the pump that might contain flammable vapors or fluids must meet the requirements of §29.1183 if they are in a designated fire zone.

(c) Other vacuum air system components in designated fire zones must be at least fire resistant.

§29.1435 Hydraulic systems.

(a) *Design.* Each hydraulic system must be designed as follows:

(1) Each element of the hydraulic system must be designed to withstand, without detrimental, permanent deformation, any structural loads that may be imposed simultaneously with the maximum operating hydraulic loads.

(2) Each element of the hydraulic system must be designed to withstand pressures sufficiently greater than those prescribed in paragraph (b) of

this section to show that the system will not rupture under service conditions.

(3) There must be means to indicate the pressure in each main hydraulic power system.

(4) There must be means to ensure that no pressure in any part of the system will exceed a safe limit above the maximum operating pressure of the system, and to prevent excessive pressures resulting from any fluid volumetric change in lines likely to remain closed long enough for such a change to take place. The possibility of detrimental transient (surge) pressures during operation must be considered.

(5) Each hydraulic line, fitting, and component must be installed and supported to prevent excessive vibration and to withstand inertia loads. Each element of the installation must be protected from abrasion, corrosion, and mechanical damage.

(6) Means for providing flexibility must be used to connect points, in a hydraulic fluid line, between which relative motion or differential vibration exists.

(b) *Tests.* Each element of the system must be tested to a proof pressure of 1.5 times the maximum pressure to which that element will be subjected in normal operation, without failure, malfunction, or detrimental deformation of any part of the system.

(c) *Fire protection.* Each hydraulic system using flammable hydraulic fluid must meet the applicable requirements of §§ 29.861, 29.1183, 29.1185, and 29.1189.

§ 29.1439 Protective breathing equipment.

(a) If one or more cargo or baggage compartments are to be accessible in flight, protective breathing equipment must be available for an appropriate crewmember.

(b) For protective breathing equipment required by paragraph (a) of this section or by any operating rule of this chapter—

(1) That equipment must be designed to protect the crew from smoke, carbon dioxide, and other harmful gases while on flight deck duty;

(2) That equipment must include—

(i) Masks covering the eyes, nose, and mouth; or

(ii) Masks covering the nose and mouth, plus accessory equipment to protect the eyes; and

(3) That equipment must supply protective oxygen of 10 minutes duration per crewmember at a pressure altitude of 8,000 feet with a respiratory minute volume of 30 liters per minute BTPD.

§ 29.1457 Cockpit voice recorders.

(a) Each cockpit voice recorder required by the operating rules of this chapter must be approved, and must be installed so that it will record the following:

(1) Voice communications transmitted from or received in the rotorcraft by radio.

(2) Voice communications of flight crewmembers on the flight deck.

(3) Voice communications of flight crewmembers on the flight deck, using the rotorcraft's interphone system.

(4) Voice or audio signals identifying navigation or approach aids introduced into a headset or speaker.

(5) Voice communications of flight crewmembers using the passenger loudspeaker system, if there is such a system, and if the fourth channel is available in accordance with the requirements of paragraph (c)(4)(ii) of this section.

(b) The recording requirements of paragraph (a)(2) of this section may be met—

(1) By installing a cockpit-mounted area microphone, located in the best position for recording voice communications originating at the first and second pilot stations and voice communications of other crewmembers on the flight deck when directed to those stations; or

(2) By installing a continually energized or voice-actuated lip microphone at the first and second pilot stations.

The microphone specified in this paragraph must be so located and, if necessary, the preamplifiers and filters of the recorder must be so adjusted or supplemented, that the recorded communications are intelligible when recorded under flight cockpit noise conditions and played back. The level of intelligibility must be approved by the

Administrator. Repeated aural or visual playback of the record may be used in evaluating intelligibility.

(c) Each cockpit voice recorder must be installed so that the part of the communication or audio signals specified in paragraph (a) of this section obtained from each of the following sources is recorded on a separate channel:

(1) For the first channel, from each microphone, headset, or speaker used at the first pilot station.

(2) For the second channel, from each microphone, headset, or speaker used at the second pilot station.

(3) For the third channel, from the cockpit-mounted area microphone, or the continually energized or voice-actuated lip microphones at the first and second pilot stations.

(4) For the fourth channel, from—

(i) Each microphone, headset, or speaker used at the stations for the third and fourth crewmembers; or

(ii) If the stations specified in paragraph (c)(4)(i) of this section are not required or if the signal at such a station is picked up by another channel, each microphone on the flight deck that is used with the passenger loudspeaker system if its signals are not picked up by another channel.

(iii) Each microphone on the flight deck that is used with the rotorcraft's loudspeaker system if its signals are not picked up by another channel.

(d) Each cockpit voice recorder must be installed so that—

(1) It receives its electric power from the bus that provides the maximum reliability for operation of the cockpit voice recorder without jeopardizing service to essential or emergency loads;

(2) There is an automatic means to simultaneously stop the recorder and prevent each erasure feature from functioning, within 10 minutes after crash impact; and

(3) There is an aural or visual means for preflight checking of the recorder for proper operation.

(e) The record container must be located and mounted to minimize the probability of rupture of the container as a result of crash impact and consequent heat damage to the record from fire.

(f) If the cockpit voice recorder has a bulk erasure device, the installation must be designed to minimize the probability of inadvertent operation and actuation of the device during crash impact.

(g) Each recorder container must be either bright orange or bright yellow.

[Amdt. 29–6, 35 FR 7293, May 9, 1970]

§29.1459 Flight recorders.

(a) Each flight recorder required by the operating rules of Subchapter G of this chapter must be installed so that:

(1) It is supplied with airspeed, altitude, and directional data obtained from sources that meet the accuracy requirements of §§29.1323, 29.1325, and 29.1327 of this part, as applicable;

(2) The vertical acceleration sensor is rigidly attached, and located longitudinally within the approved center of gravity limits of the rotorcraft;

(3) It receives its electrical power from the bus that provides the maximum reliability for operation of the flight recorder without jeopardizing service to essential or emergency loads;

(4) There is an aural or visual means for perflight checking of the recorder for proper recording of data in the storage medium; and

(5) Except for recorders powered solely by the engine-drive electrical generator, there is an automatic means to simultaneously stop a recorder that has a data erasure feature and prevent each erasure feature from functioning, within 10 minutes after any crash impact.

(b) Each nonejectable recorder container must be located and mounted so as to minimize the probability of container rupture resulting from crash impact and subsequent damage to the record from fire.

(c) A correlation must be established between the flight recorder readings of airspeed, altitude, and heading and the corresponding readings (taking into account correction factors) of the first pilot's instruments. This correlation must cover the airspeed range over which the aircraft is to be operated, the range of altitude to which the aircraft is limited, and 360 degrees of heading. Correlation may be established on the ground as appropriate.

(d) Each recorder container must:

(1) Be either bright orange or bright yellow;

(2) Have a reflective tape affixed to its external surface to facilitate its location under water; and

(3) Have an underwater locating device, when required by the operating rules of this chapter, on or adjacent to the container which is secured in such a manner that it is not likely to be separated during crash impact.

[Amdt. 29–25, 53 FR 26145, July 11, 1988; 53 FR 26144, July 11, 1988]

§ 29.1461 Equipment containing high energy rotors.

(a) Equipment containing high energy rotors must meet paragraph (b), (c), or (d) of this section.

(b) High energy rotors contained in equipment must be able to withstand damage caused by malfunctions, vibration, abnormal speeds, and abnormal temperatures. In addition—

(1) Auxiliary rotor cases must be able to contain damage caused by the failure of high energy rotor blades; and

(2) Equipment control devices, systems, and instrumentation must reasonably ensure that no operating limitations affecting the integrity of high energy rotors will be exceeded in service.

(c) It must be shown by test that equipment containing high energy rotors can contain any failure of a high energy rotor that occurs at the highest speed obtainable with the normal speed control devices inoperative.

(d) Equipment containing high energy rotors must be located where rotor failure will neither endanger the occupants nor adversely affect continued safe flight.

[Amdt. 29–3, 33 FR 971, Jan. 26, 1968]

Subpart G—Operating Limitations and Information

§ 29.1501 General.

(a) Each operating limitation specified in §§ 29.1503 through 29.1525 and other limitations and information necessary for safe operation must be established.

(b) The operating limitations and other information necessary for safe

operation must be made available to the crewmembers as prescribed in §§ 29.1541 through 29.1589.

(Secs. 313(a), 601, 603, 604, and 605 of the Federal Aviation Act of 1958 (49 U.S.C. 1354(a), 1421, 1423, 1424, and 1425); and sec. 6(c), Dept. of Transportation Act (49 U.S.C. 1655(c)))

[Amdt. 29–15, 43 FR 2327, Jan. 16, 1978]

OPERATING LIMITATIONS

§ 29.1503 Airspeed limitations: general.

(a) An operating speed range must be established.

(b) When airspeed limitations are a function of weight, weight distribution, altitude, rotor speed, power, or other factors, airspeed limitations corresponding with the critical combinations of these factors must be established.

§ 29.1505 Never-exceed speed.

(a) The never-exceed speed, $V_{NE,}$ must be established so that it is—

(1) Not less than 40 knots (CAS); and

(2) Not more than the lesser of—

(i) 0.9 times the maximum forward speeds established under § 29.309;

(ii) 0.9 times the maximum speed shown under §§ 29.251 and 29.629; or

(iii) 0.9 times the maximum speed substantiated for advancing blade tip mach number effects under critical altitude conditions.

(b) V_{NE} may vary with altitude, r.p.m., temperature, and weight, if—

(1) No more than two of these variables (or no more than two instruments integrating more than one of these variables) are used at one time; and

(2) The ranges of these variables (or of the indications on instruments integrating more than one of these variables) are large enough to allow an operationally practical and safe variation of V_{NE}.

(c) For helicopters, a stabilized power-off V_{NE} denoted as V_{NE} (power-off) may be established at a speed less than V_{NE} established pursuant to paragraph (a) of this section, if the following conditions are met:

(1) V_{NE} (power-off) is not less than a speed midway between the power-on V_{NE} and the speed used in meeting the requirements of—

(i) §29.67(a)(3) for Category A helicopters;

(ii) §29.65(a) for Category B helicopters, except multi-engine helicopters meeting the requirements of §29.67(b); and

(iii) §29.67(b) for multi-engine Category B helicopters meeting the requirements of §29.67(b).

(2) V_{NE} (power-off) is—

(i) A constant airspeed;

(ii) A constant amount less than power-on $V_{NE;}$ or

(iii) A constant airspeed for a portion of the altitude range for which certification is requested, and a constant amount less than power-on V_{NE} for the remainder of the altitude range.

(Secs. 313(a), 601, 603, 604, and 605 of the Federal Aviation Act of 1958 (49 U.S.C. 1354(a), 1421, 1423, 1424, and 1425); and sec. 6(c), Dept. of Transportation Act (49 U.S.C. 1655(c)))

[Amdt. 29–3, 33 FR 971, Jan. 26, 1968, as amended by Amdt. 29–15, 43 FR 2327, Jan. 16, 1978; Amdt. 29–24, 49 FR 44440, Nov. 6, 1984]

§29.1509 Rotor speed.

(a) *Maximum power-off (autorotation).* The maximum power-off rotor speed must be established so that it does not exceed 95 percent of the lesser of—

(1) The maximum design r.p.m. determined under §29.309(b); and

(2) The maximum r.p.m. shown during the type tests.

(b) *Minimum power-off.* The minimum power-off rotor speed must be established so that it is not less than 105 percent of the greater of—

(1) The minimum shown during the type tests; and

(2) The minimum determined by design substantiation.

(c) *Minimum power-on.* The minimum power-on rotor speed must be established so that it is—

(1) Not less than the greater of—

(i) The minimum shown during the type tests; and

(ii) The minimum determined by design substantiation; and

(2) Not more than a value determined under §29.33 (a)(1) and (c)(1).

§29.1517 Limiting height-speed envelope.

For Category A rotorcraft, if a range of heights exists at any speed, including zero, within which it is not possible to make a safe landing following power failure, the range of heights and its variation with forward speed must be established, together with any other pertinent information, such as the kind of landing surface.

[Amdt. 29–21, 48 FR 4391, Jan. 31, 1983]

§29.1519 Weight and center of gravity.

The weight and center of gravity limitations determined under §§29.25 and 29.27, respectively, must be established as operating limitations.

§29.1521 Powerplant limitations.

(a) *General.* The powerplant limitations prescribed in this section must be established so that they do not exceed the corresponding limits for which the engines are type certificated.

(b) *Takeoff operation.* The powerplant takeoff operation must be limited by—

(1) The maximum rotational speed, which may not be greater than—

(i) The maximum value determined by the rotor design; or

(ii) The maximum value shown during the type tests;

(2) The maximum allowable manifold pressure (for reciprocating engines);

(3) The maximum allowable turbine inlet or turbine outlet gas temperature (for turbine engines);

(4) The maximum allowable power or torque for each engine, considering the power input limitations of the transmission with all engines operating;

(5) The maximum allowable power or torque for each engine considering the power input limitations of the transmission with one engine inoperative;

(6) The time limit for the use of the power corresponding to the limitations established in paragraphs (b)(1) through (5) of this section; and

(7) If the time limit established in paragraph (b)(6) of this section exceeds 2 minutes—

(i) The maximum allowable cylinder head or coolant outlet temperature (for reciprocating engines); and

(ii) The maximum allowable engine and transmission oil temperatures.

(c) *Continuous operation.* The continuous operation must be limited by—

(1) The maximum rotational speed, which may not be greater than—

(i) The maximum value determined by the rotor design; or

(ii) The maximum value shown during the type tests;

(2) The minimum rotational speed shown under the rotor speed requirements in § 29.1509(c).

(3) The maximum allowable manifold pressure (for reciprocating engines);

(4) The maximum allowable turbine inlet or turbine outlet gas temperature (for turbine engines);

(5) The maximum allowable power or torque for each engine, considering the power input limitations of the transmission with all engines operating;

(6) The maximum allowable power or torque for each engine, considering the power input limitations of the transmission with one engine inoperative; and

(7) The maximum allowable temperatures for—

(i) The cylinder head or coolant outlet (for reciprocating engines);

(ii) The engine oil; and

(iii) The transmission oil.

(d) *Fuel grade or designation.* The minimum fuel grade (for reciprocating engines) or fuel designation (for turbine engines) must be established so that it is not less than that required for the operation of the engines within the limitations in paragraphs (b) and (c) of this section.

(e) *Ambient temperature.* Ambient temperature limitations (including limitations for winterization installations if applicable) must be established as the maximum ambient atmospheric temperature at which compliance with the cooling provisions of §§ 29.1041 through 29.1049 is shown.

(f) *Two and one-half minute OEI power operation.* Unless otherwise authorized, the use of 2½-minute OEI power must be limited to engine failure operation of multiengine, turbine-powered rotorcraft for not longer than 2½ minutes for any period in which that power is used. The use of 2½-minute OEI power must also be limited by—

(1) The maximum rotational speed, which may not be greater than—

(i) The maximum value determined by the rotor design; or

(ii) The maximum value shown during the type tests;

(2) The maximum allowable gas temperature;

(3) The maximum allowable torque; and

(4) The maximum allowable oil temperature.

(g) *Thirty-minute OEI power operation.* Unless otherwise authorized, the use of 30-minute OEI power must be limited to multiengine, turbine-powered rotorcraft for not longer than 30 minutes after failure of an engine. The use of 30-minute OEI power must also be limited by—

(1) The maximum rotational speed, which may not be greater than—

(i) The maximum value determined by the rotor design; or

(ii) The maximum value shown during the type tests;

(2) The maximum allowable gas temperature;

(3) The maximum allowable torque; and

(4) The maximum allowable oil temperature.

(h) *Continuous OEI power operation.* Unless otherwise authorized, the use of continuous OEI power must be limited to multiengine, turbine-powered rotorcraft for continued flight after failure of an engine. The use of continuous OEI power must also be limited by—

(1) The maximum rotational speed, which may not be greater than—

(i) The maximum value determined by the rotor design; or

(ii) The maximum value shown during the type tests.

(2) The maximum allowable gas temperature;

(3) The maximum allowable torque; and

(4) The maximum allowable oil temperature.

(i) *Rated 30-second OEI power operation.* Rated 30-second OEI power is permitted only on multiengine, turbine-powered rotorcraft, also certificated for the use of rated 2-minute OEI power, and can only be used for continued operation of the remaining engine(s) after a failure or precautionary shutdown of an engine. It must be shown that following application of 30-second OEI power, any damage will be readily detectable by the applicable inspections and other related procedures furnished in accordance with Section A29.4 of appendix A of this part and Section A33.4 of appendix A of part 33.

The use of 30-second OEI power must be limited to not more than 30 seconds for any period in which that power is used, and by—

(1) The maximum rotational speed which may not be greater than—

(i) The maximum value determined by the rotor design; or

(ii) The maximum value demonstrated during the type tests;

(2) The maximum allowable gas temperature; and

(3) The maximum allowable torque.

(j) *Rated 2-minute OEI power operation.* Rated 2-minute OEI power is permitted only on multiengine, turbine-powered rotorcraft, also certificated for the use of rated 30-second OEI power, and can only be used for continued operation of the remaining engine(s) after a failure or precautionary shutdown of an engine. It must be shown that following application of 2-minute OEI power, any damage will be readily detectable by the applicable inspections and other related procedures furnished in accordance with Section A29.4 of appendix a of this part and Section A33.4 of appendix A of part 33. The use of 2-minute OEI power must be limited to not more than 2 minutes for any period in which that power is used, and by—

(1) The maximum rotational speed, which may not be greater than—

(i) The maximum value determined by the rotor design; or

(ii) The maximum value demonstrated during the type tests;

(2) The maximum allowable gas temperature; and

(3) The maximum allowable torque.

(Secs. 313(a), 601, 603, 604, and 605 of the Federal Aviation Act of 1958 (49 U.S.C. 1354(a), 1421, 1423, 1424, and 1425); and sec. 6(c), Dept. of Transportation Act (49 U.S.C. 1655(c)))

[Doc. No. 5084, 29 FR 16150, Dec. 3, 1964, as amended by Amdt. 29–1, 30 FR 8778, July 13, 1965; Amdt. 29–3, 33 FR 971, Jan. 26, 1968; Amdt. 29–15, 43 FR 2327, Jan. 16, 1978; Amdt. 29–26, 53 FR 34220, Sept. 2, 1988; Amdt. 29–34, 59 FR 47768, Sept. 16, 1994; Amdt. 29–41, 62 FR 46173, Aug. 29, 1997]

§29.1522 Auxiliary power unit limitations.

If an auxiliary power unit that meets the requirements of TSO–C77 is installed in the rotorcraft, the limitations established for that auxiliary power unit under the TSO including the categories of operation must be specified as operating limitations for the rotorcraft.

(Secs. 313(a), 601, 603, 604, Federal Aviation Act of 1958 (49 U.S.C. 1354(a), 1421, 1423), sec. 6(c), Dept. of Transportation Act (49 U.S.C. 1655(c)))

[Amdt. 29–17, 43 FR 50602, Oct. 30, 1978]

§29.1523 Minimum flight crew.

The minimum flight crew must be established so that it is sufficient for safe operation, considering—

(a) The workload on individual crewmembers;

(b) The accessibility and ease of operation of necessary controls by the appropriate crewmember; and

(c) The kinds of operation authorized under §29.1525.

§29.1525 Kinds of operations.

The kinds of operations (such as VFR, IFR, day, night, or icing) for which the rotorcraft is approved are established by demonstrated compliance with the applicable certification requirements and by the installed equipment.

[Amdt. 29–24, 49 FR 44440, Nov. 6, 1984]

§29.1527 Maximum operating altitude.

The maximum altitude up to which operation is allowed, as limited by flight, structural, powerplant, functional, or equipment characteristics, must be established.

(Secs. 313(a), 601, 603, 604, and 605 of the Federal Aviation Act of 1958 (49 U.S.C. 1354(a), 1421, 1423, 1424, and 1425); and sec. 6(c), Dept. of Transportation Act (49 U.S.C. 1655(c)))

[Amdt. 29–15, 43 FR 2327, Jan. 16, 1978]

§29.1529 Instructions for Continued Airworthiness.

The applicant must prepare Instructions for Continued Airworthiness in accordance with appendix A to this part that are acceptable to the Administrator. The instructions may be incomplete at type certification if a program exists to ensure their completion prior to delivery of the first rotorcraft or issuance of a standard certificate of airworthiness, whichever occurs later.

[Amdt. 29–20, 45 FR 60178, Sept. 11, 1980]

MARKINGS AND PLACARDS

§ 29.1541 General.

(a) The rotorcraft must contain—

(1) The markings and placards specified in §§ 29.1545 through 29.1565; and

(2) Any additional information, instrument markings, and placards required for the safe operation of the rotorcraft if it has unusual design, operating or handling characteristics.

(b) Each marking and placard prescribed in paragraph (a) of this section—

(1) Must be displayed in a conspicuous place; and

(2) May not be easily erased, disfigured, or obscured.

§ 29.1543 Instrument markings: general.

For each instrument—

(a) When markings are on the cover glass of the instrument there must be means to maintain the correct alignment of the glass cover with the face of the dial; and

(b) Each arc and line must be wide enough, and located to be clearly visible to the pilot.

§ 29.1545 Airspeed indicator.

(a) Each airspeed indicator must be marked as specified in paragraph (b) of this section, with the marks located at the corresponding indicated airspeeds.

(b) The following markings must be made:

(1) A red radial line—

(i) For rotorcraft other than helicopters, at V_{NE}; and

(ii) For helicopters, at a V_{NE} (power-on).

(2) A red, cross-hatched radial line at V_{NE} (power-off) for helicopters, if V_{NE} (power-off) is less than V_{NE} (power-on).

(3) For the caution range, a yellow arc.

(4) For the safe operating range, a green arc.

(Secs. 313(a), 601, 603, 604, and 605 of the Federal Aviation Act of 1958 (49 U.S.C. 1354(a), 1421, 1423, 1424, and 1425); and sec. 6(c), Dept. of Transportation Act (49 U.S.C. 1655(c)))

[Doc. No. 5084, 29 FR 16150, Dec. 3, 1964, as amended by Amdt. 29–15, 43 FR 2327, Jan. 16, 1978; 43 FR 3900, Jan. 30, 1978; Amdt. 29–17, 43 FR 50602, Oct. 30, 1978]

§ 29.1547 Magnetic direction indicator.

(a) A placard meeting the requirements of this section must be installed on or near the magnetic direction indicator.

(b) The placard must show the calibration of the instrument in level flight with the engines operating.

(c) The placard must state whether the calibration was made with radio receivers on or off.

(d) Each calibration reading must be in terms of magnetic heading in not more than 45 degree increments.

§ 29.1549 Powerplant instruments.

For each required powerplant instrument, as appropriate to the type of instruments—

(a) Each maximum and, if applicable, minimum safe operating limit must be marked with a red radial or a red line;

(b) Each normal operating range must be marked with a green arc or green line, not extending beyond the maximum and minimum safe limits;

(c) Each takeoff and precautionary range must be marked with a yellow arc or yellow line;

(d) Each engine or propeller range that is restricted because of excessive vibration stresses must be marked with red arcs or red lines; and

(e) Each OEI limit or approved operating range must be marked to be clearly differentiated from the markings of paragraphs (a) through (d) of this section except that no marking is normally required for the 30-second OEI limit.

[Amdt. 29–12, 41 FR 55474, Dec. 20, 1976, as amended by Amdt. 29–26, 53 FR 34220, Sept. 2, 1988; Amdt. 29–34, 59 FR 47769, Sept. 16, 1994]

§ 29.1551 Oil quantity indicator.

Each oil quantity indicator must be marked with enough increments to indicate readily and accurately the quantity of oil.

§ 29.1553 Fuel quantity indicator.

If the unusable fuel supply for any tank exceeds one gallon, or five percent of the tank capacity, whichever is greater, a red arc must be marked on its indicator extending from the calibrated zero reading to the lowest reading obtainable in level flight.

§29.1555 Control markings.

(a) Each cockpit control, other than primary flight controls or control whose function is obvious, must be plainly marked as to its function and method of operation.

(b) For powerplant fuel controls—

(1) Each fuel tank selector valve control must be marked to indicate the position corresponding to each tank and to each existing cross feed position;

(2) If safe operation requires the use of any tanks in a specific sequence, that sequence must be marked on, or adjacent to, the selector for those tanks; and

(3) Each valve control for any engine of a multiengine rotorcraft must be marked to indicate the position corresponding to each engine controlled.

(c) Usable fuel capacity must be marked as follows:

(1) For fuel systems having no selector controls, the usable fuel capacity of the system must be indicated at the fuel quantity indicator.

(2) For fuel systems having selector controls, the usable fuel capacity available at each selector control position must be indicated near the selector control.

(d) For accessory, auxiliary, and emergency controls—

(1) Each essential visual position indicator, such as those showing rotor pitch or landing gear position, must be marked so that each crewmember can determine at any time the position of the unit to which it relates; and

(2) Each emergency control must be red and must be marked as to method of operation.

(e) For rotorcraft incorporating retractable landing gear, the maximum landing gear operating speed must be displayed in clear view of the pilot.

[Doc. No. 5084, 29 FR 16150, Dec. 3, 1964, as amended by Amdt. 29–12, 41 FR 55474, Dec. 20, 1976; Amdt. 29–24, 49 FR 44440, Nov. 6, 1984]

§29.1557 Miscellaneous markings and placards.

(a) *Baggage and cargo compartments, and ballast location.* Each baggage and cargo compartment, and each ballast location must have a placard stating any limitations on contents, including weight, that are necessary under the loading requirements.

(b) *Seats.* If the maximum allowable weight to be carried in a seat is less than 170 pounds, a placard stating the lesser weight must be permanently attached to the seat structure.

(c) *Fuel and oil filler openings.* The following apply:

(1) Fuel filler openings must be marked at or near the filler cover with—

(i) The word "fuel";

(ii) For reciprocating engine powered rotorcraft, the minimum fuel grade;

(iii) For turbine-engine-powered rotorcraft, the permissible fuel designations, except that if impractical, this information may be included in the rotorcraft flight manual, and the fuel filler may be marked with an appropriate reference to the flight manual; and

(iv) For pressure fueling systems, the maximum permissible fueling supply pressure and the maximum permissible defueling pressure.

(2) Oil filler openings must be marked at or near the filler cover with the word "oil".

(d) *Emergency exit placards.* Each placard and operating control for each emergency exit must differ in color from the surrounding fuselage surface as prescribed in §29.811(h)(2). A placard must be near each emergency exit control and must clearly indicate the location of that exit and its method of operation.

[Doc. No. 5084, 29 FR 16150, Dec. 3, 1964, as amended by Amdt. 29–3, 33 FR 971, Jan. 26, 1968; Amdt. 29–12, 41 FR 55474, Dec. 20, 1976; Amdt. 29–26, 53 FR 34220, Sept. 2, 1988]

§29.1559 Limitations placard.

There must be a placard in clear view of the pilot that specifies the kinds of operations (VFR, IFR, day, night, or icing) for which the rotorcraft is approved.

[Amdt. 29–24, 49 FR 44440, Nov. 6, 1984]

§29.1561 Safety equipment.

(a) Each safety equipment control to be operated by the crew in emergency, such as controls for automatic liferaft releases, must be plainly marked as to its method of operation.

(b) Each location, such as a locker or compartment, that carries any fire extinguishing, signaling, or other life saving equipment, must be so marked.

(c) Stowage provisions for required emergency equipment must be conspicuously marked to identify the contents and facilitate removal of the equipment.

(d) Each liferaft must have obviously marked operating instructions.

(e) Approved survival equipment must be marked for identification and method of operation.

§ 29.1565   Tail rotor.

Each tail rotor must be marked so that its disc is conspicuous under normal daylight ground conditions.

[Amdt. 29–3, 33 FR 971, Jan. 26, 1968]

ROTORCRAFT FLIGHT MANUAL

§ 29.1581   General.

(a) *Furnishing information.* A Rotorcraft Flight Manual must be furnished with each rotorcraft, and it must contain the following:

(1) Information required by §§ 29.1583 through 29.1589.

(2) Other information that is necessary for safe operation because of design, operating, or handling characteristics.

(b) *Approved information.* Each part of the manual listed in §§ 29.1583 through 29.1589 that is appropriate to the rotorcraft, must be furnished, verified, and approved, and must be segregated, indentified, and clearly distinguished from each unapproved part of that manual.

(c) [Reserved]

(d) *Table of contents.* Each Rotorcraft Flight Manual must include a table of contents if the complexity of the manual indicates a need for it.

(Secs. 313(a), 601, 603, 604, and 605 of the Federal Aviation Act of 1958 (49 U.S.C. 1354(a), 1421, 1423, 1424, and 1425); and sec. 6(c), Dept. of Transportation Act (49 U.S.C. 1655(c)))

[Amdt. 29–15, 43 FR 2327, Jan. 16, 1978]

§ 29.1583   Operating limitations.

(a) *Airspeed and rotor limitations.* Information necessary for the marking of airspeed and rotor limitations on or near their respective indicators must be furnished. The significance of each limitation and of the color coding must be explained.

(b) *Powerplant limitations.* The following information must be furnished:

(1) Limitations required by § 29.1521.

(2) Explanation of the limitations, when appropriate.

(3) Information necessary for marking the instruments required by §§ 29.1549 through 29.1553.

(c) *Weight and loading distribution.* The weight and center of gravity limits required by §§ 29.25 and 29.27, respectively, must be furnished. If the variety of possible loading conditions warrants, instructions must be included to allow ready observance of the limitations.

(d) *Flight crew.* When a flight crew of more than one is required, the number and functions of the minimum flight crew determined under § 29.1523 must be furnished.

(e) *Kinds of operation.* Each kind of operation for which the rotorcraft and its equipment installations are approved must be listed.

(f) *Limiting heights.* Enough information must be furnished to allow compliance with § 29.1517.

(g) *Maximum allowable wind.* For Category A rotorcraft, the maximum allowable wind for safe operation near the ground must be furnished.

(h) *Altitude.* The altitude established under § 29.1527 and an explanation of the limiting factors must be furnished.

(i) *Ambient temperature.* Maximum and minimum ambient temperature limitations must be furnished.

(Secs. 313(a), 601, 603, 604, and 605 of the Federal Aviation Act of 1958 (49 U.S.C. 1354(a), 1421, 1423, 1424, and 1425); and sec. 6(c), Dept. of Transportation Act (49 U.S.C. 1655(c)))

[Doc. No. 5084, 29 FR 16150, Dec. 3, 1964, as amended by Amdt. 29–3, 33 FR 971, Jan. 26, 1968; Amdt. 29–15, 43 FR 2327, Jan. 16, 1978; Amdt. 29–17, 43 FR 50602, Oct. 30, 1978; Amdt. 29–24, 49 FR 44440, Nov. 6, 1984]

§ 29.1585   Operating procedures.

(a) The parts of the manual containing operating procedures must have information concerning any normal and emergency procedures, and other information necessary for safe operation, including the applicable procedures, such as those involving minimum speeds, to be followed if an engine fails.

(b) For multiengine rotorcraft, information identifying each operating condition in which the fuel system independence prescribed in §29.953 is necessary for safety must be furnished, together with instructions for placing the fuel system in a configuration used to show compliance with that section.

(c) For helicopters for which a V_{NE} (power-off) is established under §29.1505(c), information must be furnished to explain the V_{NE} (power-off) and the procedures for reducing airspeed to not more than the V_{NE} (power-off) following failure of all engines.

(d) For each rotorcraft showing compliance with §29.1353 (c)(6)(ii) or (c)(6)(iii), the operating procedures for disconnecting the battery from its charging source must be furnished.

(e) If the unusable fuel supply in any tank exceeds 5 percent of the tank capacity, or 1 gallon, whichever is greater, information must be furnished which indicates that when the fuel quantity indicator reads "zero" in level flight, any fuel remaining in the fuel tank cannot be used safely in flight.

(f) Information on the total quantity of usable fuel for each fuel tank must be furnished.

(g) For Category B rotorcraft, the airspeeds and corresponding rotor speeds for minimum rate of descent and best glide angle as prescribed in §29.71 must be provided.

(Secs. 313(a), 601, 603, 604, and 605 of the Federal Aviation Act of 1958 (49 U.S.C. 1354(a), 1421, 1423, 1424, and 1425); and sec. 6(c), Dept. of Transportation Act (49 U.S.C. 1655(c)))

[Amdt. 29-2, 32 FR 6914, May 5, 1967, as amended by Amdt. 29-15, 43 FR 2328, Jan. 16, 1978; Amdt. 29-17, 43 FR 50602, Oct. 30, 1978; Amdt. 29-24, 49 FR 44440, Nov. 6, 1984]

§29.1587 Performance information.

Flight manual performance information which exceeds any operating limitation may be shown only to the extent necessary for presentation clarity or to determine the effects of approved optional equipment or procedures. When data beyond operating limits are shown, the limits must be clearly indicated. The following must be provided:

(a) *Category A*. For each category A rotorcraft, the Rotorcraft Flight Manual must contain a summary of the performance data, including data necessary for the application of any operating rule of this chapter, together with descriptions of the conditions, such as airspeeds, under which this data was determined, and must contain—

(1) The indicated airspeeds corresponding with those determined for takeoff, and the procedures to be followed if the critical engine fails during takeoff;

(2) The airspeed calibrations;

(3) The techniques, associated airspeeds, and rates of descent for autorotative landings;

(4) The rejected takeoff distance determined under §29.62 and the takeoff distance determined under §29.61;

(5) The landing data determined under §29.81 and §29.85;

(6) The steady gradient of climb for each weight, altitude, and temperature for which takeoff data are to be scheduled, along the takeoff path determined in the flight conditions required in §29.67(a)(1) and (a)(2):

(i) In the flight conditions required in §29.67(a)(1) between the end of the takeoff distance and the point at which the rotorcraft is 200 feet above the takeoff surface (or 200 feet above the lowest point of the takeoff profile for elevated heliports);

(ii) In the flight conditions required in §29.67(a)(2) between the points at which the rotorcraft is 200 and 1000 feet above the takeoff surface (or 200 and 1000 feet above the lowest point of the takeoff profile for elevated heliports); and

(7) Out-of-ground effect hover performance determined under §29.49 and the maximum safe wind demonstrated under the ambient conditions for data presented.

(b) *Category B*. For each category B rotorcraft, the Rotorcraft Flight Manual must contain—

(1) The takeoff distance and the climbout speed together with the pertinent information defining the flight

715

path with respect to autorotative landing if an engine fails, including the calculated effects of altitude and temperature;

(2) The steady rates of climb and hovering ceiling, together with the corresponding airspeeds and other pertinent information, including the calculated effects of altitude and temperature;

(3) The landing distance, appropriate airspeed, and type of landing surface, together with all pertinent information that might affect this distance, including the effects of weight, altitude, and temperature;

(4) The maximum safe wind for operation near the ground;

(5) The airspeed calibrations;

(6) The height-speed envelope except for rotorcraft incorporating this as an operating limitation;

(7) Glide distance as a function of altitude when autorotating at the speeds and conditions for minimum rate of descent and best glide angle, as determined in § 29.71;

(8) Out-of-ground effect hover performance determined under § 29.49 and the maximum safe wind demonstrated under the ambient conditions for data presented; and

(9) Any additional performance data necessary for the application of any operating rule in this chapter.

[Doc. No. 5084, 29 FR 16150, Dec. 3, 1964, as amended by Amdt. 29–21, 48 FR 4392, Jan. 31, 1983; Amdt. 29–24, 49 FR 44440, Nov. 6, 1984; Amdt. 29–39, 61 FR 21901, May 10, 1996; Amdt. 29–40, 61 FR 21908, May 10, 1996; Amdt. 29–44, 64 FR 45338, Aug. 19, 1999]

§ 29.1589 Loading information.

There must be loading instructions for each possible loading condition between the maximum and minimum weights determined under § 29.25 that can result in a center of gravity beyond any extreme prescribed in § 29.27, assuming any probable occupant weights.

APPENDIX A TO PART 29—INSTRUCTIONS FOR CONTINUED AIRWORTHINESS

A29.1 GENERAL

(a) This appendix specifies requirements for the preparation of Instructions for Continued Airworthiness as required by § 29.1529.

(b) The Instructions for Continued Airworthiness for each rotorcraft must include the Instructions for Continued Airworthiness for each engine and rotor (hereinafter designated "products"), for each appliance required by this chapter, and any required information relating to the interface of those appliances and products with the rotorcraft. If Instructions for Continued Airworthiness are not supplied by the manufacturer of an appliance or product installed in the rotorcraft, the Instructions for Continued Airworthiness for the rotorcraft must include the information essential to the continued airworthiness of the rotorcraft.

(c) The applicant must submit to the FAA a program to show how changes to the Instructions for Continued Airworthiness made by the applicant or by the manufacturers of products and appliances installed in the rotorcraft will be distributed.

A29.2 FORMAT

(a) The Instructions for Continued Airworthiness must be in the form of a manual or manuals as appropriate for the quantity of data to be provided.

(b) The format of the manual or manuals must provide for a practical arrangement.

A29.3 CONTENT

The contents of the manual or manuals must be prepared in the English language. The Instructions for Continued Airworthiness must contain the following manuals or sections, as appropriate, and information:

(a) *Rotorcraft maintenance manual or section.* (1) Introduction information that includes an explanation of the rotorcraft's features and data to the extent necessary for maintenance or preventive maintenance.

(2) A description of the rotorcraft and its systems and installations including its engines, rotors, and appliances.

(3) Basic control and operation information describing how the rotorcraft components and systems are controlled and how they operate, including any special procedures and limitations that apply.

(4) Servicing information that covers details regarding servicing points, capacities of tanks, reservoirs, types of fluids to be used, pressures applicable to the various systems, location of access panels for inspection and servicing, locations of lubrication points, the lubricants to be used, equipment required for servicing, tow instructions and limitations, mooring, jacking, and leveling information.

(b) *Maintenance Instructions.* (1) Scheduling information for each part of the rotorcraft and its engines, auxiliary power units, rotors, accessories, instruments, and equipment that provides the recommended periods at which they should be cleaned, inspected, adjusted, tested, and lubricated, and the degree of inspection, the applicable wear tolerances, and work recommended at these periods. However, the applicant may refer to an accessory, instrument, or equipment manufacturer as the source of this information if the applicant shows that the item has an exceptionally high degree of complexity requiring specialized maintenance techniques, test equipment, or expertise. The recommended overhaul periods and necessary cross references to the Airworthiness Limitations section of the manual must also be included. In addition, the applicant must include an inspection program that includes the frequency and extent of the inspections necessary to provide for the continued airworthiness of the rotorcraft.

(2) Troubleshooting information describing probable malfunctions, how to recognize those malfunctions, and the remedial action for those malfunctions.

(3) Information describing the order and method of removing and replacing products and parts with any necessary precautions to be taken.

(4) Other general procedural instructions including procedures for system testing during ground running, symmetry checks, weighing and determining the center of gravity, lifting and shoring, and storage limitations.

(c) Diagrams of structural access plates and information needed to gain access for inspections when access plates are not provided.

(d) Details for the application of special inspection techniques including radiographic and ultrasonic testing where such processes are specified.

(e) Information needed to apply protective treatments to the structure after inspection.

(f) All data relative to structural fasteners such as identification, discard recommendations, and torque values.

(g) A list of special tools needed.

A29.4 AIRWORTHINESS LIMITATIONS SECTION

The Instructions for Continued Airworthiness must contain a section titled Airworthiness Limitations that is segregated and clearly distinguishable from the rest of the document. This section must set forth each mandatory replacement time, structural inspection interval, and related structural inspection procedure approved under §29.571. If the Instructions for Continued Airworthiness consist of multiple documents, the section required by this paragraph must be included in the principal manual. This section must contain a legible statement in a prominent location that reads: "The Airworthiness Limitations section is FAA approved and specifies maintenance required under §§43.16 and 91.403 of the Federal Aviation Regulations unless an alternative program has been FAA approved."

[Amdt. 29–20, 45 FR 60178, Sept 11, 1980, as amended by Amdt. 29–27, 54 FR 34330, Aug. 18, 1989]

APPENDIX B TO PART 29—AIRWORTHINESS CRITERIA FOR HELICOPTER INSTRUMENT FLIGHT

I. *General.* A transport category helicopter may not be type certificated for operation under the instrument flight rules (IFR) of this chapter unless it meets the design and installation requirements contained in this appendix.

II. *Definitions.* (a) V_{YI} means instrument climb speed, utilized instead of V_Y for compliance with the climb requirements for instrument flight.

(b) V_{NEI} means instrument flight never exceed speed, utilized instead of V_{NE} for compliance with maximum limit speed requirements for instrument flight.

(c) V_{MINI} means instrument flight minimum speed, utilized in complying with minimum limit speed requirements for instrument flight.

III. *Trim.* It must be possible to trim the cyclic, collective, and directional control forces to zero at all approved IFR airspeeds, power settings, and configurations appropriate to the type.

IV. *Static longitudinal stability.* (a) *General.* The helicopter must possess positive static longitudinal control force stability at critical combinations of weight and center of gravity at the conditions specified in paragraphs IV (b) through (f) of this appendix. The stick force must vary with speed so that any substantial speed change results in a stick force clearly perceptible to the pilot. The airspeed must return to within 10 percent of the trim speed when the control force is slowly released for each trim condition specified in paragraphs IV (b) through (f) of this appendix.

(b) *Climb.* Stability must be shown in climb thoughout the speed range 20 knots either side of trim with—

(1) The helicopter trimmed at V_{YI};

(2) Landing gear retracted (if retractable); and

(3) Power required for limit climb rate (at least 1,000 fpm) at V_{YI} or maximum continuous power, whichever is less.

(c) *Cruise.* Stability must be shown throughout the speed range from 0.7 to 1.1 V_H or V_{NEI}, whichever is lower, not to exceed ±20 knots from trim with—

(1) The helicopter trimmed and power adjusted for level flight at 0.9 V_H or 0.9 V_{NEI}, whichever is lower; and

(2) Landing gear retracted (if retractable).

(d) *Slow cruise.* Stability must be shown throughout the speed range from 0.9 V_{MINI} to 1.3 V_{MINI} or 20 knots above trim speed, whichever is greater, with—

(1) The helicopter trimmed and power adjusted for level flight at 1.1 V_{MINI}; and

(2) Landing gear retracted (if retractable).

(e) *Descent.* Stability must be shown throughout the speed range 20 knots either side of trim with—

(1) The helicopter trimmed at 0.8 V_H or 0.8 V_{NEI} (or 0.8 V_{LE} for the landing gear extended case), whichever is lower;

(2) Power required for 1,000 fpm descent at trim speed; and

(3) Landing gear extended and retracted, if applicable.

(f) *Approach.* Stability must be shown throughout the speed range from 0.7 times the minimum recommended approach speed to 20 knots above the maximum recommended approach speed with—

(1) The helicopter trimmed at the recommended approach speed or speeds;

(2) Landing gear extended and retracted, if applicable; and

(3) Power required to maintain a 3° glide path and power required to maintain the steepest approach gradient for which approval is requested.

V. *Static lateral-directional stability.* (a) Static directional stability must be positive throughout the approved ranges of airspeed, power, and vertical speed. In straight, steady sideslips up to ±10° from trim, directional control position must increase in approximately constant proportion to angle of sideslip. At greater angles up to the maximum sideslip angle appropriate to the type, increased directional control position must produce increased angle of sideslip.

(b) During sideslips up to ±10° from trim throughout the approved ranges of airspeed, power, and vertical speed there must be no negative dihedral stability perceptible to the pilot through lateral control motion or force. Longitudinal cycle movement with sideslip must not be excessive.

VI. *Dynamic stability.* (a) Any oscillation having a period of less than 5 seconds must damp to 1/2 amplitude in not more than one cycle.

(b) Any oscillation having a period of 5 seconds or more but less than 10 seconds must damp to 1/2 amplitude in not more than two cycles.

(c) Any oscillation having a period of 10 seconds or more but less than 20 seconds must be damped.

(d) Any oscillation having a period of 20 seconds or more may not achieve double amplitude in less than 20 seconds.

(e) Any aperiodic response may not achieve double amplitude in less than 9 seconds.

VII. *Stability augmentation system (SAS).* (a) If a SAS is used, the reliability of the SAS must be related to the effects of its failure. The occurrence of any failure condition which would prevent continued safe flight and landing must be extremely improbable. For any failure condition of the SAS which is not shown to be extremely improbable—

(1) The helicopter must be safely controllable and capable of prolonged instrument flight without undue pilot effort. Additional unrelated probable failures affecting the control system must be considered; and

(2) The flight characteristics requirements in Subpart B of Part 29 must be met throughout a practical flight envelope.

(b) The SAS must be designed so that it cannot create a hazardous deviation in flight path or produce hazardous loads on the helicopter during normal operation or in the event of malfunction or failure, assuming corrective action begins within an appropriate period of time. Where multiple systems are installed, subsequent malfunction conditions must be considered in sequence unless their occurrence is shown to be improbable.

VIII. *Equipment, systems, and installation.* The basic equipment and installation must comply with Subpart F of Part 29 through Amendment 29-14, with the following exceptions and additions:

(a) *Flight and navigation instruments.* (1) A magnetic gyro-stabilized direction indicator instead of the gyroscopic direction indicator required by §29.1303(h); and

(2) A standby attitude indicator which meets the requirements of §§29.1303(g)(1) through (7), instead of a rate-of-turn indicator required by §29.1303(g). If standby batteries are provided, they may be charged from the aircraft electrical system if adequate isolation is incorporated. The system must be designed so that the standby batteries may not be used for engine starting.

(b) *Miscellaneous requirements.* (1) Instrument systems and other systems essential for IFR flight that could be adversely affected by icing must be provided with adequate ice protection whether or not the rotorcraft is certificated for operation in icing conditions.

(2) There must be means in the generating system to automatically de-energize and disconnect from the main bus any power source developing hazardous overvoltage.

(3) Each required flight instrument using a power supply (electric, vacuum, etc.) must have a visual means integral with the instrument to indicate the adequacy of the power being supplied.

(4) When multiple systems performing like functions are required, each system must be grouped, routed, and spaced so that physical separation between systems is provided to ensure that a single malfunction will not adversely affect more than one system.

(5) For systems that operate the required flight instruments at each pilot's station—

(i) Only the required flight instruments for the first pilot may be connected to that operating system;

(ii) Additional instruments, systems, or equipment may not be connected to an operating system for a second pilot unless provisions are made to ensure the continued normal functioning of the required instruments in the event of any malfunction of the additional instruments, systems, or equipment which is not shown to be extremely improbable;

(iii) The equipment, systems, and installations must be designed so that one display of the information essential to the safety of flight which is provided by the instruments will remain available to a pilot, without additional crew-member action, after any single failure or combination of failures that is not shown to be extremely improbable; and

(iv) For single-pilot configurations, instruments which require a static source must be provided with a means of selecting an alternate source and that source must be calibrated.

(6) In determining compliance with the requirements of §29.1351(d)(2), the supply of electrical power to all systems necessary for flight under IFR must be included in the evaluation.

(c) *Thunderstorm lights.* In addition to the instrument lights required by §29.1381(a), thunderstorm lights which provide high intensity white flood lighting to the basic flight instruments must be provided. The thunderstorm lights must be installed to meet the requirements of §29.1381(b).

IX. *Rotorcraft Flight Manual.* A Rotorcraft Flight Manual or Rotorcraft Flight Manual IFR Supplement must be provided and must contain—

(a) *Limitations.* The approved IFR flight envelope, the IFR flightcrew composition, the revised kinds of operation, and the steepest IFR precision approach gradient for which the helicopter is approved;

(b) *Procedures.* Required information for proper operation of IFR systems and the recommended procedures in the event of stability augmentation or electrical system failures; and

(c) *Performance.* If V_{YI} differs from V_Y, climb performance at V_{YI} and with maximum continuous power throughout the ranges of weight, altitude, and temperature for which approval is requested.

[Amdt. 29–21, 48 FR 4392, Jan. 31, 1983, as amended by Amdt. 29–31, 55 FR 38967, Sept. 21, 1990; 55 FR 41309, Oct. 10, 1990; Amdt. 29–40, 61 FR 21908, May 10, 1996]

APPENDIX C TO PART 29—ICING
CERTIFICATION

(a) *Continuous maximum icing.* The maximum continuous intensity of atmospheric icing conditions (continuous maximum icing) is defined by the variables of the cloud liquid water content, the mean effective diameter of the cloud droplets, the ambient air temperature, and the interrelationship of these three variables as shown in Figure 1 of this appendix. The limiting icing envelope in terms of altitude and temperature is given in Figure 2 of this appendix. The interrelationship of cloud liquid water content with drop diameter and altitude is determined from Figures 1 and 2. The cloud liquid water content for continuous maximum icing conditions of a horizontal extent, other than 17.4 nautical miles, is determined by the value of liquid water content of Figure 1, multiplied by the appropriate factor from Figure 3 of this appendix.

(b) *Intermittent maximum icing.* The intermittent maximum intensity of atmospheric icing conditions (intermittent maximum icing) is defined by the variables of the cloud liquid water content, the mean effective diameter of the cloud droplets, the ambient air temperature, and the interrelationship of these three variables as shown in Figure 4 of this appendix. The limiting icing envelope in terms of altitude and temperature is given in Figure 5 of this appendix. The interrelationship of cloud liquid water content with drop diameter and altitude is determined from Figures 4 and 5. The cloud liquid water content for intermittent maximum icing conditions of a horizontal extent, other than 2.6 nautical miles, is determined by the value of cloud liquid water content of Figure 4 multiplied by the appropriate factor in Figure 6 of this appendix.

APPENDIX C

FIGURE 1

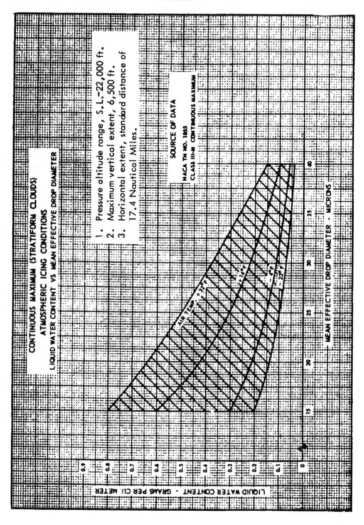

APPENDIX C
FIGURE 2

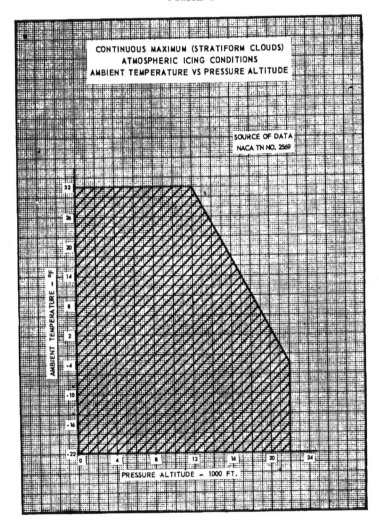

APPENDIX C
FIGURE 3

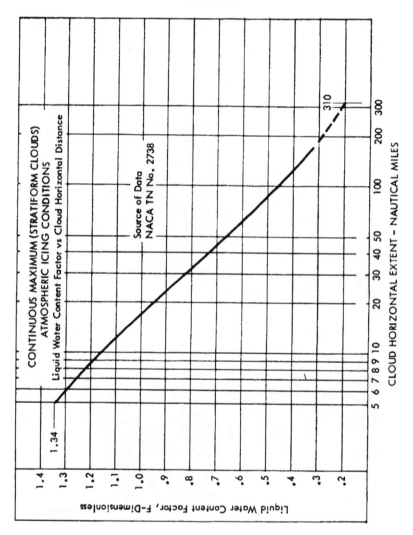

CONTINUOUS MAXIMUM (STRATIFORM CLOUDS)
ATMOSPHERIC ICING CONDITIONS
Liquid Water Content Factor vs Cloud Horizontal Distance

Source of Data
NACA TN No. 2738

CLOUD HORIZONTAL EXTENT – NAUTICAL MILES

Liquid Water Content Factor, F–Dimensionless

APPENDIX C

FIGURE 4

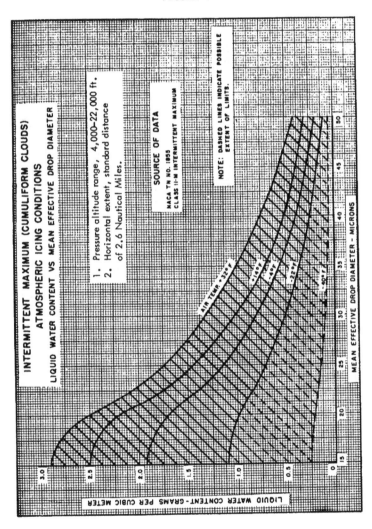

INTERMITTENT MAXIMUM (CUMULIFORM CLOUDS)
ATMOSPHERIC ICING CONDITIONS
LIQUID WATER CONTENT VS MEAN EFFECTIVE DROP DIAMETER

1. Pressure altitude range, 4,000–22,000 ft.
2. Horizontal extent, standard distance of 2.6 Nautical Miles.

SOURCE OF DATA

NACA TN NO. 1855
CLASS II-M INTERMITTENT MAXIMUM

NOTE: DASHED LINES INDICATE POSSIBLE EXTENT OF LIMITS.

MEAN EFFECTIVE DROP DIAMETER – MICRONS

LIQUID WATER CONTENT–GRAMS PER CUBIC METER

APPENDIX C
FIGURE 5

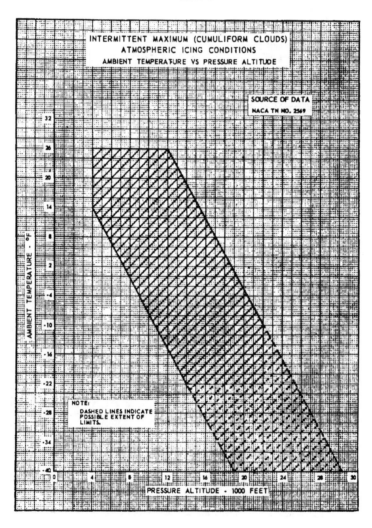

APPENDIX C

FIGURE 6

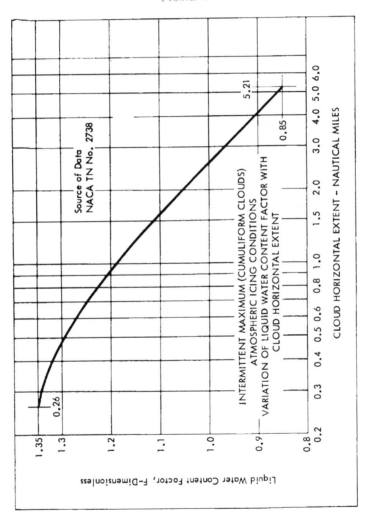

Source of Data
NACA TN No. 2738

INTERMITTENT MAXIMUM (CUMULIFORM CLOUDS)
ATMOSPHERIC ICING CONDITIONS
VARIATION OF LIQUID WATER CONTENT FACTOR WITH
CLOUD HORIZONTAL EXTENT

CLOUD HORIZONTAL EXTENT – NAUTICAL MILES

Liquid Water Content Factor, F–Dimensionless

[Amdt. 29–21, 48 FR 4393, Jan. 31, 1983]

APPENDIX D TO PART 29—CRITERIA FOR DEMONSTRATION OF EMERGENCY EVACUATION PROCEDURES UNDER § 29.803

(a) The demonstration must be conducted either during the dark of the night or during daylight with the dark of night simulated. If the demonstration is conducted indoors during daylight hours, it must be conducted inside a darkened hangar having doors and windows covered. In addition, the doors and windows of the rotorcraft must be covered if the hangar illumination exceeds that of a moonless night. Illumination on the floor or ground may be used, but it must be kept low and shielded against shining into the rotorcraft's windows or doors.

(b) The rotorcraft must be in a normal attitude with landing gear extended.

(c) Safety equipment such as mats or inverted liferafts may be placed on the floor or ground to protect participants. No other equipment that is not part of the rotorcraft's emergency evacuation equipment may be used to aid the participants in reaching the ground.

(d) Except as provided in paragraph (a) of this appendix, only the rotorcraft's emergency lighting system may provide illumination.

(e) All emergency equipment required for the planned operation of the rotorcraft must be installed.

(f) Each external door and exit and each internal door or curtain must be in the takeoff configuration.

(g) Each crewmember must be seated in the normally assigned seat for takeoff and must remain in that seat until receiving the signal for commencement of the demonstration. For compliance with this section, each crewmember must be—

(1) A member of a regularly scheduled line crew; or

(2) A person having knowledge of the operation of exits and emergency equipment.

(h) A representative passenger load of persons in normal health must be used as follows:

(1) At least 25 percent must be over 50 years of age, with at least 40 percent of these being females.

(2) The remaining, 75 percent or less, must be 50 years of age or younger, with at least 30 percent of these being females.

(3) Three life-size dolls, not included as part of the total passenger load, must be carried by passengers to simulate live infants 2 years old or younger, except for a total passenger load of fewer than 44 but more than 19, one doll must be carried. A doll is not required for a 19 or fewer passenger load.

(4) Crewmembers, mechanics, and training personnel who maintain or operate the rotorcraft in the normal course of their duties may not be used as passengers.

(i) No passenger may be assigned a specific seat except as the Administrator may require. Except as required by paragraph (1) of this appendix, no employee of the applicant may be seated next to an emergency exit, except as allowed by the Administrator.

(j) Seat belts and shoulder harnesses (as required) must be fastened.

(k) Before the start of the demonstration, approximately one-half of the total average amount of carry-on baggage, blankets, pillows, and other similar articles must be distributed at several locations in the aisles and emergency exit access ways to create minor obstructions.

(l) No prior indication may be given to any crewmember or passenger of the particular exits to be used in the demonstration.

(m) The applicant may not practice, rehearse, or describe the demonstration for the participants nor may any participant have taken part in this type of demonstration within the preceding 6 months.

(n) A pretakeoff passenger briefing may be given. The passengers may also be advised to follow directions of crewmembers, but not be instructed on the procedures to be followed in the demonstration.

(o) If safety equipment, as allowed by paragraph (c) of this appendix, is provided, either all passenger and cockpit windows must be blacked out or all emergency exits must have safety equipment to prevent disclosure of the available emergency exits.

(p) Not more than 50 percent of the emergency exits in the sides of the fuselage of a rotorcraft that meet all of the requirements applicable to the required emergency exits for that rotorcraft may be used for demonstration. Exits that are not to be used for the demonstration must have the exit handle deactivated or must be indicated by red lights, red tape, or other acceptable means placed outside the exits to indicate fire or other reasons why they are unusable. The exits to be used must be representative of all the emergency exits on the rotorcraft and must be designated by the applicant, subject to approval by the Administrator. If installed, at least one floor level exit (Type I; § 29.807(a)(1)) must be used as required by § 29.807(c).

(q) All evacuees must leave the rotorcraft by a means provided as part of the rotorcraft's equipment.

(r) Approved procedures must be fully utilized during the demonstration.

(s) The evacuation time period is completed when the last occupant has evacuated the rotorcraft and is on the ground.

[Amdt. 27-26, 55 FR 8005, Mar. 6, 1990]

PART 31—AIRWORTHINESS STANDARDS: MANNED FREE BALLOONS

AUTHORITY: 49 U.S.C. 106(g), 40113, 44701–44702, 44704.

SOURCE: Docket No. 1437, 29 FR 8258, July 1, 1964, as amended by Amdt. 31–1, 29 FR 14563, Oct. 24, 1964, unless otherwise noted.

Subpart A—General

§31.1 Applicability.

(a) This part prescribes airworthiness standards for the issue of type certificates and changes to those certificates, for manned free balloons.

(b) Each person who applies under Part 21 for such a certificate or change must show compliance with the applicable requirements of this part.

(c) For purposes of this part—

(1) A captive gas balloon is a balloon that derives its lift from a captive lighter-than-air gas;

(2) A hot air balloon is a balloon that derives its lift from heated air;

(3) The envelope is the enclosure in which the lifting means is contained;

(4) The basket is the container, suspended beneath the envelope, for the balloon occupants;

(5) The trapeze is a harness or is a seat consisting of a horizontal bar or platform suspended beneath the envelope for the balloon occupants; and

(6) The design maximum weight is the maximum total weight of the balloon, less the lifting gas or air.

[Doc. No. 1437, 29 FR 8258, July 1, 1964, as amended by Amdt. 31–3, 41 FR 55474, Dec. 20, 1976]

Subpart B—Flight Requirements

§31.12 Proof of compliance.

(a) Each requirement of this subpart must be met at each weight within the range of loading conditions for which certification is requested. This must be shown by—

(1) Tests upon a balloon of the type for which certification is requested or by calculations based on, and equal in accuracy to, the results of testing; and

(2) Systematic investigation of each weight if compliance cannot be reasonably inferred from the weights investigated.

(b) Except as provided in §31.17(b), allowable weight tolerances during flight testing are +5 percent and −10 percent.

[Amdt. 31–4, 45 FR 60179, Sept. 11, 1980]

§31.14 Weight limits.

(a) The range of weights over which the balloon may be safely operated must be established.

(b) *Maximum weight.* The maximum weight is the highest weight at which compliance with each applicable requirement of this part is shown. The maximum weight must be established so that it is not more than—

(1) The highest weight selected by the applicant;

(2) The design maximum weight which is the highest weight at which compliance with each applicable structural loading condition of this part is shown; or

(3) The highest weight at which compliance with each applicable flight requirement of this part is shown.

(c) The information established under paragraphs (a) and (b) of this section must be made available to the pilot in accordance with § 31.81.

[Amdt. 31–3, 41 FR 55474, Dec. 20, 1976]

§ 31.16 Empty weight.

The empty weight must be determined by weighing the balloon with installed equipment but without lifting gas or heater fuel.

[Amdt. 31–4, 45 FR 60179, Sept. 11, 1980]

§ 31.17 Performance: Climb.

(a) Each balloon must be capable of climbing at least 300 feet in the first minute after takeoff with a steady rate of climb. Compliance with the requirements of this section must be shown at each altitude and ambient temperature for which approval is sought.

(b) Compliance with the requirements of paragraph (a) of this section must be shown at the maximum weight with a weight tolerance of +5 percent.

[Amdt. 31–4, 45 FR 60179, Sept. 11, 1980]

§ 31.19 Performance: Uncontrolled descent.

(a) The following must be determined for the most critical uncontrolled descent that can result from any single failure of the heater assembly, fuel cell system, gas value system, or maneuvering vent system, or from any single tear in the balloon envelope between tear stoppers:

(1) The maximum vertical velocity attained.

(2) The altitude loss from the point of failure to the point at which maximum vertical velocity is attained.

(3) The altitude required to achieve level flight after corrective action is inititated, with the balloon descending at the maximum vertical velocity determined in paragraph (a)(1) of this section.

(b) Procedures must be established for landing at the maximum vertical velocity determined in paragraph (a)(1) of this section and for arresting that descent rate in accordance with paragraph (a)(3) of this section.

[Amdt. 31–4, 45 FR 60179, Sept. 11, 1980]

§ 31.20 Controllability.

The applicant must show that the balloon is safely controllable and maneuverable during takeoff, ascent, descent, and landing without requiring exceptional piloting skill.

[Amdt. 31–3, 41 FR 55474, Dec. 20, 1976]

Subpart C—Strength Requirements

§ 31.21 Loads.

Strength requirements are specified in terms of limit loads, that are the maximum load to be expected in service, and ultimate loads, that are limit loads multiplied by prescribed factors of safety. Unless otherwise specified, all prescribed loads are limit loads.

§ 31.23 Flight load factor.

In determining limit load, the limit flight load factor must be at least 1.4.

§ 31.25 Factor of safety.

(a) Except as specified in paragraphs (b) and (c) of this section, the factor of safety is 1.5.

(b) A factor of safety of at least five must be used in envelope design. A reduced factor of safety of at least two may be used if it is shown that the selected factor will preclude failure due to creep or instantaneous rupture from lack of rip stoppers. The selected factor must be applied to the more critical of the maximum operating pressure or envelope stress.

(c) A factor of safety of at least five must be used in the design of all fibrous or non-metallic parts of the rigging and related attachments of the envelope to basket, trapeze, or other means provided for carrying occupants.

The primary attachments of the envelope to the basket, trapeze, or other means provided for carrying occupants must be designed so that failure is extremely remote or so that any single failure will not jeopardize safety of flight.

(d) In applying factors of safety, the effect of temperature, and other operating characteristics, or both, that may affect strength of the balloon must be accounted for.

(e) For design purposes, an occupant weight of at least 170 pounds must be assumed.

[Doc. No. 1437, 29 FR 8258, July 1, 1964, as amended by Amdt. 31–2, 30 FR 3377, Mar. 13, 1965]

§31.27 Strength.

(a) The structure must be able to support limit loads without detrimental effect.

(b) The structure must be substantiated by test to be able to withstand the ultimate loads for at least three seconds without failure. For the envelope, a test of a representative part is acceptable, if the part tested is large enough to include critical seams, joints, and load attachment points and members.

(c) An ultimate free-fall drop test must be made of the basket, trapeze, or other place provided for occupants. The test must be made at design maximum weight on a horizontal surface, with the basket, trapeze, or other means provided for carrying occupants, striking the surface at angles of 0, 15, and 30 degrees. The weight may be distributed to simulate actual conditions. There must be no distortion or failure that is likely to cause serious injury to the occupants. A drop test height of 36 inches, or a drop test height that produces, upon impact, a velocity equal to the maximum vertical velocity determined in accordance with §31.19, whichever is higher, must be used.

[Doc. No. 1437, 29 FR 8258, July 1, 1964, as amended by Amdt. 31–4, 45 FR 60179, Sept. 11, 1980]

Subpart D—Design Construction

§31.31 General.

The suitability of each design detail or part that bears on safety must be established by tests or analysis.

§31.33 Materials.

(a) The suitability and durability of all materials must be established on the basis of experience or tests. Materials must conform to approved specifications that will ensure that they have the strength and other properties assumed in the design data.

(b) Material strength properties must be based on enough tests of material conforming to specifications so as to establish design values on a statistical basis.

§31.35 Fabrication methods.

The methods of fabrication used must produce a consistently sound structure. If a fabrication process requires close control to reach this objective, the process must be performed in accordance with an approved process specification.

§31.37 Fastenings.

Only approved bolts, pins, screws, and rivets may be used in the structure. Approved locking devices or methods must be used for all these bolts, pins, and screws, unless the installation is shown to be free from vibration. Self-locking nuts may not be used on bolts that are subject to rotation in service.

§31.39 Protection.

Each part of the balloon must be suitably protected against deterioration or loss of strength in service due to weathering, corrosion, or other causes.

§31.41 Inspection provisions.

There must be a means to allow close examination of each part that require repeated inspection and adjustment.

§ 31.43 Fitting factor.

(a) A fitting factor of at least 1.15 must be used in the analysis of each fitting the strength of which is not proven by limit and ultimate load tests in which the actual stress conditions are simulated in the fitting and surrounding structure. This factor applies to all parts of the fitting, the means of attachment, and the bearing on the members joined.

(b) Each part with an integral fitting must be treated as a fitting up to the point where the section properties become typical of the member.

(c) The fitting factor need not be used if the joint design is made in accordance with approved practices and is based on comprehensive test data.

§ 31.45 Fuel cells.

If fuel cells are used, the fuel cells, their attachments, and related supporting structure must be shown by tests to be capable of withstanding, without detrimental distortion or failure, any inertia loads to which the installation may be subjected, including the drop tests prescribed in § 31.27(c). In the tests, the fuel cells must be loaded to the weight and pressure equivalent to the full fuel quantity condition.

[Amdt. 31–3, 41 FR 55474, Dec. 20, 1976]

§ 31.46 Pressurized fuel systems.

For pressurized fuel systems, each element and its connecting fittings and lines must be tested to an ultimate pressure of at least twice the maximum pressure to which the system will be subjected in normal operation. No part of the system may fail or malfunction during the test. The test configuration must be representative of the normal fuel system installation and balloon configuration.

[Amdt. 31–3, 41 FR 55474, Dec. 20, 1976]

§ 31.47 Burners.

(a) If a burner is used to provide the lifting means, the system must be designed and installed so as not to create a fire hazard.

(b) There must be shielding to protect parts adjacent to the burner flame, and the occupants, from heat effects.

(c) There must be controls, instruments, or other equipment essential to the safe control and operation of the heater. They must be shown to be able to perform their intended functions during normal and emergency operation.

(d) The burner system (including the burner unit, controls, fuel lines, fuel cells, regulators, control valves, and other related elements) must be substantiated by an endurance test of at least 40 hours. Each element of the system must be installed and tested to simulate actual balloon installation and use.

(1) The test program for the main blast valve operation of the burner must include:

(i) Five hours at the maximum fuel pressure for which approval is sought, with a burn time for each one minute cycle of three to ten seconds. The burn time must be established so that each burner is subjected to the maximum thermal shock for temperature affected elements;

(ii) Seven and one-half hours at an intermediate fuel pressure, with a burn time for each one minute cycle of three to ten seconds. An intermediate fuel pressure is 40 to 60 percent of the range between the maximum fuel pressure referenced in paragraph (d)(1)(i) of this section and minimum fuel pressure referenced in paragraph (d)(1)(iii);

(iii) Six hours and fifteen minutes at the minimum fuel pressure for which approval is sought, with a burn time for each one minute cycle of three to ten seconds;

(iv) Fifteen minutes of operation on vapor, with a burn time for each one minute cycle of at least 30 seconds; and

(v) Fifteen hours of normal flight operation.

(2) The test program for the secondary or backup operation of the burner must include six hours of operation with a burn time for each five minute cycle of one minute at an intermediate fuel pressure.

(e) The test must also include at least three flameouts and restarts.

(f) Each element of the system must be serviceable at the end of the test.

[Doc. No. 1437, 29 FR 8258, July 1, 1964, as amended by Amdt. 31–2, 30 FR 3377, Mar. 13, 1965; Amdt. 31–7, 61 FR 18223, Apr. 24, 1996; 61 FR 20877, May 8, 1996]

§31.49 Control systems.

(a) Each control must operate easily, smoothly, and positively enough to allow proper performance of its functions. Controls must be arranged and identified to provide for convenience of operation and to prevent the possibility of confusion and subsequent inadvertent operation.

(b) Each control system and operating device must be designed and installed in a manner that will prevent jamming, chafing, or interference from passengers, cargo, or loose objects. Precaution must be taken to prevent foreign objects from jamming the controls. The elements of the control system must have design features or must be distinctly and permanently marked to minimize the possibility of incorrect assembly that could result in malfunctioning of the control system.

(c) Each balloon using a captive gas as the lifting means must have an automatic valve or appendix that is able to release gas automatically at the rate of at least three percent of the total volume per minute when the balloon is at its maximum operating pressure.

(d) Each hot air balloon must have a means to allow the controlled release of hot air during flight.

(e) Each hot air balloon must have a means to indicate the maximum envelope skin temperatures occurring during operation. The indicator must be readily visible to the pilot and marked to indicate the limiting safe temperature of the envelope material. If the markings are on the cover glass of the instrument, there must be provisions to maintain the correct alignment of the glass cover with the face of the dial.

[Doc. No. 1437, 29 FR 8258, July 1, 1964, as amended by Amdt. 31–2, 30 FR 3377, Mar. 13, 1965]

§31.51 Ballast.

Each captive gas balloon must have a means for the safe storage and con-trolled release of ballast. The ballast must consist of material that, if released during flight, is not hazardous to persons on the ground.

§31.53 Drag rope.

If a drag rope is used, the end that is released overboard must be stiffened to preclude the probability of the rope becoming entangled with trees, wires, or other objects on the ground.

§31.55 Deflation means.

There must be a means to allow emergency deflation of the envelope so as to allow a safe emergency landing. If a system other than a manual system is used, the reliability of the system used must be substantiated.

[Amdt. 31–2, 30 FR 3377, Mar. 13, 1965]

§31.57 Rip cords.

(a) If a rip cord is used for emergency deflation, it must be designed and installed to preclude entanglement.

(b) The force required to operate the rip cord may not be less than 25, or more than 75, pounds.

(c) The end of the rip cord to be operated by the pilot must be colored red.

(d) The rip cord must be long enough to allow an increase of at least 10 percent in the vertical dimension of the envelope.

§31.59 Trapeze, basket, or other means provided for occupants.

(a) The trapeze, basket, or other means provided for carrying occupants may not rotate independently of the envelope.

(b) Each projecting object on the trapeze, basket, or other means provided for carrying occupants, that could cause injury to the occupants, must be padded.

§31.61 Static discharge.

Unless shown not to be necessary for safety, there must be appropriate bonding means in the design of each balloon using flammable gas as a lifting means to ensure that the effects of static discharges will not create a hazard.

[Amdt. 31–2, 30 FR 3377, Mar. 13, 1965]

§ 31.63 Safety belts.

(a) There must be a safety belt, harness, or other restraining means for each occupant, unless the Administrator finds it unnecessary. If installed, the belt, harness, or other restraining means and its supporting structure must meet the strength requirements of Subpart C of this part.

(b) This section does not apply to balloons that incorporate a basket or gondola.

[Amdt. 31–2, 30 FR 3377, Mar. 13, 1965, as amended by Amdt. 31–3, 41 FR 55474, Dec. 20, 1976]

§ 31.65 Position lights.

(a) If position lights are installed, there must be one steady aviation white position light and one flashing aviation red (or flashing aviation white) position light with an effective flash frequency of at least 40, but not more than 100, cycles per minute.

(b) Each light must provide 360° horizontal coverage at the intensities prescribed in this paragraph. The following light intensities must be determined with the light source operating at a steady state and with all light covers and color filters in place and at the manufacturer's rated mimimum voltage. For the flashing aviation red light, the measured values must be adjusted to correspond to a red filter temperature of at least 130 °F:

(1) The intensities in the horizontal plane passing through the light unit must equal or exceed the following values:

Position light	Minimum intensity (candles)
Steady white	20
Flashing red or white	40

(2) The intensities in vertical planes must equal or exceed the following values. An intensity of one unit corresponds to the applicable horizontal plane intensity specified in paragraph (b)(1) of this section.

Angles above and below the horizontal in any vertical plane (degrees)	Minimum intensity (units)
0	1.00
0 to 5	0.90
5 to 10	0.80
10 to 15	0.70

Angles above and below the horizontal in any vertical plane (degrees)	Minimum intensity (units)
15 to 20	0.50
20 to 30	0.30
30 to 40	0.10
40 to 60	0.05

(c) The steady white light must be located not more than 20 feet below the basket, trapeze, or other means for carrying occupants. The flashing red or white light must be located not less than 7, nor more than 10, feet below the steady white light.

(d) There must be a means to retract and store the lights.

(e) Each position light color must have the applicable International Commission on Illumination chromaticity coordinates as follows:

(1) *Aviation red*—

y is not greater than 0.335; and z is not greater than 0.002.

(2) *Aviation white*—

x is not less than 0.300 and not greater than 0.540;

y is not less than $x-0.040$ or $y_o-0.010$, whichever is the smaller; and

y is not greater than $x+0.020$ nor $0.636-0.0400 x$;

Where y_o is the y coordinate of the Planckian radiator for the value of x considered.

[Doc. No. 1437, 29 FR 8258, July 1, 1964, as amended by Amdt. 31–1, 29 FR 14563, Oct. 24, 1964; Amdt. 31–4, 45 FR 60179, Sept. 11, 1980]

Subpart E—Equipment

§ 31.71 Function and installation.

(a) Each item of installed equipment must—

(1) Be of a kind and design appropriate to its intended function;

(2) Be permanently and legibly marked or, if the item is too small to mark, tagged as to its identification, function, or operating limitations, or any applicable combination of those factors;

(3) Be installed according to limitations specified for that equipment; and

(4) Function properly when installed.

(b) No item of installed equipment, when performing its function, may affect the function of any other equipment so as to create an unsafe condition.

(c) The equipment, systems, and installations must be designed to prevent hazards to the balloon in the event of a probable malfunction or failure.

[Amdt. 31–4, 45 FR 60180, Sept. 11, 1980]

Subpart F—Operating Limitations and Information

§ 31.81 General.

(a) The following information must be established:

(1) Each operating limitation, including the maximum weight determined under § 31.14.

(2) The normal and emergency procedures.

(3) Other information necessary for safe operation, including—

(i) The empty weight determined under § 31.16;

(ii) The rate of climb determined under § 31.17, and the procedures and conditions used to determine performance;

(iii) The maximum vertical velocity, the altitude drop required to attain that velocity, and altitude drop required to recover from a descent at that velocity, determined under § 31.19, and the procedures and conditions used to determine performance; and

(iv) Pertinent information peculiar to the balloon's operating characteristics.

(b) The information established in compliance with paragraph (a) of this section must be furnished by means of—

(1) A Balloon Flight Manual; or

(2) A placard on the balloon that is clearly visible to the pilot.

[Amdt. 31–4, 45 FR 60180, Sept. 11, 1980]

§ 31.82 Instructions for Continued Airworthiness.

The applicant must prepare Instructions for Continued Airworthiness in accordance with appendix A to this part that are acceptable to the Administrator. The instructions may be incomplete at type certification if a program exists to ensure their completion prior to delivery of the first balloon or issuance of a standard certificate of airworthiness, whichever occurs later.

[Amdt. 31–4, 45 FR 60180, Sept. 11, 1980]

§ 31.83 Conspicuity.

The exterior surface of the envelope must be of a contrasting color or colors so that it will be conspicuous during operation. However, multicolored banners or streamers are acceptable if it can be shown that they are large enough, and there are enough of them of contrasting color, to make the balloon conspicuous during flight.

§ 31.85 Required basic equipment.

In addition to any equipment required by this subchapter for a specific kind of operation, the following equipment is required:

(a) For all balloons:

(1) [Reserved]

(2) An altimeter.

(3) A rate of climb indicator.

(b) For hot air balloons:

(1) A fuel quantity gauge. If fuel cells are used, means must be incorporated to indicate to the crew the quantity of fuel in each cell during flight. The means must be calibrated in appropriate units or in percent of fuel cell capacity.

(2) An envelope temperature indicator.

(c) For captive gas balloons, a compass.

[Amdt. 31–2, 30 FR 3377, Mar. 13, 1965, as amended by Amdt. 31–3, 41 FR 55474, Dec. 20, 1976; Amdt. 31–4, 45 FR 60180, Sept. 11, 1980]

APPENDIX A TO PART 31—INSTRUCTIONS FOR CONTINUED AIRWORTHINESS

A31.1 GENERAL

(a) This appendix specifies requirements for the preparation of Instructions for Continued Airworthiness as required by § 31.82.

(b) The Instructions for Continued Airworthiness for each balloon must include the Instructions for Continued Airworthiness for all balloon parts required by this chapter and any required information relating to the interface of those parts with the balloon. If Instructions for Continued Airworthiness are not supplied by the part manufacturer for a balloon part, the Instructions for Continued Airworthiness for the balloon must include the information essential to the continued airworthiness of the balloon.

(c) The applicant must submit to the FAA a program to show how changes to the Instructions for Continued Airworthiness made by the applicant or by the manufacturers of balloon parts will be distributed.

A31.2 FORMAT

(a) The Instructions for Continued Airworthiness must be in the form of a manual or manuals as appropriate for the quantity of data to be provided.

(b) The format of the manual or manuals must provide for a practical arrangement.

A31.3 CONTENT

The contents of the manual or manuals must be prepared in the English language. The Instructions for Continued Airworthiness must contain the following information:

(a) Introduction information that includes an explanation of the balloon's features and data to the extent necessary for maintenance or preventive maintenance.

(b) A description of the balloon and its systems and installations.

(c) Basic control and operation information for the balloon and its components and systems.

(d) Servicing information that covers details regarding servicing of balloon components, including burner nozzles, fuel tanks, and valves during operations.

(e) Maintenance information for each part of the balloon and its envelope, controls, rigging, basket structure, fuel systems, instruments, and heater assembly that provides the recommended periods at which they should be cleaned, adjusted, tested, and lubricated, the applicable wear tolerances, and the degree of work recommended at these periods. However, the applicant may refer to an accessory, instrument, or equipment manufacturer as the source of this information if the applicant shows that the item has an exceptionally high degree of complexity requiring specialized maintenance techniques, test equipment, or expertise. The recommended overhaul periods and necessary cross references to the Airworthiness Limitations section of the manual must also be included. In addition, the applicant must include an inspection program that includes the frequency and extent of the inspections necessary to provide for the continued airworthiness of the balloon.

(f) Troubleshooting information describing probable malfunctions, how to recognize those malfunctions, and the remedial action for those malfunctions.

(g) Details of what, and how, to inspect after a hard landing.

(h) Instructions for storage preparation including any storage limits.

(i) Instructions for repair on the balloon envelope and its basket or trapeze.

A31.4 AIRWORTHINESS LIMITATIONS SECTION

The Instructions for Continued Airworthiness must contain a section titled Airworthiness Limitations that is segregated and clearly distinguishable from the rest of the document. This section must set forth each mandatory replacement time, structural inspection interval, and related structural inspection procedure, including envelope structural integrity, required for type certification. If the Instructions for Continued Airworthiness consist of multiple documents, the section required by this paragraph must be included in the principal manual. This section must contain a legible statement in a prominent location that reads: "The Airworthiness Limitations section is FAA approved and specifies maintenance required under §§ 43.16 and 91.403 of the Federal Aviation Regulations."

[Amdt. 31–4, 45 FR 60180, Sept. 11, 1980, as amended by Amdt. 31–5, 54 FR 34330, Aug. 18, 1989]

PART 33—AIRWORTHINESS STANDARDS: AIRCRAFT ENGINES

Subpart A—General

Subpart B—Design and Construction; General

Subpart C—Design and Construction; Reciprocating Aircraft Engines

Subpart D—Block Tests; Reciprocating Aircraft Engines

Subpart E—Design and Construction; Turbine Aircraft Engines

Subpart F—Block Tests; Turbine Aircraft Engines

AUTHORITY: 49 U.S.C. 106(g), 40113, 44701–44702, 44704.

SOURCE: Docket No. 3025, 29 FR 7453, June 10, 1964, unless otherwise noted.

NOTE: For miscellaneous amendments to cross references in this Part 33, see Amdt. 33–2, 31 FR 9211, July 6, 1966.

Subpart A—General

§ 33.1   Applicability.

(a) This part prescribes airworthiness standards for the issue of type certificates and changes to those certificates, for aircraft engines.

(b) Each person who applies under part 21 for such a certificate or change must show compliance with the applicable requirements of this part and the applicable requirements of part 34 of this chapter.

[Amdt. 33–7, 41 FR 55474, Dec. 20, 1976, as amended by Amdt. 33–14, 55 FR 32861, Aug. 10, 1990]

§ 33.3   General.

Each applicant must show that the aircraft engine concerned meets the applicable requirements of this part.

§ 33.4   Instructions for Continued Airworthiness.

The applicant must prepare Instructions for Continued Airworthiness in accordance with appendix A to this part that are acceptable to the Administrator. The instructions may be incomplete at type certification if a program exists to ensure their completion prior to delivery of the first aircraft with the engine installed, or upon issuance of a standard certificate of airworthiness for the aircraft with the engine installed, whichever occurs later.

[Amdt. 33–9, 45 FR 60181, Sept. 11, 1980]

§ 33.5   Instruction manual for installing and operating the engine.

Each applicant must prepare and make available to the Administrator prior to the issuance of the type certificate, and to the owner at the time of delivery of the engine, approved instructions for installing and operating the engine. The instructions must include at least the following:

(a) *Installation instructions.* (1) The location of engine mounting attachments, the method of attaching the engine to the aircraft, and the maximum allowable load for the mounting attachments and related structure.

(2) The location and description of engine connections to be attached to accessories, pipes, wires, cables, ducts, and cowling.

(3) An outline drawing of the engine including overall dimensions.

(b) *Operation instructions.* (1) The operating limitations established by the Administrator.

(2) The power or thrust ratings and procedures for correcting for nonstandard atmosphere.

(3) The recommended procedures, under normal and extreme ambient conditions for—

(i) Starting;

(ii) Operating on the ground; and

(iii) Operating during flight.

[Amdt. 33–6, 39 FR 35463, Oct. 1, 1974, as amended by Amdt. 33–9, 45 FR 60181, Sept. 11, 1980]

§ 33.7 **Engine ratings and operating limitations.**

(a) Engine ratings and operating limitations are established by the Administrator and included in the engine certificate data sheet specified in § 21.41 of this chapter, including ratings and limitations based on the operating conditions and information specified in this section, as applicable, and any other information found necessary for safe operation of the engine.

(b) For reciprocating engines, ratings and operating limitations are established relating to the following:

(1) Horsepower or torque, r.p.m., manifold pressure, and time at critical pressure altitude and sea level pressure altitude for—

(i) Rated maximum continuous power (relating to unsupercharged operation or to operation in each supercharger mode as applicable); and

(ii) Rated takeoff power (relating to unsupercharged operation or to operation in each supercharger mode as applicable).

(2) Fuel grade or specification.

(3) Oil grade or specification.

(4) Temperature of the—

(i) Cylinder;

(ii) Oil at the oil inlet; and

(iii) Turbosupercharger turbine wheel inlet gas.

(5) Pressure of—

(i) Fuel at the fuel inlet; and

(ii) Oil at the main oil gallery.

(6) Accessory drive torque and overhang moment.

(7) Component life.

(8) Turbosupercharger turbine wheel r.p.m.

(c) For turbine engines, ratings and operating limitations are established relating to the following:

(1) Horsepower, torque, or thrust, r.p.m., gas temperature, and time for—

(i) Rated maximum continuous power or thrust (augmented);

(ii) Rated maximum continuous power or thrust (unaugmented);

(iii) Rated takeoff power or thrust (augmented);

(iv) Rated takeoff power or thrust (unaugmented);

(v) Rated 30-minute OEI power;

(vi) Rated 2½-minute OEI power;

(vii) Rated continuous OEI power; and

(viii) Rated 2-minute OEI Power;

(ix) Rated 30-second OEI power; and

(x) Auxiliary power unit (APU) mode of operation.

(2) Fuel designation or specification.

(3) Oil grade or specification.

(4) Hydraulic fluid specification.

(5) Temperature of—

(i) Oil at a location specified by the applicant;

(ii) Induction air at the inlet face of a supersonic engine, including steady state operation and transient overtemperature and time allowed;

(iii) Hydraulic fluid of a supersonic engine;

(iv) Fuel at a location specified by the applicant; and

(v) External surfaces of the engine, if specified by the applicant.

(6) Pressure of—

(i) Fuel at the fuel inlet;

(ii) Oil at a location specified by the applicant;

(iii) Induction air at the inlet face of a supersonic engine, including steady state operation and transient overpressure and time allowed; and

(iv) Hydraulic fluid.

(7) Accessory drive torque and overhang moment.

(8) Component life.

(9) Fuel filtration.

(10) Oil filtration.

(11) Bleed air.

(12) The number of start-stop stress cycles approved for each rotor disc and spacer.

(13) Inlet air distortion at the engine inlet.

(14) Transient rotor shaft overspeed r.p.m., and number of overspeed occurrences.

(15) Transient gas overtemperature, and number of overtemperature occurrences.

(16) For engines to be used in supersonic aircraft, engine rotor windmilling rotational r.p.m.

[Amdt. 33–6, 39 FR 35463, Oct. 1, 1974, as amended by Amdt. 33–10, 49 FR 6850, Feb. 23, 1984; Amdt. 33–11, 51 FR 10346, Mar. 25, 1986; Amdt. 33–12, 53 FR 34220, Sept. 2, 1988; Amdt. 33–18, 61 FR 31328, June 19, 1996]

§ 33.8 Selection of engine power and thrust ratings.

(a) Requested engine power and thrust ratings must be selected by the applicant.

(b) Each selected rating must be for the lowest power or thrust that all engines of the same type may be expected to produce under the conditions used to determine that rating.

[Amdt. 33–3, 32 FR 3736, Mar. 4, 1967]

Subpart B—Design and Construction; General

§ 33.11 Applicability.

This subpart prescribes the general design and construction requirements for reciprocating and turbine aircraft engines.

§ 33.13 [Reserved]

§ 33.14 Start-stop cyclic stress (low-cycle fatigue).

By a procedure approved by the FAA, operating limitations must be established which specify the maximum allowable number of start-stop stress cycles for each rotor structural part (such as discs, spacers, hubs, and shafts of the compressors and turbines), the failure of which could produce a hazard to the aircraft. A start-stop stress cycle consists of a flight cycle profile or an equivalent representation of engine usage. It includes starting the engine, accelerating to maximum rated power or thrust, decelerating, and stopping. For each cycle, the rotor structural parts must reach stabilized temperature during engine operation at a maximum rate power or thrust and after engine shutdown, unless it is shown that the parts undergo the same stress range without temperature stabilization.

[Amdt. 33–10, 49 FR 6850, Feb. 23, 1984]

§ 33.15 Materials.

The suitability and durability of materials used in the engine must—

(a) Be established on the basis of experience or tests; and

(b) Conform to approved specifications (such as industry or military specifications) that ensure their having the strength and other properties assumed in the design data.

Secs. 313(a), 601, and 603, 72 Stat. 759, 775, 49 U.S.C. 1354(a), 1421, and 1423; sec. 6(c), 49 U.S.C. 1655(c))

[Amdt. 33–8, 42 FR 15047, Mar. 17, 1977, as amended by Amdt. 33–10, 49 FR 6850, Feb. 23, 1984]

§ 33.17 Fire prevention.

(a) The design and construction of the engine and the materials used must minimize the probability of the occurrence and spread of fire. In addition, the design and construction of turbine engines must minimize the probability of the occurrence of an internal fire that could result in structural failure, overheating, or other hazardous conditions.

(b) Except as provided in paragraphs (c), (d), and (e) of this section, each external line, fitting, and other component, which contains or conveys flammable fluid must be fire resistant. Components must be shielded or located to safeguard against the ignition of leaking flammable fluid.

(c) Flammable fluid tanks and supports which are part of and attached to the engine must be fireproof or be enclosed by a fireproof shield unless damage by fire to any non-fireproof part will not cause leakage or spillage of flammable fluid. For a reciprocating engine having an integral oil sump of less than 25-quart capacity, the oil sump need not be fireproof nor be enclosed by fireproof shield.

(d) For turbine engines type certificated for use in supersonic aircraft, each external component which conveys or contains flammable fluid must be fireproof.

(e) Unwanted accumulation of flammable fluid and vapor must be prevented by draining and venting.

(Secs. 313(a), 601, and 603, 72 Stat. 759, 775, 49 U.S.C. 1354(a), 1421, and 1423; sec. 6(c), 49 U.S.C. 1655(c))

[Amdt. 33–6, 39 FR 35464, Oct. 1, 1974, as amended by Amdt. 33–8, 42 FR 15047, Mar. 17, 1977; Amdt. 33–10, 49 FR 6850, Feb. 23, 1984]

§ 33.19   Durability.

(a) Engine design and construction must minimize the development of an unsafe condition of the engine between overhaul periods. The design of the compressor and turbine rotor cases must provide for the containment of damage from rotor blade failure. Energy levels and trajectories of fragments resulting from rotor blade failure that lie outside the compressor and turbine rotor cases must be defined.

(b) Each component of the propeller blade pitch control system which is a part of the engine type design must meet the requirements of § 35.42 of this chapter.

[Doc. No. 3025, 29 FR 7453, June 10, 1964, as amended by Amdt. 33–9, 45 FR 60181, Sept. 11, 1980; Amdt. 33–10, 49 FR 6851, Feb. 23, 1984]

§ 33.21   Engine cooling.

Engine design and construction must provide the necessary cooling under conditions in which the airplane is expected to operate.

§ 33.23   Engine mounting attachments and structure.

(a) The maximum allowable limit and ultimate loads for engine mounting attachments and related engine structure must be specified.

(b) The engine mounting attachments and related engine structure must be able to withstand—

(1) The specified limit loads without permanent deformation; and

(2) The specified ultimate loads without failure, but may exhibit permanent deformation.

[Amdt. 33–10, 49 FR 6851, Feb. 23, 1984]

§ 33.25   Accessory attachments.

The engine must operate properly with the accessory drive and mounting attachments loaded. Each engine accessory drive and mounting attachment must include provisions for sealing to prevent contamination of, or unacceptable leakage from, the engine interior. A drive and mounting attachment requiring lubrication for external drive splines, or coupling by engine oil, must include provisions for sealing to prevent unacceptable loss of oil and to prevent contamination from sources outside the chamber enclosing the drive connection. The design of the engine must allow for the examination, adjustment, or removal of each accessory required for engine operation.

[Amdt. 33–10, 49 FR 6851, Feb. 23, 1984]

§ 33.27   Turbine, compressor, fan, and turbosupercharger rotors.

(a) Turbine, compressor, fan, and turbosupercharger rotors must have sufficient strength to withstand the test conditions specified in paragraph (c) of this section.

(b) The design and functioning of engine control devices, systems, and instruments must give reasonable assurance that those engine operating limitations that affect turbine, compressor, fan, and turbosupercharger rotor structural integrity will not be exceeded in service.

(c) The most critically stressed rotor component (except blades) of each turbine, compressor, and fan, including integral drum rotors and centrifugal compressors in an engine or turbosupercharger, as determined by analysis or other acceptable means, must be tested for a period of 5 minutes—

(1) At its maximum operating temperature, except as provided in paragraph (c)(2)(iv) of this section; and

(2) At the highest speed of the following, as applicable:

(i) 120 percent of its maximum permissible r.p.m. if tested on a rig and equipped with blades or blade weights.

(ii) 115 percent of its maximum permissible r.p.m. if tested on an engine.

(iii) 115 percent of its maximum permissible r.p.m. if tested on turbosupercharger driven by a hot gas supply from a special burner rig.

(iv) 120 percent of the r.p.m. at which, while cold spinning, it is subject to operating stresses that are equivalent to those induced at the maximum operating temperature and maximum permissible r.p.m.

(v) 105 percent of the highest speed that would result from failure of the most critical component or system in a representative installation of the engine.

(vi) The highest speed that would result from the failure of any component or system in a representative installation of the engine, in combination with any failure of a component or system that would not normally be detected during a routine preflight check or during normal flight operation.

Following the test, each rotor must be within approved dimensional limits for an overspeed condition and may not be cracked.

[Amdt. 33–10, 49 FR 6851, Feb. 23, 1984]

§ 33.28 Electrical and electronic engine control systems.

Each control system which relies on electrical and electronic means for normal operation must:

(a) Have the control system description, the percent of available power or trust controlled in both normal operation and failure conditions, and the range of control of other controlled functions, specified in the instruction manual required by § 33.5 for the engine;

(b) Be designed and constructed so that any failure of aircraft-supplied power or data will not result in an unacceptable change in power or thrust, or prevent continued safe operation of the engine;

(c) Be designed and constructed so that no single failure or malfunction, or probable combination of failures of electrical or electronic components of the control system, results in an unsafe condition;

(d) Have environmental limits, including transients caused by lightning strikes, specified in the instruction manual; and

(e) Have all associated software designed and implemented to prevent errors that would result in an unacceptable loss of power or thrust, or other unsafe condition, and have the method used to design and implement the software approved by the Administrator.

[Doc. No. 24466, 58 FR 29095, May 18, 1993]

§ 33.29 Instrument connection.

(a) Unless it is constructed to prevent its connection to an incorrect instrument, each connection provided for powerplant instruments required by aircraft airworthiness regulations or necessary to insure operation of the engine in compliance with any engine limitation must be marked to identify it with its corresponding instrument.

(b) A connection must be provided on each turbojet engine for an indicator system to indicate rotor system unbalance.

(c) Each rotorcraft turbine engine having a 30-second OEI rating and a 2-minute OEI rating must have a provision for a means to:

(1) Alert the pilot when the engine is at the 30-second OEI and the 2-minute OEI power levels, when the event begins, and when the time interval expires;

(2) Determine, in a positive manner, that the engine has been operated at each rating; and

(3) Automatically record each usage and duration of power at each rating.

[Amdt. 33–5, 39 FR 1831, Jan. 15, 1974, as amended by Amdt. 33–6, 39 FR 35465, Oct. 1, 1974; Amdt. 33–18, 61 FR 31328, June 19, 1996]

Subpart C—Design and Construction; Reciprocating Aircraft Engines

§ 33.31 Applicability.

This subpart prescribes additional design and construction requirements for reciprocating aircraft engines.

§ 33.33 Vibration.

The engine must be designed and constructed to function throughout its normal operating range of crankshaft rotational speeds and engine powers without inducing excessive stress in any of the engine parts because of vibration and without imparting excessive vibration forces to the aircraft structure.

§ 33.35 Fuel and induction system.

(a) The fuel system of the engine must be designed and constructed to supply an appropriate mixture of fuel to the cylinders throughout the complete operating range of the engine under all flight and atmospheric conditions.

(b) The intake passages of the engine through which air or fuel in combination with air passes for combustion purposes must be designed and constructed to minimize the danger of ice accretion in those passages. The engine must be designed and constructed to permit the use of a means for ice prevention.

(c) The type and degree of fuel filtering necessary for protection of the engine fuel system against foreign particles in the fuel must be specified. The applicant must show that foreign particles passing through the prescribed filtering means will not critically impair engine fuel system functioning.

(d) Each passage in the induction system that conducts a mixture of fuel and air must be self-draining, to prevent a liquid lock in the cylinders, in all attitudes that the applicant establishes as those the engine can have when the aircraft in which it is installed is in the static ground attitude.

(e) If provided as part of the engine, the applicant must show for each fluid injection (other than fuel) system and its controls that the flow of the injected fluid is adequately controlled.

[Doc. No. 3025, 29 FR 7453, June 10, 1964, as amended by Amdt. 33–10, 49 FR 6851, Feb. 23, 1984]

§ 33.37 Ignition system.

Each spark ignition engine must have a dual ignition system with at least two spark plugs for each cylinder and two separate electric circuits with separate sources of electrical energy, or have an ignition system of equivalent in-flight reliability.

§ 33.39 Lubrication system.

(a) The lubrication system of the engine must be designed and constructed so that it will function properly in all flight attitudes and atmospheric conditions in which the airplane is expected to operate. In wet sump engines, this requirement must be met when only one-half of the maximum lubricant supply is in the engine.

(b) The lubrication system of the engine must be designed and constructed to allow installing a means of cooling the lubricant.

(c) The crankcase must be vented to the atmosphere to preclude leakage of oil from excessive pressure in the crankcase.

Subpart D—Block Tests; Reciprocating Aircraft Engines

§ 33.41 Applicability.

This subpart prescribes the block tests and inspections for reciprocating aircraft engines.

§ 33.42 General.

Before each endurance test required by this subpart, the adjustment setting and functioning characteristic of each component having an adjustment setting and a functioning characteristic that can be established independent of installation on the engine must be established and recorded.

[Amdt. 33–6, 39 FR 35465, Oct. 1, 1974]

§ 33.43 Vibration test.

(a) Each engine must undergo a vibration survey to establish the torsional and bending vibration characteristics of the crankshaft and the propeller shaft or other output shaft, over the range of crankshaft speed and engine power, under steady state and transient conditions, from idling speed to either 110 percent of the desired maximum continuous speed rating or 103 percent of the maximum desired takeoff speed rating, whichever is higher. The survey must be conducted using, for airplane engines, the same configuration of the propeller type which is used for the endurance test, and using, for other engines, the same configuration of the loading device type which is used for the endurance test.

(b) The torsional and bending vibration stresses of the crankshaft and the propeller shaft or other output shaft may not exceed the endurance limit stress of the material from which the shaft is made. If the maximum stress

740

in the shaft cannot be shown to be below the endurance limit by measurement, the vibration frequency and amplitude must be measured. The peak amplitude must be shown to produce a stress below the endurance limit; if not, the engine must be run at the condition producing the peak amplitude until, for steel shafts, 10 million stress reversals have been sustained without fatigue failure and, for other shafts, until it is shown that fatigue will not occur within the endurance limit stress of the material.

(c) Each accessory drive and mounting attachment must be loaded, with the loads imposed by each accessory used only for an aircraft service being the limit load specified by the applicant for the drive or attachment point.

(d) The vibration survey described in paragraph (a) of this section must be repeated with that cylinder not firing which has the most adverse vibration effect, in order to establish the conditions under which the engine can be operated safely in that abnormal state. However, for this vibration survey, the engine speed range need only extend from idle to the maximum desired takeoff speed, and compliance with paragraph (b) of this section need not be shown.

[Amdt. 33-6, 39 FR 35465, Oct. 1, 1974, as amended by Amdt. 33-10, 49 FR 6851, Feb. 23, 1984]

§ 33.45 Calibration tests.

(a) Each engine must be subjected to the calibration tests necessary to establish its power characteristics and the conditions for the endurance test specified in § 33.49. The results of the power characteristics calibration tests form the basis for establishing the characteristics of the engine over its entire operating range of crankshaft rotational speeds, manifold pressures, fuel/air mixture settings, and altitudes. Power ratings are based upon standard atmospheric conditions with only those accessories installed which are essential for engine functioning.

(b) A power check at sea level conditions must be accomplished on the endurance test engine after the endurance test. Any change in power characteristics which occurs during the endurance test must be determined.

Measurements taken during the final portion of the endurance test may be used in showing compliance with the requirements of this paragraph.

[Doc. No. 3025, 29 FR 7453, June 10, 1964, as amended by Amdt. 33-6, 39 FR 35465, Oct. 1, 1974]

§ 33.47 Detonation test.

Each engine must be tested to establish that the engine can function without detonation throughout its range of intended conditions of operation.

§ 33.49 Endurance test.

(a) *General.* Each engine must be subjected to an endurance test that includes a total of 150 hours of operation (except as provided in paragraph (e)(1)(iii) of this section) and, depending upon the type and contemplated use of the engine, consists of one of the series of runs specified in paragraphs (b) through (e) of this section, as applicable. The runs must be made in the order found appropriate by the Administrator for the particular engine being tested. During the endurance test the engine power and the crankshaft rotational speed must be kept within ±3 percent of the rated values. During the runs at rated takeoff power and for at least 35 hours at rated maximum continuous power, one cylinder must be operated at not less than the limiting temperature, the other cylinders must be operated at a temperature not lower than 50 degrees F. below the limiting temperature, and the oil inlet temperature must be maintained within ±10 degrees F. of the limiting temperature. An engine that is equipped with a propeller shaft must be fitted for the endurance test with a propeller that thrust-loads the engine to the maximum thrust which the engine is designed to resist at each applicable operating condition specified in this section. Each accessory drive and mounting attachment must be loaded. During operation at rated takeoff power and rated maximum continuous power, the load imposed by each accessory used only for an aircraft service must be the limit load specified by the applicant for the engine drive or attachment point.

(b) *Unsupercharged engines and engines incorporating a gear-driven single-*

741

speed supercharger. For engines not incorporating a supercharger and for engines incorporating a gear-driven single-speed supercharger the applicant must conduct the following runs:

(1) A 30-hour run consisting of alternate periods of 5 minutes at rated takeoff power with takeoff speed, and 5 minutes at maximum best economy cruising power or maximum recommended cruising power.

(2) A 20-hour run consisting of alternate periods of 1½ hours at rated maximum continuous power with maximum continuous speed, and ½ hour at 75 percent rated maximum continuous power and 91 percent maximum continuous speed.

(3) A 20-hour run consisting of alternate periods of 1½ hours at rated maximum continuous power with maximum continuous speed, and ½ hour at 70 percent rated maximum continuous power and 89 percent maximum continuous speed.

(4) A 20-hour run consisting of alternate periods of 1½ hours at rated maximum continuous power with maximum continuous speed, and ½ hour at 65 percent rated maximum continuous power and 87 percent maximum continuous speed.

(5) A 20-hour run consisting of alternate periods of 1½ hours at rated maximum continuous power with maximum continuous speed, and ½ hour at 60 percent rated maximum continuous power and 84.5 percent maximum continuous speed.

(6) A 20-hour run consisting of alternate periods of 1½ hours at rated maximum continuous power with maximum continuous speed, and ½ hour at 50 percent rated maximum continuous power and 79.5 percent maximum continuous speed.

(7) A 20-hour run consisting of alternate periods of 2½ hours at rated maximum continuous power with maximum continuous speed, and 2½ hours at maximum best economy cruising power or at maximum recommended cruising power.

(c) *Engines incorporating a gear-driven two-speed supercharger.* For engines incorporating a gear-driven two-speed supercharger the applicant must conduct the following runs:

(1) A 30-hour run consisting of alternate periods in the lower gear ratio of 5 minutes at rated takeoff power with takeoff speed, and 5 minutes at maximum best economy cruising power or at maximum recommended cruising power. If a takeoff power rating is desired in the higher gear ratio, 15 hours of the 30-hour run must be made in the higher gear ratio in alternate periods of 5 minutes at the observed horsepower obtainable with the takeoff critical altitude manifold pressure and takeoff speed, and 5 minutes at 70 percent high ratio rated maximum continuous power and 89 percent high ratio maximum continuous speed.

(2) A 15-hour run consisting of alternate periods in the lower gear ratio of 1 hour at rated maximum continuous power with maximum continuous speed, and ½ hour at 75 percent rated maximum continuous power and 91 percent maximum continuous speed.

(3) A 15-hour run consisting of alternate periods in the lower gear ratio of 1 hour at rated maximum continuous power with maximum continuous speed, and ½ hour at 70 percent rated maximum continuous power and 89 percent maximum continuous speed.

(4) A 30-hour run in the higher gear ratio at rated maximum continuous power with maximum continuous speed.

(5) A 5-hour run consisting of alternate periods of 5 minutes in each of the supercharger gear ratios. The first 5 minutes of the test must be made at maximum continuous speed in the higher gear ratio and the observed horsepower obtainable with 90 percent of maximum continuous manifold pressure in the higher gear ratio under sea level conditions. The condition for operation for the alternate 5 minutes in the lower gear ratio must be that obtained by shifting to the lower gear ratio at constant speed.

(6) A 10-hour run consisting of alternate periods in the lower gear ratio of 1 hour at rated maximum continuous power with maximum continuous speed, and 1 hour at 65 percent rated maximum continuous power and 87 percent maximum continuous speed.

(7) A 10-hour run consisting of alternate periods in the lower gear ratio of 1 hour at rated maximum continuous

power with maximum continuous speed, and 1 hour at 60 percent rated maximum continuous power and 84.5 percent maximum continuous speed.

(8) A 10-hour run consisting of alternate periods in the lower gear ratio of 1 hour at rated maximum continuous power with maximum continuous speed, and 1 hour at 50 percent rated maximum continuous power and 79.5 percent maximum continuous speed.

(9) A 20-hour run consisting of alternate periods in the lower gear ratio of 2 hours at rated maximum continuous power with maximum continuous speed, and 2 hours at maximum best economy cruising power and speed or at maximum recommended cruising power.

(10) A 5-hour run in the lower gear ratio at maximum best economy cruising power and speed or at maximum recommended cruising power and speed.

Where simulated altitude test equipment is not available when operating in the higher gear ratio, the runs may be made at the observed horsepower obtained with the critical altitude manifold pressure or specified percentages thereof, and the fuel-air mixtures may be adjusted to be rich enough to suppress detonation.

(d) *Helicopter engines.* To be eligible for use on a helicopter each engine must either comply with paragraphs (a) through (j) of §29.923 of this chapter, or must undergo the following series of runs:

(1) A 35-hour run consisting of alternate periods of 30 minutes each at rated takeoff power with takeoff speed, and at rated maximum continuous power with maximum continuous speed.

(2) A 25-hour run consisting of alternate periods of 2½ hours each at rated maximum continuous power with maximum continuous speed, and at 70 percent rated maximum continuous power with maximum continuous speed.

(3) A 25-hour run consisting of alternate periods of 2½ hours each at rated maximum continuous power with maximum continuous speed, and at 70 percent rated maximum continuous power with 80 to 90 percent maximum continuous speed.

(4) A 25-hour run consisting of alternate periods of 2½ hours each at 30 percent rated maximum continuous power with takeoff speed, and at 30 percent rated maximum continuous power with 80 to 90 percent maximum continuous speed.

(5) A 25-hour run consisting of alternate periods of 2½ hours each at 80 percent rated maximum continuous power with takeoff speed, and at either rated maximum continuous power with 110 percent maximum continuous speed or at rated takeoff power with 103 percent takeoff speed, whichever results in the greater speed.

(6) A 15-hour run at 105 percent rated maximum continuous power with 105 percent maximum continuous speed or at full throttle and corresponding speed at standard sea level carburetor entrance pressure, if 105 percent of the rated maximum continuous power is not exceeded.

(e) *Turbosupercharged engines.* For engines incorporating a turbosupercharger the following apply except that altitude testing may be simulated provided the applicant shows that the engine and supercharger are being subjected to mechanical loads and operating temperatures no less severe than if run at actual altitude conditions:

(1) For engines used in airplanes the applicant must conduct the runs specified in paragraph (b) of this section, except—

(i) The entire run specified in paragraph (b)(1) of this section must be made at sea level altitude pressure;

(ii) The portions of the runs specified in paragraphs (b)(2) through (7) of this section at rated maximum continuous power must be made at critical altitude pressure, and the portions of the runs at other power must be made at 8,000 feet altitude pressure; and

(iii) The turbosupercharger used during the 150-hour endurance test must be run on the bench for an additional 50 hours at the limiting turbine wheel inlet gas temperature and rotational speed for rated maximum continuous power operation unless the limiting temperature and speed are maintained during 50 hours of the rated maximum continuous power operation.

(2) For engines used in helicopters the applicant must conduct the runs specified in paragraph (d) of this section, except—

(i) The entire run specified in paragraph (d)(1) of this section must be made at critical altitude pressure;

(ii) The portions of the runs specified in paragraphs (d)(2) and (3) of this section at rated maximum continuous power must be made at critical altitude pressure and the portions of the runs at other power must be made at 8,000 feet altitude pressure;

(iii) The entire run specified in paragraph (d)(4) of this section must be made at 8,000 feet altitude pressure;

(iv) The portion of the runs specified in paragraph (d)(5) of this section at 80 percent of rated maximum continuous power must be made at 8,000 feet altitude pressure and the portions of the runs at other power must be made at critical altitude pressure;

(v) The entire run specified in paragraph (d)(6) of this section must be made at critical altitude pressure; and

(vi) The turbosupercharger used during the endurance test must be run on the bench for 50 hours at the limiting turbine wheel inlet gas temperature and rotational speed for rated maximum continuous power operation unless the limiting temperature and speed are maintained during 50 hours of the rated maximum continuous power operation.

[Amdt. 33–3, 32 FR 3736, Mar. 4, 1967, as amended by Amdt. 33–6, 39 FR 35465, Oct. 1, 1974; Amdt. 33–10, 49 FR 6851, Feb. 23, 1984]

§ 33.51 Operation test.

The operation test must include the testing found necessary by the Administrator to demonstrate backfire characteristics, starting, idling, acceleration, overspeeding, functioning of propeller and ignition, and any other operational characteristic of the engine. If the engine incorporates a multispeed supercharger drive, the design and construction must allow the supercharger to be shifted from operation at the lower speed ratio to the higher and the power appropriate to the manifold pressure and speed settings for rated maximum continuous power at the

higher supercharger speed ratio must be obtainable within five seconds.

[Doc. No. 3025, 29 FR 7453, June 10, 1964, as amended by Amdt. 33–3, 32 FR 3737, Mar. 4, 1967]

§ 33.53 Engine component tests.

(a) For each engine that cannot be adequately substantiated by endurance testing in accordance with § 33.49, the applicant must conduct additional tests to establish that components are able to function reliably in all normally anticipated flight and atmospheric conditions.

(b) Temperature limits must be established for each component that requires temperature controlling provisions in the aircraft installation to assure satisfactory functioning, reliability, and durability.

§ 33.55 Teardown inspection.

After completing the endurance test—

(a) Each engine must be completely disassembled;

(b) Each component having an adjustment setting and a functioning characteristic that can be established independent of installation on the engine must retain each setting and functioning characteristic within the limits that were established and recorded at the beginning of the test; and

(c) Each engine component must conform to the type design and be eligible for incorporation into an engine for continued operation, in accordance with information submitted in compliance with § 33.4.

[Amdt. 33–6, 39 FR 35466, Oct. 1, 1974, as amended by Amdt. 33–9, 45 FR 60181, Sept. 11, 1980]

§ 33.57 General conduct of block tests.

(a) The applicant may, in conducting the block tests, use separate engines of identical design and construction in the vibration, calibration, detonation, endurance, and operation tests, except that, if a separate engine is used for the endurance test it must be subjected to a calibration check before starting the endurance test.

(b) The applicant may service and make minor repairs to the engine during the block tests in accordance with the service and maintenance instructions submitted in compliance with §33.4. If the frequency of the service is excessive, or the number of stops due to engine malfunction is excessive, or a major repair, or replacement of a part is found necessary during the block tests or as the result of findings from the teardown inspection, the engine or its parts may be subjected to any additional test the Administrator finds necessary.

(c) Each applicant must furnish all testing facilities, including equipment and competent personnel, to conduct the block tests.

[Doc. No. 3025, 29 FR 7453, June 10, 1964, as amended by Amdt. 33–6, 39 FR 35466, Oct. 1, 1974; Amdt. 33–9, 45 FR 60181, Sept. 11, 1980]

Subpart E—Design and Construction; Turbine Aircraft Engines

§33.61 Applicability.

This subpart prescribes additional design and construction requirements for turbine aircraft engines.

§33.62 Stress analysis.

A stress analysis must be performed on each turbine engine showing the design safety margin of each turbine engine rotor, spacer, and rotor shaft.

[Amdt. 33–6, 39 FR 35466, Oct. 1, 1974]

§33.63 Vibration.

Each engine must be designed and constructed to function throughout its declared flight envelope and operating range of rotational speeds and power/thrust, without inducing excessive stress in any engine part because of vibration and without imparting excessive vibration forces to the aircraft structure.

[Doc. No. 28107, 61 FR 28433, June 4, 1996]

§33.65 Surge and stall characteristics.

When the engine is operated in accordance with operating instructions required by §33.5(b), starting, a change of power or thrust, power or thrust augmentation, limiting inlet air distortion, or inlet air temperature may not cause surge or stall to the extent that flameout, structural failure, overtemperature, or failure of the engine to recover power or thrust will occur at any point in the operating envelope.

[Amdt. 33–6, 39 FR 35466, Oct. 1, 1974]

§33.66 Bleed air system.

The engine must supply bleed air without adverse effect on the engine, excluding reduced thrust or power output, at all conditions up to the discharge flow conditions established as a limitation under §33.7(c)(11). If bleed air used for engine anti-icing can be controlled, provision must be made for a means to indicate the functioning of the engine ice protection system.

[Amdt. 33–10, 49 FR 6851, Feb. 23, 1984]

§33.67 Fuel system.

(a) With fuel supplied to the engine at the flow and pressure specified by the applicant, the engine must function properly under each operating condition required by this part. Each fuel control adjusting means that may not be manipulated while the fuel control device is mounted on the engine must be secured by a locking device and sealed, or otherwise be inaccessible. All other fuel control adjusting means must be accessible and marked to indicate the function of the adjustment unless the function is obvious.

(b) There must be a fuel strainer or filter between the engine fuel inlet opening and the inlet of either the fuel metering device or the engine-driven positive displacement pump whichever is nearer the engine fuel inlet. In addition, the following provisions apply to each strainer or filter required by this paragraph (b):

(1) It must be accessible for draining and cleaning and must incorporate a screen or element that is easily removable.

(2) It must have a sediment trap and drain except that it need not have a drain if the strainer or filter is easily removable for drain purposes.

(3) It must be mounted so that its weight is not supported by the connecting lines or by the inlet or outlet connections of the strainer or filter, unless adequate strength margins under all loading conditions are provided in the lines and connections.

(4) It must have the type and degree of fuel filtering specified as necessary

for protection of the engine fuel system against foreign particles in the fuel. The applicant must show:

(i) That foreign particles passing through the specified filtering means do not impair the engine fuel system functioning; and

(ii) That the fuel system is capable of sustained operation throughout its flow and pressure range with the fuel initially saturated with water at 80 °F (27 °C) and having 0.025 fluid ounces per gallon (0.20 milliliters per liter) of free water added and cooled to the most critical condition for icing likely to be encountered in operation. However, this requirement may be met by demonstrating the effectiveness of specified approved fuel anti-icing additives, or that the fuel system incorporates a fuel heater which maintains the fuel temperature at the fuel strainer or fuel inlet above 32 °F (0 °C) under the most critical conditions.

(5) The applicant must demonstrate that the filtering means has the capacity (with respect to engine operating limitations) to ensure that the engine will continue to operate within approved limits, with fuel contaminated to the maximum degree of particle size and density likely to be encountered in service. Operation under these conditions must be demonstrated for a period acceptable to the Administrator, beginning when indication of impending filter blockage is first given by either:

(i) Existing engine instrumentation; or

(ii) Additional means incorporated into the engine fuel system.

(6) Any strainer or filter bypass must be designed and constructed so that the release of collected contaminants is minimized by appropriate location of the bypass to ensure that collected contaminants are not in the bypass flow path.

(c) If provided as part of the engine, the applicant must show for each fluid injection (other than fuel) system and its controls that the flow of the injected fluid is adequately controlled.

(d) Engines having a 30-second OEI rating must incorporate means for automatic availability and automatic control of a 30-second OEI power.

[Amdt. 33–6, 39 FR 35466, Oct. 1, 1974, as amended by Amdt. 33–10, 49 FR 6851, Feb. 23, 1984; Amdt. 33–18, 61 FR 31328, June 19, 1996]

§ 33.68 Induction system icing.

Each engine, with all icing protection systems operating, must—

(a) Operate throughout its flight power range (including idling) without the accumulation of ice on the engine components that adversely affects engine operation or that causes a serious loss of power or thrust in continuous maximum and intermittent maximum icing conditions as defined in appendix C of Part 25 of this chapter; and

(b) Idle for 30 minutes on the ground, with the available air bleed for icing protection at its critical condition, without adverse effect, in an atmosphere that is at a temperature between 15° and 30 °F (between −9° and −1 °C) and has a liquid water content not less than 0.3 grams per cubic meter in the form of drops having a mean effective diameter not less than 20 microns, followed by a momentary operation at takeoff power or thrust. During the 30 minutes of idle operation the engine may be run up periodically to a moderate power or thrust setting in a manner acceptable to the Administrator.

[Amdt. 33–6, 39 FR 35466, Oct. 1, 1974, as amended by Amdt. 33–10, 49 FR 6852, Feb. 23, 1984]

§ 33.69 Ignitions system.

Each engine must be equipped with an ignition system for starting the engine on the ground and in flight. An electric ignition system must have at least two igniters and two separate secondary electric circuits, except that only one igniter is required for fuel burning augmentation systems.

[Amdt. 33–6, 39 FR 35466, Oct. 1, 1974]

§ 33.71 Lubrication system.

(a) *General.* Each lubrication system must function properly in the flight attitudes and atmospheric conditions in which an aircraft is expected to operate.

(b) *Oil strainer or filter.* There must be an oil strainer or filter through which all of the engine oil flows. In addition:

(1) Each strainer or filter required by this paragraph that has a bypass must be constructed and installed so that oil will flow at the normal rate through the rest of the system with the strainer or filter element completely blocked.

(2) The type and degree of filtering necessary for protection of the engine oil system against foreign particles in the oil must be specified. The applicant must demonstrate that foreign particles passing through the specified filtering means do not impair engine oil system functioning.

(3) Each strainer or filter required by this paragraph must have the capacity (with respect to operating limitations established for the engine) to ensure that engine oil system functioning is not impaired with the oil contaminated to a degree (with respect to particle size and density) that is greater than that established for the engine in paragraph (b)(2) of this section.

(4) For each strainer or filter required by this paragraph, except the strainer or filter at the oil tank outlet, there must be means to indicate contamination before it reaches the capacity established in accordance with paragraph (b)(3) of this section.

(5) Any filter bypass must be designed and constructed so that the release of collected contaminants is minimized by appropriate location of the bypass to ensure that the collected contaminants are not in the bypass flow path.

(6) Each strainer or filter required by this paragraph that has no bypass, except the strainer or filter at an oil tank outlet or for a scavenge pump, must have provisions for connection with a warning means to warn the pilot of the occurence of contamination of the screen before it reaches the capacity established in accordance with paragraph (b)(3) of this section.

(7) Each strainer or filter required by this paragraph must be accessible for draining and cleaning.

(c) *Oil tanks.* (1) Each oil tank must have an expansion space of not less than 10 percent of the tank capacity.

(2) It must be impossible to inadvertently fill the oil tank expansion space.

(3) Each recessed oil tank filler connection that can retain any appreciable quantity of oil must have provision for fitting a drain.

(4) Each oil tank cap must provide an oil-tight seal.

(5) Each oil tank filler must be marked with the word "oil."

(6) Each oil tank must be vented from the top part of the expansion space, with the vent so arranged that condensed water vapor that might freeze and obstruct the line cannot accumulate at any point.

(7) There must be means to prevent entrance into the oil tank or into any oil tank outlet, of any object that might obstruct the flow of oil through the system.

(8) There must be a shutoff valve at the outlet of each oil tank, unless the external portion of the oil system (including oil tank supports) is fireproof.

(9) Each unpressurized oil tank may not leak when subjected to a maximum operating temperature and an internal pressure of 5 p.s.i., and each pressurized oil tank may not leak when subjected to maximum operating temperature and an internal pressure that is not less than 5 p.s.i. plus the maximum operating pressure of the tank.

(10) Leaked or spilled oil may not accumulate between the tank and the remainder of the engine.

(11) Each oil tank must have an oil quantity indicator or provisions for one.

(12) If the propeller feathering system depends on engine oil—

(i) There must be means to trap an amount of oil in the tank if the supply becomes depleted due to failure of any part of the lubricating system other than the tank itself;

(ii) The amount of trapped oil must be enough to accomplish the feathering opeation and must be available only to the feathering pump; and

(iii) Provision must be made to prevent sludge or other foreign matter from affecting the safe operation of the propeller feathering system.

(d) *Oil drains.* A drain (or drains) must be provided to allow safe drainage of the oil system. Each drain must—

(1) Be accessible; and

(2) Have manual or automatic means for positive locking in the closed position.

(e) *Oil radiators*. Each oil radiator must withstand, without failure, any vibration, inertia, and oil pressure load to which it is subjected during the block tests.

[Amdt. 33–6, 39 FR 35466, Oct. 1, 1974, as amended by Amdt. 33–10, 49 FR 6852, Feb. 23, 1984]

§ 33.72 Hydraulic actuating systems.

Each hydraulic actuating system must function properly under all conditions in which the engine is expected to operate. Each filter or screen must be accessible for servicing and each tank must meet the design criteria of § 33.71.

[Amdt. 33–6, 39 FR 35467, Oct. 1, 1974]

§ 33.73 Power or thrust response.

The design and construction of the engine must enable an increase—

(a) From minimum to rated takeoff power or thrust with the maximum bleed air and power extraction to be permitted in an aircraft, without over-temperature, surge, stall, or other detrimental factors occurring to the engine whenever the power control lever is moved from the minimum to the maximum position in not more than 1 second, except that the Administrator may allow additional time increments for different regimes of control operation requiring control scheduling; and

(b) From the fixed minimum flight idle power lever position when provided, or if not provided, from not more than 15 percent of the rated takeoff power or thrust available to 95 percent rated takeoff power or thrust in not over 5 seconds. The 5-second power or thrust response must occur from a stabilized static condition using only the bleed air and accessories loads necessary to run the engine. This takeoff rating is specified by the applicant and need not include thrust augmentation.

[Amdt. 33–1, 36 FR 5493, Mar. 24, 1971]

§ 33.74 Continued rotation.

If any of the engine main rotating systems will continue to rotate after the engine is shutdown for any reason while in flight, and where means to prevent that continued rotation are not provided; then any continued rotation during the maximum period of flight, and in the flight conditions ex-

pected to occur with that engine inoperative, must not result in any condition described in § 33.75 (a) through (c).

[Doc. No. 28107, 61 FR 28433, June 4, 1996]

§ 33.75 Safety analysis.

It must be shown by analysis that any probable malfunction or any probable single or multiple failure, or any probable improper operation of the engine will not cause the engine to—

(a) Catch fire;

(b) Burst (release hazardous fragments through the engine case);

(c) Generate loads greater than those ultimate loads specified in § 33.23(a); or

(d) Lose the capability of being shut down.

[Amdt. 33–6, 39 FR 35467, Oct. 1, 1974, as amended by Amdt. 33–10, 49 FR 6852, Feb. 23, 1984]

§ 33.76 Bird ingestion.

(a) *General*. Compliance with paragraphs (b) and (c) of this section shall be in accordance with the following:

(1) All ingestion tests shall be conducted with the engine stabilized at no less than 100-percent takeoff power or thrust, for test day ambient conditions prior to the ingestion. In addition, the demonstration of compliance must account for engine operation at sea level takeoff conditions on the hottest day that a minimum engine can achieve maximum rated takeoff thrust or power.

(2) The engine inlet throat area as used in this section to determine the bird quantity and weights will be established by the applicant and identified as a limitation in the installation instructions required under § 33.5.

(3) The impact to the front of the engine from the single large bird and the single largest medium bird which can enter the inlet must be evaluated. It must be shown that the associated components when struck under the conditions prescribed in paragraphs (b) or (c) of this section, as applicable, will not affect the engine to the extent that it cannot comply with the requirements of paragraphs (b)(3) and (c)(6) of this section.

(4) For an engine that incorporates an inlet protection device, compliance with this section shall be established

with the device functioning. The engine approval will be endorsed to show that compliance with the requirements has been established with the device functioning.

(5) Objects that are accepted by the Administrator may be substituted for birds when conducting the bird ingestion tests required by paragraphs (b) and (c) of this section.

(6) If compliance with the requirements of this section is not established, the engine type certification documentation will show that the engine shall be limited to aircraft installations in which it is shown that a bird cannot strike the engine, or be ingested into the engine, or adversely restrict airflow into the engine.

(b) *Large birds.* Compliance with the large bird ingestion requirements shall be in accordance with the following:

(1) The large bird ingestion test shall be conducted using one bird of a weight determined from Table 1 aimed at the most critical exposed location on the first stage rotor blades and ingested at a bird speed of 200-knots for engines to be installed on airplanes, or the maximum airspeed for normal rotorcraft flight operations for engines to be installed on rotorcraft.

(2) Power lever movement is not permitted within 15 seconds following ingestion of the large bird.

(3) Ingestion of a single large bird tested under the conditions prescribed in this section may not cause the engine to:

(i) Catch fire;

(ii) Release hazardous fragments through the engine casing;

(iii) Generate loads greater than those ultimate loads specified under § 33.23(a); or

(iv) Lose the ability to be shut down.

(4) Compliance with the large bird ingestion requirements of this paragraph may be shown by demonstrating that the requirements of § 33.94(a) constitute a more severe demonstration of blade containment and rotor unbalance than the requirements of this paragraph.

TABLE 1 TO § 33.76.—LARGE BIRD WEIGHT
REQUIREMENTS

Engine Inlet Throat Area (A)—Square/meters (square-inches)	Bird weight kg. (lb.)
1.35 (2,092)> A	1.85 (4.07) minimum, unless a smaller bird is determined to be a more severe demonstration.
1.35 (2,029)≤ A< 3.90 (6,045)	2.75 (6.05)
3.90 (6,045)≤ A	3.65 (8.03)

(c) *Small and medium birds.* Compliance with the small and medium bird ingestion requirements shall be in accordance with the following:

(1) Analysis or component test, or both, acceptable to the Administrator, shall be conducted to determine the critical ingestion parameters affecting power loss and damage. Critical ingestion parameters shall include, but are not limited to, the affects of bird speed, critical target location, and first stage roto speed. The critical bird ingestion speed should reflect the most critical condition within the range of airspeeds used for normal flight operations up to 1,500 feet above ground level, but not less than V_1 minimum for airplanes.

(2) Medium bird engine tests shall be conducted so as to simulate a flock encounter, and will use the bird weights and quantities specified in Table 2. When only one bird is specified, that bird will be aimed at the engine core primary flow path; the other critical locations on the engine face area must be addressed, as necessary, by appropriate tests or analysis, or both. When two or more birds are specified in Table 2, the largest of those birds must be aimed at the engine core primary flow path, and a second bird must be aimed at the most critical exposed location on the first stage rotor blades. Any remaining birds must be evenly distributed over the engine face area.

(3) In addition, except for rotorcraft engines, it must also be substantiated by appropriate tests or analysis or both, that when the full fan assembly is subjected to the ingestion of the quantity and weights of bird from Table 3, aimed at the fan assembly's most critical location outboard of the

primary core flowpath, and in accordance with the applicable test conditions of this paragraph, that the engine can comply with the acceptance criteria of this paragraph.

(4) A small bird ingestion test is not required if the prescribed number of medium birds pass into the engine rotor blades during the medium bird test.

(5) Small bird ingestion tests shall be conducted so as to simulate a flock encounter using one 85 gram (0.187 lb.) bird for each 0.032 square-meter (49.6 square-inches) of inlet area, or fraction thereof, up to a maximum of 16 birds. The birds will be aimed so as to account for any critical exposed locations on the first stage rotor blades, with any remaining birds evenly distributed over the engine face area.

(6) Ingestion of small and medium birds tested under the conditions prescribed in this paragraph may not cause any of the following:

(i) More than a sustained 25-percent power or thrust loss;

(ii) The engine to be shut down during the required run-on demonstration prescribed in paragraphs (c)(7) or (c)(8) of this section;

(iii) The conditions defined in paragraph (b)(3) of this section.

(iv) Unacceptable deterioration of engine handling characteristics.

(7) Except for rotorcraft engines, the following test schedule shall be used:

(i) Ingestion so as to simulate a flock encounter, with approximately 1 second elapsed time from the moment of the first bird ingestion to the last.

(ii) Followed by 2 minutes without power level movement after the ingestion.

(iii) Followed by 3 minutes at 175-percent of the test condition.

(iv) Followed by 6 minutes at 60-percent of the test condition.

(v) Followed by 6 minutes at 40-percent of the test condition.

(vi) Followed by 1 minute at approach idle.

(vii) Followed by 2 minutes at 75-percent of the test condition.

(viii) Followed by stabilizing at idle and engine shut down.

The durations specified are times at the defined conditions with the power lever being moved between each condition in less than 10 seconds.

(8) For rotorcraft engines, the following test schedule shall be used:

(i) Ingestion so as to simulate a flock encounter within approximately 1 second elapsed time between the first ingestion and the last.

(ii) Followed by 3 minutes at 75-percent of the test condition.

(iii) Followed by 90 seconds at descent flight idle.

(iv) Followed by 30 seconds at 75-percent of the test condition.

(v) Followed by stabilizing at idle and engine shut down. The duration specified are times at the defined conditions with the power being changed between each condition in less than 10 seconds.

(9) Engines intended for use in multi-engine rotorcraft are not required to comply with the medium bird ingestion portion of this section, providing that the appropriate type certificate documentation is so endorsed.

(10) If any engine operating limit(s) is exceeded during the initial 2 minutes without power lever movement, as provided by paragraph (c)(7)(ii) of this section, then it shall be established that the limit exceedence will not result in an unsafe condition.

TABLE 2 TO § 33.76.—MEDIUM FLOCKING BIRD WEIGHT AND QUANTITY REQUIREMENTS

Engine Inlet Throat Area (A)—Square-meters (square-inches)	Bird quantity	Bird weight kg. (lb.)
0.05 (77.5)> A	none	
.05 (77.5)≤ A <0.10 (155)	1	0.35 (0.77)
0.10 (155)≤ A <0.20 (310)	1	0.45 (0.99)
0.20 (310)≤ A <0.40 (620)	2	0.45 (0.99)
0.40 (620)≤ A <0.60 (930)	2	0.70 (1.54)
0.60 (930)≤ A <1.00 (1,550)	3	0.70 (1.54)
1.00 (1,550)≤ A <1.35 (2,092)	4	0.70 (1.54)
1.35 (2,092)≤ A <1.70 (2,635)	1	1.15 (2.53)
1.70 (2,635)≤ A <2.10 (3,255)	plus 3	0.70 (1.54)
	1	1.15 (2,53)
2.10 (3,255)≤ A <2.50 (3,875)	plus 4	0.70 (1.54)
	1	1.15 (2.53)

TABLE 2 TO §33.76.—MEDIUM FLOCKING BIRD WEIGHT AND QUANTITY REQUIREMENTS—Continued

Engine Inlet Throat Area (A)—Square-meters (square-inches)	Bird quantity	Bird weight kg. (lb.)
2.50 (3,875)≤ A <3.90 (6045)	plus 5	0.70 (1.54)
	1	1.15 (2.53)
	plus 6	0.70 (1.54)
3.90 (6045)≤ A <4.50 (6975)	3	1.15 (2.53)
4.50 (6975)≤ A	4	1.15 (2.53)

TABLE 3 TO §33.76.—ADDITIONAL INTEGRITY ASSESSMENT

Engine Inlet Throat Area (A)—square-meters (square-inches)	Bird quantity	Bird weight kg. (lb.)
1.35 (2,092)> A	none	
1.35 (2,092)≤ A <2.90 (4,495)	1	1.15 (2.53)
2.90 (4,495)≤ A <3.90 (6,045)	2	1.15 (2.53)
3.90 (6,045)≤ A	1	1.15 (2.53)
	plus 6	0.70 (1.54)

[Doc. No. FAA–1998–4815, 65 FR 55854, Sept. 14, 2000]

§33.77 Foreign object ingestion—ice.

(a)–(b) [Reserved]

(c) Ingestion of ice under the conditions of paragraph (e) of this section may not—

(1) Cause a sustained power or thrust loss; or

(2) Require the engine to be shutdown.

(d) For an engine that incorporates a protection device, compliance with this section need not be demonstrated with respect to foreign objects to be ingested under the conditions prescribed in paragraph (e) of this section if it is shown that—

(1) Such foreign objects are of a size that will not pass through the protective device;

(2) The protective device will withstand the impact of the foreign objects; and

(3) The foreign object, or objects, stopped by the protective device will not obstruct the flow of induction air into the engine with a resultant sustained reduction in power or thrust greater than those values required by paragraph (c) of this section.

(e) Compliance with paragraph (c) of this section must be shown by engine test under the following ingestion conditions:

(1) Ice quantity will be the maximum accumulation on a typical inlet cowl and engine face resulting from a 2-minute delay in actuating the anti-icing system; or a slab of ice which is comparable in weight or thickness for that size engine.

(2) The ingestion velocity will simulate ice being sucked into the engine inlet.

(3) Engine operation will be maximum cruise power or thrust.

(4) The ingestion will simulate a continuous maximum icing encounter at 25 degrees Fahrenheit.

[Doc. No. 16919, 49 FR 6852, Feb. 23, 1984, as amended by Amdt. 33–19, 63 FR 14798, Mar. 26, 1998; 63 FR 53278, Oct. 5, 1998; Amdt. 33–20, 65 FR 55856, Sept. 14, 2000]

§33.78 Rain and hail ingestion.

(a) *All engines.* (1) The ingestion of large hailstones (0.8 to 0.9 specific gravity) at the maximum true air speed, up to 15,000 feet (4,500 meters), associated with a representative aircraft operating in rough air, with the engine at maximum continuous power, may not cause unacceptable mechanical damage or unacceptable power or thrust loss after the ingestion, or require the engine to be shut down. One-half the number of hailstones shall be aimed randomly over the inlet face area and the other half aimed at the critical inlet face area. The hailstones shall be ingested in a rapid sequence to simulate a hailstone encounter and the number and size of the hailstones shall be determined as follows:

(i) One 1-inch (25 millimeters) diameter hailstone for engines with inlet areas of not more than 100 square inches (0.0645 square meters).

(ii) One 1-inch (25 millimeters) diameter and one 2-inch (50 millimeters) diameter hailstone for each 150 square inches (0.0968 square meters) of inlet area, or fraction thereof, for engines with inlet areas of more than 100 square inches (0.0645 square meters).

(2) In addition to complying with paragraph (a)(1) of this section and except as provided in paragraph (b) of this section, it must be shown that each engine is capable of acceptable operation throughout its specified operating envelope when subjected to sudden encounters with the certification standard concentrations of rain and hail, as defined in appendix B to this part. Acceptable engine operation precludes flameout, run down, continued or non-recoverable surge or stall, or loss of acceleration and deceleration capability, during any three minute continuous period in rain and during any 30 second continuous period in hail. It must also be shown after the ingestion that there is no unacceptable mechanical damage, unacceptable power or thrust loss, or other adverse engine anomalies.

(b) *Engines for rotorcraft.* As an alternative to the requirements specified in paragraph (a)(2) of this section, for rotorcraft turbine engines only, it must be shown that each engine is capable of acceptable operation during and after the ingestion of rain with an overall ratio of water droplet flow to airflow, by weight, with a uniform distribution at the inlet plane, of at least four percent. Acceptable engine operation precludes flameout, run down, continued or non-recoverable surge or stall, or loss of acceleration and deceleration capability. It must also be shown after the ingestion that there is no unacceptable mechanical damage, unacceptable power loss, or other adverse engine anomalies. The rain ingestion must occur under the following static ground level conditions:

(1) A normal stabilization period at take-off power without rain ingestion, followed immediately by the suddenly commencing ingestion of rain for three minutes at takeoff power, then

(2) Continuation of the rain ingestion during subsequent rapid deceleration to minimum idle, then

(3) Continuation of the rain ingestion during three minutes at minimum idle

power to be certified for flight operation, then

(4) Continuation of the rain ingestion during subsequent rapid acceleration to takeoff power.

(c) *Engines for supersonic airplanes.* In addition to complying with paragraphs (a)(1) and (a)(2) of this section, a separate test for supersonic airplane engines only, shall be conducted with three hailstones ingested at supersonic cruise velocity. These hailstones shall be aimed at the engine's critical face area, and their ingestion must not cause unacceptable mechanical damage or unacceptable power or thrust loss after the ingestion or require the engine to be shut down. The size of these hailstones shall be determined from the linear variation in diameter from 1-inch (25 millimeters) at 35,000 feet (10,500 meters) to ¼-inch (6 millimeters) at 60,000 feet (18,000 meters) using the diameter corresponding to the lowest expected supersonic cruise altitude. Alternatively, three larger hailstones may be ingested at subsonic velocities such that the kinetic energy of these larger hailstones is equivalent to the applicable supersonic ingestion conditions.

(d) For an engine that incorporates or requires the use of a protection device, demonstration of the rain and hail ingestion capabilities of the engine, as required in paragraphs (a), (b), and (c) of this section, may be waived wholly or in part by the Administrator if the applicant shows that:

(1) The subject rain and hail constituents are of a size that will not pass through the protection device;

(2) The protection device will withstand the impact of the subject rain and hail constituents; and

(3) The subject of rain and hail constituents, stopped by the protection device, will not obstruct the flow of induction air into the engine, resulting in damage, power or thrust loss, or other adverse engine anomalies in excess of what would be accepted in paragraphs (a), (b), and (c) of this section.

[Doc. No. 28652, 63 FR 14799, Mar. 26, 1998]

§ 33.79   Fuel burning thrust augmentor.

Each fuel burning thrust augmentor, including the nozzle, must—

(a) Provide cutoff of the fuel burning thrust augmentor;

(b) Permit on-off cycling;

(c) Be controllable within the intended range of operation;

(d) Upon a failure or malfunction of augmentor combustion, not cause the engine to lose thrust other than that provided by the augmentor; and

(e) Have controls that function compatibly with the other engine controls and automatically shut off augmentor fuel flow if the engine rotor speed drops below the minimum rotational speed at which the augmentor is intended to function.

[Amdt. 33–6, 39 FR 35468, Oct. 1, 1974]

Subpart F—Block Tests; Turbine Aircraft Engines

§33.81 Applicability.

This subpart prescribes the block tests and inspections for turbine engines.

[Doc. 3025, 29 FR 7453, June 10, 1964, as amended by Amdt. 33–6, 39 FR 35468, Oct. 1, 1974]

§33.82 General.

Before each endurance test required by this subpart, the adjustment setting and functioning characteristic of each component having an adjustment setting and a functioning characteristic that can be established independent of installation on the engine must be established and recorded.

[Amdt. 36–6, 39 FR 35468, Oct. 1, 1974]

§33.83 Vibration test.

(a) Each engine must undergo vibration surveys to establish that the vibration characteristics of those components that may be subject to mechanically or aerodynamically induced vibratory excitations are acceptable throughout the declared flight envelope. The engine surveys shall be based upon an appropriate combination of experience, analysis, and component test and shall address, as a minimum, blades, vanes, rotor discs, spacers, and rotor shafts.

(b) The surveys shall cover the ranges of power or thrust, and both the physical and corrected rotational speeds for each rotor system, corresponding to operations throughout the range of ambient conditions in the declared flight envelope, from the minimum rotational speed up to 103 percent of the maximum physical and corrected rotational speed permitted for rating periods of two minutes or longer, and up to 100 percent of all other permitted physical and corrected rotational speeds, including those that are overspeeds. If there is any indication of a stress peak arising at the highest of those required physical or corrected rotational speeds, the surveys shall be extended sufficiently to reveal the maximum stress values present, except that the extension need not cover more than a further 2 percentage points increase beyond those speeds.

(c) Evaluations shall be made of the following:

(1) The effects on vibration characteristics of operating with scheduled changes (including tolerances) to variable vane angles, compressor bleeds, accessory loading, the most adverse inlet air flow distortion pattern declared by the manufacturer, and the most adverse conditions in the exhaust duct(s); and

(2) The aerodynamic and aeromechanical factors which might induce or influence flutter in those systems susceptible to that form of vibration.

(d) Except as provided by paragraph (e) of this section, the vibration stresses associated with the vibration characteristics determined under this section, when combined with the appropriate steady stresses, must be less than the endurance limits of the materials concerned, after making due allowances for operating conditions for the permitted variations in properties of the materials. The suitability of these stress margins must be justified for each part evaluated. If it is determined that certain operating conditions, or ranges, need to be limited, operating and installation limitations shall be established.

(e) The effects on vibration characteristics of excitation forces caused by fault conditions (such as, but not limited to, out-of balance, local blockage or enlargement of stator vane passages,

753

fuel nozzle blockage, incorrectly schedule compressor variables, etc.) shall be evaluated by test or analysis, or by reference to previous experience and shall be shown not to create a hazardous condition.

(f) Compliance with this section shall be substantiated for each specific installation configuration that can affect the vibration characteristics of the engine. If these vibration effects cannot be fully investigated during engine certification, the methods by which they can be evaluated and methods by which compliance can be shown shall be substantiated and defined in the installation instructions required by § 33.5.

[Doc. No. 28107, 61 FR 28433, June 4, 1996]

§ 33.85 Calibration tests.

(a) Each engine must be subjected to those calibration tests necessary to establish its power characteristics and the conditions for the endurance test specified § 33.87. The results of the power characteristics calibration tests form the basis for establishing the characteristics of the engine over its entire operating range of speeds, pressures, temperatures, and altitudes. Power ratings are based upon standard atmospheric conditions with no airbleed for aircraft services and with only those accessories installed which are essential for engine functioning.

(b) A power check at sea level conditions must be accomplished on the endurance test engine after the endurance test and any change in power characteristics which occurs during the endurance test must be determined. Measurements taken during the final portion of the endurance test may be used in showing compliance with the requirements of this paragraph.

(c) In showing compliance with this section, each condition must stabilize before measurements are taken, except as permitted by paragraph (d) of this section.

(d) In the case of engines having 30-second OEI, and 2-minute OEI ratings, measurements taken during the applicable endurance test prescribed in § 33.87(f) (1) through (8) may be used in showing compliance with the requirements of this section for these OEI ratings.

[Doc. No. 3025, 29 FR 7453, June 10, 1964, as amended by Amdt. 33–6, 39 FR 35468, Oct. 1, 1974; Amdt. 33–18, 61 FR 31328, June 19, 1996]

§ 33.87 Endurance test.

(a) *General.* Each engine must be subjected to an endurance test that includes a total of at least 150 hours of operation and, depending upon the type and contemplated use of the engine, consists of one of the series of runs specified in paragraphs (b) through (g) of this section, as applicable. For engines tested under paragraphs (b), (c), (d), (e) or (g) of this section, the prescribed 6-hour test sequence must be conducted 25 times to complete the required 150 hours of operation. Engines for which the 30-second OEI and 2-minute OEI ratings are desired must be further tested under paragraph (f) of this section. The following test requirements apply:

(1) The runs must be made in the order found appropriate by the Administrator for the particular engine being tested.

(2) Any automatic engine control that is part of the engine must control the engine during the endurance test except for operations where automatic control is normally overridden by manual control or where manual control is otherwise specified for a particular test run.

(3) Except as provided in paragraph (a)(5) of this section, power or thrust, gas temperature, rotor shaft rotational speed, and, if limited, temperature of external surfaces of the engine must be at least 100 percent of the value associated with the particular engine operation being tested. More than one test may be run if all parameters cannot be held at the 100 percent level simultaneously.

(4) The runs must be made using fuel, lubricants and hydraulic fluid which conform to the specifications specified in complying with § 33.7(c).

(5) Maximum air bleed for engine and aircraft services must be used during at least one-fifth of the runs. However, for these runs, the power or thrust or the rotor shaft rotational speed may be less than 100 percent of the value associated with the particular operation

being tested if the Administrator finds that the validity of the endurance test is not compromised.

(6) Each accessory drive and mounting attachment must be loaded. The load imposed by each accessory used only for aircraft service must be the limit load specified by the applicant for the engine drive and attachment point during rated maximum continuous power or thrust and higher output. The endurance test of any accessory drive and mounting attachment under load may be accomplished on a separate rig if the validity of the test is confirmed by an approved analysis.

(7) During the runs at any rated power or thrust the gas temperature and the oil inlet temperature must be maintained at the limiting temperature except where the test periods are not longer than 5 minutes and do not allow stabilization. At least one run must be made with fuel, oil, and hydraulic fluid at the minimum pressure limit and at least one run must be made with fuel, oil, and hydraulic fluid at the maximum pressure limit with fluid temperature reduced as necessary to allow maximum pressure to be attained.

(8) If the number of occurrences of either transient rotor shaft overspeed or transient gas overtemperature is limited, that number of the accelerations required by paragraphs (b) through (g) of this section must be made at the limiting overspeed or overtemperature. If the number of occurrences is not limited, half the required accelerations must be made at the limiting overspeed or overtemperature.

(9) For each engine type certificated for use on supersonic aircraft the following additional test requirements apply:

(i) To change the thrust setting, the power control lever must be moved from the initial position to the final position in not more than one second except for movements into the fuel burning thrust augmentor augmentation position if additional time to confirm ignition is necessary.

(ii) During the runs at any rated augmented thrust the hydraulic fluid temperature must be maintained at the limiting temperature except where the test periods are not long enough to allow stabilization.

(iii) During the simulated supersonic runs the fuel temperature and induction air temperature may not be less than the limiting temperature.

(iv) The endurance test must be conducted with the fuel burning thrust augmentor installed, with the primary and secondary exhaust nozzles installed, and with the variable area exhaust nozzles operated during each run according to the methods specified in complying with §33.5(b).

(v) During the runs at thrust settings for maximum continuous thrust and percentages thereof, the engine must be operated with the inlet air distortion at the limit for those thrust settings.

(b) *Engines other than certain rotorcraft engines.* For each engine except a rotorcraft engine for which a rating is desired under paragraph (c), (d), or (e) of this section, the applicant must conduct the following runs:

(1) *Takeoff and idling.* One hour of alternate five-minute periods at rated takeoff power and thrust and at idling power and thrust. The developed powers and thrusts at takeoff and idling conditions and their corresponding rotor speed and gas temperature conditions must be as established by the power control in accordance with the schedule established by the manufacturer. The applicant may, during any one period, manually control the rotor speed, power, and thrust while taking data to check performance. For engines with augmented takeoff power ratings that involve increases in turbine inlet temperature, rotor speed, or shaft power, this period of running at takeoff must be at the augmented rating. For engines with augmented takeoff power ratings that do not materially increase operating severity, the amount of running conducted at the augmented rating is determined by the Administrator. In changing the power setting after each period, the power-control lever must be moved in the manner prescribed in paragraph (b)(5) of this section.

(2) *Rated maximum continuous and takeoff power and thrust.* Thirty minutes at—

(i) Rated maximum continuous power and thrust during fifteen of the twenty-five 6-hour endurance test cycles; and

(ii) Rated takeoff power and thrust during ten of the twenty-five 6-hour endurance test cycles.

(3) *Rated maximum continuous power and thrust.* One hour and 30 minutes at rated maximum continuous power and thrust.

(4) *Incremental cruise power and thrust.* Two hours and 30 minutes at the successive power lever positions corresponding to at least 15 approximately equal speed and time increments between maximum continuous engine rotational speed and ground or minimum idle rotational speed. For engines operating at constant speed, the thrust and power may be varied in place of speed. If there is significant peak vibration anywhere between ground idle and maximum continuous conditions, the number of increments chosen may be changed to increase the amount of running made while subject to the peak vibrations up to not more than 50 percent of the total time spent in incremental running.

(5) *Acceleration and deceleration runs.* 30 minutes of accelerations and decelerations, consisting of six cycles from idling power and thrust to rated takeoff power and thrust and maintained at the takeoff power lever position for 30 seconds and at the idling power lever position for approximately four and one-half minutes. In complying with this paragraph, the power-control lever must be moved from one extreme poition to the other in not more than one second, except that, if different regimes of control operations are incorporated necessitating scheduling of the power-control lever motion in going from one extreme position to the other, a longer period of time is acceptable, but not more than two seconds.

(6) *Starts.* One hundred starts must be made, of which 25 starts must be preceded by at least a two-hour engine shutdown. There must be at least 10 false engine starts, pausing for the applicant's specified minimum fuel drainage time, before attempting a normal start. There must be at least 10 normal restarts with not longer than 15 minutes since engine shutdown. The re-

maining starts may be made after completing the 150 hours of endurance testing.

(c) *Rotorcraft engines for which a 30-minute OEI power rating is desired.* For each rotorcraft engine for which a 30-minute OEI power rating is desired, the applicant must conduct the following series of tests:

(1) *Takeoff and idling.* One hour of alternate 5-minute periods at rated takeoff power and at idling power. The developed powers at takeoff and idling conditions and their corresponding rotor speed and gas temperature conditions must be as established by the power control in accordance with the schedule established by the manufacturer. During any one period, the rotor speed and power may be controlled manually while taking data to check performance. For engines with augmented takeoff power ratings that involve increases in turbine inlet temperature, rotor speed, or shaft power, this period of running at rated takeoff power must be at the augmented power rating. In changing the power setting after each period, the power control lever must be moved in the manner prescribed in paragraph (c)(5) of this section.

(2) *Rated 30-minute OEI power.* Thirty minutes at rated 30-minute OEI power.

(3) *Rated maximum continuous power.* Two hours at rated maximum continuous power.

(4) *Incremental cruise power.* Two hours at the successive power lever positions corresponding with not less than 12 approximately equal speed and time increments between maximum continuous engine rotational speed and ground or minimum idle rotational speed. For engines operating at constant speed, power may be varied in place of speed. If there are significant peak vibrations anywhere between ground idle and maximum continuous conditions, the number of increments chosen must be changed to increase the amount of running conducted while being subjected to the peak vibrations up to not more than 50 percent of the total time spent in incremental running.

(5) *Acceleration and deceleration runs.* Thirty minutes of accelerations and decelerations, consisting of six cycles

from idling power to rated takeoff power and maintained at the takeoff power lever position for 30 seconds and at the idling power lever position for approximately 4½ minutes. In complying with this paragraph, the power control lever must be moved from one extreme position to the other in not more than 1 second, except that if different regimes of control operations are incorporated necessitating scheduling of the power control lever motion in going from one extreme position to the other, a longer period of time is acceptable, but not more than 2 seconds.

(6) *Starts.* One hundred starts, of which 25 starts must be preceded by at least a two-hour engine shutdown. There must be at least 10 false engine starts, pausing for the applicant's specified minimum fuel drainage time, before attempting a normal start. There must be at least 10 normal restarts with not longer than 15 minutes since engine shutdown. The remaining starts may be made after completing the 150 hours of endurance testing.

(d) *Rotorcraft engines for which a continuous OEI rating is desired.* For each rotorcraft engine for which a continuous OEI power rating is desired, the applicant must conduct the following series of tests:

(1) *Takeoff and idling.* One hour of alternate 5-minute periods at rated takeoff power and at idling power. The developed powers at takeoff and idling conditions and their corresponding rotor speed and gas temperature conditions must be as established by the power control in accordance with the schedule established by the manufacturer. During any one period the rotor speed and power may be controlled manually while taking data to check performance. For engines with augmented takeoff power ratings that involve increases in turbine inlet temperature, rotor speed, or shaft power, this period of running at rated takeoff power must be at the augmented power rating. In changing the power setting after each period, the power control lever must be moved in the manner prescribed in paragraph (c)(5) of this section.

(2) *Rated maximum continuous and takeoff power.* Thirty minutes at—

(i) Rated maximum continuous power during fifteen of the twenty-five 6-hour endurance test cycles; and

(ii) Rated takeoff power during ten of the twenty-five 6-hour endurance test cycles.

(3) *Rated continuous OEI power.* One hour at rated continuous OEI power.

(4) *Rated maximum continuous power.* One hour at rated maximum continuous power.

(5) *Incremental cruise power.* Two hours at the successive power lever positions corresponding with not less than 12 approximately equal speed and time increments between maximum continuous engine rotational speed and ground or minimum idle rotational speed. For engines operating at constant speed, power may be varied in place of speed. If there are significant peak vibrations anywhere between ground idle and maximum continuous conditions, the number of increments chosen must be changed to increase the amount of running conducted while being subjected to the peak vibrations up to not more than 50 percent of the total time spent in incremental running.

(6) *Acceleration and deceleration runs.* Thirty minutes of accelerations and decelerations, consisting of six cycles from idling power to rated takeoff power and maintained at the takeoff power lever position for 30 seconds and at the idling power lever position for approximately 4½ minutes. In complying with this paragraph, the power control lever must be moved from one extreme position to the other in not more than 1 second, except that if different regimes of control operations are incorporated necessitating scheduling of the power control lever motion in going from one extreme position to the other, a longer period of time is acceptable, but not more than 2 seconds.

(7) *Starts.* One hundred starts, of which 25 starts must be preceded by at least a 2-hour engine shutdown. There must be at least 10 false engine starts, pausing for the applicant's specified minimum fuel drainage time, before attempting a normal start. There must be at least 10 normal restarts with not longer than 15 minutes since engine shutdown. The remaining starts may

be made after completing the 150 hours of endurance testing.

(e) *Rotorcraft engines for which a 2½-minute OEI power rating is desired.* For each rotorcraft engine for which a 2½-minute OEI power rating is desired, the applicant must conduct the following series of tests:

(1) *Takeoff, 2½-minute OEI, and idling.* One hour of alternate 5-minute periods at rated takeoff power and at idling power except that, during the third and sixth takeoff power periods, only 2½ minutes need be conducted at rated takeoff power, and the remaining 2½ minutes must be conducted at rated 2½-minute OEI power. The developed powers at takeoff, 2½-minute OEI, and idling conditions and their corresponding rotor speed and gas temperature conditions must be as established by the power control in accordance with the schedule established by the manufacturer. The applicant may, during any one period, control manually the rotor speed and power while taking data to check performance. For engines with augmented takeoff power ratings that involve increases in turbine inlet temperature, rotor speed, or shaft power, this period of running at rated takeoff power must be at the augmented rating. In changing the power setting after or during each period, the power control lever must be moved in the manner prescribed in paragraph (d)(6) of this section.

(2) The tests required in paragraphs (b)(2) through (b)(6), or (c)(2) through (c)(6), or (d)(2) through (d)(7) of this section, as applicable, except that in one of the 6-hour test sequences, the last 5 minutes of the 30 minutes at takeoff power test period of paragraph (b)(2) of this section, or of the 30 minutes at 30-minute OEI power test period of paragraph (c)(2) of this section, or of the 1 hour at continuous OEI power test period of paragraph (d)(3) of this section, must be run at 2½-minute OEI power.

(f) *Rotorcraft engines for which 30-second OEI and 2-minute OEI ratings are desired.* For each rotorcraft engine for which 30-second OEI and 2-minute OEI power ratings are desired, and following completion of the tests under paragraphs (b), (c), (d), or (e) of this section, the applicant may disassemble the tested engine to the extent necessary to show compliance with the requirements of §33.93(a). The tested engine must then be reassembled using the same parts used during the test runs of paragraphs (b), (c), (d), or (e) of this section, except those parts described as consumables in the Instructions for Continued Airworthiness. The applicant must then conduct the following test sequence four times, for a total time of not less than 120 minutes:

(1) *Takeoff power.* Three minutes at rated takeoff power.

(2) *30-second OEI power.* Thirty seconds at rated 30-second OEI power.

(3) *2-minute OEI power.* Two minutes at rated 2-minute OEI power.

(4) *30-minute OEI power, continuous OEI power, or maximum continuous power.* Five minutes at rated 30-minute OEI power, rated continuous OEI power, or rated maximum continuous power, whichever is greatest, except that, during the first test sequence, this period shall be 65 minutes.

(5) *50 percent takeoff power.* One minute at 50 percent takeoff power.

(6) *30-second OEI power.* Thirty seconds at rated 30-second OEI power.

(7) *2-minute OEI power.* Two minutes at rated 2-minute OEI power.

(8) *Idle.* One minute at idle.

(g) *Supersonic aircraft engines.* For each engine type certificated for use on supersonic aircraft the applicant must conduct the following:

(1) *Subsonic test under sea level ambient atmospheric conditions.* Thirty runs of one hour each must be made, consisting of—

(i) Two periods of 5 minutes at rated takeoff augmented thrust each followed by 5 minutes at idle thrust;

(ii) One period of 5 minutes at rated takeoff thrust followed by 5 minutes at not more than 15 percent of rated takeoff thrust;

(iii) One period of 10 minutes at rated takeoff augmented thrust followed by 2 minutes at idle thrust, except that if rated maximum continuous augmented thrust is lower than rated takeoff augmented thrust, 5 of the 10-minute periods must be at rated maximum continuous augmented thrust; and

(iv) Six periods of 1 minute at rated takeoff augmented thrust each followed by 2 minutes, including acceleration and deceleration time, at idle thrust.

(2) *Simulated supersonic test.* Each run of the simulated supersonic test must be preceded by changing the inlet air temperature and pressure from that attained at subsonic condition to the temperature and pressure attained at supersonic velocity, and must be followed by a return to the temperature attained at subsonic condition. Thirty runs of 4 hours each must be made, consisting of—

(i) One period of 30 minutes at the thrust obtained with the power control lever set at the position for rated maximum continuous augmented thrust followed by 10 minutes at the thrust obtained with the power control lever set at the position for 90 percent of rated maximum continuous augmented thrust. The end of this period in the first five runs must be made with the induction air temperature at the limiting condition of transient overtemperature, but need not be repeated during the periods specified in paragraphs (g)(2)(ii) through (iv) of this section;

(ii) One period repeating the run specified in paragraph (g)(2)(i) of this section, except that it must be followed by 10 minutes at the thrust obtained with the power control lever set at the position for 80 percent of rated maximum continuous augmented thrust;

(iii) One period repeating the run specified in paragraph (g)(2)(i) of this section, except that it must be followed by 10 minutes at the thrust obtained with the power control lever set at the position for 60 percent of rated maximum continuous augmented thrust and then 10 minutes at not more than 15 percent of rated takeoff thrust;

(iv) One period repeating the runs specified in paragraphs (g)(2)(i) and (ii) of this section; and

(v) One period of 30 minutes with 25 of the runs made at the thrust obtained with the power control lever set at the position for rated maximum continuous augmented thrust, each followed by idle thrust and with the remaining 5 runs at the thrust obtained with the power control lever set at the position

for rated maximum continuous augmented thrust for 25 minutes each, followed by subsonic operation at not more than 15 percent or rated takeoff thrust and accelerated to rated takeoff thrust for 5 minutes using hot fuel.

(3) *Starts.* One hundred starts must be made, of which 25 starts must be preceded by an engine shutdown of at least 2 hours. There must be at least 10 false engine starts, pausing for the applicant's specified minimum fuel drainage time before attempting a normal start. At least 10 starts must be normal restarts, each made no later than 15 minutes after engine shutdown. The starts may be made at any time, including the period of endurance testing.

[Doc. No. 3025, 29 FR 7453, June 10, 1964, as amended by Amdt. 33–3, 32 FR 3737, Mar. 4, 1967; Amdt. 33–6, 39 FR 35468, Oct. 1, 1974; Amdt. 33–10, 49 FR 6853, Feb. 23, 1984; Amdt. 33–12, 53 FR 34220, Sept. 2, 1988; Amdt. 33–18, 61 FR 31328, June 19, 1996]

§33.88 Engine overtemperature test.

(a) Each engine must run for 5 minutes at maximum permissible rpm with the gas temperature at least 75 °F (42 °C) higher than the maximum rating's steady-state operating limit, excluding maximum values of rpm and gas temperature associated with the 30-second OEI and 2-minute OEI ratings. Following this run, the turbine assembly must be within serviceable limits.

(b) Each engine for which 30-second OEI and 2-minute OEI ratings are desired, that does not incorporate a means to limit temperature, must be run for a period of 5 minutes at the maximum power-on rpm with the gas temperature at least 75 °F (42 °C) higher than the 30-second OEI rating operating limit. Following this run, the turbine assembly may exhibit distress beyond the limits for an overtemperature condition provided the engine is shown by analysis or test, as found necessary by the Administrator, to maintain the integrity of the turbine assembly.

(c) Each engine for which 30-second OEI and 2-minute OEI ratings are desired, that incorporates a means to limit temperature, must be run for a period of 4 minutes at the maximum power-on rpm with the gas temperature at least 35 °F (20 °C) higher than the maximum operating limit. Following this run, the turbine assembly may exhibit distress beyond the limits for an overtemperature condition provided the engine is shown by analysis or test, as found necessary by the Administrator, to maintain the integrity of the turbine assembly.

(d) A separate test vehicle may be used for each test condition.

[Doc. No. 26019, 61 FR 31329, June 19, 1996]

§ 33.89   Operation test.

(a) The operation test must include testing found necessary by the Administrator to demonstrate—

(1) Starting, idling, acceleration, overspeeding, ignition, functioning of the propeller (if the engine is designated to operate with a propeller);

(2) Compliance with the engine response requirements of § 33.73; and

(3) The minimum power or thrust response time to 95 percent rated takeoff power or thrust, from power lever positions representative of minimum idle and of minimum flight idle, starting from stabilized idle operation, under the following engine load conditions:

(i) No bleed air and power extraction for aircraft use.

(ii) Maximum allowable bleed air and power extraction for aircraft use.

(iii) An intermediate value for bleed air and power extraction representative of that which might be used as a maximum for aircraft during approach to a landing.

(4) If testing facilities are not available, the determination of power extraction required in paragraph (a)(3)(ii) and (iii) of this section may be accomplished through appropriate analytical means.

(b) The operation test must include all testing found necessary by the Administrator to demonstrate that the engine has safe operating characteristics throughout its specified operating envelope.

[Amdt. 33–4, 36 FR 5493, Mar. 24, 1971, as amended by Amdt. 33–6, 39 FR 35469, Oct. 1, 1974; Amdt. 33–10, 49 FR 6853, Feb. 23, 1984]

§ 33.90   Initial maintenance inspection.

Each engine, except engines being type certificated through amendment of an existing type certificate or through supplemental type certification procedures, must undergo an approved test run that simulates the conditions in which the engine is expected to operate in service, including typical start-stop cycles, to establish when the initial maintenance inspection is required. The test run must be accomplished on an engine which substantially conforms to the final type design.

[Amdt. 33–10, 49 FR 6854, Feb. 23, 1984]

§ 33.91   Engine component tests.

(a) For those systems that cannot be adequately substantiated by endurance testing in accordance with the provisions of § 33.87, additional tests must be made to establish that components are able to function reliably in all normally anticipated flight and atmospheric conditions.

(b) Temperature limits must be established for those components that require temperature controlling provisions in the aircraft installation to assure satisfactory functioning, reliability, and durability.

(c) Each unpressurized hydraulic fluid tank may not fail or leak when subjected to maximum operating temperature and an internal pressure of 5 p.s.i., and each pressurized hydraulic fluid tank may not fail or leak when subjected to maximum operating temperature and an internal pressure not less than 5 p.s.i. plus the maximum operating pressure of the tank.

(d) For an engine type certificated for use in supersonic aircraft, the systems, safety devices, and external components that may fail because of operation at maximum and minimum operating temperatures must be identified and tested at maximum and minimum operating temperatures and while temperature and other operating conditions are cycled between maximum and minimum operating values.

[Doc. No. 3025, 29 FR 7453, June 10, 1964, as amended by Amdt. 33–6, 39 FR 35469, Oct. 1, 1974]

§ 33.92 Rotor locking tests.

If continued rotation is prevented by a means to lock the rotor(s), the engine must be subjected to a test that includes 25 operations of this means under the following conditions:

(a) The engine must be shut down from rated maximum continuous thrust or power; and

(b) The means for stopping and locking the rotor(s) must be operated as specified in the engine operating instructions while being subjected to the maximum torque that could result from continued flight in this condition; and

(c) Following rotor locking, the rotor(s) must be held stationary under these conditions for five minutes for each of the 25 operations.

[Doc. No. 28107, 61 FR 28433, June 4, 1996]

§ 33.93 Teardown inspection.

(a) After completing the endurance testing of § 33.87 (b), (c), (d), (e), or (g) of this part, each engine must be completely disassembled, and

(1) Each component having an adjustment setting and a functioning characteristic that can be established independent of installation on the engine must retain each setting and functioning characteristic within the limits that were established and recorded at the beginning of the test; and

(2) Each engine part must conform to the type design and be eligible for incorporation into an engine for continued operation, in accordance with information submitted in compliance with § 33.4.

(b) After completing the endurance testing of § 33.87(f), each engine must be completely disassembled, and

(1) Each component having an adjustment setting and a functioning characteristic that can be established independent of installation on the engine must retain each setting and functioning characteristic within the limits that were established and recorded at the beginning of the test; and

(2) Each engine may exhibit deterioration in excess of that permitted in paragraph (a)(2) of this section including some engine parts or components that may be unsuitable for further use. The applicant must show by analysis and/or test, as found necessary by the Administrator, that structural integrity of the engine including mounts, cases, bearing supports, shafts, and rotors, is maintained; or

(c) In lieu of compliance with paragraph (b) of this section, each engine for which the 30-second OEI and 2-minute OEI ratings are desired, may be subjected to the endurance testing of §§ 33.87 (b), (c), (d), or (e) of this part, and followed by the testing of § 33.87(f) without intervening disassembly and inspection. However, the engine must comply with paragraph (a) of this section after completing the endurance testing of § 33.87(f).

[Doc. No. 26019, 61 FR 31329, June 19, 1996]

§ 33.94 Blade containment and rotor unbalance tests.

(a) Except as provided in paragraph (b) of this section, it must be demonstrated by engine tests that the engine is capable of containing damage without catching fire and without failure of its mounting attachments when operated for at least 15 seconds, unless the resulting engine damage induces a self shutdown, after each of the following events:

(1) Failure of the most critical compressor or fan blade while operating at maximum permissible r.p.m. The blade failure must occur at the outermost retention groove or, for integrally-bladed rotor discs, at least 80 percent of the blade must fail.

(2) Failure of the most critical turbine blade while operating at maximum permissible r.p.m. The blade failure must occur at the outermost retention groove or, for integrally-bladed rotor discs, at least 80 percent of the blade must fail. The most critical turbine blade must be determined by considering turbine blade weight and the strength of the adjacent turbine case at case temperatures and pressures associated with operation at maximum permissible r.p.m.

(b) Analysis based on rig testing, component testing, or service experience may be substitute for one of the engine tests prescribed in paragraphs (a)(1) and (a)(2) of this section if—

(1) That test, of the two prescribed, produces the least rotor unbalance; and

(2) The analysis is shown to be equivalent to the test.

Secs. 313(a), 601, and 603, Federal Aviation Act of 1958 (49 U.S.C. 1354(a), 1421, and 1423); and 49 U.S.C. 106(g) Revised, Pub. L. 97–449, Jan. 12, 1983)

[Amdt. 33–10, 49 FR 6854, Feb. 23, 1984]

§ 33.95 Engine-propeller systems tests.

If the engine is designed to operate with a propeller, the following tests must be made with a representative propeller installed by either including the tests in the endurance run or otherwise performing them in a manner acceptable to the Administrator:

(a) Feathering operation: 25 cycles.

(b) Negative torque and thrust system operation: 25 cycles from rated maximum continuous power.

(c) Automatic decoupler operation: 25 cycles from rated maximum continuous power (if repeated decoupling and recoupling in service is the intended function of the device).

(d) Reverse thrust operation: 175 cycles from the flight-idle position to full reverse and 25 cycles at rated maximum continuous power from full forward to full reverse thrust. At the end of each cycle the propeller must be operated in reverse pitch for a period of 30 seconds at the maximum rotational speed and power specified by the applicant for reverse pitch operation.

[Doc. No. 3025, 29 FR 7453, June 10, 1964, as amended by Amdt. 33–3, 32 FR 3737, Mar. 4, 1967]

§ 33.96 Engine tests in auxiliary power unit (APU) mode.

If the engine is designed with a propeller brake which will allow the propeller to be brought to a stop while the gas generator portion of the engine remains in operation, and remain stopped during operation of the engine as an auxiliary power unit ("APU mode"), in addition to the requirements of § 33.87, the applicant must conduct the following tests:

(a) Ground locking: A total of 45 hours with the propeller brake engaged in a manner which clearly demonstrates its ability to function without adverse effects on the complete engine while the engine is operating in the APU mode under the maximum

conditions of engine speed, torque, temperature, air bleed, and power extraction as specified by the applicant.

(b) Dynamic braking: A total of 400 application-release cycles of brake engagements must be made in a manner which clearly demonstrates its ability to function without adverse effects on the complete engine under the maximum conditions of engine acceleration/deceleration rate, speed, torque, and temperature as specified by the applicant. The propeller must be stopped prior to brake release.

(c) One hundred engine starts and stops with the propeller brake engaged.

(d) The tests required by paragraphs (a), (b), and (c) of this section must be performed on the same engine, but this engine need not be the same engine used for the tests required by § 33.87.

(e) The tests required by paragraphs (a), (b), and (c) of this section must be followed by engine disassembly to the extent necessary to show compliance with the requirements of § 33.93(a) and § 33.93(b).

[Amdt. 33–11, 51 FR 10346, Mar. 25, 1986]

§ 33.97 Thrust reversers.

(a) If the engine incorporates a reverser, the endurance calibration, operation, and vibration tests prescribed in this subpart must be run with the reverser installed. In complying with this section, the power control lever must be moved from one extreme position to the other in not more than one second except, if regimes of control operations are incorporated necessitating scheduling of the power-control lever motion in going from one extreme position to the other, a longer period of time is acceptable but not more than three seconds. In addition, the test prescribed in paragraph (b) of this section must be made. This test may be scheduled as part of the endurance run.

(b) 175 reversals must be made from flight-idle forward thrust to maximum reverse thrust and 25 reversals must be made from rated takeoff thrust to maximum reverse thrust. After each reversal the reverser must be operated at full reverse thrust for a period of one minute, except that, in the case of a reverser intended for use only as a braking means on the ground, the reverser need only be operated at full reverse thrust for 30 seconds.

[Doc. No. 3025, 29 FR 7453, June 10, 1964, as amended by Amdt. 33–3, 32 FR 3737, Mar. 4, 1967]

§ 33.99 General conduct of block tests.

(a) Each applicant may, in making a block test, use separate engines of identical design and construction in the vibration, calibration, endurance, and operation tests, except that, if a separate engine is used for the endurance test it must be subjected to a calibration check before starting the endurance test.

(b) Each applicant may service and make minor repairs to the engine during the block tests in accordance with the service and maintenance instructions submitted in compliance with § 33.4. If the frequency of the service is excessive, or the number of stops due to engine malfunction is excessive, or a major repair, or replacement of a part is found necessary during the block tests or as the result of findings from the teardown inspection, the engine or its parts must be subjected to any additional tests the Administrator finds necessary.

(c) Each applicant must furnish all testing facilities, including equipment and competent personnel, to conduct the block tests.

[Doc. No. 3025, 29 FR 7453, June 10, 1964, as amended by Amdt. 33–6, 39 FR 35470, Oct. 1, 1974; Amdt. 33–9, 45 FR 60181, Sept. 11, 1980]

APPENDIX A TO PART 33—INSTRUCTIONS FOR CONTINUED AIRWORTHINESS

A33.1 GENERAL

(a) This appendix specifies requirements for the preparation of Instructions for Continued Airworthiness as required by § 33.4.

(b) The Instructions for Continued Airworthiness for each engine must include the Instructions for Continued Airworthiness for all engine parts. If Instructions for Continued Airworthiness are not supplied by the engine part manufacturer for an engine part, the Instructions for Continued Airworthiness for the engine must include the information essential to the continued airworthiness of the engine.

(c) The applicant must submit to the FAA a program to show how changes to the Instructions for Continued Airworthiness made by the applicant or by the manufacturers of engine parts will be distributed.

A33.2 FORMAT

(a) The Instructions for Continued Airworthiness must be in the form of a manual or manuals as appropriate for the quantity of data to be provided.

(b) The format of the manual or manuals must provide for a practical arrangement.

A33.3 CONTENT

The contents of the manual or manuals must be prepared in the English language. The Instructions for Continued Airworthiness must contain the following manuals or sections, as appropriate, and information:

(a) *Engine Maintenance Manual or Section.*

(1) Introduction information that includes an explanation of the engine's features and data to the extent necessary for maintenance or preventive maintenance.

(2) A detailed description of the engine and its components, systems, and installations.

(3) Installation instructions, including proper procedures for uncrating, deinhibiting, acceptance checking, lifting, and attaching accessories, with any necessary checks.

(4) Basic control and operating information describing how the engine components, systems, and installations operate, and information describing the methods of starting, running, testing, and stopping the engine and its parts including any special procedures and limitations that apply.

(5) Servicing information that covers details regarding servicing points, capacities of tanks, reservoirs, types of fluids to be used, pressures applicable to the various systems, locations of lubrication points, lubricants to be used, and equipment required for servicing.

(6) Scheduling information for each part of the engine that provides the recommended periods at which it should be cleaned, inspected, adjusted, tested, and lubricated, and the degree of inspection the applicable wear tolerances, and work recommended at these periods. However, the applicant may refer to an accessory, instrument, or equipment manufacturer as the source of this information if the applicant shows that the item has an exceptionally high degree of complexity requiring specialized maintenance techniques, test equipment, or expertise. The recommended overhaul periods and necessary cross references to the Airworthiness Limitations section of the manual must also be included. In addition, the applicant must include an inspection program that includes the frequency and extent of the inspections necessary to provide for the continued airworthiness of the engine.

(7) Troubleshooting information describing probable malfunctions, how to recognize those malfunctions, and the remedial action for those malfunctions.

(8) Information describing the order and method of removing the engine and its parts and replacing parts, with any necessary precautions to be taken. Instructions for proper ground handling, crating, and shipping must also be included.

(9) A list of the tools and equipment necessary for maintenance and directions as to their method of use.

(b) *Engine Overhaul Manual or Section.* (1) Disassembly information including the order and method of disassembly for overhaul.

(2) Cleaning and inspection instructions that cover the materials and apparatus to be used and methods and precautions to be taken during overhaul. Methods of overhaul inspection must also be included.

(3) Details of all fits and clearances relevant to overhaul.

(4) Details of repair methods for worn or otherwise substandard parts and components along with the information necessary to determine when replacement is necessary.

(5) The order and method of assembly at overhaul.

(6) Instructions for testing after overhaul.

(7) Instructions for storage preparation, including any storage limits.

(8) A list of tools needed for overhaul.

A33.4 AIRWORTHINESS LIMITATIONS SECTION

The Instructions for Continued Airworthiness must contain a section titled Airworthiness Limitations that is segregated and clearly distinguishable from the rest of the document. This section must set forth each mandatory replacement time, inspection in-

terval, and related procedure required for type certification. If the Instructions for Continued Airworthiness consist of multiple documents, the section required by this paragraph must be included in the principal manual. This section must contain a legible statement in a prominent location that reads: "The Airworthiness Limitations section is FAA approved and specifies maintenance required under §§ 43.16 and 91.403 of the Federal Aviation Regulations unless an alternative program has been FAA approved."

[Amdt. 33–9, 45 FR 60181, Sept. 11, 1980, as amended by Amdt. 33–13, 54 FR 34330, Aug. 18, 1989]

APPENDIX B TO PART 33—CERTIFICATION STANDARD ATMOSPHERIC CONCENTRATIONS OF RAIN AND HAIL

Figure B1, Table B1, Table B2, Table B3, and Table B4 specify the atmospheric concentrations and size distributions of rain and hail for establishing certification, in accordance with the requirements of § 33.78(a)(2). In conducting tests, normally by spraying liquid water to simulate rain conditions and by delivering hail fabricated from ice to simulate hail conditions, the use of water droplets and hail having shapes, sizes and distributions of sizes other than those defined in this appendix B, or the use of a single size or shape for each water droplet or hail, can be accepted, provided that applicant shows that the substitution does not reduce the severity of the test.

FIGURE B1 - Illustration of Rain and Hail Threats. Certification concentrations are obtained using Tables B1 and B2.

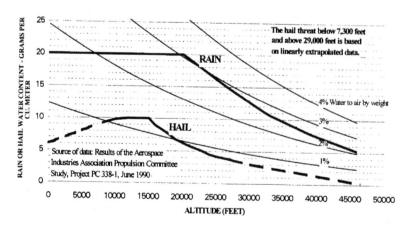

TABLE B1—CERTIFICATION STANDARD ATMOSPHERIC RAIN CONCENTRATIONS

Altitude (feet)	Rain water content (RWC) (grams water/meter³ air)
0	20.0
20,000	20.0
26,300	15.2
32,700	10.8
39,300	7.7
46,000	5.2

RWC values at other altitudes may be determined by linear interpolation.
NOTE: Source of data—Results of the Aerospace Industries Association (AIA) Propulsion Committee Study, Project PC 338–1, June 1990.

TABLE B2—CERTIFICATION STANDARD ATMOSPHERIC HAIL CONCENTRATIONS

Altitude (feet)	Hail water content (HWC) (grams water/meter³ air)
0	6.0
7,300	8.9
8,500	9.4
10,000	9.9
12,000	10.0
15,000	10.0
16,000	8.9
17,700	7.8
19,300	6.6
21,500	5.6
24,300	4.4
29,000	3.3
46,000	0.2

HWC values at other altitudes may be determined by linear interpolation. The hail threat below 7,300 feet and above 29,000 feet is based on linearly extrapolated data.
Note: Source of data—Results of the Aerospace Industries Association (AIA) Propulsion Committee (PC) Study, Project PC 338–1, June 1990.

TABLE B3—CERTIFICATION STANDARD ATMOSPHERIC RAIN DROPLET SIZE DISTRIBUTION

Rain droplet diameter (mm)	Contribution total RWC (%)
0–0.49	0
0.50–0.99	2.25
1.00–1.49	8.75
1.50–1.99	16.25
2.00–2.49	19.00
2.50–2.99	17.75
3.00–3.49	13.50
3.50–3.99	9.50
4.00–4.49	6.00
4.50–4.99	3.00
5.00–5.49	2.00
5.50–5.99	1.25
6.00–6.49	0.50
6.50–7.00	0.25

TABLE B3—CERTIFICATION STANDARD ATMOSPHERIC RAIN DROPLET SIZE DISTRIBUTION—Continued

Rain droplet diameter (mm)	Contribution total RWC (%)
Total	100.00

Median diameter of rain droplets in 2.66 mm
Note: Source of data—Results of the Aerospace Industries Association (AIA) Propulsion Committee (PC) Study, Project PC 338–1, June 1990.

TABLE B4—CERTIFICATION STANDARD ATMOSPHERIC HAIL SIZE DISTRIBUTION

Hail diameter (mm)	Contribution total HWC (%)
0–4.9	0
5.0–9.9	17.00
10.0–14.9	25.00
15.0–19.9	22.50
20.0–24.9	16.00
25.0–29.9	9.75
30.0–34.9	4.75
35.0–39.9	2.50
40.0–44.9	1.50
45.0–49.9	0.75
50.0–55.0	0.25
Total	100.00

Median diameter of hail is 16 mm
Note: Source of data—Results of the Aerospace Industries Association (AIA) Propulsion Committee (PC) Study, Project PC 338–1, June 1990.

[Doc. No. 28652, 63 FR 14799, Mar. 26, 1998]

PART 34—FUEL VENTING AND EXHAUST EMISSION REQUIREMENTS FOR TURBINE ENGINE POWERED AIRPLANES

Subpart A—General Provisions

Sec.
34.1 Definitions.
34.2 Abbreviations.
34.3 General requirements.
34.4 [Reserved]
34.5 Special test procedures.
34.6 Aircraft safety.
34.7 Exemptions.

Subpart B—Engine Fuel Venting Emissions (New and In-Use Aircraft Gas Turbine Engines)

34.10 Applicability.
34.11 Standard for fuel venting emissions.

Subpart C—Exhaust Emissions (New Aircraft Gas Turbine Engines)

34.20 Applicability.
34.21 Standards for exhaust emissions.

AUTHORITY: 42 U.S.C. 4321 *et seq.*, 7572; 49 U.S.C. 106(g), 40113, 44701–44702, 44704, 44714.

SOURCE: Docket No. 25613, 55 FR 32861, Aug. 10, 1990, unless otherwise noted.

Subpart A—General Provisions

§ 34.1 Definitions.

As used in this part, all terms not defined herein shall have the meaning given them in the Clean Air Act, as amended (42 U.S.C. 7401 et. seq.):

Act means the Clean Air Act, as amended (42 U.S.C. 7401 et. seq.).

Administrator means the Administrator of the Federal Aviation Administration or any person to whom he has delegated his authority in the matter concerned.

Administrator of the EPA means the Administrator of the Environmental Protection Agency and any other officer or employee of the Environmental Protection Agency to whom the authority involved may be delegated.

Aircraft as used in this part means any airplane as defined in 14 CFR part 1 for which a U.S. standard airworthiness certificate or equivalent foreign airworthiness certificate is issued.

Aircraft engine means a propulsion engine which is installed in, or which is manufactured for installation in, an aircraft.

Aircraft gas turbine engine means a turboprop, turbofan, or turbojet aircraft engine.

Class TP means all aircraft turboprop engines.

Class TF means all turbofan or turbojet aircraft engines or aircraft engines designed for applications that otherwise would have been fulfilled by turbojet and turbofan engines except engines of class T3, T8, and TSS.

Class T3 means all aircraft gas turbine engines of the JT3D model family.

Class T8 means all aircraft gas turbine engines of the JT8D model family.

Class TSS means all aircraft gas turbine engines employed for propulsion of aircraft designed to operate at supersonic flight speeds.

Commercial aircraft engine means any aircraft engine used or intended for use by an "air carrier" (including those engaged in "intrastate air transportation") or a "commercial operator" (including those engaged in "intrastate air transportation") as these terms are defined in the Federal Aviation Act and the Federal Aviation Regulations.

Commercial aircraft gas turbine engine means a turboprop, turbofan, or turbojet commercial aircraft engine.

Date of manufacture of an engine is the date the inspection acceptance records reflect that the engine is complete and meets the FAA approved type design.

Emission measurement system means all of the equipment necessary to transport the emission sample and measure the level of emissions. This includes the sample system and the instrumentation system.

Engine model means all commercial aircraft turbine engines which are of the same general series, displacement, and design characteristics and are approved under the same type certificate.

Exhaust emissions means substances emitted into the atmosphere from the exhaust discharge nozzle of an aircraft or aircraft engine.

Fuel venting emissions means raw fuel, exclusive of hydrocarbons in the exhaust emissions, discharged from aircraft gas turbine engines during all normal ground and flight operations.

In-use aircraft gas turbine engine means an aircraft gas turbine engine which is in service.

New aircraft turbine engine means an aircraft gas turbine engine which has never been in service.

Power setting means the power or thrust output of an engine in terms of kilonewtons thrust for turbojet and turbofan engines or shaft power in terms of kilowatts for turboprop engines.

Rated output (r0) means the maximum power/thrust available for takeoff at standard day conditions as approved for the engine by the Federal Aviation Administration, including reheat contribution where applicable, but excluding any contribution due to water injection and excluding any emergency power/thrust rating.

Rated pressure ratio (rPR) means the ratio between the combustor inlet pressure and the engine inlet pressure achieved by an engine operation at rated output.

Reference day conditions means the reference ambient conditions to which the gaseous emissions (HC and smoke) are to be corrected. The reference day conditions are as follows: Temperature=15 °C, specific humidity=0.00629 kg H_2O/kg of dry air, and pressure=101325 Pa.

Sample system means the system which provides for the transportation of the gaseous emission sample from the sample probe to the inlet of the instrumentation system.

Shaft power means only the measured shaft power output of a turboprop engine.

Smoke means the matter in exhaust emissions which obscures the transmission of light.

Smoke number (SN) means the dimensionless term quantifying smoke emissions.

Standard day conditions means standard ambient conditions as described in the United States Standard Atmosphere 1976, (i.e., temperature=15 °C, specific humidity=0.00 kg H_2O/kg dry air, and pressure=101325 Pa.)

Taxi/idle (in) means those aircraft operations involving taxi and idle between the time of landing roll-out and final shutdown of all propulsion engines.

Taxi/idle (out) means those aircraft operations involving taxi and idle between the time of initial starting of the propulsion engine(s) used for the taxi and the turn onto the duty runway.

[Doc. No. 25613, 55 FR 32861, Aug. 10, 1990; 55 FR 37287, Sept. 10, 1990, as amended by Amdt. 34–3, 64 FR 5558, Feb. 3, 1999]

§34.2 Abbreviations.

The abbreviations used in this part have the following meanings in both upper and lower case:

CO   Carbon monoxide
EPA   United States Environmental Protection Agency
FAA   Federal Aviation Administration, United States Department of Transportation
HC   Hydrocarbon(s)
HP   Horsepower
hr   Hour(s)
H_2O water
kg   Kilogram(s)
kJ   Kilojoule(s)
LTO   Landing and takeoff
min   Minute(s)
NO_x Oxides of nitrogen
Pa   Pascal(s)
rO   Rated output
rPR   Rated pressure ratio
sec   Second(s)
SP   Shaft power
SN   Smoke number
T   Temperature, degrees Kelvin
TIM   Time in mode
W   Watt(s)
°C   Degrees Celsius
%   Percent

Doc. No. 25613, 55 FR 32861, Aug. 10, 1990, as amended by Amdt. 34–3, 64 FR 5559, Feb. 3, 1999]

§34.3 General requirements.

(a) This part provides for the approval or acceptance by the Administrator or the Administrator of the EPA of testing and sampling methods, analytical techniques, and related equipment not identical to those specified in this part. Before either approves or accepts any such alternate, equivalent, or otherwise nonidentical procedures or equipment, the Administrator or the Administrator of the EPA shall consult with the other in determining whether or not the action requires rulemaking under sections 231 and 232 of the Clean Air Act, as amended, consistent with the responsibilities of the Administrator of the EPA and the Secretary of Transportation under sections 231 and 232 of the Clean Air Act.

(b) Under section 232 of the Act, the Secretary of Transportation issues regulations to ensure compliance with 40 CFR part 87. This authority has been delegated to the Administrator of the FAA (49 CFR 1.47).

(c) *U.S. airplanes.* This Federal Aviation Regulation (FAR) applies to civil airplanes that are powered by aircraft gas turbine engines of the classes specified herein and that have U.S. standard airworthiness certificates.

(d) *Foreign airplanes.* Pursuant to the definition of "aircraft" in 40 CFR 87.1(c), this FAR applies to civil airplanes that are powered by aircraft gas turbine engines of the classes specified herein and that have foreign airworthiness certificates that are equivalent to U.S. standard airworthiness certificates. This FAR applies only to those foreign civil airplanes that, if registered in the United States, would be required by applicable Federal Aviation Regulations to have a U.S. standard airworthiness certificate in order to conduct the operations intended for the airplane. Pursuant to 40 CFR 87.3(c), this FAR does not apply where it would be inconsistent with an obligation assumed by the United States to a foreign country in a treaty, convention, or agreement.

(e) Reference in this regulation to 40 CFR part 87 refers to title 40 of the Code of Federal Regulations, chapter I—Environmental Protection Agency, part 87, Control of Air Pollution from Aircraft and Aircraft Engines (40 CFR part 87).

(f) This part contains regulations to ensure compliance with certain standards contained in 40 CFR part 87. If EPA takes any action, including the issuance of an exemption or issuance of a revised or alternate procedure, test method, or other regulation, the effect of which is to relax or delay the effective date of any provision of 40 CFR

part 87 that is made applicable to an aircraft under this FAR, the Administrator of FAA will grant a general administrative waiver of its more stringent requirements until this FAR is amended to reflect the more relaxed requirements prescribed by EPA.

(g) Unless otherwise stated, all terminology and abbreviations in this FAR that are defined in 40 CFR part 87 have the meaning specified in that part, and all terms in 40 CFR part 87 that are not defined in that part but that are used in this FAR have the meaning given them in the Clean Air Act, as amended by Public Law 91–604.

(h) All interpretations of 40 CFR part 87 that are rendered by the EPA also apply to this FAR.

(i) If the EPA, under 40 CFR 87.3(a), approves or accepts any testing and sampling procedures or methods, analytical techniques, or related equipment not identical to those specified in that part, this FAR requires an applicant to show that such alternate, equivalent, or otherwise nonidentical procedures have been complied with, and that such alternate equipment was used to show compliance, unless the applicant elects to comply with those procedures, methods, techniques, and equipment specified in 40 CFR part 87.

(j) If the EPA, under 40 CFR 87.5, prescribes special test procedures for any aircraft or aircraft engine that is not susceptible to satisfactory testing by the procedures in 40 CFR part 87, the applicant must show the Administrator that those special test procedures have been complied with.

(k) Wherever 40 CFR part 87 requires agreement, acceptance, or approval by the Administrator of the EPA, this FAR requires a showing that such agreement or approval has been obtained.

(l) Pursuant to 42 U.S.C. 7573, no state or political subdivision thereof may adopt or attempt to enforce any standard respecting emissions of any air pollutant from any aircraft or engine thereof unless that standard is identical to a standard made applicable to the aircraft by the terms of this FAR.

(m) If EPA, by regulation or exemption, relaxes a provision of 40 CFR part 87 that is implemented in this FAR, no state or political subdivision thereof may adopt or attempt to enforce the terms of this FAR that are superseded by the relaxed requirement.

(n) If any provision of this FAR is rendered inapplicable to a foreign aircraft as provided in 40 CFR 87.3(c) (international agreements), and §34.3(d) of this FAR, that provision may not be adopted or enforced against that foreign aircraft by a state or political subdivision thereof.

(o) For exhaust emissions requirements of this FAR that apply beginning February 1, 1974, January 1, 1976, January 1, 1978, January 1, 1984, and August 9, 1985, continued compliance with those requirements is shown for engines for which the type design has been shown to meet those requirements, if the engine is maintained in accordance with applicable maintenance requirements for 14 CFR chapter I. All methods of demonstrating compliance and all model designations previously found acceptable to the Administrator shall be deemed to continue to be an acceptable demonstration of compliance with the specific standards for which they were approved.

(p) Each applicant must allow the Administrator to make, or witness, any test necessary to determine compliance with the applicable provisions of this FAR.

[Doc. No. 25613, 55 FR 32861, Aug. 10, 1990; 55 FR 37287, Sept. 10, 1990]

§34.4 [Reserved]

§34.5 Special test procedures.

The Administrator or the Administrator of the EPA may, upon written application by a manufacturer or operator of aircraft or aircraft engines, approve test procedures for any aircraft or aircraft engine that is not susceptible to satisfactory testing by the procedures set forth herein. Prior to taking action on any such application, the Administrator or the Administrator of the EPA shall consult with the other.

§34.6 Aircraft safety.

(a) The provisions of this part will be revised if at any time the Administrator determines that an emission standard cannot be met within the

specified time without creating a safety hazard.

(b) Consistent with 40 CFR 87.6, if the FAA Administrator determines that any emission control regulation in this part cannot be safely applied to an aircraft, that provision may not be adopted or enforced against that aircraft by any state or political subdivision thereof.

§34.7 Exemptions.

Notwithstanding part 11 of the Federal Aviation Regulations (14 CFR part 11), all petitions for rulemaking involving either the substance of an emission standard or test procedure prescribed by the EPA that is incorporated in this FAR, or the compliance date for such standard or procedure, must be submitted to the EPA. Information copies of such petitions are invited by the FAA. Petitions for rulemaking or exemption involving provisions of this FAR that do not affect the substance or the compliance date of an emission standard or test procedure that is prescribed by the EPA, and petitions for exemptions under the provisions for which the EPA has specifically granted exemption authority to the Secretary of Transportation are subject to part 11 of the Federal Aviation Regulations (14 CFR part 11). Petitions for rulemaking or exemptions involving these FARs must be submitted to the FAA.

(a) *Exemptions based on flights for short durations at infrequent intervals.* The emission standards of this part do not apply to engines which power aircraft operated in the United States for short durations at infrequent intervals. Such operations are limited to:

(1) Flights of an aircraft for the purpose of export to a foreign country, including any flights essential to demonstrate the integrity of an aircraft prior to a flight to a point outside the United States.

(2) Flights to a base where repairs, alterations or maintenance are to be performed, or to a point of storage, or for the purpose of returning an aircraft to service.

(3) Official visits by representatives of foreign governments.

(4) Other flights the Administrator determines, after consultation with the Administrator of the EPA, to be for

short durations at infrequent intervals. A request for such a determination shall be made before the flight takes place.

(b) *Exemptions for very low production engine models.* The emissions standards of this part do not apply to engines of very low production after the date of applicability. For the purpose of this part, "very low production" is limited to a maximum total production for United States civil aviation applications of no more than 200 units covered by the same type certificate after January 1, 1984. Engines manufactured under this provision must be reported to the FAA by serial number on or before the date of manufacture and exemptions granted under this provision are not transferable to any other engine.

(c) *Exemptions for new engines in other categories.* The emissions standards of this part do not apply to engines for which the Administrator determines, with the concurrence of the Administrator of the EPA, that application of any standard under § 34.21 is not justified, based upon consideration of—

(1) Adverse economic impact on the manufacturer;

(2) Adverse economic impact on the aircraft and airline industries at large;

(3) Equity in administering the standards among all economically competing parties;

(4) Public health and welfare effects; and

(5) Other factors which the Administrator, after consultation with the Administrator of the EPA, may deem relevant to the case in question.

(d) *Time-limited exemptions for in-use engines.* The emissions standards of this part do not apply to aircraft or aircraft engines for time periods which the Administrator determines, with the concurrence of the Administrator of the EPA, that any applicable standard under § 34.11(a), or § 34.31(a), should not be applied based upon consideration of—

(1) Documentation demonstrating that all good faith efforts to achieve compliance with such standard have been made;

(2) Documentation demonstrating that the inability to comply with such standard is due to circumstances be-

yond the control of the owner or operator of the aircraft; and

(3) A plan in which the owner or operator of the aircraft shows that he will achieve compliance in the shortest time which is feasible.

(e) Applications for exemption from this part shall be submitted in duplicate to the Administrator in accordance with the procedures established by the Administrator in part 11.

(f) The Administrator shall publish in the FEDERAL REGISTER the name of the organization to whom exemptions are granted and the period of such exemptions.

(g) No state or political subdivision thereof may attempt to enforce a standard respecting emissions from an aircraft or engine if such aircraft or engine has been exempted from such standard under this part.

Subpart B—Engine Fuel Venting Emissions (New and In-Use Aircraft Gas Turbine Engines)

§ 34.10 Applicability.

(a) The provisions of this subpart are applicable to all new aircraft gas turbine engines of classes T3, T8, TSS, and TF equal to or greater than 36 kilonewtons (8090 pounds) rated output, manufactured on or after January 1, 1974, and to all in-use aircraft gas turbine engines of classes T3, T8, TSS, and TF equal to or greater than 36 kilonewtons (8090 pounds) rated output manufactured after February 1, 1974.

(b) The provisions of this subpart are also applicable to all new aircraft gas turbine engines of class TF less than 36 kilonewtons (8090 pounds) rated output and class TP manufactured on or after January 1, 1975, and to all in-use aircraft gas turbine engines of class TF less than 36 kilonewtons (8090 pounds) rated output and class TP manufactured after January 1, 1975.

§ 34.11 Standard for fuel venting emissions.

(a) No fuel venting emissions shall be discharged into the atmosphere from any new or in-use aircraft gas turbine engine subject to the subpart. This paragraph is directed at the elimination of intentional discharge to the atmosphere of fuel drained from fuel nozzle manifolds after engines are shut down and does not apply to normal fuel seepage from shaft seals, joints, and fittings.

(b) Conformity with the standard set forth in paragraph (a) of this section shall be determined by inspection of the method designed to eliminate these emissions.

(c) As applied to an airframe or an engine, any manufacturer or operator may show compliance with the fuel venting and emissions requirements of this section that were effective beginning February 1, 1974 or January 1, 1975, by any means that prevents the intentional discharge of fuel from fuel nozzle manifolds after the engines are shut down. Acceptable means of compliance include one of the following:

(1) Incorporation of an FAA-approved system that recirculates the fuel back into the fuel system.

(2) Capping or securing the pressurization and drain valve.

(3) Manually draining the fuel from a holding tank into a container.

Subpart C—Exhaust Emissions (New Aircraft Gas Turbine Engines)

§ 34.20 Applicability.

The provisions of this subpart are applicable to all aircraft gas turbine engines of the classes specified beginning on the dates specified in § 34.21.

§ 34.21 Standards for exhaust emissions.

(a) Exhaust emissions of smoke from each new aircraft gas turbine engine of class T8 manufactured on or after February 1, 1974, shall not exceed a smoke number (SN) of 30.

(b) Exhaust emissions of smoke from each new aircraft gas turbine engine of class TF and of rated output of 129 kilonewtons (29,000 pounds) thrust or greater, manufactured on or after January 1, 1976, shall not exceed

$SN = 83.6 (rO) - 0.274$ (rO is in kilonewtons).

(c) Exhaust emission of smoke from each new aircraft gas turbine engine of class T3 manufactured on or after January 1, 1978, shall not exceed a smoke number (SN) of 25.

(d) Gaseous exhaust emissions from each new aircraft gas turbine engine shall not exceed:

(1) For Classes TF, T3, T8 engines greater than 26.7 kilonewtons (6000 pounds) rated output:

(i) Engines manufactured on or after January 1, 1984:

Hydrocarbons: 19.6 grams/kilonewton r0.

(ii) Engines manufactured on or after July 7, 1997.

Carbon Monoxide: 118 grams/kilonewton r0.

(iii) Engines of a type or model of which the date of manufacture of the first individual production model was on or before December 31, 1995, and for which the date of manufacture of the individual engine was on or before December 31, 1999:

Oxides of Nitrogen: $(40+2(rPR))$ grams/ kilonewtons r0.

(iv) Engines of a type or model of which the date of manufacture of the first individual production model was after December 31, 1995, or for which the date of manufacture of the individual engine was after December 31, 1999:

Oxides of Nitrogen: $(32+1.6 \ (rPR))$ grams/ kilonewtons r0.

(v) The emission standards prescribed in paragraphs (d)(1)(iii) and (iv) of this section apply as prescribed beginning July 7, 1997.

(2) For Class TSS Engines manufactured on or after January 1, 1984:

Hydrocarbons=140 $\quad (0.92)^{rPR}$ grams/ kilonewtons r0.

(e) Smoke exhaust emissions from each gas turbine engine of the classes specified below shall not exceed:

(1) Class TF of rated output less than 26.7 kilonewtons (6000 pounds) manufactured on or after August 9, 1985

$SN = 83.6(rO)^{-0.274}$ (rO is in kilonewtons) not to exceed a maximum of SN=50.

(2) Classes T3, T8, TSS, and TF of rated output equal to or greater than 26.7 kilonewtons (6000 pounds) manufactured on or after January 1, 1984

$SN = 83.6(rO)^{-0.274}$ (rO is in kilonewtons) not to exceed a maximum of SN=50.

(3) For Class TP of rated output equal to or greater than 1,000 kilowatts

manufactured on or after January 1, 1984:

$$SN=187(ro)^{-0.168} \text{ (ro is in kilowatts)}$$

(f) The standards set forth in paragraphs (a), (b), (c), (d), and (e) of this section refer to a composite gaseous emission sample representing the operating cycles set forth in the applicable sections of subpart G of this part, and exhaust smoke emissions emitted during operations of the engine as specified in the applicable sections of subpart H of this part, measured and calculated in accordance with the procedures set forth in those subparts.

[Doc. No. 25613, 55 FR 32861, Aug. 10, 1990; 55 FR 37287, Sept. 10, 1990, as amended by Amdt. 34–3, 64 FR 5559, Feb. 3, 1999]

Subpart D—Exhaust Emissions (In-use Aircraft Gas Turbine Engines)

§ 34.30 Applicability.

The provisions of this subpart are applicable to all in-use aircraft gas turbine engines certificated for operation within the United States of the classes specified, beginning on the dates specified in § 34.31.

§ 34.31 Standards for exhaust emissions.

(a) Exhaust emissions of smoke from each in-use aircraft gas turbine engine of Class T8, beginning February 1, 1974, shall not exceed a smoke number (SN) of 30.

(b) Exhaust emissions of smoke from each in-use aircraft gas turbine engine of Class TF and of rated output of 129 kilonewtons (29,000 pounds) thrust or greater, beginning January 1, 1976, shall not exceed

$$SN=83.6(rO)^{-0.274} \text{ (rO is in kilonewtons).}$$

(c) The standards set forth in paragraphs (a) and (b) of this section refer to exhaust smoke emissions emitted during operations of the engine as specified in the applicable section of subpart H of this part, and measured and calculated in accordance with the procedure set forth in this subpart.

Subparts E–F [Reserved]

Subpart G—Test Procedures for Engine Exhaust Gaseous Emissions (Aircraft and Aircraft Gas Turbine Engines)

§ 34.60 Introduction.

(a) Except as provided under § 34.5, the procedures described in this subpart shall constitute the test program used to determine the conformity of new aircraft gas turbine engines with the applicable standards set forth in this part.

(b) The test consists of operating the engine at prescribed power settings on an engine dynamometer (for engines producing primarily shaft power) or thrust measuring test stand (for engines producing primarily thrust). The exhaust gases generated during engine operation must be sampled continuously for specific component analysis through the analytical train.

(c) The exhaust emission test is designed to measure concentrations of hydrocarbons, carbon monoxide, carbon dioxide, and oxides of nitrogen, and to determine mass emissions through calculations during a simulated aircraft landing-takeoff cycle (LTO). The LTO cycle is based on time in mode data during high activity periods at major airports. The test for propulsion engines consists of at least the following four modes of engine operation: taxi/idle, takeoff, climbout, and approach. The mass emission for the modes are combined to yield the reported values.

(d) When an engine is tested for exhaust emissions on an engine dynamometer or test stand, the complete engine (with all accessories which might reasonably be expected to influence emissions to the atmosphere installed and functioning), shall be used if not otherwise prohibited by § 34.62(a)(2). Use of service air bleed and shaft power extraction to power auxiliary, gearbox-mounted components required to drive aircraft systems is not permitted.

(e) Other gaseous emissions measurement systems may be used if shown to yield equivalent results and if approved in advance by the Administrator or the Administrator of the EPA.

[Doc. No. 25613, 55 FR 32861, Aug. 10, 1990, as amended by Amdt. 34–3, 64 FR 5559, Feb. 3, 1999]

§34.61 Turbine fuel specifications.

For exhaust emission testing, fuel that meets the specifications listed in this section shall be used. Additives used for the purpose of smoke suppression (such as organometallic compounds) shall not be present.

SPECIFICATION FOR FUEL TO BE USED IN AIRCRAFT TURBINE ENGINE EMISSION TESTING

Property	Allowable range of values
Density at 15 °C	780–820.
Distillation Temperature, °C 10% Boiling Point.	155–201.
Final Boiling Point	235–285.
Net Heat of Combustion, MJ/Kg	42.86–43.50.
Aromatics, Volume %	15–23.
Naphthalenes, Volume %	1.0–3.5.
Smoke point, mm	20–28.
Hydrogen, Mass %	13.4–14.1.
Sulfur Mass %	Less than 0.3%.
Kinematic viscosity at—20 °C, mm² /sec.	2.5–6.5.

[Doc. No. FAA–1999–5018, 64 FR 5559, Feb. 3, 1999]

§34.62 Test procedure (propulsion engines).

(a)(1) The engine shall be tested in each of the following engine operating modes which simulate aircraft operation to determine its mass emission rates. The actual power setting, when corrected to standard day conditions, should correspond to the following percentages of rated output. Analytical correction for variations from reference day conditions and minor variations in actual power setting should be specified and/or approved by the Administrator:

Mode	Class		
	TP	TF, T3, T8	TSS
Taxi/idle	(*)	(*)	(*)
Takeoff	100	100	100
Climbout	90	85	65
Descent	NA	NA	15
Approach	30	30	34

*See paragraph (a) of this section.

(2) The taxi/idle operating modes shall be carried out at a power setting of 7% rated thrust unless the Administrator determines that the unique characteristics of an engine model undergoing certification testing at 7% would result in substantially different HC and CO emissions than if the engine model were tested at the manufacturers recommended idle power setting. In such cases the Administrator shall specify an alternative test condition.

(3) The times in mode (TIM) shall be as specified below:

Mode	Class		
	TP	TF, T3, T8	TSS
Taxi/idle	26.0 Min.	26.0 Min.	26.0 Min.
Takeoff	0.5	0.7	1.2
Climbout	2.5	2.2	2.0
Descent	N/A	N/A	1.2
Approach	4.5	4.0	2.3

(b) Emissions testing shall be conducted on warmed-up engines which have achieved a steady operating temperature.

[Doc. No. 25613, 55 FR 32861, Aug. 10, 1990; 55 FR 37287, Sept. 10, 1990, as amended by Amdt. 34–3, 64 FR 5559, Feb. 3, 1999]

§34.63 [Reserved]

§34.64 Sampling and analytical procedures for measuring gaseous exhaust emissions.

The system and procedures for sampling and measurement of gaseous emissions shall be as specified in Appendices 3 and 5 to the International Civil Aviation Organization (ICAO) Annex 16, Environmental Protection, Volume II, Aircraft Engine Emissions, Second Edition, July 1993, effective March 20, 1997. This incorporation by reference was approved by the Director of the Federal Register in accordance with 5 U.S.C. 552(a) and 1 CFR part 51. This document can be obtained from the International Civil Aviation Organization (ICAO), Document Sales Unit, P.O. Box 400, Succursale: Place de L'Aviation Internationale, 1000 Sherbrooke Street West, Suite 400, Montreal, Quebec, Canada H3A 2R2. Copies may be reviewed at the FAA Office of the Chief Counsel, Rules Docket, Room 916, Federal Aviation Administration Headquarters Building, 800 Independence Avenue, SW., Washington, DC, or at the FAA New England Regional Office, 12 New England Executive Park, Burlington, Massachusetts, or at the Office of Federal Register, 800 North Capitol Street, NW., Suite 700, Washington, DC.

[Doc. No. FAA–1999–5018, 64 FR 5559, Feb. 3, 1999; Amdt. 34–3, 64 FR 60336, Nov. 5, 1999]

§§ 34.65–34.70 [Reserved]

§ 34.71 Compliance with gaseous emission standards.

Compliance with each gaseous emission standard by an aircraft engine shall be determined by comparing the pollutant level in grams/kilonewton/thrust/cycle or grams/kilowatt/cycle as calculated in § 34.64 with the applicable emission standard under this part. An acceptable alternative to testing every engine is described in Appendix 6 to ICAO Annex 16, Environmental Protection, Volume II, Aircraft Engine Emissions, Second Edition, July 1993, effective July 26, 1993. This incorporation by reference was approved by the Director of the Federal Register in accordance with 5 U.S.C. 552(a) and 1 CFR part 51. This document can be obtained from, and copies may be reviewed at, the respective addresses listed in § 34.64. Other methods of demonstrating compliance may be approved by the FAA Administrator with the concurrence of the Administrator of the EPA.

[Doc. No. FAA–1999–5018, 64 FR 5559, Feb. 3, 1999; Amdt. 34–3, 64 FR 60336, Nov. 5, 1999]

Subpart H—Test Procedures for Engine Smoke Emissions (Aircraft Gas Turbine Engines)

§ 34.80 Introduction.

Except as provided under § 34.5, the procedures described in this subpart shall constitute the test program to be used to determine the conformity of new and in-use gas turbine engines with the applicable standards set forth in this part. The test is essentially the same as that described in §§ 34.60–34.62, except that the test is designed to determine the smoke emission level at various operating points representative of engine usage in aircraft. Other smoke measurement systems may be used if shown to yield equivalent results and if approved in advance by the Administrator or the Administrator of the EPA.

§ 34.81 Fuel specifications.

Fuel having specifications as provided in § 34.61 shall be used in smoke emission testing.

§ 34.82 Sampling and analytical procedures for measuring smoke exhaust emissions.

The system and procedures for sampling and measurement of smoke emissions shall be as specified in Appendix 2 to ICAO Annex 16, Volume II, Environmental Protection, Aircraft Engine Emissions, Second Edition, July 1993, effective July 26, 1993. This incorporation by reference was approved by the Director of the Federal Register in accordance with 5 U.S.C. 552(a) and 1 CFR part 51. This document can be obtained from, and copies may be reviewed at, the respective addresses listed in § 34.64.

[Doc. No. FAA–1999–5018, 64 FR 5560, Feb. 3, 1999; Amdt. 34–3, 64 FR 60336, Nov. 5, 1999]

§§ 34.83–34.88 [Reserved]

§ 34.89 Compliance with smoke emission standards.

Compliance with each smoke emission standard shall be determined by comparing the plot of SN as a function of power setting with the applicable emission standard under this part. The SN at every power setting must be such that there is a high degree of confidence that the standard will not be exceeded by any engine of the model being tested. An acceptable alternative to testing every engine is described in Appendix 6 to ICAO Annex 16, Environmental Protection, Volume II, Aircraft Engine Emissions, Second Edition, July 1993, effective July 26, 1993. This incorporation by reference was approved by the Director of the Federal Register in accordance with 5 U.S.C. 552(a) and 1 CFR part 51. This document can be obtained from the address listed in § 34.64. Other methods of demonstrating compliance may be approved by the Administrator with the concurrence of the Administrator of the EPA.

[Doc. No. FAA–1999–5018, 64 FR 5560, Feb. 3, 1999; Amdt. 34–3, 64 FR 60336, Nov. 5, 1999]

PART 35—AIRWORTHINESS STANDARDS: PROPELLERS

Subpart A—General

AUTHORITY: 49 U.S.C. 106(g), 40113, 44701–44702, 44704.

SOURCE: Docket No. 2095, 29 FR 7458, June 10, 1964, unless otherwise noted.

Subpart A—General

§ 35.1 Applicability.

(a) This part prescribes airworthiness standards for the issue of type certificates and changes to those certificates, for propellers.

(b) Each person who applies under Part 21 for such a certificate or change must show compliance with the applicable requirements of this part.

[Amdt. 35–3, 41 FR 55475, Dec. 20, 1976]

§ 35.3 Instruction manual for installing and operating the propeller.

Each applicant must prepare and make available an approved manual or manuals containing instructions for installing and operating the propeller.

[Amdt. 35–5, 45 FR 60181, Sept. 11, 1980]

§ 35.4 Instructions for Continued Airworthiness.

The applicant must prepare Instructions for Continued Airworthiness in accordance with appendix A to this part that are acceptable to the Administrator. The instructions may be incomplete at type certification if a program exists to ensure their completion prior to delivery of the first aircraft with the propeller installed, or upon issuance of a standard certificate of airworthiness for an aircraft with the propeller installed, whichever occurs later.

[Amdt. 35–5, 45 FR 60181, Sept. 11, 1980]

§ 35.5 Propeller operating limitations.

Propeller operating limitations are established by the Administrator, are included in the propeller type certificate data sheet specified in § 21.41 of this chapter, and include limitations based on the operating conditions demonstrated during the tests required by this part and any other information found necessary for the safe operation of the propeller.

[Amdt. 35–5, 45 FR 60182, Sept. 11, 1980]

Subpart B—Design and Construction

§ 35.11 Applicability.

This subpart prescribes the design and construction requirements for propellers.

§ 35.13 General.

Each applicant must show that the propeller concerned meets the design and construction requirements of this subpart.

§ 35.15 Design features.

The propeller may not have design features that experience has shown to be hazardous or unreliable. The suitability of each questionable design detail or part must be established by tests.

§ 35.17 Materials.

The suitability and durability of materials used in the propeller must—

(a) Be established on the basis of experience or tests; and

(b) Conform to approved specifications (such as industry or military specifications, or Technical Standard Orders) that ensure their having the strength and other properties assumed in the design data.

(Secs. 313(a), 601, and 603, 72 Stat. 752, 775, 49 U.S.C. 1354(a), 1421, and 1423; sec. 6(c), 49 U.S.C. 1655(c))

[Amdt. 35–4, 42 FR 15047, Mar. 17, 1977]

§ 35.19 Durability.

Each part of the propeller must be designed and constructed to minimize the development of any unsafe condition of the propeller between overhaul periods.

§ 35.21 Reversible propellers.

A reversible propeller must be adaptable for use with a reversing system in an airplane so that no single failure or malfunction in that system during normal or emergency operation will result in unwanted travel of the propeller blades to a position substantially below the normal flight low-pitch stop. Failure of structural elements need not be considered if the occurrence of such a failure is expected to be extremely remote. For the purposes of this section the term "reversing system" means that part of the complete reversing system that is in the propeller itself and those other parts that are supplied by the applicant for installation in the aircraft.

§ 35.23 Pitch control and indication.

(a) No loss of normal propeller pitch control may cause hazardous overspeeding of the propeller under intended operating conditions.

(b) Each pitch control system that is within the propeller, or supplied with the propeller, and that uses engine oil for feathering, must incorporate means to override or bypass the normally operative hydraulic system components so as to allow feathering if those components fail or malfunction.

(c) Each propeller approved for installation on a turbopropeller engine must incorporate a provision for an indicator to indicate when the propeller blade angle is below the flight low pitch position. The provision must directly sense the blade position and be arranged to cause an indicator to indicate that the blade angle is below the flight low pitch position before the blade moves more than 8° below the flight low pitch stop.

[Amdt. 35–2, 32 FR 3737, Mar. 4, 1967, as amended by Amdt. 35—5, 45 FR 60182, Sept. 11, 1980]

Subpart C—Tests and Inspections

§ 35.31 Applicability.

This subpart prescribes the tests and inspections for propellers and their essential accessories.

§ 35.33 General.

(a) Each applicant must show that the propeller concerned and its essential accessories complete the tests and inspections of this subpart without evidence of failure or malfunction.

(b) Each applicant must furnish testing facilities, including equipment, and competent personnel, to conduct the required tests.

§ 35.35 Blade retention test.

The hub and blade retention arrangement of propellers with detachable blades must be subjected to a centrifugal load of twice the maximum centrifugal force to which the propeller would be subjected during operations within the limitations established for the propeller. This may be done by either a whirl test or a static pull test.

(Secs. 313(a), 601, and 603, 72 Stat. 752, 775, 49 U.S.C. 1354(a), 1421, and 1423; sec. 6(c), 49 U.S.C. 1655(c))

[Amdt. 35–4, 42 FR 15047, Mar. 17, 1977]

§ 35.37 Fatigue limit tests.

A fatigue evalution must be made and the fatigue limits determined for each metallic hub and blade, and each primary load carrying metal component of nonmetallic blades. The fatigue evaluation must include consideration of all reasonably foreseeable vibration load patterns. The fatigue limits must account for the permissible service deteriortion (such as nicks, grooves, galling, bearing wear, and variations in material properties).

[Amdt. 35–5, 45 FR 60182, Sept. 11, 1980]

§35.39 Endurance test.

(a) *Fixed-pitch wood propellers.* Fixed-pitch wood propellers must be subjected to one of the following tests:

(1) A 10-hour endurance block test on an engine with a propeller of the greatest pitch and diameter for which certification is sought at the rated rotational speed.

(2) A 50-hour flight test in level flight or in climb. At least five hours of this flight test must be with the propeller operated at the rated rotational speed, and the remainder of the 50 hours must be with the propeller operated at not less than 90 percent of the rated rotational speed. This test must be conducted on a propeller of the greatest diameter for which certification is requested.

(3) A 50-hour endurance block test on an engine at the power and propeller rotational speed for which certification is sought. This test must be conducted on a propeller of the greatest diameter for which certification is requested.

(b) *Fixed-pitch metal propellers and ground adjustable-pitch propellers.* Each fixed-pitch metal propeller or ground adjustable-pitch propeller must be subjected to the test prescribed in either paragraph (a)(2) or (a)(3) of this section.

(c) *Variable-pitch propellers.* Compliance with this paragraph must be shown for a propeller of the greatest diameter for which certification is requested. Each variable-pitch propeller (a propeller the pitch setting of which can be changed by the flight crew or by automatic means while the propeller is rotating) must be subjected to one of the following tests:

(1) A 100-hour test on a representative engine with the same or higher power and rotational speed and the same or more severe vibration characteristics as the engine with which the propeller is to be used. Each test must be made at the maximum continuous rotational speed and power rating of the propeller. If a takeoff rating greater than the maximum continuous rating is to be established, and additional 10-hour block test must be made at the

maximum power and rotational speed for the takeoff rating.

(2) Operation of the propeller throughout the engine endurance tests prescribed in Part 33 of this subchapter.

[Doc. No. 2095, 29 FR 7458, June 10, 1964, as amended by Amdt. 35–2, 32 FR 3737, Mar. 4, 1967; Amdt. 35–3, 41 FR 55475, Dec. 20, 1976]

§35.41 Functional test.

(a) Each variable-pitch propeller must be subjected to the applicable functional tests of this section. The same propeller used in the endurance test must be used in the functional tests and must be driven by an engine on a test stand or on an aircraft.

(b) *Manually controllable propellers.* 500 complete cycles of control must be made throughout the pitch and rotational speed ranges.

(c) *Automatically controllable propellers.* 1,500 complete cycles of control must be made throughout the pitch and rotational speed ranges.

(d) *Feathering propellers.* 50 cycles of feathering operation must be made.

(e) *Reversible-pitch propellers.* Two hundred complete cycles of control must be made from lowest normal pitch to maximum reverse pitch, and, while in maximum reverse pitch, during each cycle, the propeller must be run for 30 seconds at the maximum power and rotational speed selected by the applicant for maximum reverse pitch.

[Doc. No. 2095, 29 FR 7458, June 10, 1964, as amended by Amdt. 35–3, 41 FR 55475, Dec. 20, 1976]

§35.42 Blade pitch control system component test.

The following durability requirements apply to propeller blade pitch control system components:

(a) Except as provided in paragraph (b) of this section, each propeller blade pitch control system component, including governors, pitch change assemblies, pitch locks, mechanical stops, and feathering system components, must be subjected to cyclic tests to cyclic loadings that simulate the frequency and amplitude those to which the component would be subjected during 1,000 hours of propeller operation.

(b) Compliance with paragraph (a) of this section may be shown by a rational analysis based on the results of tests on similar components.

[Amdt. 35–5, 45 FR 60182, Sept. 11, 1980]

§ 35.43 Special tests.

The Administrator may require any additional tests he finds necessary to substantiate the use of any unconventional features of design, material, or construction.

§ 35.45 Teardown inspection.

(a) After completion of the tests prescribed in this subpart, the propeller must be completely disassembled and a detailed inspection must be made of the propeller parts for cracks, wear, distortion, and any other unusual conditions.

(b) After the inspection the applicant must make any changes to the design or any additional tests that the Administrator finds necessary to establish the airworthiness of the propeller.

[Doc. No. 3095, 29 FR 7458, June 10, 1964, as amended by Amdt. 35–3, 41 FR 55475, Dec. 20, 1976]

§ 35.47 Propeller adjustments and parts replacements.

The applicant may service and make minor repairs to the propeller during the tests. If major repairs or replacement of parts are found necessary during the tests or in the teardown inspection, the parts in question must be subjected to any additional tests the Administrator finds necessary.

APPENDIX A TO PART 35—INSTRUCTIONS FOR CONTINUED AIRWORTHINESS

A35.1 GENERAL

(a) This appendix specifies requirements for the preparation of Instructions for Continued Airworthiness as required by § 35.4.

(b) The Instructions for Continued Airworthiness for each propeller must include the Instructions for Continued Airworthiness for all propeller parts. If Instructions for Continued Airworthiness are not supplied by the propeller part manufacturer for a propeller part, the Instructions for Continued Airworthiness for the propeller must include the information essential to the continued airworthiness of the propeller.

(c) The applicant must submit to the FAA a program to show how changes to the Instructions for Continued Airworthiness made by the applicant or by the manufacturers of propeller parts will be distributed.

A35.2 FORMAT

(a) The Instructions for Continued Airworthiness must be in the form of a manual or manuals as appropriate for the quantity of data to be provided.

(b) The format of the manual or manuals must provide for a practical arrangement.

A35.3 CONTENT

The contents of the manual must be prepared in the English language. The Instructions for Continued Airworthiness must contain the following sections and information:

(a) *Propeller Maintenance Section.* (1) Introduction information that includes an explanation of the propeller's features and data to the extent necessary for maintenance or preventive maintenance.

(2) A detailed description of the propeller and its systems and installations.

(3) Basic control and operation information describing how the propeller components and systems are controlled and how they operate, including any special procedures that apply.

(4) Instructions for uncrating, acceptance checking, lifting, and installing the propeller.

(5) Instructions for propeller operational checks.

(6) Scheduling information for each part of the propeller that provides the recommended periods at which it should be cleaned, adjusted, and tested, the applicable wear tolerances, and the degree of work recommended at these periods. However, the applicant may refer to an accessory, instrument, or equipment manufacturer as the source of this information if it shows that the item has an exceptionally high degree of complexity requiring specialized maintenance techniques, test equipment, or expertise. The recommended overhaul periods and necessary cross-references to the Airworthiness Limitations section of the manual must also be included. In addition, the applicant must include an inspection program that includes the frequency and extent of the inspections necessary to provide for the continued airworthiness of the propeller.

(7) Troubleshooting information describing probable malfunctions, how to recognize those malfunctions, and the remedial action for those malfunctions.

(8) Information describing the order and method of removing and replacing propeller parts with any necessary precautions to be taken.

(9) A list of the special tools needed for maintenance other than for overhauls.

(b) *Propeller Overhaul Section.* (1) Disassembly information including the order and method of disassembly for overhaul.

(2) Cleaning and inspection instructions that cover the materials and apparatus to be used and methods and precautions to be taken during overhaul. Methods of overhaul inspection must also be included.

(3) Details of all fits and clearances relevant to overhaul.

(4) Details of repair methods for worn or otherwise substandard parts and components along with information necessary to determine when replacement is necessary.

(5) The order and method of assembly at overhaul.

(6) Instructions for testing after overhaul.

(7) Instructions for storage preparation including any storage limits.

(8) A list of tools needed for overhaul.

A35.4 AIRWORTHINESS LIMITATIONS SECTION

The Instructions for Continued Airworthiness must contain a section titled Airworthiness Limitations that is segregated and clearly distinguishable from the rest of the document. This section must set forth each mandatory replacement time, inspection interval, and related procedure required for type certification. This section must contain a legible statement in a prominent location that reads: "The Airworthiness Limitations section is FAA approved and specifies maintenance required under §§ 43.16 and 91.403 of the Federal Aviation Regulations unless an alternative program has been FAA approved."

[Amdt. 35–5, 45 FR 60182, Sept. 11, 1980, as amended by Amdt. 35–6, 54 FR 34330, Aug. 18, 1989]

PART 36—NOISE STANDARDS: AIRCRAFT TYPE AND AIRWORTHINESS CERTIFICATION

Subpart A—General

Subpart B—Transport Category Large Airplanes and Jet Airplanes

Subpart C [Reserved]

Subpart D—Noise Limits for Supersonic Transport Category Airplanes

Subpart E [Reserved]

Subpart F—Propeller Driven Small Airplanes and Propeller-Driven, Commuter Category Airplanes

Subpart G [Reserved]

Subpart H—Helicopters

Subparts I–N [Reserved]

Subpart O—Operating Limitations and Information

AUTHORITY: 42 U.S.C. 4321 *et seq.*; 49 U.S.C. 106(g), 40113, 44701–44702, 44704, 44715; sec. 305, Pub. L. 96–193, 94 Stat. 50, 57; E.O. 11514, 35 FR 4247, 3 CFR, 1966–1970 Comp., p. 902.

SOURCE: Docket No. 9337, 34 FR 18364, Nov. 18, 1969, unless otherwise noted.

Subpart A—General

§ 36.1   Applicability and definitions.

(a) This part prescribes noise standards for the issue of the following certificates:

(1) Type certificates, and changes to those certificates, and standard airworthiness certificates, for subsonic transport category large airplanes, and for subsonic jet airplanes regardless of category.

(2) Type certificates and changes to those certificates, standard airworthiness certificates, and restricted category airworthiness certificates, for propeller-driven, small airplanes, and for propeller-driven, commuter category airplanes except those airplanes that are designed for "agricultural aircraft operations" (as defined in § 137.3 of this chapter, as effective on January 1, 1966) or for dispersing fire fighting materials to which § 36.1583 of this part does not apply.

(3) A type certificate and changes to that certificate, and standard airworthiness certificates, for Concorde airplanes.

(4) Type certificates, and changes to those certificates, for helicopters except those helicopters that are designated exclusively for "agricultural aircraft operations" (as defined in § 137.3 of this chapter, as effective on January 1, 1966), for dispensing fire fighting materials, or for carrying external loads (as defined in § 133.1(b) of this chapter, as effective on December 20, 1976).

(b) Each person who applies under Part 21 of this chapter for a type of airworthiness certificate specified in this part must show compliance with the applicable requirements of this part, in addition to the applicable airworthiness requirements of this chapter.

(c) Each person who applies under Part 21 of this chapter for approval of an acoustical change described in § 21.93(b) of this chapter must show that the aircraft complies with the applicable provisions of §§ 36.7, 36.9, or 36.11 of this part in addition to the applicable airworthiness requirements of this chapter.

(d) Each person who applies for the original issue of a standard airworthiness certificate for a transport category large airplane or for a jet airplane under § 21.183 must, regardless of date of application, show compliance with the following provisions of this part (including appendix B):

(1) The provisions of this part in effect on December 1, 1969, for subsonic airplanes that have not had any flight time before—

(i) December 1, 1973, for airplanes with maximum weights greater than 75,000 pounds, except for airplanes that are powered by Pratt & Whitney Turbo Wasp JT3D series engines;

(ii) December 31, 1974, for airplanes with maximum weights greater than 75,000 pounds and that are powered by Pratt & Whitney Turbo Wasp JT3D series engines; and

(iii) December 31, 1974, for airplanes with maximum weights of 75,000 pounds and less.

(2) The provisions of this part in effect on October 13, 1977, including the stage 2 noise limits, for Concorde airplanes that have not had any flight time before January 1, 1980.

(e) Each person who applies for the original issue of a standard airworthiness certificate under § 21.183, or for the original issue of a restricted category airworthiness certificate under § 21.185, for propeller-driven, commuter category airplanes for a propeller driven small airplane that has not had any flight time before January 1, 1980, must show compliance with the applicable provisions of this part.

(f) For the purpose of showing compliance with this part for transport category airplanes and jet airplanes regardless of category, the following terms have the following meanings:

(1) A "Stage 1 noise level" means a flyover, lateral or approach noise level greater than the Stage 2 noise limits prescribed in section B36.5(b) of appendix B of this part.

(2) A "Stage 1 airplane" means an airplane that has not been shown under this part to comply with the flyover, lateral, and approach noise levels required for Stage 2 or Stage 3 airplanes.

(3) A "Stage 2 noise level" means a noise level at or below the Stage 2

noise limits prescribed in section B36.5(b) of appendix B of this part but higher than the Stage 3 noise limits prescribed in section B36.5(c) of appendix B of this part.

(4) A "Stage 2 airplane" means an airplane that has been shown under this part to comply with Stage 2 noise levels prescribed in section B36.5(b) of appendix B of this part (including use of the applicable tradeoff provisions specified in section B36.6) and that does not comply with the requirements for a Stage 3 airplane.

(5) A "Stage 3 noise level" means a noise level at or below the Stage 3 noise limits prescribed in section B36.5(c) of appendix B of this part.

(6) A "Stage 3 airplane" means an airplane that has been shown under this part to comply with Stage 3 noise levels prescribed in section B36.5(c) of appendix B of this part (including use of the applicable tradeoff provisions specified in section B36.6).

(7) A "subsonic airplane" means an airplane for which the maximum operating limit speed, M_{mo}, does not exceed a Mach number of 1.

(8) A "supersonic airplane" means an airplane for which the maximum operating limit speed, M_{mo}, exceeds a Mach number of 1.

(g) For the purpose of showing compliance with this part for transport category large airplanes and jet airplanes regardless of category, each airplane may not be identified as complying with more than one stage or configuration simultaneously.

(h) For the purpose of showing compliance with this part, for helicopters in the primary, normal, transport, and restricted categories, the following terms have the specified meanings:

(1) *Stage 1 noise level* means a takeoff, flyover, or approach noise level greater than the Stage 2 noise limits prescribed in section H36.305 of appendix H of this part, or a flyover noise level greater than the Stage 2 noise limits prescribed in section J36.305 of appendix J of this part.

(2) *Stage 1 helicopter* means a helicopter that has not been shown under this part to comply with the takeoff, flyover, and approach noise levels required for Stage 2 helicopters as prescribed in section H36.305 of appendix H of this part, or a helicopter that has not been shown under this part to comply with the flyover noise level required for Stage 2 helicopters as prescribed in section J36.305 of appendix J of this part.

(3) *Stage 2 noise level* means a takeoff, flyover, or approach noise level at or below the Stage 2 noise limits prescribed in section H36.305 of appendix H of this part, or a flyover noise level at or below the Stage 2 limit prescribed in section J36.305 of appendix J of this part.

(4) *Stage 2 helicopter* means a helicopter that has been shown under this part to comply with Stage 2 noise limits (including applicable tradeoffs) prescribed in section H36.305 of appendix H of this part, or a helicopter that has been shown under this part to comply with the Stage 2 noise limit prescribed in section J36.305 of appendix J of this part.

[Doc. No. 13243, Amdt. 36–4, 40 FR 1034, Jan. 6, 1975 as amended by Amdt. 36–7, 42 FR 12370, Mar. 3, 1977; Amdt. 36–10, 43 FR 28419, June 29, 1978; Amdt. 36–11, 45 FR 67066, Oct. 9, 1980; Amdt. 36–13, 52 FR 1836, Jan. 15, 1987; Amdt. 36–14, 53 FR 3540, Feb. 5, 1988; 53 FR 7728, Mar. 10, 1988; Amdt. 36–15, 53 FR 16366, May 6, 1988; Amdt. 36–20, 57 FR 42854, Sept. 16, 1992; Amdt. 36–54, 67 FR 45211, July 8, 2002; Amdt. 36–24, 67 FR 63195, Oct. 10, 2002]

§36.2 Requirements as of date of application.

(a) Section 21.17 of this chapter notwithstanding, each person who applies for a type certificate for an aircraft covered by this part, must show that the aircraft meets the applicable requirements of this part that are effective on the date of application for that type certificate. When the time interval between the date of application for the type certificate and the issuance of the type certificate exceeds 5 years, the applicant must show that the aircraft meets the applicable requirements of this part that were effective on a date, to be selected by the applicant, not earlier than 5 years before the issue of the type certificate.

(b) Section 21.101(a) of this chapter notwithstanding, each person who applies for an acoustical change to a type design specified in §21.93(b) of this chapter must show compliance with the applicable requirements of this part that are effective on the date of application for the change in type design. When the time interval between the date of application for the change in type design and the issuance of the amended or supplemental type certificate exceeds 5 years, the applicant must show that the aircraft meets the applicable requirements of this part that were effective on a date, to be selected by the applicant, not earlier than 5 years before the issue of the amended or supplemental type certificate.

(c) If an applicant elects to comply with a standard in this part that was effective after the filing of the application for a type certificate or change to a type design, the election:

(1) Must be approved by the FAA;

(2) Must include standards adopted between the date of application and the date of the election;

(3) May include other standards adopted after the standard elected by the applicant as determined by the FAA.

[Amdt. 36–54, 67 FR 45211, July 8, 2002; Amdt. 36–24, 67 FR 63195, Oct. 10, 2002]

§ 36.3 Compatibility with airworthiness requirements.

It must be shown that the aircraft meets the airworthiness regulations constituting the type certification basis of the aircraft under all conditions in which compliance with this part is shown, and that all procedures used in complying with this part, and all procedures and information for the flight crew developed under this part, are consistent with the airworthiness regulations constituting the type certification basis of the aircraft.

[Doc. No. 9337, 34 FR 18364, Nov. 18, 1969, as amended by Amdt. 36–14, 53 FR 3540, Feb. 5, 1988]

§ 36.5 Limitation of part.

Pursuant to 49 U.S.C. 1431(b)(4), the noise levels in this part have been determined to be as low as is economically reasonable, technologically practicable, and appropriate to the type of aircraft to which they apply. No determination is made, under this part, that these noise levels are or should be acceptable or unacceptable for operation at, into, or out of, any airport.

§ 36.6 Incorporation by reference.

(a) *General.* This part prescribes certain standards and procedures which are not set forth in full text in the rule. Those standards and procedures are contained in published material which is reasonably available to the class of persons affected and has been approved for incorporation by reference by the Director of the Federal Register under 5 U.S.C. 552 (a) and 1 CFR Part 51.

(b) *Incorporated matter.* (1) Each publication, or part of a publication, which is referenced but not set forth in full-text in this part and which is identified in paragraph (c) of this section is hereby incorporated by reference and made a part of Part 36 of this chapter with the approval of the Director of the Federal Register.

(2) Incorporated matter which is subject to subsequent change is incorporated by reference according to the specific reference and to the identification statement. Adoption of any subsequent change in incorporated matter is made under Part 11 of this chapter and 1 CFR Part 51.

(c) *Identification statement.* The complete title or description which identifies each published matter incorporated by reference in this part is as follows:

(1) *International Electrotechnical Commission (IEC) Publications.* (i) IEC Publication No. 179, entitled "Precision Sound Level Meters," dated 1973.

(ii) IEC Publication No. 225, entitled "Octave, Half-Octave, Third Octave Band Filters Intended for the Analysis of Sounds and Vibrations," dated 1966.

(iii) IEC Publication No. 651, entitled "Sound Level Meters," first edition, dated 1979.

(iv) IEC Publication No. 561, entitled "Electro-acoustical Measuring Equipment for Aircraft Noise Certification," first edition, dated 1976.

(v) IEC Publication No. 804, entitled "Integrating-averaging Sound Level Meters," first edition, dated 1985.

(vi) IEC Publication 61094–3, entitled "Measurement Microphones—Part 3: Primary Method for Free-Field Calibration of Laboratory Standard Microphones by the Reciprocity Technique", edition 1.0, dated 1995.

(vii) IEC Publication 61094–4, entitled "Measurement Microphones—Part 4: Specifications for Working Standard Microphones", edition 1.0, dated 1995.

(viii) IEC Publication 61260, entitled "Electroacoustics-Octave-Band and Fractional-Octave-Band filters", edition 1.0, dated 1995.

(ix) IEC Publication 61265, entitled "Instruments for Measurement of Aircraft Noise-Performance Requirements for Systems To Measure One-Third-Octave-Band Sound pressure Levels in Noise Certification of Transport-Category Aeroplanes," edition 1.0, dated 1995.

(x) IEC Publication 60942, entitled "Electroacoustics—Sound Calibrators," edition 2.0, dated 1997.

(2) *Society of Automotive Engineers (SAE) Publications.* (i) SAE ARP 866A, entitled "Standard Values at Atmospheric Absorption as a Function of Temperature and Humidity for Use in Evaluating Aircraft Flyover Noise," dated March 15, 1975.

(d) *Availability for purchase.* Published material incorporated by reference in this part may be purchased at the price established by the publisher or distributor at the following mailing addresses:

(1) *IEC publications.*

(i) International Electrotechnical Commission, 3, rue de Varembe, Case postale 131, 1211 Geneva 20, Switzerland.

(ii) American National Standard Institute, 11 West 42nd Street, New York City, New York 10036.

(2) *SAE publications.* Society of Automotive Engineers, Inc., 400 Commonwealth Drive, Warrentown, Pennsylvania 15096.

(e) *Availability for inspection.* A copy of each publication incorporated by reference in this part is available for public inspection at the following locations:

(1) FAA Office of the Chief Counsel, Rules Docket, Room 916, Federal Aviation Administration Headquarters Building, 800 Independence Avenue, SW., Washington, DC.

(2) Department of Transportation, Branch Library, Room 930, Federal Aviation Administration Headquarters Building, 800 Independence Avenue, SW., Washington, DC.

(3) The respective Region Headquarters of the Federal Aviation Administration as follows:

(i) New England Region Headquarters, 12 New England Executive Park, Burlington, Massachusetts 01803.

(ii) Eastern Region Headquarters, Federal Building, John F. Kennedy (JFK) International Airport, Jamaica, New York 11430.

(iii) Southern Region Headquarters, 1701 Columbia Avenue, College Park, Georgia, 30337.

(iv) Great Lakes Region Headquarters, O'Hare Lake Office Center, 2300 East Devon Avenue, Des Plaines, Illinois 60018.

(v) Central Region Headquarters, Federal Building, 601 East 12th Street, Kanasa City Missouri 64106.

(vi) Southwest Region Headquarters, 2601 Meacham Boulevard, Fort Worth, Texas, 76137–4298.

(vii) Northwest Mountain Region Headquarters, 1601 Lind Avenue, Southwest, Renton, Washington 98055.

(viii) Western-Pacific Region Headquarters, 15000 Aviation Boulevard, Hawthorne, California 92007.

(ix) Alaskan Region Headquarters, 222 West 7th Avenue, #14, Anchorage, Alaska, 99513.

(x) European Office Headquarters, 15, Rue de la Loi (3rd Floor), B–1040 Brussels, Belgium.

[Amdt. 36–9, 43 FR 8739, Mar. 3, 1978, as amended by Amdt. 36–16, 53 FR 47400, Nov. 22, 1988; Amdt. 36–20, 57 FR 42854, Sept. 16, 1992; Amdt. 36–54, 67 FR 45212, July 8, 2002; Amdt. 36–24, 68 FR 1512, Jan. 10, 2003]

§36.7 Acoustical change: Transport category large airplanes and jet airplanes.

(a) *Applicability.* This section applies to all transport category large airplanes and jet airplanes for which an acoustical change approval is applied for under §21.93(b) of this chapter.

(b) *General requirements.* Except as otherwise specifically provided, for each airplane covered by this section, the acoustical change approval requirements are as follows:

(1) In showing compliance, noise levels must be measured and evaluated in accordance with the applicable procedures and conditions prescribed in Appendix A of this part.

(2) Compliance with the noise limits prescribed in section B36.5 of appendix B must be shown in accordance with the applicable provisions of sections B36.7 and B36.8 of appendix B of this part.

(c) *Stage 1 airplanes.* For each Stage 1 airplane prior to the change in type design, in addition to the provisions of paragraph (b) of this section, the following apply:

(1) If an airplane is a Stage 1 airplane prior to the change in type design, it may not, after the change in type design, exceed the noise levels created prior to the change in type design. The tradeoff provisions of section B36.6 of appendix B of this part may not be used to increase the Stage 1 noise levels, unless the aircraft qualifies as a Stage 2 airplane.

(2) In addition, for an airplane for which application is made after September 17, 1971—

(i) There may be no reduction in power or thrust below the highest airworthiness approved power or thrust, during the tests conducted before and after the change in type design; and

(ii) During the flyover and lateral noise tests conducted before the change in type design, the quietest airworthiness approved configuration available for the highest approved takeoff weight must be used.

(d) *Stage 2 airplanes.* If an airplane is a Stage 2 airplane prior to the change in type design, the following apply, in addition to the provisions of paragraph (b) of this section:

(1) *Airplanes with high bypass ratio jet engines.* For an airplane that has jet engines with a bypass ratio of 2 or more before a change in type design—

(i) The airplane, after the change in type design, may not exceed either (A) each Stage 3 noise limit by more than 3 EPNdB, or (B) each Stage 2 noise limit, whichever is lower:

(ii) The tradeoff provisions of section B36.6 of appendix B of this part may be used in determining compliance under this paragraph with respect to the Stage 2 noise limit or to the Stage 3 plus 3 EPNdB noise limits, as applicable; and

(iii) During the flyover and lateral noise test conducted before the change in type design, the quietest airworthiness approved configuration available for the highest approved takeoff weight must be used.

(2) *Airplanes that do not have high bypass ratio jet engines.* For an airplane that does not have jet engines with a bypass ratio of 2 or more before a change in type design—

(i) The airplane may not be a Stage 1 airplane after the change in type design; and

(ii) During the flyover and lateral noise tests conducted before the change in type design, the quietest airworthiness approved configuration available for the highest approved takeoff weight must be used.

(e) *Stage 3 airplanes.* If an airplane is a Stage 3 airplane prior to the change in type design, the following apply, in addition to the provisions of paragraph (b) of this section:

(1) If compliance with Stage 3 noise levels is not required before the change in type design, the airplane must—

(i) Be a Stage 2 airplane after the change in type design and compliance must be shown under the provisions of paragraph (d)(1) or (d)(2) of this section, as appropriate; or

(ii) Remain a Stage 3 airplane after the change in type design. Compliance must be shown under the provisions of paragraph (e)(2) of this section.

(2) If compliance with Stage 3 noise levels is required before the change in type design, the airplane must be a Stage 3 airplane after the change in type design.

(3) Applications on or after [August 14, 1989.] The airplane must remain a Stage 3 airplane after the change in type design.

[Amdt. 36–7, 42 FR 12371, Mar. 3, 1977; Amdt. 36–8, 43 FR 8730, Mar. 2, 1978; Amdt. 36–10, 43 FR 28420, June 29, 1978; Amdt. 36–12, 46 FR 33464, June 29, 1981; Amdt. 36–15, 53 FR 16366, May 6, 1988; 53 FR 18950, May 25, 1988; Amdt. 36–17, 54 FR 21042, May 15, 1989; Amdt. 36–54, 67 FR 45212, July 8, 2002]

§ 36.9 **Acoustical change: Propeller-driven small airplanes and propeller-driven commuter category airplanes.**

For propeller-driven small airplanes in the primary, normal, utility, acrobatic, transport, and restricted categories and for propeller-driven, commuter category airplanes for which an acoustical change approval is applied for under § 21.93(b) of this chapter after January 1, 1975, the following apply:

(a) If the airplane was type certificated under this part prior to a change in type design, it may not subsequently exceed the noise limits specified in § 36.501 of this part.

(b) If the airplane was not type certificated under this part prior to a change in type design, it may not exceed the higher of the two following values:

(1) The noise limit specified in § 36.501 of this part, or

(2) The noise level created prior to the change in type design, measured and corrected as prescribed in § 36.501 of this part.

[Amdt. 36–16, 53 FR 47400, Nov. 22, 1988; 53 FR 50157, Dec. 13, 1988; Amdt. 36–19, 57 FR 41369, Sept. 9, 1992]

§ 36.11 Acoustical change: Helicopters.

This section applies to all helicopters in the primary, normal, transport, and restricted categories for which an acoustical change approval is applied for under § 21.93(b) of this chapter on or after March 6, 1986. Compliance with the requirements of this section must be demonstrated under appendix H of this part, or, for helicopters having a maximum certificated takeoff weight of not more than 6,000 pounds, compliance with this section may be demonstrated under appendix J of this part.

(a) *General requirements.* Except as otherwise provided, for helicopters covered by this section, the acoustical change approval requirements are as follows:

(1) In showing compliance with the requirements of appendix H of this part, noise levels must be measured, evaluated, and calculated in accordance with the applicable procedures and conditions prescribed in parts B and C of appendix H of this part. For helicopters having a maximum certificated takeoff weight of not more than 6,000 pounds that alternatively demonstrate compliance under appendix J of this part, the flyover noise level prescribed in appendix J of this part must be measured, evaluated, and calculated in accordance with the applicable procedures and conditions prescribed in parts B and C of appendix J of this part.

(2) Compliance with the noise limits prescribed in section H36.305 of appendix H of this part must be shown in accordance with the applicable provisions of part D of appendix H of this part. For those helicopters that demonstrate compliance with the requirements of appendix J of this part, compliance with the noise levels prescribed in section J36.305 of appendix J of this part must be shown in accordance with the applicable provisions of part D of appendix J of this part.

(b) *Stage 1 helicopters.* Except as provided in § 36.805(c), for each Stage 1 helicopter prior to a change in type design, the helicopter noise levels may not, after a change in type design, exceed the noise levels specified in section H36.305(a)(1) of appendix H of this part where the demonstration of compliance is under appendix H of this part. The tradeoff provisions under section H36.305(b) of appendix H of this part may not be used to increase any Stage 1 noise level beyond these limits. If an applicant chooses to demonstrate compliance under appendix J of this part, for each Stage 1 helicopter prior to a change in type design, the helicopter noise levels may not, after a change in type design, exceed the Stage 2 noise levels specified in section J36.305(a) of appendix J of this part.

(c) *Stage 2 helicopters.* For each helicopter that is Stage 2 prior to a change in type design, the helicopter must be a Stage 2 helicopter after a change in type design.

[Doc. No. 26910, 57 FR 42854, Sept. 16, 1992]

Subpart B—Transport Category Large Airplanes and Jet Airplanes

§ 36.101 Noise measurement and evaluation.

For transport category large airplanes and jet airplanes, the noise generated by the airplane must be measured and evaluated under appendix A of this part or under an approved equivalent procedure.

[Amdt. 36–54, 67 FR 45212, July 8, 2002]

§ 36.103 Noise limits.

(a) For subsonic transport category large airplanes and subsonic jet airplanes compliance with this section must be shown with noise levels measured and evaluated as prescribed in appendix A of this part, and demonstrated at the measuring points, and in accordance with the test procedures under section B36.8 (or an approved equivalent procedure), stated under appendix B of this part.

(b) Type certification applications for subsonic transport category large airplanes and all subsonic jet airplanes must show that the noise levels of the airplane are no greater than the Stage 3 noise limits stated in section B36.5(c) of appendix B of this part.

[Amdt. 36–54, 67 FR 45212, July 8, 2002]

Subpart C [Reserved]

Subpart D—Noise Limits for Supersonic Transport Category Airplanes

§ 36.301 Noise limits: Concorde.

(a) *General.* For the Concorde airplane, compliance with this subpart must be shown with noise levels measured and evaluated as prescribed in Subpart B of this part, and demonstrated at the measuring points prescribed in appendix B of this part.

(b) *Noise limits.* It must be shown, in accordance with the provisions of this part in effect on October 13, 1977, that the noise levels of the airplane are reduced to the lowest levels that are economically reasonable, technologically practicable, and appropriate for the Concorde type design.

[Amdt. 36–10, 43 FR 28420, June 29, 1978, as amended by Amdt. 36–54, 67 FR 45212, July 8, 2002]

Subpart E [Reserved]

Subpart F—Propeller Driven Small Airplanes and Propeller-Driven, Commuter Category Airplanes

§ 36.501 Noise limits.

(a) Compliance with this subpart must be shown for—

(1) Propeller driven small airplanes for which application for the issuance of a new, amended, or supplemental type certificate in the normal, utility, acrobatic, transport, or restricted category is made on or after October 10, 1973; and propeller-driven, commuter category airplanes for which applica-

tion for the issuance of a type certificate in the commuter category is made on or after January 15, 1987.

(2) Propeller driven small airplanes and propeller–driven, commuter category airplanes for which application is made for the original issuance of a standard airworthiness certificate or restricted category airworthiness certificate, and that have not had any flight time before January 1, 1980 (regardless of date of application).

(3) Airplanes in the primary category:

(i) Except as provided in paragraph (a)(3)(ii) of this section, for an airplane for which application for a type certificate in the primary category is made, and was not previously certificated under appendix F of this part, compliance with appendix G of this part must be shown.

(ii) For an airplane in the normal, utility or acrobatic category that (A) has a type certificate issued under this chapter, (B) has a standard airworthiness certificate issued under this chapter, (C) has not undergone an acoustical change from its type design, (D) has not previously been certificated under appendix F or G of this part, and (E) for which application for conversion to the primary category is made, no further showing of compliance with this part is required.

(b) For aircraft covered by this subpart for which certification tests are completed before December 22, 1988, compliance must be shown with noise levels as measured and prescribed in Parts B and C of appendix F, or under approved equivalent procedures. It must be shown that the noise level of the airplane is no greater than the applicable limit set in Part D of appendix F.

(c) For aircraft covered by this subpart for which certification tests are not completed before December 22, 1988, compliance must be shown with noise levels as measured and prescribed in Parts B and C of appendix G, or under approved equivalent procedures. It must be shown that the noise level of the airplane is no greater than the applicable limits set in Part D of appendix G.

[Doc. No. 13243, 40 FR 1034, Jan. 6, 1975, as amended by Amdt. 36–13, 52 FR 1836, Jan. 15, 1987; Amdt. 36–16, 53 FR 47400, Nov. 22, 1988; Amdt. 36–19, 57 FR 41369, Sept. 9, 1992]

Subpart G [Reserved]

Subpart H—Helicopters

SOURCE: Amdt. 36–14, 53 FR 3540, Feb. 5, 1988; 53 FR 7728, Mar. 10, 1988, unless otherwise noted.

§36.801 Noise measurement.

For primary, normal, transport, or restricted category helicopters for which certification is sought under appendix H of this part, the noise generated by the helicopter must be measured at the noise measuring points and under the test conditions prescribed in part B of appendix H of this part, or under an FAA-approved equivalent procedure. For those primary, normal, transport, and restricted category helicopters having a maximum certificated takeoff weight of not more than 6,000 pounds for which compliance with appendix J of this part is demonstrated, the noise generated by the helicopter must be measured at the noise measuring point and under the test conditions prescribed in part B of appendix J of this part, or an FAA-approved equivalent procedure.

[Doc. No. 26910, 57 FR 42854, Sept. 16, 1992]

§36.803 Noise evaluation and calculation.

The noise measurement data required under §36.801 and obtained under appendix H of this part must be corrected to the reference conditions contained in part A of appendix H of this part, and evaluated under the procedures of part C of appendix H of this part, or an FAA-approved equivalent procedure. The noise measurement data required under §36.801 and obtained under appendix J of this part must be corrected to the reference conditions contained in part A of appendix J of this part, and evaluated under the procedures of part C of appendix J of this part, or an FAA-approved equivalent procedure.

[Doc. No. 26910, 57 FR 42854, Sept. 16, 1992]

§36.805 Noise limits.

(a) Compliance with the noise levels prescribed under part D of appendix H of this part, or under part D of appendix J of this part, must be shown for helicopters for which application for issuance of a type certificate in the primary, normal, transport, or restricted category is made on or after March 6, 1986.

(b) For helicopters covered by this section, except as provided in paragraph (c) or (d)(2) of this section, it must be shown either:

(1) For those helicopters demonstrating compliance under appendix H of this part, the noise levels of the helicopter are no greater than the applicable limits prescribed under section H36.305 of appendix H of this part, or

(2) For helicopters demonstrating compliance under appendix J of this part, the noise level of the helicopter is no greater than the limit prescribed under section J36.305 of appendix J of this part.

(c) For helicopters for which application for issuance of an original type certificate in the primary, normal, transport, or restricted category is made on or after March 6, 1986, and which the FAA finds to be the first civil version of a helicopter that was designed and constructed for, and accepted for operational use by, an Armed Force of the United States or the U.S. Coast Guard on or before March 6, 1986, it must be shown that the noise levels of the helicopter are no greater than the noise limits for a change in type design as specified in section H36.305(a)(1)(ii) of appendix H of this part for compliance demonstrated under appendix H of this part, or as specified in section J36.305 of appendix J of this part for compliance demonstrated under appendix J of this part. Subsequent civil versions of any such helicopter must meet the Stage 2 requirements.

(d) Helicopters in the primary category:

(1) Except as provided in paragraph (d)(2) of this section, for a helicopter

for which application for a type certificate in the primary category is made, and that was not previously certificated under appendix H of this part, compliance with appendix H of this part must be shown.

(2) For a helicopter that:

(i) Has a normal or transport type certificate issued under this chapter,

(ii) Has a standard airworthiness certificate issued under this chapter,

(iii) Has not undergone an acoustical change from its type design,

(iv) Has not previously been certificated under appendix H of this part, and

(v) For which application for conversion to the primary category is made, no further showing of compliance with this part is required.

[Doc. No. 26910, 57 FR 42855, Sept. 16, 1992]

Subparts I–N [Reserved]

Subpart O—Operating Limitations and Information

§ 36.1501 Procedures, noise levels and other information.

(a) All procedures, weights, configurations, and other information or data employed for obtaining the certified noise levels prescribed by this part, including equivalent procedures used for flight, testing, and analysis, must be developed and approved. Noise levels achieved during type certification must be included in the approved airplane (rotorcraft) flight manual.

(b) Where supplemental test data are approved for modification or extension of an existing flight data base, such as acoustic data from engine static tests used in the certification of acoustical changes, the test procedures, physical configuration, and other information and procedures that are employed for obtaining the supplemental data must be developed and approved.

[Amdt. 36–15, 53 FR 16366, May 6, 1988]

§ 36.1581 Manuals, markings, and placards.

(a) If an Airplane Flight Manual or Rotorcraft Flight Manual is approved, the approved portion of the Airplane Flight Manual or Rotorcraft Flight Manual must contain the following in-

formation, in addition to that specified under § 36.1583 of this part. If an Airplane Flight Manual or Rotorcraft Flight Manual is not approved, the procedures and information must be furnished in any combination of approved manual material, markings, and placards.

(1) For transport category large airplanes and jet airplanes, the noise level information must be one value for each flyover, lateral, and approach as defined and required by appendix B of this part, along with the maximum takeoff weight, maximum landing weight, and configuration.

(2) For propeller driven small airplanes the noise level information must be one value for flyover as defined and required by appendix F of this part, along with the maximum takeoff weight and configuration.

(b) If supplemental operational noise level information is included in the approved portion of the Airplane Flight Manual, it must be segregated, identified as information in addition to the certificated noise levels, and clearly distinguished from the information required under § 36.1581(a).

(c) The following statement must be furnished near the listed noise levels:

No determination has been made by the Federal Aviation Administration that the noise levels of this aircraft are or should be acceptable or unacceptable for operation at, into, or out of, any airport.

(d) For transport category large airplanes and jet airplanes, for which the weight used in meeting the takeoff or landing noise requirements of this part is less than the maximum weight established under the applicable airworthiness requirements, those lesser weights must be furnished, as operating limitations in the operating limitations section of the Airplane Flight Manual. Further, the maximum takeoff weight must not exceed the takeoff weight that is most critical from a takeoff noise standpoint.

(e) For propeller driven small airplanes and for propeller–driven, commuter category airplanes for which the weight used in meeting the flyover noise requirements of this part is less than the maximum weight by an amount exceeding the amount of fuel needed to conduct the test, that lesser weight must be furnished, as an operating limitation, in the operating limitations section of an approved Airplane Flight Manual, in approved manual material, or on an approved placard.

(f) For primary, normal, transport, and restricted category helicopters, if the weight used in meeting the takeoff, flyover, or approach noise requirements of appendix H of this part, or the weight used in meeting the flyover noise requirement of appendix J of this part, is less than the certificated maximum takeoff weight established under either § 27.25(a) or § 29.25(a) of this chapter, that lesser weight must be furnished as an operating limitation in the operating limitations section of the Rotorcraft Flight Manual, in FAA-approved manual material, or on an FAA-approved placard.

(g) Except as provided in paragraphs (d), (e), and (f) of this section, no operating limitations are furnished under this part.

[Doc. 13243, 40 FR 1035, Jan. 6, 1975 as amended by Amdt. 36–10, 43 FR 28420, June 29, 1978; Amdt. 36–11, 45 FR 67066, Oct. 9, 1980; Amdt. 36–13, 52 FR 1836, Jan. 15, 1987. Redesignated and amended by Amdt. 36–14, 53 FR 3540, Feb. 5, 1988; 53 FR 7728, Mar. 10, 1988; Amdt. 36–15, 53 FR 16366, May 6, 1988; 53 FR 18950, May 25, 1988; Amdt. 36–20, 57 FR 42855, Sept. 16, 1992; Amdt. 36–54, 67 FR 45212, July 8, 2002]

§ 36.1583 Noncomplying agricultural and fire fighting airplanes.

(a) This section applies to propeller-driven, small airplanes that—

(1) Are designed for "agricultural aircraft operations" (as defined in § 137.3 of this chapter, effective on January 1, 1966) or for dispensing fire fighting materials; and

(2) Have not been shown to comply with the noise levels prescribed under appendix F of this part—

(i) For which application is made for the original issue of a standard airworthiness certificate and that do not have any flight time before January 1, 1980; or

(ii) For which application is made for an acoustical change approval, for airplanes which have a standard airworthiness certificate after the change in the type design, and that do not have any flight time in the changed configuration before January 1, 1980.

(b) For airplanes covered by this section an operating limitation reading as follows must be furnished in the manner prescribed in § 36.1581:

Noise abatement: This airplane has not been shown to comply with the noise limits in FAR Part 36 and must be operated in accordance with the noise operating limitation prescribed under FAR § 91.815.

[Amdt. 36–11, 45 FR 67066, Oct. 9, 1980. Redesignated by Amdt. 36–14, 53 FR 3540, Feb. 5, 1988; Amdt. 36–18, 54 FR 34330, Aug. 18, 1989]

APPENDIX A TO PART 36—AIRCRAFT NOISE MEASUREMENT AND EVALUATION UNDER § 36.101

Sec.
A36.1 *Introduction.*
A36.2 *Noise Certification Test and Measurement Conditions.*
A36.3 *Measurement of Airplane Noise Received on the Ground.*
A36.4 *Calculations of Effective Perceived Noise Level From Measured Data.*
A36.5 *Reporting of Data to the FAA.*
A36.6 *Nomenclature: Symbols and Units.*
A36.7 *Sound Attenuation in Air.*
A36.8 *[Reserved]*
A36.9 *Adjustment of Airplane Flight Test Results.*

Section A36.1 Introduction

A36.1.1 This appendix prescribes the conditions under which airplane noise certification tests must be conducted and states the measurement procedures that must be used to measure airplane noise. The procedures that must be used to determine the noise evaluation quantity designated as effective perceived noise level, EPNL, under §§ 36.101 and 36.803 are also stated.

A36.1.2 The instructions and procedures given are intended to ensure uniformity during compliance tests and to permit comparison between tests of various types of airplanes conducted in various geographical locations.

A36.1.3 A complete list of symbols and units, the mathematical formulation of perceived noisiness, a procedure for determining atmospheric attenuation of sound, and detailed procedures for correcting noise levels from non-reference to reference conditions are included in this appendix.

Section A36.2 Noise Certification Test and Measurement Conditions

A36.2.1 *General.*
A36.2.1.1 This section prescribes the conditions under which noise certification must be conducted and the measurement procedures that must be used.

NOTE: Many noise certifications involve only minor changes to the airplane type design. The resulting changes in noise can often be established reliably without resorting to a complete test as outlined in this appendix. For this reason, the FAA permits the use of approved equivalent procedures. There are also equivalent procedures that may be used in full certification tests, in the interest of reducing costs and providing reliable results. Guidance material on the use of equivalent procedures in the noise certification of subsonic jet and propeller-driven large airplanes is provided in the current advisory circular for this part.

A36.2.2 *Test environment.*

A36.2.2.1 Locations for measuring noise from an airplane in flight must be surrounded by relatively flat terrain having no excessive sound absorption characteristics such as might be caused by thick, matted, or tall grass, shrubs, or wooded areas. No obstructions that significantly influence the sound field from the airplane must exist within a conical space above the point on the ground vertically below the microphone, the cone being defined by an axis normal to the ground and by a half-angle 80° from this axis.

NOTE: Those people carrying out the measurements could themselves constitute such obstruction.

A36.2.2.2 The tests must be carried out under the following atmospheric conditions.

(a) No precipitation;

(b) Ambient air temperature not above 95 °F (35 °C) and not below 14 °F (−10 °C), and relative humidity not above 95% and not below 20% over the whole noise path between a point 33 ft (10 m) above the ground and the airplane;

NOTE: Care should be taken to ensure that the noise measuring, airplane flight path tracking, and meteorological instrumentation are also operated within their specific environmental limitations.

(c) Relative humidity and ambient temperature over the whole noise path between a point 33 ft (10 m) above the ground and the airplane such that the sound attenuation in the one-third octave band on 8 kHz will not be more than 12 dB/100 m unless:

(1) The dew point and dry bulb temperatures are measured with a device which is accurate to ±0.9 °F (±0.5 °C) and used to obtain relative humidity; in addition layered sections of the atmosphere are used as described in section A36.2.2.3 to compute equivalent weighted sound attenuations in each one-third octave band; or

(2) The peak noy values at the time of PNLT, after adjustment to reference conditions, occur at frequencies less than or equal to 400 Hz.;

(d) If the atmospheric absorption coefficients vary over the PNLTM sound propagation path by more than ±1.6 dB/1000 ft (±0.5 dB/100m) in the 3150Hz one-third octave band

from the value of the absorption coefficient derived from the meteorological measurement obtained at 33 ft (10 m) above the surface, "layered" sections of the atmosphere must be used as described in section A36.2.2.3 to compute equivalent weighted sound attenuations in each one-third octave band; the FAA will determine whether a sufficient number of layered sections have been used. For each measurement, where multiple layering is not required, equivalent sound attenuations in each one-third octave band must be determined by averaging the atmospheric absorption coefficients for each such band at 33 ft (10 m) above ground level, and at the flight level of the airplane at the time of PNLTM, for each measurement;

(e) Average wind velocity 33 ft (10 m) above ground may not exceed 12 knots and the crosswind velocity for the airplane may not exceed 7 knots. The average wind velocity must be determined using a 30-second averaging period spanning the 10 dB-down time interval. Maximum wind velocity 33 ft (10 m) above ground is not to exceed 15 knots and the crosswind velocity is not to exceed 10 knots during the 10 dB-down time interval;

(f) No anomalous meteorological or wind conditions that would significantly affect the measured noise levels when the noise is recorded at the measuring points specified by the FAA; and

(g) Meteorological measurements must be obtained within 30 minutes of each noise test measurement; meteorological data must be interpolated to actual times of each noise measurement.

A36.2.2.3 When a multiple layering calculation is required by section A36.2.2.2(c) or A36.2.2.2(d) the atmosphere between the airplane and 33 ft (10 m) above the ground must be divided into layers of equal depth. The depth of the layers must be set to not more than the depth of the narrowest layer across which the variation in the atmospheric absorption coefficient of the 3150 Hz one-third octave band is not greater than ±1.6 dB/1000 ft (±0.5 dB/100m), with a minimum layer depth of 100 ft (30 m). This requirement must be met for the propagation path at PNLTM. The mean of the values of the atmospheric absorption coefficients at the top and bottom of each layer may be used to characterize the absorption properties of each layer.

A36.2.2.4 The airport control tower or another facility must be aproved by the FAA for use as the central location at which measurements of atmospheric parameters are representative of those conditions existing over the geographical area in which noise measurements are made.

A36.2.3 *Flight path measurement.*

A36.2.3.1 The airplane height and lateral position relative to the flight track must be determined by a method independent of normal flight instrumentation such as radar tracking, theodolite triangulation, or photographic scaling techniques, to be approved by the FAA.

A36.2.3.2 The airplane position along the flight path must be related to the noise recorded at the noise measurement locations by means of synchronizing signals over a distance sufficient to assure adequate data during the period that the noise is within 10 dB of the maximum value of PNLT.

A36.2.3.3 Position and performance data required to make the adjustments referred to in section A36.9 of this appendix must be automatically recorded at an approved sampling rate. Measuring equipment must be approved by the FAA.

Section A36.3 Measurement of Airplane Noise Received on the Ground

A36.3.1 *Definitions.*

For the purposes of section A36.3 the following definitions apply:

A36.3.1.1 *Measurement system* means the combination of instruments used for the measurement of sound pressure levels, including a sound calibrator, windscreen, microphone system, signal recording and conditioning devices, and one-third octave band analysis system.

NOTE: Practical installations may include a number of microphone systems, the outputs from which are recorded simultaneously by a multi-channel recording/analysis device via signal conditioners, as appropriate. For the purpose of this section, each complete measurement channel is considered to be a measurement system to which the requirements apply accordingly.

A36.3.1.2 *Microphone system* means the components of the measurement system which produce an electrical output signal in response to a sound pressure input signal, and which generally include a microphone, a preamplifier, extension cables, and other devices as necessary.

A36.3.1.3 *Sound incidence angle* means in degrees, an angle between the principal axis of the microphone, as defined in IEC 61094–3 and IEC 61094–4, as amended and a line from the sound source to the center of the diaphragm of the microphone.

NOTE: When the sound incidence angle is 0°, the sound is said to be received at the microphone at "normal (perpendicular) incidence;" when the sound incidence angle is 90°, the sound is said to be received at "grazing incidence."

A36.3.1.4 *Reference direction* means, in degrees, the direction of sound incidence specified by the manufacturer of the microphone, relative to a sound incidence angle of 0°, for which the free-field sensitivity level of the microphone system is within specified tolerance limits.

A36.3.1.5 *Free-field sensitivity of a microphone system* means, in volts per Pascal, for a sinusoidal plane progressive sound wave of

specified frequency, at a specified sound incidence angle, the quotient of the root mean square voltage at the output of a microphone system and the root mean square sound pressure that would exist at the position of the microphone in its absence.

A36.3.1.6 *Free-field sensitivity level of a microphone system* means, in decibels, twenty times the logarithm to the base ten of the ratio of the free-field sensitivity of a microphone system and the reference sensitivity of one volt per Pascal.

NOTE: The free-field sensitivity level of a microphone system may be determined by subtracting the sound pressure level (in decibels re 20 µPa) of the sound incident on the microphone from the voltage level (in decibels re 1 V) at the output of the microphone system, and adding 93.98 dB to the result.

A36.3.1.7 *Time-average band sound pressure level* means in decibels, ten times the logarithm to the base ten, of the ratio of the time mean square of the instantaneous sound pressure during a stated time interval and in a specified one-third octave band, to the square of the reference sound pressure of 20 µPa.

A36.3.1.8 *Level range* means, in decibels, an operating range determined by the setting of the controls that are provided in a measurement system for the recording and one-third octave band analysis of a sound pressure signal. The upper boundary associated with any particular level range must be rounded to the nearest decibel.

A36.3.1.9 *Calibration sound pressure level* means, in decibels, the sound pressure level produced, under reference environmental conditions, in the cavity of the coupler of the sound calibrator that is used to determine the overall acoustical sensitivity of a measurement system.

A36.3.1.10 *Reference level range* means, in decibels, the level range for determining the acoustical sensitivity of the measurement system and containing the calibration sound pressure level.

A36.3.1.11 *Calibration check frequency* means, in hertz, the nominal frequency of the sinusoidal sound pressure signal produced by the sound calibrator.

A36.3.1.12 *Level difference* means, in decibels, for any nominal one-third octave midband frequency, the output signal level measured on any level range minus the level of the corresponding electrical input signal.

A36.3.1.13 *Reference level difference* means, in decibels, for a stated frequency, the level difference measured on a level range for an electrical input signal corresponding to the calibration sound pressure level, adjusted as appropriate, for the level range.

A36.3.1.14 *Level non-linearity* means, in decibels, the level difference measured on any level range, at a stated one-third octave nominal midband frequency, minus the corresponding reference level difference, all input and output signals being relative to the same reference quantity.

A36.3.1.15 *Linear operating range* means, in decibels, for a stated level range and frequency, the range of levels of steady sinusoidal electrical signals applied to the input of the entire measurement system, exclusive of the microphone but including the microphone preamplifier and any other signal-conditioning elements that are considered to be part of the microphone system, extending from a lower to an upper boundary, over which the level non-linearity is within specified tolerance limits.

NOTE: Microphone extension cables as configured in the field need not be included for the linear operating range determination.

A36.3.1.16 *Windscreen insertion loss* means, in decibels, at a stated nominal one-third octave midband frequency, and for a stated sound incidence angle on the inserted microphone, the indicated sound pressure level without the windscreen installed around the microphone minus the sound pressure level with the windscreen installed.

A36.3.2 *Reference environmental conditions.*

A36.3.2.1 The reference environmental conditions for specifying the performance of a measurement system are:

(a) Air temperature 73.4 °F (23 °C);

(b) Static air pressure 101.325 kPa; and

(c) Relative humidity 50%.

A36.3.3. *General.*

NOTE: Measurements of aircraft noise that are made using instruments that conform to the specifications of this section will yield one-third octave band sound pressure levels as a function of time. These one-third octave band levels are to be used for the calculation of effective perceived noise level as described in section A36.4.

A36.3.3.1 The measurement system must consist of equipment approved by the FAA and equivalent to the following:

(a) A windscreen (See A36.3.4.);

(b) A microphone system (See A36.3.5):

(c) A recording and reproducing system to store the measured aircraft noise signals for subsequent analysis (see A36.3.6);

(d) A one-third octave band analysis system (see A36.3.7); and

(e) Calibration systems to maintain the acoustical sensitivity of the above systems within specified tolerance limits (see A36.3.8).

A36.3.3.2. For any component of the measurement system that converts an analog signal to digital form, such conversion must be performed so that the levels of any possible aliases or artifacts of the digitization process will be less than the upper boundary of the linear operating range by at least 50 dB

at any frequency less than 12.5 kHz. The sampling rate must be at least 28 kHz. An anti-aliasing filter must be included before the digitization process.

A36.3.4 *Windscreen.*

A36.3.4.1 In the absence of wind and for sinusoidal sounds at grazing incidence, the insertion loss caused by the windscreen of a stated type installed around the microphone must not exceed ±1.5 dB at nominal one-third octave midband frequencies from 50 Hz to 10 kHz inclusive.

A36.3.5 *Microphone system.*

A36.3.5.1 The microphone system must meet the specifications in sections A36.3.5.2 to A36.3.5.4. Various microphone systems may be approved by the FAA on the basis of demonstrated equivalent overall electroacoustical performance. Where two or more microphone systems of the same type are used, demonstration that at least one system conforms to the specifications in full is sufficient to demonstrate conformance.

NOTE: An applicant must still calibrate and check each system as required in section A36.3.9.

A36.3.5.2 The microphone must be mounted with the sensing element 4 ft (1.2 m) above the local ground surface and must be oriented for grazing incidence, i.e., with the sensing element substantially in the plane defined by the predicted reference flight path of the aircraft and the measuring station. The microphone mounting arrangement must minimize the interference of the supports with the sound to be measured. Figure A36–1 illustrates sound incidence angles on a microphone.

A36.3.5.3 The free-field sensitivity level of the microphone and preamplifier in the reference direction, at frequencies over at least the range of one-third-octave nominal midband frequencies from 50 Hz to 5 kHz inclusive, must be within ±1.0 dB of that at the calibration check frequency, and within ±2.0 dB for nominal midband frequencies of 6.3 kHz, 8 kHz and 10 kHz.

A36.3.5.4 For sinusoidal sound waves at each one-third octave nominal midband frequency over the range from 50 Hz to 10 kHz inclusive, the free-field sensitivity levels of the microphone system at sound incidence angles of 30°, 60°, 90°, 120° and 150°, must not differ from the free-field sensitivity level at a sound incidence angle of 0° ("normal incidence") by more than the values shown in Table A36–1. The free-field sensitivity level differences at sound incidence angles between any two adjacent sound incidence angles in Table A36–1 must not exceed the tolerance limit for the greater angle.

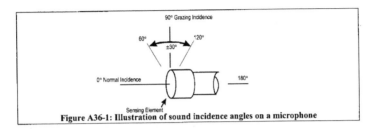

Figure A36-1: Illustration of sound incidence angles on a microphone

Nominal midband frequency kHz	Maximum difference between the free-field sensitivity level of a microphone system at normal incidence and the free-field sensitivity level at specified sound incidence angles dB Sound Incidence angle degrees				
	30	60	90	120	150
0.05 to 1.6	0.5	0.5	1.0	1.0	1.0
2.0	0.5	0.5	1.0	1.0	1.0
2.5	0.5	0.5	1.0	1.5	1.5
3.15	0.5	1.0	1.5	2.0	2.0
4.0	0.5	1.0	2.0	2.5	2.5
5.0	0.5	1.5	2.5	3.0	3.0
6.3	1.0	2.0	3.0	4.0	4.0
8.0	1.5	2.5	4.0	5.5	5.5
10.0	2.0	3.5	5.5	6.5	7.5

Table A36-1   Microphone Directional Response Requirements

A36.3.6 *Recording and reproducing systems.*

A36.3.6.1 A recording and reproducing system, such as a digital or analog magnetic tape recorder, a computer-based system or other permanent data storage device, must be used to store sound pressure signals for subsequent analysis. The sound produced by the aircraft must be recorded in such a way that a record of the complete acoustical signal is retained. The recording and reproducing systems must meet the specifications in sections A36.3.6.2 to A36.3.6.9 at the recording speeds and/or data sampling rates used for the noise certification tests. Conformance must be demonstrated for the frequency bandwidths and recording channels selected for the tests.

A36.3.6.2 The recording and reproducing systems must be calibrated as described in section A36.3.9.

(a) For aircraft noise signals for which the high frequency spectral levels decrease rapidly with increasing frequency, appropriate pre-emphasis and complementary de-emphasis networks may be included in the measurement system. If pre-emphasis is included,

over the range of nominal one-third octave midband frequencies from 800 Hz to 10 kHz inclusive, the electrical gain provided by the pre-emphasis network must not exceed 20 dB relative to the gain at 800 Hz.

A36.3.6.3 For steady sinusoidal electrical signals applied to the input of the entire measurement system including all parts of the microphone system except the microphone at a selected signal level within 5 dB of that corresponding to the calibration sound pressure level on the reference level range, the time-average signal level indicated by the readout device at any one-third octave nominal midband frequency from 50 Hz to 10 kHz inclusive must be within ±1.5 dB of that at the calibration check frequency. The frequency response of a measurement system, which includes components that convert analog signals to digital form, must be within ±0.3 dB of the response at 10 kHz over the frequency range from 10 kHz to 11.2 kHz.

NOTE: Microphone extension cables as configured in the field need not be included for the frequency response determination. This allowance does not eliminate the requirement of including microphone extension cables when performing the pink noise recording in section A36.3.9.5.

A36.3.6.4 For analog tape recordings, the amplitude fluctuations of a 1 kHz sinusoidal signal recorded within 5 dB of the level corresponding to the calibration sound pressure level must not vary by more than ±0.5 dB throughout any reel of the type of magnetic tape used. Conformance to this requirement must be demonstrated using a device that has time-averaging properties equivalent to those of the spectrum analyzer.

A36.3.6.5 For all appropriate level ranges and for steady sinusoidal electrical signals applied to the input of the measurement system, including all parts of the microphone system except the microphone, at one-third-octave nominal midband frequencies of 50 Hz, 1 kHz and 10 kHz, and the calibration check frequency, if it is not one of these frequencies, the level non-linearity must not exceed ±0.5 dB for a linear operating range of at least 50 dB below the upper boundary of the level range.

NOTE 1: Level linearity of measurement system components may be tested according to the methods described in IEC 61265 as amended.

NOTE 2: Microphone extension cables configured in the field need not be included for the level linearity determination.

A36.3.6.6 On the reference level range, the level corresponding to the calibration sound pressure level must be at least 5 dB, but no more than 30 dB less than the upper boundary of the level range.

A36.3.6.7 The linear operating ranges on adjacent level ranges must overlap by at least 50 dB minus the change in attenuation introduced by a change in the level range controls.

NOTE: It is possible for a measurement system to have level range controls that permit attenuation changes of either 10 dB or 1 dB, for example. With 10 dB steps, the minimum overlap required would be 40 dB, and with 1 dB steps the minimum overlap would be 49 dB.

A36.3.6.8 An overload indicator must be included in the recording and reproducing systems so that an overload indication will occur during an overload condition on any relevant level range.

A36.3.6.9 Attenuators included in the measurement system to permit range changes must operate in known intervals of decibel steps.

A36.3.7 *Analysis systems.*

A36.3.7.1 The analysis system must conform to the specifications in sections A36.3.7.2 to A36.3.7.7 for the frequency bandwidths, channel configurations and gain settings used for analysis.

A36.3.7.2 The output of the analysis system must consist of one-third octave band sound pressure levels as a function of time, obtained by processing the noise signals (preferably recorded) through an analysis system with the following characteristics:

(a) A set of 24 one-third octave band filters, or their equivalent, having nominal midband frequencies from 50 Hz to 10 kHz inclusive;

(b) Response and averaging properties in which, in principle, the output from any one-third octave filter band is squared, averaged and displayed or stored as time-averaged sound pressure levels;

(c) The interval between successive sound pressure level samples must be 500 ms ±5 milliseconds(ms) for spectral analysis with or without slow time-weighting, as defined in section A36.3.7.4;

(d) For those analysis systems that do not process the sound pressure signals during the period of time required for readout and/or resetting of the analyzer, the loss of data must not exceed a duration of 5 ms; and

(e) The analysis system must operate in real time from 50 Hz through at least 12 kHz inclusive. This requirement applies to all operating channels of a multi-channel spectral analysis system.

A36.3.7.3 The minimum standard for the one-third octave band analysis system is the class 2 electrical performance requirements of IEC 61260 as amended, over the range of one-third octave nominal midband frequencies from 50 Hz through 10 kHz inclusive.

NOTE: IEC 61260 specifies procedures for testing of one-third octave band analysis systems for relative attenuation, anti-aliasing filters, real time operation, level linearity, and filter integrated response (effective bandwidth).

A36.3.7.4 When slow time averaging is performed in the analyzer, the response of the one-third octave band analysis system to a sudden onset or interruption of a constant sinusoidal signal at the respective one-third octave nominal midband frequency, must be measured at sampling instants 0.5, 1, 1.5 and 2 seconds(s) after the onset and 0.5 and 1s after interruption. The rising response must be −4 ±1 dB at 0.5s, −1.75 ±0.75 dB at 1s, −1 ±0.5 dB at 1.5s and −0.5 ±0.5 dB at 2s relative to the steady-state level. The falling response must be such that the sum of the output signal levels, relative to the initial steady-state level, and the corresponding rising response reading is −6.5 ±1 dB, at both 0.5 and 1s. At subsequent times the sum of the rising and falling responses must be −7.5 dB or less. This equates to an exponential averaging process (slow time-weighting) with a nominal 1s time constant (*i.e.*, 2s averaging time).

A36.3.7.5 When the one-third octave band sound pressure levels are determined from the output of the analyzer without slow time-weighting, slow time-weighting must be simulated in the subsequent processing.

Simulated slow time-weighted sound pressure levels can be obtained using a continuous exponential averaging process by the following equation:

$$L_s\ (i,k)=10\ \log\ [(0.60653)\ 10^{0.1\ L_s[i,\ (k-1)]}\ +\ (0.39347)\ 10^{0.1\ L\ (i,\ k)}]$$

where $L_s(i,k)$ is the simulated slow time-weighted sound pressure level and $L(i,k)$ is the as-measured 0.5s time average sound pressure level determined from the output of the analyzer for the k-th instant of time and i-th one-third octave band. For k=1, the slow time-weighted sound pressure $L_s[i, (k-1=0)]$ on the right hand side should be set to 0 dB. An approximation of the continuous exponential averaging is represented by the following equation for a four sample averaging process for $k \geq 4$:

$$L_s\ (i,k)=10\ \log\ [(0.13)\ 10^{0.1\ L[i,(k-3)]}\ +\ (0.21)\ 10^{0.1\ L[i,\ (k-2)]}\ +\ (0.27)\ 10^{0.1\ L[i,\ (k-1)]}\ +\ (0.39)\ 10^{0.1\ L[i,\ k]}]$$

where $L_s\ (i,\ k)$ is the simulated slow time-weighted sound pressure level and $L\ (i,\ k)$ is the as measured 0.5s time average sound pressure level determined from the output of the analyzer for the k-th instant of time and the i-th one-third octave band.

The sum of the weighting factors is 1.0 in the two equations. Sound pressure levels calculated by means of either equation are valid for the sixth and subsequent 0.5s data samples, or for times greater than 2.5s after initiation of data analysis.

NOTE: The coefficients in the two equations were calculated for use in determining equivalent slow time-weighted sound pressure levels from samples of 0.5s time average sound pressure levels. The equations do not work with data samples where the averaging time differs from 0.5s.

A36.3.7.6 The instant in time by which a slow time-weighted sound pressure level is characterized must be 0.75s earlier than the actual readout time.

NOTE: The definition of this instant in time is needed to correlate the recorded noise with the aircraft position when the noise was emitted and takes into account the averaging period of the slow time-weighting. For each 0.5 second data record this instant in time may also be identified as 1.25 seconds after the start of the associated 2 second averaging period.

A36.3.7.7 The resolution of the sound pressure levels, both displayed and stored, must be 0.1 dB or finer.

A36.3.8 *Calibration systems.*

A36.3.8.1 The acoustical sensitivity of the measurement system must be determined using a sound calibrator generating a known sound pressure level at a known frequency. The minimum standard for the sound calibrator is the class 1L requirements of IEC 60942 as amended.

A36.3.9 *Calibration and checking of system.*

A36.3.9.1 Calibration and checking of the measurement system and its constituent components must be carried out to the satisfaction of the FAA by the methods specified in sections A36.3.9.2 through A36.3.9.10. The calibration adjustments, including those for environmental effects on sound calibrator output level, must be reported to the FAA and applied to the measured one-third-octave sound pressure levels determined from the output of the analyzer. Data collected during an overload indication are invalid and may not be used. If the overload condition occurred during recording, the associated test data are invalid, whereas if the overload occurred during analysis, the analysis must be repeated with reduced sensitivity to eliminate the overload.

A36.3.9.2 The free-field frequency response of the microphone system may be determined by use of an electrostatic actuator in combination with manufacturer's data or by tests in an anechoic free-field facility. The correction for frequency response must be determined within 90 days of each test series. The correction for non-uniform frequency response of the microphone system must be reported to the FAA and applied to the measured one-third octave band sound pressure levels determined from the output of the analyzer.

A36.3.9.3 When the angles of incidence of sound emitted from the aircraft are within ±30° of grazing incidence at the microphone (see Figure A36–1), a single set of free-field corrections based on grazing incidence is considered sufficient for correction of directional response effects. For other cases, the angle of incidence for each 0.5 second sample must be determined and applied for the correction of incidence effects.

A36.3.9.4 For analog magnetic tape recorders, each reel of magnetic tape must carry at least 30 seconds of pink random or pseudo-random noise at its beginning and end. Data obtained from analog tape-recorded signals will be accepted as reliable only if level differences in the 10 kHz one-third-octave-band are not more than 0.75 dB for the signals recorded at the beginning and end.

A36.3.9.5 The frequency response of the entire measurement system while deployed in the field during the test series, exclusive of the microphone, must be determined at a level within 5 dB of the level corresponding to the calibration sound pressure level on the level range used during the tests for each one-third octave nominal midband frequency from 50 Hz to 10 kHz inclusive, utilizing pink random or pseudo-random noise. Within six months of each test series the output of the noise generator must be determined by a method traceable to the U.S. National Institute of Standards and Technology or to an equivalent national standards laboratory as determined by the FAA. Changes in the relative output from the previous calibration at each one-third octave band may not exceed 0.2 dB. The correction for frequency response must be reported to the FAA and applied to the measured one-third octave sound pressure levels determined from the output of the analyzer.

A36.3.9.6 The performance of switched attenuators in the equipment used during noise certification measurements and calibration must be checked within six months of each test series to ensure that the maximum error does not exceed 0.1 dB.

A36.3.9.7 The sound pressure level produced in the cavity of the coupler of the sound calibrator must be calculated for the test environmental conditions using the manufacturer's supplied information on the influence of atmospheric air pressure and temperature. This sound pressure level is used to establish the acoustical sensitivity of the measurement system. Within six months of each test series the output of the sound calibrator must be determined by a method traceable to the U.S. National Institute of Standards and Technology or to an equivalent national standards laboratory as determined by the FAA. Changes in output from the previous calibration must not exceed 0.2 dB.

A36.3.9.8 Sufficient sound pressure level calibrations must be made during each test day to ensure that the acoustical sensitivity of the measurement system is known at the prevailing environmental conditions corresponding with each test series. The difference between the acoustical sensitivity levels recorded immediately before and immediately after each test series on each day may not exceed 0.5 dB. The 0.5 dB limit applies after any atmospheric pressure corrections have been determined for the calibrator output level. The arithmetic mean of the before and after measurements must be used to represent the acoustical sensitivity level of the measurement system for that test series. The calibration corrections must be reported to the FAA and applied to the measured one-third octave band sound pressure levels determined from the output of the analyzer.

A36.3.9.9 Each recording medium, such as a reel, cartridge, cassette, or diskette, must carry a sound pressure level calibration of at least 10 seconds duration at its beginning and end.

A36.3.9.10 The free-field insertion loss of the windscreen for each one-third octave nominal midband frequency from 50 Hz to 10 kHz inclusive must be determined with sinusoidal sound signals at the incidence angles determined to be applicable for correction of directional response effects per section A36.3.9.3. The interval between angles tested must not exceed 30 degrees. For a windscreen that is undamaged and uncontaminated, the insertion loss may be taken from manufacturer's data. Alternatively, within six months of each test series the insertion loss of the windscreen may be determined by a method traceable to the U.S. National Institute of Standards and Technology or an equivalent national standards laboratory as determined by the FAA. Changes in the insertion loss from the previous calibration at each one-third-octave frequency band must not exceed 0.4 dB. The correction for the free-field insertion loss of the windscreen must be reported to the FAA and applied to the measured one-third octave sound pressure levels determined from the output of the analyzer.

A36.3.10 Adjustments for ambient noise.

A36.3.10.1 Ambient noise, including both a acoustical background and electrical noise of the measurement system, must be recorded for at least 10 seconds at the measurement points with the system gain set at the levels used for the aircraft noise measurements. Ambient noise must be representative of the acoustical background that exists during the flyover test run. The recorded aircraft noise data is acceptable only if the ambient noise levels, when analyzed in the same way, and quoted in PNL (see A36.4.1.3 (a)), are at least 20 dB below the maximum PNL of the aircraft.

A36.3.10.2 Aircraft sound pressure levels within the 10 dB-down points (see A36.4.5.1) must exceed the mean ambient noise levels determined in section A36.3.10.1 by at least 3 dB in each one-third octave band, or must be adjusted using a method approved by the FAA; one method is described in the current advisory circular for this part.

Section A36.4 Calculation of Effective Perceived Noise Level From Measured Data

A36.4.1 *General.*

A36.4.1.1 The basic element for noise certification criteria is the noise evaluation measure known as effective perceived noise level, EPNL, in units of EPNdB, which is a single number evaluator of the subjective effects of airplane noise on human beings. EPNL consists of instantaneous perceived noise level, PNL, corrected for spectral irregularities, and for duration. The spectral irregularity correction, called "tone correction factor", is made at each time increment for only the maximum tone.

A36.4.1.2 Three basic physical properties of sound pressure must be measured: level, frequency distribution, and time variation. To determine EPNL, the instantaneous sound pressure level in each of the 24 one-third octave bands is required for each 0.5 second increment of time during the airplane noise measurement.

A36.4.1.3 The calculation procedure that uses physical measurements of noise to derive the EPNL evaluation measure of subjective response consists of the following five steps:

(a) The 24 one-third octave bands of sound pressure level are converted to perceived noisiness (noy) using the method described in section A36.4.2.1 (a). The noy values are combined and then converted to instantaneous perceived noise levels, PNL(k).

(b) A tone correction factor C(k) is calculated for each spectrum to account for the subjective response to the presence of spectral irregularities.

(c) The tone correction factor is added to the perceived noise level to obtain tone-corrected perceived noise levels PNLT(k), at each one-half second increment:

PNLT(k)=PNL(k) + C(k)

The instantaneous values of tone-corrected perceived noise level are derived and the maximum value, PNLTM, is determined.

(d) A duration correction factor, D, is computed by integration under the curve of tone-corrected perceived noise level versus time.

(e) Effective perceived noise level, EPNL, is determined by the algebraic sum of the maximum tone-corrected perceived noise level and the duration correction factor:

EPNL=PNLTM + D

A36.4.2 *Perceived noise level.*

A36.4.2.1 Instantaneous perceived noise levels, PNL(k), must be calculated from instantaneous one-third octave band sound pressure levels, SPL(i, k) as follows:

(a) Step 1: For each one-third octave band from 50 through 10,000 Hz, convert SPL(i, k) to perceived noisiness n(i, k), by using the mathematical formulation of the noy table given in section A36.4.7.

(b) Step 2: Combine the perceived noisiness values, n(i, k), determined in step 1 by using the following formula:

$$N(k) = n(k) + 0.15 \left\{ \left[\sum_{i=1}^{24} n(i,k) \right] - n(k) \right\}$$

$$= 0.85\, n(k) + 0.15 \sum_{i=1}^{24} n(i,k)$$

where n(k) is the largest of the 24 values of n(i, k) and N(k) is the total perceived noisiness.

(c) Step 3: Convert the total perceived noisiness, N(k), determined in Step 2 into perceived noise level, PNL(k), using the following formula:

$$PNL(k) = 40.0 + \frac{10}{\log 2} \log N(k)$$

NOTE: PNL(k) is plotted in the current advisory circular for this part.

A36.4.3 *Correction for spectral irregularities.*

A36.4.3.1 Noise having pronounced spectral irregularities (for example, the maximum discrete frequency components or tones) must be adjusted by the correction factor C(k) calculated as follows:

(a) Step 1: After applying the corrections specified under section A36.3.9, start with the sound pressure level in the 80 Hz one-third octave band (band number 3), calculate the changes in sound pressure level (or "slopes") in the remainder of the one-third octave bands as follows:

$s(3,k)$=no value
$s(4,k)$=SPL$(4,k)$−SPL$(3,k)$
•
•
$s(i,k)$=SPL(i,k)−SPL$(i-1,k)$
•
•
$s(24,k)$=SPL$(24,k)$−SPL$(23,k)$

(b) Step 2: Encircle the value of the slope, s(i, k), where the absolute value of the change in slope is greater than five; that is where:

$|\Delta s(i,k)|=|s(i,k)-s(i-1,k)|>5$

(c) Step 3:

(1) If the encircled value of the slope s(i, k) is positive and algebraically greater than the slope s(i−1, k) encircle SPL(i, k).

(2) If the encircled value of the slope s(i, k) is zero or negative and the slope s(i−1, k) is positive, encircle SPL(i−1, k).

(3) For all other cases, no sound pressure level value is to be encircled.

(d) Step 4: Compute new adjusted sound pressure levels SPL'(i, k) as follows:

(1) For non-encircled sound pressure levels, set the new sound pressure levels equal to the original sound pressure levels, SPL'(i, k)=SPL(i, k).

(2) For encircled sound pressure levels in bands 1 through 23 inclusive, set the new sound pressure level equal to the arithmetic average of the preceding and following sound pressure levels as shown below:

$SPL'(i,k)=\frac{1}{2}[SPL(i-1,k)+SPL(i+1,k)]$

(3) If the sound pressure level in the highest frequency band (i=24) is encircled, set the new sound pressure level in that band equal to:

$SPL'(24,k)=SPL(23,k)+s(23,k)$

(e) Step 5: Recompute new slope s'(i, k), including one for an imaginary 25th band, as follows:

$s'(3,k)=s'(4,k)$
$s'(4,k)$=SPL$'(4,k)$−SPL$'(3,k)$
•
•
$s'(i,k)$=SPL$'(i,k)$−SPL$'(i-1,k)$
•
•
$s'(24,k)$=SPL$'(24,k)$−SPL$'(23,k)$

$s'(25,k)=s'(24,k)$

(f) Step 6: For i, from 3 through 23, compute the arithmetic average of the three adjacent slopes as follows:

$\bar{s}(i,k)=\frac{1}{3}[s'(i,k)+s'(i+1,k)+s'(i+2,k)]$

(g) Step 7: Compute final one-third octave-band sound pressure levels, SPL′ (i,k), by beginning with band number 3 and proceeding to band number 24 as follows:

SPL′$(3,k)$=SPL(3,k)

SPL′$(4,k)$=SPL′(3,k)+$\bar{s}(3,k)$

•

•

SPL′(i,k)=SPL′(i−1,k)+$\bar{s}(i−1,k)$

•

•

SPL′$(24,k)$=SPL′(23,k)+$\bar{s}(23,k)$

(h) Setp 8: Calculate the differences, F (i,k), between the original sound pressure level and the final background sound pressure level as follows:

$F(i,k)$=SPL(i,k)-SPL′(i,k)

and note only values equal to or greater than 1.5.

(i) Step 9: For each of the relevant one-third octave bands (3 through 24), determine tone correction factors from the sound pressure level differences F (i, k) and Table A36–2.

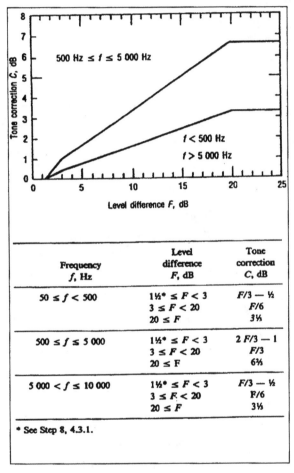

Table A36-2. Tone correction factor

Frequency f, Hz	Level difference F, dB	Tone correction C, dB
50 ≤ f < 500	1½* ≤ F < 3	F/3 — ½
	3 ≤ F < 20	F/6
	20 ≤ F	3⅓
500 ≤ f ≤ 5 000	1½* ≤ F < 3	2 F/3 — 1
	3 ≤ F < 20	F/3
	20 ≤ F	6⅔
5 000 < f ≤ 10 000	1½* ≤ F < 3	F/3 — ½
	3 ≤ F < 20	F/6
	20 ≤ F	3⅓

* See Step 8, 4.3.1.

(j) Step 10: Designate the largest of the tone correction factors, determined in Step 9, as C(k). (An example of the tone correction procedure is given in the current advisory circular for this part). Tone-corrected perceived noise levels PNLT(k) must be determined by adding the C(k) values to corresponding PNL(k) values, that is:

PNLT(k)=PNL(k)+C(k)

For any i-th one-third octave band, at any k-th increment of time, for which the tone cor-rection factor is suspected to result from something other than (or in addition to) an actual tone (or any spectral irregularity other than airplane noise), an additional analysis may be made using a filter with a bandwidth narrower than one-third of an octave. If the narrow band analysis corroborates these suspicions, then a revised value for the background sound pressure level

799

SPL'(i,k), may be determined from the narrow band analysis and used to compute a revised tone correction factor for that particular one-third octave band. Other methods of rejecting spurious tone corrections may be approved.

A36.4.3.2 The tone correction procedure will underestimate EPNL if an important tone is of a frequency such that it is recorded in two adjacent one-third octave bands. An applicant must demonstrate that either:

(a) No important tones are recorded in two adjacent one-third octave bands; or

(b) That if an important tone has occurred, the tone correction has been adjusted to the value it would have had if the tone had been recorded fully in a single one-third octave band.

A36.4.4 Maximum tone-corrected perceived noise level

A36.4.4.1 The maximum tone-corrected perceived noise level, PNLTM, must be the maximum calculated value of the tone-corrected perceived noise level PNLT(k). It must be calculated using the procedure of section A36.4.3. To obtain a satisfactory noise time history, measurements must be made at 0.5 second time intervals.

NOTE 1: Figure A36–2 is an example of a flyover noise time history where the maximum value is clearly indicated.

NOTE 2: In the absence of a tone correction factor, PNLTM would equal PNLM.

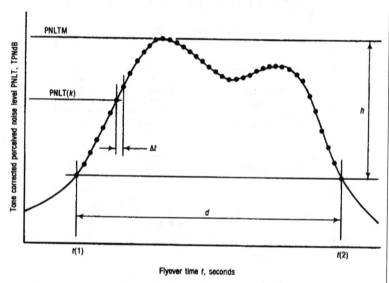

Figure A36–2. Example of perceived noise level corrected for tones as a function of aircraft flyover time

A36.4.4.2 After the value of PNLTM is obtained, the frequency band for the largest tone correction factor is identified for the two preceding and two succeeding 500 ms data samples. This is performed in order to identity the possibility of tone suppression at PNLTM by one-third octave band sharing of that tone. If the value of the tone correction factor C(k) for PNLTM is less than the average value of C(k) for the five consecutive time intervals, the average value of C(k) must be used to compute a new value for PNLTM.

A36.4.5 *Duration correction.*

A36.4.5.1 The duration correction factor D determined by the integration technique is defined by the expression:

$$D = 10 \log \left[\left(\frac{1}{T} \right) \int_{t(1)}^{t(2)} antilog \frac{PNLT}{10} dt \right] - PNLTM$$

where T is a normalizing time constant, PNLTM is the maximum value of PNLT, t(1) is the first point of time after which PNLT becomes greater than PNLTM–10, and t(2) is the point of time after which PNLT remains constantly less than PNLTM–10.

A36.4.5.2 Since PNLT is calculated from measured values of sound pressure level (SPL), there is no obvious equation for PNLT as a function of time. Consequently, the equation is to be rewritten with a summation sign instead of an integral sign as follows:

$$D = 10 \log \left[\left(\frac{1}{T} \right) \sum_{k=0}^{d/\Delta t} \Delta t . antilog \frac{PNLT(k)}{10} \right] - PNLTM$$

where Δt is the length of the equal increments of time for which PNLT(k) is calculated and d is the time interval to the nearest 0.5s during which PNLT(k) remains greater or equal to PNLTM–10.

A36.4.5.3 To obtain a satisfactory history of the perceived noise level use one of the following:

(a) Half-Second time intervals for Δt; or

(b) A shorter time interval with approved limits and constants.

A36.4.5.4 The following values for T and Δt must be used in calculating D in the equation given in section A36.4.5.2:

T=10 s, and

Δt=0.5s (or the approved sampling time interval).

Using these values, the equation for D becomes:

$$D = 10 \log \left[\sum_{k=0}^{2d} antilog \frac{PNLT(k)}{10} \right] - PNLTM - 13$$

where d is the duration time defined by the points corresponding to the values PNLTM–10.

A36.4.5.5 If in using the procedures given in section A36.4.5.2, the limits of PNLTM–10 fall between the calculated PNLT(k) values (the usual case), the PNLT(k) values defining the limits of the duration interval must be chosen from the PNLT(k) values closest to PNLTM–10. For those cases with more than one peak value of PNLT(k), the applicable limits must be chosen to yield the largest possible value for the duration time.

A36.4.6 Effective perceived noise level.

The total subjective effect of an airplane noise event, designated effective perceived noise level, EPNL, is equal to the algebraic sum of the maximum value of the tone-corrected perceived noise level, PNLTM, and the duration correction D. That is:

EPNL=PNLTM+D

where PNLTM and D are calculated using the procedures given in sections A36.4.2, A36.4.3, A36.4.4. and A36.4.5.

A36.4.7 Mathematical formulation of noy tables.

A36.4.7.1 The relationship between sound pressure level (SPL) and the logarithm of perceived noisiness is illustrated in Figure A36–3 and Table A36–3.

A36.4.7.2 The bases of the mathematical formulation are:

(a) The slopes (M(b), M(c), M(d) and M(e)) of the straight lines;

(b) The intercepts (SPL(b) and SPL(c)) of the lines on the SPL axis; and

(c) The coordinates of the discontinuities, SPL(a) and log n(a); SPL(d) and log n=–1.0; and SPL(e) and log n=log (0.3).

A36.4.7.3 Calculate noy values using the following equations:

(a)

SPL ≥ SPL (a)

n=antilog {(c)[SPL – SPL(c)]}

(b)

SPL(b) ≤ SPL < SPL(a)

n=antilog {M(b)[SPL − SPL(b)]}

(c)

SPL(e) ≤ SPL < SPL(b)

n=0.3 antilog {M(e)[SPL − SPL(e)]}

(d)

SPL(d) ≤ SPL < SPL(e)

n=0.1 antilog {M(d)[SPL − SPL(d)]}

A36.4.7.4 Table A36–3 lists the values of the constants necessary to calculate perceived noisiness as a function of sound pressure level.

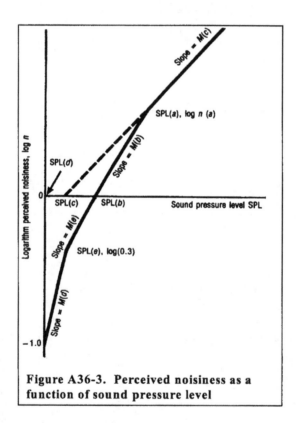

Figure A36-3. Perceived noisiness as a function of sound pressure level

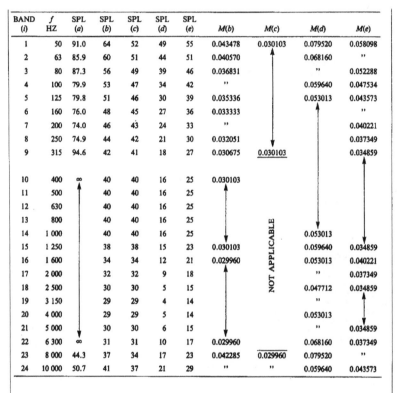

BAND (i)	f HZ	SPL (a)	SPL (b)	SPL (c)	SPL (d)	SPL (e)	M(b)	M(c)	M(d)	M(e)
1	50	91.0	64	52	49	55	0.043478	0.030103	0.079520	0.058098
2	63	85.9	60	51	44	51	0.040570		0.068160	"
3	80	87.3	56	49	39	46	0.036831		"	0.052288
4	100	79.9	53	47	34	42	"		0.059640	0.047534
5	125	79.8	51	46	30	39	0.035336		0.053013	0.043573
6	160	76.0	48	45	27	36	0.033333			"
7	200	74.0	46	43	24	33	"			0.040221
8	250	74.9	44	42	21	30	0.032051			0.037349
9	315	94.6	42	41	18	27	0.030675	0.030103		0.034859
10	400	∞	40	40	16	25	0.030103			
11	500		40	40	16	25				
12	630		40	40	16	25				
13	800		40	40	16	25		NOT APPLICABLE		
14	1 000		40	40	16	25			0.053013	
15	1 250		38	38	15	23	0.030103		0.059640	0.034859
16	1 600		34	34	12	21	0.029960		0.053013	0.040221
17	2 000		32	32	9	18			"	0.037349
18	2 500		30	30	5	15			0.047712	0.034859
19	3 150		29	29	4	14			"	
20	4 000		29	29	5	14			0.053013	
21	5 000		30	30	6	15			"	0.034859
22	6 300	∞	31	31	10	17	0.029960		0.068160	0.037349
23	8 000	44.3	37	34	17	23	0.042285	0.029960	0.079520	"
24	10 000	50.7	41	37	21	29	"	"	0.059640	0.043573

Table A36-3. Constants for mathematically formulated noy values

Section A36.5 Reporting of Data to the FAA

A36.5.1 *General.*

A36.5.1.1 Data representing physical measurements and data used to make corrections to physical measurements must be recorded in an approved permanent form and appended to the record.

A36.5.1.2 All corrections must be reported to and approved by the FAA, including corrections to measurements for equipment response deviations.

A36.5.1.3 Applicants may be required to submit estimates of the individual errors inherent in each of the operations employed in obtaining the final data.

A36.5.2 *Data reporting.*

An applicant is required to submit a noise certification compliance report that includes the following.

A36.5.2.1 The applicant must present measured and corrected sound pressure levels in one-third octave band levels that are obtained with equipment conforming to the standards described in section A36.3 of this appendix.

A36.5.2.2 The applicant must report the make and model of equipment used for measurement and analysis of all acoustic performance and meteorological data.

A36.5.2.3 The applicant must report the following atmospheric environmental data, as measured immediately before, after, or during each test at the observation points prescribed in section A36.2 of this appendix.

(a) Air temperature and relative humidity;

(b) Maximum, minimum and average wind velocities; and

(c) Atmospheric pressure.

A36.5.2.4 The applicant must report conditions of local topography, ground cover, and events that might interfere with sound recordings.

A36.5.2.5 The applicant must report the following:

(a) Type, model and serial numbers (if any) of airplane, engine(s), or propeller(s) (as applicable);

(b) Gross dimensions of airplane and location of engines;

(c) Airplane gross weight for each test run and center of gravity range for each series of test runs;

(d) Airplane configuration such as flap, airbrakes and landing gear positions for each test run;

(e) Whether auxiliary power units (APU), when fitted, are operating for each test run;

(f) Status of pneumatic engine bleeds and engine power take-offs for each test run;

(g) Indicated airspeed in knots or kilometers per hour for each test run;

(h) Engine performance data:

(1) For jet airplanes: engine performance in terms of net thrust, engine pressure ratios, jet exhaust temperatures and fan or compressor shaft rotational speeds as determined from airplane instruments and manufacturer's data for each test run;

(2) For propeller-driven airplanes: engine performance in terms of brake horsepower and residual thrust; or equivalent shaft horsepower; or engine torque and propeller rotational speed; as determined from airplane instruments and manufacturer's data for each test run;

(i) Airplane flight path and ground speed during each test run; and

(j) The applicant must report whether the airplane has any modifications or non-standard equipment likely to affect the noise characteristics of the airplane. The FAA must approve any such modifications or nonstandard equipment.

A36.5.3 *Reporting of noise certification reference conditions.*

A36.5.3.1 Airplane position and performance data and the noise measurements must be corrected to the noise certification reference conditions specified in the relevant sections of appendix B of this part. The applicant must report these conditions, including reference parameters, procedures and configurations.

A36.5.4 *Validity of results.*

A36.5.4.1 Three average reference EPNL values and their 90 percent confidence limits must be produced from the test results and reported, each such value being the arithmetical average of the adjusted acoustical measurements for all valid test runs at each measurement point (flyover, lateral, or approach). If more than one acoustic measurement system is used at any single measurement location, the resulting data for each test run must be averaged as a single meas-

urement. The calculation must be performed by:

(a) Computing the arithmetic average for each flight phase using the values from each microphone point; and

(b) Computing the overall arithmetic average for each reference condition (flyover, lateral or approach) using the values in paragraph (a) of this section and the related 90 percent confidence limits.

A36.5.4.2 For each of the three certification measuring points, the minimum sample size is six. The sample size must be large enough to establish statistically for each of the three average noise certification levels a 90 percent confidence limit not exceeding ±1.5 EPNdB. No test result may be omitted from the averaging process unless approved by the FAA.

NOTE: Permitted methods for calculating the 90 percent confidence interval are shown in the current advisory circular for this part.

A36.5.4.3 The average EPNL figures obtained by the process described in section A36.5.4.1 must be those by which the noise performance of the airplane is assessed against the noise certification criteria.

Section A36.6 Nomenclature: Symbols and Units

Symbol	Unit	Meaning
antilog	....	Antilogarithm to the base 10.
C(k)	dB	*Tone correction factor.* The factor to be added to PNL(k) to account for the presence of spectral irregularities such as tones at the k-th increment of time.
d	s	*Duration time.* The time interval between the limits of t(1) and t(2) to the nearest 0.5 second.
D	dB	*Duration correction.* The factor to be added to PNLTM to account for the duration of the noise.
EPNL	EPNdB	*Effective perceived noise level.* The value of PNL adjusted for both spectral irregularities and duration of the noise. (The unit EPNdB is used instead of the unit dB).
EPNL$_r$	EPNdB	Effective perceived noise level adjusted for reference conditions.
f(i)	Hz	*Frequency.* The geometrical mean frequency for the i-th one-third octave band.

Symbol	Unit	Meaning
F (i, k)	dB	*Delta-dB.* The difference between the original sound pressure level and the final background sound pressure level in the i-th one-third octave band at the k-th interval of time. In this case, background sound pressure level means the broadband noise level that would be present in the one-third octave band in the absence of the tone.
h	dB	*dB-down.* The value to be subtracted from PNLTM that defines the duration of the noise.
H	Percent	*Relative humidity.* The ambient atmospheric relative humidity.
i		*Frequency band index.* The numerical indicator that denotes any one of the 24 one-third octave bands with geometrical mean frequencies from 50 to 10,000 Hz.
k		*Time increment index.* The numerical indicator that denotes the number of equal time increments that have elapsed from a reference zero.
Log		Logarithm to the base 10.
log n(a)		*Noy discontinuity coordinate.* The log n value of the intersection point of the straight lines representing the variation of SPL with log n.
M(b), M(c), etc.		*Noy inverse slope.* The reciprocals of the slopes of straight lines representing the variation of SPL with log n.
n	noy	The perceived noisiness at any instant of time that occurs in a specified frequency range.
n(i,k)	noy	The perceived noisiness at the k–th instant of time that occurs in the i–th one–third octave band.
n(k)	noy	*Maximum perceived noisiness.* The maximum value of all of the 24 values of n(i) that occurs at the k-th instant of time.
N(k)	noy	*Total perceived noisiness.* The total perceived noisiness at the k-th instant of time calculated from the 24-instantaneous values of n (i, k).
p(b), p(c), etc		*Noy slope.* The slopes of straight lines representing the variation of SPL with log n.
PNL	PNdB	The perceived noise level at any instant of time. (The unit PNdB is used instead of the unit dB).

Symbol	Unit	Meaning
PNL(k)	PNdB	The perceived noise level calculated from the 24 values of SPL (i, k), at the k-th increment of time. (The unit PNdB is used instead of the unit dB).
PNLM	PNdB	*Maximum perceived noise level.* The maximum value of PNL(k). (The unit PNdB is used instead of the unit dB).
PNLT	TPNdB	*Tone-corrected perceived noise level.* The value of PNL adjusted for the spectral irregularities that occur at any instant of time. (The unit TPNdB is used instead of the unit dB).
PNLT(k)	TPNdB	The tone-corrected perceived noise level that occurs at the k-th increment of time. PNLT(k) is obtained by adjusting the value of PNL(k) for the spectral irregularities that occur at the k-th increment of time. (The unit TPNdB is used instead of the unit dB).
PNLTM	TPNdB	*Maximum tone-corrected perceived noise level.* The maximum value of PNLT(k). (The unit TPNdB is used instead of the unit dB).
PNLT$_r$	TPNdB	Tone-corrected perceived noise level adjusted for reference conditions.
s (i, k)	dB	*Slope of sound pressure level.* The change in level between adjacent one-third octave band sound pressure levels at the i-th band for the k-th instant of time.
Δs (i, k)	dB	Change in slope of sound pressure level.
s′ (i, k)	dB	Adjusted slope of sound pressure level. The change in level between adjacent adjusted one-third octave band sound pressure levels at the i-th band for the k-th instant of time.
š (i, k)	dB	Average slope of sound pressure level.
SPL	dB re 20 μPa	*Sound pressure level.* The sound pressure level that occurs in a specified frequency range at any instant of time.
SPL(a)	dB re 20 μPa	*Noy discontinuity coordinate.* The SPL value of the intersection point of the straight lines representing the variation of SPL with log n.
SPL(b) SPL (c)	dB re 20 μPa	*Noy intercept.* The intercepts on the SPL-axis of the straight lines representing the variation of SPL with log n.
SPL (i, k)	dB re 20 μPa	The sound pressure level at the k-th instant of time that occurs in the i-th one-third octave band.

Symbol	Unit	Meaning
SPL′ (i, k)	dB re .... 20 μPa	*Adjusted sound pressure level.* The first approximation to background sound pressure level in the i-th one-third octave band for the k-th instant of time.
SPL(i)	dB re .... 20 μPa	*Maximum sound pressure level.* The sound pressure level that occurs in the i-th one-third octave band of the spectrum for PNLTM.
SPL(i)$_r$	dB re .... 20 μPa	*Corrected maximum sound pressure level.* The sound pressure level that occurs in the i-th one-third octave band of the spectrum for PNLTM corrected for atmospheric sound absorption.
SPL′ (i, k)	dB re .... 20 μPa	*Final background sound pressure level.* The second and final approximation to background sound pressure level in the i-th one-third octave band for the k-th instant of time.
t	s	*Elapsed time.* The length of time measured from a reference zero.
t(1), t(2)	s	*Time limit.* The beginning and end, respectively, of the noise time history defined by h.
Δt	s	*Time increment.* The equal increments of time for which PNL(k) and PNLT(k) are calculated.
T	s	*Normalizing time constant.* The length of time used as a reference in the integration method for computing duration corrections, where T=10s.
t(°F) (°C) ...	°F, °C	*Temperature.* The ambient air temperature.
α(i)	dB/1000ft db/ 100m.	*Test atmospheric absorption.* The atmospheric attenuation of sound that occurs in the i-th one-third octave band at the measured air temperature and relative humidity.
α(i)$_o$	dB/1000ft db/ 100m.	*Reference atmospheric absorption.* The atmospheric attenuation of sound that occurs in the i-th one–third octave band at a reference air temperature and relative humidity.

Symbol	Unit	Meaning
A$_1$	Degrees	First constant climb angle (Gear up, speed of at least V$_2$+10 kt (V$_2$+19 km/h), takeoff thrust).
A$_2$	Degrees	Second constant climb angle (Gear up, speed of at least V$_2$+10 kt (V$_2$+19 km/h), after cut-back).
δ .... ε	Degrees	*Thrust cutback angles.* The angles defining the points on the takeoff flight path at which thrust reduction is started and ended respectively.
η	Degrees	Approach angle.
η$_r$	Degrees	Reference approach angle.
θ	Degrees	*Noise angle (relative to flight path).* The angle between the flight path and noise path. It is identical for both measured and corrected flight paths.
ψ	Degrees	*Noise angle (relative to ground).* The angle between the noise path and the ground. It is identical for both measured and corrected flight paths.
μ	....	Engine noise emission parameter.
μ$_r$	....	Reference engine noise emission parameter.
Δ$_1$	EPNdB	*PNLT correction.* The correction to be added to the EPNL calculated from measured data to account for noise level changes due to differences in atmospheric absorption and noise path length between reference and test conditions.
Δ$_2$	EPNdB	*Adjustment to duration correction.* The adjustment to be made to the EPNL calculated from measured data to account for noise level changes due to the noise duration between reference and test conditions.
Δ$_3$	EPNdB	*Source noise adjustment.* The adjustment to be made to the EPNL calculated from measured data to account for noise level changes due to differences between reference and test engine operating conditions.

Section A36.7   Sound Attenuation in Air

A36.7.1   The atmospheric attenuation of sound must be determined in accordance with the procedure presented in section A36.7.2.

A36.7.2   The relationship between sound attenuation, frequency, temperature, and humidity is expressed by the following equations.

A36.7.2(a)   For calculations using the English System of Units:

$$\alpha(i) = 10^{\left[2.05\log\left(f_0/1000\right)+6.33\times10^{-4}\,\theta-1.45325\right]}$$
$$+\,\eta(\delta)\times10^{\left[\log\left(f_0\right)+4.6833\times10^{-3}\,\theta-2.4215\right]}$$

and

$$\delta = \sqrt{\frac{1010}{f(0)}}\,10^{\left(\log H-1.97274664+2.288074\times10^{-2}\,\theta\right)}$$
$$\times 10^{\left(-9.589\times10^{-5}\,\theta^2+3.0\times10^{-7}\,\theta^3\right)}$$

where
$\eta(\delta)$ is listed in Table A36–4 and f_o in Table A36–5;
$\alpha(i)$ is the attenuation coefficient in dB/1000 ft;
θ is the temperature in °F; and
H is the relative humidity, expressed as a percentage.

A36.7.2(b) For calculations using the International System of Units (SI):

$$\alpha(i) = 10^{\left[2.05\log\left(f_0/1000\right)+1.1394\times10^{-3}\,\theta-1.916984\right]}$$
$$+\,\eta(\delta)\times10^{\left[\log\left(f_0\right)+8.42994\times10^{-3}\,\theta-2.755624\right]}$$

and

$$\delta = \sqrt{\frac{1010}{f_0}}\,10^{\left(\log H-1.328924+3.179768\times10^{-2}\,\theta\right)}$$
$$\times 10^{\left(-2.173716\times10^{-4}\,\theta^2+1.7496\times10^{-6}\,\theta^3\right)}$$

where
$\eta(\delta)$ is listed in Table A36–4 and f_o in Table A36–5;
$\alpha(i)$ is the attenuation coefficient in dB/100 m;
θ is the temperature in °C; and
H is the relative humidity, expressed as a percentage.

A36.7.3 The values listed in table A36–4 are to be used when calculating the equations listed in section A36.7.2. A term of quadratic interpolation is to be used where necessary.

807

Section A36.8 [Reserved]

Table A36-4. Values of $\eta(\delta)$

δ	$\eta(\delta)$	δ	$\eta(\delta)$
0.00	0.000	2.50	0.450
0.25	0.315	2.80	0.400
0.50	0.700	3.00	0.370
0.60	0.840	3.30	0.330
0.70	0.930	3.60	0.300
0.80	0.975	4.15	0.260
0.90	0.996	4.45	0.245
1.00	1.000	4.80	0.230
1.10	0.970	5.25	0.220
1.20	0.900	5.70	0.210
1.30	0.840	6.05	0.205
1.50	0.750	6.50	0.200
1.70	0.670	7.00	0.200
2.00	0.570	10.00	0.200
2.30	0.495		

Table A36-5. Values of f_0

one-third octave center frequency	f_0 (Hz)	one-third octave center frequency	f_0 (Hz)
50	50	800	800
63	63	1000	1000
80	80	1250	1250
100	100	1600	1600
125	125	2000	2000
160	160	2500	2500
200	200	3150	3150
250	250	4000	4000
315	315	5000	4500
400	400	6300	5600
500	500	8000	7100
630	630	10000	9000

Section A36.9 Adjustment of Airplane Flight Test Results.

A36.9.1 When certification test conditions are not identical to reference conditions, appropriate adjustments must be made to the measured noise data using the methods described in this section.

A36.9.1.1 Adjustments to the measured noise values must be made using one of the methods described in sections A36.9.3 and A36.9.4 for differences in the following:

(a) Attenuation of the noise along its path as affected by "inverse square" and atmospheric attenuation

(b) Duration of the noise as affected by the distance and the speed of the airplane relative to the measuring point

(c) Source noise emitted by the engine as affected by the differences between test and reference engine operating conditions

(d) Airplane/engine source noise as affected by differences between test and reference airspeeds. In addition to the effect on duration, the effects of airspeed on component noise sources must be accounted for as follows: for conventional airplane configurations, when differences between test and reference airspeeds exceed 15 knots (28 km/h) true airspeed, test data and/or analysis approved by the FAA must be used to quantify the effects of the airspeed adjustment on resulting certification noise levels.

A36.9.1.2 The "integrated" method of adjustment, described in section A36.9.4, must be used on takeoff or approach under the following conditions:

(a) When the amount of the adjustment (using the "simplified" method) is greater than 8 dB on flyover, or 4 dB on approach; or

(b) When the resulting final EPNL value on flyover or approach (using the simplified method) is within 1 dB of the limiting noise levels as prescribed in section B36.5 of this part.

A36.9.2 *Flight profiles.*

As described below, flight profiles for both test and reference conditions are defined by their geometry relative to the ground, together with the associated airplane speed relative to the ground, and the associated engine control parameter(s) used for determining the noise emission of the airplane.

A36.9.2.1 *Takeoff Profile.*

NOTE: Figure A36–4 illustrates a typical takeoff profile.

(a) The airplane begins the takeoff roll at point A, lifts off at point B and begins its first climb at a constant angle at point C. Where thrust or power (as appropriate) cutback is used, it is started at point D and completed at point E. From here, the airplane begins a second climb at a constant angle up to point F, the end of the noise certification takeoff flight path.

(b) Position K_1 is the takeoff noise measuring station and AK_1 is the distance from start of roll to the flyover measuring point. Position K_2 is the lateral noise measuring station, which is located on a line parallel to, and the specified distance from, the runway center line where the noise level during takeoff is greatest.

(c) The distance AF is the distance over which the airplane position is measured and synchronized with the noise measurements, as required by section A36.2.3.2 of this part.

A36.9.2.2 *Approach Profile.*

NOTE: Figure A36–5 illustrates a typical approach profile.

(a) The airplane begins its noise certification approach flight path at point G and touches down on the runway at point J, at a distance OJ from the runway threshold.

(b) Position K_3 is the approach noise measuring station and K_3O is the distance from the approach noise measurement point to the runway threshold.

(c) The distance GI is the distance over which the airplane position is measured and synchronized with the noise measurements, as required by section A36.2.3.2 of this part.

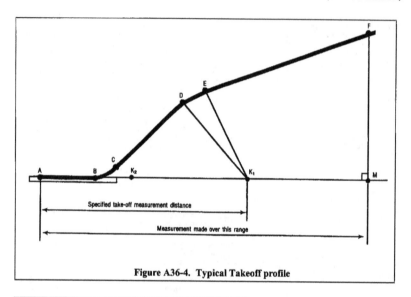

Figure A36-4. Typical Takeoff profile

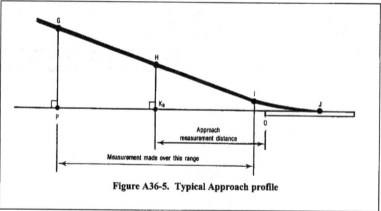

Figure A36-5. Typical Approach profile

The airplane reference point for approach measurements is the instrument landing system (ILS) antenna. If no ILS antenna is installed an alternative reference point must be approved by the FAA.

A36.9.3 *Simplified method of adjustment.*

A36.9.3.1 *General.* As described below, the simplified adjustment method consists of applying adjustments (to the EPNL, which is calculated from the measured data) for the differences between measured and reference conditions at the moment of PNLTM.

A36.9.3.2 *Adjustments to PNL and PNLT.*

(a) The portions of the test flight path and the reference flight path described below, and illustrated in Figure A36–6, include the noise time history that is relevant to the calculation of flyover and approach EPNL. In figure A36–6:

(1) XY represents the portion of the measured flight path that includes the noise time history relevant to the calculation of flyover and approach EPNL; X_rY_r represents the corresponding portion of the reference flight path.

(2) Q represents the airplane's position on the measured flight path at which the noise was emitted and observed as PNLTM at the noise measuring station K. Q_r is the corresponding position on the reference flight path, and K_r the reference measuring station. QK and Q_rK_r are, respectively, the measured

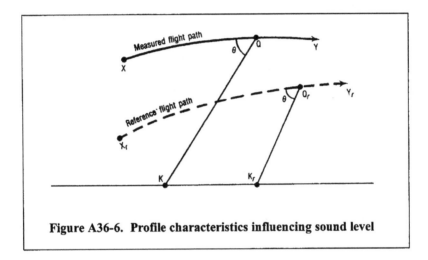

Figure A36-6. Profile characteristics influencing sound level

and reference noise propagation paths, Q_r being determined from the assumption that QK and Q_rK_r form the same angle θ with their respective flight paths.

(b) The portions of the test flight path and the reference flight path described in paragraph (b)(1) and (2), and illustrated in Figure A36–7(a) and (b), include the noise time history that is relevant to the calculation of lateral EPNL.

(1) In figure A36–7(a), XY represents the portion of the measured flight path that includes the noise time history that is relevant to the calculation of lateral EPNL; in figure A36–7(b), X_rY_r represents the corresponding portion of the reference flight path.

(2) Q represents the airplane position on the measured flight path at which the noise was emitted and observed as PNLTM at the

noise measuring station K. Q_r is the corresponding position on the reference flight path, and K_r the reference measuring station. QK and Q_rK_r are, respectively, the measured and reference noise propagation paths. In this case K_r is only specified as being on a particular Lateral line; K_r and Q_r are therefore determined from the assumptions that QK and Q_rK_r:

(i) Form the same angle θ with their respective flight paths; and

(ii) Form the same angle ψ with the ground.

NOTE: For the lateral noise measurement, sound propagation is affected not only by inverse square and atmospheric attenuation, but also by ground absorption and reflection effects which depend mainly on the angle ψ.

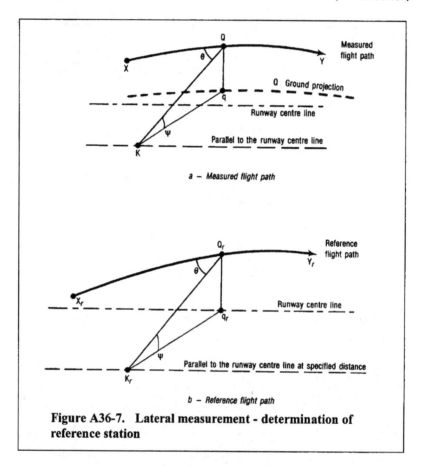

a – Measured flight path

b – Reference flight path

Figure A36-7.   Lateral measurement - determination of reference station

A36.9.3.2.1 The one-third octave band levels SPL(i) comprising PNL (the PNL at the moment of PNLTM observed at K) must be adjusted to reference levels SPL(i)$_r$ as follows:

A36.9.3.2.1(a) For calculations using the English System of Units:

$$SPL(i)_r = SPL(i) + 0.001[\alpha(i) - \alpha(i)_0]QK$$
$$+ 0.001\alpha(i)_0(QK - Q_rK_r)$$
$$+ 20\log(QK/Q_rK_r)$$

In this expression,

(1) The term $0.001[\alpha(i) - \alpha(i)_0]QK$ is the adjustment for the effect of the change in sound attenuation coefficient, and $\alpha(i)$ and $\alpha(i)_0$ are the coefficients for the test and reference atmospheric conditions respectively,

determined under section A36.7 of this appendix;

(2) The term $0.001\alpha(i)_0(QK - Q_rK_r)$ is the adjustment for the effect of the change in the noise path length on the sound attenuation;

(3) The term $20\log(QK/Q_rK_r)$ is the adjustment for the effect of the change in the noise path length due to the "inverse square" law;

(4) QK and Q_rK_r are measured in feet and $\alpha(i)$ and $\alpha(i)_0$ are expressed in dB/1000 ft.

A36.9.3.2.1(b) For calculations using the International System of Units:

$$SPL(i)_r = SPL(i) + 0.01[\alpha(i) - \alpha(i)_0]QK$$
$$+ 0.01\alpha(i)_0 (QK - Q_rK_r)$$
$$+ 20\log(QK/Q_rK_r)$$

In this expression,

(1) The term $0.01[\alpha(i) - \alpha(i)_0]QK$ is the adjustment for the effect of the change in sound attenuation coefficient, and $\alpha(i)$ and $\alpha(i)_0$ are the coefficients for the test and reference atmospheric conditions respectively, determined under section A36.7 of this appendix;

(2) The term $0.01\alpha(i)_0(QK - Q_rK_r)$ is the adjustment for the effect of the change in the noise path length on the sound attenuation;

(3) The term $20 \log(QK/Q_rK_r)$ is the adjustment for the effect of the change in the noise path length due to the inverse square law;

(4) QK and Q_rK_r are measured in meters and $\alpha(i)$ and $\alpha(i)_0$ are expressed in dB/100 m.

A36.9.3.2.1.1 *PNLT Correction.*

(a) Convert the corrected values, $SPL(i)_r$, to $PNLT_r$;

(b) Calculate the correction term Δ_1 using the following equation:

$$\Delta_1 = PNLT_r - PNLTM$$

A36.9.3.2.1.2 Add Δ_1 arithmetically to the EPNL calculated from the measured data.

A36.9.3.2.2 If, during a test flight, several peak values of PNLT that are within 2 dB of PNLTM are observed, the procedure defined in section A36.9.3.2.1 must be applied at each peak, and the adjustment term, calculated according to section A36.9.3.2.1, must be added to each peak to give corresponding adjusted peak values of PNLT. If these peak values exceed the value at the moment of PNLTM, the maximum value of such exceedance must be added as a further adjustment to the EPNL calculated from the measured data.

A36.9.3.3 *Adjustments to duration correction.*

A36.9.3.3.1 Whenever the measured flight paths and/or the ground velocities of the test conditions differ from the reference flight paths and/or the ground velocities of the reference conditions, duration adjustments must be applied to the EPNL values calculated from the measured data. The adjustments must be calculated as described below.

A36.9.3.3.2 For the flight path shown in Figure A36–6, the adjustment term is calculated as follows:

$$\Delta_2 = -7.5 \log(QK/Q_rK_r) + 10 \log(V/V_r)$$

(a) Add Δ_2 arithmetically to the EPNL calculated from the measured data.

A36.9.3.4 *Source noise adjustments.*

A36.9.3.4.1 To account for differences between the parameters affecting engine noise as measured in the certification flight tests, and those calculated or specified in the reference conditions, the source noise adjustment must be calculated and applied. The adjustment is determined from the manufacturer's data approved by the FAA. Typical data used for this adjustment are illustrated in Figure A36–8 that shows a curve of EPNL versus the engine control parameter μ, with the EPNL data being corrected to all the other relevant reference conditions (airplane mass, speed and altitude, air temperature) and for the difference in noise between the test engine and the average engine (as defined in section B36.7(b)(7)). A sufficient number of data points over a range of values of μ_r is required to calculate the source noise adjustments for lateral, flyover and approach noise measurements.

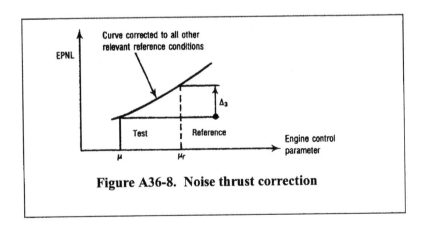

Figure A36-8. Noise thrust correction

A36.9.3.4.2 Calculate adjustment term Δ_3 by subtracting the EPNL value cor- responding to the parameter μ from the EPNL value corresponding to the parameter

μ_r. Add Δ_3 arithmetically to the EPNL value calculated from the measured data.

A36.9.3.5 *Symmetry adjustments.*

A36.9.3.5.1 A symmetry adjustment to each lateral noise value (determined at the section B36.4(b) measurement points), is to be made as follows:

(a) If the symmetrical measurement point is opposite the point where the highest noise level is obtained on the main lateral measurement line, the certification noise level is the arithmetic mean of the noise levels measured at these two points (see Figure A36–9(a));

(b) If the condition described in paragraph (a) of this section is not met, then it is assumed that the variation of noise with the altitude of the airplane is the same on both sides; there is a constant difference between the lines of noise versus altitude on both sides (see figure A36–9(b)). The certification noise level is the maximum value of the mean between these lines.

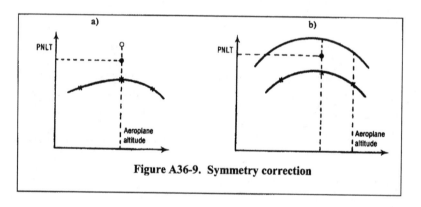

Figure A36-9. Symmetry correction

A36.9.4 *Integrated method of adjustment*

A36.9.4.1 *General.* As described in this section, the integrated adjustment method consists of recomputing under reference conditions points on the PNLT time history corresponding to measured points obtained during the tests, and computing EPNL directly for the new time history obtained in this way. The main principles are described in sections A36.9.4.2 through A36.9.4.4.1.

A36.9.4.2 *PNLT computations.*

(a) The portions of the test flight path and the reference flight path described in paragraph (a)(1) and (2), and illustrated in Figure A36–10, include the noise time history that is relevant to the calculation of flyover and approach EPNL. In figure A36–10:

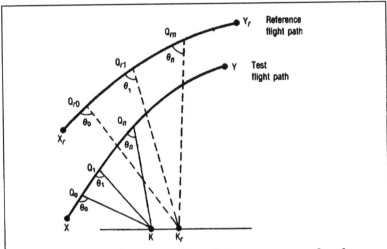

Figure A36-10. Correspondence between measured and reference flight paths for the application of the integrated method of adjustment

(1) XY represents the portion of the measured flight path that includes the noise time history relevant to the calculation of flyover and approach EPNL; X_rY_r represents the corresponding reference flight path.

(2) The points Q_0, Q_1, Q_n represent airplane positions on the measured flight path at time t_0, t_1 and t_n respectively. Point Q_1 is the point at which the noise was emitted and observed as one-third octave values $SPL(i)_1$ at the noise measuring station K at time t_1. Point Q_{r1} represents the corresponding position on the reference flight path for noise observed as $SPL(i)_{r1}$ at the reference measuring station K_r at time t_{r1}. Q_1K and $Q_{r1}K_r$ are respectively the measured and reference noise propagation paths, which in each case form the angle θ_1 with their respective flight paths. Q_{r0} and Q_{rn} are similarly the points on the reference flight path corresponding to Q_0 and Q_n on the measured flight path. Q_0 and Q_n are chosen so that between Q_{r0} and Q_{rn} all values of $PNLT_r$ (computed as described in paragraphs A36.9.4.2.2 and A36.9.4.2.3) within 10 dB of the peak value are included.

(b) The portions of the test flight path and the reference flight path described in para-

graph (b)(1) and (2), and illustrated *in Figure A36–11(a) and (b)*, include the noise time history that is relevant to the calculation of lateral EPNL.

(1) In figure A36–11(a) XY represents the portion of the measured flight path that includes the noise time history that is relevant to the calculation of lateral EPNL; in figure A36–11(b), X_rY_r represents the corresponding portion of the reference flight path.

(2) The points Q_0, Q_1 and Q_n represent airplane positions on the measured flight path at time t_0, t_1 and t_n respectively. Point Q_1 is the point at which the noise was emitted and observed as one-third octave values $SPL(i)_1$ at the noise measuring station K at time t_1. The point Q_{r1} represents the corresponding position on the reference flight path for noise observed as $SPL(i)_{r1}$ at the measuring station K_r at time t_{r1}. Q_1K and $Q_{r1}K_r$ are respectively the measured and reference noise propagation paths. Q_{r0} and Q_{rn} are similarly the points on the reference flight path corresponding to Q_0 and Q_n on the measured flight path.

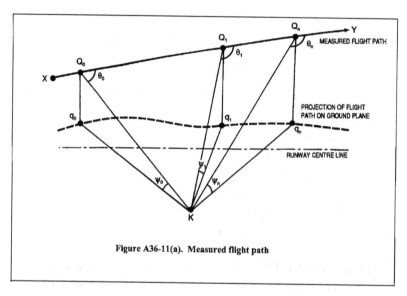

Figure A36-11(a). Measured flight path

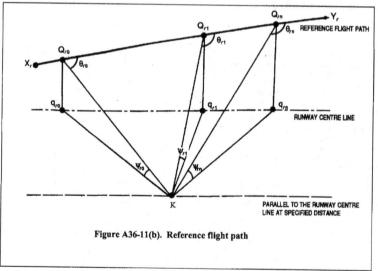

Figure A36-11(b). Reference flight path

Q_0 and Q_n are chosen to that between Q_{r0} and Q_{rn} all values of $PNLT_r$ (computed as described in paragraphs A36.9.4.2.2 and A36.9.4.2.3) within 10 dB of the peak value are included. In this case K_r is only specified as being on a particular lateral line. The position of K_r and Q_{r1} are determined from the following requirements.

(i) Q_1K and $Q_{r1}K_r$ form the same angle θ_1 with their respective flight paths; and

(ii) The differences between the angles $_1$ and $_{r1}$ must be minimized using a method, approved by the FAA. The differences between the angles are minimized since, for geometrical reasons, it is generally not possible to choose K_r so that the condition described in paragraph A36.9.4.2(b)(2)(i) is met while at the same time keeping $_1$ and $_{r1}$ equal.

NOTE: For the lateral noise measurement, sound propagation is affected not only by "inverse square" and atmospheric attenuation, but also by ground absorption and reflection effects which depend mainly on the angle.

A36.9.4.2.1 In paragraphs A36.9.4.2(a)(2) and (b)(2) the time t_{r1} is later (for $Q_{r1}K_r > Q_1K$) than t_1 by two separate amounts:

(1) The time taken for the airplane to travel the distance $Q_{r1}Q_{r0}$ at a speed V_r less the time taken for it to travel Q_1Q_0 at V;

(2) The time taken for sound to travel the distance $Q_{r1}K_r–Q_1K$.

NOTE: For the flight paths described in paragraphs A36.9.4.2(a) and (b), the use of thrust or power cut-back will result in test and reference flight paths at full thrust or power and at cut-back thrust or power. Where the transient region between these thrust or power levels affects the final result, an interpolation must be made between them by an approved method such as that given in the current advisory circular for this part.

A36.9.4.2.2 The measured values of $SPL(i)_1$ must be adjusted to the reference values $SPL(i)_{r1}$ to account for the differences between measured and reference noise path lengths and between measured and reference atmospheric conditions, using the methods of section A36.9.3.2.1 of this appendix. A corresponding value of PNL_{r1} must be computed according to the method in section A36.4.2. Values of PNL_r must be computed for times t_0 through t_n.

A36.9.4.2.3 For each value of PNL_{r1}, a tone correction factor C_1 must be determined by analyzing the reference values $SPL(i)_r$ using the methods of section A36.4.3 of this appendix, and added to PNL_{r1} to yield $PNLT_{r1}$. Using the process described in this paragraph, values of $PNLT_r$ must be computed for times t_0 through t_n.

A36.9.4.3 *Duration correction.*

A36.9.4.3.1 The values of $PNLT_r$ corresponding to those of PNLT at each one-half second interval must be plotted against time ($PNLT_{r1}$ at time t_{r1}). The duration correction must then be determined using the method of section A36.4.5.1 of this appendix, to yield $EPNL_r$.

A36.9.4.4 *Source Noise Adjustment.*

A36.9.4.4.1 A source noise adjustment, Δ_3, must be determined using the methods of section A36.9.3.4 of this appendix.

A36.9.5 FLIGHT PATH IDENTIFICATION POSITIONS

Position	Description
A	Start of Takeoff roll.
B	Lift-off.
C	Start of first constant climb.
D	Start of thrust reduction.
E	Start of second constant climb.
F	End of noise certification Takeoff flight path.
G	Start of noise certification Approach flight path.
H	Position on Approach path directly above noise measuring station.
I	Start of level-off.
J	Touchdown.
K	Noise measurement point.
K_r	Reference measurement point.
K_1	Flyover noise measurement point.
K_2	Lateral noise measurement point.
K_3	Approach noise measurement point.
M	End of noise certification Takeoff flight track.
O	Threshold of Approach end of runway.
P	Start of noise certification Approach flight track.
Q	Position on measured Takeoff flight path corresponding to apparent PNLTM at station K See section A36.9.3.2.
Q_r	Position on corrected Takeoff flight path corresponding to PNLTM at station K. See section A36.9.3.2.
V	Airplane test speed.
V_r	Airplane reference speed.

A36.9.6 FLIGHT PATH DISTANCES

Distance	Unit	Meaning
AB	Feet (meters).	Length of takeoff roll. The distance along the runway between the start of takeoff roll and lift off.
AK	Feet (meters).	Takeoff measurement distance. The distance from the start of roll to the takeoff noise measurement station along the extended center line of the runway.
AM	Feet (meters).	Takeoff flight track distance. The distance from the start of roll to the takeoff flight track position along the extended center line of the runway after which the position of the airplane need no longer be recorded.
QK	Feet (meters).	Measured noise path. The distance from the measured airplane position Q to station K.
Q_rK_r	Feet (meters).	Reference noise path. The distance from the reference airplane position Q_r to station K_r.
K_3H	Feet (meters).	Airplane approach height. The height of the airplane above the approach measuring station.

A36.9.6 FLIGHT PATH DISTANCES—Continued

Distance	Unit	Meaning
OK₃	Feet (meters).	Approach measurement distance. The distance from the runway threshold to the approach measurement station along the extended center line of the runway.
OP	Feet (meters).	Approach flight track distance. The distance from the runway threshold to the approach flight track position along the extended center line of the runway after which the position of the airplane need no longer be recorded.

[Amdt. 36–54, 67 FR 45212, July 8, 2002; Amdt. 36–24, 67 FR 63195, 63196, Oct. 10, 2002; Amdt. 36–24, 68 FR 1512, Jan. 10, 2003]

APPENDIX B TO PART 36—NOISE LEVELS FOR TRANSPORT CATEGORY AND JET AIRPLANES UNDER § 36.103

Sec.
B36.1 *Noise Measurement and Evaluation.*
B36.2 *Noise Evaluation Metric.*
B36.3 *Reference Noise Measurement Points.*
B36.4 *Test Noise Measurement Points.*
B36.5 *Maximum Noise Levels.*
B36.6 *Trade-Offs.*
B36.7 *Noise Certification Reference Procedures and Conditions.*
B36.8 *Noise Certification Test Procedures.*

Section B36.1 Noise Measurement and Evaluation

Compliance with this appendix must be shown with noise levels measured and evaluated using the procedures of appendix A of this part, or under approved equivalent procedures.

Section B36.2 Noise Evaluation Metric

The noise evaluation metric is the effective perceived noise level expressed in EPNdB, as calculated using the procedures of appendix A of this part.

Section B36.3 Reference Noise Measurement Points

When tested using the procedures of this part, except as provided in section B36.6, an airplane may not exceed the noise levels specified in section B36.5 at the following points on level terrain:

(a) Lateral full-power reference noise measurement point:

(1) For jet airplanes: The point on a line parallel to and 1,476 feet (450 m) from the runway centerline, or extended centerline, where the noise level after lift-off is at a maximum during takeoff. For the purpose of showing compliance with Stage 1 or Stage 2 noise limits for an airplane powered by more than three jet engines, the distance from the runway centerline must be 0.35 nautical miles (648 m). For jet airplanes, when approved by the FAA, the maximum lateral noise at takeoff thrust may be assumed to occur at the point (or its approved equivalent) along the extended centerline of the runway where the airplane reaches 985 feet (300 meters) altitude above ground level. A height of 1427 feet (435 meters) may be assumed for Stage 1 or Stage 2 four engine airplanes. The altitude of the airplane as it passes the noise measurement points must be within +328 to −164 feet (+100 to −50 meters) of the target altitude. For airplanes powered by other than jet engines, the altitude for maximum lateral noise must be determined experimentally.

(2) For propeller-driven airplanes: The point on the extended centerline of the runway above which the airplane, at full takeoff power, reaches a height of 2,133 feet (650 meters). For tests conducted before August 7, 2002, an applicant may use the measurement point specified in section B36.3(a)(1) as an alternative.

(b) Flyover reference noise measurement point: The point on the extended centerline of the runway that is 21,325 feet (6,500 m) from the start of the takeoff roll;

(c) Approach reference noise measurement point: The point on the extended centerline of the runway that is 6,562 feet (2,000 m) from the runway threshold. On level ground, this corresponds to a position that is 394 feet (120 m) vertically below the 3° descent path, which originates at a point on the runway 984 feet (300 m) beyond the threshold.

Section B36.4 Test noise measurement points.

(a) If the test noise measurement points are not located at the reference noise measurement points, any corrections for the difference in position are to be made using the same adjustment procedures as for the differences between test and reference flight paths.

(b) The applicant must use a sufficient number of lateral test noise measurement points to demonstrate to the FAA that the maximum noise level on the appropriate lateral line has been determined. For jet airplanes, simultaneous measurements must be made at one test noise measurement point at its symmetrical point on the other side of the runway. Propeller-driven airplanes have an inherent asymmetry in lateral noise. Therefore, simultaneous measurements must be made at each and every test noise measurement point at its symmetrical position on the opposite side of the runway. The measurement points are considered to be symmetrical if they are longitudinally within 33 feet (±10 meters) of each other.

Section B36.5 Maximum Noise Levels

Except as provided in section B36.6 of this appendix, maximum noise levels, when determined in accordance with the noise evaluation methods of appendix A of this part, may not exceed the following:

(a) For acoustical changes to Stage 1 airplanes, regardless of the number of engines, the noise levels prescribed under §36.7(c) of this part.

(b) For any Stage 2 airplane regardless of the number of engines:

(1) Flyover: 108 EPNdB for maximum weight of 600,000 pounds or more; for each halving of maximum weight (from 600,000 pounds), reduce the limit by 5 EPNdB; the limit is 93 EPNdB for a maximum weight of 75,000 pounds or less.

(2) Lateral and approach: 108 EPNdB for maximum weight of 600,000 pounds or more; for each halving of maximum weight (from 600,000 pounds), reduce the limit by 2 EPNdB; the limit is 102 EPNdB for a maximum weight of 75,000 pounds or less.

(c) For any Stage 3 airplane:

(1) Flyover.

(i) For airplanes with more than 3 engines: 106 EPNdB for maximum weight of 850,000 pounds or more; for each halving of maximum weight (from 850,000 pounds), reduce the limit by 4 EPNdB; the limit is 89 EPNdB for a maximum weight of 44,673 pounds or less;

(ii) For airplanes with 3 engines: 104 EPNdB for maximum weight of 850,000 pounds or more; for each halving of maximum weight (from 850,000 pounds), reduce the limit by 4 EPNdB; the limit is 89 EPNdB for a maximum weight of 63,177 pounds or less; and

(iii) For airplanes with fewer than 3 engines: 101 EPNdB for maximum weight of 850,000 pounds or more; for each halving of maximum weight (from 850,000 pounds), reduce the limit by 4 EPNdB; the limit is 89 EPNdB for a maximum weight of 106,250 pounds or less.

(2) Lateral, regardless of the number of engines: 103 EPNdB for maximum weight of 882,000 pounds or more; for each halving of maximum weight (from 882,000 pounds), reduce the limit by 2.56 EPNdB; the limit is 94 EPNdB for a maximum weight of 77,200 pounds or less.

(3) Approach, regardless of the number of engines: 105 EPNdB for maximum weight of 617,300 pounds or more; for each halving of maximum weight (from 617,300 pounds), reduce the limit by 2.33 EPNdB; the limit is 98 EPNdB for a maximum weight of 77,200 pounds or less.

Section B36.6 Trade-Offs

Except when prohibited by sections 36.7(c)(1) and 36.7(d)(1)(ii), if the maximum noise levels are exceeded at any one or two measurement points, the following conditions must be met:

(a) The sum of the exceedance(s) may not be greater than 3 EPNdB;

(b) Any exceedance at any single point may not be greater than 2 EPNdB, and

(c) Any exceedance(s) must be offset by a corresponding amount at another point or points.

Section B36.7 Noise Certification Reference Procedures and Conditions

(a) General conditions:

(1) All reference procedures must meet the requirements of section 36.3 of this part.

(2) Calculations of airplane performance and flight path must be made using the reference procedures and must be approved by the FAA.

(3) Applicants must use the takeoff and approach reference procedures prescribed in paragraphs (b) and (c) of this section.

(4) [Reserved]

(5) The reference procedures must be determined for the following reference conditions. The reference atmosphere is homogeneous in terms of temperature and relative humidity when used for the calculation of atmospheric absorption coefficients.

(i) Sea level atmospheric pressure of 2116 pounds per square foot (psf) (1013.25 hPa);

(ii) Ambient sea-level air temperature of 77 °F (25 °C, i.e. ISA+10 °C);

(iii) Relative humidity of 70 per cent;

(iv) Zero wind.

(v) In defining the reference takeoff flight path(s) for the takeoff and lateral noise measurements, the runway gradient is zero.

(b) Takeoff reference procedure:

The takeoff reference flight path is to be calculated using the following:

(1) Average engine takeoff thrust or power must be used from the start of takeoff to the point where at least the following height above runway level is reached. The takeoff thrust/power used must be the maximum available for normal operations given in the performance section of the airplane flight manual under the reference atmospheric conditions given in section B36.7(a)(5).

(i) For Stage 1 airplanes and for Stage 2 airplanes that do not have jet engines with a bypass ratio of 2 or more, the following apply:

(A): For airplanes with more than three jet engines—700 feet (214 meters).

(B): For all other airplanes—1,000 feet (305 meters).

(ii) For Stage 2 airplanes that have jet engines with a bypass ratio of 2 or more and for Stage 3 airplanes, the following apply:

(A): For airplanes with more than three engines—689 feet (210 meters).

(B): For airplanes with three engines—853 feet (260 meters).

(C): For airplanes with fewer than three engines—984 feet (300 meters).

(2) Upon reaching the height specified in paragraph (b)(1) of this section, airplane thrust or power must not be reduced below that required to maintain either of the following, whichever is greater:

(i) A climb gradient of 4 per cent; or

(ii) In the case of multi-engine airplanes, level flight with one engine inoperative.

(3) For the purpose of determining the lateral noise level, the reference flight path must be calculated using full takeoff power throughout the test run without a reduction in thrust or power. For tests conducted before August 7, 2002, a single reference flight path that includes thrust cutback in accordance with paragraph (b)(2) of this section, is an acceptable alternative in determining the lateral noise level.

(4) The takeoff reference speed is the all-engine operating takeoff climb speed selected by the applicant for use in normal operation; this speed must be at least V2+10kt (V2+19km/h) but may not be greater than V2+20kt (V2+37km/h). This speed must be attained as soon as practicable after lift-off and be maintained throughout the takeoff noise certification test. For Concorde airplanes, the test day speeds and the acoustic day reference speed are the minimum approved value of V2+35 knots, or the all-engines-operating speed at 35 feet, whichever speed is greater as determined under the regulations constituting the type certification basis of the airplane; this reference speed may not exceed 250 knots. For all airplanes, noise values measured at the test day speeds must be corrected to the acoustic day reference speed.

(5) The takeoff configuration selected by the applicant must be maintained constantly throughout the takeoff reference procedure, except that the landing gear may be retracted. Configuration means the center of gravity position, and the status of the airplane systems that can affect airplane performance or noise. Examples include, the position of lift augmentation devices, whether the APU is operating, and whether air bleeds and engine power take-offs are operating;

(6) The weight of the airplane at the brake release must be the maximum takeoff weight at which the noise certification is requested, which may result in an operating limitation as specified in §36.1581(d); and

(7) The average engine is defined as the average of all the certification compliant engines used during the airplane flight tests, up to and during certification, when operating within the limitations and according to the procedures given in the Flight Manual. This will determine the relationship of thrust/power to control parameters (e.g., N_1 or EPR). Noise measurements made during certification tests must be corrected using this relationship.

(c) Approach reference procedure:

The approach reference flight path must be calculated using the following:

(1) The airplane is stabilized and following a 3° glide path;

(2) For subsonic airplanes, a steady approach speed of V_{ref} + 10 kts (V_{ref} + 19 km/h) with thrust and power stabilized must be established and maintained over the approach measuring point. V_{ref} is the reference landing speed, which is defined as the speed of the airplane, in a specified landing configuration, at the point where it descends through the landing screen height in the determination of the landing distance for manual landings. For Concorde airplanes, a steady approach speed that is either the landing reference speed + 10 knots or the speed used in establishing the approved landing distance under the airworthiness regulations constituting the type certification basis of the airplane, whichever speed is greater. This speed must be established and maintained over the approach measuring point.

(3) The constant approach configuration used in the airworthiness certification tests, but with the landing gear down, must be maintained throughout the approach reference procedure;

(4) The weight of the airplane at touchdown must be the maximum landing weight permitted in the approach configuration defined in paragraph (c)(3) of this section at which noise certification is requested, except as provided in §36.1581(d) of this part; and

(5) The most critical configuration must be used; this configuration is defined as that which produces the highest noise level with normal deployment of aerodynamic control surfaces including lift and drag producing devices, at the weight at which certification is requested. This configuration includes all those items listed in section A36.5.2.5 of appendix A of this part that contribute to the noisiest continuous state at the maximum landing weight in normal operation.

Section B36.8   Noise Certification Test Procedures

(a) All test procedures must be approved by the FAA.

(b) The test procedures and noise measurements must be conducted and processed in an approved manner to yield the noise evaluation metric EPNL, in units of EPNdB, as described in appendix A of this part.

(c) Acoustic data must be adjusted to the reference conditions specified in this appendix using the methods described in appendix A of this part. Adjustments for speed and thrust must be made as described in section A36.9 of this part.

(d) If the airplane's weight during the test is different from the weight at which noise certification is requested, the required EPNL adjustment may not exceed 2 EPNdB for each takeoff and 1 EPNdB for each approach. Data approved by the FAA must be used to determine the variation of EPNL with weight for both takeoff and approach test conditions. The necessary EPNL adjustment for variations in approach flight path from the reference flight path must not exceed 2 EPNdB.

(e) For approach, a steady glide path angle of 3° ± 0.5° is acceptable.

(f) If equivalent test procedures different from the reference procedures are used, the test procedures and all methods for adjusting the results to the reference procedures must be approved by the FAA. The adjustments may not exceed 16 EPNdB on takeoff and 8 EPNdB on approach. If the adjustment is more than 8 EPNdB on takeoff, or more than 4 EPNdB on approach, the resulting numbers must be more than 2 EPNdB below the limit noise levels specified in section B36.5.

(g) During takeoff, lateral, and approach tests, the airplane variation in instantaneous indicated airspeed must be maintained within ±3% of the average airspeed between the 10 dB-down points. This airspeed is determined by the pilot's airspeed indicator. However, if the instantaneous indicated airspeed exceeds ±3 kt (±5.5 km/h) of the average airspeed over the 10 dB-down points, and is determined by the FAA representative on the flight deck to be due to atmospheric turbulence, then the flight so affected must be rejected for noise certification purposes.

NOTE: Guidance material on the use of equivalent procedures is provided in the current advisory circular for this part.

[Amdt. 36–54, 67 FR 45235, July 8, 2002; Amdt. 36–24, 67 FR 63196, Oct. 10, 2002; Amdt. 36–24, 68 FR 1512, Jan. 10, 2003]

APPENDIXES C–E TO PART 36 [RESERVED]

APPENDIX F TO PART 36—FLYOVER NOISE REQUIREMENTS FOR PROPELLER-DRIVEN SMALL AIRPLANE AND PROPELLER-DRIVEN, COMMUTER CATEGORY AIRPLANE CERTIFICATION TESTS PRIOR TO DECEMBER 22, 1988

PART A—GENERAL

Sec.
F36.1 *Scope.*

PART B—NOISE MEASUREMENT

F36.101 *General test conditions.*
F36.103 *Acoustical measurement system.*
F36.105 *Sensing, recording, and reproducing equipment.*
F36.107 *Noise measurement procedures.*
F36.109 *Data recording, reporting, and approval.*
F36.111 *Flight procedures.*

PART C—DATA CORRECTION

F36.201 *Correction of data.*
F36.203 *Validity of results.*

PART D—NOISE LIMITS

F36.301 *Aircraft noise limits.*

PART A—GENERAL

Section F36.1 *Scope.* This appendix prescribes noise level limits and procedures for measuring and correcting noise data for the propeller driven small airplanes specified in §§ 36.1 and 36.501(b).

PART B—NOISE MEASUREMENT

Sec. F36.101 *General test conditions.*

(a) The test area must be relatively flat terrain having no excessive sound absorption characteristics such as those caused by thick, matted, or tall grass, by shrubs, or by wooded areas. No obstructions which significantly influence the sound field from the airplane may exist within a conical space above the measurement position, the cone being defined by an axis normal to the ground and by a half-angle 75 degrees from this axis.

(b) The tests must be carried out under the following conditions:

(1) There may be no precipitation.

(2) Relative humidity may not be higher than 90 percent or lower than 30 percent.

(3) Ambient temperature may not be above 86 degrees F. or below 41 degrees F. at 33′ above ground. If the measurement site is within 1 n.m. of an airport thermometer the airport reported temperature may be used.

(4) Reported wind may not be above 10 knots at 33′ above ground. If wind velocities of more than 4 knots are reported, the flight direction must be aligned to within ±15 degrees of wind direction and flights with tail wind and head wind must be made in equal numbers. If the measurement site is within 1 n.m. of an airport anemometer, the airport reported wind may be used.

(5) There may be no temperature inversion or anomalous wind conditions that would significantly alter the noise level of the airplane when the noise is recorded at the required measuring point.

(6) The flight test procedures, measuring equipment, and noise measurement procedures must be approved by the FAA.

(7) Sound pressure level data for noise evaluation purposes must be obtained with acoustical equipment that complies with section F36.103 of this appendix.

Sec. F36.103 *Acoustical measurement system.* The acoustical measurement system must consist of approved equipment equivalent to the following:

(a) A microphone system with frequency response compatible with measurement and analysis system accuracy as prescribed in section F36.105 of this appendix.

(b) Tripods or similar microphone mountings that minimize interference with the sound being measured.

(c) Recording and reproducing equipment characteristics, frequency response, and dynamic range compatible with the response and accuracy requirements of section F36.105 of this appendix.

(d) Acoustic calibrators using sine wave or broadband noise of known sound pressure level. If broadband noise is used, the signal must be described in terms of its average and maximum root-mean-square (rms) value for nonoverload signal level.

Sec. F36.105 *Sensing, recording, and reproducing equipment.*

(a) The noise produced by the airplane must be recorded. A magnetic tape recorder is acceptable.

(b) The characteristics of the system must comply with the recommendations in International Electrotechnical Commission (IEC) Publication No. 179, entitled "Precision Sound Level Meters" as incorporated by reference in Part 36 under §36.6 of this part.

(c) The response of the complete system to a sensibly plane progressive sinusoidal wave of constant amplitude must lie within the tolerance limits specified in IEC Publication No. 179, dated 1973, over the frequency range 45 to 11,200 Hz.

(d) If limitations of the dynamic range of the equipment make it necessary, high frequency pre-emphasis must be added to the recording channel with the converse de-emphasis on playback. The pre-emphasis must be applied such that the instantaneous recorded sound pressure level of the noise signal between 800 and 11,200 Hz does not vary more than 20 dB between the maximum and minimum one-third octave bands.

(e) If requested by the Administrator, the recorded noise signal must be read through an "A" filter with dynamic characteristics designated "slow," as defined in IEC Publication No. 179, dated 1973. The output signal from the filter must be fed to a rectifying circuit with square law rectification, integrated with time constants for charge and discharge of about 1 second or 800 milliseconds.

(f) The equipment must be acoustically calibrated using facilities for acoustic freefield calibration and if analysis of the tape recording is requested by the Administrator, the analysis equipment shall be electronically calibrated by a method approved by the FAA.

(g) A windscreen must be employed with microphone during all measurements of aircraft noise when the wind speed is in excess of 6 knots.

Sec. F36.107 *Noise measurement procedures.*

(a) The microphones must be oriented in a known direction so that the maximum sound received arrives as nearly as possible in the direction for which the microphones are calibrated. The microphone sensing elements must be approximately 4' above ground.

(b) Immediately prior to and after each test; a recorded acoustic calibration of the system must be made in the field with an acoustic calibrator for the two purposes of checking system sensitivity and providing an acoustic reference level for the analysis of the sound level data.

(c) The ambient noise, including both acoustical background and electrical noise of the measurement systems, must be recorded and determined in the test area with the system gain set at levels that will be used for aircraft noise measurements. If aircraft sound pressure levels do not exceed the background sound pressure levels by at least 10 dB(A), approved corrections for the contribution of background sound pressure level to the observed sound pressure level must be applied.

Sec. F36.109 *Data recording, reporting, and approval.*

(a) Data representing physical measurements or corrections to measured data must be recorded in permanent form and appended to the record except that corrections to measurements for normal equipment response deviations need not be reported. All other corrections must be approved. Estimates must be made of the individual errors inherent in each of the operations employed in obtaining the final data.

(b) Measured and corrected sound pressure levels obtained with equipment conforming to the specifications described in section F36.105 of this appendix must be reported.

(c) The type of equipment used for measurement and analysis of all acoustic, airplane performance, and meteorological data must be reported.

(d) The following atmospheric data, measured immediately before, after, or during each test at the observation points prescribed in section F36.101 of this appendix must be reported:

(1) Air temperature and relative humidity.

(2) Maximum, minimum, and average wind velocities.

(e) Comments on local topography, ground cover, and events that might interfere with sound recordings must be reported.

(f) The following airplane information must be reported:

(1) Type, model and serial numbers (if any) of airplanes, engines, and propellers.

(2) Any modifications or nonstandard equipment likely to affect the noise characteristics of the airplane.

(3) Maximum certificated takeoff weights.

(4) Airspeed in knots for each overflight of the measuring point.

(5) Engine performance in terms of revolutions per minute and other relevant parameters for each overflight.

(6) Aircraft height in feet determined by a calibrated altimeter in the aircraft, approved photographic techniques, or approved tracking facilities.

(g) Aircraft speed and position and engine performance parameters must be recorded at an approved sampling rate sufficient to ensure compliance with the test procedures and conditions of this appendix.

Sec. F36.111 *Flight procedures.*

(a) Tests to demonstrate compliance with the noise level requirements of this appendix must include at least six level flights over the measuring station at a height of 1,000′ ±30′ and ±10 degrees from the zenith when passing overhead.

(b) Each test over flight must be conducted:

(1) At not less than the highest power in the normal operating range provided in an Airplane Flight Manual, or in any combination of approved manual material, approved placard, or approved instrument markings; and

(2) At stabilized speed with propellers synchronized and with the airplane in cruise configuration, except that if the speed at the power setting prescribed in this paragraph would exceed the maximum speed authorized in level flight, accelerated flight is acceptable.

PART C—DATA CORRECTION

Sec. F36.201 *Correction of data.*

(a) Noise data obtained when the temperature is outside the range of 68 degrees F. ±9 degrees F., or the relative humidity is below 40 percent, must be corrected to 77 degrees F. and 70 percent relative humidity by a method approved by the FAA.

(b) The performance correction prescribed in paragraph (c) of this section must be used. It must be determined by the method described in this appendix, and must be added algebraically to the measured value. It is limited to 5dB(A).

(c) The performance correction must be computed by using the following formula:

$$\Delta dB = 60 - 20 \, \log_{10} \left\{ (11{,}430 - D_{50} \, \frac{R/C}{V_y} + 50 \right\}$$

Where:

D_{50}=Takeoff distance to 50 feet at maximum certificated takeoff weight.
R/C=Certificated best rate of climb (fpm).
V_y=Speed for best rate of climb in the same units as rate of climb.

(d) When takeoff distance to 50′ is not listed as approved performance information, the figures of 2000 for single-engine airplanes and 1600′ for multi-engine airplanes must be used.

Sec. F36.203 *Validity of results.*

(a) The test results must produce an average dB(A) and its 90 percent confidence limits, the noise level being the arithmetic average of the corrected acoustical measurements for all valid test runs over the measuring point.

(b) The samples must be large enough to establish statistically a 90 pecent confidence limit not to exceed ±1.5 dB(A). No test result may be omitted from the averaging process, unless omission is approved by the FAA.

PART D—NOISE LIMITS

Sec. F36.301 *Aircraft noise limits.*

(a) Compliance with this section must be shown with noise data measured and corrected as prescribed in Parts B and C of this appendix.

(b) For airplanes for which application for a type certificate is made on or after October 10, 1973, the noise level must not exceed 68 dB(A) up to and including aircraft weights of 1,320 pounds (600 kg.). For weights greater than 1,320 pounds up to and including 3,630 pounds (1.650 kg.) the limit increases at the rate of 1 dB/165 pounds (1 dB/75 kg.) to 82 dB(A) at 3,630 pounds, after which it is constant at 82 dB(A). However, airplanes produced under type certificates covered by this paragraph must also meet paragraph (d) of this section for the original issuance of standard airworthiness certificates or restricted category airworthiness certificates if those airplanes have not had flight time before the date specified in that paragraph.

(c) For airplanes for which application for a type certificate is made on or after January 1, 1975, the noise levels may not exceed the noise limit curve prescribed in paragraph (b) of this section, except that 80 dB(A) may not be exceeded.

(d) For airplanes for which application is made for a standard airworthiness certificate or for a restricted category airworthiness certificate, and that have not had any flight time before January 1, 1980, the requirements of paragraph (c) of this section apply, regardless of date of application, to the original issuance of the certificate for that airplane.

[Doc. No. 13243, 40 FR 1035, Jan. 6, 1975; 40 FR 6347, Feb. 11, 1975, as amended by Amdt. 36–6, 41 FR 56064, Dec. 23, 1976; Amdt. 36–6, 42 FR 4113, Jan. 24, 1977; Amdt. 36–9, 43 FR 8754, Mar. 2, 1978; Amdt. 36–13, 52 FR 1836, Jan. 15, 1987; Amdt. 36–16, 53 FR 47400, Nov. 22, 1988]

APPENDIX G TO PART 36—TAKEOFF NOISE REQUIREMENTS FOR PROPELLER-DRIVEN SMALL AIRPLANE AND PROPELLER-DRIVEN, COMMUTER CATEGORY AIRPLANE CERTIFICATION TESTS ON OR AFTER DECEMBER 22, 1988

PART A—GENERAL

Sec.

G36.1   *Scope.*

PART B—NOISE MEASUREMENT

G36.101   *General Test Conditions.*
G36.103   *Acoustical measurement system.*
G36.105   *Sensing, recording, and reproducing equipment.*
G36.107   *Noise measurement procedures.*
G36.109   *Data recording, reporting, and approval.*
G36.111   *Flight procedures.*

PART C—DATA CORRECTIONS

G36.201   *Corrections to Test Results.*
G36.203   *Validity of results.*

PART D—NOISE LIMITS

G36.301   *Aircraft Noise Limits.*

PART A—GENERAL

Section G36.1 *Scope.* This appendix prescribes limiting noise levels and procedures for measuring noise and adjusting these data to standard conditions, for propeller driven small airplanes and propeller-driven, commuter category airplanes specified in §§ 36.1 and 36.501(c).

PART B—NOISE MEASUREMENT

Sec. G36.101 *General Test Conditions.*

(a) The test area must be relatively flat terrain having no excessive sound absorption characteristics such as those caused by thick, matted, or tall grass, by shrubs, or by wooded areas. No obstructions which significantly influence the sound field from the airplane may exist within a conical space above the measurement position, the cone being defined by an axis normal to the ground and by a half-angle 75 degrees from the normal ground axis.

(b) The tests must be carried out under the following conditions:

(1) No precipitation;

(2) Ambient air temperature between 36 and 95 degrees F (2.2 and 35 degrees C);

(3) Relative humidity between 20 percent and 95 percent, inclusively;

(4) Wind speed may not exceed 10 knots (19 km/h) and cross wind may not exceed 5 knots (9 km/h), using a 30-second average;

(5) No temperature inversion or anomalous wind condition that would significantly alter the noise level of the airplane when the nose is recorded at the required measuring point, and

(6) The meteorological measurements must be made between 4 ft. (1.2 m) and 33 ft. (10 m) above ground level. If the measurement site is within 1 n.m. of an airport meteorological station, measurements from that station may be used.

(c) The flight test procedures, measuring equipment, and noise measurement procedures must be approved by the FAA.

(d) Sound pressure level data for noise evaluation purposes must be obtained with acoustical equipment that complies with section G36.103 of this appendix.

Sec. G36.103 *Acoustical Measurement System.*

The acoustical measurement system must consist of approved equipment with the following characteristics: (a) A microphone system with frequency response compatible with measurement and analysis system accuracy as prescribed in section G36.105 of this appendix.

(b) Tripods or similar microphone mountings that minimize interference with the sound being measured.

(c) Recording and reproducing equipment characteristics, frequency response, and dynamic range compatible with the response and accuracy requirements of section G36.105 of this appendix.

(d) Acoustic calibrators using sine wave or broadband noise of known sound pressure level. If broadband noise is used, the signal must be described in terms of its average and maximum root-mean-square (rms) value for non-overload signal level.

Sec. G36.105 *Sensing, Recording, and Reproducing Equipment.*

(a) The noise produced by the airplane must be recorded. A magnetic tape recorder, graphic level recorder, or sound level meter is acceptable when approved by the regional certificating authority.

(b) The characteristics of the complete system must comply with the requirements in International Electrotechnical Commission (IEC) Publications No. 651, entitled "Sound Level Meters" and No. 561, entitled "Electroacoustical Measuring Equipment for Aircraft Noise Certification" as incorporated by reference under § 36.6 of this part. Sound level meters must comply with the requirements for Type 1 sound level meters as specified in IEC Publication No. 651.

(c) The response of the complete system to a sensibly plane progressive sinusoidal wave of constant amplitude must be within the tolerance limits specified in IEC Publication No. 651, over the frequency range 45 to 11,200 Hz.

(d) If equipment dynamic range limitations make it necessary, high frequency pre-emphasis must be added to the recording channel with the converse de-emphasis on playback. The pre-emphasis must be applied such that the instantaneous recorded sound pressure level of the noise signal between 800 and 11,200 Hz does not vary more than 20 dB between the maximum and minimum one-third octave bands.

(e) The output noise signal must be read through an "A" filter with dynamic characteristics designated "slow" as defined in IEC Publication No. 651. A graphic level recorder, sound level meter, or digital equivalent may be used.

(f) The equipment must be acoustically calibrated using facilities for acoustic free-field calibration and if analysis of the tape recording is requested by the Administrator, the analysis equipment shall be electronically calibrated by a method approved by the FAA. Calibrations shall be performed, as appropriate, in accordance with paragraphs A36.3.8 and A36.3.9 of appendix A of this part.

(g) A windscreen must be employed with the microphone during all measurements of aircraft noise when the wind speed is in excess of 5 knots (9 km/hr).

Sec. G36.107 *Noise Measurement Procedures.*

(a) The microphone must be a pressure type, 12.7 mm in diameter, with a protective grid, mounted in an inverted position such that the microphone diaphragm is 7 mm above and parallel to a white-painted metal circular plate. This white-painted metal plate shall be 40 cm in diameter and at least 2.5 mm thick. The plate shall be placed horizontally and flush with the surrounding ground surface with no cavities below the plate. The microphone must be located three-quarters of the distance from the center to the back edge of the plate along a radius normal to the line of flight of the test airplane.

(b) Immediately prior to and after each test, a recorded acoustic calibration of the system must be made in the field with an acoustic calibrator for the purposes of checking system sensitivity and providing an acoustic reference level for the analysis of the sound level data. If a tape recorder or graphic level recorder is used, the frequency response of the electrical system must be determined at a level within 10 dB of the full-scale reading used during the test, utilizing pink or pseudorandom noise.

(c) The ambient noise, including both acoustic background and electrical systems noise, must be recorded and determined in the test area with the system gain set at levels which will be used for aircraft noise measurements. If aircraft sound pressure levels do not exceed the background sound pressure levels by at least 10 dB(A), a takeoff measurement point nearer to the start of the takeoff roll must be used and the results must be adjusted to the reference measurement point by an approved method.

Sec. G36.109 *Data Recording, Reporting, and Approval.*

(a) Data representing physical measurements and adjustments to measured data must be recorded in permanent form and appended to the record, except that corrections to measurements for normal equipment response deviations need not be reported. All other adjustments must be approved. Estimates must be made of the individual errors inherent in each of the operations employed in obtaining the final data.

(b) Measured and corrected sound pressure levels obtained with equipment conforming to the specifications in section G36.105 of this appendix must be reported.

(c) The type of equipment used for measurement and analysis of all acoustical, airplane performance, and meteorological data must be reported.

(d) The following atmospheric data, measured immediately before, after, or during each test at the observation points prescribed in section G36.101 of this appendix must be reported:

(1) Ambient temperature and relative humidity.

(2) Maximum and average wind speeds and directions for each run.

(e) Comments on local topography, ground cover, and events that might interfere with sound recordings must be reported.

(f) The aircraft position relative to the takeoff reference flight path must be determined by an approved method independent of normal flight instrumentation, such as radar tracking, theodolite triangulation, or photographic scaling techniques.

(g) The following airplane information must be reported:

(1) Type, model, and serial numbers (if any) of airplanes, engines, and propellers;

(2) Any modifications or nonstandard equipment likely to affect the noise characteristics of the airplane;

(3) Maximum certificated takeoff weight;

(4) For each test flight, airspeed and ambient temperature at the flyover altitude over the measuring site determined by properly calibrated instruments;

(5) For each test flight, engine performance parameters, such as manifold pressure or power, propeller speed (rpm) and other relevant parameters. Each parameter must be determined by properly calibrated instruments. For instance, propeller RPM must be validated by an independent device accurate

to within ±1 percent, when the airplane is equipped with a mechanical tachometer.

(6) Airspeed, position, and performance data necessary to make the corrections required in section G36.201 of this appendix must be recorded by an approved method when the airplane is directly over the measuring site.

Sec. G36.111 *Flight Procedures.*

(a) The noise measurement point is on the extended centerline of the runway at a distance of 8200 ft (2500 m) from the start of takeoff roll. The aircraft must pass over the measurement point within ±10 degrees from the vertical and within 20% of the reference altitude. The flight test program shall be initiated at the maximum approved takeoff weight and the weight shall be adjusted back to this maximum weight after each hour of flight time. Each flight test must be conducted at the speed for the best rate of climb (V_y) ±5 knots (±9 km/hour) indicated airspeed. All test, measurement, and data correction procedures must be approved by the FAA.

(b) The takeoff reference flight path must be calculated for the following atmospheric conditions:

(1) Sea level atmospheric pressure of 1013.25 mb (013.25 hPa);

(2) Ambient air temperature of 59 °F (15 °C);

(3) Relative humidity of 70 percent; and

(4) Zero wind.

(c) The takeoff reference flight path must be calculated assuming the following two segments:

(1) First segment.

(i) Takeoff power must be used from the brake release point to the point at which the height of 50 ft (15m) above the runway is reached.

(ii) A constant takeoff configuration selected by the applicant must be maintained through this segment.

(iii) The maximum weight of the airplane at brake-release must be the maximum for which noise certification is requested.

(iv) The length of this first segment must correspond to the airworthiness approved value for a takeoff on a level paved runway (or the corresponding value for seaplanes).

(2) Second segment.

(i) The beginning of the second segment corresponds to the end of the first segment.

(ii) The airplane must be in the climb configuration with landing gear up, if retractable, and flap setting corresponding to normal climb position throughout this second segment.

(iii) The airplane speed must be the speed for the best rate of climb (V_y).

(iv) Maximum continuous installed power and rpm for variable pitch propeller(s) shall be used. For fixed pitch propeller(s), the maximum power and rpm that can be delivered by the engine(s) must be maintained throughout the second segment.

PART C—DATA CORRECTIONS

Sec. G36.201 *Corrections to Test Results.*

(a) These corrections account for the effects of:

(1) Differences in atmospheric absorption of sound between meteorological test conditions and reference conditions.

(2) Differences in the noise path length between the actual airplane flight path and the reference flight path.

(3) The change in the helical tip Mach number between test and reference conditions.

(4) The change in the engine power between test and reference conditions.

(b) Atmospheric absorption correction is required for noise data obtained when the test conditions are outside those specified in Figure G1. Noise data outside the applicable range must be corrected to 59 F and 70 percent relative humidity by an FAA approved method.

MEASUREMENT WINDOW FOR NO ABSORPTION CORRECTION   Figure G1

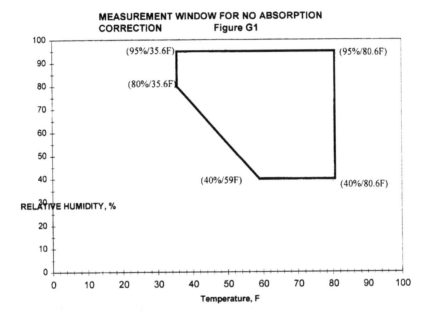

(c) Helical tip Mach number and power corrections must be made as follows:

(1) Corrections for helical tip Mach number and power corrections must be made if—

(i) The propeller is a variable pitch type; or

(ii) The propeller is a fixed pitch type and the test power is not within 5 percent of the reference power.

(2) No corrections for helical tip Mach number variation need to be made if the propeller helical tip Mach number is:

(i) At or below 0.70 and the test helical tip Mach number is within 0.014 of the reference helical tip Mach number.

(ii) Above 0.70 and at or below 0.80 and the test helical tip Mach number is within 0.007 of the reference helical tip Mach number.

(iii) Above 0.80 and the test helical tip Mach number is within 0.005 of the reference helical tip Mach number. For mechanical tachometers, if the helical tip Mach number is above 0.8 and the test helical tip Mach number is within 0.008 of the reference helical tip Mach number.

(d) When the test conditions are outside those specified, corrections must be applied by an approved procedure or by the following simplified procedure:

(1) Measured sound levels must be corrected from test day meteorological conditions to reference conditions by adding an increment equal to

Delta $(M)=(H_T \alpha - 0.7 H_R)/1000$

where H_T is the height in feet under test conditions, H_R is the height in feet under reference conditions when the aircraft is directly over the noise measurement point and α is the rate of absorption for the test day conditions at 500 Hz as specified in SAE ARP 866A, entitled "Standard Values of Atmospheric Absorption as a function of Temperature and Humidity for use in Evaluating Aircraft Flyover Noise" as incorporated by reference under §36.6.

(2) Measured sound levels in decibels must be corrected for height by algebraically adding an increment equal to Delta (1). When test day conditions are within those specified in figure G1:

Delta $(1)=22 \log (H_T/H_R)$

where H_T is the height of the test aircraft when directly over the noise measurement point and H_R is the reference height.

When test day conditions are outside those specified in figure G1:

Delta $(1)=20 \log (H_T/H_R)$

(3) Measured sound levels in decibels must be corrected for helical tip Mach number by algebraically adding an increment equal to:

Delta $(2)=k \log (M_R/M_T)$

where M_T and M_R are the test and reference helical tip Mach numbers, respectively. The constant "k" is equal to the slope of

827

the line obtained for measured values of the sound level in dB(A) versus helical tip Mach number. The value of k may be determined from approved data. A nominal value of k=150 may be used when M_T is smaller than M_R. No correction may be made using the nominal value of k when M_T is larger than M_R. The reference helical tip Mach number M_R is the Mach number corresponding to the reference conditions (RPM, airspeed, temperature) above the measurement point.

(4) Measured sound levels in decibels must be corrected for engine power by algebraically adding an increment equal to

Delta $(3) = K_3 \log (P_R / P_T)$

where P_R and P_T are the test and reference engine powers respectively obtained from the manifold pressure/torque gauges and engine rpm. The value of K_3 shall be determined from approved data from the test airplane. In the absence of flight test data and at the discretion of the Administrator, a value of $K_3=17$ may be used.

Sec. G36.203 *Validity of Results.*

(a) The measuring point must be overflown at least six times. The test results must produce an average noise level (L_{Amax}) value

within a 90 percent confidence limit. The average noise level is the arithmetic average of the corrected acoustical measurements for all valid test runs over the measuring point.

(b) The samples must be large enough to establish statistically a 90 percent confidence limit not exceeding ±1.5 dB(A). No test results may be omitted from the averaging process unless omission is approved by the FAA.

PART D—NOISE LIMITS

Sec. G36.301 *Aircraft noise limits.*

(a) Compliance with this section must be shown with noise data measured and corrected as prescribed in Parts B and C of this appendix.

(b) The noise level must not exceed 76 dB (A) up to and including aircraft weights of 1,320 pounds (600 kg). For aircraft weights greater than 1,320 pounds, the limit increases from that point with the logarithm of airplane weight at the rate of 9.83 dB (A) per doubling of weight, until the limit of 88 dB (A) is reached, after which the limit is constant up to and including 19,000 pounds (8,618 kg). Figure G2 shows noise level limits vs airplane weight.

NOISE LEVELS vs AIRPLANE WEIGHT
FIGURE G2

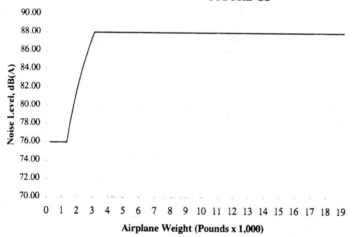

(Secs. 313(a), 603, and 611(b), Federal Aviation Act of 1958 as amended (49 U.S.C. 1354(a), 1423, and 1431(b)); sec. 6(c), Department of Transportation Act (49 U.S.C. 1655 (c)); Title I, National Environmental Policy Act of 1969 (42 U.S.C. 4321 *et seq.*); E. O. 11514, March 5, 1970 and 14 CFR 11.45).

[Amdt. 36–16, 53 FR 47400, Nov. 22, 1988; 53 FR 50157, Dec. 13, 1988, as amended by Amdt. 36–22, 64 FR 55602, Oct. 13, 1999; Amdt. 36–54, 67 FR 45236, July 8, 2002]

APPENDIX H TO PART 36—NOISE RE-QUIREMENTS FOR HELICOPTERS UNDER SUBPART H

PART A—REFERENCE CONDITIONS

Sec.

H36.1　*General.*
H36.3　*Reference Test Conditions.*
H36.5　*Symbols and Units.*

PART B—NOISE MEASUREMENT UNDER § 36.801

H36.101　*Noise certification test and measurement conditions.*
H36.103　*Takeoff test conditions.*
H36.105　*Flyover test conditions.*
H36.107　*Approach test conditions.*
H36.109　*Measurement of helicopter noise received on the ground.*
H36.111　*Reporting and correcting measured data.*
H36.113　*Atmospheric attenuation of sound.*

PART C—NOISE EVALUATION AND CALCULATION UNDER § 36.803

H36.201　*Noise evaluation in EPNdB.*
H36.203　*Calculation of noise levels.*
H36.205　*Detailed data correction procedures.*

PART D—NOISE LIMITS UNDER § 36.805

H36.301　*Noise measurement, evaluation, and calculation.*
H36.303　*[Reserved]*
H36.305　*Noise levels.*

PART A—REFERENCE CONDITIONS

Section H36.1 *General.* This appendix prescribes noise requirements for helicopters specified under § 36.1, including:

(a) The conditions under which helicopter noise certification tests under Part H must be conducted and the measurement procedures that must be used under § 36.801 to measure helicopter noise during each test;

(b) The procedures which must be used under § 36.803 to correct the measured data to the reference conditions and to calculate the noise evaluation quantity designated as Effective Perceived Noise Level (EPNL); and

(c) The noise limits for which compliance must be shown under § 36.805.

Section H36.3 *Reference Test Conditions.*

(a) *Meteorological conditions.* Aircraft position, performance data and noise measurements must be corrected to the following noise certification reference atmospheric conditions which shall be assumed to exist from the surface to the aircraft altitude:

(1) Sea level pressure of 2116 psf (76 cm mercury).

(2) Ambient temperature of 77 degrees F (25 degrees C).

(3) Relative humidity of 70 percent.

(4) Zero wind.

(b) *Reference test site.* The reference test site is flat and without line-of-sight obstructions across the flight path that encompasses the 10 dB down points.

(c) *Takeoff reference profile.* (1) Figure H1 illustrates a typical takeoff profile, including reference conditions.

(2) The reference flight path is defined as a straight line segment inclined from the starting point (1640 feet prior to the center microphone location at 65 feet above ground level) at an angle β defined by the certificated best rate of climb and V_y for minimum engine performance. The constant climb angle β is derived from the manufacturer's data (FAA-approved by the FAA) to define the flight profile for the reference conditions. The constant climb angle β is drawn through C_r and continues, crossing over station A, to the position corresponding to the end of the type certification takeoff path represented by position I_r.

(d) *Level flyover reference profile.* The beginning of the level flyover reference profile is represented by helicopter position D (Figure H2). The helicopter approaches position D in level flight 492 feet above ground level as measured at station A. Airspeed is stabilized at either 0.9 V_H or 0.45 V_H + 65 knots (0.45 V_H + 120 km/hr), whichever speed is less. Rotor speed is stabilized at the maximum continuous RPM throughout the 10 dB down time period. The helicopter crosses station A in level flight and proceeds to position J.

(e) For noise certification purposes, V_H is defined as the airspeed in level flight obtained using the minimum specification engine torque corresponding to maximum continuous power available for sea level, 25 °C ambient conditions at the relevant maximum certificated weight. The value of V_H thus defined must be listed in the Rotorcraft Flight Manual.

(f) *Approach reference profile.* (1) Figure H3 illustrates approach profile, including reference conditions.

(i) The beginning of the approach profile is represented by helicopter position E. The position of the helicopter is recorded for a sufficient distance (EK) to ensure recording of the entire interval during which the measured helicopter noise level is within 10 dB of Maximum Tone Corrected Perceived Noise Level (PNLTM), as required. EK represents a stable flight condition in terms of torque, rpm, indicated airspeed, and rate of descent resulting in a 6° ±0.5° approach angle.

(ii) The approach profile is defined by the approach angle β passing directly over the station A at a height of AH, to position K, which terminates the approach noise certification profile.

(2) The helicopter approaches position H along a constant 6° approach slope throughout the 10 dB down time period. The helicopter crosses position E and proceeds along the approach slope crossing over station A until it reaches position K.

Section H36.5 *Symbols and units.* The following symbols and units as used in this appendix for helicopter noise certification have the following meanings.

FLIGHT PROFILE IDENTIFICATION—POSITIONS

Position	Description
A	Location of the noise measuring point at the flight-track noise measuring station vertically below the reference (takeoff, flyover, or approach) flight path.
C	Start of noise certification takeoff flight path.
C_r	Start of noise certification reference takeoff flight path.
D	Start of noise certification flyover flight path.
D_r	Start of noise certification reference flyover path.
E	Start of noise certification approach flight path.
E_r	Start of noise certification reference approach flight path.
F	Position on takeoff flight path directly above noise measuring station A.
G	Position on flyover flight path directly above noise measuring station A.
H	Position on approach flight path directly above noise measuring station A.
I	End of noise type certification takeoff flight path.
I_r	End of noise type certification reference takeoff flight path.
J	End of noise type certification flyover flight path.
J_r	End of noise type certification reference flyover flight path.
K	End of noise certification approach type flight path.
K_r	End of noise type certification reference approach flight path.
L	Position on measured takeoff flight path corresponding to PNLTM at station A.
L_r	Position on reference takeoff flight path corresponding to PNLTM of station A.
M	Position on measured flyover flight path corresponding to PNLTM of station A.
M_r	Position on reference flyover flight path corresponding to PNLTM of station A.

FLIGHT PROFILE IDENTIFICATION—POSITIONS—Continued

Position	Description
N	Position on measured approach flight path corresponding to PNLTM at station A.
N_r	Position on reference approach flight path corresponding to PNLTM at station A.
S	Position on measured approach path nearest to station A.
S_r	Position on reference approach path nearest to station A.
T	Position on measured takeoff path nearest to station A.
T_r	Position on reference takeoff path nearest to station A.

FLIGHT PROFILE DISTANCES

Distance	Unit	Meaning
AF	Feet ..	*Takeoff Height.* The vertical distance between helicopter and station A.
AG	Feet ..	*Flyover Height.* The vertical distance between the helicopter and station A.
AH	Feet ..	*Approach Height.* The vertical distance between the helicopter and station A.
AL	Feet ..	*Measured Takeoff Noise Path.* The distance from station A to the measured helicopter position L.
AL_r	Feet ..	*Reference Takeoff Noise Path.* The distance from station A to the reference helicopter position L_r.
AM	Feet ..	*Measured Flyover Noise Path.* The distance from station A to the measured helicopter position M.
AM_r	Feet ..	*Reference Flyover Noise Path.* The distance from station A to helicopter position M_r on the reference flyover flight path.
AN	Feet ..	*Measured Approach Noise Path.* The distance from station A to the measured helicopter noise position N.
AN_r	Feet ..	*Reference Approach Noise Path.* The distance from station A to the reference helicopter position N_r.
AS	Feet ..	*Measured Approach Minimum Distance.* The distance from station A to the position S on the measured approach flight path.

FLIGHT PROFILE DISTANCES—Continued

Distance	Unit	Meaning
AS$_r$	Feet ..	*Reference Approach Minimum Distance.* The distance from station A to the position S$_r$ on the reference approach flight path.
AT	Feet ..	*Measured Takeoff Minimum Distance.* The distance from station A to the position T on the measured takeoff flight path.
AT$_r$	Feet ..	*Reference Takeoff Minimum Distance.* The distance from station A to the position T$_r$ on the reference takeoff flight path.
CI	Feet ..	*Takeoff Flight Path Distance.* The distance from position C at which the helicopter establishes a constant climb angle on the takeoff flight path passing over station A and continuing to position I at which the position of the helicopter need no longer be recorded.
DJ	Feet ..	*Flyover Flight Path Distance.* The distance from position D at which the helicopter is established on the flyover flight path passing over station A and continuing to position J at which the position of the helicopter need no longer be recorded.
EK	Feet ..	*Approach Flight Path Distance.* The distance from position E at which the helicopter establishes a constant angle on the approach flight path passing over station A and continuing to position K at which the position of the helicopter need no longer be recorded.

PART B—NOISE MEASUREMENT UNDER § 36.801

Section H36.101 *Noise certification test and measurement conditions.*

(a) *General.* This section prescribes the conditions under which aircraft noise certification tests must be conducted and the measurement procedures that must be used to measure helicopter noise during each test.

(b) *Test site requirements.* (1) Tests to show compliance with established helicopter noise certification levels must consist of a series of takeoffs, level flyovers, and approaches during which measurement must be taken at noise measuring stations located at the measuring points prescribed in this section.

(2) Each takeoff test, flyover test, and approach test includes simultaneous measurements at the flight-track noise measuring station vertically below the reference flight path and at two sideline noise measuring stations, one on each side of the reference flight track 492 feet (150m) from, and on a line perpendicular to, the flight track of the noise measuring station.

(3) The difference between the elevation of either sideline noise measuring station may not differ from the flight-track noise measuring station by more than 20 feet.

(4) Each noise measuring station must be surrounded by terrain having no excessive sound absorption characteristics, such as might be caused by thick, matted, or tall grass, shrubs, or wooded areas.

(5) During the period when the takeoff, flyover, or approach noise/time record indicates the noise measurement is within 10 dB of PNLTM, no obstruction that significantly influences the sound field from the aircraft may exist—

(i) For any flight-track or sideline noise measuring station, within a conical space above the measuring position (the point on the ground vertically below the microphone), the cone being defined by an axis normal to the ground and by half-angle 80° from this axis; and

(ii) For any sideline noise measuring station, above the line of sight between the microphone and the helicopter.

(6) If a takeoff or flyover test series is conducted at weights other than the maximum takeoff weight for which noise certification is requested, the following additional requirements apply:

(i) At least one takeoff test must be conducted at a weight at, or above, the maximum certification weight.

(ii) Each test weight must be within +5 percent or −10 percent of the maximum certification weight.

(iii) FAA-approved data must be used to determine the variation of EPNL with weight for takeoff test conditions.

(7) Each approach test must be conducted with the aircraft stabilized and following a 6.0 degree ±0.5 degree approach angle and must meet the requirements of section H36.107 of this part.

(8) If an approach test series is conducted at weights other than the maximum landing weight for which certification is requested, the following additional requirements apply:

(i) At least one approach test must be conducted at a weight at, or above, the maximum landing weight.

(ii) Each test weight must exceed 90 percent of the maximum landing weight.

(iii) FAA-approved data must be used to determine the variation of EPNL with weight for approach test conditions.

(9) Aircraft performance data sufficient to make the corrections required under section

H36.205 of this appendix must be recorded at an FAA-approved sampling rate using FAA approved equipment.

(c) *Weather restrictions.* The tests must be conducted under the following atmospheric conditions:

(1) No rain or other precipitation.

(2) Ambient air temperature between 36 °F and 95 °F (2.2 °C and 35 °C), inclusively, over that portion of the sound propagation path between the aircraft and a point 10 meters above the ground at the noise measuring station. The temperature and relative humidity measured at aircraft altitude and at 10 meters above ground shall be averaged and used to adjust for propagation path absorption.

(3) Relative humidity and ambient temperature over the portion of the sound propagation path between the aircraft and a point 10 meters above the ground at the noise measuring station is such that the sound attenuation in the one-third octave band centered at 8 kHz is not greater than 12 dB/100 meters and the relative humidity is between 20 percent and 95 percent, inclusively.

(4) Wind velocity as measured at 10 meters above ground does not exceed 10 knots (19 km/h) and the crosswind component does not exceed 5 knots (9 km/h). The wind shall be determined using a continuous thirty-second averaging period spanning the 10dB down time interval.

(5) No anomalous wind conditions (including turbulence) which will significantly affect the noise level of the aircraft when the noise is recorded at each noise measuring station.

(6) The wind velocity, temperature, and relative humidity measurements required under the appendix must be measured in the vicinity of noise measuring stations 10 meters above the ground. The location of the meteorological measurements must be approved by the FAA as representative of those atmospheric conditions existing near the surface over the geographical area which aircraft noise measurements are made. In some cases, a fixed meteorological station (such as those found at airports or other facilities) may meet this requirement.

(7) Temperature and relative humidity measurements must be obtained within 25 minutes of each noise test measurement. Meteorological data must be interpolated to actual times of each noise measurement.

(d) *Aircraft testing procedures.* (1) The aircraft testing procedures and noise measurements must be conducted and processed in a manner which yields the noise evaluation measure designated as Effective Perceived Noise Level (EPNL) in units of EPNdB, as prescribed in appendix A of this part.

(2) The aircraft height and lateral position relative to the centerline of the reference flight-track (which passes through the noise measuring point) must be determined by an FAA approved method which is independent of normal flight instrumentation, such as radar tracking, theodolite triangulation, laser trajectography, or photographic scaling techniques.

(3) The aircraft position along the flight path must be related to the noise recorded at the noise measuring stations by means of synchronizing signals at an approved sampling rate. The position of the aircraft must be recorded relative to the runway during the entire time period in which the recorded signal is within 10 dB of PNLTM. Measuring and sampling equipment must be approved by the FAA.

Section H36.103 *Takeoff test conditions.*

(a) This section, in addition to the applicable requirements of sections H36.101 and H36.205(b) of this appendix, applies to all takeoff noise tests conducted under this appendix to show compliance with Part 36.

(b) A test series must consist of at least six flights over the flight-track noise measuring station (with simultaneous measurements at all three noise measuring stations) as follows:

(1) An airspeed of either $V_y \pm 5$ knots or the lowest approved speed ± 5 knots for the climb after takeoff, whichever speed is greater, must be established during the horizontal portion of each test flight and maintained during the remainder of the test flight.

(2) The horizontal portion of each test flight must be conducted at an altitude of 65 feet (20 meters) above the ground level at the flight-track noise measuring station.

(3) Upon reaching a point 1,640 feet (500 meters) from the noise measuring station, the helicopter shall be stabilized at:

(i) The torque used to establish the takeoff distance for an ambient temperature at sea level of 25 °C for helicopters for which the determination of takeoff performance is required by airworthiness regulations; or

(ii) The torque corresponding to minimum installed power available for an ambient temperature at sea level of 25 °C for all other helicopters.

(4) The helicopter shall be maintained throughout the takeoff reference procedure at:

(i) The speed used ± 5 knots to establish takeoff distance for an ambient temperature at sea level of 25 °C for helicopters for which the determination of takeoff performance is required by airworthiness regulations; or

(ii) The best rate of climb speed $V_y \pm 5$ knots, or the lowest approved speed for climb after takeoff, whichever is greater, for an ambient temperature at sea level of 25 °C for all other helicopters.

(5) The rotor speed must be stabilized at the normal operating RPM ($\pm 1\%$) during the entire period of the test flight when the measured helicopter noise level is within 10 dB of PNLTM.

(6) The helicopter must pass over the flight-track noise measuring station within ±10° from the zenith.

Section H36.105 *Flyover test conditions.*

(a) This section, in addition to the applicable requirements of sections H36.101 and H36.205(c) of this appendix, applies to all flyover noise tests conducted under this appendix to show compliance with Part 36.

(b) A test series must consist of at least six flights (three in each direction) over the flight-track noise measuring station (with simultaneous measurements at all three noise measuring stations)—

(1) In level flight;

(2) At a height of 492 feet ±30 feet (150±9 meters) above the ground level at the flight-track noise measuring station; and

(3) Within ±5° from the zenith.

(c) Each flyover noise test must be conducted—

(1) At a speed of 0.9 V_H or 0.45 V_H+120 km/hr (0.45 V_H+65 kt), whichever is less, maintained throughout the measured portion of the flyover;

(2) At rotor speed stabilized at the normal operating rotor RPM (±1 percent); and

(3) With the power stabilized during the period when the measured helicopter noise level is within 10 dB of PNLTM.

(d) The airspeed shall not vary from the reference airspeed by more than ±5 knots (9 km/hr).

Section H36.107 *Approach test conditions.*

(a) This section, in addition to the requirements of sections H36.101 and H36.205(d) of this appendix, applies to all approach tests conducted under this appendix to show compliance with Part 36.

(b) A test series must consist of at least six flights over the flight-track noise measuring station (with simultaneous measurements at the three noise measuring stations)—

(1) On an approach slope of 6°±0.5°;

(2) At a height of 394±30 feet (120±9 meters) above the ground level at the flight-track noise measuring station;

(3) Within ±10° of the zenith;

(4) At stabilized airspeed equal to the certificated best rate of climb V_y, or the lowest approved speed for approach, whichever is greater, with power stabilized during the approach and over the flight path reference point, and continued to a normal touchdown; and

(5) At rotor speed stabilized at the maximum normal operating rotor RPM (±1 percent).

(c) The airspeed shall not vary from the reference airspeed by more than ±5 knots (±9 km/hr).

Section H36.109 *Measurement of helicopter noise received on the ground.*

(a) *General.* (1) The measurements prescribed in this section provide the data needed to determine the one-third octave band noise produced by an aircraft during testing, at specific noise measuring stations, as a function of time.

(2) Sound pressure level data for aircraft noise certification purposes must be obtained with FAA-approved acoustical equipment and measurement practices.

(3) Paragraphs (b), (c), and (d) of this section prescribe the required equipment specifications. Paragraphs (e) and (f) prescribe the calibration and measurement procedures required for each certification test series.

(b) *Measurement system.* The acoustical measurement system must consist of FAA-approved equipment equivalent to the following:

(1) A microphone system with frequency response and directivity which are compatible with the measurement and analysis system accuracy prescribed in paragraph (c) of this section.

(2) Tripods or similar microphone mountings that minimize interference with the sound energy being measured.

(3) Recording and reproducing equipment, the characteristics, frequency response, and dynamic range of which are compatible with the response and accuracy requirements of paragraph (c) of this section.

(4) Calibrators using sine wave, or pink noise, of known levels. When pink noise (defined in paragraph (e)(1) of this section) is used, the signal must be described in terms of its root-mean-square (rms) value.

(5) Analysis equipment with the response and accuracy which meets or exceeds the requirements of paragraph (d) of this section.

(6) Attenuators used for range changing in sensing, recording, reproducing, or analyzing aircraft sound must be capable of being operated in equal-interval decibel steps with no error between any two settings which exceeds 0.2 dB.

(c) *Sensing, recording, and reproducing equipment.* (1) The sound produced by the aircraft must be recorded in such a way that the complete information, including time history, is retained. A magnetic tape recorder is acceptable.

(2) The microphone must be a pressure-sensitive capacitive type, or its FAA-approved equivalent, such as a free-field type with incidence corrector.

(i) The variation of microphone and preamplifier system sensitivity within an angle of ±30 degrees of grazing (60–120 degrees from the normal to the diaphragm) must not exceed the following values:

Frequency (Hz)	Change in sensitivity (dB)
45 to 1,120	1
1,120 to 2,240	1.5
2,240 to 4,500	2.5
4,500 to 7,100	4
7,100 to 11,200	5

With the windscreen in place, the sensitivity variation in the plane of the microphone diaphragm shall not exceed 1.0 dB over the frequency range 45 to 11,200 Hz.

(ii) The overall free-field frequency response at 90 degrees (grazing incidence) of the combined microphone (including incidence corrector, if applicable) preamplifier, and windscreen must be determined by using either (A) an electrostatic calibrator in combination with manufacturer-provided corrections, or (B) an anechoic free-field facility. The calibration unit must include pure tones at each preferred one-third octave frequency from 50 Hz to 10,000 Hz. The frequency response (after corrections based on that determination) must be flat and within the following tolerances:

44–3,549 Hz..±0.25 dB
3,550–7,099 Hz ....±0.5 dB
7,100–11,200 Hz.....................................±1.0 dB

(iii) Specifications concerning sensitivity to environmental factors such as temperature, relative humidity, and vibration must be in conformity with the recommendations of International Electrotechnical Commission (IEC) Publication No. 179, entitled "Precision Sound Level Meters", as incorporated by reference under § 36.6 of this part.

(iv) If the wind speed exceeds 6 knots, a windscreen must be employed with the microphone during each measurement of aircraft noise. Correction for any insertion loss produced by the windscreen, as a function of frequency, must be applied to the measured data and any correction applied must be reported.

(3) If a magnetic tape recorder is used to store data for subsequent analysis, the record/replay system (including tape) must conform to the following:

(i) The electric background noise produced by the system in each one-third octave must be at least 35 dB below the standard recording level, which is defined as the level that is either 10 dB below the 3 percent harmonic distortion level for direct recording or ±40 percent deviation for frequency modulation (FM) recording.

(ii) At the standard recording level, the corrected frequency response in each selected one-third octave band between 44 Hz and 180 Hz must be flat and within ±0.75 dB, and in each band between 180 Hz and 11,200 Hz must be flat and within ±0.25 dB.

(iii) If the overall system satisfies the requirements of paragraph (c)(2)(ii) of this section, and if the limitations of the dynamic range of the equipment are insufficient to obtain adequate spectral information, high frequency pre-emphasis may be added to the recording channel with the converse de-emphasis on playback. If pre-emphasis is added, the instantaneously recorded sound-pressure level between 800 Hz and 11,200 Hz of the maximum measured noise signal must not

vary more than 20 dB between the levels of the maximum and minimum one-third octave bands.

(d) *Analysis equipment.* (1) A frequency analysis of the acoustic signal must be performed using one-third octave filters which conform to the recommendations of International Electrotechnical Commission (IEC) Publication No. 225, entitled "Octave, Half-Octave, and Third-Octave Band Filters Intended for Analysis of Sound and Vibrations," as incorporated by reference under § 36.6 of this part.

(2) A set of 24 consecutive one-third octave filters must be used. The first filter of the set must be centered at a geometric mean frequency of 50 Hz and the last filter at 10,000 Hz. The output of each filter must contain less than 0.5 dB ripple.

(3) The analyzer indicating device may be either analog or digital, or a combination of both. The preferred sequence of signal processing is:

(i) Squaring the one-third octave filter outputs;

(ii) Averaging or integrating; and

(iii) Converting linear formulation to logarithmic.

(4) Each detector must operate over a minimum dynamic range of 60 dB and perform as a root-mean-square device for sinusoidal tone bursts having crest factors of at least 3 over the following dynamic range:

(i) Up to 30 dB below full-scale reading must be accurate within ±0.5 dB;

(ii) Between 30 dB and 40 dB below full-scale reading must be accurate within ±1.0 dB; and

(iii) In excess of 40 dB below full-scale reading must be accurate within ±2.5 dB.

(5) The averaging properties of the integrator must be tested as follows:

(i) White noise must be passed through the 200 Hz one-third octave band filter and the output fed in turn to each detector/integrator. The standard deviation of the measured levels must then be determined from a statistically significant number of samples of the filtered white noise taken at intervals of not less than 5 seconds. The value of the standard deviation must be within the interval 0.48±0.06 dB for a probability limit of 95 percent. An approved equivalent method may be substituted for this test on those analyzers where the test signal cannot readily be fed directly to each detector/integrator.

(ii) For each detector/integrator, the response to a sudden onset or interruption of a constant amplitude sinusoidal signal at the respective one-third octave band center frequency must be measured at sampling times 0.5, 1.0, 1.5, and 2.0 seconds after the onset or interruption. The rising responses must be in the following amounts before the steady-state level:

0.5 seconds, 4.0±1.0 dB

1.0 seconds, 1.75±0.5 dB
1.5 seconds, 1.0±0.5 dB
2.0 seconds, 0.6±0.25 dB

(iii) The falling response must be such that the sum of the decibel readings below the initial steady-state level, and the corresponding rising response reading is 6.5± 1.0 dB, at both 0.5 and 1.0 seconds and, on subsequent records, the sum of the onset plus decay must be greater than 7.5 decibels.

NOTE 1: For analyzers with linear detection, an approximation of this response would be given by:

$$
\begin{aligned}
\text{SPL (i, k)-10 log} \quad & [0.17 \ (10^{0.1(L_{i,k}-3)}) \\
& +10.21 \ (0^{0.1(L_{i,k}-2)}) \\
& +0.24 \ (10^{0.1(L_{i,k}-1)}) \\
& +0.33 \ (10^{0.1(L_{i,k})})]
\end{aligned}
$$

When this approximation is used, the calibration signal should be established without this weighting.

NOTE 2: Some analyzers have been shown to have signal sampling rates that are insufficiently accurate to detect signals with crest factor ratios greater than three which is common to helicopter noise. Preferably, such analyzers should not be used for helicopter certification. Use of analysis systems with high signal sampling rates (greater than 40KHz) or those with analog detectors prior to digitization at the output of each one-third octave filter is encouraged.

(iv) Analyzers using true integration cannot meet the requirements of (i), (ii), and (iii) directly, because their overall average time is greater than the sampling interval. For these analyzers, compliance must be demonstrated in terms of the equivalent output of the data processor. Further, in cases where readout and resetting require a deadtime during acquisition, the percentage loss of the total data must not exceed one percent.

(6) The sampling interval between successive readouts shall not exceed 500 milliseconds and its precise value must be known to within ±1 one percent. The instant in time by which a readout is characterized shall be the midpoint of the average period where the averaging period is defined as twice the effective time constant of the analyzer.

(7) The amplitude resolution of the analyzer must be at least 0.25 dB.

(8) After all systematic errors have been eliminated, each output level from the analyzer must be accurate within ±1.0 dB of the level of the input signal. The total systematic errors for each of the output levels must not exceed ±3.0 dB. For contiguous filter systems, the systematic corrections between adjacent one-third octave channels must not exceed 4.0 dB.

(9) The dynamic range capability of the analyzer to display a single aircraft noise event, in terms of the difference between full-scale output level and the maximum noise level of the analyzer equipment, must be at least 60 dB.

(e) *Calibrations.* (1) Within five days prior to beginning each test series, the complete electronic system, as installed in field including cables, must be electronically calibrated for frequency and amplitude by the use of a pink noise signal of known amplitudes covering the range of signal levels furnished by the microphone. For purposes of this section, "pink noise" means a noise whose noise-power/unit-frequency is inversely proportional to frequency at frequencies within the range of 44 Hz to 11,200 Hz. The signal used must be described in terms of its average root-mean-square (rms) values for a nonoverload signal level. This system calibration must be repeated within five days of the end of each test series, or as required by the FAA.

(2) Immediately before and after each day's testing, a recorded acoustic calibration of the system must be made in the field with an acoustic calibrator to check the system sensitivity and provide an acoustic reference level for the sound level data analysis. The performance of equipment in the system will be considered satisfactory if, during each day's testing, the variation in the calibration value does not exceed 0.5 dB.

(3) A normal incidence pressure calibration of the combined microphone/preamplifier must be performed with pure tones at each preferred one-third octave frequency from 50 Hz to 10,000 Hz. This calibration must be completed within 90 days prior to the beginning of each test series.

(4) Each reel of magnetic tape must:

(i) Be pistonphone calibrated; and

(ii) At its beginning and end, carry a calibration signal consisting of at least a 15 second burst of pink noise, as defined in paragraph (e)(1) of this section.

(5) Data obtained from tape recorded signals are not considered reliable if the difference between the pink noise signal levels, before and after the tests in each one-third octave band, exceeds 0.75 dB.

(6) The one-third octave filters must have been demonstrated to be in conformity with the recommendations of IEC Publication 225 as incorporated by reference under §36.6 of this part, during the six calendar months preceding the beginning of each test series. However, the correction for effective bandwidth relative to the center frequency response may be determined for each filter by:

(i) Measuring the filter response to sinusoidal signals at a minimum of twenty frequencies equally spaced between the two adjacent preferred one-third octave frequencies; or

(ii) Using an FAA approved equivalent technique.

(7) A performance calibration analysis of each piece of calibration equipment, including pistonphones, reference microphones, and voltage insert devices, must have been made during the six calendar months preceding the beginning of each day's test series. Each calibration must be traceable to the National Bureau of Standards.

(f) *Noise measurement procedures.* (1) Each microphone must be oriented so that the diaphragm is substantially in the plane defined by the flight path of the aircraft and the measuring station. The microphone located at each noise measuring station must be placed so that its sensing element is approximately 4 feet above ground.

(2) Immediately before and immediately after each series of test runs and each day's testing, acoustic calibrations of the system prescribed in this section of this appendix must be recorded in the field to check the acoustic reference level for the analysis of the sound level data. Ambient noise must be recorded for at least 10 seconds and be representative of the acoustical background, including system noise, that exists during the flyover test run. During that recorded period, each component of the system must be set at the gain-levels used for aircraft noise measurement.

(3) The mean background noise spectrum must contain the sound pressure levels, which, in each preferred third octave band in the range of 50 Hz to 10,000 Hz, are the averages of the energy of the sound pressure levels in every preferred third octave. When analyzed in PNL, the resulting mean background noise level must be at least 20 PNdB below the maximum PNL of the helicopter.

(4) Corrections for recorded levels of background noise are allowed, within the limits prescribed in section H36.111(c)(3) of this appendix.

Section H36.111　Reporting and correcting measured data

(a) *General.* Data representing physical measurements, and corrections to measured data, including corrections to measurements for equipment response deviations, must be recorded in permanent form and appended to the record. Each correction must be reported and is subject to FAA approval. An estimate must be made of each individual error inherent in each of the operations employed in obtaining the final data.

(b) *Data reporting.* (1) Measured and corrected sound pressure levels must be presented in one-third octave band levels obtained with equipment conforming to the standards prescribed in section H36.109 of this appendix.

(2) The type of equipment used for measurement and analysis of all acoustic, aircraft

performance, and meteorological data must be reported.

(3) The atmospheric environmental data required to demonstrate compliance with this appendix, measured throughout the test period, must be reported.

(4) Conditions of local topography, ground cover, or events which may interfere with sound recording must be reported.

(5) The following aircraft information must be reported:

(i) Type, model, and serial numbers, if any, of aircraft engines and rotors.

(ii) Gross dimensions of aircraft and location of engines.

(iii) Aircraft gross weight for each test run.

(iv) Aircraft configuration, including landing gear positions.

(v) Airspeed in knots.

(vi) Helicopter engine performance as determined from aircraft instruments and manufacturer's data.

(vii) Aircraft flight path, above ground level in feet, determined by an FAA approved method which is independent of normal flight instrumentation, such as radar tracking, theodolite triangulation, laser trajectography, or photographic scaling techniques.

(6) Aircraft speed, and position, and engine performance parameters must be recorded at an approved sampling rate sufficient to correct to the noise certification reference test conditions prescribed in section H36.3 of this appendix. Lateral position relative to the reference flight-track must be reported.

(c) *Data corrections.* (1) Aircraft position, performance data and noise measurement must be corrected to the noise certification reference conditions as prescribed in sections H36.3 and H36.205 of this appendix.

(2) The measured flight path must be corrected by an amount equal to the difference between the applicant's predicted flight path for the certification reference conditions and the measured flight path at the test conditions. Necessary corrections relating to aircraft flight path or performance may be derived from FAA-approved data for the difference between measured and reference engine conditions, together with appropriate allowances for sound attenuation with distance. The Effective Perceived Noise Level (EPNL) correction must be less than 2.0 EPNdB for any combination of the following:

(i) The aircraft's not passing vertically above the measuring station.

(ii) Any difference between the reference flight-track and the actual minimum distance of the aircraft's ILS antenna from the approach measuring station.

(iii) Any difference between the actual approach angle and the noise certification reference approach flight path.

(iv) Any correction of the measured level flyover noise levels which accounts for any difference between the test engine thrust or power and the reference engine thrust or power.

Detailed correction requirements are prescribed in section H36.205 of this appendix.

(3) Aircraft sound pressure levels within the 10 dB-down points must exceed the mean background sound pressure levels determined under section A36.3.10.1 by at least 5 dB in each one-third octave band or be corrected under an FAA approved method to be included in the computation of the overall noise level of the aircraft. An EPNL may not be computed or reported from data from which more than four one-third octave bands in any spectrum within the 10 dB-down points have been excluded under this paragraph.

(d) *Validity of results.* (1) The test results must produce three average EPNL values within the 90 percent confidence limits, each value consisting of the arithmetic average of the corrected noise measurements for all valid test runs at the takeoff, level flyovers, and approach conditions. The 90 percent confidence limit applies separately to takeoff, flyover, and approach.

(2) The minimum sample size acceptable for each takeoff, approach, and flyover certification measurements is six. The number of samples must be large enough to establish statistically for each of the three average noise certification levels a 90 percent confidence limit which does not exceed ±1.5 EPNdB. No test result may be omitted from the averaging process, unless otherwise specified by the FAA.

(3) To comply with this appendix, a minimum of six takeoffs, six approaches, and six level flyovers is required. To be counted toward this requirement, each flight event must be validly recorded at all three noise measuring stations.

(4) The approved values of V_H and V_y used in calculating test and reference conditions and flight profiles must be reported along with measured and corrected sound pressure levels.

Section H36.113 Atmospheric attenuation of sound.

(a) The values of the one-third octave band spectra measured during helicopter noise certification tests under this appendix must conform, or be corrected, to the reference conditions prescribed in section H36.3(a). Each correction must account for any differences in the atmospheric attenuation of sound between the test-day conditions and the reference-day conditions along the sound propagation path between the aircraft and the microphone. Unless the meteorological conditions are within the test window prescribed in this appendix, the test data are not acceptable.

(b) *Attenuation rates.* The atmospheric attenuation rates of sound with distance for each one-third octave band from 50 Hz to 10,000 Hz must be determined in accordance with the formulations and tabulations of SAE ARP 866A, entitled "Standard Values of Atmospheric Absorption as a Function of Temperatures and Humidity for Use in Evaluating Aircraft Flyover Noise", as incorporated by reference under §36.6 of this part.

(c) *Correction for atmospheric attenuation.* (1) EPNL values calculated for measured data must be corrected whenever—

(i) The ambient atmospheric conditions of temperature and relative humidity do not conform to the reference conditions, 77 °F and 70%, respectively, or

(ii) The measured flight paths do not conform to the reference flight paths.

(iii) The temperature and relative humidity measured at aircraft altitude and at 10 meters above the ground shall be averaged and used to adjust for propagation path absorption.

(2) The mean attenuation rate over the complete sound propagation path from the aircraft to the microphone must be computed for each one-third octave band from 50 Hz to 10,000 Hz. These rates must be used in computing the corrections required in section H36.111(d) of this appendix.

PART C—NOISE EVALUATION AND CALCULATION UNDER §36.803

Section H36.201 Noise Evaluation in EPNdB.

(a) Effective Perceived Noise Level (EPNL), in units of effective perceived noise decibels (EPNdB), shall be used for evaluating noise level values under §36.803 of this part. Except as provided in paragraph (b) of this section, the procedures in appendix A of Part 36 must be used for computing EPNL. appendix B includes requirements governing determination of noise values, including calculations of:

(1) Instantaneous perceived noise levels;

(2) Corrections for spectral irregularities;

(3) Tone corrections;

(4) Duration corrections;

(5) Effective perceived noise levels; and

(6) Mathematical formulation of noy tables.

(b) Notwithstanding the provisions of section A36.4.3.1(a), for helicopter noise certification, corrections for spectral irregularities shall start with the corrected sound pressure level in the 50 Hz one-third octave band.

Section H36.203 Calculation of noise levels.

(a) To demonstrate compliance with the noise level limits of section H36.305, the noise values measured simultaneously at the three noise measuring points must be arithmetically averaged to obtain a single EPNdB value for each flight.

(b) The calculated noise level for each noise test series, i.e., takeoff, flyover, or approach must be the numerical average of at least six separate flight EPNdB values. The 90 percent confidence limit for all valid test runs under section H36.111(d) of this appendix applies separately to the EPNdB values for each noise test series.

Section H36.205 Detailed data correction procedures

(a) *General.* If the test conditions do not conform to those prescribed as noise certification reference conditions under section H36.305 of this appendix, the following correction procedure shall apply:

(1) If a positive value results from any difference between reference and test conditions, an appropriate positive correction must be made to the EPNL calculated from the measured data. Conditions which can result in a positive value include:

(i) Atmospheric absorption of sound under test conditions which is greater than the reference;

(ii) Test flight path at an altitude which is higher than the reference; or

(iii) Test weight which is less than maximum certification weight.

(2) If a negative value results from any difference between reference and test conditions, no correction may be made to the EPNL calculated from the measured data, unless the difference results from:

(i) An atmospheric absorption of sound under test conditions which is less than the reference; or

(ii) A test flight path at an altitude which is lower than the reference.

(3) The following correction procedures may produce one or more possible correction values which must be added algebraically to the calculated EPNL to bring it to reference conditions:

(i) The flight profiles must be determined for both reference and test conditions. The procedures require noise and flight path recording with a synchronized time signal from which the test profile can be delineated, including the aircraft position for which PNLTM is observed at the noise measuring station. For takeoff, the flight profile corrected to reference conditions may be derived from FAA approved manufacturer's data.

(ii) The sound propagation paths to the microphone from the aircraft position corresponding to PNLTM are determined for both the test and reference profiles. The SPL values in the spectrum of PNLTM must then be corrected for the effects of—

(A) Change in atmospheric sound absorption;

(B) Atmospheric sound absorption on the linear difference between the two sound path lengths; and

(C) Inverse square law on the difference in sound propagation path length. The corrected values of SPL are then converted to PNLTM from which PNLTM must be subtracted. The resulting difference represents the correction which must be added algebraically to the EPNL calculated from the measured data.

(iii) The minimum distances from both the test and reference profiles to the noise measuring station must be calculated and used to determine a noise duration correction due to any change in the altitude of aircraft flyover. The duration correction must be added algebraically to the EPNL calculated from the measured data.

(iv) From FAA approved data in the form of curves or tables giving the variation of EPNL with rotor rpm and test speed, corrections are determined and must be added to the EPNL, which is calculated from the measured data to account for noise level changes due to differences between test conditions and reference conditions.

(v) From FAA approved data in the form of curves or tables giving the variation of EPNL with approach angle, corrections are determined and must be added algebraically to the EPNL, which is calculated from measured data, to account for noise level changes due to differences between the 6 degree and the test approach angle.

(b) *Takeoff profiles.* (1) Figure H1 illustrates a typical takeoff profile, including reference conditions.

(i) The reference takeoff flight path is described in section H36.3(c).

(ii) The test parameters are functions of the helicopter's performance and weight and the atmospheric conditions of temperature, pressure, wind velocity and direction.

(2) For the actual takeoff, the helicopter approaches position C in level flight at 65 feet (20 meters) above ground level at the flight track noise measuring station and at either Vy±5 knots (±9 km/hr) or the maximum speed of the curve tangential at the ordinate of the height-speed envelope plus 3.0 knots (±5 knots), whichever speed is greater. Rotor speed is stabilized at the normal operating RPM (±1 percent), specified in the flight manual. The helicopter is stabilized in level flight at the speed for best rate of climb using minimum engine specifications (power or torque and rpm) along a path starting from a point located 1640 feet (500 meters) forward of the flight-track noise measuring station and 65 feet (20 meters) above the ground. Starting at point B, the helicopter climbs through point C to the end of the noise certification takeoff flight path represented by position I. The position of point C may vary within limits allowed by the FAA. The position of the helicopter shall be recorded for a distance (CI) sufficient to ensure recording of the entire interval during which the measured helicopter noise level is

within 10 dB of PNLTM, as required by this rule. Station A is the flight-track noise measuring station. The relationships between the measured and corrected takeoff flight profiles can be used to determine the corrections which must be applied to the EPNL calculated from the measured data.

(3) Figure H1 also illustrates the significant geometrical relationships influencing sound propagation. Position L represents the helicopter location on the measured takeoff flight path from which PNLTM is observed at station A, and L_r is the A and Nρ corresponding position on the reference sound propagation path. AL and AL_r both form the angle Φ with their respective flight paths. Position T represents the point on the measured takeoff flight path nearest station A, and T_r is the corresponding position on the reference flight path. The minimum distance to the measured and reference flight paths are indicated by the lines AT and AT_r, respectively, which are normal to their flight paths.

(c) *Level flyover profiles.* (1) The noise type certification level flyover profile is shown in Figure H2. Airspeed must be stabilized within ±5 knots of the reference airspeed given in section H36.3(d). For each run, the difference between airspeed and ground speed shall not exceed 10 knots between the 10 dB down points. Rotor speed must be stabilized at the maximum continuous RPM within one percent, throughout the 10 dB down time period. If the test requirements are otherwise met, flight direction may be reversed for each subsequent flyover, to obtain three test runs in each direction.

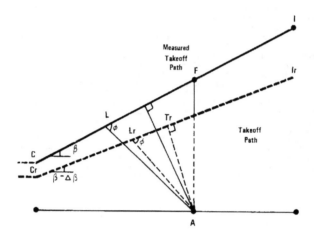

Figure H1. COMPARISON OF MEASURED AND
CORRECTED TAKEOFF PROFILES

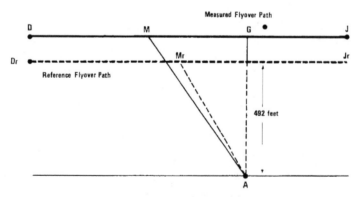

Figure H2. COMPARISON OF MEASURED AND
CORRECTED FLYOVER PROFILES

(2) Figure H2 illustrates comparative fly-over profiles when test conditions do not conform to prescribed reference conditions. The position of the helicopter shall be re-corded for a distance (DJ) sufficient to en-sure recording of the entire interval during which the measured helicopter noise level is

840

within 10 dB of PNLTM, as required. The flyover profile is defined by the height AG which is a function of the operating conditions controlled by the pilot. Position M represents the helicopter location on the measured flyover flight path for which PNLTM is observed at station A, and M_r is the corresponding position on the reference flight path.

(d) *Approach profiles.* (1) Figure H3 illustrates a typical approach profile, including reference conditions.

(2) The helicopter approaches position H along a 6° (±0.5°) average approach slope throughout the 10 dB down period. The approach procedure shall be acceptable to the FAA and shall be included in the Flight Manual.

(3) Figure H3 illustrates portions of the measured and reference approach flight paths including the significant geometrical

relationships influencing sound propagation. EK represents the measured approach path with approach angle η, and E_r and K_r represent the reference approach angle of 6°. Position N represents the helicopter location on the measured approach flight path for which PNLTM is observed at station A, and N_r is the corresponding position on the reference approach flight path. The measured and corrected noise propagation paths are AN and AN_r, respectively, both of which form the same angle with their flight paths. Position S represents the point on the measured approach flight path nearest station A, and S_r is the corresponding point on the reference approach flight path. The minimum distance to the measured and reference flight paths are indicated by the lines AS and AS_r, respectively, which are normal to their flight paths.

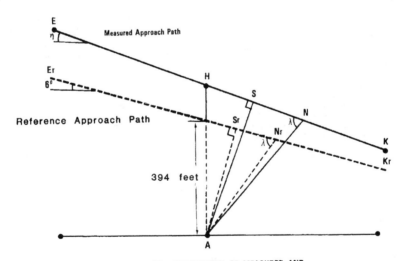

Figure H3. COMPARISON OF MEASURED AND CORRECTED APPROACH PROFILES

(e) *Correction of noise at source during level flyover.* (1) For level overflight, if any combination of the following three factors, 1) airspeed deviation from reference, 2) rotor speed deviation from reference, and 3) temperature deviation from reference, results in an advancing blade tip Mach number which deviates from the reference Mach value, then source noise adjustments shall be determined. This adjustment shall be determined

from the manufacturer supplied data approved by the FAA.

(2) Off-reference tip Mach number adjustments shall be based upon a sensitivity curve of PNLTM versus advancing blade tip Mach number, deduced from overflights carried out at different airspeeds around the reference airspeed. If the test aircraft is unable

to attain the reference value, then an extrapolation of the sensitivity curve is permitted if data cover at least a range of 0.3 Mach units. The advancing blade tip Mach number shall be computed using true airspeed, onboard outside air temperature, and rotor speed. A separate PNLTM versus advancing blade tip Mach number function shall be derived for each of the three certification microphone locations, i.e., centerline, sideline left, and sideline right. Sideline left and right are defined relative to the direction of the flight on each run. PNLTM adjustments are to be applied to each microphone datum using the appropriate PNLTM function.

(f) *PNLT corrections.* If the ambient atmospheric conditions of temperature and relative humidity are not those prescribed as reference conditions under this appendix (77 degrees F and 70 percent, respectively), corrections to the EPNL values must be calculated from the measured data under paragraph (a) of this section as follows:

(1) *Takeoff flight path.* For the takeoff flight path shown in Figure H1, the spectrum of PNLTM observed at station A for the aircraft at position L_r is decomposed into its individual SPLi values.

(i) Step 1. A set of corrected values are then computed as follows:

$$SPLic = SPLi + (\alpha i - \alpha io)AL$$
$$+ (\alpha io)AL - ALr)$$
$$+ 20 \log(AL/ALr)$$

Where SPLi and SPLic are the measured and corrected sound pressure levels, respectively, in the i-th one-third octave band. The first correction term accounts for the effects of change in atmospheric sound absorption where ai and aio are the sound absorption coefficients for the test and reference atmospheric conditions, respectively, for the -ith one-third octave band and L_r A is the measured takeoff sound propagation path. The second correction term accounts for the effects of atmospheric sound absorption on the change in the sound propagation path length where L_r A is the corrected takeoff sound propagation path. The third correction term accounts for the effects of the inverse square law on the change in the sound propagation path length.

(ii) Step 2. The corrected values of the SPLic are then converted to PNLT and a correction term calculated using as follows:

$$\Delta_1 = PNLT - PNLTM$$

Which represents the correction to be added algebraically to the EPNL calculated from the measured data.

(2) *Approach flight path.* (i) The procedure described in paragraph (f)(1) of this section for takeoff flight paths is also used for the approach flight path, except that the value for SPLic relate to the approach sound propagation paths shown in Figure H3 as follows:

$$SPLic = SPLi + (\alpha - \alpha io) AM +$$
$$\alpha(AM - AMr) + 20 \log(AM/AMr)$$

Where the lines NS and N, S_r are the measured and referenced approach sound propagation paths, respectively.

(ii) The remainder of the procedure is the same as that prescribed in paragraph (d)(1)(ii) of this section, regarding takeoff flight path.

(3) *Sideline microphones.* The procedure prescribed in paragraph (f)(1) of this section for takeoff flight paths is also used for the propagation to the sideline microphones, except that the values of SPLic relate only in the measured sideline sound propagation path as follows:

$$SPLic - SPLi + (\alpha io - \alpha + io)KX$$
$$+ \alpha io (KX - KXr) + 20 \log(KX/KXr)$$

K is the sideline measuring station where

X=L and Xr=Ln for takeoff
X=M and Xr=Mn for approach
X=N and Xr=Nr for flyover

(4) *Level flyover flight path.* The procedure prescribed in paragraph (f)(1) of this section for takeoff flight paths is also used for the level flyover flight path, except that the values of SPLic relate only to the flyover sound propagation paths as follows:

$$SPLic = SPLi + (\alpha - \alpha \text{ io}) \quad AN + \alpha \text{ io}$$
$$(AN - ANr) + 20 \log(AN/ANr)$$

(g) *Duration corrections.* (1) If the measured takeoff and approach flight paths do not conform to those prescribed as the corrected and reference flight paths, respectively, under section A36.5(d)(2) it will be necessary to apply duration corrections to the EPNL values calculated from the measured data. Such corrections must be calculated as follows:

(i) *Takeoff flight path.* For the takeoff flight path shown in Figure H1, the correction term is calculated using the formula—

$$\Delta_2 = -10 \log(AT/ATr) + 10 \log(V/Vr)$$

which represents the correction which must be added algebraically to the EPNL calculated from the measured data. The lengths AT and ATr are the measured and corrected takeoff minimum distances from the noise measuring station A to the measured and the corrected flight paths, respectively. A negative sign indicates that, for the particular case of a duration correction, the EPNL calculated from the measured data must be reduced if the measured flight path is at greater altitude than the corrected flight path.

(ii) *Approach flight path.* For the approach flight path shown in Figure H3, the correction term is calculated using the formula—

$$\Delta_2 = -10 \log(AS/ASr) + 10 \log(V/Vr)$$

where AS is the measured approach minimum distance from the noise measuring station A to the measured flight path and 394 feet is the minimum distance from station A to the reference flight path.

(iii) *Sideline microphones.* For the sideline flight path, the correction term is calculated using the formula—

$$\Delta_2 = -10 \log (KX/KXr) + 10 \log (V/Vr)$$

K is the sideline measuring station

where X=T and Xr=Tr for takeoff
where X=S and Xr=Sr for approach
where X=G and Xr=Gr for flyover

(iv) *Level flyover flight paths.* For the level flyover flight path, the correction term is calculated using the formula—

$$\Delta_2 = -10 \log (AG/AGr) + 10 \log (V/Vr)$$

where AG is the measured flyover altitude over the noise measuring station A.

(2) The adjustment procedure described in this section shall apply to the sideline microphones in the take-off, overflight, and approach cases. Although the noise emission is strongly dependent on the directivity pattern, variable from one helicopter type to another, the propagation angle θ shall be the same for test and reference flight paths. The elevation angle ψ shall not be constrained but must be determined and reported. The certification authority shall specify the acceptable limitations on ψ. Corrections to data obtained when these limits are exceeded shall be applied using FAA approved procedures.

PART D—NOISE LIMITS UNDER § 36.805

Section H36.301   Noise measurement, evaluation, and calculation

Compliance with this part of this appendix must be shown with noise levels measured, evaluated, and calculated as prescribed under Parts B and C of this appendix.

Section H36.303 [Reserved]

Section H36.305   Noise levels

(a) *Limits.* For compliance with this appendix, it must be shown by flight test that the calculated noise levels of the helicopter, at the measuring points described in section H36.305(a) of this appendix, do not exceed the following, with appropriate interpolation between weights:

(1) *Stage 1* noise limits for acoustical changes for helicopters are as follows:

(i) For takeoff, flyover, and approach calculated noise levels, the noise levels of each Stage 1 helicopter that exceed the Stage 2 noise limits plus 2 EPNdB may not, after a change in type design, exceed the noise levels created prior to the change in type design.

(ii) For takeoff, flyover, and approach calculated noise levels, the noise levels of each Stage 1 helicopter that do not exceed the Stage 2 noise limits plus 2 EPNdB may not, after the change in type design, exceed the Stage 2 noise limits plus 2 EPNdB.

(2) *Stage 2* noise limits are as follows:

(i) *For takeoff calculated noise levels*—109 EPNdB for maximum takeoff weights of 176,370 pounds or more, reduced by 3.01 EPNdB per halving of the weight down to 89 EPNdB for maximum weights of 1,764 pounds or less.

(ii) *For flyover calculated noise levels*—108 EPNdB for maximum weights of 176,370 pounds or more, reduced by 3.01 EPNdB per halving of the weight down to 88 EPNdB for maximum weights of 1,764 pounds or less.

(iii) *For approach calculated noise levels*—110 EPNdB for maximum weights of 176,370 pounds or more, reduced by 3.01 EPNdB per halving of the weight down to 90 EPNdB for maximum weight of 1,764 pounds or less.

(b) *Tradeoffs.* Except to the extent limited under §36.11(b) of this part, the noise limits prescribed in paragraph (a) of this section may be exceeded by one or two of the take-off, flyover, or approach calculated noise levels determined under section H36.203 of this appendix if

(1) The sum of the exceedances is not greater than 4 EPNdB;

(2) No exceedance is greater than 3 EPNdB; and

(3) The exceedances are completely offset by reduction in the other required calculated noise levels.

[Amdt. 36–14, 53 FR 3541, Feb. 5, 1988; 53 FR 4099, Feb. 11, 1988; 53 FR 7728, Mar. 10, 1988, as amended by Amdt. 36–54, 67 FR 45237, July 8, 2002]

APPENDIX I TO PART 36 [RESERVED]

APPENDIX J TO PART 36—ALTERNATIVE NOISE CERTIFICATION PROCEDURE FOR HELICOPTERS UNDER SUBPART H HAVING A MAXIMUM CERTIFICATED TAKEOFF WEIGHT OF NOT MORE THAN 6,000 POUNDS

PART A—REFERENCE CONDITIONS

J36.1   *General.*
J36.3   *Reference Test Conditions.*
J36.5   *[Reserved]*

PART B—NOISE MEASUREMENT PROCEDURE UNDER §36.801

J36.101   *Noise certification test and measurement conditions.*
J36.103   *[Reserved]*
J36.105   *Flyover test conditions.*
J36.107   *[Reserved]*
J36.109   *Measurement of helicopter noise received on the ground.*
J36.111   *Reporting requirements.*
J36.113   *[Reserved]*

PART C—NOISE EVALUATION AND CALCULATION UNDER §36.803

J36.201   *Noise evaluation in SEL.*
J36.203   *Calculation of noise levels.*

J36.205 *Detailed data correction procedures.*

PART D—NOISE LIMITS PROCEDURE UNDER § 36.805

J36.301 *Noise measurement, evaluation, and calculation.*
J36.303 *[Reserved]*
J36.305 *Noise limits.*

PART A—REFERENCE CONDITIONS

Section J36.1 General

This appendix prescribes the alternative noise certification requirements identified under § 36.1 of this part and subpart H of this part for helicopters in the primary, normal, transport, and restricted categories having maximum certificated takeoff weight of not more than 6,000 pounds including:

(a) The conditions under which an alternative noise certification test under subpart H of this part must be conducted and the alternative measurement procedure that must be used under § 36.801 of this part to measure the helicopter noise during the test;

(b) The alternative procedures which must be used under § 36.803 of this part to correct the measured data to the reference conditions and to calculate the noise evaluation quantity designated as Sound Exposure Level (SEL); and

(c) The noise limits for which compliance must be shown under § 36.805 of this part.

Section J36.3 Reference Test Conditions

(a) *Meteorological conditions.* The following are the noise certification reference atmospheric conditions which shall be assumed to exist from the surface to the helicopter altitude:

(1) Sea level pressure of 2116 pounds per square foot (76 centimeters mercury);
(2) Ambient temperature of 77 degrees Fahrenheit (25 degrees Celsius);
(3) Relative humidity of 70 percent; and
(4) Zero wind.

(b) *Reference test site.* The reference test site is flat and without line-of-sight obstructions across the flight path that encompasses the 10 dB down points of the A-weighted time history.

(c) *Level flyover reference profile.* The reference flyover profile is a level flight 492 feet (150 meters) above ground level as measured at the noise measuring station. The reference flyover profile has a linear flight track and passes directly over the noise monitoring station. Airspeed is stabilized at $0.9V_H$; $0.9V_{NE}$; $0.45V_H + 65$ kts ($0.45V_H + 120$ km/h); or $0.45V_{NE} + 65$ kts ($0.45V_{NE} + 120$ km/h), whichever of the four speeds is least. Rotor speed is stabilized at the power on maximum normal operating RPM throughout the 10 dB down time period.

(1) For noise certification purposes, V_H is defined as the airspeed in level flight obtained using the minimum specification engine power corresponding to maximum continuous power available for sea level, 77 degree Fahrenheit (25 degrees Celsius) ambient conditions at the relevant maximum certificated weight. The value of V_H thus defined must be listed in the Rotorcraft Flight Manual.

(2) V_{NE} is the never-exceed airspeed.

(d) The weight of the helicopter shall be the maximum takeoff weight at which noise certification is requested.

Section J36.5 [Reserved]

PART B—NOISE MEASUREMENT PROCEDURE UNDER § 36.801

Section J36.101 Noise certification test and measurement conditions

(a) *General.* This section prescribes the conditions under which helicopter noise certification tests must be conducted and the measurement procedures that must be used to measure helicopter noise during each test.

(b) *Test site requirements.* (1) The noise measuring station must be surrounded by terrain having no excessive sound absorption characteristics, such as might be caused by thick, matted, or tall grass, shrubs, or wooded areas.

(2) During the period when the flyover noise measurement is within 10 dB of the maximum A-weighted sound level, no obstruction that significantly influences the sound field from the helicopter may exist within a conical space above the noise measuring position (the point on the ground vertically below the microphone), the cone is defined by an axis normal to the ground and by half-angle 80 degrees from this axis.

(c) *Weather restrictions.* The test must be conducted under the following atmospheric conditions:

(1) No rain or other precipitation;
(2) Ambient air temperature between 36 degrees and 95 degrees Fahrenheit (2 degrees and 35 degrees Celsius), inclusively, and relative humidity between 20 percent and 95 percent inclusively, except that testing may not take place where combinations of temperature and relative humidity result in a rate of atmospheric attenuation greater than 10 dB per 100 meters (30.5 dB per 1000 ft) in the one-third octave band centered at 8 kilo-Hertz.

(3) Wind velocity that does not exceed 10 knots (19 km/h) and a crosswind component that does not exceed 5 knots (9 km/h). The wind shall be determined using a continuous averaging process of no greater than 30 seconds;

(4) Measurements of ambient temperature, relative humidity, wind speed, and wind direction must be made between 4 feet (1.2 meters) and 33 feet (10 meters) at the noise

monitoring station. Unless otherwise approved by the FAA, ambient temperature and relative humidity must be measured at the noise measuring station at the same height above the ground.

(5) No anomalous wind conditions (including turbulence) or other anomalous meteorological conditions that will significantly affect the noise level of the helicopter when the noise is recorded at the noise measuring station; and

(6) The location of the meteorological instruments must be approved by the FAA as representative of those atmospheric conditions existing near the surface over the geographical area where the helicopter noise measurements are made. In some cases, a fixed meteorological station (such as those found at airports or other facilities) may meet this requirement.

(d) *Helicopter testing procedures.* (1) The helicopter testing procedures and noise measurements must be conducted and processed in a manner which yields the noise evaluation measure designated Sound Exposure Level (SEL) as defined in section J36.109(b) of this appendix.

(2) The helicopter height relative to the noise measurement point sufficient to make corrections required under section J36.205 of this appendix must be determined by an FAA-approved method that is independent of normal flight instrumentation, such as radar tracking, theodolite triangulation, laser trajectography, or photographic scaling techniques.

(3) If an applicant demonstrates that the design characteristics of the helicopter would prevent flight from being conducted in accordance with the reference test conditions prescribed under section J36.3 of this appendix, then with FAA approval, the reference test conditions used under this appendix may vary from the standard reference test conditions, but only to the extent demanded by those design characteristics which make compliance with the reference test conditions impossible.

Section J36.103 [Reserved]

Section J36.105   Flyover test conditions

(a) This section prescribes the flight test conditions and allowable random deviations for flyover noise tests conducted under this appendix.

(b) A test series must consist of at least six flights with equal numbers of flights in opposite directions over the noise measuring station:

(1) In level flight and in cruise configuration;

(2) At a height of 492 feet ±50 feet (150 ±15 meters) above the ground level at the noise measuring station; and

(3) Within ±10 degrees from the zenith.

(c) Each flyover noise test must be conducted:

(1) At the reference airspeed specified in section J36.3(c) of this appendix, with such airspeed adjusted as necessary to produce the same advancing blade tip Mach number as associated with the reference conditions;

(i) Advancing blade tip Mach number (M_{AT}) is defined as the ratio of the arithmetic sum of blade tip rotational speed (V_R) and the helicopter true air speed (V_T) over the speed of sound (c) at 77 degrees Fahrenheit (1135.6 ft/sec or 346.13 m/sec) such that $M_{AT}=(V_R+V_T)/c$; and

(ii) The airspeed shall not vary from the adjusted reference airspeed by more than ±3 knots (±5 km/hr) or an equivalent FAA-approved variation from the reference advancing blade tip Mach number. The adjusted reference airspeed shall be maintained throughout the measured portion of the flyover.

(2) At rotor speed stabilized at the power on maximum normal operating rotor RPM (±1 percent); and

(3) With the power stabilized during the period when the measured helicopter noise level is within 10 dB of the maximum A-weighted sound level (L_{AMAX}).

(d) The helicopter test weight for each flyover test must be within plus 5 percent or minus 10 percent of the maximum takeoff weight for which certification under this part is requested.

(e) The requirements of paragraph (b)(2) of this section notwithstanding, flyovers at an FAA-approved lower height may be used and the results adjusted to the reference measurement point by an FAA-approved method if the ambient noise in the test area, measured in accordance with the requirements prescribed in section J36.109 of this appendix, is found to be within 15 dB(A) of the maximum A-weighted helicopter noise level (L_{AMAX}) measured at the noise measurement station in accordance with section J36.109 of this appendix.

Section J36.107 [Reserved]

Section J36.109   Measurement of helicopter noise received on the ground

(a) *General.* (1) The helicopter noise measured under this appendix for noise certification purposes must be obtained with FAA-approved acoustical equipment and measurement practices.

(2) Paragraph (b) of this section identifies and prescribes the specifications for the noise evaluation measurements required under this appendix. Paragraphs (c) and (d) of this section prescribe the required acoustical equipment specifications. Paragraphs (e) and (f) of this section prescribe the calibration and measurement procedures required under this appendix.

(b) *Noise unit definition.* (1) The value of sound exposure level (SEL, or as denoted by

845

symbol, L_{AE}), is defined as the level, in decibels, of the time integral of squared 'A'-weighted sound pressure (P_A) over a given time period or event, with reference to the square of the standard reference sound pressure (P_O) of 20 micropascals and a reference duration of one second.

(2) This unit is defined by the expression:

$$L_{AE} = 10\ Log_{10}\ \frac{1}{T_0}\int_{t_1}^{t_2}\left(\frac{P_A(t)}{P_0}\right)^2 dt\ dB$$

Where T_O is the reference integration time of one second and $(t_2\text{-}t_1)$ is the integration time interval.

(3) The integral equation of paragraph (b)(2) of this section can also be expressed as:

$$L_{AE} = 10\ Log_{10}\ \frac{1}{T_0}\int_{t_1}^{t_2}10^{0.1L_A(t)}dt\ dB$$

Where $L_A(t)$ is the time varying A-weighted sound level.

(4) The integration time $(t_2\text{-}t_1)$ in practice shall not be less than the time interval during which $L_A(t)$ first rises to within 10 dB(A) of its maximum value (L_{AMAX}) and last falls below 10 dB(A) of its maximum value.

(5) The SEL may be approximated by the following expression:

$L_{AE}=L_{AMAX}$ + <delta> A

where <delta> A is the duration allowance given by:

<delta> A=10 log_{10} (T)

where T=$(t_2\text{-}t_1)$/2 and L_{AMAX} is defined as the maximum level, in decibels, of the A-weighted sound pressure (slow response) with reference to the square of the standard reference sound pressure (P_0).

(c) *Measurement system.* The acoustical measurement system must consist of FAA-approved equipment equivalent to the following:

(1) A microphone system with frequency response that is compatible with the measurement and analysis system accuracy prescribed in paragraph (d) of this section;

(2) Tripods or similar microphone mountings that minimize interference with the sound energy being measured;

(3) Recording and reproducing equipment with characteristics, frequency response, and dynamic range that are compatible with the response and accuracy requirements of paragraph (d) of this section; and

(4) Acoustic calibrators using sine wave noise and, if a tape recording system is used, pink noise, of known levels. When pink noise (defined in section H36.109(e)(1) of appendix H of this part) is used, the signal must be de-scribed in terms of its root-mean-square (rms) value.

(d) *Sensing, recording, and reproducing equipment.* (1) The noise levels measured from helicopter flyovers under this appendix may be determined directly by an integrating sound level meter, or the A-weighted sound level time history may be written onto a graphic level recorder set at "slow" response from which the SEL value may be determined. With the approval of the FAA, the noise signal may be tape recorded for subsequent analysis.

(i) The SEL values from each flyover test may be directly determined from an integrating sound level meter complying with the Standards of the International Electrotechnical Commission (IEC) Publication No. 804, "Integrating-averaging Sound Level Meters," as incorporated by reference under §36.6 of this part, for a Type 1 instrument set at "slow" response.

(ii) The acoustic signal from the helicopter, along with the calibration signals specified under paragraph (e) of this section and the background noise signal required under paragraph (f) of this section may be recorded on a magnetic tape recorder for subsequent analysis by an integrating sound level meter identified in paragraph (d)(1)(i) of this section. The record/playback system (including the audio tape) of the tape recorder must conform to the requirements prescribed in section H36.109(c)(3) of appendix H of this part. The tape recorder shall comply with specifications of IEC Publication No. 561, "Electro-acoustical Measuring Equipment for Aircraft Noise Certification," as incorporated by reference under §36.6 of this part.

(iii) The characteristics of the complete system shall comply with the recommendations given in IEC Publication No. 651, "Sound Level Meters," as incorporated by reference under §36.6 of this part, with regard to the specifications concerning microphone, amplifier, and indicating instrument characteristics.

(iv) The response of the complete system to a sensibly plane progressive wave of constant amplitude shall lie within the tolerance limits specified in Table IV and Table V for Type 1 instruments in IEC Publication No. 651, "Sound Level Meters," as incorporated by reference under §36.6 of this part, for weighting curve "A" over the frequency range of 45 Hz to 11500 Hz.

(v) A windscreen must be used with the microphone during each measurement of the helicopter flyover noise. Correction for any insertion loss produced by the windscreen, as a function of the frequency of the acoustic calibration required under paragraph (e) of this section, must be applied to the measured data and any correction applied must be reported.

(e) *Calibrations.* (1) If the helicopter acoustic signal is tape recorded for subsequent analysis, the measuring system and components of the recording system must be calibrated as prescribed under section H36.109(e) of appendix H of this part.

(2) If the helicopter acoustic signal is directly measured by an integrating sound level meter:

(i) The overall sensitivity of the measuring system shall be checked before and after the series of flyover tests and at intervals (not exceeding one-hour duration) during the flyover tests using an acoustic calibrator using sine wave noise generating a known sound pressure level at a known frequency.

(ii) The performance of equipment in the system will be considered satisfactory if, during each day's testing, the variation in the calibration value does not exceed 0.5 dB. The SEL data collected during the flyover tests shall be adjusted to account for any variation in the calibration value.

(iii) A performance calibration analysis of each piece of calibration equipment, including acoustic calibrators, reference microphones, and voltage insertion devices, must have been made during the six calendar months proceeding the beginning of the helicopter flyover series. Each calibration shall be traceable to the National Institute of Standards and Technology.

(f) *Noise measurement procedures.* (1) The microphone shall be of the pressure-sensitive capacitive type designed for nearly uniform grazing incidence response. The microphone shall be mounted with the center of the sensing element 4 feet (1.2 meters) above the local ground surface and shall be oriented for grazing incidence such that the sensing element, the diaphragm, is substantially in the plane defined by the nominal flight path of the helicopter and the noise measurement station.

(2) If a tape recorder is used, the frequency response of the electrical system must be determined at a level within 10 dB of the full-scale reading used during the test, utilizing pink or pseudorandom noise.

(3) The ambient noise, including both acoustical background and electrical noise of the measurement systems shall be determined in the test area and the system gain set at levels which will be used for helicopter noise measurements. If helicopter sound levels do not exceed the background sound levels by at least 15 dB(A), flyovers at an FAA-approved lower height may be used and the results adjusted to the reference measurement point by an FAA-approved method.

(4) If an integrating sound level meter is used to measure the helicopter noise, the instrument operator shall monitor the continuous A-weighted (slow response) noise levels throughout each flyover to ensure that the SEL integration process includes, at minimum, all of the noise signal between the maximum A-weighted sound level (L_{AMAX}) and the 10 dB down points in the flyover time history. The instrument operator shall note the actual db(A) levels at the start and stop of the SEL integration interval and document these levels along with the value of L_{AMAX} and the integration interval (in seconds) for inclusion in the noise data submitted as part of the reporting requirements under section J36.111(b) of this appendix.

Section J36.111   Reporting Requirements

(a) *General.* Data representing physical measurements, and corrections to measured data, including corrections to measurements for equipment response deviations, must be recorded in permanent form and appended to the record. Each correction is subject to FAA approval.

(b) *Data reporting.* After the completion of the test the following data must be included in the test report furnished to the FAA:

(1) Measured and corrected sound levels obtained with equipment conforming to the standards prescribed in section J36.109 of this appendix;

(2) The type of equipment used for measurement and analysis of all acoustic, aircraft performance and flight path, and meteorological data;

(3) The atmospheric environmental data required to demonstrate compliance with this appendix, measured throughout the test period;

(4) Conditions of local topography, ground cover, or events which may interfere with the sound recording;

(5) The following helicopter information:

(i) Type, model, and serial numbers, if any, of helicopter, engine(s) and rotor(s);

(ii) Gross dimensions of helicopter, location of engines, rotors, type of antitorque system, number of blades for each rotor, and reference operating conditions for each engine and rotor;

(iii) Any modifications of non-standard equipment likely to affect the noise characteristics of the helicopter;

(iv) Maximum takeoff weight for which certification under this appendix is requested;

(v) Aircraft configuration, including landing gear positions;

(vi) V_H or V_{NE} (whichever is less) and the adjusted reference airspeed;

(vii) Aircraft gross weight for each test run;

(viii) Indicated and true airspeed for each test run;

(ix) Ground speed, if measured, for each run;

(x) Helicopter engine performance as determined from aircraft instruments and manufacturer's data; and

(xi) Aircraft flight path above ground level, referenced to the elevation of the noise measurement station, in feet, determined by an FAA-approved method which is independent of normal flight instrumentation, such as radar tracking, theodolite triangulation, laser trajectography, or photoscaling techniques; and

(6) Helicopter position and performance data required to make the adjustments prescribed under section J36.205 of this appendix and to demonstrate compliance with the performance and position restrictions prescribed under section J36.105 of this appendix must be recorded at an FAA-approved sampling rate.

Section J36.113 [Reserved]

PART C—NOISE EVALUATION AND CALCULATIONS UNDER § 36.803

Section J36.201　Noise Evaluation in SEL

The noise evaluation measure shall be the sound exposure level (SEL) in units of dB(A) as prescribed under section J36.109(b) of this appendix. The SEL value for each flyover may be directly determined by use of an integrating sound level meter. Specifications for the integrating sound level meter and requirements governing the use of such instrumentation are prescribed under section J36.109 of this appendix.

Section J36.203　Calculation of Noise Levels

(a) To demonstrate compliance with the noise level limits specified under section J36.305 of this appendix, the SEL noise levels from each valid flyover, corrected as necessary to reference conditions under section J36.205 of this appendix, must be arithmetically averaged to obtain a single SEL dB(A) mean value for the flyover series. No individual flyover run may be omitted from the averaging process, unless otherwise specified or approved by the FAA.

(b) The minimum sample size acceptable for the helicopter flyover certification measurements is six. The number of samples must be large enough to establish statistically a 90 percent confidence limit that does not exceed ±1.5 dB(A).

(c) All data used and calculations performed under this section, including the calculated 90 percent confidence limits, must be documented and provided under the reporting requirements of section J36.111 of this appendix.

Section J36.205　Detailed Data Correction Procedures

(a) When certification test conditions measured under part B of this appendix differ from the reference test conditions prescribed under section J36.3 of this appendix, appropriate adjustments shall be made to the measured noise data in accordance with the methods set out in paragraphs (b) and (c) of this section. At minimum, appropriate adjustments shall be made for off-reference altitude and for the difference between reference airspeed and adjusted reference airspeed.

(b) The adjustment for off-reference altitude may be approximated from:

$$\langle delta \rangle J_1 = 12.5 \log_{10}(H_T/492) \text{ dB};$$

where $\langle delta \rangle J_1$ is the quantity in decibels that must be algebraically added to the measured SEL noise level to correct for an off-reference flight path, H_T is the height, in feet, of the test helicopter when directly over the noise measurement point, and the constant (12.5) accounts for the effects on spherical spreading and duration from the off-reference altitude.

(c) The adjustment for the difference between reference airspeed and adjusted reference airspeed is calculated from:

$$\langle delta \rangle J_3 = 10 \log_{10}(V_{RA}/V_R) \text{ dB};$$

Where $\langle delta \rangle J_3$ is the quantity in decibels that must be algebraically added to the measured SEL noise level to correct for the influence of the adjustment of the reference airspeed on the duration of the measured flyover event as perceived at the noise measurement station, V_R is the reference airspeed as prescribed under section J36.3.(c) of this appendix, and V_{RA} is the adjusted reference airspeed as prescribed under section J36.105(c) of this appendix.

(d) No correction for source noise during the flyover other than the variation of source noise accounted for by the adjustment of the reference airspeed prescribed for under section J36.105(c) of this appendix need be applied.

(e) No correction for the difference between the reference ground speed and the actual ground speed need be applied.

(f) No correction for off-reference atmospheric attenuation need be applied.

(g) The SEL adjustments must be less than 2.0 dB(A) for differences between test and reference flight procedures prescribed under section J36.105 of this appendix unless a larger adjustment value is approved by the FAA.

(h) All data used and calculations performed under this section must be documented and provided under the reporting requirements specified under section J36.111 of this appendix.

PART D—NOISE LIMITS PROCEDURE UNDER § 36.805

Section J36.301　Noise Measurement, Evaluation, and Calculation

Compliance with this part of this appendix must be shown with noise levels measured, evaluated, and calculated as prescribed under parts B and C of this appendix.

Section J36.303 [Reserved]

Section J36.305 Noise Limits

For compliance with this appendix, the calculated noise levels of the helicopter, at the measuring point described in section J36.101 of this appendix, must be shown to not exceed the following (with appropriate interpolation between weights):

(a) For primary, normal, transport, and restricted category helicopters having a maximum certificated takeoff weight of not more than 6,000 pounds and noise tested under this appendix, the Stage 2 noise limit is 82 decibels SEL for helicopters with maximum certificated takeoff weight at which the noise certification is requested, of up to 1,764 pounds and increasing at a rate of 3.01 decibels per doubling of weight thereafter. The limit may be calculated by the equation:

$L_{AE(limit)}=82+3.01[\log_{10}(MTOW/1764)/\log_{10}(2)]$ dB;

where MTOW is the maximum takeoff weight, in pounds, for which certification under this appendix is requested.

(b) The procedures required in this amendment shall be done in accordance with the International Electrotechnical Commission IEC Publication No. 804, entitled "Integrating-averaging Sound Level Meters," First Edition, dated 1985. This incorporation by reference was approved by the Director of the Federal Register in accordance with 5 U.S.C. 552(a) and 1 CFR part 51. Copies may be obtained from the Bureau Central de la Commission Electrotechnique Internationale, 1, rue de Varembe, Geneva, Switzerland or the American National Standard Institute, 1430 Broadway, New York City, New York 10018, and can be inspected at the Office of the Federal Register, 800 North Capitol Street NW., suite 700, Washington, DC.

[Doc. No. 26910, 57 FR 42855, Sept. 16, 1992, as amended by Amdt. 36–20, 57 FR 46243, Oct. 7, 1992]

PART 39—AIRWORTHINESS DIRECTIVES

AUTHORITY: 49 U.S.C. 106(g), 40113, 44701.

SOURCE: Doc. No. FAA–2000–8460, 67 FR 48003, July 22, 2002, unless otherwise noted.

§39.1 Purpose of this regulation.

The regulations in this part provide a legal framework for FAA's system of Airworthiness Directives.

§39.3 Definition of airworthiness directives.

FAA's airworthiness directives are legally enforceable rules that apply to the following products: aircraft, aircraft engines, propellers, and appliances.

§39.5 When does FAA issue airworthiness directives?

FAA issues an airworthiness directive addressing a product when we find that:

(a) An unsafe condition exists in the product; and

(b) The condition is likely to exist or develop in other products of the same type design.

§39.7 What is the legal effect of failing to comply with an airworthiness directive?

Anyone who operates a product that does not meet the requirements of an applicable airworthiness directive is in violation of this section.

§39.9 What if I operate an aircraft or use a product that does not meet the requirements of an airworthiness directive?

If the requirements of an airworthiness directive have not been met, you violate §39.7 each time you operate the aircraft or use the product.

§ 39.11 What actions do airworthiness directives require?

Airworthiness directives specify inspections you must carry out, conditions and limitations you must comply with, and any actions you must take to resolve an unsafe condition.

§ 39.13 Are airworthiness directives part of the Code of Federal Regulations?

Yes, airworthiness directives are part of the Code of Federal Regulations, but they are not codified in the annual edition. FAA publishes airworthiness directives in full in the FEDERAL REGISTER as amendments to § 39.13.

EDITORIAL NOTE: For a complete list of citations to airworthiness directives published in the FEDERAL REGISTER, consult the following publications: For airworthiness directives published in the FEDERAL REGISTER since 2001, see the entries for 14 CFR 39.13 in the List of CFR Sections Affected, which appears in the "Finding Aids" section of the printed volume and on GPO Access. For citations to prior amendments, see the entries for 14 CFR 39.13 in the separate publications "List of CFR Sections Affected, 1973–1985," "List of CFR Sections Affected, 1964–1972," and "List of CFR Sections Affected, 1986–2000," and the entries for 14 CFR 507.10 in the "List of Sections Affected, 1949–1963." See also the annual editions of the Federal Register Index for subject matter references and citations to FAA airworthiness directives. For a list of aircraft service documents approved by the Director of the Federal Register for incorporation by reference in this part under 5 U.S.C. 552(a) and 1 CFR 51, see Material Approved for Incorporation by Reference, which appears in the "Finding Aids" section of the printed volume and on GPO Access.

§ 39.15 Does an airworthiness directive apply if the product has been changed?

Yes, an airworthiness directive applies to each product identified in the airworthiness directive, even if an individual product has been changed by modifying, altering, or repairing it in the area addressed by the airworthiness directive.

§ 39.17 What must I do if a change in a product affects my ability to accomplish the actions required in an airworthiness directive?

If a change in a product affects your ability to accomplish the actions required by the airworthiness directive in any way, you must request FAA approval of an alternative method of compliance. Unless you can show the change eliminated the unsafe condition, your request should include the specific actions that you propose to address the unsafe condition. Submit your request in the manner described in § 39.19.

§ 39.19 May I address the unsafe condition in a way other than that set out in the airworthiness directive?

Yes, anyone may propose to FAA an alternative method of compliance or a change in the compliance time, if the proposal provides an acceptable level of safety. Unless FAA authorizes otherwise, send your proposal to your principal inspector. Include the specific actions you are proposing to address the unsafe condition. The principal inspector may add comments and will send your request to the manager of the office identified in the airworthiness directive (manager). You may send a copy to the manager at the same time you send it to the principal inspector. If you do not have a principal inspector send your proposal directly to the manager. You may use the alternative you propose only if the manager approves it.

§ 39.21 Where can I get information about FAA-approved alternative methods of compliance?

Each airworthiness directive identifies the office responsible for approving alternative methods of compliance. That office can provide information about alternatives it has already approved.

§ 39.23 May I fly my aircraft to a repair facility to do the work required by an airworthiness directive?

Yes, the operations specifications giving some operators authority to operate include a provision that allow them to fly their aircraft to a repair facility to do the work required by an airworthiness directive. If you do not have this authority, the local Flight Standards District Office of FAA may issue you a special flight permit unless the airworthiness directive states otherwise. To ensure aviation safety, FAA may add special requirements for operating your aircraft to a place where the repairs or modifications can be accomplished. FAA may also decline to issue a special flight permit in particular cases if we determine you cannot move the aircraft safely.

§ 39.25 How do I get a special flight permit?

Apply to FAA for a special flight permit following the procedures in 14 CFR 21.199.

§ 39.27 What do I do if the airworthiness directive conflicts with the service document on which it is based?

In some cases an airworthiness directive incorporates by reference a manufacturer's service document. In these cases, the service document becomes part of the airworthiness directive. In some cases the directions in the service document may be modified by the airworthiness directive. If there is a conflict between the service document and the airworthiness directive, you must follow the requirements of the airworthiness directive.

PART 43—MAINTENANCE, PREVENTIVE MAINTENANCE, REBUILDING, AND ALTERATION

AUTHORITY: 49 U.S.C. 106(g), 40113, 44701, 44703, 44705, 44707, 44711, 44713, 44717, 44725.

SOURCE: Docket No. 1993, 29 FR 5451, Apr. 23, 1964, unless otherwise noted.

EDITORIAL NOTE: For miscellaneous technical amendments to this part 43, see Amdt. 43–3, 31 FR 3336, Mar. 3, 1966, and Amdt. 43–6, 31 FR 9211, July 6, 1966.

§ 43.1 Applicability.

(a) Except as provided in paragraph (b) of this section, this part prescribes rules governing the maintenance, preventive maintenance, rebuilding, and alteration of any—

(1) Aircraft having a U.S. airworthiness certificate;

(2) Foreign-registered civil aircraft used in common carriage or carriage of mail under the provisions of Part 121 or 135 of this chapter; and

(3) Airframe, aircraft engines, propellers, appliances, and component parts of such aircraft.

(b) This part does not apply to any aircraft for which an experimental airworthiness certificate has been issued, unless a different kind of airworthiness certificate had previously been issued for that aircraft.

(c) This part applies to all life-limited parts that are removed from a type certificated product, segregated, or controlled as provided in § 43.10.

[Doc. No. 1993, 29 FR 5451, Apr. 23, 1964, as amended by Amdt. 43–23, 47 FR 41084, Sept. 16, 1982; Amdt. 43–37, 66 FR 21066, Apr. 27, 2001; Amdt. 43–38, 67 FR 2109, Jan. 15, 2002]

§ 43.2 Records of overhaul and rebuilding.

(a) No person may describe in any required maintenance entry or form an aircraft, airframe, aircraft engine, propeller, appliance, or component part as being overhauled unless—

(1) Using methods, techniques, and practices acceptable to the Administrator, it has been disassembled, cleaned, inspected, repaired as necessary, and reassembled; and

(2) It has been tested in accordance with approved standards and technical data, or in accordance with current standards and technical data accepteble to the Administrator, which have been developed and documented by the holder of the type certificate, supplemental type certificate, or a material, part, process, or applicance approval under § 21.305 of this chapter.

(b) No person may describe in any required maintenace entry or form an aircraft, airframe, aircraft engine, propeller, appliance, or component part as being rebuilt unless it has been disassembled, cleaned, inspected, repaired as necessary, reassembled, and tested to the same tolerances and limits as a new item, using either new parts or used parts that either conform to new part tolerances and limits or to approved oversized or undersized dimensions.

[Amdt. 43–23, 47 FR 41084, Sept. 16, 1982]

§ 43.3 Persons authorized to perform maintenance, preventive maintenance, rebuilding, and alterations.

(a) Except as provided in this section and § 43.17, no person may maintain, rebuild, alter, or perform preventive maintenance on an aircraft, airframe, aircraft engine, propeller, appliance, or component part to which this part applies. Those items, the performance of which is a major alteration, a major repair, or preventive maintenance, are listed in appendix A.

(b) The holder of a mechanic certificate may perform maintenance, pre-

ventive maintenance, and alterations as provided in Part 65 of this chapter.

(c) The holder of a repairman certificate may perform maintenance and preventive maintenance as provided in Part 65 of this chapter.

(d) A person working under the supervision of a holder of a mechanic or repairman certificate may perform the maintenance, preventive maintenance, and alterations that his supervisor is authorized to perform, if the supervisor personally observes the work being done to the extent necessary to ensure that it is being done properly and if the supervisor is readily available, in person, for consultation. However, this paragraph does not authorize the performance of any inspection required by Part 91 or Part 125 of this chapter or any inspection performed after a major repair or alteration.

(e) The holder of a repair station certificate may perform maintenance, preventive maintenance, and alterations as provided in Part 145 of this chapter.

(f) The holder of an air carrier operating certificate or an operating certificate issued under Part 121 or 135, may perform maintenance, preventive maintenance, and alterations as provided in Part 121 or 135.

(g) The holder of a pilot certificate issued under Part 61 may perform preventive maintenance on any aircraft owned or operated by that pilot which is not used under Part 121, 129, or 135.

(h) Notwithstanding the provisions of paragraph (g) of this section, the Administrator may approve a certificate holder under Part 135 of this chapter, operating rotorcraft in a remote area, to allow a pilot to perform specific preventive maintenance items provided—

(1) The items of preventive maintenance are a result of a known or suspected mechanical difficulty or malfunction that occurred en route to or in a remote area;

(2) The pilot has satisfactorily completed an approved training program and is authorized in writing by the certificate holder for each item of preventive maintenance that the pilot is authorized to perform;

(3) There is no certificated mechanic available to perform preventive maintenance;

(4) The certificate holder has procedures to evaluate the accomplishment of a preventive maintenance item that requires a decision concerning the airworthiness of the rotorcraft; and

(5) The items of preventive maintenance authorized by this section are those listed in paragraph (c) of appendix A of this part.

(i) Notwithstanding the provisions of paragraph (g) of this section, in accordance with an approval issued to the holder of a certificate issued under part 135 of this chapter, a pilot of an aircraft type-certificated for 9 or fewer passenger seats, excluding any pilot seat, may perform the removal and reinstallation of approved aircraft cabin seats, approved cabin-mounted stretchers, and when no tools are required, approved cabin-mounted medical oxygen bottles, provided—

(1) The pilot has satisfactorily completed an approved training program and is authorized in writing by the certificate holder to perform each task; and

(2) The certificate holder has written procedures available to the pilot to evaluate the accomplishment of the task.

(j) A manufacturer may—

(1) Rebuild or alter any aircraft, aircraft engine, propeller, or appliance manufactured by him under a type or production certificate;

(2) Rebuild or alter any appliance or part of aircraft, aircraft engines, propellers, or appliances manufactured by him under a Technical Standard Order Authorization, an FAA-Parts Manufacturer Approval, or Product and Process Specification issued by the Administrator; and

(3) Perform any inspection required by Part 91 or Part 125 of this chapter on aircraft it manufacturers, while currently operating under a production certificate or under a currently approved production inspection system for such aircraft.

[Doc. No. 1993, 29 FR 5451, Apr. 23, 1964, as amended by Amdt. 43–4, 31 FR 5249, Apr. 1, 1966; Amdt. 43–23, 47 FR 41084, Sept. 16, 1982; Amdt. 43–25, 51 FR 40702, Nov. 7, 1986; Amdt. 43–36, 61 FR 19501, May 1, 1996; Amdt. 43–37, 66 FR 21066, Apr. 27, 2001]

§43.5 Approval for return to service after maintenance, preventive maintenance, rebuilding, or alteration.

No person may approve for return to service any aircraft, airframe, aircraft engine, propeller, or appliance, that has undergone maintenance, preventive maintenance, rebuilding, or alteration unless—

(a) The maintenance record entry required by §43.9 or §43.11, as appropriate, has been made;

(b) The repair or alteration form authorized by or furnished by the Administrator has been executed in a manner prescribed by the Administrator; and

(c) If a repair or an alteration results in any change in the aircraft operating limitations or flight data contained in the approved aircraft flight manual, those operating limitations or flight data are appropriately revised and set forth as prescribed in §91.9 of this chapter.

[Doc. No. 1993, 29 FR 5451, Apr. 23, 1964, as amended by Amdt. 43–23, 47 FR 41084, Sept. 16, 1982; Amdt. 43–31, 54 FR 34330, Aug. 18, 1989]

§43.7 Persons authorized to approve aircraft, airframes, aircraft engines, propellers, appliances, or component parts for return to service after maintenance, preventive maintenance, rebuilding, or alteration.

(a) Except as provided in this section and §43.17, no person, other than the Administrator, may approve an aircraft, airframe, aircraft engine, propeller, appliance, or component part for return to service after it has undergone maintenance, preventive maintenance, rebuilding, or alteration.

(b) The holder of a mechanic certificate or an inspection authorization may approve an aircraft, airframe, aircraft engine, propeller, appliance, or component part for return to service as provided in Part 65 of this chapter.

(c) The holder of a repair station certificate may approve an aircraft, airframe, aircraft engine, propeller, appliance, or component part for return to service as provided in Part 145 of this chapter.

(d) A manufacturer may approve for return to service any aircraft, airframe, aircraft engine, propeller, appliance, or component part which that manufacturer has worked on under § 43.3(j). However, except for minor alterations, the work must have been done in accordance with technical data approved by the Administrator.

(e) The holder of an air carrier operating certificate or an operating certificate issued under Part 121 or 135, may approve an aircraft, airframe, aircraft engine, propeller, appliance, or component part for return to service as provided in Part 121 or 135 of this chapter, as applicable.

(f) A person holding at least a private pilot certificate may approve an aircraft for return to service after performing preventive maintenance under the provisions of § 43.3(g).

[Amdt. 43–23, 47 FR 41084, Sept. 16, 1982, as amended by Amdt. 43–36, 61 FR 19501, May 1, 1996; Amdt. 43–37, 66 FR 21066, Apr. 27, 2001]

§ 43.9 Content, form, and disposition of maintenance, preventive maintenance, rebuilding, and alteration records (except inspections performed in accordance with part 91, part 123, part 125, § 135.411(a)(1), and § 135.419 of this chapter).

(a) *Maintenance record entries.* Except as provided in paragraphs (b) and (c) of this section, each person who maintains, performs preventive maintenance, rebuilds, or alters an aircraft, airframe, aircraft engine, propeller, appliance, or component part shall make an entry in the maintenance record of that equipment containing the following information:

(1) A description (or reference to data acceptable to the Administrator) of work performed.

(2) The date of completion of the work performed.

(3) The name of the person performing the work if other than the person specified in paragraph (a)(4) of this section.

(4) If the work performed on the aircraft, airframe, aircraft engine, propeller, appliance, or component part has been performed satisfactorily, the signature, certificate number, and kind of certificate held by the person approving the work. The signature con-

stitutes the approval for return to service only for the work performed.

In addition to the entry required by this paragraph, major repairs and major alterations shall be entered on a form, and the form disposed of, in the manner prescribed in appendix B, by the person performing the work.

(b) Each holder of an air carrier operating certificate or an operating certificate issued under Part 121 or 135, that is required by its approved operations specifications to provide for a continuous airworthiness maintenance program, shall make a record of the maintenance, preventive maintenance, rebuilding, and alteration, on aircraft, airframes, aircraft engines, propellers, appliances, or component parts which it operates in accordance with the applicable provisions of Part 121 or 135 of this chapter, as appropriate.

(c) This section does not apply to persons performing inspections in accordance with Part 91, 123, 125, § 135.411(a)(1), or § 135.419 of this chapter.

[Amdt. 43–23, 47 FR 41085, Sept. 16, 1982, as amended by Amdt. 43–37, 66 FR 21066, Apr. 27, 2001]

§ 43.10 Disposition of life-limited aircraft parts.

(a) *Definitions used in this section.* For the purposes of this section the following definitions apply.

Life-limited part means any part for which a mandatory replacement limit is specified in the type design, the Instructions for Continued Airworthiness, or the maintenance manual.

Life status means the accumulated cycles, hours, or any other mandatory replacement limit of a life-limited part.

(b) *Temporary removal of parts from type-certificated products.* When a life-limited part is temporarily removed and reinstalled for the purpose of performing maintenance, no disposition under paragraph (c) of this section is required if—

(1) The life status of the part has not changed;

(2) The removal and reinstallation is performed on the same serial numbered product; and

(3) That product does not accumulate time in service while the part is removed.

(c) *Disposition of parts removed from type-certificated products.* Except as provided in paragraph (b) of this section, after April 15, 2002 each person who removes a life-limited part from a type-certificated product must ensure that the part is controlled using one of the methods in this paragraph. The method must deter the installation of the part after it has reached its life limit. Acceptable methods include:

(1) *Record keeping system.* The part may be controlled using a record keeping system that substantiates the part number, serial number, and current life status of the part. Each time the part is removed from a type certificated product, the record must be updated with the current life status. This system may include electronic, paper, or other means of record keeping.

(2) *Tag or record attached to part.* A tag or other record may be attached to the part. The tag or record must include the part number, serial number, and current life status of the part. Each time the part is removed from a type certificated product, either a new tag or record must be created, or the existing tag or record must be updated with the current life status.

(3) *Non-permanent marking.* The part may be legibly marked using a non-permanent method showing its current life status. The life status must be updated each time the part is removed from a type certificated product, or if the mark is removed, another method in this section may be used. The mark must be accomplished in accordance with the instructions under §45.16 of this chapter in order to maintain the integrity of the part.

(4) *Permanent marking.* The part may be legibly marked using a permanent method showing its current life status. The life status must be updated each time the part is removed from a type certificated product. Unless the part is permanently removed from use on type certificated products, this permanent mark must be accomplished in accordance with the instructions under §45.16 of this chapter in order to maintain the integrity of the part.

(5) *Segregation.* The part may be segregated using methods that deter its installation on a type-certificated product. These methods must include, at least—

(i) Maintaining a record of the part number, serial number, and current life status, and

(ii) Ensuring the part is physically stored separately from parts that are currently eligible for installation.

(6) *Mutilation.* The part may be mutilated to deter its installation in a type certificated produce. The mutilation must render the part beyond repair and incapable of being reworked to appear to be airworthy.

(7) *Other methods.* Any other method approved or accepted by the FAA.

(d) *Transfer of life-limited parts.* Each person who removes a life-limited part from a type certificated product and later sells or otherwise transfers that part must transfer with the part the mark, tag, or other record used to comply with this section, unless the part is mutilated before it is sold or transferred.

[Doc. No. FAA–2000–8017, 67 FR 2110, Jan. 15, 2002]

§43.11 Content, form, and disposition of records for inspections conducted under parts 91 and 125 and §§135.411(a)(1) and 135.419 of this chapter.

(a) *Maintenance record entries.* The person approving or disapproving for return to service an aircraft, airframe, aircraft engine, propeller, appliance, or component part after any inspection performed in accordance with Part 91, 123, 125, §135.411(a)(1), or §135.419 shall make an entry in the maintenance record of that equipment containing the following information:

(1) The type of inspection and a brief description of the extent of the inspection.

(2) The date of the inspection and aircraft total time in service.

(3) The signature, the certificate number, and kind of certificate held by the person approving or disapproving for return to service the aircraft, airframe, aircraft engine, propeller, appliance, component part, or portions thereof.

(4) Except for progressive inspections, if the aircraft is found to be airworthy and approved for return to service, the following or a similarly worded statement—"I certify that this aircraft has been inspected in accordance with (insert type) inspection and was determined to be in airworthy condition."

(5) Except for progressive inspections, if the aircraft is not approved for return to service because of needed maintenance, noncompliance with applicable specifications, airworthiness directives, or other approved data, the following or a similarly worded statement—"I certify that this aircraft has been inspected in accordance with (insert type) inspection and a list of discrepancies and unairworthy items dated (date) has been provided for the aircraft owner or operator."

(6) For progressive inspections, the following or a similarly worded statement—"I certify that in accordance with a progressive inspection program, a routine inspection of (identify whether aircraft or components) and a detailed inspection of (identify components) were performed and the (aircraft or components) are (approved or disapproved) for return to service." If disapproved, the entry will further state "and a list of discrepancies and unairworthy items dated (date) has been provided to the aircraft owner or operator."

(7) If an inspection is conducted under an inspection program provided for in part 91, 123, 125, or § 135.411(a)(1), the entry must identify the inspection program, that part of the inspection program accomplished, and contain a statement that the inspection was performed in accordance with the inspections and procedures for that particular program.

(b) *Listing of discrepancies and placards.* If the person performing any inspection required by part 91 or 125 or § 135.411(a)(1) of this chapter finds that the aircraft is unairworthy or does not meet the applicable type certificate data, airworthiness directives, or other approved data upon which its airworthiness depends, that persons must give the owner or lessee a signed and dated list of those discrepancies. For those items permitted to be inoper-

ative under § 91.213(d)(2) of this chapter, that person shall place a placard, that meets the aircraft's airworthiness certification regulations, on each inoperative instrument and the cockpit control of each item of inoperative equipment, marking it "Inoperative," and shall add the items to the signed and dated list of discrepancies given to the owner or lessee.

[Amdt. 43–23, 47 FR 41085, Sept. 16, 1982, as amended by Amdt. 43–30, 53 FR 50195, Dec. 13, 1988; Amdt. 43–36, 61 FR 19501, May 1, 1996]

§ 43.12 Maintenance records: Falsification, reproduction, or alteration.

(a) No person may make or cause to be made:

(1) Any fraudulent or intentionally false entry in any record or report that is required to be made, kept, or used to show compliance with any requirement under this part;

(2) Any reproduction, for fraudulent purpose, of any record or report under this part; or

(3) Any alteration, for fraudulent purpose, of any record or report under this part.

(b) The commission by any person of an act prohibited under paragraph (a) of this section is a basis for suspending or revoking the applicable airman, operator, or production certificate, Technical Standard Order Authorization, FAA-Parts Manufacturer Approval, or Product and Process Specification issued by the Administrator and held by that person.

[Amdt. 43–19, 43 FR 22639, May 25, 1978, as amended by Amdt. 43–23, 47 FR 41085, Sept. 16, 1982]

§ 43.13 Performance rules (general).

(a) Each person performing maintenance, alteration, or preventive maintenance on an aircraft, engine, propeller, or appliance shall use the methods, techniques, and practices prescribed in the current manufacturer's maintenance manual or Instructions for Continued Airworthiness prepared by its manufacturer, or other methods, techniques, and practices acceptable to the Administrator, except as noted in § 43.16. He shall use the tools, equipment, and test apparatus necessary to assure completion of the work in accordance with accepted industry practices. If special equipment or test apparatus is recommended by the manufacturer involved, he must use that equipment or apparatus or its equivalent acceptable to the Administrator.

(b) Each person maintaining or altering, or performing preventive maintenance, shall do that work in such a manner and use materials of such a quality, that the condition of the aircraft, airframe, aircraft engine, propeller, or appliance worked on will be at least equal to its original or properly altered condition (with regard to aerodynamic function, structural strength, resistance to vibration and deterioration, and other qualities affecting airworthiness).

(c) *Special provisions for holders of air carrier operating certificates and operating certificates issued under the provisions of Part 121 or 135 and Part 129 operators holding operations specifications.* Unless otherwise notified by the administrator, the methods, techniques, and practices contained in the maintenance manual or the maintenance part of the manual of the holder of an air carrier operating certificate or an operating certificate under Part 121 or 135 and Part 129 operators holding operations specifications (that is required by its operating specifications to provide a continuous airworthiness maintenance and inspection program) constitute acceptable means of compliance with this section.

[Doc. No. 1993, 29 FR 5451, Apr. 23, 1964, as amended by Amdt. 43–20, 45 FR 60182, Sept. 11, 1980; Amdt. 43–23, 47 FR 41085, Sept. 16, 1982; Amdt. 43–28, 52 FR 20028, June 16, 1987; Amdt. 43–37, 66 FR 21066, Apr. 27, 2001]

§43.15 Additional performance rules for inspections.

(a) *General.* Each person performing an inspection required by Part 91, 123, 125, or 135 of this chapter, shall—

(1) Perform the inspection so as to determine whether the aircraft, or portion(s) thereof under inspection, meets all applicable airworthiness requirements; and

(2) If the inspection is one provided for in Part 123, 125, 135, or §91.409(e) of this chapter, perform the inspection in accordance with the instructions and procedures set forth in the inspection program for the aircraft being inspected.

(b) *Rotorcraft.* Each person performing an inspection required by Part 91 on a rotorcraft shall inspect the following systems in accordance with the maintenance manual or Instructions for Continued Airworthiness of the manufacturer concerned:

(1) The drive shafts or similar systems.

(2) The main rotor transmission gear box for obvious defects.

(3) The main rotor and center section (or the equivalent area).

(4) The auxiliary rotor on helicopters.

(c) *Annual and 100-hour inspections.* (1) Each person performing an annual or 100-hour inspection shall use a checklist while performing the inspection. The checklist may be of the person's own design, one provided by the manufacturer of the equipment being inspected or one obtained from another source. This checklist must include the scope and detail of the items contained in appendix D to this part and paragraph (b) of this section.

(2) Each person approving a reciprocating-engine-powered aircraft for return to service after an annual or 100-hour inspection shall, before that approval, run the aircraft engine or engines to determine satisfactory performance in accordance with the manufacturer's recommendations of—

(i) Power output (static and idle r.p.m.);

(ii) Magnetos;

(iii) Fuel and oil pressure; and

(iv) Cylinder and oil temperature.

(3) Each person approving a turbine-engine-powered aircraft for return to service after an annual, 100-hour, or progressive inspection shall, before that approval, run the aircraft engine or engines to determine satisfactory performance in accordance with the manufacturer's recommendations.

(d) *Progressive inspection.* (1) Each person performing a progressive inspection shall, at the start of a progressive inspection system, inspect the aircraft completely. After this initial inspection, routine and detailed inspections must be conducted as prescribed in the progressive inspection schedule. Routine inspections consist of visual examination or check of the appliances, the aircraft, and its components and systems, insofar as practicable without disassembly. Detailed inspections consist of a thorough examination of the appliances, the aircraft, and its components and systems, with such disassembly as is necessary. For the purposes of this subparagraph, the overhaul of a component or system is considered to be a detailed inspection.

(2) If the aircraft is away from the station where inspections are normally conducted, an appropriately rated mechanic, a certificated repair station, or the manufacturer of the aircraft may perform inspections in accordance with the procedures and using the forms of the person who would otherwise perform the inspection.

[Doc. No. 1993, 29 FR 5451, Apr. 23, 1964, as amended by Amdt. 43-23, 47 FR 41086, Sept. 16, 1982; Amdt. 43-25, 51 FR 40702, Nov. 7, 1986; Amdt. 43-31, 54 FR 34330, Aug. 18, 1989]

§ 43.16 Airworthiness Limitations.

Each person performing an inspection or other maintenance specified in an Airworthiness Limitations section of a manufacturer's maintenance manual or Instructions for Continued Airworthiness shall perform the inspection or other maintenance in accordance with that section, or in accordance with operations specifications approved by the Administrator under Parts 121, 123, or 135, or an inspection program approved under § 91.409(e).

[Amdt. 43-20, 45 FR 60183, Sept. 11, 1980, as amended by Amdt. 43-23, 47 FR 41086, Sept. 16, 1982; Amdt. 43-31, 54 FR 34330, Aug. 18, 1989; Amdt. 43-37, 66 FR 21066, Apr. 27, 2001]

§ 43.17 Maintenance, preventive maintenance, and alterations performed on U.S. aeronautical products by certain Canadian persons.

(a) *Definitions.* For purposes of this section:

Aeronautical product means any civil aircraft or airframe, aircraft engine, propeller, appliance, component, or part to be installed thereon.

Canadian aeronautical product means any civil aircraft or airframe, aircraft engine, propeller, or appliance under airworthiness regulation by the Cana-

dian Department of Transport, or component or part to be installed thereon.

U.S. aeronautical product means any civil aircraft or airframe, aircraft engine, propeller, or appliance under airworthiness regulation by the FAA, or component or part to be installed thereon.

(b) *Applicability.* This section does not apply to any U.S. aeronautical products maintained or altered under any bilateral agreement made between Canada and any country other than the United States.

(c) *Authorized persons.* (1) A person holding a valid Canadian Department of Transport license (Aircraft Maintenance Engineer) and appropriate ratings may, with respect to a U.S.-registered aircraft located in Canada, perform maintenance, preventive maintenance, and alterations in accordance with the requirements of paragraph (d) of this section and approve the affected aircraft for return to service in accordance with the requirements of paragraph (e) of this section.

(2) A company (Approved Maintenance Organization) (AMO) whose system of quality control for the maintenance, alteration, and inspection of aeronautical products has been approved by the Canadian Department of Transport, or a person who is an authorized employee performing work for such a company may, with respect to a U.S.-registered aircraft located in Canada or other U.S. aeronautical products transported to Canada from the United States, perform maintenance, preventive maintenance, and alterations in accordance with the requirements of paragraph (d) of this section and approve the affected products for return to service in accordance with the requirements of paragraph (e) of this section.

(d) *Performance requirements.* A person authorized in paragraph (c) of this section may perform maintenance (including any inspection required by § 91.409 of this chapter, except an annual inspection), preventive maintenance, and alterations, provided:

(1) The person performing the work is authorized by the Canadian Department of Transport to perform the same type of work with respect to Canadian aeronautical products;

(2) The work is performed in accordance with §§ 43.13, 43.15, and 43.16 of this chapter, as applicable;

(3) The work is performed such that the affected product complies with the applicable requirements of part 36 of this chapter; and

(4) The work is recorded in accordance with §§ 43.2(a), 43.9, and 43.11 of this chapter, as applicable.

(e) *Approval requirements.* (1) To return an affected product to service, a person authorized in paragraph (c) of this section must approve (certify) maintenance, preventive maintenance, and alterations performed under this section, except that an Aircraft Maintenance Engineer may not approve a major repair or major alteration.

(2) An AMO whose system of quality control for the maintenance, preventive maintenance, alteration, and inspection of aeronautical products has been approved by the Canadian Department of Transport, or an authorized employee performing work for such an AMO, may approve (certify) a major repair or major alteration performed under this section if the work was performed in accordance with technical data approved by the Administrator.

(f) No person may operate in air commerce an aircraft, airframe, aircraft engine, propeller, or appliance on which maintenance, preventive maintenance, or alteration has been performed under this section unless it has been approved for return to service by a person authorized in this section.

[Amdt. 43-33, 56 FR 57571, Nov. 12, 1991]

APPENDIX A TO PART 43—MAJOR ALTERATIONS, MAJOR REPAIRS, AND PREVENTIVE MAINTENANCE

(a) *Major alterations*—(1) *Airframe major alterations.* Alterations of the following parts and alterations of the following types, when not listed in the aircraft specifications issued by the FAA, are airframe major alterations:

(i) Wings.

(ii) Tail surfaces.

(iii) Fuselage.

(iv) Engine mounts.

(v) Control system.

(vi) Landing gear.

(vii) Hull or floats.

(viii) Elements of an airframe including spars, ribs, fittings, shock absorbers, bracing, cowling, fairings, and balance weights.

(ix) Hydraulic and electrical actuating system of components.

(x) Rotor blades.

(xi) Changes to the empty weight or empty balance which result in an increase in the maximum certificated weight or center of gravity limits of the aircraft.

(xii) Changes to the basic design of the fuel, oil, cooling, heating, cabin pressurization, electrical, hydraulic, de-icing, or exhaust systems.

(xiii) Changes to the wing or to fixed or movable control surfaces which affect flutter and vibration characteristics.

(2) *Powerplant major alterations.* The following alterations of a powerplant when not listed in the engine specifications issued by the FAA, are powerplant major alterations.

(i) Conversion of an aircraft engine from one approved model to another, involving any changes in compression ratio, propeller reduction gear, impeller gear ratios or the substitution of major engine parts which requires extensive rework and testing of the engine.

(ii) Changes to the engine by replacing aircraft engine structural parts with parts not supplied by the original manufacturer or parts not specifically approved by the Administrator.

(iii) Installation of an accessory which is not approved for the engine.

(iv) Removal of accessories that are listed as required equipment on the aircraft or engine specification.

(v) Installation of structural parts other than the type of parts approved for the installation.

(vi) Conversions of any sort for the purpose of using fuel of a rating or grade other than that listed in the engine specifications.

(3) *Propeller major alterations.* The following alterations of a propeller when not authorized in the propeller specifications issued by the FAA are propeller major alterations:

(i) Changes in blade design.

(ii) Changes in hub design.

(iii) Changes in the governor or control design.

(iv) Installation of a propeller governor or feathering system.

(v) Installation of propeller de-icing system.

(vi) Installation of parts not approved for the propeller.

(4) *Appliance major alterations.* Alterations of the basic design not made in accordance with recommendations of the appliance manufacturer or in accordance with an FAA Airworthiness Directive are appliance major alterations. In addition, changes in the basic design of radio communication and navigation equipment approved under type certification or a Technical Standard Order that have an effect on frequency stability, noise level, sensitivity, selectivity, distortion, spurious radiation, AVC characteristics, or

ability to meet environmental test conditions and other changes that have an effect on the performance of the equipment are also major alterations.

(b) *Major repairs*—(1) *Airframe major repairs.* Repairs to the following parts of an airframe and repairs of the following types, involving the strengthening, reinforcing, splicing, and manufacturing of primary structural members or their replacement, when replacement is by fabrication such as riveting or welding, are airframe major repairs.

(i) Box beams.

(ii) Monocoque or semimonocoque wings or control surfaces.

(iii) Wing stringers or chord members.

(iv) Spars.

(v) Spar flanges.

(vi) Members of truss-type beams.

(vii) Thin sheet webs of beams.

(viii) Keel and chine members of boat hulls or floats.

(ix) Corrugated sheet compression members which act as flange material of wings or tail surfaces.

(x) Wing main ribs and compression members.

(xi) Wing or tail surface brace struts.

(xii) Engine mounts.

(xiii) Fuselage longerons.

(xiv) Members of the side truss, horizontal truss, or bulkheads.

(xv) Main seat support braces and brackets.

(xvi) Landing gear brace struts.

(xvii) Axles.

(xviii) Wheels.

(xix) Skis, and ski pedestals.

(xx) Parts of the control system such as control columns, pedals, shafts, brackets, or horns.

(xxi) Repairs involving the substitution of material.

(xxii) The repair of damaged areas in metal or plywood stressed covering exceeding six inches in any direction.

(xxiii) The repair of portions of skin sheets by making additional seams.

(xxiv) The splicing of skin sheets.

(xxv) The repair of three or more adjacent wing or control surface ribs or the leading edge of wings and control surfaces, between such adjacent ribs.

(xxvi) Repair of fabric covering involving an area greater than that required to repair two adjacent ribs.

(xxvii) Replacement of fabric on fabric covered parts such as wings, fuselages, stabilizers, and control surfaces.

(xxviii) Repairing, including rebottoming, of removable or integral fuel tanks and oil tanks.

(2) *Powerplant major repairs.* Repairs of the following parts of an engine and repairs of the following types, are powerplant major repairs:

(i) Separation or disassembly of a crankcase or crankshaft of a reciprocating engine equipped with an integral supercharger.

(ii) Separation or disassembly of a crankcase or crankshaft of a reciprocating engine equipped with other than spur-type propeller reduction gearing.

(iii) Special repairs to structural engine parts by welding, plating, metalizing, or other methods.

(3) *Propeller major repairs.* Repairs of the following types to a propeller are propeller major repairs:

(i) Any repairs to, or straightening of steel blades.

(ii) Repairing or machining of steel hubs.

(iii) Shortening of blades.

(iv) Retipping of wood propellers.

(v) Replacement of outer laminations on fixed pitch wood propellers.

(vi) Repairing elongated bolt holes in the hub of fixed pitch wood propellers.

(vii) Inlay work on wood blades.

(viii) Repairs to composition blades.

(ix) Replacement of tip fabric.

(x) Replacement of plastic covering.

(xi) Repair of propeller governors.

(xii) Overhaul of controllable pitch propellers.

(xiii) Repairs to deep dents, cuts, scars, nicks, etc., and straightening of aluminum blades.

(xiv) The repair or replacement of internal elements of blades.

(4) *Appliance major repairs.* Repairs of the following types to appliances are appliance major repairs:

(i) Calibration and repair of instruments.

(ii) Calibration of radio equipment.

(iii) Rewinding the field coil of an electrical accessory.

(iv) Complete disassembly of complex hydraulic power valves.

(v) Overhaul of pressure type carburetors, and pressure type fuel, oil and hydraulic pumps.

(c) *Preventive maintenance.* Preventive maintenance is limited to the following work, provided it does not involve complex assembly operations:

(1) Removal, installation, and repair of landing gear tires.

(2) Replacing elastic shock absorber cords on landing gear.

(3) Servicing landing gear shock struts by adding oil, air, or both.

(4) Servicing landing gear wheel bearings, such as cleaning and greasing.

(5) Replacing defective safety wiring or cotter keys.

(6) Lubrication not requiring disassembly other than removal of nonstructural items such as cover plates, cowlings, and fairings.

(7) Making simple fabric patches not requiring rib stitching or the removal of structural parts or control surfaces. In the case of balloons, the making of small fabric repairs

to envelopes (as defined in, and in accordance with, the balloon manufacturers' instructions) not requiring load tape repair or replacement.

(8) Replenishing hydraulic fluid in the hydraulic reservoir.

(9) Refinishing decorative coating of fuselage, balloon baskets, wings tail group surfaces (excluding balanced control surfaces), fairings, cowlings, landing gear, cabin, or cockpit interior when removal or disassembly of any primary structure or operating system is not required.

(10) Applying preservative or protective material to components where no disassembly of any primary structure or operating system is involved and where such coating is not prohibited or is not contrary to good practices.

(11) Repairing upholstery and decorative furnishings of the cabin, cockpit, or balloon basket interior when the repairing does not require disassembly of any primary structure or operating system or interfere with an operating system or affect the primary structure of the aircraft.

(12) Making small simple repairs to fairings, nonstructural cover plates, cowlings, and small patches and reinforcements not changing the contour so as to interfere with proper air flow.

(13) Replacing side windows where that work does not interfere with the structure or any operating system such as controls, electrical equipment, etc.

(14) Replacing safety belts.

(15) Replacing seats or seat parts with replacement parts approved for the aircraft, not involving disassembly of any primary structure or operating system.

(16) Trouble shooting and repairing broken circuits in landing light wiring circuits.

(17) Replacing bulbs, reflectors, and lenses of position and landing lights.

(18) Replacing wheels and skis where no weight and balance computation is involved.

(19) Replacing any cowling not requiring removal of the propeller or disconnection of flight controls.

(20) Replacing or cleaning spark plugs and setting of spark plug gap clearance.

(21) Replacing any hose connection except hydraulic connections.

(22) Replacing prefabricated fuel lines.

(23) Cleaning or replacing fuel and oil strainers or filter elements.

(24) Replacing and servicing batteries.

(25) Cleaning of balloon burner pilot and main nozzles in accordance with the balloon manufacturer's instructions.

(26) Replacement or adjustment of nonstructural standard fasteners incidental to operations.

(27) The interchange of balloon baskets and burners on envelopes when the basket or burner is designated as interchangeable in the balloon type certificate data and the baskets and burners are specifically designed for quick removal and installation.

(28) The installations of anti-misfueling devices to reduce the diameter of fuel tank filler openings provided the specific device has been made a part of the aircraft type certificiate data by the aircraft manufacturer, the aircraft manufacturer has provided FAA-approved instructions for installation of the specific device, and installation does not involve the disassembly of the existing tank filler opening.

(29) Removing, checking, and replacing magnetic chip detectors.

(30) The inspection and maintenance tasks prescribed and specifically identified as preventive maintenance in a primary category aircraft type certificate or supplemental type certificate holder's approved special inspection and preventive maintenance program when accomplished on a primary category aircraft provided:

(i) They are performed by the holder of at least a private pilot certificate issued under part 61 who is the registered owner (including co-owners) of the affected aircraft and who holds a certificate of competency for the affected aircraft (1) issued by a school approved under §147.21(e) of this chapter; (2) issued by the holder of the production certificate for that primary category aircraft that has a special training program approved under §21.24 of this subchapter; or (3) issued by another entity that has a course approved by the Administrator; and

(ii) The inspections and maintenance tasks are performed in accordance with instructions contained by the special inspection and preventive maintenance program approved as part of the aircraft's type design or supplemental type design.

(31) Removing and replacing self-contained, front instrument panel-mounted navigation and communication devices that employ tray-mounted connectors that connect the unit when the unit is installed into the instrument panel, (excluding automatic flight control systems, transponders, and microwave frequency distance measuring equipment (DME)). The approved unit must be designed to be readily and repeatedly removed and replaced, and pertinent instructions must be provided. Prior to the unit's intended use, and operational check must be performed in accordance with the applicable sections of part 91 of this chapter.

(32) Updating self-contained, front instrument panel-mounted Air Traffic Control (ATC) navigational software data bases (excluding those of automatic flight control systems, transponders, and microwave frequency distance measuring equipment (DME)) provided no disassembly of the unit is required and pertinent instructions are provided. Prior to the unit's intended use, an

operational check must be performed in accordance with applicable sections of part 91 of this chapter.

(Secs. 313, 601 through 610, and 1102, Federal Aviation Act of 1958 as amended (49 U.S.C. 1354, 1421 through 1430 and 1502); (49 U.S.C. 106(g) (Revised Pub. L. 97–449, Jan. 21, 1983); and 14 CFR 11.45)

[Doc. No. 1993, 29 FR 5451, Apr. 23, 1964, as amended by Amdt. 43–14, 37 FR 14291, June 19, 1972; Amdt. 43–23, 47 FR 41086, Sept. 16, 1982; Amdt. 43–24, 49 FR 44602, Nov. 7, 1984; Amdt. 43–25, 51 FR 40703, Nov. 7, 1986; Amdt. 43–27, 52 FR 17277, May 6, 1987; Amdt. 43–34, 57 FR 41369, Sept. 9, 1992; Amdt. 43–36, 61 FR 19501, May 1, 1996]

APPENDIX B TO PART 43—RECORDING OF MAJOR REPAIRS AND MAJOR ALTERATIONS

(a) Except as provided in paragraphs (b), (c), and (d) of this appendix, each person performing a major repair or major alteration shall—

(1) Execute FAA Form 337 at least in duplicate;

(2) Give a signed copy of that form to the aircraft owner; and

(3) Forward a copy of that form to the local Flight Standards District Office within 48 hours after the aircraft, airframe, aircraft engine, propeller, or appliance is approved for return to service.

(b) For major repairs made in accordance with a manual or specifications acceptable to the Administrator, a certificated repair station may, in place of the requirements of paragraph (a)—

(1) Use the customer's work order upon which the repair is recorded;

(2) Give the aircraft owner a signed copy of the work order and retain a duplicate copy for at least two years from the date of approval for return to service of the aircraft, airframe, aircraft engine, propeller, or appliance;

(3) Give the aircraft owner a maintenance release signed by an authorized representative of the repair station and incorporating the following information:

(i) Identity of the aircraft, airframe, aircraft engine, propeller or appliance.

(ii) If an aircraft, the make, model, serial number, nationality and registration marks, and location of the repaired area.

(iii) If an airframe, aircraft engine, propeller, or appliance, give the manufacturer's name, name of the part, model, and serial numbers (if any); and

(4) Include the following or a similarly worded statement—

"The aircraft, airframe, aircraft engine, propeller, or appliance identified above was repaired and inspected in accordance with

current Regulations of the Federal Aviation Agency and is approved for return to service.

Pertinent details of the repair are on file at this repair station under Order No. ——,

Date ————————————————
Signed ————————————————

For signature of authorized representative)

Repair station name)   (Certificate No.)
————————————————."

(Address)

(c) For a major repair or major alteration made by a person authorized in §43.17, the person who performs the major repair or major alteration and the person authorized by §43.17 to approve that work shall execute a FAA Form 337 at least in duplicate. A completed copy of that form shall be—

(1) Given to the aircraft owner; and

(2) Forwarded to the Federal Aviation Administration, Aircraft Registration Branch, Post Office Box 25082, Oklahoma City, Okla. 73125, within 48 hours after the work is inspected.

(d) For extended-range fuel tanks installed within the passenger compartment or a baggage compartment, the person who performs the work and the person authorized to approve the work by §43.7 of this part shall execute an FAA Form 337 in at least triplicate. One (1) copy of the FAA Form 337 shall be placed on board the aircraft as specified in §91.417 of this chapter. The remaining forms shall be distributed as required by paragraph (a)(2) and (3) or (c)(1) and (2) of this paragraph as appropriate.

(Secs. 101, 610, 72 Stat. 737, 780, 49 U.S.C. 1301, 1430)

[Doc. No. 1993, 29 FR 5451, Apr. 23, 1964, as amended by Amdt. 43–10, 33 FR 15989, Oct. 31, 1968; Amdt. 43–29, 52 FR 34101, Sept. 7, 1987; Amdt. 43–31, 54 FR 34330, Aug. 18, 1989]

APPENDIX C TO PART 43 [RESERVED]

APPENDIX D TO PART 43—SCOPE AND DETAIL OF ITEMS (AS APPLICABLE TO THE PARTICULAR AIRCRAFT) TO BE INCLUDED IN ANNUAL AND 100-HOUR INSPECTIONS

(a) Each person performing an annual or 100-hour inspection shall, before that inspection, remove or open all necessary inspection plates, access doors, fairing, and cowling. He shall thoroughly clean the aircraft and aircraft engine.

(b) Each person performing an annual or 100-hour inspection shall inspect (where applicable) the following components of the fuselage and hull group:

(1) Fabric and skin—for deterioration, distortion, other evidence of failure, and defective or insecure attachment of fittings.

(2) Systems and components—for improper installation, apparent defects, and unsatisfactory operation.

(3) Envelope, gas bags, ballast tanks, and related parts—for poor condition.

(c) Each person performing an annual or 100-hour inspection shall inspect (where applicable) the following components of the cabin and cockpit group:

(1) Generally—for uncleanliness and loose equipment that might foul the controls.

(2) Seats and safety belts—for poor condition and apparent defects.

(3) Windows and windshields—for deterioration and breakage.

(4) Instruments—for poor condition, mounting, marking, and (where practicable) improper operation.

(5) Flight and engine controls—for improper installation and improper operation.

(6) Batteries—for improper installation and improper charge.

(7) All systems—for improper installation, poor general condition, apparent and obvious defects, and insecurity of attachment.

(d) Each person performing an annual or 100-hour inspection shall inspect (where applicable) components of the engine and nacelle group as follows:

(1) Engine section—for visual evidence of excessive oil, fuel, or hydraulic leaks, and sources of such leaks.

(2) Studs and nuts—for improper torquing and obvious defects.

(3) Internal engine—for cylinder compression and for metal particles or foreign matter on screens and sump drain plugs. If there is weak cylinder compression, for improper internal condition and improper internal tolerances.

(4) Engine mount—for cracks, looseness of mounting, and looseness of engine to mount.

(5) Flexible vibration dampeners—for poor condition and deterioration.

(6) Engine controls—for defects, improper travel, and improper safetying.

(7) Lines, hoses, and clamps—for leaks, improper condition and looseness.

(8) Exhaust stacks—for cracks, defects, and improper attachment.

(9) Accessories—for apparent defects in security of mounting.

(10) All systems—for improper installation, poor general condition, defects, and insecure attachment.

(11) Cowling—for cracks, and defects.

(e) Each person performing an annual or 100-hour inspection shall inspect (where applicable) the following components of the landing gear group:

(1) All units—for poor condition and insecurity of attachment.

(2) Shock absorbing devices—for improper oleo fluid level.

(3) Linkages, trusses, and members—for undue or excessive wear fatigue, and distortion.

(4) Retracting and locking mechanism—for improper operation.

(5) Hydraulic lines—for leakage.

(6) Electrical system—for chafing and improper operation of switches.

(7) Wheels—for cracks, defects, and condition of bearings.

(8) Tires—for wear and cuts.

(9) Brakes—for improper adjustment.

(10) Floats and skis—for insecure attachment and obvious or apparent defects.

(f) Each person performing an annual or 100-hour inspection shall inspect (where applicable) all components of the wing and center section assembly for poor general condition, fabric or skin deterioration, distortion, evidence of failure, and insecurity of attachment.

(g) Each person performing an annual or 100-hour inspection shall inspect (where applicable) all components and systems that make up the complete empennage assembly for poor general condition, fabric or skin deterioration, distortion, evidence of failure, insecure attachment, improper component installation, and improper component operation.

(h) Each person performing an annual or 100-hour inspection shall inspect (where applicable) the following components of the propeller group:

(1) Propeller assembly—for cracks, nicks, binds, and oil leakage.

(2) Bolts—for improper torquing and lack of safetying.

(3) Anti-icing devices—for improper operations and obvious defects.

(4) Control mechanisms—for improper operation, insecure mounting, and restricted travel.

(i) Each person performing an annual or 100-hour inspection shall inspect (where applicable) the following components of the radio group:

(1) Radio and electronic equipment—for improper installation and insecure mounting.

(2) Wiring and conduits—for improper routing, insecure mounting, and obvious defects.

(3) Bonding and shielding—for improper installation and poor condition.

(4) Antenna including trailing antenna—for poor condition, insecure mounting, and improper operation.

(j) Each person performing an annual or 100-hour inspection shall inspect (where applicable) each installed miscellaneous item that is not otherwise covered by this listing for improper installation and improper operation.

APPENDIX E TO PART 43—ALTIMETER
SYSTEM TEST AND INSPECTION

Each person performing the altimeter system tests and inspections required by §91.411 shall comply with the following:

(a) Static pressure system:

(1) Ensure freedom from entrapped moisture and restrictions.

(2) Determine that leakage is within the tolerances established in §23.1325 or §25.1325, whichever is applicable.

(3) Determine that the static port heater, if installed, is operative.

(4) Ensure that no alterations or deformations of the airframe surface have been made that would affect the relationship between air pressure in the static pressure system and true ambient static air pressure for any flight condition.

(b) Altimeter:

(1) Test by an appropriately rated repair facility in accordance with the following subparagraphs. Unless otherwise specified, each test for performance may be conducted with the instrument subjected to vibration. When tests are conducted with the temperature substantially different from ambient temperature of approximately 25 degrees C., allowance shall be made for the variation from the specified condition.

(i) *Scale error.* With the barometric pressure scale at 29.92 inches of mercury, the altimeter shall be subjected successively to pressures corresponding to the altitude specified in Table I up to the maximum normally expected operating altitude of the airplane in which the altimeter is to be installed. The reduction in pressure shall be made at a rate not in excess of 20,000 feet per minute to within approximately 2,000 feet of the test point. The test point shall be approached at a rate compatible with the test equipment. The altimeter shall be kept at the pressure corresponding to each test point for at least 1 minute, but not more than 10 minutes, before a reading is taken. The error at all test points must not exceed the tolerances specified in Table I.

(ii) *Hysteresis.* The hysteresis test shall begin not more than 15 minutes after the altimeter's initial exposure to the pressure corresponding to the upper limit of the scale error test prescribed in subparagraph (i); and while the altimeter is at this pressure, the hysteresis test shall commence. Pressure shall be increased at a rate simulating a descent in altitude at the rate of 5,000 to 20,000 feet per minute until within 3,000 feet of the first test point (50 percent of maximum altitude). The test point shall then be approached at a rate of approximately 3,000 feet per minute. The altimeter shall be kept at this pressure for at least 5 minutes, but not more than 15 minutes, before the test reading is taken. After the reading has been taken, the pressure shall be increased further, in the same manner as before, until the pressure corresponding to the second test point (40 percent of maximum altitude) is reached. The altimeter shall be kept at this pressure for at least 1 minute, but not more than 10 minutes, before the test reading is

taken. After the reading has been taken, the pressure shall be increased further, in the same manner as before, until atmospheric pressure is reached. The reading of the altimeter at either of the two test points shall not differ by more than the tolerance specified in Table II from the reading of the altimeter for the corresponding altitude recorded during the scale error test prescribed in paragraph (b)(i).

(iii) *After effect.* Not more than 5 minutes after the completion of the hysteresis test prescribed in paragraph (b)(ii), the reading of the altimeter (corrected for any change in atmospheric pressure) shall not differ from the original atmospheric pressure reading by more than the tolerance specified in Table II.

(iv) *Friction.* The altimeter shall be subjected to a steady rate of decrease of pressure approximating 750 feet per minute. At each altitude listed in Table III, the change in reading of the pointers after vibration shall not exceed the corresponding tolerance listed in Table III.

(v) *Case leak.* The leakage of the altimeter case, when the pressure within it corresponds to an altitude of 18,000 feet, shall not change the altimeter reading by more than the tolerance shown in Table II during an interval of 1 minute.

(vi) *Barometric scale error.* At constant atmospheric pressure, the barometric pressure scale shall be set at each of the pressures (falling within its range of adjustment) that are listed in Table IV, and shall cause the pointer to indicate the equivalent altitude difference shown in Table IV with a tolerance of 25 feet.

(2) Altimeters which are the air data computer type with associated computing systems, or which incorporate air data correction internally, may be tested in a manner and to specifications developed by the manufacturer which are acceptable to the Administrator.

(c) Automatic Pressure Altitude Reporting Equipment and ATC Transponder System Integration Test. The test must be conducted by an appropriately rated person under the conditions specified in paragraph (a). Measure the automatic pressure altitude at the output of the installed ATC transponder when interrogated on Mode C at a sufficient number of test points to ensure that the altitude reporting equipment, altimeters, and ATC transponders perform their intended functions as installed in the aircraft. The difference between the automatic reporting output and the altitude displayed at the altimeter shall not exceed 125 feet.

(d) Records: Comply with the provisions of §43.9 of this chapter as to content, form, and disposition of the records. The person performing the altimeter tests shall record on the altimeter the date and maximum altitude to which the altimeter has been tested and the persons approving the airplane for return to service shall enter that data in the airplane log or other permanent record.

TABLE I

Altitude	Equivalent pressure (inches of mercury)	Tolerance ±(feet)
—1,000	31.018	20
0	29.921	20
500	29.385	20
1,000	28.856	20
1,500	28.335	25
2,000	27.821	30
3,000	26.817	30
4,000	25.842	35
6,000	23.978	40
8,000	22.225	60
10,000	20.577	80
12,000	19.029	90
14,000	17.577	100
16,000	16.216	110
18,000	14.942	120
20,000	13.750	130
22,000	12.636	140
25,000	11.104	155
30,000	8.885	180
35,000	7.041	205
40,000	5.538	230
45,000	4.355	255
50,000	3.425	280

TABLE II—TEST TOLERANCES

Test	Tolerance (feet)
Case Leak Test	±100
Hysteresis Test:	
First Test Point (50 percent of maximum altitude)	75
Second Test Point (40 percent of maximum altitude)	75
After Effect Test	30

TABLE III—FRICTION

Altitude (feet)	Tolerance (feet)
1,000	±70
2,000	70
3,000	70
5,000	70
10,000	80
15,000	90
20,000	100
25,000	120
30,000	140
35,000	160
40,000	180
50,000	250

TABLE IV—PRESSURE-ALTITUDE DIFFERENCE

Pressure (inches of Hg)	Altitude difference (feet)
28.10	−1,727
28.50	−1,340

TABLE IV—PRESSURE-ALTITUDE DIFFERENCE—Continued

Pressure (inches of Hg)	Altitude difference (feet)
29.00	−863
29.50	−392
29.92	0
30.50	+531
30.90	+893
30.99	+974

(Secs. 313, 314, and 601 through 610 of the Federal Aviation Act of 1958 (49 U.S.C. 1354, 1355, and 1421 through 1430) and sec. 6(c), Dept. of Transportation Act (49 U.S.C. 1655(c)))

[Amdt. 43–2, 30 FR 8262, June 29, 1965, as amended by Amdt. 43–7, 32 FR 7587, May 24, 1967; Amdt. 43–19, 43 FR 22639, May 25, 1978; Amdt. 43–23, 47 FR 41086, Sept. 16, 1982; Amdt. 43–31, 54 FR 34330, Aug. 18, 1989]

APPENDIX F TO PART 43—ATC TRANSPONDER TESTS AND INSPECTIONS

The ATC transponder tests required by §91.413 of this chapter may be conducted using a bench check or portable test equipment and must meet the requirements prescribed in paragraphs (a) through (j) of this appendix. If portable test equipment with appropriate coupling to the aircraft antenna system is used, operate the test equipment for ATCRBS transponders at a nominal rate of 235 interrogations per second to avoid possible ATCRBS interference. Operate the test equipment at a nominal rate of 50 Mode S interrogations per second for Mode S. An additional 3 dB loss is allowed to compensate for antenna coupling errors during receiver sensitivity measurements conducted in accordance with paragraph (c)(1) when using portable test equipment.

(a) Radio Reply Frequency:

(1) For all classes of ATCRBS transponders, interrogate the transponder and verify that the reply frequency is 1090±3 Megahertz (MHz).

(2) For classes 1B, 2B, and 3B Mode S transponders, interrogate the transponder and verify that the reply frequency is 1090±3 MHz.

(3) For classes 1B, 2B, and 3B Mode S transponders that incorporate the optional 1090±1 MHz reply frequency, interrogate the transponder and verify that the reply frequency is correct.

(4) For classes 1A, 2A, 3A, and 4 Mode S transponders, interrogate the transponder and verify that the reply frequency is 1090±1 MHz.

(b) Suppression: When Classes 1B and 2B ATCRBS Transponders, or Classes 1B, 2B, and 3B Mode S transponders are interrogated Mode 3/A at an interrogation rate between 230 and 1,000 interrogations per second; or when Classes 1A and 2A ATCRBS Transponders, or Classes 1B, 2A, 3A, and 4 Mode S transponders are interrogated at a rate between 230 and 1,200 Mode 3/A interrogations per second:

(1) Verify that the transponder does not respond to more than 1 percent of ATCRBS interrogations when the amplitude of P2 pulse is equal to the P1 pulse.

(2) Verify that the transponder replies to at least 90 percent of ATCRBS interrogations when the amplitude of the P2 pulse is 9 dB less than the P1 pulse. If the test is conducted with a radiated test signal, the interrogation rate shall be 235±5 interrogations per second unless a higher rate has been approved for the test equipment used at that location.

(c) Receiver Sensitivity:

(1) Verify that for any class of ATCRBS Transponder, the receiver minimum triggering level (MTL) of the system is −73±4 dbm, or that for any class of Mode S transponder the receiver MTL for Mode S format (P6 type) interrogations is −74±3 dbm by use of a test set either:

(i) Connected to the antenna end of the transmission line;

(ii) Connected to the antenna terminal of the transponder with a correction for transmission line loss; or

(iii) Utilized radiated signal.

(2) Verify that the difference in Mode 3/A and Mode C receiver sensitivity does not exceed 1 db for either any class of ATCRBS transponder or any class of Mode S transponder.

(d) Radio Frequency (RF) Peak Output Power:

(1) Verify that the transponder RF output power is within specifications for the class of transponder. Use the same conditions as described in (c)(1)(i), (ii), and (iii) above.

(i) For Class 1A and 2A ATCRBS transponders, verify that the minimum RF peak output power is at least 21.0 dbw (125 watts).

(ii) For Class 1B and 2B ATCRBS Transponders, verify that the minimum RF peak output power is at least 18.5 dbw (70 watts).

(iii) For Class 1A, 2A, 3A, and 4 and those Class 1B, 2B, and 3B Mode S transponders that include the optional high RF peak output power, verify that the minimum RF peak output power is at least 21.0 dbw (125 watts).

(iv) For Classes 1B, 2B, and 3B Mode S transponders, verify that the minimum RF peak output power is at least 18.5 dbw (70 watts).

(v) For any class of ATCRBS or any class of Mode S transponders, verify that the maximum RF peak output power does not exceed 27.0 dbw (500 watts).

NOTE: The tests in (e) through (j) apply only to Mode S transponders.

(e) Mode S Diversity Transmission Channel Isolation: For any class of Mode S transponder that incorporates diversity operation,

verify that the RF peak output power transmitted from the selected antenna exceeds the power transmitted from the nonselected antenna by at least 20 db.

(f) Mode S Address: Interrogate the Mode S transponder and verify that it replies only to its assigned address. Use the correct address and at least two incorrect addresses. The interrogations should be made at a nominal rate of 50 interrogations per second.

(g) Mode S Formats: Interrogate the Mode S transponder with uplink formats (UF) for which it is equipped and verify that the replies are made in the correct format. Use the surveillance formats UF=4 and 5. Verify that the altitude reported in the replies to UF=4 are the same as that reported in a valid ATCRBS Mode C reply. Verify that the identity reported in the replies to UF=5 are the same as that reported in a valid ATCRBS Mode 3/A reply. If the transponder is so equipped, use the communication formats UF=20, 21, and 24.

(h) Mode S All-Call Interrogations: Interrogate the Mode S transponder with the Mode S-only all-call format UF=11, and the ATCRBS/Mode S all-call formats (1.6 microsecond P4 pulse) and verify that the correct address and capability are reported in the replies (downlink format DF=11).

(i) ATCRBS-Only All-Call Interrogation: Interrogate the Mode S transponder with the ATCRBS-only all-call interrogation (0.8 microsecond P4 pulse) and verify that no reply is generated.

(j) Squitter: Verify that the Mode S transponder generates a correct squitter approximately once per second.

(k) Records: Comply with the provisions of §43.9 of this chapter as to content, form, and disposition of the records.

[Amdt. 43–26, 52 FR 3390, Feb. 3, 1987; 52 FR 6651, Mar. 4, 1987, as amended by Amdt. 43–31, 54 FR 34330, Aug. 18, 1989]

PART 45—IDENTIFICATION AND REGISTRATION MARKING

Subpart A—General

Subpart B—Identification of Aircraft and Related Products

Subpart C—Nationality and Registration Marks

AUTHORITY: 49 U.S.C. 106(g), 40103, 44109, 40113–40114, 44101–44105, 44107–44108, 44110–44111, 44504, 44701, 44708–44709, 44711–44713, 44725, 45302–45303, 46104, 46304, 46306, 47122.

SOURCE: Docket No. 2047, 29 FR 3223, Mar. 11, 1964, unless otherwise noted.

Subpart A—General

§ 45.1 Applicability.

This part prescribes the requirements for—

(a) Identification of aircraft, and identification of aircraft engines and propellers that are manufactured under the terms of a type or production certificate:

(b) Identification of certain replacement and modified parts produced for installation on type certificated products; and

(c) Nationality and registration marking of U.S. registered aircraft.

[Doc. No. 2047, 29 FR 3223, Mar. 11, 1964, as amended by Amdt. 45–3, 32 FR 188, Jan. 10, 1967]

Subpart B—Identification of Aircraft and Related Products

§ 45.11 General.

(a) *Aircraft and aircraft engines.* Aircraft covered under § 21.182 of this chapter must be identified, and each person who manufacturers an aircraft engine under a type or production certificate shall identify that engine, by means of a fireproof plate that has the information specified in § 45.13 of this part marked on it by etching, stamping, engraving, or other approved method of fireproof marking. The identification plate for aircraft must be secured in such a manner that it will not likely be defaced or removed during normal service, or lost or destroyed in an accident. Except as provided in paragraphs (c) and (d) of this section, the aircraft identification plate must be secured to the aircraft fuselage exterior so that it is legible to a person on the ground, and must be either adjacent to and aft of the rear-most entrance door or on the fuselage surface near the tail surfaces. For aircraft engines, the identification plate must be affixed to the engine at an accessible location in such a manner that it will not likely be defaced or removed during normal service, or lost or destroyed in an accident.

(b) *Propellers and propeller blades and hubs.* Each person who manufactures a propeller, propeller blade, or propeller hub under the terms of a type or production certificate shall identify his product by means of a plate, stamping, engraving, etching, or other approved method of fireproof identification that is placed on it on a noncritical surface, contains the information specified in § 45.13, and will not be likely to be defaced or removed during normal service or lost or destroyed in an accident.

(c) For manned free balloons, the identification plate prescribed in paragraph (a) of this section must be secured to the balloon envelope and must be located, if practicable, where it is legible to the operator when the balloon is inflated. In addition, the basket and heater assembly must be permanently and legibly marked with the manufacturer's name, part number (or equivalent) and serial number (or equivalent).

(d) On aircraft manufactured before March 7, 1988, the identification plate required by paragraph (a) of this section may be secured at an accessible exterior or interior location near an entrance, if the model designation and builder's serial number are also displayed on the aircraft fuselage exterior. The model designation and builder's serial number must be legible to a person on the ground and must be located either adjacent to and aft of the rear-most entrance door or on the fuselage near the tail surfaces. The model designation and builder's serial number must be displayed in such a manner that they are not likely to be defaced or removed during normal service.

[Amdt. 45–3, 32 FR 188, Jan. 10, 1967 as amended by Amdt. 45–7, 33 FR 14402, Sept. 25, 1968; Amdt. 45–12, 45 FR 60183, Sept. 11, 1980; 45 FR 85597, Dec. 29, 1980; Amdt. 45–17, 52 FR 34101, Sept. 9, 1987; 52 FR 36566, Sept. 30, 1987]

§ 45.13 Identification data.

(a) The identification required by § 45.11 (a) and (b) shall include the following information:

(1) Builder's name.

(2) Model designation.

(3) Builder's serial number.

(4) Type certificate number, if any.

(5) Production certificate number, if any.

(6) For aircraft engines, the established rating.

(7) On or after January 1, 1984, for aircraft engines specified in part 34 of this chapter, the date of manufacture as defined in § 34.1 of that part, and a designation, approved by the Administrator of the FAA, that indicates compliance with the applicable exhaust emission provisions of part 34 and 40 CFR part 87. Approved designations include COMPLY, EXEMPT, and NON-US as appropriate.

(i) The designation COMPLY indicates that the engine is in compliance with all of the applicable exhaust emissions provisions of part 34. For any engine with a rated thrust in excess of 26.7 kilonewtons (6000 pounds) which is not used or intended for use in commercial operations and which is in compliance with the applicable provisions of part 34, but does not comply with the hydrocarbon emissions standard of § 34.21(d), the statement "May not be used as a commercial aircraft engine" must be noted in the permanent powerplant record that accompanies the engine at the time of manufacture of the engine.

(ii) The designation EXEMPT indicates that the engine has been granted an exemption pursuant to the applicable provision of § 34.7 (a)(1), (a)(4), (b), (c), or (d), and an indication of the type of exemption and the reason for the grant must be noted in the permanent powerplant record that accompanies the engine from the time of manufacture of the engine.

(iii) The designation NON-US indicates that the engine has been granted an exemption pursuant to § 34.7(a)(1), and the notation "This aircraft may not be operated within the United States", or an equivalent notation approved by the Administrator of the FAA, must be inserted in the aircraft logbook, or alternate equivalent document, at the time of installation of the engine.

(8) Any other information the Administrator finds appropriate.

(b) Except as provided in paragraph (d)(1) of this section, no person may remove, change, or place identification information required by paragraph (a) of this section, on any aircraft, aircraft engine, propeller, propeller blade, or propeller hub, without the approval of the Administrator.

(c) Except as provided in paragraph (d)(2) of this section, no person may remove or install any identification plate required by § 45.11 of this part, without the approval of the Administrator.

(d) Persons performing work under the provisions of Part 43 of this chapter may, in accordance with methods, techniques, and practices acceptable to the Administrator—

(1) Remove, change, or place the identification information required by paragraph (a) of this section on any aircraft, aircraft engine, propeller, propeller blade, or propeller hub; or

(2) Remove an identification plate required by § 45.11 when necessary during maintenance operations.

(e) No person may install an identification plate removed in accordance with paragraph (d)(2) of this section on any aircraft, aircraft engine, propeller, propeller blade, or propeller hub other than the one from which it was removed.

[Amdt. 45–3, 32 FR 188, Jan. 10, 1967, as amended by Amdt. 45–10, 44 FR 45379, Aug. 2, 1979; Amdt. 45–12, 45 FR 60183, Sept. 11, 1980; Amdt. 45–20, 55 FR 32861, Aug. 10, 1990; 55 FR 37287, Sept. 10, 1990]

§ 45.14 Identification of critical components.

Each person who produces a part for which a replacement time, inspection interval, or related procedure is specified in the Airworthiness Limitations section of a manufacturer's maintenance manual or Instructions for Continued Airworthiness shall permanently and legibly mark that component with a part number (or equivalent) and a serial number (or equivalent).

[Amdt. 45–16, 51 FR 40703, Nov. 7, 1986]

§45.15 Replacement and modification parts.

(a) Except as provided in paragraph (b) of this section, each person who produces a replacement or modification part under a Parts Manufacturer Approval issued under §21.303 of this chapter shall permanently and legibly mark the part with—

(1) The letters "FAA–PMA";

(2) The name, trademark, or symbol of the holder of the Parts Manufacturer Approval;

(3) The part number; and

(4) The name and model designation of each type certificated product on which the part is eligible for installation.

(b) If the Administrator finds that a part is too small or that it is otherwise impractical to mark a part with any of the information required by paragraph (a) of this section, a tag attached to the part or its container must include the information that could not be marked on the part. If the marking required by paragraph (a)(4) of this section is so extensive that to mark it on a tag is impractical, the tag attached to the part or the container may refer to a specific readily available manual or catalog for part eligibility information.

[Amdt. 45–8, 37 FR 10660, May 26, 1972, as amended by Amdt. 45–14, 47 FR 13315, Mar. 29, 1982]

§45.16 Marking of life-limited parts.

When requested by a person required to comply with §43.10 of this chapter, the holder of a type certificate or design approval for a life-limited part must provide marking instructions, or must state that the part cannot be practicably marked without compromising its integrity. Compliance with this paragraph may be made by providing marking instructions in readily available documents, such as the maintenance manual or the Instructions for Continued Airworthiness.

[Doc. No. FAA–200–8017, 67 FR 2110, Jan. 15, 2002]

Subpart C—Nationality and Registration Marks

§45.21 General.

(a) Except as provided in §45.22, no person may operate a U.S.-registered aircraft unless that aircraft displays nationality and registration marks in accordance with the requirements of this section and §§45.23 through 45.33.

(b) Unless otherwise authorized by the Administrator, no person may place on any aircraft a design, mark, or symbol that modifies or confuses the nationality and registration marks.

(c) Aircraft nationality and registration marks must—

(1) Except as provided in paragraph (d) of this section, be painted on the aircraft or affixed by any other means insuring a similar degree of permanence;

(2) Have no ornamentation;

(3) Contrast in color with the background; and

(4) Be legible.

(d) The aircraft nationality and registration marks may be affixed to an aircraft with readily removable material if—

(1) It is intended for immediate delivery to a foreign purchaser;

(2) It is bearing a temporary registration number; or

(3) It is marked temporarily to meet the requirements of §45.22(c)(1) or §45.29(h) of this part, or both.

[Doc. No. 8093, Amdt. 45–5, 33 FR 450, Jan 12, 1968, as amended by Amdt. 45–17, 52 FR 34102, Sept. 9, 1987]

§45.22 Exhibition, antique, and other aircraft: Special rules.

(a) When display of aircraft nationality and registration marks in accordance with §§45.21 and 45.23 through 45.33 would be inconsistent with exhibition of that aircraft, a U.S.-registered aircraft may be operated without displaying those marks anywhere on the aircraft if:

(1) It is operated for the purpose of exhibition, including a motion picture or television production, or an airshow;

(2) Except for practice and test fights necessary for exhibition purposes, it is

operated only at the location of the exhibition, between the exhibition locations, and between those locations and the base of operations of the aircraft; and

(3) For each flight in the United States:

(i) It is operated with the prior approval of the Flight Standards District Office, in the case of a flight within the lateral boundaries of the surface areas of Class B, Class C, Class D, or Class E airspace designated for the takeoff airport, or within 4.4 nautical miles of that airport if it is within Class G airspace; or

(ii) It is operated under a flight plan filed under either § 91.153 or § 91.169 of this chapter describing the marks it displays, in the case of any other flight.

(b) A small U.S.-registered aircraft built at least 30 years ago or a U.S.-registered aircraft for which an experimental certificate has been issued under § 21.191(d) or 21.191(g) for operation as an exhibition aircraft or as an amateur-built aircraft and which has the same external configuration as an aircraft built at least 30 years ago may be operated without displaying marks in accordance with §§ 45.21 and 45.23 through 45.33 if:

(1) It displays in accordance with § 45.21(c) marks at least 2 inches high on each side of the fuselage or vertical tail surface consisting of the Roman capital letter "N" followed by:

(i) The U.S. registration number of the aircraft; or

(ii) The symbol appropriate to the airworthiness certificate of the aircraft ("C", standard; "R", restricted; "L", limited; or "X", experimental) followed by the U.S. registration number of the aircraft; and

(2) It displays no other mark that begins with the letter "N" anywhere on the aircraft, unless it is the same mark that is displayed under paragraph (b)(1) of this section.

(c) No person may operate an aircraft under paragraph (a) or (b) of this section—

(1) In an ADIZ or DEWIZ described in Part 99 of this chapter unless it temporarily bears marks in accordance with §§ 45.21 and 45.23 through 45.33;

(2) In a foreign country unless that country consents to that operation; or

(3) In any operation conducted under Part 121, 133, 135, or 137 of this chapter.

(d) If, due to the configuration of an aircraft, it is impossible for a person to mark it in accordance with §§ 45.21 and 45.23 through 45.33, he may apply to the Administrator for a different marking procedure.

[Doc. No. 8093, Amdt. 45–5, 33 FR 450, Jan. 12, 1968, as amended by Amdt. 45–13, 46 FR 48603, Oct. 1, 1981; Amdt. 45–19, 54 FR 39291, Sept. 25, 1989; Amdt. 45–18, 54 FR 34330, Aug. 18, 1989; Amdt. 45–21, 56 FR 65653, Dec. 17, 1991; Amdt. 45–22, 66 FR 21066, Apr. 27, 2001]

§ 45.23 Display of marks; general.

(a) Each operator of an aircraft shall display on that aircraft marks consisting of the Roman capital letter "N" (denoting United States registration) followed by the registration number of the aircraft. Each suffix letter used in the marks displayed must also be a Roman capital letter.

(b) When marks that include only the Roman capital letter "N" and the registration number are displayed on limited or restricted category aircraft or experimental or provisionally certificated aircraft, the operator shall also display on that aircraft near each entrance to the cabin or cockpit, in letters not less than 2 inches nor more than 6 inches in height, the words "limited," "restricted," "experimental," or "provisional airworthiness," as the case may be.

[Doc. No. 8093, Amdt. 45–5, 33 FR 450, Jan. 12, 1968, as amended by Amdt. 45–9, 42 FR 41102, Aug. 15, 1977]

§ 45.25 Location of marks on fixed-wing aircraft.

(a) The operator of a fixed-wing aircraft shall display the required marks on either the vertical tail surfaces or the sides of the fuselage, except as provided in § 45.29(f).

(b) The marks required by paragraph (a) of this section shall be displayed as follows:

(1) If displayed on the vertical tail surfaces, horizontally on both surfaces, horizontally on both surfaces of a single vertical tail or on the outer surfaces of a multivertical tail. However, on aircraft on which marks at least 3 inches high may be displayed in accordance with § 45.29(b)(1), the marks

may be displayed vertically on the vertical tail surfaces.

(2) If displayed on the fuselage surfaces, horizontally on both sides of the fuselage between the trailing edge of the wing and the leading edge of the horizontal stabilizer. However, if engine pods or other appurtenances are located in this area and are an integral part of the fuselage side surfaces, the operator may place the marks on those pods or appurtenances.

[Amdt. 45–9, 42 FR 41102, Aug. 15, 1977]

§45.27 Location of marks; nonfixed-wing aircraft.

(a) *Rotorcraft.* Each operator of a rotorcraft shall display on that rotorcraft horizontally on both surfaces of the cabin, fuselage, boom, or tail the marks required by §45.23.

(b) *Airships.* Each operator of an airship shall display on that airship the marks required by §45.23, horizontally on—

(1) The upper surface of the right horizontal stabilizer and on the under surface of the left horizontal stabilizer with the top of the marks toward the leading edge of each stabilizer; and

(2) Each side of the bottom half of the vertical stabilizer.

(c) *Spherical balloons.* Each operator of a spherical balloon shall display the marks required by §45.23 in two places diametrically opposite and near the maximum horizontal circumference of that balloon.

(d) *Nonspherical balloons.* Each operator of a nonspherical balloon shall display the marks required by §45.23 on each side of the balloon near its maximum cross section and immediately above either the rigging band or the points of attachment of the basket or cabin suspension cables.

[Doc. No. 2047, 29 FR 3223, Mar. 11, 1964, as amended by Amdt. 45–15, 48 FR 11392, Mar. 17, 1983]

§45.29 Size of marks.

(a) Except as provided in paragraph (f) of this section, each operator of an aircraft shall display marks on the aircraft meeting the size requirements of this section.

(b) *Height.* Except as provided in paragraph (h) of this part, the nation-

ality and registration marks must be of equal height and on—

(1) Fixed-wing aircraft, must be at least 12 inches high, except that:

(i) An aircraft displaying marks at least 2 inches high before November 1, 1981 and an aircraft manufactured after November 2, 1981, but before January 1, 1983, may display those marks until the aircraft is repainted or the marks are repainted, restored, or changed;

(ii) Marks at least 3 inches high may be displayed on a glider;

(iii) Marks at least 3 inches high may be displayed on an aircraft for which an experimental certificate has been issued under §21.191(d) or 21.191(g) for operating as an exhibition aircraft or as an amateur-built aircraft when the maximum cruising speed of the aircraft does not exceed 180 knots CAS; and

(iv) Marks may be displayed on an exhibition, antique, or other aircraft in accordance with §45.22.

(2) Airships, spherical balloons, and nonspherical balloons, must be at least 3 inches high; and

(3) Rotorcraft, must be at least 12 inches high, except that rotorcraft displaying before April 18, 1983, marks required by §45.29(b)(3) in effect on April 17, 1983, and rotorcraft manufactured on or after April 18, 1983, but before December 31, 1983, may display those marks until the aircraft is repainted or the marks are repainted, restored, or changed.

(c) *Width.* Characters must be two-thirds as wide as they are high, except the number "1", which must be one-sixth as wide as it is high, and the letters "M" and "W" which may be as wide as they are high.

(d) *Thickness.* Characters must be formed by solid lines one-sixth as thick as the character is high.

(e) *Spacing.* The space between each character may not be less than one-fourth of the character width.

(f) If either one of the surfaces authorized for displaying required marks under §45.25 is large enough for display of marks meeting the size requirements of this section and the other is not, full-size marks shall be placed on the larger surface. If neither surface is large enough for full-size marks, marks as large as practicable shall be displayed on the larger of the two surfaces. If any surface authorized to be marked by § 45.27 is not large enough for full-size marks, marks as large as practicable shall be placed on the largest of the authorized surfaces.

(g) *Uniformity.* The marks required by this part for fixed-wing aircraft must have the same height, width, thickness, and spacing on both sides of the aircraft.

(h) After March 7, 1988, each operator of an aircraft penetrating an ADIZ or DEWIZ shall display on that aircraft temporary or permanent nationality and registration marks at least 12 inches high.

[Doc. No. 2047, 29 FR 3223, Mar. 11, 1964, as amended by Amdt. 45–2, 31 FR 9863, July 21, 1966; Amdt. 45–9, 42 FR 41102, Aug. 15, 1977; Amdt. 45–13, 46 FR 48604, Oct. 1, 1981; Amdt. 45–15, 48 FR 11392, Mar. 17, 1983; Amdt. 45–17, 52 FR 34102, Sept. 9, 1987; 52 FR 36566, Sept. 30, 1987]

§ 45.31 Marking of export aircraft.

A person who manufactures an aircraft in the United States for delivery thereof may display on that aircraft any marks required by the State of registry of the aircraft. However, no person may operate an aircraft so marked within the United States, except for test and demonstration flights for a limited period of time, or while in necessary transit to the purchaser.

§ 45.33 Sale of aircraft; removal of marks.

When an aircraft that is registered in the United States is sold, the holder of the Certificate of Aircraft Registration shall remove, before its delivery to the purchaser, all United States marks from the aircraft, unless the purchaser is—

(a) A citizen of the United States;

(b) An individual citizen of a foreign country who is lawfully admitted for permanent residence in the United States; or

(c) When the aircraft is to be based and primarily used in the United States, a corporation (other than a corporation which is a citizen of the United States) lawfully organized and doing business under the laws of the United States or any State thereof.

[Amdt. 45–11, 44 FR 61938, Oct. 29, 1979]

PART 47—AIRCRAFT REGISTRATION

Subpart A—General

Subpart B—Certificates of Aircraft Registration

Subpart C—Dealers' Aircraft Registration Certificate

AUTHORITY: 49 U.S.C. 106(g), 40113–40114, 44101–44108, 44110–44111, 44703–44704, 44713, 45302, 46104, 46301; 4 U.S.T. 1830.

SOURCE: Docket No. 7190, 31 FR 4495, Mar. 17, 1966, unless otherwise noted.

Subpart A—General

§47.1 Applicability.

This part prescribes the requirements for registering aircraft under section 501 of the Federal Aviation Act of 1958 (49 U.S.C. 1401). Subpart B applies to each applicant for, and holder of, a Certificate of Aircraft Registration. Subpart C applies to each applicant for, and holder of, a Dealers' Aircraft Registration Certificate.

§47.2 Definitions.

The following are definitions of terms used in this part:

Act means the Federal Aviation Act of 1958 (49 U.S.C. section 1301 *et seq.*).

Resident alien means an individual citizen of a foreign country lawfully admitted for permanent residence in the United States as an immigrant in conformity with the regulations of the Immigration and Naturalization Service of the Department of Justice (8 CFR Chapter 1).

U.S. citizen means one of the following:

(1) An individual who is a citizen of the United States or one of its possessions.

(2) A partnership of which each member is such an individual.

(3) A corporation or association created or organized under the laws of the United States or of any State, Territory, or possession of the United States, of which the president and two-thirds or more of the board of directors and other managing officers thereof are such individuals and in which at least 75 percent of the voting interest is owned or controlled by persons who are citizens of the United States or of one of its possessions.

[Amdt. 47–20, 44 FR 61939, Oct. 29, 1979]

§47.3 Registration required.

(a) Section 501(b) of the Federal Aviation Act of 1958 (49 U.S.C. 1401 (b)) defines eligibility for registration as follows:

(b) An aircraft shall be eligible for registration if, but only if—

(1)(A) it is—

(i) owned by a citizen of the United States or by an individual citizen of a foreign country who has lawfully been admitted for permanent residence in the United States; or

(ii) owned by a corporation (other than a corporation which is a citizen of the United States) lawfully organized and doing business under the laws of the United States or any State thereof so long as such aircraft is based and primarily used in the United States; and

(B) it is not registered under the laws of any foreign country; or

(2) it is an aircraft of the Federal Government, or of a State, territory, or possession of the United States or the District of Columbia or a political subdivision thereof.

(b) No person may operate on aircraft that is eligible for registration under section 501 of the Federal Aviation Act of 1958 unless the aircraft—

(1) Has been registered by its owner;

(2) Is carrying aboard the temporary authorization required by §47.31(b); or

(3) Is an aircraft of the Armed Forces.

(c) Governmental units are those named in paragraph (a) of this section and Puerto Rico.

[Doc. No. 7190, 31 FR 4495, Mar. 17, 1966, as amended by Amdt. 47–20, 44 FR 61939, Oct. 29, 1979]

§47.5 Applicants.

(a) A person who wishes to register an aircraft in the United States must submit an Application for Aircraft Registration under this part.

(b) An aircraft may be registered only by and in the legal name of its owner.

(c) Section 501(f) of the Act (49 U.S.C. 1401(f)), provides that registration is not evidence of ownership of aircraft in any proceeding in which ownership by a particular person is in issue. The FAA does not issue any certificate of ownership or endorse any information with respect to ownership on a Certificate of Aircraft Registration. The FAA issues a Certificate of Aircraft Registration to the person who appears to be the owner on the basis of the evidence of ownership submitted pursuant to §47.11 with the Application for Aircraft Registration, or recorded at the FAA Aircraft Registry.

(d) In this part, "owner" includes a buyer in possession, a bailee, or a lessee of an aircraft under a contract of conditional sale, and the assignee of that person.

[Amdt. 47–20, 44 FR 61939, Oct. 29, 1979]

§ 47.7 United States citizens and resident aliens.

(a) *U.S. citizens.* An applicant for aircraft registration under this part who is a U.S. citizen must certify to this in the application.

(b) *Resident aliens.* An applicant for aircraft registration under section 501(b)(1)(A)(i) of the Act who is a resident alien must furnish a representation of permanent residence and the applicant's alien registration number issued by the Immigration and Naturalization Service.

(c) *Trustees.* An applicant for aircraft registration under section 501(b)(1)(A)(i) of the Act that holds legal title to an aircraft in trust must comply with the following requirements:

(1) Each trustee must be either a U.S. citizen or a resident alien.

(2) The applicant must submit with the application—

(i) A copy of each document legally affecting a relationship under the trust;

(ii) If each beneficiary under the trust, including each person whose security interest in the aircraft is incorporated in the trust, is either a U.S. citizen or a resident alien, an affidavit by the applicant to that effect; and

(iii) If any beneficiary under the trust, including any person whose security interest in the aircraft is incorporated in the trust, is not a U.S. citizen or resident alien, an affidavit from each trustee stating that the trustee is not aware of any reason, situation, or relationship (involving beneficiaries or other persons who are not U.S. citizens or resident aliens) as a result of which those persons together would have more than 25 percent of the aggregate power to influence or limit the exercise of the trustee's authority.

(3) If persons who are neither U.S. citizens nor resident aliens have the power to direct or remove a trustee, either directly or indirectly through the control of another person, the trust instrument must provide that those persons together may not have more than 25 percent of the aggregate power to direct or remove a trustee. Nothing in this paragraph prevents those persons from having more than 25 percent of the beneficial interest in the trust.

(d) *Partnerships.* A partnership may apply for a Certificate of Aircraft Registration under section 501(b)(1)(A)(i) of the Act only if each partner, whether a general or limited partner, is a citizen of the United States. Nothing in this section makes ineligible for registration an aircraft which is not owned as a partnership asset but is co-owned by—

(1) Resident aliens; or

(2) One or more resident aliens and one or more U.S. citizens.

[Amdt. 47–20, 44 FR 61939, Oct. 29, 1979]

§ 47.8 Voting trusts.

(a) If a voting trust is used to qualify a domestic corporation as a U.S. citizen, the corporate applicant must submit to the FAA Aircraft Registry—

(1) A true copy of the fully executed voting trust agreement, which must identify each voting interest of the applicant, and which must be binding upon each voting trustee, the applicant corporation, all foreign stockholders, and each other party to the transaction; and

(2) An affidavit executed by each person designated as voting trustee in the voting trust agreement, in which each affiant represents—

(i) That each voting trustee is a citizen of the United States within the meaning of section 101(16) of the Act;

(ii) That each voting trustee is not a past, present, or prospective director, officer, employee, attorney, or agent of any other party to the trust agreement;

(iii) That each voting trustee is not a present or prospective beneficiary, creditor, debtor, supplier or contractor of any other party to the trust agreement;

(iv) That each voting trustee is not aware of any reason, situation, or relationship under which any other party to the agreement might influence the exercise of the voting trustee's totally independent judgment under the voting trust agreement.

(b) Each voting trust agreement submitted under paragraph (a)(1) of this section must provide for the succession of a voting trustee in the event of death, disability, resignation, termination of citizenship, or any other event leading to the replacement of any voting trustee. Upon succession, the replacement voting trustee shall immediately submit to the FAA Aircraft Registry the affidavit required by paragraph (a)(2) of this section.

(c) If the voting trust terminates or is modified, and the result is less than 75 percent control of the voting interest in the corporation by citizens of the United States, a loss of citizenship of the holder of the registration certificate occurs, and §47.41(a)(5) of this part applies.

(d) A voting trust agreement may not empower a trustee to act through a proxy.

[Amdt. 47–20, 44 FR 61939, Oct. 29, 1979]

§47.9 Corporations not U.S. citizens.

(a) Each corporation applying for registration of an aircraft under section 501(b)(1)(A)(ii) of the Act must submit to the FAA Registry with the application—

(1) A certified copy of its certificate of incorporation;

(2) A certification that it is lawfully qualified to do business in one or more States;

(3) A certification that the aircraft will be based and primarily used in the United States; and

(4) The location where the records required by paragraph (e) of this section will be maintained.

(b) For the purposes of registration, an aircraft is based and primarily used in the United States if the flight hours accumulated within the United States amount to at least 60 percent of the total flight hours of the aircraft during—

(1) For aircraft registered on or before January 1, 1980, the 6-calendar month period beginning on January 1, 1980, and each 6-calendar month period thereafter; and

(2) For aircraft registered after January 1, 1980, the period consisting in the remainder of the registration month and the succeeding 6 calendar months and each 6-calendar month period thereafter.

(c) For the purpose of this section, only those flight hours accumulated during non-stop (except for stops in emergencies or for purposes of refueling) flight between two points in the United States, even if the aircraft is

outside of the United States during part of the flight, are considered flight hours accumulated within the United States.

(d) In determining compliance with this section, any periods during which the aircraft is not validly registered in the United States are disregarded.

(e) The corporation that registers an aircraft pursuant to section 501(b)(1)(A)(ii) of the Act shall maintain, and make available for inspection by the Administrator upon request, records containing the total flight hours in the United States of the aircraft for three calendar years after the year in which the flight hours were accumulated.

(f) The corporation that registers an aircraft pursuant to section 501(b)(1)(A)(ii) of the Act shall send to the FAA Aircraft Registry, at the end of each period of time described in paragraphs (b)(1) and (2) of this section, either—

(1) A signed report containing—

(i) The total time in service of the airframe as provided in §91.417(a)(2)(i), accumulated during that period; and

(ii) The total flight hours in the United States of the aircraft accumulated during that period; or

(2) A signed statement that the total flight hours of the aircraft, while registered in the United States during that period, have been exclusively within the United States.

[Amdt. No. 47–20, 44 FR 61940, Oct. 29, 1979, as amended by Amdt. 47–24, 54 FR 34330, Aug. 18, 1989]

§47.11 Evidence of ownership.

Except as provided in §§47.33 and 47.35, each person that submits an Application for Aircraft Registration under this part must also submit the required evidence of ownership, recordable under §§49.13 and 49.17 of this chapter, as follows:

(a) The buyer in possession, the bailee, or the lessee of an aircraft under a contract of conditional sale must submit the contract. The assignee under a contract of conditional sale must submit both the contract (unless it is already recorded at the FAA Aircraft Registry), and his assignment from the original buyer, bailee, lessee, or prior assignee.

(b) The repossessor of an aircraft must submit—

(1) A certificate of repossession on FAA Form 8050-4, or its equivalent, signed by the applicant and stating that the aircraft was repossessed or otherwise seized under the security agreement involved and applicable local law;

(2) The security agreement (unless it is already recorded at the FAA Aircraft Registry), or a copy thereof certified as true under §49.21 of this chapter; and

(3) When repossession was through foreclosure proceedings resulting in sale, a bill of sale signed by the sheriff, auctioneer, or other authorized person who conducted the sale, and stating that the sale was made under applicable local law.

(c) The buyer of an aircraft at a judicial sale, or at a sale to satisfy a lien or charge, must submit a bill of sale signed by the sheriff, auctioneer, or other authorized person who conducted the sale, and stating that the sale was made under applicable local law.

(d) The owner of an aircraft, the title to which has been in controversy and has been determined by a court, must submit a certified copy of the decision of the court.

(e) The executor or administrator of the estate of the deceased former owner of an aircraft must submit a certified copy of the letters testimentary or letters of administration appointing him executor or administrator. The Certificate of Aircraft Registration is issued to the applicant as executor or administrator.

(f) The buyer of an aircraft from the estate of a deceased former owner must submit both a bill of sale, signed for the estate by the executor or administrator, and a certified copy of the letters testimentary or letters of administration. When no executor or administrator has been or is to be appointed, the applicant must submit both a bill of sale, signed by the heir-at-law of the deceased former owner, and an affidavit of the heir-at-law stating that no

application for appointment of an executor or administrator has been made, that so far as he can determine none will be made, and that he is the person entitled to, or having the right to dispose of, the aircraft under applicable local law.

(g) The guardian of another person's property that includes an aircraft must submit a certified copy of the order of the court appointing him guardian. The Certificate of Aircraft Registration is issued to the applicant as guardian.

(h) The trustee of property that includes an aircraft, as described in §47.7(c), must submit either a certified copy of the order of the court appointing the trustee, or a complete and true copy of the instrument creating the trust. If there is more than one trustee, each trustee must sign the application. The Certificate of Aircraft Registration is issued to a single applicant as trustee, or to several trustees jointly as co-trustees.

[Doc. No. 7190, 31 FR 4495, Mar. 17, 1966, as amended by Amdt. 47-20, 44 FR 61940, Oct. 29, 1979; Amdt. 47-23, 53 FR 1915, Jan. 25, 1988]

§ 47.13 Signatures and instruments made by representatives.

(a) Each signature on an Application for Aircraft Registration, on a request for cancellation of a Certificate of Aircraft Registration or on a document submitted as supporting evidence under this part, must be in ink.

(b) When one or more persons doing business under a trade name submits an Application for Aircraft Registration or a request for cancellation of a Certificate of Aircraft Registration, the application or request must be signed by, or in behalf of, each person who shares title to the aircraft.

(c) When an agent submits an Application for Aircraft Registration or a request for cancellation of a Certificate of Aircraft Registration in behalf of the owner, he must—

(1) State the name of the owner on the application or request;

(2) Sign as agent or attorney-in-fact on the application or request; and

(3) Submit a signed power of attorney, or a true copy thereof certified under §49.21 of this chapter, with the application or request.

(d) When a corporation submits an Application for Aircraft Registration or a request for cancellation of a Certificate of Aircraft Registration, it must—

(1) Have an authorized person sign the application or request;

(2) Show the title of the signer's office on the application or request; and

(3) Submit a copy of the authorization from the board of directors to sign for the corporation, certified as true under § 49.21 of this chapter by a corporate officer or other person in a managerial position therein, with the application or request, unless—

(i) The signer of the application or request is a corporate officer or other person in a managerial position in the corporation and the title of his office is stated in connection with his signature; or

(ii) A valid authorization to sign is on file at the FAA Aircraft Registry.

(e) When a partnership submits an Application for Aircraft Registration or a request for cancellation of a Certificate of Aircraft Registration, it must—

(1) State the full name of the partnership on the application or request;

(2) State the name of each general partner on the application or request; and

(3) Have a general partner sign the application or request.

(f) When co-owners, who are not engaged in business as partners, submit an Application for Aircraft Registration or a request for cancellation of a Certificate of Aircraft Registration, each person who shares title to the aircraft under the arrangement must sign the application or request.

(g) A power of attorney or other evidence of a person's authority to sign for another, submitted under this part, is valid for the purposes of this section, unless sooner revoked, until—

(1) Its expiration date stated therein; or

(2) If an expiration date is not stated therein, for not more than 3 years after the date—

(i) It is signed; or

(ii) The grantor (a corporate officer or other person in a managerial position therein, where the grantor is a corporation) certifies in writing that the authority to sign shown by the power of attorney or other evidence is still in effect.

[Doc. No. 7190, 31 FR 4495, Mar. 17, 1966, as amended by Amdt. 47–2, 31 FR 15349, Dec. 8, 1966; Amdt. 47–3, 32 FR 6554, Apr. 28, 1967; Amdt. 47–12, 36 FR 8661, May 11, 1971]

§ 47.15 Identification number.

(a) *Number required.* An applicant for Aircraft Registration must place a U.S. identification number (registration mark) on his Aircraft Registration Application, AC Form 8050–1, and on any evidence submitted with the application. There is no charge for the assignment of numbers provided in this paragraph. This paragraph does not apply to an aircraft manufacturer who applies for a group of U.S. identification numbers under paragraph (c) of this section; a person who applies for a special identification number under paragraphs (d) through (g) of this section; or a holder of a Dealer's Aircraft Registration Certificate who applies for a temporary registration number under § 47.16.

(1) *Aircraft not previously registered anywhere.* The applicant must obtain the U.S. identification number from the FAA Aircraft Registry by request in writing describing the aircraft by make, type, model, and serial number (or, if it is amateur-built, as provided in § 47.33(b)) and stating that the aircraft has not previously been registered anywhere. If the aircraft was brought into the United States from a foreign country, the applicant must submit evidence that the aircraft has never been registered in a foreign country.

(2) *Aircraft last previously registered in the United States.* Unless he applies for a different number under paragraphs (d) through (g) of this section, the applicant must place the U.S. identification number that is already assigned to the aircraft on his application and the supporting evidence.

(3) *Aircraft last previously registered in a foreign country.* Whether or not the foreign registration has ended, the applicant must obtain a U.S. identification number from the FAA Aircraft Registry for an aircraft last previously registered in a foreign country, by request in writing describing the aircraft

by make, model, and serial number, accompanied by—

(i) Evidence of termination of foreign registration in accordance with §47.37(b) or the applicant's affidavit showing that foreign registration has ended; or

(ii) If foreign registration has not ended, the applicant's affidavit stating that the number will not be placed on the aircraft until foreign registration has ended.

Authority to use the identification number obtained under paragraph (a)(1) or (3) of this section expires 90 days after the date it is issued unless the applicant submits an Aircraft Registration Application, AC Form 8050-1, and complies with §47.33 or §47.37, as applicable, within that period of time. However, the applicant may obtain an extension of this 90-day period from the FAA Aircraft Registry if he shows that his delay in complying with that section is due to circumstances beyond his control.

(b) A U.S. identification number may not exceed five symbols in addition to the prefix letter "N". These symbols may be all numbers (N10000), one to four numbers and one suffix letter (N 1000A), or one to three numbers and two suffix letters (N 100AB). The letters "I" and "O" may not be used. The first zero in a number must always be preceded by at least one of the numbers 1 through 9.

(c) An aircraft manufacturer may apply to the FAA Aircraft Registry for enough U.S. identification numbers to supply his estimated production for the next 18 months. There is no charge for this assignment of numbers.

(d) Any unassigned U.S. identification number may be assigned as a special identification number. An applicant who wants a special identification number or wants to change the identification number of his aircraft may apply for it to the FAA Aircraft Registry. The fee required by §47.17 must accompany the application.

(e) [Reserved]

(f) The FAA Aircraft Registry assigns a special identification number on AC Form 8050-64. Within 5 days after he affixes the special identification number to his aircraft, the owner must complete and sign the receipt contained in

AC Form 8050-64, state the date he affixed the number to his aircraft, and return the original form to the FAA Aircraft Registry. The owner shall carry the duplicate of AC Form 8050-64 and the present Certificate of Aircraft Registration in the aircraft as temporary authority to operate it. This temporary authority is valid until the date the owner receives the revised Certificate of Aircraft Registration issued by the FAA Aircraft Registry.

(g) [Reserved]

(h) A special identification number may be reserved for no more than 1 year. If a person wishes to renew his reservation from year to year, he must apply to the FAA aircraft Registry for renewal and submit the fee required by §47.17 for a special identification number.

[Doc. No. 7190, 31 FR 4495, Mar. 17, 1966, as amended by Amdt. 47-1, 31 FR 13314, Oct. 14, 1966; Amdt. 47-5, 32 FR 13505, Sept. 27, 1967; Amdt. 47-7, 34 FR 2480, Feb. 21, 1969; Amdt. 47-13, 36 FR 16187, Aug. 20, 1971; Amdt. 47-15, 37 FR 21528, Oct. 12, 1972; Amdt. 47-16, 37 FR 25487, Dec. 1, 1972; Amdt. 47-17, 39 FR 1353, Jan. 8, 1974; Amdt. 47-22, 47 FR 12153, Mar. 22, 1982]

§47.16 Temporary registration numbers.

(a) Temporary registration numbers are issued by the FAA to manufacturers, distributors, and dealers who are holders of Dealer's Aircraft Registration Certificates for temporary display on aircraft during flight allowed under Subpart C of this part.

(b) The holder of a Dealer's Aircraft Registration Certificate may apply to the FAA Aircraft Registry for as many temporary registration numbers as are necessary for his business. The application must be in writing and include—

(1) Sufficient information to justify the need for the temporary registration numbers requested; and

(2) The number of each Dealer's Aircraft Registration Certificate held by the applicant.

There is no charge for these numbers.

(c) The use of temporary registration numbers is subject to the following conditions:

(1) The numbers may be used and reused—

(i) Only in connection with the holder's Dealer's Aircraft Registration Certificate;

(ii) Within the limitations of §47.69 where applicable, including the requirements of §47.67; and

(iii) On aircraft not registered under Subpart B of this part or in a foreign country, and not displaying any other identification markings.

(2) A temporary registration number may not be used on more than one aircraft in flight at the same time.

(3) Temporary registration numbers may not be used to fly aircraft into the United States for the purpose of importation.

(d) The assignment of any temporary registration number to any person lapses upon the expiration of all of his Dealer's Aircraft Registration Certificates. When a temporary registration number is used on a flight outside the United States for delivery purposes, the holder shall record the assignment of that number to the aircraft and shall keep that record for at least 1 year after the removal of the number from that aircraft. Whenever the owner of an aircraft bearing a temporary registration number applies for an airworthiness certificate under Part 21 of this chapter he shall furnish that number in the application. The temporary registration number must be removed from the aircraft not later than the date on which either title or possession passes to another person.

[Amdt. 47–4, 32 FR 12556, Aug. 30, 1967]

§47.17 Fees.

(a) The fees for applications under this part are as follows:

(1) Certificate of Aircraft Registration (each aircraft)	$5.00
(2) Dealer's Aircraft Registration Certificate	10.00
(3) Additional Dealer's Aircraft Registration Certificate (issued to same dealer)	2.00
(4) Special identification number (each number)	10.00
(5) Changed, reassigned, or reserved identification number	10.00
(6) Duplicate Certificate of Registration	2.00

(b) Each application must be accompanied by the proper fee, that may be paid by check or money order to the Federal Aviation Administration.

[Doc. No. 7190, 31 FR 4495, Mar. 17, 1966; 31 FR 5483, Apr. 7, 1966, as amended by Doc. No. 8084, 32 FR 5769, Apr. 11, 1967]

§47.19 FAA Aircraft Registry.

Each application, request, notification, or other communication sent to the FAA under this part must be mailed to the FAA Aircraft Registry, Department of Transportation, Post Office Box 25504, Oklahoma City, Oklahoma 73125, or delivered to the Registry at 6400 South MacArthur Boulevard, Oklahoma City, Oklahoma.

[Doc. No. 13890, 41 FR 34009, Aug. 12, 1976]

Subpart B—Certificates of Aircraft Registration

§47.31 Application.

(a) Each applicant for a Certificate of Aircraft Registration must submit the following to the FAA Aircraft Registry—

(1) The original (white) and one copy (green) of the Aircraft Registration Application, AC Form 8050–1;

(2) The original Aircraft Bill of Sale, ACC Form 8050–2, or other evidence of ownership authorized by §§47.33, 47.35, or 47.37 (unless already recorded at the FAA Aircraft Registry); and

(3) The fee required by §47.17.

The FAA rejects an application when any form is not completed, or when the name and signature of the applicant are not the same throughout.

(b) After he complies with paragraph (a) of this section, the applicant shall carry the second duplicate copy (pink) of the Aircraft Registration Application, AC Form 8050–1, in the aircraft as temporary authority to operate it without registration. This temporary authority is valid until the date the applicant receives the certificate of the Aircraft Registration, AC Form 8050–3, or until the date the FAA denies the application, but in no case for more than 90 days after the date the applicant signs the application. If by 90 days after the date the applicant signs the application, the FAA has neither issued the Certificate of Aircraft Registration nor denied the application, the FAA aircraft Registry issues a letter of extension that serves as authority to continue to operate the aircraft without registration while it is carried in the aircraft.

(c) Paragraph (b) of this section applies to each application submitted under paragraph (a) of this section, and signed after October 5, 1967. If, after that date, an applicant signs an application and the second duplicate copy (pink) of the Aircraft Registration Application, AC Form 8050-1, bears an obsolete statement limiting its validity to 30 days, the applicant may strike out the number "30" on that form, and insert the number "90" in place thereof.

[Doc. No. 7190, 31 FR 4495, Mar. 17, 1966; 31 FR 5483, Apr. 7, 1966, as amended by Amdt. 47-6, 33 FR 11, Jan. 3, 1968; Amdt. 47-15, 37 FR 21528, Oct. 12, 1972; Amdt. 47-16, 37 FR 25487, Dec. 1, 1972]

§ 47.33 Aircraft not previously registered anywhere.

(a) A person who is the owner of an aircraft that has not been registered under the Federal Aviation Act of 1958, under other law of the United States, or under foreign law, may register it under this part if he—

(1) Complies with §§ 47.3, 47.7, 47.8, 47.9, 47.11, 47.13, 47.15, and 47.17, as applicable; and

(2) Submits with his application an aircraft Bill of Sale, AC Form 8050-2, signed by the seller, an equivalent bill of sale, or other evidence of ownership authorized by § 47.11.

(b) If, for good reason, the applicant cannot produce the evidence of ownership required by paragraph (a) of this section, he must submit other evidence that is satisfactory to the Administrator. This other evidence may be an affidavit stating why he cannot produce the required evidence, accompanied by whatever further evidence is available to prove the transaction.

(c) The owner of an amateur-built aircraft who applies for registration under paragraphs (a) and (b) of this section must describe the aircraft by class (airplane, rotorcraft, glider, or balloon), serial number, number of seats, type of engine installed, (reciprocating, turbopropeller, turbojet, or other), number of engines installed, and make, model, and serial number of each engine installed; and must state whether the aircraft is built for land or water operation. Also, he must submit as evidence of ownership an affidavit giving the U.S. identification number, and stating that the aircraft was built from

parts and that he is the owner. If he built the aircraft from a kit, the applicant must also submit a bill of sale from the manufacturer of the kit.

(d) The owner, other than the holder of the type certificate, of an aircraft that he assembles from parts to conform to the approved type design, must describe the aircraft and engine in the manner required by paragraph (c) of this section, and also submit evidence of ownership satisfactory to the Administrator, such as bills of sale, for all major components of the aircraft.

[Doc. No. 7190, 31 FR 4495, Mar. 17, 1966; 31 FR 5483, Apr. 7, 1966, as amended by Amdt. 47-16, 37 FR 25487, Dec. 1, 1972; Amdt. 47-20, 44 FR 61940, Oct. 29, 1979]

§ 47.35 Aircraft last previously registered in the United States.

(a) A person who is the owner of an aircraft last previously registered under the Federal Aviation Act of 1958, or under other law of the United States, may register it under this part if he complies with §§ 47.3, 47.7, 47.8, 47.9, 47.11, 47.13, 47.15, and 47.17, as applicable and submits with his application an Aircraft Bill of Sale, AC Form 8050-2, signed by the seller or an equivalent conveyance, or other evidence of ownership authorized by § 47.11:

(1) If the applicant bought the aircraft from the last registered owner, the conveyance must be from that owner to the applicant.

(2) If the applicant did not buy the aircraft from the last registered owner, he must submit conveyances or other instruments showing consecutive transactions from the last registered owner through each intervening owner to the applicant.

(b) If, for good reason, the applicant cannot produce the evidence of ownership required by paragraph (a) of this section, he must submit other evidence that is satisfactory to the Administrator. This other evidence may be an affidavit stating why he cannot produce the required evidence, accompanied by whatever further evidence is available to prove the transaction.

[Doc. No. 7190, 31 FR 4495, Mar. 17, 1966, as amended by Amdt. 47-16, 37 FR 25487, Dec. 1, 1972; Amdt. 47-20, 44 FR 61940, Oct. 29, 1979]

§47.37 Aircraft last previously registered in a foreign country.

(a) A person who is the owner of an aircraft last previously registered under the law of a foreign country may register it under this part if he—

(1) Complies with §§47.3, 47.7, 47.8, 47.9, 47.11, 47.13, 47.15, and 47.17, as applicable;

(2) Submits with his application a bill of sale from the foreign seller or other evidence satisfactory to the Administrator that he owns the aircraft; and

(3) Submits evidence satisfactory to the Administrator that—

(i) If the country in which the aircraft was registered has not ratified the Convention on the International Recognition of Rights in Aircraft (4 U.S.T. 1830), the foreign registration has ended or is invalid; or

(ii) If that country has ratified the convention, the foreign registration has ended or is invalid, and each holder of a recorded right against the aircraft has been satisfied or has consented to the transfer, or ownership in the country of export has been ended by a sale in execution under the terms of the convention.

(b) For the purposes of paragraph (a)(3) of this section, satisfactory evidence of termination of the foreign registration may be—

(1) A statement, by the official having jurisdiction over the national aircraft registry of the foreign country, that the registration has ended or is invalid, and showing the official's name and title and describing the aircraft by make, model, and serial number; or

(2) A final judgment or decree of a court of competent jurisdiction that determines, under the law of the country concerned, that the registration has in fact become invalid.

[Doc. No. 7190, 31 FR 4495, Mar. 17, 1966, as amended by Amdt. 47–20, 44 FR 61940, Oct. 29,1979]

§47.39 Effective date of registration.

(a) Except for an aircraft last previously registered in a foreign country, an aircraft is registered under this subpart on the date and at the time the FAA Aircraft Registry receives the documents required by §47.33 or §47.35.

(b) An aircraft last previously registered in a foreign country is registered under this subpart on the date and at the time the FAA Aircraft Registry issues the Certificate of Aircraft Registration, AC Form 8050–3, after the documents required by §47.37 have been received and examined.

[Doc. No. 7190, 31 FR 4495, Mar. 17, 1966, as amended by Amdt. 47–16, 37 FR 25487, Dec. 1, 1972]

§47.41 Duration and return of Certificate.

(a) Each Certificate of Aircraft Registration issued by the FAA under this subpart is effective, unless suspended or revoked, until the date upon which—

(1) Subject to the Convention on the International Recognition of Rights in Aircraft when applicable, the aircraft is registered under the laws of a foreign country;

(2) The registration is canceled at the written request of the holder of the certificate;

(3) The aircraft is totally destroyed or scrapped;

(4) Ownership of the aircraft is transferred;

(5) The holder of the certificate loses his U.S. citizenship;

(6) 30 days have elapsed since the death of the holder of the certificate;

(7) The owner, if an individual who is not a citizen of the United States, loses status as a resident alien, unless that person becomes a citizen of the United States at the same time; or

(8) If the owner is a corporation other than a corporation which is a citizen of the United States—

(i) The corporation ceases to be lawfully organized and doing business under the laws of the United States or any State thereof; or

(ii) A period described in §47.9(b) ends and the aircraft was not based and primarily used in the United States during that period.

(9) If the trustee in whose name the aircraft is registered—

(i) Loses U.S. citizenship;

(ii) Loses status as a resident alien and does not become a citizen of the United States at the same time; or

(iii) In any manner ceases to act as trustee and is not immediately replaced by another who meets the requirements of § 47.7(c).

(b) The Certificate of Aircraft Registration, with the reverse side completed, must be returned to the FAA Aircraft Registry—

(1) In case of registration under the laws of a foreign country, by the person who was the owner of the aircraft before foreign registration;

(2) Within 60 days after the death of the holder of the certificate, by the administrator or executor of his estate, or by his heir-at-law if no administrator or executor has been or is to be appointed; or

(3) Upon the termination of the registration, by the holder of the Certificate of Aircraft Registration in all other cases mentioned in paragraph (a) of this section.

[Doc. No. 7190, 31 FR 4495, Mar. 17, 1966; 31 FR 5483, Apr. 7, 1966, as amended by Amdt. 47-20, 44 FR 61940, Oct. 29, 1979]

§ 47.43 Invalid registration.

(a) The registration of an aircraft is invalid if, at the time it is made—

(1) The aircraft is registered in a foreign country;

(2) The applicant is not the owner;

(3) The applicant is not qualified to submit an application under this part; or

(4) The interest of the applicant in the aircraft was created by a transaction that was not entered into in good faith, but rather was made to avoid (with or without the owner's knowledge) compliance with section 501 of the Federal Aviation Act of 1958 (49 U.S.C. 1401).

(b) If the registration of an aircraft is invalid under paragraph (a) of this section, the holder of the invalid Certificate of Aircraft Registration shall return it as soon as possible to the FAA Aircraft Registry.

[Doc. No. 7190, 31 FR 4495, Mar. 17, 1966; 31 FR 5483, Apr. 7, 1966, as amended by Amdt. 47-20, 44 FR 61940, Oct. 29, 1979]

§ 47.45 Change of address.

Within 30 days after any change in his permanent mailing address, the holder of a Certificate of Aircraft Registration for an aircraft shall notify the FAA Aircraft Registry of his new address. A revised Certificate of Aircraft Registration is then issued, without charge.

§ 47.47 Cancellation of Certificate for export purpose.

(a) The holder of a Certificate of Aircraft Registration who wishes to cancel the Certificate for the purpose of export must submit to the FAA Aircraft Registry—

(1) A written request for cancellation of the Certificate describing the aircraft by make, model, and serial number, stating the U.S. identification number and the country to which the aircraft will be exported; and

(2) Evidence satisfactory to the Administrator that each holder of a recorded right has been satisfied or has consented to the transfer.

(b) The FAA notifies the country to which the aircraft is to be exported of the cancellation by ordinary mail, or by airmail at the owner's request. The owner must arrange and pay for the transmission of this notice by means other than ordinary mail or airmail.

[Amdt. 47-11, 36 FR 8661, May 11, 1971, as amended by Amdt. 47-23, 53 FR 1915, Jan. 25, 1988]

§ 47.49 Replacement of Certificate.

(a) If a Certificate of Aircraft Registration is lost, stolen, or mutilated, the holder of the Certificate of Aircraft Registration may apply to the FAA Aircraft Registry for a duplicate certificate, accompanying his application with the fee required by § 47.17.

(b) If the holder has applied and has paid the fee for a duplicate Certificate of Aircraft Registration and needs to operate his aircraft before receiving it, he may request a temporary certificate. The FAA Aircraft Registry issues a temporary certificate, by a collect telegram, to be carried in the aircraft. This temporary certificate is valid until he receives the duplicate Certicate of Aircraft Registration.

§ 47.51 Triennial aircraft registration report.

(a) Unless one of the registration activities listed in paragraph (b) of this section has occurred within the preceding 36 calendar months, the holder of each Certificate of Aircraft Registration issued under this subpart shall submit, on the form provided by the FAA Aircraft Registry and in the manner described in paragraph (c) of this section, a Triennial Aircraft Registration Report, certifying—

(1) The current identification number (registration mark) assigned to the aircraft;

(2) The name and permanent mailing address of the certificate holder;

(3) The name of the manufacturer of the aircraft and its model and serial number;

(4) Whether the certificate holder is—

(i) A citizen of the United States;

(ii) An individual citizen of a foreign country who has lawfully been admitted for permanent residence in the United States; or

(iii) A corporation (other than a corporation which is a citizen of the United States) lawfully organized and doing business under the laws of the United States or any State thereof; and

(5) Whether the aircraft is currently registered under the laws of any foreign country.

(b) The FAA Aircraft Registry will forward a Triennial Aircraft Registration Report to each holder of a Certificate of Aircraft Registration whenever 36 months has expired since the latest of the following registration activities occurred with respect to the certificate holder's aircraft:

(1) The submission of an Application for Aircraft Registration.

(2) The submission of a report or statement required by §47.9(f).

(3) The filing of a notice of change of permanent mailing address.

(4) The filing of an application for a duplicate Certificate of Aircraft Registration.

(5) The filing of an application for a change of aircraft identification number.

(6) The submission of an Aircraft Registration Eligibility, Identification, and Activity Report, Part 1, AC Form 8050–73, under former §47.44.

(7) The submission of a Triennial Aircraft Registration Report under this section.

(c) The holder of the Certificate of Aircraft Registration shall return the Triennial Aircraft Registration Report to the FAA Aircraft Registry within 60 days after issuance by the FAA Aircraft Registry. The report must be dated, legibly executed, and signed by the certificate holder in the manner prescribed by §47.13, except that any co-owner may sign for all co-owners.

(d) Refusal or failure to submit the Triennial Aircraft Registration Report with the information required by this section may be cause for suspension or revocation of the Certificate of Aircraft Registration in accordance with Part 13 of this chapter.

[Amdt. 47–21, 45 FR 20773, Mar. 31, 1980]

Subpart C—Dealers' Aircraft Registration Certificate

§47.61 Dealers' Aircraft Registration Certificates.

(a) The FAA issues a Dealers' Aircraft Registration Certificate, AC Form 8050–6, to manufacturers and dealers so as to—

(1) Allow manufacturers to make any required flight tests of aircraft.

(2) Facilitate operating, demonstrating, and merchandising aircraft by the manufacturer or dealer without the burden of obtaining a Certificate of Aircraft Registration for each aircraft with each transfer of ownership, under Subpart B of this part.

(b) A Dealers' Aircraft Registration Certificate is an alternative for the Certificate of Aircraft Registration issued under Subpart B of this part. A dealer may, under this subpart, obtain one or more Dealers' Aircraft Registration Certificates in addition to his original certificate, and he may use a Dealer's Aircraft Registration Certificate for any aircraft he owns.

[Doc. No. 7190, 31 FR 4495, Mar. 17, 1966; as amended by Amdt. 47–9, 35 FR 802, Jan. 21, 1970; Amdt. 47–16, 37 FR 25487, Dec. 1, 1972]

§47.63 Application.

A manufacturer or dealer that wishes to obtain a Dealer's Aircraft Registration Certificate, AC Form 8050–6, must submit—

(a) An Application for Dealers' Aircraft Registration Certificates, AC Form 8050–5; and

(b) The fee required by § 47.17.

[Doc. No. 7190, 31 FR 4495, Mar. 17, 1966, as amended by Amdt. 47–16, 37 FR 25487, Dec. 1, 1972]

§ 47.65 Eligibility.

To be eligible for a Dealer's Aircraft Registration Certificate, a person must have an established place of business in the United States, must be substantially engaged in manufacturing or selling aircraft, and must be a citizen of the United States, as defined by section 101(13) of the Federal Aviation Act of 1958 (49 U.S.C. 1301).

[Amdt. 47–9, 35 FR 802, Jan. 21, 1970]

§ 47.67 Evidence of ownership.

Before using his Dealer's Aircraft Registration Certificate for operating an aircraft, the holder of the certificate (other than a manufacturer) must send to the FAA Aircraft Registry evidence satisfactory to the Administrator that he is the owner of that aircraft. An Aircraft Bill of Sale, or its equivalent, may be used as evidence of ownership. There is no recording fee.

§ 47.69 Limitations.

A Dealer's Aircraft Registration Certificate is valid only in connection with use of aircraft—

(a) By the owner of the aircraft to whom it was issued, his agent or employee, or a prospective buyer, and in the case of a dealer other than a manufacturer, only after he has complied with § 47.67;

(b) Within the United States, except when used to deliver to a foreign purchaser an aircraft displaying a temporary registration number and carrying an airworthiness certificate on which that number is written;

(c) While a certificate is carried within the aircraft; and

(d) On a flight that is—

(1) For required flight testing of aircraft; or

(2) Necessary for, or incident to, sale of the aircraft.

However, a prospective buyer may operate an aircraft for demonstration purposes only while he is under the direct supervision of the holder of the Dealer's Aircraft Registration Certificate or his agent.

[Doc. No. 7190 31 FR 4495, Mar. 17, 1966; 31 FR 5483, Apr. 7, 1966, as amended by Amdt. 47–4, 32 FR 12556, Aug. 30, 1967]

§ 47.71 Duration of Certificate; change of status.

(a) A Dealer's Aircraft Registration Certificate expires 1 year after the date it is issued. Each additional certificate expires on the date the original certificate expires.

(b) The holder of a Dealer's Aircraft Registration Certificate shall immediately notify the FAA Aircraft Registry of any of the following—

(1) A change of his name;

(2) A change of his address;

(3) A change that affects his status as a citizen of the United States; or

(4) The discontinuance of his business.

PART 49—RECORDING OF AIRCRAFT TITLES AND SECURITY DOCUMENTS

49.45 Recording of releases, cancellations, discharges, and satisfactions: special requirements.

Subpart E—Encumbrances Against Air Carrier Aircraft Engines, Propellers, Appliances, and Spare Parts

49.51 Applicability.
49.53 Eligibility for recording: general requirements.
49.55 Recording of releases, cancellations, discharges, and satisfactions: special requirements.

AUTHORITY: 49 U.S.C. 106(g), 40113–40114, 44101–44108, 44110–44111, 44704, 44713, 45302, 46104, 46301; 4 U.S.T. 1830.

SOURCE: Docket No. 1996, 29 FR 6486, May 19, 1964, unless otherwise noted.

Subpart A—Applicability

§ 49.1 Applicability.

(a) This part applies to the recording of certain conveyances affecting title to, or any interest in—

(1) Any aircraft registered under section 501 of the Federal Aviation Act of 1958 (49 U.S.C. 1401);

(2) Any specifically identified aircraft engine of 750 or more rated takeoff horsepower, or the equivalent of that horsepower;

(3) Any specifically identified aircraft propeller able to absorb 750 or more rated takeoff shaft horsepower; and

(4) Any aircraft engine, propeller, or appliance maintained by or for an air carrier certificated under section 604(b) of the Federal Aviation Act of 1958 (49 U.S.C. 1424(b)), for installation or use in an aircraft, aircraft engine, or propeller, or any spare part, maintained at a designated location or locations by or for such an air carrier.

(b) Subpart B of this part governs, where applicable by its terms, conveyances subject to this part.

Subpart B—General

§ 49.11 FAA Aircraft Registry.

To be eligible for recording, a conveyance must be mailed to the FAA Aircraft Registry, Department of Transportation, Post Office Box 25504, Oklahoma City, Oklahoma 73125, or delivered to the Registry at 6400 South MacArthur Boulevard, Oklahoma City, Oklahoma.

[Doc. No. 13890, 41 FR 34010, Aug. 12, 1976]

§ 49.13 Signatures and acknowledgements.

(a) Each signature on a conveyance must be in ink.

(b) Paragraphs (b) through (f) of § 47.13 of this chapter apply to a conveyance made by, or on behalf of, one or more persons doing business under a trade name, or by an agent, corporation, partnership, coowner, or unincorporated association.

(c) No conveyance or other instrument need be acknowledged, as provided in section 503(e) of the Federal Aviation Act of 1958 (49 U.S.C. 1403(e)), in order to be recorded under this part. The law of the place of delivery of the conveyance determines when a conveyance or other instrument must be acknowledged in order to be valid for the purposes of that place.

(d) A power of attorney or other evidence of a person's authority to sign for another, submitted under this part, is valid for the purposes of this section, unless sooner revoked, until—

(1) Its expiration date stated therein; or

(2) If an expiration date is not stated thereon, for not more than 3 years after the date—

(i) It is signed; or

(ii) The grantor (a corporate officer or other person in a managerial position therein, where the grantor is a corporation) certifies in writing that the authority to sign shown by the power of attorney or other evidence is still in effect.

[Doc. No. 7190, 31 FR 4499, Mar. 17, 1966, as amended by Amdt. 49–2, 31 FR 15349, Dec. 8, 1966; Amdt. 49–6, 36 FR 8661, May 11, 1971]

§ 49.15 Fees for recording.

(a) The fees charged for recording conveyances under this part are as follows:

(1) Conveyance of aircraft—
 For each aircraft listed therein $5.00
(2) Conveyance, made for security purposes, of a specifically identified aircraft engine or propeller, or any assignment or amendment thereof, or supplement thereto, recorded under Subpart D—
 For each engine or propeller 5.00

(3) Conveyance, made for security purposes, of aircraft engines, propellers, appliances, or spare parts, maintained at a designated location or locations, or any assignment or amendment thereof, or supplement thereto, recorded under Subpart E—

For the group of items at each location 5.00

(b) There is no fee for recording a bill of sale that accompanies an application for aircraft registration and the proper fee under Part 47 of this chapter.

(c) Each conveyance must be accompanied by the proper fee, that may be paid by check or money order to the Federal Aviation Administration.

[Doc. No. 1996, 29 FR 6486, May 19, 1964, as amended by Amdt. 49–1, 31 FR 4499, Mar. 17, 1966; Doc. No. 8084, 32 FR 5769, Apr. 11, 1967]

§ 49.17 Conveyances recorded.

(a) Each instrument recorded under this part is a "conveyance" within the following definition in section 101(17) of the Federal Aviation Act of 1958 (49 U.S.C. 1301):

(17) "Conveyance" means a bill of sale, contract of conditional sale, mortgage, assignment of mortgage, or other instrument affecting title to, or interest in, property.

A notice of Federal tax lien is not recordable under this part, since it is required to be filed elsewhere by the Internal Revenue Code (26 U.S.C. 6321, 6323; 26 CFR 301.6321–1, 301.6323–1).

(b) The kinds of conveyance recordable under this part include those used as evidence of ownership under § 47.11 of this chapter.

(c) The validity of any instrument, eligible for recording under this part, is governed by the laws of the State, possession, Puerto Rico, or District of Columbia, as the case may be, in which the instrument was delivered, regardless of the location or place of delivery of the property affected by the instrument. If the place where an instrument is intended to be delivered is stated in the instrument, it is presumed that the instrument was delivered at that place. The recording of a conveyance is not a decision of the FAA that the instrument does, in fact, affect title to, or an interest in, the aircraft or other property it covers.

(d) The following rules apply to conveyances executed for security purposes and assignments thereof:

(1) A security agreement must be signed by the debtor. If the debtor is not the registered owner of the aircraft, the security agreement must be accompanied by the debtor's Application for Aircraft Registration and evidence of ownership, as prescribed in Part 47 of this chapter, unless the debtor—

(i) Holds a Dealer's Aircraft Registration Certificate and submits evidence of ownership as provided in § 47.67 of this chapter (if applicable);

(ii) Was the owner of the aircraft on the date the security agreement was signed, as shown by documents recorded at the FAA Aircraft Registry; or

(iii) Is the vendor, bailor, or lessor under a contract of conditional sale.

(2) The name of a cosigner may not appear in the security agreement as a debtor or owner. If a person other than the registered owner signs the security agreement, that person must show the capacity in which that person signs, such as "cosigner" or "guarantor".

(3) An assignment of an interest in a security agreement must be signed by the assignor and, unless it is attached to and is a part of the original agreement, must describe the agreement in sufficient detail to identify it, including its date, the names of the parties, the date of FAA recording, and the recorded conveyance number.

(4) An amendment of, or a supplement to, a conveyance executed for security purposes that has been recorded by the FAA must meet the requirements for recording the original conveyance and must describe the original conveyance in sufficient detail to identify it, including its date, the names of the parties, the date of FAA recording, and the recorded conveyance number.

(5) Immediately after a debt secured by a conveyance given for security purposes has been satisfied, or any of the encumbered aircraft have been released from the conveyance, the holder shall execute a release on AC Form 8050–41, Part II—Release, provided to him by the FAA when the conveyance was recorded by the FAA, or its equivalent, and shall send it to the FAA Aircraft Registry for recording. If the debt is secured by more than one aircraft and all

of the collateral is released, the collateral need not be described in detail in the release. However, the original conveyance must be clearly described in enough detail to identify it, including its date, the names of the parties, the date of FAA recording, and the recorded conveyance number.

(6) A contract of conditional sale, as defined in section 101(19) of the Federal Aviation Act of 1958 (49 U.S.C. 1301(19)), must be signed by all parties to the contract.

[Doc. No. 1996, 29 FR 6486, May 19, 1964, as amended by Amdt. 49–1, 31 FR 4499, Mar. 17, 1966; Amdt. 49–9, 53 FR 1915, Jan. 25, 1988]

§49.19 Effective date of filing for recordation.

A conveyance is filed for recordation upon the date and at the time it is received by the FAA Aircraft Registry.

§49.21 Return of original conveyance.

If a person submitting a conveyance for recording wants the original returned to him, he must submit a true copy with the original. After recording, the copy is kept by the FAA and the original is returned to the applicant stamped with the date and time of recording. The copy must be imprinted on paper permanent in nature, including dates, and signatures, to which is attached a certificate of the person submitting the conveyance stating that the copy has been compared with the original and that it is a true copy.

[Doc. No. 1996, 29 FR 6486, May 19, 1964, as amended by Amdt. 49–1, 31 FR 4499, Mar. 17, 1966]

Subpart C—Aircraft Ownership and Encumbrances Against Aircraft

§49.31 Applicability.

This subpart applies to the recording of the following kinds of conveyances:

(a) A bill of sale, contract of conditional sale, assignment of an interest under a contract of conditional sale, mortgage, assignment of mortgage, lease, equipment trust, notice of tax lien or of other lien, or other instrument affecting title to, or any interest in, aircraft.

(b) A release, cancellation, discharge, or satisfaction of a conveyance named in paragraph (a) of this section.

§49.33 Eligibility for recording: general requirements.

A conveyance is eligible for recording under this subpart only if, in addition to the requirements of §§49.11, 49.13, and 49.17, the following requirements are met:

(a) It is in a form prescribed by, or acceptable to, the Administrator for that kind of conveyance;

(b) It describes the aircraft by make and model, manufacturer's serial number, and United States registration number, or other detail that makes identification possible;

(c) It is an original document, or a duplicate original document, or if neither the original nor a duplicate original of a document is available, a true copy of an original document, certified under §49.21;

(d) It affects aircraft registered under section 501 of the Federal Aviation Act of 1958 (49 U.S.C. 1401); and

(e) It is accompanied by the recording fee required by §49.15, but there is no fee for recording a conveyance named in §49.31(b).

[Doc. No. 1996, 29 FR 6486, May 19, 1964, as amended by Amdt. 49–1, 31 FR 4499, Mar. 17, 1966]

§49.35 Eligibility for recording: ownership requirements.

If the seller of an aircraft is not shown on the records of the FAA as the owner of the aircraft, a conveyance, including a contract of conditional sale, submitted for recording under this subpart must be accompanied by bills of sale or similar documents showing consecutive transfers from the last registered owner, through each intervening owner, to the seller.

§49.37 Claims for salvage or extraordinary expenses.

The right to a charge arising out of a claim for compensation for salvage of an aircraft or for extraordinary expenses indispensable for preserving the aircraft in operations terminated in a foreign country that is a party to the Convention on the International Recognition of Rights in Aircraft (4 U.S.T.

1830) may be noted on the FAA record by filing notice thereof with the FAA Aircraft Registry within three months after the date of termination of the salvage or preservation operations.

Subpart D—Encumbrances Against Specifically Identified Aircraft Engines and Propellers

§ 49.41　Applicability.

This subpart applies to the recording of the following kinds of conveyances:

(a) Any lease, a notice of tax lien or other lien (except a notice of Federal tax lien referred to in § 49.17(a)), and any mortgage, equipment trust, contract of conditional sale, or other instrument executed for security purposes, which affects title to, or any interest in, any specifically identified aircraft engine of 750 or more rated takeoff horsepower, or the equivalent of that horsepower, or a specifically identified aircraft propeller capable of absorbing 750 or more rated takeoff shaft horsepower.

(b) An assignment or amendment of, or supplement to, an instrument named in paragraph (a) of this section.

(c) A release, cancellation, discharge, or satisfaction of a conveyance named in paragraph (a) or (b) of this section.

[Doc. No. 1996, 29 FR 6486, May 19, 1964, as amended by Amdt. 49-5, 35 FR 802, Jan 21, 1970]

§ 49.43　Eligibility for recording: general requirements.

A conveyance is eligible for recording under this subpart only if, in addition to the requirements of §§ 49.11, 49.13, and 49.17, the following requirements are met:

(a) It affects and describes an aircraft engine or propeller to which this subpart applies, specifically identified by make, model, horsepower, and manufacturer's serial number; and

(b) It is accompanied by the recording fee required by § 49.15, but there is no fee for recording a conveyance named in § 49.41(c).

§ 49.45　Recording of releases, cancellations, discharges, and satisfactions: special requirements.

(a) A release, cancellation, discharge, or satisfaction of an encumbrance created by an instrument recorded under this subpart must be in a form equivalent to AC Form 8050-41 and contain a description of the encumbrance, the recording information furnished to the holder at the time of recording, and the collateral released.

(b) If more than one engine or propeller, or both, are listed in an instrument, recorded under this subpart, that created an encumbrance thereon and all of them are released, they need not be listed by serial number, but the release, cancellation, discharge, or satisfaction must state that all of the encumbered engines or propellers are released. The original recorded document must be clearly identified by the names of the parties, the date of FAA recording, and the document date.

[Doc. No. 1996, 29 FR 6486, May 19, 1964, as amended by Amdt. 49-7, 37 FR 25487, Dec. 1, 1972]

Subpart E—Encumbrances Against Air Carrier Aircraft Engines, Propellers, Appliances, and Spare Parts

§ 49.51　Applicability.

This subpart applies to the recording of the following kinds of conveyances:

(a) Any lease, a notice of tax lien or other lien (except a notice of Federal tax lien referred to in § 49.17(a), and any mortgage, equipment trust, contract of conditional sale, or other instrument executed for security purposes, which affects title to, or any interest in, any aircraft engine, propeller, or appliance maintained by or on behalf of an air carrier certificated under section 604(b) of the Federal Aviation Act of 1958 (49 U.S.C. 1424(b)) for installation or use in aircraft, aircraft engines, or propellers, or any spare parts, maintained at a designated location or locations by or on behalf of such an air carrier.

(b) An assignment or amendment of, or supplement to, an instrument named in paragraph (a) of this section.

(c) A release, cancellation, discharge, or satisfaction of a conveyance named in paragraph (a) or (b) of this section.

[Doc. No. 1996, 29 FR 6486, May 19, 1964, as amended by Amdt. 49–5, 35 FR 802, Jan. 21, 1970]

§ 49.53 Eligibility for recording: general requirements.

(a) A conveyance is eligible for recording under this subpart only if, in addition to the requirements of §§ 49.11, 49.13, and 49.17, the following requirements are met:

(1) It affects any aircraft engine, propeller, appliance, or spare part, maintained by or on behalf of an air carrier certificated under section 604(b) of the Federal Aviation Act of 1958 (49 U.S.C. 1424(b));

(2) It contains or is accompanied by a statement by the air carrier certificated under that section;

(3) It specifically describes the location or locations of each aircraft engine, propeller, appliance, or spare part covered by it; and

(4) It is accompanied by the recording fee required by § 49.15, but there is no fee for recording a conveyance named in § 49.51(c).

(b) The conveyance need only describe generally, by type, the engines, propellers, appliances, or spare parts covered by it.

[Doc. No. 1996, 29 FR 6486, May 19, 1964, as amended by Amdt. 49–5, 35 FR 802, Jan. 21, 1970]

§ 49.55 Recording of releases, cancellations, discharges, and satisfactions: special requirements.

(a) A release, cancellation, discharge, or satisfaction of an encumbrance on all of the collateral listed in an instrument recorded under this subpart, or on all of the collateral at a particular location, must be in a form equivalent to AC Form 8050–41, signed by the holder of all of the collateral at the particular location, and contain a description of the encumbrance, the recording information furnished to the holder at the time of recording, and the location of the released collateral.

(b) If the encumbrance on collateral at all of the locations listed in an instrument recorded under this subpart is released, canceled, discharged, or satisfied, the locations need not be listed. However, the document must state that all of the collateral at all of the locations listed in the encumbrance has been so released, canceled, discharged, or satisfied. The original recorded document must be clearly identified by the names of the parties, the date of recording by the FAA, and the document number.

[Doc. No. 1996, 29 FR 6486, May 19, 1964, as amended by Amdt. 49–1, 31 FR 4499, Mar. 17, 1966; Amdt. 49–7, 37 FR 25487, Dec. 1, 1972]

PARTS 50–59 [RESERVED]

FINDING AIDS

A list of CFR titles, subtitles, chapters, subchapters and parts and an alphabetical list of agencies publishing in the CFR are included in the CFR Index and Finding Aids volume to the Code of Federal Regulations which is published separately and revised annually.

Material Approved for Incorporation by Reference
Table of CFR Titles and Chapters
Alphabetical List of Agencies Appearing in the CFR
List of CFR Sections Affected

Material Approved for Incorporation by Reference

(Revised as of January 1, 2003)

The Director of the Federal Register has approved under 5 U.S.C. 552(a) and 1 CFR Part 51 the incorporation by reference of the following publications. This list contains only those incorporations by reference effective as of the revision date of this volume. Incorporations by reference found within a regulation are effective upon the effective date of that regulation. For more information on incorporation by reference, see the preliminary pages of this volume.

14 CFR (PARTS 1–59)
FEDERAL AVIATION ADMINISTRATION, DEPARTMENT OF TRANSPORTATION

14 CFR

ACS Products Co
P.O. Box 152, 1585 Copper Dr., Lake Havasu City, AZ 86403-0008

SB SB92-01, dated August 15, 1992	39.13
SB SB92-01, dated August 15, 1992	39.13

Aerocon California, Inc
Western Aircraft Maintenance, 4444 Aeronca St., Boise, ID 83705

Engineering Order (E.O.) B-9975-02 dated Nov. 14, 1975	39.13
Service Letter dated May 25, 1976	39.13

Aeromot Industria Mecanico Metalurgica Itda
Grupo Aeromot, Aeromot-Industria Mecanico Metalurgica Itda., Av. Das Industrias, 1210-Bairro Anchieta, Caixa Postal 8031, 90 200-290-Porto Alegre-RS, Brazil

Service Bulletin No. 200-27-078 dated September 18, 2001	39.13
Mandatory SB No. 100-53-042, Rev. 1, dated July 3, 1997	39.13
Mandatory SB No. 100-53-042, Rev. 1, dated July 3, 1997	39.13
SB-200-79-036, dated January 30, 1997	39.13

Aerospace Lighting Corp
101-8 Colin Dr., Holbrook, NY 11741

II AL-11023M, Rev. A, dated May 20, 1994	39.13
II AL-11024M, dated March 15, 1992	39.13
II AL-11025M, dated March 15, 1992	39.13
Information Bulletin IB 90-001 dated March 30, 1990	39.13
No. IB 90-001, Rev. 1, dated August 15, 1992	39.13

Aerospace Technologies of Australia Pty Ltd
ASTA DEFENCE Private Bag No. 4, Beach Road Lara 3212, Victoria, Australia

Alert SB ANMD-27-27, Rev. 1, dated November 5, 1982	39.13
SB ANMD-53-13, Rev. 3, dated October 24, 1995	39.13
SB ANMD-55-23, Rev. 1, dated July 11, 1991	39.13
SB ANMD-55-26, Rev. 8, dated April 15, 1994	39.13
SB ANMSD-55-34, dated April 22, 1996	39.13
SB NMD-27-24, dated October 8, 1982	39.13
SB NMD-53-5, Rev. 2, dated December 6, 1995	39.13

Aerospatiale
316 Route de Bayonne 31060 Toulouse Cedex 03 France

Title 14—Aeronautics and Space

Material Approved for Incorporation by Reference

	14 CFR
SB ATR42-22-0015, Rev. 1, dated March 6, 1992	39.13
SB ATR42-22-0015, Rev. 2, dated July 29, 1993	39.13
SB ATR42-25-0075, dated September 4, 1991	39.13
SB ATR42-25-0084, dated, April 10, 1992	39.13
SB ATR42-25-0094, dated June 23, 1995	39.13
SB ATR42-27-0022, Rev. 1, dated April 14, 1988	39.13
SB ATR42-27-0048, Rev. 2, dated May 16, 1991	39.13
SB ATR42-27-0049, Rev. 2, dated May 16, 1991	39.13
SB ATR42-27-0050, dated November 22, 1990	39.13
SB ATR42-27-0051, dated November 22, 1990	39.13
SB ATR42-27-0052, Rev. 1 dated April 4, 1991	39.13
SB ATR42-27-0058, Rev. 1, dated February 27, 1992	39.13
SB ATR42-27-0058, Rev. 2, dated July 5, 1993	39.13
SB ATR42-27-0068, dated January 25, 1994	39.13
SB ATR42-27-0069, dated January 25, 1994	39.13
SB ATR42-27-0071, dated February 23, 1994	39.13
SB ATR42-27-0083, dated November 22, 1996	39.13
SB ATR42-32-0028, Rev. 3 dated Feb. 12, 1991	39.13
SB ATR42-32-0036, Rev. 1, dated February 15, 1991	39.13
SB ATR42-32-0036, Rev. 1, dated February 15, 1991	39.13
SB ATR42-32-0036, Rev. 3, dated December 12, 1991	39.13
SB ATR42-32-0036, Rev. 3, dated December 12, 1991	39.13
SB ATR42-32-0036, Rev. 3, dated December 12, 1991	39.13
SB ATR42-32-0038, Rev. 1 dated June 24, 1991	39.13
SB ATR42-32-0039, Rev. 1 dated Aug. 1, 1991	39.13
SB ATR42-32-0040, dated February 24, 1992	39.13
SB ATR42-32-0040, dated February 24, 1992	39.13
SB ATR42-32-0040, dated February 24, 1992	39.13
SB ATR42-32-0040, Rev. 1 dated January 18, 1993	39.13
SB ATR42-32-0040, Rev. 1, dated January 18, 1993	39.13
SB ATR42-32-0040, Rev. 1, dated January 18, 1993	39.13
SB ATR42-32-0081, dated July 16, 1996	39.13
SB ATR42-32-0082, dated July 16, 1996	39.13
SB ATR42-52-0072, dated October 2, 1995	39.13
SB ATR42-53-0004, Rev. 4 dated July 25, 1989	39.13
SB ATR42-53-0023, Rev. 2 dated May 25, 1989	39.13
SB ATR42-53-0031, Rev. 1 dated May 20, 1989	39.13
SB ATR42-53-0031, Rev. 2 dated May 31, 1990	39.13
SB ATR42-53-0031, Rev. 3 dated Feb. 19, 1991	39.13
SB ATR42-53-0042 dated May 3, 1989	39.13
SB ATR42-53-0042, Rev. 1 dated Apr. 22, 1991	39.13
SB ATR42-53-0043, Rev. 4 dated April 30, 1991	39.13
SB ATR42-53-0070, dated June 10, 1991	39.13
SB ATR42-53-0070, Rev. 1, dated June 12, 1992	39.13
SB ATR42-53-0070, Rev. 2, dated March 22, 1993	39.13
SB ATR42-53-0081, Rev. 1, dated December 9, 1994	39.13
SB ATR42-53-0082, dated June 6, 1994	39.13
SB ATR42-53-0093, Rev. 1, dated February 19, 1996	39.13
SB ATR42-53-0094, Rev. 2, dated February 19, 1996	39.13
SB ATR42-53-0103, dated September 23, 1996	39.13

Title 14—Aeronautics and Space

Material Approved for Incorporation by Reference

	14 CFR
SB No. 67.11 dated March 23, 1989	39.13
SB No. 67.14 dated April 18, 1990	39.13
SB No. ATR42-30-0059, Rev. 1, dated April 10, 1995	39.13
SB No. ATR42-57-0043, Rev. 1, dated April 10, 1995	39.13
SB No. ATR72-30-1023, Rev. 1, dated April 10, 1995	39.13
SB No. ATR72-57-1015, Rev. 1, dated April 10, 1995	39.13
SB No. ATR72-57-1016, Rev. 1, dated April 10, 1995	39.13
Service Bulletin 05.71R4 (Revision 4) dated December 18, 1990	39.13
Service Bulletin No. 01.14a	39.13
Service Bulletin No. 01.17a	39.13
SB 05-65 dated February 14, 1978	39.13
SB 65-81, Issue 2 dated February 14, 1976	39.13
SB No. 01.49 and Lana SA 315 SB No. 01.18	39.13
SB No. 01.49, Rev. 1 dated May 30, 1986	39.13
SB 05-14 dated February 14, 1979	39.13
SB 65-06, Issue 2 dated February 14, 1977	39.13
Imperative SB 57 dated Jan. 1991	39.13
SB 150 dated June 1991	39.13

Aerostar Aircraft Corporation

10555 Airport Drive, Coeur d'Alene Airport, Hayden Lake, Idaho 83835-8742

SB 600-121 dated Sept. 12, 1991	39.13
SB No. 746C, dated September 15, 1992	39.13
SB SB600-130, dated September 26, 1995	39.13
SB SB600-132, dated September 3, 1997	39.13
Mandatory Service Bulletin SB600-131A dated January 10, 1998	39.13
Service Bulletin SB600-134A dated March 31, 2000	39.13
SB 861 dated May 4, 1987	39.13
Special Advisory 60-7 dated Jan. 11, 1991	39.13

Aerotechnikcz s.r.o.

686 04 Kunovic, Czech Republic; telephone: +420 632 537111; Fax: +420 632 537 900

Service Bulletin SEH 13-005a dated November 18, 1999	39.13

Agusta

21017 Cascina Costa di Samarate (VA) Italy Via Giovanni Agusta 520

Alert Bollettino Tecnico 412-83 Revision A dated December 29, 2000	39.13
Alert Bollettino Tecnico No. 109-106 Revision B dated December 19, 2000.	39.13
Alert Bollettino Tecnico No. 109EP-1 Revision B dated December 19, 2000.	39.13
Alert Bollettino Tecnico No. 109EP-14 Revision A dated March 19, 2001.	39.13
Alert Bollettino Tecnico No. 109EP-30 Revision A dated July 25, 2002.	39.13
Alert Bollettino Tecnico No. 109K-22 Revision B dated December 19, 2000.	39.13
Alert Bollettino Tecnico No. 119-6 Revision A dated July 12, 2002	39.13
Bollettino Tecnico No. 109EP-16 dated December 21, 2000	39.13
Bollettino Tecnico No. 119-1 Revision A dated August 22, 2001	39.13

Title 14—Aeronautics and Space

14 CFR (PARTS 1–59)—Continued
FEDERAL AVIATION ADMINISTRATION, DEPARTMENT OF TRANSPORTATION—
Continued

14 CFR

Agusta (Costruzioni Aeronautiche Giovanni Agusta S.p.A.)
   Direzione Supporto Prodotto E Servizi, 21019 Somma Lombardo
   (VA), Via per Tornavento, 15, Italy

Alert Bollettino Tecnico No. 109EP-14 dated October 11, 2000	39.13
Bollettino Tecnico dated December 22, 1998	39.13
Bollettino Tecnico 109-103 dated November 22, 1995	39.13
Bollettino Tecnico 109EP-12 dated July 24, 2000	39.13
Bollettino Tecnico 109K-10 dated November 22, 1995	39.13
Bollettino Tecnico No. 109-96, dated March 30, 1994	39.13
Bollettino Tecnico No. 109K-16, dated April 24, 1997	39.13
Service Bulletin 109-111 dated October 14, 1999	39.13
Technical Bulletin 109EP-5 dated December 22, 1999	39.13

Air Cruisers Company
   Technical Publications Department, P.O. Box 180, Belmar, NJ
   07719-0180

SB 001-25-8, Rev. 4 dated May 24, 1990	39.13
SB 105-25-30, Rev. 1 dated August 21, 1989	39.13
SB 201-25-13 dated Sept. 17, 1990	39.13
SB 35-25-2 dated Oct. 30, 1990	39.13
SB 35-25-3 dated Oct. 22, 1990	39.13
SB 757-105-25-51, dated January 29, 1999	39.13
SB S.B. 103-25-19, Rev. 7, dated April 18, 1996	39.13
SB S.B. 201-25-17, dated June 4, 1992	39.13

Air Research Technology, Inc.
   3440 McCarthy Montreal Quebec Canada H4K

SB No. SB-1-96, Issue 1, dated April 11, 1996	39.13

Air Tractor, Inc
   P.O. Box 485, Olney, TX 76374-0150

Service Letter 90 dated May 6, 1991	39.13
Service Letter No. 138, dated July 29, 1995	39.13
Service Letter No. 76 Instructions, as referenced in Snow Engineering Co. Service Letter No. 76, dated December 12, 1988.	39.13
Process Specification 197 Revised May 3, 2002	39.13
Process Specification 197 Revised May 1, 2002	39.13
Report No. 138, dated July 29, 1995, revised August 7, 1996	39.13
Service Letter (SL) No. 134, dated November 29, 1994	39.13
Service Letter 104A, dated July 29, 1995	39.13
Service Letter 195 dated February 4, 2000	39.13
Service Letter 196 Revised dated March 7, 2000	39.13
Service Letter 197 dated June 13, 2000	39.13
Service Letter 220 May 3, 2002	39.13
Service Letter 97 Revision 1 dated October 3, 2000	39.13
Service Letter No. 140, dated November 27, 1995, Revised October 10, 1996.	39.13
Service Letter No. 165, dated May 15, 1998	39.13
Service Letter No. 197 Revision 2 dated March 26, 2001	39.13
Service Letter No. 199 dated May 30, 2000	39.13
Service Letter No. 202 Revision 2 dated March 26, 2001	39.13
Service Letter No. 203 Revision 1 dated March 26, 2001	39.13
Service Letter No. 205 Revision 3 dated March 26, 2001	39.13
SL No. 135, dated February 1, 1995	39.13

Material Approved for Incorporation by Reference

FEDERAL AVIATION ADMINISTRATION, DEPARTMENT OF TRANSPORTATION—Continued

14 CFR

Airbus Industrie

P.O. Box 33, 1 Rond Point Maurice Bellonte F-31707 Blagnac Cedex France

2.05.00/43 dated September 16, 1999	39.13
A300 Flight Manual Temporary Revision 4.02.00/08 dated April 25, 2001.	39.13
A300 Flight Manual Temporary Revision 4.02.00/09 dated April 26, 2001.	39.13
A300 Supplemental Structural Inspection Document (SSID), Rev. 2, dated June, 1994.	39.13
A300 Supplemental Structural Inspection Document, dated September 1989.	39.13
A300-54-070, Rev. 1, dated March 17, 1992	39.13
A300-57-0232, Rev. 01, dated January 12, 1998	39.13
A300-600 Flight Manual Temporary Revision 4.02.00/11 dated March 21, 2000.	39.13
A300-600 Flight Manual Temporary Revision 4.02.00/13 dated March 28, 2000.	39.13
A300-600 Flight Manual Temporary Revision 5.03.00/01 dated January 22, 2001.	39.13
A300/ AOT 71-07, dated September 8, 1998	39.13
A310 Flight Manual Temporary Revision 4.02.00/11 dated March 21, 2000.	39.13
A310 Flight Manual Temporary Revision 4.02.00/12 dated March 22, 2000.	39.13
A310 Flight Manual Temporary Revision 4.02.00/13 dated March 23, 2000.	39.13
A310 Flight Manual Temporary Revision 4.02.00/14 dated March 24, 2000.	39.13
A310 Flight Manual Temporary Revision 5.03.00/01 dated January 22, 2001.	39.13
A310 Flight Manual Temporary Revision 5.03.00/02 dated January 22, 2001.	39.13
A319/320/321 Airplane Flight Manual Temporary Rev. 9.99.99/02, Issue 02, dated April 8, 1997.	39.13
A319/320/321 Airplane Flight Manual Temporary Rev. 9.99.99/44, Issue 3, dated March 3, 1998.	39.13
A319/A321 AOT 32-15, dated July 1, 1997	39.13
A320/A321 Flight Manual Temporary Rev. 9.99.99/20, dated June 14, 1994.	39.13
A340 Airplane Flight Manual Temporary Rev. 4.03.00/14, dated October 18, 1996.	39.13
Airplane Flight Manual Temporary Revision 3.02.00/11 undated	39.13
Airplane Flight Manual Temporary Revision 3.02.00/7 undated	39.13
Airplane Flight Manual Temporary Revision 3.02.00/8 undated	39.13
Airplane Flight Manual Temporary Revision 5.02.00/60 Issue 2 dated September 14, 2001.	39.13
Airplane Flight Manual Temporary Revision 5.03.00/21 Issue 2 dated September 14, 2001.	39.13
All Operator Telex A300-22A0115 dated December 23, 1999	39.13
All Operator Telex A300-53A0350 dated October 25, 1999	39.13
All Operator Telex A300-53A0352 dated January 4, 2000	39.13

Title 14—Aeronautics and Space

Material Approved for Incorporation by Reference

FEDERAL AVIATION ADMINISTRATION, DEPARTMENT OF TRANSPORTATION—
Continued

	14 CFR
AOT 29-07, dated August 28, 1992	39.13
AOT 29-09, dated Novemer 16, 1993	39.13
AOT 29-15, dated May 30, 1995	39.13
AOT 29-21, Rev. 1, dated January 8, 1997	39.13
AOT 29-22, dated November 24, 1997	39.13
AOT 30-01, Rev. 2, dated March 6, 1995	39.13
AOT 32-04, Rev. 1 dated Oct. 22, 1991	39.13
AOT 32-14, dated February 3, 1997	39.13
AOT 32-14, Rev. 01, dated March 13, 1997	39.13
AOT 32-17, Rev. 01, dated November 6, 1997	39.13
AOT 32-19, dated July 7, 1998	39.13
AOT 34-03, dated February 20, 1996	39.13
AOT 34-04, dated July 16, 1996	39.13
AOT 36-02, dated August 23, 1995	39.13
AOT 38-01, dated December 15, 1993	39.13
AOT 49-01, Issue 3 dated April 25, 1991	39.13
AOT 52-06, dated February 4, 1994	39.13
AOT 52-07, dated July 28, 1994	39.13
AOT 52-08, Rev. 1, dated December 1, 1994	39.13
AOT 53-01, dated August 27, 1992	39.13
AOT 53-02, dated November 2, 1992	39.13
AOT 53-04, dated January 20, 1993	39.13
AOT 53-05, Rev. 1, dated August 16, 1993	39.13
AOT 53-08, Rev. 01, dated January 15, 1996	39.13
AOT 53-11, dated October 13, 1997	39.13
AOT 56-01, Rev. 1, dated April 29, 1994	39.13
AOT 57-03, Issue 2 dated June 13, 1991	39.13
AOT 57-04 dated June 21, 1991	39.13
AOT 57-08, Rev. 1, dated June 28, 1994	39.13
AOT 71-06, dated October 21, 1997	39.13
AOT 78-03, Rev. 1, dated July 20, 1994	39.13
AOT 78-05, Rev. 1, dated February 8, 1995	39.13
Change Notice 1.A. to A300-54-063 dated February 13, 1990	39.13
Change Notice 1.A. to A300-54-066 dated February 13, 1990	39.13
Change Notice 2.A. to A300-54-060 dated February 13, 1990	39.13
Change Notice OB to A300-57-165 dated November 27, 1990	39.13
Change Notice, dated July 8, 1985	39.13
Document A300 Corrosion Prevention and Control Program, dated November 1992.	39.13
Flight Manual A300/600 Rev. 4.03.00/18, dated November 4, 1996	39.13
Flight Manual A300/600 Temporary Rev. 4.03.00/19, dated November 4, 1996.	39.13
Flight Manual A310 Temporary Rev. 4.03.00/20, dated November 4, 1996.	39.13
Flight Manual A310 Temporary Rev. 4.03.00/21, dated November 4, 1996.	39.13
Flight Manual A319/320/321 Temporary Rev. 2.05.00/13, dated October 18, 1996.	39.13
Flight Operations TELEX 999.0099/98 Revision 5 dated May 21, 1999	39.13
Model A300 Temporary Rev. 5.02.00/1 dated December 4, 1991	39.13

14 CFR (PARTS 1–59)—Continued
FEDERAL AVIATION ADMINISTRATION, DEPARTMENT OF TRANSPORTATION—
Continued

	14 CFR
Model A300 Temporary Rev. 5.04.00/1 dated November 4, 1991	39.13
Model A300 Temporary Rev. 5.04.00/2 dated December 4, 1991	39.13
Model A310 Temporary Rev. 5.04.00/1 dated October 22, 1991	39.13
Model A310 Temporary Rev. 5.04.00/3 dated February 13, 1992	39.13
Model A310 Temporary Rev. 5.04.00/4 dated March 6, 1992	39.13
Model A319/320/321 Flight Manual Temporary Rev. 4.03.00/02, dated May 28, 1997.	39.13
Model A320 Airplane Flight Manual Temporary Rev. 9.99.99/90, Issue 2, dated December 22, 1992.	39.13
Operations Engineering Bulletin No. 50/1 dated November 28, 1986	39.13
Operations Engineering Bulletin No. 86/1 dated November 28, 1987	39.13
SB 300-53-0309, dated March 19, 1997	39.13
SB 320-57-1025, Rev. 05, dated June 26, 1997	39.13
SB 340-32-4087, Rev. 2, dated May 27, 1997	39.13
SB A-320-32-1061, Rev. 3, dated October 19, 1992	39.13
SB A300-22-6010, dated April 18, 1989	39.13
SB A300-22-6011, dated June 8, 1990	39.13
SB A300-22-6017, dated September 2, 1991	39.13
SB A300-22-6021, Rev. 1, dated December 24, 1993	39.13
SB A300-22-6032, Rev. 1, dated January 8, 1997	39.13
SB A300-22-6035, dated July 16, 1996	39.13
SB A300-24-0082, dated March 3, 1993	39.13
SB A300-24-0082, dated March 3, 1993	39.13
SB A300-24-6029, Rev. 1 dated Feb. 22, 1991	39.13
SB A300-25-0465, dated October 31, 1997	39.13
SB A300-25-395, as revised by Change Notice OB, dated June 2, 1985, and Change Notice OC, dated June 20, 1988 dated March 22, 1984.	39.13
SB A300-25-434 dated Oct. 22, 1990	39.13
SB A300-25-6028 dated Oct. 22, 1990	39.13
SB A300-26-055, Rev. 1, dated September 4, 1991	39.13
SB A300-26-055, Rev. 2, dated December 18, 1991	39.13
SB A300-26-6030, Rev. 02, dated April 4, 1997	39.13
SB A300-27-0188, Rev. 2, dated October 1, 1997	39.13
SB A300-27-6025, dated September 15, 1993	39.13
SB A300-27-6025, Rev. 1, dated August 31, 1994	39.13
SB A300-27-6025, Rev. 2, dated April 19, 1995	39.13
SB A300-27-6026, dated May 5, 1994	39.13
SB A300-27-6026, Rev. 1, dated August 31, 1995	39.13
SB A300-27-6028, dated December 19, 1994	39.13
SB A300-27-6035, dated November 26, 1996	39.13
SB A300-27-6036, Rev. 2, dated October 1, 1997	39.13
SB A300-27-6037, Revision 1, dated September 29, 1998	39.13
SB A300-27-6042, Revision 1, dated February 17, 1999	39.13
SB A300-28-0061, Rev. 1, dated March 14, 1992	39.13
SB A300-28-0063, Rev. 01, dated January 15, 1997	39.13
SB A300-28-0071, dated January 15, 1997	39.13
SB A300-28-055, Change Notice 3.A, dated March 16, 1992	39.13
SB A300-28-055, Rev. 3, dated December 19, 1991	39.13
SB A300-28-6031, Rev. 01, dated January 15, 1997	39.13

Material Approved for Incorporation by Reference

	14 CFR
SB A300-28-6035, Revision 3, dated August 5, 1999	39.13
SB A300-28-6054, dated January 15, 1997	39.13
SB A300-28-6055, Revision 01, dated July 24, 1998	39.13
SB A300-28A065, Rev. 1, dated February 14, 1994	39.13
SB A300-28A6033, Rev. 1, dated February 14, 1994	39.13
SB A300-29-0099, dated January 30, 1992	39.13
SB A300-29-0108, dated April 1, 1996	39.13
SB A300-29-0109, dated January 27, 1997	39.13
SB A300-29-097, Rev. 2 dated August 27, 1991	39.13
SB A300-29-2077, dated January 27, 1997	39.13
SB A300-29-6022, Rev. 2 dated August 27, 1991	39.13
SB A300-29-6024, Rev. 1 dated June 10, 1992	39.13
SB A300-29-6037, dated April 1, 1996	39.13
SB A300-29-6038, dated January 27, 1997	39.13
SB A300-32-0418, Rev. 1, dated April 29, 1996	39.13
SB A300-32-0425, Rev. 01, dated October 10, 1997	39.13
SB A300-32-0425, Revision 2, dated June 23, 1998	39.13
SB A300-32-6061, Rev. 1, dated April 29, 1996	39.13
SB A300-32-6072, Rev. 01, dated October 10, 1997	39.13
SB A300-32-6072, Revision 2, dated June 23, 1998	39.13
SB A300-33-0119, dated March 1, 1993	39.13
SB A300-33-6013, dated March 1, 1989	39.13
SB A300-33-6020, dated March 1, 1993	39.13
SB A300-35-6001, Rev. 2, dated April 30, 1991	39.13
SB A300-36-0033, dated October 17, 1994	39.13
SB A300-36-6024, dated October 17, 1994	39.13
SB A300-49-0049 dated July 12, 1991	39.13
SB A300-49-6009 dated July 12, 1991	39.13
SB A300-52-0161, dated October 3, 1994	39.13
SB A300-53- 6055, dated October 28, 1993	39.13
SB A300-53- 6056, dated February 23, 1996	39.13
SB A300-53-027, Rev. 4, dated January 30, 1981	39.13
SB A300-53-0294, dated May 17, 1993	39.13
SB A300-53-0300, dated October 28, 1993	39.13
SB A300-53-0314, dated January 14, 1997	39.13
SB A300-53-0329, Rev. 01, dated October 17, 1997	39.13
SB A300-53-0331, Revision 01, dated November 5, 1998	39.13
SB A300-53-100, Rev. 1, dated May 10, 1984	39.13
SB A300-53-100, Rev. 2, dated July 11, 1995	39.13
SB A300-53-101, Rev. 7, dated May 10, 1984	39.13
SB A300-53-103, Rev. 4 dated June 30, 1983	39.13
SB A300-53-103, Rev. 5, dated February 23, 1994	39.13
SB A300-53-112, Rev. 2, dated July 20, 1981	39.13
SB A300-53-121, Rev. 3, dated January 30, 1981	39.13
SB A300-53-126, Rev. 7 dated November 11, 1990	39.13
SB A300-53-126, Rev. 8, dated September 18, 1991	39.13
SB A300-53-127, Rev. 4, dated May 10, 1984	39.13
SB A300-53-143, Rev. 3, dated May 10, 1984	39.13
SB A300-53-146, Rev. 7 dated April 26, 1991	39.13
SB A300-53-152, Rev. 1, dated January 30, 1981	39.13

14 CFR (PARTS 1–59)—Continued
FEDERAL AVIATION ADMINISTRATION, DEPARTMENT OF TRANSPORTATION—
Continued

	14 CFR
SB A300-53-152, Rev. 4, dated March 13, 1992	39.13
SB A300-53-162, Rev. 4 dated November 12, 1990	39.13
SB A300-53-162, Rev. 5, dated March 17, 1994	39.13
SB A300-53-182, Rev. 3, dated March 16, 1994	39.13
SB A300-53-192, Rev. 7, dated July 13, 1992	39.13
SB A300-53-196, Rev. 1 dated November 12, 1990	39.13
SB A300-53-2030, Rev. 5, dated March 6, 1991	39.13
SB A300-53-2037, Rev. 1, dated April 29, 1992	39.13
SB A300-53-204, Rev. 6, dated October 11, 1993	39.13
SB A300-53-225, Rev. 2 dated May 30, 1990	39.13
SB A300-53-226, Rev. 5 dated September 7, 1991	39.13
SB A300-53-227, Rev. 1, dated April 29, 1992	39.13
SB A300-53-233, Rev. 1, dated April 18, 1991	39.13
SB A300-53-278 dated November 12, 1990	39.13
SB A300-53-278, Rev. 1, dated March 17, 1994	39.13
SB A300-53-301, dated September 28, 1995	39.13
SB A300-53-301, Rev. 1, dated February 20, 1997	39.13
SB A300-53-302, dated November 3, 1995	39.13
SB A300-53-303, dated February 23, 1996	39.13
SB A300-53-6002, Rev. 3, dated February 22, 1992	39.13
SB A300-53-6011, Rev. 3, dated February 4, 1991	39.13
SB A300-53-6018, Rev. 1, dated April 29, 1992	39.13
SB A300-53-6022, dated February 4, 1991	39.13
SB A300-53-6037, dated March 21, 1995	39.13
SB A300-53-6042, Rev. 1, dated February 20, 1995	39.13
SB A300-53-6045, dated March 21, 1995, including Change Notice O.A., dated June 1, 1995.	39.13
SB A300-53-6046, Rev. 1, dated April 5, 1994	39.13
SB A300-53-6060, dated March 19, 1997	39.13
SB A300-53-6066, dated October 16, 1996	39.13
SB A300-53-6066, Rev. 01, dated March 11, 1998	39.13
SB A300-53-6105, Rev. 01, dated October 17, 1997	39.13
SB A300-53-6107, Revision 01, dated November 5, 1998	39.13
SB A300-54- 045, Rev. 6, dated February 25, 1994	39.13
SB A300-54-0073, Rev. 1, dated March 28, 1994	39.13
SB A300-54-0084, dated April 21, 1994	39.13
SB A300-54-045, Rev. 4 dated January 31, 1990	39.13
SB A300-54-046, dated June 24, 1982	39.13
SB A300-54-060, Rev. 2 dated September 7, 1988	39.13
SB A300-54-060, Rev. 3, dated February 25, 1994	39.13
SB A300-54-063, Rev. 1 dated April 22, 1990	39.13
SB A300-54-063, Rev. 2, dated February 25, 1994	39.13
SB A300-54-066, Rev. 1 dated February 15, 1989	39.13
SB A300-54-066, Rev. 2, dated February 25, 1994	39.13
SB A300-54-6014, Rev. 1, dated March 28, 1994	39.13
SB A300-55-0044, dated October 22, 1996	39.13
SB A300-55-026, Rev. 3, dated May 10, 1984	39.13
SB A300-55-026, Rev. 4, dated February 16, 1998	39.13
SB A300-55-6008, dated December 10, 1990	39.13
SB A300-55-6010, dated April 18, 1991	39.13

Material Approved for Incorporation by Reference

	14 CFR
SB A300-55-6023, dated October 22, 1996	39.13
SB A300-57- 0167, Rev. 1, (including Appendix 1), dated May 25, 1993.	39.13
SB A300-57-0168, Rev. 3, (including Appendix 1), dated November 22, 1993.	39.13
SB A300-57-0180, Rev. 1, dated March 29, 1993	39.13
SB A300-57-0185, Rev. 1, (including Appendix 1), dated March 8, 1993.	39.13
SB A300-57-0194, Rev. 2, (including Appendix 1), dated August 19, 1993.	39.13
SB A300-57-0204, dated December 4, 1995	39.13
SB A300-57-0213, dated August 12, 1994	39.13
SB A300-57-0229, dated October 16, 1996	39.13
SB A300-57-0234, Revision 1, dated March 11, 1998	39.13
SB A300-57-0235, Revision 1, including Appendix 1, both dated February 1, 1999.	39.13
SB A300-57-026, Rev. 3, dated October 21, 1982	39.13
SB A300-57-026, Rev. 4, dated December 12, 1985	39.13
SB A300-57-109, Rev. 1, dated July 10, 1982	39.13
SB A300-57-116, Rev. 6, dated July 16, 1993	39.13
SB A300-57-128, Rev. 3, dated January 26, 1990	39.13
SB A300-57-141, Rev. 7, dated July 16, 1993	39.13
SB A300-57-145, Rev. 3 dated February 10, 1988	39.13
SB A300-57-150, Rev. 1 dated September 18, 1987	39.13
SB A300-57-165 dated May 21, 1990	39.13
SB A300-57-166, Rev. 3, (including Appendix 1), dated July 12, 1993.	39.13
SB A300-57-6005, Rev. 2, dated December 16, 1993	39.13
SB A300-57-6006, Rev. 4, dated July 25, 1994	39.13
SB A300-57-6017, Rev. 1, (includes Appendix 1) dated July 25, 1994	39.13
SB A300-57-6017, Revision 3, dated	39.13
SB A300-57-6028, Rev. 3, dated September 13, 1994	39.13
SB A300-57-6037, dated August 1, 1994	39.13
SB A300-57-6044, Rev. 2, dated September 6, 1995, including Appendix 1, dated November 25, 1994.	39.13
SB A300-57-6045, Rev. 1, dated August 3, 1994, including Appendix 1, Rev. 1, dated August 3, 1994.	39.13
SB A300-57-6045, Rev. 2, dated April 21, 1998, including Appendix 1, Rev. 02, dated April 21, 1998.	39.13
SB A300-57-6047, Rev. 01, dated October 16, 1996, including Change Notice 1.A., dated February 24, 1997.	39.13
SB A300-57-6049, dated September 9, 1994	39.13
SB A300-57-6052, Revision 1, dated July 22, 1996	39.13
SB A300-57-6053, Revision 1, dated October 31, 1995	39.13
SB A300-57-6059, dated August 12, 1994	39.13
SB A300-57-6074, dated October 16, 1996	39.13
SB A300-57-6079, Rev. 02, dated January 12, 1998	39.13
SB A300-57-6087, Revision 1, dated March 11, 1998	39.13
SB A300-57-6088, Revision 1, including Appendix 1, both dated February 1, 1999.	39.13
SB A300-57A0234, dated August 5, 1997	39.13

Title 14—Aeronautics and Space

14 CFR (PARTS 1–59)—Continued
FEDERAL AVIATION ADMINISTRATION, DEPARTMENT OF TRANSPORTATION—
Continued

	14 CFR
SB A300-57A6087, dated August 5, 1997	39.13
SB A300-6015, dated March 15, 1993	39.13
SB A300-71-6019, dated March 16, 1994	39.13
SB A300-72-6013, Revision 3, dated August 6, 1993	39.13
SB A300-72-6014, dated March 15, 1993	39.13
SB A300-72-6016, Revision 2, dated January 13, 1993	39.13
SB A300-72-6018, Rev. 1, dated December 22, 1993, including Change Notice No. O.A., dated June 17, 1993.	39.13
SB A300-72-6019, Rev. 1, dated December 22, 1993, including Change Notice No. O.A., dated June 17, 1993.	39.13
SB A300-72-6025, Revision 1, dated June 22, 1995	39.13
SB A300-72-6027, dated July 24, 1995	39.13
SB A300-76-0018, as revised by Change Notice O.A. dated February 18, 1997 dated October 12, 1995.	39.13
SB A300-76-6010, as revised by Change Notice O.A., dated February 18, 1997 dated October 12, 1995.	39.13
SB A300-76-6011, Rev. 02, dated January 6, 1997	39.13
SB A300-78-0015, Rev. 2, dated May 24, 1996, including Change Notice 2.A, dated May 24, 1996.	39.13
SB A310-22-2025, dated April 18, 1989	39.13
SB A310-22-2027, dated June 8, 1990	39.13
SB A310-22-2031, dated September 2, 1991	39.13
SB A310-22-2035, Rev. 1, dated July 13, 1994	39.13
SB A310-22-2036, dated December 14, 1993	39.13
SB A310-22-2044, Rev. 1, dated January 8, 1997	39.13
SB A310-22-2047, dated July 16, 1996	39.13
SB A310-24-2040, Rev. 1 dated June 28, 1991	39.13
SB A310-24-2065, dated November 30, 1995	39.13
SB A310-24-2065, Rev. 1, dated April 19, 1996	39.13
SB A310-25-2054 dated Oct. 22, 1990	39.13
SB A310-26-2030, Rev. 02, dated April 4, 1997	39.13
SB A310-27-2040, Rev. 2, dated January 5, 1995	39.13
SB A310-27-2042, Rev. 1, dated, December 11, 1986	39.13
SB A310-27-2046, Rev. 1, dated November 24, 1989	39.13
SB A310-27-2054, Rev. 2 dated Nov. 9, 1990	39.13
SB A310-27-2059, dated March 1, 1993	39.13
SB A310-27-2061, dated November 4, 1992	39.13
SB A310-27-2061, Revision 01, dated October 3, 1997	39.13
SB A310-27-2067, Rev. 1, dated January 5, 1995	39.13
SB A310-27-2068, Rev. 1, dated March 16, 1994	39.13
SB A310-27-2068, Rev. 2, dated April 19, 1995	39.13
SB A310-27-2070, dated May 5, 1994	39.13
SB A310-27-2074, dated November 18, 1994	39.13
SB A310-27-2081, dated November 26, 1996	39.13
SB A310-27-2082, Rev. 2, dated October 1, 1997	39.13
SB A310-27-2087, Revision 1, dated February 17, 1999	39.13
SB A310-28-2053, Rev. 01, dated January 15, 1997	39.13
SB A310-28-2058, Revision 2, dated February 22, 1995	39.13
SB A310-28-2124, dated January 15, 1997	39.13
SB A310-29-2030, Rev. 2 dated August 27, 1991	39.13

Material Approved for Incorporation by Reference

FEDERAL AVIATION ADMINISTRATION, DEPARTMENT OF TRANSPORTATION—
Continued

	14 CFR
SB A310-29-2032, Rev.1 dated June 10, 1992	39.13
SB A310-29-2076, dated April 1, 1996	39.13
SB A310-31-2098, Rev. 1, dated April 29, 1996	39.13
SB A310-32-2069, Rev. 1, dated December 13, 1994	39.13
SB A310-32-2076, Rev. 1, dated December 13, 1994	39.13
SB A310-32-2111, Rev. 01, dated October 10, 1997	39.13
SB A310-32-2111, Revision 2, dated June 23, 1998	39.13
SB A310-33-2025, dated March 1, 1993	39.13
SB A310-35-2002, Rev. 2, dated April 30, 1991	39.13
SB A310-36-2032, dated October 17, 1994	39.13
SB A310-49-2012 dated July 12, 1991	39.13
SB A310-52-2060, dated July 22, 1996	39.13
SB A310-53-2016, Revision 5, dated December 7, 1992	39.13
SB A310-53-2041, Rev. 02, dated July 2, 1996	39.13
SB A310-53-2054, Revision 2, dated May 22, 1990	39.13
SB A310-53-2057 Revision 1 dated April 30, 1992	39.13
SB A310-53-2059, Revision 1, dated January 4, 1996	39.13
SB A310-53-2069, Rev. 1, dated September 19, 1995	39.13
SB A310-53-2070, dated October 3, 1994	39.13
SB A310-53-2074, Revision 1, dated February 20, 1995	39.13
SB A310-53-2076, dated May 17, 1993	39.13
SB A310-53-2077, dated October 28, 1993	39.13
SB A310-53-2079, dated February 23, 1996	39.13
SB A310-53-2087, dated March 19, 1997	39.13
SB A310-53-2092, dated October 16, 1996	39.13
SB A310-53-2092, Rev. 01, dated March 11, 1998	39.13
SB A310-53-2101, Rev. 01, dated October 17, 1997	39.13
SB A310-54-2017, Rev. 1, dated March 28, 1994	39.13
SB A310-54-2023, dated October 15, 1993	39.13
SB A310-55-2002, Revision 4, dated April 28, 1989	39.13
SB A310-55-2004, Revision 2, dated February 7, 1991	39.13
SB A310-55-2010, dated December 10, 1990	39.13
SB A310-55-2012, dated April 18, 1991	39.13
SB A310-55-2026, dated October 22, 1996	39.13
SB A310-57-2002, Revision 1, dated July 2, 1992	39.13
SB A310-57-2002, Revision 2, dated January 4, 1996	39.13
SB A310-57-2006, Revision 3, dated May 2, 1996	39.13
SB A310-57-2032, Revision 3, dated January 4, 1996	39.13
SB A310-57-2037, Revision 3, dated January 4, 1996	39.13
SB A310-57-2038, Revision 2, dated January 4, 1996	39.13
SB A310-57-2039, dated September 24, 1990	39.13
SB A310-57-2046, Revision 4, dated October 16, 1996, including Appendix I, Revision 3, dated October 17, 1995 and Change Notice 4A, dated October 16, 1996.	39.13
SB A310-57-2047, Revision 2, dated January 22, 1997	39.13
SB A310-57-2050, dated April 23, 1990, including Change Notice O.A., dated September 29, 1992 and Change Notice O.B., dated January 6, 1995.	39.13
SB A310-57-2061, dated December 4, 1995	39.13
SB A310-57-2064, dated August 24, 1995	39.13

Title 14—Aeronautics and Space

	14 CFR
SB A310-57-2075, Rev. 01, dated January 12, 1998	39.13
SB A310-57-2078, Revision 1, dated January 11, 1999	39.13
SB A310-57-2079, Revision 1, dated January 11, 1999	39.13
SB A310-71-2021, dated March 16, 1994	39.13
SB A310-72-2017, Revision 3, dated August 6, 1993	39.13
SB A310-72-2018, Rev. 2, dated December 22, 1993	39.13
SB A310-72-2019, Rev. 2, dated December 22, 1993	39.13
SB A310-72-2020, Revision 2, dated January 13, 1993	39.13
SB A310-72-2022, dated February 16, 1993	39.13
SB A310-72-2023, Rev. 1, dated December 22, 1993	39.13
SB A310-72-2029, Revision 1, dated June 25, 1995, including Changes Notice 1.A., dated March 13, 1997 and Change Notice 1.B. dated.	39.13
SB A310-72-2031, dated July 24, 1995, including Change Notice O.A., dated October 12, 1995.	39.13
SB A310-76-2013, as revised by Change Notice O.A., dated February 18 1997 dated October 12, 1995.	39.13
SB A310-76-2014, Rev. 02, dated January 6, 1997	39.13
SB A320-24-1022, Rev. 1, dated February 27, 1990	39.13
SB A320-24-1035, Rev. 1, dated February 27, 1990	39.13
SB A320-24-1035, Rev. 2, dated June 24, 1994	39.13
SB A320-24-1044, Rev. 2 dated March 3, 1992	39.13
SB A320-24-1044, Rev. 3, dated March 12, 1993	39.13
SB A320-24-1045, Rev. 2 dated April 12, 1992	39.13
SB A320-24-1045, Rev. 3, dated June 10, 1993	39.13
SB A320-24-1054, Revision 2, dated September 22, 1993	39.13
SB A320-24-1092, dated March 26, 1997	39.13
SB A320-24-1092, Rev. 01, dated December 24, 1997	39.13
SB A320-24-1092, Rev. 02, dated March 9, 1998	39.13
SB A320-25-1086, Revision 2, dated April 27, 1999	39.13
SB A320-25-1186, Revision 2, dated April 27, 1999	39.13
SB A320-25-1199, dated March 25, 1998	39.13
SB A320-26-1031, dated March 31, 1994	39.13
SB A320-26-1032, dated March 31, 1994	39.13
SB A320-26-1037, Rev. 02, dated July 8, 1997	39.13
SB A320-27-1041, Rev. 2, dated April 20, 1994	40.13
SB A320-27-1043 dated Oct. 7, 1991	39.13
SB A320-27-1066, Revision 4, dated July 15, 1997	39.13
SB A320-27-1073, dated January 20, 1995	39.13
SB A320-27-1081, Rev. 2, dated September 6, 1995	39.13
SB A320-27-1082, dated April 25, 1995	39.13
SB A320-27-1082, Rev. 1, dated September 6, 1995	39.13
SB A320-27-1088, Rev. 03, dated December 11, 1996	39.13
SB A320-27-1096, dated March 14, 1996	39.13
SB A320-27-1096, Revision 01, dated January 14, 1998	39.13
SB A320-27-1097, Revision 01, dated July 15, 1997	39.13
SB A320-27-1097, Revision 0202, dated June 25, 1999	39.13
SB A320-27-1103, dated June 14, 1996	39.13
SB A320-27-1103, Revision 01, dated January 26, 1998	39.13
SB A320-27-1108, Revision 01, dated July 15, 1997	39.13
SB A320-27-1108, Revision 02, dated April 17, 1998	39.13

Material Approved for Incorporation by Reference

	14 CFR
SB A320-27-1108, Revision 0303, dated June 25, 1999	39.13
SB A320-28-1028, Rev. 1 dated Nov. 23, 1990	39.13
SB A320-28-1040, Rev. 1, dated April 3, 1992	39.13
SB A320-28-1040, Rev. 3, dated January 15, 1993	39.13
SB A320-28-1044, Rev. 11, dated August 26, 1997	39.13
SB A320-29-1048, Rev. 1, dated December 4, 1992	39.13
SB A320-29-1048, Rev. 2, dated September 1, 1994	39.13
SB A320-29-1058, dated July 16, 1993	39.13
SB A320-29-1058, Revision 1, dated November 28, 1994	39.13
SB A320-29-1061, dated April 13, 1993	39.13
SB A320-29-1071, dated September 21, 1995	39.13
SB A320-29-1086, dated October 19, 1998	39.13
SB A320-29-1086, Revision 1, dated March 9, 1999	39.13
SB A320-30-1036, dated May 9, 1997	39.13
SB A320-30-1036, Revision 02, dated February 4, 1998	39.13
SB A320-31-1080, Rev. 01, dated July 12, 1996	39.13
SB A320-31-1080, Rev. 02, dated October 24, 1996	39.13
SB A320-31-1088, Rev. 2, dated September 16, 1996	39.13
SB A320-32-1024, dated January 29, 1990	39.13
SB A320-32-1058; Rev. 2, dated June 16, 1993	39.13
SB A320-32-1094, Rev. 2, dated November 25, 1992	39.13
SB A320-32-1094, Rev. 3, dated June 24, 1993	39.13
SB A320-32-1100, Rev. 1, dated November 9, 1993	39.13
SB A320-32-1119, Rev. 1, dated June 13, 1994	39.13
SB A320-32-1139, Rev. 1, dated December 30, 1994	39.13
SB A320-32-1144, dated December 8, 1994	39.13
SB A320-32-1197, Revision 1, dated February 11, 1999.	39.13
SB A320-34-1024, Rev. 3 dated December 13, 1991	39.13
SB A320-35-1002, Rev. 1, dated December 3, 1990	39.13
SB A320-38-1049, dated January 22, 1997	39.13
SB A320-52-1047, dated April 25, 1994	39.13
SB A320-52-1057, dated July 26, 1994	39.13
SB A320-52-1064, Rev. 1, dated September 8, 1995	39.13
SB A320-52-1066, dated March 6, 1995	39.13
SB A320-53-1004, Rev. 1, dated July 30, 1992	39.13
SB A320-53-1005, Rev. 1, dated June 19, 1992	39.13
SB A320-53-1011, dated December 9, 1994	39.13
SB A320-53-1014, dated June 25, 1992	39.13
SB A320-53-1014, Rev. 1, dated May 26, 1993	39.13
SB A320-53-1015, Rev. 02, dated July 17, 1997	39.13
SB A320-53-1017, Rev. 1, dated September 7, 1993	39.13
SB A320-53-1021, Rev. 1, dated April 13, 1992	39.13
SB A320-53-1022, Rev. 1, dated June 18, 1992	39.13
SB A320-53-1023, dated September 23, 1992, which includes Appendix 1, dated September 23, 1992.	39.13
SB A320-53-1023, Rev. 1, dated March 23, 1993, including Appendix 1, dated September 23, 1992.	39.13
SB A320-53-1023, Rev. 7, dated November 3, 1995	39.13
SB A320-53-1023, incl Appendix 1 dated September 23, 1993	39.13
SB A320-53-1024, dated September 23, 1992	39.13

Title 14—Aeronautics and Space

Material Approved for Incorporation by Reference

	14 CFR
SB A330-25-3086 and Appendix 1, Revision 1, dated June 11, 1999	39.13
SB A330-26-3002, dated March 29, 1994	39.13
SB A330-27-3034, dated June 21, 1995	39.13
SB A330-27-3051, dated February 13, 1997	39.13
SB A330-27-3055, Revision 1, dated July 1, 1998	39.13
SB A330-28-3045, dated August 9, 1996	39.13
SB A330-28-3046, Rev. 01, dated November 12, 1996	39.13
SB A330-29-3018, dated January 17, 1996	39.13
SB A330-29-3041, dated February 25, 1997	39.13
SB A330-32-3042, Rev. 1, dated September 19, 1995	39.13
SB A330-32-3058, Revision 1, dated February 25, 1997	39.13
SB A330-32-3061, Rev. 1, dated May 6, 1997	39.13
SB A330-32-3062, Rev. 2, dated May 27, 1997	39.13
SB A330-32-3066, dated November 18, 1996	39.13
SB A330-53-3012 dated June 26, 1995	39.13
SB A330-53-3015, dated November 24, 1995	39.13
SB A330-53-3019, dated November 30, 1995	39.13
SB A330-53-3019, dated November 30, 1995	39.13
SB A330-53-3020, dated November 30, 1995	39.13
SB A330-53-3020, dated November 30, 1995	39.13
SB A330-53-3029, dated June 26, 1995	39.13
SB A330-53-3036, Revision 01, dated December 22, 1997	39.13
SB A330-53-3037, Revision 01, dated January 30, 1998	39.13
SB A330-57-3029, dated April 26, 1995, for Model A330 Series Airplanes.	39.13
SB A340- 32-4050, Rev. 1, dated May 17, 1995	39.13
SB A340-21-4046, Rev. 2, dated May 5, 1995	39.13
SB A340-25-4115 and Appendix 1, Revision 1, dated June 11, 1999	39.13
SB A340-26-4007, Rev. 1, dated May 16, 1994	39.13
SB A340-26-4007, Rev. 2, dated November 22, 1994	39.13
SB A340-27-4013, dated October 27, 1993	39.13
SB A340-27-4041, dated June 21, 1995	39.13
SB A340-27-4058, dated February 13, 1997	39.13
SB A340-27-4063, Revision 1, dated July 1, 1998	39.13
SB A340-28-4008, dated July 9, 1993	39.13
SB A340-28-4012, dated November 8, 1993	39.13
SB A340-28-4029, Rev. 1, dated September 14, 1994	39.13
SB A340-29-4018, dated January 17, 1996	39.13
SB A340-29-4041, dated February 26, 1997	39.13
SB A340-32-4050, dated April 10, 1995	39.13
SB A340-32-4058, dated April 10, 1995	39.13
SB A340-32-4058, Rev. 1, dated May 17, 1995	39.13
SB A340-32-4062, dated May 17, 1995	39.13
SB A340-32-4066, Rev. 1, dated September 19, 1995	39.13
SB A340-32-4082, Revision 01, dated February 25, 1997	39.13
SB A340-32-4086, Rev. 2, dated June 13, 1997	39.13
SB A340-32-4091, Revision 1, dated June 3, 1998	39.13
SB A340-32-4092, dated November 18, 1996	39.13
SB A340-32-4111, Revision 1, dated May 28, 1998.	39.13
SB A340-38-4013, dated January 5, 1994	39.13

Material Approved for Incorporation by Reference

	14 CFR
Service Bulletin A300-28-0077 dated July 19, 1999	39.13
Service Bulletin A300-28-0078 dated September 27, 2000	39.13
Service Bulletin A300-28-0080 dated September 28, 2000	39.13
Service Bulletin A300-28-2141, including Appendix 1 dated September 27, 2000.	39.13
Service Bulletin A300-28-6020 Revision 1 dated September 28, 1999	39.13
Service Bulletin A300-28-6057 Revision 01 dated October 1, 1998	39.13
Service Bulletin A300-28-6058 Revision 01 dated October 1, 1998	39.13
Service Bulletin A300-28-6062 dated July 19, 1999	39.13
Service Bulletin A300-28-6063 dated September 27, 2000	39.13
Service Bulletin A300-29-0101 Revision 2 dated June 28, 2000	39.13
Service Bulletin A300-29-0106 Revision 3 dated June 28, 2000	39.13
Service Bulletin A300-29-0106 Revision 4 dated March 22, 2001	39.13
Service Bulletin A300-29-0115 Revision 1 dated June 28, 2000	39.13
Service Bulletin A300-29-0118 dated April 20, 2001	39.13
Service Bulletin A300-29-6003, including Change Notice O.A., dated June 9, 1987 dated January 31, 1985.	39.13
Service Bulletin A300-29-6005 Revision 1 dated September 2, 1986	39.13
Service Bulletin A300-29-6030 Revision 2 dated June 28, 2000	39.13
Service Bulletin A300-29-6039 Revision 3 dated June 28, 2000	39.13
Service Bulletin A300-29-6039 Revision 4 dated March 22, 2001	39.13
Service Bulletin A300-29-6046 Revision 2 dated June 28, 2000	39.13
Service Bulletin A300-29-6048 Revision 1 dated July 12, 2000	39.13
Service Bulletin A300-29-6049 Revision 2 dated September 10, 2001	39.13
Service Bulletin A300-32-6069 Revision 1 dated December 29, 1999	39.13
Service Bulletin A300-32-6077 Revision 1 dated September 25, 1999	39.13
Service Bulletin A300-32A0437 dated April 5, 2000	39.13
Service Bulletin A300-32A0441, including Appendix 1 dated September 10, 2001.	39.13
Service Bulletin A300-32A6080 dated April 5, 2000	39.13
Service Bulletin A300-32A6087, including Appendix 1 dated September 10, 2001.	39.13
Service Bulletin A300-49-0049 Revision 1 dated November 28, 1991	39.13
Service Bulletin A300-49-6009 Revision 1 dated November 28, 1991	39.13
Service Bulletin A300-53-0149 Revision 14 dated September 8, 1998	39.13
Service Bulletin A300-53-0162 Revision 6 dated March 20, 1996	39.13
Service Bulletin A300-53-0209 Revision 10 dated July 5, 1999	39.13
Service Bulletin A300-53-0278 Revision 2 dated November 10, 1995	39.13
Service Bulletin A300-53-0296 Revision 1 dated September 30, 1998	39.13
Service Bulletin A300-53-0296 Revision 2 dated May 12, 1999	39.13
Service Bulletin A300-53-0297 Revision 2 dated October 31, 1995	39.13
Service Bulletin A300-53-0298 Revision 3 dated November 26, 1998	39.13
Service Bulletin A300-53-0313 Revision 1 dated April 27, 1999	39.13
Service Bulletin A300-53-0328 Revision 1 dated March 15, 2000	39.13
Service Bulletin A300-53-0332 dated November 24, 1997	39.13
Service Bulletin A300-53-0333 dated November 24, 1997	39.13
Service Bulletin A300-53-0339 Revision 1 dated July 28, 1998	39.13
Service Bulletin A300-53-148 Revision 11 dated September 8, 1998	39.13
Service Bulletin A300-53-178 Revision 10 dated September 8, 1998	39.13
Service Bulletin A300-53-6048 Revision 1 dated September 30, 1998	39.13

Title 14—Aeronautics and Space

Material Approved for Incorporation by Reference

	14 CFR
Service Bulletin A310-32A2124, including Appendix 1 dated September 10, 2001.	39.13
Service Bulletin A310-49-2012 Revision 1 dated November 28, 1991	39.13
Service Bulletin A310-53-2106 dated October 2, 1997	39.13
Service Bulletin A310-53-2106 Revision 1 dated July 28, 1998	39.13
Service Bulletin A310-53-2107 Revision 1 dated July 2, 1999	39.13
Service Bulletin A310-53-2109 dated May 5, 2000	39.13
Service Bulletin A310-53A2111, including Appendix 1 Revision 1 dated June 21, 2000.	39.13
Service Bulletin A310-54-2016 Revision 2 dated June 11, 1999	39.13
Service Bulletin A310-54-2017 Revision 3 dated June 11, 1999	39.13
Service Bulletin A310-54-2022 Revision 1 dated March 16, 1999	39.13
Service Bulletin A310-54-2033 Revision 1 dated January 3, 2001	39.13
Service Bulletin A320-22-1063 Revision 1 dated October 8, 1999	39.13
Service Bulletin A320-22-1064 dated September 15, 1998	39.13
Service Bulletin A320-22-1065 dated October 28, 1998	39.13
Service Bulletin A320-22-1067 Revision 1 dated July 7, 1999	39.13
Service Bulletin A320-22-1068 dated December 9, 1998	39.13
Service Bulletin A320-22-1069 dated February 1, 1999	39.13
Service Bulletin A320-24-1092 Revision 3 dated September 16, 1998	39.13
Service Bulletin A320-25-1215 dated April 29, 1999	39.13
Service Bulletin A320-25-1220 dated November 19, 1999	39.13
Service Bulletin A320-25-1225 dated November 19, 1999	39.13
Service Bulletin A320-27-1066 Revision 5 dated June 25, 1999	39.13
Service Bulletin A320-27-1108 Revision 4 dated November 22, 1999	39.13
Service Bulletin A320-27-1114 Revision 4 dated December 7, 1999	39.13
Service Bulletin A320-27-1117 Revision 2 dated January 18, 2000	39.13
Service Bulletin A320-27-1126, including App. 01 and 02 dated April 26, 1999.	39.13
Service Bulletin A320-27-1126, including App. 01 and 02 Revision 01 dated October 6, 1999.	39.13
Service Bulletin A320-27-1127, including App. 01 and 02 dated April 26, 1999.	39.13
Service Bulletin A320-27-1127, including App. 01 and 02 Revision 01 dated October 6, 1999.	39.13
Service Bulletin A320-27-1130 Revision 2 dated September 6, 2001	39.13
Service Bulletin A320-28-1077 dated July 9, 1999	39.13
Service Bulletin A320-29-1088 dated February 23, 1999	39.13
Service Bulletin A320-31-1106 Revision 4 dated December 21, 1999	39.13
Service Bulletin A320-32-1187 dated June 17, 1998	39.13
Service Bulletin A320-32-1187 Revision 1 dated February 17, 1999	39.13
Service Bulletin A320-32-1189 dated December 23, 1998	39.13
Service Bulletin A320-32-1199 dated January 15, 1999	39.13
Service Bulletin A320-32-1203 dated June 4, 1999	39.13
Service Bulletin A320-32-1213 Revision 2 dated February 9, 2001	39.13
Service Bulletin A320-32A1233, including Appendix 1 dated August 16, 2001.	39.13
Service Bulletin A320-34-1119 Revision 2 dated April 30, 1997	39.13
Service Bulletin A320-34-1191 dated July 12, 1999	39.13
Service Bulletin A320-34-1196 dated July 15, 1999	39.13
Service Bulletin A320-35-1003 Revision 1 dated January 28, 1993	39.13

Material Approved for Incorporation by Reference

	14 CFR
Service Bulletin A330-53-3074 Revision 1 dated May 19, 1998	39.13
Service Bulletin A330-53-3090 Revision 2 dated January 9, 2001	39.13
Service Bulletin A330-53-3094 Revision 2 dated May 28, 1998	39.13
Service Bulletin A330-54-3005 Revision 1 dated October 19, 1999	39.13
Service Bulletin A330-55A3025 Revision 1 dated September 15, 2000	39.13
Service Bulletin A330-55A3026 dated June 23, 2000	39.13
Service Bulletin A330-57-3017 Revision 2 dated October 11, 1999	39.13
Service Bulletin A330-57-3019 Revision 2 dated September 14, 2000	39.13
Service Bulletin A330-57-3021, including Appendices 01 and 02 Revision 3 dated November 5, 1999.	39.13
Service Bulletin A330-57-3053 Revision 1 dated June 15, 1999	39.13
Service Bulletin A330-57-3054 Revision 2 dated November 22, 1999	39.13
Service Bulletin A330-57-3060 Revision 1 dated December 6, 1999	39.13
Service Bulletin A330-71-3010 dated September 25, 1999	39.13
Service Bulletin A330-78-3006 Revision 5 dated March 6, 2001	39.13
Service Bulletin A330-92-3034 Revision 3 dated November 13, 2001	39.13
Service Bulletin A340-25-4131 dated October 22, 1999	39.13
Service Bulletin A340-25-4136 dated December 23, 1999	39.13
Service Bulletin A340-27-4061 Revision 2 dated May 5, 1998	39.13
Service Bulletin A340-27-4062 Revision 1 dated November 8, 1999	39.13
Service Bulletin A340-27-4072 Revision 1 dated July 21, 1999	39.13
Service Bulletin A340-27-4079 Revision 1 dated January 18, 2000	39.13
Service Bulletin A340-27-4081 dated September 24, 1999	39.13
Service Bulletin A340-28-4077 Revision 2, including Appendix 1 dated May 27, 1999.	39.13
Service Bulletin A340-28-4079 dated October 6, 1999	39.13
Service Bulletin A340-28A4087 dated July 27, 2000	39.13
Service Bulletin A340-29A4058, including Appendix 1 Revision 1 dated April 10, 2000.	39.13
Service Bulletin A340-31-4047 dated September 13, 1999	39.13
Service Bulletin A340-32-4126 dated November 2, 1998	39.13
Service Bulletin A340-32-4128 Revision 1 dated December 2, 1998	39.13
Service Bulletin A340-32-4131 Revision 1 dated June 10, 1999	39.13
Service Bulletin A340-32-4148 Revision 01 dated December 14, 1999	39.13
Service Bulletin A340-32-4157 dated July 13, 2000	39.13
Service Bulletin A340-32A4124 Revision 1 dated November 20, 1998	39.13
Service Bulletin A340-32A4176, including Appendix 1 Revision 1 dated November 23, 2001.	39.13
Service Bulletin A340-34-4022 dated April 3, 1995	39.13
Service Bulletin A340-34-4078 Revision 1 dated November 26, 1999	39.13
Service Bulletin A340-34-4089 Revision 1 dated September 28, 1999	39.13
Service Bulletin A340-34-4092 Revision 1 dated September 28, 1999	39.13
Service Bulletin A340-52-4053 dated March 2, 2001	39.13
Service Bulletin A340-52-4054 dated March 2, 2001	39.13
Service Bulletin A340-53-4072 dated June 29, 1998	39.13
Service Bulletin A340-53-4085 Revision 1 dated May 19, 1998	39.13
Service Bulletin A340-53-4105 Revision 2 dated May 25, 1998	39.13
Service Bulletin A340-54-4003 Revision 1 dated April 26, 2000	39.13
Service Bulletin A340-57-4022 dated October 8, 1999	39.13

Title 14—Aeronautics and Space

Material Approved for Incorporation by Reference

FEDERAL AVIATION ADMINISTRATION, DEPARTMENT OF TRANSPORTATION—Continued

	14 CFR
Drawing No. LW3600-180A-11, dated September 21, 1979	39.13
Drawing No. LW3600-180A-3, Revision A, dated April 30, 1979	39.13
SB No. LW3600-3, dated September 21, 1979; amended October 10, 1997.	39.13

Alexander Schleicher Segelflugzeubau GmbH and Co.,
D-36161 Poppenhausen, Federal Republic of Germany

ASH 25 M Technical Note No. 15 dated September 3, 1999	39.13
ASH 26 E Technical Note No. 8 dated August 23, 1999	39.13
ASK 21 Technical Note No. 20, dated October 16, 1987	39.13
ASK 21 Technical Note No. 22, dated November 26, 1990	39.13
ASK 21 Technical Note No. 23, dated January 29, 1991	39.13
ASK 21 Technical Note. No. 14 dated 5/16/85	39.13
ASK-21 Technical Note No. 10, dated October 10, 1983	39.13
ASK-21 Technical Note No. 13a, dated June 4, 1984	39.13
ASK21 Technical Note No. 19 dated October 22, 1986	39.13
ASW 19 Technical Note No. 2, dated September 6, 1976	39.13
ASW-12 Technical Note No. 4, dated May 10, 1989	39.13
ASW-15 Technical Note No. 23, dated April 21, 1988	39.13
ASW-17 Technical Note No. 12, dated May 8, 1989	39.13
Technical Note 5 dated July 16, 1999	39.13
Technical Note No. 17 dated 3/27/84	39.13
Technical Note No. 18, dated July 3, 1984	39.13
Technical Note No. 20, dated October 16, 1987	39.13
Technical Note No. 21 dated 11/24/81 and Technical Note No. 22 dated 11/1/82.	39.13
Technical Note No. 21, dated May 12, 1980	39.13
Technical Note No. 23 dated April 21, 1988	39.13
Technical Note No. 26, dated July 1, 1993	39.13
Technical Note No. 5, dated July 23, 1998	39.13
Technical Note No. 6, dated August 10, 1998	39.13
Technical Note No. 7, dated September 11, 1978	39.13

AlliedSignal Aerospace Company, Garrett Engine Division (See Honeywell International, Inc.)
ATTN: Data Distribution, M/S 64-3/2101-201 P.O. Box 29003, Phoenix AZ 85038-9003, Telephone: 602-365-2548

Alert SB No. TPE331-A72-7129, dated June 10, 1994	39.13
Alert SB No. TPE331-A72-7522, dated February 17, 1995	39.13
Alert Service Bulletin TFE731-A72-3641 dated November 24, 1998	39.13
Alert Service Bulletin TFE731-A72-3641 Revision 1 dated October 20, 1999.	39.13
ASB No. TFE731-A72-3432, dated April 11, 1991	39.13
ASB No. TFE731-A72-3432, dated April 11, 1991	39.13
ASB No. TFE731-A72-3432, dated April 11, 1991	39.13
ASB No. TFE731-A72-3432, Rev. 1, dated April 30, 1991	39.13
ASB No. TFE731-A72-3432, Rev. 2, dated June 3, 1991	39.13
ASB No. TFE731-A72-3432, Rev. 3, dated October 17, 1991	39.13
ASB No. TFE731-A72-3432, Rev. 4, dated August 6, 1993	39.13
ASB No. TFE731-A72-3432, Rev. 5, dated May 31, 1995	39.13
ASB No. TFE731-A72-3445, Rev. 2, dated May 31, 1995	39.13
ASB No. TFE731-A72-3504, dated November 25, 1992	39.13

Material Approved for Incorporation by Reference

14 CFR (PARTS 1–59)—Continued
FEDERAL AVIATION ADMINISTRATION, DEPARTMENT OF TRANSPORTATION—
Continued

	14 CFR
ASB No. TPE/TSE331-A72-0384, Rev. 3, dated July 1, 1987	39.13
ASB No. TPE/TSE331-A72-0384, Rev. 4, dated September 4, 1987	39.13
ASB No. TPE/TSE331-A72-0559, dated July 1, 1987	39.13
ASB No. TPE/TSE331-A72-0559, Rev. 1, dated September 4, 1987	39.13
ASB No. TPE/TSE331-A72-0559, Rev. 2, dated January 15, 1987	39.13
SB 103576-21-4054, dated January 30, 1995	39.13
SB 103576-21-4056, dated January 30, 1995	39.13
SB 103648-21-4055, dated January 30, 1995	39.13
SB 103742-21-4059, dated March 31, 1995; and	39.13
SB 103744-21-4060, dated March 31, 1995	39.13
SB 979410-80-1611, dated November 27, 1995	39.13
SB 979410-80-1611, Rev. 1, dated March 13, 1997	39.13
SB No. ALF/LF 73-1002, dated December 22, 1995	39.13
SB No. ALF502R79-9, Rev. 1, dated November 27, 1996	39.13
SB No. GTCP85-49-6919, Rev. 1, dated January 15, 1995	39.13
SB No. TFE73-731-3107, dated July 21, 1992	39.13
SB No. TFE73-731-3107, Rev. 1, dated September 23, 1992	39.13
SB No. TFE73-731-3118, dated September 3, 1992	39.13
SB No. TFE73-731-3118, Rev. 1, dated February 16, 1993	39.13
SB No. TFE731-72-3502, dated November 25, 1992	39.13
SB No. TFE731-72-3502, Rev. 1, dated December 21, 1992	39.13
SB No. TFE731-72-3502, Rev. 2, dated March 15, 1993	39.13
SB No. TFE731-72-3503, Rev. 1, dated December 21, 1992	39.13
SB No. TFE731-72-3530, Rev. 1, dated October 8, 1993, April 4, 1994.	39.13
SB No. TPE331-A72-0857, dated October 29, 1992	39.13
SB No. TPE331-A72-0858, dated October 29, 1992	39.13
SB No. TPE331-A72-0893, dated October 29, 1992	39.13
SB No. TPE331-A72-7092, dated October 29, 1992	39.13
SB No. TPE331-A72-7519, dated October 30, 1992	39.13
SB TSCP700-49-A7168, dated November 7, 1995	39.13
SB VN 411B-21, dated November 1996	39.13
ASB No. TFE731-A72-3544, dated October 8, 1993	39.13
ASB TFE731-A72-3557, dated May 12, 1994	39.13
SB M-4431	39.13
SB M-4426 (RIA-35B-34-6); Rev. 3, dated May 1998	39.13
Alert SB TFE731-A72-3569, dated May 31, 1995	39.13
Alert SB TFE731-A72-3570, dated May 31, 1995	39.13
SB LTS101A-73-20-0166, Rev. 1, dated November 21, 1994	39.13
SB LTS101A-73-20-0166, Rev. 2, dated August 1, 1995	39.13
SB T5313B/T5317-0081, Rev. 1, dated May 28, 1996	39.13
Alert SB No. TPE331-A73-0221, Rev. 2, dated October 10, 1994	39.13
Alert SB No. TPE331-A73-0226, dated October 10, 1994	39.13
Alert SB T53-L-13B-A0092, dated June 4, 1997	39.13
Alert SB T53-L-703-A0092, dated June 4, 1997	39.13
Alert SB T5313B/17A-A0092, Rev. 1, dated July 1, 1997	39.13
ASB No. TFE731-A73-5119, dated March 4, 1999	39.13
ASB No. TPE331-A72-0861, Rev. 2, dated April 23, 1997	39.13
ASB T5317A-1-A0106, dated October 23, 1998	39.13
ASB TFE731-A73-3132, dated April 9, 1997	39.13

Title 14—Aeronautics and Space

Material Approved for Incorporation by Reference

Title 14—Aeronautics and Space

Material Approved for Incorporation by Reference

	14 CFR
ATR Airplane Flight Manual, chapter 2.06.01, Temporary Revision, dated February 1999.	39.13
ATR Airplane Flight Manual, chapter 4.05.05, Temporary Revision, dated February 1999.	39.13
ATR42-400/500 Maintenance Planning Document Revision 3 dated February 1999.	39.13
ATR72 Maintenance Planning Document Revision 4 dated July 1999	39.13
Bulletin ATR42-32-0064, dated January 17, 1994	39.19
SB ATR42-21-0069, dated February 5, 1998	39.13
SB ATR42-25-0108, dated January 24, 1997	39.13
SB ATR42-25-0108, Rev. 1, dated February 28, 1997	39.13
SB ATR42-25-0108, Rev. 2, dated July 1, 1997	39.13
SB ATR42-27-0014, Rev. 2, dated December 20, 1993	39.13
SB ATR42-27-0070, dated December 20, 1993	39.13
SB ATR42-32-0070, dated April 3, 1995	39.13
SB ATR42-53-0112, dated January 20, 1998	39.13
SB ATR42-53-0112, Revision 1, dated April 22, 1998	39.13
SB ATR42-54-0019, dated March 9, 1998	39.13
SB ATR42-57-0050, dated April 17, 1998	39.13
SB ATR42-71-0010, Rev. 4, dated October 23, 1996	39.13
SB ATR72-21-1048, dated February 5, 1998	39.13
SB ATR72-25-1052, dated February 11, 1997	39.13
SB ATR72-25-1052, Rev. 1, dated July 1, 1997	39.13
SB ATR72-32-1021, dated January 17, 1994	39.13
SB ATR72-32-1028, dated September 1, 1994	39.13
SB ATR72-32-1029, dated November 4, 1994	39.13
SB ATR72-34-0090, Rev. 1, dated April 22, 1997	39.13
SB ATR72-54-1011, dated March 9, 1998	39.13
SB ATR72-57-0038, Rev. 2, dated December 18, 1997	39.13
SB ATR72-57-0040, dated April 21, 1994	39.13
SB ATR72-57-1019, dated July 7, 1997	39.13
SB ATR72-57-1019, Revision 1, dated May 12, 1998	39.13
SB ATR72-57-1020, dated March 9, 1998	39.13
SB ATR72-71-1006, Rev. 1, dated October 21, 1996	39.13
Service Bulletin ATR42-30-0063 Revision 2 dated October 1, 1999	39.13
Service Bulletin ATR42-30-0064 Revision 2 dated October 1, 1999	39.13
Service Bulletin ATR42-30-0065 Revision 2 dated October 25, 1999	39.13
Service Bulletin ATR42-52-0052 Revision 1 dated March 2, 1993	39.13
Service Bulletin ATR42-52-0058 Revision 1 dated March 1, 1995	39.13
Service Bulletin ATR42-52-0059 dated February 16, 1995	39.13
Service Bulletin ATR42-53-0070 Revision 2 dated March 22, 1993	39.13
Service Bulletin ATR42-53-0070 Revision 3 dated February 19, 1999	39.13
Service Bulletin ATR42-53-0076 Revision 2 dated October 15, 1996	39.13
Service Bulletin ATR42-53-0076 Revision 3 dated February 19, 1999	39.13
Service Bulletin ATR72-30-1032 Revision 2 dated October 1, 1999	39.13
Service Bulletin ATR72-30-1033 Revision 2 dated October 1, 1999	39.13
Service Bulletin ATR72-30-1034 Revision 2 dated October 19, 1999	39.13
Service Bulletin ATR72-52-1018 dated May 18, 1995	39.13
Service Bulletin ATR72-52-1028 dated July 5, 1993	39.13
Service Bulletin ATR72-52-1029 Revision 1 dated November 16, 1994	39.13

Title 14—Aeronautics and Space

14 CFR (PARTS 1–59)—Continued
FEDERAL AVIATION ADMINISTRATION, DEPARTMENT OF TRANSPORTATION—
Continued

	14 CFR
Service Bulletin ATR72-52-1033 dated April 28, 1995	39.13
Service Bulletin ATR72-53-1013 Revision 3 dated January 22, 1999	39.13
Service Bulletin ATR72-53-1014 Revision 2 dated October 15, 1992	39.13
Service Bulletin ATR72-53-1019 Revision 3 dated January 22, 1999	39.13
Service Bulletin ATR72-53-1020 dated October 6, 1992	39.13
Service Bulletin ATR72-53-1021 Revision 1 dated February 20, 1995	39.13
SB CAP10B No. 15, dated April 14, 1992	39.13
SB CAP10B No. 16, dated April 27, 1992	39.13
SB CAPIOB No. 13 dated May 14, 1991	39.13
SB No. 15, CAP10B-57-003, Rev. 1, dated April 3, 1996	39.13

Avions Pierre Robin
  1 route de Troyes, 21121 Darois, France

Note NAV 96-3, dated May 2, 1996.	39.13
SB No. 101, Rev. 3, dated March 5, 1992	39.13
SB No. 120, dated September 27, 1990	39.13
SB No. 135, dated May 17, 1994	39.13
SB No. 141, Rev. 1, dated November 6, 1995	39.13
SB No. 146, Rev. 1, dated September 26, 1996	39.13
SB No. 151, dated July 8, 1996	39.13
SB No. 152, dated September 30, 1996	39.13
SB No. 90, dated May 3, 1982	39.13
SB No. 97, dated April 22, 1983	39.13

Avro International Aerospace Division, British Aerospace Holdings, Inc
  P.O. Box 16039, Dulles International Airport, Washington, DC
  20041-6039

Alert Inspection SB S.B. 34-A155, Rev. 2, dated August 9, 1995	39.13
Inspection SB S.B. 24-107, dated January 25, 1995	39.13
Inspection SB S.B. 53-130, dated May 10, 1994	39.13
Inspection SB S.B. 53-131, dated March 29, 1995	39.13
SB 57-40, dated March 18, 1994	39.13
SB S.B. 24-103, dated March 24, 1994	39.13
SB S.B. 49-40, Rev. 1, dated March 17, 1994	39.13
SB S.B. 57-33, Rev. 1, dated October 29, 1993	39.13
SB S.B. 57-33, Rev. 2 dated February 16, 1994	39.13
SB S.B. 57-33, Rev. 3, dated September 16, 1994	39.13

Ayres Corp.
  P.O. Box 3090, Albany, GA 31708

SB No. SB-AG-29, dated June 15, 1992	39.13
SB No. SB-AG-32, dated February 12, 1993	39.13
SB No. SB-AG-39, dated September 17, 1996	39.13
Custom Kit No. CK-AG-29 dated December 23 1997	39.13
SB-AG-39 dated 17 September 1996	39.13
Service Bulletin SB-AG-42 dated June 16, 1999	39.13

B. Grob Flugzeugbau, Industriestrabe
  D-8948 Mindelheim-Mattsies, Germany

TM-306-17 dated 6/10/81	39.13

Ballonbau Worner GmbH
  Zirbelstrasse 57c 86154 Augsburg Federal Republic of Germany

Technical Note No. Nr. 8002-13 dated January 14, 2000	39.13

Material Approved for Incorporation by Reference

14 CFR (PARTS 1–59)—Continued
FEDERAL AVIATION ADMINISTRATION, DEPARTMENT OF TRANSPORTATION—
Continued

14 CFR

Barry Aviation, LLC
   11600 Aviation Boulevard Suite 16 West Palm Beach Florida 33412
Service Bulletin No. 1-02 dated June 10, 2002 .... 39.13
Service Bulletin No. BE-29/KR-03A/93 dated November 16, 1993 .... 39.13

Beech Aircraft Corp
   P.O. Box 85, Wichita, KS 67201-0085
Kit 58-5016-1 S as referenced in Beech SB 2439, dated May 1992   39.13
Kit No. 118-9003-1, 118-9003-3, 129-9010-1, and 129-9010-3 as speci-   39.13
   fied in Beech SB No. 2539 and Beech SB No. 2591, dated December
   1994.
Landing Gear Motor Circuit Breaker Installation Kits 101-3069-1 S,   39.13
   101-3069-3 S, 101-3069-5 S, 101-3069-7 Rev. III: Issued February
   1985 , Revised April 1995.
Mandatory SB 2416 dated July 1991 .... 39.13
Mandatory SB 2416, Rev. 1 dated Dec. 1991 .... 39.13
Pilot's Operating Handbook/FAA Approved Flight Manual, B2 Rev.,   39.13
   Part No. 130-590031-1 dated Sept. 1991.
SB 2241, Rev. 1 dated Jan. 1991 .... 39.13
SB 2255, Rev. III dated Nov. 1991 .... 39.13
SB 2255, Rev. VI, dated August 1994 .... 39.13
SB 2333 dated Oct. 1989 .... 39.13
SB 2333, Rev. 1 dated Nov. 1991 .... 39.13
SB 2360 dated Nov. 1990 .... 39.13
SB 2360 dated Nov. 1990 .... 39.13
SB 2361 dated Feb. 1991 .... 39.13
SB 2362, Rev. 1 dated Feb. 1991 .... 39.13
SB 2365 dated Jan. 1991 .... 39.13
SB 2365, Rev. 1 dated Dec. 1991 .... 39.13
SB 2380 dated Apr. 1991 .... 39.13
SB 2394 dated Dec. 1990 .... 39.13
SB 2399 dated Mar. 1991 .... 39.13
SB 2408 dated June 1991 .... 39.13
SB 2420 dated February 1992 .... 39.13
SB 2423 dated Dec. 1991 .... 39.13
SB 2428 dated Oct. 1991 .... 39.13
SB 2432 dated Feb. 1992 .... 39.13
SB 2437 dated April 1992 .... 39.13
SB 2442 dated May 1992 .... 39.13
SB 2443 and Tosington SB No. 001, both dated July 1993 .... 39.13
SB 2445 dated June 1992 .... 39.13
SB No. 2188, dated May 1987 including: instructions to Beech Kit   39.13
   Nos. 35-4016-3, 35-4016-5, 35-4016-7 and 35-4016-9; and instruc-
   tions to Beech Kit No. 35-4017-1, Kit Information Empennage &
   Aft Fuselage Inspection.
SB No. 2442, Rev. 1, dated September 1993 .... 39.13
SB No. 2444, Rev. 2, dated May 1995 .... 39.13
SB No. 2444, Rev. II, dated May 1995 .... 39.13
SB No. 2475, dated February 1993 .... 39.13
SB No. 2487, dated August 1993 .... 39.13
SB No. 2522, dated January, 1994 .... 39.13
SB No. 2562, dated August 1994 .... 39.13

Title 14—Aeronautics and Space

Material Approved for Incorporation by Reference

	14 CFR
Alert Service Bulletin 430-98-8 dated December 31, 1998	39.13
ASB No. 430-98-5, dated June 12, 1998.	39.13
Technical Bulletin 407-98-13 dated December 12, 1998	39.13
Technical Bulletin 407-98-13, dated December 12, 1998	39.13
Alert Service Bulletin 206L-99-115 Revision F dated April 14, 2001	39.13
Alert Service Bulletin No. 205-00-77 Revision A dated September 13, 2000.	39.13
Alert Service Bulletin No. 205B-00-31 Revision A dated September 13, 2000.	39.13
Alert Service Bulletin No. 212-00-107 Revision A dated September 13, 2000.	39.13
Alert Service Bulletin No. 212-00-110 Revision A dated February 15, 2001.	39.13
Alert Service Bulletin No. 212-00-184 Revision A dated April 23, 2001.	39.13
Alert Service Bulletin No. 412-00-102 Revision A dated September 13, 2000.	39.13
Alert Service Bulletin No. 412CF-00-10 Revision A dated September 13, 2000.	39.13
Alert Service Bulletin 205-00-80 Revision A dated December 20, 2000.	39.13
Alert Service Bulletin 205B-00-34 Revision A dated December 20, 2000.	39.13
Alert Service Bulletin 206-00-93 Revision A dated May 10, 2000	39.13
Alert Service Bulletin 206L-00-116 dated March 10, 2000	39.13
Alert Service Bulletin 212-00-111 Revision A dated December 20, 2000.	39.13
Alert Service Bulletin 222-00-86 dated May 19, 2000	39.13
Alert Service Bulletin 222-99-84 dated February 15, 1999	39.13
Alert Service Bulletin 222U-00-57 dated May 19, 2000	39.13
Alert Service Bulletin 222U-99-55 dated February 15, 1999	39.13
Alert Service Bulletin 230-00-18 dated May 19, 2000	39.13
Alert Service Bulletin 230-99-16 dated February 15, 1999	39.13
Alert Service Bulletin 407-99-33 Revision A dated March 10, 2000	39.13
Alert Service Bulletin 412-00-106 Revision A dated December 20, 2000.	39.13
Alert Service Bulletin 412CF-00-13 Revision A dated December 20, 2000.	39.13
Alert Service Bulletin 430-00-17 dated May 19, 2000	39.13
Alert Service Bulletin 430-99-10 dated December 16, 1999	39.13
Alert Service Bulletin 430-99-11 dated May 7, 1999	39.13
Alert Service Bulletin 430-99-13 dated December 13, 1999	39.13
Alert Service Bulletin ASB 407-99-32 dated December 7, 1999	39.13
ASB 204B-98-50, dated October 22, 1998	39.13
ASB 205-96-68, Revision A, dated May 18, 1998	39.13
ASB 205-96-69, dated September 3, 1996	39.13
ASB 205-98-71, Revision A, dated September 21, 1998	39.13
ASB 205-98-73, dated September 25, 1998	39.13
ASB 205B-96-25, dated September 3, 1996	39.13
ASB 212-96-100, Revision A, dated May 18, 1998	39.13
ASB 212-96-101, dated September 3, 1996	39.13

Material Approved for Incorporation by Reference

	14 CFR
Alert SB 412-92-57, Rev. A, dated January 30, 1992	39.13
Alert SB 412-92-61, dated May 14, 1992	39.13
Alert SB 412-93-72, Rev. A, dated	39.13
Alert SB 412-96-89, Rev. A, dated October 17, 1997	39.13
Alert SB 412CF-96-01, dated September 3, 1996	39.13
Alert SB 430-97-2, dated July 11, 1997	39.13
Alert SB No. 206-93-75, dated October 19, 1993	39.13
Alert SB No. 206-93-76, Rev. B, dated September 6, 1994	39.13
Alert SB No. 206L-88-52 dated June 10, 1988	39.13
Alert SB No. 206L-93-90, Rev. A, dated November 9, 1993	39.13
Alert SB No. 206L-94-99, Rev. A, dated May 1, 1995	39.13
Alert SB No. 214ST-95-72, dated July 24, 1995	39.13
Alert SB No. 222-85-28 dated March 21, 1985	39.13
Alert SB No. 222-85-33 dated August 13, 1985	39.13
Alert SB No. 222-86-39, Rev. A dated January 14, 1987	39.13
Alert SB No. 222-89-53 dated March 20, 1989	39.13
Alert SB No. 222U-85-3 dated March 21, 1985	39.13
Alert SB No. 222U-85-8 dated August 13, 1985	39.13
Alert SB No. 222U-86-14, Rev. A dated January 14, 1987	39.13
Alert SB No. 222U-89-27 dated March 20, 1989	39.13
Alert SB No. 412-92-65, Accomplishment Instructions, Parts I and II, dated August 17, 1992.	39.13
ASB No. 205-90-40, Revision A, dated March 21, 1991	39.13
ASB No. 205B-90-1, Revision A, dated March 21, 1991	39.13
ASB No. 205B-90-1, Revision A, dated March 21, 1991	39.13
ASB No. 212-90-64, Revision B, dated March 11, 1992	39.13
ASB No. 214-97-59, dated July 17, 1997	39.13
ASB No. 214ST-97-78, dated July 17, 1997	39.13
ASB No. 47-96-22, dated August 16, 1996	39.13
SB No. 141500-29-66 dated July 30, 1985	39.13
SB No. 143000-29-65 dated July 30, 1985	39.13

Bellanca, Inc

P.O. Box 964, Alexandria, Minnesota 56308; Telephone (612) 762-1501

Service Letter B-107, dated September 20, 1995	39.13

Bendix--AlliedSignal Aerospace Co

Bendix Wheels and Brakes Division, South Bend, IN 46628

SB 737-32-026, dated April 26, 1988	39.13
SB No. 737-32-026, dated June 27, 1998, including Attachment 1, dated January 17, 1978, and Attachment 2, dated June 27,.	39.13
SB 2601182-32-014 dated Jan. 30, 1991	39.13
SB 2601902-32-001, Rev. 2 dated Oct. 10, 1991	39.13
SB 2602012-32-001, Rev. 2 dated Oct. 10, 1991	39.13
SB 2605155-32-001, Rev. 2 dated Oct. 10, 1991	39.13
SB 2605662-32-028, Rev. 2 dated Oct. 10, 1991	39.13
Service Information Letter (SIL) 392, Rev. 1, dated November 15, 1979.	39.13

Bendix/King

Product Support Department, 400 N. Rogers Road, Olathe, KS 66062-0212

Title 14—Aeronautics and Space

14 CFR (PARTS 1–59)—Continued
FEDERAL AVIATION ADMINISTRATION, DEPARTMENT OF TRANSPORTATION—
Continued

	14 CFR
Installation Bulletin 312 dated Mar. 19, 1990	39.13
SB RIA-32A-34-47, Revision 1, dated January 1992	39.13
SB RIA-32A-34-48, dated December 1991	39.13
Software Bulletin No: GNS-XLS-SW2, dated February 1997.	39.13

BF Goodrich Co. Aircraft Evaluation Systems
3414 South 5th St., Phoenix, AZ 85040

11331-25-248 dated April 15, 1992	39.13
1474-32-14, Rev. 2 dated Jan. 15, 1992	39.13
2-1147-32-13 dated Dec. 21, 1990	39.13
2-1190-32-13 dated Dec. 21, 1990	39.13
2-1444-32-5 dated Jan. 24, 1991	39.13
2-1457-32-13 dated January 30, 1991	39.13
2-1457-32-13, Rev. 1 dated December 16, 1991; issued February 28, 1991.	39.13
2-1474-32-13, Rev. 1 dated July 9, 1992	39.13
2-1474-32-13, Rev. 2 dated Feb. 12, 1992	39.13
25-232 dated Nov. 18, 1991	39.13
25-232, Rev. 1 dated Mar. 16, 1992	39.13
4A3416-25-223 dated Oct. 1, 1991	39.13
4A3416-25-233 dated Dec. 14, 1990	39.13
Alert SB 100102-25A-244 dated Dec. 13, 1991	39.13
Alert SB 7A1299-25A274, dated December 15, 1993	39.13
SB 101630/655/656-25-269, dated October 28, 1994	39.13
SB 25-262, dated February 18, 1994	39.13
SB 4A3106/4A3153-25-258, dated March 29, 1993	39.13
SB 4A3221-25-250, dated March 12, 1993	39.13
SB 5A2917/27/63-25-278, Rev. 1, dated July 14, 1995	39.13
SB 5A2917/27/63-25-279, dated January 12, 1995	39.13
SB 7A1255-25-275, dated February 25, 1994	39.13
SB 7A1323-25-266, Rev. 1, dated September 30, 1994	39.13
SB 7A1418-25-253, dated April 28, 1993	39.13
SB 7A1418-25-253, Rev. 2, dated April 15, 1994	39.13
SB 7A1469-25-283, dated November 6, 1995	39.13
SL 1498 dated Oct. 26, 1989	39.13
SB 2-1598-32-1, dated November 5, 1999	39.13
SB 2-1600-32-2, dated November 5, 1999	39.13
Service Bulletin 2-1598-32-2 dated June 16, 2000	39.13
Service Bulletin 2-1600-32-3 dated June 16, 2000	39.13
Service Bulletin 76A-32-03 Revision 1 dated September 15, 2000	39.13
SB 2-1479-32-2, Revision 1, dated June 17, 1998	39.13
SB 2-1585-32-1, Revision 1, dated June 17, 1998	39.13
SB 3-1398-32-16, dated August 20, 1993.	39.13
SB 3-1439-32-13, dated August 20, 1993	39.13

BFGoodrich Aerospace
3100 112th Street, SW Everett Washington 98204-3500

767 Flight Attendant Manual Supplement D2000-160 dated August 16, 2000.	39.13
B767 Airplane Flight Manual Supplement D2001-025 dated February 26, 2001.	39.13

932

Material Approved for Incorporation by Reference

14 CFR

Engineering Order 23-32-767-031, including Parts List Attachment and Wire List Attachment dated August 16, 2001. — 39.13

Boeing Airplane Co

Commercial Airplane Group P.O. Box 3707, Seattle, Washington 98124-2207

Service Bulletin AEI 00-01 Revision A dated May 7, 2001 .... 39.13

Service Bulletin ATS 727-001 dated May 7, 2001 .... 39.13

SB 1211233-29-21-3, Revision 2, dated June 17, 1994 .... 39.13

SB 1211233-29-21-3, Revision 3, dated February 7, 1997 .... 39.13

SB 2156204A-26-02, dated January 17, 1992 .... 39.13

SB 2156204A-26-02, dated January 17, 1992 .... 39.13

747-24-2193 NSC 1, dated April 13, 1995, ... 39.13

747-24-2193 NSC 2, dated October 5, 1995, ... 39.13

747-24-2193 NSC 5, dated May 2, 1996, ... 39.13

737 Nondestructive Test Manual D6-37239 dated August 5, 1997 — 39.13

737 Nondestructive Test Manual D6-37239, Part 6, List of Effective Pages, dated December 5, 1998. — 39.13

737 Nondestructive Test Manual D6-37239, Part 6, Section 51-00-00, Figure 23, dated November 5, 1995. — 39.13

737 Nondestructive Test Manual D6-37239, Part 6, Section 53-10-54, dated December 5, 1998. — 39.13

747- 24-2193 NSC 6, dated March 13, 1997; 39.13

747-24-2193 NSC 3, dated November 22, 1995, ... 39.13

747-24-2193 NSC 4, dated December 21, 1995, ... 39.13

747-400 Operations Manual Bulletin 93-5, dated July 26, 1993 .... 39.13

767 Component Maintenance Manual, Section 25-66-30 Revision 2 dated November 1, 2000. — 39.13

767 Maintenance Planning Data Document D622T001-9 Revised June 1997. — 39.13

767 Operations Manual Bulletin No. 86-13 dated December 9, 1986 — 39.13

Aging Airplane SB Structural Modification and Inspection Program -- Model 737-100/-200/-200C, Rev. F, dated April 23, 1992. — 39.13

Airplane Maintenance Manual for the Model 737 Aircraft, Temporary Rev's. 12-368, 12-369, 12-370, 12-371, dated February 7, 1997. — 39.13

Alert Service Bulletin 717-27A0002 dated February 11, 2000 .... 39.13

Alert Service Bulletin 717-27A0002 Revision 2 dated March 30, 2000 — 39.13

Alert Service Bulletin 717-34A0002 dated March 30, 2000 .... 39.13

Alert Service Bulletin 727-29A0068 dated May 30, 2002 .... 39.13

Alert Service Bulletin 727-55A0090 Revision 1 dated September 20, 2001. — 39.13

Alert Service Bulletin 727-57A0145 Revision 2 dated October 24, 2002. — 39.13

Alert Service Bulletin 727-57A0179 Revision 3 dated September 2, 1999. — 39.13

Alert Service Bulletin 727-57A0179 Revision 4 dated July 13, 2000 — 39.13

Alert Service Bulletin 737-21A1129, including Appendices A and B dated June 29, 2000. — 39.13

Alert Service Bulletin 737-22A1130 dated September 24, 1998 .... 39.13

Alert Service Bulletin 737-23A1170 dated April 27, 2000 .... 39.13

Alert Service Bulletin 737-24A1148 dated December 6, 2001 .... 39.13

Alert Service Bulletin 737-24A1150 dated April 11, 2002 .... 39.13

Title 14—Aeronautics and Space

Material Approved for Incorporation by Reference

14 CFR (PARTS 1–59)—Continued
FEDERAL AVIATION ADMINISTRATION, DEPARTMENT OF TRANSPORTATION—Continued

	14 CFR
Alert Service Bulletin 747-24A2118 Revision 3 dated June 24, 1999	39.13
Alert Service Bulletin 747-25A2407 Revision 1 dated September 23, 1999.	39.13
Alert Service Bulletin 747-26A2233 Revision 1 dated November 16, 2000.	39.13
Alert Service Bulletin 747-26A2266 dated March 3, 2000	39.13
Alert Service Bulletin 747-26A2267 dated December 20, 2000	39.13
Alert Service Bulletin 747-27A2373 dated June 24, 1999	39.13
Alert Service Bulletin 747-27A2376 dated July 1, 1999	39.13
Alert Service Bulletin 747-28A2232 Revision 1 dated June 22, 2000	39.13
Alert Service Bulletin 747-28A2248 dated September 23, 2002	39.13
Alert Service Bulletin 747-30A2078 Revision 1 dated November 16, 2000.	39.13
Alert Service Bulletin 747-32A2465 Revision 1 dated July 20, 2000	39.13
Alert Service Bulletin 747-34A2638 Revision 1 dated April 8, 1999	39.13
Alert Service Bulletin 747-35A2035, Revision1, dated July 22, 1999, as revised by Boeing Service Bulletin dated September 23, 1999.	39.13
Alert Service Bulletin 747-38A2073 Revision 2 dated April 26, 2001	39.13
Alert Service Bulletin 747-52A2258 dated June 1, 1995	39.13
Alert Service Bulletin 747-53A2293 Revision 8 dated July 13, 2000	39.13
Alert Service Bulletin 747-53A2349 Revision 1 dated October 12, 2000.	39.13
Alert Service Bulletin 747-53A2390 Revision 1 dated July 6, 2000	39.13
Alert Service Bulletin 747-53A2416 Revision 1 dated May 6, 1999	39.13
Alert Service Bulletin 747-53A2417 Revision 2 dated August 10, 2000.	39.13
Alert Service Bulletin 747-53A2419 Revision 1 dated September 21, 2000.	39.13
Alert Service Bulletin 747-53A2425 dated October 29, 1998	39.13
Alert Service Bulletin 747-53A2427 dated December 17, 1998	39.13
Alert Service Bulletin 747-53A2427 Revision 1 dated October 28, 1999.	39.13
Alert Service Bulletin 747-53A2427 Revision 2 dated October 5, 2000	39.13
Alert Service Bulletin 747-53A2444 Revision 2 dated May 24, 2001	39.13
Alert Service Bulletin 747-53A2450 Revision 2, including Appendix A dated January 4, 2001.	39.13
Alert Service Bulletin 747-53A2451, including Appendix A dated October 5, 2000.	39.13
Alert Service Bulletin 747-53A2459 dated January 11, 2001	39.13
Alert Service Bulletin 747-53A2477 dated February 28, 2002	39.13
Alert Service Bulletin 747-53A2478 dated February 7, 2002	39.13
Alert Service Bulletin 747-53A2487 Revision 1 dated October 31, 2002.	39.13
Alert Service Bulletin 747-54A2184 Revision 1 dated May 6, 1999	39.13
Alert Service Bulletin 747-54A2200 dated July 7, 2000	39.13
Alert Service Bulletin 747-54A2201 dated September 28, 2000	39.13
Alert Service Bulletin 747-54A2203 dated August 31, 2000	39.13
Alert Service Bulletin 747-54A2207 dated November 16, 2000	39.13
Alert Service Bulletin 747-54A2208 dated March 29, 2001	39.13
Alert Service Bulletin 747-55A2050 dated February 28, 2002	39.13
Alert Service Bulletin 747-57A2298 Revision 3 dated January 7, 1999	39.13

Title 14—Aeronautics and Space

Material Approved for Incorporation by Reference

FEDERAL AVIATION ADMINISTRATION, DEPARTMENT OF TRANSPORTATION— Continued

	14 CFR
Alert Service Bulletin 767-27A0168 dated November 21, 2000	39.13
Alert Service Bulletin 767-27A0169 dated November 21, 2000	39.13
Alert Service Bulletin 767-27A0176 Revision 1 dated June 6, 2002	39.13
Alert Service Bulletin 767-28A0050 dated December 18, 1997	39.13
Alert Service Bulletin 767-28A0057 dated November 18, 1999	39.13
Alert Service Bulletin 767-29A0083 Revision 4 dated September 28, 2000.	39.13
Alert Service Bulletin 767-29A0090 dated December 7,2000	39.13
Alert Service Bulletin 767-30A0037 dated May 28, 2002	39.13
Alert Service Bulletin 767-32A0163 dated March 5, 1998	39.13
Alert Service Bulletin 767-32A0192 dated May 31, 2001	39.13
Alert Service Bulletin 767-33A0085 Revision 2 dated December 7, 2000.	39.13
Alert Service Bulletin 767-38A0057 dated July 13, 2000	39.13
Alert Service Bulletin 767-53A0085 Revision 1 dated July 1, 1999	39.13
Alert Service Bulletin 767-57A0074 dated May 17, 2000	39.13
Alert Service Bulletin 767-57A0074 Revision 1 dated May 17, 2000	39.13
Alert Service Bulletin 767-78A0081 Revision 2 dated April 19, 2001	39.13
Alert Service Bulletin 767-78A0088 dated April 19, 2001	39.13
Alert Service Bulletin 767-78A0089 Revision 1 dated May 30, 2002	39.13
Alert Service Bulletin 767-78A0090 Revision 1 dated July 5, 2001	39.13
Alert Service Bulletin 767-78A0091 Revision 1 dated July 5, 2001	39.13
Alert Service Bulletin 777-26A0009 dated October 23, 1997	39.13
Alert Service Bulletin 777-27A0030 dated April 1, 1999	39.13
Alert Service Bulletin 777-28A0019 dated April 27, 2000	39.13
Alert Service Bulletin 777-31A0019 Revision 4 dated April 27, 2000	39.13
Alert Service Bulletin 777-32A0024 dated August 12, 1999	39.13
Alert Service Bulletin 777-32A0025 Revision 1 dated March 8, 2001	39.13
Alert Service Bulletin 777-35A0010 dated October 4, 2001	39.13
Alert Service Bulletin 777-54A0017 dated December 21, 2001	39.13
Alert Service Bulletin 777-55A0013 Revision 1 dated January 31, 2002.	39.13
Alert Service Bulletin 777-57A0011 Revision 1 dated January 25, 2001.	39.13
Alert Service Bulletin 777-57A0022 dated August 26, 1999	39.13
Alert Service Bulletin 777-57A0029 dated December 22, 1998	39.13
Alert Service Bulletin 777-57A0034 Revision 3 dated May 4, 2000	39.13
Alert Service Bulletin 777-57A0034 Revision 4 dated July 20, 2000	39.13
Alert Service Bulletin 777-57A0034 Revision 5 dated January 25, 2001.	39.13
Alert Service Bulletin 777-57A0036 dated June 24, 1999	39.13
Alert Service Bulletin A3395 Revision 4 dated October 28, 1999	39.13
Alert Service Bulletin DC9-24A193 Revision 1 dated January 15, 2002.	39.13
Alert Service Bulletin DC9-27A362 dated February 11, 2000	39.13
Alert Service Bulletin DC9-27A362 Revision 2 dated March 30, 2000	39.13
Alert Service Bulletin DC9-57A218 dated September 20, 2000	39.13
Alert Service Bulletin MD11-24A144 dated May 2, 2000	39.13
Alert Service Bulletin MD11-24A181 dated June 27, 2000	39.13
Alert Service Bulletin MD11-25A253 dated March 10, 2000	39.13

Material Approved for Incorporation by Reference

	14 CFR
ASB 737-28A1132, dated December 2, 1998	39.13
ASB 737-28A1132, Revision 1, dated January 15, 1999	39.13
ASB 737-28A1134, Revision 1, dated June 10, 1999	39.13
ASB 737-32A1224, Revision 1, dated April 12, 1990	39.13
ASB 737-32A1314, dated April 15, 1999	39.13
ASB 737-35A1037 dated February 13, 1992	39.13
ASB 737-35A1038 dated March 19, 1992	39.13
ASB 737-52A1124, dated January 11, 1996	39.13
ASB 737-53A1152, Rev. 1 dated October 24, 1991	39.13
ASB 737-53A1160, dated October 24, 1991	39.13
ASB 737-53A1160, Rev. 1, dated April 29, 1993	39.13
ASB 737-53A1166, dated June 30, 1994, including Addendum	39.13
ASB 737-53A1177, dated November 8, 1994	39.13
ASB 737-53A1177, Rev. 1, dated September 19, 1996	39.13
ASB 737-53A1177, Rev. 2, dated July 24, 1997	39.13
ASB 737-53A1177, Rev. 3, dated September 18, 1997	39.13
ASB 737-54A1038, dated May 7, 1998, as	39.13
ASB 737-54A1038, NSC 01, dated June 18, 1998	39.13
ASB 737-55A1068, Revision 1, dated June 11, 1999	39.13
ASB 737-55A1068, Revision 1, dated June 11, 1999	39.13
ASB 737-71A1208 dated December 10, 1987	39.13
ASB 737-71A1208, Rev. 2 dated March 23, 1989	39.13
ASB 737-71A1212, dated December 22, 1987	39.13
ASB 737-73A1011, dated November 25, 1998	39.13
ASB 737-78A1055 dated April 2, 1992	39.13
ASB 737-78A1056, dated August 11, 1994	39.13
ASB 744-24A2193, Revision 1, dated June 19, 1997	39.13
ASB 747- 22A2213, Rev. 2, dated June 22, 1995	39.13
ASB 747-11A2052, dated September 11, 1997	39.13
ASB 747-21A-2312 dated May 30, 1991	39.13
ASB 747-21A2381, dated June 27, 1996;	39.13
ASB 747-22A2212, Rev. 1, dated April 27, 1995	39.13
ASB 747-22A2213, Rev. 1, dated April 27, 1995	39.13
ASB 747-23A2241, Rev. 3 dated September 5, 1991	39.13
ASB 747-24A2168 dated Sept. 24, 1991	39.13
ASB 747-24A2168, dated September 24, 1991	39.13
ASB 747-24A2168, Rev. 1 dated Dec. 5, 1991	39.13
ASB 747-24A2168, Rev. 1, dated December 5, 1991	39.13
ASB 747-24A2168, Rev. 2, dated September 24, 1992	39.13
ASB 747-24A2186, dated January 14, 1993	39.13
ASB 747-24A2190 dated November 16, 1992	39.13
ASB 747-24A2214, dated June 19, 1997	39.13
ASB 747-25A2889 dated Nov. 1, 1990	39.13
ASB 747-25A3056, dated July 12, 1993	39.13
ASB 747-25A3064, dated December 21, 1995	39.13
ASB 747-25A3095, dated April 27, 1995	39.13
ASB 747-25A3095, Rev. 1, dated September 28, 1995	39.13
ASB 747-25A3142, dated October 16, 1997	39.13
ASB 747-26A2179 dated Feb. 28, 1991	39.13
ASB 747-26A2179, Rev. 1 dated Aug. 26, 1991	39.13

14 CFR (PARTS 1–59)—Continued
FEDERAL AVIATION ADMINISTRATION, DEPARTMENT OF TRANSPORTATION—
Continued

Material Approved for Incorporation by Reference

FEDERAL AVIATION ADMINISTRATION, DEPARTMENT OF TRANSPORTATION—
Continued

	14 CFR
ASB 747-54-2100, Rev. 1, dated August 25, 1988	39.13
ASB 747-54-2100, Rev. 2, dated July 20, 1989	39.13
ASB 747-54-2100, Rev. 3, dated November 16, 1989	39.13
ASB 747-54-2101, dated April 11, 1983	39.13
ASB 747-54-2101, Rev. 1, dated June 1, 1984	39.13
ASB 747-54-2177, dated June 27, 1996	39.13
ASB 747-54-A2166, Rev. 1, dated May 1, 1997	39.13
ASB 747-54A2069, Rev. 2, dated February 1, 1980	39.13
ASB 747-54A2069, Rev. 3, dated May 23, 1980	39.13
ASB 747-54A2069, Rev. 4, dated November 26, 1980	39.13
ASB 747-54A2069, Rev. 5, dated August 21, 1980	39.13
ASB 747-54A2069, Rev. 6, dated October 22, 1982	39.13
ASB 747-54A2069, Rev. 7, dated July 28, 1988	39.13
ASB 747-54A2069, Rev. 8, dated June 9, 1994	39.13
ASB 747-54A2069, Rev. 9, dated May 29, 1997	39.13
ASB 747-54A2126, Rev. 5, dated June 26, 1997	39.13
ASB 747-54A2126, Revision 7, dated November 20, 1998	39.13
ASB 747-54A2150 dated October 5, 1992	39.13
ASB 747-54A2150, Rev. 1 dated November 13, 1992	39.13
ASB 747-54A2150, Rev. 1, dated November 13, 1992	39.13
ASB 747-54A2152, dated December 23, 1992	39.13
ASB 747-54A2152, Rev. 1, dated July 15, 1993	39.13
ASB 747-54A2153, dated December 23, 1992	39.13
ASB 747-54A2156, dated December 15, 1994	39.13
ASB 747-54A2157, dated January 12, 1995	39.13
ASB 747-54A2158, dated November 30, 1994	39.13
ASB 747-54A2159, dated November 3, 1994	39.13
ASB 747-54A2166, dated April 28, 1994	39.13
ASB 747-54A2171, dated October 31, 1994	39.13
ASB 747-54A2171, Rev. 1, dated June 27, 1996	39.13
ASB 747-54A2172, dated February 23, 1995	39.13
ASB 747-54A2179, dated June 27, 1996	39.13
ASB 747-54A2179, Rev. 1, dated November 27, 1996	39.13
ASB 747-54A2179, Rev. 2, dated December 4, 1997	39.13
ASB 747-54A2184, dated July 3, 1997	39.13
ASB 747-54A2187, dated May 22, 1997	39.13
ASB 747-57A2259, dated February 15, 1990	39.13
ASB 747-57A2259, Rev. 1, dated September 6, 1990	39.13
ASB 747-57A2259, Rev. 2, dated June 9, 1994	39.13
ASB 747-57A2266, Rev. 5, dated August 3, 1995	39.13
ASB 747-57A2302, dated April 10, 1997	39.13
ASB 747-71A2269, dated April 14, 1994	39.13
ASB 747-71A2283, dated October 10, 1996	39.13
ASB 747-73A2055 dated June 8, 1990	39.13
ASB 747-76A2083 dated Dec. 18, 1991	39.13
ASB 747-76A2083, Rev. 1 dated May 28, 1992	39.13
ASB 747-76A2083, Rev. 2, dated February 25, 1993	39.13
ASB 747-78A2112, Rev. 1, dated March 7, 1994	39.13
ASB 747-78A2113, Rev. 1, dated March 10, 1994	39.13
ASB 747-78A2115, Rev. 1, dated March 4, 1994	39.13

Title 14—Aeronautics and Space

Material Approved for Incorporation by Reference

	14 CFR
ASB 767-27A0094, Rev. 4, dated October 22, 1992	39.13
ASB 767-27A0095, Rev. 3 dated May 23, 1989	39.13
ASB 767-27A0151, Rev. 1, dated April 2, 1997	39.13
ASB 767-27AO118, Rev. 1 dated Jan. 9, 1992	39.13
ASB 767-28A0036 dated May 3, 1991	39.13
ASB 767-28A0036, Rev. 1 dated June 11, 1991	39.13
ASB 767-28A0045, Rev. 1, dated April 28, 1994	39.13
ASB 767-29A0064, Rev. 1 dated Oct. 24, 1991	39.13
ASB 767-29A0077, dated October 6, 1994	39.13
ASB 767-29A0077, Rev. 1, dated June 8, 1995	39.13
ASB 767-29A0080, dated October 12, 1995	39.13
ASB 767-31-0033 dated May 31, 1990	39.13
ASB 767-31-0038 dated April 12, 1990	39.13
ASB 767-32A0125, dated November 11, 1993	39.13
ASB 767-32A0127, dated January 29, 1996	39.13
ASB 767-32A0185, dated September 2, 1999	39.13
ASB 767-35A0028, dated September 7, 1995	39.13
ASB 767-35A0029, dated January 30, 1997	39.13
ASB 767-35A0029, Revision 1, dated June 25, 1998	39.13
ASB 767-36A0041, dated July 2, 1992	39.13
ASB 767-36A0041, dated July 2, 1992	39.13
ASB 767-54A0062, dated April 14, 1994	39.13
ASB 767-54A0094, dated May 22, 1998	39.13
ASB 767-57A0038, Rev. 1 dated November 21, 1991	39.13
ASB 767-57A0038, Rev. 2 dated February 20, 1992	39.13
ASB 767-57A0047, Rev. 1, dated May 9, 1996	39.13
ASB 767-57A0054, Revision 2, dated April 18, 1996	39.13
ASB 767-57A0054, Revision 3, dated October 30, 1997	39.13
ASB 767-57A0066, Revision 1, dated August 6, 1998	39.13
ASB 767-71A0082, dated July 6, 1995	39.13
ASB 767-71A0087, dated October 10, 1996	39.13
ASB 767-73A0033 dated June 5, 1990	39.13
ASB 767-78-0064, dated July 16, 1992	39.13
ASB 767-78-0065, dated July 16, 1992	39.13
ASB 767-78A0052, Rev. 1 dated Feb. 14, 1992	39.13
ASB 767-78A0080, dated February 25, 1999	39.13
ASB 777-23A0027, dated February 13, 1997	39.13
ASB 777-25A0035, dated December 2, 1996	39.13
ASB 777-26A0004, dated June 21, 1996	39.13
ASB 777-26A0012, dated May 1, 1997	39.13
ASB 777-27A0019, dated April 3, 1997	39.13
ASB 777-27A0029, dated March 26, 1998	39.13
ASB 777-27A0029, Revision 1, dated October 1, 1998	39.13
ASB 777-29A0022, Revision 1, dated May 21, 1999	39.13
ASB 777-31A0013, dated August 29, 1996	39.13
ASB 777-32A0015, dated September 4, 1997	39.13
ASB 777-55A0003, Rev. 1, dated June 20, 1996	39.13
ASB 777-55A0005, Revision 1, dated June 4, 1998	39.13
ASB 777-55A0005, Revision 1, dated June 4, 1998	39.13
ASB 777-57A0008, dated March 25, 1999	39.13

Title 14—Aeronautics and Space

Material Approved for Incorporation by Reference

	14 CFR
Document No. D6-48040-1, Volumes 1 and 2, Supplemental Structural Inspection Document.0 (SSID), Rev. H, dated June 1994.	39.13
Document No. D6-54996, Aging Airplane SB Structural Modification and Inspection Program--Model 707/720, Rev. E, dated March 8, 1994.	39.13
Document No. D6-54996, Aging Airplane SB Structural Modification and Inspection Program--Model 707/720, Rev. E, dated March 8, 1994.	39.13
Document Number D6-54996, Aging Airplane SB Structural Modification and Inspection Program--Model 707/720, Rev. D, dated January 23, 1992.	39.13
Flight Operations Bulletin DC-10-00-01A, MD-11-00-03A, MD-10-00-02A dated September 20, 2000.	39.13
Information Notice 757-54-0013 IN 02 dated April 8, 1999	39.13
Interim Operating Procedure 2-17 dated March 31, 2000	39.13
M-7200-00-02672, including Attachments 1 and 2 dated November 1, 2000.	39.13
Maintenance Tip 737 MT 24-003 dated May 14, 1998	39.13
MD-11 Certification Maintenance Requirements Report No. MDC-K4174 Revision P dated April 5, 1999.	39.13
MD-11 Certification Maintenance Requirements Report No. MDC-K4174 Revision Q dated December 22, 1999.	39.13
Message M-7200-98-00140, dated January 11, 1998	39.13
Message M-7200-98-01080, dated March 18, 1998	39.13
Notice of Status Change 727-53-0210 NSC 1, dated June 17, 1993	39.13
Notice of Status Change 727-53-0210 NSC 2, dated September 21, 1995.	39.13
Notice of Status Change 747-33A2252 NSC 01, dated October 10, 1996.	39.13
Notice of Status Change 747-76A2068, NSC 2 dated December 12, 1991.	39.13
Notice of Status Change 747-78A2160 NSC 1 dated June 8, 1995	39.13
Processing Spec. BAC 5159, Rev. F dated March 1, 1991	39.13
SB 2330, Rev. 2 dated Nov. 17, 1967	39.13
SB 2590, Rev. 10, dated January 31, 1991	39.13
SB 2590, Rev. 11, dated December 12, 1991	39.13
SB 2590, Rev. 7, dated September 22, 1969	39.13
SB 2590, Rev. 8, dated June 2, 1972	39.13
SB 2590, Rev. 9, dated March 14, 1975	39.13
SB 2959, Rev. 4 dated Aug. 17, 1979	39.13
SB 2983 Rev. 5, dated January 31, 1991	39.13
SB 2983 Rev. 6, dated November 12, 1992	39.13
SB 3067, Rev. 3 dated Aug. 24, 1979	39.13
SB 3183, Rev. 1 dated May 13, 1977	39.13
SB 3183, Rev. 2 dated Jan. 28, 1988	39.13
SB 3183, Rev. 4 dated July 8, 1992	39.13
SB 3240, Rev. 3 dated October 18, 1985	39.13
SB 3253, Rev. 4 dated Nov. 17, 1988	39.13
SB 3477 dated July 26, 1990	39.13
SB 3484, pages 37 and 38 dated December 12, 1991	39.13
SB 3485, pages 34 and 35 dated December 12, 1991	39.13

Title 14—Aeronautics and Space

Material Approved for Incorporation by Reference

	14 CFR
SB 737-28A1120, Revision 2, dated November 26, 1998	39.13
SB 737-28A1120, Revision 2, dated November 26, 1998	39.13
SB 737-29-1070, dated June 8, 1995	39.13
SB 737-29-1071, dated May 16, 1996	39.13
SB 737-32A1224, Revision 2, dated April 25, 1991	39.13
SB 737-38-1043, dated January 8, 1998	39.13
SB 737-49-1073 dated July 25, 1991	39.13
SB 737-52-1060 dated June 11, 1976	39.13
SB 737-52-1079, Revision 5, dated May 16, 1996	39.13
SB 737-52-1128, dated April 22, 1999	39.13
SB 737-52-1137, dated May 13, 1999	39.13
SB 737-53-1023, Revison 11, dated May 16, 1991	39.13
SB 737-53-1042, Rev. 1 dated February 4, 1977	39.13
SB 737-53-1042, Rev. 2 dated March 31, 1978	39.13
SB 737-53-1076, Rev. 2 dated February 8, 1990	39.13
SB 737-53-1076, Rev. 4 dated September 26, 1991	39.13
SB 737-53-1096, dated July 24, 1986	39.13
SB 737-53-1096, dated July 24, 1986	39.13
SB 737-53-1096, Rev. 4, dated February 14, 1991	39.13
SB 737-53-1096, Rev. 1, dated April 2, 1987	39.13
SB 737-53-1096, Rev. 1, dated April 2, 1987	39.13
SB 737-53-1096, Rev. 2, dated July 30, 1987	39.13
SB 737-53-1096, Rev. 2, dated July 30, 1987	39.13
SB 737-53-1096, Rev. 3, dated February 8, 1990	39.13
SB 737-53-1096, Rev. 3, dated February 8, 1990	39.13
SB 737-53-1096, Rev. 4, dated February 14, 1991	39.13
SB 737-53-1096, Rev. 5, dated January 16, 1992	39.13
SB 737-53-1096, Rev. 5, dated January 16, 1992	39.13
SB 737-53-1107, Revision 3, dated August 26, 1993, as revised by Notice of Status Change 737-53-1107 NSC 3, dated June 9, 1994 and Notice of Status Change 737-53-1107 NSC 4, dated September 22, 1994.	39.13
SB 737-53-1107, Revision 4, dated February 8, 1996	39.13
SB 737-53-1154, dated November 11, 1993	39.13
SB 737-531042, Rev. 3 dated December 4, 1981	39.13
SB 737-531042, Rev. 4 dated November 5, 1982	39.13
SB 737-531042, Rev. 5 dated October 5, 1984	39.13
SB 737-531042, Rev. 6 dated August 10, 1989	39.13
SB 737-531042, Rev. 7 dated October 19, 1989	39.13
SB 737-531042, Rev. 8 dated July 19, 1990	39.13
SB 737-531042, Rev. 9 dated July 25, 1991	39.13
SB 737-53A1108, Revision 1, dated March 12, 1987	39.13
SB 737-53A1108, Revision 2, dated August 13, 1987	39.13
SB 737-53A1108, Revision 3, dated March 3, 1988	39.13
SB 737-53A1108, Revision 4, dated November 17, 1988	39.13
SB 737-53A1108, Revision 5, dated October 26, 1989	39.13
SB 737-53A1166, Rev. 1, dated May 25, 1995, including Addendum	39.13
SB 737-54-1007, Rev. 1, dated March 26, 1998	39.13
SB 737-54-1009, Rev. 1, dated March 26, 1998	39.13
SB 737-54-1028 Rev. 1 dated July 11, 1991	39.13

Title 14—Aeronautics and Space

14 CFR (PARTS 1–59)—Continued
FEDERAL AVIATION ADMINISTRATION, DEPARTMENT OF TRANSPORTATION—
Continued

	14 CFR
SB 737-54A1012, Rev. 4, dated March 26, 1998	39.13
SB 737-55-1063, dated July 1, 1999	39.13
SB 737-55-1063, dated July 1, 1999	39.13
SB 737-57-1129, Rev. 1, dated October 30, 1981, as revised by Notice of Status Change 737-57-1129NSC1, dated July 23, 1982; Notice of Status Change 737-57-1129NSC2, dated April 14, 1983; Notice of Status Change 737-57-1129NSC3, dated May 18, 1995.	39.13
SB 737-57-1221, dated August 6, 1992	39.13
SB 737-57-1221, Rev. 2, dated November 17, 1994	39.13
SB 737-71-1203, Rev. 3 dated June 1, 1989	39.13
SB 737-71-1250, dated June 14, 1990	39.13
SB 737-71-1289, dated August 19, 1993	39.13
SB 737-76-1023 dated February 14, 1991	39.13
SB 737-77-1031, Rev. 1, dated May 14, 1992	39.13
SB 737-78-1048, Rev. 1 dated February 22, 1990	39.13
SB 737-78-1053, Rev. 1, dated July 1, 1993	39.13
SB 737-78-1053, Rev. 2, dated February 17, 1994	39.13
SB 737-78-1053, Rev. 3, dated June 30, 1994	39.13
SB 737-78-1058, dated July 1, 1993	39.13
SB 737-78-1058, Rev. 1, dated February 17, 1994	39.13
SB 737-78-1058, Rev. 2, dated July 7, 1994	39.13
SB 737-SL-27-82-B, dated July 13, 1993	39.13
SB 747-21-2317 dated May 30, 1991	39.13
SB 747-24-2154 dated February 7, 1991	39.13
SB 747-24-2193, dated January 26, 1995	39.13
SB 747-24A2186, Rev. 1, dated May 20, 1993	39.13
SB 747-25-2734 dated November 3, 1988	39.13
SB 747-25-2734, Rev. 1 dated May 25, 1989	39.13
SB 747-25-2754 dated March 30, 1989	39.13
SB 747-25-2807, Rev. 2 dated Aug. 22, 1991	39.13
SB 747-25-2951 dated Aug. 15, 1991	39.13
SB 747-25-3073, dated September 21, 1995	39.13
SB 747-25-3132, dated December19, 1996	39.13
SB 747-25-3132, Rev. 1, dated January 15, 1998	39.13
SB 747-25A3137, dated March 13, 1997	39.13
SB 747-25A3142, Revision 1, dated August 6, 1998	39.13
SB 747-26-2143, Rev. 1 dated Aug. 15, 1991	39.13
SB 747-26-2162 dated September 20, 1990	39.13
SB 747-26-2164 dated Feb. 14, 1991	39.13
SB 747-26-2168 dated Mar. 28. 1991	39.13
SB 747-27-2367, dated June 25, 1998	39.13
SB 747-27-2367, Revision 1, dated December 17, 1998	39.13
SB 747-27A2346, Rev. 2, dated January 12, 1995	39.13
SB 747-27A2356, Revision 1, dated August 13, 1998	39.13
SB 747-28-2146, dated August 13, 1992	39.13
SB 747-28-2153 dated July 18, 1991	39.13
SB 747-28-2154 dated June 27, 1991	39.13
SB 747-28-2160, dated July 23, 1992	39.13
SB 747-28-2160, Rev. 1, dated December 16, 1993	39.13
SB 747-28-2205, Revision 1, dated April 16, 1998	39.13

14 CFR (PARTS 1–59)—Continued
FEDERAL AVIATION ADMINISTRATION, DEPARTMENT OF TRANSPORTATION—Continued

	14 CFR
SB 747-28A2194, Rev. 1, dated January 18, 1996	39.13
SB 747-28A2209, Revision 1, dated February 18, 1999	39.13
SB 747-31-2288, dated December 17, 1998	39.13
SB 747-31-2288, Revision 1, dated January 28, 1999	39.13
SB 747-35-2074, Rev. 1 dated Dec. 12, 1991	39.13
SB 747-36-2081 dated November 29, 1990	39.13
SB 747-36-2092 dated June 28, 1990	39.13
SB 747-36A2097, Rev. 3, dated September 28, 1995	39.13
SB 747-38A2105, Rev. 1, dated March 2, 1995	39.13
SB 747-51-2048, Rev. 1, dated January 27, 1994	39.13
SB 747-52-2186, Rev. 4, dated October 24, 1991	39.13
SB 747-52-2186, Rev. 4, dated October 24, 1991	39.13
SB 747-53-2275, dated March 26, 1987	39.13
SB 747-53-2275, Rev. 1, dated August 13, 1987	39.13
SB 747-53-2275, Rev. 2, dated March 31, 1988	39.13
SB 747-53-2275, Rev. 3, dated March 29, 1990	39.13
SB 747-53-2275, Rev. 4, dated March 26, 1992	39.13
SB 747-53-2275, Rev. 5, dated January 16, 1997	39.13
SB 747-53-2283, Rev. 3 dated Nov. 1, 1989	39.13
SB 747-53-2302 dated December 13, 1990	39.13
SB 747-53-2307, Rev. 2, dated October 14, 1993	39.13
SB 747-53-2349, dated June 27, 1991	39.13
SB 747-53-2349, dated June 27, 1991	39.13
SB 747-53-2358, dated August 26, 1993	39.13
SB 747-53-2366, including the Addendum, dated August 6, 1992	39.13
SB 747-53-2367, dated December 18, 1991	39.13
SB 747-53-2367, Rev. 1, dated January 27, 1994	39.13
SB 747-53-2371, including the ADDENDUM, dated July 29, 1993	39.13
SB 747-53A2267, Rev. 3, dated March 26, 1992	39.13
SB 747-53A2275, Rev. 6, dated August 27, 1998	39.13
SB 747-53A2312, Rev. 2, dated October 8, 1992	39.13
SB 747-53A2377, Rev. 1, dated January 28, 1993	39.13
SB 747-53A2377, Rev. 2, dated October 6, 1994	39.13
SB 747-53A2378, Rev. 1, dated March 10, 1994	39.13
SB 747-53A2396, Rev. 1, dated February 22, 1996	39.13
SB 747-54-2062, Rev. 7, dated December 21, 1994	39.13
SB 747-54-2062, Rev. 8, dated August 21, 1997	39.13
SB 747-54-2063, Rev. 9 dated April 23, 1992	39.13
SB 747-54-2091, Rev. 1, dated October 22, 1984	39.13
SB 747-54-2091, Rev. 2, dated March 31, 1988	39.13
SB 747-54-2091, Rev. 5, dated April 26, 1990	39.13
SB 747-54-2091; Rev. 3, dated July 27, 1989	39.13
SB 747-54-2091; Rev. 4, dated December 14, 1989	39.13
SB 747-54-2118, dated July 25, 1986	39.13
SB 747-54-2118, Rev. 1, dated May 21, 1987	39.13
SB 747-54-2118, Rev. 2, dated April 21, 1988	39.13
SB 747-54-2118, Rev. 3, dated September 29, 1988	39.13
SB 747-54-2118, Rev. 4, dated May 11, 1989	39.13
SB 747-54-2155, Revision 2, dated June 6, 1996	39.13
SB 747-54-2160, dated September 9, 1993	39.13

Title 14—Aeronautics and Space

Material Approved for Incorporation by Reference

	14 CFR
SB 757-31-0066, Revision 1, dated December 17, 1998	39.13
SB 757-52-0042, Rev. 1, dated April 26, 1990	39.13
SB 757-52-0055 dated June 25, 1992	39.13
SB 757-53-0056, Original dated Sept. 27, 1990	39.13
SB 757-53A0060 dated Aug. 8, 1991	39.13
SB 757-54-0028, dated March 31, 1994	39.13
SB 757-54-0031, Rev. 2, dated December 19, 1996	39.13
SB 757-54-0035, dated July 17, 1997	39.13
SB 757-54A0019, Rev. 3, dated March 26, 1992	39.13
SB 757-54A0019, Rev. 4, dated May 27, 1993	39.13
SB 757-54A0019, Rev. 5, dated March 17, 1994	39.13
SB 757-54A0020, Rev. 4, dated May 27, 1993	39.13
SB 757-54A0020, Rev. 5, dated March 17, 1994	39.13
SB 757-54A0020, Rev. 6, dated July 18, 1997	39.13
SB 757-56-0007, dated May 6, 1993	39.13
SB 757-57-0027, Rev. 1 dated March 15, 1990	39.13
SB 757-57-0036 dated June 13, 1991	39.13
SB 757-57-0053, dated February 6, 1997	39.13
SB 757-57-0053, Rev. 1, dated January 15, 1998	39.13
SB 757-76-0007, Rev. 2, dated January 23, 1992	39.13
SB 757-76-0009, Revision 1, dated December 3, 1998	39.13
SB 757-76-0010, dated August 12, 1993	39.13
SB 757-76-0011, dated December 2, 1993	39.13
SB 757-78-0012, dated August 31, 1989	39.13
SB 757-78-0025 dated September 9, 1991	39.13
SB 757-78-0032, Rev. 2, dated May 12, 1994	39.13
SB 757-78-0035, Rev. 2, dated June 23, 1994	39.13
SB 767 dated July 18, 1991	39.13
SB 767, Rev. 1 dated Feb. 13, 1992	39.13
SB 767-21A0098 dated May 9, 1991	39.13
SB 767-25-0137, Rev. 1 dated May 9, 1991	39.13
SB 767-25-0216, dated February 3, 1994	39.13
SB 767-25-0218, dated December 15, 1994	39.13
SB 767-25-0244, dated December 19, 1996	39.13
SB 767-25-0244, Rev. 1, dated January 15, 1998	39.13
SB 767-27-0096, dated April 23, 1992	39.13
SB 767-27-0096, dated April 23, 1992	39.13
SB 767-27-0096, dated April 23, 1992	39.13
SB 767-27-0104 dated November 15, 1990	39.13
SB 767-27-0104, Rev. 1 dated May 30, 1991	39.13
SB 767-27-0104, Rev. 2 dated Sept. 12, 1991	39.13
SB 767-27-0108, Rev. 1, dated October 1, 1992	39.13
SB 767-27-0108, Rev. 1, dated October 1, 1992	39.13
SB 767-27-0108, Rev. 1, dated October 1, 1992	39.13
SB 767-27A0094, Rev. 5, dated June 9, 1994, and Boeing SB 767-27-0138, dated August 17, 1995.	39.13
SB 767-31-0106, Revision 1, dated December 17, 1998	39.13
SB 767-32-0128, Rev. 1, dated March 31, 1994	39.13
SB 767-32A0116, Rev. 1, dated January 13, 1994	39.13
SB 767-32A0126, Rev. 1, dated January 13, 1994	39.13

Title 14—Aeronautics and Space

14 CFR (PARTS 1–59)—Continued
FEDERAL AVIATION ADMINISTRATION, DEPARTMENT OF TRANSPORTATION—
Continued

	14 CFR
SB 767-32A0148, Rev. 1, dated October 10, 1996	39.13
SB 767-32A0151, Rev. 1, dated October 10, 1996	39.13
SB 767-32A0157, dated October 10, 1996	39.13
SB 767-33-0052, Rev. 1, dated December 8, 1994 as revised by Notice of Status Change 767-33-0052 NSC 01, dated May 9, 1996.	39.13
SB 767-36A0041, Rev. 1, dated February 25, 1993	39.13
SB 767-36A0041, Rev. 1, dated February 25, 1993	39.13
SB 767-36A0041, Rev. 2, dated October 28, 1993	39.13
SB 767-52A0053, Rev. 2, dated April 30, 1992	39.13
SB 767-52A0053, Rev. 2, dated April 30, 1992	39.13
SB 767-52A0061, Rev. 1 dated Sept. 26, 1991	39.13
SB 767-56-0002 as amended by Notice of Status Change Number 767-56-0002 NSC 1, dated July 3, 1986.	39.13
SB 767-56-0002, dated August 30, 1985	39.13
SB 767-57-0043, Rev. 1, dated May 6, 1993	39.13
SB 767-57-0043, Rev. 2, dated September 16, 1993	39.13
SB 767-57-0043, Rev. 3, dated February 2, 1995	39.13
SB 767-57A0039, Rev. 1, dated October 15, 1992	39.13
SB 767-57A0039, Rev. 1, dated October 15, 1992	39.13
SB 767-57A0064, Revision 1, dated July 9, 1998	39.13
SB 767-76-0010, Revision 1, dated February 20, 1992	39.13
SB 767-78-0046 dated July 2, 1991	39.13
SB 767-78-0046, Rev. 1 dated Sept. 17, 1992	39.13
SB 767-78-0047 dated August 22, 1991	39.13
SB 767-78-0047, Rev. 1, dated March 26, 1992	39.13
SB 767-78-0047, Rev. 2, dated January 21, 1993	39.13
SB 767-78-0047, Rev. 3, dated July 28, 1994	39.13
SB 767-78-0048 dated August 15, 1991	39.13
SB 767-78-0048, Rev. 1, dated March 26, 1992	39.13
SB 767-78-0051 dated October 9, 1991	39.13
SB 767-78-0054 dated Dec. 13, 1991	39.13
SB 767-78-0059, Rev. 2, dated June 10, 1993	39.13
SB 767-78-0059, Rev. 3, dated January 20, 1994	39.13
SB 767-78-0060, Rev. 2, dated August 19, 1993	39.13
SB 767-78-0061, Rev. 1, dated August 5, 1993	39.13
SB 767-78-0062, Rev. 2, dated June 3, 1993	39.13
SB 767-78-0062, Rev. 3, dated February 24, 1994	39.13
SB 767-78-0063 dated Dec. 13, 1991	39.13
SB 767-78-0063, Rev. 2, dated April 28, 1994	39.13
SB 767-78A0052, Rev. 2 dated May 28, 1992	39.13
SB 777-32-0016, dated January 14, 1999	39.13
SB 777-53-0006, dated May 8, 1997	39.13
SB 777-53A0018, Revision 1, dated February 11, 1999	39.13
SB Notice of Status Change 737-71-1289 NSC 03, dated October 3, 1996.	39.13
SB Notice of Status Change 737-71-1289 NSC 1, dated September 2, 1993.	39.13
SB Notice of Status Change 737-71-1289 NSC 2, dated January 26, 1995.	39.13
SB Notice of Status Change, 747-54-2118, dated October 5, 1986	39.13

952

Material Approved for Incorporation by Reference

14 CFR (PARTS 1–59)—Continued
FEDERAL AVIATION ADMINISTRATION, DEPARTMENT OF TRANSPORTATION—
Continued

	14 CFR
Service Bulletin 1541 Revision 3 dated February 15, 1967	39.13
Service Bulletin 2411 Revision 2 dated April 29, 1968	39.13
Service Bulletin 2999 Revision 3 dated January 12, 1972	39.13
Service Bulletin 2999 Revision 4 dated January 31, 1991	39.13
Service Bulletin 3499 Revision 1 dated May 17, 2001	39.13
Service Bulletin 727-25-0294 dated May 25, 2000	39.13
Service Bulletin 727-25-0295 Revision 1 dated May 17, 2001	39.13
Service Bulletin 727-52-79 Revision 4 dated June 19, 1981	39.13
Service Bulletin 727-52-79 Revision 5 dated June 17, 1983	39.13
Service Bulletin 727-52A0079 Revision 6 dated January 11, 1990	39.13
Service Bulletin 727-53-0054 Revision 1 dated November 16, 1989	39.13
Service Bulletin 727-53-0084 Revision 4 dated August 2, 1990	39.13
Service Bulletin 727-53-0186 Revision 1 dated May 21, 1992	39.13
Service Bulletin 727-53A0222 Revision 1, including Appendix A dated March 15, 2001.	39.13
Service Bulletin 727-57-0127 Revision 3 dated August 24, 1989	39.13
Service Bulletin 727-57-0177 dated December 22, 1988	39.13
Service Bulletin 727-57-0177 Revision 1 dated November 21, 1991	39.13
Service Bulletin 727-57-0177 Revision 2 dated September 16, 1993	39.13
Service Bulletin 727-57-0177 Revision 3 dated February 15, 1996	39.13
Service Bulletin 727-57-0177 Revision 4 dated October 28, 1999	39.13
Service Bulletin 727-57-0184 dated August 16, 2001	39.13
Service Bulletin 727-57A0179 Revision 5 dated December 20, 2000	39.13
Service Bulletin 727-57A0182 Revision 1 dated February 25, 1999	39.13
Service Bulletin 737-24-1128 dated April 29, 1999	39.13
Service Bulletin 737-25-1047 dated December 9, 1999	39.13
Service Bulletin 737-25-1322 Revision 2 dated February 19, 1998	39.13
Service Bulletin 737-25-1371 Revision 2 dated December 9, 1999	39.13
Service Bulletin 737-25-1404 dated May 25, 2000	39.13
Service Bulletin 737-25-1405 dated May 25, 2000	39.13
Service Bulletin 737-25-1412 Revision 1 dated May 17, 2001	39.13
Service Bulletin 737-27A1214 Revision 1 dated July 1, 1999	39.13
Service Bulletin 737-28-1164 Revision 1 dated May 10, 2001	39.13
Service Bulletin 737-32-1253 dated November 7, 1991	39.13
Service Bulletin 737-35-1049 dated September 17, 1998	39.13
Service Bulletin 737-52-1100 Revision 2 dated March 31, 1994	39.13
Service Bulletin 737-53-1173 Revision 1 dated April 25, 1996	39.13
Service Bulletin 737-53-1212, including Appendix A dated August 13, 1998.	39.13
Service Bulletin 737-53A1177 Revision 4 dated September 2, 1999	39.13
Service Bulletin 737-53A1177 Revision 5 dated February 15, 2001	39.13
Service Bulletin 737-53A1177 Revision 6 dated May 31, 2001	39.13
Service Bulletin 737-53A1177 Revision 6 dated May 31, 2001	39.13
Service Bulletin 737-53A1177 Revision 6 dated May 31, 2001	39.13
Service Bulletin 737-55-1067 dated October 19, 2000	39.13
Service Bulletin 737-55A-1064 Revision 1 dated December 7, 2000	39.13
Service Bulletin 737-55A1070, including Appendices A, B, and C Revision 1 dated May 10, 2001.	39.13
Service Bulletin 737-57-1067 Revision 4 dated November 7, 1991	39.13
Service Bulletin 737-57-1129 Revision 2 dated May 28, 1998	39.13

14 CFR (PARTS 1–59)—Continued
FEDERAL AVIATION ADMINISTRATION, DEPARTMENT OF TRANSPORTATION—Continued

	14 CFR
Service Bulletin 737-57-1139 Revision 4 dated April 16, 1992	39.13
Service Bulletin 737-57-1210 dated April 4, 1991	39.13
Service Bulletin 737-57-1253 dated December 16, 1999	39.13
Service Bulletin 737-57A1249 Revision 1, including Appendix A dated June 1, 2000.	39.13
Service Bulletin 737-57A1260 Revision 2 dated October 18, 2001	39.13
Service Bulletin 747-25-3196 Revision 1 dated May 13, 1999	39.13
Service Bulletin 747-25-3244 Revision 1 dated May 17, 2001	39.13
Service Bulletin 747-25-3253, including Appendices A, B, and C dated June 29, 2000.	39.13
Service Bulletin 747-25A3271 Revision 1 dated December 19, 2001	39.13
Service Bulletin 747-26-2233 dated May 11, 1995	39.13
Service Bulletin 747-27-2374 dated November 18, 1999	39.13
Service Bulletin 747-28A2199 Revision 1 dated October 1, 1998	39.13
Service Bulletin 747-28A2199 Revision 2 dated July 8, 1999	39.13
Service Bulletin 747-28A2212 Revision 3 dated August 3, 2000	39.13
Service Bulletin 747-31-2245 dated June 27, 1996	39.13
Service Bulletin 747-31-2246 dated May 2, 1996	39.13
Service Bulletin 747-32-2190 Revision 4 dated October 26, 1989	39.13
Service Bulletin 747-45-2007 dated March 29, 1990	39.13
Service Bulletin 747-45-2016 Revision 1 dated May 2, 1996	39.13
Service Bulletin 747-45-2016 Revision 1 dated May 2, 1996	39.13
Service Bulletin 747-52-2260 Revision 1 dated March 21, 1996	39.13
Service Bulletin 747-53-2327 Revision 2 dated September 24, 1998	39.13
Service Bulletin 747-53A2410 Revision 3 dated March 12, 1998	39.13
Service Bulletin 747-53A2417 Revision 1 dated July 23, 1998	39.13
Service Bulletin 747-53A2444 Revision 1 dated June 15, 2000	39.13
Service Bulletin 747-53A2449 Revision 1 dated May 24, 2001	39.13
Service Bulletin 747-54A2196 Revision 1 dated August 17, 2000	39.13
Service Bulletin 747-54A2200 Revision 1 dated February 15, 2001	39.13
Service Bulletin 747-54A2206 Revision 1 dated February 22, 2001	39.13
Service Bulletin 747-54A2206 Revision 2 dated May 17, 2001	39.13
Service Bulletin 747-57-2256 dated March 8, 1990	39.13
Service Bulletin 747-57-2256 Revision 1 dated November 15, 1990	39.13
Service Bulletin 747-57-2256 Revision 2 dated March 5, 1992	39.13
Service Bulletin 747-57-2256 Revision 3 dated June 21, 2001	39.13
Service Bulletin 747-57-2305 Revision 1 dated January 21, 1999	39.13
Service Bulletin 747-57A2298 Revision 2 dated October 2, 1997	39.13
Service Bulletin 747-57A2309 Revision 1 dated December 22, 1999	39.13
Service Bulletin 747-57A2310 Revision 1 dated November 23, 1999	39.13
Service Bulletin 747-57A2310 Revision 2 dated February 22, 2001	39.13
Service Bulletin 747-71-2285 dated October 8, 1998	39.13
Service Bulletin 747-71-2290 dated March 18, 1999	39.13
Service Bulletin 747-73-2052 Revision 1 dated April 23, 1992	39.13
Service Bulletin 747-76-2067 Revision 1 dated November 19, 1987	39.13
Service Bulletin 747-76A2068 Revision 3 dated August 22, 1991	39.13
Service Bulletin 747-78-2121 dated October 29, 1992	39.13
Service Bulletin 747-78-2135 dated August 31, 1995	39.13
Service Bulletin 747-78-2144 Revision 1 dated April 11, 1996	39.13
Service Bulletin 747-78-2150 Revision 1 dated July 2, 1998	39.13

Material Approved for Incorporation by Reference

	14 CFR
Service Bulletin 747-78-2153 Revision 1 dated November 27, 1996	39.13
Service Bulletin 747-78-2154 Revision 3 dated December 11, 1997	39.13
Service Bulletin 747-78-2155 Revision 2 dated November 5, 1998	39.13
Service Bulletin 747-78-2157 Revision 2 dated November 26, 1997	39.13
Service Bulletin 747-78-2158 Revision 2 dated July 29, 1999	39.13
Service Bulletin 747-78A2113 Revision 2 dated June 8, 1995	39.13
Service Bulletin 747-78A2113 Revision 3 dated September 11, 1997	39.13
Service Bulletin 747-78A2149 Revision 1 dated May 9, 1996	39.13
Service Bulletin 747-78A2149 Revision 2 dated August 29, 1996	39.13
Service Bulletin 747-78A2164 Revision 2 dated December 3, 1998	39.13
Service Bulletin 747-78A2166 Revision 1 dated October 9, 1997	39.13
Service Bulletin 757-25-0194 dated February 11, 1999	39.13
Service Bulletin 757-25-0217 dated May 25, 2000	39.13
Service Bulletin 757-25-0218 dated May 25, 2000	39.13
Service Bulletin 757-25-0223 Revision 1 dated May 17, 2001	39.13
Service Bulletin 757-25-0226, including Appendices A, B, and C dated July 3, 2000.	39.13
Service Bulletin 757-25-0228, including Appendices A, B, and C dated July 3, 2000.	39.13
Service Bulletin 757-27A0086 Revision 2 dated July 27, 1989	39.13
Service Bulletin 757-27A0127 Revision 1 dated September 2, 1999	39.13
Service Bulletin 757-28-0057 Revision 1 dated February 28, 2002	39.13
Service Bulletin 757-28-0059 Revision 1 dated February 28, 2002	39.13
Service Bulletin 757-29-0058 dated November 9, 2000	39.13
Service Bulletin 757-29-0059 dated November 9, 2000	39.13
Service Bulletin 757-35-0014 dated September 10, 1998	39.13
Service Bulletin 757-54-0013 Revision 3 dated October 23, 1997	39.13
Service Bulletin 757-54-0027 Revision 1 dated October 27, 1994	39.13
Service Bulletin 757-54-0031 Revision 4 dated November 11, 1999	39.13
Service Bulletin 757-54-0034 dated May 14, 1998	39.13
Service Bulletin 757-54-0036 dated May 14, 1998	39.13
Service Bulletin 757-57A0054 Revision 1 dated December 16, 1999	39.13
Service Bulletin 76-2019 dated June 9, 1971	39.13
Service Bulletin 767-25-0288 Revision 1 dated May 17, 2001	39.13
Service Bulletin 767-25-0290, including Appedices A, B, and C dated June 29, 2000.	39.13
Service Bulletin 767-27A0159 Revision 1 dated April 5, 2001	39.13
Service Bulletin 767-28-0059 dated December 22, 1999	39.13
Service Bulletin 767-28A0050 Revision 1 dated December 22, 1999	39.13
Service Bulletin 767-28A0053 Revision 1 dated August 5, 1999	39.13
Service Bulletin 767-29-0057 dated December 16, 1993	39.13
Service Bulletin 767-29-0057 dated December 16, 1993	39.13
Service Bulletin 767-29-0057, Notice of Status Change 1 dated November 23, 1994.	39.13
Service Bulletin 767-32A0148 Revision 2 dated November 30, 2000	39.13
Service Bulletin 767-32A0163 Revision 1 dated October 1, 1998	39.13
Service Bulletin 767-33-0093 dated December 20, 2001	39.13
Service Bulletin 767-33A0075 Revision 1 dated May 27, 1999	39.13
Service Bulletin 767-35-0033 dated September 10, 1998	39.13
Service Bulletin 767-51A0020 Revision 1 dated July 22, 1999	39.13

Title 14—Aeronautics and Space

Material Approved for Incorporation by Reference

	14 CFR
Service Letter 737-SL-12-017 dated April 10, 2002	39.13
Service Letter 737-SL-24-106, dated March 10, 1995, including Attachments I and II.	39.13
Service Letter 737-SL-24-111-B, including Attachment dated January 16, 2001.	39.13
Service Letter 737-SL-24-138, including Attachment dated May 24, 1999.	39.13
Service Letter 737-SL-27-112-B, dated February 6, 1997	39.13
Service Letter 737-SL-27-118-A, dated November 14, 1997	39.13
Service Letter 737-SL-27-118-D dated December 17, 1999	39.13
Service Letter 737-SL-27-120 dated January 28, 1998	39.13
Service Letter 737-SL-27-71-A, dated June 19, 1992, including Attachment 1.	39.13
Service Letter 737-SL-28-36 dated November 30, 1990	39.13
Service Letter 737-SL-28-36, dated November 30, 1990	39.13
Service Letter 737-SL-28-36, dated November 30, 1990; 737-SL-28-42, dated December 15, 1992; and 737-SL-28-42-A, dated July 15, 1993.	39.13
Service Letter 737-SL-28-42, dated December 15, 1992	39.13
Service Letter 737-SL-28-42-A, dated July 15, 1993	39.13
Service Letter 737-SL-29-21, dated December 16, 1982, including Attachments 1-3, dated April 15, 1982.	39.13
Service Letter 737-SL-49-14, Rev. A dated Mar. 29, 1989	39.13
Service Letter 737-SL-49-14, Rev. B dated April 20, 1989	39.13
Service Letter 747-SL-32-19, dated January 16, 1980	39.13
Service Letter 747-SL-36-089 dated August 10, 1998	39.13
Service Letter 757-SL-27-52-B dated April 30, 1990	39.13
Service Letter 757-SL-52-6 dated September 17, 1991	39.13
Service Letter 767-SL-32-067, dated August 4, 1995	39.13
Service Letter 777-SL-24-023-B, dated August 16, 1999	39.13
Service Letter 777-SL-24-024, dated August 16, 1999	39.13
Service Letter 777-SL-24-025, dated August 18, 1999	39.13
Special Attention Service Bulletin 737-24-1144 Revision 1 dated June 21, 2001.	39.13
Special Attention Service Bulletin 737-25-1403 dated May 4, 2000	39.13
Special Attention Service Bulletin 737-27-1223 dated October 21, 1999.	39.13
Special Attention Service Bulletin 737-28-0060 Revision 1 dated October 26, 2000.	39.13
Special Attention Service Bulletin 737-28-0061 Revision 1 dated October 26, 2000.	39.13
Special Attention Service Bulletin 737-28-1160 Revision 1 dated October 26, 2000.	39.13
Special Attention Service Bulletin 737-28-1164 dated August 24, 2000	39.13
Special Attention Service Bulletin 737-35-1076 dated March 1, 2001	39.13
Special Attention Service Bulletin 737-35-1077 dated March 1, 2001	39.13
Special Attention Service Bulletin 747-31-2288 Revision 2 dated November 18, 1999.	39.13
Special Attention Service Bulletin 747-32-2461 dated August 19, 1999	39.13
Special Attention Service Bulletin 747-35-2111 dated March 1, 2001	39.13
Special Attention Service Bulletin 757-25-0214 dated April 6, 2000	39.13

14 CFR (PARTS 1–59)—Continued
FEDERAL AVIATION ADMINISTRATION, DEPARTMENT OF TRANSPORTATION—Continued

	14 CFR
SB 327400-27-171, Rev. 1, dated April 14, 1995	39.13
SB 93600-27-173, dated May 17, 1995	39.13
Service Bulletin 727-53-0007 Revision 1 dated June 6, 2001	39.13
ASB 5006286-28-A5, Rev. 2, dated May 3, 1994	39.13
ASB 734187-27-A2, Rev. 1, dated September 15, 1990	39.13
ASB 734378-27-A3, Rev. 1, dated January 25, 1991	39.13
ASB 734380-27-A2, Rev. 1, dated September 15, 1990	39.13
ASB 734382-27-A3, Rev. 1, dated September 15, 1990	39.13
ASB 734384-27-A2, Rev. 1, dated September 15, 1990	39.13
ASB 734386-27-A2, Rev. 1, dated September 15, 1990	39.13
ASB 734388-27-A1, Rev. 1, dated September 15, 1990	39.13
SB ERPS13GCM-29-3, dated June 24, 1998	39.13

Boeing Commercial Aircraft Group
Long Beach Division 3855 Lakewood Boulevard Long Beach California 90846 ATTN: Data and Service Management Dept. C1-L5A (D800-0024)

	14 CFR
Alert Service Bulletin 717-27A0010 dated August 15, 2000	39.13
Alert Service Bulletin 717-27A0016, including Appendix dated April 9, 2001.	39.13
Alert Service Bulletin 717-27A0025 dated June 11, 2002	39.13
Alert Service Bulletin 717-57A0002 Revision 2 dated October 2, 2001	39.13
Alert Service Bulletin 737-73A1011 Revision 2 dated July 13, 2000	39.13
Alert Service Bulletin DC10-24A130 Revision 1 dated March 12, 2001.	39.13
Alert Service Bulletin DC10-24A137 Revision 1 dated May 31, 2001	39.13
Alert Service Bulletin DC10-24A149 Revision 2 dated April 5, 2001	39.13
Alert Service Bulletin DC10-24A164 dated June 22, 2000	39.13
Alert Service Bulletin DC10-24A170 Revision 1 dated September 25, 2001.	39.13
Alert Service Bulletin DC10-28A228, including Appendix dated December 11, 2000.	39.13
Alert Service Bulletin DC10-28A228, including Appendix Revision 1 dated July 16, 2001.	39.13
Alert Service Bulletin DC10-28A228, including Appendix Revision 2 dated December 7, 2001.	39.13
Alert Service Bulletin DC8-26A046 dated November 7, 2001	39.13
Alert Service Bulletin DC9-24A160 Revision 2 dated March 14, 2001	39.13
Alert Service Bulletin DC9-24A189 Revision 2 dated October 8, 2002	39.13
Alert Service Bulletin DC9-24A191 Revision 1 dated January 9, 2002	39.13
Alert Service Bulletin DC9-24A193 dated July 31, 2001	39.13
Alert Service Bulletin DC9-27A147 Revision 3 dated May 8, 2001	39.13
Alert Service Bulletin DC9-34A075 Revision 1 dated April 30, 2001	39.13
Alert Service Bulletin MD11-23A046 Revision 1 dated May 21, 2001	39.13
Alert Service Bulletin MD11-24A036 Revision 1 dated May 21, 2001	39.13
Alert Service Bulletin MD11-24A095 Revision 1 dated March 16, 2001.	39.13
Alert Service Bulletin MD11-24A117 dated May 18, 2000	39.13
Alert Service Bulletin MD11-24A179, including Appendix A Revision 1 dated October 31, 2000.	39.13
Alert Service Bulletin MD11-24A189 dated June 22, 2000	39.13
Alert Service Bulletin MD11-25A244 dated August 10, 2000	39.13

Title 14—Aeronautics and Space

	14 CFR
Alert Service Bulletin MD11-25A244 Revision 1 dated October 31, 2000.	39.13
Alert Service Bulletin MD11-28A058 Revision 1 dated March 29, 2001.	39.13
Alert Service Bulletin MD11-28A112, including Appendix dated December 11, 2000.	39.13
Alert Service Bulletin MD11-52A035 Revision 2 dated March 12, 2001.	39.13
Alert Service Bulletin MD11-57A067, including Appendices A and B dated July 10, 2002.	39.13
Alert Service Bulletin MD11-71A086 Revision 1 dated May 21, 2001	39.13
Alert Service Bulletin MD80-23A100 Revision 2 dated February 8, 2001.	39.13
Alert Service Bulletin MD80-25A376 dated September 21, 2000	39.13
Alert Service Bulletin MD80-27A359 dated January 29, 2001	39.13
Alert Service Bulletin MD80-27A359 Revision 1 dated March 26, 2001.	39.13
Alert Service Bulletin MD80-30A092, including Appendix dated March 14, 2001.	39.13
Alert Service Bulletin MD80-33A096 Revision 3 dated August 14, 2001.	39.13
Alert Service Bulletin MD80-33A099 Revision 3 dated January 27, 2000.	39.13
Alert Service Bulletin MD90-23A018 Revision 1 dated August 10, 2000.	39.13
Alert Service Bulletin MD90-25A070, including Evaluation Form Revision 1 dated February 26, 2002.	39.13
Alert Service Bulletin MD90-27A031 dated January 29, 2001	39.13
Alert Service Bulletin MD90-27A031 Revision 1 dated March 26, 2001.	39.13
Alert Service Bulletin MD90-30A023, including Appendix dated March 14, 2001.	39.13
Service Bulletin 717-27-0013 dated January 30, 2001	39.13
Service Bulletin 717-27-0013 Revision 1 dated February 28, 2001	39.13
Service Bulletin 717-57-0004 Revision 1 dated October 2, 2001	39.13
Service Bulletin DC9-32-315 Revision 1 dated October 24, 2000	39.13
Service Bulletin DC9-53-290 Revision 1 dated March 15, 2002	39.13
Service Bulletin MD11-24-128 Revision 3 dated May 17, 2001	39.13
Service Bulletin MD11-24-184 dated February 22, 2001	39.13
Service Bulletin MD11-24-197 dated May 16, 2001	39.13
Service Bulletin MD11-26-037 dated November 8, 2000	39.13
Service Bulletin MD80-25-377 dated March 14, 2001	39.13
Service Bulletin MD80-25-377 Revision 1 dated July 17, 2001	39.13
Service Bulletin MD80-32-309 Revision 1 dated April 25, 2001	39.13
Service Bulletin MD90-24-007 Revision 2 dated July 16, 2001	39.13
Service Bulletin MD90-24-066 Revision 1 dated February 8, 2001	39.13
Service Bulletin MD90-24-067 Revision 1 dated February 8, 2001	39.13
Service Bulletin MD90-24-068 Revision 1 dated February 8, 2001	39.13
Service Bulletin MD90-24-069 Revision 1 dated February 8, 2001	39.13
Service Bulletin MD90-24-070 Revision 1 dated February 8, 2001	39.13
Service Bulletin MD90-24-071 Revision 1 dated February 8, 2001	39.13

Material Approved for Incorporation by Reference

14 CFR (PARTS 1–59)—Continued

FEDERAL AVIATION ADMINISTRATION, DEPARTMENT OF TRANSPORTATION—
Continued

	14 CFR
Service Bulletin MD90-24-072 Revision 1 dated February 8, 2001	39.13
Service Bulletin MD90-32-031 Revision 1 dated April 25, 2001	39.13
Service Bulletin MD90-32-033 Revision 1 dated October 24, 2000	39.13
Alert Service Bulletin 109XXXX-30-38 dated August 8, 2002	39.13
Alert Service Bulletin MD11-29A057 Revision 1 dated October 21, 1999.	39.13
Alert Service Bulletin DC10-24A147 Revision 3 dated April 30, 2001	39.13
Alert Service Bulletin DC10-24A174 dated June 29, 2001	39.13
Alert Service Bulletin DC10-29A142 Revision 1 dated October 21, 1999.	39.13
Alert Service Bulletin DC8-24A068 Revision 1 dated November 1, 1999.	39.13
Alert Service Bulletin DC8-24A075 Revision 1 dated September 21, 1999.	39.13
Alert Service Bulletin DC8-24A075 Revision 2 dated May 2, 2000	39.13
Alert Service Bulletin DC8-27A275 R03 Revision 3 dated April 5, 1996.	39.13
Alert Service Bulletin DC8-30A032 Revision 2 dated September 21, 1999.	39.13
Alert Service Bulletin DC8-33A053 Revision 2 dated November 1, 1999.	39.13
Alert Service Bulletin DC8-33A070 dated November 1, 1999	39.13
Alert Service Bulletin DC9-24A072 Revision 1 dated May 22, 2000	39.13
Alert Service Bulletin DC9-24A115 Revision 1 dated April 24, 2000	39.13
Alert Service Bulletin DC9-24A135 Revision 1 dated May 1, 2000	39.13
Alert Service Bulletin DC9-32A298 R02 Revision 2 dated October 29, 1997.	39.13
Alert Service Bulletin DC9-33A037 Revision 2 dated July 27, 1999	39.13
Alert Service Bulletin DC9-33A058 Revision 2 dated January 27, 2000.	39.13
Alert Service Bulletin DC9-33A058 Revision 3 dated November 21, 2001.	39.13
Alert Service Bulletin DC9-33A062 Revision 1 dated April 24, 2000	39.13
Alert Service Bulletin DC9-33A081 Revision 1 dated November 8, 1999.	39.13
Alert Service Bulletin DC9-33A114 Revision 1 dated February 15, 2000.	39.13
Alert Service Bulletin MD11-24A111 Revision 1 dated July 27, 2000	39.13
Alert Service Bulletin MD11-24A138 Revision 1 dated June 5, 2001	39.13
Alert Service Bulletin MD11-24A157 dated August 10, 2000	39.13
Alert Service Bulletin MD11-24A178 Revision 1 dated December 17, 2001.	39.13
Alert Service Bulletin MD11-24A186 dated October 4, 2000	39.13
Alert Service Bulletin MD11-24A186 Revision 1 dated May 16, 2001	39.13
Alert Service Bulletin MD11-25A227 Revision 1 dated October 31, 2001.	39.13
Alert Service Bulletin MD80-24A124 Revision 1 dated August 24, 2000.	39.13
Alert Service Bulletin MD80-24A126 Revision 2 dated September 22, 1999.	39.13
Alert Service Bulletin MD80-24A145 Revision 1 dated June 22, 2000	39.13

Material Approved for Incorporation by Reference

FEDERAL AVIATION ADMINISTRATION, DEPARTMENT OF TRANSPORTATION—Continued

	14 CFR
Aircraft Systems Modification Drawing 537L68229 dated May 18, 1999.	39.13
Aircraft Systems Modification Drawing 537L68230 dated May 18, 1999.	39.13
Aircraft Systems Modification Drawing 537L68231 dated May 18, 1999.	39.13
Aircraft Systems Modification Drawing 537L68232 dated May 18, 1999.	39.13
Service Bulletin MDC-CNS 78-41 dated June 11, 1999	39.13
Overhaul Manual 24-20-46 Revision 8 dated August 15, 1983	39.13

Boeing Vertol Company

Boeing Center, P.O. Box 16858, Philadelphia, Pennsylvania 19142

SB 107-113, Rev. A dated November 22, 1963	39.13
SB 107-116 (R-1), Rev. B dated February 21, 1983	39.13
SB 107-182, Rev. B dated July 26, 1965	39.13
SB 107-6, Maintenance Schedule, Section 2, Temporary Rev. 31 dated February 7, 1986.	39.13
SB No. 234-32-1009 dated February 23, 1987	39.13
SBe/Boeing No. 234-63-1009 dated June 29, 1984	39.13

Bombardier Inc., Canadair, Aerospace Group

P.O. Box 6087, Station Centre-ville, Montreal, Quebec, Canada H3C 3G9

(Learjet 45) Alert Service Bulletin SB A45-30-2 dated December 18, 2000.	39.13
Advisory Wire 32-021 dated February 5, 2001	39.13
Aerospace Information Letter SIL 32-016 dated March 30, 2000	39.13
Aerospace Repair Drawing RD8-21-23 Issue 2 dated December 16, 1999.	39.13
Alert SB A600-0645, dated January 11, 1995	39.13
Alert SB A601-0443, dated January 11, 1995	39.13
Alert SB A8-27-73, dated November 25, 1993	39.13
Alert SB A8-28-20, Rev. A, dated September 10, 1996	39.13
Alert SB A8-34-117, Rev. C, dated February 14, 1997	39.13
Alert Service Bulletin A604-73-002 dated January 12, 2001	39.13
Alert Service Bulletin (Learjet 60) SB A60-35-2 dated November 4, 1999.	39.13
Alert Service Bulletin 215-A476 Revision 4 dated August 18, 2000	39.13
Alert Service Bulletin 601R-28-042 Revision A dated January 12, 2001.	39.13
Alert Service Bulletin A601-0542 dated January 12, 2001	39.13
Alert Service Bulletin A601R-24-103 Revision B dated January 26, 2001.	39.13
Alert Service Bulletin A601R-24-105 Revision A dated July 20, 2001	39.13
Alert Service Bulletin A601R-28-045 Revision A dated December 7, 2001.	39.13
Alert Service Bulletin A601R-32-079 Revision D dated December 1, 2000.	39.13
Alert Service Bulletin A601R-57-027 Revision C dated May 30, 2000	39.13
Alert Service Bulletin A601R-57-031, including Appendix A Revision A dated March 28, 2001.	39.13
Alert Service Bulletin A604-27-006 dated April 18, 2000	39.13

Title 14—Aeronautics and Space

Material Approved for Incorporation by Reference

14 CFR (PARTS 1–59)—Continued
FEDERAL AVIATION ADMINISTRATION, DEPARTMENT OF TRANSPORTATION—
Continued

Material Approved for Incorporation by Reference

14 CFR (PARTS 1–59)—Continued

FEDERAL AVIATION ADMINISTRATION, DEPARTMENT OF TRANSPORTATION—Continued

	14 CFR
SB F100-32-86, Rev. 2, dated July 3, 1997, including Appendix A, Rev. 1, dated November 1, 1996, and Appendix B, Rev. 1, dated November 1, 1996.	39.13
SB F100-32-92, dated November 14, 1997	39.13
SB F50-32-48, Rev. 4, dated June 21, 1995	39.13
SB No. M-DT 17002-32-10, Rev. 3, dated September 6, 1996	39.13
Bombardier, Inc.	
Bombardier Regional Aircraft Division 123 Garratt Boulevard Downsview Ontario M3K 1Y5 Canada	
Alert Service Bulletin A8-27-91 dated September 12, 2000	39.13
Alert Service Bulletin A8-27-91 Revision A dated November 23, 2000	39.13
Alert Service Bulletin A8-73-23 Revision A dated December 12, 2000	39.13
Alert Service Bulletin A8-73-23 Revision B dated January 30, 2001	39.13
Alert Service Bulletin A84-28-02 dated February 7, 2001	39.13
DHC-8 Alert Service Bulletin A84-32-15 dated February 4, 2002	39.13
Service Bulletin 7-27-90 dated September 3, 1999	39.13
Service Bulletin 8-25-306 dated May 5, 2000	39.13
Service Bulletin 8-25-307 dated November 13, 2000	39.13
Service Bulletin 8-35-19 dated August 17, 2000	39.13
Service Bulletin 8-52-38 dated October 10, 1995	39.13
Service Bulletin 8-52-38 Revision A dated September 19, 1997	39.13
Service Bulletin 8-52-46 dated September 30, 1998	39.13
Service Bulletin 8-52-56 Revision C dated March 10, 2000	39.13
Service Bulletin 8-52-56 Revision D dated May 18, 2000	39.13
Service Bulletin 8-52-56 Revision E dated July 20, 2000	39.13
Service Bulletin 8-52-56 Revision F dated August 29, 2000	39.13
Service Bulletin 8-52-56 Revision G dated November 7, 2000	39.13
Service Bulletin 8-52-57 dated February 23, 2000	39.13
Service Bulletin 8-52-57 Revision A dated July 28, 2000	39.13
Service Bulletin 8-52-57 Revision B dated November 14, 2000	39.13
Service Bulletin 8-52-59 dated September 18, 2000	39.13
Service Bulletin 8-52-59 Revision A dated January 3, 2001	39.13
Service Bulletin 8-53-75 dated December 6, 1999	39.13
Service Bulletin 8-57-41 Revision C dated August 4, 2000	39.13
Service Bulletin 8-61-31 dated October 17, 2000	39.13
Service Bulletin 84-28-01 Revision A dated February 8, 2001	39.13
Temporary Revision TR AWL 2-15 dated September 3, 1999	39.13
Temporary Revision TR AWL 3-78 dated November 19, 1999	39.13
Temporary Revision TR AWL-71 dated September 3, 1999	39.13
Dash 8 Airworthiness Limitations List Temporary Revision AWL 2-19 dated July 14, 2000.	39.13
Dash 8 Airworthiness Limitations List Temporary Revision AWL 3-83 dated July 14, 2000.	39.13
Dash 8 Airworthiness Limitations List Temporary Revision AWL-75 dated July 14, 2000.	39.13
Dash 8 Airworthiness Limitations List Temporary Revision AWL-76 dated July 14, 2000.	39.13
Bombardier-Rotax GmbH	
Welser Strasse 32 A-4623 Gunskirchen Austria Telephone 7246-601-232	
Mandatory Service Bulletin SB-912-022/SB-914-011 dated March 2001	39.13

Title 14—Aeronautics and Space

Material Approved for Incorporation by Reference

	14 CFR
ASB 57-A-JA 980441 Revision No. 1, dated July 7, 1998	39.13
MSB 7/5, Rev. 1, dated May 23, 1988	39.13
MSB 7/8, Rev. 3, dated May 23, 1988	39.13
SB 53-JM7297, dated May 10, 1984	39.13
SB 57-JM7298, dated May 16, 1984	39.13
Service Bulletin J41-32-072 Revision 1 May 18, 2001	39.13
Service Bulletin J41-32-075 April 18, 2001	39.13
Mandatory SB (MSB) B121/79, Rev. 1 dated Feb. 15, 1991	39.13
ASB ATP A52-30, dated March 19, 1997	39.13
SB No. 26-40-01601A, dated March 25, 1998	39.13
SB No. 71-68-01581A, Pages 1-3, dated March 25, 1998; and Pages 4-18, dated August 14, 1997.	39.13
Viscount Alert PTL 182, Issue 2, dated August 7, 1992	39.13
Alert Service Bulletin 32-A-JA-980840 Revision 3 dated May 5, 1999	39.13
Alert Service Bulletin 32-A-JA010740 Revision 2 dated July 23, 2001	39.13
Mandatory Alert Service Bulletin 53-JA-990842 Revision 1 dated February 21, 2000.	39.13
Mandatory Service Bulletin 32-JA 991140 dated April 14, 2000	39.13
SB S.B.32-150-70656A, dated December 1, 1998.	39.13
Service Bulletin 11-137-30405A dated March 26, 1998	39.13
Service Bulletin 32-PM6054 dated February 2000	39.13
Service Bulletin ATP-27-86 dated May 15, 1999	39.13
Service Bulletin ATP-30-52 Revision 1 dated June 12, 1998	39.13
Service Bulletin ATP-53-36 Revision 1 dated February 21, 2000	39.13
Service Bulletin SB.53-144 Revision 1 dated May 21, 1999	39.13
Service Bulletin SB.54-10 dated September 16, 1999	39.13
Service Bulletin SB.57-56 dated September 2, 1999	39.13
PTL 326, Issue 2, dated December 1, 1994	39.13
146 Inspection SB S.B.27-137, dated November 17, 1992	39.13
146 Inspection SB 28-18 dated March 12, 1991	39.13
146 Inspection SB 28-18 dated March 12, 1991	39.13
146 Inspection SB S.B. 27-133, dated January 31, 1992, which includes Appendix A1 to SB S.B. 27-133, dated January 31, 1992.	39.13
146 Inspection SB S.B. 27-133, dated January 31, 1992, which includes Appendix A1 to SB S.B. 27-133, dated January 31, 1992.	39.13
146 Inspection SB S.B. 27-135, dated April 23, 1992, which includes Appendices A1 and A2.	39.13
146 Inspection SB S.B. 27-135, dated April 23, 1992, which includes Appendices A1 and A2.	39.13
Airplane Flight Manual (Doc. No. ATP 004) Temp. Rev. 22, Issue 1 dated Nov. 1, 1991.	39.13
Alert PTL 264, Issue 3, dated September 1, 1992 and BAe Alert Preliminary Technical Leaflet, Issue 3, dated June 1, 1992.	39.13
Alert SB 24-A97 dated November 12, 1991	39.13
Alert SB 27-A-PM6005 Issue 1 dated March 28, 1990	39.13
Alert SB 27-A-PM6005 Issue 2 dated June 17, 1991	39.13
Alert SB 27-A-PM6007, Issue 1, dated April 10, 1992	39.13
Alert SB 27-A-PM6023, Issue No. 2, dated November 23, 1992	39.13
Alert SB 27-A-PM6025, Issue 1, dated March 23, 1994	39.13
Alert SB 27-PM6005 dated June 11, 1991	39.13
Alert SB 53-A-PM5989, Issue No. 1 dated Oct. 3, 1991	39.13

Title 14—Aeronautics and Space

Material Approved for Incorporation by Reference

14 CFR (PARTS 1–59)—Continued
FEDERAL AVIATION ADMINISTRATION, DEPARTMENT OF TRANSPORTATION—
Continued

	14 CFR
PTL 324, Issue 1 dated Feb. 10, 1990	39.13
PTL 500, dated January 1, 1993, including Appendices 1 through 4 inclusive, dated November 1992, and Appendix 5, dated October, 1992.	39.13
PTL 501, dated May 1, 1994	39.13
PTL 501, Issue 2, dated June 1, 1994, including Appendix 1, dated January 1, 1994.	39.13
Repair Drawing 572-40205, Rev. F, dated August 12, 1997	39.13
Repair Drawing 572-40208, Rev. B, dated August 12, 1997	39.13
SB 25-67-25A013A, Rev. 2 dated Oct. 18, 1991	39.13
SB Viscount Alert PTL 319 dated Mar. 14, 1990	39.13
SB 24-120, dated September 18, 1997	39.13
SB 24-279-3255A dated Nov. 16, 1990	39.13
SB 26-31 dated Feb. 25, 1991	39.13
SB 27-114-01028B dated Sept. 26, 1990	39.13
SB 27-155 dated Aug. 16, 1991	39.13
SB 28-86 dated June 28, 1991	39.13
SB 28-A-JA881143 dated Feb. 24, 1989	39.13
SB 29-JA 901242 dated June 18, 1991	39.13
SB 32-103, Rev. 1, dated February 22, 1991	39.13
SB 32-124-70491A & B, Rev. 1 dated Nov. 25, 1991	39.13
SB 32-124-70491A & B, Rev. 2 dated June 30, 1992	39.13
SB 32-144, dated December 11, 1996	39.13
SB 32-145, Rev. 1, dated October 6, 1997	39.13
SB 32-226-3257A dated May 3, 1991	39.13
SB 32-46 dated Apr. 9, 1991	39.13
SB 33-44-7670A, Rev. 1 dated April 4, 1991	39.13
SB 33-45-25A027A & B dated December 23, 1991	39.13
SB 33-45-25A027A & B dated December 23, 1991	39.13
SB 34-128-00950J dated March 22, 1991	39.13
SB 34-131-46041A dated June 24, 1991	39.13
SB 34-132-46042A dated June 24, 1991	39.13
SB 49-37-25A253A & B dated Oct. 28, 1991	39.13
SB 49-37-25A253A & B dated Oct. 28, 1991	39.13
SB 5-A-PM5987, Time Limits--Aircraft General--Corrosion Control Programme, Issue 2, dated June 30, 1992.	39.13
SB 52-89-006684, J, K, L, Rev. 2 dated June 3, 1991	39.13
SB 53-144, dated April 27, 1998	39.13
SB 53-73, Rev. 2 dated May 18, 1991	39.13
SB 53-74-3193C & D dated January 7, 1992	39.13
SB 55-15, dated April 14, 1997	39.13
SB 55-16, dated July 14, 1997	39.13
SB 57-49, dated June 4, 1996	39.13
SB 57-49, Rev. 1 dated June 19, 1997	39.13
SB 57-50, Rev. 2, dated March 20, 1997	39.13
SB 57-55, Rev. X, undated dated April 27, 1998, including	39.13
SB 57-73 dated July 30, 1991	39.13
SB 57-75 dated July 30, 1991	39.13
SB 57-76 dated Dec. 31, 1991	39.13
SB 57-76 dated Dec. 31, 1991	39.13

Title 14—Aeronautics and Space

Material Approved for Incorporation by Reference

	14 CFR
SB S.B. 32-216, Rev. 1 dated March 21, 1988	39.13
SB S.B. 57-47, dated June 15, 1995	39.13
SB S.B. 57-48, dated June 30, 1995	39.13
SB S.B. 57-73, Rev. 1, dated May 29, 1992	39.13
SB S.B. 57-73, Rev. 1, dated May 29, 1992	39.13
SB S.B.26-35, Rev. 1, dated August 30, 1995	39.13
SB S.B.26-44, dated February 25, 1999.	39.13
SB S.B.29-89-3269A dated May 22, 1992	39.13
SB SB 28-87 dated December 31, 1991	39.13
SB SB 57-33, dated August 31, 1989, including Appendix A	39.13
SB SB. 53-74-3193C & D, Rev. 1, dated March 12, 1992	39.13
SB SB. 53-74-3193C & D, Rev. 1, dated March 12, 1992	39.13
SB SB.24-288-3284A, dated February 7, 1992	39.13
SB SB.24-289-3267A, B,C,D,E,F & G, Rev. 1, dated April 10, 1992	39.13
SB SB.26-35-36179A, dated August 4, 1995	39.13
SB SB.26-36-36179B, dated June 22, 1995	39.13
SB SB.27-150-01510B, dated December 15, 1995	39.13
SB SB.27-70-00913A & B, Rev. 7, dated March 21, 1994	39.13
SB SB.27-77-00955A & C, Rev. 2, dated March 10, 1989	39.13
SB SB.29-31-01339A, dated May 24, 1993	39.13
SB SB.29-31-01339A, dated May 24, 1993	39.13
SB SB.29-31-01339A, Rev. 1, dated July 8, 1993	39.13
SB SB.32-130-70295C dated September 27, 1991	39.13
SB SB.32-143, dated August 22, 1995	39.13
SB SB.53-152, dated October 8, 1998	39.13
SB SB.53-74-3193C & D, dated January 7, 1992	39.13
SB SB.53-74-3193C & D, dated January 7, 1992	39.13
SB SB.53-74-3193C & D, Rev. 1, dated March 12, 1992	39.13
SB SB.55-014-01510A, dated December 15, 1995	39.13
SB SB.55-13-01490B, dated July 7, 1995	39.13
SB SB.78-4-9949A dated January 20, 1992	39.13
SB SB24-113-01532A, dated March 12, 1996	39.13
SB SB24-113-01532A, Rev. 1, dated June 18, 1996	39.13
SB.11-97-01285A, Rev. 1 dated April 3, 1992	39.13
Temporary Rev. (TR) 32, (Document BAe 3.3), Issue No. 2 dated July, 1996.	39.13
Temporary Rev. No. 12 (Document No. BAe 3.11) dated March 1992	39.13
Temporary Rev. No. 22 (Document No. BAe 3.3) dated April 1992	39.13
Temporary Rev. No. 23 (Document No. BAe 3.11) Issue No. 2, dated February 1994.	39.13
Temporary Rev. No. 28 (Document No. BAe 3.6) dated April 1992	39.13
Temporary Rev. No. 30 (Document No. BAe 3.3), Issue No. 2, dated February 1994.	39.13
Temporary Rev. No. 33 (Document No. BAe 3.6) dated April 1992	39.13
Temporary Rev. No. 41 (Document No. BAe 3.6), Issue No. 2, dated February 1994.	39.13
Temporary Rev. No. 42 (Document No. BAe 3.6), Issue No. 2, dated February 1994.	39.13
Temporary Rev. No. T/24, Issue 1 dated Feb. 17, 1992	39.13
Temporary Rev. No. T/24, Issue 1 dated Feb. 17, 1992	39.13

Title 14—Aeronautics and Space

Material Approved for Incorporation by Reference

Title 14—Aeronautics and Space

14 CFR (PARTS 1–59)—Continued
FEDERAL AVIATION ADMINISTRATION, DEPARTMENT OF TRANSPORTATION—
Continued

14 CFR

Cessna Aircraft Co
   Product Support P.O. Box 7706, Wichita, KS 67277
Accomplishment Instructions Attachment to Cessna SB MEB91-7R1,   39.13
   Rev. 1, dated July 2, 1993.
Accomplishment Instructions SEB90-1 Revision 3 dated March 15,   39.13
   1999.
Accomplishment Instructions SEB92-33R1, Rev. 1, dated June 25,   39.13
   1993.
Airplane Flight Manual Model 560 Citation V Serial -0001 thru -0259   39.13
   Revision 11 dated July 16, 1998.
Airplane Flight Manual Model 560 Citation V Unit -0260 and on   39.13
   Revision 7 dated July 16, 1998.
Alert Service Letter ASL560XL-33-02 dated May 4, 2001 ....   39.13
ASB 750-27-22, dated July 2, 1998 ....   39.13
Attachment to SB CQB91-1R1 dated June 21, 1991 ....   39.13
Attachment to SB for Cessna SB CQB91-8R1, Rev. 1, dated November   39.13
   6, 1992, August 31, 1993.
Citation Alert Service Letter A650-27-30, dated November 12, 1992   39.13
Citation Alert Service Letter ASL750-12-02, dated September 29, 1997   39.13
Citation SB 500-78-11, dated September 13, 1991 ....   39.13
Citation SB 750-27-10, dated January 16, 1998, including Supple-   39.13
   mental Data, dated January 16, 1998.
Citation SB SB650-24-57, dated May 15, 1997 ....   39.13
Citation Service SB550-78-03, dated September 13, 1991 ....   39.13
Citation Service SB560-78-02, dated September 13, 1991 ....   39.13
Citation Service SB650-78-05, Rev. 1, dated June 12, 1992 ....   39.13
Citation Service SBS550-78-04, dated September 13, 1991 ....   39.13
MEB85-3, Rev. 1, dated August 23, 1985, as referenced in Cessna   39.13
MEB85-3, Rev. 2, dated October 23, 1987 ....   39.13
MEB93-10R1 Accomplishment Instructions supplement to Cessna SB   39.13
   MEB93-10, Rev. 1, dated December 3, 1993.
SB 97-34-02, Rev. 1, dated December 22, 1997 ....   39.13
SB 97-53-02, dated September 15, 1997 ....   39.13
SB 98-27-02, dated May 11, 1998 ....   39.13
SB 98-27-03, dated June 1, 1998 ....   39.13
SB 98-27-05, dated June 1, 1998 ....   39.13
SB 98-27-05, Revision 1, dated August 17, 1998 ....   39.13
SB 98-27-06, dated June 15, 1998 ....   39.13
SB CAB96-15, Rev. 1, dated October 18, 1996 ....   39.13
SB CQB91-8 dated Oct. 18, 1991 ....   39.13
SB CQB96-3, dated October 18, 1996 ....   39.13
SB MEB91-7 dated Oct. 18, 1991 ....   39.13
SB MEB96-10, dated October 18, 1996 ....   39.13
SB MEB99-3, dated May 6, 1999 ....   39.13
SB SB97-28-01, dated June 6, 1997 ....   39.13
SB SB99-27-01, dated July 12, 1999. ....   39.13
SB SEB91-5, Rev. 1, dated June 14, 1991, which includes Attachment   39.13
   to SB SEB 91-5R1, Rev. 1, dated June 14, 1991.
SB SEB91-5, Rev. 1, dated June 14, 1991, which includes Attachment   39.13
   to SB SEB 91-5R1, Rev. 1, dated June 14, 1991.
SB SEB96-15, dated October 18, 1996 ....   39.13

Material Approved for Incorporation by Reference

14 CFR (PARTS 1–59)—Continued
FEDERAL AVIATION ADMINISTRATION, DEPARTMENT OF TRANSPORTATION—
Continued

	14 CFR
Service Bulletin MEB97-12 dated November 17, 1997	39.13
Service Bulletin No. CAB02-1 dated February 11, 2002	39.13
Service Bulletin SB 98-78-03 dated December 14, 1998	39.13
Service Bulletin SB0-79-01 dated January 31, 2000	39.13
Service Bulletin SB00-55-03 dated August 28, 2000	39.13
Service Bulletin SB525-24-20 dated November 16, 2000	39.13
Service Bulletin SB560-34-69 Revision 2 dated July 24, 1998	39.13
Service Bulletin SB560-34-70 dated July 14, 1998	39.13
Service Bulletin SB560XL-27-10 dated July 13, 2000	39.13
Service Bulletin SB650-32-47, including Cessna Service Bulletin Supplemental Data SB650-32-47 dated August 14, 2000.	39.13
Service Bulletin SB750-24-15, including Supplemental Data, Revision A Revision 1 dated May 24, 1999.	39.13
Service Bulletin SB750-53-19, including Supplemental Data dated January 20, 2000.	39.13
Service Bulletin SEB00-1 and Accomplishment Instructions dated January 17, 2000.	39.13
Service Bulletin SEB00-10 dated November 6, 2000	39.13
Service Bulletin SEB90-1 Revision 3 dated March 15, 1999	39.13
Service Bulletin SEB97-9 dated November 17, 1997	39.13
Service Bulletin Supplemental Data SB560XL-27-10 dated July 13, 2000.	39.13
Service Kit SK172-151 dated March 15, 1999	39.13
Service Kit SK414-19B, Revised dated March 4, 1986	39.13
Service Kit SK421-135A dated August 5, 1988	39.13
Service Kit SK421-142, dated July 2, 1993	39.13
Service Kit SK421-78A dated October 11, 1977	39.13
Service Kit SK425-44, dated November 6, 1992	39.13
Service Kit SK441-103A dated June 21, 1991	39.13
Special Service Project SSP99-27-02, dated May 18, 1999	39.13
Service Bulletin No. CQB02-1R1 Revision 1 dated April 22, 2002	39.13
SB CAB96-21, dated October 18, 1996	39.13
Service Bulletin CAB98-16 dated November 2, 1998	39.13

CFE Company
Data Distribution, MS 64-03/2101-201, P.O. Box 29003, Phoenix, AZ 85038-9003

Alert Service Bulletin CFE738-A72-8031 Rev. 1 dated June 23, 1999	39.13
Alert Service Bulletin CFE738-A72-8041 dated August 21, 2000	39.13
Alert Service Bulletin CFE738-A72-8042 Revision 1 dated September 25, 2000.	39.13
Service Bulletin CFE738-72-8043 Revision 1 dated October 2, 2000	39.13
Alert Service Bulletin CFE738-A72-8031 Revision 4 dated March 27, 2002.	39.13

CFM International
Neumann Way, Cincinnati, Ohio 45215

(CFM56-2) SB 72-620, Rev. 4, dated November 17, 1995	39.13
(CFM56-3/3B/3C) SB 72-530, Rev. 3, dated November 17, 1995	39.13
(CFM56-5) SB 72-A118, Rev. 1, dated August 1, 1997	39.13
56 SB 73-021 dated August 12/83	39.13
56 SB 73-024 dated October 14/83,	39.13
56 SB 73-034 dated August 17/84	39.13

Title 14—Aeronautics and Space

14 CFR (PARTS 1–59)—Continued
FEDERAL AVIATION ADMINISTRATION, DEPARTMENT OF TRANSPORTATION—
Continued

	14 CFR
56-2 73-109 Revision 1 dated January 7, 1998	39.13
56-2 73-110 Revision 2 dated April 29, 1999	39.13
56-2 SB 72-817, Rev. 1, dated November 25, 1997	39.13
56-2 SB 72-823, dated August 12, 1997	39.13
56-2 SB 72-825, dated January 23, 1998	39.13
56-2 SB No. 72-728, Rev. 2, dated December 21, 1994	39.13
56-2A 73-054 Revision 1 dated January 7, 1998	39.13
56-2A 73-055 Revision 1 dated April 29, 1999	39.13
56-2A 73-A058 dated August 17, 1999	39.13
56-2A SB 72-419, Rev. 2, dated November 14, 1997	39.13
56-2A SB No. 72-338, dated November 25, 1993	39.13
56-2B 73-074 Revision 1 dated January 12, 1998	39.13
56-2B 73-076 Revision 1 dated April 29, 1999	39.13
56-2B 73-A079 Revision 1 dated October 22, 1999	39.13
56-2B SB 72-561, Rev. 1, dated January 31, 1997	39.13
56-2B SB No. 72-476, dated December 7, 1993	39.13
56-3/-3B/-3C ASB No. 72-A861, Rev. 3, dated December 3, 1997	39.13
56-3/-3B/-3C SB 72-843, Rev. 1, dated November 25, 1997	39.13
56-3/-3B/-3C SB 72-855, Rev. 1, dated February 9, 1998	39.13
56-3/-3B/-3C SB 72-856, dated January 23, 1998	39.13
56-3/-3B/-3C SB 72-877, Rev. 1, dated June 15, 1998	39.13
56-3/-3B/-3C SB No. 72-863, Rev. 1, dated November 18, 1997	39.13
56-3/-3B/-3C SB No. 72-865, dated November 18, 1997	39.13
56-3/-3B/-3C SB No. 72-867, dated November 18, 1997	39.13
56-3/-3B/-3C SB No. 72-873, Rev. 1, dated February 5, 1998	39.13
56-3/3B/3C 73-125 Revision 1 dated January 7, 1998	39.13
56-3/3B/3C 73-126 Revision 1 dated April 29, 1999	39.13
56-3/3B/3C 73-A129 dated August 17, 1999	39.13
56-3/3B/3C SB No. 72-695, dated November 25, 1993	39.13
56-5 73-135 Revision 1 dated January 7, 1998	39.13
56-5 73-136 Revision 2 dated April 29, 1999	39.13
56-5 73-A143 dated June 18, 1999	39.13
56-5 SB No. 72-440, Rev. 2, dated June 23, 1995	39.13
56-5 SB No. 72-523, Rev. 1, dated January 30, 1998	39.13
56-5 SB No. 80-003, Rev. 5, dated October 25, 1994	39.13
56-5B 73-055 Revision 1 dated January 7, 1998	39.13
56-5B 73-056 Revision 2 dated April 29, 1999	39.13
56-5B 73-A062 dated June 18, 1999	39.13
56-5B SB 72-211, Rev. 1, dated January 29, 1998	39.13
56-5B SB No. 72-064, Rev. 2, dated June 23, 1995	39.13
56-5C 73-070 Revision 1 dated January 7, 1998	39.13
56-5C 73-073 Revision 2 dated April 29, 1999	39.13
56-5C 73-A078 dated June 21, 1999	39.13
56-5C SB 72-350, Rev. 1, dated January 30, 1998	39.13
56-5C SB No. 72-229, Rev. 2, dated June 23, 1995	39.13
56-7B ASB 73-A024, dated September 2, 1998	39.13
56-7B SB 72-130, dated June 29, 1998	39.13
56-7B SB 72-132, dated July 2, 1998	39.13
56-7B SB 73-016, Rev. 2, dated August 10, 1998	39.13
57 SB 73-024 Rev. 1, dated August 8/84	39.13

Material Approved for Incorporation by Reference

Title 14—Aeronautics and Space

Material Approved for Incorporation by Reference

	14 CFR
Service Bulletin SB-235-30-14 dated August 13, 1999	39.13
Service Bulletin SB-235-53-40 dated June 16, 1994	39.13
Service Bulletin SB-235-53-48 dated December 11, 1997	39.13
Supplemental Inspection Document (SID)C-212-PV-01-SID, dated June 1, 1987.	39.13

Continental Airlines, Inc.
600 Jefferson Street HQJAV Houston Texas 77002

Engineering Change/Repair Authorization 2330-02321 dated August 29, 2000.	39.13
Engineering Change/Repair Authorization 2330-02322 dated August 29, 2000.	39.13
Engineering Change/Repair Authorization 2330-02323 dated August 29, 2000.	39.13
Engineering Change/Repair Authorization 2330-02324 dated August 29, 2000.	39.13
Engineering Change/Repair Authorization 2330-02325 dated August 29, 2000.	39.13
Engineering Change/Repair Authorization 2330-02326 dated August 29, 2000.	39.13
Engineering Change/Repair Authorization 2330-02327 dated August 29, 2000.	39.13
Engineering Change/Repair Authorization 2330-02328 dated August 29, 2000.	39.13
Engineering Change/Repair Authorization 2330-02334 dated September 15, 2000.	39.13
Engineering Change/Repair Authorization 2330-02335 dated September 15, 2000.	39.13
Top Drawing 2330DA11072 Revision B dated September 15, 2000	39.13

Corporate Jets, Inc
22070 Broderick Drive, Sterling, VA 20166

Alert SB S.B. 71-A43, dated February 9, 1993	39.13
SB S.B. 26-33, dated December 8, 1992	39.13
SB S.B. 26-33, dated December 8, 1992	39.13
SB S.B. 35-36, dated January 7, 1993	39.13
SB S.B. 35-36, dated January 7, 1993	39.13
SB S.B. 57-77, dated May 20, 1993	39.13
SB S.B.71-43-3644A, dated February 8, 1993	39.13
SB SB.24-293-3501A,B,C,D,E,F, & G, Rev. 2, dated March 31, 1993	39.13
SB SB.24-293-3501A,B,C,D,E,F, & G, Rev. 2, dated March 31, 1993	39.13
SB SB.24-293-3510A,B,C,D, & E, Rev. 1, dated February 4, 1993	39.13
SB SB.24-293-3510A,B,C,D, & E, Rev. 1, dated February 4, 1993	39.13
SB SB.25-68-25A440A, dated August 19, 1992	39.13
SB SB.25-68-25A440A, dated August 19, 1992	39.13
SB SB.25-68-25A440A, dated August 19, 1993	39.13
SB SB.25-68-25A440A, dated August 19, 1993	39.13
SB SB.31-44-3645A, dated January 15, 1993	39.13

Dassault Aviation (Falcon Jet Corp.)
Customer Support Department. Teterboro Airport, Teterboro, NJ 07608

SB F50-122 (F50-53-2), dated June 25, 1986	39.13

14 CFR (PARTS 1–59)—Continued
FEDERAL AVIATION ADMINISTRATION, DEPARTMENT OF TRANSPORTATION—
Continued

Material Approved for Incorporation by Reference

14 CFR

Dassault Falcon Jet

  P.O. Box 2000 South Hackensack New Jersey 07606

Service Bulletin F900-232 Revision 1 dated November 12, 1999	39.13
Service Bulletin F900EX-93 Revision 1 dated November 12, 1999	39.13
Falcon 900 Service Bulletin No. 0232 dated March 1999	39.13
Falcon 900EX Service Bulletin No. 0093 dated March 1999	39.13
Service Bulletin F10-A291 dated June 1, 2001	39.13
Service Bulletin F50-328 dated May 31, 2000	39.13
Airplane Maintenance Manual Temporary Revision 27-504 dated October 1998.	39.13
Airplane Maintenance Manual Temporary Revision 27-514 dated February 1999.	39.13
Airplane Maintenance Manual Temporary Revision 27-514 dated February 1999.	39.13

de Havilland, Inc

  Garratt Boulevard, Downsview, Ontario M3K 1Y5, Canada

5-100 Temporary Revision (5-100) dated December 23, 1998	39.13
Alert SB A7-27-86, dated December 19, 1991	39.13
Alert SB 8-28-15, Rev. A dated April 17, 1992	39.13
Alert SB A7-32-100, dated July 7, 1993	39.13
Alert SB A7-32-97, dated November 10, 1992	39.13
Alert SB A8-24-44, dated October 23, 1992	39.13
Alert SB A8-28-16, dated May 30, 1991 and	39.13
Alert SB A8-28-16, Rev. C, dated January 31, 1992	39.13
Alert SB A8-33-30, Rev. A, dated December 18, 1992	39.13
Alert SB A8-33-30, Rev. A, dated December 18, 1992	39.13
Alert SB A8-33-33, dated May 31, 1993	39.13
Alert SB A8-53-46, Rev. A, dated May 25, 1993	39.13
Alert SB A8-55-18, dated February 5, 1993	39.13
Alert SB A8-73-14, Rev. B dated April 24, 1992	39.13
Alert SB ASB A8-35-5, Rev. A dated April 5, 1991	39.13
Alert SB. A8-32-117, dated December 11, 1992	39.13
Alert Service Bulletin S.B. A8-61-30 Revision B dated December 6, 1999.	39.13
ASB A8-28-16, Rev. B dated June 24, 1991	39.13
Beaver SB No. 2/52, dated August 30, 1998	39.13
Beaver Service Buletin No. TB/60, dated August 30, 1998	39.13
DHC-7 Maintenance Manual (PSM 1-7-2), chapter 5-60-00, Temporary Rev. (TR 5-84), dated June 15, 1994.	39.13
DHC-8 Alert SB A8-53-40, Rev. D, dated June 30, 1995	39.13
Notice of Status Change 7-53-31-1, dated April 20, 1990, for 7-53-31, dated December 15, 1989.	39.13
SB 7-29-20, dated March 20, 1992	39.13
SB 2/47, Rev. C dated Sept. 4, 1992	39.13
SB 6/298, Rev. D, dated December 20, 1991	39.13
SB 6/371, Rev. A, dated May 18, 1979	39.13
SB 7-24-69, dated October 8, 1993	39.13
SB 7-27-37 dated October 28, 1981	39.13
SB 7-27-46, Rev. A dated Nov. 19, 1982	39.13
SB 7-27-46, Rev. B dated Dec. 17, 1982	39.13
SB 7-53-15, Rev. A dated Nov. 27, 1981	39.13

Title 14—Aeronautics and Space

Material Approved for Incorporation by Reference

Material Approved for Incorporation by Reference

14 CFR (PARTS 1–59)—Continued

FEDERAL AVIATION ADMINISTRATION, DEPARTMENT OF TRANSPORTATION—
Continued

	14 CFR
Technical Note No. 873/12 (including Working Instructions No. 1 and No. 2) dated March 9, 1999.	39.13
Technical Note No. 873/13 dated June 30, 1999	39.13
Technical Note No. 873/25 dated August 30, 2001	39.13
Working Instructions No. 1 for TN 348/12 (843/12) dated September 28, 1999.	39.13

Diamond Aircraft Industries GmbH
  N.A. Otto-Strasse 5 A-2700 Wiener Neistadt Austria

Service Bulletin No. MSB36-72 dated February 1, 2002	39.13
Work Instruction No. WI-MSB36-72 dated February 1, 2002	39.13

Diamond Aircraft Industries, Inc
  690 Crumlin Sideroad, Ontario, Canada N5V 1S2; Telephone (519) 457-4000; FAX: (519) 457-4037

SB No. 51, dated March 30,1996	39.13
Work Instruction No. 21, dated March 20, 1996, as referenced in Diamond.	39.13
Alert SB No. DA20-53-01A, Rev. 0, dated June 5, 1997	39.13
Alert SB No. DA20-57-02, Rev. 0, dated March 7, 1996	39.13

Don Luscombe Aviation History Foundation
  P.O. Box 63581, Phoenix, AZ 85082, Telephone 606-693-4312

Recommendation No. 2, dated December 15, 1993, ...	39.13
Recommendation No. 2, Revised November 21, 1995	39.13
Service Recommendation No. 1, dated November 28, 1993	39.13

Dowty Propellers
  Anson Business Park, Cheltenham Road East, Gloucester GL2 9QN United Kingdom

SB 200-32-137 dated Nov. 6, 1990	39.13
SB F100-32-63, Rev. 2, dated September 23, 1993	39.13
SB F100-32-64, Rev. 1, dated February 18, 1994	39.13
SB SF340-61-57, dated February 15, 1991	39.13
SB SF340-61-58, Rev. 1, dated July 18, 1991, including Appendix A dated February 15, 1991; Appendix B, Rev. 1, dated July 18, 1991; and Appendix C, dated February 15, 1991.	39.13
SB SF340-61-61, Rev. 1, dated October 19, 1992	39.13
SB F100-32-505, Rev. 1, dated April 16, 1993	39.13
SB F100-32-506, dated June 9, 1993	39.13
SB 32-69SD, Rev. 2, dated January 20, 1993	39.13
SB 32-104E, dated January 20, 1993	39.13
SB F50-32-27, Rev. 4, dated December 18, 1992	39.13
SB 1150-27-04, dated December 5, 1996	39.13
S2000-61-75 Revision 4 dated September 28, 2000	39.13
SB No. S2000-61-75, Revision 1, dated June 11, 1999	39.13
Service Bulletin SB No. 61-1119 Revision 2 dated December 6, 2001	39.13
SB 32-77W, Rev. 4, dated February 3, 1993	39.13
SB 32-81W, Rev. 2, dated February 3, 1993	39.13
SB SF340-61-11 dated October 8, 1986	39.13
SF-340-61-A21, Rev. 4 dated October 1, 1987, including Appendices A through G.	39.13

Title 14—Aeronautics and Space

Material Approved for Incorporation by Reference

FEDERAL AVIATION ADMINISTRATION, DEPARTMENT OF TRANSPORTATION—
Continued

	14 CFR
ASB 145-27-A054, Change 01, dated February 17, 1999	39.13
ASB 145-32-A029, dated April 15, 1998	39.13
ASB 145-36-A011, dated March 19, 1999	39.13
ASB S.B. 145-31-A010, dated December 15, 1998	39.13
EMB-145 Airplane Flight Manual 145/1153, Revision 19, dated October 23, 1998.	39.13
SB 110-027-0089 dated July 19, 1991	39.13
SB 110-27-0091 dated Dec. 5, 1991	39.13
SB 120-076-0009, Change No. 4 dated Nov. 1, 1990	39.13
SB 120-24-0008, Change No. 04, dated October 3, 1995	39.13
SB 120-24-0051, Change No. 04, dated March 8, 1995	39.13
SB 120-27-0068, Change 02, dated March 20, 1998.	39.13
SB 120-30-0027, dated May 9, 1997	39.13
SB 120-57-0021, Change 1, dated September 10, 1993	39.13
SB 120-57-0021, Change 2, dated March 8, 1996	39.13
SB 120-57-0031, dated July 6, 1995	39.13
SB 145-27-0013, dated August 20, 1997	39.13
SB 145-27-0014, dated August 20, 1997	39.13
SB 145-27-0029, dated November 10, 1997	39.13
SB 145-28-0005, dated May 23, 1997	39.13
SB 145-28-0006, dated October 22, 1997	39.13
SB 145-30-0007, dated November 13, 1997	39.13
SB 145-30-0008, dated November 10, 1997	39.13
SB 145-32-0009, dated September 1, 1997	39.13
SB 145-32-0012, dated September 1, 1997	39.13
SB 145-34-0008, dated September 10, 1997	39.13
SB 145-34-0010, dated July 25, 1997, including Change No. 01, dated September 25, 1997.	39.13
SB 145-34-0026, Change No. 1, dated June 23, 1999	39.13
SB 145-36-0007, Change 03, dated December 9, 1998	39.13
SB 145-53-0004, dated July 28, 1997	39.13
SB No. 110-032-0068, dated December 20, 1985	39.13
SB No. 110-032-0071, Change No. 01, dated June 21, 1988	39.13
SB S.B. 120-54-0035, Change 02, dated May 29, 1998	39.13
Service Bulletin 120-27-0077 Revision 1 dated October 24, 1997	39.13
Service Bulletin 120-29-0047 Change 1 dated October 22, 1996	39.13
Service Bulletin 120-30-0027 Revision 2 dated December 3, 1997	39.13
Service Bulletin 120-30-0027 Revision 3 dated June 26, 1998	39.13
Service Bulletin 120-30-0027 Revision 4 dated July 13, 1999	39.13
Service Bulletin 120-30-0028 dated August 25, 1997	39.13
Service Bulletin 120-53-0064 dated October 31, 1995	39.13
Service Bulletin 145-26-0008 dated December 19, 2000	39.13
Service Bulletin 145-26-0009 dated January 26, 2001	39.13
Service Bulletin 145-29-0003 dated November 13, 1997	39.13
Service Bulletin 145-32-0036 dated February 1, 1999	39.13
Service Bulletin 145-32-0037 dated February 12, 1999	39.13
Service Bulletin 145-55-0024 dated May 25, 2000	39.13
Service Bulletin S.B. 120-27-0081 dated September 1, 2000	39.13
Service Bulletin S.B. 145-31-0010 dated March 18, 1999	39.13

Title 14—Aeronautics and Space

Material Approved for Incorporation by Reference

14 CFR

Alert Service Bulletin BO 105 ASB-BO 105-10-113 Revision 2 dated November 16, 1999.	39.13
Alert Service Bulletin EC 135-53A-004 dated August 14, 1998	39.13
Alert Service Bulletin EC 135-53A-005 Revision 3 dated September 2, 1998.	39.13
Alert Service Bulletin EC 135-62A-005 Revision 1 dated November 16, 1999.	39.13
Alert Service Bulletin MBB-BK 117-10-120 Revision 1 dated August 31, 1999.	39.13
Alert Service Bulletin MBB-BK 117-10-120 Revision 1 dated August 31, 1999.	39.13
ASB EC 135-53A-009, dated March 23, 1999	39.13
ASB EC 135-53A-010, Revision 2, dated July 22, 1999	39.13
ASB No. ASB-BO 105-10-113, dated August 11, 1999	39.13
MBB-BK117-30-106, Rev. 3, dated May 5, 1997, including Appendix	39.13
MBB-Helicopters Alert SB ASB-MBB-BK 117-20-104, Rev. 1, dated December 8, 1989.	39.13
Service Bulletin SB-MBB-BK 117-20-109 Revision 2 dated April 30, 1999.	39.13
SA 332 SB No. 01.00.47, Rev. No. 1, dated September 10, 1997	39.13
Alert Service Bulletin No. 52A004 Revision 1 dated April 19, 2001	39.13
AS 365 SB No. 01.00.40, Rev. 1, dated October 24, 1996	39.13
AS SB No. 01.20, Rev. 1, dated October 24, 1996	39.13
SA 330 SB No. 01.00.43, Rev. No. 1, dated February 14, 1996	39.13
SA 330 SB No. 01.52 R1, Rev. No. 1, dated February 14, 1996	39.13
SA 330 SB No. 01.53R1 Accomplishment Instructions, dated March 13, 1997.	39.13
SA 330 SB No. 54.20, Rev. 1, Accomplishment Instructions, dated February 27, 1996.	39.13
SA 330 SB No. 65.73 R3, dated June 22, 1995	39.13
SB 05.20, Rev. 3, dated November 14, 1996	39.13
SB 05.84, Revision 2, dated December 19, 1997	39.13
SB No. 01.00.44, dated March 26, 1996	39.13
SB No. 01.00.49 Accomplishment Instructions, dated June 30, 1997	39.13
SB No. 01.36, dated December 11, 1997	39.13
SB No. 05.00.34, Rev. 3, dated November 14, 1996	39.13
SB No. 05.00.36, Rev. 1, Accomplishment Instructions, dated December 16, 1996.	39.13
SB No. 1.00.45, dated December 11, 1997	39.13
SB No. 5.00.28, applicable to Model AS-350 helicopters	39.13
SB No. 5.00.29, applicable to Model AS-355 helicopters	39.13
SB No. 55.01, Rev. 3, dated April 25, 1997	39.13
SB No. 55.10, Rev. 2, dated April 25, 1997	39.13
SB No. 62.00.43, dated February 13, 1997	39.13
Service Bulletin 01.00.44 dated November 10, 1998	39.13
Service Bulletin 01.00.47 dated November 10, 1998	39.13
Service Bulletin 01.00.57 Revision 1 dated November 24, 1999	39.13
Service Bulletin 05.00.28 dated May 26, 1997	39.13
Service Bulletin 05.00.29 dated May 26, 1997	39.13
Service Bulletin 05.19 Revision 3 dated May 4, 1998	39.13
Service Bulletin 05.58 Revision 3 dated May 4, 1998	39.13

Material Approved for Incorporation by Reference

14 CFR (PARTS 1–59)—Continued
FEDERAL AVIATION ADMINISTRATION, DEPARTMENT OF TRANSPORTATION—
Continued

	14 CFR
SB 228-160 dated Dec. 18, 1989	39.13
SB 228-164, Rev. dated Aug. 28, 1990	39.13
SB 228-171 dated July 20, 1990	39.13
SB 228-214, dated January 28, 1994	39.13
SB 228-215, Rev. 1, dated January 31, 1995	39.13
SB 328-21-215, Rev. 1, dated June 12, 1997	39.13
SB 328-21-218, dated July 2, 1997, including Price/Material Information Sheet.	39.13
SB 328-21-227, dated July 16, 1997, including Price/Material Information Sheet, dated July 16, 1997.	39.13
SB 328-24-018, dated August 5, 1997	39.13
SB 328-24-021, dated November 25, 1997	39.13
SB 328-24-062, Rev. 1, dated June 27, 1995	39.13
SB 328-24-188, dated September 11, 1996	39.13
SB 328-25-196, dated November 12, 1996	39.13
SB 328-27-236, Rev. 1, dated November 5, 1997	39.13
SB 328-27-247, Rev. 1, dated February 19, 1998	39.13
SB 328-28-211, dated March 26, 1997	39.13
SB 328-29-205, dated February 12, 1997	39.13
SB 328-30-164, dated April 30, 1996	39.13
SB 328-31-172, dated June 18, 1996	39.13
SB 328-31-226, dated June 16, 1997, including Price/Material Information Sheet.	39.13
SB 328-32-183, dated October 9, 1996	39.13
SB 328-32-213, dated April 16, 1997	39.13
SB 328-32-248, Rev. 1, dated April 22, 1998	39.13
SB 328-53-144, Rev. 2, dated September 18, 1996	39.13
SB 328-57-020, dated October 28, 1997	39.13
SB 328-57-239, dated July 7, 1997	39.13
SB 328-57-255, dated January 21, 1998	39.13
SB 328-61-138, dated November 13, 1995	39.13
SB 328-76-152, dated May 6, 1996	39.13
SB 328-76-168, dated May 6, 1996	39.13
SB No. 1140-0000, dated September 29, 1995	39.13
SB No. SB-328-30-265, dated July 24, 1998	39.13
SB SB-328-24-061, Rev. 1, dated November 3,1994	39.13
SB SB-328-25-072, dated December 16, 1994	39.13
SB SB-328-25-114, dated July 10, 1995	39.13
SB SB-328-25-114, Rev. 1, dated April 17, 1997	39.13
SB SB-328-27-063, Rev. 1, dated January 26, 1995	39.13
SB SB-328-27-116, dated September 26, 1995	39.13
SB SB-328-27-228, Revision 1, dated December 18, 1997	39.13
SB SB-328-27-243, Revision 1, dated December 18, 1997	39.13
SB SB-328-27-263, dated June 29, 1998	39.13
SB SB-328-29-220, dated May 20, 1997	39.13
SB SB-328-29-220, Revision 1, dated May 4, 1998	39.13
SB SB-328-29-237, Revision 1, dated December 17, 1997	39.13
SB SB-328-30-020, dated March 17, 1994	39.13
SB SB-328-30-132, dated October 11, 1995	39.13
SB SB-328-32-048, dated August 11,1994	39.13

Material Approved for Incorporation by Reference

14 CFR (PARTS 1–59)—Continued
FEDERAL AVIATION ADMINISTRATION, DEPARTMENT OF TRANSPORTATION—
Continued

	14 CFR
SB SB-328-53-051, dated August 16, 1994	39.13
SB SB-328-53-184, Revision 1, dated July 2, 1997	39.13
SB SB-328-56-165, dated April 19,1996	39.13
SB SB-328-57-058, dated November 23, 1994	39.13
SB SB-328-71-086, dated March 6, 1995	39.13
SB SB-328-76-254, dated June 30, 1998	39.13
SB SB-328-76-254, dated June 30, 1998	39.13
SB SB-328-76-254, Revision 1, dated August 6, 1998	39.13
SB SB-328-76-254, Revision 1, dated August 6, 1998	39.13
SB SB-328-76-267, Revision 1, dated September 25, 1998	39.13
SB SB-328-76-267, Revision 1, dated September 25, 1998	39.13
SB SB-328-76-267, Revision 2, dated October 8, 1998	39.13
SB SB-328-76-267, Revision 2, dated October 8, 1998	39.13
Service Bulletin SB-328-27-289 dated March 3, 1999	39.13
Service Bulletin SB-328-27-293 dated November 10, 1999	39.13
Service Bulletin SB-328-27-310 dated June 10, 2000	39.13
Service Bulletin SB-328-27-359 dated March 29, 2001	39.13
Service Bulletin SB-328-55-351 dated April 10, 2001	39.13
Service Bulletin SB-328-76-268 Revision 1 dated December 9, 1998	39.13
Service Bulletin SB-328J-27-064 Revision 1 dated April 12, 2001	39.13
Service Bulletin SB-328J-29-040 dated June 8, 2000	39.13
Service Bulletin SB-328J-32-029 Revision 1 dated August 4, 2000	39.13
Service Bulletin SB-328J-55-058 Revision 1 dated April 10, 2001	39.13
Service Bulletin SB-328J-71-109 dated March 26, 2001	39.13
All Operators Telefax AOT-328J-00-006 dated October 1, 2002	39.13
Dornier 228 Service Bulletin SB-228-236 dated January 11, 2001	39.13
Service Bulletin No. SB-228-234 dated October 13, 2000	39.13
Service Bulletin SB-328-24-391 September 11, 2001	39.13
Service Bulletin SB-328-26-342 November 2, 2000	39.13
Service Bulletin SB-328J-24-120 September 12, 2001	39.13
Service Bulletin SB-328J-26-049 Revision 1 June 11, 2001	39.13

Fairchild Dornier Aircraft Corp.
P.O. Box 790490, San Antonio, TX 78279-0490

Airframe Airworthiness Limitations Manual ST-UN-M001, Revision No. C- 6, dated April 7, 1998.	39.13
Airframe Airworthiness Limitations Manual ST-UN-M003, Revision No. 5, dated April 7, 1998.	39.13
Airframe Inspection Manual ST-UN-M002, Revision No. A-6, dated December 8, 1997.	39.13
SA226 SB 226-53-007, Revision, dated February 17, 1992	39.13
SA226 SB 226-55-010 dated May 13, 1991	39.13
SA226 SB 226-55-010 Revised Dec. 13, 1991	39.13
SA226 SB 57-016, issued June 25, 1981 and revised December 9, 1981.	39.13
SA226 Series Service Letter 226-SL-005, Revised 34067	39.13
SA226 Series Service Letter 226-SL-005, and Fairchild SA227 Series Service Letter 227-SL-011, both Issued: Revised: April 28, 1993, February 12, 1991.	39.13
SA226 Series Service Letter 226-SL-014, dated October 3, 1997	39.13

Material Approved for Incorporation by Reference

14 CFR (PARTS 1–59)—Continued
FEDERAL AVIATION ADMINISTRATION, DEPARTMENT OF TRANSPORTATION—Continued

	14 CFR
SA 227 Series SL 227-SL-011 Revised August 3, 1999	39.13
SA 227 Series SL 227-SL-031 Revised February 1, 1999	39.13
SA 227 Series SL CC7-SL-021 Revised February 1, 1999	39.13
SA 227 Series SL CC7-SL-028 Issued August 12, 1999	39.13
SA226 Series Service Letter 226-SL-005, issued April 8, 1993 and revised March 2, 1995.	39.13
SA226 Series Service Letter 226-SL-005, Revised 35207	39.13
SA227 Series Service Letter 227-SL-011, issued April 8, 1993 and revised March 2, 1995.	39.13
SA227 Series Service Letter 227-SL-011, Revised 35207	39.13
SB 226-52-008	39.13
SB 226-55-005, dated August 15, 1985	39.13
SB 226-55-005, Revised, dated January 7, 1991	39.13
SB 227-55-002, dated August 15, 1985	39.13
SB 227-55-002, Revised 32429	39.13
SB No. 26-27-30-046, issued December 11, 1996	39.13
SB No. CC7-27-010, issued December 11, 1996	39.13
Service Bulletin 226-32-068 dated June 23, 2000	39.13
Service Bulletin 226-32-069, including Overhaul Instructions with Parts Breakdown dated October 24, 2001.	39.13
Service Bulletin 227-32-043 dated June 23, 2000	39.13
Service Bulletin 227-32-045, including Overhaul Instructions with Parts Breakdown dated October 24, 2001.	39.13
Service Bulletin No. 226-74-003 (FA Kit Drawing 27K82087) dated March 21, 2000.	39.13
Service Bulletin No. 227-74-001 dated July 8, 1986	39.13
Service Bulletin No. 227-74-003 (FA Kit Drawing 27K82087) dated March 21, 2000.	39.13
Service Bulletin No. 26-74-30-048 (FA Kit Drawing 26K82301) Revision 1 dated April 13, 2000.	39.13
SB 27-027 dated July 17, 1980	39.13

Falcon Jet Corp
P.O. Box 967, Little Rock, AR 72203-0967

	14 CFR
SB 900-54 (F900 31-30), dated October 14, 1994	39.13
SB 900-54, Rev. 1 (F900 31-1), dated November 17, 1994	39.13

Federal Aviation Administration
800 Independence Ave., SW., Washington, DC 20590

	14 CFR
TSO-C91 dated Oct. 21, 1971	25.1415; 29.1415
TSO-C77 dated May 20, 1963	25.1522; 29.1522

Ferranti (Jetstream Aircraft, Inc.)
P.O. Box 16029, Dulles International Airport, Washington, DC 20041-6029

	14 CFR
SB 24-20-171, dated September 1993	39.13
SB 24-20-172, dated September 1993	39.13

Flight Equipment and Engineering Ltd. (FEEL)
Technical Manager, Nissen House, Grovebury Road, Leighton Buzzard, Bedfordshire, LU7 8TB, United Kingdom

	14 CFR
SB 25-20-1287, Rev. 3, dated March 1993	39.13
SB 25-20-1294, Rev. 1, dated May 1993	39.13

Flight Structures, Inc.
4407 172nd Street NE, Arlington, Washington 98223

Title 14—Aeronautics and Space

Material Approved for Incorporation by Reference

14 CFR

SB F27/51-10, Rev. 2, dated June 12, 1993, as amended by Fokker SB Change Notification F27/51--10REV2/01, dated October 1, 1993.	39.13
SB F27/53-116, dated April 15, 1994	39.13
SB F27/54-47 dated Nov. 30, 1990	39.13
SB F27/55-66, dated December 21, 1994	39.13
SB F27/57-23, Rev. 6, dated August 13, 1991	39.13
SB F27/57-70, dated May 17, 1993	39.13
SB F27/57-74, dated November 15, 1994	39.13
SB F27/61-40, Revision 1, dated August 1, 1997	39.13
SB F28/27-180 dated July 3, 1992	39.13
SB F28/27-183, dated November 21, 1994	39.13
SB F28/32-123, Rev. 1, dated June 30, 1994	39.13
SB F28/32-149, dated August 30, 1991	39.13
SB F28/32-149, dated August 30, 1991	39.13
SB F28/32-151, Rev. 1, dated March 12, 1997	39.13
SB F28/32-153, dated November 10, 1994	39.13
SB F28/52-101, Rev. 1, dated August 24, 1992	39.13
SB F28/52-110, dated April 7, 1993	39.13
SB F28/52-112, dated February 1, 1995	39.13
SB F28/52/111, dated March 12, 1994	39.13
SB F28/53-101 dated May 31, 1991	39.13
SB F28/53-121, Rev. 1 dated Dec. 13, 1991	39.13
SB F28/53-143, dated August 30, 1996	39.13
SB F28/53-144, dated July 15, 1996	39.13
SB F28/55-029, Rev. 1, dated January 23, 1993	39.13
SB F28/55-30, Rev. 1, dated January 4, 1993	39.13
SB F28/76-20, dated January 1, 1979	39.13
SB Notification SBF50-25-069/01, dated February 15, 1995	39.13
SB SBF 100-27-032, dated September 20, 1991	39.13
SB SBF-57-017 dated Sept. 12, 1991	39.13
SB SBF100-027-041 dated Feb. 24, 1992	39.13
SB SBF100-20-001, dated January 15, 1994	39.13
SB SBF100-21-045, Rev. 1, dated November 17, 1993	39.13
SB SBF100-21-056, Rev. 1, dated November 24, 1993	39.13
SB SBF100-22-020, dated September 25, 1990	39.13
SB SBF100-22-029, dated January 6, 1992	39.13
SB SBF100-22-031 dated Sept. 9, 1991	39.13
SB SBF100-22-032, dated September 2, 1991	39.13
SB SBF100-22-037, dated May 31, 1993	39.13
SB SBF100-22-037, dated May 31, 1993	39.13
SB SBF100-24-029, dated June 28, 1993, including Nordskog Engineering Change Order 43589 Attachment.	39.13
SB SBF100-24-032, dated September 12, 1996	39.13
SB SBF100-24-032, Rev. 1, dated April 25, 1997	39.13
SB SBF100-25-061, dated March 8, 1994 and Fokker SB SBF100-25-068, dated March 31, 1994.	39.13
SB SBF100-25-064, dated February 23, 1993	39.13
SB SBF100-25-082, Revision 1, dated May 7, 1998	39.13
SB SBF100-25-083, dated April 30, 1998	39.13
SB SBF100-26-004 dated Aug. 23, 1991	39.13

Title 14—Aeronautics and Space

Material Approved for Incorporation by Reference

	14 CFR
SB SBF100-53-039, dated February 10, 1993	39.13
SB SBF100-53-052, Rev. 1, dated June 7, 1993	39.13
SB SBF100-53-067 dated July 1, 1991	39.13
SB SBF100-53-067 dated July 1, 1991	39.13
SB SBF100-53-072, dated March 12, 1993	39.13
SB SBF100-55-011 dated Oct. 1, 1991	39.13
SB SBF100-55-021, Rev. 2, dated December 27, 1993	39.13
SB SBF100-57-008, Rev. 2, dated September 22, 1995	39.13
SB SBF100-57-018, dated September 23, 1993	39.13
SB SBF100-57-029, Rev. 1, dated March 23, 1995	39.13
SB SBF100-57-030, dated December 17, 1994	39.13
SB SBF100-57-032, dated August 21, 1995	39.13
SB SBF100-57-034, dated December 20, 1996	39.13
SB SBF100-71-012, dated February 7, 1992	39.13
SB SBF100-71-016, dated February 18, 1994	39.13
SB SBF100-71-019, dated March 21, 1996,	39.13
SB SBF100-76-008 dated May 8, 1991	39.13
SB SBF100-76-010, dated October 31, 1993	39.13
SB SBF100-78-014, Revision 2, including List of Effective Pages, dated May 1, 1999, and and Attachment 1 (undated);.	39.13
SB SBF50-20-003, dated January 11, 1994	39.13
SB SBF50-25-046, Rev. 1, dated August 5, 1994	39.13
SB SBF50-25-069, dated July 13, 1994, as	39.13
SB SBF50-27-036, dated December 28, 1993	39.13
SB SBF50-27-040, dated May 10, 1996	39.13
SB SBF50-32-029, dated February 11, 1994	39.13
SB SBF50-32-033, dated December 20, 1996	39.13
SB SBF50-53-015, dated August 16, 1989	39.13
SB SBF50-53-016, dated December 20, 1989	39.13
SB SBF50-53-048, dated October 17, 1994	39.13
SB SBF50-53-053, dated February 1, 1997	39.13
SB SBF50-57-015, dated February 28, 1996	39.13
SB SBF50-57-018, dated February 28, 1996	39.13
SB SBF50-71-041, dated November 10, 1993	39.13
SB SFB100-36-027, including Appendix I, dated March 21, 1997	39.13
SB SFB100-53-087, dated November 17, 1997	39.13
SB100-24-032, Rev. 2, dated July 28, 1997	39.13
SBF100-33-015, Rev. 1, dated March 21, 1994	39.13
SBF100-52-039 dated Sept. 17, 1991	39.13
Service Bulletin F27/30-45 dated August 11, 1999	39.13
Service Bulletin F28/27-186, including Manual Change Notification MCNM F28-020 dated May 8, 2000.	39.13
Service Bulletin SBF100-23-032 dated September 22, 1999	39.13
Service Bulletin SBF100-25-088 dated October 14, 1999	39.13
Service Bulletin SBF100-26-015 dated August 15, 1999	39.13
Service Bulletin SBF100-27-076 dated July 1, 1999	39.13
Service Bulletin SBF100-32-117 dated September 27, 1999	39.13
Service Bulletin SBF100-32-118 dated October 8, 1999	39.13
Service Bulletin SBF27/25-65 Revision 1 dated March 1, 2000	39.13
Service Bulletin SBF27/30-44 dated February 20, 1998	39.13

Title 14—Aeronautics and Space

Material Approved for Incorporation by Reference

14 CFR (PARTS 1–59)—Continued
FEDERAL AVIATION ADMINISTRATION, DEPARTMENT OF TRANSPORTATION—
Continued

	14 CFR
SB 1121-27-023, dated August 14, 1996	39.13
SB 1121-27-023, Rev. 1, dated May 28, 1997	39.13
SB 1121-27-025, dated December 22, 1997	39.13
SB 1121-29-022, dated September 11, 1996	39.13
(Israel Aircraft Industries) Alert Service Bulletin 1124-27A-145 dated March 24, 2000.	39.13
Alert Service Bulletin 1123-27A-053 dated August 28, 2000	39.13
Alert Service Bulletin 1124-27A-147 dated August 28, 2000	39.13
SB 1123-27-046, dated August 14, 1996	39.13
SB 1123-27-046, Rev. 1, dated May 28, 1997	39.13
SB 1123-27-047, dated September 1, 1997	39.13
SB 1123-29-045, dated September 11, 1996	39.13
SB 1124-27-133, dated August 14, 1996	39.13
SB 1124-27-133, Rev. 1, dated May 28, 1997	39.13
SB 1124-27-136, dated September 1, 1997	39.13
SB 1124-29-132, dated September 11, 1996	39.13

Garmin International
1200 East 151st Street Olathe Kansas 66062

Service Bulletin No. 9905 Revision A dated September 17, 1999	39.13

Garrett Engine Division, AlliedSignal Inc. (See Honeywell International, Inc.)
ATTN: Data Distribution, M/S 64-3/2101-201 P.O. Box 29003, Phoenix, AZ 85038-9003

SB GTCP36-49-6549, dated February 28, 1992	39.13
SB GTCP36-49-A5973, dated May 17, 1990	39.13
SB GTCP36-49-A5973, Rev. 1, dated May 22, 1990	39.13
SB GTCP85-49-5700, dated July 20,1987	39.13
SB GTCP85-49-5700, Rev. 1, dated October 6, 1988	39.13
SB GTCP85-49-5700, Rev. 2, dated August 31, 1989	39.13
SB GTCP85-49-6706, dated December 7, 1992	39.13
SB No. TPE331-A73-0198, Rev. 1, dated Jan. 10, 1992	39.13

Garrett General Aviation Services Division
ATTN: Dept. 64-03/2101-201 P.O. Box 29003, Phoenix, Arizona 85038-9003

Alert SB TFE731-A72-3474 dated April 3, 1992	39.13
SB GTC36-49-A6642 dated May 1, 1992	39.13
SB GTC36-49-A6653 dated May 1, 1992	39.13
SB TFE731-A72-3376 dated August 19, 1988	39.13
SB TFE731-A77-3020 dated April 27, 1990	39.13
SB TPE 331-A72-0571 dated March 31, 1988	39.13
SB TSCP700-49-5892, Rev. 2 dated Oct. 10, 1990	39.13

Garrett Turbine Engine Company (See Honeywell International, Inc.)
ATTN: Data Distribution, M/S 64-3/2101-201 P.O. Box 29003, Phoenix, Arizona 85038-9003

36-49-6549, dated February 28, 1992	39.13
36-49-A5973, dated May 17, 1990	39.13
36-49-A5973, Rev. 1, dated May 22, 1990	39.13
Alert SB ATF3-A72-6113, dated February 25, 1985, ATF3-72-6114, dated February 25, 1985 and Light Maintenance Manual ATF3-6.	39.13
Alert SB ATF3-A72-6113, Rev. No. 72-133, dated February 25, 1986	39.13

Title 14—Aeronautics and Space

14 CFR (PARTS 1–59)—Continued
FEDERAL AVIATION ADMINISTRATION, DEPARTMENT OF TRANSPORTATION—Continued

	14 CFR
Alert SB ATF3-A72-6113, Rev. No. 72-135, dated February 25, 1987	39.13
Alert SB ATF3-A72-6113, Rev. No. 72-132, dated February 25, 1985	39.13
Alert SB ATF3-A72-6113, Rev. No. 72-136, dated February 25, 1988	39.13
Alert SB No. TPE/TSE331-A72-0384, Rev. 3 dated July 1, 1987	39.13
Alert SB TPE331-A72-0522, Rev. 2 dated July 1, 1987	39.13
Alert SB TPE331-A72-0559 dated July 1, 1987	39.13
Alert SB TPE331-A72-0560 dated July 1, 1987	39.13
Engine TPE/TSE 331-72-0384, ...	39.13
Engine TPE 331-72-0300, ...	39.13
Engine TPE 331-72-0351	39.13
Engine TPE 331-72-0327, ...	39.13
Engine SB TPE/TSE 331-72-0380, ...	39.13
Light Maintenance Manual Report No. 72-00-52 Rev. 6, dated November 15, 1983.	39.13
Light Maintenance Manual Report No. 72-02-32 Rev. 3, dated November 15, 1984.	39.13
Light Maintenance Manual report No. 72-03-42 Rev. 4, dated November 15, 1983.	39.13
SB TFE 731-72-3239	39.13
SB ATF3-72-6089, 30788	39.13
SB ATF3-72-6090, 30788	39.13
SB ATF3-72-6092, dated May 25, 1984;	39.13
SB ATF3-72-6092, 30827	39.13
SB TPE 331-73-0121 Rev. 2, dated 4/18/84	39.13
SB TPE 331-73-0121, Rev. 1, 30836	39.13
SB TPE331-72-0533, Rev. 2 dated March 11, 1988	39.13
SB TPE331-73-0121, Rev. 3 dated November 5, 1984	39.13
Temporary Rev. No. 72-43, 72-00-00 Trouble Shooting, dated April 16, 1984,.	39.13
Temporary Rev. No. 72-44, 72-00-00 Trouble Shooting, dated April 16, 1984;.	39.13
Temporary Rev. No. 72-44, 72-00-00 Trouble Shooting, dated April 16, 1984.	39.13
Temporary Rev. No. 72-45, 72-00-00 Trouble Shooting, dated April 16, 1984.	39.13
Temporary Rev. No. 72-88, 72-00-00, Trouble Shooting dated April 16, 1984,.	39.13
Temporary Rev. No. 72-89, 72-00-00, Trouble shooting dated April 16, 1984;.	39.13
No. 72-00-52, Rev. 6, dated November 15, 1983; Temporary Rev. No. 72-90, 72-00-00, Inspection, dated May 25, 1984; Temporary Rev. No. 72-8, 72-00-00, Trouble Shooting, dated April 16, 1984; and Temporary Rev. No. 72-89, 72-00-00, Trouble Shooting, dated April 16, 1984.	39.13
No. 72-03-32, Rev. 3, dated November 15, 1983; Temporary Rev. No. 72-45, 72-00-00, Inspection, dated May 25, 1984; Temporary Rev. No. 72-43, 72-00-00, Trouble Shooting, dated April 16, 1984; and Temporary Rev. No. 72-44, 72-00-00, Trouble Shooting, dated April 16, 1984.	39.13

Material Approved for Incorporation by Reference

14 CFR

No. 72-03-42, Rev. 4, dated November 15, 1983; Temporary Rev.   39.13
   No. 72-46, 72-00-00, Inspection, dated May 25, 1984; Temporary
   Rev. No. 72-44, 72-00-00, Trouble Shooting, dated April 16, 1984;
   and Temporary Rev. No. 72-45, 72-00-00, Trouble Shooting, dated
   April 16, 1984.

GE (General Electric) Company
  Neumann Way, Cincinnati, Ohio 45215

(CT7-TP Series) SB 72-390, Rev. 1, dated December 11, 1996	39.13
(CT7-TP Series) SB A72-393, dated November 26, 1996	39.13
(CT7-TP Series) SB No. A72-350, Rev. 3, dated June 9, 1994	39.13
6F6-80A SB 72-583, Rev. 3 dated July 24, 1991	39.13
72- 550,	39.13
72- 551	39.13
90 ASB 72-A318, dated June 27, 1997	39.13
All Operators Wire--Subject: FPI of Deep Disk Spools, Best Practices, dated August 10, 1995.	39.13
ASB 72-A357, Revision 2, dated April 21, 1998	39.13
ASB 73-A283, dated September 18, 1998	39.13
ASB 73-A283, Revision 1, dated October 30, 1998;	39.13
ASB 73-A283, Revision 2, dated November 18, 1998	39.13
CF6-50 ASB 72-a988, Revision 6, dated August 25, 1998	39.13
CF6-50 Engine Task Numbered Shop Manual Temporary Rev. 05-0011, dated November 3, 1995.	39.13
CF6-50 SB 72-1000, Rev. 1 dated Mar. 28, 1991	39.13
CF6-50 SB No. 72-1000, Rev. 2, dated September 9, 1993 and GE CF6-80A SB No. 72-583, Rev. 4, dated September 15, 1993.	39.13
CF6-50 SB No. 72-1006, Rev. 1, dated November 14, 1991	39.13
CF6-50 SB No. 72-1057, Rev. 1, dated June 17, 1993	39.13
CF6-50 SB No. 72-1059, dated February 12, 1993	39.13
CF6-50 SB No. 72-1069, dated September 12, 1994	39.13
CF6-50 SB No. 72-1108, dated November 6, 1995	39.13
CF6-50 SB No. 72-573, Rev. 5, 29844	39.13
CF6-50 Series Alert SB No. 72-A1139, dated October 17, 1997	39.13
CF6-50/45 SB 72-879 dated Oct. 30, 1990	39.13
CF6-6 ASB 72-A996, Revivion 4, dated June 9, 1998	39.13
CF6-6 SB 72-947, Rev. 4 dated Feb. 8, 1991	39.13
CF6-6 SB No. 72-1002, dated February 12, 1993	39.13
CF6-6 SB No. 72-1003, Rev. 1, dated June 17, 1993	39.13
CF6-80A ASB 72-A565, Revision 5, dated June 9, 1998	39.13
CF6-80A SB 72-459, Rev. 2 dated June 14, 1989	39.13
CF6-80A SB 72-605 dated Dec. 20, 1991	39.13
CF6-80A SB No. 72-604, Rev. 3, dated April 8, 1993	39.13
CF6-80A SB No. 72-678, dated November 6, 1995	39.13
CF6-80A Series Alert SB ASB A72-510, Rev. 2 dated Novmber 14, 1988.	39.13
CF6-80A Series Alert SB ASB A72-512, Rev. 1 dated May 24, 1988	39.13
CF6-80A Series SB 71-053, Rev. 2 dated June 26, 1990	39.13
CF6-80A, SB 72-531, Rev. 2 dated May 18, 1990	39.13
CF6-80C2 Alert SB A73-038, Rev. 1 dated January 25, 1989	39.13
CF6-80C2 Alert SB No. 72-A906, dated October 17, 1997	39.13
CF6-80C2 ASB 72-A478, Revision 4, dated June 9, 1998	39.13

Title 14—Aeronautics and Space

Material Approved for Incorporation by Reference

	14 CFR
SB CF700 dated August 30, 1983	39.13
SB CJ610 dated August 30, 1983	39.13
SB No. CF34 73-5 dated January 22, 1988	39.13
SB No. CF34 73-6 dated January 22, 1988	39.13
Service Document CF6-6, CESM 98, Rev. 2 dated Oct. 5, 1989	39.13
Service Document CF6-6, SB 72-962, Rev. 3 dated May 22, 1991	39.13
ASB A73-13, Revision 1, May 29, 1998	39.13
ASB A73-18, Revision 1, dated September 24, 1997	39.13
ASB A73-19, Revision 1, dated February 20, 1998	39.13
ASB A73-32, Revision 1, dated September 24, 1997	39.13
ASB A73-32, Revision 2, dated May 29, 1998	39.13
ASB A73-33, dated November 21, 1997	39.13
CF6-6 SB 72-971 dated Oct. 2, 1990	39.13
CF6-6 SB 72-971, Rev. 2 dated Aug. 27, 1991	39.13
CF6-6 SB 72-977 dated March 15, 1991	39.13
CF700 SB 72-154, dated December 20, 1996	39.13
SB 72-011, dated April 9, 1997	39.13
SB 72-126, Rev. 1, dated April 29, 1997	39.13
SB CF6-50 SB No. 72-1092, dated November 18, 1994	39.13
Service Bulletin 72-183, dated February 28, 1997	39.13
Service Bulletin 72-263, dated February 5, 1997	39.13
Service Bulletin 72-275, dated March 4, 1997	39.13
Service Bulletin 72-280, Rev. 3, dated April 15, 1997	39.13
Service Bulletin 72-283, Rev. 4, dated April 17, 1997	39.13
Service Bulletin 72-286, dated April 14, 1997	39.13
ASB CF34AL 73-A0025, dated July 7, 1999;	39.13
ASB CF34BJ 73-A0040, dated July 7, 1999;	39.13
SB CF34AL S/B 73-0026, dated August 12, 1999;	39.13
SB CF34BJ S/B 73-0041, dated August 12, 1999.	39.13
SB HGE 24-23, dated March 11, 1994	39.13
Alert Service Bulletin 73-A0060 dated December 23, 1999	39.13
Alert Service Bulletin 73-A0231 Revision 1 dated May 3, 1999	39.13
Alert Service Bulletin 73-A224 Revision 2 dated July 9, 1997	39.13
Alert Service Bulletin CF6-50 72-A1196 dated September 15, 2000	39.13
Alert Service Bulletin CF6-50 72-A1197 dated December 14, 2000	39.13
Alert Service Bulletin CF6-50 72-A1201 dated December 22, 2000	39.13
Alert Service Bulletin CF6-50 72-A1201 Revision 1 dated February 6, 2001.	39.13
Alert Service Bulletin CF6-80C2 72-A0848 Revision 5 dated August 3, 2000.	39.13
Alert Service Bulletin CF6-80C2 72-A0964 dated April 16, 1999	39.13
Alert Service Bulletin CF6-80C2 72-A0964 Revision 1 dated November 12, 1999.	39.13
Alert Service Bulletin CF6-80C2 72-A0964 Revision 2 dated January 24, 2000.	39.13
Alert Service Bulletin CF6-80C2 72-A0989 dated January 19, 2000	39.13
Alert Service Bulletin CF6-80E1 72-A0126 Revision 3 dated August 3, 2000.	39.13
Service Bulletin A73-19 Revision 2 dated March 9, 1999	39.13
Service Bulletin A73-33 Revision 2 dated March 9, 1999	39.13

Material Approved for Incorporation by Reference

14 CFR

SB 640 (340D) SB No. A55-7, dated March 22, 1993	39.13
SB 640 (340D)55-5, dated September 21, 1990, ...	39.13
SB 640(340D) SB No. 55-6, dated September 1, 1992	39.13
SB 640(340D)55-5, dated September 21, 1990	39.13
SID Model 340/440, Rep. No. ZS-340-1000, Rev. 1 dated April 15, 1991,.	39.13
SID Model 340/440, Rep. No. ZS-340-1000, Rev. 1 Addenda and II dated April 15, 1991.	39.13
SID Model 340/440, Rep. No. ZS-340-1000, Rev. 1 Addenda I, dated April 15, 1991.	39.13
SID Model 340/440, Rep. No. ZS-340-1000, Rev. 1 Addenda II, dated April 15, 1991,.	39.13

General Electric Company via Lockheed Martin Technology Services
10525 Chester Road, ATTN: Leader for Distribution/Microfilm Suite C Cincinnati Ohio 45215 (513) 672-8400 FAX: (513) 672-8422

Alert Service Bulletin CF6-50 72-A0958 Revision 3 dated May 25, 2001.	39.13
Alert Service Bulletin CF6-50 72-A1200 Revision 1 dated July 20, 2000.	39.13
Alert Service Bulletin CF6-50 72-A1200 Revision 2 dated November 2, 2000.	39.13
Alert Service Bulletin CF6-50 72-A1200 Revision 3 dated May 30, 2001.	39.13
Alert Service Bulletin CF6-80C2 72-A1026 dated January 17, 2001	39.13
Alert Service Bulletin No. GE90 73-A0060 Revision 3 dated September 14, 2000.	39.13
Alert Service Bulletin No. GE90 S/B 75-0031 Revision 3 dated March 30, 2001.	39.13
Martin Marietta CF6-80C2 SB No. 78-1002, Rev. 1, dated March 23, 1995.	39.13
Service Bulletin CF6-50 72-1200 dated May 8, 2000	39.13
Alert Service Bulletin CF6-50 S/B 72-A1108 Revision 5 dated October 2, 2002.	39.13
Alert Service Bulletin CF6-50 S/B 72-A1131 Revision 4 dated October 2, 2002.	39.13
Alert Service Bulletin CF6-50 S/B 72-A1157 Revision 4 dated October 2, 2002.	39.13
Alert Service Bulletin CF6-80A S/B 72-A0678 Revision 5 dated October 2, 2002.	39.13
Alert Service Bulletin CF6-80A S/B 72-A0691 Revision 5 dated October 2, 2002.	39.13
Alert Service Bulletin CF6-80A S/B 72-A0719 Revision 5 dated October 2, 2002.	39.13
Alert Service Bulletin CF6-80C2 S/B 72-A0812 Revision 4 dated October 2, 2002.	39.13
Alert Service Bulletin CF6-80C2 S/B 72-A0848 Revision 8 dated October 2, 2002.	39.13
Alert Service Bulletin CF6-80C2 S/B 72-A0934 Revision 4 dated October 2, 2002.	39.13
Alert Service Bulletin CF6-80E1 S/B 72-A0126 Revision 5 dated October 2, 2002.	39.13

Title 14—Aeronautics and Space

Material Approved for Incorporation by Reference

14 CFR

Glasflugel
c/o Hansjorg Streifeneder, Glasfaser-Flugzeug Service, Hofener Weg, D. 72582 Grabenstetten, Germany

Sailplane Flight and Service Manual Amendments: Club Libelle 205, dated October 1974;. — 39.13

Sailplane Flight and Service Manual Amendments: H301 Libelle dated May 1965;. — 39.13

Sailplane Flight and Service Manual Amendments: H301B Libelle, dated May 1965;. — 39.13

Sailplane Flight and Service Manual Amendments: Kestrel, dated April 1971. — 39.13

Sailplane Flight and Service Manual Amendments: Standard Libelle 201B, dated July 1972;. — 39.13

Sailplane Flight and Service Manual Amendments: Standard Libelle, dated October 1968;. — 39.13

Technical Note 303-18, dated March 1, 1991 .... 39.13

GQ Parachutes Ltd
Portugal Road, Woking, Surrey, GU21 5JE, England

SB No. 25-01 dated January 1989 .... 39.13

GROB Luft-und Raumfahrt
Lettenbachstrasse 9 D86874 Tussenhausen-Mattsies Federal Republic of Germany Telephone: 49 8268 998139

Service Bulletin No. MSB306-36/2 dated November 22, 2001 .... 39.13

GROB Systems, Inc
Aircraft Division, I-75 and Airport Drive, Bluffton, Ohio 45817

TM 817-36, dated September 14, 1992 .... 39.13

Installation Instructions 1078-64, dated December 11, 1996 .... 39.13

Installation Instructions No. 1078-75, dated May 15, 1998 .... 39.13

Repair Instruction No. 306-27/1 to SB TM 306-1, dated June 4, 1991 — 39.13

Repair Instruction No. 315-33/1 for SB TM 315-33 dated August 3, 1987. — 39.13

Repair Instruction No. 315-33/2 for SB TM 315-33 dated August 3, 1987. — 39.13

Repair Instruction No. 817-25 for SB TM 817-25, dated November 9, 1987. — 39.13

SB 1078-59/3, dated October 24, 1996 .... 39.13

SB 1078-64, dated December 11, 1996 .... 39.13

SB 1078-64/2, dated April 8, 1997 .... 39.13

SB 1078-66, dated February 10, 1997 .... 39.13

SB 1078-75, dated May 15, 1998 .... 39.13

SB TM 306-31, dated September 14, 1992 .... 39.13

SB TM 817-35, dated July 20, 1992 .... 39.13

SB TM 817-39, dated January 4, 1994 .... 39.13

SB TM 817-45, dated July 27, 1995 .... 39.13

SB TM-315-32 dated June 12, 1987, including Repair Instructions No. 315-32. — 39.13

TM 315-49, dated September 14, 1992 .... 39.13

TM 320-6, dated September 14, 1992 .... 39.13

Gulfstream Aerospace Corporation
P.O. Box 2206, Mail Station D-25 Savannah, GA 31402-9980

Service Kit No. 12 as referenced by American General SB ME-1A dated Feb. 21, 1991. — 39.13

Title 14—Aeronautics and Space

Material Approved for Incorporation by Reference

FEDERAL AVIATION ADMINISTRATION, DEPARTMENT OF TRANSPORTATION—Continued

	14 CFR
ASB 14SF-61-A21, Rev. 2 dated March 27, 1987	39.13
SB JFC118-10-73-14, Rev. 1 dated Oct. 26, 1990	39.13
SB JFC118-11-73-15, Rev. 1 dated Oct. 26, 1990	39.13
SB JFC118-12-73-16, Rev. 1 dated Oct. 26, 1990	39.13
SB JFC118-30-73-15, Rev. 1 dated Oct. 26, 1990	39.13
SB JFC118-31-73-14, Rev. 1 dated Oct. 26, 1990	39.13
Alert Service Bulletin No. 568F-61-A35 Revision 2 dated March 21, 2002.	39.13
Service Bulletin 247F-61-37 Revision 2 dated September 7, 2001	39.13
Alert SB ASB No. 14RF-9-61-A90, dated November 9, 1995	39.13
Alert SB ASB No. 14RF-9-61-A94, Rev. 1, dated March 6, 1996	39.13
14RF-19-61-A34, dated April 18, 1994	39.13
14RF-21-61-A53, dated April 18, 1994	39.13
14RF-9-61-A66, dated April 18, 1994	39.13
14SF-61-A73, dated April 18, 1994	39.13
6/5500/F-61-A27, dated April 18, 1994	39.13
Air SB 14RF-21-61-A39, dated October 27, 1993	39.13
Air SB 14RF-9-61-A57, dated October 27, 1993	39.13
Alert SB 14RF-19-61-A25, Rev. 2, dated July 28, 1993	39.13
Alert SB 14RF-21-61-A38, Rev. 2, dated July 28, 1993	39.13
Alert SB 14RF-9-61-A53 dated March 12, 1992	39.13
Alert SB 14RF-9-61-A53, Rev. 3, dated July 28, 1993	39.13
Alert SB 14SF-61-A59, Rev. 2, dated July 28, 1993	39.13
Alert SB 247F-61-A3, Rev. 1, dated July 28, 1993	39.13
Alert SB 54H60-61-A133, Rev. 1, dated May 29, 1997	39.13
Alert SB 54H60-61-A134, Revision 1, dated June 24, 1998	39.13
Alert SB 54H60-61-A135, dated June 24, 1998	39.13
Alert SB 6/5500/F-61-A11, Rev. 2, dated July 28, 1993	39.13
Alert SB No. 14RF-19-61-A25, Rev. 4, dated April 7, 1994	39.13
Alert SB No. 14RF-19-61-A36, Rev. 1, dated October 5, 1994	39.13
Alert SB No. 14RF-21-61-A38, Rev. 4, dated April 7, 1994	39.13
Alert SB No. 14RF-21-61-A55, Rev. 1, dated October 5, 1994	39.13
Alert SB No. 14RF-9-61-A53, Rev. 5, dated April 7, 1994	39.13
Alert SB No. 14RF-9-61-A69, Rev. 1, dated October 5, 1994	39.13
Alert SB No. 14SF-61-A59, Rev. 4, dated April 7, 1994	39.13
Alert SB No. 14SF-61-A74, Rev. 1, dated October 5, 1994	39.13
Alert SB No. 247F-61-A3, Rev. 3, dated April 7, 1994	39.13
Alert SB No. 6/5500/F-61-A11, Rev. 4, dated April 7, 1994	39.13
Alert SB No. 6/5500/F-61-A29, dated August 29, 1994	39.13
ASB No. 14RF-19-61-A25, Rev. 6, dated May 5, 1995	39.13
ASB No. 14RF-19-61-A53, Rev. 1, dated March 6, 1996	39.13
ASB No. 14RF-21-61-A38, Rev. 6, dated May 5, 1995	39.13
ASB No. 14RF-21-61-A72, Rev. 1, dated March 6, 1996	39.13
ASB No. 14RF-9-61-A53, Rev. 7, dated May 5, 1995	39.13
ASB No. 14RF-9-61-A92, Rev. 2, dated March 6, 1996	39.13
ASB No. 14SF-61-A59, Rev. 6, dated May 5, 1995	39.13
ASB No. 14SF-61-A92, Rev. 1, dated March 6, 1996	39.13
ASB No. 247F-61-A3, Rev. 5, dated May 5, 1995	39.13
ASB No. 6/5500/F-61-A11, Rev. 6, dated May 5, 1995	39.13
ASB No. 6/5500/F-61-A39, Rev. 1, dated March 6, 1996 ,	39.13

Title 14—Aeronautics and Space

Material Approved for Incorporation by Reference

	14 CFR
SB No. 73-129; Rev. 3, dated July 1, 1977	39.13
SB No. 73-150, Rev. 1, dated August 15, 1991	39.13
SB No. 73-21, Rev. 1, dated October 27,1976	39.13
SB No. 73-24, Rev. 2, dated October 15, 1974	39.13
SB No. 73-27, Rev. 1, dated September 27, 1982	39.13
SB No. 73-28, dated May 29, 1974	39.13
SB No. 73-29, Rev. 1, dated September 27, 1977	39.13
SB No. 73-3, dated January 7, 1977	39.13
SB No. 73-35, Rev. 1, dated August 29, 1975	39.13
SB No. 73-36, Rev. 3, dated July 1, 1977	39.13
SB No. 73-42, dated February 27, 1976	39.13
SB No. 73-50, Rev. 2, dated December 13, 1992	39.13
SB No. 75-10, dated September 10, 1974	39.13
SB No. 75-11, dated January 3, 1975	39.13
SB No. 75-14, dated May 23, 1975	39.13
SB No. 75-19, Rev. 3, dated August 19, 1991	39.13
SB No. 75-2, Rev. 1, dated November 8, 1979	39.13
SB No. 75-20, dated September 1, 1978	39.13
SB No. 75-22, Rev. 1, dated August 19, 1991	39.13
SB No. 75-23, dated March 31, 1988	39.13
SB No. 75-24, Rev. 1, dated August 19, 1991	39.13
SB No. 75-27, dated August 19, 1991	39.13
SB No. 75-27, dated September 10, 1974	39.13
SB No. 75-28, dated January 3, 1975	39.13
SB No. 75-28, dated May 13, 1991	39.13
SB No. 75-31, dated May 23, 1975	39.13
SB No. 75-36, Rev. 1, dated September 1, 1978	39.13
SB No. 75-37, Rev. 3, dated August 16, 1991	39.13
SB No. 75-4, Rev. 2, dated August 20, 1991	39.13
SB No. 75-41, Rev. 3, dated August 16, 1991	39.13
SB No. 75-42, Rev. 1, dated August 16, 1991	39.13
SB No. 75-43, Rev. 2, dated April 25, 1991	39.13
SB No. 75-45, Rev. 1, dated August 16, 1991	39.13
SB No. 75-48, Rev. 1, dated August 16, 1991	39.13
SB No. 75-49, dated May 13, 1991	39.13
SB No. 75-5, dated March 31, 1988	39.13
SB No. 75-6, Rev. 1, dated August 20, 1991	39.13
SB No. 75-9, Rev. 1, dated August 20, 1991	39.13
SB No. GTA9-73-139; dated February 27, 1976	39.13
SB No. GTA9-73-33, Rev. 2, dated October 31, 1978	39.13
SB No. GTA9-75- 17, dated March 31, 1988	39.13
SB No. GTA9-75-16, dated March 20, 1988	39.13
SB No. GTA9-75-17, dated March 31, 1988	39.13
SB No. GTA9-75-19, Rev. 1, dated August 21, 1991	39.13
SB No. GTA9-75-26, Rev. 1, dated August 21, 1991	39.13
SB No. GTA9-75-9, Rev. 3, dated August 15, 1992	39.13
TemporaryRev (TR) No. 61-6 to HS Maintenance Manual (MM) P5186, dated March 15, 1993.	39.13
TR No. 61-4 to HS MM P5189, dated March 15, 1993	39.13
TR No. 61-5 to HS MM P5189, dated July 27, 1993	39.13

Title 14—Aeronautics and Space

Material Approved for Incorporation by Reference

14 CFR

SB No. 165E, dated January 21, 1994 .... 39.13

SB No. 202, dated January 5, 1995 .... 39.13

SB No. HC-SB-61-227 Revision 2 dated May 8, 2000 .... 39.13

Service Bulletin No. 101D Revision D dated December 19, 1974   39.13

Service Bulletin No. 118A Revision A dated February 15, 1977 .... 39.13

Service Lette No. 69 Revision 1 dated November 30, 1971 .... 39.13

Service Manual No. 202A, dated March, 1993 .... 39.13

Standard Practices Manual, Rev. 1, dated June 1994 .... 39.13

Standard Practices Manual, 61-01-02, Rev. 1, dated June 1994 .... 39.13

SB 165D, dated August 6, 1993 .... 39.13

HB Aircraft Industries AG (Ing. Helno Brditschka Flugtechnik Ges.m.b.H.)
Dr. Adolf Scharfstr. 44, 4053 Haid, Austria; Telephone 43.7229.80904

23/2/90 dated Dec. 1990 .... 39.13

SB HB-23/17/91, dated October 28, 1991 .... 39.13

SB HB-23/18/91, dated October 28, 1991 .... 39.13

SB HB-23/19/91, dated October 5, 1991 .... 39.13

Heath Tecna Aerospace Co
19819 84th Ave. South, Kent, WA 98032

ASB ESCI-25-A1 dated Apr. 30, 1990 .... 39.13

ASB MarkI-33-A2, Revision 1, dated July 24, 1996 .... 39.13

ASB MarkI-33-A3, Revision 1, dated July 24, 1996 .... 39.13

ASB MarkI-33-A4, Revision 1, dated July 24, 1996 .... 39.13

ASB MarkI-33-A5, Revision 1, dated July 24, 1996; 39.13

ASB Spmk-33-A1, Revision 1, dated July 24, 1996 .... 39.13

ASB Spmk-33-A2, Revision 1, dated July 24, 1996 .... 39.13

SB H0364-35-001, dated March 15, 1996 .... 39.13

SB H0655-33-01, dated March 28, 1996 .... 39.13

Helicopter Technology Company, LLC
12923 South Spring Street Los Angeles CA 90061 Phone (310)523-2750 fax (310)523-2745

Mandatory Service Bulletin Notice No. 2100-2R2 dated November   39.13
14, 2000.

Hercules (Lockheed Aeronautical Systems Support Company)
Field Support Department, Department 693, Zone 0755, 2251 Lake Park Drive, Smyrna, GA 30080

188A Airplane Flight Manual, dated October 17, 1996 .... 39.13

188C Airplane Flight Manual, dated October 17, 1996 .... 39.13

SB 382-57-74 (82-688), dated January 31, 1994 (includes Attachment   39.13
1, and Appendices A and B).

Hexcel Interiors
3225 Woburn Street Bellingham, WA 98226 or Boeing Commercial Aircraft Group, Long Beach Division 3855 Lakewood Blvd, Long Beach, CA 90846 Attn: Data and Service Management Dept. C1-L5A (D800-0024)

Service Bulletin 110000-25-001 dated March 31, 2001 .... 39.13

Hiller Aircraft Corp
7980 Enterprise Drive, Newark, CA 94560-3497

Service Bulletin No. 10-4 Revision 2 dated December 20, 1999 .... 39.13

SB 36-1, Rev. 3, dated October 24, 1979 .... 39.13

Title 14—Aeronautics and Space

Material Approved for Incorporation by Reference

14 CFR (PARTS 1–59)—Continued
FEDERAL AVIATION ADMINISTRATION, DEPARTMENT OF TRANSPORTATION—Continued

	14 CFR
Service Bulletin 3505582-80-1706 dated March 8, 2000	39.13
Service Bulletin 7015327-22-4 dated March 31, 1997	39.13
Service Bulletin LT 101-72-30-0186 dated October 1, 1999	39.13
Alert Service Bulletin ALF/LF A72-1076 Revision 1 dated August 30, 2002.	39.13
Service Bulletin LT 101-73-20-0203 Revision 1 dated January 5, 2001	39.13
Alert Service Bulletin TPE331-A72-2083 Revision 1 dated May 17, 2002.	39.13
Alert Service Bulletin TPE331-A72-2087 dated October 10, 2001	39.13
Alert Service Bulletin TPE331-A72-2087 Revision 1 dated November 16, 2001.	39.13
Alert Service Bulletin TPE331-A72-2088 dated October 10, 2001	39.13
Alert Service Bulletin TPE331-A72-2088 Revision 1 dated November 16, 2001.	39.13
Alert Service Bulletin TPE331-A72-2088 Revision 2 dated February 20, 2002.	39.13
Alert Service Bulletin TPE331-A72-2092 dated October 10, 2001	39.13
Alert Service Bulletin TPE331-A72-2092 Revision 1 dated November 16, 2001.	39.13
Alert Service Bulletin TPE331-A72-2093 dated October 10, 2001	39.13
Alert Service Bulletin TPE331-A72-2093 Revision 1 dated November 16, 2001.	39.13
Alert Service Bulletin TPE331-A79-0034 Revision 3 dated October 2, 2001.	39.13
Alert Service Bulletin TPE331-A79-0034 Revision 4 dated April 5, 2002.	39.13
SB LT 101-72-30-0186 dated October 1, 1999	39.13
Service Bulletin T53-L-13B-0020 Revision 3 dated October 25, 2001	39.13
Service Bulletin T53-L-13B/D-0020 Revision 1 dated April 25, 2001	39.13
Service Bulletin T53-L-703-0020 Revision 1 dated April 25, 2001	39.13
Service Bulletin T5313B/17-0020 Revision 6 dated May 2, 2001	39.13
Service Bulletin TPE331-72-2090RWK dated October 10, 2001	39.13
Service Bulletin TPE331-72-2091RWK dated October 10, 2001	39.13
Service Bulletin TPE331-72-2094RWK dated October 10, 2001	39.13
Service Bulletin TPE331-72-2095RWK dated October 10, 2001	39.13
Service Bulletin T53-L-13B-0020 Revision 3 dated October 25, 2001	39.13
Service Bulletin T53-L-13B/D-0020 Revision 1 dated April 25, 2001	39.13
Service Bulletin T53-L-703-0020 Revision 1 dated April 25, 2001	39.13
Service Bulletin T5313B/17-0052 Revision 2 dated December 16, 1993	39.13

HR Textron

25200 W. Rye Canyon Road, Santa Clarita, CA 91355-1265

Alert Service Bulletin 41000470-67A-05 Revision 1 dated October 19, 2000.	39.13
Alert Service Bulletin 41105950-67A-01 dated October 19, 2000	39.13

Hughes Helicopters, Inc

Centinela Avenue and Teale Street, Culver City, California 90230

Service Information EN-19 dated November 14, 1984	39.13
Service Information HN-197 dated November 14, 1984	39.13
Service Information Nos. DN-130, dated November 14, 1984	39.13

International Aero Engines, AG

400 Main Street, East Hartford, CT 06108

Title 14—Aeronautics and Space

14 CFR (PARTS 1–59)—Continued
FEDERAL AVIATION ADMINISTRATION, DEPARTMENT OF TRANSPORTATION—
Continued

Material Approved for Incorporation by Reference

14 CFR

JAMCO America, Inc.
1018 80th Street, SW Everett Washington 98023

Service Bulletin 747-25-M025 dated August 30, 2000	39.13
Service Bulletin 767-25-M019 dated August 30, 2000	39.13

JanAero Devices
Airport Complex, P.O. Box 273, Fort Deposit, Alabama 36032

SB No. A-102, dated September, 1994	39.13
SB No. A-103, dated September, 1995	39.13
Service Bulletin No. A-107 dated January 8, 2001	39.13

Jensen Aircraft
9225 Country Road 140, Salida, CO 812101

Installation Instructions for Modified Lift Strut Fittings, Revision 2, dated April 20, 1984..	39.13

Jetstream Aircraft, Inc. (formerly BAe)
P.O. Box 16029, Dulles International Airport, Washington, DC 20041-6029

SB 32-41, Rev. 2, dated March 9, 1993	39.13
SB 8679-29-02 dated April 1991	39.13
SB AIR44880-29-01 dated April 1991	39.13
SB AIR44880-29-02, Rev. 1, dated March 9, 1993	39.13
Alert SB 57-A-JA 920640, dated February 19, 1993	39.13
ASB 27-A-JM7847, Rev. 1, dated April 27, 1998	39.13
Mandatory SB 74-JM 7693A, dated May 17, 1990	39.13
Mandatory SB 74-JM 7693A, Rev. 3, dated January 28, 1993	39.13
SB 22-A-JA 851231, dated April 9, 1986	39.13
SB 28-JM 7161, dated December 19, 1983	39.13
SB 29-JM 7360, Rev. No. 1, dated January 3, 1991	39.13
SB 34-JA 891143, dated March 2, 1990	39.13
SB 57-JM 5259, dated February 5, 1993	39.13
SB J41-57-019, Rev. 1, dated November 26, 1997	39.13
SB J41-57-020, dated March 20, 1997	39.13
SB J41-57-021, dated May 7, 1998	39.13
MSB B121/105, dated January 12, 1998	39.13
SB B121/106, dated January 12, 1998	39.13
Airplane Flight Manual Temporary Rev. T/40, Issue 1, dated August 3, 1994.	39.13
Airplane Flight Manual Temporary Rev. T/41, Issue 1, dated November 15, 1994.	39.13
Alert SB 24-A-JA 900443, Rev. 2, dated November 15, 1990	39.13
Alert SB 24-A-JM 7708, Rev. 1, dated May 22, 1990	39.13
Alert SB 30-A-JA 920444, dated October 30, 1992	39.13
Alert SB 32-A-JA 941245, Rev. 3, dated March 15, 1996	39.13
Alert SB 80-A-JA 911045, Rev. 1, dated November 1, 1991	39.13
Alert SB J41-52-050, dated May 6, 1997	39.13
Alert SB J41-53-028, Rev. 1, dated October 12, 1994	39.13
Alert SB J41-53-028, Rev. No. 2, dated January 17, 1995	39.13
Alert SB J41-A-27-026, Rev. 2, dated January 17, 1994	39.13
Alert SB J41-A22-005, dated July 1, 1996	39.13
Alert SB J41-A25-034, Rev. 1, dated October 30, 1993	39.13
Alert SB J41-A25-061, dated June 6, 1995	39.13

Title 14—Aeronautics and Space

14 CFR (PARTS 1–59)—Continued
FEDERAL AVIATION ADMINISTRATION, DEPARTMENT OF TRANSPORTATION—Continued

Material Approved for Incorporation by Reference

	14 CFR
SB 53-A-JA 870510, Rev. 1, dated November 10, 1987	39.13
SB 53-JM 5285, Rev. 2, dated November 12, 1992	39.13
SB 57-A-JA920540, dated September 1, 1992	39.13
SB 57-JA 921140, Rev. 1, dated February 24, 1994	39.13
SB 57-JA 921144, Rev. 1, dated April 19, 1994	39.13
SB 57-JA 930941, Rev. 2, dated November 11, 1994	39.13
SB 57-JA-921144, Rev. 1, dated April 19, 1994	39.13
SB 57-JM 5218, Rev. 4, dated October 31, 1990	39.13
SB 57-JM 5326, dated September 3, 1993	39.13
SB 57-JM5221, dated September 28, 1984 and Modification No. 5146 Ref. 7/5146, dated October 1984.	39.13
SB ATP 30-37-30143A, dated August 1, 1994	39.13
SB ATP-21-24-10306A, dated July 30, 1993	39.13
SB ATP-23-21-35288A, Rev. 2, dated February 15, 1994	39.13
SB ATP-24-55, Rev. 1, dated April 24, 1993	39.13
SB ATP-26-9, dated May 12, 1993	39.13
SB ATP-27-49-10234A, Rev. 1, dated August 14, 1993; and Rev. 2, dated November 23, 1993, June 18, 1993.	39.13
SB ATP-27-78, Rev. 1, dated January 31, 1996	39.13
SB ATP-27-80, dated April 23, 1996	39.13
SB ATP-30-35285A, dated July 15, 1994	39.13
SB ATP-30-39-30146A, dated July 29, 1994	39.13
SB ATP-30-44-35274D, dated August 12, 1994	39.13
SB ATP-32-48, Rev. 1, dated January 28, 1994	39.13
SB ATP-32-48, Rev. 3, dated July 15, 1994	39.13
SB ATP-32-51-35296A, dated May 12, 1994	39.13
SB ATP-32-53-35294A, dated July 18, 1994 (including Erratum No. 1).	39.13
SB ATP-32-53-35294A, Rev. 2, dated January 13, 1995	39.13
SB ATP-52-26-10350B, dated June 29, 1994	39.13
SB ATP-53-30-10372A, dated November 3, 1994	39.13
SB ATP-54-11, dated July 13, 1993;	39.13
SB ATP-54-11, Rev. 1, dated November 9, 1993	39.13
SB ATP-54-13-35274B, Rev. 2, dated August 18, 1994	39.13
SB ATP-57-13, Rev. 5, dated June 3, 1994	39.13
SB ATP-57-16-10313A, Rev. 1, dated July 2, 1994 (as corrected by Erratum 2, dated August 30, 1994).	39.13
SB ATP-76-16, dated October 14, 1994	39.13
SB ATP-76-18, dated June 21, 1995	39.13
SB ATP-79-23, dated August 26, 1994	39.13
SB ATP-79-24-10360A, dated September 4, 1994	39.13
SB ATP-80-06, Rev. 2, dated October 16, 1994	39.13
SB ATP-80-7-30141A, Rev. 2, dated November 4, 1994	39.13
SB ATP29-12, dated September 9, 1995,	39.13
SB ATP29-12, Temporary Rev. No. T/52, Issue 1, dated August 16, 1995.	39.13
SB ATP30-37-30143A, Rev. 1, dated September 5, 1994	39.13
SB HS748-27-124, dated November 17, 1995	39.13
SB HS748-27-126, dated February 29, 1996	39.13
SB J41-11-004, Rev. 1, dated March 23, 1994	39.13

Title 14—Aeronautics and Space

Material Approved for Incorporation by Reference

14 CFR (PARTS 1–59)—Continued
FEDERAL AVIATION ADMINISTRATION, DEPARTMENT OF TRANSPORTATION—
Continued

	14 CFR
Series 4100 Alert SB J41-A52-016, dated May 18, 1993	39.13
Series 4100 SB J41-57-003, dated October 13, 1993	39.13
Service Bulletin J41-27-059 dated May 31, 2000	39.13
Service Bulletin J41-32-068 Revision 1 dated May 12, 2000	39.13
Service Bulletin J41-53-046 dated March 15, 2000	39.13
Temporary Rev. T/42, Issue 1, dated August 12, 1994	39.13
ATP 80-06, Rev. 1, dated October 22, 1993	39.13
ATP-53-31, Rev. 1, dated December 5, 1995	39.13
ATP-54-12-35274A, dated September 28, 1993	39.13
ATP-54-13-35274B, dated October 9, 1993	39.13
ATP-54-14, dated October 14, 1993	39.13
Drawing 141R0370, Issue 3, dated May 27, 1993	39.13
Drawing 141R0370, Issue 3, dated May 27, 1993	39.13
SB ATP-54-10-35256A, Rev. 1, dated April 16, 1993	39.13
SB ATP-54-9, dated December 9, 1992	39.13
SB ATP-54-9, Rev. 1, dated May 10, 1993	39.13
SB No. B121/103, dated October 26, 1995	39.13
SB ATP-21-36, dated January 3, 1996	39.13
SB ATP-79-25-10382A, Rev. 1, dated May 25, 1995	39.13
SB 32-56, Rev. 3, dated February, 1995	39.13
SB 32-66, Rev. 2, as referenced in Jetstream Series 3100-3200 ASB 32-JA-960601, Rev. 1, Accomplishment Instructions, dated April 11, 1997 dated March 1997,.	39.13
SB No. 2314M-30-16,as referenced in Jetstream Series 3100/3200 SB 30-JA 950641, Rev. 2, dated March 18, dated December 1996,.	39.13

Korff & Co. KG
Luftfahrttechnischer Betrieb, LBA II-A 189, Dieselstrasse 5, D-63128
Dietzenbach Germany phone (49)6074/4006 fax (49)6741/4033

	14 CFR
Service Bulletin SB-KOCO 05/818 Revision 2 dated January 16, 2001	39.13
Work Instructions AW-KOCO 05/818 Revision 2 dated January 16, 2001.	39.13

Learjet, Inc.
One Learjet Way Wichita, KS 67209-2942

	14 CFR
Service Bulletin 55-32-14 dated November 9, 1999	39.13
Service Bulletin 60-32-10 Revision 1 dated June 22, 2000	39.13
45 Maintenance Manual Temporary Revision No. 30-1 dated January 2, 2001.	39.13
45 Maintenance Manual Temporary Revision No. 4-2 dated January 2, 2001.	39.13
45 Maintenance Manual Temporary Revision No. 5-2 dated January 2, 2001.	39.13
45 Temporary Flight Manual Change TFM 2000-16 dated January 8, 2001.	39.13
Airplane Modification Kit AMK No. 90-5 dated Oct. 11, 1991	39.13
Alert SB SB A31-26-3, dated July 14, 1995 and Learjet Alert SB SB A60-26-1, dated July 14, 1995.	39.13
Alert SB SB A60-21-1, dated November 1, 1993	39.13
Alert SB SB A60-28-3, dated May 12, 1995	39.13
Alert Service Bulletin SB A45-21-14 dated May 3, 2002	39.13
SB 23/24/25-28-2, dated October 6, 1995 and Learjet SB SB 35/36-28-10, dated October 6, 1995.	39.13

Title 14—Aeronautics and Space

Material Approved for Incorporation by Reference

	14 CFR
Document Number LG92ER0060, L-1011-385 Series Supplemental Inspection Document, revised January 1994.	39.13
Document Number LR 31889, Corrosion Prevention and Control Program, Tristar L-1011, dated March 15, 1991; including Errata Sheet, LR 31889, Corrosion Prevention and Control Program, TriStar L-1011, issued September 29, 1992.	39.13
Document Number LR 31889, Corrosion Prevention and Control Program, Tristar L-1011, dated March 15, 1991; including Errata Sheet, LR 31889, Corrosion Prevention and Control Program, TriStar L-1011, issued September 29, 1992.	39.13
Document Number LR 31889, Corrosion Prevention and Control Program, Tristar L-1011, Rev. A, dated April 15, 1994.	39.13
L-1011 SB 093-53-105, Rev. 1, dated November 17, 1995	39.13
L-1011 SB 093-53-258, dated February 20, 1990	39.13
L-1011 SB 093-53-268, dated April 15, 1993	39.13
L-1011 SB 093-53-268, Revision 1, dated July 2, 1996	39.13
L-1011 SB 093-53-272, dated November 12, 1996	39.13
L-1011 SB 093-55-031, dated April 26, 1996.	39.13
L-1011 SB 093-57-184, Rev. 7, dated December 6, 1994, as amended by Change Notification 093-57-184, R7-CN1, dated August 22, 1995.	39.13
L-1011 SB 093-57-196, Rev. 6, dated December 6, 1994, as amended by Change Notification 093-57-196, R6-CN1, dated August 22, 1995.	39.13
L-1011 SB 093-57-203, Rev. 4, dated March 27, 1995	39.13
L-1011 SB 093-57-203, Rev. 6, dated August 18, 1997	39.13
L-1011 SB 093-57-215, dated April 11, 1996	39.13
L-1011 SB 093-57-218, dated April 11, 1996	39.13
SB 093-25-294, Revision 2, dated April 13, 1981	39.13
SB 093-26-036, dated April 1, 1986	39.13
SB 093-26-039, dated November 11, 1992	39.13
SB 093-26-039, Rev. 1, dated April 10, 1996	39.13
SB 093-27-301, dated June 9, 1992	39.13
SB 093-27-304, Rev. 1 dated May 28, 1992	39.13
SB 093-27-306, dated January 14, 1998	39.13
SB 093-28-093, Revision 1, including List of Effective Pages, dated February 8, 1999.	39.13
SB 093-32-256, dated November 11, 1994	39.13
SB 093-51-035 dated June 28, 1990	39.13
SB 093-51-035, Rev. 1, dated December 16, 1991, as revised by L-1011 SB Change Notification 093-51-035, R1-CN1,.	39.13
SB 093-52-155, Rev. 1, dated October 23, 1989	39.13
SB 093-53-252, Rev. 2, dated April 25, 1989	39.13
SB 093-53-264 dated Oct. 4, 1991	39.13
SB 093-53-277, dated July 2, 1996	39.13
SB 093-57-184, Revision 6, dated October 28, 1991	39.13
SB 093-57-184, Revision 7, dated December 6, 1994	39.13
SB 093-57-196, Revision 5, dated October 28, 1991	39.13
SB 093-57-196, Revision 6, dated December 6, 1994	39.13
SB 093-57-203, Rev. 3, dated October 28, 1991	39.13
SB 093-57-203, Rev. 3, dated October 28, 1991	39.13
SB 093-57-203, Revision 3, dated October 28, 1991	39.13
SB 093-57-203, Revision 4, dated March 27, 1995	39.13

Title 14—Aeronautics and Space

14 CFR (PARTS 1–59)—Continued
FEDERAL AVIATION ADMINISTRATION, DEPARTMENT OF TRANSPORTATION—Continued

Material Approved for Incorporation by Reference

	14 CFR
Alert Service Bulletin DB9-25A357 Revision 1 dated March 16, 1998	39.13
Alert Service Bulletin DB9-25A357 Revision 2 dated May 28, 1998	39.13
Alert Service Bulletin DC10-24A149 Revision 1 dated July 28, 1999	39.13
Alert Service Bulletin DC10-24A161 dated October 29, 1999	39.13
Alert Service Bulletin DC10-24A162 dated July 28, 1999	39.13
Alert Service Bulletin DC10-24A163 dated July 28, 1999	39.13
Alert Service Bulletin DC10-24A165 dated April 14, 1999	39.13
Alert Service Bulletin DC10-57A143 dated December 20, 1999	39.13
Alert Service Bulletin DC10-78A056 dated January 19, 1998	39.13
Alert Service Bulletin DC10-78A056 Revision 1 dated June 4, 1998	39.13
Alert Service Bulletin DC10-78A056 Revision 2 dated February 18, 1999.	39.13
Alert Service Bulletin DC10-78A057 dated November 30, 1998	39.13
Alert Service Bulletin DC10-78A057 Revision 1 dated February 18, 1999.	39.13
Alert Service Bulletin DC10-78A057 Revision 1 dated February 18, 1999.	39.13
Alert Service Bulletin DC9-24A171 Revision 01 September 21, 1999	39.13
Alert Service Bulletin DC9-25A357 Revision 1 dated March 16, 1998	39.13
Alert Service Bulletin DC9-25A357 Revision 1 dated March 16, 1998	39.13
Alert Service Bulletin DC9-25A357 Revision 2 May 28, 1998	39.13
Alert Service Bulletin DC9-74A001 Revision 1 dated October 26, 1998.	39.13
Alert Service Bulletin MD11-24A008 Revision 2 dated March 27, 2000.	39.13
Alert Service Bulletin MD11-24A040 Revision 1 dated October 11, 1999.	39.13
Alert Service Bulletin MD11-24A041 Revision 1 dated April 26, 1999	39.13
Alert Service Bulletin MD11-24A068 Revision 1 dated March 8, 1999	39.13
Alert Service Bulletin MD11-24A071 Revision 01 dated May 20, 1999	39.13
Alert Service Bulletin MD11-24A078 Revision 1 dated June 16, 1999	39.13
Alert Service Bulletin MD11-24A097 dated April 3, 2000	39.13
Alert Service Bulletin MD11-24A116 Revision 1 dated October 11, 1999.	39.13
Alert Service Bulletin MD11-24A130 Revision 1 dated September 20, 1999.	39.13
Alert Service Bulletin MD11-24A138 dated April 3, 2000	39.13
Alert Service Bulletin MD11-24A141 dated May 17, 1999	39.13
Alert Service Bulletin MD11-24A141 Revision 1 dated August 23, 1999.	39.13
Alert Service Bulletin MD11-24A147 dated March 24, 1999	39.13
Alert Service Bulletin MD11-24A150 dated March 25, 1999	39.13
Alert Service Bulletin MD11-24A152 dated August 9, 1999	39.13
Alert Service Bulletin MD11-24A172 dated September 8, 1999	39.13
Alert Service Bulletin MD11-24A180 dated January 4, 2000	39.13
Alert Service Bulletin MD11-24A182 dated April 3, 2000	39.13
Alert Service Bulletin MD11-25A187 Revision 1 dated January 5, 2000.	39.13
Alert Service Bulletin MD11-25A194 Revision 5 dated June 21, 1999	39.13
Alert Service Bulletin MD11-25A194 Revision 6 dated January 27, 2000.	39.13

14 CFR (PARTS 1–59)—Continued
FEDERAL AVIATION ADMINISTRATION, DEPARTMENT OF TRANSPORTATION—
Continued

Material Approved for Incorporation by Reference

	14 CFR
Service Bulletin MD80-25-355 Revision 1 dated November 5, 1997	39.13
Service Bulletin MD80-29-056 dated June 18, 1996	39.13
Service Bulletin MD80-29-062 Revision 1 dated August 3, 1999	39.13
Service Bulletin MD80-53-286 dated September 3, 1999	39.13
Service Bulletin MD90-24-062 dated February 3, 2000	39.13
Service Bulletin MD90-25-015 Revision 1 dated November 5, 1997	39.13
Service Bulletin MD90-32-012 dated May 19, 1997	39.13
Service Bulletin MD90-32-012 Revision 1 dated June 6, 1998	39.13
Service Bulletin MD90-53-004 dated August 20, 1998	39.13
Service Bulletin MD90-53-018 dated September 3, 1999	39.13
Airworthiness Limitations Instructions Report No. MDC- 94K9000, Revision 3, and List of Effective Pages, dated November 1997.	39.13
Alert SB A34-57, dated December 19, 1994	39.13
Alert SB 24A090, dated July 21, 1995	39.13
Alert SB 24A090, Rev. 1, dated November 14, 1995	39.13
Alert SB 24A094, dated October 12, 1995	39.13
Alert SB 24A104, dated May 7, 1996	39.13
Alert SB 25A181, dated September 28, 1995	39.13
Alert SB 27A057, dated August 31, 1995	39.13
Alert SB 28A081, dated November 30, 1995	39.13
Alert SB 28A082, dated May 14, 1996	39.13
Alert SB 28A083, dated March 13, 1996	39.13
Alert SB 28A083, Rev. 1, including Summary, dated May 29, 1996	39.13
Alert SB 32A058, dated June 30, 1995	39.13
Alert SB 38A044, dated March 22, 1995	39.13
Alert SB 38A044, Rev. 1, dated June 30, 1995	39.13
Alert SB 54A049 R03, Rev. 3, dated May 18, 1995	39.13
Alert SB 71A073, Rev. 1, dated May 16, 1995	39.13
Alert SB A24-123 dated Mar. 19, 1991	39.13
Alert SB A24-132, Rev. 1 dated March 2, 1992	39.13
Alert SB A24-48, dated February 17, 1993	39.13
Alert SB A24-51, dated September 11, 1992	39.13
Alert SB A24-64 dated March 29, 1993	39.13
Alert SB A24-75, dated December 22, 1993	39.13
Alert SB A26-16, dated November 22, 1993	39.13
Alert SB A26-46, dated December 6, 1993	39.13
Alert SB A27-220 dated May 29, 1992	39.13
Alert SB A27-275, Rev. 1 dated February 3, 1992	39.13
Alert SB A27-29 dated June 23, 1992	39.13
Alert SB A27-30 dated August 20, 1992	39.13
Alert SB A27-325, Rev. 1 dated February 3, 1992	39.13
Alert SB A27-327, Rev. 1, dated March 9, 1992	39.13
Alert SB A27-342, dated August 4, 1994	39.13
Alert SB A27-342, Rev. 1, dated May 15, 1995	39.13
Alert SB A27-38, dated July 8, 1993	39.13
Alert SB A28-56, dated May 25, 1993	39.13
Alert SB A28-56, Rev. 1, dated June 14, 1993	39.13
Alert SB A32-237, dated April 11, 1994	39.13
Alert SB A32-238, dated July 15, 1994	39.13
Alert SB A32-47, dated July 15, 1994	39.13

Material Approved for Incorporation by Reference

Material Approved for Incorporation by Reference

	14 CFR
Report Supplemental Inspection Document No. L26-012, DC-10: (SID), Volume II, Rev. 3, dated December 1992,.	39.13
Report Supplemental Inspection Document No. L26-012, DC-10: (SID), Volume III-92, dated October 1992.	39.13
ROD Sketch 95-09-14-005, dated September 14, 1995	39.13
SB 22-111, dated May 23, 1995	39.13
SB 22-122, dated August 6, 1996	39.13
SB 22-14, dated November 30, 1994	39.13
SB 24-111, dated December 3, 1996	39.13
SB 24-121, dated February 24, 1992	39.13
SB 24-150, dated March 28, 1994	39.13
SB 24-150, Rev. 1, dated April 7, 1995	39.13
SB 24-151, dated September 29, 1994	39.13
SB 24-78, dated May 10, 1994	39.13
SB 24-94, Rev. 4, dated June 7, 1993	39.13
SB 25-116, Rev. 1 dated May 15, 1992	39.13
SB 25-331, dated December 10, 1993	39.13
SB 25-335, dated April 28, 1993	39.13
SB 25-87 dated January 23, 1992	39.13
SB 25-A364, dated October 30, 1997	39.13
SB 25A-030, dated October 30, 1997	39.13
SB 26-018, dated August 24, 1995	39.13
SB 26-025, Rev. 03, dated July 25, 1996	39.13
SB 26-025, Rev. 04, dated April 30, 1997	39.13
SB 26-025, Rev. 05, dated May 29, 1998	39.13
SB 26-25, dated May 25, 1994	39.13
SB 26-25, Rev. 1, dated September 30, 1994	39.13
SB 26-25, Rev. 2, dated April 18, 1995	39.13
SB 27-051, dated December 19, 1995	39.13
SB 27-067, dated July 31, 1997	39.13
SB 27-067, Rev. 01, dated February 24, 1998	39.13
SB 27-120, dated February 10, 1975	39.13
SB 27-152, dated August 9, 1976	39.13
SB 27-18 dated August 30, 1991	39.13
SB 27-18, Rev. 1 dated October 16, 1991	39.13
SB 27-181, Rev. 1, dated May 28, 1981	39.13
SB 27-196, Rev. 2 dated Dec. 17, 1990	39.13
SB 27-201, dated December 30, 1985	39.13
SB 27-208, dated September 5, 1989	39.13
SB 27-209, dated October 20, 1989	39.13
SB 27-222, dated November 1, 1993	39.13
SB 27-250, Rev. 2 dated Jan. 3, 1990	39.13
SB 27-301 dated June 21, 1989	39.13
SB 27-301, Rev. 1 dated May 24, 1991	39.13
SB 27-321, dated May 18, 1992	39.13
SB 27-34, dated November 1, 1993	39.13
SB 27-346, Rev. 01, dated July 29, 1997	39.13
SB 27-36, Rev. 1, dated December 9, 1994	39.13
SB 27-71, Rev. 1, dated February 14, 1973	39.13
SB 27-A067, Rev. 02, dated May 18, 1998	39.13

Title 14—Aeronautics and Space

Material Approved for Incorporation by Reference

14 CFR (PARTS 1–59)—Continued
FEDERAL AVIATION ADMINISTRATION, DEPARTMENT OF TRANSPORTATION—Continued

	14 CFR
SB 53-216, Rev. 3, dated April 23, 1993	39.13
SB 53-235, dated September 15, 1993	39.13
SB 53-253, dated March 31, 1994	39.13
SB 53-253, as amended by Change Notification 53-253 CN1, dated April 15, 1994.	39.13
SB 53-256, dated August 12, 1993	39.13
SB 53-256, Revision 1, dated November 29, 1994	39.13
SB 53-257, Rev. 1, dated February 9, 1996	39.13
SB 53-262, dated October 11, 1994	39.13
SB 53-265, dated June 13, 1994	39.13
SB 53-269, dated August 11, 1994	39.13
SB 53-276, dated September 30, 1996	39.13
SB 53-277, dated September 30, 1996	39.13
SB 53-284, dated August 20, 1996	39.13
SB 53-288, dated February 10, 1997	39.13
SB 53-31, dated January 29, 1993	39.13
SB 54-049 R01, Rev. 1, dated May 18, 1995	39.13
SB 54-049, dated March 31, 1995	39.13
SB 54-100, Rev. 1, dated September 17, 1993	39.13
SB 54-108, dated February 9, 1995	39.13
SB 54-17 dated February 24, 1992	39.13
SB 54-17, Rev. 1 dated July 16, 1992	39.13
SB 54-74, dated December 21, 1979	39.13
SB 55-14, Rev. 5, dated August 24, 1990	39.13
SB 55-14, Rev. 6, dated January 11, 1993	39.13
SB 55-20, Rev. 1, dated March 8, 1991	39.13
SB 55-20, Rev. 2, dated August 4, 1994	39.13
SB 55-23, dated December 17, 1992	39.13
SB 55-23, Rev. 1, dated December 17, 1993	39.13
SB 55-24, Rev. 1, dated August 3, 1994	39.13
SB 55-25, Rev. 1, dated August 3, 1994	39.13
SB 57-031, dated August 15, 1995	39.13
SB 57-114, Rev. 1, dated July 26, 1993	39.13
SB 57-123, dated June 8, 1993	39.13
SB 57-126, dated October 30, 1992	39.13
SB 57-129, dated August 12, 1994	39.13
SB 57-184, Rev. 1, dated December 22, 1994	39.13
SB 57-36, Rev. 7, dated December 11, 1992	39.13
SB 57-61, Rev. 2, dated August 15, 1990	39.13
SB 57-78, Revision 1, dated August 26, 1986	39.13
SB 57-79, Revision 1, dated September 21, 1979, as revised by MD DC-10 SB Change Notification 57-59, dated January 23, 1980.	39.13
SB 57-82, dated February 19, 1980	39.13
SB 71-133, Rev. 6, dated June 30, 1992	39.13
SB 71-154 dated Jan. 18, 1991	39.13
SB 78-112, Rev. 2, dated March 8, 1994	39.13
SB 80-010, dated August 22, 1997	39.13
SB 80-014, dated August 22, 1997	39.13
SB A27-250, Rev. 3 dated May 15, 1991	39.13
SB A28-14 dated Apr. 11, 1991	39.13

Title 14—Aeronautics and Space

Material Approved for Incorporation by Reference

Title 14—Aeronautics and Space

Material Approved for Incorporation by Reference

14 CFR (PARTS 1–59)—Continued
FEDERAL AVIATION ADMINISTRATION, DEPARTMENT OF TRANSPORTATION—
Continued

	14 CFR
Airplane Flight Manual MU-2B-36 Modified by STC SA2413SW, Pages 1 through 31, FAA APPROVED 2-1-78, REVISION 1 RE-ISSUED 12-18-92,.	39.13
Airplane Flight Manual MU-2B-36A, Pages 1, 2, REVISION LOG 2, 1-5, 2-10, 5-10, 5-13, and 5-23, FAA REVISION 6; REISSUED 02-28-86,.	39.13
Airplane Flight Manual MU-2B-40, Pages 1, 2, REVISION LOG 2, 1-5, 2-10, 5-10, 5-13, 5-14, and 5-24, FAA REVISION 4; REISSUED 03-25-86,.	39.13
Airplane Flight Manual MU-2B-60, Pages 1, 2, REVISION LOG 2, 1-5, 2-9, 5-10, 5-13, 5-14, and 5-24, FAA REVISION 5; REISSUED 09-24-85,.	39.13
MU-2 SB No. 089/57-002A, dated November 5, 1996	39.13
MU-2 SB No. 130A, dated July 19, 1971	39.13
MU-2 SB No. 225, dated September 29, 1995	39.13
MU-300 Diamond Service Recommendation SR 71-001, Revision 2, and List of Effective Pages, dated June 1, 1984.	39.13
MU-300 SB No. 30-007, dated January 12, 1996	39.13
SB 71-004 dated Jan. 8, 1992	39.13
SB No. 079/27-010, dated August 28, 1992	39.13
SB No. 216, dated September 11, 1992	39.13
Service Bulletin MU-2 SB No. 086/74-002 dated November 15, 1995	39.13
Service Bulletin MU-2 SB No. 226 Revision B dated October 27, 1997.	39.13
Service Bulletin MU-2 SB No. 231 dated July 2, 1997	39.13
Service Bulletin MU-2 SB No. 231 dated July 2, 1997	39.13
Service Bulletin MU-2 SB No. 232 dated July 2, 1997	39.13
Publication No. YS-MR-301, YS-11 Corrosion Control Program, dated November 1, 1993.	39.13
SB 57-77, Revision 2, dated September 14, 1994	39.13
SB 57-77, List of Effective Pages, dated September 14, 1994	39.13

Mooney Aircraft Corp
P.O. Box 72, Kerrville, TX 78029-0072

Engineering Design SB No. M20-264, dated February 1, 1998	39.13
Instructions-Retrofit Kit, part number 940095-501-1, dated March 31, 1995 and Mooney Special Letter 95-1, dated April 20, 1995.	39.13
Instructions-Retrofit Kit, part number 940095-501-1, Revised April 21, 1995.	39.13
SB M20-250B, dated December 1995	39.13
SB M20-252 dated April 6, 1992	39.13
SB M20-253A, dated December 1995	39.13
SB M20-256, dated January 24, 1995	39.13
SB M20-259, issued September 1, 1996	39.13
SB M20-265, dated April 13, 1998	39.13

Moravan, Incorporated
765 81 Otrokovice Czech Republic

Mandatory Service Bulletin Z242L/19a Revision 3, Z143L/20a dated April 30, 1999.	39.13

Morris Aviation Ltd
Statesboro Airport, Box 718, Statesboro, Georgia 30458

Title 14—Aeronautics and Space

Material Approved for Incorporation by Reference

Material Approved for Incorporation by Reference

Title 14—Aeronautics and Space

Material Approved for Incorporation by Reference

	14 CFR
Alert SB No. 5676, Rev. 1 dated September 24, 1986	39.13
Alert SB No. 5729 dated January 29, 1987	39.13
Alert SB No. 5842, Rev. 3, dated October 10, 1990, including Appendix A, dated May 26, 1989, Appendix B, Rev. 3, dated October 10, 1990, and Appendix C, dated May 26, 1989.	39.13
Alert SB No. 5913, Rev. No. 5, dated August 10, 1992, including Appendix A, Rev. No. 5, dated August 10, 1992.	39.13
Alert SB No. 5944, Rev. 2, dated June 8, 1992	39.13
Alert SB No. 6104, Rev. No. 2, dated June 18, 1993, including Attachment No. NDIP-764, dated December 8, 1992.	39.13
Alert SB No. A5913, Rev. 6, dated October 15, 1993, including Appendix A, Rev. 6, dated October 15, 1993.	39.13
Alert SB No. A5913, Rev. 6, dated October 15, 1993, including Appendix A, Rev. 6, dated October 15, 1993.	39.13
Alert SB No. A6104, Rev. 3, dated June 16, 1994, including Appendix A and Appenix B; and Attachment 1, NDIP-764, dated December 8,.	39.13
Alert SB No. A6110, Rev. 1, dated October 15, 1993	39.13
Alert SB No. A6110, Rev. 1, dated October 15, 1993	39.13
Alert SB No. A6131, dated August 24, 1993	39.13
Alert SB No. A6131, dated August 24, 1993	39.13
Alert SB No. A6202, dated February 20, 1995	39.13
Alert SB No. A6226, dated October 17, 1995	39.13
Alert SB No. A6322, dated March 19, 1998	39.13
Alert SB No. JT9D-7R4-72-480, dated April 20, 1993	39.13
Alert SB No. JT9D-7R4-72-481, dated April 20, 1993	39.13
Alert SB No. PW2000 A75-36 dated October 28, 1987	39.13
Alert SB No. PW2000 A75-38 dated December 21, 1987	39.13
Alert SB No. PW4ENG 72-328 dated September 28, 1990	39.13
All Operator Wire JT9/73-13/PSE:DAB:3-10-14-1; P & W SB JT9D-7R4-73-4 dated 5/3/83; P & W Special Instruction No. 77F-83 and P & W Aircraft Manual P/N 785057 TR 72-1.	39.13
All Operator Wire No. JT8D/72-33/CTS: CRC-5-4-5-1, dated April 5, 1995.	39.13
ASB A6232, Revision 2, including List of Effective Pages, dated June 26, 1997.	39.13
ASB JT9D-7R4-A72-524, Revision 1, including List of Effective Pages, dated June 26, 1997.	39.13
ASB No. 6053, Rev. 7, dated May 24, 1993	39.13
ASB No. 6053, Rev. 7, dated May 24, 1993	39.13
ASB No. 6272, Rev. 1, dated September 24, 1996, including NDIP-892 dated September 15, 1996 and Attachment 1, dated September 15, 1996.	39.13
ASB No. A6153, Rev. 1, dated June 8, 1994	39.13
ASB No. A6169, Rev. 1, dated June 15, 1994	39.13
ASB No. A6170, dated May 13, 1994	39.13
ASB No. A6241, Revision 2, dated June 29, 1998.	39.13
ASB No. A6332, Rev. 2, dated June 26, 1997	39.13
ASB No. A6346, dated September 10, 1998	39.13
ASB No. A6346, and List of Effective Pages, dated April 23, 1999	39.13
ASB No. JT9D-7R4-A72-524, Rev. 1, dated June 26, 1997	39.13

14 CFR (PARTS 1–59)—Continued
FEDERAL AVIATION ADMINISTRATION, DEPARTMENT OF TRANSPORTATION—
Continued

	14 CFR
ASB No. PW4ENG-A72-628, Rev. 1, dated February 17, 1998, including NDIP-894, dated November 12, 1996 and NDIP-896, dated November 7, 1996.	39.13
ASB No. PW4G-100-A72-80, Rev. 1, dated February 17, 1998, including NDIP-894, dated November 12, 1996 and NDIP-896, dated November 7, 1996.	39.13
ASB PW4NAC A71-149, Rev. 1, dated August 30, 1995	39.13
ASB PW7R4 A71-129, Rev. 1, dated August 30, 1995	39.13
Cactus Wire C042 G 930302 ZRH, dated September 2, 1993	39.13
Engine Manual No. 50A443, Section 71-00-00, dated June, 15, 1999	39.13
Engine Manual No. 50A605, Section 71-00-00, dated June 15, 1999	39.13
Engine Manual No. 50A822, Section 71-00-00, dated June 15, 1999	39.13
Engine Manual P/N 646028, Section 72-52-06, Inspection 01, Paragraph 4E dated December 1, 1986, including figure 810 dated August 1, 1984.	39.13
Engine Manual PW785058 dated June 15, 1990	39.13
Engineering Change No. 197707	Part 11, SFAR 27, Sec. 14(b)
JT8D Maintenance Manual, section 72-00, Engine Troubleshooting, page 117 dated May 1, 1990, pages 118-124 dated Sept. 1, 1986.	39.13
JT8D Maintenance Manual, section 72-00-00, Troubleshooting-02, pages 120, 121, and 122 dated Aug. 1, 1991 and pages 123, 124, 135, and 136 dated May 15, 1990.	39.13
Mandatory SB JT9D 6329, dated May 20, 1998.	39.13
NDIP-620, Rev. A, dated October 7, 1995	39.13
NDIP-691, Rev. B, dated October 7, 1995	39.13
NDIP-781, dated October 7, 1995	39.13
NDIP-829, dated October 7, 1995	39.13
NDIP-834, Rev. A, dated October 7, 1995	39.13
NDIP-856, dated October 7, 1993	39.13
Nondestructive Investigations Procedure NDIP-858, dated November 7, 1995.	39.13
SB 2417	Part 11, SFAR 27, Sec. 14(b)
SB 2531	Part 11, SFAR 27, Sec. 14(b)
SB 4835, Rev. 5 dated September 27, 1983	39.13
SB 5510, Rev. 1 dated February 13, 1984	39.13
SB 5541, Rev. 1 dated May 4, 1984	39.13
SB 5566, Rev. No. 4, dated June 23, 1988	39.13
SB 5591, Rev. No. 7, dated August 25, 1992	39.13
SB 5667, Rev. 2, dated June 11, 1992	39.13
SB 5711, Rev. 3 dated April 1, 1987	39.13
SB 5744, Rev. 1 dated Mar. 21, 1990	39.13
SB 5749, Rev. 4, dated May 10, 1993	39.13
SB 5751, Rev. 1 dated September 30, 1987	39.13
SB 5753, Rev. 2 dated December 11, 1987	39.13
SB 5805, Rev. No. 6, dated September 15, 1993	39.13
SB 5873, Rev. 1 dated December 20, 1989	39.13
SB 6076, Rev. No. 1, dated August 20, 1992	39.13
SB 6088, dated August 5, 1992	39.13

Material Approved for Incorporation by Reference

Material Approved for Incorporation by Reference

	14 CFR
Alert Service Bulletin JT8D A6336 Revision 1 dated June 29, 1999	39.13
Alert Service Bulletin JT8D A6359 dated August 31, 2001	39.13
Alert Service Bulletin JT8D A6381 dated March 15, 2000	39.13
Alert Service Bulletin JT9D-7R4-A72-563 dated July 28, 1999	39.13
Alert Service Bulletin JT9D-A6367 dated July 28, 1999	39.13
Alert Service Bulletin PW4ENG A72-722 dated September 29, 2000	39.13
Alert Service Bulletin PW4ENG A72-722 Revision 1 dated June 7, 2001.	39.13
Alert Service Bulletin PW4ENG A72-722 Revision 1 dated June 7, 2001.	39.13
Alert Service Bulletin PW4G-100-A71-18 Revision 1 dated December 9, 1999.	39.13
Alert Service Bulletin PW4G-100-A71-18 Revision 2 dated January 15, 2002.	39.13
Alert Service Bulletin PW4G-100-A71-20 dated December 9, 1999	39.13
Alert Service Bulletin PW4G-100-A71-20 Revision 1 dated January 15, 2002.	39.13
Alert Service Bulletin PW4G-100-A71-9 Revision 1 dated November 24, 1997.	39.13
Alert Service Bulletin PW4G-112-A72-233 Revision 3 dated August 3, 2001.	39.13
CIR Manual 51A357, Section 72-35-68, Inspection/Check-04, Indexes 8-11 dated March 15, 2002.	39.13
Clean, Inspection, and Repair Manual 51A357, Section 72-35-68 Inspection/Check 04 dated September 15, 2001.	39.13
Clean, Inspection, and Repair Manual 51A357, Section 72-35-68 Repair 16 dated June 15, 1996.	39.13
Internal Engineering Notice 96KC973D dated October 12, 2001	39.13
Service Bulletin JT9D 6409 dated July 27, 2001	39.13
Service Bulletin 5707 dated September 17, 1986	39.13
Service Bulletin JT8D 6291 Revision 3 dated August 31, 2001	39.13
Service Bulletin JT8D 6291 Revision 4 dated May 30, 2002	39.13
Service Bulletin JT9D-7R4-72-289 dated March 26, 1986	39.13
Service Bulletin JT9D-7R4-72-574 Revision 1 dated June 26, 2001	39.13
Service Bulletin JT9D-7R4-72-574 Revision 2 dated January 21, 2002	39.13
Service Bulletin No. 6100 Revision No. 2 dated December 9, 1998	39.13
Service Bulletin PW4ENG72-714 Revision 1 dated November 8, 2001	39.13
Service Bulletin PW4G-100-71-22 dated January 15, 2002	39.13
Temporary Revision No. 71-0018 dated November 14, 2001	39.13
Temporary Revision No. 71-0026 dated November 14, 2001	39.13
Temporary Revision No. 71-0035 dated November 14, 2001	39.13
Service Bulletin PW4G-112-A72-242 dated May 1, 2001	39.13
SB No. 73-28, Rev. 2, Dated April 15, 1977	39.13
SB No. 73-29, Rev. 1, dated September 1, 1980	39.13
SB No. 73-31, dated September 1, 1979	39.13
SB No. 73-32, Rev. 3, dated April 1, 1985	39.13
SB No. 73-5; dated April 30, 1981	39.13
SB No. 73-8; dated September 1, 1982	39.13

Pratt & Whitney Canada

1000 Marie-Victorin Boulevard East Longueuil Quebec Canada J4G1A1

14 CFR (PARTS 1–59)—Continued
FEDERAL AVIATION ADMINISTRATION, DEPARTMENT OF TRANSPORTATION—
Continued

Material Approved for Incorporation by Reference

	14 CFR
SB 21018R2, Rev. 2 dated November 25, 1991	39.13
SB 21053R2, Rev. 2, dated December 9, 1991	39.13
SB 21077, Rev. 8, dated April 4, 1998	39.13
SB 21088, Rev. 1, dated November 12, 1991	39.13
SB 21097, dated November 8, 1991	39.13
SB 21111, dated December 16, 1991	39.13
SB 21112, dated February 13, 1992	39.13
SB 21113, Rev. 1, dated May 4, 1992	39.13
SB 21364, Rev. 1, dated April 28, 1995	39.13
SB 21373, Rev. 3, dated October 11, 1996	39.13
SB 21516, dated August 14, 1997	39.13
SB 21549, dated September 18, 1997	39.13
SB JT15D 72-7296R3, Rev. 3, dated October 18, 1991	39.13
SB JT15D 72-7297R1, Rev. 1, dated May 25, 1991	39.13
SB JT15D 72-7297R1, Rev. 1, dated May 25, 1991	39.13
SB JT15D 72-7307R2, Rev. 2, dated December 19, 1991	39.13
SB JT15D, Rev. 2, dated December 19, 1991	39.13
SB JT15D, Rev. 3, dated October 18, 1991	39.13
SB No. 12134, Rev. 1, dated December 2, 1996	39.13
SB No. 13287, Rev. 1, dated December 2, 1996	39.13
SB No. 14128, Rev. No. 3, dated April 19, 1993	39.13
SB No. 14132, Rev. No. 1, dated May 12, 1993	39.13
SB No. 14142, Rev. No. 1, dated May 12, 1993	39.13
SB No. 14251, Rev. 1, dated December 2, 1996	39.13
SB No. 1538, Rev. 3, dated December 2, 1996	39.13
SB No. 20914R3, Rev. 3, dated October 15, 1991	39.13
SB No. 20957R5, Rev. 5, dated August 10, 1992	39.13
SB No. 21065R4, Rev. 4, dated February 1, 1993	39.13
SB No. 21088R1, Rev. 1, November 12, 1991	39.13
SB No. 21097, dated November 8, 1991	39.13
SB No. 21111R1, Rev. 1, dated June 22, 1992	39.13
SB No. 21112, dated February 13, 1992	39.13
SB No. 21113R1, Rev. 1, dated May 4, 1992	39.13
SB No. 21211, dated January 28, 1993	39.13
SB No. 3344, Rev. 1, dated December 3, 1996	39.13
SB No. 4143R2, Rev. 2, dated December 6, 1991	39.13
SB No. 4143R2, Rev. 2, dated December 6, 1991	39.13
SB No. 4204, dated December 10, 1996	39.13
SB No. 7257, Rev. No. 2 dated July 2, 1987	39.13
SB No. JT15D-72-7371, dated October 14, 1992	39.13
SB PW100-72--21211, Rev. 4, dated April 20, 1995	39.13
SB PW100-72-21113, Rev. 1, dated May 4, 1992	39.13
SB PW500-72-30044, Rev. 2, dated July 10, 1998	39.13
SB PW500-72-30063, Rev. 2, dated July 10, 1998	39.13
SB SB 20946R2, Rev. 2 dated May 13, 1991	39.13
Service Information Letter PW100-003, dated June 18, 1997	39.13
Service PT 6A-50 Maintenance Manual, Section 79-25-04, pages 207, 208 and 210, dated April 2, 1987.	39.13
Service PT 6A-50 Maintenance Manual, Section 79-25-04, consisting of pages 202A & B, 204 and 209 dated January 26, 1983;.	39.13

14 CFR (PARTS 1–59)—Continued
FEDERAL AVIATION ADMINISTRATION, DEPARTMENT OF TRANSPORTATION—
Continued

	14 CFR
Service PT 6A-50 Maintenance Manual, Section 79-25-04, consisting of pages 202A & B, 204 and 209 dated January 26, 1983;.	39.13
Service PT 6A-50 Maintenance Manual, Section 79-25-04, page 203, dated April 5, 1976;.	39.13
Service PT 6A-50 Maintenance Manual, Section 79-25-04, page 203, dated April 5, 1976;.	39.13
Service PT 6A-50 Maintenance Manual, Section 79-25-04, pages 205 and 206, dated January 15, 1991;.	39.13
Service PT 6A-50 Maintenance Manual, Section 79-25-04, pages 205 and 206, dated January 15, 1991;.	39.13
Service PT 6A-50 Maintenance Manual, Section 79-25-04, pages 207, 208 and 210, dated April 2, 1987.	39.13
Temporary Rev. 72-95 to Maintenance Manual Part No. 3017542 dated Jan. 16, 1991.	39.13
Temporary Rev. 72-96 to Maintenance Manual Part No. 3017542 dated Jan. 16, 1991.	39.13
Service Bulletin PT6A-72-12173 dated January 24, 2002	39.13
Service Bulletin PT6A-72-1574 Revision 2 dated October 14, 1999	39.13
Service Bulletin PT6A-72-1581 Revision 1 dated February 1, 2000	39.13
Service Bulletin PT6A-72-1588 dated February 18, 2000	39.13
Service Bulletin PT6A-72-1589 dated November 1, 2000	39.13
Service Bulletin PT6A-72-1610 Revision 2 dated October 1, 2002	39.13

Precise Flight, Inc
63120 Powell Butte Road, Bend, OR 97701

Instructions for Continued Airworthiness, Section 3.3 of Installation Report No. 50050, Revision 25, dated August 26, 1996.	39.13
SB No. PL9303001, dated March 10, 1993	39.13

Precision Airmotive Corp
3220 100th Street, SW., Bldg. E, Everett, WA 98204

SB No. A1-78, dated September, 1978 and Precision Airmotive Corp. SB No. MSA-6, dated April 6, 1994.	39.13
SB No. MSA-2, dated November 11, 1991	39.13
SB No. MSA-2, Rev. 1, dated November 11, 1991	39.13
SB No. MSA-2, Rev. 2, dated December 28, 1993	39.13
SB No. MSA-2, Rev. 3, dated October 10, 1995	39.13
SB No. MSA-7, dated September 30, 1994	39.13
SB No. MSA-8, dated July 10, 1995	39.13
SB No. MSA-9, dated October 10, 1995	39.13

PTC Aerospace
607 Bantam Road, Litchfield, CT 6759

SB 25-1192, Rev. A, dated March 16, 1992	39.13
SB 25-1330, dated July 27, 1994	39.13
SB No. 25-1233, Rev. E, dated April 15, 1994	39.13

PTI Technologies, Inc.(Purolator)
950 Rancho Conejo Boulevard, Newbury Park, CA 91320

SB FSC-912, dated December 1972	39.13

Puritan Bennett Aero Systems Company
108000 Pfluum Road, Lenexa, KS 66215

SB C351-2000-35-1, Revision 2, dated February 1998.	39.13

Material Approved for Incorporation by Reference

FEDERAL AVIATION ADMINISTRATION, DEPARTMENT OF TRANSPORTATION— Continued

	14 CFR
Kit No. 280041-00: Lanyard Retrofit Drop Out Box, Revision A01, dated October 21, 1998.	39.13
SB 174250-35-1, dated August 1994	39.13
PZL-Mielec	
Ludowego Wojska Polkiego 3, 39-300, Mielec, Poland	
Mandatory Engineering Bulletin K/02.141/90 dated Apr. 1990	39.13
PZL-RZESZOW (Wytwornia Sprzetu komunikacyjnego)	
PZL Warzawa-Okecie, AL. Krakowska 110/110, 00-973 Warsaw Po-land	
Mandatory Service Bulletin 10400030 dated June 26, 2000	39.13
Engine Servicing Instructions, section 3.3.5, page 3-11 dated February 1984,.	39.13
Engine Servicing Instructions, section 3.3.5, pages 3-12 and 3-13 dated March 1984.	39.13
Raytheon Aircraft Company	
Customer Support Dept., Adams Field, P.O. Box 3356 Little Rock, AR 72203; or 3 Bishops Square, St. Albans Road West, Hatfield, Hertfordshire, AL109NE, United Kingdom	
Update Procedures for the ET EM630 Blower Installation Instructions to Raytheon Kit No. EM630-201-1 or as referenced in Raytheon SB No. 2721.	39.13
Service Bulletin 1FA10043-0001, dated October 1997.	39.13
SB 24-317, dated December 22, 1994	39.13
SB 27-161, Rev. 1, dated July 29, 1994	39.13
SB.27-168, dated July 17, 1995	39.13
SB.29-95, dated March 24, 1995	39.13
SB.30-61-7676A, dated February 15, 1995	39.13
SB.49-45, dated May 15, 1995	39.13
SB.49-47-25A825A, dated August 1, 1995	39.13
SB.53-82-3566G, Rev. 3, dated December 14, 1995	39.13
SB.53-85-3566D, dated March 10, 1995	39.13
SB.53-85-3566D, Rev. 1, dated May 23, 1995	39.13
SB.78-14-3691A,B & E, dated June 21, 1995	39.13
SB.53-76-3627A, dated February 25, 1994	39.13
SB.53-81-3661B, dated February 25, 1994	39.13
SB.24-310-3544A & B, dated February 14, 1994	39.13
SB.25-75-25A699A, dated February 10, 1994	39.13
SB.25-75-25A699A, dated February 10, 1994	39.13
SB.25-76-25A698A & B, dated February 10, 1994	39.13
SB 24-313, dated December 19, 1994	39.13
SB 49-3018, dated August 1997	39.13
SB No. 2522, Rev. 1, dated May 1996	39.13
SB No. 2691, Rev. 1, dated October, 1996	39.13
SB No. SB 21-151-25A683C, dated July 12, 1994	39.13
SB No. SB.52-48, including Appendix A, dated June 19, 1996	39.13
SB.32-233, Rev. 1, dated July 8, 1994	39.13
SB.32-233, Rev. 2, dated July 28, 1995	39.13
SB.32-233-3597A, dated July 28, 1995	39.13
SB.54-1-3815B, dated March 26, 1996	39.13
SB.55-36-25F017A & B, dated April 15, 1996	39.13

Title 14—Aeronautics and Space

Material Approved for Incorporation by Reference

	14 CFR
Mandatory Service Bulletin SB 35-3233, dated December 1998.	39.13
Mandatory Service Bulletin SB 53-3341 Revision 1 dated May 2000	39.13
Mandatory Service Bulletin SB 53-3341 Revision 2 October, 2002	39.13
Mandatory Service Bulletin SB 53-3375 dated December 1999	39.13
Mandatory Service Bulletin SB 54-3308 dated October 2000	39.13
Mandatory Service Bulletin SB 57-3329 dated February 2000	39.13
Mandatory Service Bulletin SB.28-3104, dated September 1997.	39.13
Mandatory Service Bulletin SB27-3265 dated January 2000	39.13
Mandatory Service Bulletin SB34-3267 dated March 1999	39.13
Mandatory Service Bulletin SB34-3268 dated April 2000	39.13
Mandatory Service Bulletin SB34-3269 dated January 2000	39.13
Mandatory Service Bulletin SB34-3269 Revision 1 dated October 2000	39.13
MSB No. 2718, Rev. 1, dated June 1997	39.13
MSB 1900D No. 2643, dated August 1996	39.13
MSB 2714, dated June 1997	39.13
MSB No. 2728, dated June 1997,	39.13
MSB No. 2728, Rev. 1, dated February 1998	39.13
MSB No. 2741, Rev. 1, dated May 1997	39.13
Recommended Service Bulletin SB 23-3094 dated November 1999	39.13
Recommended Service Bulletin SB 32-3116 dated October 1999	39.13
Safety Communique No. 137, dated May, 1997	39.13
Safety Communique No. 137, Revision 1, dated December 1997;	39.13
Safety Communique No. 158, dated March 1999;	39.13
Safety Communique No. 189 Revision 1 dated January 2002	39.13
Safety Communique No. 1900-128, dated October 25, 1996	39.13
SB 2476, Rev. II, dated June 1997	39.13
SB 26-3250 Revision 1 dated July 1999	39.13
SB 49-44, dated January 20, 1995	39.13
SB.26-3197, dated April 1998	39.13
SB.34-3028, dated January 1998.	39.13
Service Bulletin 32-3391 dated August 2000	39.13
Service Bulletin 51-3336 Revision 1 dated January 2001	39.13
Service Bulletin SB 21-3108 dated November 1998	39.13
Service Bulletin SB 21-3377- Revision 1 dated July 2000	39.13
Service Bulletin SB 21-3414 Revision 1 dated July 2000	39.13
Service Bulletin SB 24-3201, dated October 1998.	39.13
Service Bulletin SB 24-3212 dated August 1999	39.13
Service Bulletin SB 24-3213 Revision 1 dated February 2000	39.13
Service Bulletin SB 27-3358 dated February 2000	39.13
Service Bulletin SB 30-3008 Revision 1 dated August 1999	39.13
Service Bulletin SB 32-3274 dated August 1999	39.13
Service Bulletin SB 32-3300 dated December 1999	39.13
Service Bulletin SB 32-3386 dated June 2000	39.13
Service Bulletin SB 34-3207 dated August 1999	39.13
Service Bulletin SB 34-3223 dated August 1999	39.13
Service Bulletin SB 34-3282 dated August 1999	39.13
Service Bulletin SB 35-3034 dated September 1998	39.13
Service Bulletin SB 35-3168 dated September 1998	39.13
Service Bulletin SB 35-3171 dated September 1998	39.13
Service Bulletin SB 53-93 Revision 2 dated April 2000	39.13

Title 14—Aeronautics and Space

Material Approved for Incorporation by Reference

14 CFR

Relative Workshop
 1645 N. Lexington Avenue, DeLand, FL 32724
Product Service Bulletin No. 091098-B, dated September 10, 1998. 39.13

REVO, Inc.
 PO Box 312 One High Street Sanford Maine 04073
B-79 R1 Revised January 5, 2000 .... 39.13
SB B-78, dated April 3, 1998 .... 39.13

Rigging Innovations, Inc.
 236-C East 3rd Street, Perris, CA 92570
SB 1513, Rev. A, dated June 22, 1992 .... 39.13

Robinson Helicopter Co.
 24747 Crenshaw Blvd., Torrance, CA 90505
KI-112 R44 Pilot's Grip Assembly Upgrade Kit instructions, dated 39.13
 December 20, 1996.
KI-114 O-360 Engine Carburetor Change Kit Instructions, Rev. A, 39.13
R22 SB No. 74, dated July 18, 1994 .... 39.13
R22 SB SB-77, dated April 25, 1995 .... 39.13
R22 SB SB-82, dated March 3, 1997 .... 39.13
R44 SB SB-21, dated April 18, 1997 .... 39.13
R44 SB SB-23, dated May 30, 1997 .... 39.13
R44 SB SB-26, dated January 31, 1998 .... 39.13
R44 Service Bulletin SB-35, dated July 26, 1999. .... 39.13
SB-4, dated January 24, 1995 .... 39.13

Rocket Engineering Corp.
 East 6247 Rutter Road, Felts Field, Spokane, WA 99212
Mandatory SB MSB95-305-1, dated August 9, 1995 .... 39.13
Alert Service Bulletin ASB CF6-80A3-NAC-A71-061 Revision 1 dated 39.13
 February 22, 2000.
Alert Service Bulletin ASB CF6-80A3-NAC-A71-064 dated April 4, 39.13
 2000.
ASB CF6-80A3-NAC-A71-060, dated January 30, 1998 .... 39.13
Service Bulletin RA34078-47, Revision 1, dated November 30, 1996. 39.13
Service Bulletin TBC-CNS 78-32 Revision 1 dated August 20, 1996 39.13
Service Bulletin TBC-CNS 78-33 Revision 1 dated August 20, 1996 39.13

Rockwell Collins
 Business and Regional Systems 400 Collins Road Northeast Cedar
 Rapids Iowa 52498
Air Transport Systems Overhaul Manual with Illustrated Parts List 39.13
 Temporary Revision No. 34-44-00-38 dated April 20, 2000.
Service Bulletin 12 (AFD-3010-31-12) Revision 2 dated August 30, 39.13
 2002.
Service Bulletin 33 (CTL-92-34-33) dated April 5, 2001 .... 39.13
Service Bulletin 621A-3-34-21 Revision 1 dated November 14, 1975 39.13
Service Bulletin No. 17 (TDR-94/94D-34-17) dated February 8, 1999 39.13
Service Bulletin No. 17 (TDR-94/94D-34-17) Revision 1 dated May 39.13
 15, 2000.
Service Bulletin No. 20 (TDR-94/94D-34-20) Revision 1 dated May 39.13
 2, 2001.
Service Bulletin No. 62, ADC-85/85A/850C/850D/850E/850F-34-62 39.13
 Revision 2 dated March 7, 2000.

Title 14—Aeronautics and Space

Material Approved for Incorporation by Reference

	14 CFR
Mandatory SB R.B. 211-73-B869, Rev. 1, dated May 24, 1996	39.13
Mandatory Service Bulletin No. RB.211-78-C931 Revision 1 dated June 13, 2000.	39.13
Mandatory Service Bulletin RB.211-72-C329 Revision 1 dated November 6, 1998.	39.13
Mandatory Service Bulletin RB.211-72-C491 Revision 1 dated October 8, 1999.	39.13
Mandatory Service Bulletin RB.211-72-C817 Revision 1 dated January 24, 2000.	39.13
Mandatory Service Bulletin RB.211-72-C817 Revision 2 dated March 7, 2001.	39.13
Mandatory Service Bulletin RB.211-72-C818 Revision 2 dated October 8, 1999.	39.13
Mandatory Service Bulletin RB.211-72-C877 dated January 29, 2000	39.13
Mandatory Service Bulletin RB.211-72-C877 Revision 1 dated March 7, 2001.	39.13
R.B. 211-73-8457, Rev. 1 dated August 7, 1987	39.13
RB.211-72-9764 Revision 3 dated January 16, 1998	39.13
RB.211-72-C878 Revision 1 dated December 10, 1999	39.13
RB.211-78-B115, Rev. 1, dated March 14, 1997	39.13
RB.211-78-C955 Revision 1 dated June 20, 2000	39.13
SB No. R.B. 211-72-9672, Rev. 1, dated November 6, 1992	39.13
SB No. Sp72-1034, Rev. 1, dated May, 1990	39.13
SB No. Sp72-1044, dated September 1992	39.13
SB OL.593-72-8951-364, Rev. 5, dated August 31, 1995	39.13
SB OL.593-72-9016-416, Rev. 1, dated December 5, 1997	39.13
SB OL.593-72-9038-417, dated June 26, 1996	39.13
SB OL.593-72-9042-422, Rev. 1, dated May 23, 1997	39.13
SB OL.593-72-9047-423, dated January 31, 1997	39.13
SB OL.593-72-9048-424, dated April 25, 1997	39.13
SB OL.593-76-9039-71, Rev. 2, dated July 23, 1997	39.13
SB R.B. 211-72-4666, Rev. 4, dated May 16, 1986	39.13
SB R.B. 211-72-4666, Supplement Page 1, dated October 14, 1977	39.13
SB R.B. 211-72-4666, Supplement Page 2, dated August 26, 1977	39.13
SB R.B. 211-72-5787, including the Supplement dated March 20, 1981,.	39.13
SB R.B. 211-72-8301, Rev. 2 dated March 27, 1987	39.13
SB R.B. 211-72-8301, Rev. 5 dated May 13, 1988	39.13
SB R.B. 211-72-9594, Rev. 5, dated February 12, 1993	39.13
SB R.B. 211-72-9764, Rev. 2, dated November 10, 1995	39.13
SB R.B. 211-72-B482, Rev. 3, dated September 27, 1996	39.13
SB R.B. 211-72-C089, Rev. 1, dated January 24, 1997	39.13
SB R.B. 211-72-C114, including Supplement dated February 6, 1997	39.13
SB R.B. 211-72-C129, Rev. 2, dated March 21, 1997	39.13
SB R.B. 211-73-8195 dated May 2, 1986	39.13
SB R.B. 211-73-8438, Rev. 1 dated July 31, 1987	39.13
SB R.B. 211-73-8502 dated August 28, 1987	39.13
SB R.B. 211-73-8534 dated September 18, 1987	39.13
SB R.B. 211-73-B048, Rev. 1 including Supplement 1, dated July 22, 1994.	39.13
SB R.B. 211-78-9822, dated October 1, 1993	39.13

Title 14—Aeronautics and Space

Material Approved for Incorporation by Reference

14 CFR (PARTS 1–59)—Continued
FEDERAL AVIATION ADMINISTRATION, DEPARTMENT OF TRANSPORTATION—
Continued

	14 CFR
Mandatory Service Bulletin TAY-72-1447 Revision 2 dated July 25, 2000.	39.13
Service Bulletin No. RB.211-72-C878 Revision 4 dated January 22, 2001.	39.13
Service Bulletin RB. 211-72-D344, including Appendices 1 through 5 Revision 4 dated March 15, 2002.	39.13

Rolls-Royce Corporation
P.O. Box 420 Indianapolis Indiana 46206-0420

Alert Service Bulletin AE 2100A-A-72-234 Revision 2 dated October 13, 2000.	39.13
Alert Service Bulletin AE 2100A-A-72-234 Revision 3 dated June 19, 2001.	39.13
Alert Service Bulletin AE 2100C-A-72-183 Revision 2 dated October 13, 2000.	39.13
Alert Service Bulletin AE 2100C-A-72-183 Revision 3 dated June 19, 2001.	39.13
Alert Service Bulletin AE 2100D3-A-72-179 Revision 2 dated October 13, 2000.	39.13
Alert Service Bulletin AE 2100D3-A-72-179 Revision 3 dated June 19, 2001.	39.13
Alert Service Bulletin AE 3007A-A-72-179 Revision 2 dated October 17, 2000.	39.13
Alert Service Bulletin AE 3007A-A-72-179 Revision 3 dated June 19, 2001.	39.13
Alert Service Bulletin AE 3007C-A-72-153 Revision 2 dated October 17, 2000.	39.13
Alert Service Bulletin AE 3007C-A-72-153 Revision 3 dated June 19, 2001.	39.13

Rolls-Royce Defence (Europe) Technical Publications Department
P.O. Box 3 Filton Bristol BS34 7QE England Telephone 011 44 7979 6060

Service Bulletin OL.593-71-9056-33 Revision 2 dated December 7, 2000.	39.13
Mandatory Service Bulletin OL.593-72-8951-364 Revision 7 dated November 23, 2001.	39.13
Mandatory Service Bulletin OL.593-73-9075-103 dated November 17, 2000.	39.13
Mandatory Service Bulletin OL.593-73-9093-109 Revision 1 dated November 23, 2001.	39.13

Rolls-Royce Deutschland GmbH
Eschenweg 11 D-15827 DAHLEWITZ Germany Phone: International Access Code 011, Country Code 49(0), 33 7086- 1768 Fax: International Access Code 011, Country Code 49, 33 7086- 3276

SB-BR700-72-900229 Revision 2 dated November 23, 2000	39.13
Service Bulletin TAY-73-1540 Revision 1 dated September 13, 2002	39.13

Rolls-Royce Ltd., Dart Service
East Kilbride, Glasgow, G74 4PY Scotland

SB No. Da72-423, Part 2, Rev. 16 dated July 13, 1984	39.13
SB No. Da72-470, Rev. 1 dated March 30, 1984	39.13
SB No. Da72-480, Rev. 4 dated December 1984	39.13
SB No. Da72-485 dated July 2, 1984	39.13
SB No. Da72-A488, Rev. 1 dated October 18, 1984	39.13

Material Approved for Incorporation by Reference

14 CFR (PARTS 1–59)—Continued
FEDERAL AVIATION ADMINISTRATION, DEPARTMENT OF TRANSPORTATION—
Continued

	14 CFR
SB 2000-57-010, dated February 25, 1997	39.13
SB 2000-57-014, Rev. 02, dated February 11, 1997	39.13
SB 2000-A25-022, Rev. 1, dated January 23, 1996	39.13
SB 340-25-181 dated March 7, 1991	39.13
SB 340-25-235, dated December 11, 1996	39.13
SB 340-25-244, dated June 13, 1997	39.13
SB 340-26-012, Rev. 1, dated October 5, 1993	39.13
SB 340-26-015, Rev. 1, dated December 8, 1995	39.13
SB 340-26-016, dated November 9, 1995	39.13
SB 340-27-079, dated December 22, 1995	39.13
SB 340-28-013 dated March 14, 1991	39.13
SB 340-30-073, dated August 18, 1997	39.13
SB 340-30-080, dated November 21, 1997	39.13
SB 340-30-081, dated November 14, 1997, including Attachment 1,Rev. 1, dated September 14, 1997.	39.13
SB 340-32-066, Rev. 1 dated Oct. 17, 1990 including Attachments 1 through 8 dated Jan. 1990 and Attachment 6, Rev. 1 dated Aug..	39.13
SB 340-32-094, dated October 29, 1993	39.13
SB 340-32-094, Rev. 1, dated March 4, 1994	39.13
SB 340-32-100, Rev. 02, dated March 25, 1996	39.13
SB 340-32-105, dated September 5, 1995	39.13
SB 340-32-107, dated January 18, 1996	39.13
SB 340-32-114, dated May 4, 1998	39.13
SB 340-32-115, dated April 7, 1998	39.13
SB 340-32-115, Rev. 01, dated August 12, 1998	39.13
SB 340-33-030, Rev. 2 dated Sept. 27, 1991	39.13
SB 340-33-040, Rev. 2, dated February 20, 1997	39.13
SB 340-33-047, dated May 16, 1997	39.13
SB 340-34-068 dated Nov. 9, 1990	39.13
SB 340-51-012, dated November 10, 1993	39.13
SB 340-52-013, Rev. 1 dated Dec. 18, 1990	39.13
SB 340-52-014 dated April 16, 1991	39.13
SB 340-53-028, dated August 20, 1992	39.13
SB 340-53-047, dated December 14, 1994	39.13
SB 340-54-027, Rev. 2 dated March 10, 1992	39.13
SB 340-55-032, dated May 22, 1995	39.13
SB 340-57-020, Rev. 1 dated April 3, 1992	39.13
SB 340-71-035, Rev. 1 dated Dec. 18, 1990	39.13
SB 340-76-031, Rev. 04, dated February 25, 1996	39.13
SB 340-76-032, Rev. 03, dated March 25, 1996	39.13
SB 340-76-032, Rev. 2, dated December 8, 1995	39.13
SB 340-76-032, Rev. 3, dated March 25, 1996	39.13
SB 340-76-033, dated March 31, 1994	39.13
SB 340-76-034, dated January 4, 1995	39.13
SB 340-76-038, dated December 8, 1995	39.13
SB 340-76-041, dated May 29, 1997, including	39.13
SB 340-76-041, Rev. 1, dated July 2, 1997	39.13
SB SAAB 340-28-016, dated October 21, 1992	39.13
SB SAAB 340-57-027, Rev. 01, dated June 30, 1995	39.13

Title 14—Aeronautics and Space

14 CFR (PARTS 1–59)—Continued
FEDERAL AVIATION ADMINISTRATION, DEPARTMENT OF TRANSPORTATION—Continued

Material Approved for Incorporation by Reference

Title 14—Aeronautics and Space

Material Approved for Incorporation by Reference

14 CFR (PARTS 1–59)—Continued
FEDERAL AVIATION ADMINISTRATION, DEPARTMENT OF TRANSPORTATION—
Continued

	14 CFR
SB SD3-53-41, Original dated May 21, 1980	39.13
SB SD3-53-48, Rev. 1 dated Jan. 5, 1983	39.13
SB SD3-55-16, Rev. 3 dated Nov. 1987	39.13
SB SD3-57-10, Rev. 1 dated Oct. 11, 1982	39.13
SB SD3-60 SHERPA-35-1, dated April 8, 1997	39.13
SB SD3-76-01, Original dated Sept. 8, 1981	39.13
SB SD330-55-19, dated February 11, 1997	39.13
SB SD360-24-18, Rev. 3 dated Nov. 29, 1990	39.13
SB SD360-33-23, dated June 1, 1992	39.13
SB SD360-55-17 dated May 7, 1991	39.13
Service Bulletin SD3-60 SHERPA-53-3, dated November 4, 1997.	39.13
Service Bulletin SD360-53-42, dated September 1996;	39.13
SB SD 330-53-66, dated July 1993	39.13
SB SD3 SHERPA 27-2, dated January 14, 1997	39.13
SB SD3 SHERPA 53-2, dated July 1993	39.13
SB SD3 SHERPA-24-1, dated May 1992	39.13
SB SD3 SHERPA-27-1, dated September 12, 1995	39.13
SB SD3 SHERPA-32-2, dated September 22, 1995	39.13
SB SD3 SHERPA-33-1, includes Attachment to SB Drawing SD3 SHERPA-33-1/A dated January 17, 1993.	39.13
SB SD3 SHERPA-53-1, Rev. 1, dated May 1993	39.13
SB SD3-27-36, dated January 14, 1997	39.13
SB SD3-57-10, Rev. 2 dated January 4, 1993	39.13
SB SD3-60 SHERPA-53-2, dated November 4, 1997	39.13
SB SD3-SHERPA-53-1, dated March 29, 1993	39.13
SB SD330-24-25, Rev. 2 dated Nov. 29, 1990	39.13
SB SD330-27-34, dated September 12, 1995	39.13
SB SD330-28-35, dated February 22, 1991	39.13
SB SD330-32-90, Rev. 2, dated June 29, 1992	39.13
SB SD330-53-65, dated March 29, 1993	39.13
SB SD330-53-65, Revison 1, dated May 1993	39.13
SB SD330-55-18, dated April 20, 1995	39.13
SB SD360 SHERPA 27-1, dated January 14, 1997	39.13
SB SD360-27-23, Rev. 1, dated April 15, 1994	39.13
SB SD360-27-24, dated September 12, 1995	39.13
SB SD360-27-26, dated January 14, 1997	39.13
SB SD360-28-20, dated February 22, 1991	39.13
SB SD360-32-33, dated August 7, 1992	39.13
SB SD360-32-34, dated September 22, 1995	39.13
SB SD360-39-04, Rev. 1, dated January 12, 1998	39.13
SB SD360-53-38, dated March 25, 1993	39.13
SB SD360-53-38, Rev. 1, dated May 1993	39.13
SB SD360-53-39, dated June 11, 1993	39.13
SB SD360-55-12, Rev. 2, dated November 1986	39.13
SB SD360-55-16, Original, dated April 1988	39.13
SB SD360-55-19, dated January 18, 1993	39.13
SD3 SHERPA SB SD3 SHERPA-55-1, dated April 20, 1995	39.13
SD3-30 SB SD3-32-90, Rev. 2, dated June 29, 1992	39.13
Service Bulletin SD3 SHERPA 27-2, dated January 14, 1997	39.13

Title 14—Aeronautics and Space

Material Approved for Incorporation by Reference

FEDERAL AVIATION ADMINISTRATION, DEPARTMENT OF TRANSPORTATION— Continued

	14 CFR
Alert SB 58B35-32, dated July 6, 1993	39.13
Alert SB 61B15-29A, Rev. A, dated May 9, 1997	39.13
Alert SB 76-65-35A, Rev. A, dated February 29, 1984	39.13
Alert SB No. 58B35-31A, Rev. A, dated February 17, 1993	39.13
Alert SB No. 64B10-4A dated July 17, 1985	39.13
Alert SB No. 64B15-8A dated October 16, 1984	39.13
Alert SB No. 76-24-8 dated January 30, 1987	39.13
Alert SB No. 76-34-6A (287A), Rev. A, dated September 12, 1996	39.13
Alert SB No. 76-52-10A, Rev. A dated August 27, 1987	39.13
Alert SB No. 76-66-20 dated July 25, 1985	39.13
Alert SB No. 76-71-7 dated 11/7/84	39.13
Alert SB, No. 61B10-48 dated Jan. 18, 1991	39.13
Alert Service Bulletin 61B20-33 dated September 3, 1999	39.13
Alert Service Bulletin 61B20-33 dated September 3, 1999	39.13
Alert Service Bulletin 76-55-16, dated May 12, 1999.	39.13
Alert Service Bulletin 76-65-35B (153B) Revision B dated October 2, 1997.	39.13
Alert Service Bulletin 76-65-50 dated May 25, 2000	39.13
Alert Service Bulletin 76-66-31 (318B) Revision B dated November 7, 2000.	39.13
Alert Service Bulletin 76-66-32A Revision A dated January 17, 2001	39.13
Composite Materials Manual paragraphs 7 & 7-A dated 1/15/82, ...	39.13
Customer Service Notice No. 76-141B (133B) dated January 15, 1985	39.13
No. CST-P-83-171 Rev. 2 dated 12/5/83	39.13
SB No. 61B15-20E	39.13
SB No. 61B15-6P	39.13
SB No. 61 B10-14 dated 12/5/83	39.13
Alert Service Bulletin 76-65-55A dated July 25, 2002	39.13
Alert Service Bulletin No. 76-34-7A (320A) Revision A dated September 17, 2001.	39.13

Slingsby Engineering Ltd.
Ings Lane, Kirbymoorside, York Y066EZ, England

Technical Instruction No. 104/T65, Issue 1 dated 9/22/82	39.13
Technical Instruction No. 100/T53 dated October 20, 1981	39.13
Technical Instruction No. 68 dated August 14, 1974	39.13
Technical Instruction No. 70 dated September 11, 1974	39.13

Socata Groupe AEROSPATIALE
Socata Product Support, Aerodrome Tarbes-Ossun-Lourdes, B P 930-F65009, Tarbes Cedex, France; Telephone 62.41.74.26; FAX: 62.41.74.32; or the Product Support Manager, U.S. AEROSPATIALE, Socata Aircraft, North Perry Airport, 7501 Pembroke Road, Pembroke Pines, Florida 33023.

Alert Service Bulletin SB 70-077-55, dated February 1999.	39.13
Mandatory Service Bulletin SB 155-27 dated April 2000	39.13
Mandatory Service Bulletin SB 155-27 dated April 2000	39.13
Mandatory Service Bulletin SB 70-087 57 Amendment 1 dated November 2000.	39.13
MSB 10-085, Amendment 2, dated April 1996	39.13
MSB 70-046-35, dated May 1998	39.13
SB 10-080 57, Amendment 2, dated November 1995	39.13
SB 10-081-57, Amendment 1, dated August 1996	39.13

Title 14—Aeronautics and Space

Material Approved for Incorporation by Reference

14 CFR (PARTS 1–59)—Continued
FEDERAL AVIATION ADMINISTRATION, DEPARTMENT OF TRANSPORTATION—
Continued

	14 CFR
Installation Instruction No. A34-10-017-E, Amendment-Index 01.a, dated August 10, 1998, as referenced in Stemme SB No. A31-10-017, Amendment-Index 02.a, dated May 20, 1998.	39.13
Procedural Instruction A17-10AP-V/2-E, Amendment-Index:01.a dated August 24, 1999.	39.13
SB A31-10-018, dated June 3, 1994	39.13
SB A31-10-021, dated June 28, 1995	39.13
SB A31-10-022, dated August 16, 1996	39.13
SB A31-10-032, Amendment-Index 02.a, dated July 10, 1998	39.13
Service Bulletin A31-10-051, Amendment-Index: 05.a dated December 6, 1999.	39.13
Service Bulletin A31-10-055 dated October 9, 2000	39.13
Service Bulletin A31-10-057 dated June 7, 2001	39.13
Service Bulletin A31-10-061 dated April 22, 2002	39.13
Technical Bulletin A31-10-003, dated February 7, 1992	39.13
SB A31-10-020, Am-index: 02.a, pages 3 and 4, dated October 7, 1996.	39.13
Service Bulletin No. A31-10-034, Amendment 01.a, Pages 3 and 4, dated July 24, 1998..	39.13

Superior Air Parts, Inc.
14280 Gillis Rd., Dallas, TX 75244-3792; Telephone (800) 487-4884, fax(214) 490-8471.

MSB 96-001, dated August 5, 1996	39.13
Mandatory SB 96-002, Rev. A, dated December 17, 1996	39.13
SB No. T95-SB001, Rev. A, dated September 29, 1995	39.13
SB No. T95-SB002, Rev. A, dated September 29, 1995	39.13

Switlik Parachute Co., Inc.
1325 East State Street, P.O. Box 1328, Trenton, NJ 8607

SB No. 25-00-19 dated September 8, 1987	39.13

Teledyne Continental Motors, Aircraft Products Division
P.O. Box 90, Mobile, Alabama 36601

LTS101B-72-50-0116 Rev. 6 dated August 14, 1992	39.13
LTS101B-72-50-0119 Rev. 2 dated June 17, 1991	39.13
LTS101B-72-50-0127 Rev. 2 dated August 14, 1992	39.13
LTS101B-72-50-0129 Rev. 3 dated August 14, 1992	39.13
M91-10, Rev. 1, dated November 27, 1991	39.13
Continental Motors Critical SB 99-6A, dated July 21, 1999	39.13
Continental Motors Mandatory SB 99-3C, dated July 27, 1999	39.13
Critical SB 93-13, dated August 12, 1993	39.13
Critical SB CSB641, dated February 1, 1994	39.13
Critical SB CSB96-8, dated June 25, 1996	39.13
Critical SB CSB97-10A, dated July 15, 1997	39.13
Mandatory SB M93-9, Rev. 1, dated March 10, 1993	39.13
Mandatory SB M85-3 dated February 4, 1985	39.13
Mandatory SB M87-26 dated December 21, 1987	39.13
Mandatory SB MSB96-10, dated August 15, 1996	39.13
Mandatory SB No. 93-12, dated May 12, 1993	39.13
Mandatory SB No. MSB645, dated April 4, 1994; and TCM SB No. 639, dated March, 1993.	39.13
Mandatory SB No. MSB94-9, dated October 21, 1994	39.13

Title 14—Aeronautics and Space

Material Approved for Incorporation by Reference

	14 CFR
SB No. 385C, dated October 3, 1975, with Supplement No. 1, dated March 18, 1977.	39.13
SB No. 454B, dated January 2, 1987	39.13
SB No. 455D, dated January 2, 1987	39.13
Service Letter 047 dated October 10, 1986	39.13
Alert SB No. A-ALF-502R 73-12, Rev. 1, dated April 7, 1992	39.13
Alert SB No. A-LT101-72-50-0163, Rev. 1, dated	39.13
CSL 063 R-1, Rev. 1 dated May 31, 1991	39.13
LTS101B-72-50-0116, Rev. 6, dated August 14, 1992	39.13
LTS101B-73-10-0127, Rev. 2, dated August 14, 1992	39.13
LTS101C-72-50- 0119, Rev. 2, dated June 17, 1991	39.13
LTS101C-73-10-0129, Rev. 3, dated August 14, 1992	39.13
Mandatory SB 525A, dated October 7, 1996	39.13
Mandatory SB No. 527C, dated April 18, 1997, including Attachments I and II, dated April 18, 1997.	39.13
Mandatory Service Bulletin No. 342D dated July 10, 2001	39.13
Mandatory Service Bulletin No. 543A Revision A August 30, 2000	39.13
Mandatory Service Bulletin No. 543A, Supplement No. 1 October 4, 2000.	39.13
MSB 505B, dated December 1, 1997	39.13
MSB 530, dated December 1, 1997	39.13
SB 475, Rev. A dated July 16, 1990	39.13
SB 484 dated Jan. 30, 1989	39.13
SB 499A dated June 14, 1991	39.13
SB 529, dated December 1, 1997	39.13
SB ALF502 72-0002, Rev. 22, dated December 23, 1992	39.13
SB ALF502 72-0004, Rev. 11, dated June 17, 1987	39.13
SB ALF502L 72-259, dated August 13, 1993	39.13
SB ALF502L 72-259, dated August 13, 1993	39.13
SB ALF502L 72-270, dated April 30, 1993	39.13
SB ALF502R 72-259 dated August 13, 1993	39.13
SB ALF502R 72-259 dated August 13, 1993	39.13
SB ALF502R 72-270, Rev. 1, dated March 31, 1992	39.13
SB LT 101-72-00-0093, Rev. 5 dated Jan. 15, 1990	39.13
SB LT101-72-50-0144, dated January 15, 1993	39.13
SB LT101-72-50-0145, dated November 27, 1991	39.13
SB LT101-72-50-0150, dated September 1, 1993	39.13
SB LTS 101C-72-00-0131 dated Sep. 17, 1990	39.13
SB LTS101B-72-50-0122, Rev. 4 dated June 17, 1991	39.13
SB No. 342A, dated May 26, 1992	39.13
SB No. 456F, dated February 8, 1993	39.13
SB No. 501, Rev. B (501B) dated Nov. 15, 1991	39.13
SB No. 524 (including Attachment), dated September 1, 1995	39.13
SB No. LT 101-72-00-0093, Rev. 2 dated May 12, 1987	39.13
SB No. LT 101-72-00-0093, Rev. 3 dated May 29, 1987	39.13
SB No. LT 101-72-30-0088, Rev. 5, dated September 25, 1992	39.13
SB No. LT 101-72-40-0103 dated January 15, 1988	39.13
SB No. LT 101-77-30-0104, Rev. 1 dated March 18, 1988	39.13
SB No. T5313B/17-0020, Rev. 4, dated July 5, 1994	39.13
SB No. T5313B/17-0052, Rev. 2, dated December 16, 1993	39.13

Title 14—Aeronautics and Space

Material Approved for Incorporation by Reference

14 CFR (PARTS 1–59)—Continued
FEDERAL AVIATION ADMINISTRATION, DEPARTMENT OF TRANSPORTATION—
Continued

14 CFR

Mandatory Service Bulletin A292-72-0207 Revision 2 dated October 23, 2000.	39.13
Service Bulletin 218 80 0093 Revision 2 dated January 14, 1999	39.13
Service Bulletin 218 80 0098 dated January 14, 1999	39.13
Service Bulletin 223 72 0070 dated January 21, 1999	39.13
Service Bulletin No. 292 73 2803 dated July 2, 1999	39.13
Service Bulletin No. 298 73 0166 dated October 5, 2001	39.13
Alert Service Bulletin A218 72 0099 Revision 1 dated June 6, 2001	39.13
Alert Service Bulletin A218 72 0100 Revision 1 dated March 13, 2001.	39.13

Twin Commander Aircraft Corp
19010 59th Dr. NE, Arlington, Washington, 98223-7832; Telephone: (360) 435-9797 FAX: (360) 435-1112

MSB 226, dated April 14, 1997	39.13
MSB 226, Rev. 1, dated July 15, 1997	39.13
SB 218, dated May 19, 1994,	39.13
SB 218, Rev. Notice 1 dated July 11, 1994,	39.13
SB 218, Rev. Notice 2, dated September 23, 1994	39.13
SB 223, dated October 24, 1996,	39.13
SB 223, Rev. 2, dated August 18, 1997	39.13
SB 223, Rev. Notice 1, dated May 8, 1997	39.13
SB 224, Rev. A, dated April 24, 1996	39.13
SB 224, Rev. C, dated July 25, 1996	39.13
SB No. 213, dated July 29, 1994	39.13

U.S. Government Printing Office
Superintendent of Documents, P.O. Box 371954 Pittsburgh PA 15250-7954 Phone: 1-866-512-1800; 202-512-1800 if calling within Washington DC metropolitan area

Design of Wood Aircraft Structures dated June 1951, Second Ed.	39.13
MIL-HDBK-17A Plastics for Aerospace Vehicles dated Jan., 1971	23.613; 25.613; 27.613; 29.613
MIL-HDBK-23A Structural Sandwich Composites dated Dec. 30, 1968	23.613; 25.613; 27.613; 29.613
MIL-HDBK-5C, Vol. 1 & Vol. 2 Metallic Materials and Elements for Flight Vehicle Structures, dated Sept. 15, 1976, as amended through Dec. 15, 1978.	23.613; 23.615; 25.693; 27.613; 29.613; 29.685
MIL-STD-6866 dated November 29, 1985	39.13

Univair Aircraft Corporation
2500 Himalaya Road, Aurora, CO 80011

Airplane Flight Manual dated October 18, 2001	39.13
SB No. 29, Rev. B, dated January 2, 1995	39.13
Service Bulletin No. 24B dated January 29, 2002	39.13
Service Bulletin No. 31 dated January 29, 2002	39.13
Service Bulletin No. 31 Revision 1 dated June 14, 2002	39.13

Ursula Hanle
Haus Schwalbenwerder, D-14728 Strodehne, Federal Republic of Germany, Telephone and FAX: +;49 (0) 33875-30389

101-25/2, dated January 21, 1998, including drawing No. 101-44-3(2), as referenced therein.	39.13

Title 14—Aeronautics and Space

VALSAN Partnership Ltd
    Aviation Products Management, Product Support Office, 39450 Third Street East, Suite 121, Palmdale, CA 93550

SB 71-006, Rev. 1, dated March 3, 1995 .... 39.13

Vazer Aerospace
    3025 Eldridge Avenue, Bellingham, WA 98226

A.M. Luton Electrical System Schematic, Drawing 20075, Rev. G 39.13
    and E, Sheets 1, 2, and 3, dated May 15, 1998.

A.M. Luton Service Information Letter No. SA-SIL-98-11-03, Electrical 39.13
    Systems, Rev. A, dated May 15, 1998.

Vulcanair S.p.A.
    Via G. Poscoli, 7, 80026 Casoria (Naples), Italy

P68 Series Service Bulletin No. 110 dated March 19, 2002 .... 39.13

P68 Series Service Bulletin No. 111 Revision 1 dated February 20, 39.13
    2002.

Service Bulletin No. 98 dated July 31, 1999 .... 39.13

Weatherly Aviation Company, Inc
    2100 Flightline Drive, suite 1, P.O. Box 68, Lincoln, California 95648

Service Note No. 15, dated July 17, 1996 .... 39.13

Williams Rolls
    2280 West Maple Road, P.O. Box 200, Walled Lake, MI 48390-0200

ASB FJ44-A72-38, dated October 21, 1997 .... 39.13

SB FJ44-72-36, dated October 21, 1997 .... 39.13

Woodward (AlliedSignal Inc.)
    Aviation Services Division, Data Distribution, Dept. 64-3/2102-1M, P.O. Box 29003, Phoenix, AZ 85038-9003; Telephone (602) 365-2548

SB No. WG4044, June 28, 1993 .... 39.13

SB No. WG64047, Rev. 4, October 3, 1994 .... 39.13

SB No.WG64050, October 3, 1994 (available from AlliedSignal) 39.13

Z.1. de l'Arsenal
    BP. 109-17303 Rochefort Cedex France

Service Bulletin SB TAA12-25-402 Revision 1 dated December 21, 39.13
    2000.

Table of CFR Titles and Chapters

(Revised as of January 1, 2003)

Title 1—General Provisions

Title 2 [Reserved]

Title 3—The President

Title 4—Accounts

Title 5—Administrative Personnel

Title 5—Administrative Personnel—Continued

Title 6 [Reserved]

Title 7—Agriculture

Title 12—Banks and Banking—Continued

Title 13—Business Credit and Assistance

Title 14—Aeronautics and Space

Title 15—Commerce and Foreign Trade

Title 20—Employees' Benefits

Title 21—Food and Drugs

Title 22—Foreign Relations

Title 25—Indians

Title 26—Internal Revenue

Title 27—Alcohol, Tobacco Products and Firearms

Title 28—Judicial Administration

Title 29—Labor

Title 32—National Defense

Title 33—Navigation and Navigable Waters

Title 34—Education

1092

Title 49—Transportation—Continued

Title 50—Wildlife and Fisheries

CFR Index and Finding Aids

Alphabetical List of Agencies Appearing in the CFR

(Revised as of January 1, 2003)

1103

List of CFR Sections Affected

All changes in this volume of the Code of Federal Regulations which were made by documents published in the FEDERAL REGISTER since January 1, 2001, are enumerated in the following list. Entries indicate the nature of the changes effected. Page numbers refer to Federal Register pages. The user should consult the entries for chapters and parts as well as sections for revisions.

For the period before January 1, 2001, see the "List of CFR Sections Affected, 1949–1963, 1964–1972, 1973–1985, and 1986–2000" published in 11 separate volumes.

14 CFR—Continued

14 CFR—Continued

2002

14 CFR

14 CFR—Continued

14 CFR—Continued

14 CFR—Continued

14 CFR—Continued

2003

(Corrections published January 10, 2003, and January 15, 2003)

14 CFR

CPSIA information can be obtained
at www.ICGtesting.com
Printed in the USA
LVHW051254170323
741852LV00005B/201